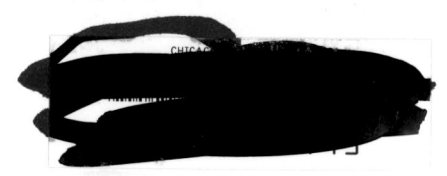

Historical Statistics of Black America

Historical Statistics of Black America

Media to Vital Statistics

Compiled & Edited by

Jessie Carney Smith • *Fisk University*
and
Carrell Peterson Horton • *Fisk University*

An International Thomson Publishing Company

NEW YORK • LONDON • BONN • BOSTON • DETROIT • MADRID
MELBOURNE • MEXICO CITY • PARIS • SINGAPORE • TOKYO
TORONTO • WASHINGTON • ALBANY NY • BELMONT CA • CINCINNATI OH

Jessie Carney Smith and Carrell Peterson Horton, *Editors*

Gale Research Inc. Staff
Mary Beth Trimper, *Production Director*
Mary Kelley, *Production Assistant*

Cynthia Baldwin, *Product Design Manager*
Sherrell Hobbs, *Desktop Publisher*
Pamela Galbreath, *Cover Design*

Editorial Code and Data Inc. Staff
Nancy Ratliff, Sherae Carroll, *Data Entry*
Gary Alampi, *Data Processing*

Library of Congress Cataloging-in-Publication Data

Historical statistics of black america: compiled and edited by Jessie Carney Smith and Carrell Peterson Horton.
p. cm.
Includes bibliographical references (p.) and index.
ISBN 0-8103-8542-2 : $125.00. -- ISBN 0-8103-9391-3 (v. 1). -- ISBN 0-8103-9392-1 (v. 2)
1. Afro-Americans--History--Statistics. I. Smith, Jessie Carney. II. Horton, Carrell.
E185.H543 1995
973'.0496073'021--dc20 94-29718
CIP

∞™ This book is printed on acid-free paper that meets the minimum requirements of American National Standard for Information Sciences—Permanence Paper for Printed Library Materials, ANSI Z39.48-1984.

Library of Congress Catalog Card Number 94-29718
ISBN 0-8103-8542-2
Vol 2 ISBN 0-8103-9392-1

Printed in the United States of America
Published simultaneously in the United Kingdom
by Gale Research International Limited
(An affiliated company of Gale Research Inc.)

I(T)P™ Gale Research Inc., an International Thomson Publishing Company.
ITP logo is a trademark under license.

10 9 8 7 6 5 4 3 2 1

TABLE OF CONTENTS

CHAPTER 1 - AGRICULTURE continued:

CHAPTER 1 - AGRICULTURE continued:

CHAPTER 1 - AGRICULTURE continued:

CHAPTER 1 - AGRICULTURE continued:

CHAPTER 1 - AGRICULTURE continued:

CHAPTER 1 - AGRICULTURE continued:

CHAPTER 1 - AGRICULTURE continued:

CHAPTER 2 - BUSINESS AND ECONOMICS continued:

CHAPTER 2 - BUSINESS AND ECONOMICS continued:

CHAPTER 2 - BUSINESS AND ECONOMICS continued:

CHAPTER 3 - CRIME, LAW ENFORCEMENT, AND LEGAL JUSTICE continued:

CHAPTER 3 - CRIME, LAW ENFORCEMENT, AND LEGAL JUSTICE continued:

CHAPTER 4 - EDUCATION continued:

CHAPTER 4 - EDUCATION continued:

CHAPTER 4 - EDUCATION continued:

CHAPTER 4 - EDUCATION continued:

CHAPTER 4 - EDUCATION continued:

CHAPTER 4 - EDUCATION continued:

CHAPTER 4 - EDUCATION continued:

CHAPTER 4 - EDUCATION continued:

CHAPTER 4 - EDUCATION continued:

CHAPTER 4 - EDUCATION continued:

CHAPTER 4 - EDUCATION continued:

CHAPTER 4 - EDUCATION continued:

CHAPTER 5 - THE FAMILY continued:

CHAPTER 5 - THE FAMILY continued:

CHAPTER 5 - THE FAMILY continued:

CHAPTER 7 - HOUSING continued:

CHAPTER 7 - HOUSING continued:

CHAPTER 9 - LABOR AND EMPLOYMENT continued:

CHAPTER 9 - LABOR AND EMPLOYMENT continued:

CHAPTER 9 - LABOR AND EMPLOYMENT continued:

CHAPTER 11 - MILITARY AND MILITARY AFFAIRS continued:

CHAPTER 14 - POPULATION continued:

CHAPTER 14 - POPULATION continued:

CHAPTER 14 - POPULATION continued:

CHAPTER 14 - POPULATION continued:

CHAPTER 14 - POPULATION continued:

CHAPTER 14 - POPULATION continued:

CHAPTER 14 - POPULATION continued:

CHAPTER 16 - RELIGION continued:

CHAPTER 16 - RELIGION continued:

CHAPTER 18 - SPORTS AND LEISURE continued:

CHAPTER 19 - VITAL STATISTICS continued:

CHAPTER 19 - VITAL STATISTICS continued:

CHAPTER 19 - VITAL STATISTICS continued:

CHAPTER 19 - VITAL STATISTICS continued:

CHAPTER 19 - VITAL STATISTICS continued:

CHAPTER 19 - VITAL STATISTICS continued:

INTRODUCTION

Historical Statistics of Black America is a work that should have enormous value as a practical resource for those who seek a chronology of the condition, status, and experiences of African Americans. Tables and text reports in this volume begin with information recorded in the eighteenth century and extend through 1975. Although some of the tables in the *Statistical Record of Black America* companion series contain historical information, the majority of the material included here represents a uniquely different presentation than those works. This volume also is somewhat different in the areas that are included and in the quantity of information available in the various areas. It was, for example, necessary to add a separate chapter on agriculture, reflecting the importance of agricultural pursuits to African Americans in earlier times. In contrast, there is less recorded information on African-American business or African Americans in sports, and even somewhat less information on the health of AfricanAmericans. The careful user can thus compare the contents of this volume with those in the *Statistical Record of Black America* and gain insight and understanding of the general context of African-American life from the time of slavery to the present.

Beyond its usefulness as a chronological record, *Historical Statistics of Black America* can be a revelation. It is one thing to know that slavery existed, was abolished, and led to new and different challenges, problems, and opportunities for African Americans and for society. It is quite another to note the social context in which all of this occurred. The reader may be surprised at what tables on lynchings reveal about its frequency over the years and the ''reasons'' for which it occurred. The reader who pays attention to the tables as they were titled in the original sources can follow along various designations given to the subjects of this volume, from ''colored'' to ''Negro'' to ''black'' to today's ''African-American.''

One particularly interesting aspect of assembling material for this volume was related to the sources of the material. Much of the information came, as has been the case with the *Statistical Record of Black America* series, from U.S. government publications, but a significant amount of material came from publications originating at African-American institutions or from African-American authors. The amount of information obtained from *The Negro Year Book* (initially published at Tuskegee Institute) and *The Negro Handbook* (edited by Florence Murray) is quite astounding. In many instances, these publications used U.S. government data as their starting point and then added new analyses which greatly increased the usefulness of the information. In addition, they often collected data on aspects of African-American life and issues confronting African Americans that other publications had not yet begun to consider. In material available to the editors, for example, the earliest record of African-American achievements in sports was found in issues of *The Negro Handbook.*

Interpreting the Data

There is an inherent risk in compiling any historical record. Unless there have been periodic compilations at previous intervals, the age of original source documents will in some cases lead researchers to very fragile documents. Such was the case here. Volumes published originally in the 1800s clearly showed their age in the fragility of their pages and in some instances in the figures they presented. This volume presents such material as it was found.

We have made every effort to assure that figures presented are accurate and that there is consistency between column and row categories and totals. There are still, however, a few instances in which inconsistencies could not be resolved and in which row or column figures do not sum to the exact total that is printed. Percent totals may also fail to sum to exactly 100 because of rounding procedures used in original sources. The differences are in all instances minor.

Acknowledgments

The editors are deeply appreciative of the cooperation of those individuals and organizations that gave us access to this vast store of information and permission to reproduce it here. Our gratitude is also extended to those who helped us compile, assemble, and organize a volume that we hope will be as useful and interesting to readers as it has been to us. For their assistance in photocopying massive amounts of materials, we give thanks to Vallie Pursley of Tennessee State University and her family, Tobey and Yolanda Pursley. To our colleagues at Fisk University we thank library staff members Jackie London for helping to locate information and Dixie Jernigan and Sharon Williams for copying tables. We also wish to thank Robert L. Johns of the Fisk faculty for recommending sources. President Henry Ponder of Fisk University continued his support of our research and publication, and we express our kind appreciation to him. For their guidance, patience, support, and magnificent layout of the tables we thank our Gale editors James E. Person, Jr., Sandra C. Davis, and Kathryn Horste.

Carrell Peterson Horton

Jessie Carney Smith

Historical Statistics of Black America

Chapter 10
MEDIA

Geographic Divisions

★ 1426 ★

Newspapers and Periodicals: Circulation, 1940

Geographic divisions	Number		Combined circulation per issue
	Operating	Reporting circulation	
United States total	210	155	1,276,600
New England	2	1	9,000
Middle Atlantic	24	18	311,700
East North Central	32	25	222,200
West North Central	21	15	89,500
South Atlantic	51	40	280,200
East South Central	34	22	134,500
West South Central	34	22	131,800
Mountain	3	3	5,600
Pacific	9	9	92,100

Source: "Combined Circulation of Newspaper, 1940, by Geographic Division," Florence Murray, ed., *The Negro Handbook*, 1942, p. 201. Published by permission. Primary source: U.S. Bureau of the Census.

News Agencies

★ 1427 ★

Newspapers and Periodicals: Combined Circulation, 1945

Classification	Number of periodicals	Combined average net circulation
Total	85	749,025
Advertising, business, and trade	9	16,400
Alumni and collegiate	15	24,428
Educational	20	126,691
Fraternal	6	28,750
General	14	255,294
Religious	13	228,962
Miscellaneous	8	68,500

Source: "Combined Circulation of Periodicals: 1940," Florence Murray, ed., *The Negro Handbook*, p. 389. Primary source: U.S. Bureau of the Census.

★ 1428 ★

News Agencies

Newspapers and Periodicals: News Gathering Agencies, 1940

Destination[1]	Papers subscribing	Combined circulation per issue
A	225[2]	900,200[2]
B	135	675,000
C	68	400,000
D	50	500,000
E	35	100,000
F	28	200,000
G	28	250,000
H	20	50,000
I	10	250,000
J	10	250,000
K	8	20,000

[Continued]

★ 1428 ★

Newspapers and Periodicals: News Gathering Agencies, 1940

[Continued]

Destination[1]	Papers subscribing	Combined circulation per issue
L	4	230,000
M	3	12,000

Source: "News Gathering Agencies: 1940," Florence Murray, ed., *The Negro Handbook*, p. 202. Primary source: U.S. Bureau of the Census. *Notes:* 1. Letters A, B, C, etc., are used to prevent disclosing the identity of any reporting agency. 2. Includes 39 white newspapers and circulation figures for same.

Print Media

★ 1429 ★

Newspapers and Periodicals: Combined Circulation, 1940

Class	Number operating	Number and circulation of reporting periodicals	
		Number	Circulation
United States total	129	78	703,600
Advertising, business and trade	12	4	2,900
Collegiate	6	4	3,000
Educational	29	20	90,700
Fraternal	16	12	38,000
General	8	2	10,000
Health, medical and scientific	5	5	10,300
Pictorial and theatrical	4	2	22,000
Religious	46	27	524,700
Miscellaneous	3	2	2,000

Source: "Combined Circulation of Periodicals: 1940," Florence Murray, ed., *The Negro Handbook*, p. 201. Primary source: U.S. Bureau of the Census.

★ 1430 ★

Print Media

Newspapers and Periodicals: Growth in Circulation, to 1940

"From 1939 to 1940 the total circulation per issue of 117 newspaper increased 23,200 or from 1,100,000 to 1,123,200. Increase were reported by newspapers published in the West North Central, South Atlantic, East South Central, West South Central, and Pacific States."

Source: "Negro Newspapers and Periodicals in the United States: As of 1940," Florence Murray, ed., *The Negro Handbook*, p. 201.

★ 1431 ★

Print Media

Newspapers in the East: Circulation, 1951

Circulation of magazines	Circulation
MARYLAND	
Baltimore	
Afro-American (wkly)	60,742
(Tues. local issue)	31,511
(Sat. local issue)	32,352
Total	124,605
MASSACHUSETTS	
Boston	
Chronicle (wkly)	5,000
Guardian (wkly)	10,000
Times (wkly)	12,000
Total	27,000
NEW JERSEY	
Newark	
New Jersey Afro-American (wkly)	14,609
New Jersey Herald News (wkly)	28,371
New Jersey Record (wkly)	-
Patterson	
North Jersey Independent (wkly)	26,498
Total	69,478
NEW YORK	
Buffalo	
Criterion, The (wkly)	2,500
Empire Star (wkly)	8,115
New York	
Age (wkly)	32,750
Amsterdam Nes (wkly)	59,849
Westchester County Press (wkly)	6,000

[Continued]

★ 1431 ★

Newspapers in the East: Circulation, 1951

[Continued]

Circulation of magazines	Circulation
Rochester	
Star (wkly)	2,825
Voice (bi-wkly)	3,267
Syracuse	
Progressive Herald (wkly)	5,500
Total	120,806
PENNSYLVANIA	
Philadelphia	
Afro-American (wkly)	18,496
Christian Review (wkly)	6,000
Independent (wkly)	24,213
Tribune (s-wkly)	20,916
Pittsburgh	
Courier (wkly)	268,447
Triangle Advocate (wkly)	2,000
Total	340,072
RHODE ISLAND	
Providence	
Chronicle (wkly)	1,541

Source: "The Negro Press, Circulation." Jessie Parkhurst Guzman, ed., *Negro Year Book: A Review of Events Affecting Negro Life, 1941-1946*, 1952, pp. 32-35. Published by Permission. Primary source: N.W. Ayer & Sons, *Directory of Newspapers and Periodicals*, 1950, and *Editor and Publisher International Yearbook*, 1951.

★ 1432 ★

Print Media

Newspapers in the Mid West: Circulation, 1951

Circulation of magazines	Circulation
ILLINOIS	
Chicago	
Defender (wkly)	155,074
World (wkly)	32,000
Globe (wkly)	35,000
East St. Louis	
Crusader, The (wkly)	-
Robbins	
Herald (wkly)	3,800
Views and Voices of Chicago and Suburbs	-
Springfield	
Illinois Chronicle (wkly)	1,200
Illinois Conservator (s-mo.)	3,500

[Continued]

★ 1432 ★

Newspapers in the Mid West: Circulation, 1951

[Continued]

Circulation of magazines	Circulation
Total	230,574
INDIANA	
Evansville	
Consolidated News (bi-weekly)	7,000
Gary	
American (wkly)	5,500
Lake County Observer (wkly)	8,000
Indianapolis	
Recorder (wkly)	11,635
Total	32,135
IOWA	
Des Moines	
Iowa Bystander (wkly)	1,863
Iowa Observer (wkly)	1,100
Total	2,863
KANSAS	
Hutchinson	
Blade (Fri.)	635
Kansas City	
Peoples Elevator (wkly)	-
Plaindealer (wkly)	15,000
Wyandotte Echo (wkly)	1,000
Wichita	
Negro Star (wkly)	1,000
Total	17,635
MICHIGAN	
Detroit	
Michigan Chronical (wkly)	21,619
Telegram (wkly)	1,100
Tribune (wkly)	18,500
Inkster	
Voice (wkly)	1,600
Total	42,719
MINNESOTA	
Minneapolis	
Spokesman (wkly)	4,318
Twin City Observer (wkly)	5,127
St. Paul	
Recorder (wkly)	3,958
Total	13,403

[Continued]

★ 1432 ★

Newspapers in the Mid West: Circulation, 1951

[Continued]

Circulation of magazines	Circulation
MISSOURI	
Kansas City	
Call (wkly)	38,892
St. Louis	
American (wkly)	18,374
Argus (wkly)	25,650
News (wkly)	3,000
Total	85,916
NEBRASKA	
Lincoln	
Voice (wkly)	843
Omaha	
Guide (wkly)	15,965
Star (wkly)	25,575
Total	42,383
OHIO	
Cincinnati	
Independent (wkly)	7,500
Union (wkly)	12,000
Cleveland	
Call and Post (wkly)	23,530
Guide (wkly)	-
Herald (wkly)	12,000
Columbus	
Ohio State News (wkly)	7,380
Sentinel (wkly)	6,232
Dayton	
Ohio Express (dly)	7,500
Citizen (wkly)	5,000
Hamilton	
Butler County American (wkly)	1,600
Youngstown	
Buckeye Review, The (wkly)	2,100
Toledo	
Script (wkly)	25,000
Total	109,842
WISCONSIN	
Milwaukee	
Globe (wkly)	975
Wisconsin Enterprise-Blade (wkly)	55,000
Total	55,975

Source: "The Negro Press, Circulation," Jessie Parkhurst Guzman, ed., pp. 32- 35. Published by permission. Primary source: N.W. Ayer & Sons, *Directory of Newspapers and Periodicals*, 1950, and *Editor and Publisher International Yearbook*, 1951.

★ 1433 ★

Print Media

Newspapers in the South: Circulation, 1951, Part I

Circulation of magazines	Circulation
ALABAMA	
Birmingham	
Baptist Leader (wkly)	3,500
Review (wkly)	18,893
World (s-wkly)	10,500
Mirror (wkly)	21,106
Alabama Weekly Review (wkly)	28,438
Mobile	
Advocate (wkly)	-
Gulf Informer (wkly)	12,643
Montgomery	
Alabama Tribune (wkly)	1,500
Tuscaloosa	
Alabama Citizen (wkly)	8,000
Tuskegee	
Herald (wkly)	2,740
Total	107,320
ARKANSAS	
Little Rock	
Arkansas Survey-Journal (wkly)	12,550
Arkansas World (wkly)	13,560
Baptist Vanguard	-
State Press (wkly)	17,656
Arkansas Flashlight (wkly)	1,500
Pine Bluff	
Negro Spokesman (wkly)	7,000
Total	52,266
DISTRICT OF COLUMBIA	
Washington	
Afro-American (s-wkly) (Tue.)	15,120
Afro-American (s-wkly) (Fri.)	19,281
Capital Times (wkly)	13,500
Gaily News (Fri.)	10,000
Nite Life (Fri.)	5,000
Total	62,901
FLORIDA	
Jacksonville	
Florida Tattler (wkly)	10,508
Progressive News (wkly)	8,650
Florida Star (wkly)	5,000
Miami	
Call, The (wkly)	-
Tropical Dispatch (wkly)	-
Florida Times	5,500

[Continued]

★ 1433 ★

Newspapers in the South: Circulation, 1951, Part I

[Continued]

Circulation of magazines	Circulation
Pensacola	
Colored Citizen (wkly)	1,100
Courier (wkly)	5,342
Tampa	
Bulletin (wkly)	780
Courier (Sat.)	1,500
Florida Sentinel (Tues.)	9,400
Total	47,780
GEORGIA	
Albany	
Enterprise (wkly)	2,242
Southwest Georgian (Sat.)	1,500
Atlanta	
World (dly)	29,500
Augusta Review	4,000
Columbus	
World (Sun.)	2,800
Macon	
World	2,500
Rome	
Enterprise (ftntly)	-
Savannah	
Tribune (wkly)	3,992
Herald	-
Total	46,534
KENTUCKY	
Louisville	
American Baptist (wkly)	1,500
Defender (wkly)	15,226
Kentucky Reporter (wkly)	1,000
Leader (wkly)	15,296
Total	33,022
LOUISIANA	
New Orleans	
Central Christian Advocate (wkly)	23,000
Informer and Sentinel (wkly)	3,890
MISSISSIPPI	
Greenville	
Delta Leader (Sun.)	3,000
Jackson	
Advocate (wkly)	5,500

[Continued]

★ 1433 ★

Newspapers in the South: Circulation, 1951, Part I

[Continued]

Circulation of magazines	Circulation
Mississippi Enterprise (wkly)	10,000
Meridian	
Echo (s-mo.)	7,500
Mound Bayou	
News-Digest (s-mo.)	4,728
New Albany	
Community Citizen (s-mo.)	1,925
Total	32,653

Source: "The Negro Press, Circulation," Jessie Parkhurst Guzman, ed., *Negro Year Book: A Review of Events Affecting Negro Life, 1941-1946*, 1952, pp. 32-35. Published by Permission. Primary source: N.W. Ayer & Sons, *Directory of Newspapers and Periodicals*, 1950, and *Editor and Publisher International Yearbook*, 1951.

★ 1434 ★

Print Media

Newspapers in the South: Circulation, 1951, Part II

Circulation of magazines	Circulation
LOUISIANA	
New Orleans	
Lousiana Weekly (wkly)	12,678
Sun (wkly)	1,000
Shreveport	
Sun (wkly)	10,680
Total	51,248
NORTH CAROLINA	
Asheville	
Southern News (wkly)	2,700
Charlotte	
Post (wkly)	5,000
Star of Zion (wkly)	8,000
Eagle	15,000
Durham	
Carolina Times (wkly)	10,385
Henderson	
Mountain News (wkly)	2,000
Raleigh	
Carolinian, The (wkly)	15,000
Wilmington	
Journal (wkly)	10,000
Total	68,085

[Continued]

★ 1434 ★

Newspapers in the South: Circulation, 1951, Part II

[Continued]

Circulation of magazines	Circulation
OKLAHOMA	
Muskogee	
Oklahoma Independent (wkly)	2,000
Oklahoma City	
Black Dispatch (wkly)	23,888
Okmulgee	
Observer (wkly)	1,800
Tulsa	
Appeal (wkly)	3,320
Oklahoma Eagle (wkly)	5,000
Total	36,008
SOUTH CAROLINA	
Charleston	
New Citizen (wkly)	2,000
Columbia	
Lighthouse and Informer (wkly)	6,400
Palmetto Leader (wkly)	4,680
Greenville	
American (wkly)	2,000
Sumter	
Samaritan Herald and Voice os Job (wkly)	1,000
Total	16,080
TENNESSEE	
Chattanooga	
Observer (wkly)	4,000
Jackson	
Christian Index, The (wkly)	6,000
Knoxville	
Flashlight Herald (wkly)	6,500
Monitor (wkly)	5,700
Memphis	
World (s-wkly) (Tues.)	16,000
(Fri.)	21,000
Nashville	
Globe and Independent (wkly)	26,000
National Baptist Union Review (wkly)	53,460
Recorder (wkly)	8,000
Total	146,660
TEXAS	
Dallas	
Express (wkly)	8,728
Fort Worth	
Defender and Baptist Herald (wkly)	3,860
Lake Como News (wkly)	2,000

[Continued]

★ 1434 ★

Newspapers in the South: Circulation, 1951, Part II

[Continued]

Circulation of magazines	Circulation
Mind (wkly)	2,000
Houston	
Defender (wkly)	3,361
Houston Informer (wkly)	7,803
Informer and Texas Freeman, The (wkly)	26,109
Negro Labor News (wkly)	2,000
Marshall	
Traveler (wkly)	1,500
San Antonio	
Register (wkly)	9,750
Waco	
Messenger (wkly)	4,000
Total	71,111
VIRGINIA	
Charlottesville	
Tribune (wkly)	3,000
Norfolk	
Journal and Guide (wkly)	63,428
Richmond	
Afro-American (wkly)	11,303
Roanoke	
Tribune (wkly)	15,000
Total	92,731
WEST VIRGINIA	
Bluefield	
Independent Observer (wkly)	2,400

Source: "The Negro Press, Circulation," Jessie Parkhurst Guzman, ed., *Negro Year Book: A Review of Events Affecting Negro Life, 1941-1946*, 1952, pp. 32-35. Published by Permission. Primary source: N.W. Ayer & Sons, *Directory of Newspapers and Periodicals*, 1950, and *Editor and Publisher International Yearbook*, 1951.

★ 1435 ★

Print Media

Newspapers in the West: Circulation, 1951

Circulation of magazines	Circulation
ARIZONA	
Phoenix	
Sun (wkly)	2,000
CALIFORNIA	
Los Angeles	
California Eagle (wkly)	20,000

[Continued]

★ 1435 ★

Newspapers in the West: Circulation, 1951

[Continued]

Circulation of magazines	Circulation
Criterion, The (wkly)	-
Neighborhood News (wkly)	-
Sentinel (wkly)	25,000
Tribune (wkly)	10,000
Spotlight (Th. & Sun.)	30,000
Star Review (Th.)	12,500
Oakland	
California Voice (wkly)	10,500
Herald (wkly)	-
San Bernardino	
Tri-County Bulletin (wkly)	-
San Diego	
Comet (wkly)	10,000
San Francisco	
Sun-Reporter (wkly)	24,480
Labor Herald (s-mo.)	85,567
Total	228,047
COLORADO	
Denver	
Colorado Statesman (wkly)	2,700
Star (wkly)	1,500
Pueblo	
Western Ideal (wkly)	1,100
Total	5,300
OREGON	
Portland	
Northwest Clarion (wkly)	15,000
WASHINGTON	
Seattle	
Northwest Enterprise (wkly)	10,500

Source: "The Negro Press, Circulation," Jessie Parkhurst Guzman, ed., *Negro Year Book: A Review of Events Affecting Negro Life, 1941-1946*, 1952, pp. 32-35. Published by permission. Primary source: N.W. Ayer & Sons, *Directory of Newspapers and Periodicals*, 1950, and *Editor and Publisher International Yearbook*, 1951.

★ 1436 ★

Print Media

Periodicals: Circulation by State, 1951

Circulation of Magazines[1]	Circulation
ALABAMA	
Tuskegee	
Service (mo.)	5,000
CALIFORNIA	
Berkeley	
Ivy Leaf (quar.)	5,000
DISTRICT OF COLUMBIA	
Washington	
Journal of Negro Education (quar.)	4,500
Journal of Negro History (quar.)	1,450
Negro History Bulletin (mo.)	9,000
Pulse (mo.)	25,000
GEORGIA	
Atlanta	
Colored Morticians Bulletin, The (mo.)	1,500
Foundation, The (quar.)	1,000
Georgia Baptist, The (s-mo.)	2,500
Macon	
Sunday School Worker (bi-mo.)	
ILLINOIS	
Chicago	
Ebony (mo.)	379,000
Negro Digest (mo.)	100,000
Negro Traveler	72,000
Tan Confessions	200,000
Peoria	
Bronze Citizen (mo.)	1,000
KENTUCKY	
Louisville	
Kentucky Negro Education Assn. Journal (bi-mo.)	1,400
MARYLAND	
Baltimore	
Colored Harvest, The (mo.)	46,000
MICHIGAN	
Detroit	
Postal Alliance, The (mo.)	10,000
MISSISSIPPI	
Bay St. Louis	
St. Augustine's Messenger (mo.)	9,400

[Continued]

★ 1436 ★

Periodicals: Circulation by State, 1951

[Continued]

Circulation of Magazines[1]	Circulation
Mound Bayou	
Taborian Star (mo.)	6,000
Yazoo City	
Central Voice, The (mo.)	2,500
NEW YORK	
New York	
Crisis (mo.)	40,000
Interracial Review (mo.)	10,000
Journal of the National Medical Association (bi-mo.)	4,032
Our World (mo.)	166,031
Voice of Mission (mo.)	2,300
NORTH CAROLINA	
Charlotte	
Quarterly Review of Higher Education Amoung Negroes (quar.)	2,000
PENNSYLVANIA	
Philadelphia	
Bronze Woman (mo.)	5,700
Kappa Alpha Psi Journal (mo).	4,000
TENNESSEE	
Memphis	
Sphinx Magazine (quar.)	14,000
Whole Truth, The (mo.)	2,000
Nashville	
American Negro Mind (mo.)	3,000
Broadcaster, The (quar.)	2,791
Message Magazine (mo.)	5,000
Modern Farmer, The (mo.)	32,500
National Baptist Voice (bi-mo.)	5,000
Review, The (quar.)	3,000
West'n Christian Recorder (s-mo.)	2,000
Union City	
Cumberland Flag, The (mo.)	500
TEXAS	
Fort Worth	
World's Messenger (mo.)	6,000
Negro Achievements (mo.)	4,000
VIRGINIA	
Manassas	
Bulletin of the National Dental Association (quar.)	1,650
Richmond	
Saint Luke Fraternal Bulletin (mo.)	1,400

[Continued]

★ 1436 ★

Periodicals: Circulation by State, 1951

[Continued]

Circulation of Magazines[1]	Circulation
WEST VIRGINIA	
Charleston	
Color (mo.)	100,483

Source: The Negro Press, Circulation." Jessie Parkhurst Guzman, ed., *Negro Year Book: A Review of Events Affecting Negro Life, 1941-1946*, 1952, p. 35. Primary source: N.W. Ayer & Sons, *Directory of Newspapers and Periodicals*, 1950. Published by permission. *Notes:* 1. Circulation figures have been derived in the main from N.W. Ayer & Sons's Directory Newspapers and Periodicals (1950).

Chapter 11
MILITARY AND MILITARY AFFAIRS

Military Crime

★ 1437 ★

Prisoners: Inmates of Military and Naval Prisons, by Race, 1943

	Total	Military	Naval
Race and Nativity			
Total	1,182	677	505
White	929	469	460
Native	918	458	460
Foreign born	11	11	..
Negro	245	200	45
Other races	8	8	..

Source: "Prisoners Received from Court, by Race, Nativity, and Age, for Principal Military and Naval Prisoners: 1943," *The Negro Handbook, 1946- 1947*, 1947, p. 167. Primary source: Reports received from U.S. Disciplinary Barracks, Fort Leavenworth, Kansas; U.S. Naval Prison, Navy Yard, Mare Island, California; U.S. Naval Prison, Navy Yard, Portsmouth, New Hampshire.

The Military Services

★ 1438 ★

Air Force and Navy: Pilots, Total and Black, in the Air Force and Navy, 1969

Service	Total Pilots	Negro Pilots	Percent Negro
Air Force	37,000	236	0.6
Navy	15,650	16	0.1
Total	52,650	252	0.5

Source: "Northrup, Thieblot, and Chernish, "Air Force and Navy Employment of Pilots by Race: May 1969," *The Racial Policies of American Industry,* Report No. 23, *The Negro in the Air Transport Industry,* 1971, p. 48. Primary source: *Chicago Tribune,* May 18, 1969.

★ 1439 ★

The Military Services

Army and Air Force: Black Officers Post-World War II, 1947

In Reg. Army June '46 and Later Increments	Appointed from Reserves		Negro Officers to Date
	Total	Negro	
June 1, 1946			12
Appointed-			
July 3, 1946	9,803	31	43
January 29, 1947	1,850	5	48
June 3, 1947	9,209	30	78
October 10, 1947[1]	5,900	32	110

Source: "Officers in the Postwar Regular Army and Air Force as of December 1947," *The Negro Handbook, 1949,* 1949, p. 252. Primary source: Unspecified release. *Notes:* 1. A note on the release states: "Except for a group of medical department officers and a small group whose applications were completely processed, this will be the last increment of officers taken into the Regular Army under provisions of Public Law 281 which expires December 31, 1947."

★ 1440 ★

The Military Services

Chaplains: Black Chaplains in 1951

Service and Denomination	1st Lt.	Captain	Major	Lt. Col.	TOTAL
ARMY:					
African Methodist Episcopal	1	9	1	1	12
African Methodist Episcopal Zion	1	5	-	-	6
Church of God, Indiana	-	1	-	-	1
Congregational Christian	2	-	1	1	4
Lutheran	-	1	-	-	1
Methodist	2	5	3	1	11
Methodist Episcopal, Colored	-	1	2	-	3
National Baptist Convention of America	-	4	-	-	4
National Baptist Convention, U.S.A.	2	10	4	1	17
Presbyterian, U.S.A.	-	8	1	-	9
Protestant Episcopal	-	1	2	-	3
TOTAL ARMY	8	45	14	4	71
NAVY:					
African Methodist Episcopal	1[1]	-	-	-	1
Presbyterian, U.S.A.	1[1]	-	-	-	1
TOTAL NAVY	2[1]	-	-	-	2
UNITED STATES AIR FORCE:					
African Methodist Episcopal	-	3	2	-	5
Methodist	-	2	-	-	2
Presbyterian, U.S.A.	1	1	-	-	2
National Baptist Convention, U.S.A.	1	3	3	1	8
Protestant Episcopal	-	-	1	-	1
TOTAL U.S.A.F.	2	9	6	1	18
GRAND TOTAL	12	54	20	5	91

Source: Adapted by the editors from "Negro Chaplains," *Negro Year Book: A Review of Events Affecting Negro Life, 1952*, pp. 266-267. Primary source: Not specifically identified.

★ 1441 ★

The Military Services

Officers and Enlisted Personnel In and Outside of Southeast Asia in 1969 and 1970

[Numbers in thousands]

Subject	Total		Negro		Percent Negro	
	1969	1970	1969	1970	1969	1970
Total	3,439	3,074	323	293	9	10
Officers	419	366	9	8	2	2
Outside Southeast Asia	354	(NA)	7	(NA)	2	(NA)
In Southeast Asia	65	(NA)	2	(NA)	3	(NA)
Enlisted men	3,020	2,708	314	284	10	11
Outside Southeast Asia	2,447	(NA)	249	(NA)	10	(NA)
In Southeast Asia	573	(NA)	65	(NA)	11	(NA)

Source: "Total and Negro officers and Enlisted Men in the Armed Forces: 1969 and 1970," Current Population Reports, Special Studies, Series P-23, No. 38. *The Social and Economic Status of the Black Population in the United States, 1970*, 1970, p. 136. Primary source: U.S. Department of Defense. *Note:* NA Not available.

★ 1442 ★

The Military Services

Officers and Enlisted Personnel by Branch of Service, 1970 and 1974

[Numbers in thousands]

Military service and status	Total		Black		Percent black	
	1970	1974	1970	1974	1970	1974
All services, total	2,861	2,151	279	298	9.8	13.8
Officer	389	302	8	9	2.2	2.8
Enlisted	2,472	1,848	271	289	11.0	15.7
Army	1,230	780	149	148	12.1	19.0
Officer	160	106	5	5	3.4	4.5
Enlisted	1,069	674	144	143	13.5	21.3
Navy	645	542	31	41	4.8	7.5
Officer	78	67	1	1	0.7	1.3
Enlisted	567	475	30	40	5.4	8.4
Marine Corps	232	189	24	31	10.2	16.5
Officer	23	19	-	-	1.3	2.4
Enlisted	209	170	23	31	11.2	18.1
Air Force	755	640	75	78	10.0	12.1

[Continued]

★ 1442 ★

Officers and Enlisted Personnel by Branch of Service, 1970 and 1974

[Continued]

Military service and status	Total		Black		Percent black	
	1970	1974	1970	1974	1970	1974
Officer	128	111	2	2	1.7	2.2
Enlisted	627	529	73	75	11.7	14.2

Source: "Officer-Enlisted Status of Armed Forces Personnel, by Type of Service: 1970 and 1974," Current Population Reports, Special Studies, Series P-23, No. 54. *The Social and Economic Status of the Black Population in the United States, 1974,* 1975, p. 156. Primary source: U.S. Department of Defense. *Notes:* - Rounds to zero. Figures for 1970 represent the total number of officers and enlisted personnel as of December 1970; figures for 1974 are as of June 1974.

★ 1443 ★

The Military Services

Officers and Enlisted Personnel: Officer-Enlisted Category of Black Armed Forces Personnel as Percent of Total personnel, 1945-1975

Military service and status	1945	1949	1964	1967	1970	1975
All services	(NA)	6.7	8.7	9.0	9.8	14.3
Officer	(NA)	0.9	1.8	2.1	2.2	3.1
Enlisted	(NA)	7.4	9.7	9.9	11.0	16.1
Army	(NA)	10.1	10.9	11.2	12.1	19.9
Officer	0.7[1]	1.9	3.3	3.4	3.4	4.8
Enlisted	10.3[1]	11.1	11.8	12.1	13.5	22.2
Air Force	(NA)	5.3	8.6	9.1	10.0	12.5
Officer	(NA)	0.6	1.5	1.8	1.7	2.5
Enlisted	(NA)	6.1	10.0	10.4	11.7	14.6
Navy	(NA)	4.0	5.3	4.3	4.8	7.2
Officer	-	-	0.3	0.3	0.7	1.4
Enlisted	4.8	4.4	5.9	4.7	5.4	8.0
Marine Corps	(NA)	2.3	7.9	10.3	10.2	16.7
Officer	(NA)	0.1	0.3	0.7	1.3	3.0
Enlisted	(NA)	2.5	8.7	9.6	11.2	18.1

Source: "Black Armed Forces Personnel as a Percent of All Armed Forces Personnel by Officer-Enlisted Status and Type of Service for Selected Years: 1945 to 1975," *The Social and Economic Status of the Black Population in the United States: An Historical View, 1790-1978,* 1979, p. 160. Primary source: U.S. Department of Defense, and U.S. Commission on Civil Rights, 1963 Report, Washington, 1963. *Notes:* - Represents zero. NA Not available. 1. Includes Air Force personnel.

★ 1444 ★

The Military Services

Officers and Enlisted Personnel: Personnel Category of Black Armed Forces Personnel, by Type of Service, 1949-1975

[Numbers in thousands]

Military service and status	1949	1964	1967	1970	1975
BLACK					
All services, total	107[1]	238	303	279	302
Officer	2	6	8	8	9
Percent of total	1.5	2.6	2.7	3.0	3.0
Enlisted	105	232	295	271	293
Army	66	118	163	149	155
Officer	1	4	5	5	5
Percent of total	2.0	3.2	3.4	3.6	3.2
Enlisted	64	114	157	144	150
Air Force	22	72	80	75	76
Officer	-	2	2	2	3
Percent of total	1.4	2.9	3.0	2.9	3.4
Enlisted	22	70	78	73	73
Navy	17	34	31	31	38
Officer	-	-	-	1	1
Percent of total	-	0.6	0.9	1.7	2.4
Enlisted	17	34	31	30	37
Marine Corps	2	15	29	24	33
Officer	-	-	-	-	1
Percent of total	0.1	0.4	0.6	1.3	1.7
Enlisted	2	15	28	23	32

Source: "Officer-Enlisted Status of Armed Forces Personnel, by Type of Service for Selected Years: 1949 to 1975," *The Social and Economic Status of the Black Population in the United States: An Historical View, 1790-1978*, p. 1979, p. 159. Primary source: U.S. Department of Defense. *Notes:* - Less than 500 or rounds to zero. 1. Detail may not add to "All services" total because warrant officers are not included in totals for the individual branches.

★ 1445 ★

The Military Services

Officers and Enlistment Personnel: Black Armed Forces Personnel, 1970-1974

[In thousands, except percent. As of December 31].

YEAR AND ITEM	Total	Officers[1]	Enlisted men	Participation in Vietnam[2]
1970, Armed Forces	2,861	389	2,472	378
Negro	279	8	271	43
Percent of total	9.8	2.2	11.0	11.5
1971, Armed Forces	2,505	359	2,146	237
Negro	267	8	259	23
Percent of total	10.7	2.3	12.1	9.5
1972, Armed Forces	2,335	329	2,006	128
Negro	278	8	270	11
Percent of total	11.9	2.4	13.5	8.7
1973, Armed Forces	2,189	308	1,881	(Z)
Negro	287	8	279	(Z)
Percent of total	13.1	2.6	14.8	(Z)
1974, Armed Forces	2,127	296	1,831	(Z)
Negro	307	9	298	(Z)
Percent of total	14.4	3.0	16.3	(Z)

Source: "Negro Men in the Armed Forces: 1962 to 1974," *Statistical Abstract of the United States, 1975*, p. 324. Primary source: Dept. of Defense, Office of Equal Opportunity, *The Negro in the Armed Forces,* and unpublished data. *Notes:* NA Not available. Z Less than 500 or 0.05 percent. 1. Includes warrant officers. 2. Beginning 1968, includes offshore.

★ 1446 ★

The Military Services

Officers and Enlistment Personnel: Black Male Armed Forces Personnel, 1965-1969

[In thousands, except percent. As of December 31].

YEAR AND ITEM	Total	Officers[1]	Enlisted men	PARTICIPATION IN VIETNAM					Vietnam battle deaths since 1961
				Total	Army	Navy[2]	Marine Corps	Air Force	
1965, Armed Forces	2,843	338	2,505	173	112	10	40	11	2
Negro	269	6	263	22	17	(Z)	4	1	(Z)
Percent of total	9.5	1.9	10.5	12.5	14.8	5.1	8.9	8.3	14.6
1966, Armed Forces	3,322	362	2,960	385	239	24	69	53	7
Negro	303	7	296	41	30	1	5	5	1
Percent of total	9.1	1.9	10.0	10.6	12.6	54.4	8.0	10.3	16.0
1967, Armed Forces	3,384	402	2,982	486	320	32	78	56	16
Negro	303	8	295	48	35	1	6	6	2

[Continued]

★ 1446 ★

Officers and Enlistment Personnel: Black Male Armed Forces Personnel, 1965-1969

[Continued]

YEAR AND ITEM	Total	Officers[1]	Enlisted men	PARTICIPATION IN VIETNAM					Vietnam battle deaths since 1961
				Total	Army	Navy[2]	Marine Corps	Air Force	
Percent of total	8.9	2.1	9.9	9.8	11.1	4.7	8.2	10.5	14.1
1968, Armed Forces	3,395	418	2,977	536	360	37	81	58	31
Negro	313	9	304	59	44	1	8	6	4
Percent of total	9.2	2.1	10.2	10.9	11.7	4.0	10.7	10.0	13.5
1969, Armed Forces	3,285	408	2,877	498	357	30	53	58	40
Negro	286	9	277	48	35	1	6	6	5
Percent of total	8.7	2.1	9.6	9.7	9.8	4.1	11.4	10.5	12.9

Source: "Negro Men in the Armed Forces: 1965 to 1969," *Statistical Abstract of the United States, 1970*, p. 258. Primary source: Dept. of Defense, Office of the Secretary; unpublished data. *Notes:* Z Less than 500. 1. Includes warrant officers. 2. Includes Coast Guard.

★ 1447 ★

The Military Services

Overseas Service: Servicemen In and Out of Southeast Asia, 1969 and 1970

[Numbers in thousands]

Subject	1969			1970		
	Total	Negro	%Negro	Total	Negro	%Negro
Total	3,439	323	9	3,074	293	10
Outside Southeast Asia	2,801	256	9	2,555	241	9
In Southeast Asia	683	67	11	519	52	10
Deaths in Southeast Asia (January 1965-December 1970)				41	5	13

Source: Adapted by the editors from "Negro Men in the Armed Forces, March 31, 1969," Current Population Reports, Special Studies, Series P-23, No. 29. *The Social and Economic Status of the Black Population in the United States, 1969,* 1972, p. 85; and "Total and Negro Men in the Armed Forces: 1970," Current Population Reports, Special Studies, Series P-23, No. 38. *The Social and Economic Status of the Black Population in the United States, 1970,* 1970, p. 135. Primary source: U.S. Department of Defense.

★ 1448 ★

The Military Services

Overseas Service: Theater of Operation of Black Army Personnel, September 1945

Pacific Theater	206,512
China-India-Burma	23,802
Alaska Area	4,726
Africa-Middle East	585
Mediterranean Theater	43,727
Persian Gulf	80
Caribbean Defense	2,763
European Theater	181,620

Source: [Untitled Table], *The Negro Handbook, 1949*, 1949, p. 242. Primary source: Not specifically identified.

★ 1449 ★

The Military Services

Overseas Service: Theater of Operation of Black Troops in 1947 and 1948

	As of Jan. 1, 1947	As of March 1948
Total	60,348	23,395
Pacific Theater	35,414	1,106
Far East		13,222
Alaskan Dept.	2,907	334
European Theater	18,000	8,022
Mediterranean Theater	2,996	[1]
Caribbean Defense	350	335
Others	681	-

Source: "Negro Troops Serving Overseas," *The Negro Handbook, 1949*, 1949, p. 243. Primary source: Unspecified "occasional" official releases. *Note:* 1. The Mediterranean Theater (Italy) was evacuated in late 1947.

★ 1450 ★

The Military Services

Reenlistments: Military First Term Reenlistments, 1970-1975

Year	Black			White		
	Total eligible for re-enlistment[1]	Reenlistments		Total eligible for re-enlistment[1]	Reenlistments	
		Number	Percent of total		Number	Percent of total
1970	64,376	8,301	13	637,906	58,756	9
1972	24,580	7,271	30	303,301[2]	53,622[2]	18[2]
1975	26,884	13,724	51	177,472[2]	61,574[2]	35[2]

Source: "First Term Reenlistments of Servicemen for Selected Years: 1964 to 1975, "*The Social and Economic Status of the Black Population in the United States: An Historical View, 1790-1978,* 1979, p. 161. Primary source: U.S. Department of Defense. *Notes:* 1. Servicemen who have earned honorable status and otherwise demonstrated the qualities necessary for career service in the Armed Forces. Only first term servicemen are included. 2. Data include persons of "other" races.

★ 1451 ★

The Military Services

Servicemen Choosing To or Not To Reenlist, 1964-1967

	Reenlistments					
	Total eligible for reenlistments[1]		Number		Percent of total eligible	
	Negro	White	Negro	White	Negro	White
1964	24,501	295,339	11,216	59,384	46	20
1965	21,948	301,849	10,041	51,552	46	17
1966	23,202	335,456	10,615	60,271	46	18
1967	32,319	378,790	9,825	56,061	30	15

Source: "First Term Reenlistments of Servicemen, 1964-1967," Current Population Reports, Special Studies, Series P-23, No. 29. *The Social and Economic Status of the Black Population in the United States, 1969,* 1969, p. 87. Primary source: U.S. Department of Defense. *Notes:* 1. Servicemen who have earned honorable status and otherwise demonstrated the qualities necessary for career service in the Armed Forces. Only first-term servicemen are included.

★ 1452 ★

The Military Services

Servicemen Choosing To or Not To Reenlist, 1968-1970

Year	Inductees		Enlistees	
	Negro	White	Negro	White
1968	15	9	(NA)	(NA)
1969	14	11	21	14
1970	14	9	18	11

Source: "Reenlistment Rates of Servicemen: 1968 to 1970," Current Population Reports, Special Studies, Series P-23, No. 38. *The Social and Economic Status of the Black Population in the United States, 1970*, 1970, p. 137. Primary source: U.S. Department of Defense. *Notes:* NA Not available. Figures are for servicemen who have earned honorable status and otherwise demonstrated the qualities necessary for career service in the Armed Forces. Only first-term servicemen are included. Figures are reenlistment rates.

★ 1453 ★

The Military Services

The Air Force: Black Officers and Enlisted Men in Technical Positions, August 1945

Officers Total = 925.

Pilots - 563	
Pilot 1-E	130
Fighter Pilot 1-E	223
Bomber Pilot 2-E	1
Pilot 2-E	100
Fighter Pilot 2-E	2
Pilot B-25	89
Pilot B-24	1
Service Pilot 1-E	9
Flight Test Maintenance Off	7
Weather Officer Pilot	1
Navigators - 130	
Navigator	58
Navigator-Bombardier	72
Bombardiers - 189	
Bombardier	189
Communications Officer - 34	
Electronics	3
Radio Officer	1
Communications Officer	23
Signal Officer	2
Message Center Off., Cryptogram	1

[Continued]

★ 1453 ★

The Air Force: Black Officers and Enlisted Men in Technical Positions, August 1945

[Continued]

Maintenance Repair Air Signal Equipment	1
Signal Equipment Maintenance Repair Officer	1
Security Officer, Cryptogram	1
Communication Inspector	1
Weather Officers - 9	
Weather Engineer Survey	2
Weather Officer	7
ENLISTED MEN	
Radio Operators	657
Crew Chiefs	379
Radar Technicians	88
Airplane Engine Mechanics	1,369
Propeller Technicians	56

Source: "Negroes in the Army Air Forces, August 31, 1945," *Negro Year Book: A Review of Events Affecting Negro Life, 1941-1946*, 1947, p. 358. Primary source: War Department releases.

★ 1454 ★

The Military Services

The Army: Army Branch of Black Officers and Enlisted Personnel in 1948

	Officers	Enlisted
Total (Army Command)	991	53,433
Armored Force	0	496
General Officers	1	
General Staff Offs.	2	
Cavalry	21	354
Coast Artillery	22	1,632
Field Artillery	41	1,955
Infantry	301	10,945
Adjutant General	2	395
Chemical Corps	4	92
Corps of Engineers	60	4,912
Corps of Chaplains	55	
Military Police	22	1,179
Finance		1
Medical Corps		2,103
Dental	25	
Medical Corps	8	
Medical Service Corps	18	

[Continued]

★ 1454 ★

The Army: Army Branch of Black Officers and Enlisted Personnel in 1948

[Continued]

	Officers	Enlisted
Veterinary Corps	1	
Ordnance	45	2,132
Quartermaster	60	5,391
Signal Corps	18	480
Transportation	155	13,770
Chief Warrant Offs.	32	
Warrant Offs. Jun. Gr.	24	
Female		
Army Nurse Corps	66	
Women's Army Corps	8	292

Source: "Negro Personnel in the Army in the Various Staffs and Arms as of March 1948," *The Negro Handbook, 1949,* 1949, p. 243. Primary source: Unspecified "occasional" official releases.

★ 1455 ★

The Military Services

The Army: Black Officers After World War II, 1946

Brigadier General	1
Colonels	6
Lieutenant Colonels	16
Majors	47
Captains	322
First Lieutenants	824
Second Lieutenants	462
Warrant and Flight Officers	84
Total	1762
In Continental United States	1242
Assigned	
Army Air Forces	557
Army Ground Forces	175
Army Areas and Mil. Dept. of Washington	222[1]
Administration and Technical Services	264
War Department in Washington	24

Source: "Negro Officers in the Army by Ranks as of Aug. 1, 1946," *The Negro Handbook, 1949,* 1949, p. 244. Primary source: War Department release. *Notes:* 1. The 222 on duty in Army Areas and the Military Department of Washington comprised instructors, trainers, officers on staff duties, members of various corps - medical, chaplain, etc., and awaiting assignment.

★ 1456 ★

The Military Services

The Army: Deployment of Black Personnel, May, 1946

	Continental	Overseas	Worldwide
Infantry	7,057	2,076	9,133
Coast and Field Artillery	1,706	1,006	2,712
Engineers	7,429	13,450	20,879
Air Corps	31,605	3,401	35,006
Transportation Corps	12,501	5,307	17,808
Quartermaster Corps	19,135	24,213	43,348
All Others	39,697	18,800	58,497
TOTAL	119,130	68,253	187,383
Officers:			
Included in above totals			2,626
Including:			
Dental Corps Officers			29
Nurses			167
Other Medical Corps Officers			43
Chaplains			91
Serving Overseas		68,253	
Including:			
Pacific Theater		35,398	
China and India-Burma Theaters		1,392	
Alaskan Department		1,144	
European Theater		22,461	
Mediterranean Theater		2,540	
Caribbean Defense Command		721	

Source: [Untitled Table], *Negro Year Book: A Review of Events Affecting Negro Life, 1941-1946*, 1947, p. 366. Primary source: Unspecified releases.

★ 1457 ★

The Military Services

The Army: Deployment of Negroes, October 1946

Continental	
Army Air Forces	29,226
Army Ground Forces	16,589
Army Areas and Military District of Washington	16,513
Administrative and Technical Services	34,900
War Department Groups	608
Total Continental US	97,836

[Continued]

★ 1457 ★

The Army: Deployment of Negroes, October 1946

[Continued]

Overseas	
US Army Forces Pacific	31,416
US Army Forces European Theater	31,408
En Route US to Theaters	3,748
US Army Forces Mediterranean Theater	3,269
Alaskan Department	2,261
Caribbean Defense Command[1]	598
Commanding General, Army Air Forces[2]	495
Total Outside Continental US	73,195
Aggregate	171,031

Source: "Negro Strength of the Army," *Negro Year Book: A Review of Events Affecting Negro Life, 1941-1946*, 1947, p. 365. Primary source: Guzman, Jessie Parkhurst (Ed.), *Negro Year Book: A Review of Events Affecting Negro Life, 1941-1946*. Tuskegee Institute, AL: Department of Records and Research, 1947. *Notes:* 1. In the main Virgin Island and Puerto Rican Negroes. 2. Physically overseas but charged to the CG Army Air Forces, Washington and not to theater strength.

★ 1458 ★

The Military Services

The Army: Officers and Army Branch of Black Personnel, 1946-1948

	As of Jan. 1, 1946	As of May 1, 1946	As of Jan. 1, 1947	As of Aug. 1, 1947	As of Mar. 1, 1948
Total	372,369	187,383	122,037	56,184	54,434
Infantry	19,198	9,133	8,705	8,478	10,945
Coast and Field Artillery	6,517	2,712	4,252	2,669	1,632
Engineers	58,659	20,879	12,728	7,231	4,912
Air Corps	51,664	35,006	32,886	[1]	
Transportation Corps		17,808	20,785	16,257	13,770
Quartermaster Corps		43,348			5,391
All Others	191,718	58,497	42,681	21,549	17,784
OFFICERS: Commissioned, Flight, Warrant, in above totals-					
Total	4,743	2,646	1,403	945	991
Including:					
Dental Corps	79	29	28	29	25
Medical Corps	331		24[2]	9	8
Nurse Corps	318	167	93	72	66
Other Med. Dept. Officers		43	40	20	18
Chaplains	143	91	57	66	55
Others			1,185	749	579

Source: "Negro Personnel in the Postwar Armed Forces," *The Negro Handbook, 1949*, 1949, p. 243. Primary source: Official Government Reports and Releases. *Notes:* 1. Air Force was separated from the Army in July 1947. 2. As of April 1, 1947.

★ 1459 ★

The Military Services

The Army: Service Grades of Black Soldiers in 1940

Service Grade	Number
Commissioned officers	5
Warrant officers	11
Enlisted men	4,435
Total	4,451

Source: Adapted by the editors from "Commissioned Officers," "Warrant Officers," and "Enlisted men," *The Negro Handbook*, 1942, p. 65. Primary source: Report of the U.S. Adjutant General.

★ 1460 ★

The Military Services

The Army: Strength in July, 1941

	White	Colored
Regular Army		
Commissioned Officers	14,694	6
Warrant Officers	750	8
National Guard		
Officers	21,573	227
Warrant Officers	253	3
Reserves		
Officers	51,474	26
Enlisted Men		
Regular Army	462,112	26,888
National Guard	266,415	1,585
Selective Service Trainees	527,338	40,662
Totals		
Regular Army	476,798	26,902
National Guard	287,985	1,815
Selective Service Men	527,338	40,662

[Continued]

★ 1460 ★

The Army: Strength in July, 1941

[Continued]

	White	Colored
Reserves	51,474	26
Grand Total	1,343,595	69,405

Source: "Negro Strength of U.S. Army (as of July 31, 1941)," *The Negro Handbook*, 1942, p. 66.

★ 1461 ★

The Military Services

The Marine Services: Black Men in the Navy, Marine Corps, and Coast Guard in the Mid to Late 1940s

	Officers	Enlisted
NAVY		
Sept. 1, 1945	52	165,000
Jan. 1, 1947	2	19,783
Aug. 1, 1947	2	20,000
MARINE CORPS		
Sept. 1945	0	16,944
Aug. 1947	0	1,900
April 1948	1[1]	1,407
COAST GUARD		
Sept. 1945	972[2]	3,627
April 1948	219[2]	942

Source: "Negro Male Personnel," *The Negro Handbook, 1949*, 1949, p. 245. Primary source: Unspecified official releases. *Notes:* 1. On active duty. 2. Includes commissioned, warrant and petty officers, 4 of whom were commissioned officers in September 1945; number of commissioned in April 1948, not stated.

★ 1462 ★

The Military Services

The Navy: Black Enlisted Men in 1939 and 1940

At the end of the fiscal year, 1939, there were only 2,807 colored men enlisted in the Navy, out of a total personnel of 116,000. Of the 10,477 commissioned and warrant officers, none was colored.

[Continued]

★ 1462 ★

The Navy: Black Enlisted Men in 1939 and 1940
[Continued]

The U.S. Navy, on June 30, 1940, had an actual enlisted strength of 139,554 men, of whom 4,007 were colored. These figures were contained in the annual report of Rear Admiral Chester W. Nimitz, chief of the Bureau of Navigation, to the Secretary of the Navy, made public in late November.

Source: "Statistics," *The Negro Handbook*, 1942, p. 81. Primary source: Murray, Florence (Ed.), *The Negro Handbook*. New York: Wendell Malliet and Co., 1942.

★ 1463 ★

The Military Services

Women: Black Nurses in the Army and Navy, July 1945 - March 1948

"As of July, 1945, of the 512 Negro nurses in the Army, 9 were captains, 115 first lieutenants, and 388 second lieutenants. The number enrolled at specific dates after the end of hostilities were: January 1, 1946, 318; May 1, 1946, 167; January 1, 1947, 93; May 1, 1947, 88; March 1, 1948, 66...It was March, 1945, six months before the end of hostilities, that the first Negro nurse was sworn into the Navy. Three others were sworn in later."

Source: "Nurses," *The Negro Handbook, 1949*, 1949, p. 276. Primary source: Not specifically identified.

★ 1464 ★

The Military Services

Women: Black WAC and Air Force Officers and Enlisted Personnel, August 1945 - November 1947

	Officers	Enlisted
Aug. 31, 1945	115	3,456
Feb. 1, 1946	44	1,190
Jan. 1, 1947	9	363
May 1, 1947	9	366
Nov. 1, 1947	7	307
March 1948	8	292
Serving with Air Force		
Aug. 1, 1947	2	102
Nov. 1, 1947	2	116

Source: "Negro Personnel of the Women's Army Corps at Specified Dates," *The Negro Handbook, 1949*, 1949, p. 276. Primary source: Unspecified official release.

★ 1465 ★

The Military Services

Women: Black WAVES, SPARS, and Navy Nurses, 1945-1948

On V-J Day there were 70 WAVES on duty (2 of whom were officers) and 4 Navy nurses. On August 1, 1947, the Navy reported 6 WAVES (no officers) on duty and 2 nurses. The 6 WAVES were still on duty in April 1948, but only 1 nurse remained, who was in the Regular Navy, the first so appointed. Five SPARS were on duty in September 1945. The corps was demobilized prior to June 30, 1946.

Source: "Women," *The Negro Handbook, 1949*, 1949, p. 245. Primary source: Unspecified official releases.

★ 1466 ★

The Military Services

Women: Black Women on Duty at End of World War II, 1945-1948

At the end of the war, 68 WAVES were on active duty in the Navy, and by the end of 1947, 6 remained in the service. They remained on duty until early in 1948. Four SPARS were on duty with the Coast Guard at the termination of hostilities and the entire corps was demobilized by June 30, 1946. At the close of hostilities (Sept. 1945) there were 3,671 WACS on duty, with 115 officers; 850 were serving overseas.

Source: "Women in the Armed Forces," *The Negro Handbook, 1949*, 1949, p. 275. Primary source: Reports of the U.S. Armed Forces.

★ 1467 ★

The Military Services

Women: Black Women's Service Participation, by Type of Service, 1966, 1970, and 1975

Military service and status	Black women			Percent Black women of total women		
	1966	1970	1975	1966	1970	1975
All services, total	2,774	4,449	15,088	8.5	10.6	15.6
Percent	100.0	100.0	100.0	(X)	(X)	(X)
Officer	15.8	9.0	4.2	3.7	3.1	4.7
Enlisted	84.2	91.0	95.8	11.2	13.9	17.4
Army	1,455	2,386	8,252	10.7	13.7	19.5
Percent	100.0	100.0	100.0	(X)	(X)	(X)
Officer	15.0	7.4	2.7	4.8	3.3	4.8

[Continued]

★ 1467 ★

Women: Black Women's Service Participation, by Type of Service, 1966, 1970, and 1975

[Continued]

Military service and status	Black women			Percent Black women of total women		
	1966	1970	1975	1966	1970	1975
Enlisted	85.0	92.6	97.3	13.8	18.2	21.3
Air Force	862	1,297	4,457	9.4	9.2	14.8
Percent	100.0	100.0	100.0	(X)	(X)	(X)
Officer	22.5	13.9	6.6	4.6	3.8	5.9
Enlisted	77.5	86.1	93.4	13.5	11.8	16.5
Navy	317	430	1,842	3.9	5.3	8.8
Percent	100.0	100.0	100.0	(X)	(X)	(X)
Officer	8.5	9.3	5.8	0.9	1.4	2.9
Enlisted	91.5	90.7	94.2	5.6	7.3	10.0
Marine Corps	140	336	537	7.1	14.0	16.8
Percent	100.0	100.0	100.0	(X)	(X)	(X)
Officer	-	1.5	3.2	(X)	(X)	(X)
Enlisted	100.0	98.5	96.8	8.3	15.8	18.3

Source: "Participation of Black Women in the Armed Forces by Type of Service: 1966, 1970, and 1975," *The Social and Economic Status of the Black Population in the United States: An Historical View, 1790-1978*, 1979, p. 160. Primary source: U.S. Department of Defense. *Note:* - Represents or rounds to zero. X Not applicable.

Personnel Characteristics

★ 1468 ★

Age Distribution of Officers and Enlisted Personnel, 1974

Age and race	Total	Officer	Enlisted
BLACK			
Total, 17 years and over (thousands)	298	9	289
Percent	100	100	100
17 to 19 years[1]	21	-	22
20 to 24 years	43	14	44
25 to 34 years	23	49	22
35 to 44 years	12	33	12
45 to 64 years	1	5	1
65 years and over	-	-	-

[Continued]

★ 1468 ★

Age Distribution of Officers and Enlisted Personnel, 1974

[Continued]

Age and race	Total	Officer	Enlisted
WHITE			
Total 17 years and over (thousands)	1,798	287	1,511
Percent	100	100	100
17 to 19 years[1]	17	-	20
20 to 24 years	38	13	43
25 to 34 years	28	51	24
35 to 44 years	15	29	12
45 to 64 years	2	7	1
65 years and over	-	-	-

Source: "Age of Armed Forces Personnel, by Officer-Enlisted Status: June 1974," Current Population Reports, Special Studies, Series P-23, No. 54. *The Social and Economic Status of the Black Population in the United States, 1974,* 1975, p. 157. Primary source: U.S. Department of Defense. *Notes:* - Represents or rounds to zero. 1. Includes a negligible number of 16 year olds.

★ 1469 ★

Personnel Characteristics

Educational Attainment of Officers and Enlisted Personnel, 1974

Level of schooling and status	Total	Black	Percent black
TOTAL			
Total (thousands)[1]	2,151	298	14
Percent	100	100	100
Not a high school graduate	17	23	19
High school graduate (only)[2]	61	66	15
Some college	8	7	11
College degree	13	3	3
With graduate degree	3	1	2
OFFICERS			
Total (thousands)[1]	302	9	3
Percent	100	100	(X)
Not a high school graduate	-	-	2
High school graduate (only)[2]	5	7	4
Some college	10	13	3
College degree	81	77	3
With graduate degree	24	17	2

[Continued]

★ 1469 ★

Educational Attainment of Officers and Enlisted Personnel, 1974

[Continued]

Level of schooling and status	Total	Black	Percent black
ENLISTED			
Total (thousands)[1]	1,848	289	16
Percent	100	100	(X)
Not a high school graduate	19	24	19
High school graduate (only)[2]	70	68	15
Some college	8	6	12
College degree	1	1	7

Source: "Educational Attainment of Armed Forces Personnel, by Officer-Enlisted Status: June 1974" Current Population Reports, Special Studies, Series P- 23, No. 54. *The Social and Economic Status of the Black Population in the United States, 1974,* 1975, p. 158. Primary source: U.S. Department of Defense. *Notes:* - Rounds to zero. X Not applicable. 1. Includes about 10,000 officers (including 235 blacks) and 15,000 enlisted men (including 2,993 blacks) whose education was unknown. 2. Includes those persons who received a General Education Development certificate.

★ 1470 ★

Personnel Characteristics

Educational Attainment: Years of School Completed for First-Time Enlistees, 1972 and 1975

Enlistment status and years of school completed	All races		Black		White	
	1972	1975	1972	1975	1972	1975
ALL SERVICES[1]						
Total, first enlistment (thousands)[2]	412	408	60	73	347	327
Percent	100	100	100	100	100	100
Less than 4 years of high school[3]	28	28	30	31	27	28
High school: 4 years	60	64	63	62	60	64
College: 1 to 3 years	9	5	6	4	9	5
College: 4 years or more	3	1	1	1	4	1
ARMY						
Total, first enlistment (thousands)[2]	182	180	28	41	152	136
Percent	100	100	100	100	100	100
Less than 4 years of high school[3]	28	34	26	35	29	34
High school: 4 years	57	59	65	60	55	59

[Continued]

★ 1470 ★

Educational Attainment: Years of School Completed for First-Time Enlistees, 1972 and 1975

[Continued]

Enlistment status and years of school completed	All races		Black		White	
	1972	1975	1972	1975	1972	1975
College: 1 to 3 years	11	5	8	4	12	5
College: 4 years or more	4	2	1	1	4	2

Source: "First Enlistment of Armed Forces Personnel, by Years of School Completed: Fiscal Years 1972 and 1975, "*The Social and Economic Status of the Black Population in the United States: An Historical View, 1790-1978,* 1979, p. 161. Primary source: U.S. Department of Defense. *Notes:* 1. Includes Air Force, Marine Corps, and Navy, not shown separately. 2. Data are for persons who have never served in the Armed Forces (non- prior service accessions). Total includes category "education unknown" not shown separately. 3. Includes high school 1 to 3 years, elementary school, and no school years completed.

★ 1471 ★

Personnel Characteristics

Health and Disease: Syphilis Among Early Draftees and Volunteers, November, 1940-April, 1941

State	White Rate per 1,000	Negro Rate per 1,000
Alabama	24.2	193.5
Arizona	50.5	298.9
Arkansas	20.6	275.6
California	21.2	184.3
Colorado	16.3	166.7
Connecticut	6.1	186.4
Delaware	15.6	229.4
Florida	46.8	401.8
Georgia	33.7	292.7
Illinois	16.2	187.9
Indiana	23.3	234.6
Iowa	11.6	145.2
Kansas	16.6	212.2
Louisiana	32.0	247.2
Maine	25.9	[1]
Maryland	26.7	341.5
Massachusetts	5.5	76.6
Michigan	11.2	150.2
Minnesota	7.1	120.0
Mississippi	29.9	284.0
Missouri	21.9	201.7
Montana	12.0	[1]
Nebraska	7.9	166.7
Nevada	17.1	[1]
New Hampshire	6.1	[1]
New Jersey	10.0	164.3
New Mexico	44.0	364.3

[Continued]

★ 1471 ★

Health and Disease: Syphilis Among Early Draftees and Volunteers, November, 1940-April, 1941

[Continued]

State	White Rate per 1,000	Negro Rate per 1,000
New York	12.5	183.6
North Carolina	29.5	240.1
North Dakota	5.9	[1]
Ohio	16.0	174.7
Oklahoma	30.6	217.7
Pennsylvania	14.7	174.5
Rhode Island	7.8	106.8
South Carolina	43.9	296.5
South Dakota	6.8	[1]
Tennessee	34.5	264.2
Texas	42.6	292.2
Utah	6.1	137.9
Virginia	25.1	[1]
Washington	16.7	[1]
West Virginia	36.7	176.3
Wisconsin	5.1	147.9
Wyoming	14.2	[1]
District of Columbia	21.4	262.7
Total	18.5	247.7

Source: "Prevalence of Syphilis Among the First Million Selectees and Volunteers by Race, and State," *The Negro Handbook, 1944*, 1944, p. 133. Primary source: U.S. Public Health Service. *Notes:* Data for Idaho, Kentucky, Oregon and Vermont are limited to the material compiled and supplied by the state health departments and did not include information on race. Based on routine serologic blood tests given during general physical examinations. 1. Returns incomplete.

Selective Service

★ 1472 ★

Characteristics of Registrants: Defects per 1,000 Registrants in 1944

Defect	Bulletin No. 1 all[1] races[3]	Bulletin No. 20[2]		
		All races	White[4]	Negro
Total	1,356.8	1,583.3	1,595.0	1,493.9
Eyes	115.7	123.5	130.5	70.6
Ears	44.5	50.1	54.0	20.0

[Continued]

★ 1472 ★

Characteristics of Registrants: Defects per 1,000 Registrants in 1944

[Continued]

Defect	Bulletin No. 1 all[1] races[3]	Bulletin No. 20[2]		
		All races	White[4]	Negro
Teeth	140.3	167.8	176.9	98.5
Mouth and gums	63.9	84.2	81.3	106.3
Nose	68.9	81.5	89.0	24.1
Throat	66.3	81.5	81.2	84.0
Lungs	16.4	16.2	17.1	8.6
Tuberculosis	5.7	9.7	10.3	5.2
Cardiovascular	100.4	83.1	84.6	71.8
Blood and blood-forming	1.0	1.3	1.4	.4
Hernia	64.6	79.7	83.0	54.5
Kidney and urinary	14.0	9.0	9.2	7.9
Abdominal viscera	12.2	44.5	48.3	14.7
Genitalia	59.0	81.3	80.0	91.5
Syphilis	27.5	30.8	11.7	176.7
Gonorrhea and other venereal	7.4	7.3	3.4	36.5
Skin	115.8	88.0	94.0	42.2
Hemorrhoids	30.6	35.1	36.5	24.8
Varicose veins	26.7	32.1	33.6	20.4
Educational deficiency	3.6	21.2	12.4	89.0
Mental deficiency	8.4	15.3	15.7	12.1
Mental disease	18.2	23.7	25.7	7.8
Neurological	22.8	22.4	23.9	11.0
Musculoskeletal	101.3	113.9	119.3	73.8
Feet	145.0	172.4	158.9	275.7
Endocrine	16.0	19.7	21.3	7.4
Neoplasms	11.3	14.1	14.2	13.0
Infectious and parasitic	.4	.6	.7	.2
Underweight, overweight, and other	48.9	73.3	76.9	46.0

Source: "Rate of All Recorded Defects Per 100,000 Registrants Examined, by Race," *Negro Year Book: A Review of Events Affecting Negro Life, 1941-1946*, 1947, p. 331. Primary source: United States Congress. Senate Subcommittee of the Committee on Education, Part 5. A Resolution Authorizing an Investigation of the Educational and Physical Fitness of the Civilian Population as Related to National Defense. Hearings, 78th Congress, 2nd Session on S. Res. 74, July 10, 11, and 12, 1944. Washington, United States Government Printing Office, 1944, p. 1627. *Notes:* 1. Based on sample of forms 200 covering 19,923 registrants examined at local boards November 1940 through May 1941. 2. Based on sample of forms 200 covering 121,966 registrants examined at local boards November 1940 through September 1941. 3. Race breakdown not available. 4. Includes all races other than Negro.

★ 1473 ★

Selective Service

Disqualifications of Selective Service Draftees, Acceptances and Rejections in 1966 and 1967

	Negro		White	
	1966	1967	1966	1967
Number examined (thousands)	173	96	1,436	622
Percent	100	100	100	100
Accepted	43	50	65	61
Rejected	58	50	35	39
Mental reasons	43	27	8	7
Medical reasons	13	17	26	30
Administrative reasons[1]	2	2	1	1
Mentally and medically disqualified	(NA)	4	(NA)	1

Source: "Results of Pre-Induction Examinations of Draftees by Selective Service, 1966 and 1967," Current Population Reports, Special Studies, Series P-23, No. 29. *The Social and Economic Status of the Black Population in the United States, 1969,* 1969, p. 84. Primary source: U.S. Department of Defense, Office of Surgeon General. *Notes:* NA Not available. Figures for 1966 and 1967 are not strictly comparable due to a change made in the Fall of 1966 in the mental and medical qualifications for service in the Armed Forces. 1. Those rejected for administrative reasons include a few aliens and persons with significant criminal records, anti-social tendencies, such as alcoholism or drug addiction, or other traits which would make them unfit in a military environment.

★ 1474 ★

Selective Service

Disqualifications: Disqualifications, by Reason for, and Acceptable Draftees, 1966

[**Number in thousands**. Includes Puerto Rico, Canal Zone, Guam, Mariana Islands, and Virgin Islands].

STATUS	1966					
	Number			Percent		
	Total	White	Negro	Total	White	Negro
Examined	1,609	1,436	173	100.0	100.0	100.0
Found acceptable	1,004	931	73	62.4	64.8	42.5
Disqualified	605	506	99	37.6	35.2	57.5
Medically disqualified only	386	365	21	24.0	25.3	12.5
Failed mental requirements only	176	108	68	10.9	7.6	39.2
Failed mental test only	111	64	47	6.9	4.5	27.1
Trainability limited	65	44	21	4.0	3.1	12.1

[Continued]

★ 1474 ★

Disqualifications: Disqualifications, by Reason for, and Acceptable Draftees, 1966

[Continued]

STATUS	1966					
	Number			Percent		
	Total	White	Negro	Total	White	Negro
Failed mental test and medically disqualified	23	16	7	1.5	1.1	4.2
Administratively disqualified	20	17	3	1.2	1.2	1.6

Source: "Status of Selective Service Draftees Examined for Military Service, 1950 to 1966, and by Race, 1966," *Statistical Abstract of the United States,* 1967, p. 269. Primary source: Dept. of the Army, Office of the Surgeon General; *Results of the Examination of Youths for Military Service, 1966, Supplement to Health of the Army. Notes:* 1. Examines who failed minimum requirements on Armed Forces Qualifications Test (AFQT) or its equivalent (ECFA) administered to Spanish-speaking examinees in Puerto Rico. 2. Examines classified as mental group IV on basis of AFQT but who failed to meet additional aptitude requirements effective in August 1958 and called Army Classification Battery (ACB) test until mid-September 1961 and Army Qualifications Battery (AQB) since then. Also includes examinees in Puerto Rico tested with ECFA who failed the English Reading Test (ERT). The AQB requirements were raised in May 1963 and lowered in November 1965; April 1966; October 1966; and December 1966.

★ 1475 ★

Selective Service

Disqualifications: Reasons for Rejection in 1944

Principal causes for rejection[1]	Number			Percent		
	Total	White[2]	Negro	Total	White[2]	Negro
Total	4,217,000	3,393,000	824,000	100.0	100.0	100.0
Manifestly disqualifying defects	443,800	383,600	60,200	10.5	11.3	7.3
Mental disease	701,700	622,400	79,300	16.6	18.3	9.6
Mental deficiency[3]	582,100	322,700	259,400	13.8	9.5	31.5
Physical defects	2,426,500	2,013,400	413,100	57.6	59.4	50.1
Musculoskeletal	316,300	281,000	35,300	7.5	8.3	4.3
Syphilis	283,800	115,000	168,800	6.7	3.4	20.5
Cardiovascular	273,300	228,700	44,600	6.5	6.7	5.4
Hernia	238,400	211,900	26,500	5.7	6.3	3.2
Neurological	214,800	192,800	22,000	5.1	5.7	2.7
Eyes	212,700	188,700	24,000	5.0	5.6	2.9
Ears	162,900	158,300	4,609	3.9	4.7	.6
Tuberculosis	113,200	101,700	11,500	2.7	3.0	1.4
Lungs	72,800	64,100	8,700	1.7	1.9	1.0
Underweight and overweight	62,200	57,900	4,300	1.5	1.7	.5
Feet	54,000	42,000	12,000	1.3	1.2	1.5
Abdominal viscera	53,600	51,200	2,400	1.3	1.5	.3
Kidney and urinary	44,200	40,100	4,100	1.0	1.2	.5
Varicose veins	42,700	38,000	4,700	1.0	1.1	.6
Genitalia	42,300	33,100	9,200	1.0	1.0	1.1
Endocrine	40,300	38,600	1,700	1.0	1.1	1.2
Teeth	36,100	33,800	2,300	.9	1.0	.3
Neoplasms	26,100	23,700	2,400	.6	.7	.3
Skin	26,000	23,100	2,900	.6	.7	.3
Nose	25,400	24,300	1,100	.6	.7	.3

[Continued]

★ 1475 ★

Disqualifications: Reasons for Rejection in 1944

[Continued]

Principal causes for rejection[1]	Number			Percent		
	Total	White[2]	Negro	Total	White[2]	Negro
Gonorrhea and other venereal	18,300	7,300	11,000	.4	.2	1.3
Hemorrhoids	17,200	14,400	2,800	.4	.4	.3
Mouth and gums	11,100	10,300	800	.3	.3	.1
Infections and parasitic	4,500	3,900	600	.1	.1	.1
Throat	4,100	3,500	600	.1	.1	.1
Blood and blood-forming	3,900	3,400	500	.1	.1	.1
Other medical	26,300	22,600	3,700	.6	.7	.4
Nonmedical	62,900	50,900	12,000	1.5	1.5	1.5

Source: "Estimated Principal Causes for Rejection of Registrants 18-37 Years of Age in Class IV-F and Classes with F Designation, June 1, 1944," *Negro Year Book: A Review of Events Affecting Negro Life, 1941-1946*, 1947, p. 329. Primary source: United States Congress. Senate, Subcommittee of the Committee on Education and Labor. A Resolution Authorizing an Investigation of the Educational and Physical Fitness of the Civilian Population as Related to National Defense. Part 5. Hearings, 78th Congress. 2d Sessions on S. Res. 74, July 10, 11, and 12, 1944. Washington, United States Government Printing Office, 1944. p. 1625. *Notes:* 1. Includes registrants in classes II-A, B and C with F designation. 2. Includes all races other than Negro. 3. Includes (1) registrants with more than one disqualifying defect who were rejected for educational deficiency prior to June 1943: (2) registrants rejected for failure to meet minimum intelligence standards beginning June 1, 1943; (3)morons, imbeciles,and idiots rejected November 1940-April 1944.

★ 1476 ★

Selective Service

Disqualifications: Reasons for Rejection in 1945

Principal Causes for Rejection[1]	Number[2]	Percent
Total	919,000	100.0
Manifestly disqualifying defects	67,700	7.4
Mental disease	97,800	10.6
Mental deficiency	308,600	33.6
Physical defects	430,600	46.9
Musculoskeletal	40,200	4.4
Cardiovascular	51,300	5.6
Hernia	29,800	3.2
Syphilis	154,800	16.8
Neurological	24,300	2.6
Eyes	26,500	2.9
Ears	5,400	0.6
Tuberculosis	13,100	1.4
Lungs	10,100	1.1
Underweight and overweight	4,400	0.5
Feet	14,800	1.6
Abdominal viscera	2,600	0.3
Kidney and urinary	5,200	0.6
Varicose veins	5,300	0.6
Genitalia	9,900	1.1
Endocrine	1,700	0.2
Teeth	2,300	0.2

[Continued]

★ 1476 ★

Disqualifications: Reasons for Rejection in 1945

[Continued]

Principal Causes for Rejection[1]	Number[2]	Percent
Neoplasms	2,700	0.3
Skin	3,500	0.4
Nose	1,100	0.1
Hemorrhoids	3,000	0.3
Gonorrhea and other venereal	11,100	1.2
Mouth and gums	800	0.1
Infections and parasitic	600	0.1
Throat	600	0.1
Blood and blood-forming	500	0.1
Other medical	2,000	0.5
Nonmedical	14,300	1.5

Source: "Estimated Principal Causes for Rejection of Registrants 18-37 Years of Age in Class IV-F and Classes with "F" Designation, August 1, 1945, (Preliminary)," *Negro Year Book: A Review of Events Affecting Negro Life, 1941-1946*, 1947, p. 330. Primary source: National Headquarters, Selective Service System. *Notes:* 1. Includes registrants in Classes II-A, B and C with "F" designation. 2. Includes (1) registrants with more than one disqualifying defect who were rejected for educational deficiency prior to June 1, 1943: (2) registrants rejected for failure to meet minimum intelligence standards beginning June 1, 1943; (3)morons, imbeciles,and idiots rejected November 1940-July 1945.

★ 1477 ★

Selective Service

Minority Group Inductees, November 1940, through July 1943

	Number	Per Cent of Minority Groups
Negroes	624,426	89.3
Chinese	9,259	1.3
Japanese	5,963	0.9
Hawaiian	537	0.1
American Indian	13,749	2.0
Filipino	9,401	1.3
Puerto Rican	14,593	2.1
Others	20,872	3.0
	698,800	100.0

Source: "Induction of Racial Groups November, 1940, through July, 1943," *The Negro Handbook, 1944*, 1944, p. 130. Primary source: Colonel Campbell C. Johnson, Executive Assistant to Director of Selective Service. Published by permission.

Veterans

★ 1478 ★

Educational Attainment of Enlisted Reservists Trained Under GI Bill

Subject	Negro	All other races
Total enlisted reservists[1]	4,732	4,558
Percent who had entered training	18	24
Type of training:		
All types	100	100
College	57	68
Below college schooling	35	23
On-the-job-training	8	10

Source: "Percent of Enlisted Reservists who Entered Training Under Veterans Administration Programs," Current Population Reports, Special Studies, Series P-23, No. 38. *The Social and Economic Status of the Black Population in the United States, 1970*, 1970, p. 138. Primary source: Veterans Administration. *Notes:* 1. Veterans who entered training under Veterans Administration Programs 6 to 12 months after return to civilian life. First term enlisted men separated from the Armed Forces, July to December 1968.

★ 1479 ★

Veterans

Employment: Veteran Status of Unemployed Men, 1972-1974

[**In thousands, except as indicated**. Annual average for periods indicated].

ITEM	TOTAL			WHITE			NEGRO AND OTHER		
	1972	1973	1974	1972	1973	1974	1972	1973	1974
Unemployed men, number:									
16 years old and over, total	2,635	2,240	2,668	2,160	1,818	2,146	475	423	521
20-34 years old, total	1,075	938	1,159	871	749	920	204	189	239
Percent of total, 16 and over	40.8	41.9	43.4	40.3	41.2	42.9	42.9	44.7	45.9
Vietnam-era veterans[1]	328	266	310	276	224	249	52	42	61
Post-Korean peacetime veterans[2]	54	40	35	49	36	29	6	4	7
Nonveterans[3]	690	632	813	545	488	641	145	143	172
Unemployed rate, men:[4]									
16 years old and over, total	4.9	4.1	4.8	4.5	3.7	4.3	8.9	7.6	9.1
20-34 years old, total	5.7	4.7	5.6	5.2	4.2	5.0	9.8	8.4	10.3
Vietnam-era veterans[1]	6.7	5.0	5.3	6.2	4.6	4.7	11.7	8.4	11.3

[Continued]

★ 1479 ★

Employment: Veteran Status of Unemployed Men, 1972-1974

[Continued]

ITEM	TOTAL			WHITE			NEGRO AND OTHER		
	1972	1973	1974	1972	1973	1974	1972	1973	1974
Post-Korean peacetime veterans[2]	2.8	2.5	2.9	2.6	2.4	2.5	5.3	4.6	9.4
Nonveterans[3]	5.8	4.9	6.0	5.2	4.3	5.4	9.6	8.6	10.1

Source: "Unemployed Men, by Age, Veterans Status, and Race: 1972 to 1974," *Statistical Abstract of the United States, 1975*, p. 332. Primary source: U.S. Bureau of the Labor Statistics, unpublished data. *Notes:* 1. Served after August 4, 1964. 2. Served between Feb. 1, 1955, and August 4, 1964. 3. Either never served in Armed Forces, or served only in peacetime prior to June 27, 1950. 4. Percent of male civilian labor force.

★ 1480 ★

Veterans

Membership in Veteran's Organizations with No Color Bar, c. 1946-47

Organization	Home Office	No. of Members	Negro Members
Veterans			
American Gold Star Mothers Inc.	Washington	8,000	?
American Veterans Committee	New York	6,000	?
Army & Navy Union USA	Atlantic City	25,000	2,000

Source: "Class A Organizations—Veterans," *The Negro Handbook, 1946-1947*, 1947, pp. 206-207. Primary source: Murray, Florence (Ed.), *The Negro Handbook, 1946-1947*. New York: Current Books, Inc., A.A. Wyn, Pub., 1947.

★ 1481 ★

Veterans

Unemployed Male Veterans 20- to 29-Years-Old, 1969 and 1970

[Annual averages]

Age and year	Negro and other races		White	
	Vietnam veterans	Nonveterans	Vietnam veterans	Nonveterans
Total, 20 to 29 years:				
1969	7.5	6.2	4.3	3.2
1970	11.6	9.5	6.4	5.5
20 to 24 years:				
1969	10.0	8.1	5.1	4.5
1970	15.1	11.9	8.7	7.4

[Continued]

★ 1481 ★

Unemployed Male Veterans 20- to 29-Years-Old, 1969 and 1970

[Continued]

Age and year	Negro and other races		White	
	Vietnam veterans	Nonveterans	Vietnam veterans	Nonveterans
25 to 29 years:				
1969	3.6	4.1	3.2	1.7
1970	7.5	6.7	4.0	3.4

Source: "Unemployment Rates of Men 20 to 29 Years Old, by Veteran-Nonveteran Status and Age: 1969 and 1970," Current Population Reports, Special Studies, Series P-23, No. 38. *The Social and Economic Status of the Black Population in the United States, 1970*, 1970, p. 138. Primary source: U.S. Department of Labor, Bureau of Labor Statistics.

Wartime Honors

★ 1482 ★

The Navy: Ships Named for Black Persons and Black Colleges, 1941-1946

Designation	Number
Named for Negro Americans who lost their lives during WW II	18[1]
Named for Negro colleges	4[1]
Named for Negro mess attendant posthumously decorated for heroism	1[2]
TOTAL	23

Source: Adapted by the editors from "Naming and Launching of Ships," *Negro Yearbook*, 1941-1946, p. 375. Primary source: Guzman, Jessie Parkhurst (Ed.), *Negro Year Book: A Review of Events Affecting Negro Life, 1941-1946*. Tuskegee Institute, AL: Department of Records and Research, 1947. *Notes:* 1. Liberty ships. 2. Destroyer.

Wartime Service

★ 1483 ★

The Civil War: Black Persons Recruited by the Government, by State, 1861-1865

State	
Alabama	4,969
Arkansas	5,526
Colorado	95
Florida	1,044
Georgia	3,486
Louisiana	24,052
Mississippi	17,869
North Carolina	5,035
South Carolina	5,462
Tennessee	20,133
Texas	47
Virginia	5,723

Source: [Untitled Table], *Negro Year Book: An Annual Encyclopedia of the Negro, 1937-1938*, 1937, p. 318. Primary source: Livermore, *Opinions of the Founders of the Republic on Negroes as Slaves, as Citizens and as Solider,* Appendix A., C. and D.; Williams, *History of the Negro Race in America*, Vol. II. Chapter II; Washington, *The Story of the Negro,* Vol. I, Chapter XV.

★ 1484 ★

Wartime Service

The Civil War: Blacks who Volunteered, by State, 1861-1865

States	
Connecticut	1,764
Delaware	954
District of Columbia	3,269
Illinois	1,811
Indiana	1,537
Iowa	440
Kansas	2,080
Kentucky	23,703
Maine	104
Maryland	8,718
Massachusetts	3,966
Michigan	1,387
Minnesota	114
Missouri	8,344

[Continued]

★ 1484 ★

The Civil War: Blacks who Volunteered, by State, 1861-1865

[Continued]

States	
New Hampshire	125
New Jersey	1,185
New York	4,125
Ohio	5,092
Pennsylvania	8,162
Rhode Island	1,837
Vermont	120
West Virginia	196
Wisconsin	165
Total	78,779

Source: "Negro Volunteer Troops by State," *Negro Year Book: An Annual Encyclopedia of the Negro, 1937-1938,* 1937, pp. 317-318. Primary source: Livermore, *Opinions of the Founders of the Republic on Negroes as Slaves, as Citizens and as Soliders,* Appendix A., C. and D.; Williams, *History of the Negro Race in America,* Vol. II. Chapter II; Washington, *The Story of the Negro,* Vol. I, Chapter XV.

★ 1485 ★

Wartime Service

The Civil War: Soldiers and Regiments, 1861-1865

Something like 178,975 Negro soldiers were employed in the Civil War. These made up 161 regiments, of which 141 were infantry, seven were cavalry, twelve were heavy artillery, and one light artillery.

The first colored regiments to be organized were the First South Carolina, in which the first enlistments were made May 9, 1862; the First Louisiana Native Guards, September 27, 1862; the Fifty-fourth Massachusetts, February 9, 1863; the Second Carolina Volunteers, February 23, 1863.

Source: "The Civil War," *Negro Year Book: An Annual Encyclopedia of the Negro, 1937-1938,* 1937, p. 317. Primary source: Livermore, *Opinions of the Founders of the Republic on Negroes as Slaves, as Citizens and as Solider,* Appendix A., C. and D.; Williams, *History of the Negro Race in America,* Vol. II. Chapter II; Washington, *The Story of the Negro,* Vol. I, Chapter XV.

★ 1486 ★

Wartime Service

The Early Wars: Black Participation in Armed Forces during 18th and 19th Centuries

War	No. Negro Troops	Comment
Revolutionary War	3,000 Army[1]	Estimate of 35 Negro soldiers in each white regiment. plus some all Negro companies/ regiments.
War of 1812	At least 2,500 (Army & Navy)	Includes 1/10 of crews for Great Lakes vessels and 2,000 Army enlistees.
War of the Rebellion	178,975 (Army)	Includes 161 regiments.
Spanish-American War	[2]	Includes 4 Negro regiments.

Source: Compiled by the editors from "Part Six, Negro Soldiers and Heroes," *Negro Year Book and Annual Encyclopedia of the Negro*, 1913, pp. 102-105. Primary source: Unspecified "official report." *Notes:* 1. Estimate. 2. Number not given.

★ 1487 ★

Wartime Service

The Korean War: Courts Martial and the Disposition of Cases, 1950-1952

Disposition	Number by Race	
	Negro	White
Accused	60	8
Charges Withdrawn	23	2
Charge reduced to AWOL	1	0
Acquitted	4	4
Sentenced	32	2
Death	1	0
Life	15	0
50 years	1	0
25 years	2	0
20 years	3	0
15 years	1	0
10 years	7	0

[Continued]

★ 1487 ★

The Korean War: Courts Martial and the Disposition of Cases, 1950-1952

[Continued]

Disposition	Number by Race	
	Negro	White
5 years	2	1
3 years	0	1

Source: "Summary of Courts Martial in Korea: Alleged Violations of 75th Article of War," *1952 Negro Year Book: A Review of Events Affecting Negro Life,* 1952, p. 149. Primary source: Not specifically identified.

★ 1488 ★

Wartime Service

The Navy: Black Officers from Pearl Harbor Day through December 1946

Male-54	
Lieutenant Commander	1
Lieutenant	4
Lieutenant, Junior Grade	19
Ensign	25
Chief Warrant Officer	3
Commanding Officer	2
Female-6	
Lieutenant, Junior Grade	1
Ensign (includes 4 nurses)	5

Source: "Negro Strength of the Navy," *Negro Year Book: A Review of Events Affecting Negro Life, 1941-1946,* 1947, p. 375. Primary source: Bureau of Naval Personnel.

★ 1489 ★

Wartime Service

World War I and II: Comparison of Black Army Personnel in World Wars I and II

By comparison, approximately 515,700 more Negroes were accepted by the Army in World War II than in World War I. Altogether, 404,348 individuals who claimed to be of Negro race served in the United States Army during World War I: 1,353 were commissioned officers, 402,971 were enlisted men, 15 were Army nurses, and 9 were field clerks. Of the total number of these troops, approximately 840 officers and 194,000 enlisted men served in the American Expeditionary Forces.

The following figures, given to the nearest hundred, represent the total number of Negroes who served in the Army of the United States from December 1, 1941, through August 31, 1945:

Male Officers	8,000
Female Officers	600
Male Enlisted Personnel	905,000
Female Enlisted Personnel	6,400
Total	920,000

Source: "Comparison of Negro Strength of the Army, World War I and II," *Negro Year Book: A Review of Events Affecting Negro Life, 1941-1946,* 1947, p. 367. Primary source: Not specifically identified.

★ 1490 ★

Wartime Service

World War I: Army Registrants and Inductions, 1917-1918

Race	Total No.	Percent of Total Registrants	Inducted June 17, 1917 to November 11, 1918	Percent of Total Registrants
Black	2,290,527	9.63	367,710	34.10
White	21,489,470	90.37	2,299,157	24.04

Source: Adapted by the editors from "Colored and White Registrants and Inductions Compared by States," *Negro Year Book: An Annual Encyclopedia of the Negro, 1918-1919,* 1919, p. 216-217. Primary source: Work, Monroe N. (Ed.), *Negro Year Book: An Annual Encyclopedia of the Negro, 1918-1919.* Tuskegee Institute, Ala.: The Negro Year Book Pub. Co., 1919.

★ 1491 ★

Wartime Service

World War II: Black Service in All Armed Forces Branches, 1941-1945

Negroes in all branches of the armed forces	7.7 percent
Negroes in the Army[1]	9.0 percent
Negroes in the Navy	5.9 percent
Negroes in the Marine Corps	3.7 percent
Negroes in the Coast Guard	2.2 percent

Source: "Accumulated Percentages of Negroes who Served in the Armed Forces in World War II," *The Negro Handbook, 1949*, 1949, p. 247. Primary source: Address at Founder's Day celebration at Hampton Institute on February 1, 1948, by Col. Campbell C. Johnson, who served as executive assistant to director of Selective Service. *Note:* 1. Including the Air Force.

Chapter 12
MISCELLANY

Attitudes, Values, and Behavior

★ 1492 ★

Attitudes/Opinions: Personal Preference of Editors of Publications for Black People of Terms to Indicate Black Ethnicity, 1973

	One choice	Two or more choices[1]	Totals
Black	16	8	24
black	8	2	10
Negro	7	5	12
Afro-American	6	2	8
African-American	0	2	2
colored	0	0	0

Source: Smythe, *The Black American Reference Book,* "Nomenclature Preferred by 46 Publications Addressed to Persons of African Descent, 1973," 1976, p. xiv. Primary source: Smythe, Mabel M., ed. *The Black American Reference Book.* Sponsored by the Phelps-Stokes Fund. Englewood Cliffs, N.J.: Prentice-Hall, Inc., 1976. *Note:* 1. Each approved term is counted once for each publication using it.

★ 1493 ★

Attitudes, Values, and Behavior

Attitudes/Opinions: Terms Preferred by Publications for Black persons to Indicate Black Ethnicity, 1973

Total Publications	Approved Terms							
	One Only		Two		Three or More		Total	
	Number	Percent	Number	Percent	Number	Percent	Number	Percent
	22	100.0	18	100.0	6	100.0	46	100.0
Terms Used:								
Black	14	63.6	16	88.9	6	100.0	36	78.3
black	8	36.4	7	38.9	5	83.3	21	45.7
Negro	-		8	44.4	6	100.0	15	32.6
Afro-American	-		5	27.8	4	66.6	9	19.6
African-American	-		-		4	66.6	4	8.7
colored	-		-		3	50.0	3	6.5

Source: Smythe, *The Black American Reference Book*, "Nomenclature Preferred by 46 Publications Addressed to Persons of African Descent, 1973," 1976, p. xiii. Primary source: Smythe, Mabel M., ed. *The Black American Reference Book.* Sponsored by the Phelps-Stokes Fund. Englewood Cliffs, N.J.: Prentice-Hall, Inc., 1976. *Notes:* Some predominantly white publications, including *The New York Times,* employ *Negro or black,* according to the writer's preference.

★ 1494 ★

Attitudes, Values, and Behavior

Attitudes: Black Judgments on Pace of Struggle for Civil Rights (in percentages), 1963, 1966, and 1969

	1963	1966	1969
THE PACE IS:			
About right	31	35	22
Too fast	3	4	7
Too slow	51	43	59

Source: Goldman, "Black Impatience," *Report from Black America*, 1969, p. 48. Primary source: *Newsweek*, July 29, 1963, August 22, 1966, and 1969 [date unspecified].

★ 1495 ★

Attitudes, Values, and Behavior

Attitudes: Middle Class Blacks' Beliefs in Selected Areas in the 1960s

	1963	1966	1969
Believe whites want to keep Negroes down	19	39	47
Don't think whites have got better	25	34	47
Don't think whites will get better	9	18	32
Feel whites will budge only if blacks force them to	16	23	44
Think blacks must band together against whites	X	13	32
Approve the idea of black power	X	26	59
Feel the NAACP is doing an excellent job	79	58	20
Feel the Urban League is doing an excellent job	37	32	19
Think violence will be necessary	9	21	33
Believe the riots have helped	X	31	50
Would like a separate black nation	0	2	18
Don't think the U.S. is worth fighting for	7	8	20

Source: Goldman, "The Black Mood II: The Middle Class," *Report from Black America*, 1969, p. 207. Primary source: *Newsweek*, July 29, 1963, August 22, 1966, and 1969 [date unspecified].

★ 1496 ★

Attitudes, Values, and Behavior

Attitudes: Negro, Colored, Black or Afro-American? Designations Preferred by Black People (in percentages), 1963, 1966, and 1969

The Most Liked	Total	The Most Disliked	Total
Negroes	38	Colored People	31
Colored	20	Blacks	25
Blacks	19	Negroes	11
Afro-American	10	Afro-American	11
Don't care	6	Don't care	6

Source: Goldman, "Our Rightful Name," *Report from Black America*, 1969, p. 155. Primary source: *Newsweek*, July 29, 1963, August 22, 1966, and 1969 [date unspecified].

★ 1497 ★

Attitudes, Values, and Behavior

Attitudes: Preferences of Black People for Integrated or Segregated Neighborhoods (in percentages), 1963, 1966, and 1969

	1963	1966	1969
PER CENT WHO PREFER:			
A mixed neighborhood	64	68	74
A Negro neighborhood	20	17	16

Source: "Goldman, "Housing: To Live Next Door," *Report from Black America*, 1969, p. 179. Primary source: *Newsweek*, July 29, 1963, August 22, 1966, and 1969 [date unspecified].

★ 1498 ★

Attitudes, Values, and Behavior

Attitudes: Willingness of Black Persons to be Civil Rights Activists (in percentages), 1963, 1966, and 1969

	1963	1966	1969
WOULD YOU:			
Sit in	49	52	40
March	51	54	44
Picket	46	49	41
Boycott a store	62	69	57
Go to jail	47	45	33

Source: "Goldman, "The Activists: Ready or Not," *Report from Black America*, 1969, p. 88. Primary source: *Newsweek*, July 29, 1963, August 22, 1966, and 1969 [date unspecified].

★ 1499 ★

Attitudes, Values, and Behavior

Middle Class Blacks' Beliefs in Selected Areas in the 1960s

	1963	1966	1969
Believe whites want to keep Negroes down	19	39	47
Don't think whites have got better	25	34	47
Don't think whites will get better	9	18	32
Feel whites will budge only if blacks force them to	16	23	44
Think blacks must band together against whites	X	13	32
Approve the idea of black power	X	26	59

[Continued]

★ 1499 ★

Middle Class Blacks' Beliefs in Selected Areas in the 1960s

[Continued]

	1963	1966	1969
Feel the NAACP is doing an excellent job	79	58	20
Feel the Urban League is doing an excellent job	37	32	19
Think violence will be necessary	9	21	33
Believe the riots have helped	X	31	50
Would like a separate black nation	0	2	18
Don't think the U.S. is worth fighting for	7	8	20

Source: Goldman, "The Black Mood in the Middle Class," *Report from Black America,* 1969, p. 207. Primary source: *Newsweek,* July 29, 1963, August 22, 1966, and 1969 [date unspecified].

Creative Works

★ 1500 ★

Publications: Books Published by Black Authors, 1898-1928

Category	Number
Social Analysis and Discussion	12
The Negro's Cultural Background	8
Historical Studies	8
Collections of Negro Poetry	3
Negro Poets	20
Fiction and Belles Lettres	27
Negro Biography	21
Negro Music	16
Magazines	7

Source: Compiled by the editors from Locke, *A Decade of Negro Self-Expression,* 1928, pp. 9-20. Bound with Slater Fund. *Occasional Papers.* Nos. 21-27. Primary source: Locke, A. *A decade of Negro Self-Expression,* [Publication information not given]: 1928; Bound in Slater Fund. *Occasional Papers.* Nos. 21-27. [Publication information not given.].

People in Institutions

★ 1501 ★

Number/Percent: Characteristics of Persons in Correctional, Mental and Dependency Institutions, 1940-1970 - I

[For definition of institutions, see text].

Year	Total	Sex		Race		
		Male	Female	White	Negro	Other
ALL INMATES						
1970[1]	2,126,719	1,126,327	1,000,392	1,785,085	318,991	22,643
1960[2,3]	1,886,967	1,116,825	770,142	1,581,611	305,356	
1950	1,566,846	949,628	617,218	1,351,152	215,694	
INMATES, 15 YEARS AND OVER						
1970[1]	1,990,644	1,040,381	950,263	1,678,055	292,191	20,398
1960[2,3]	1,736,830	1,026,305	710,525	1,455,204	281,626	
1950	1,424,434	867,455	556,979	1,221,060	203,374	
1940	1,156,298	755,290	401,008	989,839	166,459	

Source: "Inmates of Institutions by Sex, Race, Age, and Type of Institution: 1940 to 1970,; U.S. Bureau of the Census. *Historical Statistics of the United States: Colonial Times to 1970, Part I.* Bicentennial Edition, 1975, p. 43. Primary source: U.S. Bureau of the Census. *Historical Statistics of the United States: Colonial Times to 1970, Part I.* Bicentennial Edition. Washington, D.C.: Government Printing Office, 1975. *Notes:* 1. 20-percent sample. 2. 25-percent sample. 3. Denotes first year for which figures include Alaska and Hawaii.

★ 1502 ★

People in Institutions

Number/Percent: Characteristics of Persons in Correctional, Mental and Dependency Institutions, 1940-1970 - II

[For definition of institutions, see text].

Year	Age			Type of institution			
	Under 18	18-64	65 and over	Correctional	Mental	Homes for aged and dependent	Other
ALL INMATES							
1970[1]	238,090	921,014	967,615	328,020	433,890	927,514	437,295
1960[2,3]	237,588	1,034,323	615,056	346,015	630,046	469,717	441,189
1950	204,644	976,783	385,419	264,557	613,628	296,783	391,878

[Continued]

★ 1502 ★

Number/Percent: Characteristics of Persons in Correctional, Mental and Dependency Institutions, 1940-1970 - II

[Continued]

Year	Age			Type of institution			
	Under 18	18-64	65 and over	Correctional	Mental	Homes for aged and dependent	Other
INMATES, 15 YEARS AND OVER							
1970[1]	102,015	921,014	967,615	326,720	419,768	925,847	319,309
1960[2,3]	87,451	1,034,323	615,056	345,280	622,559	468,410	300,581
1950	62,232	976,783	385,419	263,896	609,805	294,085	256,648
1940	69,788	864,545	221,965	312,423	587,328	234,054	22,493

Source: "Inmates of Institutions by Sex, Race, Age, and Type of Institution: 1940 to 1970,; U.S. Bureau of the Census. *Historical Statistics of the United States: Colonial Times to 1970, Part I.* Bicentennial Edition, 1975, p. 43. Primary source: U.S. Bureau of the Census. *Historical Statistics of the United States: Colonial Times to 1970, Part I.* Bicentennial Edition. Washington, D.C.: Government Printing Office, 1975. *Notes:* 1. 20-percent sample. 2. 25-percent sample. 3. Denotes first year for which figures include Alaska and Hawaii.

★ 1503 ★

People in Institutions

Number/Percent: Persons in Correctional, Mental, and Dependency Institutions in 1940

Color and Nativity	Institutional Population	Prison or Reformatory	Local Jail or Workhouse	Mental Institutions	Home for Aged, Infirm or Needy
Total, 14 and over	1,176,993	217,919	99,249	591,365	245,026
White	1,008,090	152,994	66,042	536,629	231,538
Native	825,868	142,909	59,696	428,912	176,229
Foreign born	182,222	10,085	6,346	107,717	55,309
Nonwhite	168,903	64,925	33,207	54,736	13,488
Percent	100.0	100.0	100.0	100.0	100.0
White	85.6	70.2	66.5	90.7	94.5
Native	70.2	65.6	60.1	72.5	71.9
Foreign born	15.5	4.6	6.4	18.2	22.6
Nonwhite	14.4	29.8	33.5	9.3	5.5

Source: "Institutional Population 14 Years and Over, by Type of Institution, Color, and Nativity, for the United States, 1940," *The Negro Handbook, 1946-1947*, 1947, p. 14. Primary source: U.S. Bureau of the Census.

★ 1504 ★

People in Institutions

Number/Percent: Population in Correctional, Mental, and Other Institutions, by Gender, 1950 and 1960

[**In thousands**. 1950 excludes Alaska and Hawaii. 1960 based on 25-percent sample].

RACE OF INMATES AND TYPE OF INSTITUTION	1950			1960		
	Total	Male	Female	Total	Male	Female
Institutional population	1,567	950	617	1,887	1,117	770
By race:						
White	1,351	791	560	1,582	889	692
Negro and other	216	158	57	305	228	78
By type of institution:						
Correctional institutions[1]	265	252	13	346	330	16
Mental hospitals and residential treatment centers	614	329	285	630	336	294
Tuberculosis hospitals	76	47	29	65	46	19
Chronic disease hospitals (excluding TB and mental)	20	12	8	42	25	17
Homes for the aged and dependent	297	148	148	470	188	282
Homes and schools for the mentally handicapped	134	69	66	175	95	80
Homes and schools for the physically handicapped	21	11	10	24	13	11
Homes for dependent and neglected children	96	54	42	73	41	32
Homes for unwed mothers	3	1	2	3	1	3
Training schools for juvenile delinquents	37	24	13	46	34	12
Detention homes	4	3	1	11	8	3
Diagnostic and reception centers	(NA)	(NA)	(NA)	1	1	(Z)

Source: "Inmates of Institutions, by Race, Type of Institution, and Sex: 1950 and 1960," *Statistical Abstract of the United States, 1970,* p. 40. Primary source: Dept. of Commerce, Bureau of the Census; *U.S. Census of Population: 1950,* Vol. IV, Part 2C and *U.S. Census of Population: 1960,* Vol. II, Part PC(2)- 8A. *Note:* NA Not available. Z Less than 500.

Philanthropy

★ 1505 ★

Julius Rosenwald Fund Expenditures for Black Summer Institutes, c. 1937.

Summer Institutes	
Institutes for Preachers	20,085
Institutes for Teachers, Athens, Georgia	1,000
Institutes for Agricultural Extension Agents	33,691
Gulfside Assembly, Mississippi	$82,776

Source: "Details of Expenditures for Negro State Colleges, Summer Institutes, and High Schools," *Negro Year Book: An Annual Encyclopedia of the Negro, 1937-1938*, 1937, p. 187. Primary source: Reports of the Julius Rosenwald Fund.

★ 1506 ★

Philanthropy

Julius Rosenwald Fund Expenditures for Miscellaneous Black Programs, 1917-1936

Negro School Building Program	$5,165,281
Negro University Centers	1,276,508
Negro Colleges and High Schools	822,083
Negro Fellowships	437,615
Negro Health	857,507
Other Negro Activities	257,860
Total Negro Activities	$8,816,854

Source: "Classification of Expenditures during the Two Decades of its Life, 1917-1936," *Negro Year Book: An Annual Encyclopedia of the Negro, 1937- 1938*, 1937, p. 184. Primary source: Reports of the Julius Rosenwald Fund.

★ 1507 ★

Philanthropy

Julius Rosenwald Fund: Expenditures for Miscellaneous Black Organizations/Activities, c. 1937

A. National Agencies	
1. National Association for the Advancement of Colored People	$11,000
2. National Urban League	4,000
3. Boy Scouts of America	7,500
4. Young Men's Christian Association	
a. Evanston, Illinois	$17,500
b. Harrisburg, Pennsylvania	25,000
c. Orange, New Jersey	25,000
d. Toledo, Ohio	25,000
e. Youngstown, Ohio	25,000
f. Special Activities in Chicago	6,375
g. National Council	15,250
	139,125
B. Economic Status	
5. Conferences on Economic Status of Negroes	13,897
6. Negro Relief and Recovery	45,882
C. Miscellaneous	
7. Nursery School for Colored Children	10,000
8. Negro Musical Festival in Chicago	5,000
9. Community Employment Service, Atlanta, Georgia	21,456
	$257,860

Source: "Details of Expenditures for Other Negro Activities," *Negro Year Book: An Annual Encyclopedia of the Negro, 1937-1938,* 1937, p. 191. Primary source: Reports of the Julius Rosenwald Fund.

★ 1508 ★

Philanthropy

Julius Rosenwald Fund: Expenditures for Race Relations Activities, c. 1937

1. Fellowships in Social Studies for Southern Students	$41,107
2. Southern Regional Committee of the Social Science Research Council, grants in-aid for social studies by southern professors	3,597
3. George Peabody College for Teachers-Department of Negro School Administration	41,000
4. Y.M.C.A. Graduate School, Nashville-Library and Department of Race Relations	65,000

[Continued]

★ 1508 ★

Julius Rosenwald Fund: Expenditures for Race Relations Activities, c. 1937

[Continued]

5. Teachers College, Columbia University-Lectures on Negro Education and Race Relations	4,000
6. Commission on Interracial Cooperation	72,326
7. Study of Negro Life and Education by Dr. Schrieke	20,000
8. Studies of Mexican Schools	6,565
9. Studies of Race at the University of Hawaii	8,000
10. Special Investigation and Conferences	26,766
11. Reports and Publications	42,928
	$331,289

Source: "Details of Expenditures for Race Relations," *Negro Year Book: An Annual Encyclopedia of the Negro, 1937-1938*, 1937, p. 191. Primary source: Reports of the Julius Rosenwald Fund.

Progress

★ 1509 ★

Change in Economic Areas from 1866 to 1936

ECONOMIC PROGRESS:	1866	1936	Gain in 70 years
Homes Owned	12,000	750,000	738,000
Farms Operated	20,000	880,000	860,000
Businesses Conducted	2,100	70,000	67,900
Wealth Accumulated	$20,000,000	$2,500,000,000	$2,480,000,000

Source: "Progress in Seventy Years 1866-1936," *Negro Year Book: An Annual Encyclopedia of the Negro, 1937-1938*, 1937, p. 1. Primary source: Work, Monroe N. (Ed.), *Negro Year Book: An Annual Encyclopedia of the Negro, 1937-1938*. Tuskegee Institute, Ala.: The Negro Year Book Pub. Co., 1937.

★ 1510 ★

Progress

Change in Educational Areas from 1866 to 1936

EDUCATIONAL PROGRESS:	1866	1936	Gain in 70 years
Per Cent Literate	10	90	80
Schools for Higher Training[1]	15	800	785
Students in Public Schools	100,000	2,500,000	2,400,000
Teachers in all Schools	600	55,000	54,400
Property for Higher Education	$60,000	$65,000,000	$64,940,000
Annual Expenditures for all Edu.	$700,000	$61,700,000	$61,000,000
Raised by Negroes	$80,000	$3,500,000	$3,420,000

Source: "Progress in Seventy Years 1866-1936," *Negro Year Book: An Annual Encyclopedia of the Negro, 1937-1938,* 1937, p. 1. Primary source: Work, Monroe N. (Ed.), *Negro Year Book: An Annual Encyclopedia of the Negro, 1937-1938.* Tuskegee Institute, Ala.: The Negro Year Book Pub. Co., 1937. *Note:* 1. Includes Public High Schools.

★ 1511 ★

Progress

Change in Religious Areas from 1866 to 1936

RELIGIOUS PROGRESS:	1866	1936	Gain in 70 years
Number Churches	700	45,000	44,300
Communicants	600,000	5,300,000	4,700,000
Sunday Schools	1,000	36,000	35,000
Sunday School Pupils	50,000	2,200,000	2,150,000
Value Church Property	$1,500,000	$210,000,000	$208,500,000

Source: "Progress in Seventy Years 1866-1936," *Negro Year Book: An Annual Encyclopedia of the Negro, 1937-1938,* 1937, p. 1. Primary source: Work, Monroe N. (Ed.), *Negro Year Book: An Annual Encyclopedia of the Negro, 1937-1938.* Tuskegee Institute, Ala.: The Negro Year Book Pub. Co., 1937.

Purposeful Organizations

★ 1512 ★

Black Access: Black Membership in Arts and Peace Organizations with No Color Bar, c. 1946-47

Organization	Home Office	No. of Members	Negro Members
Arts			
American Institute of Graphic Arts	New York	620	0
American Society of Landscape Architects	Boston	439	0
Authors League of American Inc.	New York	over 4,000	?
National Sculpture Society	New York	300	?
Society of Illustrators Inc.	New York	400	1
Peace			
Fellowship of Reconciliation	New York	15,000	250
National Council for Prevention of War	Washington	125	6
Women's International League for Peace and Freedom	Washington	10,000	?

Source: "Class A Organizations—Arts and Peace," *The Negro Handbook, 1946-1947*, 1947, pp. 206-207. Primary source: Murray, Florence (Ed.), *The Negro Handbook, 1946-1947*. New York: Current Books, Inc., A.A. Wyn, Pub., 1947.

★ 1513 ★

Purposeful Organizations

Black Access: Black Membership in Educational and Social Science Organizations with No Color Bar, c. 1946-47

Organization	Home Office	No. of Members	Negro Members
Educational			
American Association for Adult Education	New York	2,423	25
American Association of Junior Colleges	Washington	600	20
American Association of University Professors	Washington	16,000	300
American College Publicity Association	Bloomington, Ind.	437	15
American Education Fellowship	New York	8,000	?
American Labor Education Service	New York	1,000	?
American Philological Association	Brunswick, Me.	966	1
Association of American Law Schools	Columbus, O.	94	2
National Education Association	Washington	275,000	?
Workers Education Bureau of America	New York	150	?
Social Science			
American Academy of Political and Social Science	Philadelphia	10,000	?

[Continued]

★ 1513 ★

Black Access: Black Membership in Educational and Social Science Organizations with No Color Bar, c. 1946-47

[Continued]

Organization	Home Office	No. of Members	Negro Members
American Geographical Society	New York	4,000	?
American Historical Association	Washington	3,628	?
The American Philosophical Association	Middletown, Conn.	850	?
American Political Science Association	Evanston	3,000	8
Association of American Geographers	Minneapolis	205	0

Source: "Class A Organizations—Educational and Social Science," *The Negro Handbook, 1946-1947*, 1947, pp. 206-207. Primary source: Murray, Florence (Ed.), *The Negro Handbook, 1946-1947.* New York: Current Books, Inc., A.A. Wyn, Pub., 1947.

★ 1514 ★

Purposeful Organizations

Black Access: Black Membership in Public and Social Welfare Organizations with No Color Bar, c. 1946-47

Organization	Home Office	No. of Members	Negro Members
Public and Social Welfare			
American Association of Social Workers	New York	10,300	?
American Civil Liberties Union	New York	6,500	?
American Sociological Society	Washington	1,200	15
American Women's Voluntary Services Inc.	New York	300,000	3,066
League for Industrial Democracy	New York	1,500	25
National Civil Service League	New York	3,000	?
National Consumers League	Cleveland	1,500	?
National Conference of Social Work	Columbus, O	5,000	?
National Farmers Union	Denver	165,000	?
National Municipal League	New York	?	?
National Organization for Public Health Nursing (reports some doubt as to nondiscrimination in three Southern agencies)	New York	11,041	?
National Recreation Association	New York	2,000	?
People's Lobby	Washington	4,350	?
Planned Parenthood Federation of America	New York	3,500	?
Southern Conference of Human Welfare	Nashville	3,000	1/5th
Union for Democratic Action	New York	5,000	?
Workers Defense League	New York	9,000	100s

Source: "Class A Organizations—Public and Social Welfare," *The Negro Handbook, 1946-1947*, 1947, pp. 206-207. Primary source: Murray, Florence (Ed.), *The Negro Handbook, 1946-1947.* New York: Current Books, Inc., A.A. Wyn, Pub., 1947.

★ 1515 ★

Purposeful Organizations

Black Membership in Conservation and Wildlife Organizations with No Color Bar, c. 1946-47

Organization	Home Office	No. of Members	Negro Members
Conservation and Wildlife			
American Forestry Association	Washington	14,000	?
American Nature Study Society	Connecticut	350	?
American Ornithologists Union	Columbus	2,000	?
American Society of Naturalists	Ann Arbor	550	0
American Society of Zoologists	Chicago	1,062	under 10
American Wildlife Institute	Washington	700	?
National Audubon Society	New York	7,500	?
Society of American Foresters	Washington	4,200	0

Source: "Class A Organizations—Conservation and Wildlife," *The Negro Handbook, 1946-1947*, pp. 206-207. Primary source: Murray, Florence (Ed.), *The Negro Handbook, 1946-1947*. New York: Current Books, Inc., A.A. Wyn, Pub., 1947.

★ 1516 ★

Purposeful Organizations

Black Membership in General Religious and Business Organizations with No Color Bar, c. 1946-47

Organization	Home Office	No. of Members	Negro Members
General Religious Agencies			
American Friends Service Committee	Philadelphia	?	?
American Missionary Association	New York	1,000,000	9,000
Council of Church Boards of Education	Washington	96	6
National Council of Catholic Men	Washington not membership org.		
National Religion and Labor Foundation	New Haven	?	?
United Council of Church Women	New York	900	?
Business			
American Institute of Accountants	New York	8,203	5
American Management Association	New York	8,400	?
American Society of Planning Officials	Chicago	1,200	?
National Association of Manufacturers	New York	12,000 firms	?

Source: "Class A Organizations—General Religious Agencies and Business," *The Negro Handbook, 1946-1947*, 1947, pp. 206-207. Primary source: Murray, Florence (Ed.), *The Negro Handbook, 1946-1947*. New York: Current Books, Inc., A.A. Wyn, Pub., 1947.

★ 1517 ★

Purposeful Organizations

Vanguard of Freedom and Temperance Groups among Freedmen by State, 1868

	Divisions	Members
District of Columbia	17	1,490
Maryland	4	151
Virginia	7	43
West Virginia	2	115
North Carolina	59	3,897
South Carolina	-	-
Georgia	9	418
Florida	1	28
Alabama	2	228
Mississippi	3	235
Louisiana	3	154
Arkansas	1	89
Missouri	2	114
Kansas	1	75
Total	111	7,427

Source: [Untitled table], *Negro Year Book: An Annual Encyclopedia of the Negro, 1916-1917*, 1918, p. 224. Primary source: Work, Monroe N. (Ed.), *Negro Year Book: An Annual Encyclopedia of the Negro, 1916-1917*. Tuskegee Institute, Ala.: The Negro Year Book Pub. Co., 1918.

Social Services

★ 1518 ★

Food Stamps: Characteristics of Food Stamp Recipients, 1974

Selected characteristics	Black		White	
	Number (thousands)	Percent	Number (thousands)	Percent
SEX OF HEAD				
Total	1,362	100	2,115	100
Male	396	29	1,001	47
Female	966	71	1,114	53
AGE OF HEAD				
Total	1,362	100	2,115	100
Under 35 years	488	36	721	34
35 to 54 years	456	33	581	27

[Continued]

★ 1518 ★

Food Stamps: Characteristics of Food Stamp Recipients, 1974

[Continued]

Selected characteristics	Black		White	
	Number (thousands)	Percent	Number (thousands)	Percent
55 to 64 years	194	14	291	14
65 years and over	224	17	522	25
SIZE OF HOUSEHOLD				
Total	1,362	100	2,115	100
One person	289	21	574	27
Two persons	254	19	483	23
Three persons	220	16	325	15
Four persons	173	13	251	12
Five persons or more	402	29	454	22
Not reported	24	2	28	1
RECEIPT OF PUBLIC ASSISTANCE				
Total	1,362	100	2,115	100
Received public assistance	979	72	1,247	59
Did not receive public assistance	383	28	868	41
HOUSEHOLD INCOME[1]				
Total	1,362	100	2,115	100
Under $2,000	431	32	639	30
$2,000 to $2,999	296	22	462	22
$3,000 to $3,999	224	16	375	18
$4,000 to $4,999	142	10	222	10
$5,000 to $5,999	105	8	117	6
$6,000 or more	132	10	262	12
Income not reported	31	2	39	2

Source: "Selected Characteristics of Households Purchasing Food Stamps in July 1974," *The Social and Economic Status of the Black Population in the United States, 1974,* 1975, p. 29. Primary source: U.S. Department of Commerce, Social and Economic Statistics Administration, Bureau of the Census. *Notes:* Statistics on food stamps are estimates from the Current Population Survey, 1974, conducted by the Bureau of the Census under the sponsorship of the Department of Health, Education, and Welfare. 1. The money income level of households shown in this table may be somewhat understated. Income data from the June control card are based on the respondent's estimate of total household money income for the preceding 12 months coded in broad, fixed income intervals.

★ 1519 ★

Social Services

Help for the Elderly: Recipients of Old-Age Assistance Benefits, 1965 and 1970

[Includes Puerto Rico and Virgin Island. Based on sample and subject to sampling variability].

CHARACTERISTIC	1965	1970
Recipients...1,000	2,119	2,033
Percent:		
White	75.3	71.5
Negro	21.6	24.4
Other[1]	3.0	4.2

Source: "Old-Age Assistance—Characteristics of Recipients: 1965 and 1970," *Statistical Abstract of the United States*, 1975, p. 389. Primary source: U.S. Social and Rehabilitation Service, *Findings of the 1965 and 1970 Survey of Old-Age Assistance Recipients.* (Part 1, Demographic and Program Characteristics.) *Note:* 1. Includes unknown.

★ 1520 ★

Social Services

Multiple Sources of Assistance: Public Assistance and Social Security Recipients, 1971

[Numbers in millions]

Subject	Negro and other races	White
Total population	25.6	179.6
Receiving public assistance income	6.4	6.9
Percent of total	25	4
Receiving Social Security income	2.7	23.8
Percent of total	11	13

Source: "Persons Receiving Public Assistance and Social Security Income in March 1971," *The Social and Economic Status of the Black Population in the United States, 1971*, 1972, p. 46. Primary source: U.S. Bureau of the Census. Current Population Reports, Special Studies, Series P-23, No. 42. *The Social and Economic Status of the Black Population in the United States,* 1971. Washington, D.C.: Government Printing Office, 1972.

★ 1521 ★

Social Services

Public Assistance: Public Assistance Recipients, 1969

[Numbers in millions]

Subject	Negro and other races	White
Total population	25.1	177.4
Receiving public assistance	4.3	6.5
Percent of total	17	4

Source: "Persons Receiving Public Assistance in 1969," *The Social and Economic Status of the Black Population in the United States, 1969,* 1970, p. 42. Primary source: U.S. Department of Commerce, Bureau of the Census and U.S. Department of Health, Education, and Welfare.

★ 1522 ★

Social Services

Social Security: Benefits, by Type, 1973

[**Beneficiaries in thousands**. Excludes special age-72 beneficiaries. Benefits in current-payment status, end of year].

TYPE OF BENEFICIARY	White	Negro and other	Negro only	TYPE OF BENEFICIARY	White	Negro and other	Negro only
NUMBER OF BENEFICIARIES							
Total[1]	26,213	3,298	2,924	Survivors of deceased workers[1]	6,148	1,018	919
Men	9,068	974	842	Widows and widowers	3,401	256	232
Women	13,493	1,290	1,170	Widowed mothers	448	124	111
Children	3,652	1,035	912	Children	2,277	635	573
Under age 18	2,832	884	779				
Disabled, age 18 and over	286	34	30				
Students, age 18-21	534	117	102	AVERAGE MONTHLY BENEFITS			
Retired workers and dependents	17,130	1,656	1,437	Retired workers	$169	$137	$135
Retired workers	14,043	1,322	1,172	Men	186	151	150
Wives and husbands	2,623	185	150	Women	149	117	117
Children	463	150	115				
Disabled workers and dependents	2,935	624	568	Disabled workers	187	160	159
Disabled workers	1,703	314	291	Men	200	172	172

[Continued]

★ 1522 ★

Social Security: Benefits, by Type, 1973

[Continued]

TYPE OF BENEFICIARY	White	Negro and other	Negro only	TYPE OF BENEFICIARY	White	Negro and other	Negro only
Wives and husbands	321	60	54	Women	157	131	130
Children	912	249	224				
				Survivors of deceased workers:			
				Aged nondisabled widows	100	125	124
				Widowed mothers	126	91	91
				Children	119	84	84

Source: "Social Security (OASDHI)—Benefits, by Type of Beneficiary and Race: 1973," *Statistical Abstract of the United States*, 1975, p. 289. Primary source: U.S. Social Security Administration, *Social Security Bulletin*, April 1975. *Note:* 1. Includes parents, not shown separately.

Chapter 13
POLITICS AND ELECTIONS

Conventions

★ 1523 ★

Constitutional Conventions, 1867-1868

State	Whites	Negroes
Alabama	83	17
Arkansas	68	7
Florida	29	17
Georgia	133	33
Louisiana	52	41
Mississippi	68	17
North Carolina	107	13
South Carolina	34	63
Texas	81	9
Virginia	80	25

Source: "Members of 1867-1868 Constitutional Conventions," Monroe N. Work, ed., *Negro Year Book: An Annual Encyclopedia of the Negro, 1925-26,* p. 238.

★ 1524 ★

Conventions

Republican Conventions – Delegates, 1912-1924

State	Number of delagates									
	Total					Negro				
	1912	1916	1920	1924	Loss delegates 1912-1924	1912	1916	1920	1924	Loss delegates 1912-1924
Alabama	24	16	14	16	8	7	1	-	-	7
Arkansas	18	15	13	14	4	4	-	-	-	4
Florida	12	8	8	10	2	4	1	4	1	3
Georgia	28	17	17	18	10	13	10	8	11	2

[Continued]

★ 1524 ★

Republican Conventions – Delegates, 1912-1924

[Continued]

State	Number of delagates									
	Total					Negro				
	1912	1916	1920	1924	Loss delegates 1912-1924	1912	1916	1920	1924	Loss delegates 1912-1924
Louisiana	20	12	12	13	7	5	6	6	6	1[1]
Mississippi	20	12	12	12	8	11	6	6	6	5
N. Carolina	24	21	22	22	2	-	-	-	-	
S. Carolina	18	11	11	11	7	11	2	2	4	7
Tennessee	24	21	22	27	3[1]	1	1	1	3	2[1]
Texas	40	26	23	23	17	6	-	-	1	5
Virginia	24	15	15	17	7	-	-	-	-	-
Total	252	174	169	183	69	62	32	27	32	30

Source: "Delegates from the South, Total and Negro to National Republican Conventions, 1912, 1916, 1920, 1924," Monroe N. Work, ed., *Negro Year Book: An Annual Encyclopedia of the Negro, 1925-26*, p. 67. *Note:* 1. Gain.

Elected and Appointed Officials

★ 1525 ★

Elected Officials by Gender and Type of Office: 1969, 1973, 1975

Subject	March 1969		March 1973		May 1975	
	Both sexes	Women	Both sexes	Women	Both sexes	Women
Total	1,125	131	2,623	340	3,503	530
Percent change over preceding date	(X)	(X)	133	160	34	56
Percent women of both sexes	(X)	12	(X)	13	(X)	15
U.S. Senators and Representatives	10	1	16	4	18	4
State legislators and executives	172	16	238	29	281	35
Mayors	29	-	83	3	135	9
Other	914	114	2,286	304	3,069	482
County	(NA)	7	211	17	305	31
Municipal	(NA)	38	974	105	1,438	203
Judicial and law enforcement	(NA)	16	334	32	387	34
Education	(NA)	53	767	150	939	214
PERCENT DISTRIBUTION						
Total	100	100	100	100	100	100
U.S. Senators and Representatives	1	1	1	1	1	1
State legislators and executives	15	12	9	9	8	7
Mayors	3	-	3	1	4	2
Other	81	87	87	89	88	91

[Continued]

★ 1525 ★

Elected Officials by Gender and Type of Office: 1969, 1973, 1975

[Continued]

Subject	March 1969		March 1973		May 1975	
	Both sexes	Women	Both sexes	Women	Both sexes	Women
County	(NA)	5	8	5	9	6
Municipal	(NA)	29	37	31	41	38
Judicial and law enforcement	(NA)	12	13	9	11	6
Education	(NA)	40	29	44	27	40

Source: "Black Elected Officials, by Sex and Type of Office: March of 1969 and 1973 and May 1975," U.S. Department of Commerce, Bureau of the Census, *The Social and Economic Status of the Black Population in the United States: An Historical View, 1790-1978*, p. 157. Published by permission. Primary source: Joint Center for Political Studies. *Note:* - Represents zero. NA Not available. X Not applicable.

★ 1526 ★

Elected and Appointed Officials

Elected Officials by Office, 1969-1975, and Geographic Area, 1975

As of April, except as indicated. Five states had no Negro elected officials in 1975: Hawaii, North Dakota, South Dakota, Utah, and Vermont.

Year, region, and state	Total	U.S. and State legislatures[1]	City and county office[1]	Law enforcement[2]	Education[3]	State	Total	U.S. and State legislatures[1]	City and county offices[1]	Law enforcement[2]	Education[3]
1969	1,185	(NA)	(NA)	(NA)	(NA)	Kans.	35	6	16	1	12
1970 (Feb.)	1,472	182	715	213	362	Ky.	59	3	39	7	10
1971 (Mar.)	1,860	216	905	274	465	La.	237	9	114	34	80
1972 (Mar.)	2,264	224	1,108	263	669	Maine	4	1	2	-	1
1973	2,621	256	1,264	334	767	Md.	83	20[5]	50	8	5
1974	2,991	256	1,602	340	793	Mass.	24	9[7]	9	-	6
						Mich.	223	18[6]	99	25	81
1975	3,503	299	1,878	387	939	Minn.	8	2	1	3	2
						Miss.	192	1	111	41	39
Northeast	1,913	129	1,142	198	444	Mo.	113	16[5]	65	15	17
North Central	869	87	476	85	221	Mont.	1	1	-	-	-
South	1,913	129	1,142	198	444	Nebr.	4	1	1	-	2
West	218	27	81	30	80	Nev	7	3	1	1	2
						N.H.	1	1	-	-	-
Ala.	161	15	75	51	20	N.J.	142	7	67	-	68
Alaska	5	1	1	-	3	N. Mex	3	1	2	-	-
Ariz	17	2	5	1	9	N.Y.	159	16[6]	28	27	88
Ark	171	4	101	1	65	N.C.	194	6	137	5	46
Calif	147	12[4]	57	18	60	Ohio	146	12[5]	94	13	27
Colo	15	4	6	4	1	Okla	68	4	43	1	20
Conn	48	6	29	4	9	Oreg	6	1	1	2	2
Del	14	3	9	-	2	Pa	122	15[5]	42	43	22
D.C.	20	1[5]	12	-	7	R.I.	3	1	2	-	-
Fla	87	3	70	6	8	S.C.	132	13	78	15	26
Ga	168	22[5]	101	8	37	Tenn	96	12[5]	70	6	8
Idaho	1	-	1	-	-	Tex	150	10[5]	61	9	70
Ill	246	21[5]	145	16	64	Va	64	2	59	3	-

[Continued]

★ 1526 ★

Elected Officials by Office, 1969-1975, and Geographic Area, 1975

[Continued]

Year, region, and state	Total	U.S. and State legislatures[1]	City and county office[1]	Law enforcement[2]	Education[3]	State	Total	U.S. and State legislatures[1]	City and county offices[1]	Law enforcement[2]	Education[3]
Ind	66	6	44	10	6	Wash	15	2	7	4	2
Iowa	13	2	4	1	6	W. Va	17	1	12	3	1
						Wis	15	3	7	1	4
						Wyo	1	-	-	-	1

Source: "Negro Elected Officials, by Office, 1969 to 1975, and by Region, and States," *Statistical Abstract of the United States*, 1975, p. 449. Primary source: Joint Center for Political Studies, Washington, D.C., *National Roster of Black Elected Officials*, annual. *Notes:* NA Not available. - Represents zero. 1. County commissioners and councilmen, mayors, vice mayors, aldermen, and other. 2. Judges, magistrates, constables, marshals, sheriffs, justices of the peace, other. 3. College boards, school boards, other. 4. Includes 3 U.S. Representatives. 5. Includes 1 U.S. Representative. 6. Includes 2 U.S. Representatives. 7Includes 1 U.S. Senator.

★ 1527 ★

Elected and Appointed Officials

Elected Officials by State, 1970

State	1970, Percent Negro	Negro elected officials					
		Total	Congress	State	City	County	Other[1]
United States	11.1	1,860	14	202	785	120	739
Maine	0.3	-	-	-	-	-	-
New Hampshire	0.3	-	-	-	-	-	-
Vermont	0.2	1	-	-	1	-	-
Massachusetts	3.1	12	1	3	6	-	2
Rhode Island	2.7	3	-	1	2	-	-
Connecticut	6.0	48	-	6	25	-	17
New York	11.9	142	2	12	16	4	108
New Jersey	10.7	78	-	4	40	4	30
Pennsylvania	8.6	57	1	11	14	1	30
Ohio	9.1	100	1	13	58	1	27
Indiana	6.9	37	-	2	16	4	15
Illinois	12.8	104	2	20	38	2	42
Michigan	11.2	155	2	18	52	32	51
Wisconsin	2.9	9	-	1	5	2	1
Minnesota	0.9	8	-	-	2	-	6
Iowa	1.2	6	-	1	-	1	4
Missouri	10.3	69	1	15	30	1	22
North Dakota	0.4	-	-	-	-	-	-
South Dakota	0.2	-	-	-	-	-	-
Nebraska	2.7	3	-	1	1	-	1
Kansas	4.8	11	-	3	6	1	1
Delaware	14.3	11	-	3	6	1	1
Maryland	17.8	44	1	18	17	-	8
District of Columbia	71.1	9	1	-	-	-	8
Virginia	18.5	52	-	3	34	5	10

[Continued]

★ 1527 ★

Elected Officials by State, 1970

[Continued]

State	1970, Percent Negro	Negro elected officials					
		Total	Congress	State	City	County	Other[1]
West Virginia	3.9	1	-	1	-	-	-
North Carolina	22.2	68	-	2	49	3	14
South Carolina	30.5	61	-	3	37	5	16
Georgia	25.9	51	-	15	20	6	10
Florida	15.3	42	-	2	33	1	6
Kentucky	7.2	45	-	3	26	1	15
Tennessee	15.8	42	-	8	11	-	23
Alabama	26.2	105	-	2	45	12	46
Mississippi	36.8	95	-	1	33	21	40
Arkansas	18.3	76	-	-	32	1	43
Louisiana	29.8	74	-	1	27	10	36
Oklahoma	6.7	61	-	5	35	-	21
Texas	12.5	45	-	3	28	-	14
Montana	0.3	-	-	-	-	-	-
Idaho	0.3	-	-	-	-	-	-
Wyoming	0.8	2	-	-	1	-	1
Colorado	3.0	7	-	3	2	-	2
New Mexico	1.9	4	-	1	3	-	-
Arizona	3.0	8	-	4	-	-	4
Utah	0.6	-	-	-	-	-	-
Nevada	5.7	4	-	1	1	-	2
Washington	2.1	9	-	3	1	-	5
Oregon	1.3	3	-	-	1	-	2
California	7.0	95	2	7	30	1	55
Alaska	3.0	2	-	2	-	-	-
Hawaii	1.0	1	-	-	1	-	-

Source: "Negro Elected Officials, by State: 1970," U.S. Bureau of the Census, *The Social and Economic Status of the Black Population in the United States, 1970,* p. 143. Published by permission. Primary source: Joint Center for Political Studies and U.S. Department of Commerce, Bureau of the census. *Notes:* Figures shown represent the total number of elected blacks holding office as of March 1971. 1. Includes law enforcement and education.

★ 1528 ★

Elected and Appointed Officials

Elected Officials, by Office: 1964-1975

Area and office	1964[1]	1970	1972	1974	1975
Total	103	1,469	2,264	2,991	3,503
U.S. Senators					
United States	-	1	1	1	1
South	-	-	-	-	-

[Continued]

★ 1528 ★

Elected Officials, by Office: 1964-1975

[Continued]

Area and office	1964[1]	1970	1972	1974	1975
U.S. Representatives					
United States	5	9	13	16	17
South	-	-	2	4	5
State legislators and executives					
United States	94	169	206	239	281
South	16	54	78	90	124
Mayors					
United States	(NA)	48	86	108	135
South	(NA)	33	44	63	82
Other[2]					
United States	(NA)	1,242	1,958	2,627	3,069
South	(NA)	616	949	1,452	1,702

Source: "Black Elected Officials, by Type of Office for Selected Years: 1964 to 1975," U.S. Department of Commerce, Bureau of the Census, *The Social and Economic Status of the Black Population in the United States: An Historical View, 1790-1978*, p. 156. Published by permission. Primary source: Joint Center for Political Studies Potomac Institute, et al. (1964 data). *Notes:* - Represents zero. NA Not available. Data for 1964 represent the total number of elected Blacks holding office at that time, not just those elected in that year. The 1970, 1972, 1974, and 1975 data represent the number of elected Blacks holding office as of the end of March 1970, March 1972, March 1974, and May 1975, respectively. 1. Detailed figures may not add to total because of different sources. 2. Includes Black county, municipal, education, and judicial and law enforcement officials.

★ 1529 ★

Elected and Appointed Officials

Elected Officials, by Sex and Office, March 1969 and May 1975

Subject	March 1969		May 1975	
	Both sexes	Women	Both sexes	Women
Total	1,125	131	3,503	530
Percent women of total	(X)	11.6	(X)	15.1
U.S. Senators and Representatives	10	1	18	4
State legislators and executives	172	16	281	35
Mayors	29	-	135	9
Other[1]	914	114	3,069	482
County	(NA)	7	305	31
Municipal	(NA)	38	1,438	203
Law enforcement	(NA)	16	387	34
Education	(NA)	53	939	214
Percent distribution				
Total	100	100	100	100
U.S. Senators and Representatives	1	1	1	1

[Continued]

★ 1529 ★

Elected Officials, by Sex and Office, March 1969 and May 1975

[Continued]

Subject	March 1969		May 1975	
	Both sexes	Women	Both sexes	Women
State legislators and executives	15	12	8	7
Mayors	3	-	4	2
Other[1]	81	87	88	91
County	(NA)	5	9	6
Municipal	(NA)	29	41	38
Law enforcement	(NA)	12	11	6
Education	(NA)	40	27	40

Source: "Black Elected Officials, by Sex and Type of Office: March 1960 and May 1975," U.S. Bureau of the Census. Current Population Reports, Special Studies, Series P-23, No. 54, *The Social and Economic Status of the Black Population in the United States, 1974*, p. 154. Primary source: Joint Center for Political Studies. Published by permission. *Notes:* - Represents zero. NA Not available. X Not applicable. 1. Includes all black elected officials not included in the first three categories.

★ 1530 ★

Elected and Appointed Officials

Elected Officials, by State, 1970

State	1970, percent Negro	Negro elected officials					
		Total	Congress	State	City	County	Other[1]
United States	11.1	1,860	14	202	785	120	739
Maine	0.3	-	-	-	-	-	-
New Hampshire	0.3	-	-	-	-	-	-
Vermont	0.2	1	-	-	1	-	-
Massachusetts	3.1	12	1	3	6	-	2
Rhode Island	2.7	3	-	1	2	-	-
Connecticut	6.0	48	-	6	25	-	17
New York	11.9	142	2	12	16	4	108
New Jersey	10.7	78	-	4	40	4	30
Pennsylvania	8.6	57	1	11	14	1	30
Ohio	9.1	100	1	13	58	1	27
Indiana	6.9	37	-	2	16	4	15
Illinois	12.8	104	2	20	38	2	42
Michigan	11.2	155	2	18	52	32	51
Wisconsin	2.9	9	-	1	5	2	1
Minnesota	0.9	8	-	-	2	-	6
Iowa	1.2	6	-	1	-	1	4
Missouri	10.3	69	1	15	30	1	22
North Dakota	0.4	-	-	-	-	-	-
South Dakota	0.2	-	-	-	-	-	-
Nebraska	2.7	3	-	1	1	-	1
Kansas	4.8	11	-	3	6	1	1
Delaware	14.3	11	-	3	6	1	1

[Continued]

★ 1530 ★

Elected Officials, by State, 1970

[Continued]

State	1970, percent Negro	Negro elected officials					
		Total	Congress	State	City	County	Other[1]
Maryland	17.8	44	1	18	17	-	8
District of Columbia	71.1	9	1	-	-	-	8
Virginia	18.5	52	-	3	34	5	10
West Virginia	3.9	1	-	1	-	-	-
North Carolina	22.2	68	-	2	49	3	14
South Carolina	30.5	61	-	3	37	5	16
Georgia	25.9	51	-	15	20	6	10
Florida	15.3	42	-	2	33	1	6
Kentucky	7.2	45	-	3	26	1	15
Tennessee	15.8	42	-	8	11	-	23
Alabama	26.2	105	-	2	45	12	46
Mississippi	36.8	95	-	1	33	21	40
Arkansas	18.3	76	-	-	32	1	43
Louisiana	29.8	74	-	1	27	10	36
Oklahoma	6.7	61	-	5	35	-	21
Texas	12.5	45	-	3	28	-	14
Montana	0.3	-	-	-	-	-	-
Idaho	0.3	-	-	-	-	-	-
Wyoming	0.8	2	-	-	1	-	1
Colorado	3.0	7	-	3	2	-	2
New Mexico	1.9	4	-	1	3	-	-
Arizona	3.0	8	-	4	-	-	4
Utah	0.6	-	-	-	-	-	-
Nevada	5.7	4	-	1	1	-	2
Washington	2.1	9	-	3	1	-	5
Oregon	1.3	3	-	-	1	-	2
California	7.0	95	2	7	30	1	55
Alaska	3.0	2	-	2	-	-	-
Hawaii	1.0	1	-	-	1	-	-

Source: "Black Elected Officials, by State: 1970," U.S. Bureau of the Census, Current Population Reports, Special Studies, Series P-23, No. 38, *The Social and Economic Status of the Black Population in the United States, 1970*. p. 143. Primary source: Joint Center for Political Studies and U.S. Department of Commerce, Bureau of the Census. *Notes:* Figures shown represent the total number of elected blacks holding office as of March 1971. 1. Includes law enforcement and education.

★ 1531 ★

Elected and Appointed Officials

Elected Officials, by State, 1972

State	1970, percent Negro	Negro elected officials					
		Total	Congress	State	City	County	Other[1]
United States	11.1	2,264	14	210	932	176	932
Maine	0.3	-	-	-	-	-	-
New Hampshire	0.3	1	-	-	-	-	1
Vermont	0.2	1	-	-	1	-	-
Massachusetts	3.1	16	1	3	7	-	5
Rhode Island	2.7	7	-	1	2	-	4
Connecticut	6.0	51	-	6	28	-	17
New York	11.9	163	2	12	16	6	127
New Jersey	10.7	121	-	5	44	4	68
Pennsylvania	8.6	63	1	11	15	1	35
Ohio	9.1	110	1	13	60	-	36
Indiana	6.9	52	-	2	28	4	18
Illinois	12.8	123	2	19	47	3	52
Michigan	11.2	179	2	18	55	37	67
Wisconsin	2.9	9	-	1	5	2	1
Minnesota	0.9	8	-	-	3	-	5
Iowa	1.2	10	-	1	2	1	6
Missouri	10.3	77	1	15	30	1	30
North Dakota	0.4	-	-	-	-	-	-
South Dakota	0.2	-	-	-	-	-	-
Nebraska	2.7	3	-	1	1	-	1
Kansas	4.8	18	-	3	5	3	7
Delaware	14.3	11	-	3	6	1	1
Maryland	17.8	54	1	18	23	-	12
District of Columbia	71.1	8	1	-	-	-	7
Virginia	18.5	54	-	3	32	15	4
West Virginia	3.9	5	-	1	4	-	-
North Carolina	22.2	103	-	2	68	3	30
South Carolina	30.5	66	-	3	41	7	15
Georgia	25.9	65	-	15	32	7	11
Florida	15.3	51	-	2	45	1	3
Kentucky	7.2	57	-	3	35	1	18
Tennessee	15.8	48	-	8	17	4	19
Alabama	26.2	83	-	2	42	16	23
Mississippi	36.8	129	-	1	40	27	61
Arkansas	18.3	97	-	-	44	-	53
Louisiana	29.8	119	-	8	28	31	52
Oklahoma	6.7	62	-	6	35	-	21
Texas	12.5	61	-	3	37	-	21
Montana	0.3	-	-	-	-	-	-
Idaho	0.3	-	-	-	-	-	-
Wyoming	0.8	2	-	-	1	-	1
Colorado	3.0	7	-	3	3	-	1
New Mexico	1.9	4	-	1	3	-	-
Arizona	3.0	10	-	4	-	-	6

[Continued]

★ 1531 ★

Elected Officials, by State, 1972

[Continued]

State	1970, percent Negro	Negro elected officials					
		Total	Congress	State	City	County	Other[1]
Utah	0.6	-	-	-	-	-	-
Nevada	5.7	4	-	1	1	-	2
Washington	2.1	9	-	3	1	-	5
Oregon	1.3	5	-	-	1	-	4
California	7.0	134	2	7	43	1	81
Alaska	3.0	3	-	2	-	-	1
Hawaii	1.0	1	-	-	1	-	-

Source: "Negro Elected Officials by State: March 1972," U.S. Bureau of the Census. Current Population Reports, Special Studies, Series P-23, No. 42, *The Social and Economic Status of the Black Population in the United States, 1971,* p. 119. Primary source: Joint Center for Political Studies and U.S. Department of Commerce, Social and Economic Statistics Administration, Bureau of the Census. *Notes:* Figures shown represent the total number of elected blacks holding office as of March 1972. - Represents zero. 1. Includes law enforcement and education.

★ 1532 ★

Elected and Appointed Officials

Elected Officials, by Type of Office and State, May 1975

State	1970 percent black	Black elected officials					
		Total	Congressional	State	City	County	Other[1]
United States	11.1	3,503	18	281	1,573	305	1,326
Northeast							
Maine	0.3	4	-	1	2	-	1
New Hampshire	0.3	1	-	1	-	-	-
Vermont	0.2	-	-	-	-	-	-
Massachusetts	3.1	24	1	8	9	-	6
Rhode Island	2.7	3	-	1	2	-	-
Connecticut	6.0	48	-	6	29	-	13
New York	11.9	159	2	14	20	8	115
New Jersey	10.7	142	-	7	60	7	68
Pennsylvania	8.6	122	1	14	40	2	65
North Central							
Ohio	9.1	146	1	11	93	1	40
Indiana	6.9	66	-	6	37	7	16
Illinois	12.8	246	2	19	133	12	80
Michigan	11.2	223	2	16	69	30	106
Wisconsin	2.9	15	-	3	5	2	5
Minnesota	0.9	8	-	2	1	-	5
Iowa	1.2	13	-	2	3	1	7
Missouri	10.3	113	1	15	62	3	32
North Dakota	0.4	-	-	-	-	-	-

[Continued]

★ 1532 ★

Elected Officials, by Type of Office and State, May 1975

[Continued]

State	1970 percent black	Black elected officials					
		Total	Congressional	State	City	County	Other[1]
South Dakota	0.2	-	-	-	-	-	-
Nebraska	2.7	4	-	1	1	-	2
Kansas	4.8	35	-	6	13	3	13
South							
Delaware	14.3	14	-	3	9	-	2
Maryland	17.8	83	1	19	47	3	13
District of Columbia	71.1	20	1	-	12	-	7
Virginia	18.5	64	-	2	42	17	3
West Virginia	3.9	17	-	1	12	-	4
North Carolina	22.2	194	-	6	125	12	51
South Carolina	30.5	132	-	13	56	22	41
Georgia	25.9	168	1	21	89	12	45
Florida	15.3	87	-	3	68	2	14
Kentucky	7.2	59	-	3	38	1	17
Tennessee	15.8	96	1	11	27	43	14
Alabama	26.2	161	-	15	58	17	71
Mississippi	36.8	192	-	1	82	29	80
Arkansas	18.3	171	-	4	80	21	66
Louisiana	29.8	237	-	9	69	45	114
Oklahoma	6.7	68	-	4	42	1	21
Texas	12.5	150	1	9	60	1	79
West							
Montana	0.3	1	-	1	-	-	-
Idaho	0.3	1	-	-	1	-	-
Wyoming	0.8	1	-	-	-	-	1
Colorado	3.0	15	-	4	6	-	5
New Mexico	1.9	3	-	1	2	-	-
Arizona	3.0	17	-	2	5	-	10
Utah	0.6	-	-	-	-	-	-
Nevada	5.7	7	-	3	-	1	3
Washington	2.1	15	-	2	7	-	6
Oregon	1.3	6	-	1	1	-	4
California	7.0	147	3	9	56	1	78
Alaska	3.0	5	-	1	-	1	3
Hawaii	1.0	-	-	-	-	-	-

Source: "Black Elected Officials, by Type of Office and State: May 1975," U.S. Bureau of the Census, Current Population Reports, Special Studies, Series P-23, No. 54, *The Social and Economic Status of the Black Population in the United States, 1974*, p. 152. Primary source: Joint Center for Political Studies and U.S. Department of Commerce, Social and Economic Statistics Administration, Bureau of the Census. *Notes:* Figures shown represent the total number of elected blacks holding office as of May 1975. - Represents zero. 1. Includes law enforcement and education.

★ 1533 ★

Elected and Appointed Officials

Elected Officials, by Type of Office, 1964-1974

Office and area	1964	1971	1973	1975
Total	103	1,860	2,621	3,503
United States Senators				
United States	-	1	1	1
South	-	-	-	-
House of Representatives				
United States	5	13	15	17
South	-	2	4	5
State legislators and executives				
United States	94	198	240	281
South	16	70	90	124
Mayors				
United States	(NA)	81	82	135
South	(NA)	47	48	82
Other[1]				
United States	(NA)	1,567	2,283	3,069
South	(NA)	763	1,239	1,702

Source: "Black Elected Officials, by Type of Office: 1964, 1971, 1973, and 1975," U.S. Bureau of the Census, Current Population Reports, Special Studies, Series P-23, No. 54, *The Social and Economic Status of the Black Population in the United States, 1974,* p. 151. Primary source: Joint Center for Political Studies, Potomac Institute, and others (1964 date) *Notes:* Figures for 1964 represent the total number of elected blacks holding office at that time, not just those elected in that year. The 1971, 1973, and 1975 figures represent the number of elected blacks holding office as of the end of March 1971, March 1973, and May 1975, respectively. - Represents zero. NA Not Available. 1. Includes all black elected officials not included in first four categories.

★ 1534 ★

Elected and Appointed Officials

Federal and State Legislators During the Reconstruction, by State: 1869-1901

State	Total, all legislators	Federal			State		
		Total	Senators	Represent-atives	Total	Senators	Represent-atives
Total	816	22	2	20	794	124	670
Alabama	78	3	-	3	75	6	69
Arkansas	14	-	-	-	14	2	12
Delaware	-	-	-	-	-	-	-

[Continued]

★ 1534 ★

Federal and State Legislators During the Reconstruction, by State: 1869-1901

[Continued]

State	Total, all legislators	Federal			State		
		Total	Senators	Represent-atives	Total	Senators	Represent-atives
District of Columbia	-	-	-	-	-	-	-
Florida	49	1	-	1	48	10	38
Georgia	41	1	-	1	40	3	37
Kentucky	-	-	-	-	-	-	-
Louisiana	122	1	-	1	121	24	97
Maryland	-	-	-	-	-	-	-
Mississippi	67	3	2	1	64	6	58
North Carolina	82	4	-	4	78	22	56
Oklahoma	-	-	-	-	-	-	-
South Carolina	218	8	-	8	210	33	177
Tennessee	12	-	-	-	12	-	12
Texas	39	-	-	-	39	4	35
Virginia	93	1	-	1	92	14	78
West Virginia	1	-	-	-	1	-	1

Source: "Number of Black Elected Federal and State Legislators Who Served Terms During the Reconstruction Period, by State: 1869 to 1901," U.S. Department of Commerce, Bureau of the Census, *The Social and Economic Status of the Black Population in the United States: An Historical View, 1790-1978,* p. 155. Published by permission. Primary source: Joint Center for Political Studies. *Notes:* - Represents zero. Data are for total number of legislators elected during the entire Reconstruction period. Persons reelected to an office during this time were counted only once.

★ 1535 ★

Elected and Appointed Officials

Legislators and Other Public Office Holders, 1962-1972

Subject	1962	1964	1966	1968	1970	1972
U.S. Senate						
United States	-	-	1	1	1	1
South	-	-	-	-	-	-
U.S. House of representatives						
United States	4	5	6	9	13	13
South	-	-	-	-	2	2
State Legislatures						
United States	52	94	148	172	198	206
South	6	16	37	53	70	78
Mayors						
United States	(NA)	(NA)	(NA)	29	81	86
South	(NA)	(NA)	(NA)	17	47	44

[Continued]

★ 1535 ★

Legislators and Other Public Office Holders, 1962-1972

[Continued]

Subject	1962	1964	1966	1968	1970	1972
Other[1]						
United States	(NA)	(NA)	(NA)	914	1,567	1,958
South	(NA)	(NA)	(NA)	468	763	949

Source: "Negro Legislators and Negro Elected to Other Public Office: 1962, 1964, 1966, 1968, and 1970," U.S. Bureau of the Census. Current Population Reports, Special Studies, Series P-23, No. 38, *The Social and Economic Status of the Black Population in the United States, 1970,* p. 142; and "Negro Legislators and Negroes Elected to Other Public Office: 1964, 1966, 1970, and 1972," U.S. Bureau of the Census. Current Population Reports, Special Studies, Series P-23, No. 42, *The Social and Economic Status of the Black Population in the United States, 1971,* p. 118. Primary source: Joint Center for Political Studies, Potomac Institute, Democratic National Committee, and Ebony Magazine. *Notes:* Figures for the years 1962, 1964, 1966, and 1968 represent the total number of elected blacks holding office at that time, not just those elected in those years. Figures for 1970 also include persons elected the first 3 months of 1971. The 1972 numbers represent elected officials holding office as of March 1972. - Represents zero. NA Not Available. 1. Includes all black elected officials not included in first four categories.

★ 1536 ★

Elected and Appointed Officials

Legislators and Other Public Office-Holders, 1962-1970

Subject	1962	1964	1966	1968	1970[1]
U.S. Senate					
United States	-	-	1	1	1
South	-	-	-	-	-
U.S. House of Representatives					
United States	4	5	6	9	13
South	-	-	-	-	2
State Legislatures					
United States	52	94	148	172	198
South	6	16	37	53	70
Mayors					
United States	(NA)	(NA)	(NA)	29	81
South	(NA)	(NA)	(NA)	17	47
Other elected officials					
United States	(NA)	(NA)	(NA)	914	1,567
South	(NA)	(NA)	(NA)	468	763

Source: "Negro Legislators and Negroes Elected to Other Public Office: 1962, 1964, 1966, 1968, and 1970," U.S. Bureau of the Census, *The Social and Economic Status of the Black Population in the United States, 1970,* p. 142. Primary source: Potomac Institute, Democratic National Committee, Ebony Magazine, and Joint Center for Political Studies. *Notes:* Figures for each year shown represent the total number of elected blacks holding office at that time, not just those elected in that year. - Represents zero. NA Not available. 1. Figures are current as of March 1971.

★ 1537 ★

Elected and Appointed Officials

Population Characteristics for Places with Black Mayors, by Region, May 1975

All places with black mayors	Total	South	North and West
Total	135	82	53
Percent	100	61	39
Size of place			
100,000 or more	11	3	8
1,000,000 or more	2	-	2
250,000 to 999,999	4	2	2
100,000 to 249,999	5	1	4
25,000 to 99,999	20	6	14
1,000 to 24,999	53	31	22
5,000 to 24,999	22	10	12
2,500 to 4,999	13	6	7
1,000 to 2,499	18	15	3
Under 1,000	51	42	9
Percent black of total population			
Total	135	82	53
75.0 or more	61	45	16
50.0 to 74.9	33	22	11
25.0 to 49.9	13	4	9
10.0 to 24.9	16	7	9
Less than 10.0	12	4	8

Source: "Total Population Size and Percent Black for Places with Black Mayors, by Region: May 1975," U.S. Bureau of the Census. Current Population Reports, Special Studies, Series P-23, No. 54, *The Social and Economic Status of the Black Population in the United States, 1974*, 1972, p. 153. Primary source: Joint Center for Political Studies and U.S. Department of Commerce, Social and Economic Statistics Administration, Bureau of the Census. *Notes:* Population size and percent black based on 1970 census figures and estimates by the mayors.

★ 1538 ★

Elected and Appointed Officials

Presidential Appointment of Black Judges: 1901-1975

Appointment period	Total	Number appointed to--	
		U.S. Federal courts	District of Columbia courts
1901-1923	1	-	1
1923-1933	1	-	1
1933-1945	3	2	1
1945-1953	4	2	2

[Continued]

★ 1538 ★

Presidential Appointment of Black Judges: 1901-1975

[Continued]

Appointment period	Total	Number appointed to-- U.S. Federal courts	District of Columbia courts
1953-1961	3	2	1
1961-1963	5	3	2
1963-1969	18	11	7
1969-1972	19	7	12
1972-1975	1	1	-

Source: "Presidential Appointment of Black Judges by Period of Appointment: 1901-1975," U.S. Department of Commerce, Bureau of the Census, *The Social and Economic Status of the Black Population in the United States: An Historical View, 1790-1978*, p. 158. Published by permission. Primary source: *The Ebony Handbook*, ed. by Ebony Editors and Doris E. Saunders, Chicago: Johnson Publishing Company, 1974. (Primary source), and U.S. Department of Justice. *Notes:* - Represents zero. For the periods shown, judges for the District of Columbia courts were appointed by the President.

★ 1539 ★

Elected and Appointed Officials

Reconstruction Legislatures, 1868-1876

Legislatures	1868-69 Whites	1868-69 Negroes	1870-71 Whites	1870-71 Negroes	1871-72 Whites	1871-72 Negroes	1873-74 Whites	1873-74 Negroes	1874-75 Whites	1874-75 Negroes	1876 Whites	1876 Negroes
Alabama												
Senate	32	1	29	4	29	4	29	4	27	6	27	6
House	74	26	73	27	86	14	73	27	71	29	77	23
Arkansas												
Senate	23	1	22	2	-	-	22	2	-	-	-	-
House	73	7	71	9	-	-	71	9	-	-	-	-
Georgia												
Senate	41	3	42	2	-	-	-	-	-	-	-	-
House	145	31	149	26	-	-	-	-	-	-	-	-
Mississippi												
Senate	-	-	29	4	-	-	28	9	-	-	32	5
House	-	-	77	31	76	39	61	55	-	-	100	16
North Carolina												
Senate	47	3	47	9	45	5	46	4	46	4	-	-
House	102	18	101	1	118	12	107	13	107	13	113	7
South Carolina												
Senate	24	9	22	11	-	-	17	16	17	16	17	16
House	48	76	49	75	-	-	63	61	63	61	70	54
Texas												
Senate	-	-	28	2	-	-	-	-	-	-	-	-
House	-	-	82	8	-	-	-	-	-	-	-	-
Virginia												
Senate	34	6	34	6	37	3	37	3	37	3	37	3
House	119	18	116	21	123	14	115	17	112	17	112	13

Source: "Negro Members of Some Reconstruction Legislatures," Monroe N. Work, ed., *Negro Year Book: An Annual Encyclopedia of the Negro, 1925-26*, p. 239.

★ 1540 ★

Elected and Appointed Officials

Reconstruction Legislatures: North Carolina and Virginia, 1876-1899

Year	Sens.	Reps.
North Carolina		
1879	2	6
1881	1	4
1883	3	5
1885	2	2
1887	3	3
1889		2
1891	1	
1893		1
1895		1
1897		1
1899	1	1
Virginia		
1876-77	3	12
1877-78	3	4
1878-79	3	4
1881-82	3	13
1883-84	3	8
1884-85	1	7
1885-86	1	1
1886-87	1	1
1887-88	1	7
1888-89	1	7
1889-90	1	4
1890-91	1	3

Source: "Negro Members of Some Reconstruction Legislatures," Monroe N.Work, ed., *Negro Year Book: An Annual Encyclopedia of the Negro, 1925-26,* p. 239.

★ 1541 ★

Elected and Appointed Officials

U.S. Legislators Elected for Each Congressional Term: 1869-1975

Congressional term	United States	South	North and West
RECONSTRUCTION PERIOD			
1869-1871	3	3	-
1871-1873	5	5	-
1873-1875	7	7	-

[Continued]

★ 1541 ★

U.S. Legislators Elected for Each Congressional Term: 1869-1975

[Continued]

Congressional term	United States	South	North and West
1875-1877	7	7	-
1877-1879	4	4	-
1879-1881	1	1	-
1881-1883	1	1	-
1883-1885	2	2	-
1885-1887	2	2	-
1887-1889	-	-	-
1889-1891	3	3	-
1891-1893	1	1	-
1893-1895	1	1	-
1895-1897	1	1	-
1897-1899	1	1	-
1899-1901	1	1	-
20TH CENTURY			
1901-1929	-	-	-
1929-1931	1	-	1
1931-1933	1	-	1
1933-1935	1	-	1
1935-1937	1	-	1
1937-1939	1	-	1
1939-1941	1	-	1
1941-1943	1	-	1
1943-1945	1	-	1
1945-1947	1	-	1
1947-1949	2	-	2
1949-1951	2	-	2
1951-1953	2	-	2
1953-1955	2	-	2
1955-1957	3	-	3
1957-1959	3	-	3
1959-1961	4	-	4
1961-1963	4	-	4
1963-1965	5	-	5
1965-1967	6	-	6
1967-1969	7	-	7
1969-1971	8	-	8

[Continued]

★ 1541 ★

U.S. Legislators Elected for Each Congressional Term: 1869-1975

[Continued]

Congressional term	United States	South	North and West
1971-1973	13	2	11
1973-1975	18	4	14

Source: "Number of Blacks Elected to the United States Congress for Each Congressional Term, by Region: 1869-1871 to 1973-1975," U.S. Department of Commerce, Bureau of the Census, *The Social and Economic Status of the Black Population in the United States: An Historical View, 1790-1978*, p. 154. Published by permission. Primary source: *The Ebony Handbook*, ed. by Ebony Editors and Doris E. Saunders, Chicago: Johnson Publishing Company, 1974. *Notes:* - Represents zero. Individual legislators may have been reelected for several terms during the periods shown. In this table, they were counted in each term for which elected. For each of the congressional periods, 1869- 1871, 1875-1877, 1877-1879, 1967-1969, and 1973-1975, there was one Black Senator elected. For all other periods shown, figures are for Representatives.

Voters and Voting

★ 1542 ★

Citizens of Voting Age in Cities with 50,000 or More Blacks, 1940

City	Total population	Negro	Per cent Negro
Total	14,689,254	1,751,148	11.9
New York, N.Y.	4,474,689	287,528	6.43
Chicago, Ill.	2,212,128	191,242	8.65
Philadelphia, Pa.	1,240,469	162,574	13.1
Washington, D.C.	474,793	126,850	26.7
Baltimore, Md.	560,251	106,472	19.0
Detroit, Mich.	971,301	99,212	10.7
New Orleans, La.	326,837	94,397	28.9
Memphis, Tenn.	200,352	83,070	41.5
Birmingham, Ala.	173,358	68,349	39.4
St. Louis, Mo.	564,257	75,085	13.3
Atlanta, Ga.	202,762	67,917	33.5
Houston, Tex.	257,238	59,352	23.1
Cleveland, Ohio	544,241	55,742	10.2
Los Angeles, Calif.	1,025,708	46,835	4.57
Pittsburgh, Pa.	429,146	40,570	9.45
Jacksonville, Fla.	114,936	40,432	35.2
Richmond, Va.	132,359	39,467	29.8
Cincinnati, Ohio	317,258	37,227	11.7

[Continued]

★ 1542 ★

Citizens of Voting Age in Cities with 50,000 or More Blacks, 1940

[Continued]

City	Total population	Negro	Per cent Negro
Indianapolis, Ind.	266,347	34,387	12.9
Dallas, Tex.	200,824	34,440	17.2

Source: "Citizens of Voting Age for the Total Population and Negroes by States: 1940," Jessie Parkhurst Guzman, ed., *Negro Year Book: A Review of Events Affecting Negro Life, 1941-1946*, p. 277.

★ 1543 ★

Voters and Voting

Citizens of Voting Age, by States – 1940

State	Citizen		
	Total	Negro	Per Cent Negro
United States	79,863,451	7,375,609	9.2
New England			
Maine	493,506	755	0.2
New Hampshire	295,859	271	0.1
Vermont	214,248	240	0.1
Massachusetts	2,575,477	30,661	1.2
Rhode Island	424,876	5,830	1.4
Connecticut	1,011,658	19,977	2.0
Middle Atlantic			
New York	8,327,563	361,555	4.3
New Jersey	2,592,978	142,156	5.5
Pennsylvania	6,031,192	298,756	5.0
East North Central			
Ohio	4,404,423	219,672	5.0
Indiana	2,198,935	80,360	3.7
Illinois	5,119,854	262,856	5.1
Michigan	3,131,722	137,138	4.4
Wisconsin	1,941,603	8,101	0.4
West North Central			
Minnesota	1,730,547	7,150	0.4
Iowa	1,608,926	11,044	0.7
Missouri	2,463,726	164,494	6.7
North Dakota	358,090	157	0.1
South Dakota	378,405	320	0.1
Nebraska	817,280	9,636	1.2
Kansas	1,144,823	42,960	3.8
South Atlantic			
Delaware	171,856	22,863	13.3
Maryland	1,153,510	183,320	15.9

[Continued]

★ 1543 ★

Citizens of Voting Age, by States – 1940

[Continued]

State	Citizen		
	Total	Negro	Per Cent Negro
District of Columbia	474,793	126,850	26.7
Virginia	1,567,517	364,224	23.2
West Virginia	1,046,107	70,048	6.7
North Carolina	1,925,483	493,108	25.6
South Carolina	989,841	383,660	38.8
Georgia	1,768,969	580,687	32.8
Florida	1,187,827	310,228	26.1
East South Central			
Kentucky	1,630,772	137,961	8.5
Tennessee	1,703,391	309,400	18.2
Alabama	1,555,369	520,981	33.5
Mississippi	1,195,079	563,715	47.2
West South Central			
Arkansas	1,098,986	270,973	24.7
Louisiana	1,364,933	473,332	34.7
Oklahoma	1,362,438	97,089	7.1
Texas	3,710,374	540,565	14.6
Mountain			
Montana	343,180	831	0.2
Idaho	305,311	460	0.2
Wyoming	150,031	691	0.5
Colorado	688,410	8,766	1.3
New Mexico	275,227	3,152	1.2
Arizona	263,346	10,042	3.8
Utah	298,160	904	0.3
Nevada	70,327	538	0.8
Pacific			
Washington	1,123,725	5,645	5.0
Oregon	717,121	1,903	0.3
California	4,455,677	89,584	2.0

Source: "Citizens of Voting Age for the Total Population and Negroes by States: 1940," Jessie Parkhurst Guzman, ed., *Negro Year Book: A Review of Events Affecting Negro Life, 1941-1946,* p. 276.

★ 1544 ★

Voters and Voting

Educational Level of Voters in Presidential Elections: 1964, 1968, 1972

Numbers in thousands.

Years of school completed	Black			White		
	1964[1]	1968	1972	1964	1968	1972
PERSONS OF VOTING AGE						
All educational levels	11,187	10,935	13,493	92,122	104,521	121,243
Elementary						
0 to 4 years	3,435[2]	1,540	1,400	12,246[2]	4,273	3,774
5 to 7 years	3,435[2]	1,869	1,708	12,246[2]	7,729	7,253
8 years	1,211	1,149	1,248	14,190	13,556	12,349
High school						
1 to 3 years	2,431	2,645	3,177	16,928	17,637	18,906
4 years	2,267	2,489	4,037	32,605	36,898	46,248
College						
1 to 3 years	575	744	1,279	9,851	12,459	17,759
4 years	537[3]	339	405	9,734[3]	7,550	9,226
5 years or more	537[3]	159	240	9,734[3]	4,419	5,728
PERCENT OF VOTING AGE POPULATION WHO REPORTED THAT THEY VOTED						
All educational levels	57.6	57.6	52.1	76.1	69.1	64.5
Elementary						
0 to 4 years	43.4[2]	39.4	35.9	53.4[2]	38.7	32.2
5 to 7 years	43.4[2]	53.2	48.5	53.4[2]	52.4	43.5
8 years	62.8	53.7	52.1	67.3	63.3	55.6
High school						
1 to 3 years	61.7	56.3	46.9	65.9	62.2	53.1
4 years	70.8	65.3	55.3	76.5	73.1	66.5
College						
1 to 3 years	73.4	74.1	63.5	82.6	79.0	76.0
4 years	81.9[3]	79.9	80.3	87.8[3]	83.6	83.1
5 years or more	81.9[3]	90.6	79.0	87.8[3]	86.7	86.9

Source: "Reported Voter Participation of Persons of Voting Age, by Years of School Completed for Presidential Elections: 1964, 1968, and 1972," U.S. Department of Commerce, Bureau of the Census, *The Social and Economic Status of the Black Population in the United States: An Historical View, 1790-1978,* p. 153. Primary source: U.S. Department of Commerce, Bureau of the Census. *Notes:* Data includes all persons 18 years old and over in Georgia and Kentucky, 19 years old and over in Alaska, 20 years old and over in Hawaii, and 21 years old and over in remaining states. For 1972 and 1974, data include all persons 28 years old and over. Data for 1964 include persons not reporting on education, not shown separately. 1. Data include persons of "other" races. 2. Data includes 0 to 7 years. 3. Data includes 4 years or more.

★ 1545 ★

Voters and Voting

Left-Wing Vote, 1948 and 1951

Assembly district	1948 Wallace vote	1950 DuBois vote
11 (Man.)	3,484	2,469
12 "	6,676	3,291
13 "	5,492	2,836
14 "	6,251	5,324
17 (Bklyn.)	5,804	2,265
Totals	27,707	16,185

Source: "Negro Support of Wallace and Du Bois Compared," Jessie Parkhurst Guzman, ed., *Negro Year Book: A Review of Events Affecting Negro Life, 1941-1946*, p. 302.

★ 1546 ★

Voters and Voting

Participation in National Elections by Population Characteristics, 1968, 1972, 1974

[**Persons in millions**. As of November. Covers civilian noninstitutional population. For 1968, persons 18 years old and over in Georgia and Kentucky, 19 and over in Alaska, 20 and over in Hawaii, and 21 and over elsewhere; for 1972 and 1974, persons 18 years old and over in all States. Includes aliens. Figures are based on a population sample and differ from those in tables 727 and 729 based on population estimates and official vote counts. Differences in percentages may also be due to overreporting of voting by persons in the sample].

CHARACTERISTIC:	1968				1972				1974			
	Persons of voting age	Persons reporting they voted		Persons reporting not voting	Persons of voting age	Persons reporting they voted		Persons reporting not voting	Persons of voting age	Persons reporting they voted		Persons reporting not voting
		Total	Percent			Total	Percent			Total	Percent	
Total	116.5	79.0	67.8	30.0	136.2	85.8	63.0	37.0	141.3	63.2	44.7	55.3
White	104.5	72.2	69.1	28.9	121.2	78.2	64.5	35.5	125.1	57.9	46.3	53.7
Negro	10.9	6.3	57.6	38.5	13.5	7.0	52.1	47.9	14.2	4.8	33.8	66.2

Source: "Participation in National Elections, by Population Characteristics: 1968, 1972, 1974," *Statistical Abstract of the United States*, 1975, p. 450. Primary source: U.S. Bureau of the Census, *Current Population Reports*, series P-20, Nos. 192 and 253, and unpublished data.

★ 1547 ★

Voters and Voting

Percent Registered and Voting in Presidential Elections, by Region 1964-1972

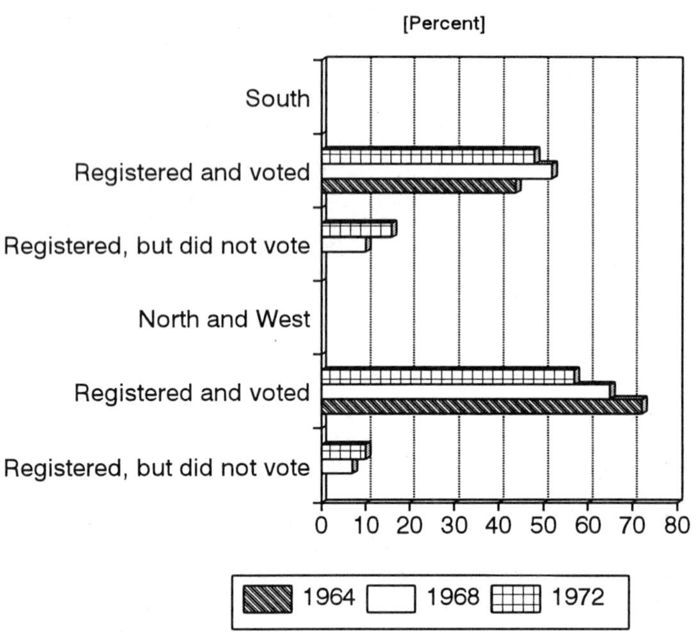

Black, by region.

Year	South		North and West	
	Registered and voted	Registered but did not vote	Registered and voted	Registered but did not vote
1964[1]	44		72	
1968	52	10	65	7
1972	48	16	57	10

Source: "Percent of Persons Voting Age Who Reported Registered and Voting, by Region, for Presidential Elections: 1964-1976," U.S. Department of Commerce, Bureau of the Census, *The Social and Economic Status of the Black Population in the United States: An Historical View, 1790-1978*, p. 145. Published by permission. Primary source: Joint Center for Political Studies. *Notes:* Data for 1964 on persons who registered but did not vote are not available. 1. Includes persons of "other" races.

★ 1548 ★

Voters and Voting

Percent Registered and Voting in Presidential Elections: 1964-1972

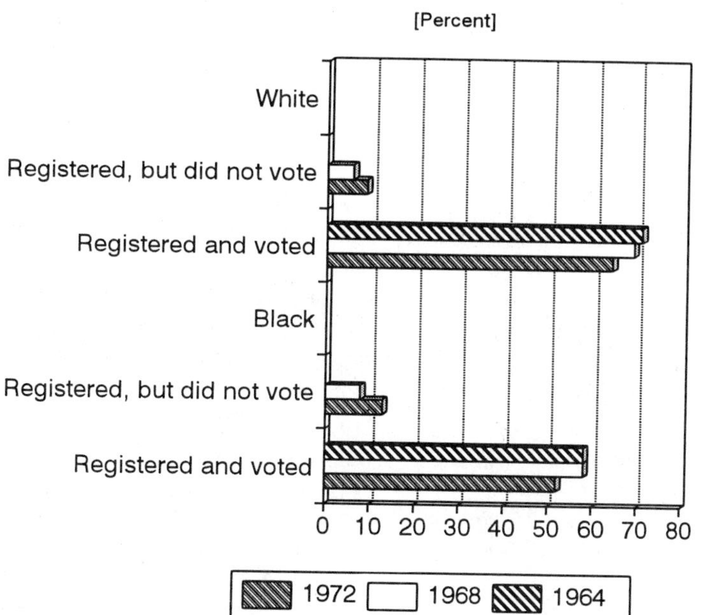

Year	Black		White	
	Registered and voted	Registered but did not vote	Registerd and voted	Registered but did not vote
1964	58		71	
1968	58	8	69	6
1972	52	13	64	9

Source: "Percent of Persons Voting Age Who Reported Registered and Voting, by Region, for Presidential Elections: 1964-1976," U.S. Department of Commerce, Bureau of the Census, *The Social and Economic Status of the Black Population in the United States: An Historical View, 1790-1978*, p. 145. Published by permission. Primary source: Joint Center for Political Studies. *Notes:* Data for 1964 on persons who registered but did not vote are not available.

★ 1549 ★

Voters and Voting

Potential Voting Population: Characteristics, 1940

Citizenship, race and nativity	Total population (all ages)			Population 21 years old and over		
	Total 1940	Male 1940	Female 1940	Total 1940	Male 1940	Female 1940
Total	131,669,275	66,061,592	65,607,683	83,996,629	42,004,816	41,991,813
Percent citizen	96.7	97.0	96.4	95.1	95.4	94.7
Percent alien and citizenship not reported	3.3	3.0	3.6	4.9	4.5	5.3
Citizen	127,354,644	64,076,972	63,277,672	79,863,451	40,111,435	39,752,016
White-Native	106,795,732	53,437,533	53,358,199	65,119,586	32,334,056	32,785,530
Naturalized	7,250,252	4,119,390	3,130,862	7,130,158	4,058,804	3,071,354
Negro-Native	12,781,577	6,224,550	6,557,027	7,346,124	3,554,389	3,791,735
Naturalized	30,013	17,637	12,376	29,485	17,403	12,082
Other races-Native	497,070	277,862	219,208	238,098	146,783	91,315
Indian	329,478	168,964	160,514	156,737	82,720	74,017
Chinese	40,262	25,702	14,560	18,812	14,328	4,484
Japanese	79,642	42,316	37,326	24,428	13,862	10,566
Filipino	45,132	39,441	5,691	37,178	35,276	1,902
Hindu	910	498	412	189	105	84
All other	1,646	941	705	754	492	262
Alien	3,479,652	1,589,784	1,889,868	3,335,392	1,517,151	1,818,241
White-first papers	914,489	575,716	338,773	900,461	568,326	332,135
No papers	2,429,325	926,307	1,503,018	2,304,996	865,178	1,439,818
Negro-first papers	10,045	5,997	4,048	9,955	5,970	3,985
No papers	33,976	15,620	18,356	32,923	15,136	17,787
Other races-foreign born	91,817	66,144	25,673	87,057	62,541	24,516
Indian	4,491	2,463	2,028	3,943	2,191	1,752
Chinese	37,242	31,687	5,555	33,869	28,813	5,056
Japanese	47,305	29,651	17,654	46,548	29,243	17,305
Filipino	431	282	149	388	261	127
Hindu	1,495	1,419	76	1,477	1,405	72
All other	853	642	211	832	628	204
Citizenship not reported	834,979	394,836	440,143	797,786	376,230	421,556
White	825,072	389,602	435,470	788,335	371,202	417,133
Negro	9,907	5,234	4,673	9,451	5,028	4,423

Source: "Potential Voting Population, by Citizenship, Race, and Nativity, for the United States: 1940," Florence Murray, ed., *The Negro Handbook*, 1942, p. 193.

★ 1550 ★

Voters and Voting

Qualified Voters in Southern States, 1951

State	Qualified
Alabama	50,000
Arkansas	50,000
Georgia	120,000
Florida	108,000
Louisiana	30,000
Mississippi	20,000
North Carolina	100,000
South Carolina	35,000
Tennessee	50,000
Texas	275,000
Virginia	76,000
Total	914,000

Source: "Qualified Negro Voters in Southern States, 1951," Jessie Parkhurst Guzman, ed., *Negro Year Book: A Review of Events Affecting Negro Life, 1941-1946*, p. 307.

★ 1551 ★

Voters and Voting

Reasons for Not Voting or Registering, by Region, 1974

(Numbers in thousands)

Reason for not voting or registering	Black			White		
	United States	South	North and West	United States	South	North and West
Total persons who reported that they did not vote[1]	9,389	5,182	4,206	67,213	23,224	43,989
Persons who reported registered but not voting[2]	2,577	1,657	920	19,755	8,016	11,739
Reported reason for not voting						
Percent	100	100	100	100	100	100
Not interested	22	21	23	20	22	19
Dislikes politics	9	7	13	15	13	16
Unable to go to polls	45	47	41	33	33	33
Out of town or away from home	8	8	7	16	15	16
Other reasons[3]	17	17	17	17	18	16
Persons reported not registered[4]	5,169	2,794	2,375	38,622	12,667	25,954
Reported reason for not registering						
Percent	100	100	100	100	100	100
Not a citizen, residence requirement not satisfied	6	3	8	13	10	14
Not interested	42	46	38	37	43	34

[Continued]

★ 1551 ★

Reasons for Not Voting or Registering, by Region, 1974

[Continued]

Reason for not voting or registering	Black			White		
	United States	South	North and West	United States	South	North and West
Dislikes politics	6	3	9	10	7	11
Unable to register	8	10	7	4	4	4
Registration inconvenient or didn't know how	8	9	7	7	7	8
Recently moved, have not registered	7	4	10	11	10	12
Other reasons	14	14	14	12	13	11

Source: "Reasons for Not Voting or Registering for Persons who Reported That They Did Not Vote, Region: 1974," U.S. Bureau of the Census, Current Population Reports, Special Studies, Series P-23, No. 54, *The Social and Economic Status of the Black Population in the United States, 1974*, p. 148. Primary source: U.S. Department of Commerce, Social and Economic Statistics Administration, Bureau of the Census. *Notes:* 1. Includes 1,228,000 blacks and 7,020,000 whites in the United States (not shown separately) who did not report on registration. 2. Includes only those who reported a reason for not voting; excludes 415,000 blacks and 1,816,000 whites who did not know or report a reason. 3. Includes a negligible number of persons who reported "machines not working or lines too long," and "didn't know of election." 4. Includes 497,000 blacks and 2,036,000 whites (not shown separately) who did not know or report a reason for not registering.

★ 1552 ★

Voters and Voting

Registration for General Elections: 1964-1974

Numbers in thousands.

Subject	Presidential election			Congressional election		
	1964	1968	1972	1966	1970	1974
BLACK						
All persons of voting age						
United States	10,340	10,935	13,493	10,533	11,472	14,175
South	5,849[1]	5,991	6,950	5,684	6,196	7,401
North and West	5,403[1]	4,944	6,543	4,849	5,277	6,774
Number who reported that they registered						
United States	(NA)	7,238	8,837	6,345	6,971	7,778
South	(NA)	3,690	4,450	3,008	3,565	4,107
North and West	(NA)	3,548	4,387	3,337	3,406	3,671
Percent of voting-age population						
United States	(NA)	66	65	60	61	55
South	(NA)	62	64	53	58	55
North and West	(NA)	72	67	69	65	54
WHITE						
All persons of voting age						
United States	99,353	104,521	121,243	101,205	107,997	125,132
South	26,580	28,834	35,413	28,612	30,839	37,074
North and West	72,771	75,687	85,830	72,593	77,158	88,058

[Continued]

★ 1552 ★

Registration for General Elections: 1964-1974

[Continued]

Subject	Presidential election			Congressional election		
	1964	1968	1972	1966	1970	1974
Number who reported that they registered						
United States	(NA)	78,835	88,987	72,517	74,672	79,490
South	(NA)	20,416	24,707	18,392	20,081	22,611
North and West	(NA)	58,419	64,279	54,125	54,591	56,879
Percent of voting-age population						
United States	(NA)	75	73	72	69	64
South	(NA)	71	70	64	65	61
North and West	(NA)	77	75	75	71	65

Source: "Reported Registration of Persons of Voting Age, by Region for General Elections: 1964 to 1974," U.S. Department of Commerce, Bureau of the Census, *The Social and Economic Status of the Black Population in the United States: An Historical View, 1790-1978,* p. 150. Primary source: U.S. Department of Commerce, Bureau of the Census. *Notes:* Data include all persons 18 years old and over in Georgia and Kentucky, 19 years old and over in Alaska, 20 years old and over in Hawaii, and 21 years old and over in the remaining States. For 1972 and 1974, data include all persons 18 years old and over. NA Not available. 1. Includes persons of "other" races.

★ 1553 ★

Voters and Voting

Voter Participation and Registration by Age and Education, 1974

(Numbers in thousands)

Years of school completed and race	All persons	Reported voted		Reported registered	
		Number	Percent of total	Number	Percent of total
Black					
Both sexes	14,175	4,786	34	7,778	55
Elementary: Less than 7 years	2,776	831	30	1,468	53
8 years	1,072	380	35	628	59
High school: 1 to 3 years	3,110	921	30	1,577	51
4 years	4,496	1,451	32	2,356	52
College: 1 to 3 years	1,728	700	41	1,032	60
4 years or more	993	504	51	718	72
White					
Both sexes	125,132	57,918	46	79,490	64
Elementary: Less than 7 years	9,203	2,476	27	4,254	46
8 years	10,957	4,630	42	6,745	62
High school: 1 to 3 years	18,407	6,851	37	10,181	55
4 years	46,675	21,522	46	29,471	63
College: 1 to 3 years	21,580	10,946	51	14,685	68
4 years or more	18,310	11,494	63	14,154	77

Source: "Reported Voter Participation and Registration of Persons of Voting Age, by Years of School Completed: November 1974," U.S. Bureau of the Census, Current Population Reports, Special Studies, Series P-23, No. 54, *The Social and Economic Status of the Black Population in the United States, 1974,* p. 149. Primary source: U.S. Department of Commerce, Social and Economic Statistics Administration, Bureau of the Census.

★ 1554 ★

Voters and Voting

Voter Participation and Registration by Region, 1974

(Numbers in thousands)

Area and age	Black			White		
	All persons	Percent reported registered	Percent reported voting	All persons	Percent reported registered	Percent reported voting
United States						
18 years and over	14,175	55	34	125,132	64	46
18 to 24 years	3,113	34	16	22,187	43	25
25 to 44 years	5,443	56	34	45,304	61	44
45 to 64 years	3,910	67	46	38,583	75	58
65 years and over	1,710	63	39	19,058	71	53
South						
18 years and over	7,401	55	30	37,074	61	37
18 to 24 years	1,674	37	16	6,510	41	19
25 to 44 years	2,627	57	31	13,670	59	35
45 to 64 years	2,038	65	40	11,263	72	48
65 years and over	1,063	63	33	5,631	68	44
North and West						
18 years and over	6,774	54	38	88,058	65	50
18 to 24 years	1,439	30	17	15,676	44	28
25 to 44 years	2,816	54	37	31,636	62	48
45 to 64 years	1,872	69	53	27,320	76	62
65 years and over	647	64	48	13,427	72	57

Source: "Reported Voter Participation and Registration of Persons of Voting Age, by Age and Region: 1974," U.S. Bureau of the Census, Current Population Reports, Special Studies, Series P-23, No. 54, *The Social and Economic Status of the Black Population in the United States, 1974*, p. 147. Primary source: U.S. Department of Commerce, Social and Economic Statistics Administration, Bureau of the Census.

★ 1555 ★

Voters and Voting

Voter Participation by Region and Election, 1968-1974

(Numbers in thousands)

Subject	Congressional election		Presidential election	
	1970	1974	1968	1972
Number who reported that they voted				
United States	4,992	4,786	6,300	7,033
South	2,278	2,219	3,094	3,324
North and West	2,714	2,567	3,206	3,707

[Continued]

★ 1555 ★

Voter Participation by Region and Election, 1968-1974

[Continued]

Subject	Congressional election		Presidential election	
	1970	1974	1968	1972
Percent of voting-age population who reported that they voted				
United States	44	34	58	52
South	37	30	52	48
North and West	51	38	65	57
Percent of registered population who reported that they voted				
United States	72	62	87	80
South	64	54	84	75
North and West	80	70	90	85
White				
Number who reported that they voted				
United States	60,426	57,918	72,213	78,167
South	14,313	13,850	17,853	20,201
North and West	46,113	44,069	54,362	57,966
Percent of voting-age population who reported that they voted				
United States	56	46	69	64
South	46	37	62	57
North and West	60	50	72	68
Percent of registered population who reported that they voted				
United States	81	73	92	88
South	71	61	87	82
North and West	84	77	93	90

Source: "Reporter Voter Participation of Persons of Voting Age, by Region: 1968, 1970, 1972, and 1974," U.S. Bureau of the Census, Current Population Reports, Special Studies, Series P-23, No. 54, *The Social and Economic Status of the Black Population in the United States, 1974*, p. 145. Primary source: U.S. Department of Commerce, Social and Economic Statistics Administration, Bureau of the Census.

★ 1556 ★

Voters and Voting

Voter Participation by Region, 1964-1970

(Numbers in millions)

Subject	Negro				White			
	1964	1966	1968	1970	1964	1966	1968	1970
All persons of voting age	10.3	10.5	10.9	11.5	99.4	101.2	104.5	108.0
North and West	5.4	4.8	4.9	5.3	72.8	72.6	75.7	77.2
South	5.8	5.7	6.0	6.2	26.6	28.6	28.8	30.8
Number who reported that they voted								
United States	6.0	4.4	6.3	5.0	70.2	57.8	72.2	60.4
North and West	3.9	2.5	3.2	2.7	54.4	44.8	54.4	46.1
South	2.6	1.9	3.1	2.3	15.8	12.9	17.9	14.3
Percent who reported that they voted								
United States	59	42	58	44	71	57	69	56
North and West	72[1]	52	65	51	75	62	72	60
South	44[1]	33	52	37	60	45	62	46

Source: "Reporter Voting Participation for Persons of Voting Age, by Region: 1964, 1966, 1968, and 1970," U.S. Bureau of the Census, Current Population Reports, Special Studies, Series P-23, No. 42, *The Social and Economic Status of the Black Population in the United States, 1971*, p. 117. Primary source: U.S. Department of Commerce, Social and Economic Statistics Administration, Bureau of the Census. *Note:* 1. For Negro and other races.

★ 1557 ★

Voters and Voting

Voter Participation in General Elections: 1964-1974

Numbers in thousands.

Subject	Presidential election			Congressional election		
	1964	1968	1972	1966	1970	1974
BLACK						
Number who reported that they voted						
United States	6,048	6,300	7,033	4,398	4,992	4,786
South	2,576[1]	3,094	3,324	1,870	2,278	2,219
North and West	3,891[1]	3,206	3,707	2,528	2,714	2,567
Percent of voting-age population who reported that they voted						
United States	58	58	52	42	44	34
South	44[1]	52	48	33	37	30
North and West	72[1]	65	57	52	51	38
Percent of registered population who reported that they voted						
United States	(NA)	87	80	69	72	62

[Continued]

★ 1557 ★

Voter Participation in General Elections: 1964-1974

[Continued]

Subject	Presidential election			Congressional election		
	1964	1968	1972	1966	1970	1974
South	(NA)	84	75	62	64	54
North and West	(NA)	90	85	76	80	70
WHITE						
Number who reported that they voted						
United States	70,204	72,213	78,167	57,757	60,426	57,918
South	15,813	17,853	20,201	12,922	14,313	13,850
North and West	54,392	54,362	57,966	44,835	46,113	44,069
Percent of voting-age population who reported that they voted						
United States	71	69	64	57	56	46
South	59	62	57	45	46	37
North and West	75	72	68	62	60	50
Percent of registered population who reported that hey voted						
United States	(NA)	92	88	80	81	73
South	(NA)	87	82	70	71	61
North and West	(NA)	93	90	83	84	77

Source: "Reported Voter Participation of Persons of Voting Age, by Region for General Elections: 1964 to 1974," U.S. Department of Commerce, Bureau of the Census, *The Social and Economic Status of the Black Population in the United States: An Historical View, 1790-1978,* p. 151. Primary source: U.S. Department of Commerce, Bureau of the Census. *Notes:* NA Not available. Data includes all persons 18 years old and over in Georgia and Kentucky, 19 years old and over in Alaska, 20 years old and over in Hawaii, and 21 years old and over in remaining states. For 1972 and 1974, data include all persons 28 years old and over. 1. Includes persons of "other" races.

★ 1558 ★

Voters and Voting

Voter Participation in Presidential Elections: 1964, 1968, 1972

Numbers in thousands.

Age	Black			White		
	1964	1968	1972	1966	1970	1974
PERSONS OF VOTING AGE						
Total, 18 years old and over	10,340	10,935	13,493	99,353	104,521	121,243
18 to 24 years	1,115	1,255	2,994	8,715	9,820	21,339
25 to 44 years	4,596	4,713	5,130	40,196	40,855	43,394
45 to 64 years	3,364	3,515	3,757	34,519	36,519	38,201
65 years old and over	1,266	1,363	1,613	15,924	16,989	18,307

[Continued]

★ 1558 ★

Voter Participation in Presidential Elections: 1964, 1968, 1972

[Continued]

Age	Black			White		
	1964	1968	1972	1966	1970	1974
PERCENT OF VOTING AGE POPULATION WHO REPORTED THAT THEY VOTED						
Total, 18 years old and over	58.5	57.6	52.1	70.7	69.1	64.5
18 to 24 years	44.2	38.9	34.7	52.1	52.8	51.9
25 to 44 years	61.5	60.3	55.6	70.1	67.7	64.0
45 to 64 years	64.1	64.5	61.9	77.2	76.1	71.9
65 years old and over	45.3	49.9	50.6	68.1	67.4	64.8

Source: "Reported Voter Participation of Persons of Voting Age, by Age for Presidential Elections: 1964, 1968, and 1972," U.S. Department of Commerce, Bureau of the Census, *The Social and Economic Status of the Black Population in the United States: An Historical View, 1790-1978*, p. 152. Primary source: U.S. Department of Commerce, Bureau of the Census. *Notes:* Data includes all persons 18 years old and over in Georgia and Kentucky, 19 years old and over in Alaska, 20 years old and over in Hawaii, and 21 years old and over in remaining states. For 1972 and 1974, data include all persons 28 years old and over.

★ 1559 ★

Voters and Voting

Voter Participation of Voting-Age Persons by Region, 1966 and 1970

Numbers in thousands.

Subject	Negro		White	
	1966	1970	1966	1970
All persons of voting age	10,533	11,472	101,205	107,997
North and west	4,849	5,277	72,593	77,158
South	5,684	6,196	28,612	30,839
Number who reported that they voted				
United States	4,398	4,992	57,757	60,426
North and west	2,528	2,714	44,835	46,113
South	1,870	2,278	12,922	14,313
Percent who reported that they voted				
United States	42	44	57	56
North and west	52	51	62	60
South	33	37	45	46

Source: "Reported Voter Participation for Persons of Voting Age, by Region: 1966 and 1970," U.S. Bureau of the Census, *The Social and Economic Status of the Black Population in the United States, 1970*, p. 141. Primary source: U.S. Department of Commerce, Bureau of the Census.

★ 1560 ★

Voters and Voting

Voter Registration by Region and Election, 1968-1974

(Numbers in thousands)

Subject	Congressional election		Presidential election	
	1970	1974	1968	1972
Black				
All persons of voting age				
United States	11,472	14,175	10,935	13,493
South	6,196	7,401	5,991	6,950
North and West	5,277	6,774	4,944	6,543
Number who reported that they registered				
United States	6,971	7,778	7,238	8,837
South	3,565	4,107	3,690	4,450
North and West	3,406	3,671	3,548	4,387
Percent of voting-age population				
United States	61	55	66	65
South	58	55	62	64
North and West	65	54	72	67
White				
All persons of voting age				
United States	107,997	125,132	104,521	121,243
South	30,839	37,074	28,834	35,413
North and West	77,158	88,058	75,687	85,830
Number who reported that they registered				
United States	74,672	79,490	78,835	88,987
South	20,081	22,611	20,416	24,707
North and West	54,591	56,879	58,419	64,279
Percent of voting-age population				
United States	69	64	75	73
South	65	61	71	70
North and West	71	65	77	75

Source: "Reported Voter Registration of Persons of Voting Age, by Region: 1968, 1970, 1972, and 1974," U.S. Bureau of the Census, Current Population Reports, Special Studies, Series P-23, No. 54, *The Social and Economic Status of the Black Population in the United States, 1974,* p. 146. Primary source: U.S. Department of Commerce, Social and Economic Statistics Administration, Bureau of the Census.

★ 1561 ★

Voters and Voting

Voter Registration by Region – 1966, 1968, 1970

(Numbers in thousands)

Subject	Negro			White		
	1966	1968	1970	1966	1968	1970
All persons of voting age	10,533	10,935	11,473	101,205	104,521	107,997
North and West	4,849	4,944	5,277	72,593	75,687	77,158
South	5,684	5,991	6,196	28,612	28,834	30,839
Number who reported they had registered						
United States	6,345	7,238	6,971	72,517	78,835	74,672
North and West	3,337	3,548	3,406	54,125	58,419	54,591
South	3,008	3,690	3,565	18,392	20,416	20,081
Percent of voting age population						
United States	60	66	61	72	75	69
North and West	69	72	65	75	77	71
South	53	62	58	64	71	65

Source: "Reporter Voter Registration for Persons of Voting Age, by Region: 1966, 1968, and 1970," U.S. Bureau of the Census, Current Population Reports, Special Studies, Series P-23, No. 42, *The Social and Economic Status of the Black Population in the United States, 1971,* p. 116. Primary source: U.S. Department of Commerce, Social and Economic Statistics Administration, Bureau of the Census.

★ 1562 ★

Voters and Voting

Voter Registration in Eleven Southern States, 1960 to 1971

In thousands, except percent. For 1960 to 1970, covers population 18 years old and over in Georgia, and 21 and over elsewhere; for 1971, covers population 18 years old and over for all the southern states.

Item	Total	Ala.	Ark.	Fla.	Ga.	La.	Miss.	N.C.	S.C.	Tenn.	Tex.	Va.
1960												
White	12,276	860	518	1,819	1,020	993	478	1,861	481	1,300	2,079	867
Negro	1,463	66	73	183	180	159	22	210	58	185	227	100
Percent white[1]	61.1	63.6	60.9	69.3	56.8	76.9	63.9	92.1	57.1	73.0	42.5	46.1
Percent Negro[1,2]	29.1	13.7	38.0	39.4	29.3	31.1	5.2	39.1	13.7	59.1	35.5	23.1
1964												
White	14,264	946	621	2,200	1,340	1,037	525	1,942	703	1,297	2,602	1,050
Negro	2,164	111	95	300	270	165	29	258	144	218	375	200
1966												
White	14,310	1,192	598	2,093	1,378	1,072	471	1,654	718	1,375	2,600	1,159
Negro	2,689	250	115	303	300	243	175	282	191	225	400	205
1968												
White	15,702	1,117	640	2,195	1,524	1,133	691	1,579	587	1,448	3,532	1,256
Negro	3,112	273	130	292	344	350	251	305	189	228	540	255
1970												
White	16,985	1,311	728	2,495	1,615	1,143	690	1,640	668	1,600	3,599	1,496

[Continued]

★ 1562 ★

Voter Registration in Eleven Southern States, 1960 to 1971

[Continued]

Item	Total	Ala.	Ark.	Fla.	Ga.	La.	Miss.	N.C.	S.C.	Tenn.	Tex.	Va.
Negro	3,357	315	153	302	395	319	286	305	221	242	550	269
1971												
White	17,378	1,370	674	3,065[3]	1,598	1,330[3]	671	1,911[3]	681[3]	1,542	3,700	1,550
Negro	3,449	290	165	349[3]	450	388[3]	268	35.1[3]	233[3]	245	575	275
Percent white[1]	65.0	78.5	61.4	69.9[3]	68.8	74.0[3]	69.7	65.2[3]	50.2[3]	67.3	56.8	59.6
Percent Negro[1,2]	58.6	54.7	80.9	53.2[3]	64.2	58.9[3]	59.4	49.8[3]	49.2[3]	565.6	68.2	52.0

Source: "White and Negro Voter Registration in 11 Southern States: 1960 to 1971," *Statistical Abstract of the United States*, 1975, p. 449. Primary source: Voter Education Project, Inc., Atlanta, Ga., *Voter Registration in the South. Notes:* 1. Of voting age population. 2. Includes other minority races. 3. 1974 data.

★ 1563 ★

Voters and Voting

Voters in Presidential Election: Eleven Southern States, 1916

States	Votes cast				Estimated number of males of voting age in 1916			*	**	***
	Democrat	Republican	All others	Total	White	Negro	Total			
Alabama	99,546	28,662	2,950	131,158	337,000	233,000	570,000	29.5	35.9	23.0
Arkansas	112,148	47,148	9,014	168,310	320,000	125,000	445,000	35.0	52.6	37.8
Florida	55,984	14,611	10,208	80,803	152,000	104,000	256,000	36.7	53.1	31.5
Georgia	125,845	11,225	20,920	156,690	398,000	293,000	691,000	31.6	39.8	23.0
Kentucky	269,990	241,854	8,103	519,947	550,000	76,000	626,000	49.7	94.5	83.0
Louisiana	79,875	6,466	6,641	92,982	277,000	190,000	467,000	28.8	33.5	19.8
Mississippi	80,422	4,253	1,484	86,159	218,000	250,000	468,000	36.8	39.5	18.6
N. Carolina	168,383	120,988	541	289,912	398,000	156,000	554,000	42.3	72.8	52.3
S. Carolina	61,846	1,550	135	63,531	187,000	179,000	366,000	33.0	33.9	17.3
Tennessee	153,282	116,223	2,689	272,194	468,000	122,000	590,000	32.7	58.1	46.1
Texas	286,514	64,990	20,984	372,461	975,000	184,000	1,159,000	29.3	38.2	32.1
Virginia	102,824	49,356	1,910	154,090	400,000	166,000	566,000	25.7	38.5	27.2

Source: Untitled table. Monroe N. Work, ed., *Negro Year Book: An Annual Encyclopedia of the Negro, 1918-1919*, p. 64. *Notes:* *Per cent that total Democratic votes cast was of the total No. of whites of voting age. **Per cent that total votes cast by whites and Negroes in all parties was of the total number of whites of voting age. F ***Per cent that total votes cast by white and Negroes in all parties was of the total number of whites and Negroes of voting age.

★ 1564 ★

Voters and Voting

Voting Age Population by State and Race, 1974

In thousands. As of November. Resident population; includes aliens.

State	Total, 18 years old and over		18-24 years		25-44 years		45-64 years		65 years and over	
	All races	Black	All races	Black	All races	Black	All races	Black	All races	Black
U.S.	144,928	14,646[1]	26,807	3,308[1]	52,754	5,626[1]	43,374	3,955[1]	21,994	1,756[1]
Alabama	2,392	537	454	115	860	169	705	157	373	96
Alaska	206	[1]	53	[1]	97	[1]	47	[1]	9	[1]
Arizona	1,442	35	276	8	532	14	422	9	212	4
Arkansas	1,417	209	242	42	485	60	422	59	268	48
California	14,509	973	2,728	222	5,528	411	4,256	254	1,997	86
Colorado	1,719	51	370	15	678	22	465	10	206	4
Connecticut	2,124	116	341	25	784	55	683	28	316	8
Delaware	391	49	77	12	151	19	115	13	48	5
District of Columbia	526	369	102	78	208	156	144	102	72	33
Florida	5,799	699	924	152	1,837	271	1,756	195	1,282	81
Georgia	3,227	743	639	177	1,266	269	903	198	419	99
Hawaii	571	[1]	125	[1]	228	[1]	164	[1]	54	[1]
Idaho	519	[1]	100	[1]	187	[1]	155	[1]	77	[1]
Illinois	7,646	913	1,371	203	2,792	389	2,337	232	1,146	89
Indiana	3,603	233	686	54	1,335	91	1,058	63	524	25
Iowa	2,002	[1]	357	[1]	683	[1]	600	[1]	362	[1]
Kansas	1,601	71	308	19	546	25	464	17	283	10
Kentucky	2,296	154	438	36	820	49	674	44	364	25
Louisiana	2,457	659	507	157	908	230	703	176	339	96
Maine	700	[1]	123	[1]	242	[1]	210	[1]	125	[1]
Maryland	2,781	461	522	105	1,090	189	830	122	339	45
Massachusetts	4,086	120	769	31	1,425	52	1,229	27	663	10
Michigan	6,037	673	1,185	165	2,259	257	1,787	185	806	66
Minnesota	2,634	[1]	509	[1]	956	[1]	735	[1]	434	[1]
Mississippi	1,495	459	307	106	518	140	418	125	252	88
Missouri	3,296	311	581	70	1,149	115	970	83	596	43
Montana	484	[1]	92	[1]	172	[1]	148	[1]	72	[1]
Nebraska	1,068	[1]	201	[1]	367	[1]	307	[1]	193	[1]
Nevada	382	[1]	65	[1]	158	[1]	118	[1]	41	[1]
New Hampshire	550	[1]	97	[1]	206	[1]	160	[1]	87	[1]
New Jersey	5,099	510	818	111	1,843	222	1,682	130	756	47
New Mexico	731	[1]	154	[1]	283	[1]	207	[1]	87	[1]
New York	12,700	1,487	2,110	302	4,583	670	3,995	390	2,012	125
North Carolina	3,635	705	736	171	1,362	240	1,060	203	477	91
North Dakota	431	[1]	89	[1]	143	[1]	128	[1]	71	[1]
Ohio	7,281	637	1,350	138	2,666	246	2,204	179	1,061	74
Oklahoma	1,879	110	339	26	659	36	550	29	331	19
Oregon	1,587	[1]	284	[1]	572	[1]	477	[1]	254	[1]
Pennsylvania	8,336	683	1,400	138	2,817	258	2,767	201	1,352	86
Rhode Island	691	[1]	131	[1]	231	[1]	217	[1]	112	[1]
South Carolina	1,831	474	396	118	691	163	522	132	222	61
South Dakota	464	[1]	90	[1]	149	[1]	141	[1]	84	[1]
Tennessee	2,881	399	531	89	1,071	134	851	113	428	63

[Continued]

★ 1564 ★

Voting Age Population by State and Race, 1974

[Continued]

State	Total, 18 years old and over		18-24 years		25-44 years		45-64 years		65 years and over	
	All races	Black	All races	Black	All races	Black	All races	Black	All races	Black
Texas	8,050	928	1,614	218	3,046	346	2,262	239	1,128	125
Utah	746	[1]	175	[1]	287	[1]	196	[1]	88	[1]
Vermont	316	[1]	62	[1]	116	[1]	87	[1]	51	[1]
Virginia	3,331	548	672	119	1,275	193	970	164	414	72
Washington	2,377	48	453	14	885	19	683	12	356	3
West Virginia	1,238	41	211	7	417	10	400	13	210	11
Wisconsin	3,121	82	596	23	1,102	37	915	17	508	5
Wyoming	244	[1]	47	[1]	89	[1]	75	[1]	33	[1]

Source: "Estimated Population of Voting Age, by Age and Race-States: 1974," *Statistical Abstract of the United States*, 1975, p. 453. Primary source: U.S. Bureau of the Census, *Current Population Reports*, series P-25, No. 526. *Notes:* 1. Data not shown where less than 50,000 black population living in the state; therefore state breakdown does not add to total.

★ 1565 ★

Voters and Voting

Voting Age Population, Estimated by State, 1960-1974

In thousands. As of November 1. Includes Armed Forces stationed in each state.

State	1960[1]		1964[1]	1970[1]		1972[2]		1974[2]		Black
	Total	Black		1968[1]	Total	Black	Total	Black	Total	
U.S.	109,674	10,098	114,085	120,285	124,498	11,935	140,068	13,992	144,929	14,645
Alabama	1,850	480	1,919	1,993	2,042	452	2,314	503	2,392	537
Alaska	139[3]	4[3]	153[3]	166[3]	178[3]	6[3]	197	6	206	(s)
Arizona	760	23	878	975	1,056	26	1,295	32	1,442	35
Arkansas	1,049	191	1,108	1,143	1,180	174	1,354	192	1,417	209
California	9,895	420	11,047	11,885	12,376	760	13,969	922	14,509	973
Colorado	1,056	23	1,142	1,251	1,328	36	1,586	46	1,719	51
Connecticut	1,608	61	1,724	1,826	1,886	94	2,089	116	2,124	116
Delaware	272	34	292	314	326	40	378	47	391	49
District of Columbia	513	245	513	495	483	314	530	362	526	369
Florida	3,176	468	3,623	4,124	4,451	529	5,242	621	5,799	699
Georgia	2,507[2]	614[2]	2,634[2]	2,851[2]	2,985	677[2]	3,098	700	3,227	743
Hawaii	371[4]	3[4]	404[4]	439[4]	473[4]	5[4]	536	6	571	(s)
Idaho	377	1	379	397	418	1	491	1	519	(s)
Illinois	6,298	584	6,422	6,667	6,795	747	7,532	893	7,646	913
Indiana	2,799	149	2,845	3,003	3,104	185	3,496	224	3,603	233
Iowa	1,666	14	1,625	1,673	1,712	16	1,936	21	2,002	(s)
Kansas	1,334	51	1,318	1,346	1,380	56	1,553	67	1,601	71
Kentucky	1,950[2]	134[2]	1,964[2]	2,063[2]	2,136[2]	140[2]	2,204	147	2,296	154
Louisiana	1,813	512	1,894	2,002	2,058	534	2,373	616	2,457	659
Maine	588	2	585	592	601	1	683	2	700	(s)
Maryland	1,867	284	2,065	2,271	2,372	372	2,690	441	2,781	461
Massachusetts	3,266	66	3,349	3,459	3,538	92	3,968	115	4,086	120

[Continued]

★ 1565 ★

Voting Age Population, Estimated by State, 1960-1974

[Continued]

State	1960[1]		1964[1]	1970[1]		1972[2]		1974[2]		Black
	Total	Black		1968[1]	Total	Black	Total	Black	Total	
Michigan	4,598	402	4,719	5,032	5,200	530	5,868	647	6,037	673
Minnesota	2,017	12	2,050	2,154	2,248	18	2,546	23	2,634	(s)
Mississippi	1,177	418	1,207	1,229	1,253	379	1,435	416	1,495	459
Missouri	2,706	220	2,709	2,813	2,913	254	3,228	304	3,296	311
Montana	395	1	402	403	410	1	469	1	484	(s)
Nebraska	868	16	879	881	906	20	1,030	25	1,068	(s)
Nevada	184	8	260	284	303	14	357	17	382	(s)
New Hampshire	376	1	398	427	452	1	520	2	550	(s)
New Jersey	3,919	302	4,142	4,358	4,507	412	4,997	499	5,099	510
New Mexico	504	9	530	539	561	9	671	11	731	(s)
New York	10,965	890	11,066	11,336	11,543	1,229	12,663	1,486	12,700	1,487
North Carolina	2,585	537	2,723	2,921	3,043	569	3,496	665	3,635	705
North Dakota	357	1	362	354	360	1	413	2	431	(s)
Ohio	5,888	446	5,962	6,252	6,419	525	7,123	623	7,281	637
Oklahoma	1,431	82	1,471	1,540	1,605	88	1,809	105	1,879	110
Oregon	1,079	10	1,141	1,231	1,308	14	1,503	18	1,587	(s)
Pennsylvania	7,122	496	7,100	7,273	7,412	567	8,193	664	8,336	683
Rhode Island	540	10	545	573	596	13	671	17	691	(s)
South Carolina	1,272	371	1,333	1,427	1,487	377	1,748	438	1,831	474
South Dakota	395	1	395	384	389	1	447	1	464	(s)
Tennessee	2,110	313	2,212	2,325	2,410	323	2,758	373	2,881	399
Texas	5,605	644	5,889	6,327	6,658	735	7,655	879	8,050	928
Utah	479	2	512	551	583	3	699	5	746	(s)
Vermont	231	(z)	232	252	265	(z)	306	1	316	(s)
Virginia	2,349	434	2,539	2,717	2,823	458	3,202	523	3,331	548
Washington	1,727	27	1,754	1,975	2,078	38	2,306	48	2,377	48
West Virginia	1,075	48	1,049	1,061	1,077	37	1,221	39	1,238	41
Wisconsin	2,372	39	2,434	2,543	2,615	60	2,991	77	3,121	82
Wyoming	192	1	192	190	198	1	229	2	244	(s)

Source: "Estimated Population of Voting Age—States: 1960 to 1974," *Statistical Abstract of the United States*, 1975, p. 452. Primary source: U.S. Bureau of the Census, *Current Population Reports*, series P-25, No. 526, and unpublished data. *Notes:* S Data not shown where less than 50,000 black population (all ages) living in the State. Z Less than 500. 1. Population age 21 and over, except as noted. 2. Population age 18 and over. 3. Population age 19 and over. 4. Population age 20 and over.

★ 1566 ★

Voters and Voting

Voting Age Population, by Region and State, 1940

Race and citizenship	Total population (All ages)	Population 21 years old and over
Foreign-born		
White	11,419,138[1]	11,123,950[1]
Citizen	7,250,252	7,130,158
Alien	3,343,814	3,205,457
Negro	12,865,518[1]	7,427,938[1]
Citizen	12,811,590	7,375,609
Alien	44,021	42,878
Other nonwhite races	588,887	325,155
Citizen	497,070	238,098
Alien	91,817	87,057

Source: "Negro Population of Voting Age in the United States: by Regions and States: 1940 and 1930," Florence Murray, ed. *The Negro Handbook, 1946-47,* p. 14. *Note:* 1. Includes persons for whom citizenship was not reported.

★ 1567 ★

Voters and Voting

Voting Age and Citizenship, 1940

Population	Negro	All classes	Percent Negro
All ages	12,865,518[1]	131,669,275	9.8
21 years and over	7,427,938	83,996,629	8.8
Citizens, 21 years and over	7,375,609	79,863,451	9.2
Alien	52,329	3,335,392	1.6

Source: "Population of Voting Age and Citizenship, for Negroes and Total Population for the United States: 1940," Jessie Parkhurst Guzman, ed., *Negro Year Book: A Review of Events Affecting Negro Life, 1941-1946,* p. 275. *Note:* 1. Includes persons for whom citizenship was not reported.

★ 1568 ★

Voters and Voting

Voting Age, School Age, and Illiterates: by States, 1913

States	Number of voting age	Number school age	Per cent attending school	Number of Negro illiterates 10 yrs. of age and over	Per cent Negroes 10 yrs. of age and over illiterate
United States	2,458,873	3,422,157	47.3	2,227,731	30.4
New England states	22,074	15,539	65.6	4,341	7.8
Maine	476	355	63.1	93	8.0
New Hampshire	200	138	55.8	51	10.6
Vermont	975	251	52.2	69	4.8
Massachusetts	12,591	8,797	66.5	2,584	8.1
Rhode Island	3,967	2,277	62.5	752	9.5
Connecticut	4,765	3,721	67.1	792	6.3
Middle Atlantic	138,750	95,194	57.5	27,811	7.9
New York	45,877	27,192	55.9	5,768	5.0
New Jersey	28,001	21,832	59.1	7,405	9.9
Pennsylvania	64,272	46,170	57.8	14,638	9.1
East North Central	107,170	72,837	61.0	28,071	11.0
Ohio	39,188	27,830	61.9	10,460	11.1
Maryland	20,651	15,560	62.3	6,959	13.7
Illinois	39,983	24,825	58.7	9,713	10.5
Michigan	6,266	3,994	64.1	826	5.7
Wisconsin	1,082	628	63.2	113	4.5
West North Central	83,219	64,085	58.1	30,436	14.9
Minnesota	3,390	1,189	65.7	215	3.4
Iowa	5,443	3,866	64.5	1,272	10.3
Missouri	52,921	41,682	54.7	23,062	17.4
North Dakota	311	103	58.3	26	4.8
South Dakota	341	184	66.3	38	5.5
Nebraska	3,225	1,512	61.5	482	7.2
Kansas	17,588	15,549	64.6	5,341	12.0
South Atlantic	955,364	1,504,019	47.0	969,432	32.5
Delaware	9,050	10,078	57.7	6,345	25.6
Maryland	63,968	73,230	52.5	42,289	23.4
District of Columbia	27,621	25,593	59.3	10,814	13.5
Virginia	159,593	242,413	47.2	48,950	30.0
West Virginia	22,757	18,481	53.1	10,347	20.3
North Carolina	146,752	264,025	54.2	156,303	31.9
South Carolina	169,155	331,429	45.8	226,242	38.7
Georgia	265,814	439,485	42.1	308,639	36.5
Florida	89,659	101,285	44.1	59,503	25.5
East South Central	642,460	944,880	47.3	681,507	34.8
Kentucky	75,694	81,976	53.7	57,900	27.6
Tennessee	119,142	163,397	47.2	98,541	27.3
Alabama	213,923	327,176	40.7	265,628	40.1
Mississippi	233,701	372,331	51.8	259,438	35.6
West South Central	488,815	715,597	43.8	483,022	33.1
Arkansas	111,365	159,431	48.6	86,398	26.4
Louisiana	174,211	254,580	28.9	254,148	48.4

[Continued]

★ 1568 ★

Voting Age, School Age, and Illiterates: by States, 1913

[Continued]

States	Number of voting age	Number school age	Per cent attending school	Number of Negro illiterates 10 yrs. of age and over	Per cent Negroes 10 yrs. of age and over illiterate
Oklahoma	36,841	48,718	63.8	17,858	17.7
Texas	166,398	252,868	51.7	124,618	24.6
Mountain	8,992	4,170	60.7	1,497	8.0
Montana	851	300	61.3	114	7.0
Idaho	328	80	-	37	6.4
Wyoming	1,325	286	49.7	102	5.0
Colorado	4,283	2,468	62.7	856	8.6
New Mexico	644	363	59.0	191	14.2
Arizona	764	416	60.3	122	7.2
Utah	568	196	77.1	49	4.8
Nevada	229	52	-	26	5.5
Pacific	12,029	5,836	60.9	1,614	6.3
Washington	3,120	906	56.8	239	4.3
Oregon	766	198	53.0	46	3.4
California	8,143	2,936	62.0	1,329	7.1

Source: "Negroes of Voting Age, School Age, and Illiterates by States," Monroe N. Work, ed., *Negro Year Book: An Annual Encyclopedia of the Negro*, pp. 266-267.

★ 1569 ★

Voters and Voting

Voting Age, by Sex and Region, 1920

Division and state	Number voting age						Per cent distribution			
	Males		Females		Total		Males		Females	
	White	Negro	White	Negro	White	Negro	White	Negro	White	Negro
United States	28,442,400	2,792,006	26,671,061	2,730,469	55,113,461	5,522,475	90.6	8.9	90.5	9.3
New England										
Maine	240,895	492	232,790	384	473,685	876	99.6	0.2	99.7	0.2
New Hampshire	140,880	229	139,650	159	280,530	388	99.8	0.2	99.9	0.1
Vermont	110,159	198	106,515	144	216,674	352	99.8	0.2	99.9	0.1
Massachusetts	1,154,369	15,550	1,223,985	14,682	2,378,354	30,232	98.5	1.3	98.8	1.2
Rhode Island	176,073	3,396	185,709	3,158	361,782	6,554	98.0	1.9	98.3	1.7
Connecticut	416,307	7,263	407,296	6,480	823,603	13,743	98.1	1.7	98.4	1.6
Middle Atlantic										
New York	3,177,406	69,259	3,183,943	73,283	6,361,349	142,544	97.6	2.1	97.7	2.2
New Jersey	921,957	37,511	898,771	38,160	1,820,728	75,671	96.0	3.9	95.9	4.1
Pennsylvania	2,481,133	103,137	2,364,508	88,089	4,845,641	191,226	95.9	4.0	96.4	3.6
East North Central										
Ohio	1,775,424	70,853	1,654,973	56,087	3,430,597	126,940	96.1	3.8	96.7	3.3
Indiana	880,164	28,651	845,285	25,284	1,725,449	53,935	96.8	3.2	97.1	2.9
Illinois	1,958,116	67,846	1,854,489	60,604	3,812,605	128,450	96.5	3.3	96.8	3.2
Michigan	1,163,745	25,887	1,004,322	17,520	2,168,067	43,407	97.6	2.2	98.1	1.7
Wisconsin	795,265	2,144	723,708	1,465	1,518,973	3,609	99.4	0.3	99.5	0.2

[Continued]

★ 1569 ★

Voting Age, by Sex and Region, 1920

[Continued]

Division and state	Number voting age						Per cent distribution			
	Males		Females		Total		Males		Females	
	White	Negro	White	Negro	White	Negro	White	Negro	White	Negro
West North Central										
Minnesota	731,857	3,838	637,535	2,828	1,369,392	6,666	99.1	0.5	99.2	0.4
Iowa	730,477	6,930	685,082	5,629	1,415,559	12,568	99.0	0.9	99.2	0.8
Missouri	974,483	63,452	942,381	57,876	1,916,864	121,328	93.8	6.1	94.2	5.8
North Dakota	176,167	207	143,225	129	319,392	336	98.9	0.1	98.9	0.1
South Dakota	184,106	315	151,516	205	335,622	520	97.5	0.2	97.1	0.1
Nebraska	383,501	5,378	343,151	4,059	726,652	9,437	98.3	1.4	98.6	1.2
Kansas	514,015	19,562	472,173	17,448	986,188	37,010	96.2	3.7	94.6	3.6
South Atlantic										
Delaware	60,875	9,657	57,484	8,456	118,359	18,113	86.3	13.7	87.2	12.8
Maryland	360,412	73,086	359,600	68,905	720,012	142,091	83.1	16.8	83.9	16.1
District of Columbia	105,401	33,822	125,779	39,626	231,180	73,448	75.4	24.2	76.0	23.9
Virginia	437,083	176,036	418,040	175,193	855,123	251,231	71.2	28.7	70.4	29.5
West Virginia	373,663	29,826	327,443	21,319	701,106	51,145	92.6	7.4	93.9	6.1
North Carolina	433,875	167,240	429,180	175,516	863,055	342,756	71.9	27.7	70.7	28.9
South Carolina	205,533	183,474	197,263	193,456	402,796	376,930	52.8	47.1	50.5	49.5
Georgia	428,759	282,779	417,269	292,551	846,028	575,330	60.2	39.7	58.8	41.2
Florida	185,187	95,092	169,959	85,916	355,146	171,008	66.0	33.9	66.4	33.6
East South Central										
Kentucky	584,721	73,091	560,804	70,790	1,145,525	143,881	88.9	11.1	88.8	11.2
Tennessee	488,515	120,947	480,929	124,448	969,444	245,395	80.1	19.8	79.4	20.6
Alabama	357,822	215,915	344,209	225,215	702,131	441,130	62.4	37.6	60.4	39.5
Mississippi	215,098	225,700	206,561	227,963	421,659	453,663	48.7	51.1	47.5	52.4
West South Central										
Arkansas	328,115	123,939	296,788	118,295	624,903	242,244	72.6	27.4	71.5	28.5
Louisiana	290,374	178,623	273,643	180,628	564,017	359,251	61.8	38.0	60.2	39.7
Oklahoma	497,552	40,110	423,301	36,221	920,853	76,331	90.4	7.3	89.8	7.7
Texas	1,086,862	196,055	957,408	188,373	2,044,270	384,428	84.6	15.3	83.5	16.4
Mountain										
Montana	179,526	754	132,538	508	312,064	1,262	97.2	0.4	97.6	0.4
Idaho	130,256	463	99,732	236	229,988	699	98.0	0.3	98.6	0.2
Wyoming	67,667	678	45,015	387	112,682	1,065	96.9	1.0	98.1	0.8
Colorado	297,728	4,237	256,070	3,869	553,798	8,106	98.0	1.4	98.2	1.5
New Mexico	93,326	4,046	77,831	763	161,157	4,809	91.0	3.9	94.2	0.9
Arizona	94,909	5,075	69,720	1,484	164,629	6,559	86.8	4.6	87.9	1.0
Utah	117,387	652	106,242	452	223,629	1,104	97.1	0.5	98.5	0.4
Nevada	30,591	167	17,329	110	47,920	277	91.8	0.5	91.7	0.6
Pacific										
Washington	465,714	3,105	366,809	2,103	832,523	5,208	96.6	0.6	97.8	0.6
Oregon	264,302	937	221,228	683	485,530	1,620	97.5	0.3	98.8	0.2
California	1,174,678	14,393	1,031,880	13,451	2,206,558	27,539	93.9	.2	96.7	1.3

Source: "Males and Females of Voting Age in 1920," Monroe N. Work, ed., *Negro Year Book: An Annual Encyclopedia of the Negro, 1925-26*, pp. 456-457.

★ 1570 ★

Voters and Voting

Voting Results in 10 Ohio Cities, 1948 and 1950

City	1950			1948		
	Ferguson (D.)	Taft (R)	% Dem.	Truman (D)	Dewey (R)	% Dem
Cleveland	41,024	21,295	65	41,307	17,307	70
Cincinnati	15,936	8,847	64	22,082	9,987	69
Columbus	9,713	6,200	61	10,474	6,083	63
Toledo	5,990	4,142	59	8,536	4,372	66
Dayton	10,194	4,751	68	12,646	5,713	69
Akron	6,997	3,133	69	8,012	2,621	75
Springfield	4,638	3,887	54.4	4,668	3,506	57
Youngstown	8,285	3,341	71	14,585	4,033	78
Canton	.2,598	715	78	3,060	598	84
Massillon	1,019	466	69	1,376	471	74
Totals	106,394	56,777	65	126,746	54,691	69

Source: "Negro Vote in 10 Ohio Cities, 1950 and 1948," Jessie Parkhurst Guzman, ed., *Negro Year Book: A Review of Events Affecting Negro Life, 1941-1946,* p. 302.

★ 1571 ★

Voters and Voting

Voting-Age Population, by Region, 1972

Age	United States	North-east	North Central	South	West
18 years and over	10.0	8.5	7.6	16.4	4.6
Under 25 years	13.6	11.4	10.1	22.3	6.1
25 to 44 years	10.6	10.5	8.4	15.9	5.1
45 to 64 years	8.9	7.0	6.7	15.4	4.0
65 years and over	7.9	5.1	5.3	15.2	2.8

Source: "Projected Black Population as a Percent of the Voting-Age Population in the United States and Regions, by Age: 1972," U.S. Bureau of the Census. Current Population Reports, Special Studies, Series P-23, No. 42, *The Social and Economic Status of the Black Population in the United States, 1971,* p. 120. Primary source: U.S. Department of Commerce, Social and Economic Statistics Administration, Bureau of the Census.

★ 1572 ★

Voters and Voting

Voting-Age Population: Projected, 1972

(Numbers in thousands)

States	Total, 18 years old and over	Black population, 18 years and over	Percent black
United States, total	139,642	13,992	10.0
Maine	666	2	0.3
New Hampshire	521	2	0.4
Vermont	309	1	0.3
Massachusetts	3,955	115	2.9
Rhode Island	673	17	2.5
Connecticut	2,106	116	5.5
New York	12,773	1,486	11.6
New Jersey	5,025	499	9.9
Pennsylvania	8,161	664	8.1
Ohio	7,185	623	8.7
Indiana	3,509	224	6.4
Illinois	7,542	893	11.8
Michigan	5,874	647	11.0
Wisconsin	2,955	77	2.6
Minnesota	2,560	23	0.9
Iowa	1,909	21	1.1
Missouri	3,266	304	9.3
North Dakota	402	2	0.5
South Dakota	434	1	0.2
Nebraska	1,022	25	2.4
Kansas	1,541	67	4.3
Delaware	371	47	12.7
Maryland	2,688	441	16.4
District of Columbia	518	362	69.9
Virginia	3,197	523	16.4
West Virginia	1,182	39	3.3
North Carolina	3,463	665	19.2
South Carolina	1,706	438	25.7
Georgia	3,104	700	22.6
Florida	5,105	621	12.2
Kentucky	2,206	147	6.7
Tennessee	2,713	373	13.7
Alabama	2,274	503	22.1
Mississippi	1,403	416	29.7
Arkansas	1,310	192	14.7
Louisiana	2,339	616	26.3
Oklahoma	1,812	105	5.8
Texas	7,681	879	11.4
Montana	460	1	0.2
Idaho	479	1	0.2
Wyoming	225	2	0.9
Colorado	1,558	46	3.0
New Mexico	636	11	1.7

[Continued]

★ 1572 ★

Voting-Age Population: Projected, 1972

[Continued]

States	Total, 18 years old and over	Black population, 18 years and over	Percent black
Arizona	1,239	32	2.6
Utah	689	5	0.7
Nevada	348	17	4.9
Washington	2,371	48	2.0
Oregon	1,500	18	1.2
California	13,945	922	6.6
Alaska	200	6	3.0
Hawaii	531	6	1.1

Source: "The Projected 1972 Total and Black Population of Voting Age by State," U.S. Bureau of the Census, Current Population Reports, Special Studies, Series P-23, No. 42, *The Social and Economic Status of the Black Population in the United States, 1971*, p. 121. Primary source: U.S. Department of Commerce, Social and Economic Statistics Administration, Bureau of the Census.

Chapter 14
POPULATION

Age Composition

★ 1573 ★

Age Distribution of the Black Population, 1920

Age Period	Age Distribution, Negroes 1920					
	Total	Male	Female	Percent distribution		
				Total	Male	Female
United States:						
All ages	10,463,131	5,209,436	5,253,695	100.0	100.0	100.0
Under 5 years	1,143,699	568,633	575,066	10.9	10.9	10.9
Under 1 year	227,207	112,660	115,000	2.2	2.2	2.2
5 to 9 years	1,266,207	631,341	634,866	12.1	12.1	12.1
10 to 14 years	1,236,914	616,251	620,663	11.8	11.8	11.8
15 to 19 years	1,083,215	513,416	569,799	10.4	9.9	10.8
20 to 44 years	3,996,083	1,902,613	2,093,470	38.2	36.5	39.8
45 years and over	1,713,510	963,672	749,838	16.4	18.5	14.3
Age unknown	23,503	13,510	9,993	-	-	-
18 to 44 years	4,424,417	2,106,879	2,327,538	42.4	40.4	44.3
21 years and over	5,522,475	2,792,006	2,730,469	52.8	53.6	52.0
Urban Population						
All ages	3,559,473	1,737,820	1,821,653	100.0	100.0	100.0
Under 5 years	268,069	131,798	136,271	-	-	-
Under 1 year	57,332	28,183	29,149	7.5	7.6	7.5
5 to 9 years	291,762	142,780	148,982	8.2	8.2	8.2
10 to 14 years	291,094	137,844	153,250	8.2	7.9	8.4
15 to 19 years	310,522	138,893	171,629	8.7	8.0	9.4
20 to 44 years	1,762,692	848.421	914,271	49.5	48.8	50.1
45 years and over	621,935	330,667	291,268	17.5	19.9	16.0
Age unknown	13,399	7,417	5,982	-	-	-
Rural Population:						
All ages	6,903,658	3,471,616	3,432,042	100.0	100.0	100.0
Under 5 years	875,630	436,835	438,795	12.7	12.6	12.8
Under 1 year	170,328	84,474	85,851	-	-	-
5 to 9 years	974,445	488,561	485,884	14.1	14.1	14.2

[Continued]

★ 1573 ★

Age Distribution of the Black Population, 1920

[Continued]

Age Period	Age Distribution, Negroes 1920					
	Total	Male	Female	Percent distribution		
				Total	Male	Female
10 to 14 years	945,820	478,407	467,413	13.7	13.8	13.6
15 to 19 years	772,693	374,523	398,170	11.2	10.8	11.6
20 to 44 years	2,233,391	1,054,192	1,179,199	32.4	30.4	34.4
45 years and over	1,091,575	633,005	458,570	15.8	18.2	13.4
Age unknown	10,104	6,093	41,100	-	-	-

Source: "Age Distribution, Negroes 1920." Work, Monroe N., ed., *Negro Year Book: An Annual Encyclopedia of the Negro, 1925-26*, p. 432.

★ 1574 ★

Age Composition

Age Distribution, by Certain Years, for the Black Population, by Gender and for Cities with at least 50,000 Blacks, 1930 - I

Age	Atlanta		Baltimore		Birmingham		Chicago	
	Male	Female	Male	Female	Male	Female	Male	Female
All ages	39,923	50,152	70,043	72,063	46,582	52,495	115,488	118,415
Up to 29 years	24,146	30,528	36,956	40,818	27,251	32,803	56,986	64,212
Under 1 years	651	667	1,138	1,106	817	840	1,750	1,730
1 year	562	611	1,100	1,152	799	818	1,630	1,632
2 years	759	792	1,269	1,296	840	890	1,798	1,789
3 years	758	757	1,313	1,343	984	948	1,781	1,873
4 years	771	762	1,279	1,278	929	852	1,772	1,801
5 years	761	773	1,280	1,357	909	895	1,699	1,931
6 years	775	832	1,268	1,373	943	979	1,626	1,774
7 years	841	793	1,245	1,320	915	960	1,707	1,685
8 years	867	921	1,215	1,432	891	1,024	1,695	1,744
9 years	876	875	1,242	1,321	873	974	1,615	1,665
10 years	940	900	1,250	1,277	962	964	1,565	1,708
11 years	724	745	920	1,051	715	760	1,372	1,445
12 years	791	969	975	1,192	799	819	1,252	1,417
13 years	768	887	873	1,009	763	825	1,233	1,408
14 years	794	891	806	1,070	792	877	1,246	1,456
15 years	786	910	810	1,081	761	941	1,233	1,296
16 years	776	1,073	945	1,154	818	1,077	1,239	1,482
17 years	779	1,070	954	1,178	806	1,047	1,390	1,521
18 years	859	1,288	1,069	1,362	813	1,216	1,449	1,928
19 years	793	1,249	1,115	1,408	792	1,175	1,579	2,047

[Continued]

★ 1574 ★

Age Distribution, by Certain Years, for the Black Population, by Gender and for Cities with at least 50,000 Blacks, 1930 - I

[Continued]

Age	Atlanta		Baltimore		Birmingham		Chicago	
	Male	Female	Male	Female	Male	Female	Male	Female
20 years	872	1,567	1,108	1,562	818	1,408	1,576	2,442
21 years	852	1,016	1,275	1,371	873	1,207	2,048	2,290
22 years	921	1,380	1,476	1,665	1,038	1,400	2,186	2,836
23 years	829	1,339	1,518	1,642	1,069	1,402	2,427	3,032
24 years	806	1,275	1,590	1,769	1,077	1,481	2,728	3,268
25 years	986	1,474	1,676	1,783	1,214	1,544	2,822	3,383
26 years	716	1,156	1,369	1,447	964	1,331	2,814	3,254
27 years	776	1,066	1,482	1,483	1,006	1,308	2,986	3,227
28 years	911	1,280	1,724	1,730	1,189	1,439	3,278	3,651
29 years	846	1,125	1,672	1,606	1,082	1,402	3,500	3,524
60 to 79 years	1,426	1,838	2,806	2,069	1,346	1,466	3,175	3,863
60 years	365	457	646	685	308	295	641	680
61 years	46	46	134	145	67	78	215	227
62 years	93	93	198	203	118	101	269	299
63 years	87	102	192	167	93	83	262	278
64 years	80	77	161	134	75	94	202	246
65 years	198	249	374	407	172	196	376	449
66 years	36	49	80	96	39	43	129	139
67 years	45	66	100	112	38	53	141	176
68 years	64	65	125	137	65	66	121	191
69 years	53	87	120	127	45	61	131	181
70 years	115	182	193	300	88	119	167	277
71 years	20	33	50	44	23	32	58	95
72 years	33	48	91	104	41	47	92	107
73 years	29	34	59	68	33	23	77	98
74 years	26	33	53	62	26	25	53	75
75 years	61	124	80	129	54	70	82	143
76 years	22	22	51	48	21	19	49	49
77 years	16	22	32	18	11	10	36	41
78 years	26	30	34	45	16	30	34	63
79 years	11	19	33	38	13	21	40	49

Source: "Age Distribution by Single Years Up to 29, and From 60 to 79 Years for the Negro Population, by Sex, for the 15 Cities Having At Least 50,000 Negroes: 1930." U.S. Bureau of the Census, *Negroes in the United States, 1920-1932*, p. 144.

★ 1575 ★

Age Composition

Age Distribution, by Certain Years, for the Black Population, by Gender and for Cities with at least 50,000 Blacks, 1930 - II

Age	Cleveland		Detroit		Houston		Memphis	
	Male	Female	Male	Female	Male	Female	Male	Female
All ages	36,180	35,719	62,239	57,827	30,160	33,177	44,859	51,691
Up to 29 years	18,530	20,345	32,897	34,655	16,428	19,841	23,155	28,659
Under 1 years	624	616	1,046	1,016	449	427	671	666
1 year	593	585	940	949	419	450	615	593
2 years	635	685	1,101	1,082	491	492	732	756
3 years	705	727	1,121	1,183	498	432	763	738
4 years	629	659	1,106	1,074	466	464	756	772
5 years	649	718	1,103	1,128	471	530	701	739
6 years	638	671	1,038	1,028	484	535	727	788
7 years	632	655	975	974	493	526	764	770
8 years	617	692	1,033	997	551	539	746	762
9 years	591	603	997	928	450	522	7448	744
10 years	539	619	892	962	467	520	735	795
11 years	492	457	752	765	394	398	556	611
12 years	495	488	776	779	404	456	632	683
13 years	436	450	647	756	388	421	557	618
14 years	453	494	752	747	396	468	607	717
15 years	395	470	628	665	358	518	582	700
16 years	427	494	672	721	393	582	566	801
17 years	485	472	634	798	469	593	654	873
18 years	453	569	716	866	512	718	746	1,144
19 years	508	606	759	995	517	783	728	1,124
20 years	521	699	868	1,229	581	922	788	1,329
21 years	602	668	1,089	1,141	577	766	796	1,037
22 years	662	803	1,269	1,456	714	908	936	1,302
23 years	641	782	1,370	1,510	751	986	919	1,320
24 years	788	896	1,492	1,654	806	1,048	1,043	1,377
25 years	860	991	1,622	1,826	799	1,011	1,109	1,533
26 years	727	886	1,643	1,658	764	899	966	1,390
27 years	814	862	1,818	1,794	692	913	929	1,208
28 years	1,004	1,028	2,026	2,033	862	1,049	1,099	1,494
29 years	915	1,000	2,112	1,941	812	965	984	1,275
60 to 79 years	871	940	972	1,151	915	972	2,026	2,218
60 years	189	177	221	214	196	222	504	540
61 years	53	50	58	53	56	45	112	81
62 years	79	74	86	91	68	91	134	140

[Continued]

★ 1575 ★

Age Distribution, by Certain Years, for the Black Population, by Gender and for Cities with at least 50,000 Blacks, 1930 - II

[Continued]

Age	Cleveland		Detroit		Houston		Memphis	
	Male	Female	Male	Female	Male	Female	Male	Female
63 years	79	73	79	87	71	58	127	153
64 years	62	66	64	77	65	49	109	103
65 years	90	105	113	138	94	117	287	272
66 years	31	35	37	32	30	41	62	53
67 years	28	24	41	48	42	38	75	82
68 years	40	43	36	50	37	35	94	93
69 years	29	38	25	40	30	31	63	62
70 years	56	82	52	82	66	78	153	232
71 years	18	18	14	24	12	16	31	40
72 years	26	37	24	31	24	18	52	52
73 years	17	32	14	20	12	28	36	43
74 years	14	22	19	31	15	17	29	33
75 years	18	23	29	60	37	47	61	118
76 years	9	10	17	20	18	8	37	36
77 years	11	9	14	11	15	9	15	15
78 years	13	12	17	28	16	12	26	40
79 years	9	10	12	14	11	12	19	30

Source: "Age Distribution by Single Years Up to 29, and From 60 to 79 Years for the Negro Population, by Sex, for the 15 Cities Having At Least 50,000 Negroes: 1930." U.S. Bureau of the Census, *Negroes in the United States, 1920-1932,* p. 144.

★ 1576 ★

Age Composition

Age Distribution, by Certain Years, for the Black Population, by Gender and for Cities with at least 50,000 Blacks, 1930 - III

Age	New Orleans		New York		Philadelphia	
	Male	Female	Male	Female	Male	Female
All ages	59,732	69,900	156,968	170,738	108,483	111,116
Up to 29 years	33,821	40,397	82,924	95,462	56,483	63,162
Under 1 years	1,085	1,062	2,569	2,607	1,773	1,700
1 year	1,078	1,108	2,692	2,503	1,675	1,729
2 years	1,166	1,173	2,825	2,828	1,972	1,990
3 years	1,214	1,202	2,725	2,880	2,026	1,968
4 years	1,230	1,200	2,620	2,671	1,865	1,960
5 years	1,203	1,254	2,606	2,734	1,955	1,918

[Continued]

★ 1576 ★

Age Distribution, by Certain Years, for the Black Population, by Gender and for Cities with at least 50,000 Blacks, 1930 - III

[Continued]

Age	New Orleans		New York		Philadelphia	
	Male	Female	Male	Female	Male	Female
6 years	1,322	1,342	2,444	2,569	1,848	2,003
7 years	1,242	1,327	2,382	2,476	1,932	1,930
8 years	1,223	1,301	2,280	2,418	1,943	1,996
9 years	1,183	1,173	2,182	2,274	1,886	1,889
10 years	1,075	1,148	2,091	2,238	1,798	1,864
11 years	864	979	1,758	1,886	1,456	1,608
12 years	982	1,061	1,1811	,1963	1,529	1,583
13 years	898	1,103	1,608	1,789	1,345	1,517
14 years	1,007	1,163	1,719	1,799	1,357	1,469
15 years	938	1,094	1,572	1,753	1,295	1,485
16 years	979	1,258	1,566	1,900	1,379	1,636
17 years	996	1,274	1,742	2,111	1,349	1,675
18 years	1,024	1,360	2,024	2,931	1,411	2,075
19 years	1,022	1,395	2,265	3,256	1,574	2,079
20 years	1,030	1,705	2,567	3,994	1,555	2,418
21 years	1,046	1,407	3,081	3,626	1,814	2,149
22 years	1,191	1,653	3,441	4,509	2,102	2,673
23 years	1,296	1,728	3,619	4,905	2,059	2,678
24 years	1,233	1,685	3,947	4,960	2,282	2,797
25 years	1,315	1,781	4,478	5,620	2,573	3,007
26 years	1,183	1,547	4,032	4,714	2,266	2,622
27 years	1,184	1,558	4,341	4,838	2,598	2,769
28 years	1,314	1,730	4,831	5,584	2,998	3,146
29 years	1,298	1,626	5,097	5,126	2,868	2,879
60 to 79 years	1,941	2,8859	3,298	4,716	3,259	3,494
60 years	381	517	731	962	727	771
61 years	127	126	187	214	196	166
62 years	176	218	313	321	250	248
63 years	138	170	275	308	225	232
64 years	140	169	202	254	218	211
65 years	248	333	379	567	393	426
66 years	67	121	124	189	106	103
67 years	81	116	128	222	119	133
68 years	79	120	122	229	169	154
69 years	69	132	138	233	123	129
70 years	113	232	154	360	218	269

[Continued]

★ 1576 ★

Age Distribution, by Certain Years, for the Black Population, by Gender and for Cities with at least 50,000 Blacks, 1930 - III

[Continued]

Age	New Orleans		New York		Philadelphia	
	Male	Female	Male	Female	Male	Female
71 years	36	63	67	92	69	65
72 years	61	98	97	128	92	109
73 years	39	70	64	110	65	72
74 years	27	69	66	98	63	64
75 years	57	121	80	160	85	139
76 years	31	43	54	87	46	69
77 years	30	35	34	40	30	37
78 years	26	66	46	69	43	53
79 years	15	40	37	73	22	44

Source: "Age Distribution by Single Years Up to 29, and From 60 to 79 Years for the Negro Population, by Sex, for the 15 Cities Having At Least 50,000 Negroes: 1930." U.S. Bureau of the Census, *Negroes in the United States, 1920-1932*, p. 144.

★ 1577 ★

Age Composition

Age Distribution, by Certain Years, for the Black Population, by Gender and for Cities with at least 50,000 Blacks, 1930 - IV

Age	Pittsburgh		Richmond		St. Louis		Washington	
	Male	Female	Male	Female	Male	Female	Male	Female
All ages	27,962	27,021	24,354	28,634	45,832	47,748	62,225	69,843
Up to 29 years	14,235	15,397	13,446	16,176	21,933	25,069	33,005	37,393
Under 1 years	444	468	394	417	654	650	921	926
1 year	478	461	403	452	619	603	926	944
2 years	501	522	458	469	641	680	1,044	959
3 years	514	499	471	527	706	732	1,124	1,049
4 years	511	536	491	494	715	634	1,021	1,092
5 years	531	508	504	510	743	711	1,101	1,099
6 years	480	532	538	519	678	663	1,064	1,098
7 years	488	526	527	559	717	707	1,040	1,093
8 years	508	510	524	594	711	689	1,065	1,119
9 years	447	505	529	585	692	677	1,044	1,115
10 years	450	517	494	571	656	715	996	1,125
11 years	356	404	440	465	532	571	883	918
12 years	406	396	502	496	594	624	879	1,062
13 years	347	391	428	447	538	604	801	972

[Continued]

★ 1577 ★

Age Distribution, by Certain Years, for the Black Population, by Gender and for Cities with at least 50,000 Blacks, 1930 - IV

[Continued]

Age	Pittsburgh		Richmond		St. Louis		Washington	
	Male	Female	Male	Female	Male	Female	Male	Female
14 years	403	398	421	490	502	624	873	975
15 years	353	374	375	478	591	612	846	977
16 years	364	430	407	590	566	672	872	1,094
17 years	360	435	400	543	592	687	969	1,105
18 years	358	464	452	637	600	857	1,039	1,362
19 years	396	509	414	608	687	819	1,031	1,380
20 years	401	521	399	601	665	989	1,102	1,575
21 years	441	509	414	542	751	880	1,217	1,404
22 years	473	592	451	623	812	1,100	1,371	1,553
23 years	500	579	394	589	878	1,169	1,406	1,676
24 years	542	632	432	566	885	1,219	1,376	1,726
25 years	579	622	442	646	962	1,318	1,560	1,819
26 years	559	634	387	510	918	1,231	1,214	1,460
27 years	622	597	407	516	997	1,119	1,380	1,493
28 years	680	664	469	592	1,130	1,274	1,391	1,672
29 years	743	662	479	540	1,201	1,239	1,449	1,551
60 to 79 years	909	846	1,022	1,296	1,778	1,944	2,862	3,601
60 years	203	155	212	247	373	338	603	743
61 years	53	40	63	50	128	106	143	157
62 years	80	80	87	89	168	140	217	230
63 years	75	51	41	81	109	134	182	214
64 years	52	48	58	59	93	116	129	167
65 years	128	108	132	197	210	218	369	530
66 years	28	33	45	44	63	56	90	85
67 years	35	32	35	39	60	80	128	126
68 years	36	27	39	75	87	111	132	188
69 years	31	34	45	52	63	92	130	164
70 years	55	69	84	110	111	157	201	293
71 years	14	11	24	40	33	34	62	67
72 years	40	33	40	41	50	73	99	95
73 years	9	24	27	17	33	44	82	77
74 years	17	21	24	21	40	52	64	83
75 years	28	37	28	63	65	75	83	170
76 years	7	10	12	18	25	36	39	65
77 years	5	4	5	16	20	27	29	41

[Continued]

★ 1577 ★

Age Distribution, by Certain Years, for the Black Population, by Gender and for Cities with at least 50,000 Blacks, 1930 - IV

[Continued]

Age	Pittsburgh		Richmond		St. Louis		Washington	
	Male	Female	Male	Female	Male	Female	Male	Female
78 years	7	14	10	22	22	26	47	66
79 years	6	15	11	15	25	29	33	40

Source: "Age Distribution by Single Years Up to 29, and From 60 to 79 Years for the Negro Population, by Sex, for the 15 Cities Having At Least 50,000 Negroes: 1930." U.S. Bureau of the Census, *Negroes in the United States, 1920-1932*, p. 144.

★ 1578 ★

Age Composition

Age by Certain Years, for the Black Population, by Gender and for States with at least 100,000 Blacks, 1930 - I

Age	New York		New Jersey		Pennsylvania		Ohio	
	Male	Female	Male	Female	Male	Female	Male	Female
All ages	199,485	213,329	102,929	105,899	218,412	212,845	159,128	150,176
60 years	1,002	1,246	813	778	1,570	1,425	1,172	976
61 years	301	310	239	208	457	373	399	310
62 years	465	467	341	302	664	550	540	462
63 years	420	426	311	300	589	482	489	408
64 years	331	367	278	245	491	434	460	414
65 years	565	763	454	474	905	807	694	616
66 years	175	269	160	127	286	241	268	237
67 years	218	303	174	168	295	320	294	249
68 years	204	333	193	215	394	325	358	269
69 years	226	303	166	176	331	293	294	294
70 years	268	484	294	301	507	541	439	499
71 years	110	135	98	72	170	149	163	142
72 years	150	179	128	136	260	251	257	199
73 years	116	156	104	86	141	179	173	189
74 years	116	137	66	86	176	159	192	174
75 years	146	234	128	181	245	309	238	262
76 years	82	135	76	73	134	146	145	137
77 years	58	82	52	64	84	87	99	92
78 years	78	108	66	78	102	129	135	120
79 years	64	106	42	59	65	100	96	96

Source: "Age Distribution by Single Years From 60 to 79, for the Negro Population, by Sex, for States Having At Least 100,000 Negroes: 1930." U.S. Bureau of the Census, *Negroes in the United States, 1920-1932*, p. 110.

★ 1579 ★

Age Composition

Age by Certain Years, for the Black Population, by Gender and for States with at least 100,000 Blacks, 1930 - II

Age	Indiana		Illinois		Michigan		Missouri	
	Male	Female	Male	Female	Male	Female	Male	Female
All ages	57,088	54,914	164,425	164,547	88,936	80,517	111,929	111,911
60 years	515	394	1,149	1,103	386	344	1,183	986
61 years	192	146	374	352	122	104	380	297
62 years	230	187	49	472	179	165	542	433
63 years	204	189	480	450	170	169	512	413
64 years	191	191	412	415	144	137	405	352
65 years	339	321	690	702	218	238	793	656
66 years	126	98	240	236	91	71	285	257
67 years	139	137	281	298	106	98	279	252
68 years	163	125	282	312	104	98	351	333
69 years	173	133	262	291	76	88	287	273
70 years	229	201	359	471	115	146	475	510
71 years	89	78	129	161	46	47	146	116
72 years	115	105	205	183	57	77	252	210
73 years	70	76	155	169	37	46	163	154
74 years	100	77	138	156	50	51	189	171
75 years	92	133	176	280	66	97	283	307
76 years	71	68	115	116	54	38	150	121
77 years	49	33	73	88	36	31	103	91
78 years	70	56	99	115	38	54	150	130
79 years	49	47	90	85	26	32	118	93

Source: "Age Distribution by Single Years From 60 to 79, for the Negro Population, by Sex, for States Having At Least 100,000 Negroes: 1930." U.S. Bureau of the Census, *Negroes in the United States, 1920-1932*, p. 110.

★ 1580 ★

Age Composition

Age by Certain Years, for the Black Population, by Gender and for States with at least 100,000 Blacks, 1930 - III

Age	Maryland		District of Columbia		Virginia		West Virginia	
	Male	Female	Male	Female	Male	Female	Male	Female
All ages	140,506	135,873	62,225	69,843	321,545	328,620	60,873	54,020
60 years	1,438	1,375	603	743	3,598	3,424	426	265
61 years	366	324	143	157	766	632	113	78
62 years	580	484	217	230	1,256	1,088	171	121
63 years	502	399	182	214	1,133	1,029	145	101

[Continued]

★ 1580 ★

Age by Certain Years, for the Black Population, by Gender and for States with at least 100,000 Blacks, 1930 - III

[Continued]

Age	Maryland		District of Columbia		Virginia		West Virginia	
	Male	Female	Male	Female	Male	Female	Male	Female
64 years	486	358	129	167	1,020	907	148	120
65 years	963	868	369	530	2,307	2,382	225	166
66 years	269	257	90	85	682	609	106	75
67 years	322	280	128	126	707	572	92	81
68 years	890	349	132	188	896	856	104	80
69 years	327	290	130	164	682	646	96	55
70 years	619	704	201	293	1,627	1,806	129	129
71 years	159	123	62	67	352	325	54	39
72 years	307	209	99	95	656	597	75	54
73 years	198	170	82	77	527	400	50	33
74 years	182	153	64	83	489	369	53	48
75 years	297	325	83	170	852	985	60	73
76 years	159	134	39	65	350	316	31	29
77 years	86	66	29	41	270	216	28	23
78 years	122	129	47	66	319	311	24	33
79 years	92	111	33	40	218	201	25	33

Source: "Age Distribution by Single Years From 60 to 79, for the Negro Population, by Sex, for States Having At Least 100,000 Negroes: 1930." U.S. Bureau of the Census, *Negroes in the United States, 1920-1932*, p. 110.

★ 1581 ★

Age Composition

Age by Certain Years, for the Black Population, by Gender and for States with at least 100,000 Blacks, 1930 - IV

Age	North Carolina		South Carolina		Georgia		Florida	
	Male	Female	Male	Female	Male	Female	Male	Female
All ages	446,500	472,147	379,300	414,381	512,451	557,674	215,148	216,680
60 years	3,542	3,444	4,465	3,707	7,008	5,558	2,130	1,506
61 years	884	641	819	556	1,160	783	431	287
62 years	1,326	1,0550	1,273	872	1,950	1,312	657	476
63 years	1,311	1,085	1,325	737	1,856	1,283	657	457
64 years	1,179	959	1,055	746	1,637	1,065	569	396
65 years	2,277	2,261	2,603	2,378	3,875	3,360	1,289	1,000
66 years	750	574	555	463	935	679	350	232
67 years	773	602	602	414	928	716	357	267
68 years	929	818	811	697	1,250	1,052	433	342
69 years	720	600	600	497	944	757	346	234

[Continued]

★ 1581 ★

Age by Certain Years, for the Black Population, by Gender and for States with at least 100,000 Blacks, 1930 - IV

[Continued]

Age	North Carolina		South Carolina		Georgia		Florida	
	Male	Female	Male	Female	Male	Female	Male	Female
70 years	1,593	1,785	1,537	1,724	2,495	2,671	692	713
71 years	440	332	299	237	470	363	158	130
72 years	707	559	584	419	806	652	260	210
73 years	492	437	409	276	544	464	190	123
74 years	547	414	356	288	558	420	163	121
75 years	916	1,000	758	919	1,290	1,568	360	363
76 years	407	323	274	244	474	397	159	116
77 years	270	193	170	121	308	254	75	75
78 years	348	296	258	223	476	400	140	132
79 years	228	200	178	140	255	230	96	61

Source: "Age Distribution by Single Years From 60 to 79, for the Negro Population, by Sex, for States Having At Least 100,000 Negroes: 1930." U.S. Bureau of the Census, *Negroes in the United States, 1920-1932*, p. 110.

★ 1582 ★

Age Composition

Age by Certain Years, for the Black Population, by Gender and for States with at least 100,000 Blacks, 1930 - V

Age	Kentucky		Tennessee		Alabama		Mississippi	
	Male	Female	Male	Female	Male	Female	Male	Female
All ages	113,501	112,539	232,569	245,077	457,690	498,338	498,338	511,380
60 years	1,557	1,453	3,000	2,551	5,242	4,557	6,606	5,217
61 years	358	323	582	461	1,111	751	1,176	774
62 years	588	556	907	770	1,681	1,201	1,928	1,232
63 years	555	456	866	743	1,470	1,265	1,790	1,147
64 years	537	459	797	686	1,360	1,036	1,567	1,046
65 years	1,116	963	1,785	1,643	3,218	2,985	3,952	3,016
66 years	366	317	487	356	833	642	893	605
67 years	375	347	570	433	803	642	924	622
68 years	453	411	621	591	1,105	1,030	1,160	908
69 years	368	300	511	412	746	685	813	614
70 years	812	804	1,139	1,278	2,080	2,364	2,379	2,323
71 years	237	152	256	227	395	356	397	305
72 years	347	259	462	360	722	620	729	630
73 years	246	214	304	267	460	368	522	378
74 years	246	172	371	238	460	416	550	395
75 years	425	498	613	737	1,083	1,301	1,287	1,383
76 years	189	180	266	234	414	365	456	333

[Continued]

★ 1582 ★

Age by Certain Years, for the Black Population, by Gender and for States with at least 100,000 Blacks, 1930 - V

[Continued]

Age	Kentucky		Tennessee		Alabama		Mississippi	
	Male	Female	Male	Female	Male	Female	Male	Female
77 years	144	102	172	124	257	197	310	193
78 years	170	175	210	220	403	426	412	392
79 years	92	111	153	153	221	217	239	214

Source: "Age Distribution by Single Years From 60 to 79, for the Negro Population, by Sex, for States Having At Least 100,000 Negroes: 1930." U.S. Bureau of the Census, *Negroes in the United States, 1920-1932*, p. 110.

★ 1583 ★

Age Composition

Age by Certain Years, for the Black Population, by Gender and for States with at least 100,000 Blacks, 1930 - VI

Age	Arkansas		Louisiana		Oklahoma		Texas	
	Male	Female	Male	Female	Male	Female	Male	Female
All ages	236,909	241,554	379,173	397,153	86,818	85,380	422,608	432,356
60 years	2,672	2,080	3,807	3,542	772	548	4,347	3,881
61 years	557	371	797	596	247	137	1,150	828
62 years	921	545	1,329	1,011	299	193	1,667	1,258
63 years	859	605	1,195	958	353	222	1,645	1,281
64 years	773	548	1,049	849	302	191	1,413	1,014
65 years	1,653	1,197	2,353	2,224	478	378	2,599	2,165
66 years	143	304	648	568	168	130	821	703
67 years	455	316	653	522	204	135	933	671
68 years	550	466	792	794	203	156	955	828
69 years	432	329	632	582	228	127	743	552
70 years	977	935	1,414	1,661	286	247	1,519	1,627
71 years	219	145	299	267	89	58	357	294
72 years	388	262	549	516	159	95	657	481
73 years	271	204	332	313	105	79	453	385
74 years	295	178	371	367	116	63	460	336
75 years	525	508	816	990	160	148	928	949
76 years	234	155	334	300	116	59	374	292
77 years	150	93	230	183	67	45	250	188
78 years	199	160	311	357	84	70	382	344
79 years	123	108	210	181	51	46	242	193

Source: "Age Distribution by Single Years From 60 to 79, for the Negro Population, by Sex, for States Having At Least 100,000 Negroes: 1930." U.S. Bureau of the Census, *Negroes in the United States, 1920-1932*, p. 110.

★ 1584 ★

Age Composition

Black Men and Women Under 25 Years of Age, Classified by Year of Age, in the South, 1910 - I

Age	Negro population 1910							
	The South		South Atlantic Division					
			Delaware		Maryland		District of Columbia	
	Male	Female	Male	Female	Male	Female	Male	Female
All ages	4,339,625	4,409,802	16,011	15,170	114,749	117,501	42,615	51,831
Under 25 years	2,595,339	2,701,848	8,246	8,008	60,173	63,207	18,942	22,704
Under 1 year	116,230	117,862	325	321	2,660	2,650	732	726
1 year	101,799	101,918	255	252	2,195	2,200	638	683
2 years	121,443	120,807	318	314	2,545	2,729	730	747
3 years	121,838	124,815	296	321	2,565	2,760	758	776
4 years	125,190	124,429	324	363	2,790	2,893	723	777
5 years	118,470	120,424	336	347	2,525	2,646	735	758
6 years	121,402	124,337	322	354	2,627	2,712	723	761
7 years	117,914	117,493	313	347	2,609	2,625	734	756
8 years	117,247	119,316	323	343	2,486	2,656	658	763
9 years	103,929	104,025	313	317	2,412	2,511	644	660
10 years	114,884	111,249	363	341	2,517	2,558	713	769
11 years	90,019	90,419	321	286	2,203	2,249	629	675
12 years	123,037	122,199	394	363	2,631	2,643	711	863
13 years	102,392	103,341	364	337	2,381	2,516	646	743
14 years	108,382	109,058	429	342	2,412	2,485	685	777
15 years	94,418	97,365	344	328	2,134	2,298	658	819
16 years	98,437	108,732	337	309	2,288	2,440	712	915
17 years	91,985	94,690	311	328	2,240	2,356	735	877
18 years	99,401	112,306	344	338	2,315	2,660	791	1,162
19 years	81,506	91,876	312	277	2,183	2,484	821	1,130
20 years	83,063	111,074	317	361	2,068	2,531	818	1,245
21 years	89,285	85,636	319	237	2,272	2,028	913	1,087
22 years	90,244	101,718	337	324	2,443	2,626	1,006	1,326
23 years	81,097	94,602	296	293	2,351	2,448	997	1,478
24 years	81,727	93,157	333	325	2,321	2,503	1,032	1,431
25 years and over	1,729,905	1,695,915	7,699	7,049	54,328	54,023	23,490	28,837
Age unknown	14,381	12,039	66	53	248	271	183	290

Source: "Negro Males and Females Under 15 Years of Age, Classified by Single Years of Age, by Southern States: 1910." U.S. Bureau of the Census, *Negro Population, 1790-1915*, p. 193.

★ 1585 ★

Age Composition

Black Men and Women Under 25 Years of Age, Classified by Year of Age, in the South, 1910 - II

Age	Negro population 1910 South Atlantic Division									
	Virginia		West Virginia		North Carolina		South Carolina		Georgia	
	Male	Female	Male	Female	Male	Female	Male	Female	Male	Female
All ages	330,542	340,554	36,607	27,566	339,581	358,262	408,078	427,765	580,263	596,724
Under 25 years	196,260	203,363	18,310	15,828	217,394	229,208	268,505	282,038	359,135	376,904
Under 1 year	8,888	9,013	740	731	11,316	11,536	12,977	12,957	16,449	16,543
1 year	7,218	7,444	636	617	9,600	9,726	11,399	11,305	14,704	14,730
2 years	8,830	8,895	699	712	10,753	10,843	13,228	13,159	17,367	17,186
3 years	8,784	9,099	764	688	10,561	10,907	12,926	13,343	17,328	17,682
4 years	9,207	9,177	695	692	11,049	11,006	13,940	13,478	17,777	17,632
5 years	8,768	8,923	621	673	10,173	10,360	12,525	12,758	16,317	16,936
6 years	8,768	8,836	625	715	10,906	11,428	13,225	13,531	17,457	17,965
7 years	9,289	9,319	617	622	9,942	9,858	12,192	12,363	16,415	16,281
8 years	8,637	9,073	610	659	9,889	10,078	12,488	12,471	16,326	16,745
9 years	8,196	8,314	542	590	8,752	8,765	10,873	10,641	14,571	14,281
10 years	8,754	8,600	564	561	9,506	9,289	12,747	12,145	16,419	15,768
11 years	7,132	7,044	503	511	7,558	7,879	9,119	9,226	12,656	12,638
12 years	9,636	9,493	577	562	10,203	10,172	13,574	13,561	17,386	17,500
13 years	7,918	7,905	519	512	8,708	8,616	10,437	10,648	14,548	14,355
14 years	8,492	8,451	578	537	8,679	8,806	11,408	11,476	15,601	15,158
15 years	7,358	7,767	523	514	7,870	8,106	9,412	9,993	13,453	13,387
16 years	7,553	8,369	603	570	8,087	8,842	10,477	11,727	13,072	15,251
17 years	7,237	7,418	659	541	7,916	7,867	8,961	9,451	10,823	13,058
18 years	7,636	8,209	951	636	8,263	9,187	10,624	11,646	12,647	15,436
19 years	6,584	6,916	985	593	6,616	7,499	7,968	8,859	10,728	12,068
20 years	6,094	7,445	839	663	6,482	8,256	8,423	11,763	11,405	16,087
21 years	6,629	6,515	1,084	633	6,806	7,221	8,341	8,106	11,990	11,301
22 years	6,836	7,537	1,102	786	6,349	8,306	7,635	9,715	12,423	13,885
23 years	5,969	6,887	1,141	745	5,685	7,541	6,823	8,889	10,762	12,596
24 years	5,877	6,714	1,133	765	5,725	7,114	6,783	8,827	10,511	12,335
25 years and over	133,542	136,660	18,165	11,668	120,908	127,922	138,608	144,957	219,677	218,615
Age unknown	740	531	132	70	1,279	1,132	965	770	1,451	1,205

Source: "Negro Males and Females Under 15 Years of Age, Classified by Single Years of Age, by Southern States: 1910." U.S. Bureau of the Census, *Negro Population, 1790-1915,* p. 193.

★ 1586 ★

Age Composition

Black Men and Women Under 25 Years of Age, Classified by Year of Age, in the South, 1910 - III

Age	South Atlantic Division		East South Central Division							
	Florida		Kentucky		Tennessee		Alabama		Mississippi	
	Male	Female	Male	Female	Male	Female	Male	Female	Male	Female
All ages	161,362	147,307	131,492	130,164	233,710	239,378	447,794	460,488	502,796	506,691
Under 25 years	86,245	88,190	66,716	67,915	133,232	138,087	269,230	281,625	307,752	316,652
Under 1 year	3,589	3,753	2,568	2,608	5,800	5,906	12,017	12,227	13,651	13,678
1 year	3,192	3,140	2,235	2,229	4,880	4,846	10,343	10,561	12,227	11,922
2 years	3,865	3,811	2,497	2,579	5,772	5,772	13,002	12,763	14,712	14,510
3 years	3,780	3,991	2,616	2,655	5,915	5,892	13,067	13,484	15,268	15,326
4 years	3,986	4,007	2,784	2,770	5,878	5,919	13,379	13,148	15,291	15,106
5 years	3,818	3,795	2,554	2,478	5,501	5,761	12,538	12,978	14,861	15,002
6 years	4,051	4,114	2,675	2,803	5,945	5,856	12,220	12,510	14,516	14,871
7 years	3,796	3,668	2,646	2,550	5,525	5,477	12,465	12,800	13,789	13,899
8 years	3,877	3,908	2,597	2,701	5,656	5,720	12,306	12,480	14,168	14,095
9 years	3,384	3,400	2,550	2,533	5,140	5,264	10,801	10,836	12,515	12,229
10 years	3,706	3,611	2,704	2,654	5,435	5,293	12,029	11,663	13,768	13,121
11 years	2,778	2,849	2,337	2,405	4,569	4,645	9,212	9,133	10,741	10,508
12 years	3,936	3,701	2,889	2,747	5,967	5,771	13,154	12,668	14,907	14,338
13 years	2,970	3,209	2,720	2,797	5,204	5,188	10,809	10,591	12,309	12,254
14 years	3,246	3,282	2,890	2,841	5,663	5,609	11,426	11,444	13,009	13,064
15 years	2,737	2,924	2,603	2,814	5,038	5,088	9,965	9,968	11,307	11,401
16 years	2,968	3,470	2,852	2,971	5,363	5,829	10,588	11,259	12,036	12,492
17 years	2,692	3,078	2,714	2,744	5,494	5,361	9,793	9,528	11,428	10,704
18 years	3,356	3,664	3,026	3,013	5,847	6,109	9,734	11,860	11,404	13,182
19 years	2,831	3,171	2,651	2,775	4,963	5,271	7,263	9,172	8,294	10,279
20 years	3,145	3,763	2,690	3,084	5,013	6,094	7,759	11,739	8,894	12,809
21 years	3,461	3,097	2,648	2,625	4,980	5,054	8,936	8,686	9,973	9,474
22 years	3,795	3,737	2,984	2,894	2,745	5,622	9,451	10,498	10,121	11,470
23 years	3,531	3,483	2,719	2,833	4,455	5,484	8,457	9,922	9,112	10,424
24 years	3,755	3,564	2,567	2,812	4,484	5,256	8,515	9,707	9,451	10,494
25 years and over	73,774	58,416	64,185	61,695	99,790	100,652	177,131	177,517	193,390	188,523
Age unknown	1,343	701	591	554	683	639	1,433	1,346	1,654	1,516

Source: "Negro Males and Females Under 15 Years of Age, Classified by Single Years of Age, by Southern States: 1910." U.S. Bureau of the Census, *Negro Population, 1790-1915*, p. 193.

★ 1587 ★

Age Composition

Black Men and Women Under 25 Years of Age, Classified by Year of Age, in the South, 1910 - IV

Age	West South Central Division							
	Arkansas		Louisiana		Oklahoma		Texas	
	Male	Female	Male	Female	Male	Female	Male	Female
All ages	223,323	219,568	353,824	360,050	71,937	65,675	344,941	345,108
Under 25 years	129,689	135,401	207,571	217,757	40,851	41,130	207,088	213,771
Under 1 year	5,289	5,515	8,695	8,740	1,718	1,826	8,816	9,132
1 year	4,959	5,116	7,709	7,888	1,660	1,601	7,949	7,658
2 years	6,140	6,029	9,646	9,655	1,854	1,849	9,485	9,254
3 years	5,995	6,187	9,870	10,183	1,886	1,978	9,459	9,543
4 years	6,073	6,027	9,947	10,106	1,910	1,904	9,437	9,324
5 years	5,881	5,967	10,014	9,919	1,882	1,777	9,421	9,346
6 years	6,141	6,504	10,048	10,347	1,971	1,907	9,182	9,123
7 years	5,749	5,852	9,732	9,511	1,823	1,842	10,278	9,723
8 years	5,972	6,108	9,691	9,797	1,900	1,891	9,663	9,828
9 years	5,244	5,134	8,535	8,391	1,647	1,629	7,809	8,530
10 years	5,487	5,393	9,215	8,870	1,721	1,763	9,236	8,850
11 years	4,475	4,408	6,992	7,117	1,387	1,455	7,407	7,301
12 years	5,728	5,847	10,109	9,955	1,748	1,777	9,487	9,238
13 years	5,140	5,289	8,066	8,313	1,518	1,589	8,135	8,479
14 years	5,252	5,570	8,549	8,731	1,641	1,609	8,452	8,876
15 years	4,742	4,887	7,348	7,955	1,430	1,445	7,496	7,671
16 years	5,082	5,387	7,448	8,814	1,430	1,550	7,541	8,537
17 years	4,970	4,876	7,069	7,595	1,534	1,404	7,409	7,504
18 years	5,236	6,016	7,760	8,689	1,637	1,667	7,830	8,832
19 years	4,266	4,847	6,547	7,643	1,417	1,460	7,077	7,432
20 years	4,137	5,602	6,623	9,120	1,382	1,544	6,974	8,968
21 years	4,794	4,307	7,074	6,889	1,485	1,343	7,580	7,033
22 years	4,583	4,961	7,579	8,404	1,430	1,410	7,425	8,217
23 years	4,127	4,673	6,558	7,705	1,330	1,447	6,784	7,754
24 years	4,227	4,809	6,747	7,420	1,510	1,463	6,756	7,618
25 years and over	93,049	83,660	144,996	141,324	30,743	24,297	136,425	130,100
Age unknown	585	507	1,257	969	343	248	1,428	1,237

Source: "Negro Males and Females Under 15 Years of Age, Classified by Single Years of Age, by Southern States: 1910." U.S. Bureau of the Census, *Negro Population, 1790-1915*, p. 193.

★ 1588 ★

Age Composition

Black Population by 5-Year Age Periods by Gender, 1910, 1920, and 1930 - I

Age	Total			Male			Female		
	1930	1920	1910	1930	1920	1910	1930	1920	1910
All ages	11,891,143	10,463,131	9,827,763	5,855,669	5,209,436	4,855,881	6,035,474	5,253,695	4,941,882
Under 5 years	1,230,306	1,143,699	1,263,288	611,231	568,633	629,320	618,975	575,066	633,968
Under 1 year	232,378	227,660	252,368	115,388	112,660	125,459	116,990	115,000	126,927
1 year	222,536	210,558	219,240	110,284	104,664	109,357	112,252	105,894	109,883
2 years	252,585	225,939	260,037	125,695	112,265	130,191	126,890	113,674	129,845
3 years	264,314	240,978	264,547	130,378	118,573	130,526	133,936	122,405	134,021
4 years	258,393	238,564	267,078	129,486	120,471	133,786	128,907	118,093	133,292
5 to 9 years	1,368,381	1,266,207	1,246,553	679,748	631,748	619,175	688,633	634,866	627,378
10 to 14 years	1,251,542	1,236,914	1,155,266	623,228	616,251	578,074	628,314	620,663	577,192
15 to 19 years	1,250,528	1,083,215	1,060,416	595,646	513,416	507,945	654,882	569,799	522,471
20 to 24 years	1,203,191	1,054,847	1,030,795	553,622	487,169	482,157	649,569	567,678	548,638
25 to 29 years	1,071,787	909,739	881,227	500,520	424,352	421,805	571,267	485,387	459,422
30 to 34 years	864,514	697,865	668,089	416,869	331,579	332,163	447,645	366,286	335,926
35 to 39 years	890,900	773,931	633,931	430,472	383,587	320,450	460,428	390,344	312,999
40 to 44 years	687,423	559,701	455,413	339,329	275,926	229,680	348,094	283,775	225,733
45 to 49 years	630,065	551,589	385,909	323,162	320,506	199,928	306,903	231,083	185,981
50 to 54 years	504,590	399,110	326,070	277,532	227,995	179,387	227,058	171,115	146,683
55 to 59 years	309,397	229,980	209,622	174,367	129,153	115,900	135,030	100,827	94,532
60 to 64 years	242,169	200,118	186,502	133,349	112,137	101,149	108,820	87,981	85,353
65 to 69 years	155,177	137,035	123,550	82,843	76,184	67,956	72,334	60,851	55,594
70 to 74 years	99,096	91,579	78,839	50,896	47,411	40,584	48,200	44,168	38,255
75 to 79 years	58,711	52,352	44,018	29,219	27,172	22,667	29,492	25,180	21,351
80 to 84 years	33,377	28,122	25,579	15,343	13,049	11,696	18,034	15,073	13,883
85 to 89 years	14,948	12,281	11,166	6,864	5,620	5,164	8,084	6,661	6,002
90 to 94 years	6,332	5,847	5,850	2,516	2,340	2,394	3,81	3,507	3,456
95 to 99 years	2,611	2,562	2,447	1,073	1,087	1,017	1,538	1,475	1,430
100 years and over	2,467	2,935	2,675	776	1,018	1,004	1,691	1,917	1,671
Unknown	13,731	23,503	31,040	7,064	13,510	17,076	6,667	9,993	13,964

Source: "Negro Population by 5-Year Age Periods, by Sex, for the United States: 1930, 1920, and 1910." U.S. Bureau of the Census, *Negroes in the United States, 1920-1932*, p. 90.

★ 1589 ★

Age Composition

Black Population by 5-Year Age Periods by Gender, 1910, 1920, and 1930 - II

Age	Percent distribution								
	Total			Male			Female		
	1930	1920	1910	1930	1920	1910	1930	1920	1910
All ages	100.0	100.0	100.0	100.0	100.0	100.0	100.0	100.0	100.0
Under 5 years	10.3	10.9	12.9	10.4	10.9	12.9	10.3	10.9	12.8
Under 1 year	2.0	2.2	2.6	2.0	2.2	2.6	1.9	2.2	2.6
1 year	1.9	2.0	2.2	1.9	2.0	2.2	1.9	2.0	2.2
2 years	2.1	2.2	2.6	2.1	2.2	2.7	2.1	2.2	2.6
3 years	2.2	2.3	2.7	2.2	2.3	2.7	2.2	2.3	2.7
4 years	2.2	2.3	2.7	2.2	2.3	2.7	2.1	2.2	42.7
5 to 9 years	11.5	12.1	12.7	11.6	12.1	12.7	11.4	12.1	12.7
10 to 14 years	10.5	11.8	11.8	10.6	11.8	11.8	10.4	11.8	11.7
15 to 19 years	10.5	10.4	10.8	10.2	9.9	10.4	10.9	10.8	11.2
20 to 24 years	10.1	10.1	10.5	9.5	9.4	9.9	10.8	10.8	11.1
25 to 29 years	9.0	8.7	9.0	8.5	8.1	8.6	9.5	9.2	9.3
30 to 34 years	7.3	6.7	6.8	7.1	6.4	6.8	7.4	7.0	6.8
35 to 39 years	7.5	7.4	6.4	7.4	7.4	6.6	7.6	7.4	6.3
40 to 44 years	5.8	5.3	4.6	5.8	5.3	4.7	5.8	5.4	4.6
45 to 49 years	5.3	5.3	3.9	5.5	6.2	4.1	5.1	4.4	3.8
50 to 54 years	4.2	3.8	3.3	4.7	4.4	3.7	3.8	3.3	3.0
55 to 59 years	2.6	2.2	2.1	3.0	2.5	2.4	2.2	1.9	1.9
60 to 64 years	2.0	1.9	1.9	2.3	2.2	2.1	1.8	1.7	1.7
65 to 69 years	1.3	1.3	1.3	1.4	1.5	1.4	1.2	1.2	1.1
70 to 74 years	.8	.9	.8	.9	.9	.8.	8.	.8	.8
75 to 79 years	.5	.5	.4	.5	.5	.5	.5	.5	.4
80 to 84 years	.3	.3	.3	.3	.3	.2	.3	.3	.3
85 to 89 years	.1	.1	.1	.1	.1	.1	.1	.1	.1
90 to 94 years	.1	.1	.1	.1	-	-	.1	.1	.1
95 to 99 years	-	-	-	-	-	-	-	-	-
100 years and over	-	-	-	-	-	-	-	-	-
Unknown	.1	.2	.3.	1.	3.	3.	.1	.2	.3

Source: "Negro Population by 5-Year Age Periods, by Sex, for the United States: 1930, 1920, and 1910." U.S. Bureau of the Census, *Negroes in the United States, 1920-1932*, p. 90.

★ 1590 ★

Age Composition

Black Population by Year of Age to 29, by Gender and States, 1930 - I

Age	Alabama		Arizona		Arkansas		California		Colorado	
	Male	Female	Male	Female	Male	Female	Male	Female	Male	Female
Under 1 year	10,077	10,429	80	73	4,761	4,948	469	502	69	81
1 year	9,537	9,748	75	78	4,288	4,450	489	510	75	84
2 years	11,134	11,222	84	86	4,960	5,085	563	506	72	62
3 years	11,387	11,774	77	86	5,367	5,514	551	575	79	81
4 years	11,343	11,185	80	74	5,284	5,300	563	555	94	76
5 years	11,879	11,858	79	81	5,569	5,502	640	584	73	82
6 years	12,146	12,184	75	80	5,677	5,848	608	575	72	85
7 years	11,786	11,835	82	91	5,373	5,732	582	632	66	79
8 years	12,126	12,100	86	82	5,554	5,652	617	613	78	83
9 years	11,024	10,770	85	90	5,323	5,363	583	594	80	77
10 years	11,989	11,853	84	86	5,868	5,747	589	578	73	79
11 years	9,204	9,263	62	68	4,756	4,824	501	547	64	83
12 years	11,489	11,133	72	78	5,608	5,487	507	571	81	81
13 years	10,445	10,500	75	58	4,906	5,126	493	497	65	75
14 years	11,499	11,559	75	69	5,376	5,213	548	591	77	79
15 years	10,670	11,116	75	54	5,031	5,130	491	511	53	75
16 years	11,659	12,094	92	64	5,192	5,553	511	567	80	90
17 years	11,299	10,758	75	66	5,067	5,093	521	565	58	91
18 years	10,117	12,645	104	65	5,095	6,305	535	680	77	84
19 years	8,042	10,816	114	79	4,632	5,447	557	627	85	90
20 years	8,389	12,801	130	73	4,427	6,260	506	684	79	91
21 years	8,955	9,186	134	59	5,074	4,700	621	682	66	105
22 years	9,463	11,028	169	71	4,773	5,313	629	772	67	107
23 years	8,441	10,397	172	96	4,298	5,169	613	730	78	108
24 years	8,265	10,148	138	86	4,259	4,983	664	810	94	97
25 years	8,648	10,685	135	85	4,285	5,082	713	871	92	115
26 years	6,811	8,480	150	99	3,565	4,469	651	854	86	117
27 years	5,976	7,411	102	103	3,473	3,841	724	807	82	95
28 years	7,358	8,762	123	111	3,835	4,491	769	949	85	110
29 years	6,103	7,284	154	101	3,386	3,736	873	957	99	114

Source: "Negro Population Classified by Single Years of Age Up to 29, by Sex, and by States: 1930." U.S. Bureau of the Census, *Negroes in the United States, 1920-1932*, pp. 108-109.

★ 1591 ★

Age Composition

Black Population by Year of Age to 29, by Gender and States, 1930 - II

Age	Connecticut		Delaware		District of Columbia		Florida	
	Male	Female	Male	Female	Male	Female	Male	Female
Under 1 year	283	287	283	265	921	926	3,671	3,678
1 year	260	283	248	255	926	944	3,524	3,594
2 years	320	290	273	291	1,044	959	4,115	4,212
3 years	285	339	262	304	1,124	1,049	4,440	4,550
4 years	311	311	325	281	1,021	1,092	4,345	4,312
5 years	305	315	301	306	1,101	1,099	4,424	4,476
6 years	283	301	353	342	1,064	1,098	4,640	4,803
7 years	267	279	313	315	1,040	1,093	4,471	4,668
8 years	290	281	352	344	1,065	1,119	4,507	4,735
9 years	281	298	303	319	1,044	1,115	4,282	4,444
10 years	272	294	351	369	996	1,125	4,596	4,551
11 years	223	232	264	256	883	918	3,655	3,759
12 years	227	246	336	302	879	1,062	4,451	4,483
13 years	199	247	240	283	801	972	3,916	4,104
14 years	201	206	294	290	873	975	4,244	4,357
15 years	206	243	267	295	846	977	3,859	4,234
16 years	225	222	311	299	872	1,094	4,071	4,629
17 years	225	230	315	297	969	1,105	3,895	4,486
18 years	227	271	299	316	1,039	1,362	4,335	5,112
19 years	208	259	311	275	1,031	1,380	3,842	4,892
20 years	220	280	313	345	1,102	1,575	3,877	5,564
21 years	217	258	317	245	1,217	1,404	4,393	4,676
22 years	228	337	346	256	1,371	1,553	4,672	5,365
23 years	239	302	291	254	1,406	1,676	4,605	5,298
24 years	280	308	306	315	1,376	1,726	4,598	5,354
25 years	294	318	293	293	1,560	1,819	4,848	5,525
26 years	265	284	252	266	1,214	1,460	4,022	4,675
27 years	287	288	279	248	1,380	1,493	4,065	4,390
28 years	303	308	320	269	1,391	1,672	4,622	5,084
29 years	372	298	334	265	1,449	1,551	4,228	4,491

Source: "Negro Population Classified by Single Years of Age Up to 29, by Sex, and by States: 1930." U.S. Bureau of the Census, *Negroes in the United States, 1920-1932*, pp. 108-109.

★ 1592 ★

Age Composition

Black Population by Year of Age to 29, by Gender and States, 1930 - III

Age	Georgia		Idaho		Illinois		Indiana		Iowa	
	Male	Female	Male	Female	Male	Female	Male	Female	Male	Female
Under 1 year	10,890	11,152	3	2	2,486	2,443	836	818	119	139
1 year	10,109	10,397	4	3	2,355	2,366	836	832	125	124
2 years	11,939	12,123	1	2	2,596	2,567	973	948	132	142
3 years	12,123	12,542	5	3	2,579	2,733	942	1,002	138	162
4 years	12,375	12,366	2	5	2,595	2,658	991	964	137	173
5 years	12,792	13,048	4	2	2,557	2,781	1,017	981	131	146
6 years	13,713	14,143	3	7	2,500	2,653	1,006	984	162	168
7 years	13,093	13,468	7	-	2,510	2,529	935	1,022	150	137
8 years	13,867	14,203	2	5	2,595	2,642	1,001	1,058	193	168
9 years	12,793	12,906	9	-	2,460	2,533	1,012	951	160	148
10 years	14,218	13,998	3	5	2,470	2,672	922	960	160	133
11 years	11,227	11,081	2	3	2,087	2,182	758	849	130	131
12 years	14,118	14,000	4	3	2,045	2,167	863	859	142	139
13 years	12,641	12,836	2	4	1,977	2,184	760	831	137	132
14 years	13,485	12,789	6	3	2,086	2,241	847	828	141	163
15 years	12,567	13,460	3	5	1,974	2,116	815	786	128	150
16 years	13,182	14,631	4	2	2,082	2,343	867	889	139	141
17 years	12,571	13,473	3	-	2,167	2,294	817	906	143	157
18 years	13,537	15,541	6	6	2,284	2,837	863	1,030	125	153
19 years	11,898	13,356	8	3	2,391	2,875	846	927	144	134
20 years	11,630	15,757	4	2	2,368	3,300	911	1,097	141	133
21 years	10,615	11,059	3	6	2,896	3,083	943	943	132	126
22 years	10,419	12,835	4	3	3,024	3,706	1,022	1,064	137	146
23 years	9,078	11,788	6	2	3,280	3,929	963	1,107	138	148
24 years	8,432	10,721	6	4	3,540	4,138	1,023	1,111	131	131
25 years	9,294	12,010	1	1	3,762	4,271	1,139	1,216	119	128
26 years	6,751	8,834	5	5	3,645	4,077	1,025	1,131	148	122
27 years	6,363	7,808	5	8	3,853	4,031	1,059	1,039	137	134
28 years	7,632	9,613	5	4	4,140	4,568	1,118	1,236	133	136
29 years	6,246	7,701	6	5	4,490	4,442	1,308	1,312	145	150

Source: "Negro Population Classified by Single Years of Age Up to 29, by Sex, and by States: 1930." U.S. Bureau of the Census, *Negroes in the United States, 1920-1932*, pp. 108-109.

★ 1593 ★

Age Composition

Black Population by Year of Age to 29, by Gender and States, 1930 - IV

Age	Kansas		Kentucky		Louisiana		Maine		Maryland	
	Male	Female	Male	Female	Male	Female	Male	Female	Male	Female
Under 1 year	463	479	1,751	1,749	7,993	8,096	10	11	2,523	2,523
1 year	475	460	1,652	1,631	7,604	7,754	8	9	2,493	2,490
2 years	556	541	1,940	1,945	8,627	8,648	14	10	2,747	2,811
3 years	569	554	1,958	1,935	9,050	9,369	16	5	2,907	2,872
4 years	549	536	2,069	1,957	8,928	8,917	15	13	2,814	2,826
5 years	607	591	2,166	2,128	9,126	9,311	10	6	2,873	2,965
6 years	569	591	2,263	2,201	9,695	9,906	5	9	2,985	3,043
7 years	583	621	2,169	2,142	9,177	9,275	9	10	2,832	2,967
8 years	582	614	2,227	2,300	9,702	9,674	11	12	2,902	3,175
9 years	622	639	2,111	2,116	8,613	8,603	11	6	2,857	2,965
10 years	593	604	2,121	2,151	9,542	9,397	15	14	2,90	2,903
11 years	541	541	1,812	1,911	7,356	7,583	10	7	2,371	2,418
12 years	557	512	2,049	2,042	9,049	8,940	7	14	2,511	2,669
13 years	520	588	1,890	1,990	7,793	8,210	6	8	2,419	2,475
14 years	545	607	2,149	2,166	8,240	8,690	8	11	2,361	2,540
15 years	523	582	1,918	2,009	7,738	8,136	6	7	2,274	2,411
16 years	520	533	2,144	2,207	7,833	8,889	10	8	2,576	2,512
17 years	523	539	2,043	2,115	7,440	8,388	5	5	2,531	2,509
18 years	545	611	2,140	2,167	8,086	9,406	10	4	2,539	2,804
19 years	520	538	1,956	2,063	7,095	9,332	11	8	2,634	2,627
20 years	541	596	1,944	2,130	7,227	9,891	9	4	2,516	2,785
21 years	540	480	2,016	1,894	7,377	7,648	2	1	2,771	2,435
22 years	513	537	1,925	2,073	7,893	8,792	5	8	2,887	2,846
23 years	526	561	1,838	2,009	7,101	8,515	8	6	2,798	2,731
24 years	594	598	1,925	2,062	6,948	8,158	8	5	2,869	2,773
25 years	569	574	1,859	2,055	7,564	8,975	9	10	2,814	2,765
26 years	536	525	1,589	1,894	6,220	7,367	6	10	2,369	2,290
27 years	536	526	1,665	1,716	5,826	6,809	8	5	2,456	2,297
28 years	533	568	1,874	1,941	6,489	7,622	6	7	2,777	2,608
29 years	601	586	1,802	1,807	5,707	6,462	8	12	2,649	2,424

Source: "Negro Population Classified by Single Years of Age Up to 29, by Sex, and by States: 1930." U.S. Bureau of the Census, *Negroes in the United States, 1920-1932*, pp. 108-109.

★ 1594 ★

Age Composition

Black Population by Year of Age to 29, by Gender and States, 1930 - V

Age	Massachusetts		Michigan		Minnesota		Mississippi		Missouri	
	Male	Female	Male	Female	Male	Female	Male	Female	Male	Female
Under 1 year	437	422	1,506	1,462	54	52	10,974	10,948	1,644	1,612
1 year	423	456	1,341	1,371	59	61	10,455	10,383	1,587	1,554
2 years	478	472	1,575	1,562	69	54	11,921	11,987	1,664	1,728
3 years	510	496	1,623	1,709	76	63	12,999	13,187	1,776	1,799
4 years	540	474	1,533	1,549	62	65	12,314	12,267	1,823	1,643
5 years	504	542	1,557	1,644	66	61	13,212	13,279	1,801	1,790
6 years	577	540	1,467	1,473	64	64	13,186	13,226	1,804	1,832
7 years	519	523	1,380	1,450	59	75	12,589	12,451	1,891	1,884
8 years	495	551	1,513	1,487	73	77	13,091	12,909	1,885	1,823
9 years	525	525	1,408	1,353	70	66	11,682	11,600	1,900	1,766
10 years	539	495	1,300	1,387	65	60	13,589	12,706	1,826	1,855
11 years	463	460	1,084	1,124	73	64	10,155	10,088	1,490	1,532
12 years	498	488	1,021	1,118	60	63	12,723	12,288	1,661	1,763
13 years	436	429	1,018	1,098	57	48	10,772	10,682	1,561	1,596
14 years	451	439	1,117	1,120	65	57	12,057	11,839	1,546	1,688
15 years	426	426	970	1,008	62	56	11,353	11,076	1,633	1,689
16 years	395	400	1,024	1,047	56	72	12,224	12,203	1,697	1,774
17 years	400	379	953	1,139	39	69	12,149	10,759	1,743	1,720
18 years	373	445	1,034	1,208	60	60	11,268	13,970	1,700	2,076
19 years	355	419	1,162	1,343	65	76	8,758	11,133	1,707	1,996
20 years	347	395	1,211	1,658	61	63	9,518	14,180	1,683	2,271
21 years	366	405	1,541	1,531	65	78	10,145	9,710	1,791	2,001
22 years	364	419	1,781	1,898	58	74	10,346	11,662	1,887	2,284
23 years	360	401	1,902	2,011	71	59	9,275	10,466	1,960	2,351
24 years	335	406	2,038	2,160	56	65	8,852	10,207	1,981	2,456
25 years	361	430	2,187	2,342	74	62	9,904	11,597	2,037	2,611
26 years	338	420	2,204	2,126	70	58	7,455	8,798	1,895	2,420
27 years	383	394	2,470	2,294	74	61	6,665	7,578	2,011	2,224
28 years	424	457	2,724	2,624	73	83	8,100	9,400	2,180	2,477
29 years	407	421	2,820	2,505	88	89	6,267	7,054	2,379	2,456

Source: "Negro Population Classified by Single Years of Age Up to 29, by Sex, and by States: 1930." U.S. Bureau of the Census, *Negroes in the United States, 1920-1932*, pp. 108-109.

★ 1595 ★

Age Composition

Black Population by Year of Age to 29, by Gender and States, 1930 - VI

Age	Montana		Nebraska		Nevada		New Hampshire		New Jersey	
	Male	Female	Male	Female	Male	Female	Male	Female	Male	Female
Under 1 year	6	6	110	107	4	4	6	4	1,975	1,970
1 year	9	7	91	97	1	1	3	3	1,865	1,847
2 years	4	6	117	103	2	4	4	10	2,029	1,983
3 years	10	3	118	111	2	-	5	6	2,094	2,107
4 years	9	6	95	97	1	2	2	5	1,041	1,979
5 years	4	6	114	110	3	3	6	2	2,100	2,079
6 years	5	7	112	107	-	5	5	3	1,912	2,004
7 years	1	10	102	104	3	1	5	7	1,962	1,958
8 years	7	7	103	126	4	1	4	4	1,917	2,078
9 years	11	4	115	108	1	2	3	6	1,897	1,917
10 years	10	7	100	86	3	2	2	5	1,913	1,898
11 years	10	11	95	71	-	2	5	2	1,487	1,598
12 years	8	6	101	109	-	3	7	5	1,693	1,710
13 years	6	13	95	85	1	1	5	6	1,442	1,580
14 years	9	10	93	95	1	-	5	6	1,608	1,669
15 years	4	6	81	91	-	3	8	6	1,410	1,593
16 years	9	4	102	97	3	1	3	5	1,559	1,770
17 years	3	6	103	83	1	2	10	5	1,504	1,772
18 years	9	7	88	123	2	1	6	6	1,609	2,016
19 years	7	3	81	113	-	2	8	6	1,582	1,980
20 years	10	9	80	112	3	2	13	7	1,680	2,245
21 years	4	5	116	107	3	1	14	6	1,801	2,020
22 years	11	12	112	125	4	4	11	3	2,091	2,380
23 years	9	7	82	116	1	3	9	4	2,072	2,332
24 years	8	3	113	159	4	4	14	5	2,173	2,501
25 years	12	15	132	133	4	5	5	2	2,270	2,565
26 years	11	4	118	135	3	4	8	5	1,976	2,347
27 years	6	8	144	137	4	38	7	7	2,168	2,307
28 years	11	10	136	147	4	8	12	3	2,257	2,493
29 years	11	12	162	160	4	5	7	2	2,485	2,556

Source: "Negro Population Classified by Single Years of Age Up to 29, by Sex, and by States: 1930." U.S. Bureau of the Census, *Negroes in the United States, 1920-1932*, pp. 108-109.

★ 1596 ★

Age Composition

Black Population by Year of Age to 29, by Gender and States, 1930 - VII

Age	New Mexico		New York		North Carolina		North Dakota		Ohio	
	Male	Female	Male	Female	Male	Female	Male	Female	Male	Female
Under 1 year	22	23	3,246	3,370	10,779	10,739	4	2	2,687	2,639
1 year	22	17	3,386	3,197	10,331	10,868	4	3	2,528	2,539
2 years	32	20	3,526	3,579	11,563	11,799	1	2	2,790	2,929
3 years	28	22	3,447	3,593	12,213	12,501	5	1	2,945	3,088
4 years	36	27	3,318	3,454	12,154	11,748	6	2	2,816	2,884
5 years	27	24	3,303	3,474	13,438	13,319	6	2	2,915	3,049
6 years	24	26	3,135	3,280	13,346	13,725	1	2	2,831	2,965
7 years	31	31	3,067	3,159	12,425	12,860	2	2	2,747	2,876
8 years	26	29	2,976	3,121	13,271	13,290	2	-	2,900	3,092
9 years	23	32	2,846	2,956	12,164	12,305	2	2	2,740	2,844
10 years	27	28	2,779	2,915	12,829	12,692	3	1	2,703	2,791
11 years	21	21	2,333	2,461	10,428	10,453	-	1	2,234	2,365
12 years	32	28	2,411	2,597	12,521	12,507	4	1	2,411	2,390
13 years	18	27	2,103	2,364	11,105	11,303	1	1	2,215	2,256
14 years	21	26	2,260	2,401	11,932	11,993	2	1	2,264	2,457
15 years	22	21	2,127	2,293	11,234	11,521	3	2	2,082	2,357
16 years	30	30	2,035	2,561	11,617	12,558	4	3	2,199	2,417
17 years	29	26	2,260	2,809	11,468	11,255	5	1	2,275	2,307
18 years	25	30	2,613	3,724	11,724	12,939	2	1	2,242	2,703
19 years	26	20	2,958	4,092	9,803	11,047	5	-	2,442	2,734
20 years	28	24	3,278	4,941	9,800	12,105	4	3	2,426	2,939
21 years	33	28	3,861	4,543	9,336	9,466	-	3	2,778	2,630
22 years	17	23	4,329	5,589	8,949	10,866	1	9	2,930	3,189
23 years	21	26	4,573	5,906	7,910	9,657	3	2	2,869	3,132
24 years	17	19	4,983	5,971	7,576	9,309	1	6	3,196	3,303
25 years	12	27	5,454	6,725	7,563	9,619	1	2	3,294	3,674
26 years	24	25	4,973	5,715	5,989	7,567	1	-	2,979	3,164
27 years	18	18	5,364	5,799	5,807	6,716	3	5	3,325	3,166
28 years	33	28	5,940	6,663	6,599	7,861	10	1	3,725	3,616
29 years	34	26	6,263	6,179	5,637	6,485	4	4	3,812	3,611

Source: "Negro Population Classified by Single Years of Age Up to 29, by Sex, and by States: 1930." U.S. Bureau of the Census, *Negroes in the United States, 1920-1932*, pp. 108-109.

★ 1597 ★

Age Composition

Black Population by Year of Age to 29, by Gender and States, 1930 - VIII

Age	Oklahoma		Oregon		Pennsylvania		Rhode Island		South Carolina	
	Male	Female	Male	Female	Male	Female	Male	Female	Male	Female
Under 1 year	1,636	1,667	8	15	3,663	3,722	88	105	8,692	9,063
1 year	1,553	1,554	8	14	3,662	3,706	99	110	8,477	8,722
2 years	1,791	1,736	11	7	4,126	4,096	100	107	9,875	10,016
3 years	1,761	1,911	8	14	4,144	4,188	105	99	10,224	10,549
4 years	1,854	1,874	9	13	3,959	4,079	102	93	10,388	10,294
5 years	1,868	1,906	7	12	4,144	4,135	116	111	11,416	11,416
6 years	2,035	2,120	11	15	4,011	4,181	97	119	12,040	12,342
7 years	1,963	1,882	11	13	3,930	4,067	104	116	11,311	11,561
8 years	2,086	2,042	13	9	4,040	4,141	108	102	12,161	12,424
9 years	1,956	1,934	12	24	3,929	4,054	100	96	10,875	10,750
10 years	2,057	1,977	16	12	3,756	3,869	90	97	12,153	11,919
11 years	1,701	1,695	10	12	3,081	3,343	99	89	9,097	9,113
12 years	1,947	1,906	10	11	3,262	3,398	108	92	12,660	12,405
13 years	1,621	1,676	11	14	2,888	3,180	95	93	10,275	10,655
14 years	1,796	1,920	14	12	3,047	3,204	82	93	11,289	11,557
15 years	1,734	1,805	13	9	2,766	3,122	78	87	10,201	10,915
16 years	1,852	1,945	10	17	2,085	3,422	73	103	11,025	12,250
17 years	1,857	1,858	11	16	2,951	3,415	64	79	10,059	10,197
18 years	1,890	2,188	14	19	3,095	4,023	73	99	11,023	12,491
19 years	1,766	1,916	12	7	3,306	4,028	67	84	8,497	9,771
20 years	1,730	2,070	13	20	3,243	4,441	77	62	8,732	11,373
21 years	1,770	1,708	14	8	3,590	3,858	77	66	7,747	7,590
22 years	1,683	1,934	14	23	3,964	4,712	53	65	6,993	8,613
23 years	1,553	1,864	19	17	4,064	4,724	58	85	5,780	7,771
24 years	1,585	1,996	15	18	4,352	4,947	66	65	5,280	7,133
25 years	1,566	1,719	21	18	4,740	5,231	73	61	5,913	7,984
26 years	1,375	1,633	10	13	4,287	4,703	67	80	3,959	5,668
27 years	1,437	1,576	19	12	4,807	4,787	66	52	3,700	4,904
28 years	1,614	1,713	25	16	5,441	5,541	81	68	4,695	6,250
29 years	1,429	1,533	20	21	5,568	5,248	69	73	3,601	4,625

Source: "Negro Population Classified by Single Years of Age Up to 29, by Sex, and by States: 1930." U.S. Bureau of the Census, *Negroes in the United States, 1920-1932*, pp. 108-109.

★ 1598 ★

Age Composition

Black Population by Year of Age to 29, by Gender and States, 1930 - IX

Age	South Dakota		Tennessee		Texas		Utah		Vermont	
	Male	Female	Male	Female	Male	Female	Male	Female	Male	Female
Under 1 year	6	5	4,212	4,187	8,149	8,473	14	8	7	9
1 year	1	8	3,814	3,876	8,039	8,152	11	8	8	6
2 years	5	2	4,423	4,755	8,836	8,737	6	10	11	7
3 years	3	7	4,676	4,683	9,003	9,044	11	10	2	8
4 years	2	8	4,836	4,842	8,804	8,883	7	4	10	7
5 years	7	3	4,768	4,964	9,565	9,415	7	7	8	2
6 years	4	8	5,075	5,310	9,630	9,976	8	8	3	7
7 years	3	4	4,936	4,990	10,027	10,152	7	9	4	5
8 years	6	8	5,226	5,174	9,934	10,003	11	6	2	4
9 years	2	8	4,970	4,995	9,457	9,350	5	9	6	7
10 years	4	9	5,260	5,091	10,044	9,792	9	10	4	4
11 years	7	3	4,277	4,256	7,957	7,828	3	10	4	6
12 years	3	7	5,097	9,453	9,255	9	11	5	8	
13 years	7	4	4,561	4,538	8,360	8,498	6	8	5	5
14 years	4	7	4,935	5,070	8,755	9,128	13	7	5	8
15 years	7	4	4,692	4,956	8,409	9,276	5	3	2	6
16 years	4	4	4,975	5,337	8,893	10,007	4	2	5	5
17 years	11	6	5,127	5,141	8,882	9,375	2	2	5	10
18 years	7	5	5,350	6,046	8,998	10,732	11	4	4	10
19 years	7	7	4,809	5,402	8,404	9,720	3	8	7	8
20 years	4	5	4,774	6,239	8,550	11,382	3	3	6	4
21 years	5	5	4,526	4,660	8,839	8,444	7	4	5	3
22 years	5	12	4,522	5,643	8,783	9,984	10	9	5	2
23 years	7	6	4,151	5,205	8,191	9,559	5	8	4	2
24 years	8	8	4,364	5,204	8,163	9,674	11	9	4	4
25 years	7	6	4,497	5,575	8,307	9,697	9	10	4	1
26 years	6	5	3,654	4,624	7,214	8,390	11	5	6	1
27 years	10	2	3,380	3,932	7,073	8,037	8	9	3	-
28 years	3	4	4,059	4,870	7,589	8,823	6	9	6	-
29 years	4	5	3,576	4,182	7,202	7,860	12	9	5	3

Source: "Negro Population Classified by Single Years of Age Up to 29, by Sex, and by States: 1930." U.S. Bureau of the Census, *Negroes in the United States, 1920-1932,* pp. 108-109.

★ 1599 ★

Age Composition

Black Population by Year of Age to 29, by Gender and States, 1930 - X

Age	Virginia		Washington		West Virginia		Wisconsin		Wyoming	
	Male	Female	Male	Female	Male	Female	Male	Female	Male	Female
Under 1 year	6,467	6,541	42	30	1,181	1,099	74	102	7	3
1 year	6,160	6,434	37	41	1,143	1,138	78	68	6	3
2 years	7,275	7,321	33	48	1,255	1,259	76	96	7	5
3 years	7,385	7,787	43	45	1,206	1,351	88	98	9	7
4 years	7,686	7,606	40	41	1,203	1,269	90	80	5	11
5 years	8,387	8,200	47	48	1,296	1,317	99	95	2	8
6 years	8,590	8,617	43	51	1,331	1,321	95	89	4	7
7 years	8,571	8,598	42	44	1,180	1,341	80	107	6	9
8 years	8,744	8,855	38	43	1,292	1,356	96	97	8	3
9 years	8,137	8,375	45	47	1,230	101	101	9	13	
10 years	8,700	8,557	50	38	1,211	1,231	86	86	3	12
11 years	7,214	7,101	47	39	950	1,069	90	77	8	5
12 years	8,347	8,319	44	36	1,053	1,049	80	74	8	5
13 years	7,362	7,594	43	34	975	995	72	88	9	5
14 years	7,807	7,892	51	39	938	973	67	68	6	9
15 years	7,355	7,608	41	35	852	1,038	42	59	6	8
16 years	7,611	7,855	42	55	916	1,045	65	74	3	5
17 years	7,325	7,363	41	41	976	1,051	64	69	10	9
18 years	7,599	7,621	33	39	1,037	1,147	68	68	7	4
19 years	6,542	6,564	48	41	9,24	1,123	90	97	7	9
20 years	5,996	6,877	52	42	993	1,230	77	103	9	9
21 years	5,816	5,554	45	39	1,047	966	103	95	10	6
22 years	5,886	6,062	43	43	1,143	1,185	104	93	5	11
23 years	4,971	5,537	44	57	1,155	1,118	107	119	11	5
24 years	4,658	5,210	45	49	1,195	1,195	142	123	15	14
25 years	4,707	5,510	36	48	1,141	1,159	146	129	10	7
26 years	3,863	4,489	46	38	991	1,105	122	131	8	5
27 years	3,817	4,324	48	33	1,086	1,015	145	122	7	10
28 years	4,324	5,029	55	40	1,368	1,134	165	141	8	7
29 years	4,004	4,411	73	49	1,459	1,223	154	141	15	6

Source: "Negro Population Classified by Single Years of Age Up to 29, by Sex, and by States: 1930." U.S. Bureau of the Census, *Negroes in the United States, 1920-1932*, pp. 108-109.

★ 1600 ★

Age Composition

Black and Other Classes of Population by Gender and Age, 1910

Age Period and Sex	Population: 1910									
	Total	Negro	White						Indian	Chinese, Japanese and all other
			Total	Native				Foreign born		
				Total	Native parentage	Mixed parentage	Foreign parentage			
	Number									
Both Sexes										
All ages	91,972,266	9,827,763	81,731,957	68,386,412	49,488,575	5,981,526	12,916,311	13,345,545	265,683	146,863
Under 5 years	10,631,364	1,263,288	9,322,914	9,220,407	6,516,282	854,278	1,819,847	102,507	40,384	4,778
Under 1 year	2,217,342	252,386	1,955,605	1,948,870	1,369,140	172,974	406,756	6,735	8,216	1,135
5 to 14 years	18,867,772	2,401,819	16,393,581	15,736,742	11,185,298	1,607,330	2,944,114	656,839	67,934	4,438
15 to 24 years	18,120,587	2,091,211	15,954,802	13,850,660	9,771,977	1,387,574	2,691,109	2,104,142	50,330	24,244
25 to 44 years	26,809,875	2,638,178	24,036,529	18,156,550	12,946,441	1,547,087	3,663,022	5,879,979	60,175	74,993
45 to 64 years	13,424,089	1,108,103	12,249,904	8,857,386	6,740,000	486,351	1,631,035	3,392,518	32,925	33,157
65 years and over	3,949,521	294,124	3,640,003	2,456,654	2,201,068	95,987	159,599	1,183,349	12,986	2,411
Age unknown	169,055	31,040	134,224	108,013	97,509	2,919	7,585	26,211	949	2,842
Male										
All ages	47,332,277	4,885,881	42,178,245	34,654,457	25,229,218	2,968,446	6,456,793	7,523,788	135,133	133,018
Under 5 years	5,380,596	629,320	4,728,650	4,676,710	3,326,237	432,860	917,613	51,940	20,202	2,424
Under 1 year	1,123,409	125,459	993,242	989,715	696,200	87,793	205,722	3,527	4,127	581
5 to 14 years	9,525,876	1,197,249	8,291,470	7,959,515	5,669,886	810,227	1,479,402	331,955	34,548	2,609
15 to 24 years	9,107,572	990,102	8,070,098	6,894,424	4,885,442	682,402	1,326,580	1,175,674	25,877	21,495
25 to 44 years	14,054,482	1,304,098	12,650,614	9,207,844	6,642,210	747,242	1,818,392	3,442,770	30,840	68,930
45 to 64 years	7,163,332	595,554	6,518,282	4,623,547	3,547,325	246,736	829,486	1,894,735	17,055	32,441
65 years and over	1,985,976	152,482	1,825,019	1,218,011	1,089,349	47,438	81,224	607,008	6,130	2,345
Age unknown	114,443	17,076	94,112	74,406	68,769	1,541	4,096	19,706	481	2,774
Female										
All ages	44,639,989	4,941,882	39,553,712	33,731,955	24,259,357	3,013,080	6,459,518	5,821,757	130,550	13,845
Under 5 years	5,250,768	633,968	4,594,264	4,543,697	3,220,045	421,418	902,231	50,567	20,182	2,354
Under 1 year	1,093,933	126,927	962,363	959,155	672,940	85,181	201,031	3,208	4,089	554
5 to 14 years	9,341,896	1,204,570	8,102,111	7,777,227	5,515,412	797,103	1,464,712	324,884	33,386	1,829
15 to 24 years	9,013,015	1,101,109	7,884,704	6,956,236	4,886,535	705,172	1,364,529	928,468	24,453	2,749
25 to 44 years	12,755,393	1,334,080	11,385,915	8,948,706	6,304,231	799,845	1,844,630	2,437,209	29,335	6,063
45 to 64 years	6,260,757	512,549	5,731,622	4,233,839	3,192,675	239,615	801,549	1,497,783	15,870	716
65 years and over	1,963,548	141,642	1,814,984	1,238,643	1,111,719	48,549	78,375	576,341	6,856	66
Age unknown	54,612	13,964	40,112	33,607	28,740	1,378	3,489	6,505	468	68
	Percentage Distribution by Age Periods									
Both Sexes										
All ages	100.0	100.0	100.0	100.0	100.0	100.0	100.0	100.0	100.0	100.0
Under 5 years	11.6	12.9	11.4	13.5	13.2	14.3	14.1	0.8	15.2	3.3
Under 1 year	2.4	2.6	2.4	2.8	2.8	2.9	3.1	0.1	3.1	0.8
5 to 14 years	20.5	24.4	20.1	23.0	22.6	26.9	22.8	4.9	25.6	3.0
15 to 24 years	19.7	21.3	19.5	20.3	19.7	23.2	20.8	15.8	18.9	16.5
25 to 44 years	29.1	26.8	29.4	26.5	26.2	25.9	28.4	44.1	22.6	51.1
45 to 64 years	14.6	11.3	15.0	13.0	13.6	8.1	12.6	25.4	12.4	22.6
65 years and over	4.3	3.0	4.5	3.6	4.4	1.6	1.2	8.9	4.9	1.6
Age unknown	0.2	0.3	0.2	0.2	0.2	[1]	0.1	0.2	0.4	1.9

[Continued]

★ 1600 ★

Black and Other Classes of Population by Gender and Age, 1910

[Continued]

Age Period and Sex	Population: 1910									
	Total	Negro	White						Indian	Chinese, Japanese and all other
			Total	Native				Foreign born		
				Total	Native parentage	Mixed parentage	Foreign parentage			
Male										
All ages	100.0	100.0	100.0	100.0	100.0	100.0	100.0	100.0	100.0	100.0
Under 5 years	11.4	12.9	11.2	13.5	13.2	14.6	14.2	0.7	14.9	1.8
Under 1 year	2.4	2.6	2.4	2.9	2.8	3.0	3.2	[1]	3.1	0.4
5 to 14 years	20.1	24.5	19.7	23.0	22.5	27.3	22.9	4.4	25.6	2.0
15 to 24 years	19.2	20.3	19.1	19.9	19.4	23.0	20.5	15.6	19.1	16.2
25 to 44 years	29.7	26.7	30.0	26.6	26.3	25.2	28.2	45.8	22.8	51.8
45 to 64 years	15.1	12.2	15.5	13.3	14.1	8.3	12.8	25.2	12.6	24.4
65 years and over	4.2	3.1	4.3	3.5	4.3	1.6	1.3	8.1	4.5	1.8
Age unknown	0.2	0.3	0.2	0.2	0.3	0.1	0.1	0.3	0.4	2.1
Female										
All ages	100.0	100.0	100.0	100.0	100.0	100.0	100.0	100.0	100.0	100.0
Under 5 years	11.8	12.8	11.6	13.5	13.3	14.0	14.0	0.9	15.5	17.0
Under 1 year	2.5	2.6	2.4	2.8	2.8	2.8	3.1	0.1	3.1	4.0
5 to 14 years	20.9	24.4	20.5	23.1	22.7	26.5	22.7	5.6	25.6	13.2
15 to 24 years	20.2	22.3	19.9	20.6	20.1	23.4	21.1	15.9	18.7	19.9
25 to 44 years	28.6	27.0	28.8	26.5	26.0	26.5	28.6	41.9	22.5	43.8
45 to 64 years	14.0	10.4	14.5	12.6	13.2	8.0	12.4	25.7	12.2	5.2
65 years and over	4.4	2.9	4.6	3.7	4.6	1.6	1.2	9.9	5.3	0.5
Age unknown	0.1	0.3	0.1	0.1	0.1	[1]	0.1	0.1	0.4	0.5
	Males to 1,000 Females									
Age Period										
All ages	1,060	989	1,066	1,027	1,040	985	1,000	1,292	1,035	9,608
Under 5 years	1,025	993	1,029	1,029	1,033	1,027	1,017	1,027	1,001	1,030
Under 1 year	1,026	988	1,032	1,032	1,034	1,030	1,023	1,100	1,009	1,048
5 to 14 years	1,020	994	1,023	1,023	1,028	1,016	1,010	1,022	1,035	1,426
15 to 24 years	1,010	899	1,024	991	1,000	968	972	1,266	1,058	7,819
25 to 44 years	1,102	978	1,111	1,029	1,054	934	986	1,413	1,051	11,369
45 to 64 years	1,144	1,162	1,137	1,092	1,111	1,030	1,035	1,265	1,075	45,309
65 years and over	1,011	1,077	1,006	983	980	977	1,036	1,053	894	[2]
Age unknown	2,096	1,223	2,346	2,214	2,393	1,118	1,174	3,029	1,028	[2]

Source: "Negro and Other Classes of Population, Classified by Sex and Age Periods: 1910." U.S. Bureau of the Census, *Negro Population, 1790-1915*, p. 170. *Notes:* 1. Less than one-tenth of 1 per cent. 2. Ratio not shown, the number of females being less than 100.

★ 1601 ★

Age Composition

Black and White Males of Militia Age, 1910

Racial class	Male population of militia age: 1910						
	United States	The South				The North	The West
		Total	South Atlantic division	East South Central division	West South Central division		
Number 18 to 44 years of age							
All classes	20,473,684	5,846,414	2,405,895	1,627,471	1,813,048	12,716,180	1,911,090
Negro	1,985,415	1,690,720	779,085	510,592	401,043	278,334	16,361
White	18,351,870	4,138,331	1,624,216	1,116,158	1,397,957	12,411,473	1,802,066
Native	13,880,182	2,910,504	1,520,380	1,093,776	1,296,348	8,684,498	1,285,180
Foreign born	4,471,688	227,827	103,836	22,382	101,609	3,726,975	516,886
Percentage 18 to 44 years of age							
All classes	43.3	39.2	39.2	38.3	39.9	44.5	49.7
Negro	40.6	39.0	38.4	38.8	40.3	53.7	59.0
White	43.5	39.3	39.6	38.1	39.8	44.3	49.4
Native	40.1	38.7	38.7	38.0	39.2	40.0	45.8
Foreign born	59.4	53.5	60.1	44.3	50.1	59.6	61.4
Percentage distribution by racial class							
All classes	100.0	100.0	100.0	100.0	100.0	100.0	100.0
Negro	9.7	28.9	32.4	31.4	22.1	2.2	0.9
White	89.6	70.8	67.5	68.6	77.1	97.6	94.3
Native	67.8	66.9	63.2	67.2	71.5	68.3	67.2
Foreign born	21.8	3.9	4.3	1.4	5.6	29.3	27.0

Source: "Negro and White Males of Militia Age, by Sections and Southern Divisions: 1910." U.S. Bureau of the Census. *Negro Population, 1790-1915,* p. 191.

★ 1602 ★

Age Composition

Black, White, and Foreign-Born White Population Classified by Broad Age Periods, 1910

Age Period	Population											
	All classes			Negro			Native white			Foreign-born white		
	1910	1900	1890	1910	1900	1890	1910	1900	1890	1910	1900	1890
	Number											
All ages	91,972,266	75,994,575	62,622,250	9,827,763	8,833,994	7,470,040	68,386,412	56,595,379	45,862,023	13,345,545	10,213,817	9,121,867
Under 5 years	10,631,364	9,170,628	7,634,693	1,263,288	1,215,655	1,047,574[1]	9,220,407	7,867,583	6,493,019	102,507	52,369	86,629
5 to 14 years	18,867,772	16,954,357	14,607,507	2,401,819	2,294,748	2,127,195[1]	15,736,742	14,138,807	11,820,410	656,839	458,757	644,730
15 to 24 years	18,120,587	14,891,105	12,754,239	2,091,211	1,951,194	1,602,666	13,850,660	11,397,005	9,685,145	2,104,142	1,481,228	1,438,669
25 to 44 years	26,809,875	21,297,427	16,858,086	2,638,178	2,103,989	1,677,109	18,156,550	14,665,552	11,351,992	5,879,979	4,414,590	3,745,105
45 to 64 years	13,424,089	10,399,976	8,188,272	1,108,103	958,234	767,999	8,857,386	6,549,888	4,895,125	3,392,518	2,831,646	2,499,813
65 years and over	3,949,524	3,080,498	2,417,288	294,124	261,363	211,684	2,456,654	1,856,372	1,519,808	1,183,349	950,347	682,304
Age unknown	169,055	200,584	162,165	31,040	48,811	35,813	108,013	120,172	96,524	26,211	24,880	24,617
	Percentage distribution by age periods											
All ages	100.0	100.0	100.0	100.0	100.0	100.0	100.0	100.0	100.0	100.0	100.0	100.0
Under 5 years	11.6	12.1	12.2	12.9	13.8	14.0[1]	13.5	13.9	14.2	0.8	0.5	0.9
5 to 14 years	20.5	22.3	23.3	24.4	26.0	28.5[1]	23.0	25.0	25.8	4.9	4.5	7.1
15 to 24 years	19.7	19.6	20.4	21.3	22.1	21.5	20.3	20.1	21.1	15.8	14.5	15.8
25 to 44 years	29.1	28.0	26.9	26.8	23.8	22.5	26.5	25.9	24.8	44.1	43.2	41.1
45 to 64 years	14.6	13.7	13.1	11.3	10.8	10.3	13.0	11.6	10.7	25.4	27.7	27.4
65 years and over	4.3	4.1	3.9	3.0	3.0	2.8	3.6	3.3	3.3	8.9	9.3	7.5
Age unknown	0.2	0.3	0.3	0.3	0.6	0.5	0.2	0.2	0.2	0.2	0.2	0.3

Source: "Negro, Native White, and Foreign-Born White Population, Classified by Broad Age Periods: 1910, 1900, and 1890." U.S. Bureau of the Census, *Negro Population, 1790-1915*, p. 171. *Notes:* 1. These figures are estimates. The Negro population under 15 years of age was shown by the 1890 census and was 3,174,769 but the number under 5 and the number from 5 to 14 were not distinguished. This distribution was, however, made for the total colored population, the figures being 1,055,045 and 2,142,367, respectively. Applying to the figure for the Negroes under 15 the same proportions for the two age groups as were found for the total colored, the figures and percentages given in the table have been calculated. There is no appreciable error, since the Negroes constitute the great bulk of the colored and since there is no very material difference between the Negroes and the other colored with respect to the distribution of the persons under 15 between the two age groups.

★ 1603 ★

Age Composition

Classification by Age Periods of Black Population in Geographical Areas, 1910 - I

Age period	Negro Population: 1910 Number						
	Total	Rural	Urban				
			Total	Cities of 2,500 to 25,000	Cities of 25,000 to 100,000	Cities of 100,000 to 500,000	Cities of 500,000 and over
	United States						
All ages	9,827,763	7,138,534	2,689,229	1,063,628	602,040	626,946	396,615
Under 5 years	1,263,288	1,034,208	229,080	103,345	48,799	47,911	29,025
5 to 14 years	2,401,819	1,947,600	454,219	211,911	98,821	94,262	49,225
15 to 24 years	2,091,211	1,512,912	578,299	234,989	132,615	134,308	76,387

[Continued]

★ 1603 ★

Classification by Age Periods of Black Population in Geographical Areas, 1910 - I

[Continued]

Age period	Negro Population: 1910 Number						
	Total	Rural	Urban				
			Total	Cities of 2,500 to 25,000	Cities of 25,000 to 100,000	Cities of 100,000 to 500,000	Cities of 500,000 and over
25 to 44 years	2,638,178	1,652,804	985,374	336,336	226,249	244,432	178,357
45 to 64 years	1,108,103	756,844	351,259	135,595	76,425	85,984	53,255
65 years and over	294,124	216,689	77,435	35,272	15,705	17,478	8,980
Age unknown	31,040	17,477	13,563	6,180	3,426	2,571	1,386
The South							
All ages	8,749,427	6,894,972	1,854,455	850,721	454,851	464,134	84,740
Under 5 years	1,176,331	1,009,690	166,641	85,701	37,251	37,061	6,628
5 to 14 years	2,238,537	1,898,791	339,746	176,001	76,954	74,224	12,567
15 to 24 years	1,882,319	1,464,273	418,046	192,328	104,239	103,659	17,820
25 to 44 years	2,217,273	1,581,247	636,026	262,907	168,028	172,861	32,230
45 to 64 years	951,853	720,342	231,511	102,727	54,499	61,447	12,838
65 years and over	256,694	203,949	52,745	26,071	10,968	13,254	2,452
Age unknown	26,420	16,680	9,740	4,986	2,912	1,628	214
The North							
All ages	1,027,674	232,708	794,966	201,704	140,370	141,026	311,866
Under 5 years	83,729	23,857	59,872	16,853	11,139	9,483	22,397
5 to 14 years	157,097	47,377	109,720	34,447	21,004	17,611	36,658
15 to 24 years	200,049	46,615	153,434	40,722	27,292	26,853	58,567
25 to 44 years	398,484	67,049	331,435	68,609	55,169	61,530	146,127
45 to 64 years	148,078	34,730	113,348	31,092	20,774	21,065	40,417
65 years and over	35,973	12,331	23,642	8,871	4,568	3,675	6,528
Age unknown	4,264	749	3,515	1,110	424	809	1,172
The West							
All ages	50,662	10,854	39,808	11,203	6,819	21,786	-
Under 5 years	3,228	661	2,567	791	409	1,367	-
5 to 14 years	6,185	1,432	4,753	1,463	863	2,427	-
15 to 24 years	8,843	2,024	6,819	1,939	1,084	3,796	-
25 to 44 years	22,421	4,508	17,913	4,820	3,052	10,041	-
45 to 64 years	8,172	1,772	6,400	1,776	1,152	3,472	-

[Continued]

★ 1603 ★

Classification by Age Periods of Black Population in Geographical Areas, 1910 - I

[Continued]

Age period	Negro Population: 1910 Number						
	Total	Rural	Urban				
			Total	Cities of 2,500 to 25,000	Cities of 25,000 to 100,000	Cities of 100,000 to 500,000	Cities of 500,000 and over
65 years and over	1,457	409	1,048	330	169	549	-
Age unknown	356	48	308	84	90	134	-

Source: "Classification by Age Periods of the Negro Population Living in Urban and Rural Communities, and in Classes of Cities, by Sections: 1910." U.S. Bureau of the Census. *Negro Population, 1790-1915*, p. 187.

★ 1604 ★

Age Composition

Classification by Age Periods of Black Population in Geographical Areas, 1910 - II

Age period	Negro Population: 1910 Percentage distribution by age periods						
	Total	Rural	Urban				
			Total	Cities of 2,500 to 25,000	Cities of 25,000 to 100,000	Cities of 100,000 to 500,000	Cities of 500,000 and over
United States							
All ages	100.00	100.0	100.0	100.0	100.0	100.0	100.0
Under 5 years	12.9	14.5	8.5	9.7	8.1	7.6	7.3
5 to 14 years	24.4	27.3	16.9	19.9	16.4	15.0	12.4
15 to 24 years	21.3	21.2	21.5	22.1	22.0	21.4	19.3
25 to 44 years	26.8	23.2	36.6	31.6	37.6	39.0	45.0
45 to 64 years	11.3	10.6	13.1	12.7	12.7	13.7	13.4
65 years and over	3.0	3.0	2.9	3.3	2.6	2.8	2.3
Age unknown	0.3	0.2	0.5	0.6	0.6	0.4	0.3
The South							
All ages	100.0	100.0	100.0	100.0	100.0	100.0	100.0
Under 5 years	13.4	14.6	9.0	10.1	8.2	8.0	7.8
5 to 14 years	25.6	27.5	18.3	20.7	16.9	16.0	14.8
15 to 24 years	21.5	21.2	22.5	22.6	22.9	22.3	21.0
25 to 44 years	25.3	22.9	34.3	30.9	30.9	37.2	38.0
45 to 64 years	10.9	10.4	12.5	12.1	12.0	13.2	15.1
65 years and over	2.9	3.0	2.8	3.1	2.4	2.9	2.9

[Continued]

★ 1604 ★

Classification by Age Periods of Black Population in Geographical Areas, 1910 - II

[Continued]

Age period	Negro Population: 1910 Percentage distribution by age periods						
			Urban				
	Total	Rural	Total	Cities of 2,500 to 25,000	Cities of 25,000 to 100,000	Cities of 100,000 to 500,000	Cities of 500,000 and over
Age unknown	0.3	0.2	0.5	0.6	0.6	0.4	0.3
				The North			
All ages	100.0	100.0	100.0	100.0	100.0	100.0	100.0
Under 5 years	8.1	10.3	7.5	8.4	7.9	6.7	7.2
5 to 14 years	15.3	20.4	13.8	17.1	15.0	12.5	11.8
15 to 24 years	19.5	20.0	19.3	20.2	19.4	19.0	18.8
25 to 44 years	38.8	28.8	41.7	34.0	39.3	43.6	46.9
45 to 64 years	14.4	14.9	14.3	15.4	14.8	14.9	13.0
65 years and over	3.5	5.3	3.0	4.4	3.3	2.6	2.1
Age unknown	0.4	0.3	0.4	0.6	0.3	0.6	0.4
				The West			
All ages	100.0	100.0	100.0	100.0	100.0	100.0	-
Under 5 years	6.4	6.1	6.4	7.1	6.0	6.3	-
5 to 14 years	12.2	13.2	11.9	13.1	12.7	11.1	-
15 to 24 years	17.5	18.6	17.1	17.3	15.9	17.4	-
25 to 44 years	44.3	41.5	45.0	43.0	44.8	46.1	-
45 to 64 years	16.1	16.3	16.1	15.9	16.9	15.9	-
65 years and over	2.9	3.8	2.6	2.9	2.5	2.5	-
Age unknown	0.7	0.4	0.8	0.7	1.3	0.6	-

Source: "Classification by Age Periods of the Negro Population Living in Urban and Rural Communities, and in Classes of Cities, by Sections: 1910." U.S. Bureau of the Census. *Negro Population, 1790-1915*, p. 187.

★ 1605 ★

Age Composition

Classification of Black Population by Age Periods, by Sections, and in the South, 1900 and 1910 - I

Section, Division, and State	Negro population						
	All ages	Under 5 years	5 to 9 years	10 to 14 years	15 to 19 years	20 to 24 years	25 to 29 years
				1910			
UNITED STATES	9,827,763	1,263,288	1,246,553	1,155,266	1,060,416	1,030,795	881,227
THE SOUTH	8,749,427	1,176,331	1,164,557	1,073,980	970,716	911,603	749,782
South Atlantic division	4,112,488	570,516	555,036	513,239	457,053	426,876	341,665
East South Central division	2,652,513	347,803	343,812	320,476	294,183	274,935	230,624
West South Central division	1,984,426	258,012	265,709	240,265	219,480	209,792	177,493
THE NORTH	1,027,674	83,729	78,892	78,205	86,126	113,923	124,832
THE WEST	50,662	3,228	3,104	3,081	3,574	5,269	6,613
South Atlantic division:							
Delaware	31,181	3,089	3,315	3,540	3,228	3,142	2,583
Maryland	232,250	25,987	25,809	24,595	24,398	23,591	21,023
District of Columbia	94,446	7,290	7,192	7,211	8,620	11,333	11,572
Virginia	671,096	86,555	88,123	83,395	75,047	66,503	52,324
West Virginia	64,173	6,974	6,274	5,424	6,575	8,891	8,265
North Carolina	697,843	107,297	100,151	89,416	80,253	69,485	52,293
South Carolina	835,843	128,712	123,067	114,341	99,118	85,305	63,247
Georgia	1,176,987	167,498	163,294	152,029	129,923	123,295	98,274
Florida	308,669	37,114	37,811	33,288	30,891	35,331	32,084
East South Central division:							
Kentucky	261,656	25,541	26,087	26,984	28,163	27,856	24,148
Tennessee	473,088	56,580	55,845	53,344	54,363	51,187	42,188
Alabama	908,282	123,991	121,935	112,129	99,130	93,670	78,334
Mississippi	1,009,487	141,691	139,945	128,019	112,527	102,222	85,954
West South Central division:							
Arkansas	442,891	57,330	58,552	52,679	50,309	46,220	39,488
Louisiana	713,874	92,439	95,985	85,917	76,868	74,119	63,677
Oklahoma	137,612	18,186	18,269	16,208	14,974	14,344	12,601
Texas	690,049	90,057	92,903	85,461	77,329	75,109	61,727
				1900			
United States	8,833,994	1,215,655	1,202,758	1,091,990	982,022	969,172	737,479
THE SOUTH							
South Atlantic division	3,729,017	545,284	527,900	476,108	423,855	400,667	286,748
East South Central division	2,499,886	348,061	348,997	316,984	283,363	273,069	204,948

[Continued]

★ 1605 ★

Classification of Black Population by Age Periods, by Sections, and in the South, 1900 and 1910 - I

[Continued]

Section, Division, and State	Negro population						
	All ages	Under 5 years	5 to 9 years	10 to 14 years	15 to 19 years	20 to 24 years	25 to 29 years
West South Central division	1,694,066	242,448	245,304	219,122	185,981	182,919	141,688
THE NORTH	880,771	77,794	78,233	77,597	86,506	108,993	100,587
THE WEST	30,254	2,068	2,324	2,179	2,317	3,524	3,508
South Atlantic division:							
Delaware	30,697	3,622	3,548	3,401	3,243	3,253	2,628
Maryland	235,064	28,116	27,586	26,539	25,312	25,247	20,303
District of Columbia	86,702	7,278	7,475	7,301	8,970	11,650	9,682
Virginia	660,722	90,322	91,469	85,609	76,424	66,278	46,714
West Virginia	43,499	4,793	4,403	4,079	5,033	6,585	5,032
North Carolina	624,469	96,945	89,833	81,296	74,751	65,656	43,776
South Carolina	782,321	125,254	119,669	106,982	93,535	82,082	54,399
Georgia	1,034,813	157,201	153,516	134,540	112,431	111,663	82,143
Florida	230,730	31,743	30,401	26,361	24,156	28,253	22,071
East South Central division:							
Kentucky	284,706	31,706	33,280	33,155	31,333	30,946	25,586
Tennessee	480,243	62,388	63,022	59,343	55,989	53,110	39,900
Alabama	827,307	119,275	118,403	105,926	93,246	90,314	66,023
Mississippi	907,630	134,692	134,292	118,560	102,795	98,699	73,439
West South Central division:							
Arkansas	366,856	51,255	51,793	46,714	41,231	40,853	30,861
Louisiana	650,804	92,759	93,447	82,803	69,091	68,705	55,719
Oklahoma	55,684	7,916	7,570	6,908	6,285	5,726	4,438
Texas	620,722	90,518	92,494	82,697	69,374	67,635	50,670

Source: "Negro Population, Classified by Age Periods, by Sections, Southern Divisions, and Southern States: 1910 and 1900." U.S. Bureau of the Census, *Negro Population, 1790-1915*, p. 192.

★ 1606 ★

Age Composition

Classification of Black Population by Age Periods, by Sections, and in the South, 1900 and 1910 - II

Section, Division, and State	Negro population					
	30 to 34 years	35 to 44 years	45 to 54 years	55 to 64 years	65 years and over	Age unknown
			1910			
UNITED STATES	668,089	1,088,862	711,979	396,124	294,124	31,040
THE SOUTH	557,466	910,025	607,895	343,958	256,694	26,420
South Atlantic division	253,860	421,374	279,676	162,623	119,140	11,430
East South Central division	171,477	278,306	191,801	108,199	82,481	8,416
West South Central division	132,129	210,345	136,418	73,136	55,073	6,574
THE NORTH	104,600	169,052	98,341	49,737	35,973	4,264
THE WEST	6,023	9,785	5,743	2,429	1,457	356
South Atlantic division:						
Delaware	2,233	4,154	2,903	1,635	1,240	119
Maryland	16,570	30,097	20,822	11,264	8,575	519
District of Columbia	8,963	15,255	9,088	4,492	2,957	473
Virginia	40,358	72,406	51,730	29,863	23,521	1,271
West Virginia	5,754	8,484	4,187	1,886	1,257	202
North Carolina	38,240	61,526	46,260	29,083	21,428	2,411
South Carolina	46,194	75,811	46,216	30,280	21,817	1,735
Georgia	71,459	115,255	77,110	44,235	31,959	2,656
Florida	24,089	38,386	21,360	9,885	6,386	2,044
East South Central division:						
Kentucky	19,294	34,000	24,494	13,441	10,503	1,145
Tennessee	31,848	50,969	37,930	21,357	16,155	1,322
Alabama	55,845	90,450	68,415	34,834	26,770	2,779
Mississippi	64,490	102,887	60,962	38,567	29,053	3,170
West South Central division:						
Arkansas	29,729	46,066	34,411	16,188	10,827	1,092
Louisiana	47,489	79,455	46,232	27,581	21,886	2,226
Oklahoma	9,662	14,744	9,688	5,042	3,303	591
Texas	45,249	70,080	46,087	24,325	19,057	2,665
			1900			
UNITED STATES	524,607	841,903	617,371	340,863	261,363	48,811
THE SOUTH	444,709	713,990	537,826	299,315	232,217	41,466
South Atlantic division	205,472	342,794	248,740	144,525	111,321	15,603
East South Central division	141,938	222,312	174,614	95,882	75,917	13,801

[Continued]

★ 1606 ★

Classification of Black Population by Age Periods, by Sections, and in the South, 1900 and 1910 - II

[Continued]

Section, Division, and State	Negro population					
	30 to 34 years	35 to 44 years	45 to 54 years	55 to 64 years	65 years and over	Age unknown
West South Central division	97,299	148,884	114,472	58,908	44,979	12,062
THE NORTH	76,637	122,427	76,529	40,236	28,311	6,921
THE WEST	3,261	5,486	3,016	1,312	835	424
South Atlantic division:						
Delaware	2,015	3,724	2,521	1,467	1,079	196
Maryland	14,754	27,751	18,936	10,883	7,565	2,072
District of Columbia	6,883	12,232	8,462	3,977	2,712	80
Virginia	35,730	65,997	48,530	28,158	23,126	2,355
West Virginia	3,264	4,537	2,709	1,338	961	765
North Carolina	30,364	50,150	43,661	25,476	19,576	2,985
South Carolina	39,040	64,808	44,886	28,727	21,778	1,161
Georgia	57,912	90,469	64,408	37,104	29,056	4,370
Florida	15,510	23,126	14,627	7,395	5,468	1,619
East South Central division:						
Kentucky	18,181	32,745	22,527	12,600	9,660	2,987
Tennessee	28,087	43,829	36,078	20,173	14,760	3,564
Alabama	45,044	66,363	62,540	30,137	25,093	4,943
Mississippi	50,626	79,375	53,469	32,972	26,404	2,307
West South Central division:						
Arkansas	20,957	31,211	27,912	12,612	8,446	3,011
Louisiana	38,039	60,427	42,971	24,600	19,898	2,345
Oklahoma	3,110	5,236	4,052	2,264	1,542	637
Texas	35,193	52,010	39,537	19,432	15,093	6,069

Source: "Negro Population, Classified by Age Periods, by Sections, Southern Divisions, and Southern States: 1910 and 1900." U.S. Bureau of the Census, *Negro Population, 1790-1915*, p. 192.

★ 1607 ★

Age Composition

Median Age Population by Race, Gender and Nativity, 1790-1970 - I

Year	All races			White			Negro		
	Total	Male	Female	Total	Male	Female	Total	Male	Female
1970	28.1	26.8	29.3	28.9	27.6	30.2	22.4	21.0	23.6
1960*	29.5	28.7	30.3	30.3	29.4	31.1	23.5	22.3	24.5
1960	29.6	28.7	30.4	30.3	29.5	31.2	23.5	22.3	24.5
1950	30.2	29.9	30.5	30.8	30.4	31.1	26.1	25.8	26.4
1940	29.0	29.1	29.0	29.5	29.5	29.5	25.3	25.34	25.3
1930	26.5	26.7	26.2	26.9	27.1	26.6	23.5	23.7	23.3
1920	25.3	25.8	24.7	25.6	26.1	25.1	22.3	22.8	22.0
1910	24.1	24.6	23.5	24.5	24.9	23.9	20.8	21.0	20.7
1900	22.9	23.3	22.4	23.4	23.8	22.9	19.5	19.5	19.5
1890	22.0	22.3	21.6	22.5	22.9	22.1	18.1	17.9	18.3
1880	20.9	21.2	20.7	21.4	21.6	21.1	NA	NA	NA
1870	20.2	20.2	20.1	20.4	20.6	20.3	18.3	17.8	18.8
1860	19.4	19.8	19.1	19.7	20.1	19.3	17.5	17.5	17.5
1850	18.9	19.2	18.6	19.2	19.5	18.8	17.4	17.3	17.4
1840	17.8	17.9	17.8	17.9	18.0	17.8	17.6	17.5	17.6
1830	17.2	17.2	17.3	17.3	17.2	17.3	17.2	17.1	17.3
1820	16.7	16.6	16.8	16.6	16.5	16.6	17.2	17.2	17.4
1810	-	-	-	16.0	15.9	16.1	-	-	-
1800	-	-	-	16.0	15.7	16.3	-	-	-
1790	-	-	-	-	[1]	-	-	-	-

Source: "Median Age of the Population, by Race, Sex, and Nativity: 1790 to 1970." U.S. Bureau of the Census, *Historical Statistics of the United States: Colonial Times to 1970, Part I*, p. 19. *Notes:* * Denotes first year for which figures include Alaska and Hawaii. NA Not available. 1. Median falls in the open-ended age group, 16 years and over, which includes 50.3 percent of the white male population.

★ 1608 ★

Age Composition

Median Age Population by Race, Gender and Nativity, 1790-1970 - II

Year	Other races			Foreign-born white		
	Total	Male	Female	Total	Male	Female
1970	24.7	24.4	24.9	54.6	54.5	54.7
1960*	24.3	25.2	23.2	57.7	58.4	57.1
1960	24.5	25.5	23.4	57.7	58.2	57.2
1950	24.5	26.9	21.8	56.1	59.0	55.5
1940	24.1	27.6	19.9	51.0	51.4	50.5

[Continued]

★ 1608 ★

Median Age Population by Race, Gender and Nativity, 1790-1970 - II

[Continued]

Year	Other races			Foreign-born white		
	Total	Male	Female	Total	Male	Female
1930	23.3	25.9	18.6	43.9	44.1	43.7
1920	26.1	30.4	20.5	40.0	40.1	39.9
1910	26.5	29.2	19.8	37.2	36.9	37.6
1900	27.3	30.9	20.3	38.5	38.8	38.1
1890	28.9	33.2	27.2	37.1	37.1	37.0
1880	NA	NA	Na	38.3	38.5	38.0
1870	28.1	29.1	23.0	34.6	35.3	33.9
1860	26.1	27.5	20.5	-	-	-
1850	-	-	-	-	-	-
1840	-	-	-	-	-	-
1830	-	-	-	-	-	-
1820	-	-	-	-	-	-
1810	-	-	-	-	-	-
1800	-	-	-	-	-	-
1790	-	-	-	-	-	-

Source: "Median Age of the Population, by Race, Sex, and Nativity: 1790 to 1970." U.S. Bureau of the Census, *Historical Statistics of the United States: Colonial Times to 1970, Part I*, p. 19. *Notes:* NA Not available. * Denotes first year for which figures include Alaska and Hawaii.

★ 1609 ★

Age Composition

Median Age by States of the Black Population in 1910 and 1900, and of the Black, Indian, and Mongolian Population in 1880 and 1890 - I

States Having at Least 1,000 Negroes in 1910	Median age of Negro population: 1910
United States	20.8
South Carolina	17.5
North Carolina	18.1
Georgia	18.9
Mississippi	19.0
Alabama	19.7
Texas	19.9
Virginia	20.1
Arkansas	20.2
Louisiana	20.3

[Continued]

★ 1609 ★

Median Age by States of the Black Population in 1910 and 1900, and of the Black, Indian, and Mongolian Population in 1880 and 1890 - I

[Continued]

States Having at Least 1,000 Negroes in 1910	Median age of Negro population: 1910
Oklahoma	20.3
Tennessee	21.5
Florida	22.1
Maryland	23.4
Delaware	23.8
West Virginia	23.9
Kentucky	24.2
Kansas	26.1
Missouri	27.1
Vermont	27.1
District of Columbia	27.2
New Jersey	27.4
Pennsylvania	27.5
Indiana	27.6
Iowa	27.7
Maine	27.9
Massachusetts	28.9
New York	28.2
Connecticut	28.3
Wyoming	28.3
New Mexico	28.4
Illinois	28.6
Ohio	28.6
Rhode Island	28.6
Nebraska	29.2
Wisconsin	29.3
Michigan	29.4
Arizona	29.6
California	29.7
Colorado	30.2
Minnesota	30.7
Washington	30.9
Utah	31.1

[Continued]

★ 1609 ★

Median Age by States of the Black Population in 1910 and 1900, and of the Black, Indian, and Mongolian Population in 1880 and 1890 - I

[Continued]

States Having at Least 1,000 Negroes in 1910	Median age of Negro population: 1910
Montana	32.0
Oregon	33.1

Source: "Median Age, by States, of the Negro Population: 1910 and 1900 - and of the Negro, Indian, and Mongolian Population: 1890 and 1880." U.S. Bureau of the Census, *Negro Population, 1790-1915,* p. 180.

★ 1610 ★

Age Composition

Median Age by States of the Black Population in 1910 and 1900, and of the Black, Indian, and Mongolian Population in 1880 and 1890 - II

States Having at Least 1,000 Negroes in 1910	Median age of Negro population: 1900
United States	19.4
South Carolina	17.0
North Carolina	17.8
Texas	18.0
Georgia	18.1
Mississippi	18.1
Alabama	18.5
Arkansas	18.8
Louisiana	18.9
Virginia	18.9
Oklahoma[1]	19.0
Tennessee	19.8
Florida	20.3
Maryland	21.7
Kentucky	21.8
Delaware	22.3
West Virginia	22.3
Kansas	22.8
Missouri	23.5
Indiana	24.8

[Continued]

★ 1610 ★

Median Age by States of the Black Population in 1910 and 1900, and of the Black, Indian, and Mongolian Population in 1880 and 1890 - II

[Continued]

States Having at Least 1,000 Negroes in 1910	Median age of Negro population: 1900
District of Columbia	25.3
New Jersey	25.3
Pennsylvania	25.5
Ohio	25.6
Iowa	25.7
Arizona	25.9
Connecticut	26.1
Illinois	26.3
Nebraska	26.3
New York	26.4
Michigan	26.8
New Mexico	26.8
Massachusetts	26.9
Maine	27.1
Rhode Island	27.3
California	28.1
Wisconsin	28.2
Colorado	29.1
Minnesota	29.1
Washington	30.1
Montana	30.5
Oregon	30.7

Source: "Median Age, by States, of the Negro Population: 1910 and 1900 - and of the Negro, Indian, and Mongolian Population: 1890 and 1880." U.S. Bureau of the Census, *Negro Population, 1790-1915*, p. 180. *Note:* 1. Includes population of Indian Territory for 1900.

★ 1611 ★

Age Composition

Median Age by States of the Black Population in 1910 and 1900, and of the Black, Indian, and Mongolian Population in 1880 and 1890 - III

States Having at Least 1,000 Negroes in 1910	Median age of Negro Indian, and Mongolian population: 1890
United States	18.3
South Carolina	16.1
Texas	16.6
Mississippi	16.8
North Carolina	16.8
Georgia	17.1
Alabama	17.4
Arkansas	17.4
Virginia	17.7
Louisiana	17.9
Tennessee	18.1
Florida	18.4
Kentucky	19.5
Kansas	19.8
West Virginia	20.3
Maryland	20.5
Missouri	20.7
Wisconsin	20.8
Delaware	21.3
Indiana	22.4
Iowa	22.9
District of Columbia	23.2
New Mexico	23.3
Ohio	23.4
Nebraska	23.5
Oklahoma	23.5
Illinois	23.8
Michigan	24.0
Minnesota	24.4
Pennsylvania	24.5
New Jersey	24.6
Connecticut	26.2
New York	26.8
Maine	26.9

[Continued]

★ 1611 ★

Median Age by States of the Black Population in 1910 and 1900, and of the Black, Indian, and Mongolian Population in 1880 and 1890 - III

[Continued]

States Having at Least 1,000 Negroes in 1910	Median age of Negro Indian, and Mongolian population: 1890
Massachusetts	27.0
Colorado	28.1
Arizona	28.3
Rhode Island	28.3
Washington	28.4
Montana	30.9
California	32.8
Oregon	32.9

Source: "Median Age, by States, of the Negro Population: 1910 and 1900 - and of the Negro, Indian, and Mongolian Population: 1890 and 1880." U.S. Bureau of the Census, *Negro Population, 1790-1915*, p. 180.

★ 1612 ★

Age Composition

Median Age by States of the Black Population in 1910 and 1900, and of the Black, Indian, and Mongolian Population in 1880 and 1890 - IV

States Having at Least 1,000 Negroes in 1910	Median age of Negro Indian, and Mongolian population: 1880
United States	18.0
Texas	15.8
Mississippi	16.1
South Carolina	16.2
Georgia	16.4
North Carolina	16.4
Alabama	16.7
Arkansas	16.7
Tennessee	16.9
Virginia	17.2
Florida	17.3

[Continued]

★ 1612 ★

Median Age by States of the Black Population in 1910 and 1900, and of the Black, Indian, and Mongolian Population in 1880 and 1890 - IV

[Continued]

States Having at Least 1,000 Negroes in 1910	Median age of Negro Indian, and Mongolian population: 1880
Louisiana	18.4
Kentucky	18.5
Kansas	19.1
Missouri	19.2
West Virginia	19.3
Maryland	20.0
Delaware	20.1
Wisconsin	20.4
Minnesota	21.0
Indiana	21.1
Vermont	21.3
Michigan	21.5
Ohio	21.6
Illinois	22.0
Iowa	22.0
New Mexico	22.2
Nebraska	22.6
District of Columbia	23.3
New Jersey	23.9
Pennsylvania	24.0
Maine	25.2
Colorado	25.8
Connecticut	25.8
New York	25.9
Massachusetts	26.3
Rhode Island	27.3
California	30.1

Source: "Median Age, by States, of the Negro Population: 1910 and 1900 - and of the Negro, Indian, and Mongolian Population: 1890 and 1880." U.S. Bureau of the Census, *Negro Population, 1790-1915*, p. 180.

★ 1613 ★

Age Composition

Percent Distribution by Age, Color, and Gender for the Urban, Rural-Farm, and Rural Non-farm Population, 1920 and 1930 - I

Area and Age	All Classes					
	Total		Male		Female	
	1930	1920	1930	1920	1930	1920
URBAN						
All ages	100.0	100.0	100.0	100.0	100.0	100.0
Under 5 years	8.2	9.7	8.4	9.8	8.0	9.6
5 to 9 years	9.0	9.3	9.2	9.3	8.9	9.3
10 to 14 years	8.6	8.6	8.7	8.5	8.6	8.7
15 to 19 years	8.7	8.2	8.4	7.8	9.0	8.5
20 to 24 years	9.3	9.4	8.9	8.9	9.7	9.9
25 to 29 years	9.0	9.8	8.8	9.7	9.1	9.8
30 to 34 years	8.4	8.7	8.4	8.9	8.4	8.5
35 to 39 years	8.4	8.2	8.5	8.6	8.2	7.8
40 to 44 years	7.2	6.6	7.4	6.8	6.9	6.5
45 to 49 years	6.1	5.9	6.4	6.2	5.9	5.6
50 to 54 years	5.1	4.8	5.2	5.0	4.9	4.7
55 to 59 years	3.9	3.5	3.9	3.5	3.8	3.4
60 to 64 years	3.1	2.8	3.0	2.8	3.1	2.8
65 to 69 years	2.2	1.8	2.1	1.8	2.3	1.9
70 to 74 years	1.5	1.2	1.4	1.1	1.6	1.3
75 to 79 years	.8	.7	.7	.7	.9	.8
80 to 84 years	.4	.3	.3	.3	.4	.4
85 years and over	.2	.2	.2	.1	.2	.2
Unknown	.1	.2	.1	.2	.1	.1
RURAL-FARM						
All ages	100.0	100.0	100.0	100.0	100.0	100.0
Under 5 years	11.1	12.7	10.7	12.4	11.5	13.0
5 to 9 years	12.5	13.1	12.1	12.8	13.0	13.4
10 to 14 years	12.4	12.7	12.2	12.6	12.7	12.8
15 to 19 years	11.3	10.4	11.5	10.4	11.1	10.5
20 to 24 years	8.1	7.9	8.3	7.7	7.9	8.2
25 to 29 years	6.0	6.8	5.9	6.5	6.2	7.1
30 to 34 years	5.5	6.0	5.3	5.8	5.9	6.2
35 to 39 years	5.9	6.1	5.6	6.0	6.2	6.2
40 to 44 years	5.5	5.1	5.3	5.0	5.6	5.2
45 to 49 years	5.2	4.9	5.2	5.2	5.1	4.6
50 to 54 years	4.6	4.0	4.9	4.4	4.3	3.7
55 to 59 years	3.7	3.1	4.0	3.4	3.3	2.8
60 to 64 years	2.9	2.7	3.3	3.0	2.6	2.3
65 to 69 years	2.1	1.9	2.4	2.2	1.8	1.6
70 to 74 years	1.5	1.2	1.7	1.4	1.3	1.1

[Continued]

★ 1613 ★

Percent Distribution by Age, Color, and Gender for the Urban, Rural-Farm, and Rural Non-farm Population, 1920 and 1930 - I

[Continued]

Area and Age	All Classes					
	Total		Male		Female	
	1930	1920	1930	1920	1930	1920
75 to 79 years	.9	.7	.9	.7	.8	.7
80 to 84 years	.4	.4	.4	.3	.4	.4
85 years and over	.2	.2	.2	.2	.2	.2
Unknown	-	.1	-	.1	-	.1
RURAL-NONFARM						
All ages	100.0	100.0	100.0	100.0	100.0	100.0
Under 5 years	10.5	11.6	10.4	11.3	10.6	11.8
5 to 9 years	11.1	11.2	10.9	10.9	11.2	11.5
10 to 14 years	9.8	10.0	9.6	9.7	9.9	10.3
15 to 19 years	8.9	8.6	8.6	8.2	9.3	9.0
20 to 24 years	8.5	8.4	8.2	8.2	8.8	8.7
25 to 29 years	7.8	8.2	7.7	8.1	7.9	8.3
30 to 34 years	7.1	7.3	7.1	7.4	7.0	7.2
35 to 39 years	7.0	7.1	7.1	7.4	6.8	6.7
40 to 44 years	6.0	5.7	6.2	5.9	5.7	5.5
45 to 49 years	5.3	5.2	5.6	5.6	5.1	4.7
50 to 54 years	4.6	4.3	4.8	4.5	4.4	4.0
55 to 59 years	3.7	3.4	3.9	3.5	3.6	3.3
60 to 64 years	3.1	3.0	3.2	3.1	3.1	3.0
65 to 69 years	2.5	2.3	2.5	2.3	2.5	2.3
70 to 74 years	1.9	1.7	2.0	1.7	1.9	1.8
75 to 79 years	1.2	1.1	1.2	1.2	1.2	1.1
80 to 84 years	.6	.5	.6	.5	.6	.5
85 years and over	.3	.3	.3	.2	.3	.3
Unknown	.1	.2	.1	.2	.1	.1

Source: "Percent Distribution by 5-Year Age Periods, by Color, and Sex for the Urban, Rural-Farm, and Rural-Nonfarm Population of the United States: 1930 and 1920." U.S. Bureau of the Census, *Negroes in the United States, 1920- 1932*, p. 96.

★ 1614 ★

Age Composition

Percent Distribution by Age, Color, and Gender for the Urban, Rural-Farm, and Rural Non-farm Population, 1920 and 1930 - II

Area and Age	Negro				White				Other Races			
	Male		Female		Male		Female		Male		Female	
	1930	1920	1930	1920	1930	1920	1930	1920	1930	1920	1930	1920
URBAN												
All ages	100.0	100.0	100.0	100.0	100.0	100.0	100.0	100.0	100.0	100.0	100.0	100.0
Under 5 years	8.6	7.6	7.9	7.5	8.3	9.9	7.9	9.8	12.1	7.0	15.1	17.9
5 to 9 years	9.3	8.2	8.8	8.2	9.1	9.4	8.8	9.4	11.9	4.2	14.7	10.6
10 to 14 years	7.9	7.9	7.8	8.4	8.8	8.6	8.6	8.7	8.5	3.0	10.5	7.1
15 to 19 years	7.9	8.0	9.3	9.4	8.5	7.8	9.0	8.5	8.1	5.5	9.7	8.0
20 to 24 years	9.7	10.9	11.8	12.5	8.8	8.8	9.6	9.7	10.8	9.2	9.7	12.5
25 to 29 years	10.9	11.2	12.0	12.1	8.6	9.6	8.9	9.7	11.3	9.4	9.3	13.8
30 to 34 years	9.6	9.1	9.5	9.2	8.3	8.9	8.3	8.4	8.6	11.5	7.4	10.0
35 to 39 years	9.8	10.3	9.4	9.6	8.5	8.4	8.1	7.7	7.8	12.4	6.7	7.4
40 to 44 years	7.5	7.4	6.8	0.7	7.5	6.7	6.9	6.4	6.2	10.3	4.8	5.2
45 to 49 years	6.5	7.3	5.7	5.2	6.4	6.1	5.9	5.6	5.1	8.1	4.1	2.9
50 to 54 years	4.9	4.7	4.0	3.8	5.2	5.0	5.0	4.7	3.4	6.9	2.7	1.7
55 to 59 years	2.8	2.5	2.3	2.2	4.0	3.6	4.0	3.5	2.3	5.1	1.9	.9
60 to 64 years	1.9	1.9	1.8	1.8	3.1	2.9	3.3	2.9	1.6	3.7	1.4	.7
65 to 69 years	1.1	1.2	1.2	1.2	2.2	1.8	2.4	2.0	.9	1.7	.9	.4
70 to 74 years	.7	.7	.7	.8	1.5	1.2	1.7	1.3	.5	.9	.5	.3
75 to 79 years	.4	.4	.4	.5	.8	.7	.9	.8	.3	.2	.3	.1
80 to 84 years	.2	.2	.3	.3	.3	.3	.5	.4	.1	.1	.2	.1
85 years and over	.1	.1	.2	.2	.2	.1	.2	.2	.1	-	.2	.1
Unknown	.2	.4	.2	.3	.1	.2.	.1	.1	.3	.5	.1	.3
RURAL-FARM												
All ages	100.0	100.0	100.0	100.0	100.0	100.0	100.0	100.0	100.0	100.0	100.0	100.0
Under 5 years	12.4	13.3	12.7	13.4	10.3	12.2	11.2	12.9	13.6	14.0	16.1	16.9
5 to 9 years	14.3	15.1	14.3	15.0	11.7	12.4	12.6	13.1	14.2	11.7	16.6	14.3
10 to 14 years	14.0	15.0	13.6	14.5	11.9	12.1	12.5	12.5	11.1	9.5	12.5	11.1
15 to 19 years	12.8	11.3	12.7	11.9	11.3	10.2	10.8	10.2	10.4	8.2	11.1	9.0
20 to 24 years	8.7	7.7	9.4	9.3	8.1	7.7	7.5	7.9	9.7	7.4	8.8	8.5
25 to 29 years	5.8	5.7	6.7	7.1	5.9	6.7	6.1	7.1	7.9	6.1	7.2	8.2
30 to 34 years	4.4	4.4	5.2	5.4	5.4	6.0	6.0	6.4	6.0	7.0	5.9	6.2
35 to 39 years	4.8	5.3	5.8	6.0	5.8	6.1	6.3	6.2	5.5	8.1	5.7	5.9
40 to 44 years	4.0	3.9	4.7	4.5	5.6	5.2	5.8	5.3	5.0	7.5	4.3	4.9
45 to 49 years	4.5	5.4	4.5	3.9	5.4	5.2	5.3	4.7	4.9	6.2	3.5	3.9
50 to 54 years	4.7	4.2	3.5	2.9	5.0	4.4	4.6	3.8	3.8	4.4	2.5	2.9
55 to 59 years	3.2	2.5	2.1	1.7	4.2	3.6	3.6	3.0	2.7	3.1	1.8	2.1
60 to 64 years	2.6	2.4	1.7	1.5	3.4	3.2	2.8	2.5	2.0	2.5	1.4	1.8
65 to 69 years	1.6	1.7	1.1	1.0	2.6	2.3	2.0	1.8	1.3	1.8	.9	1.4
70 to 74 years	1.0	1.0	.8	.8	1.9	1.4	1.4	1.2	.8	1.1	.7	1.1
75 to 79 years	.6	.5	.5	.4	1.0	.8	.8	.8	.5	.6	.4	.7

[Continued]

★ 1614 ★

Percent Distribution by Age, Color, and Gender for the Urban, Rural-Farm, and Rural Non-farm Population, 1920 and 1930 - II

[Continued]

Area and Age	Negro				White				Other Races			
	Male		Female		Male		Female		Male		Female	
	1930	1920	1930	1920	1930	1920	1930	1920	1930	1920	1930	1920
80 to 84 years	.3	.3	.3	.3	.4	.3	.4	.4	.3	.3	.3	.5
85 years and over	.2	.2	.3	.3	.2	.2	.2	.2	.2	.3	.2	.5
Unknown	-	.1	-	.1	-	.1	-	-	.1	.2	.1	.2
RURAL-NONFARM												
All ages	100.0	100.0	100.0	100.0	100.0	100.0	100.0	100.0	100.0	100.0	100.0	100.0
Under 5 years	10.4	10.5	10.9	11.1	10.3	11.4	10.4	11.9	13.3	11.1	16.9	14.9
5 to 9 years	11.1	11.2	11.7	11.8	10.9	10.9	11.0	11.4	12.7	9.9	15.8	13.5
10 to 14 years	9.6	10.4	10.1	11.0	9.6	9.6	9.9	10.2	9.2	8.2	11.3	10.8
15 to 19 years	9.6	9.3	10.8	10.7	8.5	8.1	9.1	8.8	8.2	7.8	9.9	9.0
20 to 24 years	10.6	10.9	11.1	11.6	7.9	7.9	8.6	8.4	10.8	8.1	9.1	8.7
25 to 29 years	9.1	9.2	9.1	9.5	7.5	8.0	7.8	8.1	10.4	7.1	8.1	8.3
30 to 34 years	7.2	6.8	6.9	6.9	7.1	7.5	7.1	7.2	7.9	7.9	6.5	6.3
35 to 39 years	7.3	7.6	7.0	7.0	7.1	7.4	6.8	6.7	7.3	8.7	5.9	5.6
40 to 44 years	5.7	5.3	5.4	5.1	6.3	6.0	5.8	5.5	5.6	7.6	4.3	4.7
45 to 49 years	5.4	6.0	4.8	4.1	5.6	5.6	5.1	4.8	4.6	6.2	3.5	3.8
50 to 54 years	4.6	4.2	3.8	3.2	4.9	4.6	4.5	4.1	3.1	4.7	2.5	3.2
55 to 59 years	2.9	2.4	2.3	2.0	4.0	3.6	3.7	3.4	2.2	3.6	1.8	2.4
60 to 64 years	2.3	2.1	2.0	1.9	3.3	3.2	3.2	3.1	1.6	3.2	1.5	2.4
65 to 69 years	1.5	1.5	1.4	1.4	2.7	2.4	2.6	2.4	1.1	2.3	1.0	2.0
70 to 74 years	1.0	1.0	1.0	1.1	2.1	1.8	2.0	1.8	.7	1.4	.7	1.5
75 to 79 years	.6	.7	.7	.6	1.3	1.2	1.3	1.2	.5	.8	.5	1.1
80 to 84 years	.4	.3	.4	.4	.6	.5	.7	.6	.3	.5	.3	.7
85 years and over	.3	.3	.3	.3	.3	.2	.3	.3	.2	.5	.3	.8
Unknown	.1	.3	.1	.2	.1	.2	.1	.1	.2	.5	.1	.4

Source: "Percent Distribution by 5-Year Age Periods, by Color, and Sex for the Urban, Rural-Farm, and Rural-Nonfarm Population of the United States: 1930 and 1920." U.S. Bureau of the Census, *Negroes in the United States, 1920- 1932*, p. 96.

★ 1615 ★

Age Composition

Percentage Black in the Population by Age Periods, Sections, and Southern Divisions, 1900 and 1910 - I

Age period	Percentage Negro in the Population of Age Specified					
	United States		The South			
			Total		South Atlantic division	
	1910	1900	1910	1900	1910	1900
All ages	10.7	11.6	29.8	32.3	33.7	35.7
Under 5 years	11.9	13.3	29.0	32.8	34.4	37.7
5 to 9 years	12.8	13.6	31.1	33.8	36.4	38.3
10 to 14 years	12.7	13.5	31.8	33.9	36.8	38.2
15 to 19 years	11.7	13.0	30.9	33.3	35.4	37.3
20 to 24 years	11.4	13.3	31.7	34.7	35.8	38.0
25 to 29 years	10.8	11.3	30.9	32.4	34.2	35.1
30 to 34 years	9.6	9.4	28.2	29.9	33.1	32.4
35 to 44 years	9.2	9.1	28.8	29.4	31.8	32.3
45 to 54 years	8.5	9.7	27.5	29.3	30.0	31.3
55 to 64 years	7.8	8.5	24.9	28.4	27.2	30.2
65 years and over	7.4	8.5	26.1	30.3	27.1	30.8
Age unknown	18.4	24.3	48.3	53.5	54.3	55.1

Source: "Percentage Negro in the Population, Classified by Age Periods, by Sections and Southern Divisions: 1900 and 1910." U.S. Bureau of the Census, *Negro Population 1790-1915*, p. 177.

★ 1616 ★

Age Composition

Percentage Black in the Population by Age Periods, Sections, and Southern Divisions, 1900 and 1910 - II

Age period	Percentage Negro in the Population of Age Specified						The West	
	The South				The North			
	East South Central division		West South Central division					
	1910	1900	1910	1900	1910	1900	1910	1900
All ages	31.5	33.1	22.6	25.9	1.8	1.9	0.7	0.7
Under 5 years	30.0	33.0	20.9	25.3	1.4	1.5	0.5	0.5
5 to 9 years	32.1	34.4	23.6	26.8	1.5	1.6	0.5	0.6
10 to 14 years	33.1	34.4	23.6	26.8	1.5	1.6	0.5	0.6
15 to 19 years	32.5	33.9	23.2	26.2	1.6	1.9	0.6	0.6
20 to 24 years	33.8	35.6	24.2	28.2	2.1	2.4	0.8	0.9

[Continued]

★ 1616 ★

Percentage Black in the Population by Age Periods, Sections, and Southern Divisions, 1900 and 1910 - II

[Continued]

Age period	Percentage Negro in the Population of Age Specified							
	The South				The North		The West	
	East South Central division		West South Central division					
	1910	1900	1910	1900	1910	1900	1910	1900
25 to 29 years	33.6	34.0	24.0	26.7	2.5	2.4	0.9	0.9
30 to 34 years	30.9	31.1	21.9	24.4	2.4	2.1	1.0	0.9
35 to 44 years	31.2	30.3	22.4	23.5	2.3	2.0	1.0	0.9
45 to 54 years	30.0	30.9	21.5	24.1	1.8	1.8	0.8	0.8
55 to 64 years	26.9	29.4	19.1	23.7	1.5	1.8	0.6	0.6
65 years and over	27.7	31.3	22.3	27.9	1.3	1.3	0.5	0.5
Age unknown	55.5	56.3	35.6	48.7	4.8	7.2	1.3	1.6

Source: "Percentage Negro in the Population, Classified by Age Periods, by Sections and Southern Divisions: 1900 and 1910." U.S. Bureau of the Census, *Negro Population 1790-1915*, p. 177.

★ 1617 ★

Age Composition

Percentage Distribution of Blacks by Age Periods and Geographical Areas, 1910 - I

Age period	Percentage Distribution by Age Periods of Negro Males and Females: 1910					
	United States		The South			
			Total		South Atlantic division	
	Males	Females	Male	Females	Male	Females
All ages	100.0	100.0	100.0	100.0	100.0	100.0
Under 5 years	12.9	12.8	13.5	13.4	14.0	13.8
5 to 9 years	12.7	12.7	13.3	13.3	13.6	13.4
10 to 14 years	11.8	11.7	12.4	12.1	12.7	12.3
15 to 19 years	10.4	11.2	10.7	11.5	10.7	11.5
20 to 24 years	9.9	11.1	9.8	11.0	9.8	11.0
25 to 29 years	8.6	9.3	8.2	8.9	7.9	8.7
30 to 34 years	6.8	6.8	6.3	6.4	6.1	6.2
35 to 44 years	11.3	10.9	10.5	10.3	10.3	10.2
45 to 54 years	7.8	6.7	7.5	6.4	7.1	6.5
55 to 64 years	4.4	3.6	4.3	3.5	4.4	3.5
65 years and over	3.1	2.9	3.1	2.8	3.1	2.7
Age unknown	0.3	0.3	0.3	0.3	0.3	0.2

Source: "Percentage Distribution, by Age Periods, of Negro Males and Females, by Sections and Southern Divisions: 1910." U.S. Bureau of the Census, *Negro Population, 1790-1915*, p. 174.

★ 1618 ★

Age Composition

Percentage Distribution of Blacks by Age Periods and Geographical Areas, 1910 - II

Age period	Percentage Distribution by Age Periods of Negro Males and Females: 1910							
	The South				The North		The West	
	East South Central division		West South Central division					
	Males	Females	Males	Females	Males	Females	Males	Females
All ages	100.0	100.0	100.0	100.0	100.0	100.0	100.0	100.0
Under 5 years	13.2	13.0	12.9	13.1	8.0	8.3	5.6	7.3
5 to 9 years	13.0	12.9	13.3	13.4	7.5	7.9	5.5	6.9
10 to 14 years	12.3	11.9	12.0	12.2	7.3	7.9	5.4	6.9
15 to 19 years	10.8	11.4	10.6	11.5	7.8	9.0	6.1	8.2
20 to 24 years	9.7	11.0	10.0	11.2	10.4	11.8	10.2	10.7
25 to 29 years	8.3	9.1	8.7	9.2	12.0	12.3	13.0	13.1
30 to 34 years	6.3	6.6	6.7	6.6	10.5	9.9	12.6	11.0
35 to 44 years	10.4	10.6	10.8	10.4	17.5	15.4	20.6	17.8
45 to 54 years	7.8	6.6	7.7	6.1	10.1	9.0	12.2	10.2
55 to 64 years	4.5	3.7	4.1	3.3	5.0	4.6	5.2	4.3
65 years and over	3.3	3.0	2.9	2.7	3.5	3.5	2.9	2.8
Age unknown	0.3	0.3	0.4	0.3	0.5	0.3	0.8	0.6

Source: "Percentage Distribution, by Age Periods, of Negro Males and Females, by Sections and Southern Divisions: 1910." U.S. Bureau of the Census, *Negro Population, 1790-1915*, p. 174.

★ 1619 ★

Age Composition

Percentage Distribution, by Age, of the Population, by Section, Division, and Racial Class: 1910 - I

Section, Division, and Racial Class	Percentage Distribution by Age Periods: 1910 Urban population						
	All ages[1]	Under 5 years	5 to 14 years	15 to 24 years	25 to 44 years	45 to 64 years	65 years and over
UNITED STATES							
Negro	100.0	8.5	16.9	21.5	36.6	13.1	2.9
Native white:							
Native parentage	100.0	11.5	19.5	20.5	29.9	14.0	4.3
Foreign or mixed parentage	100.0	15.0	23.9	21.7	27.7	10.7	1.1
Foreign-born white	100.0	0.8	5.2	17.1	45.6	23.9	7.3

[Continued]

★ 1619 ★

Percentage Distribution, by Age, of the Population, by Section, Division, and Racial Class: 1910 - I

[Continued]

Section, Division, and Racial Class	Percentage Distribution by Age Periods: 1910 Urban population						
	All ages[1]	Under 5 years	5 to 14 years	15 to 24 years	25 to 44 years	45 to 64 years	65 years and over
THE SOUTH							
Negro	100.0	9.0	18.3	22.5	34.3	12.5	2.8
Native white:							
Native parentage	100.0	11.4	20.0	21.5	30.8	12.8	3.2
Foreign or mixed parentage	100.0	10.1	18.1	19.0	33.9	16.8	2.0
Foreign-born white	100.0	1.0	5.8	14.2	40.4	26.9	11.5
SOUTH ATLANTIC DIVISION							
Negro	100.0	9.2	18.5	22.7	33.8	12.6	2.7
Native white:							
Native parentage	100.0	11.2	19.4	21.2	30.8	13.5	3.6
Foreign or mixed parentage	100.0	11.9	19.8	18.8	30.8	16.3	2.3
Foreign-born white	100.0	0.8	5.6	15.6	42.6	24.7	10.3
EAST SOUTH CENTRAL DIVISION							
Negro	100.0	8.5	17.5	22.2	34.9	13.2	3.1
Native white:							
Native parentage	100.0	11.4	20.1	21.8	30.5	12.8	3.2
Foreign or mixed parentage	100.0	6.3	13.8	18.4	39.5	19.9	2.0
Foreign-born white	100.0	0.4	3.5	9.8	35.1	33.5	17.5
WEST SOUTH CENTRAL DIVISION							
Negro	100.0	9.1	19.0	22.5	34.6	11.4	2.8
Native white:							
Native parentage	100.0	11.7	20.9	21.6	31.0	11.7	2.6
Foreign or mixed parentage	100.0	10.0	18.6	19.7	34.5	15.4	1.7
Foreign-born white	100.0	1.4	6.8	14.2	39.6	27.1	10.6
THE NORTH							
Negro	100.0	7.5	13.8	19.3	41.7	14.3	3.0
Native white:							
Native parentage	100.0	11.6	19.7	20.3	29.1	14.2	4.7
Foreign or mixed parentage	100.0	15.6	24.6	21.7	26.7	10.2	1.0
Foreign-born white	100.0	0.8	5.3	17.5	45.6	23.5	7.1
THE WEST							
Negro	100.0	6.4	11.9	17.1	45.0	16.1	2.6

[Continued]

★ 1619 ★

Percentage Distribution, by Age, of the Population, by Section, Division, and Racial Class: 1910 - I

[Continued]

Section, Division, and Racial Class	Percentage Distribution by Age Periods: 1910 Urban population						
	All ages[1]	Under 5 years	5 to 14 years	15 to 24 years	25 to 44 years	45 to 64 years	65 years and over
Native white:							
Native parentage	100.0	10.1	17.0	19.8	34.0	14.7	3.9
Foreign or mixed parentage	100.0	11.1	19.7	22.8	33.8	11.2	1.3
Foreign-born white	100.0	0.7	3.8	12.9	47.4	27.0	7.7

Source: "Percentage Distribution by Age Periods of the Urban and Rural Negro and White Population, by Sections and Southern Divisions: 1910." U.S. Bureau of the Census, *Negro Population, 1790-1915*, p. 183. *Note:* 1. Includes persons of unknown age.

★ 1620 ★

Age Composition

Percentage Distribution, by Age, of the Population, by Section, Division, and Racial Class: 1910 - II

Section, Division, and Racial Class	Percentage Distribution by Age Periods: 1910 Rural population						
	All ages[1]	Under 5 years	5 to 14 years	15 to 24 years	25 to 44 years	45 to 64 years	65 years and over
UNITED STATES							
Negro	100.0	14.5	27.3	21.2	23.2	10.6	3.0
Native white:							
Native parentage	100.0	14.2	24.3	19.3	24.1	13.4	4.5
Foreign or mixed parentage	100.0	12.6	24.4	21.4	27.4	12.2	1.8
Foreign-born white	100.0	0.7	4.1	12.4	40.1	29.5	12.8
THE SOUTH							
Negro	100.0	14.6	27.5	21.2	22.9	10.4	3.0
Native white:							
Native parentage	100.0	15.3	25.6	20.0	23.6	12.0	3.4
Foreign or mixed parentage	100.0	14.1	25.3	20.4	25.6	12.3	2.2
Foreign-born white	100.0	1.5	7.2	14.9	39.3	26.5	10.1
SOUTH ATLANTIC DIVISION							
Negro	100.0	15.2	28.1	21.1	22.2	10.2	3.0
Native white:							
Native parentage	100.0	14.8	25.1	19.7	23.8	12.7	3.8
Foreign or mixed parentage	100.0	13.7	20.6	17.1	27.9	16.7	3.9
Foreign-born white	100.0	1.0	5.1	17.1	45.0	21.9	9.4

[Continued]

★ 1620 ★

Percentage Distribution, by Age, of the Population, by Section, Division, and Racial Class: 1910 - II

[Continued]

Section, Division, and Racial Class	Percentage Distribution by Age Periods: 1910 Rural population						
	All ages[1]	Under 5 years	5 to 14 years	15 to 24 years	25 to 44 years	45 to 64 years	65 years and over
EAST SOUTH CENTRAL DIVISION							
Negro	100.0	14.2	26.8	21.3	23.4	10.9	3.1
Native white:							
Native parentage	100.0	15.2	25.4	19.9	23.6	12.2	3.6
Foreign or mixed parentage	100.0	8.7	17.6	17.5	31.8	20.1	4.2
Foreign-born white	100.0	0.7	4.5	9.6	33.2	33.0	18.7
WEST SOUTH CENTRAL DIVISION							
Negro	100.0	14.1	27.3	21.4	23.8	10.3	2.8
Native white:							
Native parentage	100.0	16.1	26.6	20.4	23.6	10.8	2.5
Foreign or mixed parentage	100.0	15.2	28.2	22.0	23.8	9.4	1.3
Foreign-born white	100.0	1.9	8.8	14.6	37.4	27.8	9.3
THE NORTH							
Negro	100.0	10.3	20.4	20.0	28.8	14.9	5.3
Native white:							
Native parentage	100.0	13.2	23.3	18.7	24.1	14.9	5.8
Foreign or mixed parentage	100.0	12.3	24.3	21.6	27.4	12.4	1.9
Foreign-born white	100.0	0.6	3.8	11.6	39.0	30.5	14.3
THE WEST							
Negro	100.0	6.1	13.2	18.6	41.5	16.3	3.8
Native white:							
Native parentage	100.0	13.7	22.5	19.0	27.4	13.4	3.7
Foreign or mixed parentage	100.0	13.6	24.5	21.4	28.6	10.4	1.4
Foreign-born white	100.0	0.8	4.0	14.5	46.0	26.6	7.6

Source: "Percentage Distribution by Age Periods of the Urban and Rural Negro and White Population, by Sections and Southern Divisions: 1910." U.S. Bureau of the Census, *Negro Population, 1790-1915*, p. 183. *Note:* 1. Includes persons of unknown age.

★ 1621 ★

Age Composition

Population by 5-Year Age Periods, by Race, and Sections, 1930

Age	Total	Negro	White	Other races	Percent distribution Negro	Percent distribution White
			UNITED STATES			
All ages	122,775,046	11,891,143	108,864,207	2,019,696	100.0	100.0
Under 5 years	11,444,390	1,230,206	9,927,396	286,788	10.3	9.1
5 to 9 years	12,607,609	1,368,381	10,956,144	283,084	11.5	10.1
10 to 14 years	12,004,877	1,251,542	10,546,282	207,053	10.5	9.7
15 to 19 years	11,552,115	1,250,528	10,111,584	190,003	10.5	9.3
20 to 24 years	10,870,378	1,203,191	9,466,155	201,032	10.1	8.7
25 to 29 years	9,833,608	1,071,787	8,573,696	188,125	9.0	7.9
30 to 34 years	9,120,421	864,514	8,109,766	146,141	7.3	7.4
35 to 39 years	9,208,645	890,900	8,183,620	134,125	7.5	7.5
40 to 44 years	7,990,195	687,423	7,198,507	104,265	5.8	6.6
45 to 49 years	7,042,279	630,065	6,322,989	89,225	5.3	5.8
50 to 54 years	5,975,804	504,590	5,409,056	62,158	4.2	5.0
55 to 59 years	4,645,677	309,397	4,293,107	43,173	2.6	3.9
60 to 64 years	3,751,221	242,169	3,476,993	32,059	2.0	3.2
65 to 69 years	2,770,605	155,177	2,594,840	20,588	1.3	2.4
70 to 74 years	1,950,004	99,096	1,838,050	12,858	.8	1.7
75 to 79 years	1,106,390	58,711	1,039,862	7,817	.5	1.0
80 to 84 years	534,676	33,377	496,803	4,496	.3	.5
85 years and over	272,130	26,358	242,028	3,744	.2	.2
Unknown	94,022	13,731	77,329	2,962	.1	.1
			THE SOUTH			
All ages	37,857,633	9,361,577	27,673,879	822,177	100.0	100.0
Under 5 years	4,152,716	1,016,579	3,017,349	118,788	10.9	10.9
5 to 9 years	4,536,133	1,150,248	3,264,359	121,526	12.3	11.8
10 to 14 years	4,145,954	1,069,120	2,985,163	91,671	11.4	10.8
15 to 19 years	4,010,733	1,063,846	2,857,176	89,711	11.4	10.3
20 to 24 years	3,604,321	953,787	2,566,877	83,657	10.2	9.3
25 to 29 years	3,001,560	774,708	2,157,552	69,300	8.3	7.8
30 to 34 years	2,549,672	599,236	1,898,612	51,824	6.4	6.9
35 to 39 years	2,516,921	630,877	1,837,148	48,896	6.7	6.7
40 to 44 years	2,081,684	495,604	1,548,583	37,497	5.3	5.6
45 to 49 years	1,890,769	469,050	1,387,574	34,145	5.0	5.0
50 to 54 years	1,625,244	390,051	1,211,800	23,393	4.2	4.4
55 to 59 years	1,188,700	239,306	931,942	17,452	2.6	3.4
60 to 64 years	923,301	195,897	713,793	13,611	2.1	2.6
65 to 69 years	646,576	125,331	512,771	8,474	1.3	1.9
70 to 74 years	470,285	80,889	384,424	5,255	.9	1.4
75 to 79 years	276,285	47,731	225,424	3,130	.5	.8
80 to 84 years	136,002	27,709	106,334	1,869	.3	.4
85 years and over	72,795	22,076	49,307	1,412	.2	.2
Unknown	27,339	9,442	17,331	566	.1	.1

[Continued]

★ 1621 ★

Population by 5-Year Age Periods, by Race, and Sections, 1930

[Continued]

Age	Total	Negro	White	Other races	Percent distribution	
					Negro	White
			THE NORTH			
All ages	73,021,191	2,409,219	70,388,367	223,605	100.0	100.0
Under 5 years	6,319,029	205,753	6,084,368	28,908	8.5	8.6
5 to 9 years	6,979,970	209,381	6,744,716	25,873	8.7	9.6
10 to 14 years	6,831,165	174,430	6,638,899	17,836	7.2	9.4
15 to 19 years	6,538,659	178,518	6,344,131	16,010	7.4	9.0
20 to 24 years	6,262,367	239,506	5,998,787	24,074	9.9	8.5
25 to 29 years	5,863,239	285,507	5,550,334	27,308	11.9	7.9
30 to 34 years	5,641,966	253,325	5,367,450	21,191	10.5	7.6
35 to 39 years	5,736,747	246,718	5,471,626	18,403	10.2	7.8
40 to 44 years	5,032,724	180,936	4,838,945	12,843	7.5	6.9
45 to 49 years	4,373,324	151,271	4,212,356	9,697	6.3	6.0
50 to 54 years	3,701,165	107,100	3,587,424	6,641	4.4	5.1
55 to 59 years	2,956,461	65,434	2,886,254	4,773	2.7	4.1
60 to 64 years	2,419,602	43,166	2,372,936	3,500	1.8	3.4
65 to 69 years	1,817,214	27,808	1,786,965	2,441	1.2	2.5
70 to 74 years	1,268,605	16,945	1,250,147	1,513	.7	1.8
75 to 79 years	714,740	10,285	703,409	1,046	.4	1.0
80 to 84 years	343,976	5,222	338,239	515	.2	.5
85 years and over	172,148	3,995	167,685	468	.2	.2
Unknown	48,090	3,919	43,696	475	.2	.1
			THE WEST			
All ages	11,896	120,347	10,801,961	973,914	100.0	100.0
Under 5 years	972,645	7,874	825,679	139,092	6.5	7.6
5 to 9 years	1,091,506	8,752	947,069	135,685	7.3	8.8
10 to 14 years	1,027,758	7,992	922,220	97,546	6.6	8.5
15 to 19 years	1,002,723	8,164	910,277	84,282	6.8	8.4
20 to 24 years	1,003,690	9,898	900,491	93,301	8.2	8.3
25 to 29 years	968,809	11,572	865,810	91,427	9.6	8.0
30 to 34 years	928,783	11,953	843,704	73,126	9.9	7.8
35 to 39 years	954,977	13,305	874,846	66,826	11.1	8.1
40 to 44 years	875,787	10,883	810,979	53,925	9.0	7.5
45 to 49 years	778,186	9,744	723,059	45,383	8.1	6.7
50 to 54 years	649,395	7,439	609,832	32,124	6.2	5.6
55 to 59 years	500,516	4,657	474,911	20,948	3.9	4.4
60 to 64 years	408,318	3,106	390,264	14,948	2.6	3.6
65 to 69 years	306,815	2,038	295,104	9,673	1.7	2.7
70 to 74 years	210,471	1,262	203,119	6,090	1.0	1.9
75 to 79 years	115,365	695	111,029	3,641	.6	1.0
80 to 84 years	54,698	356	52,230	2,112	.3	.5

[Continued]

★ 1621 ★

Population by 5-Year Age Periods, by Race, and Sections, 1930

[Continued]

Age	Total	Negro	White	Other races	Percent distribution	
					Negro	White
85 years and over	27,187	287	25,036	1,864	.2	.2
Unknown	18,593	370	16,302	1,921	.3	.2

Source: "Population by 5-Year Age Periods, by Color, by Sections: 1930." U.S. Bureau of the Census, *Negroes in the United States, 1920-1932*, p. 88.

★ 1622 ★

Age Composition

Population by Age Periods, Sections, and Southern Divisions: 1900, 1910 - I

Age period	Negro population					
	United States		The South			
			Total		South Atlantic division	
	1910	1900	1910	1900	1910	1900
	Number					
All ages	9,827,763	8,833,994	8,740,427	7,922,969	4,112,488	3,720,017
Under 5 years	1,263,288	1,215,655	1,176,331	1,135,793	570,516	545,284
5 to 9 years	1,246,553	1,202,758	1,164,557	1,122,201	555,036	527,900
10 to 14 years	1,155,266	1,091,990	1,073,980	1,012,214	513,239	476,108
15 to 19 years	1,060,416	982,022	970,716	893,199	457,053	423,855
20 to 24 years	1,030,795	969,172	911,603	856,655	426,876	400,667
25 to 29 years	881,227	737,479	749,782	633,384	341,665	286,748
30 to 34 years	668,089	524,607	557,466	444,709	253,860	205,472
35 to 44 years	1,088,862	841,903	910,025	713,990	421,374	342,794
45 to 54 years	711,979	617,371	607,895	537,826	279,676	248,740
55 to 64 years	396,124	340,863	343,958	299,315	162,623	144,525
65 years and over	294,124	261,363	256,694	232,217	119,140	111,331
Age unknown	31,040	48,811	26,420	41,466	11,430	15,603
	Percentage Distribution by Age Periods					
All ages	100.0	100.0	100.0	100.0	100.0	100.0
Under 5 years	12.9	13.8	13.4	14.3	13.9	14.0
5 to 9 years	12.7	13.6	13.3	14.2	13.5	14.2
10 to 14 years	11.8	12.4	12.3	12.8	12.5	12.8
15 to 19 years	10.8	11.1	11.1	11.3	11.1	11.4

[Continued]

★ 1622 ★

Population by Age Periods, Sections, and Southern Divisions: 1900, 1910 - I

[Continued]

Age period	Negro population					
	United States		The South			
			Total		South Atlantic division	
	1910	1900	1910	1900	1910	1900
20 to 24 years	10.5	11.0	10.4	10.8	10.4	10.7
25 to 29 years	9.0	8.3	8.6	8.0	8.3	7.7
30 to 34 years	6.8	5.9	6.4	5.6	6.2	5.5
35 to 44 years	11.1	9.5	10.4	9.0	10.2	9.2
45 to 54 years	7.2	7.0	6.9	6.8	6.8	6.7
55 to 64 years	4.0	3.9	3.9	3.8	4.0	3.9
65 years and over	3.0	3.0	2.9	2.9	2.9	3.0
Age unknown	0.3	0.6	0.3	0.5	0.3	0.4

Source: "Negro Population Classified by Age Periods, by Sections and Southern Divisions: 1910 and 1900." U.S. Bureau of the Census, *Negro Population, 1790-1915*, p. 174.

★ 1623 ★

Age Composition

Population by Age Periods, Sections, and Southern Divisions: 1900, 1910 - II

Age period	Negro Population							
	The South							
	East South Central division		West South Central division		The North		The West	
	1910	1900	1910	1900	1910	1900	1910	1900
	Number							
All ages	2,652,513	2,499,886	1,984,426	1,604,066	1,027,674	880,771	50,662	30,254
Under 5 years	347,803	348,061	258,012	242,448	83,729	77,794	3,228	2,068
5 to 9 years	343,812	348,997	265,709	245,304	78,892	78,233	3,104	2,324
10 to 14 years	320,476	316,984	240,765	219,122	78,205	77,597	3,081	2,179
15 to 19 years	294,183	283,363	219,480	185,981	86,126	86,506	3,574	2,317
20 to 24 years	274,935	273,069	209,792	182,919	113,923	108,993	5,269	3,524
25 to 29 years	230,624	204,948	177,493	141,688	124,832	100,587	6,613	3,508
30 to 34 years	171,477	141,938	132,129	97,299	104,600	76,637	6,023	3,261
35 to 44 years	278,306	222,312	210,345	148,884	169,052	122,427	9,785	5,486
45 to 54 years	191,801	174,614	136,418	114,472	98,341	76,529	5,743	3,016
55 to 64 years	108,199	95,882	73,136	58,908	49,737	40,236	2,429	1,312
65 years and over	82,481	75,917	55,073	44,979	35,973	28,311	1,457	835
Age unknown	8,416	13,801	6,574	12,062	4,264	6,921	356	424

[Continued]

★ 1623 ★

Population by Age Periods, Sections, and Southern Divisions: 1900, 1910 - II

[Continued]

Age period	Negro Population							
	The South						The West	
	East South Central division		West South Central division		The North			
	1910	1900	1910	1900	1910	1900	1910	1900
	Percentage Distribution by Age Periods							
All ages	100.0	100.0	100.0	100.0	100.0	100.0	100.0	100.0
Under 5 years	13.1	13.9	13.0	14.3	8.1	8.8	6.4	6.8
5 to 9 years	13.0	14.0	13.4	14.5	7.7	8.9	6.1	7.7
10 to 14 years	12.1	12.7	12.1	12.9	7.6	8.8	6.1	7.2
15 to 19 years	11.1	11.3	11.1	11.0	8.4	9.8	7.1	7.7
20 to 24 years	10.4	10.9	10.6	10.8	11.1	12.4	10.4	11.6
25 to 29 years	8.7	8.2	8.9	8.4	12.1	114.	13.1	11.6
30 to 34 years	6.5	5.7	6.7	5.7	10.2	8.7	11.9	10.8
35 to 44 years	10.5	8.9	10.6	8.8	16.4	13.9	19.3	18.1
45 to 54 years	7.2	7.0	6.9	6.8	9.6	8.7	11.3	10.0
55 to 64 years	4.1	3.8	3.7	3.5	4.8	4.6	4.8	4.3
65 years and over	3.1	3.0	2.8	2.7	3.5	3.2	2.9	2.8
Age unknown	0.3	0.6	0.3	0.7	0.4	0.8	0.7	1.4

Source: "Negro Population Classified by Age Periods, by Sections and Southern Divisions: 1910 and 1900." U.S. Bureau of the Census, *Negro Population, 1790-1915*, p. 174.

★ 1624 ★

Age Composition

Population by Age, Gender, Race, and Nativity, 1790 to 1970 - I

Year	Total	Under 5 years	5-9 years	10-14 years	15-19 years	20-24 years	25-29 years	30-34 years
TOTAL								
1970[1]	203,211,926	17,154,337	19,956,247	20,789,468	19,070,348	16,371,021	13,476,993	11,430,436
1960*	179,323,175	20,320,901	18,691,780	16,773,492	13,219,243	10,800,761	10,869,124	11,949,186
1960	178,464,236	20,205,746	18,592,413	16,689,953	13,147,223	10,726,632	10,803,977	11,881,172
1950	150,697,361	16,163,571	13,199,685	11,119,268	10,616,598	11,481,828	12,242,260	11,517,007
1940	131,669,275	10,541,524	10,684,622	11,745,935	12,333,523	11,587,835	11,096,638	10,242,388
1930	122,775,046	11,444,390	12,607,609	12,004,877	11,552,115	10,870,877	9,833,608	9,120,421
1920	105,710,620	11,573,230	11,394,075	10,641,137	9,430,556	9,277,021	9,086,491	8,071,193
1910	91,972,266	10,631,364	9,760,632	9,107,140	9,063,603	9,056,984	8,180,003	6,972,185
1900	75,994,575	9,170,628	8,874,123	8,080,234	7,556,089	7,335,016	6,529,441	5,555,039
1890[2]	62,622,250	7,634,693	7,573,998	7,033,509	6,557,563	6,196,676	5,227,777	4,578,630
1880	50,155,783	6,914,516	6,479,660	5,715,186	5,011,415	5,087,772	4,080,621	3,368,943
1870[3]	38,558,371	5,514,713	4,814,713	4,786,189	4,040,588	3,748,299	3,075,118	2,562,829
1860	31,443,321	4,842,496	4,171,200	3,720,780	3,361,495	5,716,400[16]	5,726,400[16]	4,021,248[17]
1850	23,191,876	3,497,773	3,241,268	2,890,629	2,529,792	4,277,318[16]	4,277,318[16]	2,825,819[17]
MALE								
1970[1]	98,912,192	8,745,499	10,168,496	10,590,737	9,633,847	7,917,269	6,621,567	5,595,790
1960*	88,331,494	10,329,729	9,504,368	8,524,289	6,633,661	5,272,340	5,333,075	5,846,224
1960	87,864,510	10,270,966	9,453,586	8,481,598	6,592,215	5,225,940	5,298,813	5,811,157
1950	74,833,239	8,236,164	6,714,555	5,660,399	5,311,342	5,606,293	5,972,078	5,624,723
1940	66,061,592	5,354,808	5,418,823	5,952,329	6,180,153	5,692,392	5,450,662	5,070,312

[Continued]

★ 1624 ★

Population by Age, Gender, Race, and Nativity, 1790 to 1970 - I

[Continued]

Year	Total	Under 5 years	5-9 years	10-14 years	15-19 years	20-24 years	25-29 years	30-34 years
1930	62,137,080	5,806,174	6,381,108	6,068,777	5,757,825	5,336,815	4,860,180	4,561,786
1920	53,900,431	5,857,461	5,753,001	5,369,306	4,673,792	4,527,045	4,538,233	4,130,783
1910	47,332,277	5,380,596	4,924,123	4,601,753	4,527,282	4,580,290	4,244,348	3,656,768
1900	38,816,448	4,633,612	4,479,396	4,083,041	3,750,451	3,624,580	3,323,543	2,901,321
1890[2]	32,067,880	3,884,869	3,830,352	3,574,787	3,248,711	3,104,893	2,698,311	2,425,664
1880	25,518,820	3,507,709	3,275,131	2,907,481	2,476,088	2,554,684	2,109,741	1,744,308
1870[3]	19,493,565	2,797,257	2,437,442	2,435,585	1,989,695	1,835,946	1,515,671	1,273,683
1860	16,085,204	2,449,547	2,109,545	1,900,868	1,650,012	2,911,558[16]	2,911,558[16]	2,129,017[17]
1850	11,837,660	1,769,460	1,640,407	1,473,116	1,237,680	2,194,469[16]	2,194,469[16]	1,490,135[17]
FEMALE								
1970[1]	104,299,734	8,408,838	9,787,751	10,198,731	9,436,501	8,453,752	6,855,426	5,834,646
1960*	90,991,681	9,991,172	9,187,412	8,249,203	6,585,582	5,528,4221	5,536,049	6,102,962
1960	90,599,726	9,934,780	9,138,827	8,208,355	6,555,008	5,500,692	5,505,164	6,070,015
1950	75,864,122	7,927,407	6,485,130	5,458,869	5,305,256	5,875,535	6,270,182	5,892,284
1940	65,607,683	5,186,716	5,265,799	5,793,606	6,153,370	5,895,443	5,645,976	5,172,076
1930	60,637,966	5,638,216	6,226,501	5,936,100	5,794,290	5,533,563	4,973,428	4,558,635
1920	51,810,189	5,715,769	5,645,074	5,271,831	4,756,764	4,749,976	4,548,258	3,940,410
1910	44,639,989	5,250,768	4,836,509	4,505,387	4,536,321	4,476,694	3,935,655	3,315,417
1900	37,178,127	4,537,016	4,394,727	3,997,193	3,805,638	3,710,436	3,205,898	2,654,718
1890[2]	30,554,370	3,749,824	3,743,646	3,458,722	3,308,852	3,091,783	2,529,466	2,152,966
1880	24,636,963	3,406,807	3,204,529	2,807,705	2,535,327	2,533,088	1,970,880	1,624,635
1870[3]	19,064,806	2,717,456	2,377,271	2,350,604	2,050,893	1,912,353	1,559,447	1,289,196
1860	15,358,117	2,392,949	2,061,655	1,819,912	1,711,483	2,814,842[16]	2,814,842[16]	1,892,231[17]
1850	11,354,216	1,728,313	1,600,861	1,417,513	1,292,112	2,082,849[16]	2,082,849[16]	1,335,684[17]
WHITE, MALE								
1970[1]	86,720,987	7,374,333	8,633,093	9,033,725	8,291,270	6,940,820	5,849,792	4,925,069
1960*	78,367,149	8,849,181	8,202,157	7,456,573	5,837,093	4,645,822	4,721,783	5,218,188
1960	78,153,040	8,823,480	8,182,144	7,440,898	5,817,598	4,614,204	4,702,477	5,200,541
1950	67,129,192	7,244,211	5,915,130	4,944,535	4,685,826	5,002,782	5,349,707	5,080,610
1940	59,448,548	4,701,470	4,744,537	5,259,007	5,515,920	5,113,642	4,892,013	4,573,316
1930	55,922,528	5,158,439	5,662,102	5,415,256	5,132,461	4,746,792	4,324,314	4,115,726
1920	48,430,655	5,260,714	5,099,205	4,735,150	4,141,831	4,094,301	4,018,576	3,776,266
1910	42,178,245	4,728,650	4,285,366	4,006,104	3,999,143	4,070,955	3,792,224	3,297,169
1900	34,201,735	4,011,455	3,862,349	3,519,303	3,258,090	3,145,481	2,942,882	2,619,446
1890[2]	28,206,332	3,351,104	3,276,983	3,044,058	2,818,914	2,740,864	2,407,153	2,200,973
1880	22,130,900	2,949,449	2,756,201	2,483,572	2,150,068	2,219,317	1,838,054	1,548,077
1870[3]	17,029,088	2,398,615	2,103,986	2,103,425	1,731,015	1,591,909	1,328,232	1,131,799
1860	13,811,387	2,091,460	1,788,711	1,590,472	1,400,536	2,497,210[16]	2,497,210[16]	1,867,378[17]
1850	10,026,402	1,472,053	1,372,438	1,225,575	1,041,116	1,869,092[16]	1,869,092[16]	1,288,682[17]
1840[4]	7,255,534	1,270,743	1,024,505	879,530	756,106	1,322,453[16]	1,322,453[16]	866,452[17]
1830[4]	5,360,451	972,980	782,075	669,734	573,196	956,487[16]	956,487[16]	592,535[17]
1820[4]	3,995,133	1,345,058[18]	1,345,058[18]	612,535[5]	776,030[6,19]	776,030[6,19]	776,030[6,19]	766,283[7,17]
1810[4]	2,987,571	1,035,058[18]	1,035,058[18]	468,083[5]	547,597[6,19]	547,597[6,19]	547,597[6,19]	571,997[7,17]
1800[4]	2,204,421	764,118[18]	764,118[18]	353,071[5]	393,156[6,19]	393,156[6,19]	393,156[6,19]	431,589[7,17]
1790[4]	1,615,625	802,327[8,21]	802,327[8,21]	802,327[8,21]	802,327[8,21]	802,327[8,21]	802,327[8,21]	802,327[21]
WHITE, FEMALE								
1970[1]	91,027,988	7,048,807	8,264,333	8,647,392	8,079,090	7,341,007	5,962,122	5,042,368
1960*	80,464,583	8,509,371	7,885,385	7,182,319	5,771,136	4,824,957	4,833,802	5,370,642
1960	80,301,916	8,484,716	7,866,039	7,167,491	5,761,253	4,811,363	4,819,304	5,356,568
1950	67,812,836	6,940,293	5,681,442	4,749,994	4,644,695	5,176,405	5,575,097	5,275,721
1940	58,766,322	4,528,035	4,584,414	5,093,688	5,448,127	5,226,507	5,012,257	4,633,162
1930	54,364,212	4,983,730	5,499,561	5,279,168	5,116,318	4,865,877	4,384,684	4,094,186
1920	46,390,260	5,113,207	4,988,040	4,634,172	4,172,324	4,166,765	4,047,389	3,562,524
1910	39,553,712	4,594,264	4,189,807	3,912,304	2,969,248	3,915,456	3,464,912	2,970,107
1900	32,607,461	3,908,497	3,775,977	3,439,935	3,285,099	3,189,563	2,820,098	2,384,998
1890[2]	26,777,558	3,228,544	3,196,185	2,947,914	2,856,433	2,707,603	2,239,534	1,943,859
1880	21,272,070	2,850,702	2,686,218	2,397,959	2,201,582	2,183,155	1,703,647	1,431,177
1870[3]	16,560,289	2,321,177	2,047,729	2,033,036	1,780,021	1,643,119	1,353,320	1,133,266
1860	13,111,150	2,025,985	1,739,387	1,523,281	1,452,045	2,420,139[16]	2,420,139[16]	1,636,213[17]
1850	9,526,666	1,424,405	1,331,690	1,176,554	1,087,600	1,758,469[16]	1,758,469[16]	1,128,257[17]
1840[4]	6,940,161	1,203,319	986,940	836,630	792,223	1,253,490[16]	1,253,490[16]	779,120[17]
1830[4]	5,171,115	921,934	750,741	638,856	596,254	918,411[16]	918,411[16]	555,531[17]
1820[4]	3,866,804	1,280,570[18]	1,280,570[18]	605,375[5]	781,371[6,19]	781,371[19]	781,371[19]	736,600[7,17]
1810[4]	2,874,433	981,421[18]	981,421[18]	448,322[5]	561,956[6,19]	561,956[6,19]	561,956[6,19]	544,256[7,17]

[Continued]

★ 1624 ★

Population by Age, Gender, Race, and Nativity, 1790 to 1970 - I

[Continued]

Year	Total	Under 5 years	5-9 years	10-14 years	15-19 years	20-24 years	25-29 years	30-34 years
1800[4]	2,100,068	715,197[18]	715,197|18	323,648[5]	401,499[6,19]	401,499[6,19]	401,499[6,19]	411,694[7,17]
1790[4]	1,556,839[10]	-	-	-	-	-	-	-
FOREIGN-BORN WHITE, MALE								
1970[1]	3,982,797	41,809	94,967	122,194	149,214	184,966	212,082	236,906
1960•	4,057,502	46,307	76,961	112,140	92,606	121,207	149,510	184,949
1960	4,500,434	46,120	76,684	111,895	92,399	120,582	149,090	184,663
1950	5,098,370	31,735	31,430	32,930	47,640	86,140	154,555	147,275
1940	6,011,015	4,219	10,937	27,114	82,391	98,917	193,647	342,991
1930	7,502,491	17,232	71,872	90,104	183,215	368,631	571,039	693,851
1920	7,528,322	22,857	85,774	167,152	259,270	456,988	792,088	946,818
1910	7,523,788	51,940	150,652	181,303	351,754	823,920	990,576	888,668
1900	5,515,285	26,567	73,727	157,632	271,381	456,186	589,521	660,702
1890[2]	4,951,858	44,040	126,070	201,159	257,658	476,224	602,545	549,099
1880	3,521,635	31,256	61,803	120,740	184,320	274,038	365,094	419,769
1870[3]	2,942,579	42,322	88,322	104,726	157,050	306,735	379,577	368,420
FOREIGN-BORN WHITE, FEMALE								
1970[1]	4,750,973	40,097	89,354	120,721	149,534	229,069	277,961	299,307
1960•	4,786,490	45,022	75,273	110,061	98,620	155,965	189,889	248,375
1960	4,778,835	44,826	74,965	109,863	98,413	155,336	189,107	247,287
1950	4,997,045	31,815	30,605	30,330	44,605	121,415	198,090	174,980
1940	5,408,123	4,102	10,647	26,637	82,394	110,592	230,629	366,100
1930	6,480,914	16,777	70,501	88,430	193,891	378,557	543,893	626,959
1920	6,184,432	22,127	84,110	164,210	268,672	469,856	662,275	704,657
1910	5,821,757	50,567	147,857	177,027	322,007	606,461	672,120	617,047
1900	4,698,532	25,802	73,465	153,933	290,365	463,296	507,708	512,981
1890[2]	4,170,009	42,589	122,281	195,220	263,637	441,150	469,694	393,221
1880	3,038,044	31,115	60,894	117,699	194,492	254,217	306,022	342,862
1870[3]	2,551,133	41,590	85,911	100,812	168,376	302,333	328,949	321,175
NEGRO, MALE								
1970[1]	10,748,316	1,219,567	1,377,355	1,406,715	1,201,605	839,848	657,544	568,086
1960[12,]•	9,097,704	1,362,831	1,195,123	989,360	740,971	569,398	547,941	563,502
1960[12]	9,090,095	1,362,000	1,194,593	989,150	740,196	567,483	546,779	562,859
1950[13]	7,269,170	947,740	761,430	674,480	591,550	563,730	579,880	510,970
1940	6,269,038	621,689	643,781	661,351	630,079	550,193	550,613	467,887
1930	5,855,669	611,231	679,748	623,228	595,646	553,622	500,520	416,869
1920	5,209,436	568,638	631,341	616,251	513,416	487,169	424,352	331,579
1910	4,885,881	629,320	619,175	578,074	507,945	482,157	421,805	332,163
1900	4,386,547	604,487	600,410	548,642	473,750	458,921	360,597	262,130
1890[2]	3,725,561	529,985[14]	549,405[14]	526,450[14]	422,258	350,392	272,044	203,361
1880	3,253,115[16]	-	-	-	-	-	-	-
1870[3]	2,393,263	396,812	331,795	329,339	251,822	232,490	175,069	130,517
1860	2,216,744	354,999	317,999	307,374	245,104	394,185[16]	394,185[16]	247,378[17]
1850	1,811,258	297,407	267,969	247,541	196,564	325,377[16]	325,377[16]	201,453[17]
1840[4]	1,432,998	478,868[18]	478,868[18]	444,011[16,19]	444,011[16,19]	270,707[17,20]	270,707[17,20]	247,378[17]
1830	1,166,276	394,994[18]	394,994[18]	355,646[16,19]	355,646[16,19]	213,235[17,20]	213,235[17,20]	201,453[17]
1820[4]	900,762	391,511[18,19]	391,511[18,19]	227,100[19,20]	227,100[19,20]	187,173[7,17]	187,173[7,17]	187,173[7,17]
NEGRO, FEMALE								
1970[1]	11,831,973	1,213,071	1,370,073	1,403,154	1,221,440	974,372	770,713	684,849
1960[12,]•	9,750,915	1,359,569	1,195,515	983,572	756,020	642,315	630,858	663,092
1960[12]	9,746,972	1,358,732	1,195,013	983,302	755,837	641,897	630,322	662,699
1950[13]	7,757,505	942,880	768,400	677,965	677,965	634,815	669,295	592,570
1940	6,596,480	627,391	650,765	669,309	674,527	645,034	615,671	524,992
1930	6,035,474	618,975	688,633	628,314	654,882	649,569	571,267	447,645
1920	5,253,695	575,066	634,866	620,663	569,799	567,678	485,387	366,286
1910	4,941,882	633,968	627,378	577,192	552,471	548,638	459,422	335,926
1900	4,447,447	611,168	602,348	543,348	508,272	510,251	376,882	262,477
1890[2]	3,744,479	517,589[14]	544,089[14]	507,251[14]	448,860	381,156	287,507	206,616
1880	3,327,678[15]	-	-	-	-	-	-	-
1870[3]	2,486,746	394,609	328,036	315,972	268,728	266,364	203,980	154,232
1860	2,225,086	364,085	319,807	294,273	256,489	389,418[16]	389,418[16]	253,220[17]
1850	1,827,550	303,908	269,171	240,959	204,512	324,380[16]	324,380[16]	207,427[17]
1840[4]	1,440,760	476,527[18]	476,527[18]	446,709[16,19]	446,709[16,19]	281,507[17,20]	281,507[17,20]	281,507[17,20]
1830	1,162,366	394,994[18]	394,994[18]	356,908[16,19]	356,908[16,19]	218,327[17,20]	218,327[17,20]	218,327[17,20]

[Continued]

★ 1624 ★

Population by Age, Gender, Race, and Nativity, 1790 to 1970 - I

[Continued]

Year	Total	Under 5 years	5-9 years	10-14 years	15-19 years	20-24 years	25-29 years	30-34 years
1820[4]	870,800	370,242[18,19]	370,242[18,19]	231,186[19,20]	231,186[19,20]	179,874[7,17]	179,874[7,17]	179,874[,17]
OTHER, MALE								
1970[1]	1,442,889	151,599	158,048	150,297	140,972	136,601	114,231	102,635
1960[12*]	857,707	118,812	102,276	84,592	63,920	56,364	59,861	60,361
1960[12]	612,962	86,651	71,504	57,800	42,478	43,656	46,016	43,721
1950[13]	401,525	48,045	36,145	36,690	30,440	35,930	34,690	25,985
1940	344,006	31,649	30,505	31,971	34,154	28,557	29,036	29,109
1930	358,883	36,504	39,258	30,293	29,718	36,401	35,346	28,191
1920	260,340	28,114	22,455	17,905	18,545	21,300	19,580	22,938
1910	268,151	22,626	19,582	17,575	20,194	27,178	30,319	27,436
1900	228,166	17,670	16,637	15,096	18,611	20,178	20,064	19,745
1890[2]	135,987	3,780[14]	3,964[14]	4,279[14]	7,539	13,637	19,114	21,330
1880	134,805[15]	-	-	-	-	-	-	-
1870[3]	71,214	1,830	1,661	2,821	6,585	11,547	12,371	11,317
1860	57,073	3,088	2,835	3,022	4,372	20,163[16]	20,163[16]	14,261[17]
OTHER, FEMALE								
1970[1]	1,439,773	146,960	153,345	148,185	135,971	138,373	122,591	107,429
1960[12*]	781,670	115,094	98,834	81,118	60,161	55,245	66,264	68,690
1960[12]	556,008	84,393	70,204	55,792	39,552	41,500	50,547	50,124
1950[12]	309,545	47,195	35,875	31,480	28,725	31,950	29,140	21,820
1940	244,881	31,290	30,620	30,609	30,716	23,902	18,048	13,922
1930	238,280	35,511	38,307	28,618	23,090	18,117	17,477	16,804
1920	166,234	27,496	22,168	16,996	14,641	15,533	15,482	11,600
1910	144,445	22,536	19,374	15,891	14,602	12,600	11,321	9,384
1900	123,219	17,351	16,402	13,910	12,267	10,622	8,918	7,243
1890[2]	82,333	3,691[14]	3,372[14]	4,557[14]	3,559	3,024	52,425	2,491
1880	37,215[15]	-	-	-	-	-	-	-
1870	17,771	1,670	1,506	1,596	2,144	2,870	2,147	1,698
1860	21,881	2,879	2,461	2,358	2,949	5,285[16]	5,285[16]	2,798[17]

Source: "Population, by Age, Sex, Race, and Nativity: 1790 to 1970." U.S. Bureau of the Census, *Historical Statistics of the United States: Colonial Times to 1970, Part I*, pp. 15-18. *Notes:* * Denotes first year for which figures include Alaska and Hawaii. - Represents zero. 1. Excludes 23,372 persons for whom age is not available. See series A 1-5, footnote 3. 2. Exclusive of 325,464 persons enumerated in the Indian Territory and on Indian reservations. See series A 105-118 footnote 7, for composition by race and sex. 3. Excludes 1,260,078 persons (747,915 white and 512,163 Negro) for whom age is not available. See series A 1-5, footnote 5, and series A 91- 104, footnote 4. 4. Totals differ slightly from corrected totals shown in series A 91- 104. Corrections by age are not available. 5. 10-15 years old. 6. 16-25 years old. 7. 26-44 years old. 8. Under 16 years old. 9. 16 years old and over. 10. Age for 1790 available only for white males. 11. 15-percent sample data. 12. 25-percent sample data. 13. 20-percent sample data. 14. Estimates based on population under 15 and age distribution of Negro and other races. 15. Age for 1880 available only for all races, white, and for Negro and other races combined. 16. Data includes persons 20 to 29 years old. 17. Data includes persons 30 to 39 years old. 18. Data includes persons under 5 to 9 years old. 19. Data includes persons 15 to 24 years old. 20. Data includes persons 25 to 34 years old. 21. Data includes persons under 5 years old to 39 years old.

★ 1625 ★

Age Composition

Population by Age, Gender, Race, and Nativity, 1790 to 1970 - II

Year	35-39 years	40-44 years	45-49 years	50-54 years	55-59 years	60-64 years	65 years and over	Age not stated
TOTAL								
1970[1]	11,106,851	11,980,954	12,115,939	11,104,018	9,973,028	8,616,784	20,065,502	-
1960*	12,481,109	11,600,243	10,879,485	9,605,954	8,429,865	7,142,452	16,559,580	-
1960	12,414,091	11,545,677	10,834,998	9,591,934	8,402,132	7,123,256	16,525,032	-
1950	11,246,386	10,203,973	9,070,465	8,272,188	7,235,120	6,059,475	12,269,537	-
1940	9,545,377	8,787,843	8,255,225	7,256,846	5,843,865	4,728,340	9,019,314	-
1930	9,208,645	7,990,195	7,042,279	5,975,804	4,645,677	3,751,221	6,633,805	94,022
1920	7,775,281	6,345,557	5,763,620	4,734,873	3,549,124	2,982,548	4,933,215	148,699
1910	6,396,100	5,261,587	4,469,197	3,900,791	2,786,951	2,267,150	3,949,524	169,055
1900	4,964,781	4,247,166	3,454,612	2,942,829	2,211,172	1,791,363	3,080,498	200,584

[Continued]

★ 1625 ★

Population by Age, Gender, Race, and Nativity, 1790 to 1970 - II

[Continued]

Year	35-39 years	40-44 years	45-49 years	50-54 years	55-59 years	60-64 years	65 years and over	Age not stated
1890[2]	3,866,161	3,185,518	2,731,640	2,326,262	1,672,336	1,458,034	2,417,288	162,165
1880	3,000,419	2,468,811	2,089,445	1,839,883	1,271,434	1,104,219	1,723,459	-
1870[3]	2,314,976	1,939,712	1,578,932	1,367,96	876,552	778,971	1,153,649	5,161
1860	4,021,248[20]	2,614,330[16]	2,614,330[16]	1,585,879[17]	1,585,879[17]	1,347,982[18]	1,347,982[18]	51,511
1850	2,825,819[20]	1,846,660[16]	1,846,660[16]	1,109,540[17]	1,109,540[17]	958,792[18]	958,792[18]	14,285
MALE								
1970[1]	5,412,423	5,818,813	5,851,334	5,347,916	4,765,821	4,026,972	8,415,708	-
1960*	6,079,512	5,675,881	5,357,925	4,734,829	4,127,245	3,409,319	7,503,097	-
1960	6,044,485	5,646,279	5,331,969	4,714,262	4,110,628	3,398,572	7,484,040	-
1950	5,517,544	5,070,269	4,526,366	4,128,648	3,630,046	3,037,833	5,796,974	-
1940	4,745,659	4,419,135	4,209,269	3,752,750	3,011,364	2,397,816	4,406,120	-
1930	4,679,860	4,136,459	3,671,924	3,131,645	2,425,992	1,941,508	3,325,211	51,816
1920	4,074,361	3,285,543	3,117,550	2,535,545	1,880,065	1,581,800	2,483,976	92,875
1910	3,367,016	2,786,350	2,378,916	2,110,013	1,488,437	1,185,966	1,985,976	114,443
1900	2,616,865	2,255,916	1,837,836	1,564,622	1,145,257	917,167	1,555,418	127,423
1890[2]	2,051,044	1,654,604	1,418,102	1,208,922	871,663	758,710	1,233,719	103,529
1880	1,527,159	1,243,773	1,078,695	966,702	674,927	584,858	867,564	-
1870[3]	1,179,866	999,021	889,578	740,360	469,495	407,491	578,230	3,795
1860	2,129,017[20]	1,392,223|16	1,392,223[16]	835,350[17]	835,350[17]	679,194[18]	679,194[18]	27,890
1850	1,490,135[20]	967,573[16]	967,573[16]	575,685[17]	575,685[17]	479,962[18]	479,962[18]	9,173
FEMALE								
1970[1]	5,694,428	6,162,141	6,264,605	5,756,102	5,207,207	4,589,812	11,649,794	-
1960*	6,401,597	5,924,362	5,521,560	4,871,125	4,302,620	3,733,133	9,056,483	-
1960	6,369,606	5,899,398	5,503,029	4,857,672	4,291,504	3,724,684	9,040,992	-
1950	5,728,842	5,133,704	4,544,099	4,143,540	3,605,074	3,021,637	6,472,563	-
1940	4,799,718	4,368,708	4,045,956	3,504,096	1,832,501	2,330,524	4,613,194	-
1930	4,528,785	3,853,736	3,370,355	2,844,159	2,219,685	1,809,713	3,308,594	42,206
1920	3,700,920	3,060,014	2,646,070	2,199,328	1,669,059	1,400,748	2,450,144	55,824
1910	3,029,084	2,475,237	2,090,281	1,790,778	1,298,514	1,081,184	1,963,548	54,612
1900	2,347,916	1,991,250	1,616,776	1,378,207	1,065,915	874,196	1,525,080	73,161
1890[2]	1,815,117	1,530,914	1,313,538	1,117,340	800,673	699,324	1,183,569	58,636
1880	1,473,260	1,225,038	1,010,750	873,181	596,507	519,361	855,895	-
1870[3]	1,135,610	949,691	739,354	627,609	407,057	371,480	575,419	1,366
1860	1,892,231[20]	1,222,107[16]	1,222,107[16]	750,529[17]	750,529[17]	668,788[18]	668,788[18]	23,621
|850	1,335,684[20]	879,087[16]	879,087[16]	533,855[17]	533,855[17]	478,830[18]	478,830[18]	5,112
WHITE, MALE								
1970[1]	4,784,375	5,194,497	5,257,619	4,832,555	4,310,921	3,647,243	7,645,675	-
1960*	5,446,833	5,117,038	4,828,179	4,286,023	3,728,599	3,121,664	6,908,016	-
1960	5,429,784	5,102,661	4,817,693	4,278,441	3,722,948	3,117,954	6,902,217	-
1950	4,955,941	4,573,529	4,080,174	3,756,125	3,350,888	2,829,399	5,360,336	-
1940	4,254,368	3,995,190	3,842,613	3,451,717	2,790,046	2,232,453	4,082,256	-
1930	4,225,332	3,772,619	3,327,142	2,835,808	2,239,604	1,799,730	3,122,827	43,376
1920	3,665,341	2,987,412	2,779,175	2,293,604	1,740,661	1,461,619	2,298,475	78,325
1910	3,024,002	2,537,219	2,161,848	1,915,860	1,363,821	1,076,753	1,825,019	94,112
1900	2,360,348	2,055,176	1,651,972	1,396,035	1,040,235	825,213	1,415,924	97,826
1890[2]	1,831,443	1,495,923	1,271,113	1,083,091	793,301	686,462	1,124,304	80,646
1880	1,353,221	1,111,763	962,027	856,178	610,080	516,416	777,477	-
1870[3]	1,048,443	881,637	751,745	654,500	424,553	358,940	518,090	2,199
1860	1,867,378[20]	1,224,086[16]	1,224,086[16]	740,429[17]	740,429[17]	597,032[18]	597,032[18]	14,073
1850	1,288,682[20]	840,222[16]	840,222[16]	498,660[17]	498,660[17]	411,411[18]	411,411[18]	7,153
1840[4]	866,452[20]	536,606[16]	536,606[16]	314,528[17]	314,528[17]	278,966[18]	278,966[18]	6,100
1830[4]	592,535[20]	367,840[16]	367,840[16]	229,284[17]	229,284[17]	211,002[18]	211,002[18]	5,318
1820[4]	766,283[7,17]	766,283[7,17]	766,283[7,17]	495,065[21]	495,065[21]	495,065[21]	495,065[21]	-
1810[4]	571,997[7,17]	571,997[7,17]	571,997[7,17]	364,836[21]	364,836[21]	364,836[21]	364,836[21]	-

[Continued]

★ 1625 ★

Population by Age, Gender, Race, and Nativity, 1790 to 1970 - II

[Continued]

Year	35-39 years	40-44 years	45-49 years	50-54 years	55-59 years	60-64 years	65 years and over	Age not stated
1800[4]	431,589[7,17]	431,589[7,17]	431,589[7,17]	262,487[21]	262,487[21]	262,487[21]	262,487[21]	-
1790[4]	813,298[9,19]	813,298[9,19]	813,298[9,19]	813,298[9,19]	813,298[9,19]	813,298[9,19]	813,298[9,19]	-
WHITE, FEMALE								
1970[1]	4,936,494	5,412,335	5,587,023	5,169,302	4,695,581	4,157,467	10,684,667	-
1960*	5,694,008	5,305,982	4,956,983	4,407,505	3,897,612	3,429,009	8,395,872	-
1960	5,679,699	5,295,312	4,948,901	4,401,423	3,893,296	3,426,023	8,390,528	-
1950	5,102,532	4,616,761	4,089,180	3,779,314	3,344,844	2,823,207	6,013,351	-
1940	4,262,292	3,940,893	3,690,893	3,228,590	2,636,799	2,184,240	4,297,175	-
1930	4,052,936	3,494,273	3,054,428	2,609,935	2,079,697	1,697,047	3,117,146	35,226
1920	3,300,464	2,768,135	2,408,865	2,023,662	1,565,010	1,309,814	2,284,551	45,338
1910	2,707,843	2,243,053	1,899,214	1,639,453	1,200,385	992,570	1,814,984	40,112
1900	2,100,227	1,796,967	1,453,706	1,237,946	980,982	795,445	1,390,795	47,226
1890[2]	1,608,487	1,369,725	1,178,107	1,007,858	738,358	636,648	1,077,808	40,495
1880	1,295,271	1,078,972	899,865	771,714	544,835	460,892	766,081	-
1870[3]	998,877	833,618	654,870	549,743	370,218	327,739	512,692	864
1860	1,636,213[20]	1,058,246[16]	1,058,246[16]	659,246[17]	659,246[17]	585,523[18]	585,523[18]	11,085
1850	1,128,257[20]	748,566[16]	748,566[16]	459,511[17]	459,511[17]	408,460[18]	408,460[18]	3,154
1840[4]	779,120[20]	502,183[16]	502,183[16]	304,852[17]	304,852[17]	281,404[18]	281,404[18]	-
1830[4]	555,531[20]	356,046[16]	356,046[16]	223,504[17]	223,504[17]	209,838[18]	209,838[18]	-
1820[4]	736,600[7,20]	736,600[7,20]	462,888[17]	462,888[17]	462,888[17]	463,888[17]	436,888[17]	-
1810[4]	544,256[7,20]	544,256[7,20]	338,478[17]	338,478[17]	338,478[17]	338,478[17]	338,478[17]	-
1800[4]	411,694[7,20]	411,694[7,20]	248,030[17]	248,030[17]	248,030[17]	248,030[17]	248,030[17]	-
1790[4]	-	-	-	-	-	-	-	-
FOREIGN-BORN WHITE, MALE								
1970[1]	232,179	247,359	272,021	219,606	282,728	351,105	1,335,661	-
1960*	243,569	204,179	293,870	396,801	514,193	521,795	1,549,415	-
1960	243,122	203,839	293,465	396,254	513,546	521,186	1,547,589	-
1950	244,470	383,225	534,395	627,215	703,470	715,185	1,358,705	-
1940	530,164	656,782	816,955	833,342	735,848	573,300	1,054,408	-
1930	933,999	992,135	907,537	737,822	565,334	491,843	871,210	6,667
1920	1,008,677	803,195	744,423	651,546	503,789	392,629	679,384	13,732
1910	812,007	751,519	656,455	526,256	380,110	331,914	607,008	19,706
1900	672,804	557,300	468,466	440,079	345,241	285,783	493,760	16,136
1890[2]	493,471	475,106	433,466	382,987	278,485	254,101	360,817	16,630
1880	432,957	384,931	340,863	318,045	206,820	170,841	210,158	-
1870[3]	359,484	328,020	260,805	215,717	115,553	98,703	115,857	1,288
FOREIGN-BORN WHITE, FEMALE								
1970[1]	282,098	317,950	333,321	250,963	323,164	398,068	1,639,366	-
1960*	293,022	226,832	318,702	413,841	507,576	538,949	1,564,363	-
1960	292,123	226,353	318,373	413,346	507,045	538,581	1,563,217	-
1950	282,565	403,795	523,085	598,190	621,545	599,620	1,336,405	-
1940	518,231	606,288	686,950	682,226	582,902	495,575	1,004,850	-
1930	768,432	753,765	702,515	607,308	483,142	434,050	808,645	4,049
1920	729,128	624,904	555,252	515,831	404,933	323,102	648,843	6,532
1910	596,086	551,956	489,905	398,799	313,410	295,669	576,341	6,505
1900	504,762	408,812	371,754	363,313	297,762	259,248	456,587	8,744
1890[2]	377,121	384,848	354,349	326,233	246,646	223,546	321,487	7,987
1880	356,308	327,959	290,078	259,042	166,294	139,622	191,440	-
1870[3]	308,508	272,729	192,729	192,021	154,061	87,983	82,228	104,172
NEGRO, MALE								
1970[1]	540,539	543,737	520,095	458,526	404,704	334,425	675,570	-
1960[12]*	569,133	508,082	479,629	406,991	365,302	258,918	540,523	-
1960[12]	568,530	507,715	479,437	406,796	365,205	258,875	540,477	-

[Continued]

★ 1625 ★

Population by Age, Gender, Race, and Nativity, 1790 to 1970 - II

[Continued]

Year	35-39 years	40-44 years	45-49 years	50-54 years	55-59 years	60-64 years	65 years and over	Age not stated
1950[13]	530,210	468,595	418,690	350,255	264,085	195,155	412,400	-
1940	462,559	400,249	343,251	283,120	207,220	154,245	308,801	-
1930	430,472	339,329	323,162	277,532	174,367	133,349	189,530	7,064
1920	383,587	275,926	320,506	227,995	129,153	112,137	173,881	13,510
1910	320,450	229,680	199,928	179,387	115,090	101,149	152,482	17,076
1900	233,371	179,090	168,495	155,188	97,323	85,961	133,025	25,157
1890[2]								18,435
1880	-	-	-	-	-	-	-	-
1870[3]	123,129	101,580	85,010	83,941	44,237	47,811	59,701	11
1860	247,453[20]	162,220[16]	162,220[16]	93,106[17]	93,106[17]	80,615[18]	80,615[18]	13,764
1850	201,453[20]	127,351[16]	127,351[16]	77,025[17]	77,025[17]	68,551[18]	68,551[18]	2,020
1840[4]	173,534[16]	173,534[16]	173,534[16]	173,534[16]	65,878[18]	65,878[18]	65,878[18]	-
1830	141,151[16]	141,151[16]	141,151[16]	141,151[16]	54,071[18]	54,071[18]	54,071[18]	-
1820[4]	187,173[20]	187,173[20]	187,173[20]	187,173[20]	94,978[17]	94,978[17]	94,978[17]	-
NEGRO, FEMALE								
1970[1]	655,188	654,128	602,684	530,941	468,824	399,352	883,184	-
1960[12]*	652,195	578,429	533,714	444,591	393,439	290,249	627,357	-
1960[12]	651,926	578,212	533,621	444,494	393,392	290,201	627,324	-
1950[13]	608,650	503,960	444,215	351,980	251,280	189,685	454,225	-
1940	523,274	414,847	344,556	267,315	189,999	141,659	307,141	-
1930	460,428	348,094	306,903	227,058	135,030	108,820	183,189	6,667
1920	390,344	283,775	231,083	171,115	100,827	87,981	158,832	9,993
1910	312,999	225,733	185,981	146,683	94,532	85,353	141,642	13,964
1900	241,316	188,126	157,889	135,799	81,853	75,726	128,338	23,654
1890[2]	363,723[20]	363,723[20]	242,378[21]	242,378[21]	123,559[22]	123,559[22]	104,373	17,378
1880	-	-	-	-	-	-	-	-
1870[3]	135,709	115,240	83,958	77,421	36,620	43,503	62,357	17
1860	253,220[20]	162,299[16]	162,299[16]	90,587[17]	90,587[17]	82,414[18]	82,414[18]	12,494
1850	207,427[20]	130,521[16]	130,521[16]	74,344[17]	74,344[17]	70,370[18]	70,370[18]	1,958
1840[4]	169,575[16]	169,575[16]	169,575[16]	169,575[16]	169,575[16]	66,442[18]	66,442[18]	-
1830	136,214[16]	136,214[16]	136,214[16]	136,214[16]	136,214[16]	55,498[18]	55,498[18]	-
1820[4]	179,874[7,20]	179,874[7,20]	179,874[7,20]	179,874[7,20]	89,498[17]	89,498[17]	89,498[17]	-
OTHER, MALE								
1970[1]	87,509	80,579	73,620	56,835	50,196	45,304	94,463	-
1960[12]*	59,119	46,508	44,820	42,769	44,732	25,533	48,040	-
1960[12]	41,866	31,642	30,061	30,064	33,617	18,628	35,258	-
1950[13]	26,985	27,470	25,300	20,370	14,655	14,310	24,510	-
1940	28,732	23,696	18,405	17,913	14,098	11,118	15,063	-
1930	24,056	24,511	21,620	18,305	12,021	8,429	12,854	1,376
1920	25,433	22,205	17,869	13,946	10,251	8,044	10,715	1,040
1910	22,564	19,451	17,140	14,766	9,526	8,064	8,475	3,255
1900	23,146	21,650	17,369	13,399	7,699	5,993	6,469	4,440
1890[2]							2,104	4,448
1880	-	-	-	-	-	-	-	-
1870[3]	7,794	6,804	2,823	1,919	705	740	439	1,585
1860	14,261[20]	5,917[16]	5,917[16]	1,815[17]	1,815[17]	1,547[18]	1,547[18]	58
OTHER, FEMALE								
1970[1]	102,746	95,678	74,898	55,859	42,802	32,993	81,943	-
1960[12]*	57,439	41,103	31,736	25,027	31,021	17,568	32,370	-
1960[12]	40,072	27,252	21,234	17,278	23,851	12,031	22,178	-
1950[13]	17,480	13,665	12,615	11,460	8,855	6,460	12,825	-
1940	14,152	12,968	11,257	8,191	5,703	4,625	8,878	-
1930	15,421	11,369	9,024	7,166	4,958	3,846	8,259	313
1920	10,112	8,104	6,122	4,551	3,222	2,953	6,761	493
1910	8,242	6,451	5,086	4,642	3,597	3,261	6,922	536

[Continued]

★ 1625 ★

Population by Age, Gender, Race, and Nativity, 1790 to 1970 - II

[Continued]

Year	35-39 years	40-44 years	45-49 years	50-54 years	55-59 years	60-64 years	65 years and over	Age not stated
1900	6,373	6,157	5,181	4,462	3,080	3,025	5,947	2,281
1890[2]	4,096[24]	4,096[24]	2,535[22]	2,535[22]	1,432[23]	1,432[23]	1,388	763
1880	-	-	-	-	-	-	-	-
1870	1,024	833	526	445	219	238	370	485
1860	2,798[20]	1,562[16]	1,562|16	696[17]	696[17]	851[18]	851[18]	42

Source: "Population, by Age, Sex, Race, and Nativity: 1790 to 1970." U.S. Bureau of the Census, *Historical Statistics of the United States: Colonial Times to 1970, Part I*, pp. 15-18. *Notes:* * Denotes first year for which figures include Alaska and Hawaii. - Represents zero. 1. Excludes 23,372 persons for whom age is not available. See series A 1-5, footnote 3. 2. Exclusive of 325,464 persons enumerated in the Indian Territory and on Indian reservations. See series A 105-118 footnote 7, for composition by race and sex. 3. Excludes 1,260,078 persons (747,915 white and 512,163 Negro) for whom age is not available. See series A 1-5, footnote 5, and series A 91- 104, footnote 4. 4. Totals differ slightly from corrected totals shown in series A 91- 104. Corrections by age are not available. 5. 10-15 years old. 6. 16-25 years old. 7. 26-44 years old. 8. Under 16 years old. 9. 16 years old and over. 10. Age for 1790 available only for white males. 11. 15-percent sample data. 12. 25-percent sample data. 13. 20-percent sample data. 14. Estimates based on population under 15 and age distribution of Negro and other races. 15. Age for 1880 available only for all races, white, and for Negro and other races combined. 16. Data includes persons 40 to 49 years old. 17. Data includes persons 50 to 59 years old. 18. Data includes persons 60 years old and over. 19. Data includes persons 35 years old and over. 20. Data includes persons 35 to 39 years old. 21. Data includes persons 45 years old and over. 22. Data includes persons 45 to 54 years old. 23. Data includes persons 55 to 64 years old. 24. Data includes persons 35 to 44 years old.

★ 1626 ★

Age Composition

Population by Race and 5-Year Age Periods, 1930 and 1920 - I

Age	All Classes		Negro		White		Other Races	
	1930	1920	1930	1920	1930	1920	1930	1920
All ages	122,775,046	105,710,620	11,891,143	10,463,131	108,864,207	94,820,915	2,019,696	426,574
Under 5 years	11,444,390	11,573,230	1,230,206	1,143,699	9,927,396	10,373,921	286,788	55,610
5 to 9 years	12,607,609	11,398,075	1,368,381	1,266,207	10,956,144	10,087,245	283,084	44,623
10 to 14 years	12,004,877	10,641,137	1,251,542	1,236,914	10,546,282	9,369,322	207,053	34,901
15 to 19 years	10,870,378	9,277,021	1,203,191	1,054,847	9,466,155	8,185,341	201,032	36,833
25 to 29 years	9,833,608	9,086,491	1,071,787	909,739	8,573,696	8,141,690	188,125	35,062
30 to 34 years	9,120,421	8,071,193	864,514	697,865	8,109,766	7,338,790	146,141	34,538
35 to 39 years	9,208,645	7,775,281	890,900	773,931	8,183,620	6,965,805	134,125	35,545
40 to 44 years	7,990,195	6,345,557	687,423	559,701	7,198,507	5,755,547	104,265	30,309
45 to 49 years	7,042,279	5,763,620	630,065	551,589	6,322,989	5,188,040	89,225	23,991
50 to 54 years	5,975,804	4,734,873	504,590	399,110	5,409,056	4,317,266	62,158	18,497
55 to 59 years	4,645,677	3,549,124	309,397	229,980	4,293,107	3,305,671	43,173	13,473
60 to 64 years	3,751,221	2,982,548	242,169	200,118	3,476,993	2,771,433	32,059	10,997
65 to 69 years	2,770,605	2,068,475	155,177	137,035	2,594,840	1,924,296	20,588	7,144
70 to 74 years	1,950,004	1,395,036	99,096	91,579	1,838,050	1,298,738	12,858	4,719
75 to 79 years	1,106,390	856,560	58,711	52,352	1,039,862	801,678	7,817	2,530
80 to 84 years	534,676	402,779	33,377	28,122	496,803	373,066	4,496	1,591
85 to 89 years	205,469	156,539	14,948	12,281	188,414	143,536	2,107	722
90 to 94 years	51,664	39,980	6,332	5,847	44,453	33,713	879	420
95 to 99 years	11,033	9,579	2,611	2,562	7,981	6,831	441	186

[Continued]

★ 1626 ★

Population by Race and 5-Year Age Periods, 1930 and 1920 - I

[Continued]

Age	All Classes		Negro		White		Other Races	
	1930	1920	1930	1920	1930	1920	1930	1920
100 years and over	3,964	4,267	2,467	2,935	1,180	1,168	317	164
Unknown	94,022	148,699	13,731	23,508	77,329	123,663	2,962	1,533

Source: "Population Classified by Color and 5-Year Age Periods, for the United States: 1930 and 1920." U.S. Bureau of the Census, *Negroes in the United States, 1920-1932*, p. 89.

★ 1627 ★

Age Composition

Population by Race and 5-Year Age Periods, 1930 and 1920 - II

Age	Percent Distribution							
	All Classes		Negro		White		Other Races	
	1930	1920	1930	1920	1930	1920	1930	1920
All ages	100.0	100.0	100.0	100.0	100.0	100.0	100.0	100.0
Under 5 years	9.3	10.9	10.3	10.9	9.1	10.9	14.2	13.0
5 to 9 years	10.3	10.8	11.5	12.1	10.1	10.6	14.0	10.5
10 to 14 years	9.8	10.1	10.5	11.8	9.7	9.9	10.3	8.2
15 to 19 years	9.4	8.9	10.5	10.4	9.3	8.8	9.4	7.8
20 to 24 years	8.9	8.8	10.1	10.1	8.7	8.6	10.0	8.6
25 to 29 years	8.0	8.6	9.0	8.7	7.9	8.6	9.3	8.2
30 to 34 years	7.4	7.6	7.3	6.7	7.4	7.7	7.2	8.1
35 to 39 years	7.5	7.4	7.5	7.4	7.5	7.3	6.6	8.3
40 to 44 years	6.5	6.0	5.8	5.3	6.6	6.1	5.2	7.1
45 to 49 years	5.7	5.5	5.3	5.3	5.8	5.5	4.4	5.6
50 to 54 years	4.9	4.5	4.2	3.8	5.0	4.6	3.1	4.3
55 to 59 years	3.8	3.4	2.6	2.2	3.9	3.5	2.1	3.3
60 to 64 years	3.1	2.8	2.0	1.9	3.2	2.9	1.6	2.6
65 to 69 years	2.3	2.0	1.3	1.3	2.4	2.0	1.0	1.7
70 to 74 years	1.6	1.3	.8	.9	1.7	1.4	.6	1.1
75 to 79 years	.9	.8	.5	.5	1.0	.8	.4	.6
80 to 84 years	.4	.4	.3	.3	.5	.4	.2	.4
85 to 89 years	.2	.1	.1	.1	.2	.2	.1	.2
90 to 94 years	-	-	.1	.1	-	-	-	.1
95 to 99 years	-	-	-	-	-	-	-	-
100 years and over	-	-	-	-	-	-	-	-
Unknown	.1	.1	.1	.2	.1	.1	.1	.4

Source: "Population Classified by Color and 5-Year Age Periods, for the United States: 1930 and 1920." U.S. Bureau of the Census, *Negroes in the United States, 1920-1932*, p. 89.

★ 1628 ★

Age Composition

Urban and Rural Black and White Population by Broad Age Periods, 1910

Age period	Urban Population: 1910					Rural Population: 1910				
	All classes	Negro	Native white: Native parentage	Native white: Foreign or mixed parentage	Foreign born white	All classes	Negro	Native white: Native parentage	Native white: Foreign or mixed parentage	Foreign-born white
	Number									
All ages[1]	42,623,383	2,689,229	17,849,644	12,346,900	9,635,369	49,348,883	7,138,534	31,638,931	6,559,937	3,710,176
Under 5 years	4,200,291	229,080	2,044,886	1,846,699	75,372	6,431,073	1,034,208	4,501,396	827,426	27,135
5 to 14 years	7,401,325	454,219	3,486,880	2,950,392	503,771	11,466,447	1,947,600	7,698,418	1,601,052	153,068
15 to 24 years	8,573,829	578,299	3,659,032	2,673,889	1,644,462	9,546,758	1,512,912	6,112,945	1,404,794	450,680
25 to 44 years	14,168,853	985,374	5,330,953	3,415,057	4,390,378	12,641,022	1,652,804	7,615,488	1,795,052	1,489,601
45 to 64 years	6,487,864	351,259	2,495,622	1,318,912	2,299,020	6,936,225	756,844	4,244,378	798,474	1,093,498
65 years and over	1,693,010	77,435	771,790	135,454	706,918	2,256,514	216,689	1,429,278	120,132	476,431
	Percentage Distribution by Age Periods									
All ages	100.0	100.0	100.0	100.0	100.0	100.0	100.0	100.0	100.0	100.0
Under 5 years	9.9	8.5	11.5	15.0	0.8	13.0	14.5	14.2	12.6	0.7
5 to 14 years	17.4	16.9	19.5	23.9	5.2	23.2	27.3	24.3	24.4	4.1
15 to 24 years	20.1	21.5	20.5	21.7	17.1	19.3	21.2	19.3	21.4	12.4
25 to 44 years	33.2	36.6	29.9	27.7	45.6	25.6	23.2	24.1	27.4	40.1
45 to 64 years	15.2	13.1	14.0	10.7	23.9	14.1	10.6	13.4	12.2	29.5
65 years and over	4.0	2.9	4.3	1.1	7.3	4.6	3.0	4.5	1.8	12.8

Source: "Urban and Rural Negro and White Population, Classified by Broad Age Periods: 1910." U.S. Bureau of the Census, *Negro Population, 1790-1915*, p. 181. *Note:* 1. Includes persons of unknown age.

★ 1629 ★

Age Composition

Urban, Rural-Farm, and Rural-Nonfarm Black Population, 5-Year Age Periods and Sections, 1930

Age	Urban	Rural: Total	Rural: Rural-farm	Rural: Rural-nonfarm	Percent Distribution: Urban	Percent Distribution: Rural
	UNITED STATES					
All ages	5,193,913	6,697,230	4,680,523	2,016,707	100.0	100.0
Under 5 years	427,607	802,599	588,846	213,753	8.2	12.0
5 to 9 years	468,357	900,024	670,165	229,859	9.0	13.4
10 to 14 years	407,867	843,675	645,112	198,563	7.9	12.6
15 to 19 years	447,155	803,373	597,578	205,795	8.6	12.0
20 to 24 years	560,215	642,976	423,663	219,313	10.8	9.6

[Continued]

★ 1629 ★

Urban, Rural-Farm, and Rural-Nonfarm Black Population, 5-Year Age Periods and Sections, 1930

[Continued]

Age	Urban	Rural			Percent Distribution	
		Total	Rural-farm	Rural-nonfarm	Urban	Rural
25 to 29 years	596,430	475,357	291,400	183,957	11.5	7.1
30 to 34 years	496,472	368,042	225,679	142,363	9.6	5.5
35 to 39 years	498,065	392,835	248,319	144,516	9.6	5.9
40 to 44 years	369,429	317,994	205,354	112,640	7.1	4.7
45 to 49 years	316,590	313,475	209,878	103,597	6.1	4.7
50 to 54 years	228,556	276,034	191,244	84,790	4.4	4.1
55 to 59 years	132,940	176,457	123,604	52,583	2.6	2.6
60 to 64 years	95,784	146,385	102,457	43,928	1.8	2.2
65 to 69 years	60,533	94,644	64,749	29,895	1.2	1.4
70 to 74 years	36,650	62,446	41,400	21,046	.7	.9
75 to 79 years	21,327	37,384	24,248	13,136	.4	.6
80 to 84 years	11,666	21,711	14,001	7,710	.4	.3
85 years and over	8,932	17,426	11,145	6,281	.2	.3
Unknown	9,338	4,393	1,681	2,712	.2	.1
THE SOUTH						
All ages	2,966,325	6,395,252	4,608,788	1,786,466	100.0	100.0
Under 5 years	242,220	774,359	581,424	192,935	8.2	12.1
5 to 9 years	280,569	869,679	662,083	207,596	9.5	13.6
10 to 14 years	253,466	815,654	637,124	178,530	8.5	12.8
15 to 19 years	287,828	776,018	596,038	185,980	9.7	12.1
20 to 24 years	336,686	617,101	417,802	199,299	11.4	9.6
25 to 29 years	324,501	450,207	286,902	163,305	10.9	7.0
30 to 34 years	255,110	344,126	221,611	122,515	8.6	5.4
35 to 39 years	262,337	368,540	243,646	124,894	8.8	5.8
40 to 44 years	197,862	297,742	201,048	96,694	6.7	4.7
45 to 49 years	174,145	294,905	205,601	89,304	5.9	4.6
50 to 54 years	129,403	260,648	187,445	73,203	4.4	4.1
55 to 59 years	73,765	165,541	120,735	44,806	2.5	2.6
60 to 64 years	57,621	138,276	100,145	38,131	1.9	2.2
65 to 69 years	36,491	88,840	63,104	25,736	1.9	1.4
70 to 74 years	22,447	58,442	40,305	18,137	.8	.9
75 to 79 years	13,007	34,724	23,568	11,156	.4	.5
80 to 84 years	7,473	20,326	13,682	6,644	.3	.3
85 years and over	5,785	16,291	10,888	5,403	.2	.3
Unknown	5,609	3,833	1,635	2,198	.2	.1
THE NORTH						
All ages	2,128,329	280,890	65,601	215,289	100.0	100.0
Under 5 years	179,197	26,556	6,746	19,810	8.4	9.5

[Continued]

★ 1629 ★

Urban, Rural-Farm, and Rural-Nonfarm Black Population, 5-Year Age Periods and Sections, 1930

[Continued]

Age	Urban	Rural			Percent Distribution	
		Total	Rural-farm	Rural-nonfarm	Urban	Rural
5 to 9 years	180,831	28,550	7,346	21,204	8.5	10.2
10 to 14 years	148,084	26,346	7,322	19,024	7.0	9.4
15 to 19 years	152,777	25,741	6,979	18,762	7.2	9.2
20 to 24 years	215,385	24,121	5,423	18,698	10.1	8.6
25 to 29 years	262,175	23,332	4,102	19,230	12.3	8.3
30 to 34 years	231,322	21,993	3,682	18,311	10.9	7.8
35 to 39 years	224,596	22,122	4,222	17,900	10.6	7.9
40 to 44 years	162,434	18,502	3,889	14,613	7.6	6.6
45 to 49 years	134,231	17,040	3,848	13,192	6.3	6.1
50 to 54 years	92,926	14,174	3,442	10,732	4.4	5.0
55 to 59 years	55,264	10,170	2,642	7,528	2.6	3.6
60 to 64 years	35,578	7,588	2,149	5,439	1.7	2.7
65 to 69 years	22,362	5,446	1,538	3,908	1.1	1.9
70 to 74 years	13,156	3,789	1,031	2,758	.6	1.3
75 to 79 years	7,772	2,513	653	1,860	.4	.9
80 to 84 years	3,903	1.319	302	1,017	.2	.5
85 years and over	2,924	1,071	243	828	.1	.4
Unknown	3,402	517	42	475	.2	.2
THE WEST						
All ages	99,259	21,088	6,136	14,952	100.0	100.0
Under 5 years	6,190	1,684	676	1,008	6.2	8.0
5 to 9 years	6,957	1,795	736	1,059	7.0	8.5
10 to 14 years	6,317	1,675	666	1,009	6.4	7.9
15 to 19 years	6,550	1,614	561	1,053	6.6	7.7
20 to 24 years	8,144	1,754	438	1,316	8.2	8.3
25 to 29 years	9,754	1,818	396	1,422	9.8	8.6
30 to 34 years	10,030	1,923	386	1,537	10.1	9.1
35 to 39 years	11,132	2,173	451	1,722	11.2	10.3
40 to 44 years	9,123	1,750	417	1,333	9.2	8.3
45 to 49 years	8,214	1,530	429	1,101	8.3	7.3
50 to 54 years	6,227	1,212	357	855	6.3	5.7
55 to 59 years	3,911	746	227	519	3.9	3.5
60 to 64 years	2,585	521	163	358	2.6	2.5
65 to 69 years	1,680	358	107	251	1.7	1.7
70 to 74 years	1,047	215	64	151	1.1	1.0
75 to 79 years	548	147	27	120	.6	.7
80 to 84 years	290	66	17	49	.3	.3

[Continued]

★ 1629 ★

Urban, Rural-Farm, and Rural-Nonfarm Black Population, 5-Year Age Periods and Sections, 1930

[Continued]

Age	Urban	Rural			Percent Distribution	
		Total	Rural-farm	Rural-nonfarm	Urban	Rural
85 years and over	223	64	14	50	.2	.3
Unknown	327	43	4	39	.3	.2

Source: "Urban, Rural-Farm, and Rural-Nonfarm Population by 5-Year Age Periods, by Sections: 1930." U.S. Bureau of the Census, *Negroes in the United States, 1920-1932*, p. 89.

Black Belt

★ 1630 ★

Areas of Increasing, Decreasing, and Stationary Black Population, 1900-1910

Section or Division	Number of counties 1910	Number of Counties or Combinations of Counties[1]				
		Total	In which the Negro population-			Having no Negro population in 1910 or in 1900.
			Increased, 1900-1910	Decreased, 1900-1910	Did not change 1900-1910	
United States	2,953	2,751	1,433	1,229	44	45
The South	1,351	1,214	662	533	4	15
South Atlantic	534	347	138	208	1	-
East South Central	361	347	138	208	1	-
West South Central	456	376	226	133	2	15
The North	1,265	1,236	582	603	29	22
The West	337	301	189	93	11	8

Source: Untitled table. U.S. Bureau of the Census, *Negro Population, 1790-1915*, p. 111. Primary source: U.S. Census. *Notes:* 1. In cases where boundaries of counties were changed during the decade 1900-1910, country areas and populations have been combined and computations made for the combined area. The entire state of Oklahoma is classified as a single area.

★ 1631 ★

Black Belt

Black Belt Counties, 1930, 1900, and 1860

Years	Number of counties	Area in Square Miles	Total Population		Rural Population	
			White	Negro	White	Negro
1860	240	167,046	1,242,228	2,171,687	1,145,651	2,101,927
1900	283	166,083	2,199,685	4,075,705	1,783,410	3,741,583
1930	190	106,581	1,619,589	2,752,796	1,237,219	2,445,643

Source: "Black Belt Counties-1860, 1900, 1930." Work, Monroe N., ed., *Negro Year Book: An Annual Encyclopedia of the Negro, 1937-38,* p. 254.

★ 1632 ★

Black Belt

Black Population in Counties in the South by Percent Black, by Divisions, and States, 1910, 1920, and 1930

Division, State, and Year	Total	Negro Population in Counties in Which the Percent Negro Was-					Total	Percent of the Total Negro Population in Counties in Which The Percent Negro Was-				
		Less than 12.5[1]	12.5 to 24.9	25 to 49.9	50 to 74.9	75 or more		Less than 12.5[1]	12.5 to 24.9	25 to 49.9	50 to 74.9	75 or more
The South:												
1930	9,361,577	604,956	1,708,008	4,310,181	2,363,181	375,320	100.0	6.5	18.2	46.0	25.2	4.0
1920	8,912,231	516,972	1,269,519	3,874,519	2,546,955	704,485	100.0	5.8	14.2	43.5	28.6	7.9
1910	8,749,427	401,024	1,013,764	3,402,155	2,870,001	1,062,483	100.0	4.6	11.6	38.9	32.8	12.1
SOUTH ATLANTIC:												
1930	4,421,388	211,770	741,217	2,286,141	1,149,316	32,944	100.0	4.8	16.8	51.7	26.0	0.7
1920	4,325,120	155,637	534,438	2,002,456	1,544,611	87,978	100.0	3.6	12.4	46.3	35.7	2.0
1910	4,112,488	119,336	385,290	1,619,774	1,800,468	187,620	100.0	2.9	9.4	39.4	43.8	4.6
EAST SOUTH CENTRAL:												
1930	2,658,238	157,668	456,866	923,582	817,461	302,661	100.0	5.9	17.2	34.7	30.8	11.4
1920	2,523,532	155,424	338,241	953,036	571,616	505,215	100.0	6.2	13.4	37.8	22.7	20.0
1910	2,652,513	131,209	347,831	896,393	571,549	705,549	100.0	4.9	13.1	33.8	21.5	26.6
WEST SOUTH CENTRAL:												
1930	2,281,951	235,518	509,925	1,100,458	396,335	39,715	100.0	10.3	22.3	48.2	17.4	1.7
1920	2,063,579	205,911	396,840	918,808	430,728	111,292	100.0	10.0	19.2	44.5	20.9	5.4
1910	1,984,426	150,479	280,643	885,988	498,002	169,314	100.0	7.6	14.1	44.6	25.1	8.5
SOUTH ATLANTIC:												
Delaware:												
1930	32,602	18,471	14,131	-	-	-	100.0	56.7	43.3	-	-	-
1920	30,335	16,325	14,010	-	-	-	100.0	53.8	46.2	-	-	-
1910	31,181	-	31,181	-	-	-	100.0	-	100.0	-	-	-
Maryland:												
1930	276,379	24,322	182,115	69,942	-	-	100.0	8.8	65.9	25.3	-	-
1920	244,479	22,617	135,562	86,300	-	-	100.0	9.3	55.4	35.3	-	-
1910	232,250	23,743	108,049	91,886	8,572	-	100.0	10.2	46.5	39.6	3.7	-
District of Columbia:												
1930	132,068	-	-	132,068	-	-	100.0	-	-	100.0	-	-
1920	109,966	-	-	109,966	-	-	100.0	-	-	100.0	-	-
1910	94,446	-	-	94,446	-	-	100.0	-	-	100.0	-	-
Virginia:												
1930	650,165	38,128	88,137	367,363	152,780	3,757	100.0	5.9	13.6	56.5	23.5	0.6
1920	690,017	28,223	59,590	434,309	164,292	3,603	100.0	4.1	8.6	62.9	23.8	.5
1910	671,096	23,358	61,753	314,888	271,097	-	100.0	3.5	9.2	46.9	40.4	-

[Continued]

★ 1632 ★

Black Population in Counties in the South by Percent Black, by Divisions, and States, 1910, 1920, and 1930

[Continued]

Division, State, and Year	Total	Negro Population in Counties in Which the Percent Negro Was-					Total	Percent of the Total Negro Population in Counties in Which The Percent Negro Was-				
		Less than 12.5[1]	12.5 to 24.9	25 to 49.9	50 to 74.9	75 or more		Less than 12.5[1]	12.5 to 24.9	25 to 49.9	50 to 74.9	75 or more
West Virginia:												
1930	114,893	66,870	48,023	-	-	-	100.0	58.2	41.8	-	-	-
1920	86,345	42,716	43,029	-	-	-	100.0	49.5	50.5	-	-	-
1910	64,173	30,736	18,770	14,667	-	-	100.0	47.9	29.2	22.9	-	-
North Carolina:												
1930	918,647	41,827	160,277	566,951	149,592	-	100.0	4.6	17.4	61.7	16.3	-
1920	763,407	33,348	122,933	430,685	176,441	-	100.0	4.4	16.1	56.4	23.1	-
1910	697,843	29,001	87,104	415,218	166,520	-	100.0	4.2	12.5	59.5	23.9	-
South Carolina:												
1930	793,681	-	48,361	298,885	446,435	-	100.0	-	6.1	37.7	56.2	-
1920	864,719	-	19,027	222,913	572,156	50,623	100.0	-	2.2	25.8	66.2	5.9
1910	835,843	-	12,098	124,274	619,748	79,723	100.0	-	1.4	14.9	74.1	9.5
Georgia:												
1930	1,071,125	19,756	78,823	590,928	352,431	29,187	100.0	1.8	7.4	55.2	32.9	2.7
1920	1,206,365	11,163	83,173	505,434	572,843	33,752	100.0	.9	6.9	41.9	47.5	2.8
1910	2,176,987	11,304	39,944	389,767	655,915	80,057	100.0	1.0	3.4	33.1	55.7	6.8
Florida:												
1930	431,828	2,396	121,350	260,004	48,078	-	100.0	.6	28.1	60.2	11.1	-
1920	329,487	1,245	56,514	212,849	58,879	-	100.0	.4	17.2	64.6	17.9	-
1910	308,669	1,194	26,391	174,628	78,616	27,840	100.0	.4	8.5	56.5	25.5	9.0
EAST SOUTH CENTRAL:												
Kentucky:												
1930	226,040	71,962	142,374	11,704	-	-	100.0	31.8	63.0	5.2	-	-
1920	235,938	69,496	125,507	40,935	-	-	100.0	29.5	53.2	17.3	-	-
1910	261,656	58,799	153,160	49,697	-	-	100.0	22.5	58.2	19.0	-	-
Tennessee:												
1930	477,646	72,350	160,785	206,189	38,322	-	100.0	15.1	33.7	43.2	8.0	-
1920	451,758	72,083	92,739	246,451	40,485	-	100.0	16.0	20.5	54.6	9.0	-
1910	473,088	58,061	89,796	284,819	17,710	22,702	100.0	12.3	19.0	60.2	3.7	4.8
Alabama:												
1930	944,834	11,281	99,356	453,334	266,328	114,535	100.0	1.2	10.5	48.0	28.2	12.1
1920	900,652	11,861	82,926	419,572	200,930	185,363	100.0	1.3	9.2	46.6	22.3	20.6
1910	908,282	12,062	69,266	339,555	200,208	287,191	100.0	1.3	7.6	37.4	22.0	31.6
Mississippi:												
1930	1,009,718	2,075	54,351	252,355	512,811	188,126	100.0	.2	5.4	25.0	50.8	18.6
1920	935,184	1,984	37,069	246,078	330,201	319,852	100.0	.2	4.0	26.3	35.3	34.2
1910	1,009,487	2,287	35,609	222,322	353,613	395,656	100.0	.2	3.5	22.0	25.0	39.2
WEST SOUTH CENTRAL:												
Arkansas:												
1930	478,463	19,914	32,709	237,558	156,916	31,366	100.0	4.2	6.8	49.7	32.8	6.6
1920	472,220	22,900	28,931	201,915	156,267	62,207	100.0	4.8	6.1	42.8	33.1	13.2
1910	442,891	25,387	19,000	172,359	131,977	94,168	100.0	5.7	4.3	38.9	29.8	21.3
Louisiana:												
1930	776,326	578	53,905	523,255	190,239	8,349	100.0	.1	6.9	67.4	24.5	1.1
1920	700,257	-	40,284	385,180	225,708	49,085	100.0	-	5.8	55.0	32.2	7.0
1910	713,874	-	51,260	305,907	281,561	75,146	100.0	-	7.2	42.9	39.4	10.5
Oklahoma:												
1930	172,198	107,365	50,797	14,036	-	-	100.0	62.3	29.5	8.2	-	-
1920	149,408	79,552	54,146	15,710	-	-	100.0	53.2	36.2	10.5	-	-
1910	137,612	58,004	26,908	52,700	-	-	100.0	42.2	19.6	38.3	-	-
Texas:												
1930	854,964	107,661	372,514	325,609	49,180	-	100.0	12.6	43.6	38.1	5.8	-
1920	741,694	103,459	273,479	316,003	48,753	-	100.0	13.9	36.9	42.6	6.6	-
1910	690,049	67,088	183,475	355,022	84,464	-	100.0	9.7	26.6	51.4	12.2	-

Source: "Negro Population in Counties in the South Classified According to Percent Negro, by Divisions, and States: 1930, 1920, and 1910." U.S. Bureau of the Census, *Negroes in the United States, 1920-1932*, p. 73. *Note:* 1. Includes counties reporting no Negro population.

★ 1633 ★

Black Belt

Center of the Black Population, 1790-1920

Census Yr	Location of Center							Decennial Movement in Miles
	North Latitude			West Longitude			Approximate location by important towns	
1790	37	4	8	77	51	21	25 miles west-southwest of Petersburg, Dinwiddie County, Va.	
1880	34	42	14	85	6	56	10.4 miles east of Lafayette, Walker County, Ga.	443 MI SW
1890	34	36	18	85	26	49	15.7 miles southwest of Lafayette, Walker County, Ga.	20.5 MI SW
1900	34	31	16	85	34	35	10.7 miles northeast of Fort Payne, Dekalb County, Ala.	9.5 MI SW
1910	34	30	0	85	40	43	5.4 miles north-northeast of Fort Payne, Dekalb County, Ala.	5.8 MI W-SW
1920	34	46	52	85	30	48	1.8 miles north-northeast of Rising Fawn, Ga.	21.5 MI NE

Source: "Center of the Negro Population: 1790, 1880-1920." Monroe Work, *Negro Yearbook, 1925-26*, p. 441.

★ 1634 ★

Black Belt

Counties Classified According to Black Population by Sections and Southern Divisions, 1930 - I

Section and Division	Total number of counties	Reporting no Negro population	Reporting Negro Population				
			Total	Under 1,000			
				Total	Under 100	100 to 500	500 to 1,000
United States	3,100[1]	245	2,355	1,666	1,009	440	217
THE SOUTH	1,415	20	1,395	428	142	161	125
South Atlantic	581	2	579	102	23	40	39
East South Central	364	-	364	117	28	50	39
West South Central	470	18	452	209	91	71	47
THE NORTH	1,274	156	1,118	914	611	224	79
THE WEST	411	69	342	324	256	55	13

Source: "Counties Classified According to Negro Population, by Sections, and Southern Divisions: 1930." U.S. Bureau of the Census, *Negroes in the United States, 1920-1932*, p. 71. *Notes:* 1. Includes Baltimore city, St. Louis city, 24 independent cities in Virginia, and that part of Yellowstone National Park in Wyoming.

★ 1635 ★

Black Belt

Counties Classified According to Black Population by Sections and Southern Divisions, 1930 - II

Section And Division	Reporting Negro Population 1,000 or more						
	Total	1,000 to 5,000	5,000 to 10,000	10,000 to 25,000	25,000 to 50,000	50,000 to 100,000	100,000 and over
United States	1,189	581	971	266	46	15	10
THE SOUTH	967	429	243	238	42	9	6
South Atlantic	477	215	120	117[1]	19	3	3
East South Central	247	113	52	64	12	4	2
West South Central	243	101	71	57	11	2	1
THE NORTH	204	137	27	27	3	6	4
THE WEST	18	15	1	1	1	-	-

Source: "Counties Classified According to Negro Population, by Sections, and Southern Divisions: 1930." U.S. Bureau of the Census, *Negroes in the United States, 1920-1932*, p. 71. *Notes:* 1. Includes Baltimore city, St. Louis city, 24 independent cities in Virginia, and that part of Yellowstone National Park in Wyoming.

★ 1636 ★

Black Belt

Counties Reporting Black Inhabitants by Sections, Divisions, and States, 1930

DIVISION AND STATE	Total number of counties	COUNTIES REPORTING	
		Negro inhabitants	No Negro inhabitants
United States	3,100[1]	2,855	245
The North	1,274	1,118	156
The South	1,415	1,395	20
The West	411	342	69
GEOGRAPHIC DIVISIONS:			
New England	67	66	1
Middle Atlantic	150	149	1
East North Central	436	400	36
West North Central	621	503	118
South Atlantic	581	579	2
East South Central	364	364	-
West South Central	470	452	18
Mountain	278	220	58
Pacific	133	122	11
NEW ENGLAND:			
Maine	16	16	-
New Hampshire	10	10	-
Vermont	14	13	1
Massachusetts	14	14	-
Rhode Island	5	5	-
Connecticut	8	8	-
MIDDLE ATLANTIC:			
New York	62	62	-

DIVISION AND STATE	Total number of counties	COUNTIES REPORTING	
		Negro inhabitants	No Negro inhabitants
WEST NORTH CENTRAL-Continued			
North Dakota	53	33	20
South Dakota	69	45	24
Nebraska	93	65	28
Kansas	105	99	6
SOUTH ATLANTIC:			
Delaware	3	3	-
Maryland	24	24	-
District of Columbia	1	1	-
Virginia	124	124	-
West Virginia	55	54	1
North Carolina	100	100	-
South Carolina	46	46	-
Georgia	161	160	1
Florida	67	67	-
EAST SOUTH CENTRAL:			
Kentucky	120	120	-
Tennessee	95	95	-
Alabama	67	67	-
Mississippi	82	82	-
WEST SOUTH CENTRAL:			
Arkansas	75	72	3
Louisiana	64	64	-
Oklahoma	77	73	4

[Continued]

★ 1636 ★

Counties Reporting Black Inhabitants by Sections, Divisions, and States, 1930

[Continued]

DIVISION AND STATE	Total number of counties	COUNTIES REPORTING Negro inhabitants	COUNTIES REPORTING No Negro inhabitants	DIVISION AND STATE	Total number of counties	COUNTIES REPORTING Negro inhabitants	COUNTIES REPORTING No Negro inhabitants
New Jersey	21	21	-	Texas	254	243	11
Pennsylvania	67	66	1				
				MOUNTAIN:			
EAST NORTH CENTRAL:				Montana	56	45	11
Ohio	88	87	1	Idaho	44	30	14
Indiana	92	86	6	Wyoming	24	22	2
Illinois	102	96	6	Colorado	63	54	9
Michigan	83	76	7	New Mexico	31	28	3
Wisconsin	71	55	16	Arizona	14	13	1
				Utah	29	13	16
WEST NORTH CENTRAL:				Nevada	17	15	2
Minnesota	87	71	16				
Iowa	99	87	12	PACIFIC:			
Missouri	115	103	12	Washington	39	33	6
				Oregon	36	32	4
				California	58	57	1

Source: "Number of Counties Reporting Negro Inhabitants, 1930, by Sections, Divisions, and States." U.S. Bureau of the Census, *Negroes in the United States, 1920-1932*, p. 70. *Notes:* 1. Includes Baltimore city, St. Louis city, 24 independent cities in Virginia, and that part of Yellowstone National Park in Wyoming.

★ 1637 ★

Black Belt

Counties with 50 Percent or More Black Population by Divisions and States, Number and Area in Square Miles, 1910, 1920, and 1930 - I

Division And State	Number of Counties 1930	1920	1910	Increase or decrease (-) 1920-30	1910-20
The South	191	221	264	-30	-43
South Atlantic	107	130	156	-23	-26
East South Central	55	54	61	1	-7
West South Central	29	37	47	-8	-10
SOUTH ATLANTIC:					
Maryland	-	-	1	-	-1
Virginia	21	23	32	-2	-9
North Carolina	0	12	14	-3	-2
South Carolina	25	32	33	-7	-1
Georgia	48	58	66	-10	-8
Florida	4	5	10	-1	-5
EAST SOUTH CENTRAL:					
Tennessee	2	2	2	-	-
Alabama	18	18	21	-	-3
Mississippi	35	34	38	1	-4
WEST SOUTH CENTRAL:					
Arkansas	9	11	14	-2	-3

[Continued]

★ 1637 ★

Counties with 50 Percent or More Black Population by Divisions and States, Number and Area in Square Miles, 1910, 1920, and 1930 - I

[Continued]

Division And State	Number of Counties				
	1930	1920	1910	Increase or decrease (-)	
				1920-30	1910-20
Louisiana	16	22	25	-6	-3
Texas	4	4	8	-	-4

Source: "Number and Area of Counties in Which the Negro Population was 50 Percent or More of Total Population, by Divisions, and States: 1930, 1920, and 1910." U.S. Bureau of the Census, *Negroes in the United States, 1920- 1932,* p. 71.

★ 1638 ★

Black Belt

Counties with 50 Percent or More Black Population by Divisions and States, Number and Area in Square Miles, 1910, 1920, and 1930 - II

Division And State	Area of Counties in Square Miles							
	1930	1920	1910	Increase or decrease (-)		Percent of total area of specified section, division, or State		
				1920-30	1910-20	1930	1920	1910
The South	105,315	122,532	147,219	-17,217	-24,687	12.0	14.0	16.8
South Atlantic	50,932	63,883	76,584	-12,951	-12,701	18.9	23.7	28.5
East South Central	36,048	35,598	40,721	450	-5,123	20.1	19.8	22.7
West South Central	18,335	23,051	29,914	-4,716	-6,863	4.3	5.4	7.0
SOUTH ATLANTIC:								
Maryland	-	-	464	-	-464	-	-	4.7
Virginia	7,650	7,882	11,375	-232	-3,493	19.0	19.6	28.3
North Carolina	4,480	6,019	6,044	-1,539	-25	9.2	12.3	12.4
South Carolina	16,452	20,777	23,316	-4,325	-2,539	53.9	68.1	76.5
Georgia	19,791	24,999	27,418	-5,208	-2,419	33.7	42.6	46.7
Florida	2,559	4,206	7,967	-1,647	-3,761	4.7	7.7	14.5
EAST SOUTH CENTRAL:								
Tennessee	1,126	1,126	1,126	-	-	2.7	2.7	2.7
Alabama	14,432	14,428	16,678	4	-2,250	28.1	28.1	32.5
Mississippi	20,490	20,044	22,917	446	-2,873	44.2	43.2	49.4
WEST SOUTH CENTRAL:								
Arkansas	5,934	7,244	9,556	-1,310	-2,312	11.3	13.8	18.2
Louisiana	10,224	13,151	15,207	-2,927	-2,056	22.5	29.0	33.5
Texas	2,177	2,656	5,151	-479	-2,495	.8	1.0	2.0

Source: "Number and Area of Counties in Which the Negro Population was 50 Percent or More of Total Population, by Divisions, and States: 1930, 1920, and 1910." U.S. Bureau of the Census, *Negroes in the United States, 1920- 1932,* p. 71.

★ 1639 ★

Black Belt

County Areas of Black Population by Rates of Black Increase or Decrease, Southern States, 1900-1910

Rate of Increase, 1900-1910	Southern Counties or Combinations of Counties[1]								
	Number	Area		Negro population					
		Square miles	Percentage distribution	Number		Percentage distribution		Increase, 1900-1910[2]	
				1910	1900	1910	1900	Number	Per cent
Total, all counties	1,214	878,326	100.0	8,749,427	7,922,969	100.0	100.0	826,458	10.4
Counties having less than 100 Negroes at each census	143	136,973	15.6	2,690	2,775	[3]	[3]	-85	-3.1
Area of increasing Negro population	603	493,058	56.1	6,491,951	5,435,313	74.2	68.6	1,056,638	19.4
Increasing above average-									
Increase 18 per cent or more	254	287,685	32.8	2,531,665	1,781,533	28.9	22.5	750,132	42.1
Increase 13 to 18 per cent	82	48,162	5.5	994,647	860,301	11.4	10.9	134,256	15.6
Increase 10.5 to 13 per cent	40	20,561	2.3	352,822	315,894	4.0	4.0	36,928	11.7
Increase below average-									
Increase 8 to 10.5 per cent	47	29,050	3.3	669,329	614,958	7.6	7.8	54,371	8.8
Increase 2.5 to 8 per cent	117	72,410	8.2	1,459,576	1,384,180	16.7	17.5	75,396	5.4
Increase 0.0 to 2.5 per cent	63	35,190	4.0	483,912	478,357	5.5	6.0	5,555	1.2
Area of decreasing Negro population	468	248,295	28.3	2,254,786	2,484,881	25.8	31.4	-230,095	-9.3
Decrease 0.0 to 2.5 per cent	56	30,748	3.5	390,999	395,961	4.5	5.0	-4,062	-1.3
Decrease 2.5 to 7.5 per cent	106	61,310	7.0	801,504	843,396	9.2	10.6	-41,892	-5.0
Decrease 7.5 per cent or more	306	156,237	17.8	1,062,283	1,245,524	12.1	15.7	-183,241	-14.7
Area increasing more than the average (10.5 per cent or more)	376	356,408	40.6	3,879,134	2,957,818	44.3	37.3	921,316	31.1
Area increasing less than the average or decreasing	695	384,945	48.8	4,867,603	4,962,376	55.6	62.6	-94,773	-1.9
Area of relatively rapid increase 913 per cent or more)	336	335,847	38.2	3,526,312	2,641,924	40.3	33.3	884,388	33.5
Area of approximately average increase (8 to 13 per cent)	87	49,611	5.6	1,022,151	930,852	11.7	11.7	91,299	9.8
Area of low increase (less than 8 per cent) or decrease	648	355,895	40.5	4,198,274	4,347,418	48.0	54.9	-149,144	-3.4
Area of approximately stationary population (increase or decrease less than 2.5 per cent)	119	65,938	7.5	874,911	847,318	10.0	11.0	593	0.1
Area decreasing more than 2.5 per cent	412	217,547	24.8	1,863,787	2,863,787	21.3	26.4	-225,133	-10.8

Source: "Country Areas and Negro Populations Classified According to Rates to Negro Increase or Decrease, for Southern States: 1900-1910." U.S. Bureau of the Census, *Negro Population, 1790-1915*, p. 112. *Notes:* 1. A minus sign (-) denotes decrease. 2. Less than one-tenth of 1 per cent.

Black Towns and Settlements

★ 1640 ★

Black Settlements in the United States, 1912

City	Population
Alabama:	
Benson (Elmore County)	400
Southern Improvement Company Settlement (Macon Co.)	350
Indiana:	
Bassett Settlement (Howard County)	-
Cabin Creek Settlement (Randolph County)	-
Greenville Settlement (Randolph County)	-
Lost Creek Settlement (Vigo County)	-

[Continued]

★ 1640 ★

Black Settlements in the United States, 1912

[Continued]

City	Population
Roberts Settlement (Hamilton County)	-
Weaver Settlement (Grant County)	-
Michigan:	
Calvin Township (Cass County)	800
New Jersey:	
Snow Hill (Camden County)	1,250
Whitesboro (Cape May County)	100
Ohio:	
Long (Darke County)	500
Wilberforce (Greene County)	300

Source: "The Principal Towns and Settlements in the United States." Work, Monroe N., ed., *Negro Year Book and Annual Encyclopedia of the Negro*, p. 166.

★ 1641 ★

Black Towns and Settlements

Black Settlements in the United States, 1913

City	
SETTLEMENTS	
Alabama:	
Benson (Elmore County)	400
Southern Improvement Company Settlement (Macon Co.)	350
Colorado:	
Deerfield	-
Indiana:	
Bassett Settlement (Howard County)	-
Cabin Creek Settlement (Randolph County)	-
Grenville Settlement (Randolph County)	-
Lost Creek Settlement (Vigo County)	-
Roberts Settlement (Hamilton County)	-
Weaver Settlement (Grant County)	-
Michigan:	
Calvin Township (Cass County)	800
Nebraska:	
Brownlee (Cherry County)	-
New Jersey:	
Snow Hill (Camden County)	1,250
Whitesboro (Cape May County)	100
Ohio:	
Long (Drake County)	500
McIntyre (Jefferson County)	-

[Continued]

★ 1641 ★

Black Settlements in the United States, 1913

[Continued]

City	
Randolph (Mercer County)	-
Wilberforce (Greene County)	300

Source: "Black Towns and Settlements in the United States." Work, Monroe N., ed., *Negro Year Book: An Annual Encyclopedia of the Negro*, pp. 218-219.

★ 1642 ★

Black Towns and Settlements

Black Settlements in the United States, 1918

City	
SETTLEMENTS	
Alabama:	
Baldwin Farms (Macon County)	
Venson (Elmore County)	400
Small Farms, (Limestone County)	
Southern Improvement Company Settlement (Macon Co.)	350
Colorado:	
Deerfield	
Indiana:	
Bassett Settlement (Howard County)	
Cabin Creek Settlement (Randolph County)	
Greenville Settlement (Randolph County)	
Lost Creek Settlement (Vigo County)	
Roberts Settlement (Grant County)	
Michigan:	
Calvin Township (Cass County)	800
Mississippi:	
Des Velente	800
Chambers	
New Africa	
Nebraska:	
Brownlee (Cherry County)	
New Jersey:	
Snow Hill (Camden County)	1,250
Ohio:	
Long (Drake County)	500
McIntyre (Jefferson County)	
Randolph (Mercer County)	
Wilberforce (Greene County)	300

Source: "Black Towns and Settlements in the United States." Work, Monroe N., ed., *Negro Year Book: An Annual Encyclopedia of the Negro 1916-1917*, pp. 317-318.

★ 1643 ★

Black Towns and Settlements

Black Settlements in the United States, 1925

City	
SETTLEMENTS	
Alabama:	
Baldwin Farms (Macon County)	
Benson (Elmore County)	200
Moffatts	
Small Farms (Limestone County)	
Southern Improvement Company Settlements (Macon Co.)	
Arkansas:	
Peace	
Colorado:	
Dearfield	
Indiana:	
Bassett Settlement (Howard County)	
Cabin Creek Settlement (Randolph County)	
Greenville Settlement (Randolph Co.)	
Lost Creek Settlement (Vigo County)	
Roberts Settlement (Hamilton County)	
Weaver Settlement (Grant County)	
Michigan:	
Calvin Township (Cass County)	800
Mississippi:	
Des Velente	800
Chambers	
New Africa	
Nebraska:	
Brownlee (Cherry County)	
New Jersey:	
Snow Hill (Camden County)	1,250
Ohio:	
Long (Darke County)	500
McIntyre (Jefferson County)	
Randolph (Mercer County)	
Wilberforce (Green County)	300

Source: "Black Towns and Settlements in the United States." Work, Monroe N., ed., *Negro Year Book: An Annual Encyclopedia of the Negro 1925-26*, pp. 386-387.

★ 1644 ★

Black Towns and Settlements

Black Towns in the United States, 1912

City	Population
TOWNS	
Alabama:	
Cedarlake (near Decatur)	300
Greenwood Village (Macon County)	300
Hobson City (near Anniston)	300 or 400
Plateau (near Mobile)	200
Arkansas:	
Thomasville	-
California:	
Allensworth	-
Florida:	
Eatonville	200
Georgia:	
Burroughs (Chatham County)	200
Illinois:	
Brooklyn	1,600
Iowa:	
Buxton (1,000 whites)	5,000
Kansas:	
Nicodemus (Graham County)	300
Mississippi:	
Mound Bayou	700
Renoya (Bolivar County)	150
New Jersey:	
Gouldtown (Cumberland County)	250
Springtown (Cumberland County)	200
North Carolina:	
Columbia Heights (a suburb or Winston-Salem)	-
Oklahoma:	
Boley	3,000
Clearview	300
Porter	637
Grayson	411
Langston	339
Lima	200
Mantu	100
Redbird	500
Rentiesville	411
Taft	352
Tatum	200
Tallahassee	350
Vernon	150
Texas:	
Mill City (near Dallas)	300

Source: "The Principal Negro Towns and Settlements in the United States." Work, Monroe, N., ed., *Negro Year Book and Annual Encyclopedia of the Negro*, p. 165-166.

★ 1645 ★

Black Towns and Settlements

Black Towns in the United States, 1913

City	Population
TOWNS	
Alabama:	
Cedarlake (Morgan Co.)	300
Greenwood Village (Macon County)	300
Hobson City (near Anniston)	344
Pleateau (near Mobile)	1,500
Arkansas:	
Thomasville	
California:	
Abila	
Allensworth	
Bowles	
Victorville (San Bernardino County)	
Florida:	
Eatonville	200
Georgia:	
Archery (Sumter County)	
Burroughs (Chatham County)	200
Cannonville (Troup County)	200
Greenough (Mitchell County)	
Odd Fellow City (near Macon)	
Leroy (Burke County)	
Illinois:	
Brooklyn	1,600
Iowa:	
Buxton (1,000 whites)	5,000
Kansas:	
Nicodemus (Graham County)	300
Maryland:	
Lincoln (near Washington, DC)	
Mississippi:	
Expose (Marion County)	
Mound Bayou (Bolivar County)	700
Renova (Bolivar County)	150
New Jersey:	
Gouldtown (Cumerland County)	250
Whitesboro (near Cape May)	100
Springtown (Cumberland County)	200
New Mexico: Blackdom	
North Carolina:	
Columbia Heights (a suburb of Winston-Salem)	
Method (near Raleigh)	
Oberlin (suburb of Raleigh)	
Oklahoma:	
Boley	3,000
Clearview	300
Porter	697

[Continued]

★ 1645 ★

Black Towns in the United States, 1913

[Continued]

City	Population
Grayson	411
Langston	339
Lima	200
Mantu	100
Redbird	500
Rentiesville	411
Taft	352
Tatum	200
Tullahassee	350
Vernon	150
Tennessee:	
New Bedford (near Chattanooga)	
Texas:	
Booker (Red River County)	
Mill City (near Dallas)	300
Oldham (Houston County)	
Roberts	
Union City	
Virginia:	
Jonesboro (near Richmond)	
Ocean Grove (near Norfolk)	
SETTLEMENTS	
Alabama:	
Benson (Elmore County)	400
Southern Improvement Company Settlement (Macon Co.)	350
Colorado:	
Deerfield	
Indiana:	
Bassett Settlement (Howard County)	
Cabin Creek Settlement (Randolph County)	
Greenville Settlement (Randolph County)	
Lost Creek Settlement (Vigo County)	
Roberts Settlement (Hamilton County)	
Weaver Settlement (Grant County)	
Michigan:	
Calvin Township (Cass County)	800
Nebraska:	
Brownlee (Cherry County)	
New Jersey	
Snow Hill (Camden County)	1,250
Ohio:	
Long (Darke County)	500

[Continued]

★ 1645 ★

Black Towns in the United States, 1913

[Continued]

City	Population
McIntyre (Jefferson County)	
Randolph (Mercer County)	
Wilberforce (Greene County)	300

Source: "Negro Towns and Settlements in the United States." Work, Monroe N., ed., *Negro Year Book: An Annual Encyclopedia of the Negro*, pp. 298-299.

★ 1646 ★

Black Towns and Settlements

Black Towns in the United States, 1916

City	Population
TOWNS	
Alabama:	
Cedarlake (Morgan Co.)	300
Greenwood Village (Macon County)	300
Hobson City (near Anniston)	344
Pleateau (near Mobile)	1,500
Arkansas:	
Edmonson	
Thomasville	
California:	
Abila	
Allensworth	
Bowles	
Victorville (San Bernardino County)	
Florida:	
Eatonville	200
New Monrovia (near West Palm Beach)	
Georgia:	
Archery (Sumter County)	
Burroughs (Chatham County)	200
Cannonville (Troup County)	200
Greenough (Mitchell County)	
Odd Fellow City (near Macon)	
Leroy (Burke County)	
Illinois:	
Brooklyn	1,600
Iowa:	
Buxton (1,000 whites)	5,000
Kansas:	
Nicodemus (Graham County)	300

[Continued]

★ 1646 ★

Black Towns in the United States, 1916

[Continued]

City	Population
Kentucky:	
Camp Nelson, New Zion (near Georgetown)	
Maryland:	
Lincoln (near Washington, DC)	
Mississippi:	
Expose (Marion County)	
Mound Bayou (Bolivar County)	700
Renova (Bolivar County)	150
New Jersey:	
Gouldtown (Cumerland County)	250
Whitesboro (near Cape May)	100
Springtown (Cumberland County)	200
New Mexico:	
Blackdom	
North Carolina:	
Columbia Heights (a suburb of Winston-Salem)	
Method (near Raleigh)	
Oberlin (suburb of Raleigh)	
Oklahoma:	
Boley	3,000
Clearview	300
Porter	637
Grayson	411
Langston	339
Lima	200
Mantu	100
Redbird	600
Rentiesville	352
Taft	200
Tatum	350
Tullahassee	150
Vernon	
Tennessee:	
Hortense, (Dickenson County)	
New Bedford (near Chattanooga)	
Texas:	
Booker (Red River County)	
Mill City (near Dallas)	300

[Continued]

★ 1646 ★

Black Towns in the United States, 1916

[Continued]

City	Population
Oldham (Houston County)	
Roberts	
Union City	
Virginia:	
Jonesboro (near Richmond)	
Ocean Grove (near Norfolk)	
Titustown (near Norfolk)	
West Virginia:	
Institute, (Kanawha County)	600

Source: "Negro Towns and Settlements in the United States." Work, Monroe N., ed., *Negro Year Book: An Annual Encyclopedia of the Negro 1916-1917*, 1918.

★ 1647 ★

Black Towns and Settlements

Black Towns in the United States, 1925

City	Population
TOWNS	
Alabama:	
Cedarlake (Morgan Co.)	300
Greenwood Village (Macon County)	500
Hobson City (near Anniston)	34
Pleateau (near Mobile)	
Shepherdsville (Dallas County)	1,500
Arkansas:	
Biscoe	700
Edmondson	300
Thomasville	
California:	
Abila	
Allensworth	
Bowles	
Victorville (San Bernardino County)	
Florida:	
Eatonville	200
New Monrovia (near West Palm Beach)	
Georgia:	
Archery (Sumter County)	200
Burroughs (Chatham County)	200

[Continued]

★ 1647 ★

Black Towns in the United States, 1925

[Continued]

City	Population
Cannonville (Troup County)	
Greenough (Mitchell County)	
Odd Fellow City (near Macon)	
Leroy (Burke County)	
Illinois:	
Brooklyn	3,000
Robbins	500
Iowa:	
Buxton (1,000 whites)	5,000
Kansas:	
Nicodemus (Graham County)	300
Kentucky:	
Camp Nelson, New Zion (near Georgetown)	
Maryland:	
Lincoln (near Washington, DC)	
Highland Beach	
North Brentwood	500
Michigan:	
Idlewild (lake County)	
Marlborough	
Mississippi:	
Expose (Marion County)	
Mound Bayou (Bolivar County)	700
Renova (Bolivar County)	150
New Jersey:	
Gouldtown (Cumerland County)	250
Whitesboro (near Cape May)	100
Springtown (Cumberland County)	200
New Mexico:	
Blackdom	
North Carolina:	
Columbia Heights (a suburb of Winston-Salem)	
Method (near Raleigh)	
Oberlin (suburb of Raleigh)	
Oklahoma:	
Boley	3,000
Bookertee	
Clearview	300
Porter	637
Grayson	411
Langston	339
Lima	200
Mantu	100
Redbird	500
Rentiesville	411
Taft	352
Tatum	200

[Continued]

★ 1647 ★

Black Towns in the United States, 1925

[Continued]

City	Population
Tullahassee	350
Vernon	150
South Carolina:	
Booker Washington Heights (new Columbia)	
Tennessee:	
Hortense, (Dickenson County)	
New Bedford (near Chattanooga)	
Texas:	
Andy (Cherokee County)	
Booker (Red River County)	
Independence Heights (near Houston)	
Mill City (near Dallas)	
Oldham (Houston County)	300
Roberts	
Union City	
Virginia:	
Coardtown (Accomac County)	400
Hare Valley (Northampton County)	500
Ocean Grove (near Norfolk)	
Titustown (near Norfolk)	
Truxton (near Norfolk)	
West Virginia:	
Institute, (Kanawha County)	600

Source: "Negro Towns and Settlements in the United States." Work, Monroe N., ed., *Negro Year Book: An Annual Encyclopedia of the Negro 1925-26*, pp. 38-386.

Black and Mulatto Population

★ 1648 ★

American Black and Mulatto Population in the Western Hemisphere, 1940

	Negro Population	Per Cent of Total	Mulatto Population	Per Cent of Total	Total Population All Races
North of Mexico:					
Greenland	0	00	[2]	[2]	18,000
Alaska	150	.21	[2]	[2]	72,361
Canada	20,559	1.80	[2]	[2]	11,422,000
United States	12,765,518[1]	9.80	[2]	[2]	131,669,275
TOTAL	12,886,227	9.00	[2]	[2]	143,181,636

[Continued]

★ 1648 ★

American Black and Mulatto Population in the Western Hemisphere, 1940

[Continued]

	Negro Population	Per Cent of Total	Mulatto Population	Per Cent of Total	Total Population All Races
Mexico, Antilles, Central America:					
Mexico	80,000	.41	40,000	.20	19,446,065
Antilles	5,500,000	39.29	3,000,000	21.43	14,000,000
Guatemala	4,011	.12	2,000	.06	3,284,269
British Honduras	15,000	25.55	20,000	34.03	58,7559
Honduras	55,275	4.99	10,000	.90	1,107,859
El Salvador	100	.0001	100	.0001	1,744,535
Nicaragua	90,000	6.52	40,000	2.88	1,380,387
Costa Rica	26,900	4.09	20,000	.14	656,129
Panama	82,871	13.12	271,208	42.912	631,549
TOTAL	5,854,157	13.84	3,403,308	8.04	42,309,452
South America:					
Columbia	405,076	4.50	2,205,382	24.31	9,206,283
Venezuela	100,000	2.79	1,000,000	27.93	3,580,000
British Guiana	100,000	29.30	80,000	23.44	541,237
Dutch Guiana	17,000	9.55	20,000	11.23	177,980
French Guiana	1,000	.25	1,000	.25	40,000
Ecaudaor	50,000	2.00	150,000	6.00	2,500,000
Peru	29,054	.41	80,000	.71	7,023,111
Bolivia	7,800	.26	5,000	.15	3,300,000
Brazil	5,789,924	14.00	8,276,321	20.01	41,356,605
Paraguay	5,000	.52	5,000	.52	960,000
Uruguay	10,000	.46	50,000	2.30	2,145,545
Chile	1,000	.02	3,000	.06	5,023,539
Argentina	5,000	.038	10,000	.076	13,129,723
TOTAL	6,520,854	7.34	11,885,703	13.38	88,784,023
SUMMARY:					
North of Mexico	12,866,227	9.00	[2]	[2]	143,181,638
Mexico, Antilles and Central America	5,854,157	13.84	3,403,308	8.04	42,309,452
South America	6,520,854	7.34	11.885,703	13.40	88,784,023
Total in Americas in 1940	25,261,238	9.21	15,289,011	5.56	274,275,111

Source: "American Negro and Mulatto Population in the Western Hemisphere, 1940." Guzman, Jessie Parkhurst, ed., *Negro Year Book: A Review of Events Affecting Negro Life, 1941-1946*, p. 198. *Notes:* Adapted from Angel Rosenblatt, la Poblacion indigene de America, desde 1492 hasta la actualidad, Institucion Cultural Espanola, Buenos Aires, 1945. This table is taken from an article by Frank Tannenbaum in Political Science Quarterly, March 1946. 1. United States Census Report, 1940. 2. Included under Negroes.

★ 1649 ★

Black and Mulatto Population

Black Population Classified as Black and Mulatto, by Divisions and States, 1870, 1890, and 1910 - I

Division and State	Negro Population								
	1910			1890			1870		
	Total	Black	Mulatto	Total	Black	Mulatto	Total	Black	Mulatto
United States	9,827,763	7,777,077	2,050,686	7,488,676	6,337,980	1,132,060	4,880,009	4,295,960	584,049
GEOGRAPHIC DIVISIONS:									
New England	66,306	44,156	22,150	44,580	30,001	14,579	31,705	22,625	9,080
Middle Atlantic	417,870	335,901	81,969	225,326	177,174	48,152	148,033	126,044	21,989
East North Central	300,836	201,027	99,809	207,023	130,024	76,999	130,497	92,372	38,125
West North Central	242,662	173,031	69,631	224,089	167,307	56,782	142,583	119,703	22,880
South Atlantic	4,112,488	3,256,669	855,819	3,262,690	2,823,905	438,785	2,216,705	1,985,984	230,721
East South Central	2,652,513	2,145,458	507,055	2,119,797	1,830,762	289,762	1,464,252	1,302,024	162,228
West South Central	21,467	15,332	6,135	12,971	8,334	4,637	1,555	1,082	473
Pacific	29,195	19,063	10,132	14,110	8,143	5,967	4,825	3,027	1,798
NEW ENGLAND:									
Maine	1,363	737	626	1,190	507	683	1,606	1,014	592
New Hampshire	564	356	208	614	248	366	580	436	144
Vermont	1,621	1,185	436	937	521	416	924	677	247
Massachusetts	38,055	24,100	13,955	22,144	14,108	8,036	13,947	9,686	4,261
Rhode Island	9,529	6,350	3,179	7,393	5,396	1,997	4,980	3,820	1,160
Connecticut	15,174	11,428	3,746	12,302	9,221	3,081	9,668	6,992	2,676
MIDDLE ATLANTIC:									
New York	134,191	103,583	30,608	70,092	54,852	15,240	52,081	46,498	5,583
New Jersey	89,760	75,553	14,207	47,638	40,436	7,202	30,658	27,105	3,553
Pennsylvania	193,919	156,765	37,154	107,596	81,886	25,710	65,294	52,441	12,853
EAST NORTH CENTRAL:									
Ohio	111,452	72,203	39,249	87,113	50,078	37,035	63,213	45,374	17,839
Indiana	60,320	45,767	14,553	45,215	31,557	13,658	24,560	17,548	7,012
Illinois	109,049	72,221	36,828	57,028	40,346	16,682	28,762	21,419	7,343
Michigan	17,115	9,079	8,036	15,223	7,036	8,187	11,849	6,434	5,415
Wisconsin	2,900	1,757	1,143	2,444	1,007	1,437	2,113	1,597	516
WEST NORTH CENTRAL:									
Minnesota	7,084	4,468	2,616	3,683	1,981	1,702	759	514	245
Iowa	14,973	11,329	3,644	10,685	7,503	3,182	5,762	4,669	1,093
Missouri	157,452	112,762	44,690	150,184	114,739	35,445	118,071	100,412	17,659
North Dakota	617	460	157	373	153	220	94[3]	71[3]	23[3]
South Dakota	817	521	296	541	310	231	94[3]	71[3]	23[3]
Nebraska	7,689	5,602	2,087	8,913	6,091	2,822	789	738	51
Kansas	54,030	37,889	16,141	49,710	36,530	13,180	17,108	13,299	3,809
SOUTH ATLANTIC:									
Delaware	31,181	27,475	3,706	28,386	24,837	3,549	22,794	20,570	2,224
Maryland	232,250	189,098	43,152	215,657	181,296	34,361	175,391	151,463	23,928
District of Columbia	94,446	61,494	32,952	75,572	55,736	19,836	43,404	35,372	8,032
Virginia	671,096	448,186	222,910	635,438	512,997	122,441	512,841	440,593	72,248
West Virginia	64,173	43,294	20,879	32,600	23,336	9,354	17,980	13,640	4,340
North Carolina	697,843	553,720	144,123	561,018	483,817	77,201	391,650	354,209	37,441
South Carolina	835,843	701,462	134,381	688,934	621,781	67,153	415,814	387,985	27,829
Georgia	1,176,987	972,782	204,205	858,815	773,682	85,142	545,142	501,814	43,328

[Continued]

★ 1649 ★

Black Population Classified as Black and Mulatto, by Divisions and States, 1870, 1890, and 1910 - I

[Continued]

Division and State	Negro Population								
	1910			1890			1870		
	Total	Black	Mulatto	Total	Black	Mulatto	Total	Black	Mulatto
Florida	308,669	259,158	49,511	166,180	146,423	19,757	91,689	80,338	11,351
EAST SOUTH CENTRAL:									
Kentucky	261,656	195,713	65,943	268,071	216,085	51,986	222,210	177,499	44,711
Tennessee	473,088	354,391	118,697	430,678	356,215	74,463	322,331	292,029	30,302
Alabama	908,282	756,872	151,410	678,489	601,069	77,420	475,510	433,698	41,812
Mississippi	1,009,487	838,482	171,005	742,559	657,393	85,166	444,201	398,798	45,403
WEST SOUTH CENTRAL:									
Arkansas	442,891	361,520	81,371	309,117	269,487	39,630	122,169	109,831	12,338
Louisiana	713,874	561,297	152,577	559,193	468,240	90,953	364,210	307,610	56,600
Oklahoma	137,612	98,269	39,343	21,609[2]	2,156	817	-	-	-
Texas	690,049	565,354	124,695	488,171	422,447	65,724	253,475	225,658	27,817
MOUNTAIN:									
Montana	1,834	1,223	611	1,490	1,086	404	183	137	46
Idaho	651	425	226	201	100	101	60	60	-
Wyoming	2,235	1,942	293	922	671	251	183	96	87
Colorado	11,453	7,815	3,638	6,215	4,056	2,159	456	272	184
New Mexico	1,628	1,189	439	1,956	970	986	172	116	56
Arizona	2,009	1,561	448	1,357	932	425	26	26	-
Utah	1,144	854	290	588	379	209	118	85	33
Nevada	513	323	190	242	140	102	357	290	67
PACIFIC:									
Washington	6,058	4,218	1,840	1,602	1,044	558	207	56	151
Oregon	1,492	1,058	434	1,186	557	629	346	259	87
California	21,645	13,787	7,858	11,322	6,542	4,780	4,272	2,712	1,560

Source: "Negro Population, Classified as Black and Mulatto, by Divisions and States: 1910, 1890, 1870." U.S. Bureau of the Census, *Negro Population, 1790-1915,* p. 218. *Notes:* 1. Per cent not shown where base is less than 100. 2. Includes 18,636 Negroes enumerated in Indian Territory, not distinguished as black or mulatto. 3. Data includes North and South Dakota.

★ 1650 ★

Black and Mulatto Population

Black Population Classified as Black and Mulatto, by Divisions and States, 1870, 1890, and 1910 - II

Division and State	Per Cent of Total Negro Population					
	1910		1890		1870	
	Black	Mulatto	Black	Mulatto	Black	Mulatto
United States	79.1	20.9	84.8	15.2	88.0	12.0
GEOGRAPHIC DIVISIONS:						
New England	66.6	33.4	67.3	32.7	71.4	28.6
Middle Atlantic	80.4	19.6	78.6	21.4	85.1	14.9

[Continued]

★ 1650 ★

Black Population Classified as Black and Mulatto, by Divisions and States, 1870, 1890, and 1910 - II

[Continued]

Division and State	Per Cent of Total Negro Population					
	1910		1890		1870	
	Black	Mulatto	Black	Mulatto	Black	Mulatto
East North Central	66.8	33.2	62.8	37.2	70.8	29.2
West North Central	71.3	28.7	74.7	25.3	84.0	16.0
South Atlantic	79.2	20.8	86.6	13.4	89.6	10.4
East South Central	80.9	19.1	86.4	13.6	88.9	11.1
West South Central	79.9	20.1	85.5	14.5	86.9	13.1
Pacific	71.4	28.6	64.3	35.7	69.6	30.4
NEW ENGLAND:						
Maine	54.1	45.9	42.6	57.4	63.1	36.9
New Hampshire	63.1	36.9	40.4	59.6	75.2	24.8
Vermont	73.1	26.9	55.6	44.4	73.3	26.7
Massachusetts	63.3	36.7	63.7	36.3	69.4	30.6
Rhode Island	66.6	33.4	73.0	27.0	76.7	23.3
Connecticut	75.3	24.7	75.0	25.0	72.3	27.7
MIDDLE ATLANTIC:						
New York	77.2	22.8	78.3	21.7	89.3	10.7
New Jersey	84.2	15.8	84.9	15.1	88.4	11.6
Pennsylvania	80.8	19.2	76.1	23.9	80.3	19.7
EAST NORTH CENTRAL:						
Ohio	64.8	35.2	57.5	42.5	71.8	28.2
Indiana	75.9	24.1	69.8	30.2	71.4	28.6
Illinois	66.2	33.8	70.7	29.3	74.5	25.5
Michigan	53.0	47.0	46.2	53.8	54.3	45.7
Wisconsin	60.6	39.4	41.2	58.8	75.6	24.4
WEST NORTH CENTRAL:						
Minnesota	63.1	36.9	53.8	46.2	67.7	32.3
Iowa	75.7	24.3	70.2	29.8	81.0	19.0
Missouri	71.6	28.4	76.4	23.6	85.0	15.0
North Dakota	74.6	25.4	41.0	59.0	[1,3]	[1,3]
South Dakota	63.8	36.2	57.3	42.7	[1,3]	[1,3]
Nebraska	72.9	27.1	68.3	31.7	93.5	6.5
Kansas	70.1	29.9	73.5	26.5	77.7	22.3
SOUTH ATLANTIC:						
Delaware	88.1	11.9	87.5	12.5	90.2	9.8
Maryland	81.4	18.6	84.1	15.9	86.4	13.6
District of Columbia	65.1	34.9	73.8	26.2	81.5	18.5
Virginia	66.8	33.2	80.7	19.3	85.8	14.1
West Virginia	67.5	32.5	71.4	28.6	75.9	24.1
North Carolina	79.3	20.7	86.2	13.8	90.4	9.6
South Carolina	83.9	16.1	90.3	9.7	93.3	6.7

[Continued]

★ 1650 ★

Black Population Classified as Black and Mulatto, by Divisions and States, 1870, 1890, and 1910 - II

[Continued]

Division and State	Per Cent of Total Negro Population					
	1910		1890		1870	
	Black	Mulatto	Black	Mulatto	Black	Mulatto
Georgia	82.7	17.3	90.1	9.9	92.1	7.9
Florida	84.0	16.0	88.1	11.9	87.6	12.4
EAST SOUTH CENTRAL:						
Kentucky	74.8	25.2	80.6	19.4	79.9	20.1
Tennessee	74.9	25.1	82.7	17.3	90.6	9.4
Alabama	83.3	16.7	88.6	11.4	91.2	8.8
Mississippi	83.1	16.9	88.5	11.5	89.8	10.2
WEST SOUTH CENTRAL:						
Arkansas	81.6	18.4	87.2	12.8	89.9	10.1
Louisiana	78.6	21.4	83.7	16.3	84.5	15.5
Oklahoma	71.4	28.6	72.5	27.5	-	-
Texas	81.9	18.1	86.5	13.5	89.0	11.0
MOUNTAIN:						
Montana	66.7	33.3	72.9	27.1	74.9	25.1
Idaho	65.3	34.7	49.8	50.2	[1]	-
Wyoming	86.9	13.1	72.8	27.2	52.5	47.5
Colorado	68.2	31.8	65.3	34.7	59.6	40.4
New Mexico	73.0	27.0	49.6	50.4	67.4	32.6
Arizona	77.7	22.3	68.7	31.3	[1]	-
Utah	74.7	25.3	64.5	35.5	72.0	28.0
Nevada	63.0	37.0	57.9	42.1	81.2	18.8
PACIFIC:						
Washington	69.6	30.4	65.3	34.8	27.1	72.9
Oregon	70.9	29.1	47.0	53.0	74.9	25.1
California	63.7	36.3	57.8	42.2	63.5	36.5

Source: "Negro Population, Classified as Black and Mulatto, by Divisions and States: 1910, 1890, 1870." U.S. Bureau of the Census, *Negro Population, 1790-1915*, p. 218. *Notes:* 1. Per cent not shown where base is less than 100. 2. Includes 18,636 Negroes enumerated in Indian Territory, not distinguished as black or mulatto. 3. Data includes North and South Dakota.

★ 1651 ★

Black and Mulatto Population

Black and Mulatto Elements of the Population, Percent of Total, 1850-1920

Census Year	Negro Population			Per Cent of Total	
	Total	Black	Mulatto	Black	Mulatto
1920	10,463,131	8,802,577	1,660,554	84.1	15.9
1910	9,827,763	7,777,077	2,050,686	79.1	20.9
1890	7,488,676	6,337,980	1,132,060	84.8	15.2
1870	4,880,009	4,295,960	584,049	88.0	12.0
1860	4,441,830	3,853,467	588,363	86.8	13.2
1850	3,638,808	3,233,057	405,751	88.8	11.2

Source: "Black and Mulatto Population, 1850-1920." Work, Monroe N., ed., *Negro Year Book: An Annual Encyclopedia of the Negro, 1925-26*. p. 429. Primary source: U.S. Census.

★ 1652 ★

Black and Mulatto Population

Black and Mulatto Elements of the Population, Percentage and Section, 1850-1920

Section	Total	Black	Mulatto		Mulattoes to 1000 blacks
			Number	Per Cent	
			1850		
United States	3,638,808	3,233,057	405,751	11.2	126
The South	3,352,198	3,017,490	334,708	10.0	111
The North	285,369	214,617	70,752	24.8	329
The West	1,241	950	291	23.4	306
			1870		
United States	4,880,009	2,295,960	584,960	12.0	136
The South	4,420,811	3,391,107	489,704	11.1	125
The North	452,818	360,744	92,074	20.3	255
The West	6,380	4,109	2,271	35.6	553
			1890		
United States	7,488,686[1]	6,337,980	1,132,060	15.2	179
The South	6,760,577[1]	5,816,997	924,944	13.7	159
The North	701,018	504,506	196,512	28.0	390
The West	27,081	16,477	10,604	39.2	644

[Continued]

★ 1652 ★

Black and Mulatto Elements of the Population, Percentage and Section, 1850-1920

[Continued]

Section	Total	Black	Mulatto		Mulattoes to 1000 blacks
			Number	Per Cent	
			1910		
United States	9,827,763	7,777,077	2,050,686	20.9	264
The South	8,749,427	6,988,567	1,760,567	20.1	252
The North	1,027,674	754,115	273,559	26.6	363
The West	50,662	34,395	16,267	32.1	473
			1920		
United States	10,463,131	8,802,577	1,660,554	15.9	189
The South	8,912,231	7,514,724	1,397,507	15.7	186
The North	1,472,309	1,228,848	243,461	16.5	198
The West	78,591	59,005	19,586	24.9	366

Source: "Black and Mulatto Elements Negro Population United States." Work, Monroe N., ed., *Negro Year Book: An Annual Encyclopedia of the Negro, 1937- 38,* p. 247. *Notes:* 1. Includes 18,636 Negroes enumerated in Indian Territory not distinguished as black or mulatto.

★ 1653 ★

Black and Mulatto Population

Black and Mulatto Population Increases, 1850-1910

Section	Negro Population				
	Total	Black	Mulatto		Mulattoes to 1,000 blacks
			Number	Percent	
			1910		
United States	9,827,763	7,777,077	2,050,686	20.9	264
The South	8,749,427	6,988,567	1,760,860	20.1	252
The North	1,027,674	754,115	273,559	26.6	363
The West	50,662	34,395	10,267	32.1	473
			1890		
United States	7,488,676[1]	6,337,980	1,132,060	15.2	179
The South	6,760,577[1]	5,816,997	924,944	13.7	159
The North	701,018	504,506	196,512	28.0	390
The West	27,081	16,477	10,604	39.2	644
			1870		
United States	4,880,009	4,295,960	584,049	12.0	136
The South	4,420,811	3,931,107	489,704	11.1	125

[Continued]

★ 1653 ★

Black and Mulatto Population Increases, 1850-1910

[Continued]

Section	Negro Population				Mulattoes to 1,000 blacks
	Total	Black	Mulatto		
			Number	Percent	
The North	452,818	360,744	92,074	20.3	255
The West	6,380	4,109	2,271	35.6	553
			1850		
United States	3,638,808	3,233,057	405,751	11.2	126
The South	3,352,198	3,017,490	334,708	10.0	111
The North	285,369	214,617	70,752	24.8	329
The West	1,241	950	291	23.4	306

Source: "Increase of the Negro Population." U.S. Bureau of the Census, *Negro Population, 1790-1915*, p. 210. *Notes:* 1. Includes 18,636 Negroes enumerated in Indiana Territory, not distinguished as black or mulatto.

★ 1654 ★

Black and Mulatto Population

Black and Mulatto Population by Sex and Sex Ratio by Divisions and States, 1930

Division and State	Black and Mulatto Population: 1910											
	Black						Mulatto					
	Total	Male	Female	Excess of-		Males to 1,000 females	Total	Male	Female	Excess of-		Males to 1,000 females
				Males	Females					Males	Females	
UNITED STATES	7,777,077	3,922,332	3,854,746	67,587	-	1,018	2,050,686	963,549	1,087,137	-	123,588	886
GEOGRAPHIC DIVISIONS:												
New England	44,156	21,737	22,419	-	682	970	22,150	11,046	11,104	-	58	995
Middle Atlantic	335,901	165,079	170,822	-	5,743	966	81,969	38,387	43,582	-	5,195	881
East North Central	201,027	107,294	93,733	13,561	-	1,145	99,809	49,137	50,672	-	1,535	970
West North Central	173,031	92,134	80,897	11,237	-	1,139	69,631	33,730	35,901	-	2,171	940
South Atlantic	3,256,669	1,629,697	1,626,972	2,725	-	1,002	855,819	400,111	455,708	-	55,597	878
East South Central	2,145,458	1,081,064	1,064,394	16,670	-	1,016	507,055	234,728	272,327	-	37,599	862
West South Central	1,586,440	805,910	780,530	25,380	-	1,033	397,986	188,115	209,871	-	21,756	896
Mountain	15,332	8,697	6,635	2,062	-	1,311	6,135	3,069	3,066	3	-	1,001
Pacific	19,063	10,720	8,343	2,377	-	1,285	10,132	5,226	4,906	320	-	1,065
NEW ENGLAND:												
Maine	737	385	352	33	-	1,094	626	315	311	4	-	1,013
New Hampshire	356	167	189	-	22	884	208	121	87	34	-	[1]
Vermont	1,185	916	269	647	-	3,405	436	257	179	78	-	1,436
Massachusetts	24,100	11,652	12,448	-	796	936	13,955	7,096	6,859	237	-	1,035
Rhode Island	6,350	3,124	3,226	-	102	968	3,179	1,521	1,658	-	137	917
Connecticut	11,428	5,493	5,935	-	442	926	3,746	1,736	2,010	-	274	864
MIDDLE ATLANTIC:												
New York	103,583	50,009	53,574	-	3,565	933	30,608	14,025	16,583	-	2,558	846
New Jersey	75,553	36,914	38,639	-	1,725	955	14,207	6,688	7,519	-	831	889
Pennsylvania	156,765	78,156	78,609	-	453	994	37,154	17,674	19,480	-	1,806	907
EAST NORTH CENTRAL:												
Ohio	72,203	38,664	33,539	5,125	-	1,153	39,249	19,331	19,918	-	587	971
Indiana	45,767	23,935	21,832	2,103	-	1,096	14,553	7,109	7,444	-	335	955
Illinois	72,221	38,851	33,370	5,481	-	1,164	36,828	18,058	18,770	-	712	962
Michigan	9,079	4,941	4,138	803	-	1,194	8,036	4,066	3,970	96	-	1,024

[Continued]

★ 1654 ★

Black and Mulatto Population by Sex and Sex Ratio by Divisions and States, 1930

[Continued]

Division and State	Black and Mulatto Population: 1910											
	Black						Mulatto					
	Total	Male	Female	Excess of-		Males to 1,000 females	Total	Male	Female	Excess of-		Males to 1,000 females
				Males	Females					Males	Females	
Wisconsin	1,757	903	854	49	-	1,057	1,143	573	570	3	-	1,005
WEST NORTH CENTRAL:												
Minnesota	4,468	2,689	1,779	910	-	1,512	2,616	1,494	1,122	372	-	1,332
Iowa	11,329	6,282	5,047	1,235	-	1,245	3,644	1,838	1,806	323	-	1,018
Missouri	112,762	56,277	53,485	5,792	-	1,108	44,690	21,212	23,478	-	2,266	903
North Dakota	460	286	174	112	-	1,644	157	95	62	33	-	[1]
South Dakota	521	304	217	87	-	1,401	296	164	132	32	-	1,242
Nebraska	5,602	3,175	2,427	748	-	1,308	2,087	1,084	1,003	81	-	1,081
Kansas	37,889	20,121	17,768	2,353	-	1,132	16,141	7,843	8,298	-	455	945
SOUTH ATLANTIC:												
Delaware	27,475	14,235	13,240	995	-	1,075	3,706	1,776	1,930	-	154	920
Maryland	189,098	94,910	94,188	722	-	1,008	43,152	19,839	23,313	-	3,474	851
District of Columbia	61,494	28,254	33,240	-	4,986	850	32,952	14,361	18,591	-	4,230	772
Virginia	448,186	225,365	222,821	2,544	-	1,011	222,910	105,177	117,733	-	12,556	893
West Virginia	43,294	25,630	17,664	7,966	-	1,451	20,879	10,977	9,902	1,075	-	1,109
North Carolina	553,720	272,290	281,421	-	9,122	968	144,123	67,282	76,841	-	9,559	876
South Carolina	701,462	345,142	356,320	-	11,178	969	134,381	62,936	71,445	-	8,509	881
Georgia	972,782	486,012	486,770	-	758	998	204,205	94,251	109,954	-	15,703	857
Florida	259,158	137,850	121,308	16,542	-	1,136	49,511	23,512	25,999	-	2,487	904
EAST SOUTH CENTRAL:												
Kentucky	195,713	101,071	94,642	6,429	-	1,068	65,943	30,421	35,522	-	5,101	856
Tennessee	354,391	179,678	174,713	4,965	-	1,028	118,697	54,032	64,665	-	10,633	836
Alabama	756,872	377,869	379,003	-	1,134	997	151,410	69,925	81,485	-	11,560	858
Mississippi	838,482	422,446	416,036	6,410	-	1,015	171,005	80,350	90,655	-	10,305	886
WEST SOUTH CENTRAL:												
Arkansas	361,520	184,637	176,883	7,754	-	1,044	81,371	38,686	42,685	-	3,999	906
Louisiana	561,297	282,094	279,203	2,891	-	1,010	152,577	71,730	80,847	-	9,117	887
Oklahoma	98,269	52,360	45,909	6,451	-	1,141	39,343	19,577	19,766	-	189	990
Texas	565,354	286,819	278,535	8,284	-	1,030	124,695	58,122	66,573	-	8,451	873
MOUNTAIN:												
Montana	1,223	726	497	229	-	1,461	611	332	279	53	-	1,190
Idaho	425	269	156	113	-	1,724	226	129	97	32	-	[1]
Wyoming	1,942	1,374	568	806	-	2,419	293	170	123	47	-	1,382
Colorado	7,815	4,1117	3,698	419	-	1,113	3,638	1,750	1,888	-	138	927
New Mexico	1,189	673	516	157	-	1,304	439	218	221	-	3	986
Arizona	1,561	820	741	79	-	1,107	448	234	214	20	-	1,093
Utah	854	536	318	218	-	1,686	290	155	135	20	-	1,148
Nevada	323	182	141	41	-	1,291	190	81	109	-	28	743
PACIFIC:												
Washington	4,218	2,680	1,538	1,142	-	1,742	1,840	1,056	784	272	-	1,347
Oregon	1,058	662	396	266	-	1,672	434	245	189	56	-	1,296
California	13,787	7,378	6,409	969	-	1,151	7,858	3,925	3,933	-	8	998

Source: "Black and Mulatto Population, Classified by Sex, with Excess of Males or Females, and Sex Ratio, by Divisions and States: 1910." U.S. Bureau of the Census, *Negro Population, 1790-1915.* p. 222. *Note:* 1. Ratio not shown where the number of females is less than 100.

★ 1655 ★

Black and Mulatto Population

Black and Mulatto Population, Urban and Rural, by Gender, Divisions, and States, 1910

Division and State	Negro Population: 1910											
	Urban						Rural					
	Both sexes		Male		Female		Both sexes		Male		Female	
	Black	Mulatto	Black	Mulatto	Black	Mulatto	Black	Mulatto	Black	Mulatto	Black	Mulatto
UNITED STATES	1,957,709	731,520	952,085	327,399	1,005,624	404,121	5,819,368	1,319,166	2,970,247	636,150	2,849,121	683,016
GEOGRAPHIC DIVISIONS:												
New England	41,342	19,535	20,228	9,468	21,114	10,067	2,814	2,615	1,509	1,578	1,305	1,037
Middle Atlantic	270,946	68,300	130,050	31,403	140,896	36,897	64,955	13,669	35,029	6,984	29,926	6,685
East North Central	155,398	75,144	81,765	36,118	73,633	39,026	45,629	24,665	25,529	13,019	20,100	11,646
West North Central	113,481	50,820	59,451	24,358	54,030	26,462	59,550	18,811	32,683	9,372	26,867	9,439
South Atlantic	652,247	257,273	308,584	112,035	343,663	145,238	2,604,422	598,546	1,321,113	288,076	1,283,309	310,470
East South Central	373,417	135,680	180,024	58,179	193,393	77,501	1,772,041	371,375	901,040	176,549	871,001	194,826
West South Central	324,386	111,452	157,831	49,293	166,555	62,159	1,262,054	286,534	648,079	138,822	613,975	147,712
Mountain	10,867	4,579	5,729	2,189	5,138	2,390	4,465	1,556	2,968	880	1,497	676
Pacific	15,625	8,737	8,423	4,356	7,202	4,381	3,438	1,395	2,297	870	1,141	525
NEW ENGLAND:												
Maine	528	396	277	174	251	222	209	230	108	141	101	89
New Hampshire	270	86	110	49	160	37	86	122	57	72	29	50
Vermont	1,059	282	841	163	218	119	126	154	75	94	51	60
Massachusetts	22,952	12,291	11,044	6,057	11,908	6,234	1,148	1,664	608	1,039	540	625
Rhode Island	6,009	3,046	2,932	1,447	3,077	1,599	341	133	192	74	149	59
Connecticut	10,524	3,434	5,024	1,578	5,500	1,856	904	312	469	158	435	154
MIDDLE ATLANTIC:												
New York	89,488	27,028	42,028	12,615	47,460	15,383	14,095	2,610	7,981	1,410	6,114	1,200
New Jersey	54,962	10,465	25,932	4,850	29,030	5,615	20,591	3,742	10,982	1,838	9,609	1,904
Pennsylvania	126,496	29,837	62,090	13,938	64,406	15,899	30,269	7,317	16,066	3,736	14,203	3,581
EAST NORTH CENTRAL:												
Ohio	54,565	27,717	28,866	13,208	25,699	14,509	17,638	11,532	9,798	6,123	7,840	5,409
Indiana	36,746	11,679	11,895	5,590	17,851	6,089	9,021	2,874	5,040	1,519	2,981	1,355
Illinois	55,472	30,066	29,438	14,577	26,034	15,489	16,749	6,762	9,413	3,481	7,336	3,281
Michigan	7,276	4,880	3,893	2,362	3,383	2,518	1,803	3,156	1,048	1,704	755	1,452
Wisconsin	1,339	802	673	381	666	421	418	341	230	192	188	149
WEST NORTH CENTRAL:												
Minnesota	4,117	2,401	2,502	1,362	1,615	1,039	351	215	187	132	164	83
Iowa	7,066	2,720	3,881	1,334	3,185	1,386	4,263	924	2,401	504	1,862	420
Missouri	72,042	32,420	37,343	15,275	34,699	17,145	40,720	12,270	21,934	5,937	18,786	6,333
North Dakota	230	76	147	50	83	26	230	81	139	45	91	36
South Dakota	277	135	161	67	116	68	244	161	143	97	101	64
Nebraska	4,844	1,777	2,712	914	2,132	863	758	310	463	170	295	140
Kansas	24,905	11,291	12,705	5,356	12,200	5,935	12,984	4,850	7,416	2,487	5,568	2,363
SOUTH ATLANTIC:												
Delaware	10,064	1,093	4,913	479	5,151	614	17,411	2,613	9,322	1,297	8,089	1,316
Maryland	77,148	22,082	36,292	9,654	40,856	12,428	111,950	21,070	58,618	10,185	53,332	10,885
District of Columbia	61,494	32,952	28,254	14,361	33,240	18,591	-	-	-	-	-	-
Virginia	95,447	62,771	44,950	27,854	50,497	34,917	352,739	160,139	180,415	77,323	172,324	82,816
West Virginia	10,163	5,217	5,463	2,482	4,700	2,735	33,131	15,662	20,167	8,495	8,495	7,167
North Carolina	90,404	25,571	41,896	10,900	48,508	14,671	463,316	119,552	230,403	56,382	232,913	62,170
South Carolina	71,945	29,757	33,095	12,884	38,850	16,873	629,624	104,624	312,047	50,052	317,470	54,572
Georgia	167,375	57,451	78,931	24,300	88,444	33,151	805,407	146,754	407,081	69,951	398,326	76,803
Florida	68,207	20,379	34,790	9,121	33,417	11,258	190,951	29,132	103,060	14,391	87,891	14,741
EAST SOUTH CENTRAL:												
Kentucky	74,010	32,621	36,734	14,452	37,276	18,169	121,703	33,322	64,337	15,969	57,366	17,353
Tennessee	106,142	44,364	51,301	19,074	54,841	25,290	248,249	74,333	128,377	34,958	119,872	69,375
Alabama	119,920	36,683	58,000	15,579	61,920	21,104	636,952	114,727	319,869	54,346	317,083	60,381
Mississippi	73,345	22,012	33,089	9,074	39,356	12,938	765,137	148,993	388,457	71,276	376,680	77,717
WEST SOUTH CENTRAL:												
Arkansas	43,528	15,619	21,535	7,177	21,993	8,442	317,992	65,752	163,102	31,509	154,890	34,243
Louisiana	113,134	47,711	53,267	20,575	59,867	27,163	448,163	104,866	228,827	51,155	219,336	53,711
Oklahoma	25,906	11,076	14,063	5,434	11,843	5,642	72,363	28,267	38,297	14,143	34,066	14,124
Texas	141,818	37,046	68,966	16,107	72,852	20,939	423,536	87,649	217,853	42,015	205,683	45,034

[Continued]

★ 1655 ★

Black and Mulatto Population, Urban and Rural, by Gender, Divisions, and States, 1910

[Continued]

Division and State	Negro Population: 1910											
	Urban						Rural					
	Both sexes		Male		Female		Both sexes		Male		Female	
	Black	Mulatto	Black	Mulatto	Black	Mulatto	Black	Mulatto	Black	Mulatto	Black	Mulatto
MOUNTAIN:												
Montana	930	525	543	287	387	238	293	86	183	45	110	41
Idaho	262	164	163	89	99	75	163	62	106	40	57	22
Wyoming	869	172	458	81	411	91	1,073	121	916	89	157	32
Colorado	6,380	2,979	3,274	1,372	3,106	1,607	1,435	659	843	378	592	281
New Mexico	650	145	335	58	315	87	539	294	338	160	201	134
Arizona	1,034	276	489	137	515	139	527	172	331	97	196	75
Utah	678	281	426	147	252	134	176	9	110	8	66	1
Nevada	64	37	41	18	23	19	259	153	141	63	118	90
PACIFIC:												
Washington	3,214	1,485	1,909	829	1,305	656	1,064	355	771	227	223	128
Oregon	933	331	580	176	353	155	125	103	82	69	43	34
California	11,478	6,921	5,934	3,351	5,544	3,570	2,369	937	1,414	574	865	363

Source: "Urban and Rural Black and Mulatto Population Classified by Sex, by Divisions and States: 1910." U.S. Bureau of the Census, *Negro Population, 1790-1915*, p. 227.

★ 1656 ★

Black and Mulatto Population

Distribution by Gender of the Black and Mulatto Population: United States and Divisions, 1860

Division and state	Negro population: 1860					
	Both sexes		Male		Female	
	Black	Mulatto	Black	Mulatto	Black	Mulatto
United States	3,853,478	588,352	1,936,315	280,430	1,917,163	307,922
Geographic divisions:						
New England	17,663	7,048	8,416	3,303	9,247	3,745
Middle Atlantic	100,905	30,385	48,053	13,917	52,852	16,468
East North Central	33,862	29,837	17,501	14,761	16,361	15,076
West North Central	95,900	24,640	48,549	11,527	47,351	13,113
South Atlantic	1,813,497	244,701	906,127	116,931	907,370	127,770
East South Central	1,231,477	162,241	619,241	77,470	612,236	85,413
West South Central	557,376	87,177	286,439	41,433	270,937	45,744
Mountain	148	87	90	58	58	29
Pacific	2,650	1,594	1,899	1,030	751	564
New England:						
Maine	693	634	351	308	342	326
New Hampshire	241	253	123	130	118	123
Vermont	517	192	276	95	241	97
Massachusetts	6,531	3,071	3,055	1,414	3,476	1,657
Rhode Island	2,955	997	1,369	462	1,586	535
Connecticut	6,726	1,901	3,242	894	3,484	1,007

[Continued]

★ 1656 ★

Distribution by Gender of the Black and Mulatto Population: United States and Divisions, 1860

[Continued]

Division and state	Negro population: 1860					
	Both sexes		Male		Female	
	Black	Mulatto	Black	Mulatto	Black	Mulatto
Middle Atlantic:						
New York	41,224	7,781	19,491	3,687	21,733	4,094
New Jersey	21,874	3,462	10,721	1,598	11,153	1,864
Pennsylvania	37,807	19,142	17,841	8,632	19,966	10,510
East North Central:						
Ohio	19,982	16,691	10,271	8,171	9,711	8,520
Indiana	5,981	5,447	3,102	2,689	2,879	2,758
Illinois	4,041	3,587	2,031	1,778	2,010	1,809
Michigan	3,424	3,375	1,842	1,725	1,582	1,650
Wisconsin	434	737	255	398	179	339
West North Central:						
Minnesota	90	169	39	87	51	82
Iowa	501	568	275	291	226	277
Missouri	94,915	23,588	48,052	11,005	46,863	12,583
Nebraska	35	47	17	24	18	23
Kansas	359	268	166	120	193	148
South Atlantic:						
Delaware	18,648	2,979	9,261	1,488	9,387	1,491
Maryland	146,218	24,913	72,633	11,426	73,585	13,487
District of Columbia	8,883	5,433	3,708	2,206	5,175	3,227
Virginia	455,443	93,464	232,657	44,547	222,786	48,917
North Carolina	316,724	44,798	159,241	22,108	157,483	22,690
South Carolina	384,006	28,314	187,566	13,553	196,440	14,761
Georgia	426,794	38,904	212,164	18,698	214,630	20,206
Florida	56,781	5,896	28,897	2,905	27,884	2,991
East South Central:						
Kentucky	188,809	47,358	95,954	22,156	92,855	25,202
Tennessee	241,141	41,878	120,199	19,709	120,942	22,169
Alabama	401,342	36,428	201,550	17,470	199,792	18,958
Mississippi	400,185	37,219	201,538	18,135	198,647	19,084
West South Central:						
Arkansas	97,123	14,136	49,266	6,980	47,857	7,156
Louisiana	302,592	47,781	157,725	22,531	114,867	25,250
Texas	157,661	25,260	79,448	11,922	78,213	13,338
Mountain:						
Colorado	33	13	28	9	5	4
New Mexico	46	39	22	23	24	16
Utah	42	17	21	10	21	7

[Continued]

★ 1656 ★

Distribution by Gender of the Black and Mulatto Population: United States and Divisions, 1860

[Continued]

Division and state	Negro population: 1860					
	Both sexes		Male		Female	
	Black	Mulatto	Black	Mulatto	Black	Mulatto
Nevada	27	18	19	16	8	2
Pacific:						
Washington	27	3	24	2	3	1
Oregon	66	62	44	32	22	30
California	2,557	1,529	1,831	996	726	533

Source: "Black and Mulatto Population, Free and Slave, Classified by Sex, by Divisions, and States: 1860," U.S. Bureau of the Census, *Negro Population in the United States, 1790-1915*, p. 220.

★ 1657 ★

Black and Mulatto Population

Distribution by Gender of the Black and Mulatto Populations, United States and Divisions, 1910

Section	Negro Population: 1910			
	Total	Black	Mulatto	Percentage mulatto
		MALE		
United States	4,885,881	3,922,332	963,549	19.7
The South	4,339,625	3,516,671	822,954	19.0
The North	518,544	386,244	132,300	25.5
The West	27,712	19,417	8,295	29.9
		FEMALE		
United States	4,941,882	3,854,745	1,087,137	22.0
The South	4,409,802	3,471,896	937,906	21.3
The North	509,130	367,871	141,259	27.7
The West	22,950	14,978	7,972	34.7
		MALES TO 1,000 FEMALES		
United States	989	1,018	886	-
The South	984	1,013	877	-

[Continued]

★ 1657 ★

Distribution by Gender of the Black and Mulatto Populations, United States and Divisions, 1910

[Continued]

Section	Negro Population: 1910			
	Total	Black	Mulatto	Percentage mulatto
The North	1,018	1,050	937	-
The West	1,207	1,296	1,041	-

Source: Untitled Table. U.S. Bureau of the Census, *Negro Population, 1790-1915*, p. 212.

★ 1658 ★

Black and Mulatto Population

Excess of Males Over Females in the Black and Mulatto Urban and Rural Populations, 1910

Class of Community	Negro Population: 1910					
	Total		Black		Mulatto	
	Excess of males	Excess of females	Excess of males	Excess of females	Excess of males	Excess of females
Total	-	56,001	67,587	-	-	123,588
Urban population	-	130,261	-	53,539	-	76,722
Places of 500,000 or more	-	16,941	-	9,134	-	7,807
Places of 100,000 to 500,000	-	31,598	-	9,581	-	22,017
Places of 25,000 to 100,000	-	29,468	-	13,477	-	15,991
Places of 10,000 to 25,000	-	20,920	-	9,546	-	12,374
Places of 2,500 to 10,000	-	31,334	-	12,801	-	18,533
Rural population	74,260	-	121,126	-	-	46,866

Source: Untitled Table. U.S. Bureau of the Census, *Negro Population, 1790-1915*, p. 214.

★ 1659 ★

Black and Mulatto Population

Excess of Males and Females in the Black and Mulatto Populations in the United States and Divisions, 1910

Section	Blacks and Mulattoes: 1910					
	Excess of males		Excess of females		Males to 1,000 females	
	Black population	Mulatto population	Black population	Mulatto population	Black population	Mulatto population
United States	65,587	-	-	123,588	1,018	886
The South	44,775	-	-	114,952	1,013	877
The North	18,373	-	-	8,059	1,050	937
The West	4,439	-	323	-	1,296	1,041

Source: Untitled Table. U.S. Bureau of the Census, *Negro Population, 1790-1915*, p. 212.

★ 1660 ★

Black and Mulatto Population

Free Black and Mulatto Population of Selected Areas by State and Country of Birth, 1850

Place of Birth	Free Colored Population: 1850											
	Connecticut			Louisiana			New York City			New Orleans		
	Blacks	Mulattoes	Total	Blacks	Mulattoes	Total	Blacks	Mulattoes	Total	Blacks	Mulattoes	Total
Alabama	2	-	2	16	46	62	4	1	5	13	41	54
Arkansas	-	-	-	-	4	4	-	-	-	-	-	-
Connecticut	4,671	1,406	6,077	-	3	3	242	77	319	-	-	-
Delaware	9	1	10	-	1	1	159	30	189	-	1	1
District of Columbia	5	-	5	7	23	30	-	-	-	6	21	27
Florida	1	3	4	8	26	34	4	7	11	8	20	28
Georgia	11	8	19	5	13	18	18	14	32	2	11	13
Indiana	-	-	-	-	1	1	-	1	1	-	1	1
Illinois	-	-	-	6	11	17	-	-	-	-	5	5
Kentucky	1	-	1	31	77	108	10	4	14	21	57	78
Louisiana	2	-	2	2,488	12,714	15,202	22	5	27	1,303	6,820	8,123
Maine	1	-	1	-	1	1	10	4	14	-	-	-
Maryland	67	14	81	56	45	101	580	170	750	27	47	74
Massachusetts	141	47	188	4	7	11	111	30	141	2	7	9
Mississippi	1	-	1	30	59	89	8	3	11	9	50	59
Missouri	-	-	-	3	16	19	2	-	2	3	13	17
New Hampshire	-	-	-	-	1	1	4	-	4	-	1	1
New Jersey	80	15	95	2	-	2	1,234	246	1,480	1	-	1
New York	447	125	572	12	32	44	6,469	1,887	8,356	10	31	41
North Carolina	13	4	17	22	31	63	81	23	104	10	10	20
Ohio	-	1	1	3	20	23	7	9	16	3	19	22
Pennsylvania	75	38	113	10	33	43	513	169	682	9	33	42
Rhode Island	118	41	159	-	1	1	46	9	55	-	1	1
South Carolina	6	5	11	40	47	87	62	33	95	17	32	49
Tennessee	-	-	-	17	27	44	2	-	2	8	20	28

[Continued]

★ 1660 ★

Free Black and Mulatto Population of Selected Areas by State and Country of Birth, 1850

[Continued]

Place of Birth	Free Colored Population: 1850											
	Connecticut			Louisiana			New York City			New Orleans		
	Blacks	Mulattoes	Total	Blacks	Mulattoes	Total	Blacks	Mulattoes	Total	Blacks	Mulattoes	Total
Texas		-	-	-	8	15	23	-	-	-	-	-
Vermont	2	1	3	-	-	-	6	7	13	-	-	-
Virginia	53	13	66	225	223	449	712	166	878	153	225	378
Germany	-	-	-	1	4	5	-	-	-	1	3	4
Mexico	1	-	1	3	33	36	-	-	-	2	31	33
South America	2	-	2	-	2	2	2	2	4	-	2	2
West Indies	41	11	52	167	494	661	93	54	147	151	496	647
England	2	1	3	-	3	3	16	9	25	-	3	3
France	2	-	2	9	17	26	5	11	16	6	13	19
Ireland	-	-	-	-	6	6	-	-	-	-	6	6
Spain	-	-	-	-	7	7	8	2	10	-	7	7
Portugal	2	-	2	-	-	-	3	5	8	-	-	-
China	1	-	1	-	1	1	-	-	-	-	1	1
Africa	4	1	5	146	10	156	17	-	17	114	7	121
Other countries and unknown	134	63	197	59	19	78	299	88	387	24	22	46
Total	5,895	1,798	7,693	3,379	14,083	17,462	10,749	3,066	13,815	1,903	8,058	9,961

Source: "Free Colored Black and Mulatto Population of Selected Areas Classified by State and Country of Birth." U.S. Bureau of the Census, *Negro Population, 1790-1915*, p. 64. *Notes:* Out of 7,693 free colored persons in Connecticut, 1,798 were mulattoes, of whom 48 were born in the slave States. Out of 13,815 free colored in New York City 3,066 were mulattoes. Thus, in both instances, the mulattoes constituted less than one-fourth of the free colored population. About one-fifth of the free colored in New York were born in the present slave States. - *Compendium of the Seventh Census, p. 80.*

★ 1661 ★

Black and Mulatto Population

Increase in Black and Mulatto Elements of the Population, 1850-1870

Section	Total	Black	Mulatto	Total	Black	Mulatto	Mulattoes to 1,000 Blacks
United States	1,241,201	1,062,903	178,298	34.1	32.9	43.9	168
The South	1,068,613	913,617	154,966	31.8	30.3	46.3	170
The North	167,449	146,127	21,322	58.7	68.1	30.2	146
The West	5,139	3,159	1,980	414.1	331.7	680.4	627
1870-1890							
United States	2,590,031	2,042,020	548,011	53.5	47.5	93.8	268
The South	2,321,130	1,885,890	435,240	52.5	48.0	88.9	231
The North	248,200	143,762	104,328	54.8	39.9	113.4	726
The West	20,701	12,368	8,333	324.5	801.0	366.9	674
1890-1910							
United States	2,357,723	1,439,097	918,626	31.2	22.7	81.1	638
The South	326,656	249,609	77,047	46.6	49.5	39.2	309
The North	2,007,486	1,171,570	835,916	29.7	20.1	90.4	714
The West	23,581	17,918	5,663	87.1	108.7	53.4	316

[Continued]

★ 1661 ★

Increase in Black and Mulatto Elements of the Population, 1850-1870

[Continued]

Section	Total	Black	Mulatto	Total	Black	Mulatto	Mulattoes to 1,000 Blacks
				1910-1920			
United States	635,368	1,025,500	-390,132	6.5	13.2	-19.0	-382
The South	162,804	562,157	-363,353	1.9	7.5	-20.6	-690
The North	444,635	474,733	-30,098	43.2	62.9	-11.0	-64
The West	27,929	24,610	3,319	55.1	71.5	20.4	123
				1850-1920			
United States	6,824,323	5,569,520	1,254,803	187.5	172.3	309.3	225
The South	5,560,033	4,497,234	1,062,799	165.8	149.0	317.5	236
The North	1,186,940	1,014,231	173,709	415.9	472.6	245.5	171
The West	77,350	58,055	19,295	6232.8	6111.0	6596.2	333

Source: "Increase Black and Mulatto Elements Negro Population by 20 Year Periods, 1850-1910 and the 10 Year Period, 1910-1920." Work, Monroe, N., ed., *Negro Year Book: An Annual Encyclopedia of the Negro, 1937-38*, p. 247.

★ 1662 ★

Black and Mulatto Population

Increase in Black and Mulatto Population, by Divisions and States, 1870-1890, 1890-1910, and 1870-1910 - I

Division and State	Increase of Black and Mulatto Population Number					
	1890-1910		1870-1890		1870-1910	
	Black	Mulatto	Black	Mulatto	Black	Mulatto
UNITED STATES	1,439,097	918,626	2,042,020	548,011	3,481,117	1,466,637
GEOGRAPHIC DIVISIONS:						
New England	14,155	7,571	7,376	5,499	21,531	13,070
Middle Atlantic	158,727	33,817	51,130	26,163	209,857	59,980
East North Central	71,003	22,810	37,652	38,874	108,655	61,684
West North Central	5,724	12,849	47,604	33,902	53,328	46,751
South Atlantic	432,764	417,034	837,921	208,064	1,270,685	625,098
East South Central	314,696	218,020	528,738	126,807	843,434	344,827
West South Central	424,110[1]	200,862[1]	519,231[1]	100,369[1]	943,341	301,231
Mountain	6,998	1,498	7,252	4,164	14,250	5,662
Pacific	10,920	4,165	5,116	4,169	16,036	8,334
NEW ENGLAND:						
Maine	230	-57	-597	91	-277	34
New Hampshire	108	-158	-188	222	-80	64
Vermont	664	20	-156	169	508	189
Massachusetts	9,992	5,919	4,422	3,775	14,414	9,694

[Continued]

★ 1662 ★

Increase in Black and Mulatto Population, by Divisions and States, 1870-1890, 1890-1910, and 1870-1910 - I

[Continued]

Division and State	Increase of Black and Mulatto Population Number					
	1890-1910		1870-1890		1870-1910	
	Black	Mulatto	Black	Mulatto	Black	Mulatto
Rhode Island	954	1,182	1,576	837	2,530	2,019
Connecticut	2,207	665	2,229	405	4,436	1,070
MIDDLE ATLANTIC:						
New York	48,731	15,368	8,354	9,657	57,085	25,025
New Jersey	35,117	7,005	13,331	3,649	48,448	10,654
Pennsylvania	74,879	11,444	29,445	12,857	104,324	24,301
EAST NORTH CENTRAL:						
Ohio	22,125	2,214	4,704	19,196	26,829	21,410
Indiana	14,210	895	14,009	6,646	28,219	7,541
Illinois	31,875	20,146	18,927	9,339	50,802	29,485
Michigan	2,043	-151	602	2,772	2,645	2,621
Wisconsin	750	-294	-590	921	160	627
WEST NORTH CENTRAL:						
Minnesota	2,487	914	1,467	1,457	3,954	2,371
Iowa	3,826	462	2,834	2,089	6,660	2,551
Missouri	-1,977	9,245	14,327	17,786	12,350	27,031
North Dakota	307	-63	392[1]	428[1]	910[1]	430[1]
South Dakota	211	65	392[1]	428[1]	910[1]	430[1]
Nebraska	-489	-735	5,353	2,771	4,864	2,036
Kansas	1,359	2,961	23,231	9,371	24,590	12,332
SOUTH ATLANTIC:						
Delaware	2,638	157	4,267	1,325	6,905	1,482
Maryland	7,802	8,791	29,833	10,433	37,635	19,224
District of Columbia	5,758	13,116	20,364	11,894	26,122	24,920
Virginia	-64,811	100,469	72,404	50,193	7,593	150,662
West Virginia	19,958	11,525	9,696	5,014	29,654	16,539
North Carolina	69,903	66,922	129,608	39,760	199,511	106,682
South Carolina	79,681	67,228	233,796	39,324	313,477	106,552
Georgia	199,100	119,072	271,868	41,805	470,968	160,877
Florida	112,735	29,754	66,085	8,406	178,820	38,160
EAST SOUTH CENTRAL:						
Kentucky	-20,372	13,957	38,586	7,275	18,214	21,232
Tennessee	-1,824	44,234	64,186	44,161	62,362	88,395
Alabama	155,803	73,990	167,371	35,608	323,174	109,598
Mississippi	181,089	85,839	285,595	39,763	439,684	125,602
WEST SOUTH CENTRAL:						
Arkansas	92,033	41,741	159,656	27,292	251,689	69,033

[Continued]

★ 1662 ★

Increase in Black and Mulatto Population, by Divisions and States, 1870-1890, 1890-1910, and 1870-1910 - I

[Continued]

Division and State	Increase of Black and Mulatto Population Number					
	1890-1910		1870-1890		1870-1910	
	Black	Mulatto	Black	Mulatto	Black	Mulatto
Louisiana	93,057	61,624	160,630	34,353	253,687	95,977
Oklahoma	96,113[1]	38,526[1]	-	-	98,269	39,343
Texas	142,907	58,971	196,789	37,907	339,696	96,878
MOUNTAIN:						
Montana	137	207	949	358	1,086	565
Idaho	325	125	40	101	365	226
Wyoming	1,271	42	575	164	1,846	206
Colorado	3,759	1,479	3,784	1,975	7,543	3,454
New Mexico	219	-547	854	930	1,073	383
Arizona	629	23	906	425	1,535	448
Utah	475	81	294	176	769	257
Nevada	183	88	-150	35	33	123
PACIFIC:						
Washington	3,174	1,282	988	407	4,162	1,689
Oregon	501	-195	298	542	799	347
California	7,245	3,078	3,830	3,220	11,075	6,298

Source: "Increase in Black and Mulatto Population, by Divisions and States: 1870-1890, 1890-1910, and 1870-1910." U.S. Bureau of the Census, *Negro Population, 1790-1915*, p. 219. *Notes:* Includes 2,156 blacks and 817 mulattos enumerated in Oklahoma Territory in 1890, but does not include 18,636 Negroes enumerated in Indian Territory who were not classified as black and mulatto. 1. Data includes North and South Datota.

★ 1663 ★

Black and Mulatto Population

Increase in Black and Mulatto Population, by Divisions and States, 1870-1890, 1890-1910, and 1870-1910 - II

Division and State	Increase of Black and Mulatto Population Per cent								
	1890-1910			1870-1890			1870-1910		
	Total Negro population	Black	Mulatto	Total Negro population	Black	Mulatto	Total Negro population	Black	Mulatto
UNITED STATES	31.2	22.7	81.1	53.5	47.5	93.8	101.4	81.0	251.1
GEOGRAPHIC DIVISIONS:									
New England	48.7	47.2	51.9	40.6	32.6	60.6	199.1	95.2	143.9
Middle Atlantic	85.5	89.6	70.2	52.2	40.6	119.0	182.3	166.5	272.8
East North Central	45.3	54.6	29.6	58.6	40.8	102.0	130.5	117.6	161.8
West North Central	8.3	3.4	22.6	57.2	39.8	148.2	70.2	44.6	204.3
South Atlantic	26.0	15.3	95.0	47.2	42.2	90.2	85.5	64.0	270.9

[Continued]

★ 1663 ★

Increase in Black and Mulatto Population, by Divisions and States, 1870-1890, 1890-1910, and 1870-1910 - II

[Continued]

Division and State	Increase of Black and Mulatto Population Per cent								
	1890-1910			1870-1890			1870-1910		
	Total Negro population	Black	Mulatto	Total Negro population	Black	Mulatto	Total Negro population	Black	Mulatto
East South Central	25.1	17.2	75.4	44.8	40.6	78.2	81.2	64.8	212.6
West South Central	44.0	36.5	101.9	86.3	80.7	103.7	168.2	146.7	311.3
Mountain	65.5	84.0	32.3	734.1	670.2	880.3	1,280.5	1,317.0	1,197.0
Pacific	106.9	134.1	69.8	192.4	169.0	231.9	505.1	529.8	463.5
NEW ENGLAND:									
Maine	14.5	45.4	-8.3	-25.9	-50.0	15.4	-15.1	-27.3	5.7
New Hampshire	-8.1	43.5	-43.2	5.9	-43.1	154.2	-2.8	-18.3	44.4
Vermont	73.0	127.4	4.8	1.4	-23.0	68.4	75.4	75.0	76.5
Massachusetts	71.9	70.8	73.7	58.8	45.7	88.6	172.9	148.8	227.5
Rhode Island	28.9	17.7	59.2	48.5	41.3	72.2	91.3	66.2	174.1
Connecticut	23.3	22.2	21.6	27.2	31.9	15.1	57.0	63.4	40.0
MIDDLE ATLANTIC:									
New York	91.4	88.8	100.8	34.6	18.0	173.0	157.7	122.8	448.2
New Jersey	88.4	86.8	97.3	55.4	49.2	102.7	192.8	178.7	299.9
Pennsylvania	80.2	91.4	44.5	64.8	56.1	100.0	197.0	198.9	189.1
EAST NORTH CENTRAL:									
Ohio	27.9	44.2	6.0	37.8	10.4	107.6	76.3	59.1	120.0
Indiana	33.4	45.0	6.6	84.1	79.8	94.8	145.6	160.8	107.5
Illinois	91.2	79.0	120.8	98.3	88.4	127.2	279.1	237.2	401.5
Michigan	12.4	29.0	-1.8	28.5	9.4	51.2	44.4	41.1	48.4
Wisconsin	18.7	74.5	-20.5	15.7	-36.9	178.5	37.2	10.0	121.5
WEST NORTH CENTRAL:									
Minnesota	92.3	125.5	53.7	385.2	285.4	594.7	833.3	769.3	967.8
Iowa	40.1	51.0	14.5	85.4	60.7	191.1	159.9	142.6	233.4
Missouri	4.8	-1.7	26.1	27.2	14.3	100.7	33.4	12.3	153.1
North Dakota	65.4	200.8	-28.6	-28.6[1]	-28.6[1]	-28.6[1]	-28.6[1]	-28.6[1]	-28.6[1]
South Dakota	51.0	68.1	28.1	28.1[1]	28.1[1]	28.1[1]	28.1[1]	28.1[1]	28.1[1]
Nebraska	-13.7	-8.0	-26.0	1,029.7	725.3	-	874.5	659.1	-
Kansas	8.7	3.7	22.5	190.6	174.7	246.0	215.8	184.9	323.8
SOUTH ATLANTIC:									
Delaware	9.8	10.6	4.4	24.5	20.7	59.6	36.8	33.6	66.6
Maryland	7.7	4.3	25.6	23.0	19.7	43.6	32.4	24.8	80.3
District of Columbia	25.0	10.3	66.1	74.1	57.6	147.0	117.6	73.8	310.3
Virginia	5.6	-12.6	82.1	23.9	16.4	69.5	30.9	1.7	208.5
West Virginia	96.3	85.5	123.2	81.8	71.1	115.5	256.9	217.4	381.1
North Carolina	24.4	14.4	86.7	43.2	36.6	106.2	78.2	56.3	284.9
South Carolina	21.3	12.8	100.1	65.7	60.3	141.3	101.0	80.8	382.9
Georgia	37.0	25.7	139.9	57.5	54.2	96.5	115.9	93.9	371.3
Florida	85.7	77.0	150.6	81.2	82.3	74.1	236.6	222.6	336.2

[Continued]

★ 1663 ★

Increase in Black and Mulatto Population, by Divisions and States, 1870-1890, 1890-1910, and 1870-1910 - II

[Continued]

Division and State	Increase of Black and Mulatto Population Per cent								
	1890-1910			1870-1890			1870-1910		
	Total Negro population	Black	Mulatto	Total Negro population	Black	Mulatto	Total Negro population	Black	Mulatto
EAST SOUTH CENTRAL:									
Kentucky	-2.4	-9.4	26.8	20.6	21.7	16.3	17.8	10.3	47.5
Tennessee	9.8	-0.5	59.4	33.6	22.0	145.7	46.8	21.4	291.7
Alabama	33.9	25.9	95.6	42.7	38.6	85.2	91.0	74.5	262.1
Mississippi	35.9	27.5	100.8	67.2	64.8	87.6	127.3	110.3	276.6
WEST SOUTH CENTRAL:									
Arkansas	43.3	34.2	105.3	153.0	145.4	221.2	262.2	299.2	559.5
Louisiana	27.7	19.9	67.8	53.5	52.2	60.7	96.0	82.5	169.6
Oklahoma	536.8	-	-	-	-	-	-	-	-
Texas	41.4	33.8	89.7	92.6	87.2	136.3	172.2	150.5	348.3
MOUNTAIN:									
Montana	23.1	12.6	51.2	714.2	692.7	-	902.2	792.7	-
Idaho	233.9	325.0	123.8	-	-	-	-	-	-
Wyoming	142.4	189.4	16.7	403.8	-	-	1,121.3	-	-
Colorado	84.3	92.7	68.5	1,262.9	1,391.2	1,073.4	2,411.6	2,773.2	1,877.2
New Mexico	-16.8	22.6	-55.5	1,037.2	736.2	-	846.5	925.0	-
Arizona	48.0	125.3	38.8	398.3	-	-	869.5	-	-
Utah	94.6	125.3	38.8	398.3	-	-	869.5	-	-
Nevada	112.0	130.7	86.3	-32.2	-51.7	-	43.7	11.4	-
PACIFIC:									
Washington	278.2	304.0	229.7	673.9	-	269.5	2,826.6	-	1,118.5
Oregon	25.8	89.9	-31.0	242.8	115.1	-	331.2	308.5	-
California	91.2	110.7	64.4	165.0	141.2	206.4	406.7	408.4	403.7

Source: "Increase in Black and Mulatto Population, by Divisions and States: 1870-1890, 1890-1910, and 1870-1910." U.S. Bureau of the Census, *Negro Population, 1790-1915*, p. 219. *Notes:* Includes 2,156 blacks and 817 mulattos enumerated in Oklahoma Territory in 1890, but does not include 18,636 Negroes enumerated in Indian Territory who were not classified as black and mulatto. 1. Data includes North and South Dakota.

★ 1664 ★

Black and Mulatto Population

Males to 1,000 Females in the Black and Mulatto Population Classified as Urban and Rural, 1910

Section	Negro Population: 1910					
	Urban		Rural		Percentage mulatto	
	Black	Mulatto	Black	Mulatto	Urban	Rural
			BOTH SEXES			
United States	1,957,709	731,520	5,810,368	1,319,166	27.2	18.5
The South	1,350,167	504,405	5,638,517	1,256,455	27.2	18.2
The North	581,167	213,799	172,948	59,760	26.9	25.7
The West	26,492	13,316	7,903	2,951	33.4	23.7
			MALE			
United States	952,085	327,390	2,970,247	636,150	25.6	17.6
The South	646,439	219,507	2,870,232	603,447	25.3	17.4
The North	281,494	101,347	94,750	30,953	26.5	24.6
The West	14,152	6,545	5,265	1,750	31.6	24.9
			FEMALE			
United States	1,005,624	404,121	2,849,121	683,016	28.7	19.3
The South	703,611	284,898	2,768,285	635,008	28.8	19.1
The North	289,673	112,452	78,198	28,807	28.0	26.9
The West	12,340	6,771	2,638	1,201	35.4	31.3

Source: Untitled Table. U.S. Bureau of the Census, *Negro Population, 1790-1915,* p. 213.

★ 1665 ★

Black and Mulatto Population

Mixed-Blood Population, 1890

In 1890, the black population of mixed blood was classified as mulattoes, quadroons, and octoroons. The Eleventh Census reported that "These figures are of little value. Indeed, as an indication of the extent to which the races have mingled, they are misleading." The aggregate number in the several classes as returned in 1890 was as follows: blacks 6,337,980; mulattoes, 956,989; quadroons, 105,135; octoroons, 69,936. In this year also, the census enumerators operated under the following instructions: Be particularly careful to distinguish between blacks, mulattoes, quadroons, and octoroons. The word "black" should be used to describe those persons who have three-fourths or more black blood; "mulatto," those persons who have these-eights to five-eights black blood; "quadroon," those persons who have one-fourth black blood; and "octoroon," those persons who have one-eighth or any trace of black blood.

Source: "Color-Black and Mulatto Elements." U.S. Bureau of the Census, *Negro Population, 1790-1915*, p. 207.

★ 1666 ★

Black and Mulatto Population

Percent Change in Black and Mulatto Population in the U.S., Puerto Rico, Hawaii, Alaska, and Military Services Abroad

Area	Negro Population: 1910						
	Total	Black	Mulatto		Percentage in each area		Mulattoes per 1,000 blacks, 1910
			Number	Percent	Black population	Mulatto to population	
Area of enumeration	10,215,482	7,828,695	2,386,787	23.4	100.0	100.0	305
United States	9,827,763	7,777,077	2,050,686	20.9	99.3	85.9	264
Puerto Rico	385,437	50,245	335,192	87.0	0.6	14.0	6,671
Hawaii	695	158	537	77.3	[1]	[1]	3,399[2]
Alaska	209	124	85	40.7	[1]	[1]	684[2]
Military and naval service abroad	1,378	1,091	287	20.8	[1]	[1]	263

Source: Untitled Table. U.S. Bureau of the Census, *Negro Population, 1790-1915*, p. 23. *Notes:* 1. Less than one-tenth of 1 per cent. 2. Number of blacks less than 1,000.

★ 1667 ★

Black and Mulatto Population

Percentage Mulatto by Gender in the Urban and Rural Populations, 1910

Color and Sex	Negro Population: 1910						
	Urban communities						Rural communities
	Total	Places of 500,000 or more	Places of 100,000 to 500,000	Places of 25,000 to 100,000	Places of 10,000 to 25,000	Places of 2,500 to 10,000	
	Number						
Negro:							
Both sexes	2,689,229	396,615	626,946	602,040	408,362	655,266	7,138,534
Male	1,279,484	189,837	297,674	286,286	193,721	311,966	3,606,397
Female	1,409,745	206,778	329,272	315,754	214,641	343,300	3,532,137
Black:							
Both sexes	1,957,709	295,134	429,709	449,907	301,026	481,933	5,819,368
Male	952,085	143,000	210,064	218,215	146,240	234,566	2,970,247
Female	1,005,624	152,134	219,645	231,692	154,786	247,367	2,849,121
Mulatto:							
Both sexes	731,520	101,481	197,237	152,133	107,336	173,333	1,319,166
Male	327,339	46,837	87,610	68,071	47,481	77,400	636,150
Female	404,121	54,644	109,627	84,062	59,855	95,933	683,016
	Percentage Mulatto						
Both sexes	27.2	25.6	31.5	25.3	26.3	26.5	18.5
Male	25.6	24.7	29.4	23.8	24.5	24.8	17.6
Female	28.7	26.4	33.3	26.6	27.9	27.9	19.3
	Males to 1,000 Females						
Negro	908	918	904	907	903	909	1,021
Black	947	940	956	942	945	948	1,043
Mulatto	810	857	799	810	793	807	931

Source: Untitled Table. U.S. Bureau of the Census, *Negro Population, 1790-1915,* p. 214.

★ 1668 ★

Black and Mulatto Population

Percentage Mulatto in the Black Urban and Rural Population, and Percentage Urban, and Males to 1,000 Females in the Black and Mulatto Urban and Rural Population by Divisions and States, 1910 - I

Division and State	Negro Population: 1910											
	Percentage mulatto						Percentage urban					
	Urban communities			Rural communities			Both sexes		Male		Female	
	Both sexes	Male	Female	Both sexes	Male	Female	Black	Mulatto	Black	Mulatto	Black	Mulatto
UNITED STATES	27.2	25.6	28.7	18.5	17.6	19.3	25.2	35.7	24.3	34.0	26.1	37.2
GEOGRAPHIC DIVISIONS:												
New England	32.1	31.9	32.3	48.2	51.5	44.3	93.6	88.2	93.1	85.7	94.2	90.7
Middle Atlantic	20.1	19.5	20.8	17.4	16.6	18.3	80.7	83.3	78.8	81.8	82.5	84.7
East North Central	32.6	30.6	34.6	35.1	33.8	36.7	77.3	75.3	76.2	73.5	78.6	77.0
West North Central	30.9	29.1	32.9	24.0	22.3	26.0	65.6	73.0	64.5	72.2	66.8	73.7
South Atlantic	28.3	26.6	29.7	18.7	17.9	19.5	20.0	30.1	18.9	28.0	21.1	31.9
East South Central	26.7	24.4	28.6	17.3	16.4	18.3	17.4	26.8	16.7	24.8	18.2	28.5
West South Central	25.6	23.8	27.2	18.5	17.6	19.4	20.4	28.0	19.6	26.2	21.3	29.6
Mountain	29.6	27.6	31.7	25.8	22.9	31.1	70.9	74.6	65.9	71.3	77.4	78.0
Pacific	35.9	34.1	37.8	28.9	27.5	31.5	82.0	86.2	78.6	83.4	86.3	89.3
NEW ENGLAND:												
Maine	42.9	38.6	46.9	52.4	56.6	46.8	71.6	63.3	71.9	55.2	71.3	71.4
New Hampshire	24.2	30.8	18.8	58.7	55.8	[1]	75.8	41.3	65.9	40.5	84.7	[1]
Vermont	21.0	16.2	35.3	55.0	55.6	54.1	89.4	64.7	91.8	63.4	81.0	66.5
Massachusetts	34.9	35.4	34.4	59.2	63.1	53.6	95.2	88.1	94.8	85.4	95.7	90.9
Rhode Island	33.6	33.0	34.2	28.1	27.8	28.4	94.6	95.8	93.9	95.1	95.4	96.4
Connecticut	24.6	23.9	25.2	25.7	25.2	26.1	92.1	91.7	91.5	90.9	92.7	92.3
MIDDLE ATLANTIC:												
New York	23.8	23.1	24.5	15.6	15.0	16.4	86.4	91.5	84.0	89.9	88.6	92.8
New Jersey	16.0	15.8	16.2	15.4	14.3	16.5	72.7	73.7	70.2	72.5	75.1	74.7
Pennsylvania	19.1	18.3	19.8	19.5	18.9	20.1	80.7	80.3	79.4	78.9	81.9	81.6
EAST NORTH CENTRAL:												
Ohio	33.7	31.4	36.1	39.5	38.5	40.8	75.6	70.6	74.7	63.3	76.6	72.8
Indiana	24.1	22.8	25.4	24.2	23.2	25.4	80.3	80.3	78.9	78.6	81.8	81.8
Illinois	35.1	33.1	37.3	28.8	27.0	30.9	76.8	81.6	75.8	80.7	78.0	82.5
Michigan	40.1	37.8	42.7	63.6	61.9	65.8	80.1	60.7	78.8	58.1	81.8	63.4
Wisconsin	37.5	36.1	38.7	44.9	45.5	44.2	76.2	70.2	74.5	66.5	78.0	73.9
WEST NORTH CENTRAL:												
Minnesota	36.8	35.2	39.1	38.0	41.4	33.6	92.1	91.8	93.0	91.2	90.8	92.6
Iowa	27.8	25.6	30.3	17.3	17.3	18.4	62.4	74.6	61.8	72.6	63.1	76.7
Missouri	31.0	29.0	33.1	23.2	21.3	25.2	63.9	72.5	63.0	72.0	64.9	73.0
North Dakota	24.8	25.4	23.9	26.0	24.5	28.3	50.0	48.4	51.4	[1]	47.7	[1]
South Dakota	32.8	29.4	37.0	29.8	40.4	38.8	53.2	45.6	53.0	40.9	53.5	51.5
Nebraska	26.8	25.2	28.8	29.0	26.9	32.2	86.5	85.1	85.4	84.3	87.8	86.0
Kansas	31.2	29.7	32.7	27.2	25.1	29.8	65.7	70.0	63.1	68.3	68.7	71.5
SOUTH ATLANTIC:												
Delaware	9.8	8.9	10.7	13.0	12.2	14.0	36.6	29.5	34.5	27.0	38.9	31.8
Maryland	22.3	21.0	23.3	15.8	14.8	17.0	40.8	51.2	38.2	48.7	43.4	53.3
District of Columbia	34.9	33.7	35.9	-	-	-	100.0	100.0	100.0	100.0	100.0	100.0
Virginia	39.7	38.3	40.9	31.2	30.0	32.5	21.3	28.2	19.9	26.5	22.7	29.7
West Virginia	33.9	31.2	36.8	32.1	29.6	35.6	23.5	25.0	21.3	22.6	26.6	27.6
North Carolina	22.0	20.6	23.2	20.4	19.7	21.1	16.3	17.7	15.4	16.2	17.2	19.1
South Carolina	29.3	28.0	30.3	14.3	13.8	14.7	10.3	22.1	9.6	20.5	10.9	23.6
Georgia	25.6	23.5	27.3	15.4	14.7	16.2	17.2	28.1	16.2	25.8	18.2	30.1
Florida	23.0	20.8	25.2	13.2	12.3	14.4	26.3	41.2	25.2	38.8	27.5	43.3

[Continued]

★ 1668 ★

Percentage Mulatto in the Black Urban and Rural Population, and Percentage Urban, and Males to 1,000 Females in the Black and Mulatto Urban and Rural Population by Divisions and States, 1910 - I

[Continued]

Division and State	Negro Population: 1910											
	Percentage mulatto						Percentage urban					
	Urban communities			Rural communities			Both sexes		Male		Female	
	Both sexes	Male	Female	Both sexes	Male	Female	Black	Mulatto	Black	Mulatto	Black	Mulatto
EAST SOUTH CENTRAL:												
Kentucky	30.6	28.2	32.8	21.5	19.9	23.2	37.8	49.5	36.3	47.5	39.4	51.1
Tennessee	29.5	27.1	31.6	23.0	21.4	24.7	30.0	37.4	28.6	35.3	31.4	39.1
Alabama	23.4	21.2	25.4	15.3	14.5	16.0	15.8	24.2	15.3	22.3	16.3	25.9
Mississippi	23.1	21.1	24.7	16.3	15.5	17.1	8.7	12.9	8.0	11.3	9.5	14.3
WEST SOUTH CENTRAL:												
Arkansas	26.4	25.0	27.7	17.1	16.2	18.1	12.0	19.2	11.7	18.6	12.4	19.8
Louisiana	29.7	27.9	31.2	19.0	18.3	19.7	20.2	31.3	18.9	28.7	21.4	33.6
Oklahoma	29.9	27.9	32.3	28.1	27.0	29.3	26.4	28.2	26.9	27.8	25.8	28.5
Texas	20.7	18.9	22.3	17.1	16.2	18.2	25.1	29.7	24.0	27.7	26.2	31.5
MOUNTAIN:												
Montana	36.1	34.6	38.1	22.7	19.7	27.2	76.0	87.9	74.8	86.4	77.9	85.3
Idaho	38.5	35.3	43.1	27.6	27.4	[1]	61.6	72.6	60.6	69.0	63.5	[1]
Wyoming	16.5	15.0	18.1	10.1	8.9	16.9	44.7	58.7	33.3	47.6	72.4	74.0
Colorado	31.8	29.5	34.1	31.5	31.0	32.2	81.6	81.9	79.5	78.4	84.0	85.1
New Mexico	18.2	14.8	21.6	35.3	32.1	40.0	54.7	33.0	49.8	26.6	61.0	39.4
Arizona	21.1	21.9	20.3	24.6	22.7	27.7	66.2	61.6	59.6	58.5	73.5	65.0
Utah	29.3	25.7	34.7	4.9	6.8	[1]	79.4	96.9	79.5	94.8	79.2	99.3
Nevada	36.6	[1]	[1]	37.1	30.9	43.3	19.8	19.5	22.5	[1]	16.3	17.4
PACIFIC:												
Washington	31.6	30.3	33.5	26.1	22.7	35.5	76.2	80.7	71.2	78.5	84.9	83.7
Oregon	26.2	23.3	30.5	45.2	45.7	[1]	88.2	76.3	87.6	71.8	89.1	82.0
California	37.6	36.1	39.2	28.9	28.4	29.6	83.3	88.1	80.4	85.4	86.5	90.8

Source: "Percentage Mulatto in the Urban and Rural Negro Population, and Percentage Urban, and Males to 1,000 Females in the Urban and Rural Black and Mulatto Population, by Divisions and States: 1910." U.S. Bureau of the Census, *Negro Population, 1790-1915*, p. 228. *Notes:* 1. Per cent not shown where base is less than 100. 2. Ratio not shown, the number of females being less than 100.

★ 1669 ★

Black and Mulatto Population

Percentage Mulatto in the Black Urban and Rural Population, and Percentage Urban, and Males to 1,000 Females in the Black and Mulatto Urban and Rural Population by Divisions and States, 1910 - II

Division and State	Negro Population: 1910 Males to 1,000 females			
	Urban communities		Rural communities	
	Black	Mulatto	Black	Mulatto
UNITED STATES	947	810	1,043	931
GEOGRAPHIC DIVISIONS:				
New England	958	940	1,156	1,522
Middle Atlantic	923	851	1,171	1,045
East North Central	1,110	925	1,270	1,118
West North Central	1,100	920	1,216	993
South Atlantic	808	771	1,029	928
East South Central	932	751	1,034	906
West South Central	948	793	1,056	940
Mountain	1,115	916	1,983	1,302
Pacific	1,170	994	2,013	1,657
NEW ENGLAND:				
Maine	1,104	784	1,069	[2]
New Hampshire	688	[2]	[2]	[2]
Vermont	3,858	1,370	[2]	[2]
Massachusetts	927	972	1,126	1,662
Rhode Island	953	905	1,289	[2]
Connecticut	913	850	1,078	1,026
MIDDLE ATLANTIC:				
New York	886	820	1,305	1,175
New Jersey	893	864	1,143	965
Pennsylvania	964	877	1,131	1,043
EAST NORTH CENTRAL:				
Ohio	1,123	910	1,250	1,132
Indiana	1,058	918	1,266	1,121
Illinois	1,131	941	1,283	1,061
Michigan	1,151	938	1,388	1,174
Wisconsin	1,011	905	1,223	1,289
WEST NORTH CENTRAL:				
Minnesota	1,549	1,311	1,140	[2]
Iowa	1,219	962	1,289	1,200
Missouri	1,076	891	1,168	937
North Dakota	[2]	[2]	[2]	[2]
South Dakota	1,388	[2]	1,416	[2]
Nebraska	1,272	1,059	1,569	1,214
Kansas	1,041	902	1,332	1,052

[Continued]

★ 1669 ★

Percentage Mulatto in the Black Urban and Rural Population, and Percentage Urban, and Males to 1,000 Females in the Black and Mulatto Urban and Rural Population by Divisions and States, 1910 - II

[Continued]

Division and State	Negro Population: 1910 Males to 1,000 females			
	Urban communities		Rural communities	
	Black	Mulatto	Black	Mulatto
SOUTH ATLANTIC:				
Delaware	954	780	1,152	986
Maryland	888	777	1,099	936
District of Columbia	850	772	[2]	[2]
Virginia	890	798	1,047	934
West Virginia	1,162	907	1,556	1,185
North Carolina	864	743	983	907
South Carolina	852	764	983	917
Georgia	892	733	1,022	911
Florida	1,041	810	1,173	976
EAST SOUTH CENTRAL:				
Kentucky	985	795	1,122	920
Tennessee	935	754	1,071	883
Alabama	937	738	1,009	900
Mississippi	864	701	1,031	917
WEST SOUTH CENTRAL:				
Arkansas	979	850	1,053	920
Louisiana	800	758	1,043	952
Oklahoma	1,187	963	1,124	1,001
Texas	947	769	1,059	921
MOUNTAIN:				
Montana	1,403	1,206	1,664	[2]
Idaho	[2]	[2]	[2]	[2]
Wyoming	1,114	[2]	5,834	[2]
Colorado	1,054	[2]	1,682	1,194
New Mexico	897	986	1,689	[2]
Arizona	1,690	1,097	[2]	[2]
Utah	[2]	[2]	1,195	[2]
Nevada				
PACIFIC:				
Washington	1,463	1,264	3,309	1,773
Oregon	1,643	1,135	[2]	[2]
California	1,070	939	1,669	1,581

Source: "Percentage Mulatto in the Urban and Rural Negro Population, and Percentage Urban, and Males to 1,000 Females in the Urban and Rural Black and Mulatto Population, by Divisions and States: 1910." U.S. Bureau of the Census, *Negro Population, 1790-1915*, p. 228. *Notes:* 1. Per cent not shown where base is less than 100. 2. Ratio not shown, the number of females being less than 100.

★ 1670 ★

Black and Mulatto Population

Proportion Mulatto in the Urban and Rural Population, United States and Divisions, 1910

Section	Negro Population: 1910					
	Urban		Rural		Percentage mulatto	
	Black	Mulatto	Black	Mulatto	Urban	Rural
			BOTH SEXES			
United States	1,957,709	731,520	5,810,368	1,319,166	27.2	18.5
The South	1,350,167	504,405	5,638,517	1,256,455	27.2	18.2
The North	581,167	213,799	172,948	59,760	26.9	25.7
The West	26,492	13,316	7,903	2,951	33.4	23.7
			MALE			
United States	952,085	327,390	2,970,247	636,150	25.6	17.6
The South	646,439	219,507	2,870,232	603,447	25.3	17.4
The North	281,494	101,347	94,750	30,953	26.5	24.6
The West	14,152	6,545	5,265	1,750	31.6	24.9
			FEMALE			
United States	1,005,624	404,121	2,849,121	683,016	28.7	19.3
The South	703,611	284,898	2,768,285	635,008	28.8	19.1
The North	289,673	112,452	78,198	28,807	28.0	26.9
The West	12,340	6,771	2,638	1,201	35.4	31.3

Source: Untitled Table. U.S. Bureau of the Census, *Negro Population, 1790-1915*, p. 213.

★ 1671 ★

Black and Mulatto Population

Proportion Mulatto of the Population by Age, 1860, 1870, and 1910

Racial Class	Males to 1,000 Females		
	1910	1870	1860
Total population	1,060	1,022	1,047
Negro	989	962	996
Black	1,018	970	1,010
Mulatto	886	908	909

[Continued]

★ 1671 ★

Proportion Mulatto of the Population by Age, 1860, 1870, and 1910

[Continued]

Racial Class	Males to 1,000 Females		
	1910	1870	1860
White	1,066	1,028	1,053
Native	1,027	1,006	1,037
Native parentage	1,040	-	-
Foreign or mixed parentage	995	-	-
Foreign-born	1,292	1,153	1,151
Indian	1,035	950	1,190
Chinese	14,301	12,841	18,581
Japanese	6,941	[1]	-

Source: Untitled Table. U.S. Bureau of the Census, *Negro Population, 1790-1915*, p. 212. *Note:* 1. Number of females less than 100.

★ 1672 ★

Black and Mulatto Population

Proportion Mulatto of the Population by Age, 1910

Age	Percentage Mulatto in the Negro Population: 1910							
	United States		The South		The North		The West	
	Male	Female	Male	Female	Male	Female	Male	Female
All ages	19.7	22.0	19.0	21.3	25.5	27.7	29.9	34.7
Under 5 years	22.0	22.5	21.3	21.8	31.0	31.2	40.7	38.8
Under 1 year	24.0	24.2	23.3	23.5	32.0	32.2	43.0	39.5
5 to 9 years	20.5	21.5	19.9	20.8	29.2	29.3	36.8	27.1
15 to 19 years	20.4	22.6	19.7	22.0	27.9	29.0	36.7	38.6
20 to 44 years	19.0	22.6	18.1	21.8	24.1	27.1	27.6	34.0
45 years and over	17.4	20.3	16.5	19.5	22.9	25.5	27.8	31.6
Age unknown	17.0	18.7	16.6	18.5	18.6	19.7	21.2	18.2

Source: Untitled Table. U.S. Bureau of the Census, *Negro Population, 1790-1915*, p. 212.

★ 1673 ★

Black and Mulatto Population

Proportion Mulatto, of the Population by Gender, 1860, 1870, 1910

Year And Class of Population	Negro Population[1]							
	Both sexes	Male	Female	Excess-		Males to 1,000 females	Percentage distribution by color	
				Of males	Of females		Male	Females
1910 Total	9,827,763	4,885,881	4,941,882	-	56,001	989	100.0	100.0
Black	7,777,077	3,922,332	3,854,745	67,587	-	1,018	80.3	78.0
Mulatto	2,050,686	963,549	1,087,137	-	123,588	886	19.7	22.0
1870 Total	4,880,009	2,393,263	2,486,746	-	93,483	62	100.0	100.0
Black	4,295,960	2,115,367	2,180,593	-	65,226	970	88.4	87.7
Mulatto	584,049	277,896	306,153	-	28,257	908	11.6	12.3
1860 Total	4,441,830	2,216,744	2,225,086	-	8,342	996	100.0	100.0
Black	3,853,467	1,936,536	1,916,931	19,605	-	1,010	87.4	86.2
Mulatto	588,363	280,208	308,155	-	27,947	909	12.6	13.8

Source: Untitled Table. U.S. Bureau of the Census, *Negro Population, 1790-1915*, p. 211. *Notes:* 1. The classification by sex of the black and mulatto population was not made in the report for 1890; nor in the report for 1850, except for the free colored in Connecticut, Louisiana, New York City, and New Orleans.

★ 1674 ★

Black and Mulatto Population

Proportion of Children in the Black and Mulatto Population, 1910

Sex	Percentage Under 5 Years of Age in the Negro Population: 1910		
	Total	Black	Mulatto
Both sexes	12.9	12.6	13.7
Male	12.9	12.5	14.4
Female	12.8	12.7	13.1

Source: Untitled Table. U.S. Bureau of the Census, *Negro Population, 1790-1915*, p. 213.

Distribution by Gender

★ 1675 ★

Annual Estimates of Population by Gender and Race, 1900 to 1970 - I

Year	Total	Sex		Race		
		Male	Female	White	Negro	Other
1970	204,879	100,266	104,613	179,491	22,787	2,600
1969	202,677	99,287	103,390	177,782	22,431	2,464
1968	200,706	98,426	102,280	176,246	22,117	2,343
1967	198,712	97,564	101,148	174,695	21,780	2,237
1966	196,560	96,620	99,941	172,998	21,434	2,129
1965	194,303	95,609	98,694	171,205	21,064	2,034
1964	191,889	94,518	97,371	169,257	20,672	1,960
1963	189,242	93,303	95,939	167,104	20,255	1,882
1962	186,538	92,066	94,472	164,885	19,852	1,801
1961	183,691	90,740	92,952	162,533	19,437	1,721
1960	180,671	89,320	91,352	160,023	19,006	1,642
1959[3]	177,830	87,995	89,834	157,655	20,175[4]	20,175[4]
1959	177,073	87,621	89,453	157,368	19,706[4]	19,706[4]
1958	174,141	86,236	87,905	154,922	19,220[4]	19,220[4]
1957	171,274	84,892	86,382	152,512	18,762[4]	18,762[4]
1956	168,221	83,434	84,786	149,923	18,298[4]	18,298[4]
1955	165,275	82,030	83,246	147,428	17,847[4]	17,847[4]
1954	162,391	80,647	81,744	144,981	17,409[4]	17,409[4]
1953	159,565	79,295	80,270	142,573	16,991[4]	16,991[4]
1952	156,954	78,061	78,893	140,344	16,909[4]	16,909[4]
1951	154,287	76,792	77,496	138,049	16,238[4]	16,238[4]
1950	151,684	75,539	76,146	135,814	15,870[4]	15,870[4]
1949	149,188	74,335	74,853	133,598	15,590[4]	15,590[4]
1948	146,631	73,130	73,502	131,308	15,323[4]	15,323[4]
1947	144,126	71,946	72,180	129,059	15,067[4]	15,067[4]
1946	141,389	70,631	70,757	126,565	14,824[4]	14,824[4]
1945	139,928	70,035	69,893	125,266	14,662[4]	14,662[4]
1944	138,397	69,378	69,020	124,009	14,388[4]	14,388[4]
1943	136,739	68,546	68,194	122,605	14,134[4]	14,134[4]
1942	134,860	67,597	67,263	120,992	13,868[4]	13,868[4]
1941	133,402	66,920	66,482	119,731	13,671[4]	13,671[4]
1940	132,122	66,352	65,770	118,629	13,494[4]	13,494[4]
1939	130,880	65,713	65,166	117,524	13,355[4]	13,355[4]
1938	129,825	65,235	64,590	116,592	13,233[4]	13,233[4]
1937	128,825	64,790	64,035	115,706	13,118[4]	13,118[4]

[Continued]

★ 1675 ★

Annual Estimates of Population by Gender and Race, 1900 to 1970 - I

[Continued]

Year	Total	Sex		Race		
		Male	Female	White	Negro	Other
1936	128,053	64,460	63,594	115,022	13,031[4]	13,031[4]
1935	127,250	64,110	63,140	114,309	12,941[4]	12,941[4]

Source: "Annual Estimates of the Population, by Sex and Race: 1900 to 1970." U.S. Bureau of the Census. *Historical Statistics of the United States: Colonial Times to 1970, Part I*, Bicentennial Edition, p. 9. *Notes:* 1. Estimates including Armed Forces overseas, in thousands: 1917 - 103,414; 1918 - 104,550; 1919 - 105,063. 2. Estimates including Armed Forces overseas, in thousands: 1917 - 52,934; 1918 - 53,316; 1919 - 53,658. 3. Denotes first year for which figures include Alaska and Hawaii. 4. Data includes Negro and other races.

★ 1676 ★

Distribution by Gender

Annual Estimates of Population by Gender and Race, 1900 to 1970 - II

Year	Total	Sex		Race	
		Male	Female	White	Negro and other
1934	126,374	63,726	62,648	113,527	12,847
1933	125,579	63,384	62,195	112,815	12,764
1932	124,840	63,070	61,770	112,154	12,686
1931	124,040	62,726	61,314	111,433	12,606
1930	123,077	62,297	60,780	110,559	12,518
1929	121,767	61,680	60,087	109,383	12,384
1928	120,509	61,101	59,408	108,244	12,265
1927	119,035	60,397	58,638	106,941	12,094
1926	117,397	59,588	57,809	105,468	11,929
1925	115,829	58,813	57,016	104,061	11,768
1924	114,109	57,985	56,124	102,512	11,597
1923	111,947	56,861	55,086	100,510	11,437
1922	110,049	55,886	54,163	98,768	11,281
1921	108,538	55,292	53,246	97,416	11,122
1920	106,461	54,291	52,170	95,510	10,951
1919	104,514[1]	53,103[2]	51,411	93,684	10,830
1918	103,208[1]	51,974[2]	51,234	92,352	10,856
1917	103,268[1]	52,788[2]	50,480	92,435	10,833
1916	101,961	52,234	49,727	91,196	10,765
1915	100,546	51,573	48,973	89,848	10,698
1914	99,111	50,883	48,228	88,480	10,631

[Continued]

★ 1676 ★

Annual Estimates of Population by Gender and Race, 1900 to 1970 - II

[Continued]

Year	Total	Sex		Race	
		Male	Female	White	Negro and other
1913	97,225	49,957	47,268	86,705	10,520
1912	95,335	49,025	46,310	84,928	10,407
1911	93,863	48,290	45,573	83,524	10,339
1910	92,407	47,554	44,853	82,137	10,270
1909	90,490	46,545	43,945	80,339	10,151
1908	88,710	45,594	43,116	78,658	10,052
1907	87,008	44,682	42,326	77,055	9,953
1906	85,450	43,841	41,609	75,583	9,867
1905	83,822	42,965	40,857	74,059	9,763
1904	82,166	42,089	40,077	72,520	9,646
1903	80,632	41,262	39,370	71,084	9,548
1902	79,163	40,483	38,680	69,722	9,441
1901	77,584	39,649	37,935	68,267	9,317
1900	76,094	38,867	37,227	66,900	9,194

Source: "Annual Estimates of the Population, by Sex and Race: 1900 to 1970." U.S. Bureau of the Census. *Historical Statistics of the United States: Colonial Times to 1970, Part I*, Bicentennial Edition, p. 9. *Notes:* 1. Estimates including Armed Forces overseas, in thousands: 1917 - 103,414; 1918 - 104,550; 1919 - 105,063. 2. Estimates including Armed Forces overseas, in thousands: 1917 - 52,934; 1918 - 53,316; 1919 - 53,658. 3. Denotes first year for which figures include Alaska and Hawaii.

★ 1677 ★

Distribution by Gender

Black Males and Females 21 Years of Age and Over in Urban and Rural Communities, and Black Males 18 to 44 Years by Divisions and States, 1910 - I

DIVISION AND STATE	NEGROES 21 YEARS OF AGE AND OVER: 1910				
	Total	Male			Female
		Total	In urban communities	In rural communities	
UNITED STATES	4,886,615	2,458,873	811,945	1,646,928	2,427,742
GEOGRAPHIC DIVISIONS:					
New England	43,896	22,074	20,170	1,904	21,822
Middle Atlantic	280,865	138,750	113,137	25,613	142,115
East North Central	199,868	107,170	83,991	23,179	92,698
West North Central	155,497	88,219	58,938	24,281	72,278
South Atlantic	1,924,939	955,364	250,083	705,281	969,575
East South Central	1,288,157	642,460	146,339	496,121	645,697

[Continued]

★ 1677 ★

Black Males and Females 21 Years of Age and Over in Urban and Rural Communities, and Black Males 18 to 44 Years by Divisions and States, 1910 - I

[Continued]

DIVISION AND STATE	NEGROES 21 YEARS OF AGE AND OVER: 1910				
	Total	Male			Female
		Total	In urban communities	In rural communities	
West South Central	956,610	488,815	123,640	365,175	467,795
Mountain	15,678	8,992	6,010	2,982	6,686
Pacific	21,105	12,029	9,637	2,392	9,076
NEW ENGLAND:					
Maine	877	476	296	180	401
New Hampshire	376	200	116	84	176
Vermont	1,252	975	879	96	277
Massachusetts	25,239	12,591	11,610	981	12,648
Rhode Island	6,245	3,067	2,899	168	3,178
Connecticut	9,907	4,765	4,370	395	5,142
MIDDLE ATLANTIC:					
New York	95,177	45,877	39,600	6,277	49,300
New Jersey	58,467	28,601	20,832	7,769	29,866
Pennsylvania	127,221	64,272	52,705	11,567	62,949
EAST NORTH CENTRAL:					
Ohio	72,871	39,188	29,787	9,401	33,683
Indiana	39,037	20,651	16,769	3,882	18,386
Illinois	74,355	39,983	32,103	7,880	34,372
Michigan	11,584	6,266	4,509	1,757	5,318
Wisconsin	2,021	1,082	823	259	939
WEST NORTH CENTRAL:					
Minnesota	5,451	3,390	3,163	227	2,061
Iowa	9,567	5,443	3,665	1,778	4,124
Missouri	100,978	52,921	37,468	15,453	48,057
North Dakota	469	311	168	143	158
South Dakota	561	341	171	170	220
Nebraska	5,594	3,225	2,763	462	2,369
Kansas	32,877	17,588	11,540	6,048	15,289
SOUTH ATLANTIC:					
Delaware	17,331	9,050	3,574	5,476	8,281
Maryland	127,862	63,963	30,294	33,669	63,899
District of Columbia	62,070	27,621	27,621	-	34,449
Virginia	324,437	159,593	43,548	116,045	164,844
West Virginia	37,424	22,757	5,223	17,534	14,667
North Carolina	305,988	146,752	27,600	119,152	159,236
South Carolina	350,419	169,155	24,728	114,427	181,264
Georgia	536,751	266,814	60,115	206,699	269,937

[Continued]

★ 1677 ★

Black Males and Females 21 Years of Age and Over in Urban and Rural Communities, and Black Males 18 to 44 Years by Divisions and States, 1910 - I

[Continued]

DIVISION AND STATE	NEGROES 21 YEARS OF AGE AND OVER: 1910				
	Total	Male			Female
		Total	In urban communities	In rural communities	
Florida	162,657	89,659	27,380	62,279	72,998
EAST SOUTH CENTRAL:					
Kentucky	149,107	75,694	33,556	42,138	73,413
Tennessee	241,849	119,142	43,903	75,239	122,707
Alabama	431,599	213,923	44,146	169,777	217,676
Mississippi	465,602	233,701	24,734	208,967	231,901
WEST SOUTH CENTRAL:					
Arkansas	214,282	111,365	17,438	93,927	102,917
Louisiana	346,922	174,211	43,293	130,918	172,711
Oklahoma	67,049	36,841	12,252	24,589	30,208
Texas	328,357	166,398	50,657	115,741	161,959
MOUNTAIN:					
Montana	1,404	851	665	186	553
Idaho	515	328	217	111	187
Wyoming	1,819	1,325	400	925	494
Colorado	8,144	4,283	3,441	842	3,861
New Mexico	1,085	644	288	356	441
Arizona	1,399	764	458	306	635
Utah	881	568	489	79	313
Nevada	431	229	52	177	202
PACIFIC:					
Washington	4,817	3,120	2,288	832	1,697
Oregon	1,209	766	648	118	443
California	15,079	8,143	6,701	1,442	6,936

Source: "Negro Males and Females 21 Years of Age and Over, Negro Males 21 Years and Over in Urban and Rural Communities, and Negro Males (of Militia Age, 18 to 44 Years), by Divisions and States: 1910." U.S. Bureau of the Census, *Negro Population, 1790-1915*, p. 200.

★ 1678 ★

Distribution by Gender

Black Males and Females 21 Years of Age and Over in Urban and Rural Communities, and Black Males 18 to 44 Years by Divisions and States, 1910 - II

DIVISION AND STATE	PERCENT NEGRO IN TOTAL MALE POPULATION 21 YEARS OF AGE AND OVER: 1910			NEGRO MALES OF MILITIA AGE 18 TO 44 YEARS: 1910	
	Total	In urban communities	In rural communities	Number	Per cent of total males of militia age
UNITED STATES	9.1	6.1	12.1	1,985,415	9.7
GEOGRAPHIC DIVISIONS:					
New England	1.1	1.2	0.5	17,325	1.2
Middle Atlantic	2.3	2.7	1.5	115,040	2.5
East North Central	1.9	2.8	0.9	81,757	2.0
West North Central	2.4	4.6	1.1	64,212	2.5
South Atlantic	31.1	28.0	32.4	779,085	32.4
East South Central	30.6	31.8	30.3	510,592	31.4
West South Central	21.6	21.0	21.8	401,043	22.1
Mountain	1.0	1.8	0.5	7,011	1.0
Pacific	0.7	1.0	0.3	9,350	0.8
NEW ENGLAND:					
Maine	0.2	0.3	0.2	330	0.2
New Hampshire	0.1	0.2	0.1	137	0.2
Vermont	0.9	1.7	0.2	895	1.2
Massachusetts	1.2	1.2	1.2	10,054	1.3
Rhode Island	1.9	1.8	2.7	2,357	1.9
Connecticut	1.4	1.4	1.0	3,552	1.4
MIDDLE ATLANTIC:					
New York	1.6	1.8	1.0	38,488	1.8
New Jersey	3.7	3.6	3.9	23,099	3.9
Pennsylvania	2.8	3.7	1.3	52,453	2.9
EAST NORTH CENTRAL:					
Ohio	2.6	3.5	1.5	29,269	2.7
Indiana	2.5	4.6	0.9	15,530	2.7
Illinois	2.3	2.9	1.2	31,702	2.4
Michigan	0.7	1.1	0.4	4,459	0.7
Wisconsin	0.2	0.3	0.1	797	0.2
WEST NORTH CENTRAL:					
Minnesota	0.5	1.1	0.1	2,743	0.6
Iowa	0.8	1.7	0.4	4,011	0.8
Missouri	5.4	8.3	3.0	41,411	5.7
North Dakota	0.2	0.8	0.1	250	0.2
South Dakota	0.2	0.6	0.1	271	0.2
Nebraska	0.9	2.7	0.2	2,600	1.0
Kansas	3.5	7.4	1.7	12,896	3.5
SOUTH ATLANTIC:					
Delaware	14.6	11.7	17.5	6,911	15.5
Maryland	17.4	15.8	19.1	49,386	18.2
District of Columbia	26.6	26.6	-	22,472	28.7
Virginia	30.5	31.6	30.1	125,692	31.5
West Virginia	6.7	7.4	6.5	21,134	7.7

[Continued]

★ 1678 ★

Black Males and Females 21 Years of Age and Over in Urban and Rural Communities, and Black Males 18 to 44 Years by Divisions and States, 1910 - II

[Continued]

DIVISION AND STATE	PERCENT NEGRO IN TOTAL MALE POPULATION 21 YEARS OF AGE AND OVER: 1910			NEGRO MALES OF MILITIA AGE 18 TO 44 YEARS: 1910	
	Total	In urban communities	In rural communities	Number	Per cent of total males of militia age
North Carolina	29.0	33.8	28.1	115,547	29.5
South Carolina	50.5	42.1	52.3	144,019	52.0
Georgia	43.0	39.9	44.0	217,970	43.8
Florida	41.9	40.6	42.4	75,954	44.2
EAST SOUTH CENTRAL:					
Kentucky	12.5	20.3	9.6	58,306	12.7
Tennessee	21.6	33.3	17.9	93,709	22.1
Alabama	41.7	41.6	41.7	166,099	41.4
Mississippi	54.7	43.3	56.5	192,478	55.7
WEST SOUTH CENTRAL:					
Arkansas	28.1	28.3	28.1	88,627	28.4
Louisiana	42.0	31.1	47.5	144,430	42.7
Oklahoma	8.2	11.5	7.2	30,148	8.4
Texas	16.6	18.0	16.0	137,838	17.1
MOUNTAIN:					
Montana	0.5	1.3	0.2	613	0.5
Idaho	0.3	0.8	0.1	253	0.3
Wyoming	2.1	2.2	2.1	1,253	2.3
Colorado	1.6	2.5	0.6	3,241	1.6
New Mexico	0.7	2.1	0.4	474	0.6
Arizona	1.0	2.0	0.6	568	1.0
Utah	0.5	1.0	0.1	445	0.5
Nevada	0.6	0.9	0.5	164	0.6
PACIFIC:					
Washington	0.7	0.9	0.4	2,538	0.7
Oregon	0.3	0.5	0.1	613	0.3
California	0.9	1.2	0.4	6,199	0.9

Source: "Negro Males and Females 21 Years of Age and Over, Negro Males 21 Years and Over in Urban and Rural Communities, and Negro Males (of Militia Age, 18 to 44 Years), by Divisions and States: 1910." U.S. Bureau of the Census, *Negro Population, 1790-1915*, p. 200.

★ 1679 ★

Distribution by Gender

Black Population Classified by Gender and Quinquennial Age Periods, 1900 and 1910 - I

AGE PERIOD	NEGRO POPULATION					
	1910			1900		
	Both sexes	Male	Female	Both sexes	Male	Female
All ages	9,827,763	4,885,881	4,941,882	8,833,994	4,386,547	4,447,447
Under 5 years	1,263,288	629,320	633,968	1,215,655	604,487	611,168
Under 1 year	252,386	125,459	126,927	244,510	121,329	123,181
5 to 9 years	1,246,553	619,175	627,378	1,202,758	600,410	602,348
10 to 14 years	1,155,266	578,074	577,192	1,091,990	548,642	543,348
15 to 19 years	1,060,416	507,945	552,471	982,022	473,750	508,272
20 to 24 years	1,030,795	482,157	548,638	969,172	458,921	510,251
25 to 29 years	881,227	421,805	459,422	737,479	360,597	367,882
30 to 34 years	668,089	332,163	355,926	524,607	262,130	262,477
35 to 39 years	633,449	320,450	312,999	474,687	233,371	241,316
40 to 44 years	455,413	229,680	225,733	367,216	179,090	188,126
45 to 49 years	385,909	199,928	185,981	326,384	168,495	157,889
50 to 54 years	326,070	179,387	146,683	290,987	155,188	135,799
55 to 59 years	209,622	115,090	94,532	179,176	97,323	81,853
60 to 64 years	186,502	101,149	85,353	161,687	85,961	75,726
65 to 69 years	123,550	67,956	55,594	102,671	56,018	46,653
70 to 74 years	78,839	40,584	38,255	72,382	36,235	36,147
75 to 79 years	44,018	22,667	21,351	40,420	20,475	19,945
80 to 84 years	25,579	11,696	13,883	25,527	11,655	13,872
85 to 89 years	11,166	5,164	6,002	10,083	4,713	5,370
90 to 94 years	5,850	2,394	3,456	5,293	2,085	3,208
95 to 99 years	2,447	1,017	1,430	2,434	958	1,476
100 years and over	2,675	1,004	1,671	2,553	886	1,667
Age unknown	31,040	17,076	13,964	48,811	25,157	23,654

Source: "Negro Population Classified by Sex and Quinquennial Age Periods: 1910 and 1900." U.S. Bureau of the Census, *Negro Population, 1790-1915,* p. 164. *Note:* 1. Less than one-tenth of 1 per cent.

★ 1680 ★

Distribution by Gender

Black Population Classified by Gender and Quinquennial Age Periods, 1900 and 1910 - II

AGE PERIOD	NEGRO POPULATION								
	Percentage distribution by age period						Percentage increase by age period: 1900-1910		
	1910			1900					
	Both sexes	Male	Female	Both sexes	Male	Female	Both sexes	Male	Female
All ages	100.0	100.0	100.0	100.0	100.0	100.0	11.2	11.4	11.1
Under 5 years	12.9	12.9	12.8	13.8	13.8	13.7	3.9	4.1	3.7
Under 1 year	2.6	2.6	2.6	2.8	2.8	2.8	3.2	3.4	3.0
5 to 9 years	12.7	12.7	12.8	13.8	13.8	13.7	3.9	3.1	4.2
10 to 14 years	11.8	11.8	11.7	12.4	12.5	12.2	5.8	5.4	6.2
15 to 19 years	10.8	10.4	11.2	11.1	10.8	11.4	8.0	7.2	8.7
20 to 24 years	10.5	9.9	11.1	11.0	10.6	11.5	6.4	5.1	7.5
25 to 29 years	9.0	8.6	9.3	8.3	8.2	8.5	19.5	17.0	21.9
30 to 34 years	6.8	6.8	6.8	5.9	6.0	5.9	27.4	26.7	28.0
35 to 39 years	6.4	6.6	6.3	5.4	5.3	5.4	33.4	37.3	29.7
40 to 44 years	4.6	4.7	4.6	4.2	4.1	4.2	24.0	28.2	20.0
45 to 49 years	3.9	4.1	3.8	3.7	3.8	3.6	18.2	18.7	17.8
50 to 54 years	3.3	3.7	3.0	3.3	3.5	3.1	12.1	15.6	8.0
55 to 59 years	2.1	2.4	1.9	2.0	2.2	1.8	17.0	18.3	15.5
60 to 64 years	1.9	2.1	1.7	1.8	2.0	1.7	15.3	17.7	12.7
65 to 69 years	1.3	1.4	1.1	1.2	1.3	1.0	20.3	21.3	19.2
70 to 74 years	0.8	0.8	0.8	0.8	0.8	0.8	8.9	12.0	5.8
75 to 79 years	0.4	0.5	0.4	0.5	0.5	0.4	8.9	10.7	7.0
80 to 84 years	0.3	0.2	0.3	0.3	0.3	0.3	0.2	0.4	0.1
85 to 89 years	0.1	0.1	0.1	0.1	0.1	0.1	10.7	9.6	11.8
90 to 94 years	0.1	[1]	0.1	0.1	[1]	0.1	10.5	14.8	7.7
95 to 99 years	[1]	[1]	[1]	[1]	[1]	[1]	0.5	6.2	-3.1
100 years and over	[1]	[1]	[1]	[1]	[1]	[1]	4.8	13.3	0.2
Age unknown	0.3	0.3	0.3	0.6	0.6	0.5	-36.4	-32.1	-41.0

Source: "Negro Population Classified by Sex and Quinquennial Age Periods: 1910 and 1900." U.S. Bureau of the Census, *Negro Population, 1790-1915*, p. 164. *Note:* 1. Less than one-tenth of 1 per cent.

★ 1681 ★

Distribution by Gender

Black Population Classified by Gender and Year of Age, and Number in Each Year of Age per 100,000 Under 1 Year, 1900 and 1910

AGE	NEGRO POPULATION											
	1910			1900			Per 100,000 under 1 year of age					
							1910			1900		
	Both sexes	Male	Female	Both sexes	Male	Female	Both sexes	Male	Female	Both sexes	Male	Female
All ages	9,827,763	4,885,881	4,941,882	8,833,994	4,386,547	4,447,447	3,893,943	3,893,956	3,893,480	3,612,937	3,615,416	3,610,494
Under 1 year	252,386	125,459	126,927	244,510	121,329	123,181	100,000	100,000	100,000	100,000	100,000	100,000
1 year	219,240	190,357	109,883	231,940	115,102	116,838	86,867	87,166	86,572	94,859	94,868	94,851
2 years	260,037	130,192	129,845	248,922	124,334	124,585	103,031	103,773	102,299	101,804	102,477	101,142
3 years	264,547	130,526	134,021	244,083	120,671	123,412	104,818	104,039	105,589	99,825	99,458	100,188
4 years	267,078	133,786	133,292	246,200	123,051	123,149	105,821	106,637	105,015	100,691	101,419	99,974
5 years	255,703	126,709	128,994	245,385	122,168	123,217	101,314	100,996	101,628	100,358	100,692	100,029
6 years	262,815	129,804	133,011	251,875	124,929	129,946	104,132	103,463	104,793	103,012	102,967	103,056
7 years	251,742	125,950	125,792	241,767	120,747	121,020	99,745	100,391	99,106	98,878	99,520	98,246
8 years	252,473	124,937	127,536	245,996	122,726	123,270	100,034	99,584	100,480	100,608	101,151	100,072
9 years	223,820	111,775	112,045	217,735	109,840	107,895	88,682	89,093	88,275	89,050	90,531	87,591
10 years	242,509	122,880	119,629	241,487	122,701	118,786	96,087	97,944	94,250	98,764	101,131	96,432
11 years	195,048	97,062	97,986	193,865	97,293	96,572	77,282	77,366	77,199	79,287	80,189	78,398
12 years	261,300	131,267	130,033	237,494	119,589	117,905	103,532	104,629	102,447	97,131	98,566	95,717
13 years	221,861	110,226	111,635	207,501	103,776	103,725	87,905	87,858	87,952	84,864	85,533	84,205
14 years	234,548	116,639	117,909	211,643	105,283	106,360	92,932	92,970	92,895	86,558	86,775	86,344
15 years	207,555	101,921	105,634	198,494	97,899	100,595	82,237	81,238	83,224	81,180	80,689	81,664
16 years	224,403	106,679	117,724	205,537	98,771	106,766	88,913	85,031	92,749	84,061	81,408	86,674
17 years	203,847	100,185	103,662	186,663	91,137	95,526	80,768	79,855	81,671	76,342	75,116	77,549
18 years	231,307	108,316	122,991	211,345	100,703	110,642	91,648	86,336	96,899	86,436	83,000	89,821
19 years	193,304	90,844	102,460	179,983	85,240	94,743	76,591	72,409	80,724	73,610	70,225	76,914
20 years	215,625	92,494	123,131	222,417	98,956	123,461	85,435	73,724	97,009	90,964	81,560	100,227
21 years	196,600	100,178	96,429	179,596	92,440	87,147	77,897	79,849	75,967	73,451	76,197	70,747
22 years	216,269	101,974	114,295	200,961	95,076	105,885	85,690	81,281	90,048	82,189	78,362	85,959
23 years	200,705	92,960	107,745	182,805	85,731	97,074	79,523	74,096	84,887	74,764	70,660	78,806
24 years	201,596	94,551	107,045	183,393	86,709	96,684	79,876	75,364	84,336	75,004	71,466	78,489
25 years	218,093	101,523	116,570	209,908	99,446	110,462	86,412	80,921	91,840	85,848	81,964	89,675
26 years	177,605	83,100	94,505	148,041	71,458	76,583	70,370	66,237	74,456	60,546	58,896	62,171
27 years	159,423	77,595	81,828	133,358	66,528	66,830	63,166	61,849	64,469	54,541	54,833	54,253
28 years	192,795	93,921	98,874	141,024	70,528	70,406	76,389	74,862	77,898	57,676	58,130	57,230
29 years	133,311	65,666	67,645	105,148	52,637	52,511	52,820	52,341	53,294	43,003	43,384	42,629
30 years	233,557	114,699	118,858	192,436	95,910	96,526	92,540	91,423	93,643	78,703	79,050	78,361
31 years	89,743	45,572	44,171	66,996	34,518	32,478	35,558	36,324	34,800	27,400	28,450	26,366
32 years	128,545	63,470	65,075	90,999	45,186	45,813	50,932	50,590	51,270	37,217	37,243	37,192
33 years	106,042	52,894	53,148	84,141	41,818	42,323	42,016	42,160	41,873	34,412	34,467	34,358
34 years	110,202	55,528	54,674	90,035	44,698	45,337	43,664	44,260	43,075	36,823	36,840	36,805
35 years	184,182	94,561	89,621	150,710	74,496	76,214	72,976	75,372	70,608	61,638	61,400	61,872
36 years	115,720	57,054	58,666	79,976	38,629	41,347	45,850	45,476	46,220	32,709	31,838	33,566
37 years	96,694	48,830	47,864	71,489	35,245	36,214	38,312	38,921	37,710	29,238	29,049	29,423
38 years	136,025	68,778	67,247	91,648	44,834	46,814	53,896	54,821	52,081	37,482	36,952	38,004
39 years	100,828	51,227	49,601	80,864	40,167	40,697	39,950	40,832	39,078	33,072	33,106	33,038
40 years	186,178	93,149	93,029	167,046	79,300	87,746	73,767	74,247	73,293	68,319	65,359	71,223
41 years	56,545	29,794	26,751	42,358	21,901	20,457	22,404	23,748	21,076	17,324	18,051	16,607
42 years	84,809	43,041	41,768	59,604	29,431	30,173	33,603	34,307	32,907	24,377	24,257	24,495
43 years	63,616	31,532	32,084	46,191	22,723	23,206	25,206	25,133	25,278	18,891	18,728	19,052
44 years	64,265	32,164	32,101	52,017	25,735	26,282	25,463	25,637	25,291	21,274	21,211	21,336
45 years	129,838	66,921	62,917	112,275	55,595	56,680	51,444	53,341	49,569	45,918	45,822	46,014
46 years	58,210	30,580	27,630	49,743	27,110	22,633	23,064	24,374	21,768	20,344	22,344	18,374
47 years	53,808	28,528	25,280	48,463	26,305	22,158	21,320	22,739	19,917	19,820	21,681	17,988
48 years	80,337	40,258	40,079	61,383	31,232	30,151	31,831	32,089	31,576	25,104	25,742	24,477
49 years	63,716	33,641	30,075	54,520	28,253	26,287	25,245	26,814	23,695	23,298	23,286	21,324
50 years	142,123	73,147	68,976	138,280	67,914	70,366	56,312	58,304	54,343	56,554	55,675	57,124

[Continued]

★ 1681 ★

Black Population Classified by Gender and Year of Age, and Number in Each Year of Age per 100,000 Under 1 Year, 1900 and 1910

[Continued]

AGE	NEGRO POPULATION											
	1910			1900			Per 100,000 under 1 year of age					
							1910			1900		
	Both sexes	Male	Female	Both sexes	Male	Female	Both sexes	Male	Female	Both sexes	Male	Female
51 years	39,305	22,906	16,399	33,203	19,247	13,956	15,573	18,258	12,920	13,579	15,863	11,330
52 years	57,500	33,491	24,069	46,661	26,922	19,739	22,806	26,695	18,963	19,083	22,189	16,024
53 years	40,728	23,753	16,975	34,409	19,899	14,510	16,137	18,933	13,374	14,073	16,401	11,779
54 years	46,354	26,090	20,264	38,434	21,206	17,228	18,366	20,796	15,965	15,719	17,478	13,986
55 years	68,408	36,621	31,787	64,973	34,013	30,960	27,105	29,190	25,044	26,573	28,034	25,134
56 years	45,350	25,854	19,496	35,086	20,281	14,805	17,969	20,608	15,360	14,350	16,716	12,019
57 years	30,205	17,360	12,845	24,392	13,935	10,457	11,968	13,387	10,120	9,976	11,485	8,489
58 years	38,222	20,293	17,929	28,065	14,806	13,259	15,144	16,175	14,125	11,478	12,203	10,764
59 years	27,437	14,962	12,475	26,660	14,288	12,372	10,871	11,926	9,828	10,903	11,776	10,044
60 years	96,575	49,275	47,300	92,756	46,011	46,745	38,265	39,276	37,266	37,935	37,923	37,948
61 years	18,685	10,565	8,120	13,696	8,006	5,690	7,403	8,421	6,397	5,601	6,599	4,619
62 years	25,927	14,893	11,034	19,367	11,204	8,163	10,273	11,871	8,693	7,921	9,234	6,627
63 years	23,976	14,115	9,861	17,987	10,676	7,311	9,500	11,251	7,769	7,356	8,709	5,935
64 years	21,339	12,301	9,038	17,881	10,064	7,817	8,455	9,805	7,121	7,313	8,295	6,346
65 years	56,886	29,683	27,203	47,437	24,452	22,985	22,539	23,660	21,432	19,401	20,153	18,660
66 years	16,871	10,132	6,739	14,181	8,549	5,632	6,685	8,076	5,300	5,800	7,046	4,572
67 years	15,837	9,322	6,515	13,388	8,022	5,366	6,275	7,430	5,133	5,475	6,612	4,356
68 years	19,695	10,663	9,032	14,612	7,924	6,688	7,804	8,499	7,116	5,976	6,531	5,429
69 years	14,261	8,156	6,105	13,053	7,071	5,982	5,650	6,501	4,810	5,338	5,823	4,856
70 years	42,899	20,594	22,305	43,132	20,224	22,908	16,997	16,415	17,573	17,640	16,669	18,597
71 years	7,805	4,314	3,491	5,916	3,271	2,645	3,092	3,439	2,750	2,420	2,696	2,147
72 years	11,592	6,397	5,195	9,140	4,994	4,146	4,593	5,099	4,093	3,738	4,116	3,366
73 years	8,358	4,706	3,652	6,725	3,750	2,975	3,312	3,751	2,877	2,750	3,091	2,415
74 years	8,185	4,573	3,612	7,469	3,996	3,473	3,243	3,645	2,846	3,055	3,294	2,819
75 years	21,005	10,139	10,866	20,433	9,737	10,696	8,323	8,082	8,561	8,357	8,025	8,683
76 years	7,529	4,137	3,392	5,847	3,204	2,643	2,983	3,297	2,672	2,391	2,641	2,146
77 years	4,721	2,799	1,922	4,080	2,268	1,812	1,871	2,231	1,514	1,669	1,869	1,471
78 years	6,754	3,485	3,269	5,430	2,879	2,551	2,676	2,778	2,575	2,221	2,373	2,071
79 years	4,009	2,107	1,902	4,630	2,387	2,243	1,588	1,679	1,498	1,894	1,967	1,821
80 years	15,054	6,434	8,620	16,431	6,977	9,454	5,965	5,128	6,791	6,720	5,750	7,675
81 years	2,537	1,264	1,273	2,091	1,128	963	1,005	1,008	1,003	855	930	782
82 years	2,989	1,487	1,502	2,802	1,461	1,341	1,184	1,185	1,183	1,146	1,204	1,089
83 years	2,393	1,195	1,198	1,974	1,007	967	948	953	944	807	830	785
84 years	2,606	1,316	1,290	2,229	1,082	1,147	1,033	1,049	1,016	912	892	931
85 years	4,961	2,142	2,819	4,633	1,976	2,657	1,966	1,707	2,221	1,895	1,629	2,157
86 years	1,907	948	959	1,592	841	751	756	756	756	651	693	610
87 years	1,757	890	867	1,448	743	705	696	709	683	592	612	572
88 years	1,335	643	692	1,288	637	651	529	513	545	527	525	528
89 years	1,206	541	665	1,122	516	606	478	431	524	459	425	492
90 years	3,718	1,393	2,325	3,648	1,342	2,306	1,473	1,110	1,832	1,492	1,106	1,872
91 years	563	276	287	395	189	206	223	220	226	162	156	167
92 years	622	300	322	496	222	274	246	239	254	203	183	222
93 years	514	216	298	382	163	219	204	172	235	156	134	178
94 years	433	209	224	372	169	203	172	167	176	152	139	165
95 years	1,092	420	672	923	346	577	433	335	529	377	285	268
96 years	379	176	203	388	168	220	150	140	160	159	138	179
97 years	267	118	149	295	124	171	106	94	117	121	102	139
98 years	480	210	270	475	167	308	190	167	213	194	138	250
99 years	229	93	136	353	153	200	91	74	107	144	126	162

[Continued]

★ 1681 ★

Black Population Classified by Gender and Year of Age, and Number in Each Year of Age per 100,000 Under 1 Year, 1900 and 1910

[Continued]

AGE	NEGRO POPULATION											
	1910			1900			Per 100,000 under 1 year of age					
							1910			1900		
	Both sexes	Male	Female	Both sexes	Male	Female	Both sexes	Male	Female	Both sexes	Male	Female
100 years and over	2,675	1,004	1,671	2,553	886	1,667	1,060	800	1,317	1,044	730	1,353
Age unknown	31,040	17,076	13,964	48,811	25,157	23,654	12,299	13,611	11,002	19,963	20,735	19,203

Source: "Negro Population Classified by Sex and Single Years of Age, and Number in Each Year of Age Per 100,000 Under 1 Year: 1910 and 1900." U.S. Bureau of the Census, *Negro Population, 1790-1915*, pp. 161-162.

★ 1682 ★

Distribution by Gender

Black Population Classified by Gender, Gender Ratio, 1880-1910, and Gender for White Classes, 1910 by Sections and Southern Divisions

SECTION AND DIVISION	NEGRO POPULATION: 1910					MALES TO 1,000 FEMALES						
	Both sexes	Male	Female	Excess of-		Negro population				White population: 1910		
				Male	Females	1910	1900	1890	1880	Total	Native	Foreign born
United States	9,827,763	4,885,881	4,941,882	-	56,001	989	986	995	978	1,066	1,027	1,292
The South	8,749,427	4,339,625	4,409,802	-	70,177	984	982	990	975	1,052	1,041	1,420
South Atlantic	4,112,488	2,029,808	2,082,680	-	52,872	975	969	979	968	1,032	1,018	1,469
East South Central	2,652,513	1,315,792	1,336,721	-	20,929	984	989	993	973	1,036	1,031	1,392
West South Central	1,984,426	994,025	990,401	3,624	-	1,004	999	1,012	997	1,093	1,079	1,388
The North	1,027,674	518,544	509,130	9,414	-	1,018	1,017	1,030	997	1,050	1,007	1,235
The West	50,662	27,712	22,950	4,762	-	1,207	1,306	1,575	1,414	1,262	1,153	1,845

Source: "Negro Population Classified by Sex, 1910; Negro Sex Ratio for White Classes, 1910: by Sections and Southern Divisions." U.S. Bureau of the Census, *Negro Population, 1790-1915*, p. 149.

★ 1683 ★

Distribution by Gender

Black Population Cumulated by States, Ranged by Gender Ratio, 1890-1910 - I

STATES RANGED IN ORDER BY SEX RATIO	NEGRO POPULATION, CUMULATED BY STATES, BY SEX RATIOS 1910			
	Males to 1,000 females	Population	Cumulated population	
			Number	Percent
United States	989	9,827,763	-	-
1 Dist. of Columbia	822	94,446	94,446	1.0
2 Connecticut	910	15,174	109,620	1.1
3 New York	913	134,191	243,811	2.5
4 New Jersey	945	89,760	333,571	3.4
5 North Carolina	948	697,843	1,031,414	10.5
6 Rhode Island	951	9,529	1,040,943	10.6
7 South Carolina	954	835,843	1,876,786	19.1
8 Massachusetts	971	38,055	1,914,841	19.5
9 Virginia	971	672,096	2,585,937	26.3
10 Alabama	972	908,282	3,494,219	35.6
11 Georgia	972	1,176,987	4,671,206	47.5
12 Tennessee	976	473,088	5,144,294	52.3
13 Maryland	977	232,250	5,376,544	54.7
14 Pennsylvania	977	193,919	5,570,463	56.7
15 Louisiana	983	713,874	6,284,337	63.9
16 Mississippi	992	1,009,487	7,293,824	74.2
17 Texas	1,000	690,049	7,983,873	81.2
18 Kentucky	1,010	261,656	8,245,529	83.9
19 Arkansas	1,017	442,891	8,688,420	88.4
20 Wisconsin	1,037	2,900	8,691,320	88.4
21 New Hampshire	1,043	564	8,691,884	88.4
22 Missouri	1,046	157,452	8,849,336	90.0
23 Colorado	1,050	11,453	8,860,789	90.2
24 Nevada	1,052	513	8,861,302	90.2
25 Delaware	1,055	31,181	8,892,483	90.5
26 Maine	1,056	1,363	8,893,846	90.5
27 Indiana	1,060	60,320	8,954,166	91.1
28 Kansas	1,073	54,030	9,008,196	91.7
29 Ohio	1,085	111,452	9,119,648	92.8
30 Illinois	1,091	109,049	9,228,697	93.9
31 California	1,093	21,645	9,250,342	94.1
32 Florida	1,095	308,669	9,559,011	97.3
33 Oklahoma	1,095	137,612	9,696,623	98.7
34 Arizona	1,104	2,009	9,698,632	98.7
35 Michigan	1,111	17,115	9,715,747	98.9
36 Iowa	1,185	14,973	9,730,720	99.0
37 New Mexico	1,209	1,628	9,732,348	99.0
38 Nebraska	1,242	7,689	9,740,037	99.1
39 West Virginia	1,328	64,173	9,804,210	99.8

[Continued]

★ 1683 ★

Black Population Cumulated by States, Ranged by Gender Ratio, 1890-1910 - I

[Continued]

STATES RANGED IN ORDER BY SEX RATIO	NEGRO POPULATION, CUMULATED BY STATES, BY SEX RATIOS 1910			
	Males to 1,000 females	Population	Cumulated population	
			Number	Percent
40 South Dakota	1,341	817	9,805,027	99.8
41 Montana	1,363	1,834	9,806,861	99.8
42 Minnesota	1,442	7,084	9,813,945	99.9
43 Utah	1,525	1,144	9,815,089	99.9
44 Oregon	1,550	1,492	9,816,581	99.9
45 Idaho	1,573	651	9,817,232	99.9
46 Washington	1,609	6,058	9,823,290	100.0
47 North Dakota	1,614	617	9,823,907	100.0
48 Wyoming	2,234	2,235	9,826,142	100.0
49 Vermont	2,618	1,621	9,827,763	100.0

Source: "Negro Population Cumulated by States, Ranged in Order by Sex Ratio: 1910, 1900, and 1890." U.S. Bureau of the Census, *Negro Population, 1790- 1915.* p. 151. *Notes:* 1. Includes populate of Indian Territory. 2. Number of females less than 100 in Nevada for 1900 and 1890, and in Idaho for 1890.

★ 1684 ★

Distribution by Gender

Black Population Cumulated by States, Ranged by Gender Ratio, 1890-1910 - II

SEX RANGED IN ORDER BY SEX RATIO	NEGRO POPULATION, CUMULATED BY STATES, BY SEX RATIOS 1900			
	Males to 1,000 females	Population	Cumulated population	
			Number	Percent
United States	986	8,833,994	-	-
1 Dist. of Columbia	793	86,702	86,702	1.0
2 New York	886	99,232	185,934	2.1
3 Rhode Island	893	9,092	195,026	2.2
4 Connecticut	908	15,226	210,252	2.4
5 New Jersey	935	69,844	280,096	3.2
6 North Carolina	946	624,469	904,565	10.2
7 Massachusetts	952	31,974	936,539	10.6
8 Virginia	959	660,722	1,597,261	18.1
9 South Carolina	962	782,321	2,379,582	26.9
10 Maryland	968	235,064	2,614,646	29.6
11 Georgia	971	1,034,813	3,649,459	41.3
12 New Hampshire	976	662	3,650,121	41.3
13 Alabama	979	827,307	4,477,428	50.7
14 Louisiana	983	650,804	5,128,232	58.1
15 Tennessee	986	480,243	5,608,475	63.5

[Continued]

★ 1684 ★

Black Population Cumulated by States, Ranged by Gender Ratio, 1890-1910 - II

[Continued]

SEX RANGED IN ORDER BY SEX RATIO	NEGRO POPULATION, CUMULATED BY STATES, BY SEX RATIOS 1900			
	Males to 1,000 females	Population	Cumulated population	
			Number	Percent
16 Kentucky	996	284,706	5,893,181	66.7
17 Mississippi	998	907,630	6,800,811	77.0
18 Texas	999	620,722	7,421,533	84.0
19 Missouri	1,015	161,234	7,582,767	85.8
20 Arkansas	1,021	366,856	7,949,623	90.0
21 Pennsylvania	1,024	156,845	8,106,468	91.8
22 Maine	1,032	1,319	8,107,787	91.8
23 Delaware	1,035	30,697	8,138,484	92.1
24 Kansas	1,042	52,003	8,190,487	92.7
25 Oklahoma[1]	1,060	55,684	8,246,171	93.3
26 Ohio	1,065	96,901	8,343,072	94.4
27 Indiana	1,068	57,505	8,400,577	95.1
28 Michigan	1,082	15,816	8,416,393	95.3
29 Florida	1,087	230,730	8,647,123	97.9
30 California	1,092	11,045	8,658,168	98.0
31 Colorado	1,092	8,570	8,666,738	98.1
32 Illinois	1,129	85,078	8,751,816	99.1
33 Nebraska	1,161	6,269	8,758,085	99.1
34 Iowa	1,182	12,693	8,770,778	99.3
35 Vermont	1,220	826	8,771,604	99.3
36 Wisconsin	1,262	2,542	8,774,146	99.3
37 Idaho	1,307	293	8,774,439	99.3
38 Minnesota	1,336	4,959	8,779,398	99.4
39 West Virginia	1,373	43,499	8,822,897	99.9
40 South Dakota	1,409	465	8,823,362	99.9
41 Montana	1,493	1,523	8,824,855	99.9
42 North Dakota	1,531	286	8,825,171	99.9
43 Nevada[2]	1,577	134	9,925,305	99.9
44 Oregon	1,582	1,105	8,826,410	99.9
45 Washington	1,718	2,514	8,828,924	99.9
46 New Mexico	1,743	1,610	8,830,534	100.0
47 Wyoming	2,042	940	8,831,474	100.0
48 Utah	2,083	672	8,832,146	100.0
49 Arizona	2,810	1,848	8,833,994	100.0

Source: "Negro Population Cumulated by States, Ranged in Order by Sex Ratio: 1910, 1900, and 1890." U.S. Bureau of the Census, *Negro Population, 1790- 1915.* p. 151. *Notes:* 1. Includes populate of Indian Territory. 2. Number of females less than 100 in Nevada for 1900 and 1890, and in Idaho for 1890.

★ 1685 ★

Distribution by Gender

Black Population Cumulated by States, Ranged by Gender Ratio, 1890-1910 - III

STATES RANGED IN ORDER BY SEX RATIO	NEGRO POPULATION, CUMULATED BY STATES, BY SEX RATIOS 1890			
	Males to 1,000 females	Population	Cumulated population	
			Number	Percent
United States	995	7,488,676	-	-
1 Dist. of Columbia	806	75,572	75,572	1.0
2 Rhode Island	849	7,393	82,965	1.1
3 New York	916	70,092	153,057	2.0
4 Connecticut	931	12,302	165,359	2.2
5 Virginia	958	635,438	800,797	10.7
6 Maryland	961	215,657	1,016,454	13.6
7 North Carolina	963	561,018	1,577,472	21.1
8 Massachusetts	966	22,144	1,599,616	21.4
9 New Jersey	966	47,638	1,647,254	22.0
10 Louisiana	983	559,193	2,206,447	29.5
11 Tennessee	983	430,678	2,637,125	35.2
12 South Carolina	985	688,934	3,326,059	44.4
13 Alabama	987	678,489	4,004,548	53.5
14 Kentucky	993	268,071	4,272,619	57.1
15 Georgia	1,003	858,815	5,131,434	68.5
16 Mississippi	1,005	742,559	5,873,993	78.4
17 Missouri	1,007	150,184	6,024,177	80.4
18 Texas	1,011	488,171	6,512,348	87.0
19 Florida	1,021	166,180	6,678,528	89.2
20 Kansas	1,032	49,710	6,728,238	89.8
21 Pennsylvania	1,035	107,596	6,835,834	91.3
22 Delaware	1,038	28,386	6,864,220	91.7
23 Arkansas	1,059	309,117	7,173,337	95.8
24 Maine	1,066	1,190	7,174,527	95.8
25 Ohio	1,072	87,113	7,261,640	97.0
26 Indiana	1,084	45,215	7,306,855	97.6
27 Michigan	1,103	15,223	7,322,078	97.8
28 New Hampshire	1,110	614	7,322,692	97.8
29 Vermont	1,110	937	7,323,629	97.8
30 Illinois	1,122	57,028	7,380,657	98.6
31 Iowa	1,149	10,685	7,391,342	98.7
32 Oklahoma[1]	1,171	21,609	7,412,951	99.0
33 West Virginia	1,224	32,690	7,445,641	99.4
34 Wisconsin	1,261	2,444	7,448,085	99.5
35 California	1,276	11,322	7,459,407	99.6
36 Colorado	1,378	6,215	7,465,622	99.7
37 Idaho[2]	1,422	201	7,465,823	99.7
38 North Dakota	1,422	373	7,466,196	99.7
39 Minnesota	1,429	3,683	7,469,879	99.7

[Continued]

★ 1685 ★

Black Population Cumulated by States, Ranged by Gender Ratio, 1890-1910 - III

[Continued]

STATES RANGED IN ORDER BY SEX RATIO	NEGRO POPULATION, CUMULATED BY STATES, BY SEX RATIOS 1890			
	Males to 1,000 females	Population	Cumulated population	
			Number	Percent
40 Nebraska	1,429	8,913	7,478,792	99.9
41 New Mexico	1,658	1,956	7,480,748	99.9
42 Oregon	1,677	1,186	7,481,934	99.9
43 Utah	2,000	588	7,482,522	99.9
44 Nevada[2]	2,025	242	7,482,764	99.9
45 South Dakota	2,039	541	7,483,305	99.9
46 Washington	2,217	1,602	7,484,907	99.9
47 Montana	2,410	1,490	7,486,397	100.0
48 Wyoming	2,415	922	7,487,319	100.0
49 Arizona	6,375	1,357	7,488,676	100.0

Source: "Negro Population Cumulated by States, Ranged in Order by Sex Ratio: 1910, 1900, and 1890." U.S. Bureau of the Census, *Negro Population, 1790- 1915*. p. 151. *Notes:* 1. Includes populate of Indian Territory. 2. Number of females less than 100 in Nevada for 1900 and 1890, and in Idaho for 1890.

★ 1686 ★

Distribution by Gender

Black Population and Gender Ratios of Counties Having 50 Percent or More or 50 Percent or Less of the Black Population, by Sections Southern Divisions, and Southern States, 1930

SECTION, DIVISION, AND STATE	NEGRO POPULATION IN-				MALES PER 100 FEMALES IN NEGRO POPULATION IN-	
	Counties 50 percent or more Negro		Counties less than 50 percent Negro		Counties 50 percent or more Negro	Counties less than 50 percent Negro
	Male	Female	Male	Female		
United States	1,338,069	1,400,363	4,517,600	4,635,111	95.6	97.5
THE SOUTH	1,338,069	1,400,363	3,245,522	3,377,623	95.6	96.1
South Atlantic	572,476	609,784	1,584,055	1,655,073	93.9	95.7
East South Central	548,749	571,373	752,803	785,313	96.0	95.9
West South Central	216,844	219,206	908,664	937,237	98.9	97.0
THE NORTH	-	-	1,210,707	1,198,512	-	101.0
THE WEST	-	-	61,371	58,976	-	104.1
SOUTH ATLANTIC:						
Delaware	-	-	16,983	15,619	-	108.7
Maryland	-	-	140,506	135,873	-	103.4
District of Columbia	-	-	62,225	69,843	-	89.1
Virginia	79,255	77,282	242,290	251,338	102.6	96.4

[Continued]

★ 1686 ★

Black Population and Gender Ratios of Counties Having 50 Percent or More or 50 Percent or Less of the Black Population, by Sections Southern Divisions, and Southern States, 1930

[Continued]

SECTION, DIVISION, AND STATE	NEGRO POPULATION IN-				MALES PER 100 FEMALES IN NEGRO POPULATION IN-	
	Counties 50 percent or more Negro		Counties less than 50 percent Negro		Counties 50 percent or more Negro	Counties less than 50 percent Negro
	Male	Female	Male	Female		
West Virginia	-	-	60,873	54,020	-	112.7
North Carolina	73,339	76,253	373,161	395,894	96.2	94.3
South Carolina	212,305	234,130	166,995	180,251	90.7	92.6
Georgia	184,291	197,327	329,160	360,347	93.4	91.3
Florida	23,286	24,792	191,862	191,888	93.9	100.0
EAST SOUTH CENTRAL:						
Kentucky	-	-	113,501	112,539	-	100.9
Tennessee	19,337	18,985	213,232	226,092	101.9	94.3
Alabama	182,919	197,944	274,225	289,746	92.4	94.6
Mississippi	346,493	354,444	151,845	156,936	97.8	96.8
WEST SOUTH CENTRAL:						
Arkansas	94,064	94,218	142,845	147,336	99.8	97.0
Louisiana	98,688	99,900	280,485	297,253	98.8	94.4
Oklahoma	-	-	86,818	85,380	-	101.7
Texas	24,092	25,088	398,516	407,268	96.0	97.9

Source: "Black Population and Sex Ratios of Counties Having 50 Percent or More Negroes and Counties Having Less than 50 Percent Negro Population, by Sections, Southern Divisions, and Southern States: 1930." U.S. Bureau of the Census, *Negroes in the United States, 1920-1932*, p. 80.

★ 1687 ★

Distribution by Gender

Black Population by Gender with Number of Males Per 100 Females, by Divisions and States, 1900-1930 - I

DIVISION AND STATE	1930				1920		1910		1900	
	Male	Female	Excess of-							
			Males	Females	Male	Female	Male	Female	Male	Female
United States	5,855,669	6,035,474	-	179,805	5,209,436	5,253,695	4,885,881	4,941,882	4,386,547	4,447,447
GEOGRAPHIC DIVISIONS:										
New England	46,963	47,123	-	160	40,155	38,896	32,783	33,523	28,579	30,520
Middle Atlantic	520,826	532,073	-	11,247	301,147	299,036	203,466	214,404	159,711	166,210
East North Central	475,368	455,082	20,286	-	273,026	241,528	156,431	144,405	134,445	123,397
West North Central	167,550	164,234	3,316	-	143,762	134,759	125,864	116,798	121,272	116,637
South Atlantic	2,156,531	2,264,837	-	108,326	2,133,377	2,191,743	2,029,808	2,082,680	1,835,525	1,893,492
East South Central	1,301,552	1,356,686	-	55,134	1,243,795	1,279,737	1,315,792	1,336,721	1,243,082	1,256,804
West South Central	1,125,508	1,156,443	-	30,935	1,029,457	1,034,122	994,025	990,401	846,797	847,269
Mountain	16,312	13,913	2,399	-	19,726	11,075	11,766	9,701	9,104	6,486
Pacific	45,059	45,063	-	4	24,991	22,799	15,946	13,249	8,032	6,632
NEW ENGLAND:										
Maine	597	499	98	-	716	594	700	663	670	649
New Hampshire	524	266	258	-	333	288	288	276	327	335

[Continued]

★ 1687 ★

Black Population by Gender with Number of Males Per 100 Females, by Divisions and States, 1900-1930 - I

[Continued]

DIVISION AND STATE	1930				1920		1910		1900	
	Male	Female	Excess of-		Male	Female	Male	Female	Male	Female
			Males	Females						
Vermont	310	258	52	-	320	252	1,173	448	454	372
Massachusetts	26,097	26,268	-	171	22,912	22,554	18,748	19,307	15,591	16,383
Rhode Island	4,862	5,051	-	189	5,096	4,940	4,645	4,884	4,290	4,802
Connecticut	14,573	14,781	-	208	10,778	10,268	7,229	7,945	7,247	7,979
MIDDLE ATLANTIC:										
New York	199,485	213,329	-	13,844	95,418	103,065	64,034	70,157	46,618	52,614
New Jersey	102,929	105,899	-	2,970	57,432	59,700	43,602	46,158	33,745	36,099
Pennsylvania	218,412	212,845	5,567	-	148,297	136,271	95,830	98,089	79,348	77,497
EAST NORTH CENTRAL:										
Ohio	159,128	150,176	8,952	-	100,160	86,027	57,995	53,457	49,985	46,916
Indiana	57,068	54,914	2,154	-	41,817	38,993	31,044	29,276	29,701	27,804
Illinois	164,425	164,547	-	122	93,835	88,439	56,909	52,140	45,121	39,957
Michigan	88,936	80,517	8,419	-	34,249	25,833	9,007	8,108	8,220	7,596
Wisconsin	5,811	4,928	883	-	2,965	2,236	1,476	1,424	1,418	1,124
WEST NORTH CENTRAL:										
Minnesota	5,005	4,440	565	-	4,851	3,958	4,183	2,901	2,836	2,123
Iowa	9,987	8,393	594	-	10,121	8,884	8,120	6,853	6,875	5,818
Missouri	111,929	111,911	18	-	90,991	87,250	80,489	76,963	81,206	80,028
North Dakota	243	134	109	-	276	191	381	236	173	113
South Dakota	343	303	40	-	475	357	468	349	272	193
Nebraska	7,063	6,689	374	-	7,309	5,933	4,259	3,430	3,368	2,901
Kansas	33,980	32,364	1,616	-	29,739	28,186	27,964	26,066	26,542	25,461
SOUTH ATLANTIC:										
Delaware	16,983	15,619	1,364	-	15,655	14,680	16,011	15,170	15,616	15,081
Maryland	140,506	135,873	4,633	-	123,453	121,026	114,749	117,501	115,617	119,447
District of Columbia	62,225	69,843	-	7,618	50,855	59,111	42,615	51,831	38,348	48,354
Virginia	321,545	328,620	-	7,075	342,536	347,481	330,542	340,554	323,459	337,263
West Virginia	60,873	54,020	6,853	-	47,129	39,216	36,607	27,556	25,167	18,332
North Carolina	446,500	472,147	-	25,647	373,965	389,442	339,581	358,262	303,624	320,845
South Carolina	379,300	414,381	-	35,081	422,185	442,534	408,078	427,765	383,626	398,695
Georgia	513,451	557,674	-	44,223	590,443	615,922	580,263	596,724	509,869	524,944
Florida	215,148	216,680	-	1,532	167,156	162,331	161,362	147,307	120,199	110,531
EAST SOUTH CENTRAL:										
Kentucky	113,501	112,539	962	-	118,548	117,390	131,492	130,164	142,073	142,633
Tennessee	232,569	245,077	-	12,508	222,639	229,119	233,710	239,378	238,388	241,855
Alabama	457,144	487,690	-	30,546	439,779	460,873	447,794	460,488	409,237	418,070
Mississippi	498,338	511,380	-	13,042	462,829	472,355	502,796	506,691	453,384	454,246
WEST SOUTH CENTRAL:										
Arkansas	236,909	241,554	-	4,645	236,895	235,325	223,323	219,568	185,342	181,514
Louisiana	379,173	397,153	-	17,980	344,794	355,463	353,824	360,050	322,664	328,140
Oklahoma	86,818	85,380	1,438	-	76,294	73,114	71,937	65,675	28,656	27,028
Texas	422,608	432,356	-	9,748	371,474	370,220	344,941	345,108	310,135	310,587
Mountain:										
Montana	710	546	164	-	962	696	1,058	776	912	611
Idaho	395	273	122	-	585	335	398	253	166	127
Wyoming	699	551	148	-	863	512	1,544	691	631	309
Colorado	5,739	6,089	-	350	5,834	5,484	5,867	5,586	4,473	4,097
New Mexico	1,531	1,319	212	-	4,593	1,140	891	737	1,023	587
Arizona	6,352	4,397	1,955	-	5,859	2,146	1,054	955	1,363	485

[Continued]

★ 1687 ★

Black Population by Gender with Number of Males Per 100 Females, by Divisions and States, 1900-1930 - I

[Continued]

DIVISION AND STATE	1930				1920		1910		1900	
	Male	Female	Excess of-							
			Males	Females	Male	Female	Male	Female	Male	Female
Utah	609	499	110	-	834	612	691	453	454	218
Nevada	277	239	38	-	196	150	263	250	82	52
PACIFIC:										
Washington	3,797	3,043	754	-	3,957	2,926	3,736	2,322	1,589	925
Oregon	1,210	1,024	186	-	1,197	947	907	585	677	428
California	40,052	40,996	-	944	19,837	18,926	11,303	10,342	5,766	5,279

Source: "Negro Population by Sex, With Number of Males Per 100 Females, by Divisions, and States: 1900 to 1930." U.S. Bureau of the Census, *Negroes in the United States, 1920-1932*, p. 82.

★ 1688 ★

Distribution by Gender

Black Population by Gender with Number of Males Per 100 Females, by Divisions and States, 1900-1930 - II

DIVISION AND STATE	MALES PER 100 FEMALES			
	1930	1920	1910	1900
United States	97.0	99.2	98.9	98.6
GEOGRAPHIC DIVISIONS:				
New England	99.7	103.2	97.8	93.6
Middle Atlantic	97.9	100.7	94.9	96.1
East North Central	104.5	113.0	108.3	109.0
West North Central	102.0	106.7	107.8	104.0
South Atlantic	95.2	97.3	97.5	96.9
East South Central	95.9	97.2	98.4	98.9
West South Central	97.3	99.5	100.4	99.9
Mountain	117.2	178.1	121.3	140.4
Pacific	100.0	109.6	120.4	121.1
NEW ENGLAND:				
Maine	119.6	120.5	105.6	103.2
New Hampshire	197.0	115.6	104.3	97.6
Vermont	120.2	127.0	261.8	122.0
Massachusetts	99.3	101.6	97.1	95.2
Rhode Island	96.3	103.2	95.1	89.3
Connecticut	98.6	105.0	91.0	90.8
MIDDLE ATLANTIC:				
New York	93.5	92.6	91.3	88.6
New Jersey	97.2	96.2	94.5	93.5
Pennsylvania	102.6	108.8	97.7	102.4

[Continued]

★ 1688 ★

Black Population by Gender with Number of Males Per 100 Females, by Divisions and States, 1900-1930 - II

[Continued]

DIVISION AND STATE	MALES PER 100 FEMALES			
	1930	1920	1910	1900
EAST NORTH CENTRAL:				
Ohio	106.0	116.4	108.5	106.5
Indiana	103.9	107.2	106.0	106.8
Illinois	99.9	106.1	109.1	112.9
Michigan	110.5	132.6	111.1	108.2
Wisconsin	117.9	132.6	103.7	126.2
WEST NORTH CENTRAL:				
Minnesota	112.7	122.6	144.2	133.6
Iowa	107.1	113.9	118.2	118.7
Missouri	100.0	104.3	104.6	101.5
North Dakota	181.3	144.5	161.4	153.1
South Dakota	113.2	133.1	134.1	140.9
Nebraska	105.6	123.2	124.2	116.1
Kansas	105.0	105.5	107.3	104.2
SOUTH ATLANTIC:				
Delaware	108.7	106.6	105.5	103.5
Maryland	103.4	102.0	97.7	96.8
District of Columbia	89.1	86.0	82.2	79.3
Virginia	97.8	98.6	97.1	95.9
West Virginia	112.7	120.2	132.8	137.3
North Carolina	94.6	96.0	94.8	94.6
South Carolina	91.5	95.4	95.4	96.2
Georgia	92.1	95.9	97.2	97.1
Florida	99.3	103.0	109.5	108.7
EAST SOUTH CENTRAL:				
Kentucky	100.9	101.0	101.0	99.6
Tennessee	94.9	97.2	97.6	98.6
Alabama	93.7	95.4	97.2	97.9
Mississippi	97.4	98.0	99.2	99.8
WEST SOUTH CENTRAL:				
Arkansas	98.1	100.7	101.7	102.1
Louisiana	95.5	97.0	98.3	98.3
Oklahoma	101.7	104.3	109.5	106.0
Texas	97.7	100.3	100.0	99.9
Mountain:				
Montana	130.0	138.2	136.3	149.2
Idaho	144.7	174.6	157.3	130.7
Wyoming	126.9	168.6	223.4	204.2
Colorado	94.3	106.4	105.0	109.2
New Mexico	116.1	402.9	120.9	174.3

[Continued]

★ 1688 ★

Black Population by Gender with Number of Males Per 100 Females, by Divisions and States, 1900-1930 - II

[Continued]

DIVISION AND STATE	MALES PER 100 FEMALES			
	1930	1920	1910	1900
Arizona	144.5	273.0	110.4	281.0
Utah	122.0	136.3	152.5	208.3
Nevada	115.9	130.7	105.2	-
PACIFIC:				
Washington	124.8	135.2	160.9	171.8
Oregon	118.2	126.4	155.0	158.2
California	97.7	104.9	109.3	109.2

Source: "Negro Population by Sex, With Number of Males Per 100 Females, by Divisions, and States: 1900 to 1930." U.S. Bureau of the Census, *Negroes in the United States, 1920-1932*, p. 82.

★ 1689 ★

Distribution by Gender

Black Population by Gender, with Males Per 100 Females in Cities Having 10,000 or More Blacks, 1910, 1920, 1930, and Males Per 100 Females in the White Population, 1930

CITY	NEGRO POPULATION						MALES PER 100 FEMALES					
	1930		1920		1910		Negro Population			White population, 1930		
	Male	Female	Male	Female	Male	Female	1930	1920	1910	Total	Native	Foreign-born
Total, all cities having 10,000 or more Negro inhabitants	1,596,113	1,739,836	1,070,952	1,123,746	737,020	824,297	91.7	95.3	89.4	99.4	96.7	110.1
Cities of the South	828,432	954,789	642,680	710,062	508,214	587,013	86.8	90.5	86.6	95.7	94.5	118.8
Cities of the North and West	767,681	785,047	428,272	413,694	228,806	237,284	97.8	103.5	96.4	100.3	97.3	109.7
CITIES OF THE SOUTH												
Asheville, N.C.	6,379	7,876	3,135	4,010	2,363	2,996	81.0	78.2	78.9	87.2	86.8	104.4
Atlanta, Ga.	39,923	50,152	28,993	33,803	23,219	28,683	79.6	85.8	81.0	83,3	81,6	124.1
Augusta, Ga.	10,698	13,492	10,610	11,972	8,160	10,184	79.3	88.6	80.1	94.9	94.5	115.2
Baltimore, Md.	70,043	72,063	52,889	55,433	39,054	45,695	97.2	95.4	85.5	96.6	95.2	108.3
Baton Rouge, La.	4,862	5,993	3,775	4,785	3,430	4,469	78.1	78.9	76.8	94.4	93.5	129.1
Beaumont, Tex.	8,967	9,584	6,597	6,613	3,276	3,620	93.6	99.8	90.5	102.7	101.5	137.2
Bessemer, Ala.	5,593	6,098	5,370	5,191	3,176	3,034	91.7	103.4	104.7	97.2	96.5	122.3
Birmingham, Ala.	46,582	52,495	34,160	36,070	25,662	26,643	88.7	94.7	96.3	97.5	96.5	124.8
Charleston, S.C.	11,955	16,107	14,801	17,525	13,714	17,342	74.2	84.5	79.1	92.3	80.9	126.3
Charlottes, N.C.	11,437	13,726	6,810	7,831	5,201	6,551	83.3	87.0	79.4	95.8	95.1	154.4
Chattanooga, Tenn.	15,690	17,599	9,567	9,322	8,848	9,094	89.2	102.6	97.3	95.4	95.0	122.2
Columbia, S.C.	8,484	11,035	6,630	7,825	5,226	6,320	76.9	84.7	82.7	93.8	93.1	144.9
Columbus, Ga.	6,079	8,078	4,039	5,054	3,287	4,357	75.3	79.9	75.4	88.9	88.4	164.4
Dallas, Tex.	18,101	20,641	11,828	12,195	8,680	9,344	87.7	97.0	92.9	94.5	93.7	124.1
Durham, N.C.	8,616	10,101	3,637	4,017	3,106	3,763	85.3	90.5	82.5	92.5	92.1	140.7
Fort Worth, Tex.	10,560	11,674	8,010	7,886	6,781	6,499	90.5	101.6	104.3	96.3	95.8	127.3
Galveston, Tex.	6,402	6,824	5,027	4,861	3,881	4,155	93.8	103.4	93.4	112.0	106.4	160.5
Greenville, S.C.	4,843	6,028	3,817	4,367	2,829	3,490	80.3	87.4	81.1	88.0	87.3	136.4
Greensboro, N.C.	6,470	7,580	2,817	3,156	2,556	3,144	85.4	89.3	81.6	93.5	93.0	139.6
Houston, Tex.	30,160	33,177	16,394	17,566	11,218	12,711	90.9	93.3	88.3	101.5	100.4	124.9
Jackson, Miss.	9,140	10,283	4,403	5,533	4,752	5,802	88.9	79.6	81.9	91.9	91.0	190.4
Jacksonville, Fla.	22,225	25,971	20,222	21,298	14,556	14,737	85.6	94.9	98.8	95.7	94.2	127.0
Knoxville, Tenn.	8,131	8,962	5,434	5,888	3,600	4,038	90.7	92.6	89.2	93.4	93.2	119.1
Lexington, Ky.	6,132	6,627	5,945	6,505	5,075	5,936	92.5	91.4	85.5	91.8	91.0	150.8
Little Rock, Ark.	8,889	10,809	8,292	9,185	7,060	7,479	82.2	80.3	94.4	92.1	91.6	119.0
Louisville, Ky.	22,742	24,612	19,094	20,993	19,602	20,920	92.4	91.0	93.7	92.8	92.2	109.7
Macon, Ga.	10,274	12,884	10,867	12,226	8,305	9,845	79.7	88.9	84.4	89.6	89.1	125.2
Memphis, Tenn.	44,859	51,691	28,935	32,246	25,259	27,182	86.8	89.7	92.9	93.6	92.7	124.5
Meridan, Miss.	4,915	6,437	3,620	4,713	4,273	5,048	76.4	77.0	84.6	89.3	88.8	133.6
Miami, Fla.	11,902	13,214	4,579	4,691	1,137	1,121	90.1	97.6	101.4	99.7	98.5	111.8
Mobile, Ala.	11,051	13,463	11,102	12,804	10,344	12,419	82.1	86.7	83.3	97.8	94.8	187.9
Monroe, La.	4,751	5,361	2,528	3,012	2,331	2,989	88.6	83.9	78.0	105.6	104.5	142.7

[Continued]

★ 1689 ★

Black Population by Gender, with Males Per 100 Females in Cities Having 10,000 or More Blacks, 1910, 1920, 1930, and Males Per 100 Females in the White Population, 1930

[Continued]

CITY	NEGRO POPULATION						MALES PER 100 FEMALES					
	1930		1920		1910		Negro Population			White population, 1930		
	Male	Female	Male	Female	Male	Female	1930	1920	1910	Total	Native	Foreign-born
Montgomery, Ala.	13,054	16,916	8,553	11,274	8,293	11,029	77.2	75.9	75.2	94.9	94.3	132.8
Nashville, Tenn.	19,464	23,372	16,173	19,460	16,229	20,294	83.3	83.1	80.0	89.6	89.3	113.1
New Orleans, La.	59,732	69,900	46,919	54,011	40,946	48,316	85.5	86.9	84.7	93.8	91.7	134.2
Newport News, Va.	6,442	6,839	7,654	6,423	3,714	3,545	94.2	119.2	104.8	110.7	108.7	141.0
Norfolk, Va.	20,790	23,152	21,794	21,598	11,887	13,152	89.8	100.9	90.4	106.3	105.0	131.8
Oklahoma City, Okla.	7,171	7,491	4,151	4,090	3,534	3,012	95.7	101.5	117.3	102.8	102.2	139.7
Petersburg, Va.	5,734	6,866	6,174	7,434	4,831	6,183	83.5	83.1	78.1	87.5	86.9	120.7
Port Arthur, Tex.	4,934	5,069	2,030	1,880	968	525	97.3	108.0	184.4	114.1	111.2	219.1
Portsmouth, Va.	8,941	9,908	11,635	11,610	5,542	6,075	90.2	100.2	91.2	108.1	108.0	111.6
Raleigh, N.C.	5,817	6,758	4,180	4,364	3,275	4,097	86.1	95.8	79.9	93.8	93.3	138.3
Richmond, Va.	24,354	28,634	24,696	29,345	21,472	25,261	85.1	84.2	85.0	89.4	88.7	115.7
Roanoke, Va.	5,755	6,613	4,455	4,876	3,650	4,274	87.0	91.4	85.4	93.8	93.3	137.4
San Antonio, Tex.	8,184	9,794	6,842	7,499	4,909	5,807	83.6	91.2	84.5	99.7	99.0	110.9
Savannah, Ga.	17,315	21,581	18,566	20,613	15,218	18,028	80.2	90.1	84.4	92.8	91.3	125.5
Shreveport, La.	12,223	14,996	8,176	9,309	6,226	7,670	81.5	87.8	81.2	96.3	95.6	123.3
Tampa, Fla.	10,072	11,100	5,614	5,917	4,431	4,520	90.7	94.9	98.0	98.3	94.3	118.9
Tulsa, Olka.	7,241	7,962	4,366	4,512	990	969	90.9	96.8	102.2	99.5	98.8	135.8
Vicksburg, Miss.	5,225	6,690	3,869	5,279	5,231	6,822	78.1	73.3	76.7	92.1	90.6	140.8
Washington, D.C.	62,225	69,843	50,855	59,111	42,615	51,831	89.1	86.0	82.2	91.4	89.8	109.6
Wilmington, Del.	6,056	6,024	5,568	5,178	4,390	4,691	100.5	107.5	93.6	93.6	96.9	121.1
Wilmington, N.C.	5,855	7,251	6,241	7,220	5,482	6,625	80.7	86.4	82.7	91.5	90.8	129.3
Winston-Salem, N.C.	15,173	17,393	10,232	10,503	4,410	4,677	87.2	97.4	94.3	93.3	93.0	133.9
CITIES OF THE NORTH AND WEST												
Akron, Ohio	5,748	5,332	3,554	2,026	357	300	107.8	175.4	119.0	103.8	101.1	123.6
Atlantic City, N.J.	7,527	8,084	5,251	5,695	4,851	4,983	93.1	92.2	97.4	89.6	87.1	100.2
Boston, Mass.	10,223	10,351	8,295	8,055	6,664	6,900	98.8	103.0	96.6	96.0	96.8	94.2
Buffalo, N.Y.	7,064	6,499	2,522	1,989	933	840	108.7	126.8	111.1	98.3	95.6	109.2
Camden, N.J.	5,676	5,664	4,304	4,196	2,949	3,127	100.2	102.6	94.3	100.2	98.2	110.6
Chicago, Ill.	115,488	118,415	55,943	53,515	22,685	21,418	97.5	104.5	105.9	102.5	98.0	115.9
Cincinnati, Ohio	23,914	23,904	15,145	14,934	9,905	9,734	100.0	101.4	101.8	93.6	92.5	105.9
Cleveland, Ohio	36,180	35,719	18,733	15,718	4,341	4,107	101.3	119.2	105.7	102.9	98.8	114.7
Columbus, Ohio	17,126	15,648	11,788	10,393	6,784	5,955	109.4	113.4	113.9	95.9	94.3	123.4
Dayton, Ohio	8,608	8,469	4,776	4,249	2,475	2,367	101.6	112.4	104.6	98.4	97.0	119.6
Detroit, Mich.	62,239	57,827	23,605	17,233	2,985	2,756	107.6	137.0	108.3	109.9	104.7	124.6
East St. Louis, Ill.	5,743	5,793	3,908	3,529	3,233	2,649	99.1	110.7	122.0	102.0	100.4	123.5
Gary, Ind.	9,393	8,529	2,991	2,308	242	141	110.1	129.6	171.6	117.2	105.7	162.2
Indianapolis, Ind.	21,263	22,704	17,378	17,300	10,803	11,013	93.7	100.5	98.1	94.2	93.4	113.8
Jersey City, N.J.	6,229	6,346	4,099	3,901	3,020	2,940	98.2	105.1	102.7	101.3	99.0	109.2
Kansas City, Kans.	9,628	10,244	7,130	7,275	4,622	4,664	94.0	98.0	99.1	100.6	99.1	120.0
Kansas City, Mo.	18,599	19,975	15,472	15,247	11,885	11,681	93.1	101.5	101.7	94.7	93.1	119.2
Los Angeles, Calif.	18,349	20,545	7,389	8,190	3,682	3,917	89.3	90.2	94.0	95.5	93.1	108.6
Newark, N.J.	19,280	19,600	8,552	8,425	4,477	4,998	98.4	101.5	89.6	102.4	98.7	112.5
New York, N.Y.	156,968	170,738	72,351	80,116	42,143	49,566	91.9	90.3	85.0	100.6	97.8	105.9
Bronx Borough	6,302	6,628	2,269	2,534	1,911	2,206	95.1	89.5	86.6	99.3	97.7	102.1
Brooklyn Borough	32,835	36,086	15,197	16,715	10,245	12,463	91.0	90.9	82.2	100.7	97.4	107.0
Manhattan Borough	108,229	116,441	51,912	57,221	28,024	32,510	92.9	90.7	86.2	101.5	98.3	106.8
Queens Borough	8,347	10,262	2,238	2,882	1,440	1,758	81.3	77.7	81.9	99.5	97.5	118.9
Richmond Borough	1,255	1,321	735	764	523	629	95.0	96.2	83.1	107.7	104.1	118.9
Omaha, Nebr.[1]	5,607	5,516	5,598	4,717	2,811	2,332	101.6	118.7	120.5	97.5	95.4	110.7
Philadelphia, Pa.	108,483	111,116	67,132	67,097	39,431	45,028	97.6	100.1	87.6	98.4	97.1	103.3
Pittsburgh, Pa.	27,962	27,021	19,913	17,812	13,351	12,272	103.5	111.8	108.8	98.1	95.5	111.2
St. Louis, Mo.	45,832	47,748	35,359	34,495	22,168	21,792	96.0	102.5	101.7	95.4	93.1	115.5
Toledo, Ohio	6,967	6,293	3,184	2,507	937	940	110.7	127.0	99.7	102.7	100.0	124.8
Youngstown, Ohio	7,585	6,967	3,900	2,762	1,072	864	108.9	141.2	124.1	103.5	97.8	127.9

Source: "Negro Population by Sex, with Males Per 100 Females for the 80 Cities Having 10,000 or More Negro Inhabitants, 1930, 1920, and 1910, and Males Per 100 Females in the White Population: 1930." U.S. Bureau of the Census, *Negroes in the United States, 1920-1932*, p. 85. *Note:* 1. Figures for 1910 include South Omaha.

★ 1690 ★

Distribution by Gender

Black and White Population, Urban and Rural, by Gender with Number of Males Per 100 Females by Divisions, 1920 and 1930

DIVISION AND RACIAL CLASS	URBAN POPULATION						RURAL POPULATION					
	1930			1920			1930			1920		
	Male	Female	Males per 100 females	Male	Female	Males per 100 females	Male	Female	Males per 100 females	Male	Female	Males per 100 females
United States:												
Negro	2,479,158	2,714,755	91.3	1,737,820	1,821,653	95.4	3,376,511	3,320,719	101.7	3,471,616	3,432,042	101.2
White	31,162,570	31,674,035	98.4	25,373,627	25,246,457	100.5	24,001,284	22,026,318	109.0	23,057,028	21,143,803	109.0
NEW ENGLAND:												
Negro	40,289	41,154	97.9	36,098	35,318	102.2	6,674	5,969	111.8	4,057	3,578	113.4
White	3,030,778	3,194,330	94.9	2,846,476	2,942,482	96.7	941,687	898,318	104.8	781,435	745,686	104.8
MIDDLE ATLANTIC:												
Negro	460,125	478,939	96.1	257,592	259,840	99.1	60,701	53,134	114.2	43,555	39,196	111.1
White	9,669,838	9,757,110	99.1	8,054,951	8,086,704	99.6	2,970,996	2,774,160	107.1	2,835,537	2,664,648	106.4
EAST NORTH CENTRAL:												
Negro	428,801	419,826	102.1	236,592	212,281	111.5	46,567	35,256	132.1	36,434	29,247	124.6
White	7,967,900	7,912,408	100.7	6,405,597	6,186,939	103.5	4,403,675	3,993,680	110.3	4,342,452	4,003,874	108.5
WEST NORTH CENTRAL:												
Negro	128,105	131,090	97.7	108,127	104,464	103.5	39,445	33,144	119.0	35,635	30,295	117.6
White	2,573,237	2,695,008	95.5	2,246,069	2,264,529	99.2	3,994,028	3,611,214	110.6	4,047,675	3,667,114	110.4
SOUTH ATLANTIC:												
Negro	675,013	787,891	85.7	543,188	601,183	90.4	1,481,518	1,476,966	100.3	1,590,189	1,590,560	100.0
White	2,061,376	2,170,444	95.0	1,573,226	1,618,862	97.2	3,650,071	3,467,393	105.3	3,320,064	3,136,788	105.8
EAST SOUTH CENTRAL:												
Negro	350,955	408,211	86.0	269,319	301,997	89.2	950,597	948,475	100.2	974,476	977,740	99.7
White	980,023	1,038,859	94.3	695,478	727,082	95.7	2,663,383	2,542,349	104.8	2,531,034	2,413,953	104.9
WEST SOUTH CENTRAL:												
Negro	347,049	397,206	87.4	257,107	278,175	92.4	778,459	759,237	102.5	772,350	755,947	102.2
White	1,657,494	1,685,949	98.3	1,231,595	1,197,019	102.9	2,995,071	2,761,467	108.5	2,972,282	2,714,831	109.5
MOUNTAIN:												
Negro	10,613	10,419	101.9	8,536	8,142	104.8	5,699	3,494	163.1	11,190	2,933	381.5
White	677,431	675,852	100.2	609,590	581,285	104.9	1,059,276	891,027	118.9	1,108,119	913,905	121.3
PACIFIC:												
Negro	38,208	40,019	95.5	21,261	20,253	105.0	6,851	5,044	135.8	3,730	2,546	146.5
White	2,544,493	2,544,075	100.0	1,710,645	1,641,555	104.2	1,323,097	1,086,710	121.8	1,118,430	883,004	126.7

Source: "Negro and White Population, Urban and Rural, by Sex, with the Number of Males Per 100 Females, by Divisions: 1930 and 1920." U.S. Bureau of the Census, *Negroes in the United States, 1920-1932*, p. 81.

★ 1691 ★

Distribution by Gender

Gender Ratio of the Black Population in Urban Communities, 1910

	NEGRO POPULATION: 1910						
	Urban communities						Rural communities
	Total	Places of 500,000 or more	Places of 100,000 to 500,000	Places of 25,000 to 100,000	Places of 10,000 to 25,000	Places of 2,500 to 10,000	
Both sexes	2,689,229	396,615	626,946	602,040	408,362	655,266	7,138,534
Male	1,279,484	189,837	297,674	286,286	193,721	311,966	3,606,397
Female	1,409,745	206,778	329,272	315,754	214,641	343,300	3,532,137
Excess-							
Of males	-	-	-	-	-	-	74,260
Of females	130,261	16,941	31,598	29,468	20,920	31,334	-
Males to 1,000 females	908	918	904	907	903	909	1,021

Source: Untitled Table. U.S. Bureau of the Census, *Negro Population, 1790-1915*, p. 152.

★ 1692 ★

Distribution by Gender

Gender Ratios of the Urban and Rural Population by Sections, and Southern Divisions, 1930

SECTION AND DIVISION	MALES PER 100 FEMALES					
	Negro population	White population				
		Total	Native			Foreign born
			Total	Native parentage	Foreign or mixed parentage	
	URBAN POPULATION					
United States	91.3	98.4	96.0	97.3	93.7	111.0
THE SOUTH	86.2	96.0	95.1	95.5	91.2	122.3
South Atlantic	85.7	95.0	93.9	94.1	92.1	117.5
East South Central	86.0	94.3	93.7	94.3	85.8	129.4
West South Central	87.4	98.3	97.5	98.0	92.4	130.7
THE NORTH	98.7	98.7	96.1	97.7	94.0	109.5
THE WEST	96.8	100.1	96.7	98.9	92.1	121.2
	TOTAL RURAL POPULATION					
United States	101.7	109.0	107.6	107.1	110.7	134.0

[Continued]

★ 1692 ★

Gender Ratios of the Urban and Rural Population by Sections, and Southern Divisions, 1930

[Continued]

SECTION AND DIVISION	MALES PER 100 FEMALES					
	Negro population	White population				
		Total	Native			Foreign born
			Total	Native parentage	Foreign or mixed parentage	
THE SOUTH	100.8	106.1	105.8	105.6	112.2	149.2
South Atlantic	100.3	105.3	104.8	104.6	110.6	158.3
East South Central	100.2	104.8	104.6	104.6	108.8	160.6
West South Central	102.5	108.5	108.1	107.9	113.8	137.4
THE NORTH	120.3	109.2	107.7	107.0	109.7	126.6
THE WEST	147.0	120.5	116.0	116.2	115.6	164.3
	RURAL-FARM POPULATION					
United States	101.2	112.7	111.6	110.4	120.0	139.4
THE SOUTH	100.9	108.2	108.1	107.9	116.3	134.7
South Atlantic	100.1	107.2	107.1	107.1	115.6	134.0
East South Central	100.3	106.8	106.8	106.7	122.1	148.8
West South Central	103.1	110.6	110.4	110.1	115.7	133.2
THE NORTH	121.2	115.5	114.3	112.4	120.4	134.4
THE WEST	127.8	123.4	119.4	119.1	120.3	160.6
	RURAL-NONFARM POPULATION					
United States	102.8	104.7	102.9	103.0	102.4	130.4
THE SOUTH	100.5	102.7	102.0	101.8	108.2	160.2
South Atlantic	100.7	103.0	102.0	101.7	109.2	165.2
East South Central	100.1	100.3	100.0	100.0	199.3	168.9
West South Central	100.5	104.3	103.9	103.6	109.8	145.4
THE NORTH	120.0	103.4	101.5	101.9	100.4	121.6
THE WEST	155.9	118.1	113.2	113.8	111.3	167.5

Source: "Sex Ratios of Negro and White Populations, Urban and Rural, by Sections, and Southern Divisions: 1930." U.S. Bureau of the Census, *Negroes in the United States, 1920-1932*, p. 80.

★ 1693 ★

Distribution by Gender

Males and Females: Gender Ratio for Classes of Cities by Divisions, 1910 - I

DIVISION AND RACIAL CLASS	POPULATION OF PLACES HAVING IN 1910 A POPULATION OF-								
	2,500 to 10,000			10,000 to 25,000			25,000 to 100,000		
	Male	Female	Males to 1,000 females	Male	Female	Males to 1,000 females	Male	Female	Males to 1,000 females
United States:									
Negro	311,966	343,300	909	193,721	214,641	903	286,286	315,754	907
White	3,951,056	3,847,145	1,027	2,627,246	2,559,332	1,027	3,851,950	3,774,973	1,020
New England:									
Negro	4,831	4,091	1,181	2,789	3,180	877	7,434	8,343	891
White	631,865	632,325	999	459,609	470,533	977	796,308	824,774	965
Middle Atlantic:									
Negro	13,795	14,988	920	16,095	17,067	943	25,693	27,463	936
White	832,038	801,454	1,038	688,834	647,326	1,033	1,031,004	1,025,780	1,005
East North Central:									
Negro	19,063	18,796	1,014	15,454	15,017	1,029	21,626	19,736	1,096
White	933,369	933,345	1,000	691,618	673,308	1,027	773,249	738,485	1,047
West North Central:									
Negro	17,265	17,260	1,000	11,225	10,788	1,041	15,484	14,591	1,061
White	509,523	495,847	1,028	219,755	212,717	1,033	397,727	373,590	1,065
South Atlantic:									
Negro	119,739	135,832	882	62,968	72,238	872	111,552	129,361	862
White	252,653	254,585	992	152,409	1156,973	971	237,657	233,458	1,018
East South Central:									
Negro	73,518	84,760	867	40,113	46,771	858	37,820	44,324	853
White	151,099	159,948	963	66,231	67,203	986	101,432	105,647	960
West South Central:									
Negro	60,765	64,902	936	42,247	46,868	901	63,166	68,628	920
White	254,432	243,250	1,046	135,966	128,751	1,056	261,794	242,137	1,081
Mountain:									
Negro	1,832	1,624	1,128	1,451	1,328	1,093	1,983	1,802	1,100
White	190,388	162,176	1,174	75,608	63,395	1,193	118,719	106,934	1,110
Pacific:									
Negro	1,158	1,047	1,106	1,379	1,384	996	1,528	1,506	1,015
White	195,689	167,215	1,170	157,216	139,126	1,130	134,060	124,168	1,080

Source: "Negro and White Males and Females and Sex Ratio for Classes of Cities, by Divisions: 1910." U.S. Bureau of the Census, *Negro Population, 1790- 1915*, p. 154.

★ 1694 ★

Distribution by Gender

Males and Females: Gender Ratio for Classes of Cities by Divisions, 1910 - II

DIVISION AND RACIAL CLASS	POPULATION OF PLACES HAVING IN 1910 A POPULATION OF-					
	100,000 to 500,000			500,000 and over		
	Male	Female	Males to 1,000 females	Male	Female	Males to 1,000 females
United States:						
Negro	297,674	329,272	904	189,837	206,778	918
White	4,124,897	3,992,220	1,033	5,574,530	5,528,564	1,008
New England:						
Negro	7,978	8,667	921	6,664	6,900	966
White	453,538	465,319	975	321,802	333,894	964
Middle Atlantic:						
Negro	10,945	11,409	959	94,925	106,866	888
White	865,181	861,763	1,004	3,314,750	3,325,791	907
East North Central:						
Negro	34,714	33,585	1,034	27,026	25,525	1,059
White	978,878	968,418	1,011	1,385,770	1,305,212	1,062
West North Central:						
Negro	17,667	16,061	1,100	22,168	21,792	1,017
White	442,316	412,129	1,073	323,392	319,096	1,013
South Atlantic:						
Negro	87,306	105,775	825	39,054	45,695	855
White	205,631	214,237	960	228,816	244,571	936
East South Central:						
Negro	86,752	95,039	913	-	-	-
White	207,413	208,767	994	-	-	-
West South Central:						
Negro	40,946	48,316	847	-	-	-
White	121,916	127,487	956	-	-	-
Mountain:						
Negro	2,652	2,774	956	-	-	-
White	103,959	103,112	1,008	-	-	-
Pacific:						
Negro	8,714	7,646	1,140	-	-	-
White	746,065	630,988	1,182	-	-	-

Source: "Negro and White Males and Females and Sex Ratio for Classes of Cities, by Divisions: 1910." U.S. Bureau of the Census, *Negro Population, 1790- 1915*, p. 154.

★ 1695 ★

Distribution by Gender

Males and Females: Gender Ratio in the Urban and Rural Population by Divisions, 1900, 1910

DIVISION AND RACIAL CLASS	RURAL POPULATION						URBAN POPULATION					
	1910			1900			1910			1900		
	Male	Female	Males to 1,000 females	Male	Female	Males to 1,000 females	Male	Female	Males to to 1,000 females	Male	Female	Males to 1,000 females
United States												
Negro	3,606,397	3,532,137	1,021	3,448,850	3,379,172	1,021	1,279,484	1,409,745	908	937,697	1,068,275	878
White	22,048,566	19,851,478	1,111	19,907,997	18,183,209	1,095	20,129,679	19,702,234	1,022	14,293,738	14,424,252	991
New England:												
Negro	3,087	2,342	1,318	2,925	2,644	1,106	29,696	31,181	952	25,654	27,876	920
White	564,484	526,063	1,073	573,786	541,125	1,,606	2,663,122	2,726,845	977	2,156,335	2,255,780	956
Middle Atlantic:												
Negro	42,013	36,611	1,148	42,128	36,024	1,169	161,453	177,793	908	117,853	130,186	903
White	2,884,541	2,621,990	1,100	2,728,626	2,564,936	1,064	6,711,807	6,662,114	1,007	4,858,337	4,958,963	980
East North Central:												
Negro	38,548	31,746	1,214	42,460	35,261	1,204	117,883	112,659	1,046	91,985	88,136	1,044
White	4,460,277	4,085,693	1,092	4,522,733	4,150,732	1,090	4,762,884	4,618,768	1,031	3,509,714	3,526,874	995
West North Central:												
Negro	42,055	36,306	1,158	51,867	46,679	1,111	83,809	83,492	1,041	69,405	69,958	992
White	4,051,171	3,594,358	1,127	3,845,352	3,414,541	1,126	1,892,713	1,813,379	1,044	1,423,018	1,382,906	1,029
South Atlantic:												
Negro	1,609,189	1,593,779	1,010	1,522,403	1,510,242	1,008	420,619	488,901	860	313,122	383,250	817
White	3,021,412	2,869,201	1,053	2,629,429	2,542,080	1,034	1,077,166	1,103,824	976	752,540	782,009	962
East South Central:												
Negro	1,077,589	1,065,827	1,011	1,064,191	1,049,427	1,014	238,203	270,894	879	178,891	207,377	863
White	2,401,427	2,288,159	1,050	2,195,957	2,104,385	1,044	526,175	538,565	977	368,881	375,624	982
West South Central:												
Negro	786,901	761,687	1,033	716,301	695,609	1,030	207,124	228,714	906	130,496	151,660	860
White	2,735,979	2,469,779	1,108	2,104,427	1,803,776	1,111	774,108	741,625	1,044	386,881	385,981	1,002
Mountain:												
Negro	3,848	2,173	1,771	4,052	1,704	2,378	7,918	7,528	1,052	5,052	4,782	1,056
White	923,474	672,690	1,373	607,874	445,105	1,336	488,674	435,617	1,122	276,568	250,308	1,105
Pacific:												
Negro	3,167	1,666	1,901	2,523	1,582	1,595	12,779	11,583	1,103	5,509	5,050	1,091
White	1,005,801	723,545	1,390	669,813	526,529	1,329	1,233,030	1,061,497	1,162	561,464	505,807	1,110

Source: "Negro and White Males and Females and Sex Ratio, in the Urban and Rural Population, by Divisions: 1910, 1900." U.S. Bureau of the Census, *Negro Population, 1790-1915*, p. 154.

★ 1696 ★

Distribution by Gender

Males to 1,000 Females in the Black Population 15 Years of Age and Over, 1910

SECTION AND CLASS OF COMMUNITY	MALES TO 1,000 FEMALES IN THE NEGRO POPULATION 15 YEARS OF AGE AND OVER: 1910						
	Total	Single	Married, widowed, or divorced				Marital condition unknown
			Total	Married	Widowed	Divorced	
UNITED STATES							
Rural communities	1,033	1,380	908	998	493	678	1,551
Urban communities	895	1,179	776	955	312	519	1,701
Cities of 2,500 to 25,000	887	1,152	778	955	319	468	2,107
Cities of 25,000 to 100,000	896	1,230	771	947	321	505	1,386
Cities of 100,000 and over	903	1,220	776	960	301	600	1,351

[Continued]

★ 1696 ★

Males to 1,000 Females in the Black Population 15 Years of Age and Over, 1910

[Continued]

SECTION AND CLASS OF COMMUNITY	MALES TO 1,000 FEMALES IN THE NEGRO POPULATION 15 YEARS OF AGE AND OVER: 1910						
	Total	Single	Married, widowed, or divorced				Marital condition unknown
			Total	Married	Widowed	Divorced	
THE SOUTH							
Rural communities	1,023	1,356	904	996	482	648	1,494
Urban communities	851	1,104	748	940	292	430	1,705
Cities of 2,500 to 25,000	854	1,089	757	944	297	396	2,178
Cities of 25,000 to 100,000	857	1,163	743	932	297	413	1,277
Cities of 100,000 and over	840	1,080	741	941	280	521	1,139
THE NORTH							
Rural communities	1,256	1,875	1,011	1,059	755	1,553	2,876
Urban communities	988	1,379	835	986	366	762	1,688
Cities of 2,500 to 25,000	1,013	1,375	863	998	423	829	1,737
Cities of 25,000 to 100,000	1,020	1,427	865	993	423	855	1,682
Cities of 100,000 and over	969	1,367	816	979	330	697	1,660
THE WEST							
Rural communities	2,133	5,170	1,207	1,278	867	[1]	[1]
Urban communities	1,123	2,044	842	1,010	343	673	[1]
Cities of 2,500 to 25,000	1,129	1,939	851	1,019	384	646	[1]
Cities of 25,000 to 100,000	1,100	1,878	843	987	376	[1]	[1]
Cities of 100,000 and over	1,128	2,158	838	1,012	312	646	[1]

Source: "Males to Females in the Negro Population 15 Years of Age and Over: 1910." U.S. Bureau of the Census, *Negro Population, 1790-1915*, p. 258. *Note:* 1. Ratio not shown, the number of females being less than 100.

★ 1697 ★

Distribution by Gender

Males to 1,000 Females in the Black Population by Age, Class of Community, and Marital Status, 1910

AGE PERIOD AND CLASS OF COMMUNITY	MALES TO 1,000 FEMALES IN THE NEGRO POPULATION						
	Total	Single	Married, widowed, or divorced				Marital condition unknown
			Total	Married	Widowed	Divorced	
15 years of age and over-							
Urban communities	895	1,197	776	955	312	519	1,701
Rural communities	1,033	1,380	908	998	493	678	1,551
15 to 19 years:							
Urban communities	781	903	100	103	66	56	992

[Continued]

★ 1697 ★

Males to 1,000 Females in the Black Population by Age, Class of Community, and Marital Status, 1910

[Continued]

AGE PERIOD AND CLASS OF COMMUNITY	MALES TO 1,000 FEMALES IN THE NEGRO POPULATION						
	Total	Single	Married, widowed, or divorced				Marital condition unknown
			Total	Married	Widowed	Divorced	
Rural communities	967	1,168	120	121	91	101	1,167
20 to 24 years:							
Urban communities	777	1,201	453	485	189	230	1,593
Rural communities	930	1,714	572	593	327	362	1,754
25 to 34 years:							
Urban communities	899	1,479	750	842	271	427	2,364
Rural communities	978	1,810	872	914	488	599	2,145
35 to 44 years:							
Urban communities	1,002	1,801	911	1,131	307	619	2,391
Rural communities	1,033	1,721	993	1,080	493	738	1,902
45 to 64 years:							
Urban communities	986	1,663	942	1,489	332	936	1,262
Rural communities	1,255	1,601	1,242	1,522	539	1,154	1,370
65 years and over:							
Urban communities	824	1,143	810	2,387	362	1,361	766
Rural communities	1,185	1,228	1,183	2,430	497	1,942	1,256
Age unknown:							
Urban communities	1,209	1,590	925	1,401	302	[1]	2,213
Rural communities	1,234	1,516	1,047	1,368	406	500	2,472

Source: "Males to 1,000 Females in the Negro Population: 1910." U.S. Bureau of the Census, *Negro Population, 1790-1915*, p. 254. *Note:* 1. Ratio not shown, the number of females being less than 100.

★ 1698 ★

Distribution by Gender

Males to 1,000 Females in the Black Population, 1830-1910

AGE PERIOD	MALES TO 1,000 FEMALES IN THE NEGRO POPULATION							
	1910	1900	1890	1870	1860	1850	1840	1830
All ages	988	986	995	962	996	991	995	1,003
Age unknown	1,223	1,064	1,096	[1]	1,102	1,032	[1]	-
Known age	988	986	995	962	996	9.1	995	1,003
Under 5 years	993	989	-	1,006	975	979	-	-
Under 1 year	988	985	-	991	948	958	-	-
5 to 9 years	987	997	-	1,011	994	996	-	-
10 to 14 years	1,002	1,010	1,038	1,042	1,045	1,027	-	-
15 to 19 years	919	932	941	937	956	961	-	-
20 years and over	999	989	982	919	1,000	991	-	-
Under 10 years	990	993	1,017	1,008	984	987	1,005	1,018
10 to 19 years	961	972	992	994	1,003	997	-	-
20 to 29 years	897	924	931	867	1,012	1,003	-	-

[Continued]

★ 1698 ★

Males to 1,000 Females in the Black Population, 1830-1910

[Continued]

AGE PERIOD	MALES TO 1,000 FEMALES IN THE NEGRO POPULATION							
	1910	1900	1890	1870	1860	1850	1840	1830
30 to 39 years	1,006	984	-	875	977	971	-	-
40 to 49 years	1,043	1,005	-	937	1,000	976	-	-
50 to 59 years	1,221	1,160	-	1,124	1,028	1,036	-	-
60 to 69 years	1,200	1,160	-	1,108	1,026	1,019	-	-
70 to 79 years	1,061	1,011	-	942	952	937	-	-
80 to 89 years	848	851	-	804	816	877	-	-
90 to 99 years	698	650	-	633	734	760	-	-
10 to 23 years	938	952	-	-	-	-	994	996
24 to 35 years	951	965	-	-	-	-	962	977
35 to 54 years	1,068	1,023	-	-	-	-	1,023	1,036
55 to 99 years	1,150	1,110	-	1,071	-	-	990	967
100 years and over	601	531	-	536	700	687	1,104	958

Source: "Males to 1,000 Females in the Negro Population." U.S. Bureau of the Census, *Negro Population, 1790-1915*, p. 16. *Note:* 1. Ratio not shown, the number of females being less than 100.

★ 1699 ★

Distribution by Gender

Males to 1,000 Females in the Urban Black Population by Classes of Cities, 1910

RACIAL CLASS	MALES TO 1,000 FEMALES: 1910						
	Urban population						Rural population
	Total	Places of 500,000 or more	Places of 100,000 to 500,000	Places of 25,000 to 100,000	Places of 10,000 to 25,000	Places of 2,500 to 10,000	
Negro	908	918	904	907	903	909	1,021
White	1,022	1,008	1,032	1,020	1,027	1,027	1,111
Native	973	964	980	975	971	977	1,072
Native parentage	993	981	1,016	996	987	985	1,067
Mixed parentage	933	941	931	925	923	936	1,068
Foreign parentage	951	957	939	947	947	963	1,111
Foreign born	1,189	1,096	1,222	1,201	1,305	1,363	1,611

Source: Untitled Table. U.S. Bureau of the Census, *Negro Population, 1790-1915*, p. 153.

★ 1700 ★

Distribution by Gender

Number and Ratio of Males to Females in the Black Population by Divisions and States, 1880-1910 - I

DIVISION AND STATE	MALES AND FEMALES IN THE NEGRO POPULATION									
	1910				1900		1890		1880	
	Male	Female	Excess of- Males	Excess of- Females	Male	Female	Male	Female	Male	Female
UNITED STATES	4,885,881	4,941,882	-	56,001	4,386,547	4,447,447	3,735,603	3,735,073	3,253,115	3,327,678
GEOGRAPHIC DIVISIONS:										
New England	32,783	33,523	-	740	28,579	30,520	21,633	22,947	19,223	20,702
Middle Atlantic	203,466	214,404	-	10,938	159,711	166,210	111,644	113,682	90,891	98,601
East North Central	156,431	144,405	12,026	-	134,445	123,397	108,096	98,927	95,093	88,205
West North Central	125,864	116,798	9,066	-	121,272	116,637	114,288	109,801	101,922	100,401
South Atlantic	2,029,808	2,082,680	-	52,872	1,835,525	1,893,492	1,613,769	1,648,921	1,446,862	1,494,340
East South Central	1,315,792	1,336,721	-	20,929	1,243,082	1,256,804	1,056,343	1,063,454	949,225	975,771
West South Central	994,025	990,401	3,624	-	846,797	847,269	693,264	684,826	542,956	544,749
Mountain	11,766	9,701	2,065	-	9,104	6,486	8,372	4,599	2,997	2,025
Pacific	15,946	13,249	2,697	-	8,032	6,632	8,194	5,916	3,946	2,884
NEW ENGLAND:										
Maine	700	663	37	-	670	649	614	576	765	686
New Hampshire	298	276	12	-	327	335	323	291	341	344
Vermont	1,173	448	725	-	454	372	493	444	566	491
Massachusetts	18,748	19,307	-	559	15,591	16,383	10,879	11,265	9,049	9,648
Rhode Island	4,645	4,884	-	239	4,290	4,802	3,394	3,999	2,952	3,536
Connecticut	7,229	7,945	-	716	7,247	7,979	5,930	6,372	5,550	5,997
MIDDLE ATLANTIC:										
New York	64,034	70,157	-	6,123	46,618	52,614	33,503	36,589	30,852	34,252
New Jersey	43,602	46,158	-	2,556	33,745	36,099	23,410	24,228	18,846	20,007
Pennsylvania	95,830	98,089	-	2,259	79,348	77,497	54,731	52,805	41,193	44,342
EAST NORTH CENTRAL:										
Ohio	57,995	53,457	4,538	-	49,985	46,916	45,076	42,037	40,962	38,938
Indiana	31,044	29,276	1,768	-	29,701	27,804	23,523	21,692	20,267	18,961
Illinois	56,909	52,140	4,769	-	45,121	39,957	30,148	26,880	24,507	21,861
Michigan	9,007	8,108	899	-	8,220	7,596	7,986	7,237	7,836	7,264
Wisconsin	1,476	1,424	52	-	1,418	1,124	1,363	1,081	1,521	1,181
WEST NORTH CENTRAL:										
Minnesota	4,183	2,901	1,282	-	2,836	2,123	2,167	1,516	905	659
Iowa	8,120	6,853	1,267	-	6,875	5,818	5,712	4,973	5,191	4,325
Missouri	80,489	76,963	3,526	-	81,206	80,028	75,336	74,848	72,153	73,197
North Dakota	381	236	145	-	173	113	219	154	] 225	176
South Dakota	468	349	119	-	272	193	363	178		
Nebraska	4,259	3,430	829	-	3,368	2,901	5,243	3,670	1,296	1,089
Kansas	27,964	26,006	1,898	-	26,542	25,461	25,248	24,462	22,152	20,955
SOUTH ATLANTIC:										
Delaware	16,011	15,170	841	-	15,616	15,081	14,455	13,931	13,327	13,115
Maryland	114,749	117,501	-	2,752	115,617	119,447	105,684	109,973	102,505	107,725
District of Columbia	42,615	51,831	-	9,216	38,348	48,354	33,721	41,851	26,238	33,358
Virginia	330,542	340,554	-	10,012	323,459	337,263	310,828	324,610	308,935	322,681
West Virginia	36,607	27,566	9,041	-	25,167	18,332	17,991	14,699	13,482	12,404
North Carolina	339,581	358,262	-	18,681	303,624	320,845	275,230	285,788	262,363	268,914
South Carolina	408,078	427,765	-	19,687	383,626	398,695	341,821	347,113	297,787	306,545
Georgia	580,263	596,724	-	16,461	509,869	524,944	430,072	428,743	359,157	365,976
Florida	161,362	147,307	14,055	-	120,199	110,531	83,967	82,213	63,068	63,622
EAST SOUTH CENTRAL:										
Kentucky	131,492	130,164	1,328	-	142,073	142,633	133,547	134,524	133,798	137,653
Tennessee	233,710	239,378	-	5,668	238,388	241,855	213,521	217,157	197,467	205,684

[Continued]

★ 1700 ★

Number and Ratio of Males to Females in the Black Population by Divisions and States, 1880-1910 - I

[Continued]

DIVISION AND STATE	MALES AND FEMALES IN THE NEGRO POPULATION									
	1910				1900		1890		1880	
	Male	Female	Excess of- Males	Excess of- Females	Male	Female	Male	Female	Male	Female
Alabama	447,794	460,488	-	12,694	409,237	418,070	366,997	341,492	295,001	305,102
Mississippi	502,796	506,691	-	3,895	453,384	454,246	372,278	370,281	322,959	327,332
WEST SOUTH CENTRAL:										
Arkansas	223,323	219,568	3,755	-	185,342	181,514	159,014	150,103	107,331	103,335
Louisiana	353,824	360,050	-	6,226	322,664	328,140	277,134	282,059	238,879	244,776
Oklahoma[1]	71,937	65,675	6,262	-	28,656	27,028	11,655	9,954	-	-
Texas	344,941	345,108	-	167	310,135	310,587	245,461	242,710	196,746	196,638
MOUNTAIN:										
Montana	1,058	776	282	-	912	611	1,053	437	191	155
Idaho	398	253	145	-	166	127	118	83	39	14
Wyoming	1,544	691	853	-	631	309	652	270	160	138
Colorado	5,867	5,586	281	-	4,473	4,097	3,602	2,613	1,433	1,002
New Mexico	891	737	154	-	1,023	587	1,220	736	638	377
Arizona	1,054	955	99	-	1,363	485	1,173	184	104	51
Utah	691	453	238	-	454	218	392	196	124	108
Nevada	263	250	13	-	82	52	162	80	308	180
PACIFIC:										
Washington	3,736	2,322	1,414	-	1,589	925	1,104	498	209	116
Oregon	907	585	322	-	677	428	743	443	270	217
California	11,303	10,342	961	-	5,766	5,279	6,347	4,975	3,467	2,551

Source: "Number of Males and Females and Ratio of Males to Females in the Negro Population, by Divisions and States: 1910, 1900, 1890, and 1880." U.S. Bureau of the Census, *Negro Population, 1790-1915,* p. 150. *Notes:* 1. Includes population of Indian Territory for 1900 and 1890. 2. Ratio not shown where the number of females is less than 100.

★ 1701 ★

Distribution by Gender

Number and Ratio of Males to Females in the Black Population by Divisions and States, 1880-1910 - II

DIVISION AND STATE	MALES AND FEMALES IN THE NEGRO POPULATION Males to 1,000 females			
	1910	1900	1890	1880
UNITED STATES	989	986	995	978
GEOGRAPHIC DIVISIONS:				
New England	978	936	943	929
Middle Atlantic	949	961	982	922
East North Central	1,083	1,090	1,093	1,078
West North Central	1,078	1,040	1,041	1,015
South Atlantic	975	969	979	968
East South Central	984	989	993	973
West South Central	1,004	999	1,012	997
Mountain	1,213	1,404	1,820	1,480

[Continued]

★ 1701 ★

Number and Ratio of Males to Females in the Black Population by Divisions and States, 1880-1910 - II

[Continued]

DIVISION AND STATE	MALES AND FEMALES IN THE NEGRO POPULATION Males to 1,000 females			
	1910	1900	1890	1880
Pacific	1,204	1,211	1,385	1,368
NEW ENGLAND:				
Maine	1,056	1,032	1,066	1,115
New Hampshire	1,043	976	1,110	991
Vermont	2,618	1,220	1,110	1,153
Massachusetts	971	952	966	938
Rhode Island	951	893	849	835
Connecticut	910	908	931	925
MIDDLE ATLANTIC:				
New York	913	886	916	901
New Jersey	945	935	966	942
Pennsylvania	977	1,024	1,035	929
EAST NORTH CENTRAL:				
Ohio	1,085	1,065	1,072	1,052
Indiana	1,060	1,068	1,084	1,069
Illinois	1,091	1,129	1,122	1,121
Michigan	1,111	1,082	1,103	1,079
Wisconsin	1,037	1,262	1,261	1,288
WEST NORTH CENTRAL:				
Minnesota	1,442	1,336	1,429	1,373
Iowa	1,185	1,182	1,149	1,200
Missouri	1,046	1,015	1,007	986
North Dakota	1,614	1,531	1,422	-
South Dakota	1,341	1,409	2,039	-
Nebraska	1,242	1,161	1,429	1,190
Kansas	1,073	1,042	1,032	1,057
SOUTH ATLANTIC:				
Delaware	1,055	1,035	1,038	1,016
Maryland	977	968	961	952
District of Columbia	822	793	806	787
Virginia	971	959	958	957
West Virginia	1,328	1,373	1,224	1,087
North Carolina	948	946	963	976
South Carolina	954	962	985	971
Georgia	972	971	1,003	981
Florida	1,095	1,087	1,021	991
EAST SOUTH CENTRAL:				
Kentucky	1,010	996	993	972

[Continued]

★ 1701 ★

Number and Ratio of Males to Females in the Black Population by Divisions and States, 1880-1910 - II

[Continued]

DIVISION AND STATE	MALES AND FEMALES IN THE NEGRO POPULATION Males to 1,000 females			
	1910	1900	1890	1880
Tennessee	976	986	983	960
Alabama	972	979	987	967
Mississippi	992	998	1,005	987
WEST SOUTH CENTRAL:				
Arkansas	1,017	1,021	1,059	1,039
Louisiana	983	983	983	976
Oklahoma[1]	1,095	1,060	1,171	-
Texas	1,000	999	1,011	1,001
MOUNTAIN:				
Montana	1,363	1,493	2,410	1,232
Idaho	1,573	1,307	2	2
Wyoming	2,234	2,042	2,415	1,159
Colorado	1,050	1,092	1,378	1,430
New Mexico	1,209	1,743	1,658	1,692
Arizona	1,104	2,810	6,375	2
Utah	1,525	2,083	2,000	1,148
Nevada	1,052	2	2	1,711
PACIFIC:				
Washington	1,609	1,718	2,217	1,802
Oregon	1,550	1,582	1,677	1,244
California	1,093	1,092	1,276	1,359

Source: "Number of Males and Females and Ratio of Males to Females in the Negro Population, by Divisions and States: 1910, 1900, 1890, and 1880." U.S. Bureau of the Census, *Negro Population, 1790-1915,* p. 150. *Notes:* 1. Includes population of Indian Territory for 1900 and 1890. 2. Ratio not shown where the number of females is less than 100.

★ 1702 ★

Distribution by Gender

Population by Gender and Age: 1870-1975

Numbers in thousands.

Sex and age	1870	1910	1940	1960	1970	1975
Total Black population	4,880	9,798	12,866	18,849	22,580	24,372
SEX						
Male	2,393	4,856	6,269	9,098	10,748	11,607
Female	2,487	4,942	6,596	9,751	11,832	12,766
Males per 100 females	96.2	98.3	95.0	93.3	90.8	90.9

[Continued]

★ 1702 ★

Population by Gender and Age: 1870-1975

[Continued]

Sex and age	1870	1910	1940	1960	1970	1975
AGE						
All ages	100	100	100	100	100	100
Under 5 years	16	13	10	14	11	10
5 to 9 years	13	13	10	13	12	10
10 to 14 years	13	12	10	10	12	12
15 to 19 years	11	11	10	8	11	11
20 to 24 years	46[1]	10	9	6	8	9
25 to 34 years	46[1]	16	17	13	12	13
35 to 44 years	46[1]	11	14	12	11	10
45 to 54 years	46[1]	7	10	10	9	9
55 to 64 years	46[1]	4	5	7	7	7
65 years and over	46[1]	3	5	6	7	7
Age not reported	-	-	(X)	(X)	(X)	(X)
Median age	18.5	20.8	25.1	23.5	22.4	23.4

Source: "Black Population by Sex and Age for Selected Years: 1870 to 1975," U.S. Department of Commerce, Bureau of the Census. *The Social and Economic Status of the Black Population in the United States: An Historical View, 1790-1978*, p. 16. Primary source: U.S. Department of Commerce, Bureau of the Census. *Notes:* Data for 1975 are estimates of the resident population as of April 1. - represents or rounds to zero. X Not applicable. 1. Data includes ages 20 years and over.

★ 1703 ★

Distribution by Gender

Population by Gender and Race, 1790-1970 - I

Year	Male						
	All races	White	Negro[1]	Other races			
				Total[2]	Indian	Japanese	Chinese
1970[3]	98,912,192	86,720,987	10,748,316	1,442,889	388,691	271,300	228,565
1960[6]	88,331,494	78,367,149	9,113,408	850,937	263,369	224,828	135,549
1960	87,864,510	78,153,040	9,105,702	605,768	255,677	124,323	115,849
1950	74,833,239	67,129,192	7,298,722	405,325	178,824	76,649	77,008
1940	66,061,592	59,448,548	6,269,038	344,006	171,427	71,967	57,389
1930	62,137,080	55,922,528	5,855,669	358,883	170,350	81,771	59,802
1920	53,900,431	48,430,655	5,209,436	260,340	125,068	72,707	53,891
1910	47,332,277	42,178,245	4,885,881	268,151	135,133	63,070	66,856
1900	38,816,448	34,201,735	4,386,547	228,166	119,484	23,341	85,341
1890	32,237,101	28,270,379	3,735,603	231,119	125,719	1,780	103,620
1880	25,518,820	22,130,900	3,253,115	134,805	33,985	134	100,686
1870[4]	19,493,565	17,029,088	2,393,263	71,214	12,534	47	58,633
1860	16,085,204	13,811,387	2,216,744	57,073	23,924	-	33,149
1850	11,837,660	10,026,402	1,811,258	-	-	-	-

[Continued]

★ 1703 ★

Population by Gender and Race, 1790-1970 - I

[Continued]

Year	Male						
	All races	White	Negro[1]	Other races			
				Total[2]	Indian	Japanese	Chinese
1840	8,688,532	7,255,544	1,432,988	-	-	-	-
1830	6,532,489	5,366,213	1,166,276	-	-	-	-
1820	4,896,605	3,995,809	900,796	-	-	-	-
1810	5	2,988,130	1	-	-	-	-
1800	5	2,195,305	1	-	-	-	-
1790	5	1,615,434	1	-	-	-	-

Source: "Population, by Sex and Race: 1900 to 1970." U.S. Bureau of the Census. *Historical Statistics of the United States: Colonial Times to 1970, Part I*, Bicentennial Edition, p. 9. *Notes:* 1. Sex not reported before 1820. Total for both sexes: 1790 - 757,208; 1800 - 1,002,037; 1810 - 1,377,808. Total slave population: 1790 - 697,681; 1800 - 893,602; 1810 - 1,191,362; 1820 - 1,538,022; 1830 - 2,009,043; 1840 - 2,487,355; 1850 - 3,204,313; 1860 - 3,953,760. For slave population by sex 1820-1860, see series A 119-134. 2. Includes races not shown separately, of which Filipinos are most numerous. Filipino males: 1910 - 144; 1920 - 5,232; 1930 - 42,268; 1940 - 39,723; 1950 - 46,101; 1960 (conterminous U.S.) - 67,351; 1960 (including Alaska and Hawaii) - 112,286; 1960 (conterminous U.S.) - 67,351; 1960 (including Alaska and Hawaii) - 112,286; 970 - 189,498. Filipino females: 1910 - 16; 1920 - 371; 1930 - 2,940; 1940 - 5,840; 1950 - 15,535; 1960 (conterminous U.S.) - 39,075; 1960 (including Alaska and Hawaii) - 64,024; 1970 - 153,562. 3. The population of other races (i.e., neither white nor Negro) was overstated by about 327,000 in the 1970 census. See text for series A 91- 104. Excludes 23,372 persons for whom sex and race are not available. See series A 1-5, footnote 3. 4. Revisions to include adjustments for undernumeration in the Southern States show a total (both sexes) of 34,337,292 for white and 5,392,172 for Negro. 5. Data by sex not available. See series A 1-5 for total population. 6. Denotes first year for which figures include Alaska and Hawaii.

★ 1704 ★

Distribution by Gender

Population by Gender and Race, 1790-1970 - II

Year	Female						
	All races	White	Negro[1]	Other races			
				Total[2]	Indian	Japanese	Chinese
1970[3]	104,299,734	91,027,988	11,831,973	1,439,773	404,039	319,990	206,497
1960[6]	90,991,681	80,464,583	9,758,423	768,675	260,222	239,504	101,743
1960	90,599,726	80,301,916	9,754,415	543,395	252,998	135,736	83,109
1950	75,864,122	67,812,836	7,743,564	307,722	164,586	65,119	40,621
1940	65,607,683	58,766,322	6,596,480	244,881	162,542	54,980	20,115
1930	60,637,966	54,364,212	6,035,474	238,280	162,047	57,063	15,152
1920	51,810,189	46,390,260	5,253,695	166,234	119,369	38,303	7,748
1910	44,639,989	39,553,712	4,941,882	144,395	130,550	9,087	4,675
1900	37,178,127	32,607,461	4,447,447	123,219	117,712	985	4,522
1890	30,710,613	26,830,879	3,753,073	126,661	122,534	259	3,868
1880	24,636,963	21,272,070	3,327,678	37,215	32,422	14	4,779
1870[4]	19,064,806	16,560,289	2,486,746	17,771	13,197	8	4,566
1860	15,358,117	13,111,150	2,225,086	21,881	20,097	-	1,784
1850	11,354,216	9,526,666	1,827,550	-	-	-	-
1840	9,380,921	6,940,261	1,440,660	-	-	-	-

[Continued]

★ 1704 ★

Population by Gender and Race, 1790-1970 - II

[Continued]

Year	Female						
	All races	White	Negro[1]	Other races			
				Total[2]	Indian	Japanese	Chinese
1830	6,333,531	5,171,165	1,162,366	-	-	-	-
1820	4,741,848	3,870,988	870,860	-	-	-	-
1810	5	2,873,943	1	-	-	-	-
1800	5	2,111,141	1	-	-	-	-
1790	5	1,556,572	1	-	-	-	-

Source: "Population, by Sex and Race: 1900 to 1970." U.S. Bureau of the Census. *Historical Statistics of the United States: Colonial Times to 1970, Part I*, Bicentennial Edition, p. 9. *Notes:* 1. Sex not reported before 1820. Total for both sexes: 1790 - 757,208; 1800 - 1,002,037; 1810 - 1,377,808. Total slave population: 1790 - 697,681; 1800 - 893,602; 1810 - 1,191,362; 1820 - 1,538,022; 1830 - 2,009,043; 1840 - 2,487,355; 1850 - 3,204,313; 1860 - 3,953,760. For slave population by sex 1820-1860, see series A 119-134. 2. Includes races not shown separately, of which Filipinos are most numerous. Filipino males: 1910 - 144; 1920 - 5,232; 1930 - 42,268; 1940 - 39,723; 1950 - 46,101; 1960 (conterminous U.S.) - 67,351; 1960 (including Alaska and Hawaii) - 112,286; 1960 (conterminous U.S.) - 67,351; 1960 (including Alaska and Hawaii) - 112,286; 970 - 189,498. Filipino females: 1910 - 16; 1920 - 371; 1930 - 2,940; 1940 - 5,840; 1950 - 15,535; 1960 (conterminous U.S.) - 39,075; 1960 (including Alaska and Hawaii) - 64,024; 1970 - 153,562. 3. The population of other races (i.e., neither white nor Negro) was overstated by about 327,000 in the 1970 census. See text for series A 91- 104. Excludes 23,372 persons for whom sex and race are not available. See series A 1-5, footnote 3. 4. Revisions to include adjustments for undernumeration in the Southern States show a total (both sexes) of 34,337,292 for white and 5,392,172 for Negro. 5. Data by sex not available. See series A 1-5 for total population. 6. Denotes first year for which figures include Alaska and Hawaii.

★ 1705 ★

Distribution by Gender

Population by Gender, Residence, and Race, 1790-1950 - I

Year	Total by sex		Residence by sex[1]								
			Both sexes			Male			Female		
	Male	Female	Urban	Rural nonfarm	Rural farm	Urban	Rural nonfarm	Rural farm	Urban	Rural nonfarm	Rural farm
1950 (1950 urban def.)[2]	74,833	75,864	96,468	31,181	23,048	46,892	15,863	12,079	49,576	15,318	10,970
1950 (1940 urban def.)[2]	-	-	88,927	38,693	23,077	43,117	19,622	12,094	45,810	19,071	10,983
1940	66,062	65,608	74,424	27,029	30,216	36,364	13,758	15,940	88,060	13,272	14,276
1930[2]	62,137	60,638	68,955	23,663	30,158	34,155	12,118	15,864	34,800	11,545	14,293
1920	53,900	51,810	54,158	20,159	31,393	27,203	10,337	16,360	27,101	9,710	14,999
1910	47,332	44,640	41,999	49,973[5]	49,973[5]	21,496	25,836[6]	25,836[6]	21,127	23,513[7]	23,513[7]
1900	38,816	37,178	30,160	45,835[5]	45,835[5]	15,087	23,780[6]	23,780[6]	15,294	21,885[7]	21,885[7]
1890	32,237	30,711	22,106	40,841[5]	40,841[5]	-	-	-	-	-	-
1880	25,519	24,637	14,130	36,026[5]	36,026[5]	-	-	-	-	-	-
1870	19,494	19,065	9,902	28,656[5]	28,656[5]	-	-	-	-	-	-
1860	16,085	15,358	6,217	25,227[5]	25,227[5]	-	-	-	-	-	-
1850	11,838	11,354	3,544	19,648[5]	19,648[5]	-	-	-	-	-	-
1840	8,689	8,881	1,845	15,224[5]	15,224[5]	-	-	-	-	-	-
1830	6,530	6,336	1,127	11,739[5]	11,739[5]	-	-	-	-	-	-
1820	4,897	4,742	693	8,945[5]	8,945[5]	-	-	-	-	-	-
1810	-	-	525	6,714[5]	6,714[5]	-	-	-	-	-	-

[Continued]

★ 1705 ★

Population by Gender, Residence, and Race, 1790-1950 - I

[Continued]

Year	Total by sex		Residence by sex[1]								
			Both sexes			Male			Female		
	Male	Female	Urban	Rural nonfarm	Rural farm	Urban	Rural nonfarm	Rural farm	Urban	Rural nonfarm	Rural farm
1800	-	-	322	4,986[5]	4,986[5]	-	-	-	-	-	-
1790	-	-	202	3,728[5]	3,728[5]	-	-	-	-	-	-

Source: "Population, by Sex, Residence, and Color: 1790-1950." U.S. Bureau of the Census, *Historical Statistics of the United States: Colonial Times to 1957*, p. 9. *Notes:* 1. Residence for both sexes tabulated according to the old urban (or 1940) definition (series A 36-38) from 1790 to 1940, and for male and for female separately for 1930 and 1940. Tabulations of residence for male and for female from 1900 to 1920 are according to the definitions current at those censuses. 2. See text for series A 34-50 for explanation of definitions. 3. Figures for color by sex in 1930 revised to include Mexicans as white. Mexicans were classified as nonwhite in the 1930 reports. 4. Adjustment for undernumeration in the South (see series A 20 above) shows a population of 39,818,000 of whom 34,337,000 were white and 5,481,000 were nonwhite. 5. Data includes rural non-farm and rural farm for both sexes. 6. Data includes Rural non-farm and rural farm for males. 7. Data includes Rural non-farm and rural farm for females.

★ 1706 ★

Distribution by Gender

Population by Gender, Residence, and Race, 1790-1950 - II

Year	Color by sex					
	Both sexes		Male		Female	
	White	Non white	White	Non white	White	Non white
1950 (1950 urban def.)[2]	134,942	15,755	67,129	7,704	67,813	8,051
1950 (1940 urban def.)[2]	-	-	-	-	-	-
1940	118,215	13,454	59,449	6,613	58,766	6,841
1930[2]	110,287	12,488	55,923	6,215	54,364	6,274
1920	94,821	10,890	48,431	5,470	46,390	5,420
1910	81,732	10,240	42,178	5,154	39,554	5,086
1900	66,809	9,185	34,202	4,615	82,607	4,571
1890	55,101	7,846	28,270	3,967	26,831	3,880
1880	43,403	6,753	22,181	3,388	21,272	3,365
1870	33,589[4]	4,969[4]	17,029	2,464	16,560	2,505
1860	26,923	4,521	13,811	2,274	13,111	2,247
1850	19,553	3,639	10,026	1,811	9,527	1,828
1840	14,196	2,874	7,256	1,433	6,940	1,441
1830	10,537	2,329	5,363	1,165	5,174	1,162
1820	7,867	1,772	3,998	899	3,869	873
1810	5,862	1,378	2,988	-	2,874	-

[Continued]

★ 1706 ★

Population by Gender, Residence, and Race, 1790-1950 - II

[Continued]

Year	Color by sex					
	Both sexes		Male		Female	
	White	Non white	White	Non white	White	Non white
1800	4,306	1,002	2,195	-	2,111	-
1790	3,172	757	1,615	-	1,557	-

Source: "Population, by Sex, Residence, and Color: 1790-1950." U.S. Bureau of the Census, *Historical Statistics of the United States: Colonial Times to 1957*, p. 9. *Notes:* 1. Residence for both sexes tabulated according to the old urban (or 1940) definition (series A 36-38) from 1790 to 1940, and for male and for female separately for 1930 and 1940. Tabulations of residence for male and for female from 1900 to 1920 are according to the definitions current at those censuses. 2. See text for series A 34-50 for explanation of definitions. 3. Figures for color by sex in 1930 revised to include Mexicans as white. Mexicans were classified as nonwhite in the 1930 reports. 4. Adjustment for undernumeration in the South (see series A 20 above) shows a population of 39,818,000 of whom 34,337,000 were white and 5,481,000 were nonwhite.

★ 1707 ★

Distribution by Gender

Urban and Rural Black Population by Gender With Number of Males Per 100 Females and Percent Urban, by Sections, Divisions, and States, 1930 - I

SECTION, DIVISION, AND STATE	URBAN POPULATION			RURAL POPULATION			MALES PER 100 FEMALES		PERCENT URBAN OF TOTAL POPULATION		
	Total	Male	Female	Total	Male	Female	Urban	Rural	Total	Male	Female
United States	5,193,913	2,479,158	2,714,755	6,697,230	3,376,511	3,320,719	91.3	101.7	43.7	42.3	45.0
The North	2,128,329	1,057,320	1,071,009	280,890	153,387	127,503	98.7	120.3	88.3	87.3	89.4
The South	2,966,325	1,373,017	1,593,308	6,395,252	3,210,574	3,184,678	86.2	100.8	31.7	30.0	33.3
The West	99,259	48,821	50,438	21,088	12,550	8,538	96.8	147.0	82.5	79.6	85.5
GEOGRAPHIC DIVISIONS:											
New England	81,443	40,289	41,154	12,643	6,674	5,969	97.9	111.8	86.6	85.8	87.3
Middle Atlantic	939,064	460,125	478,939	113,835	30,701	53,134	96.1	114.2	89.2	88.3	90.0
East North Central	848,627	428,801	419,826	81,823	46,567	35,256	102.1	132.1	91.2	90.2	92.3
West North Central	259,195	128,105	131,090	72,589	39,445	33,144	97.7	119.0	78.1	76.5	79.8
South Atlantic	1,462,904	675,013	787,891	2,958,484	1,481,518	1,476,966	85.7	100.3	33.1	31.3	34.8
East South Central	759,166	350,955	408,211	1,899,072	950,597	948,475	86.0	100.2	28.6	27.0	30.1
West South Central	744,255	347,049	397,206	1,537,696	788,459	759,237	87.4	102.5	32.6	30.8	34.3
Mountain	21,032	10,613	10,419	9,193	5,699	3,494	101.9	163.1	69.6	65.1	74.9
Pacific	78,227	38,208	40,019	11,895	6,851	5,044	95.5	135.8	86.8	84.8	88.8
NEW ENGLAND:											
Maine	703	363	340	393	234	159	106.8	147.2	64.1	60.8	68.1
New Hampshire	594	420	174	196	104	92	241.4	-	75.2	80.2	65.4
Vermont	213	114	99	355	196	159	-	123.3	37.5	36.8	38.4
Massachusetts	46,323	22,817	23,506	6,042	3,280	2,762	97.1	118.8	88.5	87.4	89.5
Rhode Island	9,079	4,428	4,651	834	434	400	95.2	108.5	91.6	91.1	92.1
Connecticut	24,531	12,147	12,384	4,823	2,426	2,397	98.1	101.2	83.6	83.4	83.8
MIDDLE ATLANTIC:											
New York	390,499	187,862	202,637	22,315	11,623	10,692	92.7	108.7	94.6	94.2	95.0

[Continued]

★ 1707 ★

Urban and Rural Black Population by Gender With Number of Males Per 100 Females and Percent Urban, by Sections, Divisions, and States, 1930 - I

[Continued]

SECTION, DIVISION, AND STATE	URBAN POPULATION			RURAL POPULATION			MALES PER 100 FEMALES		PERCENT URBAN OF TOTAL POPULATION		
	Total	Male	Female	Total	Male	Female	Urban	Rural	Total	Male	Female
New Jersey	174,985	85,321	89,664	33,843	17,608	16,235	95.2	108.5	83.8	82.9	84.7
Pennsylvania	373,580	186,942	186,638	57,677	31,470	26,207	100.2	120.1	86.6	85.6	87.7

Source: "Urban and Rural Negro Population by Sex, With Number of Males Per 100 Females, and Percent Urban, by Sections, Divisions, and States: 1930." U.S. Bureau of the Census, *Negroes in the United States, 1920-1932*, p. 83.

★ 1708 ★

Distribution by Gender

Urban and Rural Black Population by Gender With Number of Males Per 100 Females and Percent Urban, by Sections, Divisions, and States, 1930 - II

SECTION, DIVISION, AND STATE	URBAN POPULATION			RURAL POPULATION			MALES PER 100 FEMALES		PERCENT URBAN OF TOTAL POPULATION		
	Total	Male	Female	Total	Male	Female	Urban	Rural	Total	Male	Female
EAST NORTH CENTRAL:											
Ohio	271,972	138,224	133,748	37,332	20,904	16,428	103.3	127.2	87.9	86.9	89.1
Indiana	103,042	51,788	51,254	8,940	5,280	3,660	101.0	144.3	92.0	90.7	93.3
Illinois	304,036	150,386	153,650	24,936	14,039	10,897	97.9	128.8	92.4	91.5	93.4
Michigan	159,704	83,121	76,583	9,749	5,815	3,934	108.5	147.8	94.2	93.5	95.1
Wisconsin	9,873	5,282	4,591	866	529	337	115.1	157.0	91.9	90.9	93.2
WEST NORTH CENTRAL:											
Minnesota	9,110	4,816	4,294	335	189	146	112.2	129.5	95.6	96.2	96.7
Iowa	15,185	7,749	7,436	2,195	1,238	957	104.2	129.4	87.4	86.2	88.6
Missouri	169,954	83,527	86,427	53,886	28,402	25,484	96.6	111.5	75.9	74.7	77.2
North Dakota	216	133	83	161	110	51	-	-	57.3	54.7	61.9
South Dakota	337	171	166	309	172	137	103.0	125.6	52.2	49.9	54.8
Nebraska	13,112	6,675	6,437	640	388	252	103.7	154.0	95.4	94.5	96.2
Kansas	51,281	25,034	26,247	15,063	8,946	6,117	95.4	146.2	77.3	73.7	81.1
SOUTH ATLANTIC:											
Delaware	15,037	7,583	7,499	17,565	9,445	8,120	100.5	116.3	46.1	44.4	48.0
Maryland	159,654	78,421	81,233	116,725	62,085	54,640	96.5	113.6	57.8	55.8	59.8
District of Columbia	132,068	62,225	69,843	-	-	-	89.1	-	100.0	100.0	100.0
Virginia	213,401	99,273	114,128	436,764	222,272	214,492	87.0	103.6	32.8	30.9	34.7
West Virginia	31,224	15,586	15,638	83,669	45,287	38,382	99.7	118.0	27.2	25.6	28.9
North Carolina	246,237	112,494	133,743	672,410	334,006	338,404	84.1	98.7	26.8	25.2	28.3
South Carolina	138,354	60,319	78,035	655,327	318,981	336,346	77.3	94.8	17.4	15.9	18.8
Georgia	316,637	140,573	176,064	754,488	372,878	381,610	79.8	97.7	29.6	27.4	31.6
Florida	210,292	98,584	111,708	221,536	116,564	104,972	88.3	111.0	48.7	45.8	51.6
EAST SOUTH CENTRAL:											
Kentucky	116,561	56,086	60,475	109,479	57,415	52,064	92.7	110.3	51.6	49.4	53.7
Tennessee	240,168	111,506	128,663	237,478	121,064	116,414	86.7	104.0	50.3	47.9	52.5
Alabama	268,450	123,127	145,323	676,384	334,017	342,367	84.7	97.6	28.4	26.9	29.8
Mississippi	133,987	60,237	73,750	875,731	438,101	437,630	81.7	100.1	13.3	12.1	14.4
WEST SOUTH CENTRAL:											
Arkansas	89,162	40,844	48,318	389,301	196,965	193,236	84.5	101.5	18.6	17.2	20.0
Louisiana	257,463	118,439	139,024	518,863	260,734	258,129	85.2	101.0	33.2	31.2	35.0
Oklahoma	67,801	32,470	35,331	104,397	54,348	50,049	91.9	108.6	39.4	37.4	41.4
Texas	329,829	155,296	174,533	525,135	267,312	257,823	89.0	103.7	38.6	36.7	40.4
MOUNTAIN:											
Montana	1,027	556	471	229	154	75	118.0	-	81.8	78.3	86.3
Idaho	502	276	226	166	119	47	122.1	-	75.1	69.9	82.8
Wyoming	859	453	406	391	246	145	111.6	169.7	68.7	64.8	73.7
Colorado	10,471	4,965	5,506	1,357	774	583	90.2	132.8	88.5	86.5	90.4
New Mexico	1,718	872	846	1,132	659	473	103.1	139.3	60.3	57.0	64.1
Arizona	5,147	2,783	2,364	5,602	3,569	2,033	117.7	175.6	47.9	43.8	53.8
Utah	944	520	424	164	89	75	122.6	-	85.2	85.4	85.0
Nevada	364	188	175	152	89	63	106.8	-	70.5	67.9	73.6
PACIFIC:											
Washington	5,818	3,167	2,651	1,022	630	392	119.5	160.7	85.1	83.4	87.1

[Continued]

★ 1708 ★

Urban and Rural Black Population by Gender With Number of Males Per 100 Females and Percent Urban, by Sections, Divisions, and States, 1930 - II

[Continued]

SECTION, DIVISION, AND STATE	URBAN POPULATION			RURAL POPULATION			MALES PER 100 FEMALES		PERCENT URBAN OF TOTAL POPULATION		
	Total	Male	Female	Total	Male	Female	Urban	Rural	Total	Male	Female
Oregon	1,890	993	897	344	217	127	110.7	170.9	84.6	82.1	87.6
California	70,519	34,048	36,471	10,529	6,004	4,525	93.4	132.7	87.0	85.0	89.9

Source: "Urban and Rural Negro Population by Sex, With Number of Males Per 100 Females, and Percent Urban, by Sections, Divisions, and States: 1930." U.S. Bureau of the Census, *Negroes in the United States, 1920-1932*, p. 83.

★ 1709 ★

Distribution by Gender

Women 15 to 44 Years of Age and Children in or Outside Cities of 25,000 or More by Divisions or States, 1910

DIVISION AND STATE	NEGRO POPULATION: 1910						CHILDREN UNDER 5 PER 1,000 WOMEN 15 TO 44 YEARS OF AGE: 1910					
	Women 15 to 44 years of age			Children under 5 years of age			Negro population			White population		
	Total	In cities of 25,000 or more	Outside of cities 25,000 or more	Total	In cities of 25,000 or more	Outside of cities 25,000 or more	Total	In cities of 25,000 or more	Outside of cities 25,000 or more	Total	In cities of 25,000 or more	Outside of cities 25,000 or more
UNITED STATES	2,435,189	525,748	1,909,441	1,263,288	125,735	1,137,533	519	239	596	484	368	552
GEOGRAPHIC DIVISIONS:												
New England	18,833	13,908	4,925	5,876	3,915	1,961	312	281	308	395	375	416
Middle Atlantic	131,605	94,374	37,231	35,298	21,854	13,444	268	232	361	431	392	488
East North Central	81,994	49,521	32,473	23,428	10,599	12,829	286	214	395	442	375	484
West North Central	64,766	33,182	31,584	19,127	6,651	12,476	295	200	395	492	325	544
South Atlantic	989,583	169,439	820,141	570,516	43,082	527,434	577	254	643	589	363	645
East South Central	649,752	85,368	564,384	347,803	19,879	327,924	535	233	581	626	350	667
West South Central	484,697	71,377	413,320	258,012	17,979	240,033	532	252	581	644	365	687
Mountain	6,038	2,867	3,171	1,350	531	819	224	185	258	530	344	579
Pacific	7,921	5,712	2,209	1,878	1,245	633	237	218	287	378	266	485
NEW ENGLAND:												
Maine	332	103	229	117	21	96	352	204	419	434	326	451
New Hampshire	149	11	138	40	6	34	268	545	246	401	373	410
Vermont	252	-	252	102	-	102	405	-	405	439	-	439
Massachusetts	11,053	9,020	2,033	3,448	2,566	882	312	284	434	378	371	393
Rhode Island	2,592	2,093	499	862	618	244	333	295	489	391	374	431
Connecticut	4,455	2,681	1,774	1,307	704	603	293	263	340	409	405	414
MIDDLE ATLANTIC:												
New York	45,629	38,594	7,035	10,061	7,684	2,377	220	200	338	386	382	396
New Jersey	27,124	13,726	13,398	7,922	3,556	4,366	292	259	326	424	427	421
Pennsylvania	58,852	42,054	16,798	17,315	10,614	6,701	294	252	399	492	398	562
EAST NORTH CENTRAL:												
Ohio	29,632	17,822	11,810	8,921	3,943	4,978	301	221	422	421	368	458
Indiana	16,342	9,601	6,741	4,763	2,256	2,507	291	235	372	438	323	467
Illinois	30,823	18,847	11,976	8,248	3,731	4,517	268	198	377	437	382	492
Michigan	4,347	2,681	1,666	1,285	569	716	296	212	430	462	383	502
Wisconsin	850	570	280	211	100	111	248	175	396	482	393	518
WEST NORTH CENTRAL:												
Minnesota	1,889	1,686	203	382	300	82	202	178	404	483	323	565
Iowa	3,708	1,353	2,355	1,245	370	875	336	273	372	461	332	487
Missouri	43,156	23,790	19,366	12,299	4,356	7,943	285	183	410	464	315	551
North Dakota	147	-	147	37	-	37	252	-	252	670	-	670
South Dakota	216	-	216	60	-	60	278	-	278	576	-	576
Nebraska	2,213	1,772	441	477	336	141	216	190	320	516	349	554
Kansas	13,437	4,581	8,856	4,627	1,289	3,338	344	281	377	504	359	523

[Continued]

★ 1709 ★

Women 15 to 44 Years of Age and Children in or Outside Cities of 25,000 or More by Divisions or States, 1910

[Continued]

DIVISION AND STATE	NEGRO POPULATION: 1910						CHILDREN UNDER 5 PER 1,000 WOMEN 15 TO 44 YEARS OF AGE: 1910					
	Women 15 to 44 years of age			Children under 5 years of age			Negro population			White population		
	Total	In cities of 25,000 or more	Outside of cities 25,000 or more	Total	In cities of 25,000 or more	Outside of cities 25,000 or more	Total	In cities of 25,000 or more	Outside of cities 25,000 or more	Total	In cities of 25,000 or more	Outside of cities 25,000 or more
SOUTH ATLANTIC:												
Delaware	7,437	2,673	4,764	3,089	577	2,512	415	216	527	422	404	440
Maryland	58,631	27,385	31,246	25,987	6,628	19,359	443	242	620	431	360	497
District of Columbia	31,166	31,166	-	7,290	7,290	-	234	234	-	299	299	-
Virginia	158,798	32,638	126,160	86,555	8,739	77,816	545	268	617	577	375	617
West Virginia	15,050	981	14,069	6,974	229	6,745	463	233	479	638	374	659
North Carolina	162,377	7,309	155,068	107,297	2,505	104,792	661	343	676	675	453	682
South Carolina	196,806	14,021	182,785	128,712	4,026	124,686	654	287	682	647	372	669
Georgia	282,888	40,802	242,086	167,498	10,083	157,415	592	247	650	647	385	695
Florida	76,430	12,464	63,966	37,114	3,005	34,109	486	241	533	600	420	633
EAST SOUTH CENTRAL:												
Kentucky	66,986	17,213	49,773	25,541	3,405	22,136	381	198	445	583	325	636
Tennessee	120,951	37,869	83,082	56,580	8,484	48,096	468	224	579	609	341	656
Alabama	220,984	30,286	190,698	123,991	7,990	116,001	561	264	608	691	421	729
Mississippi	240,831	-	240,831	141,691	-	141,691	588	-	588	677	-	677
WEST SOUTH CENTRAL:												
Arkansas	108,391	4,667	103,724	57,330	1,095	56,235	529	235	542	700	343	713
Louisiana	175,313	33,024	142,289	92,439	8,805	83,634	527	267	588	612	371	728
Oklahoma[3]	31,783	4,178	27,605	18,186	1,251	16,935	572	299	613	664	338	686
Texas	196,210	29,508	139,702	90,057	6,828	83,229	532	231	596	625	368	668
MOUNTAIN:												
Montana	485	65	420	105	7	98	216	108	233	488	345	510
Idaho	158	-	158	40	-	40	253	-	253	599	-	599
Wyoming	479	-	479	109	-	109	228	-	228	549	-	549
Colorado	3,407	2,523	884	708	485	223	208	192	252	438	301	532
New Mexico	429	-	429	150	-	150	350	-	350	633	-	633
Arizona	606	-	606	156	-	156	257	-	257	555	-	555
Utah	309	279	30	56	39	17	181	140	567	649	454	762
Nevada	165	-	165	26	-	26	158	-	158	395	-	395
PACIFIC:												
Washington	1,517	1,087	430	289	180	109	191	166	253	431	214	653
Oregon	375	306	69	70	45	25	187	147	362	403	267	477
California	6,029	4,319	1,710	1,519	1,020	499	252	236	292	347	277	418

Source: "Women 15 to 44 Years of Age, and Children Under 5 Years, in the Total Population, and in the Population Living Outside of Cities of 25,000 or More Inhabitants, by Divisions and States: 1910." U.S. Bureau of the Census, *Negro Population, 1790-1915*. Washington, D.C.: Government Printing Office, 1918, p. 295.

★ 1710 ★

Distribution by Gender

Women 15 to 44 Years of Age, Children Under 5 in Cities, and Changes in Children Per 1,000 Women, 1900 and 1910 - I

CITY	WOMEN 15 TO 44 YEARS OF AGE			
	Negro		White	
	1910	1900	1910	1900
Atlanta, Ga.	17,524	12,348	28,425	14,670
Augusta, Ga.	6,276	5,874	6,235	5,639
Baltimore, Md.	27,385	26,158	125,906	112,773
Birmingham, Ala.	16,537	5,675	20,929	5,564
Boston, Mass.	4,376	3,556	177,409	152,339
Charleston, S.C.	10,251	9,802	7,282	6,423
Charlotte, N.C.	3,784	[1]	5,967	[1]
Chattanooga, Tenn.	5,787	4,026	7,423	4,605
Chicago, Ill.	14,296	9,548	567,465	434,047
Cincinnati, Ohio	6,343	4,609	95,230	85,714
Columbia, S.C.	3,770	[1]	4,031	[1]
Columbus, Ohio	3,698	2,290	46,464	32,233
Dallas, Tex.	6,223	3,013	20,581	8,964
Fort Worth, Tex.	4,200	1,366	15,566	5,813
Houston, Tex.	8,121	4,802	14,639	7,410
Indianapolis, Ind.	6,697	4,702	58,623	42,709
Jacksonville, Fla.	9,587	4,990	7,838	3,218
Kansas City, Mo.	7,896	5,914	64,274	41,453
Lexington, Ky.	3,398	3,171	6,734	4,603
Little Rock, Ark.	4,667	4,355	8,785	6,217
Louisville, Ky.	12,727	12,099	49,983	45,063
Macon, Ga.	5,653	[1]	6,025	[1]
Memphis, Tenn.	17,496	14,822	21,300	13,418
Mobile, Ala.	7,377	5,320	7,804	5,714
Montgomery, Ala.	6,372	5,532	5,008	3,511
Nashville, Tenn.	12,066	9,654	20,334	13,790
New Orleans, La.	28,355	23,176	65,833	54,234
New York, N.Y.	33,895	22,462	1,270,461	903,485
Norfolk, Va.	8,302	6,571	11,824	6,902
Philadelphia, Pa.	29,150	22,038	386,611	326,065
Pittsburgh, Pa.	7,666	5,640	132,321	110,563
Portsmouth, Va.	3,573	[1]	4,877	[1]
Richmond, Va.	15,087	10,450	22,228	14,133
St. Louis, Mo.	13,818	11,060	176,800	143,101
San Antonio, Tex.	3,600	2,247	23,040	11,869
Savannah, Ga.	11,349	9,570	8,445	6,811

[Continued]

★ 1710 ★

Women 15 to 44 Years of Age, Children Under 5 in Cities, and Changes in Children Per 1,000 Women, 1900 and 1910 - I

[Continued]

CITY	WOMEN 15 TO 44 YEARS OF AGE			
	Negro		White	
	1910	1900	1910	1900
Shreveport, La.	4,669	1	3,698	1
Washington, D.C.	31,166	28,634	64,794	52,537
Wilmington, N.C.	3,525	1	3,530	1

Source: "Women 15 to 44 Years of Age, Children Under 5 Years, and Increase or Decrease of Children Per 1,000 Women, by Cities of 25,000 or More Inhabitants Having in 1910 a Negro Population of 10,000 or More: 1910 and 1900." U.S. Bureau of the Census, *Negro Population, 1790-1915*, p. 293. *Note:* 1. Data for 1900 not available.

★ 1711 ★

Distribution by Gender

Women 15 to 44 Years of Age, Children Under 5 in Cities, and Changes in Children Per 1,000 Women, 1900 and 1910 - II

CITY	CHILDREN UNDER 5 YEARS OF AGE			
	Negro		White	
	1910	1900	1910	1900
Atlanta, Ga.	4,622	3,316	10,964	5,312
Augusta, Ga.	1,326	1,708	2,182	2,099
Baltimore, Md.	6,628	6,705	45,356	43,807
Birmingham, Ala.	4,598	1,421	9,604	2,203
Boston, Mass.	942	936	62,746	56,415
Charleston, S.C.	2,985	3,062	2,681	2,224
Charlotte, N.C.	1,225	1	2,756	1
Chattanooga, Tenn.	1,488	1,097	2,449	1,610
Chicago, Ill.	2,472	1,611	221,270	188,730
Cincinnati, Ohio	1,148	996	28,023	28,825
Columbia, S.C.	1,041	1	1,529	1
Columbus, Ohio	836	574	13,497	9,556
Dallas, Tex.	1,271	718	6,775	3,344
Fort Worth, Tex.	1,063	361	5,887	2,410
Houston, Tex.	1,790	1,144	4,986	2,975
Indianapolis, Ind.	1,557	1,167	17,139	13,396
Jacksonville, Fla.	2,234	1,543	2,608	1,196
Kansas City, Mo.	1,211	1,076	17,376	12,357
Lexington, Ky.	681	753	1,821	1,151
Little Rock, Ark.	1,095	1,166	3,010	2,316

[Continued]

★ 1711 ★

Women 15 to 44 Years of Age, Children Under 5 in Cities, and Changes in Children Per 1,000 Women, 1900 and 1910 - II

[Continued]

CITY	CHILDREN UNDER 5 YEARS OF AGE			
	Negro		White	
	1910	1900	1910	1900
Louisville, Ky.	2,458	2,747	16,390	16,152
Macon, Ga.	1,512	1	2,363	1
Memphis, Tenn.	3,729	4,568	7,024	5,087
Mobile, Ala.	1,863	1,429	2,772	1,992
Montgomery, Ala.	1,529	1,639	1,844	1,281
Nashville, Tenn.	2,721	2,480	7,451	4,882
New Orleans, La.	7,624	7,184	24,413	22,878
New York, N.Y.	6,676	4,566	500,248	392,651
Norfolk, Va.	2,008	1,918	4,185	2,675
Philadelphia, Pa.	6,863	5,328	146,045	125,790
Pittsburgh, Pa.	2,240	1,830	55,546	49,090
Portsmouth, Va.	1,064	1	2,279	1
Richmond, Va.	4,019	2,747	7,583	4,988
St. Louis, Mo.	2,685	2,403	57,399	54,620
San Antonio, Tex.	895	718	9,080	4,943
Savannah, Ga.	2,623	2,399	3,382	2,570
Shreveport, La.	1,181	1	1,365	1
Washington, D.C.	7,290	7,278	19,361	15,802
Wilmington, N.C.	1,280	1	1,547	1

Source: "Women 15 to 44 Years of Age, Children Under 5 Years, and Increase or Decrease of Children Per 1,000 Women, by Cities of 25,000 or More Inhabitants Having in 1910 a Negro Population of 10,000 or More: 1910 and 1900." U.S. Bureau of the Census, *Negro Population, 1790-1915*, p. 293. *Note:* 1. Data for 1900 not available.

★ 1712 ★

Distribution by Gender

Women 15 to 44 Years of Age, Children Under 5 in Cities, and Changes in Children Per 1,000 Women, 1900 and 1910 - III

CITY	CHILDREN UNDER 5 PER 1,000 WOMEN 15 TO 44 YEARS OF AGE					
	Negro		White		Increase (+) or decrease (-): 1900-1910	
	1910	1900	1910	1900	Negro	White
Atlanta, Ga.	264	269	386	362	-5	+24
Augusta, Ga.	211	291	350	372	-80	-22
Baltimore, Md.	242	256	360	388	-14	-28
Birmingham, Ala.	278	250	459	396	+28	+63

[Continued]

★ 1712 ★

Women 15 to 44 Years of Age, Children Under 5 in Cities, and Changes in Children Per 1,000 Women, 1900 and 1910 - III

[Continued]

CITY	CHILDREN UNDER 5 PER 1,000 WOMEN 15 TO 44 YEARS OF AGE					
	Negro		White		Increase (+) or decrease (-): 1900-1910	
	1910	1900	1910	1900	Negro	White
Boston, Mass.	215	263	354	370	-48	-16
Charleston, S.C.	291	312	368	346	-21	+22
Charlotte, N.C.	324	-	462	-	-	-
Chattanooga, Tenn.	257	272	330	350	-15	-20
Chicago, Ill.	173	169	390	435	+4	-45
Cincinnati, Ohio	181	216	294	336	-35	-42
Columbia, S.C.	276	-	379	-	-	-
Columbus, Ohio	226	251	290	297	-25	-7
Dallas, Tex.	204	238	329	373	-34	-44
Fort Worth, Tex.	253	264	378	415	-11	-37
Houston, Tex.	220	238	341	401	-18	-60
Indianapolis, Ind.	232	248	292	314	-16	-22
Jacksonville, Fla.	233	309	333	372	-76	-39
Kansas City, Mo.	153	182	270	298	-29	-28
Lexington, Ky.	200	237	270	250	-37	+20
Little Rock, Ark.	235	268	343	373	-33	-30
Louisville, Ky.	193	227	328	358	-34	-30
Macon, Ga.	267	-	392	-	-	-
Memphis, Tenn.	213	308	330	379	-95	-49
Mobile, Ala.	253	269	355	349	-16	+6
Montgomery, Ala.	240	296	368	365	-56	+3
Nashville, Tenn.	226	257	366	354	-31	+12
New Orleans, La.	269	310	371	422	-41	-51
New York, N.Y.	197	203	394	435	-6	-41
Norfolk, Va.	242	292	354	388	-50	-34
Philadelphia, Pa.	235	242	378	386	-7	-8
Pittsburgh, Pa.	292	324	420	444	-32	-24
Portsmouth, Va.	298	-	467	-	-	-
Richmond, Va.	266	263	341	353	+3	-12
St. Louis, Mo.	194	217	325	382	-23	-57
San Antonio, Tex.	249	320	394	416	-71	-22
Savannah, Ga.	231	251	400	377	-20	+23
Shreveport, La.	253	-	369	-	-	-

[Continued]

★ 1712 ★

Women 15 to 44 Years of Age, Children Under 5 in Cities, and Changes in Children Per 1,000 Women, 1900 and 1910 - III

[Continued]

CITY	CHILDREN UNDER 5 PER 1,000 WOMEN 15 TO 44 YEARS OF AGE					
	Negro		White		Increase (+) or decrease (-): 1900-1910	
	1910	1900	1910	1900	Negro	White
Washington, D.C.	234	254	299	302	-20	-3
Wilmington, N.C.	363	-	438	-	-	-

Source: "Women 15 to 44 Years of Age, Children Under 5 Years, and Increase or Decrease of Children Per 1,000 Women, by Cities of 25,000 or More Inhabitants Having in 1910 a Negro Population of 10,000 or More: 1910 and 1900." U.S. Bureau of the Census, *Negro Population, 1790-1915*, p. 293.

Free Blacks

★ 1713 ★

Free Black Population of Maryland by County, 1790-1860

County	1860	1850	1840	1830	1820	1810	1800	1790
Allegany	467	412	215	222	195	113	101	12
Anne Arundel	4864	4602	5083	4076	3382	2536	1833	804
Baltimore	29911	29075	21453	17888	12489	7208	4307	927
Calvert	1841	1530	1474	1213	694	388	307	136
Caroline	2786	2788	1720	1652	1390	1001	602	421
Carroll	1225	974	898	-	-	-	-	-
Cecil	2918	2623	2551	2249	1783	947	373	163
Charles	1068	913	819	851	567	412	571	404
Dorchester	4684	3848	3987	3000	2496	2661	2365	528
Frederick	4957	3760	2985	2716	1777	783	473	213
Harford	3644	2777	2436	2058	1387	2221	1344	775
Howard	1395	-	-	-	-	-	-	-
Kent	3411	3143	2491	2266	2067	1979	1786	655
Montgomery	1552	1311	1313	1266	922	677	262	294
Prince George's	1198	1138	1080	1202	1096	4929	648	164
Queen Anne's	3372	3278	2541	2866	2138	2738	1025	618
St. Mary's	1866	1633	1393	1179	894	636	622	343
Somerset	4571	3483	2646	2239	1954	1058	586	268
Talbot	2964	2593	2340	2483	2234	2103	1591	1076
Washington	1677	1828	1580	1082	627	483	342	64
Worcester	3571	3014	3073	2430	1638	1054	449	178
Totals	83942	74723	62078	52938	39730	53927	19587	8043

Source: "Free Colored Population of Maryland, 1790-1860," James M. Wright, *The Free Negro in Maryland*, p. 88.

★ 1714 ★

Free Blacks

Increase in Freemen and Free Blacks in Maryland, 1755, 1790, 1860 - I

	Number of freemen			Number of free Negroes			Per cent increase			
							Freemen		Free Negroes	
	1755	1790	1860	1755	1790	1860	1755-1790	1790-1860	1775-1790	1790-1860
Eastern Shore	50364	69048	120171	684	3907	28277	37.0	74.0	471.0	623
Southern Maryland	34486	58043	72159	764	2145	13784	67.7	24.3	180.7	542
Baltimore County	25291[1]	31805	261153	369[1]	927	29911	254.0[1]	721.1	439.0[1]	3126.6
Western Maryland	25291[1]	57796	146377	369[1]	1064	11970	254.0[1]	153.0	439.0[1]	1015.6
Whole state	110141	216692	599860	1817	8043	83942	96.7	176.8	342.0	943.6

Source: "Comparing Increase of All Freemen With That of the Free Negroes," James M. Wright, *The Free Negro in Maryland, 1634-1860*, p. 90. *Note:* 1. Data includes Baltimore County and Western Maryland.

★ 1715 ★

Free Blacks

Increase in Freemen and Free Blacks in Maryland, 1755, 1790, 1860 - II

	Negro per cent of total		Negro per cent of freemen		
	1755-1790	1790-1860	1755	1790	1860
Eastern Shore	18.8	47.6	1.35	5.65	23.43
Southern Maryland	5.8	82.4	2.21	3.69	19.08
Baltimore County	2.5[1]	12.6	1.45[1]	2.91	11.4
Western Maryland	2.5[1]	12.3	1.45[1]	1.84	8.18
Whole state	5.8	19.8	1.64	3.71	13.99

Source: "Comparing Increase of All Freemen With That of the Free Negroes," James M. Wright, *The Free Negro in Maryland, 1634-1860*, p. 90. *Note:* 1. Data includes Baltimore County and Western Maryland.

★ 1716 ★

Free Blacks

Population Changes of Free Blacks in Maryland and the United States, 1790-1860

	Maryland	U.S.
1790-1800	143.5%	
1800-1810	73.2	
1810-1820	17.1	25.23%
1820-1830	33.24	36.20
1830-1840	17.26	20.87

[Continued]

★ 1716 ★

Population Changes of Free Blacks in Maryland and the United States, 1790-1860

[Continued]

	Maryland	U.S.
1840-1850	19.44	12.46
1850-1860	12.00	10.97

Source: Untitled table, James M. Wright, *The Free Negro in Maryland*, p. 80. Primary source: *History and Statistics of Maryland, Seventh Census of United States*, p. 20. *Preliminary Report of Eight Census of United States*, p. 7. *Note:* The total increase for the half century was 147.4 per cent.

★ 1717 ★

Free Blacks

Population Changes of Free Blacks in North Carolina, 1790-1860

Year	Free black population
1790	4,975
1800	7,043
1810	10,266
1820	14,612
1830	19,543
1840	22,732
1850	27,463
1860	30,463

Source: Untitled table, James M. Wright, et. al., The James Sprunt Historical Publications, Vol. 17., *The Free Negro in North Carolina*, p. 23.

★ 1718 ★

Free Blacks

Population Changes of Free Blacks in North Carolina, by County, 1790-1860

County	Number of free blacks	County	Number of free blacks
Alamance	422	Jackson	6
Alexander	24	Johnston	195
Alleghany	33	Jones	113
Anson	152	Lenoir	178
Ashe	142	Lincoln	81
Bertie	319	McDowell	273

[Continued]

★ 1718 ★

Population Changes of Free Blacks in North Carolina, by County, 1790-1860

[Continued]

County	Number of free blacks	County	Number of free blacks
Bladen	435	Macon	115
Brunswick	260	Madison	17
Buncombe	111	Martin	451
Burke	221	Mecklenburg	293
Cabarrus	115	Montgomery	46
Caldwell	114	Moore	184
Camden	274	Nash	687
Carteret	153	New Hanover	640
Caswell	282	Northampton	659
Catawba	32	Orange	528
Chatham	306	Onslow	162
Cherokee	38	Pasquotank	1,507
Chowan	150	Perquimans	395
Cleveland	109	Person	318
Columbus	355	Pitt	127
Craven	1,332	Polk	106
Cumberland	109	Randolph	432
Currituck	223	Richmond	345
Davidson	149	Robeson	1,462
Davie	161	Rockingham	409
Duplin	371	Rowan	136
Edgecombe	389	Rutherford	123
Forsyth	218	Sampson	488
Franklin	566	Stanly	45
Gaston	111	Stokes	86
Gates	361	Surry	184
Granville	1,123	Tyrrell	143
Greene	154	Union	53
Guilford	693	Wake	1,446
Halifax	2,452	Warren	402
Harnett	103	Washington	299
Haywood	14	Watauga	81
Henderson	85	Wayne	737
Hertford	1,112	Wilkes	261
Hyde	257	Wilson	281
Iredell	26	Yancey	67

Source: Untitled table, James M. Wright, et. al., The James Sprunt Historical Publications, Vol. 17., *The Free Negro in North Carolina*, p. 24.

Geographical Areas: Cities/Urban, and Rural

★ 1719 ★

Blacks in Urban and Rural Communities by Divisions and States, 1890, 1900, and 1910 - I

DIVISION AND STATE	NEGRO POPULATION					
	Urban			Rural		
	1910	1900	1890	1910	1900	1890
UNITED STATES	2,689,229	2,005,972	1,481,142	7,138,534	6,828,022	6,007,534
GEOGRAPHIC DIVISIONS:						
New England	60,877	53,530	39,567	5,429	5,569	5,013
Middle Atlantic	339,246	247,769	153,346	78,624	78,152	71,980
East North Central	230,542	180,121	124,213	70,294	77,721	82,810
West North Central	164,301	139,363	116,145	78,361	98,546	107,944
South Atlantic	909,520	696,372	566,519	3,202,968	3,032,645	2,696,171
East South Central	509,097	386,268	273,971	2,143,416	2,113,618	1,845,826
West South Central	435,838	282,156	192,745	1,548,588	1,411,910	1,185,345
Mountain	15,446	9,834	6,733	6,021	5,756	6,238
Pacific	24,362	10,559	7,903	4,833	4,105	6,207
NEW ENGLAND:						
Maine	924	918	792	439	401	398
New Hampshire	356	419	300	208	243	314
Vermont	1,341	444	460	280	382	477
Massachusetts	35,243	29,867	20,427	2,812	2,107	1,717
Rhode Island	9,055	8,423	7,014	474	669	379
Connecticut	13,958	13,459	10,574	1,216	1,767	1,728
MIDDLE ATLANTIC:						
New York	117,486	81,356	51,364	16,705	17,876	18,728
New Jersey	65,427	46,128	25,043	24,333	23,716	22,595
Pennsylvania	156,333	120,285	76,939	37,586	36,560	30,657
EAST NORTH CENTRAL:						
Ohio	82,282	64,986	51,124	29,170	31,915	35,989
Indiana	48,425	42,274	28,839	11,895	15,231	16,376
Illinois	85,538	60,993	34,076	23,511	24,085	22,952
Michigan	12,156	10,009	8,734	4,959	5,807	6,489
Wisconsin	2,141	1,859	1,440	759	683	1,004
WEST NORTH CENTRAL:						
Minnesota	6,518	4,495	3,286	566	464	397
Iowa	9,786	8,097	6,635	5,187	4,596	4,050
Missouri	104,462	89,247	70,636	52,990	71,987	79,548
North Dakota	306	125	81	311	161	292
South Dakota	412	195	149	405	270	392
Nebraska	6,621	5,441	7,188	1,068	828	1,725

[Continued]

★ 1719 ★

Blacks in Urban and Rural Communities by Divisions and States, 1890, 1900, and 1910 - I

[Continued]

DIVISION AND STATE	NEGRO POPULATION					
	Urban			Rural		
	1910	1900	1890	1910	1900	1890
Kansas	36,196	31,763	28,170	17,834	20,240	21,540
SOUTH ATLANTIC:						
Delaware	11,157	11,537	9,428	20,024	19,160	18,958
Maryland	99,230	93,849	79,392	133,020	141,215	136,265
District of Columbia	94,446	86,702	75,572	-	-	-
Virginia	158,218	124,799	117,092	512,878	535,923	518,346
West Virginia	15,380	8,761	6,327	48,793	34,738	26,363
North Carolina	115,975	76,169	55,695	581,868	548,300	505,323
South Carolina	101,702	84,358	64,049	734,141	697,963	624,885
Georgia	224,826	161,061	123,862	952,161	873,752	734,953
Florida	88,586	49,136	35,102	220,083	181,594	131,078
EAST SOUTH CENTRAL:						
Kentucky	106,631	100,145	75,274	155,025	184,561	192,797
Tennessee	150,506	131,144	94,898	322,582	349,099	335,780
Alabama	156,603	98,154	69,607	751,679	729,153	608,882
Mississippi	95,357	56,825	34,192	914,130	850,805	708,367
WEST SOUTH CENTRAL:						
Arkansas	59,147	37,171	25,491	383,744	329,685	283,626
Louisiana	160,845	116,954	87,094	553,029	533,850	472,099
Oklahoma[3]	36,982	8,702	679	100,630	46,982	20,930
Texas	178,864	119,329	79,481	511,185	501,393	408,690
MOUNTAIN:						
Montana	1,455	931	628	379	592	862
Idaho	426	71	-	225	222	201
Wyoming	1,041	489	327	1,194	451	595
Colorado	9,359	7,052	5,009	2,094	1,518	1,206
New Mexico	795	581	274	833	1,029	1,682
Arizona	1,310	330	94	699	1,518	1,263
Utah	959	343	294	185	329	294
Nevada	101	37	107	412	97	135
PACIFIC:						
Washington	4,699	1,606	978	1,359	908	624
Oregon	1,264	878	597	228	227	589
California	18,399	8,075	6,328	3,246	2,970	4,994

Source: "Negroes in Urban and Rural Communities, by Divisions and States: 1910, 1900, and 1890." U.S. Bureau of the Census, *Negro Population, 1790-1915*, p. 92. *Notes:* 1. Less than one-tenth of 1 per cent. 2. Includes population of Indian Territory for 1900 and 1890.

★ 1720 ★

Geographical Areas: Cities/Urban, and Rural

Blacks in Urban and Rural Communities by Divisions and States, 1890, 1900, and 1910 - II

DIVISION AND STATE	NEGRO POPUALTION PERCENTAGE						PERCENTAGE NEGRO					
	Urban			Rural			In total urban population			In total rural population		
	1910	1900	1890	1910	1900	1890	1910	1900	1890	1910	1900	1890
UNITED STATES	27.4	22.7	19.8	72.6	77.3	80.2	6.3	6.5	6.5	14.5	15.1	14.9
GEOGRAPHIC DIVISIONS:												
New England	91.8	90.6	88.8	8.2	9.4	11.2	1.1	1.2	1.1	0.5	0.5	0.4
Middle Atlantic	81.2	76.0	68.1	18.8	24.0	31.9	2.5	2.5	2.1	1.4	1.5	1.3
East North Central	76.6	69.9	60.0	23.4	30.1	40.0	2.4	2.5	2.4	0.8	0.9	1.0
West North Central	67.7	58.6	51.8	32.3	41.4	48.2	4.2	4.7	5.0	1.0	1.3	1.6
South Atlantic	22.1	18.7	17.4	77.9	81.3	82.6	29.4	31.2	32.8	35.2	36.9	37.8
East South Central	19.2	15.5	12.9	80.8	84.5	87.1	32.3	34.2	33.5	31.4	32.9	32.9
West South Central	22.0	16.7	14.0	78.9	83.3	86.0	22.3	26.7	26.9	22.7	25.8	29.4
Mountain	72.0	63.1	51.9	28.0	36.9	48.1	1.6	1.8	1.9	0.4	0.5	0.7
Pacific	83.4	72.0	56.0	16.6	28.0	44.0	1.0	0.9	1.0	0.3	0.3	0.6
NEW ENGLAND:												
Maine	67.8	69.6	66.6	32.2	30.4	33.4	0.2	0.3	0.3	0.1	0.1	0.1
New Hampshire	63.1	63.3	48.9	36.9	36.7	51.1	0.1	0.2	0.2	0.1	0.1	0.2
Vermont	82.7	53.8	49.1	17.3	46.2	50.9	0.8	0.3	0.4	0.1	0.2	0.2
Massachusetts	92.6	93.4	92.2	7.4	6.6	7.8	1.1	1.2	1.0	1.2	0.9	0.7
Rhode Island	95.0	92.6	94.9	5.0	7.4	5.1	1.7	2.1	2.1	2.6	3.2	2.0
Connecticut	92.0	88.4	86.0	8.0	11.6	14.0	1.4	1.7	1.7	1.1	1.5	1.4
MIDDLE ATLANTIC:												
New York	87.6	82.0	73.3	12.4	18.0	26.7	1.6	1.5	1.3	0.9	0.9	0.9
New Jersey	72.9	66.0	52.6	27.1	34.0	47.4	3.4	3.5	2.9	3.9	4.3	4.0
Pennsylvania	80.6	76.6	71.5	19.4	23.3	28.5	3.4	3.5	3.0	1.2	1.3	1.1
EAST NORTH CENTRAL:												
Ohio	73.8	67.1	58.7	26.2	32.9	41.3	3.1	3.3	3.4	1.4	1.5	1.7
Indiana	80.3	73.5	63.8	19.7	26.5	36.2	4.2	4.9	4.9	0.8	0.9	1.0
Illinois	78.4	71.7	59.8	21.6	28.3	40.2	2.5	2.3	2.0	1.1	1.1	1.1
Michigan	71.0	63.3	57.4	29.0	36.7	42.6	0.9	1.1	1.2	0.3	0.4	0.5
Wisconsin	73.8	73.1	58.9	26.2	26.9	41.1	0.2	0.2	0.3	0.1	0.1	0.1
WEST NORTH CENTRAL:												
Minnesota	92.0	90.6	89.2	8.0	9.4	10.8	0.8	0.8	0.7	[1]	[1]	[1]
Iowa	65.4	63.8	62.1	34.6	36.2	37.9	1.4	1.4	1.6	0.3	0.3	0.3
Missouri	66.3	55.4	47.0	33.7	44.6	53.0	7.5	7.9	8.2	2.8	3.6	4.4
North Dakota	49.6	43.7	21.7	50.4	56.3	78.3	0.5	0.5	0.8	0.1	0.1	0.2
South Dakota	50.4	41.9	27.5	49.6	58.1	72.5	0.5	0.5	0.5	0.1	0.1	0.1
Nebraska	86.1	86.8	80.6	13.9	13.2	19.4	2.1	2.2	2.5	0.1	0.1	0.2
Kansas	67.0	61.1	56.7	33.0	38.9	43.4	7.3	9.6	10.3	1.5	1.8	1.9
SOUTH ATLANTIC:												
Delaware	35.8	37.6	33.2	64.2	62.4	66.8	11.5	13.5	13.3	19.0	19.4	19.5
Maryland	42.7	39.9	36.8	57.3	60.1	63.2	15.1	15.9	16.0	20.9	23.7	24.9

[Continued]

★ 1720 ★

Blacks in Urban and Rural Communities by Divisions and States, 1890, 1900, and 1910 - II

[Continued]

DIVISION AND STATE	NEGRO POPUALTION PERCENTAGE						PERCENTAGE NEGRO					
	Urban			Rural			In total urban population			In total rural population		
	1910	1900	1890	1910	1900	1890	1910	1900	1890	1910	1900	1890
District of Columbia	100.0	100.0	100.0	-	-	-	28.5	31.1	32.8	-	-	-
Virginia	23.6	18.9	18.4	76.4	81.1	81.6	33.2	36.7	41.4	32.4	35.4	37.7
West Virginia	24.0	20.1	19.4	76.0	79.9	80.6	6.7	7.0	7.8	4.9	4.2	3.9
North Carolina	16.6	12.2	9.9	83.4	87.8	90.1	36.4	40.8	48.1	30.8	32.1	33.6
South Carolina	12.2	10.8	9.3	87.8	89.2	90.7	45.2	49.3	55.1	56.9	59.7	60.4
Georgia	19.1	15.6	14.4	80.9	84.4	85.6	41.7	46.5	48.1	46.0	46.7	46.5
Florida	28.7	21.3	21.1	71.3	78.7	78.9	40.4	45.9	45.4	41.2	43.1	41.7
EAST SOUTH CENTRAL:												
Kentucky	40.8	35.2	28.1	59.2	64.8	71.9	19.2	21.4	21.1	8.9	11.0	12.8
Tennessee	31.8	27.3	22.0	68.2	72.7	78.0	34.1	40.1	39.8	18.5	20.6	22.0
Alabama	17.2	11.9	10.3	82.8	88.1	89.7	42.3	45.3	45.7	42.5	45.2	44.7
Mississippi	9.4	6.3	4.6	90.6	93.7	95.4	46.0	47.3	48.9	57.5	59.4	58.1
WEST SOUTH CENTRAL:												
Arkansas	13.4	10.1	8.2	86.6	89.9	91.8	29.2	33.3	34.8	28.0	27.5	26.9
Louisiana	22.5	18.0	15.6	77.5	82.0	84.4	32.4	31.9	30.7	47.7	52.5	56.6
Oklahoma[3]	26.9	15.6	3.1	73.1	84.4	96.9	11.6	14.9	7.2	7.5	6.4	8.4
Texas	25.9	19.2	16.3	74.1	80.8	83.7	19.1	22.9	22.7	17.3	19.8	21.7
MOUNTAIN:												
Montana	79.3	61.1	42.1	20.7	38.9	57.9	1.1	1.1	1.6	0.2	0.4	0.8
Idaho	65.4	24.2	-	34.6	75.8	100.0	0.6	0.7	-	0.1	0.1	0.2
Wyoming	46.6	52.0	35.5	53.4	48.0	64.5	2.4	1.8	1.5	1.2	0.7	1.4
Colorado	81.7	82.3	80.6	18.3	17.7	19.4	2.3	2.7	2.7	0.5	0.5	0.5
New Mexico	48.8	36.1	14.0	51.2	63.9	86.0	1.7	1.2	2.7	0.3	0.6	1.1
Arizona	65.2	17.9	6.9	34.8	82.1	93.1	2.1	1.7	1.1	0.5	1.5	1.6
Utah	83.3	51.0	50.0	16.2	49.0	50.0	0.6	0.3	0.4	0.1	0.2	0.2
Nevada	19.7	27.6	44.2	80.3	72.4	55.8	0.8	0.5	0.7	0.6	0.3	0.4
PACIFIC:												
Washington	77.6	63.9	61.0	22.4	36.1	39.0	0.8	0.8	0.8	0.3	0.3	0.3
Oregon	84.7	79.5	50.3	15.3	20.5	49.7	0.4	0.7	0.7	0.1	0.1	0.3
California	85.0	73.1	55.9	15.0	26.9	44.1	1.3	1.0	1.1	0.4	0.4	0.8

Source: "Negroes in Urban and Rural Communities, by Divisions and States: 1910, 1900, and 1890." U.S. Bureau of the Census, *Negro Population, 1790-1915*, p. 92. *Notes:* 1. Less than one-tenth of 1 per cent. 2. Includes population of Indian Territory for 1900 and 1890.

★ 1721 ★

Geographical Areas: Cities/Urban, and Rural

Changes in Black Population in 43 Cities Having a Black Population of 10,000 or More, 1910

CITY	NEGRO POPULATION		NEGRO INCREASE 1900 TO 1910[1]		PERCENTAGE NEGRO IN TOTAL POPULATION	
	1910	1900	Number	Percent	1910	1900
Washington, D.C.	94,446	86,702	7,744	8.9	28.5	31.1
New York, N.Y.	91,709	60,666	31,043	51.2	1.9	1.8
New Orleans, La.	89,262	77,714	11,548	14.9	26.3	27.1
Baltimore, Md.	84,749	79,258	5,491	6.9	15.2	15.6
Philadelphia, Pa.	84,459	62,613	21,846	34.9	5.5	4.8
Memphis, Tenn.	52,411	49,910	2,531	5.1	40.0	48.8
Birmingham, Ala.	52,306	16,575	35,730	215.6	39.4	43.1
Atlanta, Ga.	51,902	35,727	16,175	45.3	33.5	39.8
Richmond, Va.	46,733	32,230	14,503	45.0	36.6	37.9
Chicago, Ill.	44,103	30,150	13,953	46.3	2.0	1.8
St. Louis, Mo.	43,960	35,516	8,444	23.8	6.4	6.2
Louisville, Ky.	40,522	39,139	1,383	3.5	18.1	19.1
Nashville, Tenn.	36,523	30,044	6,479	21.6	33.1	37.2
Savannah, Ga.	33,246	28,090	5,156	18.4	51.1	51.8
Charleston, S.C.	31,056	31,522	-466	-1.5	52.8	56.6
Jacksonville, Fla.	29,293	16,236	13,057	80.4	50.8	57.1
Pittsburgh, Pa.	25,623	20,355	5,268	25.9	4.8	4.5
Norfolk, Va.	25,039	20,230	4,809	23.8	37.1	43.4
Houston, Tex.	23,929	14,608	9,321	63.8	30.4	32.7
Kansas City, Mo.	23,566	17,567	5,999	34.1	9.5	10.7
Mobile, Ala.	22,763	17,045	5,718	33.5	44.2	44.3
Indianapolis, Ind.	21,816	15,931	5,885	36.9	9.3	9.4
Cincinnati, Ohio	19,639	14,482	5,157	35.6	5.4	4.4
Montgomery, Ala.	19,322	17,229	2,093	12.1	50.7	56.8
Augusta, Ga.	18,344	18,487	-143	-0.8	44.7	46.9
Macon, Ga.	18,150	11,550	6,600	57.1	44.6	49.6
Dallas, Tex.	18,024	9,035	8,989	99.5	19.6	21.2
Chattanooga, Tenn.	17,942	13,122	4,830	36.7	40.2	43.5
Little Rock, Ark.	14,539	14,694	-155	-1.1	31.6	38.4
Shreveport, La.	13,896	8,542	5,354	62.7	49.6	53.3
Boston, Mass.	13,564	11,591	1,973	17.0	2.0	2.1
Fort Worth, Tex.	13,280	4,249	9,031	212.5	18.1	15.9
Columbus, Ohio	12,739	8,201	4,538	55.3	7.0	6.5
Wilmington, N.C.	12,107	10,407	1,700	16.3	47.0	49.6
Vicksburg, Miss.	12,053	8,147	3,906	47.9	57.9	54.9
Charlotte, N.C.	11,752	7,151	4,601	64.3	34.6	39.5
Portsmouth, Va.	11,617	5,625	5,992	106.5	35.0	32.3
Columbia, S.C.	11,546	9,858	1,688	17.1	43.9	46.7

[Continued]

★ 1721 ★

Changes in Black Population in 43 Cities Having a Black Population of 10,000 or More, 1910

[Continued]

CITY	NEGRO POPULATION		NEGRO INCREASE 1900 TO 1910[1]		PERCENTAGE NEGRO IN TOTAL POPULATION	
	1910	1900	Number	Percent	1910	1900
Petersburg, Va.	11,014	10,751	263	2.4	45.7	49.3
Lexington, Ky.	11,011	10,130	881	8.7	31.4	38.4
San Antonio, Tex.	10,716	7,538	3,178	42.2	11.1	14.1
Jackson, Miss.	10,554	4,447	6,107	137.3	49.6	56.9
Pensacola, Fla.	10,214	8,561	1,653	19.3	44.4	48.2

Source: "Untitled Table." U.S. Bureau of the Census, *Negro Population, 1790- 1915*, p. 93. *Note:* 1. A minus sign (-) denotes decrease.

★ 1722 ★

Geographical Areas: Cities/Urban, and Rural

Changes in Black Population in Cities Having in 1920 more than 25,000 Blacks, 1900-1920

City	Negro Population			Increase in Negro Population 1910-1920		Increase in Negro Population 1900-1910	
	1920	1910	1900	Number	Per Cent	Number	Per Cent
Total	1,508,061	1,060,510	825,364	447,551	42.2	235,146	28.5
New York, N.Y	152,467	91,709	60,666	60,758	66.3	31,043	51.2
Philadelphia, Pa	134,229	84,459	62,613	49,770	58.9	21,846	34.9
Washington, D.C	109,966	94,446	86,702	15,520	16.4	7,744	8.9
Chicago, Ill	109,458	44,103	30,150	65,355	148.2	13,953	46.3
Baltimore, Md	108,322	84,749	79,258	23,573	27.8	5,491	6.9
New Orleans, La	100,930	89,262	77,714	11,668	13.1	11,548	14.9
Birmingham, Ala	70,230	52,305	16,575	17,925	34.3	35,730	215.6
St. Louis, Mo	69,850	43,960	35,516	25,894	58.9	8,444	23.8
Atlanta, Ga	62,796	51,902	35,727	10,894	21.0	16,175	45.3
Memphis, Tenn	61,181	52,441	49,910	8,740	16.7	2,531	5.0
Richmond, Va	54,041	46,733	32,230	7,308	15.6	14,503	45.8
Norfolk, Va	43,392	25,039	20,230	18,353	73.3	4,809	23.1
Jacksonville, Fla	41,520	29,293	16,236	12,227	41.7	13,057	80.4
Detroit, Mich	40,838	5,741	4,111	35,097	611.3	1,630	39.6
Louisville, Ky	40,087	40,522	39,139	-435	-1.1	1,383	3.5
Savannah, Ga	39,179	33,246	28,090	5,933	17.8	5,156	18.4
Pittsburgh, Pa	37,725	25,623	20,355	12,102	47.2	5,268	25.9
Nashville, Tenn	35,633	36,523	30,044	-890	-2.4	6,479	21.6
Indianapolis, Ind	34,678	21,816	15,931	12,862	59.0	5,885	36.9
Cleveland, Ohio	34,451	8,448	5,988	26,003	307.8	2,460	41.1
Houston, Tex	33,960	23,929	14,608	10,031	41.9	9,321	63.8
Charleston, S.C	32,326	31,056	31,522	1,270	4.1	-466	-1.5

[Continued]

★ 1722 ★

Changes in Black Population in Cities Having in 1920 more than 25,000 Blacks, 1900-1920

[Continued]

City	Negro Population			Increase in Negro Population			
				1910-1920		1900-1910	
	1920	1910	1900	Number	Per Cent	Number	Per Cent
Kansas City, Mo	30,719	23,566	17,567	7,153	30.4	599	34.1
Cincinnati, Ohio	30,079	19,639	14,482	10,440	53.2	5,157	35.6

Source: "Negro Population and Increase in Negro Population of Cities Having, in 1920 More than 25,000 Negro Inhabitants: 1920, 1910, 1900." Work, Monroe N., ed., *Negro Year Book: An Annual Encyclopedia of the Negro, 1925-26*, p. 443.

★ 1723 ★

Geographical Areas: Cities/Urban, and Rural

Cities with 10,000 or More Blacks in 1930 with Comparative Figures for 1910 and 1920

CITY	NEGRO POPULATION							Percent of total population			PERCENT INCREASE OR DECREASE (-) IN WHITE POPULATION	
	1930	1920	1910	Increase or decrease (-) 1920 to 1930		1910 to 1920						
				Number	Percent	Number	Percent	1930	1920	1910	1920-1930[1]	1910-1920
New York, N.Y.	327,706	152,467	91,709	175,239	114.9	60,758	66.3	4.7	2.7	1.9	20.7	16.9
Chicago, Ill.	233,903	109,458	44,103	124,445	113.7	65,355	148.2	6.9	4.1	2.0	20.5	21.0
Philadelphia, Pa.	219,599	134,229	84,459	85,370	63.6	49,770	58.9	11.3	7.4	5.5	2.4	15.4
Baltimore, Md.	142,106	108,322	84,749	33,784	31.2	23,573	27.8	17.7	14.8	15.2	5.9	32.1
Washington, D.C.	132,068	109,966	94,446	22,102	20.1	15,520	16.4	27.1	25.1	28.5	8.3	38.4
New Orleans, La.	129,632	100,930	89,262	28,702	28.4	11,668	13.1	28.3	26.1	26.3	14.9	14.6
Detroit, Mich.	120,066	40,838	5,741	79,228	194.0	35,097	611.3	7.7	4.1	1.2	51.4	107.0
Birmingham, Ala.	99,077	70,230	52,305	28,847	41.1	17,925	34.3	38.2	39.3	39.4	47.9	35.1
Memphis, Tenn.	96,550	61,181	52,441	35,369	57.8	8,740	16.7	38.1	37.7	40.0	54.8	28.7
St. Louis, Mo.	93,580	69,854	43,960	23,726	34.0	25,894	58.9	11.4	9.0	6.4	3.5	9.4
Atlanta, Ga.	90,075	62,796	51,902	27,279	43.4	10,894	21.0	33.3	31.3	33.5	30.8	34.0
Cleveland, Ohio	71,899	34,451	8,448	37,448	108.7	26,003	307.8	8.0	4.3	1.5	8.6	38.1
Houston, Tex.	63,337	33,960	23,929	29,377	86.5	10,031	41.9	21.7	24.6	30.4	116.3	90.2
Pittsburgh, Pa.	54,983	37,725	25,623	17,258	45.7	12,102	47.2	8.2	6.4	4.8	11.6	8.3
Richmond, Va.	52,988	54,041	46,733	-1,053	-1.9	7,308	15.6	29.0	31.5	36.6	10.5	45.4
Jacksonville, Fla.	48,196	41,520	29,293	6,676	16.1	12,227	41.7	37.2	45.3	50.8	62.7	76.4
Cincinnati, Ohio	47,818	30,079	19,639	17,739	59.0	10,440	53.2	10.6	7.5	5.4	8.6	7.9
Louisville, Ky.	47,354	40,087	40,522	7,267	18.1	-435	-1.1	15.4	17.1	18.1	33.7	6.2
Indianapolis, Ind.	43,967	34,678	21,816	9,289	26.8	12,862	59.0	12.1	11.0	9.3	14.5	31.9
Norfolk, Va.	43,942	43,392	25,039	550	1.3	18,353	73.3	33.9	37.5	37.1	18.4	70.5
Nashville, Tenn.	42,836	35,633	36,523	7,203	20.2	-890	-2.4	27.8	30.1	33.1	34.2	12.0
Savannah, Ga.	38,896	39,179	33,246	-283	-.7	5,933	17.8	45.7	47.1	51.1	4.6	38.5
Los Angeles, Calif.	38,894	15,579	7,599	23,315	149.7	7,980	105.0	3.1	2.7	2.4	107.6	79.1
Newark, N.J.	38,880	16,977	9,475	21,903	129.0	7,502	79.2	8.8	4.1	2.7	1.4	17.6
Dallas, Tex.	38,742	24,023	18,024	14,719	61.3	5,999	33.3	14.9	15.1	19.6	63.4	82.2
Kansas City, Mo.	38,574	30,719	23,566	7,855	25.6	7,153	30.4	9.6	9.5	9.5	22.7	30.6
Chattanooga, Tenn.	33,289	18,889	17,942	14,400	76.2	947	5.3	27.8	32.6	40.2	121.8	46.3
Columbus, Ohio	32,774	22,181	12,739	10,593	47.8	9,442	74.1	11.3	9.4	7.0	20.0	27.3
Wintson-Salem, N.C.	32,566	20,735	9,087	11,831	57.1	11,648	128.2	43.3	42.8	40.0	54.5	103.2
Montgomery, Ala.	29,970	19,827	19,322	10,143	51.2	505	2.6	45.4	45.6	50.7	52.8	25.7
Charleston, S.C.	28,062	32,326	31,056	-4,264	-13.2	1,270	4.1	45.1	47.6	52.8	-4.0	28.2
Shreveport, La.	27,219	17,485	13,896	9,734	55.7	3,589	25.8	35.5	39.9	49.6	86.9	87.0
Charlotte, N.C.	25,163	14,641	11,752	10,522	71.9	2,889	24.6	30.4	31.6	34.6	81.4	42.4
Miami, Fla.	25,116	9,270	2,258	15,846	170.9	7,012	310.5	22.7	31.3	41.3	321.6	531.6
Mobile, Ala.	24,514	23,906	22,763	608	2.5	1,143	5.0	35.9	39.3	44.2	18.3	28.2
Augusta, Ga.	24,190	22,582	18,344	1,608	7.1	4,238	23.1	40.1	43.0	44.7	20.4	32.0
Macon, Ga.	23,158	23,093	18,150	65	.3	4,943	27.2	43.0	43.6	44.6	2.6	32.8
Fort Worth, Tex.	22,234	15,896	13,280	6,338	39.9	2,616	19.7	13.6	14.9	18.1	59.5	50.9
Tampa, Fla.	21,172	11,531	8,951	9,641	83.6	2,580	28.8	20.9	22.3	23.7	99.5	39.1

[Continued]

★ 1723 ★

Cities with 10,000 or More Blacks in 1930 with Comparative Figures for 1910 and 1920

[Continued]

CITY	NEGRO POPULATION										PERCENT INCREASE OR DECREASE (-) IN WHITE POPULATION	
	1930	1920	1910	Increase or decrease (-)				Percent of total population				
				1920 to 1930		1910 to 1920						
				Number	Percent	Number	Percent	1930	1920	1910	1920-1930[1]	1910-1920
Boston, Mass.	20,574	16,350	13,564	4,224	25.8	2,786	20.5	2.6	2.2	2.0	3.9	11.4
Kansas City, Kans.	19,872	14,405	9,286	5,467	38.0	5,119	55.1	16.3	14.2	11.3	17.6	18.8
Little Rock, Ark.	19,698	17,477	14,539	2,221	12.7	2,938	20.2	24.1	26.8	31.6	30.0	51.8
Columbia, S.C.	19,519	14,455	11,546	5,064	35.0	2,909	25.2	37.8	38.5	43.9	38.9	56.2
Jackson, Miss.	19,423	9,936	10,554	9,487	95.5	-618	-5.9	40.2	43.5	49.6	124.0	20.3
Portsmouth, Va.	18,849	23,245	11,617	-4,396	-18.9	11,628	100.1	41.2	42.7	35.9	-13.9	44.2
Durham, N.C.	18,717	7,654	6,869	11,063	144.5	785	11.4	36.0	35.2	37.7	136.9	23.6
Beaumont, Tex.	18,551	13,210	6,896	5,341	40.4	6,314	91.6	32.1	32.7	33.4	41.6	98.0
San Antonio, Tex.	17,978	14,341	10,716	3,637	25.4	3,625	33.8	7.8	8.9	11.1	24.1	71.1
Gary, Ind.	17,922	5,299	383	12,623	238.2	4,916	1,238.6	17.8	9.6	2.3	58.4	205.1
Knoxville, Tenn.	17,093	11,302	7,638	5,791	51.2	3,664	48.0	16.2	14.5	21.0	33.4	131.7
Dayton, Ohio	17,077	9,025	4,842	8,052	89.2	4,183	86.4	8.5	5.9	4.2	28.1	28.5
Atlantic City, N.J.	15,611	10,946	9,834	4,665	42.6	1,112	11.3	23.6	21.6	21.3	27.3	9.5
Tulsa, Okla.	15,203	8,878	1,959	6,325	71.2	6,919	353.2	10.8	12.3	10.8	97.6	292.7
Oklahoma City, Okla.	14,662	8,241	6,546	6,421	77.9	1,695	25.9	7.9	9.0	10.2	106.1	44.1
Youngstown, Ohio	14,552	6,662	1,936	7,890	118.4	4,726	244.1	8.6	5.0	2.4	23.6	62.9
Asheville, N.C.	14,255	7,145	5,359	7,110	99.5	1,786	33.3	28.4	25.1	28.6	68.3	59.3
Columbus, Ga.	14,157	9,093	7,644	5,064	55.7	1,449	19.0	32.8	29.2	37.2	31.5	70.7
Greensboro, N.C.	14,050	5,973	5,710	8,077	135.2	263	4.6	26.2	30.1	35.9	184.6	36.4
Buffalo, N.Y.	13,563	4,511	1,773	9,052	200.7	2,738	154.4	2.4	.9	.4	11.3	19.0
Newsport News, Va.	13,281	14,077	7,259	-796	-5.7	6,818	93.9	38.6	39.5	35.9	-1.6	66.0
Toledo, Ohio	13,260	5,691	1,877	7,569	133.0	3,814	203.2	4.6	2.3	1.1	16.7	42.5
Galveston, Tex.	13,226	9,888	8,036	3,338	33.8	1,852	23.0	25.0	22.3	21.7	8.0	18.8
Wilmington, N.C.	13,106	13,461	12,017	-355	-2.6	1,354	11.2	40.6	40.3	47.0	-3.7	46.0
Lexington, Ky.	12,759	12,450	11,011	309	2.5	1,439	13.1	27.9	30.0	31.4	13.4	20.8
Petersburg, Va.	12,600	13,608	11,014	-1,008	-7.4	2,594	23.6	44.1	43.0	45.7	-8.2	32.7
Jersey City, N.J.	12,575	8,000	5,960	4,575	57.2	2,040	34.2	4.0	2.7	2.2	4.8	10.8
Raleigh, N.C.	12,575	8,544	7,372	4,031	47.2	1,172	15.9	33.6	35.0	38.4	56.2	34.0
Roanoke, Va.	12,368	9,331	7,924	3,037	32.5	1,407	17.8	17.9	18.4	22.7	37.0	54.0
Wilmington, Del.	12,080	10,746	9,081	1,334	12.4	1,665	18.3	11.3	9.8	10.4	-5.0	26.9
Vicksburg, Miss.	11,915	9,148	12,053	2,767	30.2	-2,905	-24.1	51.9	50.6	57.9	23.5	1.9
Bessemer, Ala.	11,691	10,561	6,210	1,130	10.7	4,351	70.1	56.4	56.6	57.2	11.3	74.5
East St. Louis, Ill.	11,536	7,437	5,882	4,099	55.1	1,555	26.4	15.5	11.1	10.0	5.8	12.6
Meridian, Miss.	11,352	8,343	9,321	3,009	36.1	-978	-10.5	35.5	35.7	40.0	36.9	7.8
Camden, N.J.	11,340	8,500	6,076	2,840	33.4	2,424	39.9	9.6	7.3	6.4	-0.4	21.9
Omaha, Nebr.	11,123	10,315	5,143	808	7.8	5,172	100.6	5.2	5.4	3.4	11.8	24.9
Akron, Ohio	11,080	5,580	657	5,500	98.6	4,923	749.2	4.3	2.7	1.0	20.2	196.4
Greenville, S.C.	10,871	8,184	6,319	2,687	32.8	1,865	29.5	37.3	35.4	40.1	22.3	58.6
Baton Rouge, La.	10,675	8,560	7,899	2,115	24.7	661	8.4	34.7	39.3	53.0	51.7	89.2
Monroe, La.	10,112	5,540	5,320	4,572	82.5	220	4.1	38.9	43.7	52.1	122.2	46.0
Port Arthur, Tex.	10,003	3,910	1,493	6,093	155.8	2,417	161.9	19.7	17.6	19.5	112.7	197.2

Source: "Cities Having a Negro Population of 10,000 or More in 1930, with Comparative Figures for 1920 and 1910, and Percent Increase in White Population, 1910 to 1930." U.S. Bureau of the Census, *Negroes in the United States, 1920-1932*, p. 55. *Notes:* 1. The figures for the white population in 1920 for cities having 100,000 or more inhabitants and 100 or more Mexicans in 1930, were adjusted for (comparison with 1930 only) by deducting the estimated number of persons who would have been classified as Mexicans under the 1930 classification.

★ 1724 ★

Geographical Areas: Cities/Urban, and Rural

Density of the Population, 1910

STATE[1]	Area in square miles	POPULATION PER SQUARE MILE: 1910				
		Total			Rural	
		Negro	White	All classes	Negro	White
United States	2,973,890	3.3	27.5	30.9	2.4	14.1
District of Columbia	60	1,574.1	3,935.5	5,517.8	-	-
South Carolina	30,495	27.4	22.3	49.7	24.1	18.2
Maryland	9,941	23.4	106.9	130.3	13.4	50.7
Mississippi	46,362	21.8	17.0	38.8	19.7	14.5
Georgia	58,725	20.0	24.4	44.4	16.2	19.0
Alabama	51,279	17.7	24.0	41.7	14.7	19.8
Virginia	40,262	16.7	34.5	51.2	12.7	26.6
Delaware	1,965	15.9	87.1	103.0	10.2	43.4
Louisiana	45,409	15.7	20.7	36.5	12.2	13.3
North Carolina	48,740	14.3	30.8	45.3	11.9	26.6
New Jersey	7,514	11.9	325.5	337.7	3.2	80.6
Tennessee	41,687	11.3	41.1	52.4	7.7	34.1
Rhode Island	1,067	8.9	499.1	508.5	0.4	16.4
Arkansas	52,525	8.4	21.5	30.0	7.3	18.8
Kentucky	40,181	6.5	50.5	57.0	3.9	39.3
Florida	54,861	5.6	8.1	13.7	4.0	5.7
Massachusetts	8,039	4.7	413.6	418.8	0.3	29.6
Pennsylvania	44,832	4.3	166.6	171.0	0.8	66.8
Connecticut	4,820	3.1	228.0	231.3	0.3	23.6
New York	47,654	2.8	188.2	191.2	0.4	40.0
Ohio	40,740	2.7	114.3	117.0	0.7	50.9
West Virginia	24,022	2.7	48.2	50.8	2.0	50.9
Texas	262,398	2.6	12.2	14.8	1.9	9.3
Missouri	68,727	2.3	45.6	47.9	0.8	26.8
Oklahoma	69,414	2.0	20.8	23.9	1.4	16.8
Illinois	56,043	1.9	98.6	100.6	0.4	38.2
Indiana	36,045	1.7	73.2	74.9	0.3	42.9

Source: Untitled table. U.S. Bureau of the Census, *Negro Population, 1790-1915,* p. 40. *Notes:* 1. States having Negro population less than 1 per square mile are omitted. These states are as follows: Arizona, California, Colorado, Idaho, Iowa, Kansas, Maine, Michigan, Minnesota, Nebraska, Nevada, New Hampshire, New Mexico, North Dakota, Oregon, South Dakota, Utah, Vermont, Washington, Wisconsin, Wyoming.

★ 1725 ★

Geographical Areas: Cities/Urban, and Rural

Distribution of Population, by Urban-Rural: 1890-1970

Year and race	Total population (thousands)	Percent residing in--			Foreign born		Native	
		Urban areas	Rural areas		Number (thousands)	Percent of total population	Number (thousands)	Percent born in South[1]
			Total	Farm				
BLACK								
1890	7,489	20	80	(NA)	20	-	7,469	93[2]
1910	9,828	27	73	(NA)	40	-	9,787	93
1940	12,866	49	51	35	84	1	12,782	88[2]
1950	15,045	62	38	21	114	1	14,931	83[2]
1960	18,849	73	27	8	125	1	18,723	75
1970	22,539	81	19	2	253	1	22,286	49
WHITE								
1890	55,101	38	62	(NA)	9,122	17	45,979	28
1910	81,732	49	51	(NA)	13,346	16	68,386	29
1940	118/,702	57	43	22	11,419	10	107,282	30
1950	134,478	64	36	15	10,095	8	124,383	30
1960	158,838	70	30	7	9,294	6	149,544	30
1970	178,119	72	28	4	8,734	5	169,385	29

Source: "Distribution of the Population, Urban-Rural Residency and Nativity for Selected Years: 1970 to 1975," U.S. Department of Commerce, Bureau of the Census. *The Social and Economic Status of the Black Population in the United States: An Historical View, 1790-1978*, p. 14. Primary source: U.S. Department of Commerce, Bureau of the Census. *Notes:* - Represents or rounds to zero. NA Not available. The current definition of urban population includes urbanized areas and places of 2,500 or more outside urbanized areas. This concept has been in effect since 1950 when substantial revisions were made. 1. Census Bureau evaluation studies for recent censuses (1960 and 1970) show that the figures for Blacks born in the South have been seriously understated. 2. Partially estimated.

★ 1726 ★

Geographical Areas: Cities/Urban, and Rural

Fourteen Cities with Largest Black Population, 1940, and Largest Nonwhite Population, 1947

Urban Places	Nonwhite Population 1947	Negro Population 1940	Percent Nonwhite Population 1947	Percent Negro Population 1940
New York, N.Y.	819,450	458,444	9.0	6.1
Chicago, Ill.	447,370	277,731	10.0	8.2
Philadelphia, Pa.	439,410	250,880	13.0	13.0
Detroit, Mich.	348,245	149,119	13.0	9.2
Washington, D.C.	285,988	187,266	24.0	28.2
Baltimore, Md.	284,383	165,843	22.0	19.3
Los Angeles, Calif.	240,375	63,774	6.0	4.2

[Continued]

★ 1726 ★

Fourteen Cities with Largest Black Population, 1940, and Largest Nonwhite Population, 1947

[Continued]

Urban Places	Nonwhite Population 1947	Negro Population 1940	Percent Nonwhite Population 1947	Percent Negro Population 1940
St. Louis, Mo.	239,470	108,765	15.0	13.3
Birmingham, Ala.	209,760	108,938	42.0	40.7
New Orleans, la.	166,824	149,034	28.0	30.1
Memphis, Tenn.	163,742	121,498	41.0	41.5
Atlanta, Ga.	142,885	104,553	29.0	34.6
Pittsburgh, Pa.	131,052	62,216	6.0	9.3
Dallas, Tex.	70,708	50,407	15.0	17.1

Source: "Fourteen Cities with Largest Negro Population in 1940 and Largest Nonwhite Population in 1947." Murray, Florence, ed., *The Negro Handbook, 1949*, p. 8.

★ 1727 ★

Geographical Areas: Cities/Urban, and Rural

Number and Percentage in the Black and White Urban and Rural Population by Sections and Southern Divisions, 1910 - I

RACIAL CLASS	POPULATION: 1910						
	United States	The South				The North	The West
		Total	South Atlantic division	East South Central division	West South Central division		
URBAN							
All classes	42,623,383	6,623,838	3,092,153	1,574,229	1,957,456	32,699,705	3,329,840
Negro	2,689,229	1,854,455	909,520	509,097	435,838	794,966	39,808
White	39,831,913	4,761,463	2,180,990	1,064,740	1,515,733	31,851,632	3,218,818
Native	30,196,544	4,374,967	1,989,234	1,006,808	1,378,925	23,304,578	2,516,999
Native parentage	17,849,644	3,675,281	1,675,819	856,826	1,142,636	12,564,943	1,609,420
Mixed parentage	3,554,980	263,411	108,506	58,820	96,085	2,956,676	334,893
Foreign parentage	8,791,920	436,275	204,909	91,162	140,204	7,782,959	572,686
Foreign born	9,635,369	386,496	191,756	57,932	136,808	8,547,054	701,819
RURAL							
All classes	49,348,883	22,765,492	9,102,742	6,835,672	6,827,078	23,087,410	3,495,981
Negro	7,138,534	6,894,972	3,202,968	2,143,416	1,548,588	232,708	10,854
White	41,900,044	15,785,957	5,890,613	4,689,586	5,205,758	22,788,577	3,325,510
Native	38,189,868	15,446,282	5,791,814	4,660,661	4,993,807	20,014,615	2,728,971
Native parentage	31,638,931	14,885,865	5,665,386	4,595,666	4,624,813	14,787,092	1,965,974
Mixed parentage	2,426,546	234,294	56,886	32,242	145,166	1,884,123	308,129

[Continued]

★ 1727 ★

Number and Percentage in the Black and White Urban and Rural Population by Sections and Southern Divisions, 1910 - I

[Continued]

RACIAL CLASS	POPULATION: 1910						
		The South					
	United States	Total	South Atlantic division	East South Central division	West South Central division	The North	The West
Foreign parentage	4,124,391	325,123	60,542	32,753	223,828	3,343,400	454,868
Foreign born	3,710,176	339,675	98,799	28,925	211,951	2,773,962	596,539

Source: "Number and Percentage, Urban and Rural, in the Negro and White Population Classes, by Sections and Southern Divisions: 1910." U.S. Bureau of the Census, *Negro Population, 1790-1915*, p. 90.

★ 1728 ★

Geographical Areas: Cities/Urban, and Rural

Number and Percentage in the Black and White Urban and Rural Population by Sections and Southern Divisions, 1910 - II

RACIAL CLASS	POPULATION: 1910						
		The South					
	United States	Total	South Atlantic division	East South Central division	West South Central division	The North	The West
	PERCENTAGE URBAN						
All classes	46.3	22.5	25.4	18.7	22.3	58.6	48.8
Negro	27.4	21.2	22.1	19.2	22.0	77.4	78.6
White	47.8	23.2	27.0	18.5	22.6	58.3	49.2
Native	44.2	22.1	25.6	17.8	21.6	53.8	48.0
Native parentage	36.1	19.8	22.8	15.7	19.8	45.9	45.0
Mixed parentage	59.4	52.9	65.6	64.6	39.8	61.1	52.8
Foreign parentage	68.1	57.2	74.7	73.6	38.5	70.0	55.7
Foreign born	72.2	53.2	66.0	66.7	39.2	75.5	54.1
	PERCENTAGE RURAL						
All classes	53.7	77.5	74.6	81.3	77.7	41.4	51.2
Negro	72.6	78.8	77.9	80.8	78.0	22.6	21.4
White	51.3	76.8	73.0	81.5	77.4	41.7	50.8
Native	55.8	77.9	74.4	82.2	78.4	46.2	52.0
Native parentage	63.9	80.2	77.2	84.3	80.2	54.1	55.0
Mixed parentage	40.6	47.1	25.3	35.4	60.2	38.9	47.2

[Continued]

★ 1728 ★

Number and Percentage in the Black and White Urban and Rural Population by Sections and Southern Divisions, 1910 - II

[Continued]

RACIAL CLASS	POPULATION: 1910						
	United States	The South				The North	The West
		Total	South Atlantic division	East South Central division	West South Central division		
Foreign parentage	31.9	42.8	34.4	26.4	61.5	30.0	44.3
Foreign born	27.8	46.8	34.0	33.3	60.8	24.5	45.9

Source: "Number and Percentage, Urban and Rural, in the Negro and White Population Classes, by Sections and Southern Divisions: 1910." U.S. Bureau of the Census, *Negro Population, 1790-1915*, p. 90.

★ 1729 ★

Geographical Areas: Cities/Urban, and Rural

Percentage Urban in Population by Gender, Age Periods, Sections, and Southern Divisions, 1910 - I

AGE	PERCENTAGE URBAN: 1910					
	The United States		The South			
			Total		South Atlantic	
	Negro	Native White	Negro	Native White	Negro	Native White
BOTH SEXES						
All ages	27.4	44.2	21.2	22.1	22.1	25.6
Under 5 years	18.1	42.2	14.2	17.2	14.7	20.8
5 to 14 years	18.9	40.9	15.2	17.9	15.7	21.1
15 to 24 years	27.7	45.7	22.2	23.0	23.4	26.7
25 to 44 years	37.4	48.2	28.7	27.2	30.2	30.7
45 to 64 years	31.7	43.1	24.3	24.1	35.9	27.3
65 years and over	26.3	36.9	20.5	20.5	20.6	23.4
Age unknown	43.7	62.0	36.9	42.6	42.1	43.2
MALE						
All ages	26.2	43.0	20.0	21.4	20.7	24.8
Under 5 years	18.0	42.0	14.1	17.1	14.6	20.3
5 to 14 years	18.3	40.4	14.7	17.5	15.2	20.7
15 to 24 years	25.6	44.2	20.3	22.1	21.2	25.8
25 to 44 years	36.6	47.0	27.5	26.7	28.8	30.0
45 to 64 years	29.3	40.8	21.9	22.5	23.3	25.5
65 years and over	22.9	33.6	17.5	18.3	17.3	21.1
Age unknown	43.5	63.0	36.2	44.9	41.2	41.7

[Continued]

★ 1729 ★

Percentage Urban in Population by Gender, Age Periods, Sections, and Southern Divisions, 1910 - I

[Continued]

AGE	PERCENTAGE URBAN: 1910					
	The United States		The South			
			Total		South Atlantic	
	Negro	Native White	Negro	Native White	Negro	Native White
	FEMALE					
All ages	28.5	45.4	22.4	22.8	23.5	26.4
Under 5 years	18.3	42.4	14.3	17.3	14.7	20.9
5 to 14 years	19.6	41.4	15.7	18.3	16.3	21.5
15 to 24 years	29.5	47.3	24.0	23.9	25.3	27.6
25 to 44 years	38.1	49.4	29.8	27.7	31.5	31.4
45 to 64 years	34.5	45.5	27.2	25.9	28.9	29.2
65 years and over	30.0	40.2	23.9	22.7	24.3	25.6
Age unknown	44.0	59.9	37.6	38.4	43.4	45.4

Source: "Percentage Urban in the Negro and Native White Population, Classified by Sex and Age Periods, by Sections and Southern Divisions: 1910. U.S. Bureau of the Census, *Negro Population, 1790-1915,* p. 184.

★ 1730 ★

Geographical Areas: Cities/Urban, and Rural

Percentage Urban in Population by Gender, Age Periods, Sections, and Southern Divisions, 1910 - II

AGE	PERCENTAGE URBAN: 1910						The West	
	The South				The North			
	East South Central		West South Central					
	Negro	Native White	Negro	Native White	Negro	Native White	Negro	Native White
	BOTH SEXES							
All ages	19.2	17.8	22.0	21.6	77.4	53.8	78.6	48.0
Under 5 years	12.4	13.2	15.4	16.5	71.5	54.7	79.5	41.3
5 to 14 years	13.4	14.1	16.3	17.5	69.8	52.1	76.8	41.8
15 to 24 years	19.9	18.8	22.9	22.3	76.7	55.6	77.2	49.4
25 to 44 years	26.1	22.5	29.0	27.0	83.2	56.7	79.9	53.0
45 to 64 years	22.4	19.6	23.7	24.1	76.5	50.3	78.3	49.6
65 years and over	19.4	15.1	22.0	22.1	65.7	42.3	71.9	47.4
Age unknown	31.6	33.1	34.4	48.2	82.4	69.2	86.5	63.7
	MALE							
All ages	18.1	17.2	20.8	21.1	75.8	52.6	74.7	46.2
Under 5 years	12.3	13.1	15.3	16.4	71.2	54.6	78.9	41.3

[Continued]

★ 1730 ★

Percentage Urban in Population by Gender, Age Periods, Sections, and Southern Divisions, 1910 - II

[Continued]

AGE	PERCENTAGE URBAN: 1910						The West	
	The South				The North			
	East South Central		West South Central					
	Negro	Native White	Negro	Native White	Negro	Native White	Negro	Native White
5 to 14 years	12.9	13.7	15.9	17.2	68.8	51.6	76.0	41.2
15 to 24 years	18.3	18.0	21.0	21.2	73.6	54.0	70.0	46.9
25 to 44 years	25.2	22.1	28.0	26.7	81.9	55.4	75.8	51.0
45 to 64 years	20.3	18.3	21.4	22.6	74.6	48.2	74.8	46.0
65 years and over	16.6	13.2	19.1	20.0	60.7	38.7	66.9	41.8
Age unknown	30.8	36.4	34.1	51.9	81.8	69.8	85.1	62.2
				FEMALE				
All ages	20.3	18.4	23.1	22.2	79.0	55.0	83.3	50.0
Under 5 years	12.5	13.3	15.5	16.6	71.8	54.9	80.1	41.3
5 to 14 years	13.9	14.4	16.8	17.8	70.9	52.6	77.7	42.4
15 to 24 years	21.3	19.5	24.6	23.4	79.5	57.3	84.5	52.2
25 to 44 years	27.0	22.9	30.1	27.4	84.5	57.9	85.4	55.5
45 to 64 years	24.9	21.1	26.6	26.0	78.7	52.5	83.4	54.5
65 years and over	22.4	17.1	25.1	24.4	70.9	45.8	78.1	54.8
Age unknown	32.5	28.4	34.9	39.3	83.3	67.9	88.5	68.5

Source: "Percentage Urban in the Negro and Native White Population, Classified by Sex and Age Periods, by Sections and Southern Divisions: 1910. U.S. Bureau of the Census, *Negro Population, 1790-1915*, p. 184.

★ 1731 ★

Geographical Areas: Cities/Urban, and Rural

Population Change, 1940-1947, and Nonwhite Population in 34 Selected Metropolitan Districts: Civilian, April 1947, and Total, April 1940

Metropolitan District	Civilian Population 1947	Total Population 1940	Nonwhite Civilian Population[1] 1947
Akron, Ohio	423,539	349,705	27,343
Allentown-Bethlehem-Easton, Pa.	337,683	325,142	4,371
Atlanta, Ga.	498,109	442,294	142,885
Baltimore, Md.	1,306,040	1,046,692	284,383
Birmingham, Ala.	502,398	407,851	209,760
Boston, Mass.	2,549,700	2,350,514	51,750
Chicago, Ill.	4,644,640	4,499,126	447,370
Columbus, Ohio	432,304	365,796	40,795
Dallas, Texas	470,052	376,548	70,708

[Continued]

★ 1731 ★

Population Change, 1940-1947, and Nonwhite Population in 34 Selected Metropolitan Districts: Civilian, April 1947, and Total, April 1940

[Continued]

Metropolitan District	Civilian Population 1947	Total Population 1940	Nonwhite Civilian Population[1] 1947
Denver, Colo.	471,460	384,372	18,436
Detroit, Mich.	2,702,398	2,295,867	348,245
Los Angeles, Calif.	3,916,875	2,904,596	240,375
Lowell-Lawrence-Haverhill, Mass.	347,820	334,969	1,333
Memphis, Tenn.	402,752	332,477	163,742
Minneapolis-St. Paul, Minn.	1,006,278	911,077	11,739
New Haven, Conn.	352,036	308,228	11,873
New Orleans, La.	601,608	540,030	166,824
New York-Northeastern New Jersey	12,684,411	11,690,520	1,015,002
New York Division	9,250,875	8,707,666	819,450
New Jersey Division	3,433,536	2,982,854	195,552
Norfolk-Portsmouth-Newport New, Va.	471,034	330,396	141,658
Philadelphia, Pa.	3,372,690	2,898,644	439,410
Pittsburgh, Pa.	2,100,092	1,994,060	131,052
Portland, Oreg.	534,422	406,406	11,269
Rochester, N.Y.	463,915	411,970	7,903
Salt Lake City, Utah	245,175	204,488	4,830
San Antonio, Texas	417,010	319,010	25,466
San Francisco-Oakland, Calif.	1,989,891	1,428,525	102,465
Scranton-Wilkes-Barre, Pa.	536,458	629,581	564
Seattle, Wash.	602,910	452,639	24,090
St. Louis, Mo.	1,584,044	1,367,977	239,470
Toledo, Ohio	383,418	341,663	20,196
Tulsa, Ohio	213,276	188,562	22,323
Washington, D.C.	1,205,220	907,816	285,988
Worcester, Mass.	308,589	306,194	1,305
Youngstown, Ohio	380,897	372,428	29,915

Source: "Population Increase Between 1940 and 1947, and Nonwhite Population, for 34 Selected Metropolitan Districts: Civilian Population, April 1947 and Total Population, April 1940." Murray, Florence, ed., *The Negro Handbook, 1949*, p. 7. *Notes:* 1. Negroes constituted 95.6 percent of the nonwhite population in 1940. Mexicans are classified as white; Negroes, Indians, Japanese, Chinese and others as nonwhite.

★ 1732 ★

Geographical Areas: Cities/Urban, and Rural

Population Changes in 50 Cities of 100,000 or More and Percentage Black and Foreign-born White, 1910

CITY	POPULATION: 1910						
	All classes[1]	Negro	White			Percentage	
			Total	Native	Foreign born	Negro	Foreign born white
Total	20,302,138	1,023,561	19,220,211	13,405,035	5,815,176	5.0	25.0
Nashville, Tenn.	110,364	36,523	73,831	70,838	2,993	33.1	2.7
Atlanta, Ga.	154,839	51,902	102,861	98,451	4,410	33.5	2.8
Richmond, Va.	127,628	46,733	80,879	76,794	4,085	36.6	3.2
Birmingham, Ala.	132,685	52,305	80,369	74,669	5,700	39.4	4.3
Memphis, Tenn.	131,105	52,441	78,590	72,123	6,467	40.0	4.9
Washington, D.C.	331,069	94,446	236,128	211,777	24,351	28.5	7.4
Louisville, Ky.	223,928	40,522	183,390	165,954	17,436	18.1	7.8
New Orleans, La.	339,075	89,262	249,403	221,717	27,686	26.3	8.2
Indianapolis, Ind.	233,650	21,816	211,780	192,013	19,767	9.3	8.5
Columbus, Ohio	181,511	12,739	168,709	152,424	16,285	7.0	9.0
Kansas City, Mo.	248,381	23,566	224,677	190,350	25,327	9.5	10.2
Dayton, Ohio	116,577	4,842	111,707	97,860	13,847	4.2	11.9
Baltimore, Md.	558,485	84,749	473,387	396,344	77,043	15.2	13.8
Cincinnati, Ohio	363,591	19,639	343,919	287,127	56,792	5.4	15.6
Albany, N.Y.	100,253	1,037	99,171	81,006	18,165	1.0	18.1
Denver, Colo.	213,381	5,426	207,071	168,130	38,941	2.5	18.2
St. Louis, Mo.	687,029	43,960	642,488	516,782	125,706	6.4	18.3
Los Angeles, Cal.	319,198	7,599	305,307	244,723	60,584	2.4	19.0
Toledo, Ohio	168,497	1,877	166,567	134,530	32,037	1.1	19.0
Spokane, Wash.	104,402	723	103,071	81,851	21,220	0.7	20.3
Portland, Oreg.	207,214	1,045	198,952	155,172	43,780	0.5	21.1
Omaha, Nebr.	124,096	4,426	119,580	92,512	27,068	3.6	21.8
Syracuse, N.Y.	137,249	1,124	136,101	105,320	30,781	0.8	22.4
Oakland, Cal.	150,174	3,055	141,956	105,134	36,822	2.0	24.5
Philadelphia, Pa.	1,549,008	84,459	1,463,371	1,080,793	382,578	5.5	24.7
Grand Rapids, Mich.	112,571	665	111,879	83,544	28,335	0.6	25.2
Seattle, Wash.	237,194	2,296	227,753	166,918	60,835	1.0	25.6
Pittsburgh, Pa.	533,905	25,623	508,008	367,572	140,436	4.8	26.3
St. Paul, Minn.	214,744	3,144	211,516	154,992	56,524	1.5	26.3
Rochester, N.Y.	218,149	879	217,205	158,212	58,993	0.4	27.0
Scranton, Pa.	129,867	567	129,288	94,176	35,112	0.4	27.0
Buffalo, N.Y.	423,715	1,773	421,809	303,365	118,444	0.4	28.0
Minneapolis, Minn.	301,408	2,592	298,672	212,734	85,938	0.9	28.5
Jersey City, N.J.	267,779	5,960	261,659	183,962	77,607	2.2	29.0
Milwaukee, Wis.	373,857	980	372,809	261,353	111,456	0.3	29.8

[Continued]

★ 1732 ★

Population Changes in 50 Cities of 100,000 or More and Percentage Black and Foreign-born White, 1910

[Continued]

CITY	POPULATION: 1910						
	All classes[1]	Negro	White			Percentage	
			Total	Native	Foreign born	Negro	Foreign born white
San Francisco, Cal.	416,912	1,642	400,014	269,140	130,874	0.4	31.4
Newark, N.J.	347,469	9,475	337,742	227,087	110,655	2.7	31.8
New Haven, Conn.	133,605	2,561	129,944	87,160	42,784	2.7	32.0
Cambridge, Mass.	104,839	4,707	100,017	65,409	34,608	4.5	33.0
Worcester, Mass.	145,986	1,241	144,664	96,172	48,492	0.9	33.2
Detroit, Mich.	465,766	5,741	459,926	303,361	156,565	1.2	33.6
Providence, R.I.	224,326	5,316	218,623	142,320	76,303	2.4	34.0
Cleveland, Ohio	560,663	8,448	551,925	356,222	195,703	1.5	34.9
Bridgeport, Conn.	102,054	1,332	100,650	64,470	36,180	1.3	35.5
Chicago, Ill.	2,185,283	44,103	2,139,057	1,357,840	781,217	2.0	35.7
Boston, Mass.	670,585	13,564	655,696	414,974	240,722	2.0	35.9
Paterson, N.J.	125,600	1,539	123,969	78,571	45,398	1.2	36.1
New York, N.Y.	4,765,883	91,709	4,669,162	2,741,459	1,927,703	1.9	40.4
Lowell, Mass.	106,294	133	106,102	62,645	43,457	0.1	40.9
Fall River, Mass.	119,295	355	118,857	67,983	50,874	0.3	42.6

Source: "Untitled Table." U.S. Bureau of the Census, *Negro Population, 1790- 1915,* p. 93. *Note:* 1. Includes Indians, Chinese, Japanese, and other colored.

★ 1733 ★

Geographical Areas: Cities/Urban, and Rural

Population by Size of Community, Age Periods, and Sections, 1900 and 1910 - I

AGE	NEGRO POPULATION Number							
	Total		In cities under 25,000 and rural districts		In cities of 25,000-100,000		In cities of 100,000 and over	
	1910	1900	1910	1900	1910	1900	1910	1900
	UNITED STATES							
All ages	9,827,763	8,833,994	8,202,162	7,697,295	602,040	468,445	1,023,561	668,254
Under 5 years	1,263,288	1,215,655	1,137,553	1,121,763	48,799	40,461	76,936	53,431
5 to 14 years	2,401,819	2,294,748	2,159,511	2,102,476	98,821	86,929	143,487	105,343
15 to 24 years	2,091,211	1,951,194	1,747,901	1,693,417	132,615	108,376	210,695	149,401
25 to 44 years	2,638,178	2,103,989	1,989,140	1,691,967	226,249	158,681	422,789	253,341
45 to 64 years	1,108,103	958,234	892,439	812,926	76,425	58,363	139,239	86,945
65 years and over	294,124	261,363	251,961	233,137	15,705	11,471	26,458	16,755
Age unknown	31,040	48,811	23,657	41,609	3,426	4,164	3,957	3,038

[Continued]

★ 1733 ★

Population by Size of Community, Age Periods, and Sections, 1900 and 1910 - I

[Continued]

AGE	NEGRO POPULATION Number							
	Total		In cities under 25,000 and rural districts		In cities of 25,000-100,000		In cities of 100,000 and over	
	1910	1900	1910	1900	1910	1900	1910	1900
THE SOUTH								
All ages	8,749,427	7,922,969	7,745,693	7,224,092	454,851	366,154	548,883	332,723
Under 5 years	1,176,331	1,135,793	1,095,391	1,075,286	37,251	32,025	43,689	28,482
5 to 14 years	2,238,537	2,134,415	2,074,792	2,004,337	76,954	70,234	86,791	59,844
15 to 24 years	1,882,319	1,749,854	1,656,601	1,588,118	104,239	86,333	121,479	75,403
25 to 44 years	2,217,273	1,792,083	1,844,154	1,557,501	168,028	121,519	205,091	113,063
45 to 64 years	951,853	837,141	823,069	747,659	54,499	44,256	74,285	45,226
65 years and over	256,694	232,217	230,020	213,939	10,968	8,711	15,706	9,567
Age unknown	26,420	41,466	21,666	37,252	2,912	3,076	1,842	1,138
THE NORTH								
All ages	1,027,674	880,771	434,412	455,688	140,370	97,260	452,892	327,823
Under 5 years	83,729	77,794	40,710	45,244	11,139	8,141	31,880	24,409
5 to 14 years	157,097	155,830	81,824	95,529	21,004	16,008	54,269	44,293
15 to 24 years	200,049	195,499	87,337	101,671	27,292	21,172	85,420	72,656
25 to 44 years	398,484	299,651	135,658	127,632	55,169	34,849	207,657	137,170
45 to 64 years	148,078	116,765	65,822	62,797	20,774	13,427	61,482	40,541
65 years and over	35,973	28,311	21,202	18,679	4,568	2,650	10,203	6,982
Age unknown	4,264	6,921	1,859	4,136	424	1,013	1,981	1,772
THE WEST								
All ages	50,662	30,254	22,057	17,515	6,819	5,031	21,786	7,708
Under 5 years	3,228	2,068	1,452	1,233	409	295	1,367	540
5 to 14 years	6,185	4,503	2,895	2,610	863	687	2,427	1,206
15 to 24 years	8,843	5,841	3,963	3,628	1,084	871	3,796	1,342
25 to 44 years	22,421	12,255	9,328	6,834	3,052	2,313	10,041	3,108
45 to 64 years	8,172	4,328	3,548	2,470	1,152	680	3,472	1,178
65 years and over	1,457	835	739	519	169	110	549	206
Age unknown	356	424	132	221	90	75	134	128

Source: "Negro Population Living in Classes of Communities, Classified by Broad Age Periods, by Sections: 1910 and 1900." U.S. Bureau of the Census, *Negro Population, 1790-1915,* p. 188.

★ 1734 ★

Geographical Areas: Cities/Urban, and Rural

Population by Size of Community, Age Periods, and Sections, 1900 and 1910 - II

AGE	NEGRO POPULATION Percentage Distribution by Age							
	Total		In cities under 25,000 and rural districts		In cities of 25,000 - 100,000		In cities of 100,000 and over	
	1910	1900	1910	1900	1910	1900	1910	1900
UNITED STATES								
All ages	100.0	100.0	100.0	100.0	100.0	100.0	100.0	100.0
Under 5 years	12.9	13.8	13.9	14.6	8.1	8.6	7.5	8.0
5 to 14 years	24.4	26.0	26.3	27.3	16.4	18.6	14.0	15.8
15 to 24 years	21.3	22.1	21.3	22.0	22.0	23.1	20.6	22.4
25 to 44 years	26.8	23.8	24.3	22.0	37.6	33.9	41.3	37.9
45 to 64 years	11.3	10.8	10.9	10.6	12.7	12.5	13.6	13.0
65 years and over	3.0	3.0	3.1	3.0	2.6	2.4	2.6	2.5
Age unknown	0.3	0.6	0.3	0.5	0.6	0.9	0.4	0.5
THE SOUTH								
All ages	100.0	100.0	100.0	100.0	100.0	100.0	100.0	100.0
Under 5 years	13.4	14.3	14.1	14.9	8.2	8.7	8.0	8.6
5 to 14 years	25.6	26.9	26.8	27.7	16.9	19.2	15.8	18.0
15 to 24 years	21.5	22.1	21.4	22.0	22.9	23.6	22.1	22.7
25 to 44 years	25.3	22.6	23.8	21.6	36.9	33.2	37.4	34.0
45 to 64 years	10.9	10.6	10.6	10.3	12.0	12.1	13.5	13.6
65 years and over	2.9	2.9	3.0	3.0	2.4	2.4	2.9	2.9
Age unknown	0.3	0.5	0.3	0.5	0.6	0.8	0.3	0.3
THE NORTH								
All ages	100.0	100.0	100.0	100.0	100.0	100.0	100.0	100.0
Under 5 years	8.1	8.8	9.4	9.9	7.9	8.4	7.0	7.4
5 to 14 years	15.3	17.7	18.8	21.0	15.0	16.5	12.0	13.5
15 to 24 years	19.5	22.2	20.1	22.3	19.4	21.8	18.9	22.2
25 to 44 years	38.8	34.0	31.2	28.0	39.3	35.8	45.9	41.8
45 to 64 years	14.4	13.3	15.2	13.8	14.8	13.8	13.6	12.4
65 years and over	3.5	3.2	4.9	4.1	3.3	2.7	2.3	2.1
Age unknown	0.4	0.8	0.4	0.9	0.3	1.0	0.4	0.5
THE WEST								
All ages	100.0	100.0	100.0	100.0	100.0	100.0	100.0	100.0
Under 5 years	6.4	6.8	6.6	7.1	6.0	5.9	6.3	7.0
5 to 14 years	12.2	14.9	13.1	14.9	12.7	13.7	11.1	15.6
15 to 24 years	17.5	19.3	18.0	20.7	15.9	17.3	17.4	17.4
25 to 44 years	44.3	40.5	42.3	39.0	44.8	46.0	46.1	40.3
45 to 64 years	16.1	14.3	16.1	14.1	16.9	13.5	15.9	15.3

[Continued]

★ 1734 ★

Population by Size of Community, Age Periods, and Sections, 1900 and 1910 - II

[Continued]

AGE	NEGRO POPULATION Percentage Distribution by Age							
	Total		In cities under 25,000 and rural districts		In cities of 25,000 - 100,000		In cities of 100,000 and over	
	1910	1900	1910	1900	1910	1900	1910	1900
65 years and over	2.9	2.8	3.4	3.0	2.5	2.2	2.5	2.7
Age unknown	0.7	1.4	0.6	1.3	1.3	1.5	0.6	1.7

Source: "Negro Population Living in Classes of Communities, Classified by Broad Age Periods, by Sections: 1910 and 1900." U.S. Bureau of the Census, *Negro Population, 1790-1915*, p. 188.

★ 1735 ★

Geographical Areas: Cities/Urban, and Rural

Population by Type of Residence, Gender, and Race, 1880

Year	All races			White		Negro		Other races	
	Total	Male	Female	Male	Female	Male	Female	Male	Female
RURAL NONFARM									
1970 (1970 urban def.)[1]	45,586,707	22,683,834	22,902,873	20,537,870	20,722,994	1,865,126	1,899,159	280,838	280,720
1960 (1960 urban def.)[2,4]	40,567,121	20,598,091	19,969,030	18,547,804	17,970,872	1,804,715	1,769,962	245,572	228,196
1960 (1960 urban def.)[2]	40,291,215	20,435,131	19,856,084	18,455,737	17,915,558	1,800,610	1,768,704	178,784	171,822
1950 (1950 urban def.)	31,181,325	15,862,847	15,318,478	14,489,275	13,981,064	1,256,115	1,235,262	117,457	102,152
1950 (1940 urban def.)	38,693,358	19,622,272	19,071,086	18,028,680	17,505,535	(NA)	(NA)	(NA)	(NA)
1940 (1940 urban def.)	27,029,385	13,757,516	13,271,869	12,627,240	12,151,345	1,053,699	1,055,931	76,577	64,593
1930 (1930 urban def.)	23,662,710	12,117,945	11,544,765	11,012,799	10,487,663	1,022,066	994,641	83,080	62,461
1920 (1920 urban def.)	20,047,377	10,337,060	9,710,317	9,352,304	8,775,727	918,382	885,313	66,374	49,277
RURAL FARM									
1970 (1970 urban def.)	8,292,150	4,260,965	4,031,185	4,002,398	3,774,179	223,241	223,868	35,326	33,138
1960 (1960 urban def.)[2,4]	13,474,771	6,986,175	6,488,596	6,177,614	5,698,719	747,075	734,910	61,486	54,967
1960 (1960 urban def.)[2]	13,461,466	6,978,998	6,482,468	6,175,864	5,697,223	747,070	734,901	56,064	50,344
1950 (1950 urban def.)	23,048,350	12,078,610	10,969,740	10,390,023	9,325,231	1,592,841	1,565,460	95,746	79,049
1950 (1940 urban def.)	23,076,539	12,093,697	10,982,842	10,403,230	9,336,719	(NA)	(NA)	(NA)	(NA)
1940 (1940 urban def.)	30,216,188	15,940,370	14,275,818	13,516,607	11,946,855	2,285,916	2,216,384	137,847	112,579
1930 (1930 urban def.)	30,157,513	15,864,375	14,293,138	13,371,441	11,854,804	2,354,445	2,326,078	138,489	112,256
1920 (1920 urban def.)	31,358,640	16,360,059	14,998,581	13,704,724	12,368,076	2,553,234	2,546,729	102,101	83,776

Source: "Population, by Type of Residence, Sex, and Race: 1880." U.S. Bureau of the Census, *Historical Statistics of the United States; Colonial Times to 1970, Part I*, Bicentennial Edition, p. 13. *Notes:* NA Not available. 1. Complete-count data for total, urban, and rural; 20-percent sample data for rural nonfarm and rural farm. See text for series A 91-104 for discussion of 1970 data by race. Complete-count figures exclude 23,372 persons for whom data are not available. See series A 1-5, footnote 3. 2. Complete-count data for total, urban, and rural; 25-percent sample data for rural nonfarm and rural farm. 3. Definition modified to exclude population in incorporated places and New England towns in the 2,500-3,999 size range. 4. Denotes first year for which figures include Alaska and Hawaii.

★ 1736 ★

Geographical Areas: Cities/Urban, and Rural

Population by Type of Residence, Sex, and Race, 1880-1970

Year	All races			White		Negro		Other races	
	Total	Male	Female	Male	Female	Male	Female	Male	Female
TOTAL									
1970[1]	203,211,926	98,912,192	104,299,734	86,720,987	91,027,988	10,748,316	11,831,973	1,442,889	1,439,773
1960[2,4]	179,323,175	88,331,494	90,991,681	78,367,149	80,464,583	9,113,408	9,758,423	850,937	768,675
1960[2]	178,464,236	87,864,510	90,599,726	78,153,040	80,301,916	9,105,702	9,754,415	605,768	543,395
1950	150,697,361	74,833,239	75,864,122	67,129,192	67,812,836	7,298,722	7,743,564	405,325	307,722
1940	131,669,275	66,061,592	65,607,683	59,448,548	58,766,322	6,269,038	6,596,480	344,006	244,881
1930	122,775,046	62,137,080	60,637,966	55,922,528	54,364,212	5,855,669	6,035,474	358,883	238,280
1920	105,710,620	53,900,431	51,810,189	48,430,655	46,390,260	5,209,436	5,253,695	260,340	166,234
1910	91,972,266	47,332,277	44,639,989	42,178,245	39,553,712	4,885,881	4,941,882	268,151	144,395
1900[3]	75,994,575	38,816,448	37,178,127	34,201,735	32,607,461	4,386,547	4,447,447	228,166	123,219
1890[3]	62,947,714	32,237,101	30,710,613	28,270,379	26,830,879	7,488,676[7]	7,488,676[7]	357,780[8]	357,780[8]
1880[3]	50,155,783	50,155,783[5]	50,155,783[5]	43,402,970[6]	43,402,970[6]	6,580,793[7]	6,580,793[7]	172,020[8]	172,020[8]
URBAN									
1970 (1970 urban def.)[1]	149,324,930	71,958,564	77,366,366	62,210,243	66,562,997	8,657,231	9,710,087	1,091,090	1,093,282
1960 (1960 urban def.)[2,4]	125,268,750	60,733,005	64,535,745	53,631,145	56,797,187	6,557,123	7,250,517	544,737	488,041
1960 (1960 urban def.)[2]	124,699,022	60,436,481	64,262,541	53,510,814	56,691,185	6,553,529	7,247,735	372,138	323,621
1950 (1950 urban def.)	96,467,686	46,891,782	49,575,904	42,249,894	44,506,541	4,449,766	4,942,842	192,122	126,521
1950 (1940 urban def.)	88,927,464	43,117,270	45,810,194	38,697,282	40,970,582	(NA)	(NA)	(NA)	(NA)
1940 (1940 urban def.)	74,423,702	36,363,706	38,059,996	33,304,701	34,668,122	2,929,423	3,324,165	129,582	67,709
1930 (1930 urban def.)	68,954,823	34,154,760	34,800,063	31,538,288	32,021,745	2,479,158	2,714,755	137,314	63,563
1920 (1920 urban def.)	54,304,603	27,203,312	27,101,291	25,373,627	25,246,457	1,737,820	1,821,653	91,865	33,181
1910 (1910 urban def.)	42,623,383	21,496,181	21,127,202	20,129,679	19,702,234	1,279,484	1,409,745	87,018	15,223
1900 (1906 urban def.)	30,583,411	15,190,726	15,392,685	14,187,311	14,318,835	936,731	1,067,390	66,684	6,460
1900 (1906 urban def.)	28,372,392	14,083,330	14,289,062	13,176,238	13,317,892	844,797	955,453	62,295	5,717
1890 (1906 urban def.)	22,559,367	11,283,148	11,276,219	10,525,811	10,485,556	1,482,651[7]	1,482,651[7]	65,349[8]	65,349[8]
1890 (1906 urban def.)	20,693,924	10,349,963	10,343,961	9,676,685	9,640,865	1,317,062[7]	1,317,062[7]	59,312[8]	59,312[8]
1880 (1906 urban def.)	13,184,902	13,184,902[5]	13,184,902[5]	12,297,612[6]	12,297,612[6]	849,721[7]	849,721[7]	37,569[8]	37,569[8]
RURAL									
1970 (1970 urban def.)[1]	53,886,996	26,953,628	26,933,368	24,510,744	24,464,991	2,091,085	2,121,886	351,799	346,491
1960 (1960 urban def.)[2,4]	54,054,425	27,598,489	26,455,936	24,736,004	23,667,396	2,556,285	2,507,906	306,200	280,634
1960 (1960 urban def.)[2]	53,765,214	27,428,029	26,337,185	24,642,226	23,610,731	2,552,173	2,506,680	233,630	219,774
1950 (1950 urban def.)	54,229,675	27,941,457	26,288,218	24,879,298	23,306,295	2,848,956	2,800,722	213,203	181,201
1950 (1940 urban def.)	61,769,897	31,715,969	30,053,928	28,431,910	26,842,254	(NA)	(NA)	(NA)	(NA)
1940 (1940 urban def.)	57,245,573	29,697,886	27,547,687	26,143,847	24,098,200	3,339,615	3,272,315	214,424	177,172
1930 (1930 urban def.)	53,820,223	27,982,320	25,837,903	24,384,240	22,342,467	3,376,511	3,320,719	221,569	174,717
1920 (1920 urban def.)	51,406,017	26,697,119	24,708,898	23,057,028	21,143,803	3,471,616	3,432,042	168,475	133,053
1910 (1910 urban def.)	49,348,883	25,836,096	23,512,787	22,048,566	19,851,478	3,606,397	3,532,137	181,133	129,172
1900 (1906 urban def.)	45,411,164	23,625,722	21,785,442	20,014,424	18,288,626	3,449,816	3,380,057	161,482	116,759
1900 (1906 urban def.)[3]	47,622,183	24,733,118	22,889,065	21,025,497	19,289,569	3,541,750	3,481,994	165,871	117,502
1890 (1906 urban def.)	40,388,347	20,953,953	19,434,394	17,744,568	16,345,323	6,006,025[7]	6,006,025[7]	292,431[8]	292,431[8]
1890 (1906 urban def.)[3]	42,253,790	21,287,138	20,366,652	18,593,694	17,190,014	6,171,614[7]	6,171,614[7]	298,468[8]	298,468[8]
1880 (1906 urban def.([3]	36,970,881	36,970,881[5]	36,970,881[5]	31,105,358[6]	31,105,358[6]	5,731,072[7]	5,731,072[7]	134,451[8]	134,451[8]
1970 (1970 urban def.)[1]	45,586,707	22,683,834	22,902,873	20,537,870	20,722,994	1,865,126	1,899,159	280,838	280,720
1960 (1960 urban def.)[2,4]	40,567,121	20,598,091	19,969,030	18,547,804	17,970,872	1,804,715	1,769,962	245,572	228,196
1960 (1960 urban def.)[2]	40,291,215	20,435,131	19,856,084	18,455,737	17,915,558	1,800,610	1,768,704	178,784	171,822
1950 (1950 urban def.)	31,181,325	15,862,847	15,318,478	14,489,275	13,981,064	1,256,115	1,235,262	117,457	102,152
1950 (1940 urban def.)	38,693,358	19,622,272	19,071,086	18,028,680	17,505,535	(NA)	(NA)	(NA)	(NA)

[Continued]

★ 1736 ★

Population by Type of Residence, Sex, and Race, 1880-1970

[Continued]

Year	All races			White		Negro		Other races	
	Total	Male	Female	Male	Female	Male	Female	Male	Female
1940 (1940 urban def.)	27,029,385	13,757,516	13,271,869	12,627,240	12,151,345	1,053,699	1,055,931	76,577	64,593
1930 (1930 urban def.)	23,662,710	12,117,945	11,544,765	11,012,799	10,487,663	1,022,066	994,641	83,080	72,461
1920 (1920 urban def.)	20,047,377	10,337,060	9,710,317	9,352,304	8,775,727	918,382	885,313	66,374	49,277
RURAL FARM									
1970 (1970 urban def.)[1]	8,292,150	4,260,965	4,031,185	4,002,398	3,774,179	223,241	223,868	35,326	33,138
1960 (1960 urban def.)[2,4]	13,474,771	6,986,175	6,488,596	6,177,614	5,698,719	747,075	734,910	61,486	54,967
1960 (1960 urban def.)[2]	13,461,466	6,978,998	6,482,468	6,175,864	5,697,223	747,070	734,901	56,064	50,344
1950 (1950 urban def.)	23,048,350	12,078,610	10,969,740	10,390,023	9,325,231	1,592,841	1,565,460	95,746	79,049
1950 (1940 urban def.)	23,076,539	12,093,697	10,982,842	10,403,230	9,336,719	(NA)	(NA)	(NA)	(NA)
1940 (1940 urban def.)	30,216,188	15,940,370	14,275,818	13,516,607	11,946,855	2,285,916	2,216,384	137,847	112,579
1930 (1930 urban def.)	30,157,513	15,864,375	14,293,138	13,371,441	11,854,804	2,354,445	2,326,078	138,489	112,256
1920 (1920 urban def.)	31,358,640	16,360,059	14,998,581	13,704,724	12,368,076	2,553,234	2,546,729	102,101	83,776

Source: "Population, by Type of Residence, Sex, and Race: 1880-1970." U.S. Bureau of the Census, *Historical Statistics of the United States: Colonial Times to 1970, Part I*, Bicentennial Edition, p. 12. *Notes:* NA Not available. 1. Complete-count data for total, urban, and rural; 20-percent sample data for rural nonfarm and rural farm. See text for series A 91-103 for discussion of 1970 data by race. Complete-count figures exclude 23,372 persons for whom data are not available. See series A 1-5, footnote 3. 2. Complete-count data for total, urban, and rural; 25-percent sample data for rural nonfarm and rural farm. 3. Definition modified to exclude population in incorporated places and New England towns in the 2,500-3,999 size range. 4. Denotes first year for which include Alaska and Hawaii. 5. Data includes male and female of all races. 6. Data includes white males and females. 7. Data includes Negro males and females. 8. Data includes males and females for other races.

★ 1737 ★

Geographical Areas: Cities/Urban, and Rural

Population for Cities of 100,000 or More, 1940

City	White	Negro
Akron, Ohio	232,482	12,260
Albany, N.Y.	127,564	2,929
Atlanta, Ga.	197,686	104,533
Baltimore, Md.	692,705	165,843
Birmingham, Ala.	158,622	108,938
Boston, Mass.	745,466	23,679
Bridgeport, Conn.	143,314	3,767
Buffalo, N.Y.	557,618	17,694
Cambridge, Mass.	105,855	4,858
Camden, N.J.	104,995	12,478
Canton, Ohio	104,319	4,041
Charlotte, N.C.	69,475	31,403
Chattanooga, Tenn.	91,742	36,404
Chicago, Ill.	3,114,564	277,731
Cincinnati, Ohio	399,853	55,593
Cleveland, Ohio	793,417	84,504
Columbus, Ohio	270,183	35,765
Dallas, Texas	244,246	50,407
Dayton, Ohio	190,414	20,273
Denver, Colo.	313,810	7,836
Des Moines, Iowa	153,426	6,360

[Continued]

★ 1737 ★

Population for Cities of 100,000 or More, 1940

[Continued]

City	White	Negro
Detroit, Mich.	1,472,662	149,119
Duluth, Minn.	100,659	314
Elizabeth, N.J.	104,910	4,941
Erie, Pa.	115,565	1,375
Fall River, Mass.	114,909	402
Flint, Mich.	144,858	6,599
Fort Wayne, Ind.	115,877	2,517
Fort Worth, Texas	152,345	25,254
Gary, Ind.	91,246	20,394
Grand Rapids, Mich.	161,567	2,660
Hartford, Conn.	159,119	7,090
Houston, Texas	297,959	86,302
Indianapolis, Ind.	335,755	51,142
Jacksonville, Fla.	111,247	61,782
Jersey City, N.J.	287,598	13,416
Kansas City, Kans.	100,390	21,033
Kansas City, Mo.	357,346	41,574
Knoxville, Tenn.	95,474	16,094
Long Beach, Calif.	162,582	610
Los Angeles, Calif.	1,406,430	63,774
Louisville, Ky.	271,867	47,158
Lowell, Mass.	101,252	94
Memphis, Tenn.	171,406	121,498
Miami, Fla.	135,192	36,857
Milwaukee, Wis.	578,177	8,821
Minneapolis, Minne.	487,099	4,646
Nashville, Tenn.	120,072	47,318
Newark, N.J.	383,534	45,760
New Bedford, Mass.	105,927	4,297
New Haven, Conn.	154,262	6,235
New Orleans, La.	344,775	149,034
New York, N.Y.	6,977,501	458,444
Bronx Borough	1,370,319	23,529
Brooklyn Borough	2,587,951	107,263
Manhattan Borough	1,577,625	298,365
Queens Borough	1,270,731	25,890
Richmond Borough	170,875	3,397
Norfolk, Va.	98,248	45,893
Oakland, Calif.	287,936	8,462
Oklahoma City, Okla.	184,715	19,344
Omaha, Nebr.	211,640	12,015
Paterson, N.J.	135,300	4,268
Peoria, Ill.	102,202	2,826
Philadelphia, Pa.	1,678,577	250,880
Pittsburgh, Pa.	609,236	62,216
Portland, Oreg.	299,707	1,931
Providence, R.I.	246,904	6,388

[Continued]

★ 1737 ★

Population for Cities of 100,000 or More, 1940

[Continued]

City	White	Negro
Reading, Pa.	108,646	1,905
Richmond, Va.	131,706	61,251
Rochester, N.Y.	321,554	3,262
Sacramento, Calif.	99,808	1,468
St. Louis, Mo.	706,794	108,765
St. Paul, Minn.	283,399	4,139
Salt lake City, Utah	148,699	694
San Antonio, Texas	234,022	19,235
San Diego, Calif.	196,946	4,143
San Francisco, Calif.	602,701	4,846
Scranton, Pa.	139,647	754
Seattle, Wash.	354,101	3,789
Somerville, Mass.	101,887	262
South Bend, Ind.	97,662	3,555
Spokane, Wash.	120,897	644
Springfield, Mass.	146,361	3,144
Syracuse, N.Y.	203,640	2,082
Tacoma, Wash.	107,611	650
Tampa, Fla.	85,043	23,331
Toledo, Ohio	267,589	14,597
Trenton, N.J.	115,357	9,308
Tulsa, Okla.	126,352	15,151
Utica, N.Y.	99,989	514
Washington, D.C.	474,326	187,266
Wichita, Kans.	109,186	5,686
Wilmington, Del.	98,175	14,256
Worcester, Mass.	192,263	1,353
Yonkers, N.Y.	138,441	4,108
Youngstown, Ohio	153,056	14,615

Source: "Population, Negro and White, for Cities of 100,000 or More: 1940." Murray, Florence, ed., *The Negro Handbook*, p. 190.

★ 1738 ★

Geographical Areas: Cities/Urban, and Rural

Population, Urban, by Size of City and Urban Place, and Rural, 1930

AREA	POPULATION									
	All classes[1]		Negro		White[2]					
					Total		Native		Foreign born	
	1930	1920	1930	1920	1920	1920	1930	1920	1930	1920
	NUMBER									
United States	122,775,046	105,710,620	11,891,143	10,463,131	108,864,207	94,820,915	95,497,800	81,108,161	13,366,407	13,712,754
Urban territory	68,954,823	54,304,603	5,193,913	3,559,473	62,836,605	50,620,084	52,109,746	40,263,101	10,726,859	10,356,983
Places of 2,500 to 10,000	10,614,746	9,591,747	726,574	667,848	9,692,504	8,903,499	8,831,361	7,823,402	861,143	1,080,097
Places of 10,000 to 25,000	9,097,200	6,942,742	627,851	480,778	8,383,915	6,450,414	7,363,200	5,465,029	1,020,715	985,385
Places of 25,000 to 100,000	12,917,141	10,340,788	957,698	726,271	11,781,664	9,594,234	10,075,800	7,847,635	1,705,864	1,746,599

[Continued]

★ 1738 ★

Population, Urban, by Size of City and Urban Place, and Rural, 1930

[Continued]

AREA	POPULATION									
	All classes[1]		Negro		White[2]					
					Total		Native		Foreign born	
	1930	1920	1930	1920	1920	1920	1930	1920	1930	1920
Places of 100,000 to 500,000	15,497,194	11,060,025	1,533,613	958,378	13,719,573	10,073,615	11,769,442	8,172,626	1,950,131	1,900,989
Places of 500,000 and over	20,828,542	16,369,301	1,348,177	726,198	19,258,949	15,598,322	14,069,943	10,954,409	5,189,006	4,643,913
Rural territory	53,820,223	51,406,017	6,697,230	6,903,658	46,027,602	44,200,831	43,388,054	40,845,060	2,639,548	3,355,771
PERCENT DISTRIBUTION BY AREA										
United States	100.0	100.0	100.0	100.0	100.0	100.0	100.0	100.0	100.0	100.0
Urban territory	56.2	51.4	43.7	34.0	57.7	53.4	54.6	49.6	80.3	75.5
Places of 2,500 to 10,000	8.6	9.1	6.1	6.4	8.9	9.4	9.2	9.6	6.4	7.9
Places of 10,000 to 25,000	7.4	6.6	5.3	4.6	7.7	6.8	7.7	6.7	7.6	7.2
Places of 25,000 to 100,000	10.5	9.8	8.1	6.9	10.8	10.1	10.6	9.7	12.8	12.7
Places of 100,000 to 500,000	12.6	10.5	12.9	9.2	12.6	10.6	12.3	10.1	14.6	13.9
Places of 500,000 and over	17.0	15.5	11.3	6.9	17.7	16.5	14.7	13.5	38.8	33.9
Rural territory	43.8	48.6	56.3	66.0	42.3	46.6	45.4	50.4	19.7	24.5
PERCENT DISTRIBUTION BY RACIAL CLASS										
United States	100.0	100.0	9.7	9.9	88.7	89.7	77.8	76.7	10.9	13.0
Urban territory	100.0	100.0	7.5	6.6	91.1	93.2	75.6	74.1	15.6	19.1
Places of 2,500 to 10,000	100.0	100.0	6.8	7.0	91.3	92.8	83.2	81.6	8.1	11.3
Places of 10,000 to 25,000	100.0	100.0	6.9	6.9	92.2	92.9	80.9	78.7	11.2	14.2
Places of 25,000 to 100,000	100.0	100.0	7.4	7.0	91.2	92.8	78.0	75.9	13.9	16.9
Places of 100,000 to 500,000	100.0	100.0	9.9	8.7	88.5	91.1	75.9	73.9	12.6	17.2
Places of 500,000 and over	100.0	100.0	6.5	4.4	92.5	95.3	67.6	66.9	24.9	28.4
Rural territory	100.0	100.0	12.4	13.4	85.5	86.0	80.6	79.5	4.9	6.5

Source: "Negro and White Population, Urban (by Classes of Cities and Other Urban Places) and Rural, for the United States: 1930." U.S. Bureau of the Census, *Negroes in the United States, 1920-1932*, p. 49. *Notes:* 1. Includes "other races." 2. The white population in 1920 included 700,541 persons (estimated) who would have been classified as Mexicans in 1930.

★ 1739 ★

Geographical Areas: Cities/Urban, and Rural

Urban Population by Type of Residence, Gender, and Race, 1950 to 1970

Year	All races			White		Negro		Other races	
	Total	Male	Female	Male	Female	Male	Female	Male	Female
URBANIZED AREAS - TOTAL									
1970[1]	118,446,566	57,035,148	61,411,418	48,751,475	52,200,027	7,384,180	8,308,505	899,493	902,886
1960[3]	95,848,487	46,494,210	49,354,277	40,706,094	43,063,841	5,352,291	5,905,276	435,825	385,160
1960	95,497,151	46,310,655	49,186,496	40,646,972	43,014,130	5,350,802	5,904,446	312,881	267,920
1950[2]	69,249,148	33,670,714	35,578,434	30,160,082	31,764,954	3,338,340	3,715,560	154,320	103,680
URBANIZED AREAS - CENTRAL CITIES									
1970[1]	63,921,684	30,409,942	33,511,742	23,642,104	25,904,467	6,151,899	6,992,899	615,939	614,376
1960[3]	57,975,132	27,927,624	30,047,508	22,976,282	24,650,950	4,606,147	5,095,965	345,195	300,593
1960	57,680,938	27,777,916	29,903,022	22,935,746	24,611,212	4,605,401	5,095,392	236,769	196,418
1950[2]	48,377,240	23,432,038	24,945,202	20,402,408	21,639,560	2,886,420	3,221,310	129,690	85,500

[Continued]

★ 1739 ★

Urban Population by Type of Residence, Gender, and Race, 1950 to 1970

[Continued]

Year	All races			White		Negro		Other races	
	Total	Male	Female	Male	Female	Male	Female	Male	Female
URBANIZED AREAS - URBAN FRINGE									
1970[1]	54,524,882	26,625,206	27,899,676	25,109,371	26,295,560	1,232,281	1,315,606	283,554	288,51
1960[3]	37,873,355	18,566,586	19,306,769	17,729,812	18,412,891	746,144	809,311	90,630	84,56
1960	37,816,213	18,532,739	19,283,474	17,711,226	18,402,918	745,401	809,054	76,112	71,50
1950[2]	20,871,908	10,238,676	10,633,232	9,757,674	10,125,394	451,920	494,250	24,630	18,18
OTHER URBAN									
1970[1]	30,878,364	14,923,416	15,954,948	13,458,768	14,362,970	1,273,051	1,401,582	191,597	190,39
1960[3]	29,420,263	14,238,795	15,181,468	12,925,051	13,733,346	1,204,832	1,345,241	108,912	102,881
1960	29,201,871	14,125,826	15,076,045	12,863,842	13,677,055	1,202,727	1,343,289	59,257	55,701
1950[2]	27,218,538	13,221,068	13,997,470	12,089,812	12,741,587	1,090,110	1,226,880	34,950	27,06

Source: "Urban Population, by Type of Residence, Sex, and Race: 1950 to 1970." U.S. Bureau of the Census, *Historical Statistics of the United States: Colonial Times to 1970, Part I*, Bicentennial Edition, p. 13. *Notes:* 1. See text for series A 91-104 for discussion of 1970 data by race. Excludes 23,372 persons for whom data are not available. See series A 1-5, footnote 3. 2. Complete-count data for all races and for white; 3 1/3 percent sample for Negro and for other races. 3. Denotes first year for which figures include Alaska and Hawaii.

★ 1740 ★

Geographical Areas: Cities/Urban, and Rural

Urban and Rural Black Population by Gender with Percentage Urban, by Divisions and States, 1910

DIVISION AND STATE	NEGRO POPULATION: 1910										
	Urban communities			Rural communities			Males to 1,000 females		Percentage urban		
	Both sexes	Male	Female	Both sexes	Male	Female	Urban communities	Rural communities	Both sexes	Male	Female
UNITED STATES	2,689,229	1,279,484	1,409,745	7,138,534	3,606,397	3,532,137	908	1,021	27.4	26.2	28.5
GEOGRAPHIC DIVISIONS:											
New England	60,877	29,696	31,181	5,429	3,087	2,342	952	1,318	91.8	90.6	93.0
Middle Atlantic	339,246	161,453	177,793	78,624	42,013	36,611	908	1,148	81.2	79.4	82.9
East North Central	230,542	117,883	112,659	70,294	38,548	31,746	1,046	1,214	76.6	75.4	78.0
West North Central	164,301	83,809	80,492	78,361	42,055	36,306	1,041	1,158	67.7	66.6	68.9
South Atlantic	909,520	420,619	488,901	3,202,968	1,609,189	1,593,779	860	1,010	22.1	20.7	23.5
East South Central	509,097	238,203	270,894	2,143,416	1,077,589	1,065,827	879	1,011	19.2	18.1	20.3
West South Central	435,838	207,124	228,714	1,548,588	786,901	761,687	906	1,033	22.0	20.8	23.1
Mountain	15,446	7,918	7,528	6,021	3,848	2,173	1,052	1,771	72.0	67.3	77.6
Pacific	24,362	12,779	11,583	4,833	3,167	1,666	1,103	1,901	83.4	80.1	87.4
NEW ENGLAND:											
Maine	924	451	473	439	249	190	953	1,311	67.8	64.4	71.3
New Hampshire	356	159	197	208	129	79	807	[1]	63.1	55.2	71.4
Vermont	1,341	1,004	337	280	169	111	2,979	1,523	82.7	85.6	75.2
Massachusetts	35,243	17,101	18,142	2,812	1,647	1,165	943	1,414	92.6	91.2	94.0
Rhode Island	9,055	4,379	4,676	474	266	208	936	1,279	95.0	94.3	95.7
Connecticut	13,958	6,602	7,356	1,216	627	589	897	1,065	92,0	91.3	92.6
MIDDLE ATLANTIC:											
New York	117,486	54,643	62,843	16,705	9,391	7,314	870	1,284	87.6	85.3	89.6
New Jersey	65,427	30,782	34,645	24,333	12,820	11,513	888	1,114	72.9	70.6	75.1
Pennsylvania	156,333	76,028	80,305	37,586	19,802	17,784	947	1,113	80.6	79.3	81.9
EAST NORTH CENTRAL:											
Ohio	82,282	42,074	40,208	29,170	15,921	13,249	1,046	1,202	73.8	72.5	75.2
Indiana	48,425	24,485	23,940	11,895	6,559	5,336	1,023	1,229	80.3	78.9	81.8
Illinois	85,538	44,015	41,523	23,511	12,894	10,617	1,060	1,214	78.4	77.3	79.6
Michigan	12,156	6,255	5,901	4,959	2,752	2,207	1,060	1,247	71.0	69.4	72.8

[Continued]

★ 1740 ★

Urban and Rural Black Population by Gender with Percentage Urban, by Divisions and States, 1910

[Continued]

DIVISION AND STATE	NEGRO POPULATION: 1910										
	Urban communities			Rural communities			Males to 1,000 females		Percentage urban		
	Both sexes	Male	Female	Both sexes	Male	Female	Urban communities	Rural communities	Both sexes	Male	Female
Wisconsin	2,141	1,054	1,087	759	422	337	970	1,252	73.8	71.4	76.3
WEST NORTH CENTRAL:											
Minnesota	6,518	3,864	2,654	566	319	247	1,456	1,291	92.0	92.4	91.5
Iowa	9,786	5,215	4,571	5,187	2,905	2,282	1,141	1,273	65.4	64.2	66.7
Missouri	104,462	52,618	51,844	52,990	27,871	25,119	1,015	1,110	66.3	65.4	67.4
North Dakota	306	197	109	311	184	127	1,807	1,449	49.6	51.7	46.2
South Dakota	412	228	184	405	240	165	1,239	1,455	50.4	48.7	52.7
Nebraska	6,621	3,626	2,995	1,068	633	435	1,211	1,455	86.1	85.1	87.3
Kansas	36,196	18,061	18,135	17,834	9,903	7,931	996	1,249	67.0	64.6	69.6
SOUTH ATLANTIC:											
Delaware	11,157	5,392	5,765	20,024	10,619	9,405	935	1,129	35.8	33.7	38.0
Maryland	99,230	45,946	53,284	133,020	68,803	64,217	862	1,071	42.7	40.0	45.3
District of Columbia	94,446	42,615	51,831	-	-	-	822	-	100.0	100.0	100.0
Virginia	158,218	72,804	85,414	512,878	257,738	255,140	852	1,010	23.6	22.0	25.1
West Virginia	15,380	7,945	7,435	48,793	28,662	20,131	1,069	1,424	24.0	21.7	27.0
North Carolina	115,975	52,796	63,179	581,868	286,785	295,083	836	972	16.6	15.5	17.6
South Carolina	101,702	45,979	55,723	734,141	362,099	372,042	825	973	12.2	11.3	13.0
Georgia	224,826	103,231	121,595	952,161	477,032	475,129	849	1,004	19.1	17.8	20.4
Florida	88,586	43,911	44,675	220,083	117,451	102,632	983	1,144	28.7	27.2	30.3
EAST SOUTH CENTRAL:											
Kentucky	106,631	51,186	55,445	155,025	80,306	74,719	923	1,075	40.8	38.9	42.6
Tennessee	150,506	70,375	80,131	322,582	163,335	159,247	878	1,026	31.8	30.1	33.5
Alabama	156,603	73,579	83,024	751,679	374,215	377,464	886	991	17.2	16.4	18.0
Mississippi	95,357	43,063	52,294	914,130	459,733	454,397	823	1,012	9.4	8.6	10.3
WEST SOUTH CENTRAL:											
Arkansas	59,147	28,712	30,435	383,744	194,611	189,133	943	1,029	13.4	12.9	13.9
Louisiana	160,845	73,842	87,003	553,029	279,982	273,047	849	1,025	22.5	20.9	24.2
Oklahoma	36,982	19,497	17,485	100,630	52,440	48,190	1,115	1,088	26.9	27.1	26.6
Texas	178,864	85,073	93,791	511,185	259,868	251,317	907	1,034	25.9	24.7	27.2
MOUNTAIN:											
Montana	1,455	830	625	379	228	151	1,328	1,510	79.3	78.4	80.5
Idaho	426	252	174	225	146	79	1,448	[1]	65.4	63.3	68.8
Wyoming	1,041	530	502	1,194	1,005	189	1,074	5,317	46.6	34.9	72.6
Colorado	9,359	4,646	4,713	2,094	1,221	873	986	1,399	81.7	79.2	84.4
New Mexico	795	393	402	833	498	335	978	1,487	48.8	44.1	54.5
Arizona	1,310	626	684	699	428	271	915	1,579	65.2	59.4	71.6
Utah	959	573	386	185	118	67	1,484	[1]	83.8	82.9	85.2
Nevada	101	59	42	412	204	208	-	981	19.7	22.4	16.8
PACIFIC:											
Washington	4,609	2,738	1,961	1,359	998	361	1,396	2,765	77.6	73.3	84.5
Oregon	1,264	756	508	228	151	77	1,488	[1]	84.7	83.4	86.8
California	18,399	9,285	9,114	3,246	2,018	1,228	1,019	1,643	85.0	82.1	88.1

Source: "Urban and Rural Negro Population Classified by Sex, with Sex Ratio and Percentage Urban, by Divisions and States: 1910." U.S. Bureau of the Census, *Negro Population, 1790-1915*, p. 155. *Note:* 1. Ratio not shown where the number of females is less than 100.

★ 1741 ★

Geographical Areas: Cities/Urban, and Rural

Urban and Rural Black Population by Gender, Age Periods, Sections, and Southern Divisions, 1910 - I

SEX AND AGE PERIOD	NEGRO POPULATION: 1910					
	United States		The South			
			Total		South Atlantic division	
	Urban	Rural	Urban	Rural	Urban	Rural
	NUMBER					
BOTH SEXES						
All ages	2,689,229	7,138,534	1,854,455	6,894,972	909,520	3,202,968
Under 5 years	229,080	1,034,208	166,646	1,009,690	83,710	486,806
5 to 14 years	454,219	1,947,600	339,746	1,898,791	167,954	900,321
15 to 24 years	578,299	1,512,912	418,046	1,464,273	206,667	677,262
25 to 44 years	985,374	1,652,804	636,026	1,581,247	307,169	709,730
45 to 64 years	351,259	756,844	231,511	720,342	114,604	327,695
65 years and over	77,435	216,689	52,745	203,949	24,599	94,541
Age unknown	13,563	17,477	9,740	16,680	4,817	6,613
MALE						
All ages	1,279,484	3,606,397	865,946	3,473,679	420,619	1,609,189
Under 5 years	113,158	516,162	82,557	503,943	41,510	242,591
5 to 14 years	218,721	978,528	163,791	953,885	80,705	451,932
15 to 24 years	253,239	736,863	180,588	710,575	88,229	328,243
25 to 44 years	477,609	826,489	298,366	786,031	142,510	352,263
45 to 64 years	174,362	421,192	112,102	400,021	54,287	179,116
65 years and over	34,973	117,509	23,332	110,053	10,741	51,274
Age unknown	7,422	9,654	5,210	9,171	2,637	3,770
FEMALE						
All ages	1,409,745	3,532,137	988,509	3,421,293	488,901	1,593,779
Under 5 years	115,922	518,046	84,084	505,747	42,200	244,215
5 to 14 years	235,498	969,072	175,955	944,906	87,249	448,389
15 to 24 years	325,060	776,049	237,458	753,698	118,438	349,019
25 to 44 years	507,765	826,315	337,660	795,216	164,659	357,467
45 to 64 years	176,897	335,652	119,409	320,321	60,317	148,579
65 years and over	42,462	99,180	29,413	93,896	13,858	43,267
Age unknown	6,141	7,823	4,530	7,509	2,180	2,843
	PERCENTAGE DISTRIBUTION BY AGE PERIODS					
BOTH SEXES						
All ages	100.0	100.0	100.0	100.0	100.0	100.0
Under 5 years	8.5	14.5	9.0	14.6	9.2	15.2
5 to 14 years	16.9	27.3	18.3	27.5	18.5	28.1
15 to 24 years	21.5	21.2	22.5	21.2	22.7	21.1

[Continued]

★ 1741 ★

Urban and Rural Black Population by Gender, Age Periods, Sections, and Southern Divisions, 1910 - I

[Continued]

SEX AND AGE PERIOD	NEGRO POPULATION: 1910					
	United States		The South			
			Total		South Atlantic division	
	Urban	Rural	Urban	Rural	Urban	Rural
25 to 44 years	36.6	23.2	34.3	22.9	33.8	22.2
45 to 64 years	13.1	10.6	12.5	10.4	12.6	10.2
65 years and over	2.9	3.0	2.8	3.0	2.7	3.0
Age unknown	0.5	0.2	0.5	0.2	0.5	0.2
MALE						
All ages	100.0	100.0	100.0	100.0	100.0	100.0
Under 5 years	8.8	14.3	9.5	14.5	9.9	15.1
5 to 14 years	17.1	27.1	18.9	27.5	19.2	28.1
15 to 24 years	19.8	20.4	20.9	20.5	21.0	20.4
25 to 44 years	37.3	22.9	34.5	22.6	33.9	21.9
45 to 64 years	13.6	11.7	12.9	11.5	12.9	11.1
65 years and over	2.7	3.3	2.7	3.2	2.6	3.2
Age unknown	0.6	0.3	0.6	0.3	0.6	0.2
FEMALE						
All ages	100.0	100.0	100.0	100.0	100.0	100.0
Under 5 years	8.2	14.7	8.5	14.8	8.6	15.3
5 to 14 years	16.7	27.4	17.8	27.6	17.8	28.1
15 to 24 years	23.1	22.0	24.0	22.0	24.2	21.9
25 to 44 years	36.0	23.4	34.2	23.2	33.7	22.4
45 to 64 years	12.5	9.5	12.1	9.4	12.3	9.3
65 years and over	3.0	2.8	3.0	2.7	2.8	2.7
Age unknown	0.4	0.2	0.5	0.2	0.4	0.2

Source: "Urban and Rural Negro Population, Classified by Sex and Age Periods, by Sections and Southern Divisions: 1910. U.S. Bureau of the Census, *Negro Population, 1790-1915*, p. 182.

★ 1742 ★

Geographical Areas: Cities/Urban, and Rural

Urban and Rural Black Population by Gender, Age Periods, Sections, and Southern Divisions, 1910 - II

SEX AND AGE PERIOD	NEGRO POPULATION: 1910							
	The South				The North		The West	
	East South Central division		West South Central division					
	Urban	Rural	Urban	Rural	Urban	Rural	Urban	Rural
	NUMBER							
BOTH SEXES								
All ages	509,097	2,143,416	435,838	1,548,588	794,966	232,708	39,808	10,854
Under 5 years	43,105	304,698	39,826	218,186	59,872	23,857	2,567	661
5 to 14 years	89,109	575,179	82,683	423,291	109,720	47,377	4,735	1,432
15 to 24 years	113,114	456,004	98,265	331,007	153,434	46,615	6,819	2,024
25 to 44 years	177,844	502,563	151,013	368,954	331,435	67,049	17,913	4,508
45 to 64 years	67,249	232,751	49,658	159,896	113,348	34,730	6,400	1,772
65 years and over	16,016	66,465	12,130	42,943	23,642	12,331	1,048	409
Age unknown	2,660	5,756	2,263	4,311	3,515	749	308	48
MALE								
All ages	238,203	1,077,589	207,124	786,901	392,841	125,703	20,697	7,015
Under 5 years	21,355	152,547	19,692	108,805	29,380	11,893	1,221	326
5 to 14 years	42,937	289,774	40,149	212,179	52,642	23,919	2,288	724
15 to 24 years	49,511	220,806	42,848	161,526	69,493	24,936	3,158	1,352
25 to 44 years	83,019	246,437	72,837	187,331	169,546	37,360	9,697	3,098
45 to 64 years	32,914	129,332	24,901	91,573	58,641	19,953	3,619	1,218
65 years and over	7,125	35,674	5,466	23,105	11,104	7,190	537	266
Age unknown	1,342	3,019	1,231	2,382	2,035	452	177	31
FEMALE								
All ages	270,894	1,065,827	228,714	761,687	402,125	107,005	19,111	3,839
Under 5 years	21,750	152,151	20,134	109,381	30,492	11,964	1,346	335
5 to 14 years	46,172	285,405	42,534	211,112	57,078	23,458	2,465	708
15 to 24 years	63,603	235,189	55,417	169,481	83,941	21,679	3,661	672
25 to 44 years	94,825	256,126	78,176	181,623	161,889	29,689	8,216	1,410
45 to 64 years	34,335	103,419	24,757	68,323	54,707	14,777	2,781	554
65 years and over	8,891	30,791	6,664	19,838	12,538	5,141	511	143
Age unknown	1,318	2,737	1,032	1,929	1,480	297	131	17
	PERCENTAGE DISTRIBUTION BY AGE PERIODS							
BOTH SEXES								
All ages	100.0	100.0	100.0	100.0	100.0	100.0	100.0	100.0
Under 5 years	8.5	14.2	9.1	14.1	7.5	10.3	6.4	6.1
5 to 14 years	17.5	26.8	19.0	27.3	13.8	20.4	11.9	13.2

[Continued]

★ 1742 ★

Urban and Rural Black Population by Gender, Age Periods, Sections, and Southern Divisions, 1910 - II

[Continued]

SEX AND AGE PERIOD	NEGRO POPULATION: 1910							
	The South				The North		The West	
	East South Central division		West South Central division					
	Urban	Rural	Urban	Rural	Urban	Rural	Urban	Rural
15 to 24 years	22.2	21.3	22.5	21.4	19.3	20.0	17.1	18.6
25 to 44 years	34.9	23.4	34.6	23.8	41.7	28.8	45.0	41.5
45 to 64 years	13.2	10.9	11.4	10.3	14.3	14.9	16.1	16.3
65 years and over	3.1	3.1	2.8	2.8	3.0	5.3	2.6	3.8
Age unknown	0.5	0.3	0.5	0.3	0.4	0.3	0.8	0.4
MALE								
All ages	100.0	100.0	100.0	100.0	100.0	100.0	100.0	100.0
Under 5 years	9.0	14.2	9.5	13.8	7.5	9.5	5.9	4.6
5 to 14 years	18.0	26.9	19.4	27.0	13.4	19.0	11.1	10.3
15 to 24 years	20.8	20.5	20.7	20.5	17.7	19.8	15.3	19.3
25 to 44 years	34.9	22.9	35.2	23.8	43.2	29.7	46.9	44.2
45 to 64 years	13.8	12.0	12.0	11.6	14.9	15.9	17.5	17.4
65 years and over	3.0	3.3	2.6	2.9	2.8	5.7	2.6	3.8
Age unknown	0.6	0.3	0.6	0.3	0.5	0.4	0.9	0.4
FEMALE								
All ages	100.0	100.0	100.0	100.0	100.0	100.0	100.0	100.0
Under 5 years	8.0	14.3	8.8	14.4	7.6	11.2	7.0	8.7
5 to 14 years	17.0	26.8	18.6	27.7	14.2	21.9	12.9	18.4
15 to 24 years	23.5	22.1	24.2	22.3	20.9	20.3	19.2	17.5
25 to 44 years	35.0	24.0	34.2	23.8	40.3	27.7	43.0	36.7
45 to 64 years	12.7	9.7	10.8	9.0	13.6	13.8	14.6	14.4
65 years and over	3.3	2.9	2.9	2.6	3.1	4.8	2.7	3.7
Age unknown	0.5	0.3	0.5	0.3	0.4	0.3	0.7	0.4

Source: "Urban and Rural Negro Population, Classified by Sex and Age Periods, by Sections and Southern Divisions: 1910. U.S. Bureau of the Census, *Negro Population, 1790-1915*, p. 182.

★ 1743 ★

Geographical Areas: Cities/Urban, and Rural

Urban and Rural Population and Percentage Urban by State, 1910

DIVISION AND STATE	POPULATION: 1910					
	Urban		Rural		Percentage urban	
	Negro	White	Negro	White	Negro	White
UNITED STATES	2,689,229	39,831,913	7,138,534	41,900,044	27.4	48.7
GEOGRAPHIC DIVISIONS:						
New England	60,877	5,389,967	5,429	1,090,547	91.8	83.2
Middle Atlantic	339,246	13,373,921	78,624	5,506,531	81.2	70.8
East North Central	230,542	9,381,652	70,294	8,545,970	76.6	52.3
West North Central	164,301	3,706,092	78,361	7,645,529	67.7	32.6
South Atlantic	909,520	2,180,900	3,202,968	5,890,613	22.1	27.0
East South Central	509,097	1,064,740	2,143,416	4,689,586	19.2	18.5
West South Central	435,838	1,515,733	1,548,588	5,205,758	22.0	22.6
Mountain	15,446	924,291	6,021	1,596,164	72.0	36.7
Pacific	24,362	2,294,527	4,833	1,729,426	83.4	57.0
NEW ENGLAND:						
Maine	924	380,292	439	359,703	67.8	51.4
New Hampshire	356	254,664	208	175,242	63.1	59.2
Vermont	1,341	167,579	280	186,719	82.7	47.3
Massachusetts	35,243	3,087,146	2,812	237,780	92.6	92.8
Rhode Island	9,055	515,011	474	17,481	95.0	96.7
Connecticut	13,958	985,275	1,216	113,622	92.0	89.7
MIDDLE ATLANTIC:						
New York	117,486	7,061,043	16,705	1,905,802	87.6	78.7
New Jersey	65,427	1,840,560	24,333	605,334	72.9	75.3
Pennsylvania	156,333	4,472,318	37,586	2,995,395	80.6	59.9
EAST NORTH CENTRAL:						
Ohio	82,282	2,582,143	29,170	2,072,754	73.8	55.5
Indiana	48,425	1,095,026	11,895	1,544,935	80.3	41.5
Illinois	85,538	3,388,881	23,511	2,138,081	78.4	61.3
Michigan	12,156	1,314,186	4,959	1,471,061	71.0	47.2
Wisconsin	2,141	1,001,416	759	1,319,139	73.8	43.2
WEST NORTH CENTRAL:						
Minnesota	6,518	843,322	566	1,215,905	92.0	41.0
Iowa	9,786	670,035	5,187	1,539,156	65.4	30.2
Missouri	104,462	1,293,554	52,990	1,841,378	66.3	41.3
North Dakota	306	62,765	311	507,090	49.6	11.0
South Dakota	412	76,070	405	487,701	50.4	13.5
Nebraska	6,621	303,767	1,068	876,526	86.1	25.7
Kansas	36,146	456,579	17,834	1,177,773	67.0	27.9
SOUTH ATLANTIC:						
Delaware	11,157	85,903	20,024	85,199	35.8	50.2
Maryland	99,230	558,582	133,020	504,057	42.7	52.6
District of Columbia	94,446	236,128	-	-	100.0	100.0
Virginia	158,218	318,159	512,878	1,071,650	23.6	22.9
West Virginia	15,380	212,783	48,793	944,034	24.0	18.4
North Carolina	115,975	202,548	581,868	1,298,073	16.6	13.5
South Carolina	101,702	123,089	734,141	556,072	12.2	18.1

[Continued]

★ 1743 ★

Urban and Rural Population and Percentage Urban by State, 1910

[Continued]

DIVISION AND STATE	POPULATION: 1910					
	Urban		Rural		Percentage urban	
	Negro	White	Negro	White	Negro	White
Georgia	224,826	313,606	952,161	1,118,196	19.1	21.9
Florida	88,586	130,302	220,083	313,332	28.7	29.4
EAST SOUTH CENTRAL:						
Kentucky	106,631	448,727	155,025	1,579,224	40.8	22.1
Tennessee	150,506	290,431	322,582	1,421,001	31.8	17.0
Alabama	156,603	213,756	751,679	1,015,076	17.2	17.4
Mississippi	95,357	111,826	914,130	674,285	9.4	14.2
WEST SOUTH CENTRAL:						
Arkansas	59,147	143,326	383,744	987,700	13.4	12.7
Louisiana	160,845	335,175	553,029	605,911	22.5	35.6
Oklahoma	36,982	278,698	100,610	1,165,833	26.9	19.3
Texas	178,864	758,534	511,185	2,446,314	25.9	23.7
MOUNTAIN:						
Montana	1,455	130,531	379	230,049	79.3	36.2
Idaho	426	68,604	225	250,617	65.4	21.5
Wyoming	1,041	41,444	1,194	98,874	46.6	29.5
Colorado	9,359	394,156	2,094	389,259	81.7	50.3
New Mexico	795	45,588	843	259,006	48.8	15.0
Arizona	1,310	60,355	699	111,113	65.2	35.2
Utah	959	170,884	185	195,699	83.8	46.6
Nevada	101	12,729	412	61,547	19.7	17.1
PACIFIC:						
Washington	4,699	590,181	1,359	518,930	77.6	53.2
Oregon	1,254	297,095	228	357,995	84.7	45.4
California	18,399	1,407,251	3,246	852,421	85.0	62.3

Source: "Untitled Table." U.S. Bureau of the Census, *Negro Population, 1790- 1915,* p. 91.

★ 1744 ★

Geographical Areas: Cities/Urban, and Rural

Urban and Rural Population by Race, Section, and Southern Division, 1930 - I

RACIAL CLASS	United States	THE SOUTH				The North	The West
		Total	South Atlantic division	East South Central division	West South Central division		
URBAN POPULATION							
All classes[1]	68,954,823	12,904,248	5,698,122	2,778,687	4,427,439	49,057,772	6,992,803
Negro	5,193,913	2,966,325	1,462,904	759,166	744,255	2,128,329	99,259
White	62,836,605	9,594,145	4,231,820	2,018,882	3,343,443	46,800,609	6,441,851

[Continued]

★ 1744 ★

Urban and Rural Population by Race, Section, and Southern Division, 1930 - I

[Continued]

RACIAL CLASS	United States	THE SOUTH Total	South Atlantic division	East South Central division	West South Central division	The North	The West
Native	52,109,746	9,231,423	4,009,090	1,977,070	3,245,263	37,403,036	5,475,287
Foreign born	10,726,859	362,722	222,730	41,812	98,180	9,397,573	966,564
TOTAL RURAL POPULATION							
All classes[1]	53,820,223	24,953,385	10,095,467	7,108,527	7,749,391	23,963,419	4,903,419
Negro	6,697,230	6,395,252	2,958,484	1,899,072	1,537,696	280,890	21,088
White	46,027,602	18,079,734	7,117,464	5,205,732	5,756,732	23,587,758	4,360,110
Native	43,388,054	17,910,281	7,035,916	5,189,879	5,684,486	21,598,778	3,878,995
Foreign-born	2,639,548	169,453	81,548	15,853	72,052	1,988,980	481,115
RURAL-FARM POPULATION[2]							
All classes[1]	30,157,513	16,271,330	5,878,956	5,084,435	5,307,939	11,661,452	2,224,731
Negro	4,680,523	4,608,786	1,940,501	1,481,742	1,186,543	65,601	6,136
White	24,884,834	11,343,125	3,921,849	3,599,723	3,821,553	11,556,489	1,985,220
Native	23,800,747	11,274,220	3,905,523	3,593,474	3,775,223	10,762,898	1,763,629
Foreign born	1,084,087	68,905	16,326	6,249	46,330	793,591	221,591
RURAL-NONFARM POPULATION[3]							
All classes[1]	23,662,710	8,682,055	4,216,511	2,024,092	2,441,452	12,301,967	2,678,688
Negro	2,016,707	1,786,466	1,017,983	417,330	351,153	215,289	14,952
White	21,142,768	6,736,609	3,195,615	1,606,009	1,934,985	12,031,269	2,374,890
Native	19,587,307	6,636,061	3,130,393	1,596,405	1,909,263	10,835,880	2,115,366
Foreign born	1,555,461	100,548	65,222	9,604	25,722	1,195,389	259,524

Source: "Urban and Rural Population, by Racial Classes, by Sections, and Southern Divisions: 1930." U.S. Bureau of the Census, *Negroes in the United States, 1920-1932,* p. 51. *Notes:* 1. Includes "Other races." 2. The rural farm population as shown for 1930 comprises all persons living on farms in rural areas, that is incorporated places of less than 2,500 inhabitants, and in territory outside of incorporated places. 3. The rural-nonfarm population, sometimes termed the "village" population, includes, in general, all persons living outside cities or other incorporated places having 2,500 inhabitants or more who do not live on farms.

★ 1745 ★

Geographical Areas: Cities/Urban, and Rural

Urban and Rural Population by Race, Section, and Southern Division, 1930 - II

RACIAL CLASS	United States	THE SOUTH				The North	The West
		Total	South Atlantic division	East South Central division	West South Central division		
PERCENT URBAN							
All classes[1]	56.2	34.1	36.1	28.1	36.4	67.2	58.8
Negro	43.7	31.7	33.1	28.6	32.6	88.3	82.5
White	57.7	34.7	37.3	27.9	36.7	66.5	59.6
Native	54.6	34.0	36.3	27.6	36.3	63.4	58.5
Foreign born	80.3	68.2	73.2	72.5	57.7	82.5	66.8
PERCENT RURAL							
All classes[1]	43.8	65.9	63.9	71.9	63.6	32.8	41.2
Negro	56.3	68.3	66.9	71.4	67.4	11.7	17.5
White	42.3	65.3	62.7	72.1	63.3	33.5	40.4
Native	45.4	66.0	63.7	72.4	63.7	36.6	41.5
Foreign-born	19.7	31.8	26.8	27.5	42.3	17.5	33.2
PERCENT RURAL-FARM							
All classes[1]	24.6	43.0	37.2	51.4	43.6	16.0	18.7
Negro	39.4	49.2	43.9	55.7	52.0	2.7	5.1
White	22.9	41.0	34.6	49.8	42.0	16.4	18.4
Native	24.9	41.5	35.4	50.1	42.3	18.2	18.9
Foreign born	8.1	12.9	5.4	10.8	27.2	7.0	15.3
PERCENT RURAL-NONFARM							
All classes[1]	19.3	22.9	26.7	20.5	20.0	16.8	22.5
Negro	17.0	19.1	23.0	15.7	15.4	8.9	12.4
White	19.4	24.3	28.2	22.2	21.3	17.1	22.0
Native	20.5	24.4	28.3	22.3	21.4	18.4	22.6
Foreign born	11.6	18.9	21.4	16.7	15.1	10.5	17.9

Source: "Urban and Rural Population, by Racial Classes, by Sections, and Southern Divisions: 1930." U.S. Bureau of the Census, *Negroes in the United States, 1920-1932*, p. 51. *Notes:* 1. Includes "Other races." 2. The rural farm population as shown for 1930 comprises all persons living on farms in rural areas, that is incorporated places of less than 2,500 inhabitants, and in territory outside of incorporated places. 3. The rural-nonfarm population, sometimes termed the "village" population, includes, in general, all persons living outside cities or other incorporated places having 2,500 inhabitants or more who do not live on farms.

★ 1746 ★

Geographical Areas: Cities/Urban, and Rural

Urban and Rural Population by Sections, Divisions, and States, 1930

SECTION, DIVISION, AND STATE	URBAN		RURAL		PERCENT URBAN	
	Negro	White	Negro	White	Negro	White
United States	5,193,913	62,836,605	6,697,230	46,027,602	43.7	57.7
The North	2,128,329	46,800,609	280,890	23,587,758	88.3	66.5
The South	2,966,325	9,594,145	6,395,252	18,079,734	31.4	34.7
The West	99,259	6,441,851	21,088	4,360,110	82.5	59.6
GEOGRAPHIC DIVISIONS:						
New England	81,443	6,225,108	12,643	1,840,005	86.6	77.2
Middle Atlantic	939,064	19,426,948	113,835	5,745,156	89.2	77.2
East North Central	848,627	15,880,308	81,823	8,397,355	91.2	65.4
West North Central	259,195	5,268,245	72,589	7,605,242	78.1	40.9
South Atlantic	1,462,904	4,231,820	2,958,484	7,117,464	33.1	37.3
East South Central	759,166	2,018,882	1,899,072	5,205,732	28.6	27.9
West South Central	744,255	3,343,443	1,537,696	5,756,538	32.6	36.7
Mountain	21,032	1,353,283	9,193	1,950,303	69.6	41.0
Pacific	78,227	5,088,568	11,895	2,409,807	86.8	67.9
NEW ENGLAND						
Maine	703	320,296	393	474,887	64.1	40.3
New Hampshire	594	272,376	196	191,974	75.2	58.7
Vermont	213	118,510	355	240,455	37.5	33.0
Massachusetts	46,323	3,781,458	6,042	411,468	88.5	90.2
Rhode Island	9,079	625,856	834	51,160	91.6	92.4
Connecticut	24,531	1,106,612	4,832	470,061	83.6	70.2
MIDDLE ATLANTIC:						
New York	390,499	10,112,383	22,315	2,037,910	94.6	83.2
New Jersey	174,985	3,161,384	33,943	667,825	83.8	82.6
Pennsylvania	373,580	6,153,181	57,677	3,039,421	86.6	66.9
EAST NORTH CENTRAL:						
Ohio	271,972	4,229,930	37,332	2,101,206	87.9	66.8
Indiana	103,042	1,682,994	8,940	1,433,142	92.0	54.0
Illinois	304,036	5,300,343	24,936	1,966,018	92.4	72.9
Michigan	159,704	3,126,763	9,749	1,523,408	94.2	67.2
Wisconsin	9,873	1,540,278	866	1,373,581	91.9	52.9
WEST NORTH CENTRAL:						
Minnesota	9,110	1,245,518	335	1,293,455	96.5	49.1
Iowa	15,185	960,517	2,196	1,487,865	87.4	39.2
Missouri	169,954	1,683,348	53,886	1,715,539	75.9	49.5
North Dakota	216	112,443	161	558,800	57.3	16.8
South Dakota	337	129,992	309	539,461	52.2	19.4
Nebraska	13,112	469,679	640	884,023	95.3	34.7
Kansas	51,283	666,748	15,063	1,126,099	77.3	37.2
SOUTH ATLANTIC:						
Delaware	15,037	108,043	17,565	97,651	46.1	52.5

[Continued]

★ 1746 ★

Urban and Rural Population by Sections, Divisions, and States, 1930

[Continued]

SECTION, DIVISION, AND STATE	URBAN		RURAL		PERCENT URBAN	
	Negro	White	Negro	White	Negro	White
Maryland	159,654	814,348	116,725	539,822	57.8	60.1
District of Columbia	132,068	353,914	-	-	100.0	100.0
Virginia	213,401	571,656	435,764	1,198,749	32.8	32.3
West Virginia	31,224	460,165	83,669	1,153,769	27.2	28.5
North Carolina	246,237	563,478	672,410	1,671,470	26.8	25.2
South Carolina	138,354	232,641	655,327	711,399	17.4	24.6
Georgia	316,637	578,550	754,488	1,258,424	29.6	31.5
Florida	210,292	549,025	221,536	486,180	48.7	53.0
EAST SOUTH CENTRAL:						
Kentucky	116,561	682,356	109,479	1,706,008	51.6	28.6
Tennessee	240,168	656,248	237,478	1,482,371	50.3	30.7
Alabama	268,450	475,660	676,384	1,225,115	28.4	28.0
Mississippi	133,987	204,618	875,731	792,238	13.3	20.5
WEST SOUTH CENTRAL:						
Arkansas	89,162	293,459	389,301	1,081,447	18.6	21.3
Louisiana	257,463	574,249	518,863	743,911	33.2	43.6
Oklahoma	67,801	736,429	104,397	1,386,995	39.4	34.7
Texas	329,829	1,739,306	525,135	2,544,185	38.6	40.6
MOUNTAIN:						
Montana	1,027	178,408	229	338,919	81.8	34.5
Idaho	502	128,002	166	309,560	75.1	29.3
Wyoming	859	66,610	391	147,457	68.7	31.1
Colorado	10,471	489,947	1,357	471,170	88.5	51.0
New Mexico	1,718	93,171	1,132	238,584	60.3	28.1
Arizona	5,147	102,011	5,602	162,367	47.9	38.6
Utah	944	262,427	164	233,528	85.2	52.9
Nevada	364	32,707	152	48,718	70.5	40.2
PACIFIC:						
Washington	5,818	862,576	1,022	658,523	85.1	56.7
Oregon	1,890	482,374	344	454,655	84.6	51.5
California	70,519	3,743,618	10,529	1,296,629	87.0	74.3

Source: "Negro and White Population, Urban, Rural, by Sections, Divisions, and States: 1930." U.S. Bureau of the Census, *Negroes in the United States, 1920-1932*, p. 52.

★ 1747 ★

Geographical Areas: Cities/Urban, and Rural

Urban and Rural Population in Classes of Cities by Race, 1910

CLASS OF COMMUNITY	POPULATION: 1910							
	All classes	Negro	White					
			Total	Native				Foreign born
				Total	Native parentage	Mixed parentage	Foreign parentage	
NUMBER								
United States	91,972,266	9,827,763	81,731,957	68,386,412	49,488,575	5,981,526	12,916,311	13,345,54
Urban communities	42,623,383	2,689,229	39,831,913	30,196,544	17,849,644	3,554,980	8,791,920	9,635,36
Cities of 2,500 to 10,000	8,470,359	655,266	7,798,201	6,620,540	4,872,584	614,978	1,132,978	1,177,66
Cities of 10,000 to 25,000	5,609,208	408,362	5,186,578	4,207,860	2,827,915	446,063	933,882	978,71
Cities of 25,000 to 100,000	8,241,678	602,040	7,626,923	5,963,109	3,779,057	665,863	1,518,189	1,663,81
Cities of 100,000 to 500,000	8,790,297	626,946	8,117,117	6,173,049	3,422,040	821,365	1,929,644	1,944,06
Cities of 500,000 and over	11,511,841	396,615	11,103,094	7,231,986	2,948,048	1,006,711	3,277,227	3,871,10
Rural communities	49,348,883	7,138,534	41,900,044	38,189,868	31,638,931	2,426,546	4,124,391	3,710,17
PERCENTAGE DISTRIBUTION, BY CLASS OF COMMUNITY								
United States	100.0	100.0	100.0	100.0	100.0	100.0	100.0	100
Urban communities	46.3	27.4	48.7	44.2	36.1	59.4	68.1	72
Cities of 2,500 to 10,000	9.2	6.7	9.5	9.7	9.8	10.3	8.8	8.
Cities of 10,000 to 25,000	6.1	4.2	6.3	6.2	5.7	7.5	7.2	7
Cities of 25,000 to 100,000	9.0	6.1	9.3	8.7	7.6	11.1	11.8	12.
Cities of 100,000 to 500,000	9.6	6.4	9.9	9.0	6.9	13.7	14.9	14.
Cities of 500,000 and over	12.5	4.0	13.6	10.6	6.0	16.8	25.4	29.
Rural communities	53.7	72.6	51.3	55.8	63.9	40.6	31.9	27.
PERCENTAGE DISTRIBUTION, BY RACIAL CLASS								
United States	100.0	10.7	88.9	74.4	53.8	6.5	14.0	14.
Urban communities	100.0	6.3	93.5	70.8	41.9	8.3	20.6	22.
Cities of 2,500 to 10,000	100.0	7.7	92.1	78.2	57.5	7.3	13.4	13.
Cities of 10,000 to 25,000	100.0	7.3	92.5	75.0	50.4	8.0	16.6	17.
Cities of 25,000 to 100,000	100.0	7.3	92.5	72.4	45.9	8.1	18.4	20.
Cities of 100,000 to 500,000	100.0	7.1	92.3	70.2	38.9	9.3	22.0	22.
Cities of 500,000 and over	100.0	3.4	96.4	62.8	25.6	8.7	28.5	33
Rural communities	100.0	14.5	84.9	77.4	64.1	4.9	8.4	7.

Source: "Population, Urban and Rural, and in Classes of Cities, by Racial Classes: 1910." U.S. Bureau of the Census, *Negro Population, 1790-1915*, p. 88.

Geographical Areas: Colonies

★ 1748 ★

Estimated Population of American Colonies, 1610 to 1780 - I

Colony	1780	1770	1760	1750	1740	1730	1720	1710
WHITE AND NEGRO								
Total	2,780,369	2,148,076	1,593,625	1,170,760	905,563	629,445	466,185	331,711
Maine[1]	49,133	31,257	20,000	-	-	-	-	-
New Hampshire[2]	87,802	62,396	39,093	27,505	23,256	10,755	9,375	5,681
Vermont[3]	47,620	10,000	-	-	-	-	-	-
Plymouth[4]	-	-	-	-	-	-	-	-
Massachusetts[1,2,4]	268,627	235,308	202,600	188,000	151,613	114,116	91,008	62,390
Rhode Island[2]	52,946	58,196	45,471	33,226	25,255	16,950	11,680	7,573
Connecticut[2]	206,701	183,881	142,470	111,280	89,580	75,530	58,830	39,450
New York[2]	210,541	162,920	117,138	76,696	63,665	48,594	36,919	21,625
New Jersey[2]	139,627	117,431	93,813	71,393	51,373	37,510	29,818	19,872
Pennsylvania[2]	327,305	240,057	183,703	119,666	85,637	51,707	30,962	24,450
Delaware[2]	45,385	35,496	33,250	27,704	19,870	9,170	5,385	3,645
Maryland[2]	245,474	202,599	162,267	141,073	116,093	91,113	66,133	42,741
Virginia[2]	538,004	447,016	339,726	231,033	180,440	114,000	87,757	78,281
North Carolina[2]	270,133	197,200	110,442	72,984	51,760	30,000	21,270	15,120
South Carolina[2]	180,000	124,244	94,074	64,000	45,000	30,000	17,048	10,883
Georgia[2]	56,071	23,375	9,578	5,200	2,021	-	-	-
Kentucky[5]	45,000	15,700	-	-	-	-	-	-
Tennessee[6]	10,000	1,000	-	-	-	-	-	-
NEGRO								
Total	575,420	459,822	325,806	236,420	150,024	91,021	68,839	44,866
Maine[1]	458	475	300	-	-	-	-	-
New Hampshire[2]	541	654	600	550	500	200	170	150
Vermont[3]	50	25	-	-	-	-	-	-
Massachusetts[1,2]	4,822	4,754	4,566	4,075	3,035	2,780	2,150	1,310
Rhode Island[2]	2,671[7]	3,761	3,468	3,347	2,408	1,648	543	375
Connecticut[2]	5,885[7]	5,698	3,783	3,010	2,598	1,490	1,093	750
New York[2]	21,054	19,112	16,340	11,014	8,996	6,956	5,740	2,811
New Jersey[2]	10,460	8,220	6,567	5,354	4,366	3,008	2,385	1,332
Pennsylvania[2]	7,855	5,761	4,409	2,872	2,055	1,241	2,000	1,575
Delaware[2]	2,996	1,836	1,733	1,496	1,035	478	700	500
Maryland[2]	80,515	63,818	49,004	43,450	24,031	17,220	12,499	7,945
Virginia[2]	220,582	187,605	140,570	101,452	60,000	30,000	26,559	23,118
North Carolina[2]	91,000	69,600	33,554	19,800	11,000	6,000	3,000	900

[Continued]

★ 1748 ★

Estimated Population of American Colonies, 1610 to 1780 - I

[Continued]

Colony	1780	1770	1760	1750	1740	1730	1720	1710
South Carolina[2]	97,000	75,178	57,334	39,000	30,000	20,000	12,000	4,100
Georgia[2]	20,831	10,625	3,578	1,000	-	-	-	-
Kentucky[5]	7,200	2,500	-	-	-	-	-	-
Tennessee[6]	1,500	200	-	-	-	-	-	-

Source: "Estimated Population of American Colonies: 1610 to 1780." U.S. Bureau of the Census, *Historical Statistics of the United States: Colonial Times to 1970, Part II*, Bicentennial Edition, p. 1168. *Notes:* 1. For 1660-1750, Maine counties included with Massachusetts. Maine was a part of Massachusetts until it became a separate State in 1820. 2. One of the original 13 States. 3. Admitted to statehood in 1791. 4. Plymouth became a part of the Province of Massachusetts in 1691. 5. Admitted to statehood in 1792. 6. Admitted to statehood in 1796. 7. Includes some Indians. 8. Includes 20 Negroes.

★ 1749 ★

Geographical Areas: Colonies

Estimated Population of American Colonies, 1610 to 1780 - II

Colony	1700	1690	1680	1670	1660	1650	1640	1630
WHITE AND NEGRO								
Total	250,888	210,372	151,507	111,935	75,058	50,368	26,634	4,646
Maine[1]	-	-	-	-	-	1,000	900	400
New Hampshire[2]	4,958	4,164	2,047	1,805	1,555	1,305	1,055	500
Vermont[3]	-	-	-	-	-	-	-	-
Plymouth[4]	-	7,424	6,400	5,333	1,980	1,566	1,020	390
Massachusetts[1,2,4]	55,941	49,504	39,752	30,000	20,082	14,037	8,932	506
Rhode Island[2]	5,894	4,224	3,017	2,155	1,539	785	300	-
Connecticut[2]	25,970	21,645	17,246	12,603	7,980	4,139	1,472	-
New York[2]	19,107	13,909	9,830	5,754	4,936	4,116	1,930	350
New Jersey[2]	14,010	8,000	3,400	1,000	-	-	-	-
Pennsylvania[2]	17,950	11,450	680	-	-	-	-	-
Delaware[2]	2,470	1,482	1,005	700	540	185	-	-
Maryland[2]	29,604	24,024	17,904	13,226	8,426	4,504	583	-
Virginia[2]	58,560	53,046	43,596	35,309	27,020	18,731	10,442	2,500
North Carolina[2]	10,720	7,600	6,540	3,850	1,000	-	-	-
South Carolina[2]	5,704	3,900	1,200	200	-	-	-	-
Georgia[2]	-	-	-	-	-	-	-	-
Kentucky[5]	-	-	-	-	-	-	-	-
Tennessee[6]	-	-	-	-	-	-	-	-
NEGRO								
Total	27,817	16,729	6,971	4,535	2,920	1,600	597	60
Maine[1]	-	-	-	-	-	-	-	-
New Hampshire[2]	130	100	75	65	50	40	30	-
Vermont[3]	-	-	-	-	-	-	-	-

[Continued]

★ 1749 ★

Estimated Population of American Colonies, 1610 to 1780 - II

[Continued]

Colony	1700	1690	1680	1670	1660	1650	1640	1630
Massachusetts[1,2]	800	400	170	160	422	295	150	-
Rhode Island[2]	300	250	175	115	65	25	-	-
Connecticut[2]	450	200	50	35	25	20	15	-
New York[2]	2,256	1,670	1,200	690	600	500	232	10
New Jersey[2]	840	450	200	60	-	-	-	-
Pennsylvania[2]	430	270	25	-	-	-	-	-
Delaware[2]	135	82	55	40	30	15	-	-
Maryland[2]	3,227	2,162	1,611	1,190	758	300	20	-
Virginia[2]	16,390	9,345	3,000	2,000	950	405	150	50
North Carolina[2]	415	300	210	150	20	-	-	-
South Carolina[2]	2,444	1,500	200	30	-	-	-	-

Source: "Estimated Population of American Colonies: 1610 to 1780." U.S. Bureau of the Census, *Historical Statistics of the United States: Colonial Times to 1970, Part II*, Bicentennial Edition, p. 1168. *Notes:* 1. For 1660-1750, Maine counties included with Massachusetts. Maine was a part of Massachusetts until it became a separate State in 1820. 2. One of the original 13 States. 3. Admitted to statehood in 1791. 4. Plymouth became a part of the Province of Massachusetts in 1691. 5. Admitted to statehood in 1792. 6. Admitted to statehood in 1796. 7. Includes some Indians. 8. Includes 20 Negroes.

Geographical Areas: Counties

★ 1750 ★

Area of Counties and Number and Increase of the Black Population by Percentage, 1900-1920 - I

RATE OF INCREASE: 1900-1910	COUNTIES OF COMBINATIONS OF COUNTIES IN WHICH THE NEGRO POPULATION INCREASED OR DECREASED, 1900 TO 1910, BY PERCENTAGE SPECIFIED							
	The South	South Atlantic division	East South Central division	West South Central division	South Atlantic division: Delaware	South Atlantic division: Maryland	South Atlantic division: District of Columbia	South Atlantic division: Virginia
	INCREASE OF NEGRO POPULATION: 1900 TO 1910							
Total, all counties	826,458	383,471	152,627	290,360	484	-2,814	7,744	10,374
Counties having less than 100 Negroes at each census	-85	-186	18	83	-	-	-	6
Area of increasing Negro population	1,056,638	455,093	262,965	338,580	1,176	7,660	7,744	37,751
Increase above average-								
Increase 18 per cent or more	750,132	297,665	187,876	264,591	-	-	-	20,165
Increase 13 to 18 per cent	134,256	65,017	25,785	43,454	1,176	-	-	5,042
Increase 10.5 to 13 per cent	36,928	23,674	4,887	8,367	-	550	-	7,752
Increase below average-								
Increase 8 to 10.5 per cent	54,371	22,507	23,136	8,728	-	1,465	7,744	-
Increase 2.5 to 8 per cent	75,396	42,985	20,446	11,965	-	5,491	-	3,767
Increase 0.0 to 2.5 per cent	5,555	3,245	835	1,475	-	154	-	1,025
Area of decreasing Negro population	-230,095	-71,436	-110,365	-48,303	-692	-10,474	-	-27,383
Decrease 0.0 to 2.5 per cent	-4,962	-2,933	-1,279	-750	-177	-217	-	-898
Decrease 2.5 to 7.5 per cent	-41,892	-16,471	-19,473	-5,948	-515	-629	-	-5,697
Decrease 7.5 per cent or more	-183,241	-52,032	-89,604	-41,605	-	-9,628	-	-20,788

[Continued]

★ 1750 ★

Area of Counties and Number and Increase of the Black Population by Percentage, 1900-1920 - I

[Continued]

RATE OF INCREASE: 1900-1910	The South	South Atlantic division	East South Central division	West South Central division	South Atlantic division: Delaware	Maryland	District of Columbia	Virginia
	COUNTIES OF COMBINATIONS OF COUNTIES IN WHICH THE NEGRO POPULATION INCREASED OR DECREASED, 1900 TO 1910, BY PERCENTAGE SPECIFIED							
Area increasing more than the average (10.5 per cent or more)	921,316	386,356	218,548	316,412	1,176	550	-	32,959
Area increasing less than the average, or decreasing	-94,773	-2,699	-65,939	-26,135	-692	-3,364	7,744	-22,591
Area of relatively rapid increase 913 per cent or more)	884,388	362,682	213,661	308,045	1,176	-	-	25,207
Area of approximately average increase (8 to 13 per cent)	91,229	46,181	28,023	17,095	-	2,015	7,744	7,752
Area of low increase (less than 8 per cent) or decrease	-149,144	-25,206	-89,075	-34,863	-692	-4,829	-	-22,591
Area of approximately stationary population (increase or decrease less than 2.5 per cent)	593	312	-444	725	-177	-63	-	127
Area decreasing more than 2.5 per cent	-225,133	-68,503	-109,077	-47,553	-515	-10,257	-	-26,485
	PERCENTAGE OF INCREASE OF NEGRO POPULATION: 1900 TO 1910							
Total, all counties	10.4	10.3	6.1	17.1	1.6	-1.2	8.9	1.6
Counties having less than 100 Negroes at each census	-3.1	-30.5	3.1	5.2	-	-	-	2
Area of increasing Negro population	19.4	16.3	18.9	26.9	17.4	7.1	8.9	11.1
Increase above average-								
Increase 18 per cent or more	42.1	34.1	43.1	56.1	-	-	-	21.4
Increase 13 to 18 per cent	15.6	15.6	15.4	15.8	17.4	-	-	16.8
Increase 10.5 to 13 per cent	11.7	11.7	11.2	12.0	-	13.0	-	11.2
Increase below average-								
Increase 8 to 10.5 per cent	8.8	8.9	8.8	8.9	-	8.4	8.9	-
Increase 2.5 to 8 per cent	5.4	5.7	5.0	5.4	-	6.9	-	4.6
Increase 0.0 to 2.5 per cent	1.2	1.2	1.1	1.2	-	2.2	-	1.6
Area of decreasing Negro population	-9.3	-7.6	-10.0	-11.1	-2.9	-8.2	-	-8.5
Decrease 0.0 to 2.5 per cent	-1.3	-1.4	-1.2	-0.9	-2.3	-0.9	-	-1.8
Decrease 2.5 to 7.5 per cent	-5.0	-5.3	-4.7	-5.0	-3.2	-4.5	-	-5.3
Decrease 7.5 per cent or more	-14.7	-12.3	-15.2	-17.6	-	-10.8	-	-12.6
Area increasing more than the average (10.5 per cent or more)	31.1	25.9	33.8	38.7	17.4	13.0	-	17.1
Area increasing less than the average, or decreasing	-1.9	-0.1	-3.6	-3.0	-2.9	-1.5	8.9	-4.8
Area of relatively rapid increase 913 per cent or more)	33.5	28.1	35.4	41.2	17.4	-	-	20.3
Area of approximately average increase (8 to 13 per cent)	9.8	10.1	9.1	10.2	-	9.3	8.9	11.2
Area of low increase (less than 8 per cent) or decrease	-3.4	-1.3	-5.6	-4.5	-2.9	-2.3	-	-4.8
Area of approximately stationary population (increase or decrease less than 2.5 per cent)	0.1	0.1	-0.2	0.4	-2.3	-0.2	-	0.1
Area decreasing more than 2.5 per cent	-10.8	-9.3	-10.9	-13.4	-3.2	-9.9	-	-9.7

Source: "Area of Counties, and Number and Increase of the Negro Population, Classified by Percentage." U.S. Bureau of the Census, *Negro Population, 1790-1915,* p. 122. *Notes:* 1. In cases where boundaries of counties were changed during the decade 1900-1910, county areas and populations have been combined and computations made for the combined area. The entire state of Oklahoma is classified as a single area. 2. Per cent not shown where base is less than 100.

★ 1751 ★

Geographical Areas: Counties

Area of Counties and Number and Increase of the Black Population by Percentage, 1900-1920 - II

RATE OF INCREASE: 1900-1910	South Atlantic division: West Virginia	North Carolina	South Carolina	Georgia	Florida	East South Central division: Kentucky	Tennessee	Alabama	Mississippi
	COUNTIES OF COMBINATIONS OF COUNTIES IN WHICH THE NEGRO POPULATION INCREASED OR DECREASED, 1900 TO 1910, BY PERCENTAGE SPECIFIED								
	INCREASE OF NEGRO POPULATION: 1900 TO 1910								
Total, all counties	20,674	73,374	53,522	142,174	77,939	-23,050	-7,155	80,975	101,857
Counties having less than 100 Negroes at each census	-104	-26	-	-62	-	-46	17	47	-
Area of increasing Negro population	22,921	79,891	65,960	151,318	80,672	7,009	23,459	103,356	129,141
Increase above average-									
Increase 18 per cent or more	22,321	47,144	19,725	113,539	75,221	3,961	9,863	80,100	93,952
Increase 13 to 18 per cent	245	19,152	21,667	15,757	1,978	-	215	7,255	18,315
Increase 10.5 to 13 per cent	149	1,725	9,198	4,055	245	356	90	2,046	2,395

[Continued]

★ 1751 ★

Area of Counties and Number and Increase of the Black Population by Percentage, 1900-1920 - II

[Continued]

RATE OF INCREASE: 1900-1910	COUNTIES OF COMBINATIONS OF COUNTIES IN WHICH THE NEGRO POPULATION INCREASED OR DECREASED, 1900 TO 1910, BY PERCENTAGE SPECIFIED								
	South Atlantic division					East South Central division			
	West Virginia	North Carolina	South Carolina	Georgia	Florida	Kentucky	Tennessee	Alabama	Mississippi
Increase below average-									
Increase 8 to 10.5 per cent	119	3,607	2,940	4,842	1,790	651	7,609	8,678	6,198
Increase 2.5 to 8 per cent	9	7,798	12,394	12,269	1,257	2,035	5,670	5,235	7,506
Increase 0.0 to 2.5 per cent	78	465	486	856	181	6	12	42	775
Area of decreasing Negro population	-2,143	-6,491	-12,438	-9,082	-2,733	-30,013	-30,631	-22,428	-27,284
Decrease 0.0 to 2.5 per cent	-5	-523	-232	-856	-25	-54	-273	-604	-348
Decrease 2.5 to 7.5 per cent	-70	-2,431	-5,048	-1,962	-119	-2,452	-,4017	-8,326	-4,678
Decrease 7.5 per cent or more	-2,068	-3,537	-7,158	-6,264	-2,589	-27,507	-26,341	-13,498	-22,258
Area increasing more than the average (10.5 per cent or more)	22,715	68,021	50,140	133,351	77,444	4,317	10,168	89,401	114,662
Area increasing less than the average, or decreasing	-1,937	5,379	3,382	8,855	495	-27,321	-17,340	-8,473	-12,805
Area of relatively rapid increase 913 per cent or more)	22,566	66,296	40,942	129,296	77,199	3,961	10,078	87,355	112,267
Area of approximately average increase (8 to 13 per cent)	268	5,332	12,138	8,897	2,035	1,007	7,699	10,724	8,593
Area of low increase (less than 8 per cent) or decrease	-2,056	1,772	442	4,043	-1,295	-27,972	-24,949	-17,151	-19,003
Area of approximately stationary population (increase or decrease less than 2.5 per cent)	73	-58	254	-	156	-48	-261	-562	427
Area decreasing more than 2.5 per cent	-2,138	-5,968	-12,206	-8,226	-2,708	-29,959	-30,358	-21,824	-26,936
	PERCENTAGE OF INCREASE OF NEGRO POPULATION: 1900 TO 1910								
Total, all counties	47.5	11.7	6.8	13.7	33.8	-8.1	-1.5	9.8	11.2
Counties having less than 100 Negroes at each census	-24.2	[2]	-	-41.9	-	-11.5	10.0	[2]	-
Area of increasing Negro population	73.2	15.5	10.5	17.4	40.8	10.2	10.8	21.9	20.4
Increase above average-									
Increase 18 per cent or more	99.3	27.6	22.9	28.9	68.7	39.2	43.3	41.6	44.7
Increase 13 to 18 per cent	14.5	16.1	15.2	15.0	16.1	15.8	15.7	16.3	15.1
Increase 10.5 to 13 per cent	11.1	11.8	11.8	12.5	10.9	10.8	12.3	11.6	14.0
Increase below average-									
Increase 8 to 10.5 per cent	8.6	9.3	9.1	8.5	8.9	8.9	8.3	9.2	8.8
Increase 2.5 to 8 per cent	7.3	5.5	5.6	6.1	4.3	4.3	5.7	5.0	4.8
Increase 0.0 to 2.5 per cent	1.8	1.5	0.7	1.0	0.7	0.4	0.8	0.2	1.4
Area of decreasing Negro population	-18.2	-6.0	-8.0	-5.6	-8.3	-13.9	-11.7	-6.3	-10.0
Decrease 0.0 to 2.5 per cent	-1.7	-1.4	-1.2	-1.3	-1.1	-1.6	-1.1	-1.3	-1.1
Decrease 2.5 to 7.5 per cent	-3.0	-6.1	-5.9	-4.2	-4.8	-4.6	-5.0	-4.3	-5.4
Decrease 7.5 per cent or more	-22.7	-11.7	-14.4	-12.4	-9.2	-17.3	-16.6	-11.5	-14.5
Area increasing more than the average (10.5 per cent or more)	89.1	22.4	16.4	25.1	62.4	32.2	40.9	35.1	32.4
Area increasing less than the average, or decreasing	-11.0	1.7	0.7	1.8	0.5	-10.1	-3.8	-1.5	-2.3
Area of relatively rapid increase 913 per cent or more)	93.4	22.9	18.0	26.0	63.4	39.2	41.7	36.8	33.8
Area of approximately average increase (8 to 13 per cent)	9.8	10.0	11.0	10.0	9.1	9.5	8.3	9.6	9.3
Area of low increase (less than 8 per cent) or decrease	-12.7	0.6	0.1	0.9	-1.5	-10.6	-6.9	-3.6	-3.9
Area of approximately stationary population (increase or decrease less than 2.5 per cent)	1.6	-0.1	0.3	-	0.6	-1.0	-1.0	-0.9	0.5
Area decreasing more than 2.5 per cent	-18.6	-8.6	-9.0	-8.5	-8.9	-14.1	-12.8	-7.0	-11.2

Source: "Area of Counties, and Number and Increase of the Negro Population, Classified by Percentage." U.S. Bureau of the Census, *Negro Population, 1790-1915,* p. 122. *Notes:* 1. In cases where boundaries of counties were changed during the decade 1900-1910, county areas and populations have been combined and computations made for the combined area. The entire state of Oklahoma is classified as a single area. 2. Per cent not shown where base is less than 100.

★ 1752 ★

Geographical Areas: Counties

Area of Counties and Number and Increase of the Black Population by Percentage, 1900-1920 - III

RATE OF INCREASE: 1900-1910	COUNTIES OF COMBINATIONS OF COUNTIES IN WHICH THE NEGRO POPULATION INCREASED OR DECREASED, 1900 TO 1910, BY PERCENTAGE SPECIFIED			
	Arkansas	Louisiana	Oklahoma	Texas
	INCREASE OF NEGRO POPULATION: 1900 TO 1910			
Total, all counties	76,035	63,070	81,928	69,327
Counties having less than 100 Negroes at each census	-96	-	-	179
Area of increasing Negro population	79,452	77,609	81,928	99,591
Increase above average-				
Increase 18 per cent or more	63,753	34,242	81,928	84,668
Increase 13 to 18 per cent	12,530	26,867	-	4,057
Increase 10.5 to 13 per cent	755	4,546	-	3,066
Increase below average-				
Increase 8 to 10.5 per cent	801	5,421	-	2,506
Increase 2.5 to 8 per cent	1,417	5,862	-	4,686
Increase 0.0 to 2.5 per cent	196	671	-	608
Area of decreasing Negro population	-3,321	-14,539	-	-30,443
Decrease 0.0 to 2.5 per cent	-53	-367	-	-330
Decrease 2.5 to 7.5 per cent	-719	-1,505	-	-3,724
Decrease 7.5 per cent or more	-2,549	-12,667	-	-26,389
Area increasing more than the average (10.5 per cent or more)	77,038	65,655	81,928	91,791
Area increasing less than the average, or decreasing	-907	-2,585	-	-22,643
Area of relatively rapid increase 913 per cent or more)	76,283	61,109	81,928	88,725
Area of approximately average increase (8 to 13 per cent)	1,556	9,967	-	5,572
Area of low increase (less than 8 per cent) or decrease	-1,708	-8,006	-	-25,149
Area of approximately stationary population (increase or decrease less than 2.5 per cent)	143	304	-	278
Area decreasing more than 2.5 per cent	-3,268	-14,172	-	-30,113
	PERCENTAGE OF INCREASE OF NEGRO POPULATION: 1900 TO 1910			
Total, all counties	20.7	9.7	147.1	11.2
Counties having less than 100 Negroes at each census	-27.2	-	-	14.5
Area of increasing Negro population	23.5	15.5	147.1	27.6
Increase above average-				
Increase 18 per cent or more	31.7	57.2	147.1	54.6
Increase 13 to 18 per cent	15.7	15.8	-	15.7
Increase 10.5 to 13 per cent	12.7	11.8	-	12.1
Increase below average-				
Increase 8 to 10.5 per cent	9.1	8.7	-	9.3
Increase 2.5 to 8 per cent	5.7	5.2	-	5.6
Increase 0.0 to 2.5 per cent	1.1	1.1	-	1.4
Area of decreasing Negro population	-11.9	-9.8	-	-11.8
Decrease 0.0 to 2.5 per cent	-0.9	-1.2	-	-0.7
Decrease 2.5 to 7.5 per cent	-6.0	-5.4	-	-4.8
Decrease 7.5 per cent or more	-25.3	-14.0	-	-19.5
Area increasing more than the average (10.5 per cent or more)	26.9	24.5	147.1	44.5
Area increasing less than the average, or decreasing	-1.1	-0.7	-	-5.5
Area of relatively rapid increase 913 per cent or more)	27.2	26.6	147.1	49.0
Area of approximately average increase (8 to 13 per cent)	10.5	9.9	-	10.6
Area of low increase (less than 8 per cent) or decrease	-2.4	-2.5	-	-6.5

[Continued]

★ 1752 ★

Area of Counties and Number and Increase of the Black Population by Percentage, 1900-1920 - III

[Continued]

RATE OF INCREASE: 1900-1910	COUNTIES OF COMBINATIONS OF COUNTIES IN WHICH THE NEGRO POPULATION INCREASED OR DECREASED, 1900 TO 1910, BY PERCENTAGE SPECIFIED			
	Arkansas	Louisiana	Oklahoma	Texas
Area of approximately stationary population (increase or decrease less than 2.5 per cent)	0.6	0.3	-	0.3
Area decreasing more than 2.5 per cent	-14.7	-11.9	-	-14.1

Source: "Area of Counties, and Number and Increase of the Negro Population, Classified by Percentage." U.S. Bureau of the Census, *Negro Population, 1790-1915,* p. 122. *Notes:* 1. In cases where boundaries of counties were changed during the decade 1900-1910, county areas and populations have been combined and computations made for the combined area. The entire state of Oklahoma is classified as a single area. 2. Per cent not shown where base is less than 100.

★ 1753 ★

Geographical Areas: Counties

Distribution of Counties According to County Type and Percent Black of County Population, 1930 - I

County type	Total counties given	Percent Negroes are of county population									
		Under 10.0		10.0-19.9		20.0-9.9		30.0-39.9		40.0-49.9	
		Number	Percent	Number	Percent	Number	Percent	Number	Percent	Number	Percent
Economy											
Non-farm	124	16	12.9	27	21.8	38	30.6	25	20.1	11	8.9
Farm other than cotton	314	65	20.7	69	21.9	54	17.2	50	15.9	48	15.3
Cotton	528	52	9.9	78	14.8	77	14.6	19	178.2	75	14.2
Industrialization[1]											
Non-farm	124	16	12.9	27	21.8	38	36.6	25	26.1	11	8.9
Industrial farm	364	46	12.6	83	22.8	65	17.9	64	17.6	63	17.3
Non-industrial farm	478	71	14.8	64	13.4	66	13.8	77	16.1	60	12.5
Urbanization											
Metropolitan	66	9	13.6	12	18.1	20	30.3	13	19.7	8	12.1
Other non-farm[2]	58	7	12.1	15	25.8	18	31.0	12	20.7	3	5.1
Farm:											
City, 10,000-24,999 population	78	7	9.0	17	21.8	11	14.1	15	19.2	15	19.2
Town, 2,500-9,999 population	335	40	11.9	76	22.7	57	17.0	52	15.5	48	14.3
Rural	429	70	16.3	54	12.6	63	14.7	74	17.2	60	14.0
Total	966	133	13.8	174	18.0	169	17.5	166	17.2	134	13.9

Source: "Distribution of Counties According to Percent Negroes Are of County Population and County Type." U.S. Office of Education, *Socio-Economic Approach to Educational Problems,* Edited by Ina Corinne Brown, p. 126. *Notes:* 1. The non-farm counties in this group include metropolitan counties having cities of 25,000 population or more and other non-farm counties having no city of 25,000 population or more, but less than 25 percent of gainfully employed males in agriculture. The industrial farm counties include those with retail trade centers and those with at least 10 percent of the gainfully employed males in mining and manufacturing. 2. Counties having no city of 25,000 population or more, but less than 25 percent of gainfully employed males in agriculture.

★ 1754 ★

Geographical Areas: Counties

Distribution of Counties According to County Type and Percent Black of County Population, 1930 - II

County type	Percent Negroes are of county population								Median percent Negroes
	50.0-59.9		60.0-69.9		70.0-79.9		80.0-89.9		
	Number	Percent	Number	Percent	Number	Percent	Number	Percent	
Economy									
Non-farm	6	4.8	1	0.8	...	...	...	...	25.0
Farm other than cotton	19	6.0	7	2.2	2	0.6	...	...	24.3
Cotton	57	10.8	56	10.6	37	7.0	5	0.9	36.3
Industrialization[1]									
Non-farm	6	4.8	1	.8	...	...	...	...	25.0
Industrial farm	20	5.4	17	4.7	6	1.6	...	...	28.1
Non-industrial farm	56	11.7	46	9.6	33	6.9	5	1.0	34.9
Urbanization									
Metropolitan	4	6.1	...	...	...	...	...	...	26.0
Other non-farm[2]	2	3.4	1	1.7	...	...	...	...	23.9
Farm:									
City, 10,000-24,999 population	6	7.7	3	3.8	4	5.1	...	...	32.7
Town, 2,500-9,999 population	19	8.7	20	5.9	12	3.5	1	.3	29.0
Rural	41	9.6	40	9.3	23	5.3	4	.9	33.7
Total	82	8.5	64	6.6	39	4.0	5	.5	20.4

Source: "Distribution of Counties According to Percent Negroes Are of County Population and County Type." U.S. Office of Education, *Socio-Economic Approach to Educational Problems,* Edited by Ina Corinne Brown, p. 126. *Notes:* 1. The non-farm counties in this group include metropolitan counties having cities of 25,000 population or more and other non-farm counties having no city of 25,000 population or more, but less than 25 percent of gainfully employed males in agriculture. The industrial farm counties include those with retail trade centers and those with at least 10 percent of the gainfully employed males in mining and manufacturing. 2. Counties having no city of 25,000 population or more, but less than 25 percent of gainfully employed males in agriculture.

★ 1755 ★

Geographical Areas: Counties

Distribution of Counties According to County Type and Percent Black of Urban Population, 1930 - I

County type	Total counties given	Percent of Negro population that is urban									
		0.0		0.1-9.9		10.0-19.9		20.0-29.9		30.9-39.9	
		Number	Percent	Number	Percent	Number	Percent	Number	Percent	Number	Percent
Economy											
Non-farm	124	16	12.9	4	3.2	2	1.6	5	4.0	9	7.3
Farm other than cotton	314	167	53.1	11	3.5	25	7.8	45	14.3	22	7.0
Cotton	528	256	48.4	50	9.5	95	18.0	57	10.7	35	6.6

[Continued]

★ 1755 ★

Distribution of Counties According to County Type and Percent Black of Urban Population, 1930 - I

[Continued]

County type	Total counties given	Percent of Negro population that is urban									
		0.0		0.1-9.9		10.0-19.9		20.0-29.9		30.9-39.9	
		Number	Percent	Number	Percent	Number	Percent	Number	Percent	Number	Percent
Industrialization[1]											
Non-farm	124	16	2.9	4	3.2	2	1.6	5	4.0	9	7.3
Industrial farm	364	87	23.9	20	5.4	75	20.6	74	20.3	44	12.1
Non-industrial farm	478	336	70.2	41	8.6	45	9.4	28	5.9	13	2.7
Urbanization											
Metropolitan	66	...	...	...	...	...	...	...	...	4	6.1
Other non-farm[2]	58	16	27.6	4	6.9	2	3.4	5	8.6	5	8.6
Farm:											
City, 10,000-24,999 population	78	...	...	...	...	10	12.8	20	25.6	17	21.8
Town, 2,500-9,999 population	335	...	...	55	16.4	110	32.8	82	24.5	40	11.9
Rural	429	423	98.6	6	1.4	...	...	...	...	...	...
Total	966	439	45.4	65	6.7	122	12.6	107	11.1	66	6.8

Source: "Distribution of Counties According to Percent of Negro Population That is Urban and County Type." U.S. Office of Education, *Socio-Economic Approach to Educational Problems,* Edited by Ina Corinne Brown, p. 126. *Notes:* 1. The non-farm counties in this group include metropolitan counties having cities of 25,000 population or more and other non-farm counties having no city of 25,000 population or more, but less than 25 percent of gainfully employed males in agriculture. The industrial farm counties include those with retail trade centers and those with at least 10 percent of the gainfully employed males in mining and manufacturing. 2. Counties having no city of 25,000 population or more, but less than 25 percent of gainfully employed males in agriculture.

★ 1756 ★

Geographical Areas: Counties

Distribution of Counties According to County Type and Percent Black of Urban Population, 1930 - II

County type	Percent of Negro population that is urban											
	40.0-49.9		50.0-59.9		60.0-69.9		70.0-79.9		80.0-89.9		90.0-100.0	
	Number	Percent	Number	Percent	Number	Percent	Number	Percent	Number	Percent	Number	Percent
Economy												
Non-farm	10	8.0	14	11.2	12	9.7	16	12.9	23	18.5	13	10.4
Farm other than cotton	13	4.1	19	6.0	9	2.9	2	.6	1	.3	...	...
Cotton	18	3.4	9	1.7	5	.9	2	.4	1	.2	...	...
Industrialization[1]												
Non-farm	10	8.0	14	11.2	12	9.7	16	12.9	23	18.5	13	10.4
Industrial farm	25	6.9	22	6.0	11	3.0	4	1.1	2	.5	...	...
Non-industrial farm	6	1.3	6	1.3	3	.6	...	...	...	...	...	...
Urbanization												
Metropolitan	3	4.5	10	15.1	6	9.1	10	15.1	21	31.8	12	18.2
Other non-farm[2]	7	12.1	4	6.9	6	10.3	6	10.3	2	3.4	1	1.7
Farm:												
City, 10,000-24,999 population	15	19.2	7	8.9	6	7.7	1	1.3	2	2.6	...	...
Town, 2,500-9,999 population	16	4.8	21	6.3	8	2.4	3	.9	...	...	...	...

[Continued]

★ 1756 ★

Distribution of Counties According to County Type and Percent Black of Urban Population, 1930 - II

[Continued]

County type	Percent of Negro population that is urban											
	40.0-49.9		50.0-59.9		60.0-69.9		70.0-79.9		80.0-89.9		90.0-100.0	
	Number	Percent	Number	Percent	Number	Percent	Number	Percent	Number	Percent	Number	Percent
Rural	...	...	...	...	...	...	...	...	...	...	...	...
Total	41	4.2	42	4.3	26	2.7	20	2.0	25	2.6	13	1.3

Source: "Distribution of Counties According to Percent of Negro Population That is Urban and County Type." U.S. Office of Education, *Socio-Economic Approach to Educational Problems,* Edited by Ina Corinne Brown, p. 126. *Notes:* 1. The non-farm counties in this group include metropolitan counties having cities of 25,000 population or more and other non-farm counties having no city of 25,000 population or more, but less than 25 percent of gainfully employed males in agriculture. The industrial farm counties include those with retail trade centers and those with at least 10 percent of the gainfully employed males in mining and manufacturing. 2. Counties having no city of 25,000 population or more, but less than 25 percent of gainfully employed males in agriculture.

★ 1757 ★

Geographical Areas: Counties

Distribution of Counties According to County Type and Percent Black of Urban Population, 1930 - III

County type	Percent of counties having some Negro population urban
Economy	
Non-farm	87.1
Farm other than cotton	46.9
Cotton	51.6
Industrialization[1]	
Non-farm	87.1
Industrial farm	76.1
Non-industrial farm	29.8
Urbanization	
Metropolitan	100.0
Other non-farm[2]	72.4
Farm:	
City, 10,000-24,999 population	100.0
Town, 2,500-9,999 population	100.0

[Continued]

★ 1757 ★

Distribution of Counties According to County Type and Percent Black of Urban Population, 1930 - III

[Continued]

County type	Percent of counties having some Negro population urban
Rural	1.4
Total	54.6

Source: "Distribution of Counties According to Percent of Negro Population That is Urban and County Type." U.S. Office of Education, *Socio-Economic Approach to Educational Problems,* Edited by Ina Corinne Brown, p. 126. *Notes:* 1. The non-farm counties in this group include metropolitan counties having cities of 25,000 population or more and other non-farm counties having no city of 25,000 population or more, but less than 25 percent of gainfully employed males in agriculture. The industrial farm counties include those with retail trade centers and those with at least 10 percent of the gainfully employed males in mining and manufacturing. 2. Counties having no city of 25,000 population or more, but less than 25 percent of gainfully employed males in agriculture.

★ 1758 ★

Geographical Areas: Counties

Distribution of Counties According to Percent Change in Black Population and County Type, 1920-1930 - I

County type	Total counties given	Percent change in Negro population (1920-30) Decreased							
		30.0 or over		20.0-29.9		10.0-19.9		0.0-0.9	
		Number	Percent	Number	Percent	Number	Percent	Number	Percent
Economy									
Non-farm	116	2	1.7	1	0.9	9	7.7	11	9.5
Farm other than cotton	307	14	4.5	42	13.7	75	24.4	70	22.8
Cotton	521	39	7.5	44	8.4	84	16.1	127	24.4
Industrialization[1]									
Non-farm	116	2	1.7	1	.9	9	7.7	11	9.5
Industrial farm	358	16	4.5	25	7.0	57	15.9	96	26.8
Non-industrial farm	470	37	7.9	61	13.0	102	21.7	101	21.5
Urbanization									
Metropolitan	66	...	...	...	...	3	4.5	6	9.1
Other non-farm[2]	50	2	4.0	1	2.0	6	12.0	5	10.0
Farm:									
City, 10,000-24,999 population	78	...	...	4	5.1	5	6.4	20	25.6

[Continued]

★ 1758 ★

Distribution of Counties According to Percent Change in Black Population and County Type, 1920-1930 - I

[Continued]

County type	Total counties given	Percent change in Negro population (1920-30) Decreased							
		30.0 or over		20.0-29.9		10.0-19.9		0.0-0.9	
		Number	Percent	Number	Percent	Number	Percent	Number	Percent
Town, 2,500-9,999 population	331	13	3.9	23	6.9	67	20.2	83	25.1
Rural	419	40	9.5	59	14.1	87	20.8	94	22.4
Total	944	55	5.8	87	9.2	168	17.8	208	22.0

Source: "Distribution of Counties According to Percent Change in Negro Population (1920-30) and County Type." U.S. Office of Education, *Socio- Economic Approach to Educational Problems,* Edited by Ina Corinne Brown, p. 125. *Notes:* 1. The non-farm counties in this group include metropolitan counties having cities of 25,000 population or more and other non-farm counties having no city of 25,000 population or more, but less than 25 percent of gainfully employed males in agriculture. The industrial farm counties include those with retail trade centers and those with at least 10 percent of the gainfully employed males in mining and manufacturing. 2. Counties having no city of 25,000 population or more, but less than 25 percent of gainfully employed males in agriculture.

★ 1759 ★

Geographical Areas: Counties

Distribution of Counties According to Percent Change in Black Population and County Type, 1920-1930 - II

County type	Percent change in Negro population (1920-30) Increased											
	0.0-9.9		10.0-19.9		20.0-29.9		30.0-39.9		40.0-49.9		50.0 or over	
	Number	Percent	Number	Percent	Number	Percent	Number	Percent	Number	Percent	Number	Percent
Economy												
Non-farm	18	15.5	15	12.9	16	13.8	11	9.5	8	6.9	25	21.6
Farm other than cotton	43	14.0	30	9.8	17	5.5	2	.7	4	1.3	10	3.3
Cotton	103	19.8	60	11.5	30	5.8	18	3.4	4	.8	12	2.3
Industrialization[1]												
Non-farm	18	15.5	15	12.9	16	13.8	11	9.5	8	6.9	25	21.6
Industrial farm	60	16.7	46	12.8	29	8.1	11	3.1	6	1.7	12	3.4
Non-industrial farm	86	18.3	44	9.4	18	3.8	9	1.9	2	.4	10	2.1
Urbanization												
Metropolitan	10	15.2	10	15.2	9	13.6	6	9.1	5	7.6	17	25.7
Other non-farm[2]	8	16.0	5	10.0	7	14.0	5	10.0	3	6.0	8	16.0
Farm:												
City, 10,000-24,999 population	19	24.4	7	9.0	12	15.4	5	6.4	3	3.8	3	3.8
Town, 2,500-9,999 population	58	17.5	46	13.9	19	5.7	6	1.8	2	.6	14	4.2
Rural	69	16.5	37	8.8	16	3.8	9	2.1	3	.7	5	1.2
Total	164	17.4	105	11.1	63	6.7	31	3.3	16	1.7	47	5.0

Source: "Distribution of Counties According to Percent Change in Negro Population (1920-30) and County Type." U.S. Office of Education, *Socio- Economic Approach to Educational Problems,* Edited by Ina Corinne Brown, p. 125. *Notes:* 1. The non-farm counties in this group include metropolitan counties having cities of 25,000 population or more and other non-farm counties having no city of 25,000 population or more, but less than 25 percent of gainfully employed males in agriculture. The industrial farm counties include those with retail trade centers and those with at least 10 percent of the gainfully employed males in mining and manufacturing. 2. Counties having no city of 25,000 population or more, but less than 25 percent of gainfully employed males in agriculture.

★ 1760 ★

Geographical Areas: Counties

Distribution of Counties According to Percent Change in Black Population and County Type, 1920-1930 - III

County type	Percent change in Negro population (1920-30)	
	Median	Not given
Economy		
Non-farm	21.0	8
Farm other than cotton	-6.8	7
Cotton	-2.7	7
Industrialization[1]		
Non-farm	21.0	8
Industrial farm	-1.6	6
Non-industrial farm	-6.5	8
Urbanization		
Metropolitan	24.2	...
Other non-farm[2]	15.0	8
Farm:		
City, 10,000-24,999 population	5.3	...
Town, 2,500-9,999 population	-2.5	4
Rural	-7.5	10
Total	-2.2	22

Source: "Distribution of Counties According to Percent Change in Negro Population (1920-30) and County Type." U.S. Office of Education, *Socio- Economic Approach to Educational Problems,* Edited by Ina Corinne Brown, p. 125. *Notes:* 1. The non-farm counties in this group include metropolitan counties having cities of 25,000 population or more and other non-farm counties having no city of 25,000 population or more, but less than 25 percent of gainfully employed males in agriculture. The industrial farm counties include those with retail trade centers and those with at least 10 percent of the gainfully employed males in mining and manufacturing. 2. Counties having no city of 25,000 population or more, but less than 25 percent of gainfully employed males in agriculture.

★ 1761 ★

Geographical Areas: Counties

Distribution of Counties by State and County Types, 1930 - I

State	Total counties typed	Counties with 5 percent or more Negroes	County type Basic economy: Nonfarm		Farm: other than cotton		Farm: Cotton	
			Total counties	Counties with 5 percent Negroes	Total counties	Counties with 4 percent Negroes	Total counties	Counties with 4 percent Negroes
Alabama	67	61	3	3	1	1	63	57
Arkansas	75	45	3	3	8	1	64	41
Delaware	3	3	1	1	2	2	...	...
District of Columbia	1	1	1	1	...	...	...	...
Florida	67	66	24	24	32	32	11	10
Georgia	161	148	14	14	23	17	124	117
Kentucky	120	60	9	5	110	54	1	1
Louisiana	64	64	8	8	19	19	37	37
Maryland	23	19	5	3	18	16	...	...
Mississippi	82	82	6	6	3	3	73	73
North Carolina	100	86	10	10	61	47	29	29
Oklahoma	25	25	4	4	3	3	18	18
South Carolina	46	46	4	4	5	5	37	37
Tennessee	95	57	5	5	69	35	21	17
Texas	104	104	12	12	3	3	89	89
Virginia	100	84	12	12	86	70	2	2
West Virginia	15	15	9	9	6	6	...	...
Total	1,148	966	130	124	449	314	569	528

Source: "Distribution of Counties by States and County Types." U.S. Office of Education, *Socio-Economic Approach to Educational Problems,* Edited by Ina Corinne Brown, p. 156.

★ 1762 ★

Geographical Areas: Counties

Distribution of Counties by State and County Types, 1930 - II

State	County type Industrialization: Nonfarm		Industrial farm		Nonindustrial farm	
	Total counties	Counties with 5 percent Negroes	Total counties	Counties with 5 percent Negroes	Total counties	Counties with 5 percent Negroes
Alabama	3	3	24	23	40	35
Arkansas	3	3	28	15	44	27
Delaware	1	1	2	2	...	...
District of Columbia	1	1	...	...	...	...
Florida	24	24	29	29	14	13

[Continued]

★ 1762 ★

Distribution of Counties by State and County Types, 1930 - II

[Continued]

State	County type Industrialization					
	Nonfarm		Industrial farm		Nonindustrial farm	
	Total counties	Counties with 5 percent Negroes	Total counties	Counties with 5 percent Negroes	Total counties	Counties with 5 percent Negroes
Georgia	14	14	67	63	80	71
Kentucky	9	5	38	18	73	37
Louisiana	8	8	20	20	36	36
Maryland	5	3	12	10	6	6
Mississippi	6	6	17	17	59	59
North Carolina	10	10	50	45	40	31
Oklahoma	4	4	12	12	9	9
South Carolina	4	4	20	20	22	22
Tennessee	5	5	32	17	58	35
Texas	12	12	42	42	50	50
Virginia	12	12	35	25	53	47
West Virginia	9	9	6	6	...	...
Total	130	124	434	364	584	478

Source: "Distribution of Counties by States and County Types." U.S. Office of Education, *Socio-Economic Approach to Educational Problems,* Edited by Ina Corinne Brown, p. 156.

★ 1763 ★

Geographical Areas: Counties

Distribution of Counties by State and County Types, 1930 - III

State	County type Urbanization									
	Metropolitan		Other nonfarm		Farm: City, 10,000-24,999 population		Farm: Town, 2,500-9,999 population		Rural	
	Total counties	Counties with 5 percent Negroes	Total counties	Counties with 5 percent Negroes	Total counties	Counties with 5 percent Negroes	Total counties	Counties with 5 percent Negroes	Total counties	Counties with 5 percent Negroes
Alabama	3	3	...	...	8	8	23	20	33	30
Arkansas	2	2	1	1	5	4	36	25	31	13
Delaware	1	1	...	...	...	...	1	1	1	1
District of Columbia	1	1	...	...	...	...	...	...	...	...
Florida	7	7	17	17	4	4	15	15	24	23
Georgia	5	5	9	9	5	5	42	41	100	88
Kentucky	6	3	3	2	5	5	29	24	77	26
Louisiana	4	4	4	4	3	3	27	27	26	26
Maryland	3	1	2	2	2	2	9	8	7	6
Mississippi	2	2	4	4	8	8	22	22	46	46
North Carolina	7	7	3	3	13	13	32	31	45	32
Oklahoma	3	3	1	1	4	4	12	12	5	5
South Carolina	4	4	...	...	5	5	22	22	15	15
Tennessee	5	5	...	...	2	1	34	26	54	25
Texas	10	10	2	2	10	10	46	46	36	36
Virginia	6	6	6	6	5	5	17	14	66	53
West Virginia	2	2	7	7	1	1	1	1	4	4
Total	71	66	59	58	80	78	368	335	570	429

Source: "Distribution of Counties by States and County Types." U.S. Office of Education, *Socio-Economic Approach to Educational Problems,* Edited by Ina Corinne Brown, p. 156.

★ 1764 ★

Geographical Areas: Counties

Distribution of Counties by State and Percent Black of the County Population, 1930 - I

State	Total number of counties	Percent Negroes were of county population							
		50.0-9.9		10.0-19.9		20.0-29.9		30.0-39.9	
		Number	Percent	Number	Percent	Number	Percent	Number	Percent
Alabama	61	4	6.6	11	18.0	11	18.0	9	14.8
Arkansas	45	6	13.3	6	13.3	7	15.6	9	20.0
Delaware	3	...	...	2	66.7	1	33.3	...	...
District of Columbia	1	...	...	...	...	1	100.0	...	...
Florida	66	1	1.5	12	18.2	20	30.3	21	31.8
Georgia	148	10	6.8	16	10.8	16	10.8	32	21.6
Kentucky	60	26	43.3	28	46.7	5	8.3	1	1.7
Louisiana	64	1	1.6	5	7.8	16	25.0	15	23.4
Maryland	19	1	5.3	4	21.1	6	31.6	6	31.6
Mississippi	82	2	2.4	7	8.5	13	15.9	12	14.6
North Carolina	86	10	11.6	15	17.4	10	11.6	20	23.3
Oklahoma	25	11	44.0	7	28.0	6	24.0	1	4.0
South Carolina	46	...	...	2	4.3	5	10.9	3	6.5
Tennessee	57	24	42.1	15	26.3	9	15.8	5	8.8
Texas	103[1]	19	18.4	25	24.3	28	27.2	16	15.5
Virginia	84	7	8.3	14	16.7	16	19.0	15	17.9
West Virginia	15	9	60.0	5	33.3	1	6.7	...	...
Total	965	131	13.6	174	18.0	171	17.7	165	17.1

Source: "Distribution of Counties by States and Percent That Negroes Were of Total County Population in 1930." U.S. Office of Education, *Socio-Economic Approach to Educational Problems,* Edited by Ina Corinne Brown, p. 157. *Notes:* 1. Does not include King County in which there were fewer than 100 Negroes.

★ 1765 ★

Geographical Areas: Counties

Distribution of Counties by State and Percent Black of the County Population, 1930 - II

State	Percent Negroes were of county population										Median
	40.0-49.9		50.0-59.9		60.0-69.9		70.0-79.9		80.0-89.9		
	Number	Percent	Number	Percent	Number	Percent	Number	Percent	Number	Percent	
Alabama	8	13.1	7	11.5	...	...	8	13.1	3	4.9	30.5
Arkansas	8	17.8	2	4.4	6	13.3	1	2.2	...	...	33.9
Delaware	...	...	...	...	...	...	...	...	...	...	...
District of Columbia	...	...	...	...	...	...	...	...	...	...	...
Florida	8	12.1	3	4.5	1	1.5	...	...	...	...	30.0
Georgia	26	17.6	20	13.5	22	14.9	6	4.1	...	...	40.0
Kentucky	...	...	...	...	...	...	...	...	...	...	11.4
Louisiana	11	17.2	7	10.9	5	7.8	4	6.3	...	...	36.7
Maryland	2	10.5	...	...	...	...	...	...	...	...	27.5
Mississippi	13	15.9	11	13.4	8	9.6	14	17.1	2	2.4	45.4
North Carolina	22	25.6	6	7.0	3	3.5	...	...	...	...	34.0
Oklahoma	...	...	...	...	...	...	...	...	...	...	52.2
South Carolina	11	23.9	9	19.6	12	26.1	4	8.7	...	...	52.2
Tennessee	2	3.5	...	...	1	1.8	1	1.8	...	...	13.0

[Continued]

★ 1765 ★

Distribution of Counties by State and Percent Black of the County Population, 1930 - II

[Continued]

State	Percent Negroes were of county population										
	40.0-49.9		50.0-59.9		60.0-69.9		70.0-79.9		80.0-89.9		
	Number	Percent	Number	Percent	Number	Percent	Number	Percent	Number	Percent	Median
Texas[1]	11	10.7	2	1.9	2	1.9	...	...	...	...	22.7
Virginia	12	14.3	15	17.9	4	4.8	1	1.2	...	...	33.3
West Virginia	...	...	...	...	...	...	...	...	...	...	8.3
Total	134	13.9	82	8.5	64	6.6	39	4.0	5	0.5	30.4

Source: "Distribution of Counties by States and Percent That Negroes Were of Total County Population in 1930." U.S. Office of Education, *Socio-Economic Approach to Educational Problems,* Edited by Ina Corinne Brown, p. 157. *Notes:* 1. Does not include King County in which there were fewer than 100 Negroes.

★ 1766 ★

Geographical Areas: Counties

Distribution of Counties by State and Percent Change in Black Population, 1920-1930 - I

State	Total number of counties	Percent change in Negro population: 1920-1930 Decrease of-									
		40.0 or over		30.0-39.9		20.0-29.9		10.0-19.9		0.0-9.9	
		Number	Percent	Number	Percent	Number	Percent	Number	Percent	Number	Percent
Alabama	61	...	...	...	...	4	6.5	6	9.8	17	27.9
Arkansas	45	...	...	2	4.4	4	8.9	10.0	22.2	9	20.0
Delaware	3	...	...	...	...	...	...	...	...	1	33.3
District of Columbia	1	...	...	...	...	...	...	...	...	...	...
Florida	66	4	6.1	3	4.5	4	6.1	8	12.1	6	9.1
Georgia	148	14	9.4	18	12.2	24	16.2	29	19.6	30	20.3
Kentucky	60	...	...	2	3.3	15	25.0	20	33.3	11	18.3
Louisiana	64	1	1.6	3	4.7	1	1.6	8	12.5	17	26.6
Maryland	19	...	...	...	...	...	...	5	26.3	9	47.3
Mississippi	82	...	...	2	2.4	..	...	4	4.9	19	23.2
North Carolina	86	...	...	...	...	1	1.2	2	2.3	8	9.3
Oklahoma	25	1	4.0	...	...	2	8.0	3	12.0	5	20.0
South Carolina	46	...	...	1	2.2	6	13.0	14	30.4	15	32.6
Tennessee	57	2	3.5	1	1.8	10	17.5	17	29.8	8	14.0
Texas	104	...	...	...	...	6	5.8	14	13.5	23	22.1
Virginia	84	...	...	...	...	12	14.3	24	28.5	30	35.7
West Virginia	15	...	...	...	...	...	...	1	6.7	1	6.7
Total	966	22	2.3	32	3.3	89	9.2	165	17.1	209	21.6

Source: "Distribution of Counties by States and Percent of Change in Negro Population: 1920-1930." U.S. Office of Education, *Socio-Economic Approach to Educational Problems,* Edited by Ina Corinne Brown, p. 156.

★ 1767 ★

Geographical Areas: Counties

Distribution of Counties by State and Percent Change in Black Population, 1920-1930 - II

State	Percent change in Negro population: 1920-1930											
	Increase of-										50.0 and over	
	0.0-9.9		10.0-19.9		20.0-29.9		30.0-39.9		40.0-49.9			
	Number	Percent	Number	Percent	Number	Percent	Number	Percent	Number	Percent	Number	Percent
Alabama	25	41.0	4	6.5	2	3.3	2	3.3	1	1.6	...	...
Arkansas	7	15.6	5	11.1	3	6.7	3	6.7	2	4.4	...	...
Delaware	1	33.3	1	33.3	...	...	...	...	...	...	...	...
District of Columbia	...	...	...	...	1	100.0	...	...	...	...	...	...
Florida	2	3.0	8	12.1	2	3.0	...	...	2	3.0	14	21.2
Georgia	16	10.8	3	2.0	6	4.0	1	.7	1	.7	1	.7
Kentucky	5	8.3	4	6.7	1	1.7	...	...	1	1.7	1	1.7
Louisiana	13	20.3	5	7.8	8	12.5	4	6.2	...	...	4	6.2
Maryland	1	5.3	2	10.5	1	5.3	1	5.3	...	...	...	...
Mississippi	23	28.0	16	19.5	8	9.6	7	8.5	2	2.4	1	1.2
North Carolina	23	26.7	26	30.2	11	12.8	6	7.0	4	4.7	5	5.8
Oklahoma	3	12.0	4	16.0	1	4.0	...	...	...	...	6	24.0
South Carolina	6	13.0	3	6.5	1	2.2	...	...	...	...	...	...
Tennessee	10	17.5	4	7.0	3	5.3	1	1.8	1	1.8	...	...
Texas	19	18.2	15	14.4	8	7.7	5	4.8	...	...	11	10.6
Virginia	11	13.1	4	4.8	3	3.6	...	...	...	...	...	...
West Virginia	...	...	2	13.3	4	26.6	1	6.7	2	13.3	4	26.6
Total	165	17.1	106	11.0	63	6.5	31	3.2	16	1.7	47	4.8

Source: "Distribution of Counties by States and Percent of Change in Negro Population: 1920-1930." U.S. Office of Education, *Socio-Economic Approach to Educational Problems,* Edited by Ina Corinne Brown, p. 156.

★ 1768 ★

Geographical Areas: Counties

Distribution of Counties by State and Percent Change in Black Population, 1920-1930 - III

State	Percent change in Negro population: 1920-1930		
	Median percent	Not given	
		Number	Percent
Alabama	1.4	...	...
Arkansas	-2.8	...	...
Delaware	...	...	...
District of Columbia	...	...	...
Florida	7.5	13	19.7
Georgia	-14.7	5	3.4
Kentucky	-13.5	...	...
Louisiana	1.5	...	...
Maryland	-5.0	...	...
Mississippi	7.0	...	...
North Carolina	13.5	...	...
Oklahoma	5.0	...	...
South Carolina	-8.7	...	...

[Continued]

★ 1768 ★

Distribution of Counties by State and Percent Change in Black Population, 1920-1930 - III

[Continued]

State	Percent change in Negro population: 1920-1930		
	Median percent	Not given	
		Number	Percent
Tennessee	-10.9	...	...
Texas	3.9	3	2.9
Virginia	-8.0	...	...
West Virginia	28.7	...	...
Total	-2.1	21	2.2

Source: "Distribution of Counties by States and Percent of Change in Negro Population: 1920-1930." U.S. Office of Education, *Socio-Economic Approach to Educational Problems,* Edited by Ina Corinne Brown, p. 156.

★ 1769 ★

Geographical Areas: Counties

Distribution of Counties by State and Percent Urban Black Population, 1930 - I

State	Total Number of counties	Percent Negro population that was urban							
		None		0.1-9.9		10.0-19.9		20.0-29.9	
		Number	Percent	Number	Percent	Number	Percent	Number	Percent
Alabama	61	30	49.2	3	4.9	8	13.1	7	11.5
Arkansas	45	13	28.9	9	20.0	10	22.2	7	15.6
Delaware	3	...	...	1	33.3	...	...	1	33.3
District of Columbia	1	...	...	...	...	...	...	...	...
Florida	66	29	43.9	2	3.0	1	1.5	8	12.1
Georgia	148	89	60.1	6	4.0	14	9.5	13	8.8
Kentucky	60	26	43.3	...	...	3	5.0	4	6.7
Louisiana	64	28	43.8	4	6.2	11	17.2	9	14.1
Maryland	19	6	31.6	3	15.8	5	26.3	3	15.8
Mississippi	82	46	56.1	4	4.9	13	15.9	8	9.6
North Carolina	86	33	38.4	7	8.1	15	17.4	9	10.5
Oklahoma	25	5	20.0	3	12.0	4	16.0	3	12.0
South Carolina	46	14	30.4	8	17.4	15	32.6	5	10.9
Tennessee	57	25	43.9	1	1.7	3	5.3	9	15.8
Texas	103[1]	36	35.0	6	5.8	15	14.5	14	13.6
Virginia	84	54	64.3	3	3.6	3	3.6	7	8.3
West Virginia	15	4	26.7	3	20.0	1	6.6	...	...
Total	965	438	45.4	63	6.5	121	12.5	107	11.1

Source: "Distribution of Counties by States and Percent of Negro Population That Was Urban in 1930." U.S. Office of Education, *Socio-Economic Approach to Educational Problems,* Edited by Ina Corinne Brown, p. 157. *Notes:* 1. Does not include King County in which there were fewer than 100 Negroes.

★ 1770 ★

Geographical Areas: Counties

Distribution of Counties by State and Percent Urban Black Population, 1930 - II

State	Percent Negro population that was urban							
	30.0-39.9		40.0-49.9		50.0-59.9		60.0-69.9	
	Number	Percent	Number	Percent	Number	Percent	Number	Percent
Alabama	6	9.8	2	3.3	1	1.6	2	3.3
Arkansas	2	4.4	1	2.2	...	...	1	2.2
Delaware	...	...	...	...	...	...	...	...
District of Columbia	...	...	...	...	...	...	...	...
Florida	6	9.1	1	1.5	6	9.1	6	9.1
Georgia	7	4.7	5	3.4	4	2.7	3	2.0
Kentucky	5	8.3	7	11.7	7	11.7	2	3.3
Louisiana	4	6.2	4	6.2	2	3.1	1	1.6
Maryland	1	5.2	...	...	...	...	...	...
Mississippi	3	3.7	3	3.7	2	2.4	1	1.2
North Carolina	8	9.3	3	3.5	2	2.3	4	4.7
Oklahoma	2	8.0	5	20.0	1	4.0	...	...
South Carolina	2	4.3	...	...	2	4.3	...	...
Tennessee	6	10.5	1	1.7	5	8.8	2	3.5
Texas[1]	12	11.7	4	3.9	4	3.9	2	1.9
Virginia	3	3.6	3	3.6	4	4.7	2	2.4
West Virginia	...	...	3	20.0	2	13.3	1	6.6
Total	67	6.9	42	4.4	42	4.4	27	2.8

Source: "Distribution of Counties by States and Percent of Negro Population That Was Urban in 1930." U.S. Office of Education, *Socio-Economic Approach to Educational Problems,* Edited by Ina Corinne Brown, p. 157. *Notes:* 1. Does not include King County in which there were fewer than 100 Negroes.

★ 1771 ★

Geographical Areas: Counties

Distribution of Counties by State and Percent Urban Black Population, 1930 - III

State	Percent Negro population that was urban						Percent of counties having some urban Negro population
	80.0-79.9		80.0-89.9		90.0-100		
	Number	Percent	Number	Percent	Number	Percent	
Alabama	1	1.6	1	1.6	...	...	50.8
Arkansas	...	...	2	4.4	...	...	71.1
Delaware	1	33.3	...	...	...	...	100.0
District of Columbia	...	...	...	...	1	100.0	...
Florida	2	3.0	2	3.0	3	4.5	56.1
Georgia	5	3.4	2	1.4	...	...	39.9
Kentucky	3	5.0	2	3.3	1	1.7	56.7
Louisiana	...	...	...	...	1	1.6	56.2

[Continued]

★ 1771 ★

Distribution of Counties by State and Percent Urban Black Population, 1930 - III

[Continued]

State	Percent Negro population that was urban						Percent of counties having some urban Negro population
	80.0-79.9		80.0-89.9		90.0-100		
	Number	Percent	Number	Percent	Number	Percent	
Maryland	...	...	...	...	1	5.2	68.4
Mississippi	2	2.4	...	...	...	...	43.9
North Carolina	3	3.5	2	2.3	...	...	61.6
Oklahoma	...	...	2	8.0	...	...	80.0
South Carolina	...	...	...	...	...	...	69.6
Tennessee	1	1.7	3	5.3	1	1.7	56.1
Texas[1]	1	1.0	5	4.8	4	3.9	65.0
Virginia	1	1.2	4	4.7	...	...	35.7
West Virginia	...	...	...	...	1	6.6	73.3
Total	20	2.1	25	2.6	13	1.3	54.6

Source: "Distribution of Counties by States and Percent of Negro Population That Was Urban in 1930." U.S. Office of Education, *Socio-Economic Approach to Educational Problems,* Edited by Ina Corinne Brown, p. 157. *Notes:* 1. Does not include King County in which there were fewer than 100 Negroes.

★ 1772 ★

Geographical Areas: Counties

Number and Area of Counties with Changes in Black Population, 1900-1910

DIVISION AND STATE	COUNTIES OR COMBINATIONS OF COUNTIES[1]											
	Number				Area							
					Square miles				Percentage distribution			
	Total	Percentage Negro increased, 1900-1910	Percentage Negro decreased, 1900-1910	No Negro population or less than 100, 1900-1910	Total	Percentage Negro increased, 1900-1910	Percentage Negro decreased, 1900-1910	No Negro population or less than 100, 1900-1910	Total	Percentage Negro increased, 1900-1910	Percentage Negro decreased, 1900-1910	No Negro population or less than 100, 1900-1910
The South	1,214	276	795	143	878,326	275,908	465,445	136,973	100.0	31.4	53.0	15.6
South Atlantic	491	131	343	17	269,071	88,525	174,433	6,113	100.0	32.9	64.8	2.3
East South Central	347	68	264	15	179,509	44,176	130,795	4,538	100.0	24.6	72.9	2.5
West South Central	376	77	188	111	429,746	143,207	160,217	126,322	100.0	33.3	37.3	29.4
South Atlantic:												
Delaware	3	1	2	-	1,965	913	1,052	-	100.0	46.5	53.6	-
Maryland	24	-	24	-	9,941	-	9,941	-	100.0	-	100.0	-
District of Columbia	1	-	1	-	60	-	60	-	100.0	-	100.0	-
Virginia	110	12	96	2	40,262	3,830	35,593	839	100.0	9.5	88.4	2.1
West Virginia	55	12	31	12	24,022	5,256	14,411	4,355	100.0	21.9	60.0	18.1
North Carolina	96	24	71	1	48,740	12,526	35,916	298	100.0	25.7	73.7	0.6
South Carolina	34	7	27	-	30,495	4,985	25,510	-	100.0	16.3	83.7	-
Georgia	123	48	73	2	58,725	21,648	36,456	621	100.0	36.9	62.1	1.1
Florida	45	27	18	0	54,861	39,367	15,494	-	100.0	71.8	28.2	-
East South Central:												
Kentucky	119	11	98	10	40,181	4,871	32,578	2,732	100.0	12.1	81.1	6.8
Tennessee	95	10	81	4	41,687	3,406	37,105	1,176	100.0	8.2	89.0	2.8
Alabama	62	23	38	1	51,279	18,641	32,008	630	100.0	36.4	62.4	1.2
Mississippi	72	24	47	-	46,362	17,258	29,104	-	100.0	37.2	62.8	-
West South Central:												
Arkansas	73	15	49	9	52,525	10,066	36,498	5,951	100.0	19.2	69.5	11.3
Louisiana	59	9	50	-	45,409	10,035	35,374	-	100.0	22.1	77.9	-

[Continued]

★ 1772 ★

Number and Area of Counties with Changes in Black Population, 1900-1910

[Continued]

DIVISION AND STATE	COUNTIES OR COMBINATIONS OF COUNTIES[1]											
	Number				Area							
					Square miles				Percentage distribution			
	Total	Percentage Negro increased, 1900-1910	Percentage Negro decreased, 1900-1910	No Negro population or less than 100, 1900-1910	Total	Percentage Negro increased, 1900-1910	Percentage Negro decreased, 1900-1910	No Negro population or less than 100, 1900-1910	Total	Percentage Negro increased, 1900-1910	Percentage Negro decreased, 1900-1910	No Negro population or less than 100, 1900-1910
Oklahoma	1	1	-	-	69,414	69,414	-	-	100.0	100.0	-	-
Texas	243	52	89	102	262,398	53,692	88,345	120,361	100.0	20.5	33.7	45.9

Source: "Number and Area of Counties in Which the Percentage Negro Increased and in Which It Decreased: 1900-1910." U.S. Bureau of the Census, *Negro Population, 1790-1915*, p. 132. *Notes:* 1. In cases where boundaries of counties were changed during the decade 1900-1910, County areas and population have been combined and computation made for the combined area. The entire state of Oklahoma in classified as a single area.

★ 1773 ★

Geographical Areas: Counties

Number and Area of Southern Counties 50 Percent or More Black by Divisions and States, 1890-1910 - I

DIVISION OR STATE	COUNTIES IN WHICH THE PROPORTION NEGRO IN THE POPULATION IN THE YEAR SPECIFIED WAS 50 PER CENT OR MORE — Number of counties						
					Increase or decrease[1]		
	1910	1900	1890	1880	1900-1910	1890-1900	1880-1890
The South	264	286	282	300	-22	4	-18
South Atlantic	156	165	156	168	-9	-9	-12
East South Central	61	63	62	69	-2	1	-7
West South Central	47	58	64	63	-11	-6	1
South Atlantic:							
Delaware	-	-	-	-	-	-	-
Maryland	1	2	2	3	-1	-	-1
District of Columbia	-	-	-	-	-	-	-
Virginia	32	36	39	46	-4	-3	-7
West Virginia	-	-	-	-	-	-	-
North Carolina	14	18	16	22	-4	2	-6
South Carolina	33	30	26	25	3	4	1
Georgia	66	67	63	63	-1	4	-
Florida	10	12	10	9	-2	2	1
East South Central:							
Kentucky	-	-	-	-	-	-	-
Tennessee	2	3	3	5	-1	-	-2
Alabama	21	22	20	24	-1	2	-4
Mississippi	38	38	39	40	-	-1	-1
West South Central:							
Arkansas	14	15	15	13	-1	-	2
Louisiana	25	31	33	36	-6	-2	-3

[Continued]

★ 1773 ★

Number and Area of Southern Counties 50 Percent or More Black by Divisions and States, 1890-1910 - I

[Continued]

DIVISION OR STATE	COUNTIES IN WHICH THE PROPORTION NEGRO IN THE POPULATION IN THE YEAR SPECIFIED WAS 50 PER CENT OR MORE Number of counties						
					Increase or decrease[1]		
	1910	1900	1890	1880	1900-1910	1890-1900	1880-1890
Oklahoma	-	-	-	-	-	-	-
Texas	8	12	16	14	-4	-4	2

Source: "Number and Area of Southern Counties in Which the Proportion Negro in the Population was 50 Per Cent or More, by Divisions and States: 1910, 1900, 1890, and 1880." U.S. Bureau of the Census, *Negro Population, 1790- 1915*, p. 125. *Note:* 1. Minus sign (-) denotes decrease.

★ 1774 ★

Geographical Areas: Counties

Number and Area of Southern Counties 50 Percent or More Black by Divisions and States, 1890-1910 - II

DIVISION OR STATE	COUNTIES IN WHICH THE PROPORTION NEGRO IN THE POPULATION IN THE YEAR SPECIFIED WAS 50 PER CENT OR MORE Area of counties in square miles										
					Increase or decrease[1]			Percentage of total area of specified section, division, or state			
	1910	1900	1890	1880	1900-1910	1890-1900	1880-1890	1910	1900	1890	1880
The South	147,219	166,742	167,230	176,764	-19,523	-488	-9,534	16.8	19.0	19.0	20.2
South Atlantic	76,584	83,485	80,067	87,093	-6,901	3,418	-7,026	28.5	31.1	29.8	32.4
East South Central	40,721	42,936	41,960	46,340	-2,215	976	-4,380	22.7	23.9	23.4	25.8
West South Central	29,914	40,321	45,203	43,331	-10,407	-4,882	1,872	7.0	9.4	10.5	10.2
South Atlantic:											
Delaware	-	-	-	-	-	-	-	-	-	-	-
Maryland	464	673	678	1,070	-209	-5	-392	4.7	6.8	6.9	10.9
District of Columbia	-	-	-	-	-	-	-	-	-	-	-
Virginia	11,375	12,705	12,669	15,293	-1,330	36	-2,624	28.3	31.7	31.6	38.1
West Virginia	-	-	-	-	-	-	-	-	-	-	-
North Carolina	6,044	8,453	7,844	12,230	-2,409	609	-4,386	12.4	17.4	16.1	25.2
South Carolina	23,316	23,090	23,450	23,710	226	-300	-260	76.5	76.5	77.7	78.6
Georgia	27,418	28,577	26,262	26,460	-1,159	2,315	-198	46.7	48.5	44.5	44.9
Florida	7,967	9,987	9,164	8,330	-2,020	823	834	14.5	18.4	16.9	15.4
East South Central:											
Kentucky	-	-	-	-	-	-	-	-	-	-	-
Tennessee	1,126	1,907	1,928	2,810	-781	-21	-882	2.7	4.6	4.6	6.7
Alabama	16,678	17,648	16,056	19,160	-970	1,592	-3,104	32.5	34.2	31.2	37.2
Mississippi	22,917	23,381	23,976	24,370	-464	-595	-394	49.4	50.5	51.7	52.6
West South Central:											
Arkansas	9,556	10,529	10,385	8,790	-973	144	1,595	18.2	19.8	19.6	16.6
Louisiana	15,207	20,058	21,148	22,961	-4,851	-1,000	-1,813	33.5	44.2	46.6	50.6

[Continued]

★ 1774 ★

Number and Area of Southern Counties 50 Percent or More Black by Divisions and States, 1890-1910 - II

[Continued]

DIVISION OR STATE	COUNTIES IN WHICH THE PROPORTION NEGRO IN THE POPULATION IN THE YEAR SPECIFIED WAS 50 PER CENT OR MORE Area of counties in square miles										
	1910	1900	1890	1880	Increase or decrease[1]			Percentage of total area of specified section, division, or state			
					1900-1910	1890-1900	1880-1890	1910	1900	1890	1880
Oklahoma	-	-	-	-	-	-	-	-	-	-	-
Texas	5,151	9,734	13,670	11,580	-4,583	-3,936	2,090	2.0	3.7	5.2	4.4

Source: "Number and Area of Southern Counties in Which the Proportion Negro in the Population was 50 Per Cent or More, by Divisions and States: 1910, 1900, 1890, and 1880." U.S. Bureau of the Census, *Negro Population, 1790- 1915*, p. 125. *Note:* 1. Minus sign (-) denotes decrease.

★ 1775 ★

Geographical Areas: Counties

Percent Change in Total Population and Black Population by County Type, 1920-1930

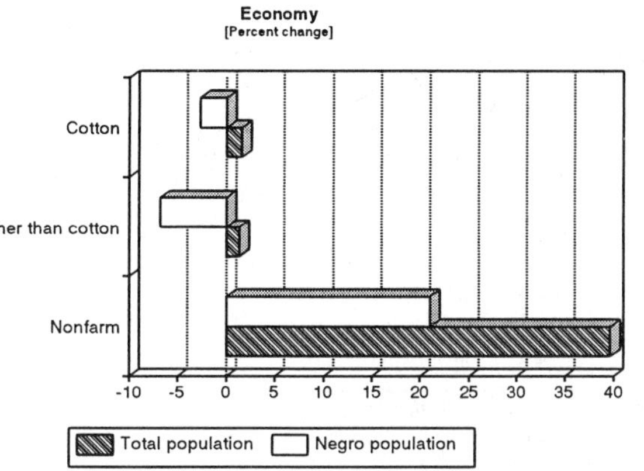

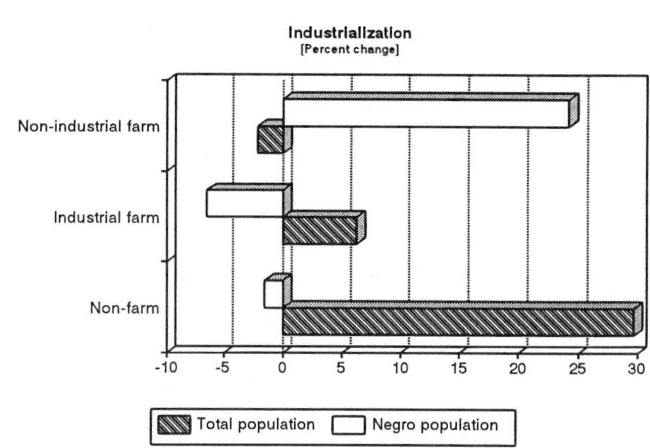

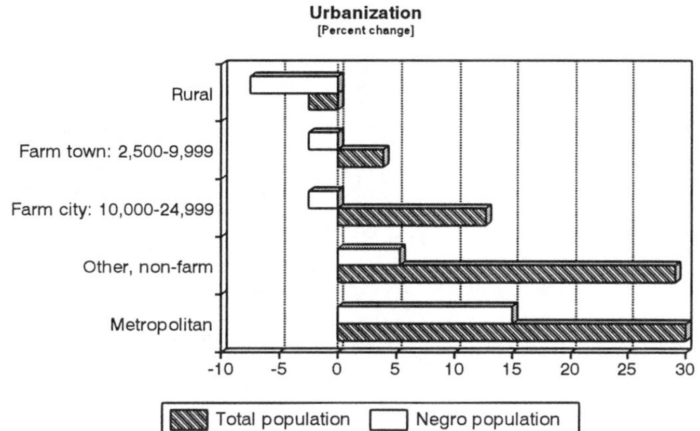

	COUNTY TYPE											TOTAL COUNTIES
	ECONOMY			INDUSTRIALIZATION			URBANIZATION					
	Nonfarm	Farm other than cotton	Cotton	Non-farm	Industrial farm	Non-industrial farm	Metropolitan	Other non-farm	Farm: City 10,000-24,999	Farm: Town 2,500-9,999	Rural	
Total population	39.7	1.3	1.5	29.7	6.2	-2.2	30.0	29.1	12.7	3.9	-2.5	3.2
Negro population	21.0	-6.8	-2.7	-1.6	-6.5	24.2	15.0	5.3	-2.5	-2.5	-7.5	-2.2

Source: "Percent Change in Total Population and in Negro Population, 1920-1930, in Relation to County Type." U.S. Office of Education, *Socio-Economic Approach to Educational Problems*, Edited by Ina Corinne Brown, p. 48.

★ 1776 ★

Geographical Areas: Counties

Population Change by Counties, 1900-1910 and 1910-1920 - I

Section	Number of counties 1910	Number of Counties or combinations of Counties[1]				
		Total	In which Negro population			Having no Negro population 1910 or in 1900
			Increased 1900 1910	Decreased 1900 1910	Did not change 1900 1910	
United States	2,953	2,751	1,443	1,229	44	45
The South	1,351	1,214	662	533	4	15
The North	1,265	1,236	582	603	29	22
The West	337	301	189	93	11	8

Source: "Increase or Decrease [in] Negro Population by Counties 1900-1910 and 1910-1920." Work, Monroe N., ed., *Negro Year Book: An Annual Encyclopedia of the Negro, 1925-26*, p. 444. *Notes:* 1. In case where boundaries of counties were changed during the decade, 1900-1910 and 1910-1920 county areas and population have been combined and computations made for the combined area. The entire State of Oklahoma was classified as a single area for 1900-1910; for 1910-1920 the counties of this State were classified.

★ 1777 ★

Geographical Areas: Counties

Population Change by Counties, 1900-1910 and 1910-1920 - II

Section	Number of counties 1920	Number of Counties or combinations of Counties[1]				
		Total	In which Negro population			Having no Negro population 1910 or in 1920
			Increased 1900 1920	Decreased 1900 1920	Did not change 1900 1920	
United States	3,065	3,038	1,272	1,664	41	61
The South	1,391	1,364	522	824	5	13
The North	1,272	1,272	559	663	28	22
The West	402	402	191	177	8	26

Source: "Increase or Decrease [in] Negro Population by Counties 1900-1910 and 1910-1920." Work, Monroe N., ed., *Negro Year Book: An Annual Encyclopedia of the Negro, 1925-26*, p. 444. *Notes:* 1. In case where boundaries of counties were changed during the decade, 1900-1910 and 1910-1920 county areas and population have been combined and computations made for the combined area. The entire State of Oklahoma was classified as a single area for 1900-1910; for 1910-1920 the counties of this State were classified.

★ 1778 ★

Geographical Areas: Counties

Population in Counties in Which Black Population Was 50 Percent or More by Divisions and States, 1880-1910 - I

DIVISION OR STATE	COUNTIES IN WHICH THE NEGRO POPULATION CONSTITUTED 50 PER CENT OF MORE OF THE TOTAL POPULATION Negro Population							
	1910	1900	1890	1880	Percentage of total Negro population of division or state			
					1910	1900	1890	1880
The South	3,932,484	4,057,619	3,555,970	3,392,235	44.9	51.2	52.6	57.0
South Atlantic	1,988,088	2,006,301	1,790,847	1,790,391	48.3	53.8	54.9	60.9
East South Central	1,277,080	1,325,226	1,102,348	1,071,915	48.1	53.0	52.0	55.7
West South Central	667,316	726,092	663,775	529,929	33.6	42.9	48.2	48.7
South Atlantic:								
Delaware	-	-	-	-	-	-	-	-
Maryland	8,572	14,791	13,200	25,234	3.7	6.3	6.1	12.0
District of Columbia	-	-	-	-	-	-	-	-
Virginia	271,097	286,733	292,784	366,750	40.4	43.4	46.1	58.1
West Virginia	-	-	-	-	-	-	-	-
North Carolina	166,520	198,237	175,255	235,290	23.9	31.7	31.2	44.3
South Carolina	699,471	662,991	594,257	533,648	83.7	84.7	86.3	88.3
Georgia	735,972	708,765	610,733	541,269	62.5	68.5	71.1	74.6
Florida	106,456	134,784	104,618	88,200	34.5	58.4	63.0	69.6
East South Central:								
Kentucky	-	-	-	-	-	-	-	-
Tennessee	40,412	123,535	97,674	109,707	8.5	25.7	22.7	27.2
Alabama	487,399	505,576	405,941	435,795	53.7	61.1	59.8	72.6
Mississippi	749,269	696,115	597,733	526,413	74.2	76.7	80.5	81.0
West South Central:								
Arkansas	226,145	187,866	161,188	97,559	51.1	51.2	52.1	46.3
Louisiana	356,707	418,148	376,273	334,550	50.0	64.3	67.3	69.2
Oklahoma	-	-	-	-	-	-	-	-
Texas	84,464	120,078	126,314	97,820	12.2	19.3	25.9	24.9

Source: "Negro and White Population of Counties in Which the Proportion Negro in the Population was 50 Per Cent or More, by Divisions and States: 1910, 1900, 1890, and 1880." U.S. Bureau of the Census, *Negro Population, 1790- 1915*, p. 126.

★ 1779 ★

Geographical Areas: Counties

Population in Counties in Which Black Population Was 50 Percent or More by Divisions and States, 1880-1910 - II

DIVISION OR STATE	COUNTIES IN WHICH THE NEGRO POPULATION CONSTITUTED 50 PER CENT OF MORE OF THE TOTAL POPULATION White population							
	1910	1900	1890	1880	Percentage of total white population of division or state			
					1910	1900	1890	1880
The South	2,094,964	2,163,731	1,876,611	1,862,669	10.2	13.1	14.2	17.6
South Atlantic	1,236,542	1,219,672	1,062,175	1,082,551	15.3	18.2	19.0	23.3
East South Central	498,985	546,196	476,088	513,478	8.7	10.8	11.1	14.0
West South Central	359,437	397,863	338,348	266,640	5.3	8.3	10.3	11.9
South Atlantic:								
Delaware	-	-	-	-	-	-	-	-
Maryland	7,813	13,094	11,850	20,786	0.7	1.4	1.4	2.9
District of Columbia	-	-	-	-	-	-	-	-
Virginia	201,575	202,027	197,553	254,099	14.5	16.9	19.4	28.8
West Virginia	-	-	-	-	-	-	-	-
North Carolina	123,841	152,251	120,609	164,799	8.3	12.0	11.4	19.0
South Carolina	403,227	342,669	297,562	269,149	59.4	61.4	64.4	68.8
Georgia	434,209	423,042	370,291	329,297	30.3	35.8	37.8	40.3
Florida	65,877	86,589	64,310	44,421	14.8	29.1	28.6	31.1
East South Central:								
Kentucky	-	-	-	-	-	-	-	-
Tennessee	15,742	84,882	67,475	78,526	0.9	5.5	5.0	6.9
Alabama	198,572	205,486	157,755	199,004	16.2	20.5	18.9	30.1
Mississippi	284,671	255,828	250,858	235,948	36.3	39.9	46.0	49.2
West South Central:								
Arkansas	104,389	90,336	79,681	49,277	9.2	9.6	9.7	8.3
Louisiana	194,319	220,339	176,349	156,653	20.6	30.2	31.6	34.4
Oklahoma	-	-	-	-	-	-	-	-
Texas	60,729	87,188	82,318	60,710	1.9	3.6	4.7	5.1

Source: "Negro and White Population of Counties in Which the Proportion Negro in the Population was 50 Per Cent or More, by Divisions and States: 1910, 1900, 1890, and 1880." U.S. Bureau of the Census, *Negro Population, 1790- 1915,* p. 126.

★ 1780 ★

Geographical Areas: Counties

Population of Counties in Which Black Population was 50 Percent or More of Total Population by Divisions and States, 1900 to 1930 - I

DIVISION AND STATE	NEGRO POPULATION							
	1930	1920	1910	1900	Percent of total Negro population of division or State			
					1930	1920	1910	1900
The South	2,738,432	3,251,440	3,932,484	4,057,619	29.3	36.5	44.9	51.2
South Atlantic	1,182,260	1,632,589	1,988,088	2,006,301	26.7	37.7	48.3	53.8
East South Central	1,120,122	1,076,831	1,277,080	1,325,226	42.1	42.7	48.1	53.0
West South Central	436,050	542,020	667,316	726,092	19.1	26.3	33.6	42.9
SOUTH ATLANTIC:								
Delaware	-	-	-	-	-	-	-	-
Maryland	-	-	8,572	14,791	-	-	3.7	6.3
District of Columbia	-	-	-	-	-	-	-	-
Virginia	156,537	167,895	271,097	286,733	24.1	24.3	40.4	43.4
West Virginia	-	-	-	-	-	-	-	-
North Carolina	149,592	176,441	166,520	198,237	16.3	23.1	23.9	31.7
South Carolina	446,435	622,779	699,471	662,991	56.2	72.0	83.7	84.7
Georgia	381,618	606,595	735,972	708,765	35.6	50.3	62.5	68.5
Florida	48,078	58,879	106,456	134,784	11.1	17.9	34.5	58.4
EAST SOUTH CENTRAL:								
Kentucky	-	-	-	-	-	-	-	-
Tennessee	38,322	40,485	40,412	123,535	8.0	9.0	8.5	25.7
Alabama	380,863	386,293	487,399	505,576	40.3	42.9	53.7	61.1
Mississippi	700,937	650,053	749,269	696,115	69.4	69.5	74.2	76.7
WEST SOUTH CENTRAL:								
Arkansas	188,282	218,474	226,145	187,866	39.4	46.3	51.1	51.2
Louisiana	198,588	274,793	356,707	418,148	25.6	39.2	50.0	64.3
Oklahoma	-	-	-	-	-	-	-	-
Texas	49,180	48,753	84,464	120,078	5.8	6.6	12.2	19.3

Source: "Negro and White Population of Counties in Which the Negro Population was 50 Percent or More of Total Population." U.S. Bureau of the Census, *Negroes in the United States, 1920-1932*, p. 72.

★ 1781 ★

Geographical Areas: Counties

Population of Counties in Which Black Population was 50 Percent or More of Total Population by Divisions and States, 1900 to 1930 - II

DIVISION AND STATE	NEGRO POPULATION							
	1930	1920	1910	1900	Percent of total white population of division or State			
					1930	1920	1910	1900
The South	1,595,564	1,815,245	2,094,964	2,163,731	5.8	7.5	10.2	13.1
South Atlantic	780,786	1,059,774	1,236,542	1,219,672	6.9	11.0	15.3	18.2
East South Central	546,754	444,976	498,985	546,196	7.6	7.0	8.7	10.8
West South Central	268,024	310,495	359,437	397,863	2.9	3.8	5.3	8.3
SOUTH ATLANTIC:								
Delaware	-	-	-	-	-	-	-	-
Maryland	-	-	7,813	13,094	-	-	0.7	1.4
District of Columbia	-	-	-	-	-	-	-	-
Virginia	116,847	123,669	201,575	202,027	6.6	7.6	14.5	16.9
West Virginia	-	-	-	-	-	-	-	-
North Carolina	108,292	136,295	123,841	152,251	4.8	7.6	8.3	12.0
South Carolina	279,645	377,719	403,227	342,669	29.6	46.1	59.4	61.4
Georgia	241,699	384,390	434,209	423,042	13.2	22.8	30.3	35.8
Florida	34,303	37,701	65,877	86,589	3.3	5.9	14.8	29.1
EAST SOUTH CENTRAL:								
Kentucky	-	-	-	-	-	-	-	-
Tennessee	16,632	16,399	15,742	84,882	.8	.9	.9	5.5
Alabama	195,641	171,286	198,572	205,486	11.5	11.8	16.2	20.5
Mississippi	334,481	257,291	284,671	255,828	33.6	30.1	36.2	39.9
WEST SOUTH CENTRAL:								
Arkansas	101,385	97,438	104,389	90,336	7.4	7.6	9.2	9.6
Louisiana	131,246	178,942	194,319	220,339	10.0	163.	20.6	30.2
Oklahoma	-	-	-	-	-	-	-	-
Texas	35,393	34,115	60,729	87,188	.8	1.0	.9	3.6

Source: "Negro and White Population of Counties in Which the Negro Population was 50 Percent or More of Total Population." U.S. Bureau of the Census, *Negroes in the United States, 1920-1932,* p. 72.

★ 1782 ★

Geographical Areas: Counties

Proportion Black and Black Population Per Square Mile in 53 Counties with 75 Percent Black Population, 1910

COUNTIES IN ORDER OF DECREASING PERCENTAGE NEGRO	NEGRO POPULATION	
	Per cent in total population	Number per square mile
Issaquena, Miss.	94.2	24.5
Tensas, La.	91.5	24.7
Tunica, Miss.	90.7	40.4
East Carroll, La.	89.3	24.7
Sharkey, Miss.	89.0	31.4
Coahoma, Miss.	88.8	57.3
Madison, La.	88.6	14.5
Lowndes, Ala.	88.2	38.0
Bolivar, Miss.	87.4	48.6
Beaufort, S.C.	86.9	28.7
Greene, Ala.	86.7	31.0
Lee, Ga.	85.6	30.6
Washington, Miss.	85.0	47.4
Macon, Ala.	84.6	35.9
Crittenden, Ark.	84.6	32.6
Leflore, Miss.	84.4	53.5
Bullock, Ala.	84.0	41.6
Noxubee, Miss.	84.0	35.1
Concordia, La.	83.6	16.7
Burke, Ga.	82.4	23.5
West Feliciana, La.	81.9	31.3
Wilcox, Ala.	81.6	30.8
Dallas, Ala.	81.5	45.5
Madison, Miss.	81.5	37.6
Sumter, Ala.	81.3	25.7
Sunflower, Miss.	80.9	33.7
Chicot, Ark.	80.4	29.1
Holmes, Miss.	79.8	37.4
Desha, Ark.	79.4	16.2
Hale, Ala.	78.9	34.0
Phillips, Ark.	78.6	38.1
Perry, Ala.	78.5	33.2
Lee Ark.	78.4	31.6
Jefferson, Miss.	78.4	28.2
Claiborne, Miss.	78.2	27.8
Quitman, Ga.	78.1	24.9
Russell, Ala.	77.9	30.8
Stewart, Ga.	77.8	25.2
Berkley, S.C.	77.6	14.7
Marengo, Ala.	77.3	31.9
McIntosh, Ga.	77.3	10.6
Bossier, La.	77.0	19.4
Wilkinson, Miss.	76.9	20.8

[Continued]

★ 1782 ★

Proportion Black and Black Population Per Square Mile in 53 Counties with 75 Percent Black Population, 1910

[Continued]

COUNTIES IN ORDER OF DECREASING PERCENTAGE NEGRO	NEGRO POPULATION	
	Per cent in total population	Number per square mile
Calhoun, S.C.	76.6	32.6
Quitman, Miss.	76.5	22.4
Jefferson, Fla.	76.2	22.4
Yazoo, Miss.	76.1	34.2
De Soto, Miss.	76.0	37.0
Fairfield, S.C.	76.0	28.2
Leon, Fla.	75.8	20.6
Terrell, Ga.	75.5	51.6
Dougherty, Ga.	75.1	35.2
Fayette, Tenn.	75.0	36.7

Source: "Proportion Negro and Negro Population Per Square Mile for the 53 Counties in Which the Proportion Negro was 75 Per Cent: 1910." U.S. Bureau of the Census, *Negro Population 1790-1915*, p. 131.

★ 1783 ★

Geographical Areas: Counties

Southern County Areas by Percentage Black and by Divisions, 1880-1910 - I

DIVISION AND YEAR	SOUTHERN STATES					
	All counties	Counties in which the percentage Negro was-				
		Less than 12.5[1]	12.5 to 24.9	25 to 49.9	50 to 74.9	75 or more
	AREA IN SQUARE MILES					
The South:						
1910	878,326	391,273	123,581	216,253	113,138	34,081
1900	878,835	399,658	105,778	206,657	129,950	36,792
1890	878,835	404,682	99,933	206,990	130,171	37,059
1880	873,095	368,859	128,178	199,294	143,875	32,889
South Atlantic:						
1910	269,071	52,484	41,564	98,439	68,972	7,612
1900	268,620	59,109	35,935	90,091	75,379	8,106
1890	268,620	65,792	35,960	86,801	71,590	8,477
1880	268,620	60,234	37,567	83,726	79,773	7,320
East South Central:						
1910	179,509	59,559	34,278	44,951	21,112	19,609
1900	179,630	54,311	30,355	52,028	22,215	20,721

[Continued]

★ 1783 ★

Southern County Areas by Percentage Black and by Divisions, 1880-1910 - I

[Continued]

DIVISION AND YEAR	SOUTHERN STATES					
	All counties	Counties in which the percentage Negro was-				
		Less than 12.5[1]	12.5 to 24.9	25 to 49.9	50 to 74.9	75 or more
1890	179,630	53,328	33,260	51,082	23,645	18,315
1880	179,630	47,970	35,890	49,430	30,840	15,500
West South Central:						
1910	429,746	279,230	47,739	72,863	23,054	6,860
1900	430,585	286,238	39,488	64,538	32,356	7,955
1890	430,585	285,562	30,713	69,107	34,936	10,267
1880	424,845	260,655	54,721	66,138	33,262	10,069

Source: "Southern County Areas Classified According to Specific Percentage Negro in the Population, by Divisions: 1910, 1900, 1890, and 1880." U.S. Bureau of the Census, *Negro Population, 1790-1915*, p. 128. *Notes:* 1. Includes counties reporting no Negro population. 2. Minus sign (-) denotes decrease.

★ 1784 ★

Geographical Areas: Counties

Southern County Areas by Percentage Black and by Divisions, 1880-1910 - II

DIVISION AND YEAR	SOUTHERN STATES					
	All counties	Counties in which the percentage Negro was-				
		Less than 12.5[1]	12.5 to 24.9	25 to 49.9	50 to 74.9	75 or more
	PERCENTAGE DISTRIBUTION OF AREA					
The South:						
1910	100.0	44.5	14.1	24.6	12.9	3.9
1900	100.0	45.5	12.0	23.5	14.8	4.2
1890	100.0	46.0	11.4	23.6	14.8	4.2
1880	100.0	42.2	14.7	22.8	16.5	3.8
South Atlantic:						
1910	100.0	19.5	15.4	36.6	25.6	2.8
1900	100.0	22.0	13.4	33.5	28.1	3.0
1890	100.0	24.5	13.4	32.3	26.7	3.2
1880	100.0	22.4	14.0	31.2	29.7	2.7
East South Central:						
1910	100.0	33.2	19.1	25.0	11.8	10.9
1900	100.0	30.2	16.9	29.0	12.4	11.5
1890	100.0	29.7	18.5	28.4	13.2	10.2
1880	100.0	26.7	20.0	27.5	17.2	8.6

[Continued]

★ 1784 ★

Southern County Areas by Percentage Black and by Divisions, 1880-1910 - II

[Continued]

DIVISION AND YEAR	SOUTHERN STATES					
	All counties	Counties in which the percentage Negro was-				
		Less than 12.5[1]	12.5 to 24.9	25 to 49.9	50 to 74.9	75 or more
West South Central:						
1910	100.0	65.0	11.1	17.0	5.4	1.6
1900	100.0	66.5	9.2	15.0	7.5	1.8
1890	100.0	66.3	7.1	16.0	8.1	2.4
1880	100.0	61.4	12.9	15.6	7.8	2.4

Source: "Southern County Areas Classified According to Specific Percentage Negro in the Population, by Divisions: 1910, 1900, 1890, and 1880." U.S. Bureau of the Census, *Negro Population, 1790-1915*, p. 128. *Notes:* 1. Includes counties reporting no Negro population. 2. Minus sign (-) denotes decrease.

★ 1785 ★

Geographical Areas: Counties

Southern County Areas by Percentage Black and by Divisions, 1880-1910 - III

DIVISION AND YEAR	SOUTHERN STATES					
	All counties	Counties in which the percentage Negro was-				
		Less than 12.5[1]	12.5 to 24.9	25 to 49.9	50 to 74.9	75 or more
	INCREASE OR DECREASE OF AREA IN SQUARE MILE[2]S					
The South:						
1910	-509	-8,385	17,803	9,596	-16,812	-2,711
1900	-	-5,024	5,845	-333	-221	-267
1890	5,740	35,823	-28,245	7,696	-13,704	4,170
1880	-	-	-	-	-	-
South Atlantic:						
1910	451	-6,625	5,629	8,348	-6,407	-494
1900	-	-6,683	-25	3,290	3,789	-371
1890	-	5,558	-1,607	3,075	-8,183	1,157
1880	-	-	-	-	-	-
East South Central:						
1910	-121	5,248	3,923	-7,077	-1,103	-1,112
1900	-	983	-2,905	946	-1,430	2,406
1890	-	5,358	-2,630	1,652	-7,195	2,815
1880	-	-	-	-	-	-
West South Central:						
1910	-839	-7,008	8,251	8,325	-9,302	-1,105
1900	-	676	8,775	-4,569	-2,580	-2,302

[Continued]

★ 1785 ★

Southern County Areas by Percentage Black and by Divisions, 1880-1910 - III

[Continued]

DIVISION AND YEAR	SOUTHERN STATES					
	All counties	Counties in which the percentage Negro was-				
		Less than 12.5[1]	12.5 to 24.9	25 to 49.9	50 to 74.9	75 or more
1890	5,740	24,907	-24,008	2,969	1,674	198
1880	-	-	-	-	-	-

Source: "Southern County Areas Classified According to Specific Percentage Negro in the Population, by Divisions: 1910, 1900, 1890, and 1880." U.S. Bureau of the Census, *Negro Population, 1790-1915*, p. 128. *Notes:* 1. Includes counties reporting no Negro population. 2. Minus sign (-) denotes decrease.

★ 1786 ★

Geographical Areas: Counties

Southern County Areas by Percentage Black in Population, by Divisions and States, 1910 - I

DIVISION AND STATE	SOUTHERN STATES: 1910					
	All counties	Counties which the percentage Negro was-				
		Less than 12.5[1]	12.5 to 24.9	25 to 49.9	50 to 74.9	75 or more
	NUMBER OF COUNTIES					
The South	1,351	540	202	345	211	53
South Atlantic	534	124	73	181	143	13
East South Central	361	153	75	72	32	29
West South Central	456	263	54	92	36	11
South Atlantic:						
Delaware	3	-	3	-	-	-
Maryland	24	6	6	11	1	-
District of Columbia	1	-	-	1	-	-
Virginia	117	22	22	41	32	-
West Virginia	55	51	3	1	-	-
North Carolina	98	25	17	42	14	-
South Carolina	43	-	2	8	29	4
Georgia	146	19	12	49	59	7
Florida	47	1	8	28	8	2
East South Central:						
Kentucky	119	82	31	6	-	-
Tennessee	96	59	20	15	1	1
Alabama	67	10	13	23	10	11
Mississippi	79	2	11	28	21	17
West South Central:						
Arkansas	75	36	6	19	9	5

[Continued]

★ 1786 ★

Southern County Areas by Percentage Black in Population, by Divisions and States, 1910 - I

[Continued]

DIVISION AND STATE	SOUTHERN STATES: 1910					
	All counties	Counties which the percentage Negro was-				
		Less than 12.5[1]	12.5 to 24.9	25 to 49.9	50 to 74.9	75 or more
Louisiana	60	-	10	25	19	6
Oklahoma	76	62	8	6	-	-
Texas	245	165	30	42	8	-

Source: "Southern County Areas Classified According to Specific Percentage Negro in the Population by Divisions and States: 1910." U.S. Bureau of the Census, *Negro Population, 1790-1915,* p. 127. *Note:* 1. Includes counties reporting no Negro population.

★ 1787 ★

Geographical Areas: Counties

Southern County Areas by Percentage Black in Population, by Divisions and States, 1910 - II

DIVISION AND STATE	SOUTHERN STATES: 1910					
	All counties	Counties which the percentage Negro was-				
		Less than 12.5[1]	12.5 to 24.9	25 to 49.9	50 to 74.9	75 or more
	AREA IN SQUARE MILES					
The South	878,326	391,273	123,581	216,253	113,138	34,081
South Atlantic	269,071	52,484	41,564	98,439	68,972	7,612
East South Central	179,509	59,559	34,278	44,951	21,112	19,609
West South Central	429,746	279,230	47,739	72,863	23,054	6,860
South Atlantic:						
Delaware	1,965	-	1,965	-	-	-
Maryland	9,941	3,347	1,789	4,341	464	-
District of Columbia	60	-	-	60	-	-
Virginia	40,262	10,161	6,838	11,888	11,375	-
West Virginia	24,022	22,192	1,297	533	-	-
North Carolina	48,740	10,841	8,065	23,789	6,044	-
South Carolina	30,495	-	1,687	5,492	19,975	3,341
Georgia	58,725	5,485	4,472	21,350	24,447	2,971
Florida	54,861	458	15,450	30,986	6,667	1,300
East South Central:						
Kentucky	40,181	27,798	10,337	2,046	-	-
Tennessee	41,687	23,633	9,451	7,477	508	618
Alabama	51,279	7,171	8,654	18,776	8,315	8,363

[Continued]

★ 1787 ★

Southern County Areas by Percentage Black in Population, by Divisions and States, 1910 - II

[Continued]

DIVISION AND STATE	SOUTHERN STATES: 1910					
	All counties	Counties which the percentage Negro was-				
		Less than 12.5[1]	12.5 to 24.9	25 to 49.9	50 to 74.9	75 or more
Mississippi	46,362	957	5,836	16,652	12,289	10,628
West South Central:						
Arkansas	52,525	25,554	3,790	13,625	6,327	3,229
Louisiana	45,409	-	12,660	17,542	11,576	3,631
Oklahoma	69,414	58,036	7,317	4,061	-	-
Texas	262,398	195,640	23,972	37,635	5,151	-

Source: "Southern County Areas Classified According to Specific Percentage Negro in the Population by Divisions and States: 1910." U.S. Bureau of the Census, *Negro Population, 1790-1915*, p. 127. *Note:* 1. Includes counties reporting no Negro population.

★ 1788 ★

Geographical Areas: Counties

Southern County Areas by Percentage Black in Population, by Divisions and States, 1910 - III

DIVISION AND STATE	SOUTHERN STATES: 1910					
	All counties	Counties which the percentage Negro was-				
		Less than 12.5[1]	12.5 to 24.9	25 to 49.9	50 to 74.9	75 or more
	PERCENTAGE OF TOTAL AREA OF DIVISION OR STATE					
The South	100.0	44.5	14.1	24.6	12.9	3.9
South Atlantic	100.0	19.5	15.4	36.6	25.6	2.8
East South Central	100.0	33.2	19.1	25.0	11.8	10.9
West South Central	100.0	65.0	11.1	17.0	5.4	1.6
South Atlantic:						
Delaware	100.0	-	100.0	-	-	-
Maryland	100.0	33.7	18.0	43.7	4.7	-
District of Columbia	100.0	-	-	100.0	-	-
Virginia	100.0	25.2	17.0	29.5	28.3	-
West Virginia	100.0	92.4	5.4	2.2	-	-
North Carolina	100.0	22.2	16.5	48.8	12.4	-
South Carolina	100.0	-	5.5	18.0	65.5	11.0
Georgia	100.0	9.3	7.6	36.4	41.5	5.1
Florida	100.0	0.8	28.2	56.5	12.2	2.4

[Continued]

★ 1788 ★

Southern County Areas by Percentage Black in Population, by Divisions and States, 1910 - III

[Continued]

DIVISION AND STATE	SOUTHERN STATES: 1910					
	All counties	Counties which the percentage Negro was-				
		Less than 12.5[1]	12.5 to 24.9	25 to 49.9	50 to 74.9	75 or more
East South Central:						
Kentucky	100.0	69.2	25.7	5.1	-	-
Tennessee	100.0	56.7	22.7	17.9	1.2	1.5
Alabama	100.0	14.0	16.9	36.6	16.2	16.3
Mississippi	100.0	2.1	12.6	35.9	26.5	22.9
West South Central:						
Arkansas	100.0	48.7	7.2	25.9	12.0	6.1
Louisiana	100.0	-	27.9	38.6	25.5	8.0
Oklahoma	100.0	83.6	10.5	5.9	-	-
Texas	100.0	74.6	9.1	14.3	2.0	-

Source: "Southern County Areas Classified According to Specific Percentage Negro in the Population by Divisions and States: 1910." U.S. Bureau of the Census, *Negro Population, 1790-1915,* p. 127. *Note:* 1. Includes counties reporting no Negro population.

★ 1789 ★

Geographical Areas: Counties

Southern County Areas by Percentage Black, by Divisions and States, 1930 - I

DIVISION AND STATE	Total number of counties	NUMBER OF COUNTIES IN WHICH THE PERCENT OF NEGRO POPULATION WAS-				
		Less than 12.5[1]	12.5 to 24.9	25 to 49.9	50 to 74.9	75 or more
The South	1,415	694	227	393	172	19
South Atlantic	581	149	96	229	104	3
East South Central	364	171	73	65	41	14
West South Central	470	284	58	99	27	2
SOUTH ATLANTIC:						
Delaware	3	1	2	-	-	-
Maryland	24	7	7	10	-	-
District of Columbia	1	-	-	1	-	-
Virginia	124	34	24	45	20	1
West Virginia	55	51	4	-	-	-
North Carolina	100	29	17	45	9	-
South Carolina	46	-	4	17	25	-
Georgia	161	24	21	68	46	2
Florida	67	3	17	43	4	-

[Continued]

★ 1789 ★

Southern County Areas by Percentage Black, by Divisions and States, 1930 - I

[Continued]

DIVISION AND STATE	Total number of counties	NUMBER OF COUNTIES IN WHICH THE PERCENT OF NEGRO POPULATION WAS-				
		Less than 12.5[1]	12.5 to 24.9	25 to 49.9	50 to 74.9	75 or more
EAST SOUTH CENTRAL:						
Kentucky	120	93	25	2	-	-
Tennessee	95	66	18	9	2	-
Alabama	67	10	16	23	12	6
Mississippi	82	2	14	31	27	8
WEST SOUTH CENTRAL:						
Arkansas	75	37	8	21	8	1
Louisiana	64	1	12	35	15	1
Oklahoma	77	69	6	2	-	-
Texas	254	177	32	41	4	-

Source: "Southern County Areas Classified According to Specific Percentage Negro in the Population, by Divisions, and States: 1930." U.S. Bureau of the Census, *Negroes in the United States, 1920-1932*, p. 72. *Note:* 1. Includes counties reporting no Negro population.

★ 1790 ★

Geographical Areas: Counties

Southern County Areas by Percentage Black, by Divisions and States, 1930 - II

DIVISION AND STATE	Total area in miles	AREA IN SQUARE MILES OF COUNTIES IN WHICH THE PERCENT OF NEGRO POPULATION WAS-				
		Less than 12.5[1]	12.5 to 24.9	25 to 49.9	50 to 74.9	75 or more
The South	878,328	415,510	130,834	226,669	93,918	11,397
South Atlantic	269,073	61,249	46,348	110,544	49,462	1,470
East South Central	179,509	65,992	35,466	42,003	27,055	8,993
West South Central	429,746	288,269	49,020	74,122	17,401	934
SOUTH ATLANTIC:						
Delaware	1,965	435	1,530	-	-	-
Maryland	9,941	3,681	2,464	3,796	-	-
District of Columbia	62	-	-	62	-	-
Virginia	40,262	13,488	5,806	13,318	7,462	188
West Virginia	24,022	22,014	2,008	-	-	-
North Carolina	48,740	12,278	8,565	23,417	4,480	-
South Carolina	30,495	-	3,098	10,945	16,452	-
Georgia	58,725	7,292	7,982	23,660	18,509	1,282
Florida	54,861	2,061	14,895	35,346	2,559	-

[Continued]

★ 1790 ★

Southern County Areas by Percentage Black, by Divisions and States, 1930 - II

[Continued]

DIVISION AND STATE	Total area in miles	AREA IN SQUARE MILES OF COUNTIES IN WHICH THE PERCENT OF NEGRO POPULATION WAS- Less than 12.5[1]	12.5 to 24.9	25 to 49.9	50 to 74.9	75 or more
EAST SOUTH CENTRAL:						
Kentucky	40,181	31,115	7,974	1,092	-	-
Tennessee	41,687	26,814	8,951	4,796	1,126	-
Alabama	51,279	7,106	11,493	18,248	10,030	4,402
Mississippi	46,362	957	7,048	17,867	15,899	4,591
WEST SOUTH CENTRAL:						
Arkansas	52,525	25,987	5,621	14,983	5,352	582
Louisiana	45,400	1,501	9,802	23,882	9,872	352
Oklahoma	69,414	62,581	5,645	1,188	-	-
Texas	262,398	198,200	27,952	34,069	2,177	-

Source: "Southern County Areas Classified According to Specific Percentage Negro in the Population, by Divisions, and States: 1930." U.S. Bureau of the Census, *Negroes in the United States, 1920-1932*, p. 72. *Note:* 1. Includes counties reporting no Negro population.

★ 1791 ★

Geographical Areas: Counties

Southern County Areas by Percentage Black, by Divisions and States, 1930 - III

DIVISION AND STATE	Total land area	PERCENT DISTRIBUTION IN AREA OR DIVISION OR STATE IN WHICH THE PERCENT OF NEGRO POPULATION WAS- Less than 12.5[1]	12.5 to 24.9	25 to 49.9	50 to 74.9	75 or more
The South	100.0	47.3	14.9	25.8	10.7	1.3
South Atlantic	100.0	22.8	17.2	41.1	18.4	0.5
East South Central	100.0	36.8	19.8	23.4	15.1	5.0
West South Central	100.0	67.1	11.4	17.2	4.0	.2
SOUTH ATLANTIC:						
Delaware	100.0	22.1	77.9	-	-	-
Maryland	100.0	37.0	24.8	38.2	-	-
District of Columbia	100.0	-	-	100.0	-	-
Virginia	100.0	33.5	14.4	33.1	18.5	.5
West Virginia	100.0	91.6	8.4	-	-	-
North Carolina	100.0	25.2	17.6	48.0	9.2	-
South Carolina	100.0	-	10.2	35.9	53.9	-
Georgia	100.0	12.4	13.6	40.3	31.5	2.2
Florida	100.0	3.8	27.2	64.4	4.7	-

[Continued]

★ 1791 ★

Southern County Areas by Percentage Black, by Divisions and States, 1930 - III

[Continued]

DIVISION AND STATE	Total land area	PERCENT DISTRIBUTION IN AREA OR DIVISION OR STATE IN WHICH THE PERCENT OF NEGRO POPULATION WAS-				
		Less than 12.5[1]	12.5 to 24.9	25 to 49.9	50 to 74.9	75 or more
EAST SOUTH CENTRAL:						
Kentucky	100.0	77.4	19.8	2.7	-	-
Tennessee	100.0	64.3	21.5	11.5	2.7	-
Alabama	100.0	13.9	22.4	35.6	19.6	8.6
Mississippi	100.0	2.1	15.2	38.5	34.3	9.9
WEST SOUTH CENTRAL:						
Arkansas	100.0	49.5	10.7	28.5	10.2	1.1
Louisiana	100.0	3.3	21.6	52.6	21,7	.8
Oklahoma	100.0	90.2	8.1	1.7	-	-
Texas	100.0	75.5	10.7	13.0	.8	-

Source: "Southern County Areas Classified According to Specific Percentage Negro in the Population, by Divisions, and States: 1930." U.S. Bureau of the Census, *Negroes in the United States, 1920-1932*, p. 72. *Note:* 1. Includes counties reporting no Negro population.

Geographical Areas: Sections, Divisions, States

★ 1792 ★

Black and White Population by States at Each Census, 1790-1910; Indian and Other 1900 and 1910 - I

DIVISION AND STATE	NEGRO, WHITE, INDIAN, AND OTHER POPULATION, 1910 and 1900									
	1910					1900				
	Total	Negro	White	Indian	Other[1]	Total	Negro	White	Indian	Other[1]
UNITED STATES	91,972,266	9,827,763	81,731,957	265,683	146,863	75,994,575	8,833,994	66,809,196	237,196	114,189
GEOGRAPHIC DIVISIONS:										
New England	6,552,681	66,306	6,480,514	2,076	3,785	5,592,017	59,099	5,527,026	1,600	4,292
Middle Atlantic	19,315,892	417,870	18,880,452	7,717	9,853	15,454,678	325,921	15,110,862	6,959	10,936
East North Central	18,250,621	300,836	17,927,622	18,255	3,908	15,985,581	257,842	15,710,053	15,027	2,659
West North Central	11,637,921	242,662	11,351,621	41,406	2,232	10,347,423	237,909	10,065,817	42,339	1,358
South Atlantic	12,194,895	4,112,488	8,072,603	9,054	1,750	10,443,480	3,729,017	6,706,058	6,585	1,820
East South Central	8,409,901	2,652,513	5,754,326	2,612	450	7,547,757	2,499,886	5,044,847	2,590	434
West South Central	8,784,534	1,984,426	6,721,491	76,767	1,850	6,532,290	1,694,066	4,771,065	65,574	1,585
Mountain	2,633,517	21,467	2,520,455	75,338	16,257	1,674,657	15,590	1,579,855	66,155	13,057
Pacific	4,192,304	29,195	4,023,873	32,458	106,778	2,416,692	14,664	2,293,613	30,367	78,048
NEW ENGLAND:										
Maine	742,371	1,363	739,995	892	121	694,466	1,319	692,226	798	123
New Hampshire	430,572	564	429,906	34	68	411,588	662	410,791	22	113
Vermont	355,956	1,621	354,298	26	11	343,641	826	324,771	5	39
Massachusetts	3,366,416	38,055	3,324,926	688	2,747	2,805,346	31,974	2,769,764	587	3,021

[Continued]

★ 1792 ★

Black and White Population by States at Each Census, 1790-1910; Indian and Other 1900 and 1910 - I

[Continued]

DIVISION AND STATE	NEGRO, WHITE, INDIAN, AND OTHER POPULATION, 1910 and 1900									
	1910					1900				
	Total	Negro	White	Indian	Other[1]	Total	Negro	White	Indian	Other[1]
Rhode Island	542,610	9,529	532,492	284	305	428,556	9,092	419,050	35	379
Connecticut	1,114,756	15,174	1,098,897	152	533	908,420	15,226	892,424	153	617
MIDDLE ATLANTIC:										
New York	9,113,614	134,191	8,966,845	6,046	6,532	7,268,894	99,232	7,156,881	5,257	7,524
New Jersey	2,537,167	89,760	2,445,894	168	1,345	1,883,669	69,844	1,812,317	63	1,445
Pennsylvania	7,665,111	193,919	7,467,713	1,503	1,976	6,302,115	156,845	6,141,664	1,639	1,967
EAST NORTH CENTRAL:										
Ohio	4,767,121	111,452	4,654,897	127	645	4,157,545	96,901	4,060,204	42	398
Indiana	2,700,876	60,320	2,639,961	279	316	2,516,462	57,506	2,458,502	243	212
Illinois	5,638,591	109,049	5,526,962	188	2,392	4,821,550	85,078	4,734,873	16	1,583
Michigan	2,810,173	17,115	2,785,247	7,519	292	2,420,982	15,816	2,398,563	6,554	249
Wisconsin	2,333,860	2,900	2,320,555	10,142	263	2,069,042	2,542	2,057,911	8,372	217
WEST NORTH CENTRAL:										
Minnesota	2,075,708	7,084	2,059,227	9,053	344	1,752,394	4,959	1,737,036	9,182	217
Iowa	2,224,771	14,973	2,209,191	471	136	2,231,853	12,693	2,218,667	382	111
Missouri	3,293,335	157,452	3,134,932	313	638	3,106,655	161,234	2,944,843	130	458
North Dakota	577,058	617	569,855	6,486	98	319,146	286	311,712	6,968	180
South Dakota	583,888	817	563,771	19,137	163	401,570	465	380,714	20,225	166
Nebraska	1,192,214	7,689	1,180,293	3,502	730	1,066,300	6,269	1,056,526	3,322	183
Kansas	1,690,949	54,030	1,634,352	2,444	123	1,470,495	52,003	1,416,319	2,130	43
SOUTH ATLANTIC:										
Delaware	202,322	31,181	171,102	5	34	184,735	30,697	153,977	9	52
Maryland	1,295,346	232,250	1,062,639	55	402	1,188,044	235,064	952,424	3	553
District of Columbia	331,069	94,446	236,128	68	427	278,718	86,702	191,532	22	462
Virginia	2,061,612	671,096	1,389,809	539	168	1,854,184	660,722	1,192,855	354	253
West Virginia	1,221,119	64,173	1,156,817	36	93	958,800	43,499	915,233	12	56
North Carolina	2,206,287	697,843	1,500,511	7,851	82	1,893,810	624,469	1,263,603	5,687	51
South Carolina	1,515,400	835,843	679,161	331	65	1,340,316	782,321	557,807	121	67
Georgia	2,609,121	1,716,987	1,431,802	95	237	2,216,331	1,034,813	1,181,294	19	205
Florida	752,619	308,669	443,634	74	242	528,542	230,730	297,333	358	121
EAST SOUTH CENTRAL:										
Kentucky	2,289,905	261,656	2,027,951	234	64	2,147,174	284,706	1,862,309	102	57
Tennessee	2,184,789	473,088	1,711,432	216	53	2,020,616	480,243	1,540,186	108	79
Alabama	2,138,093	908,282	1,228,832	909	70	1,828,697	827,307	1,001,152	177	61
Mississippi	1,797,114	1,009,487	786,111	1,253	263	1,551,270	907,630	641,200	2,203	237
WEST SOUTH CENTRAL:										
Arkansas	1,574,449	442,891	1,131,026	460	72	1,311,564	366,856	944,580	66	62
Louisiana	1,656,388	713,874	941,086	780	648	1,381,625	650,804	729,612	593	616
Oklahoma[2]	1,657,155	137,612	1,444,531	74,825	187	790,391	55,684	670,204	64,445	58
Texas	3,896,542	690,049	3,204,848	702	943	3,048,710	620,722	2,426,669	470	849
MOUNTAIN:										
Montana	376,053	1,834	360,580	10,745	2,894	243,329	1,523	226,283	11,343	4,180
Idaho	325,594	651	319,221	3,488	2,234	161,772	293	154,495	4,226	2,758
Wyoming	145,965	2,235	140,318	1,486	1,926	92,531	940	89,051	1,688	854
Colorado	799,024	11,453	783,415	1,482	2,674	539,700	8,570	529,046	1,437	647
New Mexico	327,301	1,628	304,594	20,573	506	195,310	1,610	180,207	13,144	349
Arizona	204,354	2,009	171,468	29,201	1,676	122,931	1,848	92,903	26,480	1,700
Utah	373,351	1,144	366,583	3,123	2,501	276,749	672	272,465	2,623	989
Nevada	81,875	513	74,276	5,240	1,846	42,335	134	35,405	5,216	1,580

[Continued]

★ 1792 ★

Black and White Population by States at Each Census, 1790-1910; Indian and Other 1900 and 1910 - I

[Continued]

DIVISION AND STATE	NEGRO, WHITE, INDIAN, AND OTHER POPULATION, 1910 and 1900									
	1910					1900				
	Total	Negro	White	Indian	Other[1]	Total	Negro	White	Indian	Other[1]
PACIFIC:										
Washington	1,141,990	6,058	1,109,111	10,997	15,824	518,103	2,514	496,304	10,039	9,246
Oregon	672,765	1,492	655,090	5,090	11,093	413,536	1,105	394,582	4,951	12,898
California	2,377,549	21,645	2,259,672	16,371	79,861	1,485,053	11,045	1,402,727	15,377	55,904

Source: "Population by States: Black and White, At Each Census, 1790-1910; Indian and Other, 1910 and 1900." U.S. Bureau of the Census, *Negro Population, 1790-1915*, pp. 43-45. *Notes:* 1. Chinese, Japanese, and all other. 2. Includes Indian Territory for 1900 and 1890.

★ 1793 ★

Geographical Areas: Sections, Divisions, States

Black and White Population by States at Each Census, 1790-1910; Indian and Other 1900 and 1910 - II

DIVISION AND STATE	NEGRO AND WHITE POPULATION AT EACH CENSUS, 1790 TO 1910									
	1890[1]		1880		1870		1860		1850	
	Negro	White	Negro	White	Negro	White	Negro	White	Negro	White
UNITED STATES	7,488,676	55,101,258	6,580,793	43,402,970	4,880,009	33,589,377	4,441,830	26,922,537	3,638,808	19,533,068
GEOGRAPHIC DIVISIONS:										
New England	44,580	4,653,191	39,925	3,968,789	31,705	3,455,043	24,711	3,110,480	23,021	2,705,095
Middle Atlantic	225,326	12,468,794	189,492	10,305,055	148,033	8,662,226	131,290	7,327,548	126,741	5,771,994
East North Central	207,023	13,253,725	183,298	11,012,047	130,497	8,987,512	63,699	6,855,644	45,195	4,478,065
West North Central	224,089	8,660,088	202,323	5,949,376	142,583	3,710,991	120,540	2,044,325	90,412	789,923
South Atlantic	3,262,690	5,592,149	2,941,202	4,654,112	2,216,705	3,635,238	2,058,198	3,305,107	1,860,871	2,818,219
East South Central	2,119,797	4,305,668	1,924,966	3,657,593	1,464,252	2,939,091	1,394,360	2,626,376	1,122,790	2,240,481
West South Central	1,378,090	3,295,636	1,087,705	2,243,722	739,854	1,288,880	644,553	1,102,490	368,537	571,714
Mountain	12,971	1,117,363	5,022	614,821	1,555	301,848	235	164,092	72	72,855
Pacific	14,110	1,754,644	6,830	997,455	4,825	608,548	4,244	386,475	1,169	104,722
NEW ENGLAND:										
Maine	1,190	659,263	1,451	646,852	1,606	624,809	1,327	626,947	1,356	581,813
New Hampshire	614	375,840	685	346,229	580	317,697	494	325,579	520	317,456
Vermont	937	331,418	1,057	331,218	924	329,613	709	314,369	718	313,402
Massachusetts	22,144	2,215,373	18,697	1,763,782	13,947	1,443,156	9,602	1,221,432	9,064	985,450
Rhode Island	7,393	337,859	6,488	269,939	4,980	212,219	3,952	170,649	3,670	143,875
Connecticut	12,302	733,438	11,547	610,769	9,668	527,549	8,627	451,504	7,693	363,099
MIDDLE ATLANTIC:										
New York	70,092	5,923,955	65,104	5,016,022	52,081	4,330,210	49,005	3,831,590	49,069	3,048,325
New Jersey	47,638	1,396,581	38,853	1,092,017	30,658	875,407	25,336	646,699	24,046	465,509
Pennsylvania	107,596	5,148,258	85,535	4,197,016	65,294	3,456,609	56,949	2,849,259	53,626	2,258,160
EAST NORTH CENTRAL:										
Ohio	87,113	3,584,805	79,900	3,117,920	63,213	2,601,946	36,673	2,302,808	25,279	1,955,050
Indiana	45,215	2,146,736	39,228	1,938,798	24,560	1,655,837	11,428	1,338,710	11,262	977,154
Illinois	57,028	3,768,472	46,368	3,031,151	28,762	2,511,096	7,628	1,704,291	5,436	846,034
Michigan	15,223	2,072,884	15,100	1,614,560	11,849	1,167,282	6,799	736,142	2,588	395,071
Wisconsin	2,444	1,680,828	2,702	1,309,618	2,113	1,051,351	1,171	773,693	635	304,756
WEST NORTH CENTRAL:										
Minnesota	3,683	1,296,408	1,564	776,884	759	438,257	259	169,395	39	6,038
Iowa	10,685	1,901,090	9,516	1,614,600	5,762	1,188,207	1,069	673,779	333	191,881

[Continued]

★ 1793 ★

Black and White Population by States at Each Census, 1790-1910; Indian and Other 1900 and 1910 - II

[Continued]

DIVISION AND STATE	NEGRO AND WHITE POPULATION AT EACH CENSUS, 1790 TO 1910									
	1890[1]		1880		1870		1860		1850	
	Negro	White	Negro	White	Negro	White	Negro	White	Negro	White
Missouri	150,184	2,528,458	145,350	2,022,826	118,071	1,603,146	118,503	1,063,489	90,040	592,004
North Dakota	373	182,407	113[1]	36,192[2]						
South Dakota	541	328,010	288[2]	96,955[2]						
Nebraska	8,913	1,047,096	2,385	449,764	789	122,117	82	28,696	-	-
Kansas	49,710	1,376,619	43,107	952,155	17,108	346,377	627	106,390	-	-
SOUTH ATLANTIC:										
Delaware	28,386	140,066	26,442	120,160	22,794	102,221	21,627	90,589	20,363	71,169
Maryland	215,657	826,493	210,230	724,693	175,391	605,497	171,131	515,918	165,091	417,943
District of Columbia	76,572	154,695	59,596	118,006	43,404	88,278	14,316	60,763	13,746	37,941
Virginia	635,438	1,020,122	631,616	880,858	512,841	712,089	548,907	1,047,299	526,861	894,800
West Virginia	32,690	730,077	25,886	592,537	17,980	424,033	-	-	-	-
North Carolina	561,018	1,055,382	531,277	867,242	391,650	678,470	361,522	629,942	316,011	553,028
South Carolina	688,934	462,008	604,332	391,105	415,814	289,667	412,320	291,300	393,944	274,563
Georgia	858,815	978,357	725,133	816,906	545,142	638,926	465,698	591,550	384,613	521,572
Florida	166,180	224,949	126,690	142,605	91,689	96,057	62,677	77,746	40,242	47,203
EAST SOUTH CENTRAL:										
Kentucky	268,071	1,590,462	271,451	1,377,179	222,210	1,098,692	236,167	919,484	220,992	761,413
Tennessee	430,678	1,336,637	403,151	1,138,831	322,331	936,119	283,019	826,722	245,881	756,836
Alabama	678,489	833,718	600,103	662,185	475,510	521,384	437,770	526,271	345,109	426,514
Mississippi	742,559	544,851	650,291	479,398	444,201	382,896	437,404	353,899	310,808	295,718
WEST SOUTH CENTRAL:										
Arkansas	309,117	818,752	210,666	591,531	122,169	362,115	111,259	324,143	47,708	162,189
Louisiana	559,193	555,395	483,655	454,954	364,210	362,065	350,373	357,456	262,271	255,491
Oklahoma[2]	21,609	172,554	-	-	-	-	-	-	-	-
Texas	488,171	1,745,935	393,384	1,197,237	253,475	564,700	182,921	420,891	58,558	154,034
MOUNTAIN:										
Montana	1,490	127,690	346	35,385	183	18,306	-	-	-	-
Idaho	201	82,117	53	29,013	60	10,618	-	-	-	-
Wyoming	922	59,324	298	19,437	183	8,726	-	-	-	-
Colorado	6,215	404,534	2,435	191,126	456	39,221	46	34,231	-	-
New Mexico	1,956	142,918	1,015	108,721	172	90,393	85	82,924	22	61,525
Arizona	1,357	55,734	155	35,160	26	9,581	-	-	-	-
Utah	588	205,925	232	142,423	118	86,044	59	40,125	50	11,330
Nevada	242	39,121	488	53,556	357	38,959	45	6,812	-	-
PACIFIC:										
Washington	1,602	340,829	325	67,199	207	22,195	30	11,138	-	-
Oregon	1,186	301,982	487	163,075	346	86,929	128	52,160	207	13,087
California	11,322	1,111,833	6,018	767,181	4,272	499,424	4,086	323,177	962	91,635

Source: "Population by States: Black and White, At Each Census, 1790-1910; Indian and Other, 1910 and 1900." U.S. Bureau of the Census, *Negro Population, 1790-1915*, pp. 43-45. *Notes:* 1. Includes persons specially enumerated in 1890 in Indian Territory and on Indian reservations - Negroes, 18636; whites, 117,368. 2. Dakota Territory. 3. Includes Indian Territory for 1900 and 1890.

★ 1794 ★

Geographical Areas: Sections, Divisions, States

Black and White Population by States at Each Census, 1790-1910; Indian and Other 1900 and 1910 - III

DIVISION AND STATE	NEGRO AND WHITE POPULATION AT EACH CENSUS, 1790 TO 1910											
	1840		1830		1820		1810		1800		1790	
	Negro	White	Negro	White	Negro	White	Negro	White	Negro	White	Negro	White
UNITED STATES	2,873,648	14,189,705	2,328,642	10,532,060	1,771,656	7,886,797	1,377,808	5,862,073	1,002,037	4,306,446	757,208	3,172,006
GEOGRAPHIC DIVISIONS:												
New England	22,657	2,212,165	21,379	1,933,338	20,927	1,639,144	19,906	1,452,067	18,652	1,214,359	16,987	992,421
Middle Atlantic	119,667	4,406,593	103,835	3,483,829	89,797	2,610,048	82,331	1,932,371	64,414	1,338,151	50,437	908,195
East North Central	29,345	2,895,383	15,883	1,454,135	7,691	785,028	3,454	268,870	635	50,371	-	-
West North Central	60,002	366,812	25,660	114,795	10,569	56,017	3,618	17,227	-	-	-	-
South Atlantic	1,597,317	2,327,982	1,529,283	2,116,469	1,273,399	1,787,664	1,080,800	1,594,091	859,690	1,426,804	673,462	1,178,344
East South Central	830,306	1,745,139	501,587	1,314,382	288,057	902,432	145,454	563,136	58,646	276,761	16,322	93,046
West South Central	214,354	235,631	131,015	115,112	81,216	86,464	42,245	34,311	-	-	-	-
Mountain	-	-	-	-	-	-	-	-	-	-	-	-
Pacific	-	-	-	-	-	-	-	-	-	-	-	-
NEW ENGLAND:												
Maine	1,355	500,438	1,192	398,263	929	297,406	969	227,736	818	150,901	538	96,002
New Hampshire	538	284,036	607	268,721	786	243,375	970	213,490	860	182,998	788	141,097
Vermont	730	291,218	881	279,771	903	235,078	750	217,145	557	153,908	271	85,154
Massachusetts	8,669	729,030	7,049	603,359	6,740	516,547	6,737	465,303	6,452	416,393	5,463	373,324
Rhode Island	3,243	105,587	3,578	93,621	3,602	79,457	3,717	73,214	3,684	65,438	4,355	64,470
Connecticut	8,122	301,856	8,072	289,603	7,967	267,281	6,763	255,179	6,281	244,721	5,572	232,374
MIDDLE ATLANTIC:												
New York	50,031	2,378,890	44,945	1,873,663	39,367	1,333,445	40,350	918,699	31,320	557,731	25,978	314,142
New Jersey	21,718	351,588	20,557	300,266	20,017	257,558	18,694	226,868	16,824	194,325	14,185	169,954
Pennsylvania	47,918	1,676,115	38,333	1,309,900	30,413	1,019,045	23,287	786,804	16,270	586,095	10,274	424,099
EAST NORTH CENTRAL:												
Ohio	17,345	1,502,122	9,574	928,329	4,723	576,711	1,899	228,861	337	45,028	-	-
Indiana	7,168	678,698	3,632	339,399	1,420	145,758	630	23,890	298	5,343	-	-
Illinois	3,929	472,254	2,384	155,061	1,374	53,837	781	11,501	-	-	-	-
Michigan	707	211,560	293	31,346	174	8,722	144	4,618	-	-	-	-
Wisconsin	196	30,749	-	-	-	-	-	-	-	-	-	-
WEST NORTH CENTRAL:												
Minnesota	-	-	-	-	-	-	-	-	-	-	-	-
Iowa	188	42,924	-	-	-	-	-	-	-	-	-	-
Missouri	59,814	323,888	25,660	114,795	10,569	56,017	3,618	17,227	-	-	-	-
North Dakota	-	-	-	-	-	-	-	-	-	-	-	-
South Dakota	-	-	-	-	-	-	-	-	-	-	-	-
Nebraska	-	-	-	-	-	-	-	-	-	-	-	-
Kansas	-	-	-	-	-	-	-	-	-	-	-	-
SOUTH ATLANTIC:												
Delaware	19,524	58,561	19,147	57,601	17,467	55,282	17,313	55,361	14,421	49,852	12,786	46,310
Maryland	151,815	318,204	155,932	291,108	147,127	260,223	145,429	235,117	125,222	216,326	111,079	208,649
District of Columbia	13,055	30,657	12,271	27,563	10,425	22,614	7,944	16,079	4,027	10,066	-	-
Virginia	498,829	740,968	517,105	694,300	462,031	603,335	423,086	551,514	365,920	514,280	305,493	442,117
West Virginia	-	-	-	-	-	-	-	-	-	-	-	-
North Carolina	268,549	484,870	265,114	472,843	219,629	419,200	179,090	376,410	140,339	337,764	105,547	288,204
South Carolina	335,314	259,084	323,322	257,863	265,301	237,440	200,919	214,196	149,336	196,255	108,895	140,178
Georgia	283,697	407,695	220,017	296,806	151,419	189,570	107,019	145,414	60,425	102,261	29,662	52,886
Florida	26,534	28,943	16,345	18,385	-	-	-	-	-	-	-	-
EAST SOUTH CENTRAL:												
Kentucky	189,575	590,253	170,130	517,787	129,491	434,826	82,274	324,237	41,082	179,873	12,544	61,133
Tennessee	188,583	640,627	146,158	535,746	82,844	339,979	45,852	215,875	13,893	91,709	3,778	31,913
Alabama	255,571	335,185	119,121	190,406	42,450	85,451	-	-	-	-	-	-
Mississippi	196,577	179,074	66,178	70,443	33,272	42,176	17,328	23,024	3,671	5,179	-	-
WEST SOUTH CENTRAL:												
Arkansas	20,400	77,174	4,717	25,671	1,676	12,597	-	-	-	-	-	-
Louisiana	193,954	158,457	126,298	89,441	79,540	73,867	42,245	34,311	-	-	-	-
Oklahoma[1]	-	-	-	-	-	-	-	-	-	-	-	-
Texas	-	-	-	-	-	-	-	-	-	-	-	-

[Continued]

★ 1794 ★

Black and White Population by States at Each Census, 1790-1910; Indian and Other 1900 and 1910 - III

[Continued]

DIVISION AND STATE	NEGRO AND WHITE POPULATION AT EACH CENSUS, 1790 TO 1910											
	1840		1830		1820		1810		1800		1790	
	Negro	White	Negro	White	Negro	White	Negro	White	Negro	White	Negro	White
MOUNTAIN:												
Montana	-	-	-	-	-	-	-	-	-	-	-	-
Idaho	-	-	-	-	-	-	-	-	-	-	-	-
Wyoming	-	-	-	-	-	-	-	-	-	-	-	-
Colorado	-	-	-	-	-	-	-	-	-	-	-	-
New Mexico	-	-	-	-	-	-	-	-	-	-	-	-
Arizona	-	-	-	-	-	-	-	-	-	-	-	-
Utah	-	-	-	-	-	-	-	-	-	-	-	-
Nevada	-	-	-	-	-	-	-	-	-	-	-	-
PACIFIC:												
Washington	-	-	-	-	-	-	-	-	-	-	-	-
Oregon	-	-	-	-	-	-	-	-	-	-	-	-
California	-	-	-	-	-	-	-	-	-	-	-	-

Source: "Population by States: Black and White, At Each Census, 1790-1910; Indian and Other, 1910 and 1900." U.S. Bureau of the Census, *Negro Population, 1790-1915*, pp. 43-45. *Note:* 1. Includes Indian Territory for 1900 and 1890.

★ 1795 ★

Geographical Areas: Sections, Divisions, States

Change in Black Population in Southern States, 1900-1910

DIVISION OR STATE	INCREASE OR DECREASE OF NEGRO POPULATION IN SOUTHERN STATES: 1900-1910											
	All counties		Counties or combinations of counties in which the percentage Negro in 191[1]									
			Less than 12.5		12.5 to 24.9		25 to 49.9		50 to 74.9		75 or more	
	Increase	Decrease	Increase	Decrease	Increase	Decrease	Increase	Decrease	Increase	Decrease	Increase	Decrease
	NUMBER											
The South	826,458	-	73,077	-	93,886	-	418,229	-	199,001	-	42,265	-
South Atlantic	383,471	-	2,404	-	34,301	-	216,745	-	132,743	-	-	2,722
East South Central	152,627	-	-	18,266	-	996	116,228	-	25,473	-	30,189	-
West South Central	290,360	-	88,939	-	60,581	-	85,256	-	40,786	-	14,798	-
South Atlantic:												
Delaware	484	-	-	-	484	-	-	-	-	-	-	-
Maryland	-	2,814	-	313	4,662	-	-	6,087	-	1,076	-	-
District of Columbia	7,744	-	-	-	-	-	7,744	-	-	-	-	-
Virginia	10,374	-	-	1,954	-	1,785	6,027	-	8,086	-	-	-
West Virginia	20,674	-	5,906	-	6,070	-	8,698	-	-	-	-	-
North Carolina	73,374	-	52	-	5,369	-	51,910	-	16,043	-	-	-
South Carolina	53,522	-	-	-	977	-	14,730	-	43,574	-	-	5,759
Georgia	142,174	-	-	1,200	5,150	-	78,971	-	55,437	-	3,816	-
Florida	77,939	-	-	87	13,374	-	54,752	-	10,679	-	-	779
East South Central:												
Kentucky	-	23,050	-	7,941	-	10,339	-	4,770	-	-	-	-
Tennessee	-	7,155	-	9,010	-	6,160	6,365	-	630	-	1,020	-
Alabama	80,975	-	-	1,209	15,152	-	66,986	-	11,586	-	-	11,540
Mississippi	101,857	-	-	106	351	-	47,647	-	13,256	-	40,709	-
West South Central:												
Arkansas	76,035	-	-	1,033	3,231	-	27,932	-	22,064	-	23,841	-
Louisiana	63,070	-	-	-	18,907	-	33,924	-	19,282	-	-	9,043
Oklahoma	81,928	-	81,928	-	-	-	-	-	-	-	-	-
Texas	69,327	-	8,044	-	38,443	-	23,400	-	-	560	-	-
	PER CENT											
The South	10.4	-	18.0	-	10.5	-	13.8	-	7.6	-	4.4	-

[Continued]

★ 1795 ★

Change in Black Population in Southern States, 1900-1910

[Continued]

DIVISION OR STATE	INCREASE OR DECREASE OF NEGRO POPULATION IN SOUTHERN STATES: 1900-1910											
	All counties		Counties or combinations of counties in which the percentage Negro in 191[1]									
			Less than 12.5		12.5 to 24.9		25 to 49.9		50 to 74.9		75 or more	
	Increase	Decrease	Increase	Decrease	Increase	Decrease	Increase	Decrease	Increase	Decrease	Increase	Decrease
South Atlantic	10.3	-	2.1	-	9.9	-	14.6	-	8.1	-	-	2.0
East South Central	6.1	-	-	12.3	-	0.3	14.8	-	4.7	-	4.5	-
West South Central	17.1	-	63.0	-	31.7	-	11.3	-	9.1	-	9.6	-
South Atlantic:												
Delaware	1.6	-	-	-	1.6	-	-	-	-	-	-	-
Maryland	-	1.2	-	1.3	4.5	-	-	6.2	-	11.2	-	-
District of Columbia	8.9	-	-	-	-	-	8.9	-	-	-	-	-
Virginia	1.6	-	-	7.7	-	2.8	1.8	-	3.5	-	-	-
West Virginia	47.5	-	23.8	-	47.8	-	145.7	-	-	-	-	-
North Carolina	11.7	-	0.2	-	6.6	-	14.3	-	10.7	-	-	-
South Carolina	6.8	-	-	-	8.8	-	15.0	-	7.0	-	-	10.6
Georgia	13.7	-	-	10.2	15.8	-	21.4	-	9.8	-	7.1	-
Florida	33.8	-	-	6.8	110.1	-	45.3	-	15.7	-	-	2.7
East South Central:												
Kentucky	-	8.1	-	11.9	-	6.3	-	8.8	-	-	-	-
Tennessee	-	1.5	-	13.4	-	6.4	2.3	-	3.7	-	4.7	-
Alabama	9.8	-	-	9.6	24.7	-	25.2	-	6.1	-	-	3.9
Mississippi	11.2	-	-	4.4	1.1	-	25.7	-	4.0	-	11.5	-
West South Central:												
Arkansas	20.7	-	-	3.9	20.5	-	18.4	-	21.5	-	33.9	-
Louisiana	9.7	-	-	-	62.2	-	12.4	-	7.4	-	-	10.7
Oklahoma	147.1	-	147.1	-	-	-	-	-	-	-	-	-
Texas	11.2	-	13.6	-	26.5	-	7.1	-	-	0.7	-	-

Source: "Increase or Decrease of Negro Population in Southern States Classified by Proportion Negro in the Population in 1910, by Southern Divisions and States: 1900-1910." U.S. Bureau of the Census, *Negro Population, 1790- 1915*, p. 130.

★ 1796 ★

Geographical Areas: Sections, Divisions, States

Density of Black and White Population, Total and Rural by Sections and Southern Divisions, 1930

SECTION AND DIVISION	Land area in square miles	POPULATION PER SQUARE MILE				
		Total			Rural	
		All classes	Negro	White	Negro	White
United States	2,973,776	41.3	4.0	38.6	2.3	15.5
THE SOUTH	878,328	43.1	10.7	31.5	7.3	20.6
South Atlantic	269,073	58.7	16.4	42.2	11.0	26.5
East South Central	179,509	55.1	14.8	40.2	10.6	29.0
West South Central	429,746	28.3	5.3	21.2	3.6	13.4
THE NORTH	918,344	79.5	2.6	76.6	0.3	25.7
THE WEST	1,777,104	10.1	.1	9.2	1	3.7

Source: "Density of Negro and White Population, Total and Rural, by Sections, and Southern Divisions: 1930." U.S. Bureau of the Census, *Negroes in the United States, 1920-1932*, p. 7. *Note:* 1. Less than 1/10 of 1 percent.

★ 1797 ★

Geographical Areas: Sections, Divisions, States

Distribution of Population by Sections, Divisions, and States, 1790-1930 - I

SECTION, DIVISION, AND STATE	1930				1920				1910		1900	
	Total	Negro	White	Other races	Total	Negro	White[1]	Other races[1]	Negro	White[1]	Negro	White
United States	122,775,046	11,891,143	108,864,207	2,019,696	105,710,620	10,463,131	94,120,374	1,127,115	9,827,763	81,364,447	8,833,994	66,809,196
The North	73,021,191	2,409,219	70,388,367	223,605	63,681,845	1,472,309	62,085,612	123,924	1,027,674	54,627,598	880,771	46,413,758
The South	37,857,633	9,361,577	27,673,879	822,177	33,125,803	8,912,231	23,731,899	481,673	3,749,427	20,316,253	7,922,969	16,521,970
The West	11,896,222	120,347	10,801,961	973,914	8,902,972	78,591	8,302,863	521,518	50,662	6,420,596	30,254	3,873,468
GEOGRAPHIC DIVISIONS:												
New England	8,166,341	94,086	8,065,113	7,142	7,400,909	79,051	7,315,995	5,863	66,306	6,480,468	59,099	5,527,026
Middle Atlantic	26,260,750	1,052,899	25,172,104	35,747	22,261,144	600,183	21,638,625	22,336	417,870	18,879,881	325,921	15,110,862
East North Central	25,297,185	930,450	24,277,663	89,072	21,475,543	514,554	20,931,279	29,710	300,836	17,926,513	257,842	15,710,053
West North Central	13,296,915	331,784	12,873,487	91,644	12,544,249	278,521	12,199,713	66,015	244,662	11,340,736	237,909	10,065,817
South Atlantic	15,793,589	4,421,388	11,349,284	22,917	13,990,272	4,325,120	9,648,556	16,596	4,112,488	8,071,473	3,729,017	6,706,058
East South Central	9,887,214	2,658,238	7,224,614	4,362	8,893,307	2,523,532	6,367,166	2,609	2,652,513	5,754,154	2,409,886	5,044,847
West South Central	12,176,830	2,281,951	9,009,981	794,898	10,242,224	2,063,579	7,716,177	462,468	1,984,426	6,490,426	1,694,066	4,771,065
Mountain	3,701,789	30,225	3,303,586	367,978	3,336,101	30,801	3,071,405	233,895	21,467	2,445,515	15,590	1,579,855
Pacific	8,194,433	90,122	7,498,375	605,936	5,566,871	47,790	5,231,458	287,623	29,195	3,975,081	14,664	2,293,613
NEW ENGLAND:												
Maine	797,423	1,096	795,183	1,144	768,014	1,310	765,693	1,011	1,363	739,991	1,319	692,226
New Hampshire	465,293	790	464,350	153	443,083	621	442,330	132	564	429,906	662	410,791
Vermont	359,611	568	358,965	78	352,428	572	351,916	40	1,621	354,298	826	342,771
Massachusetts	4,249,614	52,365	4,192,926	4,323	3,852,356	45,466	3,803,467	3,423	38,055	3,324,897	31,974	2,769,764
Rhode Island	687,497	9,913	677,016	568	604,397	10,036	593,976	385	9,529	532,488	9,092	419,050
Connecticut	1,606,903	29,354	1,576,673	876	1,380,631	21,046	1,358,713	872	15,174	1,098,888	15,226	892,424
MIDDLE ATLANTIC:												
New York	12,588,066	412,814	12,150,293	24,959	10,385,227	198,483	10,170,548	16,196	134,191	8,966,525	99,232	7,156,881
New Jersey	4,041,334	208,828	3,829,209	3,297	3,155,900	117,132	3,036,832	1,936	89,760	2,445,820	69,844	1,812,317
Pennsylvania	9,631,350	431,257	9,192,602	7,491	8,720,017	284,568	8,431,245	4,204	193,919	7,467,536	156,845	6,141,664
EAST NORTH CENTRAL:												
Ohio	6,646,697	309,304	6,331,136	6,257	5,759,394	186,187	5,570,951	2,256	111,452	4,654,758	96,901	4,060,204
Indiana	3,238,503	111,982	3,116,136	10,385	2,930,390	80,810	2,848,346	1,234	60,320	2,639,876	57,505	2,458,502
Illinois	7,630,654	328,972	7,266,361	35,321	6,485,280	182,274	6,294,999	8,007	109,049	5,526,241	85,078	4,734,873
Michigan	4,842,325	169,453	4,650,171	22,701	3,668,412	60,082	3,600,283	8,047	17,115	2,785,135	15,816	2,398,563
Wisconsin	2,939,006	10,739	2,913,859	14,408	2,632,067	5,201	2,616,700	10,166	2,900	2,320,503	2,542	2,057,911
WEST NORTH CENTRAL:												
Minnesota	2,563,953	9,445	2,538,973	15,535	2,387,125	8,809	2,368,586	9,730	7,084	2,059,143	4,959	1,737,036
Iowa	2,470,939	17,380	2,448,382	5,177	2,404,021	19,005	2,381,293	3,723	14,973	2,208,682	12,693	2,218,667
Missouri	3,629,367	223,840	3,398,887	6,640	3,404,055	178,241	3,221,661	4,153	157,452	3,133,570	161,234	2,944,843
North Dakota	680,845	377	671,243	9,225	646,872	467	639,912	6,493	617	569,845	286	311,712
South Dakota	692,849	646	669,453	22,750	636,547	832	619,052	16,663	817	563,747	465	380,714
Nebraska	1,377,963	13,752	1,353,702	10,509	1,296,372	13,242	1,276,473	6,657	7,689	1,179,994	6,269	1,056,526
Kansas	1,880,990	66,344	1,792,847	21,808	1,769,257	57,925	1,692,736	18,596	54,030	1,625,755	52,003	1,416,319
SOUTH ATLANTIC:												
Delaware	238,380	32,602	205,694	84	223,003	30,335	192,585	83	31,181	171,100	30,697	153,977
Maryland	1,631,526	276,379	1,354,170	977	1,449,661	244,479	1,204,690	492	232,250	1,062,627	235,064	952,424
District of Columbia	486,869	132,068	353,914	887	437,571	109,966	326,825	780	94,446	236,113	86,702	191,532
Virginia	2,421,851	650,165	1,770,405	1,281	2,309,187	690,017	1,617,871	1,299	671,096	1,389,802	660,722	1,192,855
West Virginia	1,729,205	114,893	1,613,934	378	1,463,701	86,345	1,377,180	176	64,173	1,156,811	43,499	915,233
North Carolina	3,170,276	918,647	2,234,948	16,681	2,559,123	763,407	1,783,769	11,947	697,843	1,500,508	624,469	1,263,603
South Carolina	1,738,765	793,681	944,040	1,044	1,683,724	864,719	818,532	473	835,843	679,159	782,321	557,807
Georgia	2,908,506	1,071,125	1,836,974	407	2,895,832	1,206,365	1,689,070	397	1,176,987	1,432,786	1,034,813	1,181,294
Florida	1,468,211	431,828	1,035,205	1,178	968,470	329,487	638,034	949	308,669	443,567	230,730	297,333
EAST SOUTH CENTRAL:												
Kentucky	2,614,589	226,040	2,388,364	185	2,416,630	235,938	2,180,462	230	261,656	2,027,926	284,706	1,862,309
Tennessee	2,616,556	477,646	2,138,619	291	2,337,885	451,758	1,885,939	188	473,088	1,711,417	480,243	1,540,186
Alabama	2,646,248	944,834	1,700,775	639	2,348,174	900,652	1,446,958	564	908,282	1,228,789	827,307	1,001,152
Mississippi	2,009,821	1,009,718	996,856	3,247	1,790,618	935,184	853,807	1,627	1,009,487	786,022	907,630	641,200
WEST SOUTH CENTRAL:												
Arkansas	1,854,482	478,463	1,374,906	1,113	1,752,204	472,220	1,279,479	505	442,891	1,130,878	366,856	944,580
Louisiana	2,101,593	776,326	1,318,160	7,107	1,798,509	700,257	1,093,991	4,261	713,874	939,789	650,804	729,612
Oklahoma[4]	2,396,040	172,198	2,123,424	100,418	2,028,283	149,408	1,813,217	65,658	137,612	1,441,577	55,684	670,204
Texas	5,824,715	854,964	4,283,491	686,260	4,663,228	741,694	3,529,490	392,044	690,049	2,978,382	620,722	2,426,669
MOUNTAIN:												
Montana	537,606	1,256	517,327	19,023	548,889	1,658	533,991	13,240	1,834	360,491	1,523	226,283
Idaho	445,032	668	437,562	6,802	431,866	920	424,540	6,406	651	319,074	293	154,495
Wyoming	225,565	1,250	214,067	10,248	194,402	1,375	188,146	4,881	2,235	139,990	940	89,051
Colorado	1,035,791	11,828	961,117	62,846	939,629	11,318	909,763	18,548	11,453	780,146	8,570	529,046
New Mexico	423,317	2,850	331,755	88,712	360,350	5,733	301,879	52,738	1,628	283,574	1,610	180,207
Arizona	435,573	10,749	264,378	160,446	334,162	8,005	202,985	123,172	2,009	122,360	1,848	92,903
Utah	507,847	1,108	495,955	10,784	449,396	1,446	440,699	7,251	1,144	366,425	672	272,465
Nevada	91,058	516	81,425	9,117	77,407	346	69,402	7,659	513	73,455	134	35,405

[Continued]

★ 1797 ★

Distribution of Population by Sections, Divisions, and States, 1790-1930 - I

[Continued]

SECTION, DIVISION, AND STATE	1930				1920				1910		1900	
	Total	Negro	White	Other races	Total	Negro	White[1]	Other races[1]	Negro	White[1]	Negro	White
PACIFIC:												
Washington	1,563,396	6,840	1,521,099	35,457	1,356,621	6,833	1,319,393	30,345	6,058	1,108,967	2,514	496,304
Oregon	953,786	2,234	937,029	14,523	783,389	2,144	768,530	12,715	1,492	654,833	1,105	394,582
California	5,677,251	81,048	5,040,247	555,956	3,426,861	38,763	3,143,535	244,563	21,645	2,211,281	11,045	1,402,727

Source: "Negro and White Population, by Sections, Divisions, and States: 1790 to 1930." U.S. Bureau of the Census, *Negroes in the United States, 1920-1932*, pp. 9-11. *Notes:* 1. Figures for white population in 1920 and 1910 are adjusted by deducting the estimated number of Mexicans and adding to "All Others." 2. Includes persons specially enumerated in 1890 in Indian Territory and on Indian reservations - Negroes, 18,636; whites, 117,368. 3. Dakota Territory. 4. Includes population of Indian Territory for 1900 and 1890.

★ 1798 ★

Geographical Areas: Sections, Divisions, States

Distribution of Population by Sections, Divisions, and States, 1790-1930 - II

SECTION, DIVISION, AND STATE	1890[2]		1880		1870		1860		1850	
	Negro	White	Negro	White	Negro	White	Negro	White	Negro	White
United States	7,488,676	55,101,258	6,580,793	43,402,970	4,880,009	33,589,377	4,441,830	26,922,537	3,638,808	19,553,068
The North	701,018	39,035,798	615,038	31,235,267	452,818	24,815,772	340,240	19,337,997	285,369	13,745,077
The South	6,760,577	13,193,453	5,953,903	10,555,427	4,420,811	7,863,209	4,097,111	7,033,973	3,352,198	5,630,414
The West	27,081	2,872,007	11,852	1,612,276	6,380	910,396	4,479	550,567	1,241	177,577
GEOGRAPHIC DIVISIONS:										
New England	44,580	4,653,191	39,925	3,968,789	31,705	3,455,043	24,711	3,110,480	23,021	2,705,095
Middle Atlantic	225,326	12,468,794	189,492	10,305,055	148,033	8,662,226	131,290	7,327,548	126,741	5,771,994
East North Central	207,023	13,253,725	183,298	11,012,047	130,497	8,987,512	63,699	6,855,644	45,195	4,478,065
West North Central	224,089	8,660,088	202,323	5,949,376	142,583	3,710,991	120,540	2,044,325	90,412	789,923
South Atlantic	3,262,690	5,592,149	2,941,202	4,654,112	2,216,705	3,635,238	2,058,198	3,305,107	1,860,871	2,818,219
East South Central	2,119,797	4,305,668	1,924,996	3,657,593	1,464,252	2,939,091	1,394,360	2,626,376	1,122,790	2,240,481
West South Central	1,378,090	3,295,636	1,087,705	2,243,722	739,854	1,288,880	644,553	1,102,490	368,537	571,714
Mountain	12,971	1,117,363	5,022	614,821	1,555	301,848	235	164,092	72	72,855
Pacific	14,110	1,754,644	6,830	997,455	4,825	608,548	4,244	386,475	1,169	104,722
NEW ENGLAND:										
Maine	1,190	659,263	1,451	646,852	1,606	624,809	1,327	626,947	1,356	581,813
New Hampshire	614	375,840	685	346,229	580	317,697	494	325,579	520	317,456
Vermont	937	331,418	1,057	331,218	924	329,613	709	314,369	718	313,402
Massachusetts	22,144	2,215,373	18,697	1,763,782	13,947	1,443,156	9,602	1,221,432	9,064	985,450
Rhode Island	7,393	337,859	6,488	269,939	4,980	212,219	3,952	170,649	3,670	143,875
Connecticut	12,302	733,438	11,547	610,769	9,668	527,549	8,627	451,504	7,693	363,099
MIDDLE ATLANTIC:										
New York	70,092	5,923,955	65,104	5,016,022	52,081	4,330,210	49,005	3,831,590	49,069	3,048,325
New Jersey	47,638	1,396,581	38,853	1,092,017	30,658	875,407	25,336	646,699	24,046	465,509
Pennsylvania	107,596	5,148,258	85,535	4,197,016	65,294	3,456,609	56,949	2,849,259	53,626	2,258,160
EAST NORTH CENTRAL:										
Ohio	87,113	3,584,805	79,900	3,117,920	63,213	2,601,946	36,673	2,302,808	25,279	1,955,050
Indiana	45,215	2,146,736	39,228	1,938,798	24,560	1,655,837	11,428	1,338,710	11,262	977,154
Illinois	57,028	3,768,472	46,368	3,031,151	28,762	2,511,096	7,628	1,704,291	5,436	846,034
Michigan	15,223	2,072,884	15,100	1,614,560	11,849	1,167,282	6,799	736,142	2,583	395,071
Wisconsin	2,444	1,680,828	2,702	1,309,618	2,113	1,051,351	1,171	773,693	635	304,756
WEST NORTH CENTRAL:										
Minnesota	3,683	1,296,408	1,564	776,884	759	438,257	259	169,395	39	6,038
Iowa	10,658	1,901,090	9,516	1,614,600	5,762	1,188,207	1,069	673,779	333	191,881
Missouri	150,184	2,528,458	145,350	2,022,826	118,071	1,603,146	118,503	1,063,489	90,040	592,004
North Dakota	373	182,407	113[3]	36,192[3]		12,887[3]	[3]	2,576[3]	-	-
South Dakota	541	328,010	288[3]	96,955[3]						
Nebraska	8,913	1,047,096	2,385	449,764	789	122,117	82	28,696	-	-
Kansas	49,710	1,376,619	43,107	952,155	17,108	346,377	627	106,390	-	-

[Continued]

★ 1798 ★

Distribution of Population by Sections, Divisions, and States, 1790-1930 - II

[Continued]

SECTION, DIVISION, AND STATE	1890[2]		1880		1870		1860		1850	
	Negro	White	Negro	White	Negro	White	Negro	White	Negro	White
SOUTH ATLANTIC:										
Delaware	28,386	140,066	26,442	120,160	22,794	102,221	21,627	90,589	20,363	71,169
Maryland	215,657	826,493	210,230	724,693	175,391	605,497	171,131	515,918	165,091	417,943
District of Columbia	75,572	154,695	59,596	118,006	43,404	88,278	14,316	60,763	13,746	37,941
Virginia	635,438	1,020,122	631,616	880,858	512,841	712,089	548,907	1,047,299	526,861	894,800
West Virginia	32,690	730,077	25,886	592,537	17,980	424,033	-	-	-	-
North Carolina	561,018	1,055,382	531,277	867,242	391,650	678,470	361,522	629,942	316,011	553,028
South Carolina	688,934	462,008	604,332	391,105	415,814	289,667	412,320	291,300	393,944	274,563
Georgia	858,815	978,357	725,133	816,906	545,142	638,926	465,698	591,550	384,613	521,572
Florida	166,180	224,949	126,690	142,605	91,689	96,057	62,677	77,746	40,242	47,203
EAST SOUTH CENTRAL:										
Kentucky	268,071	1,590,462	271,451	1,377,179	222,210	1,098,692	236,167	919,484	220,992	761,413
Tennessee	430,678	1,336,637	403,151	1,138,831	322,231	936,119	283,019	826,722	245,881	756,836
Alabama	678,489	833,718	600,103	662,185	475,510	521,384	437,770	526,271	345,109	426,514
Mississippi	742,559	544,851	650,291	479,398	444,201	382,896	437,404	353,899	310,808	295,718
WEST SOUTH CENTRAL:										
Arkansas	309,117	818,752	210,666	591,531	122,169	362,115	111,259	324,143	47,708	162,189
Louisiana	559,193	558,395	483,655	454,954	364,210	362,065	350,373	357,456	262,271	255,491
Oklahoma[4]	21,609	172,554	-	-	-	-	-	-	-	-
Texas	488,171	1,745,935	393,384	1,197,237	253,475	564,700	182,921	420,891	58,558	154,034
MOUNTAIN:										
Montana	1,490	127,690	346	35,385	183	18,306	-	-	-	-
Idaho	201	82,117	53	29,013	60	10,618	-	-	-	-
Wyoming	922	59,324	298	19,437	183	8,726	-	-	-	-
Colorado	6,215	404,534	2,435	191,126	456	39,221	46	34,231	-	-
New Mexico	1,956	142,918	1,015	108,721	172	90,393	85	82,924	22	61,525
Arizona	1,357	55,734	155	35,160	26	9,581	-	-	-	-
Utah	588	205,925	232	142,423	118	86,044	59	40,125	50	11,330
Nevada	242	39,121	488	53,556	357	38,959	45	6,812	-	-
PACIFIC:										
Washington	1,602	340,829	325	67,199	207	22,195	30	11,138	-	-
Oregon	1,186	301,982	487	163,075	346	86,929	128	52,160	207	13,087
California	11,322	1,111,833	6,018	767,181	4,272	499,424	4,086	323,177	962	91,635

Source: "Negro and White Population, by Sections, Divisions, and States: 1790 to 1930." U.S. Bureau of the Census, *Negroes in the United States, 1920-1932*, pp. 9-11. *Notes:* 1. Figures for white population in 1920 and 1910 are adjusted by deducting the estimated number of Mexicans and adding to "All Others." 2. Includes persons specialty enumerated in 1890 in Indian Territory and on Indian reservations - Negroes, 18,636; whites, 117,368. 3. Dakota Territory. 4. Includes population of Indian Territory for 1900 and 1890.

★ 1799 ★

Geographical Areas: Sections, Divisions, States

Distribution of Population by Sections, Divisions, and States, 1790-1930 - III

SECTION, DIVISION, AND STATE	1840		1830		1820		1810		1800		1790	
	Negro	White	Negro	White	Negro	White	Negro	White	Negro	White	Negro	White
United States	2,873,648	14,189,705	2,328,642	10,532,060	1,771,656	7,886,797	1,377,808	5,862,073	1,002,037	4,306,446	757,208	3,172,006
The North	231,671	9,880,953	166,757	6,986,097	128,984	5,090,237	109,309	3,670,535	83,701	2,602,881	67,424	1,900,616
The South	2,641,977	4,308,752	2,161,885	3,545,963	1,642,672	2,776,560	1,268,499	2,191,538	918,336	1,703,565	689,784	1,271,390
GEOGRAPHIC DIVISIONS:												
New England	22,657	2,212,165	21,379	1,933,338	20,927	1,639,144	19,906	1,452,067	18,652	1,214,359	16,987	992,421
Middle Atlantic	119,667	4,406,593	103,835	3,483,829	89,797	2,610,048	82,331	1,932,371	64,414	1,338,151	50,437	908,195
East North Central	29,345	2,895,383	15,883	1,454,135	7,619	785,208	3,454	268,870	635	50,371	-	-
West North Central	60,002	366,812	25,660	114,795	10,569	56,017	3,618	17,227	-	-	-	-
South Atlantic	1,597,317	2,327,982	1,529,283	2,116,469	1,273,399	1,787,664	1,080,800	1,594,091	859,690	1,426,804	673,462	1,178,344
East South Central	830,306	1,745,139	501,587	1,314,382	288,057	902,432	145,454	563,136	58,646	276,761	16,322	93,046
West South Central	214,354	235,631	131,015	115,112	81,216	86,464	42,245	34,311	-	-	-	-
NEW ENGLAND:												
Maine	1,355	500,438	1,192	398,263	929	297,406	969	227,736	818	150,901	538	96,002

[Continued]

★ 1799 ★

Distribution of Population by Sections, Divisions, and States, 1790-1930 - III

[Continued]

SECTION, DIVISION, AND STATE	1840		1830		1820		1810		1800		1790	
	Negro	White	Negro	White	Negro	White	Negro	White	Negro	White	Negro	White
New Hampshire	538	284,036	607	268,721	786	243,375	970	213,490	860	182,998	788	141,097
Vermont	730	281,218	881	279,771	903	235,078	750	217,145	557	153,908	271	85,154
Massachusetts	8,669	729,030	7,049	603,359	6,740	516,547	6,737	465,303	6,452	416,393	5,463	373,324
Rhode Island	3,243	105,587	3,578	93,621	3,602	79,457	3,717	73,214	3,684	65,438	4,355	64,470
Connecticut	8,122	301,856	8,072	289,603	7,967	267,281	6,763	255,179	6,281	244,721	5,572	232,374
MIDDLE ATLANTIC:												
New York	50,031	2,378,890	44,945	1,873,663	39,367	1,333,445	40,350	918,699	31,320	557,731	25,978	314,142
New Jersey	21,718	351,588	20,557	300,266	20,017	257,558	18,694	226,868	16,824	194,325	14,185	169,954
Pennsylvania	47,918	1,676,115	38,333	1,309,900	30,413	1,019,045	23,287	786,804	16,270	586,095	10,274	424,099
EAST NORTH CENTRAL:												
Ohio	17,345	1,502,122	9,574	928,329	4,723	576,711	1,899	228,861	337	45,028	-	-
Indiana	7,168	678,698	3,632	339,399	1,420	145,758	630	23,890	298	5,343	-	-
Illinois	3,929	472,254	2,384	155,061	1,374	53,837	781	11,501	-	-	-	-
Michigan	707	211,560	293	31,346	174	8,722	144	4,618	-	-	-	-
Wisconsin	196	30,749	-	-	-	-	-	-	-	-	-	-
WEST NORTH CENTRAL:												
Iowa	188	42,924	-	-	-	-	-	-	-	-	-	-
Missouri	59,814	323,888	25,660	114,795	10,569	56,017	3,618	17,227	-	-	-	-
SOUTH ATLANTIC:												
Delaware	19,524	58,561	19,147	57,601	17,467	55,282	17,313	55,361	14,421	49,852	12,786	46,310
Maryland	151,815	318,204	155,932	291,108	147,127	260,223	145,429	235,117	125,222	216,326	111,079	208,649
District of Columbia	13,055	30,657	12,271	27,563	10,425	22,614	7,944	16,079	4,027	10,066	-	-
Virginia	498,829	740,968	517,105	694,300	462,031	603,335	423,086	551,514	365,920	514,280	305,493	442,117
West Virginia	-	-	-	-	-	-	-	-	-	-	-	-
North Carolina	268,549	484,870	265,144	472,843	219,629	419,200	179,090	376,410	140,339	337,764	105,547	288,204
South Carolina	335,314	259,084	323,322	257,863	265,301	237,440	200,919	214,196	149,336	196,255	108,895	140,178
Georgia	283,697	407,695	220,017	296,806	151,419	189,570	107,019	145,414	60,425	102,261	29,662	52,886
Florida	26,534	27,943	16,345	18,385	-	-	-	-	-	-	-	-
EAST SOUTH CENTRAL:												
Kentucky	189,575	590,253	170,130	517,787	129,491	434,826	82,274	324,237	41,082	179,873	12,544	61,133
Tennessee	188,583	640,627	146,158	535,746	82,844	339,979	45,852	215,875	13,893	91,709	3,778	31,913
Alabama	255,571	335,185	119,121	190,406	42,450	85,451	-	-	-	-	-	-
Mississippi	196,577	179,074	66,178	70,443	33,272	42,176	17,328	23,024	3,671	5,179	-	-
WEST SOUTH CENTRAL:												
Arkansas	20,400	77,174	4,717	25,671	1,676	12,597	-	-	-	-	-	-
Louisiana	193,954	158,457	126,298	89,441	79,540	73,867	42,245	34,311	-	-	-	-

Source: "Negro and White Population, by Sections, Divisions, and States: 1790 to 1930." U.S. Bureau of the Census, *Negroes in the United States, 1920-1932*, pp. 9-11. *Notes:* 1. Figures for white population in 1920 and 1910 are adjusted by deducting the estimated number of Mexicans and adding to "All Others." 2. Includes persons specialty enumerated in 1890 in Indian Territory and on Indian reservations - Negroes, 18,636; whites, 117,368. 3. Dakota Territory. 4. Includes population of Indian Territory for 1900 and 1890.

★ 1800 ★

Geographical Areas: Sections, Divisions, States

Distribution of Population, by Region: 1790-1975

Area and race	1790	1870	1910	1940	1960	1970	1975
BLACK							
United States (millions)	1	5	10	13	19	23	24
Percent, total	100	100	100	100	100	100	100
South	91	91	89	77	60	53	52
North	9	9	10	22	34	39	39
Northeast	9	4	5	11	16	19	18
North Central	-	6	6	11	18	20	20
West	-	-	1	1	6	8	9

[Continued]

★ 1800 ★

Distribution of Population, by Region: 1790-1975

[Continued]

Area and race	1790	1870	1910	1940	1960	1970	1975
WHITE							
United States (millions)	3	34	82	118	159	178	183
Percent, total	100	100	100	100	100	100	100
South	40	23	25	27	27	28	30
North	60	74	67	62	56	54	52
Northeast	60	36	31	29	26	25	24
North Central	-	38	36	33	30	29	28
West	-	3	8	11	16	18	18
BLACK AS A PERCENT OF THE TOTAL POPULATION							
United States	19	13	11	10	11	11	11
South	35	36	30	24	21	19	19
North	3	2	2	4	7	8	9
Northeast	3	1	2	4	7	9	9
North Central	-	2	2	4	7	8	8
West	-	1	1	1	4	5	6

Source: "Distribution of the Population, by Region for Selected Years: 1970 to 1975," U.S. Department of Commerce, Bureau of the Census. *The Social and Economic Status of the Black Population in the United States: An Historical View, 1790-1978,* p. 13. Primary source: U.S. Department of Commerce, Bureau of the Census. Current Population Survey. *Note:* - Represents or rounds to zero.

★ 1801 ★

Geographical Areas: Sections, Divisions, States

Geographic Division of Population by Race, Nativity, Sections, and Divisions, 1930 - I

SECTION AND DIVISION	Total population	NEGRO			WHITE		
		Total	Native	Foreign born	Total	Native	Foreign born
NUMBER							
United States	123,775,046	11,891,143	11,792,523	98,620	108,864,207	95,497,800	13,366,407
THE SOUTH	37,857,633	9,361,577	9,347,049	14,528	27,673,879	27,141,704	532,175
South Atlantic	15,793,589	4,421,388	4,408,804	12,584	11,349,284	11,045,006	304,278
East South Central	9,887,214	2,658,238	2,657,706	532	7,224,614	7,166,949	57,665
West South Central	12,176,830	2,281,951	2,280,539	1,412	9,099,981	8,929,749	170,232
THE NORTH	73,021,191	2,409,219	2,327,183	82,036	70,388,367	59,001,814	11,386,553
New England	8,166,341	94,086	82,300	11,786	8,065,113	6,230,803	1,834,310
Middle Atlantic	26,260,750	1,052,899	988,334	64,565	25,172,104	19,903,062	5,269,042
East North Central	25,297,185	930,450	925,293	5,157	24,277,663	21,053,739	3,223,924

[Continued]

★ 1801 ★

Geographic Division of Population by Race, Nativity, Sections, and Divisions, 1930 - I

[Continued]

SECTION AND DIVISION	Total population	NEGRO			WHITE		
		Total	Native	Foreign born	Total	Native	Foreign born
West North Central	13,296,915	331,784	331,256	528	12,873,487	11,814,210	1,059,277
THE WEST	11,896,222	120,347	118,291	2,056	10,801,961	9,354,282	1,447,679
Mountain	3,701,789	39,225	30,038	187	3,303,586	3,015,672	287,914
Pacific	8,194,433	90,122	88,253	1,869	7,498,375	6,338,610	1,159,765
PERCENT DISTRIBUTION							
United States	100.0	100.0	100.0	100.0	100.0	100.0	100.0
THE SOUTH	30.8	78.7	79.3	14.7	25.4	28.4	4.0
South Atlantic	12.9	37.2	37.4	12.8	10.4	11.6	2.3
East South Central	8.1	22.4	22.5	.5	6.6	7.5	.4
West South Central	9.9	19.2	19.3	1.4	8.4	9.4	1.3
THE NORTH	59.5	20.3	19.7	83.2	64.7	61.8	85.2
New England	6.7	.8	.7	12.0	7.4	6.5	13.7
Middle Atlantic	21.4	8.9	8.4	65.5	23.1	20.8	39.4
East North Central	20.6	7.8	7.8	5.2	22.3	22.0	24.1
West North Central	10.8	2.8	2.8	.5	11.8	12.4	7.9
THE WEST	9.7	1.0	1.0	2.1	9.9	9.8	10.8
Mountain	3.0	.3	.3	.2	3.0	3.2	2.2
Pacific	6.7	.8	.7	1.9	6.9	6.6	8.7

Source: "Geographic Distribution of Population by Race and Nativity, by Sections, and Divisions: 1930." U.S. Bureau of the Census, *Negroes in the United States, 1920-1932*, p. 4. *Notes:* 1. Includes Filipino, Hindu, Korean, Hawaiian, Malay, Siamese, and Samoan. 2. Less than 1/10 of 1 percent.

★ 1802 ★

Geographical Areas: Sections, Divisions, States

Geographic Division of Population by Race, Nativity, Sections, and Divisions, 1930 - II

SECTION AND DIVISION	MEXICAN			Indian	Chinese	Japanese	All other[1]
	Total	Native	Foreign born				
NUMBER							
United States	1,422,533	805,535	616,998	332,397	74,954	138,834	50,978
THE SOUTH	698,090	429,494	268,596	116,836	4,194	1,126	1,931
South Atlantic	691	232	459	19,060	1,869	393	940
East South Central	1,403	724	679	2,106	743	46	64

[Continued]

★ 1802 ★

Geographic Division of Population by Race, Nativity, Sections, and Divisions, 1930 - II

[Continued]

SECTION AND DIVISION	MEXICAN			Indian	Chinese	Japanese	All other[1]
	Total	Native	Foreign born				
West South Central	695,996	428,538	267,458	95,670	1,582	687	963
THE NORTH	104,986	36,076	68,910	78,237	25,877	6,039	8,466
New England	107	39	68	2,466	3,794	352	423
Middle Atlantic	6,757	1,528	5,229	7,709	14,005	3,662	3,614
East North Central	58,317	17,104	41,213	19,317	6,340	1,022	3,576
West North Central	39,805	17,045	22,400	48,245	1,738	1,003	853
THE WEST	619,457	339,965	279,492	137,324	44,883	31,669	40,581
Mountain	249,314	162,818	86,496	102,083	3,252	11,418	1,911
Pacific	370,143	177,147	192,996	35,241	41,631	120,251	38,670
PERCENT DISTRIBUTION							
United States	100.0	100.0	100.0	100.0	100.0	100.0	100.0
THE SOUTH	49.1	53.3	43.5	35.1	5.6	0.8	3.8
South Atlantic	[2]	[2]	.1	5.7	2.5	.3	1.8
East South Central	.1	.1	.1	.6	1.0	[2]	.1
West South Central	48.9	53.2	43.3	28.8	2.1	0.5	1.9
THE NORTH	7.4	4.5	11.2	23.5	34.5	4.3	16.6
New England	[2]	[2]	[2]	.7	5.1	.3	.8
Middle Atlantic	.5	.2	.8	2.3	18.7	2.6	7.1
East North Central	4.1	2.1	6.7	6.0	8.5	.7	7.0
West North Central	2.8	2.2	3.6	14.5	2.3	.7	1.7
THE WEST	43.5	42.2	45.3	41.3	59.9	94.8	79.6
Mountain	17.5	20.2	14.0	30.7	4.3	8.2	3.7
Pacific	26.0	22.0	31.3	10.6	55.5	86.6	75.9

Source: "Geographic Distribution of Population by Race and Nativity, by Sections, and Divisions: 1930." U.S. Bureau of the Census, *Negroes in the United States, 1920-1932,* p. 4. *Notes:* 1. Includes Filipino, Hindu, Korean, Hawaiian, Malay, Siamese, and Samoan. 2. Less than 1/10 of 1 percent.

★ 1803 ★

Geographical Areas: Sections, Divisions, States

Increase in Population by Sections and Divisions, 1920 to 1930

SECTION AND DIVISION	INCREASE OR DECREASE (-)					
	Number		Percent		Percent distribution	
	Negro	White	Negro	White	Negro	White
United States	1,428,012	14,743,833	13.6	15.7	100.0	100.0
THE SOUTH	449,346	3,941,980	5.0	16.6	31.5	26.7
South Atlantic	96,268	1,700,728	2.2	17.6	6.7	11.5
East South Central	134,706	857,448	5.3	13.5	9.4	5.8
West South Central	218,372	1,383,804	10.6	17.9	15.3	9.4
THE NORTH	936,910	8,302,755	63.6	13.4	65.6	56.3
New England	15,035	749,118	19.0	10.2	1.1	5.1
Middle Atlantic	452,716	3,533,479	75.4	16.3	31.7	24.0
East North Central	415,896	3,346,384	80.8	16.0	29.1	22.7
West North Central	53,263	673,774	19.1	5.5	3.7	4.6
THE WEST	41,756	2,499,098	53.1	30.1	2.9	17.0
Mountain	-576	232,181	-1.9	7.6	[1]	1.6
Pacific	42,332	2,266,917	88.6	43.3	3.0	15.4

Source: "Increase in Negro and White Population, by Sections, and Divisions: 1920 to 1930." U.S. Bureau of the Census, *Negroes in the United States, 1920-1932*, p. 7. *Note:* 1. Less than 1/10 of 1 percent.

★ 1804 ★

Geographical Areas: Sections, Divisions, States

Increases by 20-Year Periods in Population by Sections and Southern Divisions, 1790-1930 - I

PERIOD	INCREASE OF POPULATION					
	United States		The South			
			Total		South Atlantic division	
	Negro	White	Negro	White	Negro	White
	NUMBER					
1910-30	2,063,380	27,499,760	612,150	7,357,626	308,900	3,277,811
1890-1910	2,339,087	26,263,189	1,988,850	7,122,800	849,798	2,479,324
1870-90	2,608,667	21,511,881	2,339,766	5,330,244	1,045,985	1,596,911
1850-70	1,241,201	14,036,309	1,068,613	2,232,794	355,834	817,019
1830-50[1]	1,310,166	9,105,690	1,190,313	2,084,451	331,588	701,750
1810-30	950,834	4,675,305	893,386	1,354,415	448,483	522,378
1790-1810	620,600	2,690,067	578,715	920,148	407,338	415,747

[Continued]

★ 1804 ★

Increases by 20-Year Periods in Population by Sections and Southern Divisions, 1790-1930 - I

[Continued]

PERIOD	INCREASE OF POPULATION					
	United States		The South			
			Total		South Atlantic division	
	Negro	White	Negro	White	Negro	White
	PERCENT					
1910-30	21.0	33.8	7.0	36.2	7.5	40.6
1890-1910	31.2	47.7	29.4	54.0	26.0	44.2
1870-90	53.5	64.0	52.9	67.8	47.2	53.8
1850-70	34.1	71.8	31.9	39.7	19.1	29.0
1830-50	56.3	85.6	55.1	58.8	21.7	32.2
1810-30	69.0	79.8	70.4	61.8	41.5	32.8
1790-1810	82.0	84.8	83.9	72.4	60.5	35.3

Source: "Increase by 20-Year Periods for Negro and White Population, by Sections, and Southern Divisions: 1790-1930." U.S. Bureau of the Census, *Negroes in the United States, 1920-1932,* p. 4. *Notes:* 1. Total population for 1830 included 5,318 white persons on public ships in the service of the United States, not credited to any division or State.

★ 1805 ★

Geographical Areas: Sections, Divisions, States

Increases by 20-Year Periods in Population by Sections and Southern Divisions, 1790-1930 - II

PERIOD	INCREASE OF POPULATION							
	The South				The North		The West	
	East South Central division		West South Central division					
	Negro	White	Negro	White	Negro	White	Negro	White
	NUMBER							
1910-30	5,725	1,470,460	297,525	2,609,355	1,381,545	15,760,769	69,685	4,381,365
1890-1910	532,716	1,448,486	606,336	3,194,990	326,656	15,591,800	23,581	3,548,589
1870-90	655,545	1,366,577	638,236	2,006,756	248,200	14,220,026	20,701	1,961,611
1850-70	341,462	698,610	371,317	717,166	167,449	11,070,695	5,139	732,819
1830-50[1]	621,203	926,099	237,522	456,602	118,612	6,758,980	1,241	177,577
1810-30	356,133	751,246	88,770	80,801	57,448	3,315,562	-	-
1790-1810	129,132	470,090	42,245	34,311	41,885	1,769,919	-	-
	PERCENT							
1910-30	0.2	25.6	15.0	40.2	134.4	28.9	137.5	68.2
1890-1910	25.1	33.6	44.0	96.9	46.6	39.9	87.1	123.6
1870-90	44.8	46.5	86.3	155.7	54.8	57.3	324.5	215.5
1850-70	30.4	31.2	100.8	125.4	58.7	80.5	414.1	412.7
1830-50	123.8	70.5	181.3	396.7	71.1	96.7	-	-

[Continued]

★ 1805 ★

Increases by 20-Year Periods in Population by Sections and Southern Divisions, 1790-1930 - II

[Continued]

PERIOD	INCREASE OF POPULATION							
	The South				The North		The West	
	East South Central division		West South Central division					
	Negro	White	Negro	White	Negro	White	Negro	White
1810-30	244.8	133.4	210.1	235.5	52.6	90.3	-	-
1790-1810	791.2	505.2	-	-	62.1	93.1	-	-

Source: "Increase by 20-Year Periods for Negro and White Population, by Sections, and Southern Divisions: 1790-1930." U.S. Bureau of the Census, *Negroes in the United States, 1920-1932*, p. 4. *Notes:* 1. Total population for 1830 included 5,318 white persons on public ships in the service of the United States, not credited to any division or State.

★ 1806 ★

Geographical Areas: Sections, Divisions, States

Increases in Population, by Sections, Divisions, and States, 1790-1930

SECTION, DIVISION, AND STATE	1920-30				1910-20		1870-1910		1830-70		1790-1830	
	Negro		White									
	Number	Percent	Number	Percent	Negro	White	Negro	White	Negro	White	Negro	White
United States	1,428,012	13.6	14,743,833	15.7	635,368	12,755,927	4,947,754	47,775,070	2,551,367	23,057,317	1,571,434	7,360,054
The North	936,910	63.6	8,302,755	13.4	444,635	7,548,014	574,856	29,811,826	286,061	17,829,675	99,333	5,085,481
The South	449,346	5.0	3,941,980	16.6	162,804	3,415,646	4,328,616	12,453,044	2,258,926	4,317,246	1,472,101	2,274,573
The West	41,756	53.1	2,499,098	30.1	27,929	1,882,267	44,282	5,510,200	6,380	910,396	-	-
GEOGRAPHIC DIVISIONS:												
New England	15,053	19.0	749,118	10.2	12,745	835,527	34,601	3,025,425	10,326	1,521,705	4,392	940,917
Middle Atlantic	452,716	75.4	3,533,479	16.3	182,313	2,758,744	269,837	10,217,655	44,198	5,178,397	53,398	2,575,634
East North Central	415,896	80.8	3,346,384	16.0	213,718	3,004,766	170,339	8,939,001	114,614	7,533,377	15,883	1,454,135
West North Central	53,263	19.1	673,774	5.5	35,859	858,977	100,079	7,629,745	116,923	3,596,196	25,660	114,795
South Atlantic	96,268	2.2	1,700,728	17.6	212,632	1,577,083	1,895,783	4,436,235	687,422	1,518,769	855,821	938,125
East South Central	134,706	5.3	857,448	13.5	-128,981	613,012	1,188,261	2,815,063	962,665	1,624,709	485,265	1,221,336
West South Central	218,372	10.6	1,383,804	17.9	79,153	1,225,551	1,244,572	5,201,746	608,839	1,173,768	131,015	115,112
Mountain	-576	-1.9	232,181	7.6	9,334	625,890	19,912	2,143,667	1,555	301,848	-	-
Pacific	42,332	88.6	2,266,917	43.3	18,595	1,256,377	24,370	3,366,533	4,825	608,548	-	-
NEW ENGLAND:												
Maine	-214	-16.3	29,490	3.9	-53	25,702	-243	115,182	414	226,546	654	302,261
New Hampshire	169	27.2	22,020	5.0	57	12,424	-16	112,209	-27	48,976	-181	127,624
Vermont	-4	-0.7	7,149	2.0	-1,049	-2,482	697	24,685	43	49,842	610	194,617
Massachusetts	6,899	15.2	389,459	10.2	7,411	478,108	24,108	1,881,741	6,898	839,797	1,586	230,035
Rhode Island	-123	-1.2	83,040	14.0	507	61,488	4,549	320,269	1,402	118,598	-777	29,151
Connecticut	8,308	39.5	217,960	16.0	5,872	259,825	5,506	571,339	1,596	237,946	2,500	57,229
MIDDLE ATLANTIC:												
New York	214,331	108.0	1,979,745	19.5	64,292	1,204,023	82,110	4,663,315	7,136	2,456,547	18,967	1,559,521
New Jersey	91,696	78.3	792,377	26.1	27,372	591,012	59,102	1,570,413	10,101	575,141	6,372	130,312
Pennsylvania	146,689	51.5	761,357	9.0	90,649	963,709	128,625	4,010,927	26,961	2,146,709	28,059	885,801
EAST NORTH CENTRAL:												
Ohio	123,117	66.1	760,185	13.6	74,735	916,193	48,239	2,052,812	53,639	1,673,617	9,574	928,329
Indiana	31,172	38.6	267,790	9.4	20,490	208,470	35,760	984,039	20,928	1,316,438	3,632	339,399
Illinois	146,698	80.5	971,362	15.4	73,225	768,758	80,287	3,015,145	26,378	2,356,035	2,384	155,061
Michigan	109,371	182.0	1,049,888	29.2	42,967	815,148	5,266	1,617,853	11,556	1,135,936	293	31,346
Wisconsin	5,538	106.5	297,159	11.4	2,301	296,197	787	1,269,152	2,113	1,051,351	-	-
WEST NORTH CENTRAL:												
Minnesota	636	7.2	170,387	7.2	1,725	309,443	6,325	1,620,886	759	438,257	-	-
Iowa	-1,625	-8.6	67,089	2.8	4,032	172,611	9,211	1,020,475	5,762	1,188,207	-	-
Missouri	45,599	25.6	177,226	5.5	20,789	88,091	39,381	1,530,424	92,411	1,488,351	25,660	114,795
North Dakota	-90	-19.3	31,331	4.9	-150	70,067						
South Dakota	-186	-22.4	50,401	8.1	15	55,305						
Nebraska	510	3.9	77,229	6.1	5,553	96,479	6,900	1,057,877	789	122,117	-	-
Kansas	8,419	14.5	100,111	5.9	3,895	66,981	36,922	1,279,378	17,108	346,377	-	-
SOUTH ATLANTIC:												
Delaware	2,267	7.5	13,109	6.8	-846	21,486	8,387	68,879	3,647	44,620	6,361	11,291

[Continued]

★ 1806 ★

Increases in Population, by Sections, Divisions, and States, 1790-1930

[Continued]

SECTION, DIVISION, AND STATE	1920-30				1910-20		1870-1910		1830-70		1790-1830	
	Negro		White									
	Number	Percent	Number	Percent	Negro	White	Negro	White	Negro	White	Negro	White
Maryland	31,900	13.0	149,480	12.4	12,229	142,063	56,859	457,130	19,459	314,389	44,853	82,459
District of Columbia	22,102	20.1	27,089	8.3	15,520	90,712	51,042	147,835	31,133	60,715	12,271	27,563
Virginia	-39,852	-5.8	152,534	9.4	18,921	228,069	158,255	677,713	-4,264	17,789	211,612	252,183
West Virginia	28,548	33.1	236,754	17.2	22,172	220,369	46,193	732,778	17,980	424,033	-	-
North Carolina	155,240	20.3	451,179	25.3	65,564	283,261	306,193	822,038	126,506	205,627	159,597	184,639
South Carolina	-71,038	-8.2	125,508	15.3	28,876	139,373	420,029	389,492	92,492	31,804	214,427	117,685
Georgia	-135,240	-11.2	147,904	8.8	29,378	257,284	631,845	792,860	325,125	342,120	190,355	243,920
Florida	102,341	31.1	397,171	68.2	20,818	194,467	216,980	347,510	75,344	77,672	16,345	18,385
EAST SOUTH CENTRAL:												
Kentucky	-9,898	-4.2	207,902	9.5	-25,718	152,536	39,446	929,234	52,080	580,905	157,586	456,654
Tennessee	25,888	5.7	252,680	13.4	-21,330	174,522	150,757	775,298	176,173	400,373	142,380	503,833
Alabama	44,182	4.9	253,817	17.5	-7,630	218,169	432,772	707,405	356,389	330,978	119,121	190,406
Mississippi	74,534	8.0	143,049	16.8	-74,303	67,785	565,286	403,126	378,023	312,453	66,178	70,443
WEST SOUTH CENTRAL:												
Arkansas	6,243	1.3	95,427	7.5	29,329	148,601	320,722	768,763	117,452	336,444	4,717	25,671
Louisiana	76,069	10.9	224,169	20.5	-13,617	154,202	349,664	577,724	237,912	272,624	126,298	89,441
Oklahoma	22,790	15.3	310,207	17.1	11,796	371,140	137,612	1,441,577	-	-	-	-
Texas	113,270	15.3	754,001	21.4	51,645	551,108	436,574	2,413,682	253,475	564,700	-	-
MOUNTAIN:												
Montana	-402	-24.2	-16,664	-3.1	-176	173,500	1,651	342,185	183	18,306	-	-
Idaho	-252	-27.4	13,022	3.1	269	105,466	591	308,456	60	10,618	-	-
Wyoming	-125	-9.1	25,921	13.8	-860	48,156	2,052	131,264	183	8,726	-	-
Colorado	510	4.5	51,354	5.6	-135	129,617	10,997	740,925	456	39,221	-	-
New Mexico	-2,883	-50.3	29,876	9.9	4,106	18,305	1,456	193,181	172	90,393	-	-
Arizona	2,744	34.3	61,393	30.2	5,996	80,625	1,983	112,779	26	9,581	-	-
Utah	-338	-23.4	55,256	12.5	302	74,274	1,026	280,381	118	86,044	-	-
Nevada	170	49.1	12,023	17.3	-167	-4,053	156	34,496	357	38,959	-	-
PACIFIC:												
Washington	-43	-0.6	201,706	15.3	825	210,426	5,851	1,086,772	207	22,195	-	-
Oregon	90	4.2	168,499	21.9	652	113,697	1,146	567,904	346	86,929	-	-
California	42,285	109.1	1,896,712	60.3	17,118	932,254	17,373	1,711,857	4,272	499,424	-	-

Source: "Increases in the Negro and White Population, by Sections, Divisions, and States: by Periods, 1790-1930." U.S. Bureau of the Census, *Negroes in the United States, 1920-1932*, p. 12. *Note:* 1. Dakota Territory.

★ 1807 ★

Geographical Areas: Sections, Divisions, States

Percent Distribution of Black Population by Sections and Southern Divisions, 1790 to 1930

STATE	NEGRO POPULATION			Percent increase or decrease (-) in white population, 1920-30
	Total number, 1930	Increase or decrease (-), 1920-30		
		Number	Percent	
Total	11,891,143	1,428,012	13.6	15.7
Michigan	169,453	109,371	182.0	29.2
California	81,048	42,285	109.1	60.3
New York	412,814	214,331	108.0	19.5
Wisconsin	10,739	5,538	106.5	11.4
Illinois	328,972	146,698	80.5	15.4
New Jersey	208,828	91,696	78.3	26.1

[Continued]

★ 1807 ★

Percent Distribution of Black Population by Sections and Southern Divisions, 1790 to 1930

[Continued]

STATE	NEGRO POPULATION			Percent increase or decrease (-) in white population, 1920-30
	Total number, 1930	Increase or decrease (-), 1920-30		
		Number	Percent	
Ohio	309,304	123,117	66.1	13.6
Pennsylvania	431,257	146,689	51.5	9.0
Nevada	516	170	49.1	17.3
Connecticut	29,354	8,308	39.5	16.0
Indiana	111,982	31,172	38.6	9.4
Arizona	10,749	2,744	34.3	30.2
West Virginia	114,893	28,548	33.1	17.2
Florida	431,828	102,341	31.1	62.2
New Hampshire	790	169	27.2	5.0
Missouri	223,840	45,599	25.6	5.5
North Carolina	918,647	155,240	20.3	25.3
District of Columbia	132,068	22,102	20.1	8.3
Oklahoma	172,198	22,790	15.3	17.1
Texas	854,964	113,270	15.3	21.4
Massachusetts	52,365	6,899	15.2	10.2
Kansas	66,344	8,419	14.5	5.9
Maryland	276,379	31,900	13.0	12.4
Louisiana	776,326	76,069	10.9	20.5
Mississippi	1,009,718	74,534	8.0	16.8
Delaware	32,602	2,267	7.5	6.8
Minnesota	9,445	636	7.2	7.2
Tennessee	477,646	25,888	5.7	13.4
Alabama	944,834	44,182	4.9	17.5
Colorado	11,828	510	4.5	5.6
Oregon	2,234	90	4.2	21.9
Nebraska	13,752	510	3.9	6.1
Arkansas	478,463	6,243	1.3	7.5
Washington	6,840	-43	-.6	15.3
Vermont	568	-4	-.7	2.0
Rhode Island	9,913	-123	-1.2	14.0
Kentucky	226,040	-9,898	-4.2	9.5
Virginia	650,165	-39,852	-5.8	9.4
South Carolina	793,681	-71,038	-8.2	15.3
Iowa	17,380	-1,625	-8.6	2.8
Wyoming	1,250	-125	-9.1	13.8
Georgia	1,071,125	-135,240	-11.2	8.8

[Continued]

★ 1807 ★

Percent Distribution of Black Population by Sections and Southern Divisions, 1790 to 1930

[Continued]

STATE	NEGRO POPULATION			Percent increase or decrease (-) in white population, 1920-30
	Total number, 1930	Increase or decrease (-), 1920-30		
		Number	Percent	
Maine	1,096	-214	-16.3	3.9
North Dakota	377	-90	-19.3	4.9
South Dakota	646	-186	-22.4	8.1
Utah	1,108	-338	-23.4	12.5
Montana	1,256	-402	-24.2	-3.1
Idaho	668	-252	-27.4	3.1
New Mexico	2,850	-2,883	-50.3	9.9

Source: "Percent Distribution of Negro Population by Sections, and Southern Divisions: 1970 to 1930." U.S. Bureau of the Census, *Negroes in the United States, 1920-1932*, p. 7.

★ 1808 ★

Geographical Areas: Sections, Divisions, States

Population Change by State, 1900-1910

STATE	Negro population 1910	Negro increase 1900-1910[1]	PERCENTAGE INCREASE: 1900-1910[1]	
			Negro population	White population
Total	9,827,763	993,769	11.2	22.3
Nevada	513	379	282.8	109.8
Oklahoma	137,612	81,928	147.1	115.5
Washington	6,058	3,544	141.0	123.5
Wyoming	2,235	1,295	137.8	57.6
Idaho	651	358	122.2	106.6
North Dakota	617	331	115.7	82.8
Vermont	1,621	795	96.2	3.4
California	21,645	10,600	96.0	61.1
South Dakota	817	352	75.7	48.1
Utah	1,144	472	70.2	34.5
West Virginia	64,173	20,674	47.5	26.4
Minnesota	7,084	2,125	42.9	18.5
New York	134,191	34,959	35.2	25.3
Oregon	1,492	387	35.0	66.0
Florida	308,669	77,939	33.8	49.2

[Continued]

★ 1808 ★

Population Change by State, 1900-1910

[Continued]

STATE	Negro population 1910	Negro increase 1900-1910[1]	PERCENTAGE INCREASE: 1900-1910[1]	
			Negro population	White population
Colorado	11,453	2,883	33.6	48.1
New Jersey	89,760	19,916	28.5	35.0
Illinois	109,049	23,971	28.2	16.7
Pennsylvania	193,919	37,074	23.6	21.6
Nebraska	7,689	1,420	22.7	11.7
Arkansas	442,891	76,035	20.7	19.7
Montana	1,834	311	20.4	59.3
Massachusetts	38,055	6,081	19.0	20.0
Iowa	14,973	2,280	18.0	-0.4
Ohio	111,452	14,551	15.0	14.6
Wisconsin	2,900	358	14.1	12.8
Georgia	1,176,987	142,174	13.7	21.2
North Carolina	697,843	73,374	11.7	18.7
Mississippi	1,009,487	101,857	11.2	22.6
Texas	690,049	69,327	11.2	32.1
Alabama	908,282	80,975	9.8	22.7
Louisiana	713,874	63,070	9.7	29.0
District of Columbia	94,446	7,744	8.9	23.3
Arizona	2,009	161	8.7	84.6
Michigan	17,115	1,299	8.2	16.1
South Carolina	835,843	53,522	6.8	21.8
Indiana	60,320	2,815	4.9	7.4
Rhode Island	9,529	437	4.8	27.1
Kansas	54,030	2,027	3.9	15.4
Maine	1,363	44	3.3	6.9
Delaware	31,181	484	1.6	11.1
Virginia	671,096	10,374	1.6	16.5
New Mexico	1,628	18	1.1	69.0
Connecticut	15,174	-52	-0.3	23.1
Maryland	232,250	-2,814	-1.2	11.6
Tennessee	473,088	-7,155	-1.5	11.1
Missouri	157,452	-3,782	-2.3	6.5
Kentucky	261,656	-23,050	-8.1	8.9
New Hampshire	564	-98	-14.8	4.7

Source: "Untitled Table." U.S. Bureau of the Census, *Negro Population, 1790- 1915,* p. 38. *Note:* 1. A minus sign (-) denotes decrease.

★ 1809 ★

Geographical Areas: Sections, Divisions, States

Population Ranked by State and Black Percentage of Total Population, 1930

State	Negro percent age of population	Negro Population			White Population		
		Number	Cumulated by States		Number	Cumulated by States	
			Number	Percent		Number	Percent
Mississippi	50.2	1,009,718	1,009,718	8.5	996,856	996,856	0.9
South Carolina	45.6	793,681	1,803,399	15.2	944,040	1,940,896	1.8
Louisiana	36.9	776,326	2,579,725	21.7	1,318,160	3,259,056	3.0
Georgia	36.8	1,071,125	3,650,850	30.7	1,836,974	5,096,030	4.7
Alabama	35.7	944,834	4,595,684	38.6	1,700,775	6,796,805	6.2
Florida	29.4	431,828	5,027,512	42.3	1,035,205	7,832,010	7.2
North Carolina	29.0	918,647	5,946,159	50.0	2,234,948	10,066,958	9.2
District of Columbia	27.1	132,068	6,078,227	51.1	353,914	10,420,872	9.6
Virginia	26.8	650,165	6,728,392	56.6	1,779,405	12,191,277	11.2
Arkansas	25.8	478,463	7,206,855	60.6	1,374,906	13,566,183	12.5
Tennessee	18.3	477,646	7,684,501	64.6	2,138,619	15,704,802	14.4
Maryland	16.9	276,379	7,960,880	66.9	1,354,170	17,058,972	15.7
Texas	14.7	954,964	8,815,844	74.1	4,283,491	21,342,463	19.6
Delaware	13.7	32,602	8.848,446	74.4	205,694	21,548,157	19.8
Kentucky	8.6	226,040	9,074,486	76.3	2,388,364	23,936,521	22.0
Oklahoma	7.2	172,198	9,246,684	77.8	7,123,424	26,059,945	23.9
West Virginia	6.6	114,893	9,361,577	78.7	1,613,934	27,673,879	25.4
Missouri	6.2	223,840	9,585,417	80.6	3,398,887	31,072,766	28.5
New Jersey	5.2	208,828	9,794,245	82.4	3,829,209	34,901,975	32.1
Ohio	4.7	309,304	10,103,549	85.0	6,331,136	41,233,111	37.9
Pennsylvania	4.5	431,257	10,534,806	88.6	9,192,602	50,425,713	46.3
Illinois	4.3	329,972	10,863,778	91.4	7,266,361	57,692,074	53.0
Indiana	3.5	111,982	10,975,760	92.3	3,116,136	60,808,210	55.9
Kansas	3.5	66,344	11,042,104	92.9	1,792,847	62,601,057	57.5
Michigan	3.5	169,453	11,211,557	94.3	4,650,171	67,251,228	61.8
New York	3.3	412,814	11,624,371	97.8	12,150,293	79,401,521	72.9
Arizona	2.5	10,749	11,635,120	97.8	264,378	79,665,899	73.2
Connecticut	1.8	29,354	11,664,474	98.1	1,576,673	81,242,572	74.6
California	1.4	81,048	11,745,522	98.8	5,040,247	86,282,819	79.3
Rhode Island	1.4	9.913	11,755,435	98.9	677,016	86,959,835	79.9
Massachusetts	1.2	52,365	11,807,800	99.3	4,192,926	91,152,761	83.7
Colorado	1.1	11,828	11,819,628	99.4	961,117	92,113,878	84.6
Nebraska	1.0	13,752	11,833,380	99.5	1,353,702	93,467,580	85.9
Iowa	.7	17,380	11,850,760	99.7	2,448,382	95,915,962	88.1
New Mexico	.7	2,850	11,853,610	99.7	331,755	96,247,717	88.4
Nevada	.6	516	11,854,126	99.7	81,425	96,329,142	88.5
Wyoming	.6	1,250	11,855,376	99.7	214,067	96,543,209	88.7
Minnesota	.4	9,445	11,864,821	99.8	2,538,973	99,082,182	91.0

[Continued]

★ 1809 ★

Population Ranked by State and Black Percentage of Total Population, 1930

[Continued]

State	Negro percent age of population	Negro Population: Number	Negro Population: Cumulated by States: Number	Negro Population: Cumulated by States: Percent	White Population: Number	White Population: Cumulated by States: Number	White Population: Cumulated by States: Percent
Washington	.4	6,840	11,871,661	99.8	1,521,090	100,603,281	92.4
Wisconsin	.4	10,739	11,882,400	99.9	2,913,859	103,517,140	95.1
Idaho	.2	668	11,883,068	99.9	437,562	103,954,702	95.5
Montana	.2	1,256	11,884,324	99.9	517,327	104,472,029	96.0
New Hampshire	.2	790	11,885,114	99.9	464,350	104,936,379	96.4
Oregon	.2	2,234	11,887,348	100.0	937,029	105,873,408	97.3
Utah	.2	1,108	11,888,456	100.0	495,955	106,369,363	97.7
Vermont	.2	568	11,889,024	100.0	385,965	106,728,328	98.0
Maine	.1	1,096	11,890,120	100.0	795,183	107,523,511	86.8
North Dakota	.1	377	11,890,497	100.0	671,243	108,194,754	99.4
South Dakota	.1	646	11,891,143	100.0	669,453	108,864,207	100.0

Source: "Negro and White Population, by States, Ranked According to Negro Percentage of Total Population: 1930." U.S. Bureau of the Census, *Negroes in the United States, 1920-1932*, p. 14.

★ 1810 ★

Geographical Areas: Sections, Divisions, States

Population by Regions, Gender, Race, Residence, Age, and Nativity, 1790-1970 - I

Region and year	Total population	Sex[1]: Male	Sex[1]: Female	Race: White	Race: Negro	Race: Other races	Residence[2]: Urban	Residence[2]: Rural	Urban: White	Urban: Negro and other	Rural: White	Rural: Negro and other
NORTHEAST												
1970	49,041	23,563	25,478	44,311	4,344	386	39,450	9,591	34,883	4,567	9,427	163
1960	44,678	21,726	22,952	41,522	3,028	127	35,840	8,838	32,836	3,004	8,686	151
1950	39,478	19,347	20,131	37,399	2,018	61	31,378	8,105	29,427	1,946	7,972	133
1940	35,977	17,865	18,111	34,567	1,370	40	27,568	8,409	26,303	1,265	8,264	145
1930	34,427	17,213	17,214	33,237	1,147	43	26,707	7,720	25,652	1,055	7,585	135
1920	29,662	14,879	14,783	28,958	679	25	22,404	7,258	21,931	607	7,027	97
1910	25,869	13,078	12,790	25,361	484	23	18,563	7,305	18,311	410	7,050	97
1900	21,047	10,525	10,522	20,638	385	24	13,911	7,136	13,817	312	6,821	96
1890	17,407	8,681	8,726	17,122	270	15	10,266	7,141	-	-	-	-
1880	14,507	7,161	7,347	14,274	229	4	7,370	7,137	-	-	-	-
1870	12,299	6,080	6,219	12,117	180	2	5,448	6,851	-	-	-	-
1860	10,594	5,266	5,329	10,438	156	(Z)	3,787	6,807	-	-	-	-
1850	8,627	4,339	4,287	8,477	150	-	2,289	6,338	-	-	-	-
1840	6,761	3,397	3,364	6,619	142	-	1,253	5,508	-	-	-	-
1830[3]	5,542	2,784	2,751	5,417	125	-	785	4,758	-	-	-	-

[Continued]

★ 1810 ★

Population by Regions, Gender, Race, Residence, Age, and Nativity, 1790-1970 - I

[Continued]

Region and year	Total population	Sex[1]		Race			Residence[2]					
							Urban	Rural	Urban		Rural	
		Male	Female	White	Negro	Other races			White	Negro and other	White	Negro and other
1820	4,360	2,187	2,169	4,246	114	-	480	3,880	-	-	-	-
1810	3,487	1,714	1,670	3,384	102	-	380	3,107	-	-	-	-
1800	2,636	1,303	1,248	2,553	83	-	245	2,391	-	-	-	-
1790	1,968	961	940	1,901	67	-	160	1,809	-	-	-	-
NORTH CENTRAL												
1970	56,572	27,563	29,009	51,641	4,572	359	40,481	16,091	35,773	4,708	15,868	223
1960	51,619	25,472	26,147	48,003	3,446	170	35,481	16,138	32,085	3,396	15,917	220
1950	44,461	22,179	22,282	42,119	2,228	114	28,491	15,970	26,354	2,137	15,765	205
1940	40,143	20,268	19,876	38,640	1,420	83	23,437	16,706	22,159	1,278	16,481	225
1930	38,594	19,690	18,904	37,151	1,262	181	22,351	16,243	21,149	1,203	16,003	240
1920	34,020	17,494	16,526	33,164	793	62	17,776	16,244	17,103	674	16,061	182
1910	29,889	15,486	14,403	29,279	543	66	13,487	16,401	13,088	403	16,191	206
1900	26,333	13,589	12,744	25,776	496	61	10,165	16,168	9,843	324	15,933	233
1890	22,410	11,619	10,792	21,914	431	65	7,418	14,992	-	-	-	-
1880	17,364	9,016	8,348	16,961	386	17	4,198	13,166	-	-	-	-
1870[4]	12,981	6,705	6,262	12,699	273	10	2,702	10,279	-	-	-	-
1860	9,097	4,743	4,354	8,900	184	13	1,263	7,833	-	-	-	-
1850	5,404	2,814	2,589	5,268	136	-	499	4,904	-	-	-	-
1840	3,352	1,758	1,594	3,262	89	-	129	3,222	-	-	-	-
1830	1,610	838	772	1,569	42	-	42	1,569	-	-	-	-
1820	859	453	406	841	18	-	10	850	-	-	-	-
1810	292	151	135	286	7	-	3	290	-	-	-	-
1800	51	27	23	50	1	-	-	51	-	-	-	-
SOUTH												
1970	62,795	30,588	32,308	50,420	11,970	405	40,540	22,255	32,212	8,328	18,208	4,048
1960	54,973	27,065	27,908	43,477	11,312	185	32,160	22,813	25,472	6,688	18,004	4,809
1950	47,197	23,424	23,774	36,850	10,225	122	22,956	24,241	18,034	4,922	18,816	5,426
1940	41,666	20,795	20,871	31,659	9,905	103	15,290	26,375	11,659	3,631	19,999	6,376
1930	37,858	19,015	18,843	27,674	9,362	822	12,904	24,953	9,594	3,310	18,080	6,874
1920	33,126	16,773	16,352	24,132	8,912	81	9,300	23,826	7,043	2,261	17,089	6,733
1910	29,389	14,924	14,465	20,547	8,749	92	6,623	22,767	4,761	1,862	15,786	6,980
1900	24,524	12,405	12,119	16,522	7,923	79	4,421	20,103	3,052	1,369	13,470	6,633
1890[5]	20,028	10,118	9,910	13,193	6,761	74	3,261	16,767	-	-	-	-
1880	16,517	8,272	8,244	10,555	5,954	7	2,017	14,500	-	-	-	-
1870	12,288	6,091	6,197	7,863	4,421	4	1,497	10,791	-	-	-	-
1860	11,133	5,655	5,478	7,034	4,097	2	1,067	10,067	-	-	-	-
1850	8,983	4,552	4,430	5,630	3,352	-	744	8,239	-	-	-	-
1840	6,951	3,528	3,423	4,309	2,642	-	463	6,488	-	-	-	-
1830	5,708	2,900	2,808	3,546	2,162	-	301	5,407	-	-	-	-

[Continued]

★ 1810 ★

Population by Regions, Gender, Race, Residence, Age, and Nativity, 1790-1970 - I

[Continued]

Region and year	Total population	Sex[1]		Race			Residence[2]					
							Urban	Rural	Urban		Rural	
		Male	Female	White	Negro	Other races			White	Negro and other	White	Negro and other
1820	4,419	2,255	2,163	2,776	1,644	-	204	4,216	-	-	-	-
1810	3,461	1,123	1,069	2,191	1,268	-	143	3,318	-	-	-	-
1800	2,622	874	830	1,704	918	-	78	2,544	-	-	-	-
1790	1,961	655	616	1,271	690	-	42	1,919	-	-	-	-
WEST[6]												
1970	34,804	17,199	17,606	31,377	1,695	1,732	28,854	5,950	25,905	2,949	5,472	478
1960	28,053	14,067	13,986	25,830	1,086	1,137	21,787	6,266	20,035	1,752	5,795	471
1950	20,190	9,884	9,677	18,574	571	416	14,027	6,163	12,941	707	5,633	280
1940	14,379	7,134	6,750	13,350	171	363	8,409	5,969	7,851	276	5,498	257
1930	12,324	6,218	5,678	10,802	120	974	7,199	5,125	6,442	551	4,360	543
1920	9,214	4,754	4,149	8,567	79	258	4,773	4,440	4,543	143	4,023	193
1910	7,082	3,844	2,982	6,544	51	231	3,391	3,691	3,219	111	3,325	170
1900	4,309	2,298	1,794	3,873	30	188	1,718	2,591	1,594	70	2,279	148
1890	3,134	1,820	1,283	2,872	27	203	1,161	1,974	-	-	-	-
1880	1,801	1,070	698	1,612	12	144	544	1,257	-	-	-	-
1870	991	609	381	910	6	74	256	735	-	-	-	-
1860	619	422	197	551	4	64	99	520	-	-	-	-
1850	179	132	47	178	1	-	11	167	-	-	-	-

Source: "Population by Regions, Sex, Race, Residence, Age, and Nativity: 1790- 1970." U.S. Bureau of the Census, *Historical Statistics of the United States: Colonial Times to 1970, Part I*, Bicentennial Edition, p. 22. *Notes:* - Represents zero. Z Less than 500. 1. For 1790-1810, white persons only. 2. Series A 178 and A 179, 1950-1970, based on current definition of urban and rural; 1790-1940, based on 1940 definition. Series A 180-183, 1950-1970, based on current definition; 1930-1940, based on 1940 definition and 1900-1920 based on 1920 definition. See text for series A 43-56. 3. Includes 5,602 persons for whom sex, race, and age detail are not available. 4. Sex and age detail for the Dakota Territory not available. 5. Age detail excludes all persons residing in Indian Territory or on Indian reservations. 6. Total population, series A 172, and urban and rural population, series A 178 and A 179, include Alaska beginning 1890, and Hawaii beginning 1900. Sex, race, age, and nativity detail, series A 173-177 and A 180-194, include Alaska and Hawaii beginning 1960. 7. Ages not reported and ages unknown are not included. Prior to 1850 age detail for white only. Age detail columns have changed for early censuses as follows: 1790: Under 16 years and over 16 years, for males only; 1800-1820: Under 10 years, 10-15 years, 16-25 years, 26-44 years, and 45 and over; 1830-1860: Under 5 years, 5-14 years, 15-29 years, 30-59 years, 60-79 years, 80 and over. See also footnote 5. 8. Nativity data for 1850-1930 are based on complete-count data; data for 1940-1970 are sample data. For the 1850 and 1860 censuses, nativity detail for slaves was not compiled; nativity unknown or not reported is not included.

★ 1811 ★

Geographical Areas: Sections, Divisions, States

Population by Regions, Gender, Race, Residence, Age, and Nativity, 1790-1970 - II

Region and year	Age[7]						Nativity[8]				
							White			Negro and other races	
							Native born		Foreign born		
	Under 5 years	5-14 years	15-24 years	25-44 years	45-64 years	65 years and over	Native stock	Foreign stock		Native born	Foreign born
NORTHEAST											
1970	3,991	9,359	8,015	11,570	10,905	5,199	31,051	9,573	3,776	4,300	342
1960	4,656	8,093	5,506	12,029	9,895	4,498	26,822	10,274	4,432	3,011	143
1950	3,766	5,603	5,481	12,269	8,912	3,446	21,468	10,611	5,184	1,976	103
1940	2,391	5,546	6,381	11,280	7,784	2,594	18,131	10,560	6,021	1,328	82
1930	2,905	6,448	6,031	10,679	6,416	1,949	14,617	11,518	7,109	1,090	93
1920	3,107	5,638	4,950	9,284	5,200	1,453	12,434	9,741	6,783	641	63
1910	2,691	4,686	4,940	8,183	4,101	1,235	11,076	7,644	6,641	472	36
1900	2,244	4,018	3,913	6,584	3,227	1,018	9,918	5,981	4,739	385	24
1890	1,781	3,399	3,513	5,126	2,662	881	8,891	4,356	3,875	272	13
1880	1,646	3,080	2,861	4,035	2,187	700			2,808	227	6
1870	1,506	2,735	2,409	3,393	1,741	512			2,517	178	3
1860	1,448	2,387	3,042	3,103	561	52			2,019	151	5
1850	1,136	2,037	2,596	2,396	411	48			1,324	146	2
1840	1,017	1,626	1,965	1,685	293	33	-	-	-	-	-
1830[3]	866	1,410	1,598	1,277	234	25	-	-	-	-	-
1820	1,335	655	847	843			-	-	-	-	-
1810	1,121	528	641	655			-	-	-	-	-
1800	846	402	461	513			-	-	-	-	-
1790							-	-	-	-	-
NORTH CENTRAL											
1970	4,837	11,662	9,786	13,067	11,493	5,727	43,620	6,299	1,780	4,773	93
1960	6,009	10,212	6,682	13,222	10,415	5,078	38,532	7,237	2,237	3,578	40
1950	4,677	6,940	6,280	13,083	9,508	3,973	31,458	7,807	2,683	2,309	24
1940	3,087	6,457	7,043	11,974	8,501	3,081	27,155	8,284	3,349	1,493	10
1930	3,414	7,363	6,771	11,596	7,035	2,415	23,051	9,582	4,347	1,332	13
1920	3,561	6,652	5,889	10,309	5,781	1,787	19,266	9,303	4,595	843	13
1910	3,219	5,881	5,877	8,740	4,654	1,462	16,276	8,323	4,680	600	10
1900	3,039	5,818	5,092	7,507	3,680	1,143	14,149	7,476	4,151	550	7
1890	2,744	5,168	4,551	6,072	2,928	855	12,252	5,608	4,053	490	7
1880	2,370	4,273	3,616	4,448	2,133	525			2,912	398	5
1870[4]	1,958	3,381	2,587	3,285	1,444	313			2,331	280	2
1860	1,523	2,345	2,620	2,297	289	18			1,543	69	1
1850	883	1,451	1,553	1,277	154	11			650	48	(Z)
1840	631	911	945	690	80	6	-	-	-	-	-
1830	331	453	435	308	38	3	-	-	-	-	-
1820	318	130	163	152			-	-	-	-	-
1810	113	44	51	53			-	-	-	-	-
1800	20	8	9	9			-	-	-	-	-
SOUTH											
1970	5,389	12,736	11,346	14,783	12,498	6,043	46,564	2,718	1,220	12,195	96
1960	6,416	11,527	8,020	14,038	10,389	4,582	40,298	2,258	913	11,445	50

[Continued]

★ 1811 ★

Population by Regions, Gender, Race, Residence, Age, and Nativity, 1790-1970 - II

[Continued]

Region and year	Age[7]						Nativity[8]				
							White			Negro and other races	
							Native born		Foreign born		
	Under 5 years	5-14 years	15-24 years	25-44 years	45-64 years	65 years and over	Native stock	Foreign stock		Native born	Foreign born
1950	5,573	8,739	7,623	13,763	8,246	3,253	34,209	1,794	739	10,316	28
1940	4,007	8,336	8,131	12,113	6,778	2,300	29,647	1,484	626	9,993	14
1930	4,152	8,682	7,615	10,150	5,628	1,630	25,888	1,638	801	9,468	18
1920	4,034	8,111	6,442	8,770	4,447	1,271	21,832	1,453	847	8,972	21
1910	4,053	7,132	6,015	7,560	3,591	983	18,561	1,260	726	8,828	14
1900	3,464	6,306	5,152	5,870	2,889	765	14,862	1,097	563	7,990	11
1890[5]	2,791	5,455	4,105	4,633	2,004	603	11,843	830	521	6,825	9
1880	2,690	4,486	3,283	3,937	1,748	467			442	5,955	6
1870	1,920	3,275	2,621	2,844	1,315	317			396	4,421	4
1860	1,793	3,066	3,206	2,605	377	38			392	258	1
1850	1,464	2,546	2,578	2,055	299	35			240	234	2
1840	826	1,191	1,215	929	135	13	-	-	-	-	-
1830	695	979	1,011	740	110	11	-	-	-	-	-
1820	973	433	548	508			-	-	-	-	-
1810	783	344	418	408			-	-	-	-	-
1800	613	267	324	322			-	-	-	-	-
1790							-	-	-	-	-
WEST[6]											
1970	2,937	6,989	6,295	8,574	6,914	3,096	24,997	4,564	1,955	2,937	354
1960	3,239	5,634	3,812	7,609	5,357	2,401	20,108	4,015	1,711	2,010	212
1950	2,148	3,036	2,715	6,095	3,970	1,598	13,670	3,366	1,489	886	96
1940	1,057	2,091	2,365	4,305	3,022	1,043	9,191	2,830	1,424	464	70
1930	973	2,119	2,006	3,728	2,336	715	6,844	2,850	1,727	278	97
1920	870	1,638	1,427	2,916	1,602	422	4,890	2,190	1,487	225	111
1910	668	1,168	1,289	2,327	1,078	269	3,575	1,671	1,298	171	111
1900	424	812	734	1,337	604	154	2,021	1,092	761	132	85
1890	318	586	586	1,028	414	78	1,490	710	673	230	98
1880	208	357	340	593	237	32			397	52	103
1870	128	208	168	370	101	12			250	17	63
1860	79	95	217	216	10	1			179	4	(Z)
1850	15	26	80	52	3	(Z)			27	1	(Z)

Source: "Population by Regions, Sex, Race, Residence, Age, and Nativity: 1790- 1970." U.S. Bureau of the Census, *Historical Statistics of the United States: Colonial Times to 1970, Part I,* Bicentennial Edition, p. 22. *Notes:* - Represents zero. Z Less than 500. 1. For 1790-1810, white persons only. 2. Series A 178 and A 179, 1950-1970, based on current definition of urban and rural; 1790-1940, based on 1940 definition. Series A 180-183, 1950-1970, based on current definition; 1930-1940, based on 1940 definition and 1900-1920 based on 1920 definition. See text for series A 43-56. 3. Includes 5,602 persons for whom sex, race, and age detail are not available. 4. Sex and age detail for the Dakota Territory not available. 5. Age detail excludes all persons residing in Indian Territory or on Indian reservations. 6. Total population, series A 172, and urban and rural population, series A 178 and A 179, include Alaska beginning 1890, and Hawaii beginning 1900. Sex, race, age, and nativity detail, series A 173-177 and A 180-194, include Alaska and Hawaii beginning 1960. 7. Ages not reported and ages unknown are not included. Prior to 1850 age detail for white only. Age detail columns have changed for early censuses as follows: 1790: Under 16 years and over 16 years, for males only; 1800-1820: Under 10 years, 10-15 years, 16-25 years, 26-44 years, and 45 and over; 1830-1860: Under 5 years, 5-14 years, 15-29 years, 30-59 years, 60-79 years, 80 and over. See also footnote 5. 8. Nativity data for 1850-1930 are based on complete-count data; data for 1940-1970 are sample data. For the 1850 and 1860 censuses, nativity detail for slaves was not compiled; nativity unknown or not reported is not included.

★ 1812 ★

Geographical Areas: Sections, Divisions, States

Population of Selected States: 1870-1975

Numbers in thousands. Data shown for 15 states with largest Black population in 1970.

Selected states	Decennial census					1975 estimates
	1870	1910	1940	1960	1970	
Total, United States	4,880	9,828	12,866	18,872	22,580	24,435
Total, Selected States	3,720	7,600	9,989	14,582	17,184	18,563
Alabama	476	908	983	980	903	920
California	4	22	124	884	1,400	1,601
Florida	92	309	514	880	1,042	1,179
Georgia	545	1,177	1,085	1,123	1,187	1,288
Illinois	29	109	387	1,037	1,426	1,534
Louisiana	364	714	849	1,039	1,087	1,134
Michigan	12	17	208	718	991	1,080
Mississippi	444	1,009	1,075	916	816	841
New York	52	134	571	1,418	2,169	2,382
North Carolina	392	698	981	1,116	1,126	1,193
Ohio	63	111	339	786	970	1,034
Pennsylvania	65	194	470	853	1,017	1,049
South Carolina	416	836	814	829	789	867
Texas	253	690	924	1,187	1,399	1,530
Virginia	513	671	661	816	861	931
BLACK POPULATION AS A PERCENT OF TOTAL POPULATION IN EACH STATE						
Total, Selected States	16	15	13	13	14	14
Alabama	48	42	35	30	26	25
California	1	1	2	6	7	8
Florida	49	41	27	18	15	14
Georgia	46	45	35	28	26	26
Illinois	1	2	5	10	13	14
Louisiana	50	43	36	32	30	30
Michigan	1	1	4	9	11	12
Mississippi	54	56	49	42	37	36
New York	1	1	4	8	12	13
North Carolina	37	32	27	24	22	22
Ohio	2	2	5	8	9	10
Pennsylvania	2	3	5	8	9	9
South Carolina	59	55	43	35	30	31
Texas	31	18	14	12	12	13
Virginia	42	33	25	21	19	19

Source: "Black Population of Selected States: 1870 to 1975," U.S. Department of Commerce, Bureau of the Census. *The Social and Economic Status of the Black Population in the United States: An Historical View, 1790-1978*, p. 17. Primary source: U.S. Department of Commerce, Bureau of the Census. *Notes:* The 1975 data on the Black population by state are estimates of the July 1 resident population based on experimental techniques and are subject to an unknown level of error.

★ 1813 ★

Geographical Areas: Sections, Divisions, States

Population per Square Mile, 1910, 1920, 1930, and Rural Population, 1930

STATE	Land area in square miles, 1930	TOTAL POPULATION									RURAL POPULATION	
		Negro			White			All classes			1930	
		1930	1920	1910	1930	1920	1910	1930	1920	1910	Negro	White
United States	2,973,776	4.0	3.5	3.3	36.6	31.7	27.4	41.3	35.5	30.9	2.3	15.5
District of Columbia	62	2,130.1	1,773.6	1,574.1	5,708.3	5,271.4	3,935.2	7,852.7	7,292.9	5,517.8	-	-
Maryland	9,941	27.8	24.6	23.4	136.2	121.2	106.9	164.1	145.8	130.3	11.7	54.3
New Jersey	7,514	27.8	15.6	11.9	509.6	404.2	325.5	537.8	420.0	337.7	4.5	88.9
South Carolina	30,495	26.0	28.4	27.4	31.0	26.8	22.3	57.0	55.2	49.7	21.5	23.3
Mississippi	46,362	21.8	20.2	21.8	21.5	18.4	17.0	43.4	38.6	38.8	18.9	17.1
North Carolina	48,740	18.8	15.7	14.3	45.9	36.6	30.8	65.0	52.5	45.3	13.8	34.3
Alabama	51,279	18.4	17.6	17.7	33.2	28.2	24.0	51.6	45.8	41.7	13.2	23.9
Georgia	58,725	18.2	20.5	20.0	31.3	28.8	24.4	49.5	49.3	44.4	12.8	21.4
Louisiana	45,409	17.1	15.4	15.7	29.0	24.1	20.7	46.3	39.6	36.5	11.4	16.4
Delaware	1,965	16.6	15.4	15.9	104.7	98.0	87.1	121.3	113.5	103.0	8.9	49.7
Virginia	40,262	16.1	17.1	16.7	44.0	40.2	34.5	60.2	57.4	51.2	10.8	29.8
Tennessee	41,687	11.5	10.8	11.3	51.3	45.2	41.1	62.8	56.1	52.4	5.7	35.6
Pennsylvania	44,832	9.6	6.3	4.3	205.0	188.1	166.6	214.8	194.5	171.0	1.3	67.8
Rhode Island	1,067	9.3	9.4	8.9	634.5	556.7	499.1	644.3	566.4	508.5	.8	47.9
Arkansas	52,525	9.1	9.0	8.4	26.2	24.4	21.5	35.3	33.4	30.0	7.4	20.6
New York	47,654	8.7	4.2	2.8	255.0	213.4	188.2	264.2	217.9	191.2	.5	42.8
Florida	54,861	7.9	6.0	5.6	18.9	11.6	8.1	26.8	17.7	13.7	4.0	8.9
Ohio	40,740	7.6	4.6	2.7	155.4	136.7	114.3	163.1	141.4	117.0	.9	51.6
Massachusetts	8,039	6.5	5.7	4.7	521.6	473.1	413.6	528.6	479.2	418.8	.8	51.2
Connecticut	4,820	6.1	4.4	3.1	327.1	281.9	228.0	333.4	286.4	231.3	1.0	97.5
Illinois	56,043	5.9	3.3	1.9	129.7	112.3	98.6	136.2	115.7	100.6	.4	35.1
Kentucky	40,181	5.6	5.9	6.5	59.4	54.3	50.5	65.1	60.1	57.0	2.7	42.5
West Virginia	24,022	4.8	3.6	2.7	67.2	57.3	48.2	72.0	60.9	50.8	3.5	48.0
Missouri	68,727	3.3	2.6	2.3	49.5	46.9	45.6	52.8	49.5	47.9	.8	25.0
Texas	262,398	3.3	2.8	2.6	16.3	13.5	11.4	22.2	17.8	14.8	2.0	9.7
Indiana	36,045	3.1	2.2	1.7	86.5	79.0	73.2	89.8	81.3	74.9	.2	39.8
Michigan	57,480	2.9	1.0	.3	80.9	62.6	48.5	84.2	63.8	48.9	.2	26.5
Oklahoma	69,414	2.5	2.2	2.0	30.6	26.1	20.8	34.5	29.2	23.9	1.5	20.0

Source: "Negro and White Population Per Square Mile, 1930, 1920, and 1910, and Rural Population, by States, 1930." U.S. Bureau of the Census, *Negroes in the United States, 1920-1932*, p. 8.

★ 1814 ★

Geographical Areas: Sections, Divisions, States

States Arranged by Percent Increase in Black Population, 1920 to 1930

STATE	NEGRO POPULATION			Percent increase or decrease (-) in white population, 1920-30
	Total number, 1930	Increase or decrease (-), 1920-30		
		Number	Percent	
Total	11,891,143	1,428,012	13.6	15.7
Michigan	169,453	109,371	182.0	29.2
California	81,048	42,285	109.1	60.3
New York	412,814	214,331	108.0	19.5
Wisconsin	10,739	5,538	106.5	11.4
Illinois	328,972	146,698	80.5	15.4
New Jersey	208,828	91,696	78.3	26.1
Ohio	309,304	123,117	66.1	13.6
Pennsylvania	431,257	146,689	51.5	9.0
Nevada	516	170	49.1	17.3
Connecticut	29,354	8,308	39.5	16.0
Indiana	111,982	31,172	38.6	9.4
Arizona	10,749	2,744	34.3	30.2
West Virginia	114,893	28,548	33.1	17.2
Florida	431,828	102,341	31.1	62.2
New Hampshire	790	169	27.2	5.0
Missouri	233,840	45,599	25.6	5.5
North Carolina	918,647	155,240	20.3	25.3
District of Columbia	132,068	22,102	20.1	8.3
Oklahoma	172,198	22,790	15.3	17.1
Texas	854,964	113,270	15.3	21.4
Massachusetts	52,365	6,899	15.2	10.2
Kansas	66,344	8,419	14.5	5.9
Maryland	276,379	31,900	13.0	12.4
Louisiana	776,326	76,069	10.9	20.5
Mississippi	1,009,718	74,534	8.0	16.8
Delaware	32,602	636	7.5	6.8
Minnesota	9,445	636	7.2	7.2
Tennessee	477,646	25,888	5.7	13.4
Alabama	944,834	44,182	4.9	17.5
Colorado	11,828	510	4.5	5.6
Oregon	2,234	90	4.3	21.9
Nebraska	13,752	510	3.9	6.1
Arkansas	478,463	6,243	1.3	7.5
Washington	6,840	-43	-.6	15.3
Vermont	568	-4	-.7	2.0
Rhode Island	9,913	-123	-1.2	14.0

[Continued]

★ 1814 ★

States Arranged by Percent Increase in Black Population, 1920 to 1930

[Continued]

STATE	NEGRO POPULATION			Percent increase or decrease (-) in white population, 1920-30
	Total number, 1930	Increase or decrease (-), 1920-30		
		Number	Percent	
Kentucky	226,040	-9,898	-4.2	9.5
Virginia	650,165	-39,852	-5.8	9.4
South Carolina	793,681	-71,038	-8.2	15.3
Iowa	17,380	-1,625	-8.6	2.8
Wyoming	1,250	-125	-9.1	13.8
Georgia	1,071,125	-135,240	-11.2	8.8
Maine	1,096	-214	-16.3	3.9
North Dakota	377	-90	-19.3	4.9
South Dakota	646	-186	-22.4	8.1
Utah	1,108	-338	-23.4	12.5
Montana	1,256	-402	-24.2	-3.1
Idaho	668	-252	-27.4	3.1
New Mexico	2,850	-2,883	-50.3	9.9

Source: "States Arranged by Percent Increase in Negro Population: 1920 to 1930." U.S. Bureau of the Census, *Negroes in the United States, 1920-1932*, p. 7.

★ 1815 ★

Geographical Areas: Sections, Divisions, States

Total Population by Sections and Southern Divisions, 1830 to 1930

ECTION AND DIVISION	POPULATION										
	1930	1920	1910	1900	1890	1880	1870	1860	1850	1840	1830
						TOTAL					
United States	122,775,046	105,710,620	91,972,266	75,994,575	62,947,714	50,155,783	38,558,371	31,443,321	23,191,876	17,069,453[1]	12,866,020[1]
HE SOUTH	37,857,633	33,125,803	29,389,330	24,523,527	20,028,059	16,516,568	12,288,020	11,133,361	8,982,612	6,950,729	5,707,848
South Atlantic	15,793,589	13,990,272	12,194,895	10,443,480	8,857,922	7,597,197	5,853,610	5,364,703	4,679,090	3,925,299	364,575
East South Central	9,887,214	8,893,307	8,400,901	7,547,757	6,429,154	5,585,151	4,404,445	4,020,991	3,363,271	2,575,445	181,596
West South Central	12,176,830	10,242,224	8,784,534	6,532,290	4,740,983	3,334,220	2,029,965	1,747,667	940,251	449,985	24,612
HE NORTH	73,021,191	63,681,845	55,757,115	47,379,699	39,817,386	31,871,518	25,279,841	19,690,984	14,030,446	10,112,624	7,152,854
HE WEST	11,896,222	8,902,972	6,825,821	4,091,349	3,102,269	1,767,697	990,510	618,976	178,818	-	-
						NEGRO					
United States	11,891,143	10,463,131	9,827,763	8,833,994	7,488,676	6,580,793	4,880,009	4,441,830	3,633,808	2,873,648	2,328,643
HE SOUTH	9,361,577	8,912,231	8,749,427	7,922,969	6,760,577	5,953,903	4,420,811	4,097,111	3,352,198	2,641,977	2,161,885
South Atlantic	4,421,388	4,325,120	4,112,488	3,729,017	3,262,690	2,941,202	2,216,705	2,058,198	1,860,871	1,597,317	1,529,283
East South Central	2,658,238	2,523,532	2,652,513	2,499,886	2,119,797	1,924,996	1,464,252	1,394,360	1,122,790	830,306	501,587
West South Central	2,281,951	2,063,579	1,984,426	1,694,066	1,378,090	1,087,705	739,854	644,553	368,537	214,354	131,015
HE NORTH	2,409,219	1,472,309	1,027,674	880,771	701,018	615,038	452,818	340,240	285,369	231,671	166,757
HE WEST	120,347	78,591	50,662	30,254	27,081	11,852	6,380	4,479	1,241	-	-

[Continued]

★ 1815 ★

Total Population by Sections and Southern Divisions, 1830 to 1930

[Continued]

SECTION AND DIVISION	POPULATION 1930	1920	1910	1900	1890	1880	1870	1860	1850	1840	1830
	PERCENT DISTRIBUTION OF TOTAL POPULATION										
United States	100.0	100.0	100.0	100.0	100.0	100.0	100.0	100.0	100.0	100.0	100.0
THE SOUTH	30.8	31.3	32.0	32.3	31.8	32.9	31.9	35.4	38.7	40.7	44.4
South Atlantic	12.9	13.2	13.3	13.7	14.1	15.1	15.2	17.1	20.2	23.0	28.3
East South Central	8.1	8.4	9.1	9.9	10.2	11.1	11.4	12.8	14.5	15.1	14.1
West South Central	9.9	9.7	9.6	8.6	7.5	6.6	5.3	5.6	4.1	2.6	1.9
THE NORTH	59.5	60.2	60.6	62.3	63.3	63.5	65.5	62.6	60.5	59.2	55.6
THE WEST	9.7	8.4	7.4	5.4	4.9	3.5	2.6	2.0	.8	-	-
	PERCENT DISTRIBUTION OF NEGRO POPULATION										
United States	100.0	100.0	100.0	100.0	100.0	100.0	100.0	100.0	100.0	100.0	100.0
THE SOUTH	78.7	85.2	89.0	89.7	90.3	90.5	90.6	92.2	92.1	91.9	92.8
South Atlantic	37.2	41.3	41.8	42.2	43.6	44.7	45.4	46.3	51.1	55.6	65.7
East South Central	22.4	24.1	27.0	28.2	28.3	29.3	30.0	31.4	30.9	28.9	21.5
West South Central	19.2	19.7	20.2	19.2	18.4	16.5	15.2	14.5	10.1	7.5	5.6
THE NORTH	20.3	14.1	10.5	10.0	9.4	9.3	9.3	7.7	7.8	8.1	7.2
THE WEST	1.0	.8	.5	.3	.4	.2	.1	.1	[2]	-	-

Source: "Total and Negro Population by Sections, and Southern Divisions: 1830 to 1930." U.S. Bureau of the Census, *Negroes in the United States, 1920-1932*, p. 5. *Notes:* 1. Includes white persons (6,100 in 1840 5,318 in 1830) on public ships in the service of the United States, not credited to any division or State. 2. Less than 1/10 of 1 percent.

Households

★ 1816 ★

Characteristics of Households, 1970, 1975

Characteristic	Number (1,000) 1970	Number (1,000) 1975	Percent Distribution 1970	Percent Distribution 1975
White				
Total	56,602	62,945	100.0	100.0
Family households	46,166	49,334	81.6	78.4
Married couple	41,029	42,951	72.5	68.2
Male householder[1]	1,038	1,257	1.8	2.0
Female householder[1]	4,099	5,126	7.2	8.1
Nonfamily households	10,436	13,612	18.4	21.6
Male householder	3,406	5,038	6.0	8.0
Female householder	7,030	8,574	12.4	13.6
Black				
Total	6,223	7,262	100.0	100.0
Family households	4,856	5,468	78.0	75.3

[Continued]

★ 1816 ★

Characteristics of Households, 1970, 1975

[Continued]

Characteristic	Number (1,000)		Percent Distribution	
	1970	1975	1970	1975
Married couple	3,317	3,343	53.3	46.0
Male householder[1]	181	211	2.9	2.9
Female householder[1]	1,358	1,915	21.8	26.4
Nonfamily households	1,367	1,793	22.0	24.7
Male householder	564	791	9.1	10.9
Female householder	803	1,002	12.9	13.8

Source: "White and Black Households, by Type: 1970 to 1987," *Statistical Abstract*, 1989, p. 46. Primary source: U.S. Bureau of the Census, *Census of Population: 1970, Persons of Spanish Origin*, PC(2)- 1C; *Current Population Reports*, series P-20, No. 424 and earlier reports. *Note:* 1. No spouse present.

★ 1817 ★

Households

Size of Households, 1790-1970 - I

Year	Race of head		
	White	Negro	Other
1970	56,248	6,053	573
1969	55,394	5,870	541
1968	54,188	5,728	530
1967	52,826	6,018[5]	6,018[5]
1966	52,135	5,954[5]	5,954[5]
1965	51,441	5,808[5]	5,808[5]
1960[1]*	47,868	5,153[5]	1,153[5]
1950[1]	38,429	3,822[5]	3,822[5]
1940	31,680	3,142	127
1930	26,983[2]	2,804	118
1920	21,826	2,431	95
1910	(NA)	2,173	(NA)
1900	14,064	1,834	66
1890	11,255	1,411	24

Source: "Households, by Race, Sex, and Age of Head: 1890 to 1970." U.S. Bureau of the Census, *Historical Statistics of the United States: Colonial Times to 1970, Part I*, Bicentennial Edition, p. 42. *Notes:* *Denotes first year for which figures include Alaska and Hawaii. NA Not available. 1. Based on 20-percent sample of census returns. 2. Figures for race of head revised to include Mexicans as white. Mexicans were classified as other races in the 1930 reports. 3. Total for males includes 18,345 persons of unknown age and total for females, 6,567 of unknown age. 4. Number of female heads in each age group estimated from data on white and Negro heads with marital status and age reported. 5. Data includes Negro and Other.

★ 1818 ★

Households

Size of Households, 1790-1970 - II

Year	Male head					
	Total	Under 25 years	25-34 years	35-44 years	45-54 years	55 years and over
1970	49,588	3,485	10,328	10,286	10,278	15,211
1969	48,927	3,360	9,990	10,250	10,177	15,149
1968	48,121	3,150	9,457	10,452	10,096	14,968
1967	47,082	3,023	9,234	10,486	9,969	14,372
1966	46,517	3,046	8,952	10,467	9,904	14,146
1965	46,027	2,918	8,912	10,449	9,726	14,022
1960[1]*	43,873	2,369	8,964	10,480	9,194	12,866
1950[1]	35,863	1,850	8,139	8,676	7,274	9,925
1940	29,680	1,260	6,539	7,286	6,716	7,879
1930	26,112[3]	1,266	5,879	7,082	5,743	6,123
1920	(NA)	(NA)	(NA)	(NA)	(NA)	(NA)
1910	(NA)	(NA)	(NA)	(NA)	(NA)	(NA)
1900	14,023	(NA)	(NA)	(NA)	(NA)	(NA)
1890	10,857	572	2,962	2,883	2,184	2,256

Source: "Households, by Race, Sex, and Age of Head: 1890 to 1970." U.S. Bureau of the Census, *Historical Statistics of the United States: Colonial Times to 1970, Part I*, Bicentennial Edition, p. 42. *Notes:* *Denotes first year for which figures include Alaska and Hawaii. NA Not available. 1. Based on 20-percent sample of census returns. 2. Figures for race of head revised to include Mexicans as white. Mexicans were classified as other races in the 1930 reports. 3. Total for males includes 18,345 persons of unknown age and total for females, 6,567 of unknown age. 4. Number of female heads in each age group estimated from data on white and Negro heads with marital status and age reported.

★ 1819 ★

Households

Size of Households, 1790-1970 - III

Year	Female head					
	Total	Under 25 years	25-34 years	35-44 years	45-54 years	55 years and over
1970	13,287	820	1,324	1,401	1,959	7,782
1969	12,877	706	1,291	1,489	1,973	7,417
1968	12,323	679	1,141	1,480	1,869	7,157
1967	11,763	540	1,084	1,433	1,845	6,861
1966	11,575	506	1,071	1,413	1,839	6,748
1965	11,224	484	984	1,521	1,760	6,475
1960[1]*	9,151	330	803	1,227	1,607	5,184
1950[1]	6,389	164	541	935	1,264	3,486
1940	5,269	113	470	879	1,144	2,663

[Continued]

★ 1819 ★

Size of Households, 1790-1970 - III

[Continued]

Year	Female head					
	Total	Under 25 years	25-34 years	35-44 years	45-54 years	55 years and over
1930	3,793[3]	120[4]	371[4]	685[4]	862[4]	1,749[4]
1920	(NA)	(NA)	(NA)	(NA)	(NA)	(NA)
1910	(NA)	(NA)	(NA)	(NA)	(NA)	(NA)
1900	(NA)	(NA)	(NA)	(NA)	(NA)	(NA)
1890	1,833	59	230	387	466	691

Source: "Households, by Race, Sex, and Age of Head: 1890 to 1970." U.S. Bureau of the Census, *Historical Statistics of the United States: Colonial Times to 1970, Part I*, Bicentennial Edition, p. 42. *Notes:* *Denotes first year for which figures include Alaska and Hawaii. NA Not available. 1. Based on 20-percent sample of census returns. 2. Figures for race of head revised to include Mexicans as white. Mexicans were classified as other races in the 1930 reports. 3. Total for males includes 18,345 persons of unknown age and total for females, 6,567 of unknown age. 4. Number of female heads in each age group estimated from data on white and Negro heads with marital status and age reported.

Marital Status

★ 1820 ★

Distribution of Population 35 to 44 Years by Marital Status, Gender, and Region: 1890-1975

Area and year	Men				Women			
	Total (thousands)	Percent of total			Total (thousands)	Percent of total		
		Single	Married	Widowed and divorced		Single	Married	Widowed and divorced
SOUTH								
1890[1]	293	10	85	6	319	7	75	18
1910[1]	454	10	82	8	456	6	75	18
1940[2]	600	12	82	5	665	7	75	18
1960	571	11	84	5	673	7	81	13
1970	521	12	82	6	643	9	77	14
1975	528	10	81	9	650	9	73	17
NORTH AND WEST								
1890[1]	50	21	73	6	45	10	70	19
1910[1]	96	23	69	8	83	11	70	19
1940[2]	315	22	73	6	300	9	74	17
1960	506	11	82	6	558	7	79	13

[Continued]

★ 1820 ★

Distribution of Population 35 to 44 Years by Marital Status, Gender, and Region: 1890-1975

[Continued]

Area and year	Men				Women			
	Total (thousands)	Percent of total			Total (thousands)	Percent of total		
		Single	Married	Widowed and divorced		Single	Married	Widowed and divorced
1970	570	12	80	8	669	8	76	16
1975	513	12	81	6	682	7	73	20

Source: "Percent Distribution of the Black Population 35 to 44 Years Old, by Marital Status, Sex, for Selected Years: 1890 to 1975," U.S. Department of Commerce, Bureau of the Census. *The Social and Economic Status of the Black Population in the United States: An Historical View, 1790-1978,* p. 111. Primary source: U.S. Department of Commerce, Bureau of the Census. *Notes:* 1. Data include a small number of persons whose marital status was not reported. 2. Data include persons of "other" races.

★ 1821 ★

Marital Status

Marital Status of Population 35 to 44 Years by Gender: 1890-1975

Marital status, sex, and race	1890[1]	1910[1]	1940[2]	1960	1970	1975
BLACK						
Men						
Total, 35 to 44 years (thousands)	344	550	915	1,077	1,088	1,043
Percent	100	100	100	100	100	100
Single	11	12	15	11	12	11
Married	83	80	79	83	81	81
Widowed	5	7	4	2	2	1
Divorced	-	1	2	4	5	7
Women						
Total, 35 to 44 years (thousands)	364	539	965	1,231	1,312	1,333
Percent	100	100	100	100	100	100
Single	7	7	8	7	9	8
Married	75	74	74	80	76	73
Widowed	17	17	15	7	7	7
Divorced	1	2	3	6	8	11
WHITE						
Men						
Total, 35 to 44 years (thousands)	3,327	5,561	8,250	10,556	10,023	9,745
Percent	100	100	100	100	100	100
Single	15	17	14	8	7	8

[Continued]

★ 1821 ★

Marital Status of Population 35 to 44 Years by Gender: 1890-1975

[Continued]

Marital status, sex, and race	1890[1]	1910[1]	1940[2]	1960	1970	1975
Married	81	79	83	89	89	87
Widowed	3	3	1	1	1	-
Divorced	-	1	2	2	3	5
Women						
Total, 35 to 44 years (thousands)	2,978	4,951	8,203	11,007	10,370	10,073
Percent	100	100	100	100	100	100
Single	10	12	11	6	5	4
Married	81	81	82	88	87	86
Widowed	8	7	5	3	3	2
Divorced	1	1	3	4	5	7

Source: "Marital Status of the Population 35 to 44 Years Old, by Sex, for Selected Years: 1890 to 1975," U.S. Department of Commerce, Bureau of the Census. *The Social and Economic Status of the Black Population in the United States: An Historical View, 1790-1978*, p. 110. Primary source: U.S. Department of Commerce, Bureau of the Census. *Notes:* - Represents or rounds to zero. 1. Total includes a small number of persons whose marital status was not reported. 2. Data for Black include persons of "other" races.

★ 1822 ★

Marital Status

Marital Status of the Population, by Gender: 1890-1975

Marital status, sex, and race	1890[1]	1910[1]	1940	1960	1970	1975
BLACK						
Men						
Total, 14 years and over (thousands)	2,098	3,043	4,342	5,713	7,020	7,509
Percent	100	100	100	100	100	100
Single	40	36	33	30	33	38
Married	56	57	61	63	57	53
Widowed	4	6	6	5	4	4
Divorced	-	1	1	2	3	4
Women						
Total, 14 years old and over (thousands)	2,154	3,093	4,649	6,375	8,121	9,046
Percent	100	100	100	100	100	100
Single	30	27	24	22	29	31
Married	55	57	59	60	53	49
Widowed	15	15	16	14	13	13
Divorced	1	1	2	4	5	7

[Continued]

★ 1822 ★

Marital Status of the Population, by Gender: 1890-1975

[Continued]

Marital status, sex, and race	1890[1]	1910[1]	1940	1960	1970	1975
WHITE						
Men						
Total, 14 years and over (thousands)	18,430	29,024	44,744	55,072	63,574	67,655
Percent	100	100	100	100	100	100
Single	42	39	33	25	28	28
Married	54	56	61	70	67	66
Widowed	4	4	4	3	3	2
Divorced	-	1	1	2	3	3
Women						
Total, 14 years and over (thousands)	17,355	26,800	44,560	58,060	68,875	73,312
Percent	100	100	100	100	100	100
Single	32	30	26	19	22	22
Married	57	59	61	67	62	62
Widowed	11	10	11	12	12	12
Divorced	-	1	2	3	4	5

Source: "Marital Status of the Population 14 Years Old and Over, by Sex, for Selected Years: 1890 to 1975," U.S. Department of Commerce, Bureau of the Census. *The Social and Economic Status of the Black Population in the United States: An Historical View, 1790-1978,* p. 109. Primary source: U.S. Department of Commerce, Bureau of the Census. *Notes:* Data for 1890, 1910, and 1940 are for persons 15 years old and over. - Represents or rounds to zero. 1. Total includes a small number of persons whose marital status was not reported.

Migration

★ 1823 ★

Estimated Intercensal Migration of the Population by Race and States, 1870-1970

State	Components of change method (Bureau of the Census)			Survival-rate method (see text for sources)								
	1960-1970	1950-1960	1940-1950	1950-1960	1940-1950	1930-1940	1920-1930	1910-1920	1900-1910	1890-1900	1880-1890	1870-1880
TOTAL WHITE AND POPULATION[1]												
New England:												
Maine	-69	-67	-27	-70.5	-35.8	-1.2	-39.3	-8.3	10.6	4.1	-15.9	-33.3
New Hampshire	69	12	2	-2.1	-9.1	9.1	-10.2	-3.6	3.2	20.4	20.7	10.1
Vermont	15	-38	-19	-38.4	-23.8	-18.7	-20.6	-17.6	-3.7	-2.4	-13.3	-26.2
Massachusetts	74	-96	23	-154.0	-29.5	-69.5	22.1	192.2	307.3	334.9	295.7	140.2
Rhode Island	13	-26.	11	-36.5	2.7	-2.3	11.4	12.8	66.1	45.9	42.5	27.9
Connecticut	214	234	113	-172.7	89.5	39.2	64.1	122.1	112.7	90.8	72.9	22.4

[Continued]

★ 1823 ★

Estimated Intercensal Migration of the Population by Race and States, 1870-1970

[Continued]

State	Components of change method (Bureau of the Census)			Survival-rate method (see text for sources)								
	1960-1970	1950-1960	1940-1950	1950-1960	1940-1950	1930-1940	1920-1930	1910-1920	1900-1910	1890-1900	1880-1890	1870-1880
Middle Atlantic:												
New York	-101	210	270	1.2	83.8	396.3	1,062.1	467.4	1,061.0	604.8	395.4	61.7
New Jersey	488	578	294	409.9	200.7	-28.2	442.3	278.2	376.1	218.3	151.3	48.4
Pennsylvania	-378	-475	-355	-594.0	-447.2	-301.0	-252.9	51.9	444.6	262.0	285.1	19.1
East North Central:												
Ohio	-126	407	245	265.9	151.6	-56.6	214.7	499.4	207.7	77.7	41.9	-12.9
Indiana	-16	61	97	21.0	56.7	10.6	-.9	16.0	-54.4	33.4	-8.67	-70.2
Illinois	-43	124	75	-10.1	-22.1	-60.8	414.0	255.6	223.0	340.0	170.3	-59.0
Michigan	27	155	336	88.0	251.4	17.1	549.6	465.2	117.2	62.0	172.3	161.4
Wisconsin	4	-53	-84	85.2	-95.1	-10.9	-17.9	37.6	9.2	84.3	100.8	9.0
West North Central:												
Minnesota	-25	-98	-173	-109.2	-160.9	36.0	-106.2	59.1	72.6	148.4	264.1	156.2
Iowa	-183	-234	-196	-220.7	-178.8	-73.4	-167.2	-18.3	-207.5	21.7	-5.6	85.1
Missouri	2	-134	-190	-150.0	-168.6	-20.8	-98.7	-134.7	-163.8	-17.2	56.4	-30.4
North Dakota	-94	-105	-121	-91.0	-109.4	-105.8	-76.3	-46.0	137.3	63.8	243.4[3]	86.8[3]
South Dakota	-94	-95	-79	-76.1	-71.2	-101.4	-45.0	-31.2	86.9	.3	243.4[3]	86.8[3]
Nebraska	-73	-117	-135	-102.4	-123.0	-139.5	-78.1	-34.5	-28.8	-153.9	362.5	204.4
Kansas	-130	-44	-91	-29.6	-86.8	-163.8	-83.1	-74.5	20.0	-149.8	159.7	366.8
South Atlantic:												
Delaware	38	63	21	51.1	14.5	16.0	-3.5	5.1	2.7	-1.2	4.3	-2.3
Maryland	385	321	270	231.1	213.3	87.0	10.2	43.1	-8.3	8.2	10.7	-11.2
District of Columbia	-100	-160	49	-115.1	78.5	157.8	27.3	97.0	41.0	34.3	36.1	18.1
Virginia	141	15	169	-2.0	152.0	.2	-231.6	-27.7	-73.7	-91.5	-80.9	-51.1
West Virginia	-265	-446	-235	-401.6	-210.8	-73.6	-53.8	-1.7	46.1	17.2	-4.8	24.0
North Carolina	-94	-328	-258	-277.6	-202.8	-85.4	-7.9	-74.3	-80.4	-88.8	-57.7	-14.4
South Carolina	-149	-222	-230	-179.1	172.4	-102.5	-256.9	-80.9	-80.6	-75.5	-35.9	25.7
Georgia	51	-212	-290	-169.7	-224.3	134.1	-414.9	-98.1	-41.7	-56.1	-19.5	-40.0
Florida	1,326	1,616	578	1,385.6	510.9	280.3	297.6	101.6	103.5	36.9	51.1	12.1
East South Central:												
Kentucky	-153	-390	-366	-350.2	-319.2	-93.5	-206.1	-167.1	-177.8	-65.1	-96.8	-47.2
Tennessee	-45	-274	-143	-252.6	-102.8	-14.9	-113.8	-131.2	-156.9	-95.4	-77.7	-91.8
Alabama	-233	-369	-342	-332.3	-271.0	-165.3	-149.2	-113.9	-47.8	-40.4	-11.5	-60.7
Mississippi	-267	-433	-433	-369.6	-349.9	-90.3	-101.6	-199.3	-46.4	-44.5	-60.6	-5.6
West South Central:												
Arkansas	-71	-433	-415	-353.0	-320.4	-128.8	-191.8	-74.7	-27.2	-82.8	75.1	84.0
Louisiana	-130	-49	-147	-39.0	-112.1	5.7	-23.2	-64.7	10.6	1.4	-3.0	-12.0
Oklahoma	13	-219	-434	-196.0	-356.1	-269.4	-51.8	62.4	491.5	501.3	44.5	NA
Texas	146	121	73	174.5	132.9	-72.9	243.5	114.3	131.1	147.7	151.2	308.5
Mountain:												
Montana	-58	-25	-40	-25.3	-42.2	-19.3	-72.9	90.1	96.5	63.5	70.6	12.1
Idaho	-42	-40	-27	39.3	-29.6	-20.5	-50.6	37.3	104.1	39.8	34.2	11.7
Wyoming	-39	-20	-1	-18.7	-4.6	-.1	-1.2	20.7	33.3	15.6	28.7	7.2
Colorado	215	164	41	132.4	32.4	1.0	-16.6	39.8	159.8	51.9	146.8	119.1
New Mexico	-130	52	16	51.7	9.8	18.6	-22.9	-20.2	63.1	1.2	6.4	-3.3
Arizona	228	329	137	289.3	117.4	-3.5	23.5	75.4	50.7	21.4	10.9	19.8
Utah	-11	9	9	4.9	6.4	-30.5	-30.8	-.2	24.9	8.9	17.9	16.7
Nevada	144	86	34	74.9	28.8	12.5	6.9	-6.4	32.9	-5.1	15.6	6.6
Pacific:												
Washington	249	87	392	49.5	351.3	109.2	81.6	97.5	464.7	80.4	205.4	28.7
Oregon	159	16	286	1.2	244.0	94.1	96.5	56.0	189.9	43.0	85.9	39.0
California	2,113	3,142	2,658	2,573.1	2,339.1	974.6	1,695.2	804.1	694.1	172.7	214.2	129.6
Alaska	16	41	-	48.0	-	-	-	-	-	-	-	-
Hawaii	11	3	-	47.9	-	-	-	-	-	-	-	-

[Continued]

★ 1823 ★

Estimated Intercensal Migration of the Population by Race and States, 1870-1970

[Continued]

State	Components of change method (Bureau of the Census)			Survival-rate method (see text for sources)								
	1960-1970	1950-1960	1940-1950	1950-1960	1940-1950	1930-1940	1920-1930	1910-1920	1900-1910	1890-1900	1880-1890	1870-1880
NATIVE WHITE POPULATION[4]												
New England:												
Maine	-69	-69	-27	-71.4	-41.6	-2.2	-46.6	-22.7	-18.4	-20.6	-40.8	-46.5
New Hampshire	68	11	-1	-2.7	-12.6	8.3	14.4	-12.8	-15.7	-2.5	-7.1	-7.1
Vermont	14	-38	-20	-38.1	-25.8	-14.6	-25.2	-19.7	-17.2	-10.9	-21.9	-24.7
Massachusetts	23	-122	8	185.0	-73.8	-45.6	-101.7	-6.0	-23.3	46.9	31.9	13.5
Rhode Island	4	-28	9	-34.2	-.2	.8	-8.7	-10.5	5.1	3.3	2.4	4.1
Connecticut	166	195	98	106.6	49.0	30.2	6.4	18.7	10.9	5.4	2.8	-6.5
Middle Atlantic:												
New York	-638	-72	-6	-392.6	-270.8	140.3	138.1	-76.5	-74.9	-18.6	-146.4	-167.4
New Jersey	336	466	231	214.5	88.6	-18.8	179.3	72.0	71.4	46.3	9.4	-8.9
Pennsylvania	-423	-552	-467	-657.9	-531.3	-260.9	-380.2	-199.4	-178.1	-60.2	-70.0	-105.2
East North Central:												
Ohio	-191	274	110	116.8	28.5	-58.6	58.2	233.4	-40.4	-29.6	-96.7	-92.8
Indiana	-58	17	57	-24.6	15.0	7.1	-43.3	-33.1	-111.9	-7.6	-120.4	-101.2
Illinois	-215	-64	-142	-229.6	-202.9	-58.7	80.3	-36.2	-198.9	44.0	-170.7	-192.5
Michigan	-124	28	146	-57.7	51.7	18.1	239.9	181.5	-35.9	-26.8	-19.7	25.8
Wisconsin	-29	-82	-96	-120.8	-110.3	-10.0	-53.2	-37.3	-103.3	-25.7	-75.6	-78.8
West North Central:												
Minnesota	-39	-102	-175	-111.1	-163.1	27.1	-113.6	-1.2	-61.4	25.9	37.2	38.2
Iowa	-189	-236	-198	-218.3	-180.9	-70.5	-164.0	-45.6	-249.1	-29.9	-108.2	2.7
Missouri	-25	-161	-222	-173.7	-197.4	-36.8	-141.4	-173.7	-228.1	-50.0	2.4	-43.2
North Dakota	-94	-103	-119	87.5	103.6	-99.1	-72.8	-46.3	81.8	20.4	126.0[3]	43.5[3]
South Dakota	-92	-90	-74	-74.0	-17.3	-96.8	-46.1	-33.7	59.6	-26.5	126.0[3]	43.5[3]
Nebraska	-76	-121	-139	-106.0	-125.9	-135.5	-81.1	-53.2	-62.4	-159.2	244.3	139.2
Kansas	-139	-49	-96	-33.6	-90.1	-156.2	-84.6	-86.9	-18.2	-156.6	106.3	290.1
South Atlantic:												
Delaware	32	57	17	43.6	11.2	12.8	-3.8	.3	-3.0	-3.7	-11.	-2.6
Maryland	290	284	231	187.6	167.6	72.2	-4.5	16.8	-26.9	-5.8	-29.4	-16.1
District of Columbia	-137	-213	-14	-165.4	6.7	101.2	5.5	69.3	22.2	20.1	18.1	8.6
Virginia	206	85	194	58.4	169.1	33.7	-111.7	-9.5	-35.6	-25.8	-33.6	-16.5
West Virginia	-247	-406	-219	-361.3	-193.0	-66.7	-62.7	-29.3	-6.2	3.5	-12.3	18.1
North Carolina	81	-121	-95	-109.9	-81.6	-27.1	5.2	-47.7	-54.4	-41.7	-19.8	-7.6
South Carolina	44	-4	-24	-.7	-15.7	-8.7	-52.4	-8.0	-10.5	-10.8	-17.5	9.1
Georgia	198	-8	-49	-10.8	38.2	-44.2	-155.1	-27.4	-30.8	31.4	35.1	20.8
Florida	1,340	1,516	564	1,152.8	438.7	208.4	221.1	84.5	46.6	10.1	24.8	7.3
East South Central:												
Kentucky	-158	-375	-349	-334.8	-299.1	-83.8	-188.4	-153.1	-159.9	-58.9	-85.6	-39.6
Tennessee	1	-217	-97	-201.6	-68.6	24.4	-100.6	-103.2	-127.3	-76.7	-64.9	67.0
Alabama	-5	-145	-140	-142.5	-108.6	-101.0	-69.7	-45.3	-32.8	-41.1	-12.1	-25.9
Mississippi	10	-110	-108	-104.8	-94.3	-32.0	-33.8	-70.3	-19.0	-35.8	-47.7	-22.7
West South Central:												
Arkansas	38	-283	-259	--243.8	-207.1	-95.5	-144.4	-74.4	-55.2	-77.6	25.3	53.0
Louisiana	26	43	-2	23.0	-4.7	15.3	2.9	17.8	15.8	9.2	-12.2	-11.8
Oklahoma	-4	-193	-361	-179.5	-319.5	-253.4	-51.2	54.5	414.2	404.3	39.6	NA
Texas	92	147	173	155.3	134.4	-1.7	197.5	-28.4	60.5	95.5	90.9	233.9
Mountain:												
Montana	-57	-23	-36	-23.5	-41.9	-14.8	-66.9	75.4	51.0	37.1	39.8	8.2
Idaho	-44	-41	-28	-39.5	-30.7	20.8	-49.5	31.5	81.9	31.0	24.6	8.5
Wyoming	-39	-19	-2	-17.0	-5.6	2.2	-1.8	19.9	19.8	11.7	19.1	5.5
Colorado	187	149	32	110.1	21.1	7.4	17.6	29.2	108.8	33.1	101.1	86.7
New Mexico	-120	53	17	43.3	3.8	22.5	17.2	-32.0	52.7	-2.3	2.7	-5.9
Arizona	248	339	135	255.5	97.6	12.4	31.8	39.9	25.7	15.1	7.2	11.7
Utah	-16	8	6	-2.0	1.0	-27.5	-31.5	-7.6	2.8	-2.5	2.7	.6
Nevada	136	80	31	66.0	24.2	13.8	5.1	-6.1	21.5	-3.9	-10.0	.8

[Continued]

★ 1823 ★

Estimated Intercensal Migration of the Population by Race and States, 1870-1970

[Continued]

State	Components of change method (Bureau of the Census)			Survival-rate method (see text for sources)								
	1960-1970	1950-1960	1940-1950	1950-1960	1940-1950	1930-1940	1920-1930	1910-1920	1900-1910	1890-1900	1880-1890	1870-1880
Pacific:												
Washington	220	69	375	27.8	303.9	100.3	49.2	51.9	311.4	54.0	133.2	20.8
Oregon	145	10	278	-4.5	222.9	90.4	74.3	38.2	132.0	29.2	57.4	25.7
California	1,528	2,788	2,373	1,964.6	1,874.7	899.5	1,244.5	537.7	425.2	96.3	109.6	56.0
Alaska	22	42	-	41.1	-	-	-	-	-	-	-	-
Hawaii	58	55	-	44.5	-	-	-	-	-	-	-	-
FOREIGN-BORN WHITE POPULATION[4]												
New England:												
Maine	-	-	-	-.4	5.9	.8	7.5	14.3	28.9	24.4	25.0	13.4
New Hampshire	-	-	-	(Z)	3.3	1.0	4.0	9.2	18.9	22.7	27.9	17.1
Vermont	-	-	-	-.3	2.0	-4.0	4.7	3.0	12.7	8.6	8.6	-1.4
Massachusetts	-	-	-	14.2	33.6	-26.6	120.9	191.3	324.8	278.0	259.3	123.7
Rhode Island	-	-	-	-2.6	1.7	-3.6	21.0	22.7	60.3	41.1	88.9	22.9
Connecticut	-	-	-	37.6	27.5	6.8	52.1	98.1	123.2	82.9	69.0	28.1
Middle Atlantic:												
New York	-	-	-	150.0	11.0	120.1	751.3	480.9	1,100.2	589.7	532.0	221.5
New Jersey	-	-	-	103.2	58.5	-18.9	196.0	181.6	286.2	154.2	133.5	54.4
Pennsylvania	-	-	-	3.4	-5.5	60.4	25.6	168.7	589.8	282.9	334.3	115.6
East North Central:												
Ohio	-	-	-	41.7	16.5	-18.8	65.8	196.5	232.5	102.1	133.4	77.3
Indiana	-	-	-	10.3	9.5	-5.0	19.3	28.8	53.4	32.9	29.9	24.3
Illinois	-	-	-	60.2	1.0	-51.5	214.4	222.0	398.3	273.4	332.6	124.8
Michigan	-	-	-	35.7	36.4	-29.0	223.6	245.1	151.1	88.3	193.2	134.0
Wisconsin	-	-	-	12.1	3.4	-1.9	30.9	72.7	112.0	107.0	176.3	86.5
West North Central:												
Minnesota	-	-	-	-1.7	-.5	7.8	6.9	58.1	131.7	116.5	225.4	116.5
Iowa	-	-	-	-3.4	1.1	-2.6	-1.3	23.7	39.4	50.1	102.1	80.2
Missouri	-	-	-	4.5	3.0	-3.3	6.7	11.8	63.3	32.8	58.1	17.2
North Dakota	-	-	-	-3.9	-5.8	-6.6	-3.4	.3	55.2	38.6	117.4[3]	43.0[3]
South Dakota	-	-	-	-2.2	-.2	-4.4	1.2	2.5	27.0	12.7	117.4[3]	43.0[3]
Nebraska	-	-	-	(Z)	-.2	-4.6	3.0	13.4	32.0	7.7	110.9	64.1
Kansas	-	-	-	1.6	1.1	-7.5	-4.4	7.0	35.6	7.4	50.7	62.0
South Atlantic:												
Delaware	-	-	-	2.9	.8	.8	-.3	5.3	6.0	3.1	5.1	1.7
Maryland	-	-	-	18.6	15.7	4.1	9.7	19.4	30.0	20.6	26.2	12.4
District of Columbia	-	-	-	-.9	10.7	9.1	5.8	9.3	9.1	5.5	4.7	3.3
Virginia	-	-	-	10.7	13.4	3.4	-2.7	9.0	11.3	5.1	6.2	2.9
West Virginia	-	-	-	-3.5	-1.1	-2.8	-3.9	12.1	37.0	8.0	4.0	3.8
North Carolina	-	-	-	3.6	6.1	1.6	2.7	2.2	2.3	1.5	.6	1.1
South Carolina	-	-	-	2.5	2.3	.6	-.2	1.6	2.0	.7	.3	.9
Georgia	-	-	-	6.2	5.1	.5	.2	4.0	5.4	2.5	3.3	1.1
Florida	-	-	-	152.9	65.0	22.0	22.4	13.9	16.2	3.4	10.5	3.4
East South Central:												
Kentucky	-	-	-	1.2	2.7	-.7	-1.0	2.7	4.4	6.0	11.2	5.5
Tennessee	-	-	-	1.0	4.0	1.0	.7	1.3	4.7	.4	5.9	-.2
Alabama	-	-	-	1.8	3.0	-.5	1.1	2.2	7.0	2.4	6.3	1.3
Mississippi	-	-	-	-.6	2.5	.2	1.1	.7	3.4	1.7	.3	-.6
West South Central:												
Arkansas	-	-	-	-0.6	2.8	(Z)	-.6	0.8	5.5	2.6	5.1	5.6
Louisiana	-	-	-	4.3	6.4	-1.1	-.6	4.3	10.9	13.8	5.8	1.2
Oklahoma	-	-	-	2.2	2.3	-2.9	-2.4	7.1	22.6	17.8	2.7	(NA)
Texas	-	-	-	38.7	65.8	-76.1	36.4	137.4	80.8	45.0	47.6	53.6
Mountain:												
Montana	-	-	-	-1.8	-.5	-4.4	-5.9	14.8	35.2	26.4	30.9	4.0
Idaho	-	-	-	(Z)	.7	-.3	-.9	5.6	21.9	8.9	9.5	3.3

[Continued]

★ 1823 ★

Estimated Intercensal Migration of the Population by Race and States, 1870-1970

[Continued]

State	Components of change method (Bureau of the Census)			Survival-rate method (see text for sources)								
	1960-1970	1950-1960	1940-1950	1950-1960	1940-1950	1930-1940	1920-1930	1910-1920	1900-1910	1890-1900	1880-1890	1870-1880
Wyoming	-	-	-	-.8	-.3	-2.1	.6	1.4	12.3	4.0	9.6	1.7
Colorado	-	-	-	11.3	5.1	-7.3	.3	9.9	47.9	18.7	45.6	32.4
New Mexico	-	-	-	4.3	3.7	-5.4	-2.7	7.8	10.4	3.5	3.6	2.6
Arizona	-	-	-	26.8	13.0	-19.4	-10.2	29.8	24.8	6.4	3.8	8.2
Utah	-	-	-	6.4	4.2	-3.2	1.0	7.1	21.6	11.4	15.2	16.1
Nevada	-	-	-	3.6	1.7	-1.5	1.6	-.2	11.1	-1.1	-5.7	5.8
Pacific:												
Washington	-	-	-	15.0	29.6	7.7	32.3	44.4	149.8	26.4	72.2	8.0
Oregon	-	-	-	3.3	14.3	3.3	22.1	17.2	57.5	13.8	28.5	13.4
California	-	-	-	388.2	265.4	33.8	414.2	250.3	259.1	76.4	104.7	73.6
Alaska	-	-	-	1.7	-	-	-	-	-	-	-	-
Hawaii	-	-	-	2.2	-	-	-	-	-	-	-	-
NEGRO POPULATION												
New England:												
Maine	-2	2	5	1.4	-.1	.2	-.2	.1	.2	.3	-.1	-.2
New Hampshire	5	1	5	.7	.2	-.3	.2	(Z)	(Z)	.1	(Z)	.1
Vermont	5	5	5	(Z)	.1	-.2	(Z)	-.9	.8	-.1	(Z)	(Z)
Massachusetts	33	20	12	16.8	10.6	2.7	2.9	6.9	5.9	9.9	4.4	3.0
Rhode Island	2	1	1	.3	1.2	.6	-.7	.6	.6	1.5	1.2	.8
Connecticut	38	37	15	.28.5	12.9	2.2	5.2	5.3	.5	2.5	1.1	.8
Middle Atlantic:												
New York	396	255	266	243.8	243.6	135.9	172.8	63.1	35.8	33.8	9.9	7.6
New Jersey	120	107	61	92.2	53.6	9.5	67.0	24.5	18.5	17.7	8.4	2.9
Pennsylvania	25	75	107	60.4	89.6	20.3	101.7	82.5	32.9	39.2	20.8	8.7
East North Central:												
Ohio	45	129	131	107.4	106.7	20.7	90.7	69.4	15.6	5.2	5.2	2.6
Indiana	32	42	39	35.3	32.1	8.6	23.2	20.3	4.1	8.1	3.9	6.6
Illinois	127	182	203	159.2	179.8	49.4	119.3	69.8	23.5	22.7	8.4	8.7
Michigan	124	122	186	109.9	163.3	28.0	86.1	38.7	1.9	.4	-1.2	1.6
Wisconsin	27	29	14	23.5	11.9	1.0	4.4	2.2	.5	3.0	.1	1.3
West North Central:												
Minnesota	7	5	4	3.6	2.7	1.0	.6	2.1	2.3	5.9	1.5	1.5
Iowa	2	2	2	.9	1.0	-.4	-1.9	3.9	2.1	1.6	.4	2.3
Missouri	14	24	31	19.2	25.7	19.2	35.9	27.2	1.0	(Z)	-4.0	-4.3
North Dakota	1	1	5	.3	.1	-.1	-.1	.3	4.9	(Z)	(Z)	.3
South Dakota	5	5	5	.2	.2	-.1	-.2	(Z)	.3	14.0	(Z)	.3
Nebraska	2	4	4	3.6	3.0	.6	(Z)	5.2	1.6	-2.3	7.3	1.2
Kansas	-1	2	4	2.4	2.3	-.1	6.0	5.4	2.6	-.6	2.7	14.7
South Atlantic:												
Delaware	4	6	4	4.6	2.4	2.4	.5	-.6	-.4	-.7	.3	-1.4
Maryland	79	31	37	24.9	29.9	10.7	5.0	7.0	-11.4	-6.5	-7.5	-7.5
District of Columbia	36	51	61	51.3	61.2	47.5	16.0	18.3	9.8	8.7	13.4	6.2
Virginia	-79	-74	-29	-71.1	-30.6	-36.9	-117.2	-27.2	-49.3	-70.8	-53.4	-37.6
West Virginia	-20	-41	-17	-36.8	-16.7	-4.1	12.8	15.5	15.3	5.8	3.6	2.1
North Carolina	-175	-204	-164	-171.3	-127.3	-60.0	-15.7	-28.9	-28.4	-48.7	-38.4	-7.9
South Carolina	-197	-218	-208	-180.8	-159.0	-94.4	-204.3	-74.5	-72.0	-65.5	-18.6	15.7
Georgia	-154	-205	-243	-165.1	-191.2	-90.3	-260.0	-74.7	-16.2	-27.3	12.3	-20.3
Florida	-32	96	12	79.8	7.2	49.9	54.2	3.2	40.7	23.4	15.8	1.4
East South Central:												
Kentucky	1	-16	-18	-16.6	-22.8	-9.1	-16.6	-16.6	-22.3	-12.2	-22.4	-13.1
Tennessee	-51	-59	-48	-52.2	-38.2	8.6	-14.0	-29.3	-34.3	-19.0	-18.7	-24.6
Alabama	-231	-224	-204	-191.6	-165.4	-63.8	-80.7	-70.8	-22.1	-1.7	-5.8	-36.1
Mississippi	-279	-323	-326	-264.2	258.2	-58.2	-68.8	-129.6	-30.9	-10.4	-13.2	17.6
West South Central:												
Arkansas	-112	-150	-158	-108.6	-116.1	-33.3	-46.3	-1.0	22.5	-7.9	44.7	25.4
Louisiana	-163	-93	-147	-66.2	-113.8	-8.4	-25.5	-51.2	-16.2	-21.6	3.3	-1.3

[Continued]

★ 1823 ★

Estimated Intercensal Migration of the Population by Race and States, 1870-1970

[Continued]

State	Components of change method (Bureau of the Census)			Survival-rate method (see text for sources)								
	1960-1970	1950-1960	1940-1950	1950-1960	1940-1950	1930-1940	1920-1930	1910-1920	1900-1910	1890-1900	1880-1890	1870-1880
Oklahoma	-3	-21	-47	-18.8	-38.9	-13.0	1.9	.8	54.8	79.3	2.3	(NA)
Texas	-4	-33	-107	-19.6	-67.2	4.9	9.7	5.2	-10.2	7.1	12.6	21.0
Mountain:												
Montana	[5]	[5]	[5]	(Z)	.1	(Z)	-.2	-.1	.3	-	-	-
Idaho	[5]	[5]	[5]	.1	.3	(Z)	-.1	.3	.3	-	-	-
Wyoming	[5]	-1	2	-.8	1.3	-.2	-.1	-.6	1.2	-	-	-
Colorado	16	13	7	11.0	6.1	.9	.8	.7	3.1	-	-	-
New Mexico	-4	4	2	4.1	2.3	1.5	-2.9	4.1	(NA)	-	-	-
Arizona	-4	4	6	7.0	6.7	3.5	1.9	5.8	.2	-	-	-
Utah	1	1	1	.5	1.1	.2	-.3	.4	.5	-	-	-
Nevada	6	6	3	5.3	2.8	.2	.2	-.1	.4	-	-	-
Pacific:												
Washington	10	8	21	6.7	17.8	1.2	.2	1.1	3.4	-	-	-
Oregon	4	3	8	2.4	6.9	.5	.2	.7	.5	-	-	-
California	272	255	289	220.4	258.9	41.2	36.4	16.1	9.8	-	-	-
Alaska	[5]	[5]	-	5.2	-	-	-	-	-	-	-	-
Hawaii	1	[5]	-	1.2	-	-	-	-	-	-	-	-

Source: "Estimated Net Intercensal Migration of Total, Native White, Foreign- Born White, and Negro Population, by States: 1870 to 1970." U.S. Bureau of the Census, *Historical Statistics of the United States: Colonial Times to 1970, Part I*, pp. 93-95. *Notes:* NA Not available. Z Less than 50. 1. For 1870-1890, only white population in Mountain and Pacific States; no estimates made for Negroes. 2. Less than 1,000. 3. Includes data for both Dakotas. 4. For component of change method, 1950-1970, total white population; no estimates separately for native white and foreign-born white. 5. Less than 500.

★ 1824 ★

Migration

Estimated Net Intercensal Migration of Blacks, by Region: 1870-1970

Numbers in thousands. Plus sign (+) denotes net in-migration; minus sign (-) denotes net out-migration.

Intercensal period	South	North			West
		Total	Northeast	North Central	
1870-1880	-60	+60	+24	+36	(NA)
1880-1890	-70	+70	+46	+24	(NA)
1890-1900	-168	+168	+105	+63	(NA)
1900-1910	-170	+151	+95	+56	+20
1910-1920	-454	+426	+182	+244	+28
1920-1930	-749	+713	+349	+364	+36
1930-1940	-347	+299	+171	+128	+49
1940-1950	-1,599	+1,081	+463	+618	+339

[Continued]

★ 1824 ★

Estimated Net Intercensal Migration of Blacks, by Region: 1870-1970

[Continued]

Intercensal period	South	North			West
		Total	Northeast	North Central	
1950-1960	-1,473	+1,037	+496	+541	+293[1]
1960-1970	-1,380	+994	+612	+382	+301

Source: "Estimated Net Intercensal Migration of Blacks, by Region: 1870 to 1970," U.S. Department of Commerce, Bureau of the Census. *The Social and Economic Status of the Black Population in the United States: An Historical View, 1790-1978,* p. 15. Published by permission. Primary source: U.S. Department of Commerce, Bureau of the Census; and, Everett S. Lee, et al. *Population Redistribution and Economic Growth: United States, 1870-1950,* Vol. I, The American Philosophical Society, Philadelphia 1957. *Notes:* NA Not available. The net migration estimates for the period 1870-1940 were developed by the national census survival rate method; the estimates for 1940-1970 were prepared by the vital statistics method. See "References for Tables" for further information. 1. Figure revised since prior publication.

★ 1825 ★

Migration

Gain of North and West Loss of South by Interstate Migration, 1870-1920

Decennial Year	Born South and living in North and West		Born North and West and living in South		Net gain of Northland West and loss of South	
	Number at end each decade	10 year increase	Number at end each decade	10 year increase	Gain at end each decade	10 year increase
1870	149,100	-	15,583	-	133,517	-
1880	198,029	48,929	22,039	64,056	175,990	42,473
1890	241,855	43,826	23,268	1,229	118,587	-57,403
1900	349,651	107,796	30,397	7,129	319,254	200,667
1910	440,534	90,883	41,489	11,092	399,045	79,791
1920	780,794	340,160	47,223	5,734	733,571	334,596

Source: "Gain North and West and Loss of South by Interstate Migration 1870- 1920." Work, Monroe N., ed. *Negro Year Book: An Annual Encyclopedia of the Negro, 1925-26,* p. 438.

★ 1826 ★

Migration

Increase in Number and Percent of Blacks in the South in Urban and Rural Communities, 1890, 1900, 1910, 1920 - I

Year	Number		Per cent	
	Urban	Rural	Urban	Rural
1920	2,250,899	6,661,332	25.3	74.7
1910	1,854,455	6,894,972	21.2	78.8
1900	1,364,796	6,558,173	17.2	82.8
1890	1,033,235	5,727,342	15.3	84.7

Source: "Increase in Number and in Percent of Negroes in the South Living in Urban and Rural Communities, 1890, 1900, 1910, 1920." Work, Monroe N., ed., *Negro Year Book: An Annual Encyclopedia of the Negro, 1925-26*, p. 442.

★ 1827 ★

Migration

Increase in Number and Percent of Blacks in the South in Urban and Rural Communities, 1890, 1900, 1910, 1920 - II

Decade	Increase[1]			
	Number		Per cent	
	Urban	Rural	Urban	Rural
1910-1920	396,444	-233,640	21.3	-3.4
1900-1910	489,659	-336,800	35.8	-5.1
1890-1900	331,561	830,831	32.0	14.5

Source: "Increase in Number and in Percent of Negroes in the South Living in Urban and Rural Communities, 1890, 1900, 1910, 1920." Work, Monroe N., ed., *Negro Year Book: An Annual Encyclopedia of the Negro, 1925-26*, p. 442. *Note:* 1. A minus (-) sing indicates a decrease.

★ 1828 ★

Migration

Internal Migration of Population Surviving from Preceding Census Date by States, 1870-1950

State	1940 to 1950	1930 to 1940	1920 to 1930	1910 to 1920	1900 to 1910	1890 to 1900	1880 to 1890	1870 to 1880
NATIVE WHITE POPULATION								
New England:								
Maine	-41.6	-2.2	-46.6	-22.7	-18.4	-20.6	-40.8	-46.5
New Hampshire	-12.6	8.3	-14.4	-12.8	-15.7	-2.5	-7.1	-7.1
Vermont	-25.8	-14.6	-25.2	-19.7	-17.2	-10.9	-21.9	-24.7
Massachusetts	-73.8	-45.6	-101.7	-6.0	-23.3	46.9	31.9	13.5
Rhode Island	-0.2	0.8	-8.7	-10.5	5.1	3.3	2.4	4.1
Connecticut	49.0	30.2	6.4	18.7	-10.9	5.4	2.8	-6.5
Middle Atlantic:								
New York	-270.8	140.3	138.1	-76.5	-74.9	-18.6	-146.4	-167.4
New Jersey	88.6	-18.8	179.3	72.0	71.4	46.3	9.4	-8.9
Pennsylvania	-531.3	-260.9	-380.2	-199.4	-178.1	-60.2	-70.0	-105.2
East North Central:								
Ohio	28.5	-58.6	58.2	233.4	-40.4	-29.6	-96.7	-92.8
Indiana	15.0	7.1	-43.3	-33.1	-111.9	-7.6	-120.4	-101.2
Illinois	-202.9	-58.7	80.3	-36.2	-198.9	44.0	-170.7	-192.5
Michigan	51.7	18.1	239.9	181.5	-35.9	-26.8	-19.7	25.8
Wisconsin	-110.3	-10.0	-53.2	-37.3	-103.3	-25.7	-75.6	78.8
West North Central:								
Minnesota	163.1	27.1	-113.6	-1.2	-61.4	25.9	37.2	38.2
Iowa	-180.9	-70.5	-164.0	-45.9	-249.1	-29.9	-108.2	2.7
Missouri	-197.4	-36.8	-141.4	-173.7	-228.1	-50.0	2.4	-43.2
North Dakota	-103.6	-99.1	-72.8	-46.3	81.8	20.4	126.0[4]	43.5[4]
South Dakota	-71.8	-96.8	-46.1	-33.7	59.6	-26.5	126.0[4]	43.5[4]
Nebraska	-125.9	-135.5	-81.1	-53.2	-62.4	-159.2	244.3	139.2
Kansas	-90.1	-156.2	-84.6	-86.9	-18.2	-156.6	106.3	290.1
South Atlantic:								
Delaware	11.2	12.8	-3.8	0.3	-3.0	-3.7	-1.1	-2.6
Maryland	167.6	72.2	-4.5	16.8	-26.9	-5.8	-29.4	-16.1
District of Columbia	6.7	101.2	5.5	69.3	22.2	20.1	18.1	8.6
Virginia	169.1	33.7	-111.7	-9.5	-35.6	-25.8	-33.6	-16.5
West Virginia	-193.0	-66.7	-62.7	-29.3	-6.2	3.5	-12.3	18.1
North Carolina	-81.6	-27.1	5.2	-47.7	-54.4	-41.7	-19.8	-7.6
South Carolina	15.7	-8.7	-52.4	-8.0	-10.5	10.8	-17.5	9.1
Georgia	-38.2	-44.2	155.1	-27.4	-30.8	-31.4	-35.1	-20.8
Florida	438.7	208.4	221.1	84.5	46.6	10.1	24.8	7.3
East South Central:								
Kentucky	-299.1	-83.8	-188.4	-153.1	-159.0	-58.9	-85.6	-39.6
Tennessee	-68.6	-24.4	-100.6	-103.2	-127.3	-76.7	-64.9	-67.0
Alabama	-108.6	-101.0	-69.7	-45.3	-32.8	-41.1	-12.1	-25.9
Mississippi	-94.3	-32.0	-33.8	-70.3	-19.0	-35.8	-47.7	-22.7

[Continued]

★ 1828 ★

Internal Migration of Population Surviving from Preceding Census Date by States, 1870-1950

[Continued]

State	1940 to 1950	1930 to 1940	1920 to 1930	1910 to 1920	1900 to 1910	1890 to 1900	1880 to 1890	1870 to 1880
West South Central:								
Arkansas	-207.1	-95.5	-144.4	-74.4	-55.2	-77.6	25.3	53.0
Louisiana	-4.7	15.3	2.9	-17.8	15.8	9.2	-12.2	-11.8
Oklahoma	-319.5	-253.4	-51.2	54.5	414.2	404.3	39.6	2
Texas	134.4	-1.7	197.5	-28.4	60.5	95.5	90.9	233.9
Mountain:								
Montana	-41.9	-14.8	-66.9	75.4	51.0	37.1	39.8	3.2
Idaho	-30.7	20.8	-49.5	31.5	81.9	31.0	24.6	3.5
Wyoming	-5.6	2.2	-1.8	19.9	19.8	11.7	19.1	5.5
Colorado	21.1	7.4	-17.6	29.2	108.8	33.1	101.1	86.7
New Mexico	3.8	22.5	-17.2	-32.0	52.7	-2.3	2.7	-5.9
Arizona	97.6	12.4	31.8	39.9	25.7	15.1	7.2	11.7
Utah	1.0	-27.5	-31.5	-7.6	2.8	-2.5	2.7	0.6
Nevada	24.2	13.8	5.1	-6.1	21.5	-3.9	10.0	0.8
Pacific:								
Washington	303.9	100.3	49.2	51.9	311.4	54.0	133.2	20.8
Oregon	222.9	90.4	74.3	38.2	132.0	29.2	57.4	25.7
California	1,874.7	899.5	1,244.5	537.7	425.2	96.3	109.6	56.0
FOREIGN-BORN WHITE POPULATION								
New England:								
Maine	5.9	0.8	7.5	14.3	28.9	24.4	25.0	13.4
New Hampshire	3.3	1.0	4.0	9.2	18.9	22.7	27.9	17.1
Vermont	2.0	-4.0	4.7	3.0	12.7	8.6	8.6	-1.4
Massachusetts	33.6	-26.6	120.9	191.3	324.8	278.0	259.3	123.7
Rhode Island	1.7	-3.6	21.0	22.7	60.3	41.1	38.9	22.9
Connecticut	27.5	6.8	52.5	98.1	123.2	82.9	69.0	28.1
Middle Atlantic:								
New York	111.0	120.1	751.3	480.9	1,100.2	589.7	532.0	221.5
New Jersey	58.5	-18.9	196.0	181.6	286.2	154.2	133.5	54.4
Pennsylvania	-5.5	-60.4	25.6	168.7	589.8	282.9	334.3	115.6
East North Central:								
Ohio	16.5	-18.8	65.8	196.5	232.5	102.1	133.4	77.3
Indiana	9.5	-5.0	19.3	28.8	53.4	32.9	29.9	24.3
Illinois	1.0	-51.5	214.4	222.0	398.3	273.4	332.6	124.8
Michigan	36.4	-29.0	223.6	245.1	151.1	88.3	193.2	134.0
Wisconsin	3.4	-1.9	30.9	72.7	112.0	107.0	176.3	86.5
West North Central:								
Minnesota	-0.5	7.8	6.9	58.1	131.7	116.5	225.4	116.5
Iowa	1.1	-2.6	-1.3	23.7	39.4	50.1	102.1	80.2

[Continued]

★ 1828 ★

Internal Migration of Population Surviving from Preceding Census Date by States, 1870-1950

[Continued]

State	1940 to 1950	1930 to 1940	1920 to 1930	1910 to 1920	1900 to 1910	1890 to 1900	1880 to 1890	1870 to 1880
Missouri	3.0	-3.3	6.7	11.8	63.3	32.8	58.1	17.2
North Dakota	-5.8	-6.6	-3.4	0.3	55.2	38.6	117.4[4]	43.0[4]
South Dakota	-0.2	-4.4	1.2	2.5	27.0	12.7	117.4[4]	43.0[4]
Nebraska	-0.2	-4.6	3.0	13.4	32.0	7.7	110.9	64.1
Kansas	1.1	-7.5	-4.4	7.0	35.6	7.4	50.7	62.0
South Atlantic:								
Delaware	0.8	0.8	-0.3	5.3	6.0	3.1	5.1	1.7
Maryland	15.7	4.1	9.7	19.4	30.0	20.6	26.2	12.4
District of Columbia	10.7	9.1	5.8	9.3	9.1	5.5	4.7	3.3
Virginia	13.4	3.4	-2.7	9.0	11.3	5.1	6.2	2.9
West Virginia	-1.1	-2.8	-3.9	12.1	37.0	8.0	4.0	3.8
North Carolina	6.1	1.6	2.7	2.2	2.3	1.5	0.6	1.1
South Carolina	2.3	0.6	-0.2	1.6	2.0	0.7	0.3	0.9
Georgia	5.1	0.5	0.2	4.0	5.4	2.5	3.3	1.1
Florida	65.0	22.0	22.4	13.9	16.2	3.4	10.5	3.4
East South Central:								
Kentucky	2.7	-0.7	-1.0	2.7	4.4	6.0	11.2	5.5
Tennessee	4.0	1.0	0.7	1.3	4.7	0.4	5.9	-0.2
Alabama	3.0	-0.5	1.1	2.2	7.0	2.4	6.3	1.3
Mississippi	2.5	-0.2	1.1	0.7	3.4	1.7	0.3	-0.6
West South Central:								
Arkansas	2.8	[2]	-0.6	0.8	5.5	2.6	5.1	5.6
Louisiana	6.4	-1.1	-0.6	4.3	10.9	13.8	5.8	1.2
Oklahoma	2.3	-2.9	-2.4	7.1	22.6	17.8	2.7	[2]
Texas	65.8	-76.1	36.4	137.5	80.8	45.0	47.6	53.6
Mountain:								
Montana	-0.5	-4.4	-5.9	14.8	35.2	26.4	30.9	4.0
Idaho	0.7	-0.3	-0.9	5.6	21.9	8.9	9.5	3.3
Wyoming	-0.3	-2.1	0.6	1.4	12.3	4.0	9.6	1.7
Colorado	5.1	-7.3	0.3	9.9	47.9	18.7	45.6	32.4
New Mexico	3.7	-5.4	-2.7	7.8	10.4	3.5	3.6	2.6
Arizona	13.0	-19.4	-10.2	29.8	24.8	6.4	3.3	8.2
Utah	4.2	-3.2	1.0	7.1	21.6	11.4	15.2	16.1
Nevada	1.7	-1.5	1.6	-0.2	11.1	-1.1	-5.7	5.8
Pacific:								
Washington	29.6	7.7	32.3	44.4	149.8	26.4	72.2	8.0
Oregon	14.3	3.3	22.1	17.2	57.5	13.8	28.5	13.4
California	265.4	33.8	414.2	250.3	259.1	76.4	104.7	73.6

[Continued]

★ 1828 ★

Internal Migration of Population Surviving from Preceding Census Date by States, 1870-1950

[Continued]

State	1940 to 1950	1930 to 1940	1920 to 1930	1910 to 1920	1900 to 1910	1890 to 1900	1880 to 1890	1870 to 1880
NEGRO POPULATION								
New England:								
Maine	-0.1	0.2	-0.2	0.1	0.2	0.3	-0.1	-0.2
New Hampshire	0.2	-0.3	0.2	[3]	[3]	0.1	[3]	0.1
Vermont	0.1	-0.2	[3]	-0.9	0.8	-0.1	[3]	[3]
Massachusetts	10.6	2.7	2.9	6.9	5.9	9.9	4.4	3.0
Rhode Island	1.2	0.6	-0.7	0.6	0.6	1.5	1.2	0.8
Connecticut	12.9	2.2	5.2	5.3	0.5	2.5	1.1	0.8
Middle Atlantic:								
New York	243.6	135.9	172.8	63.1	35.8	33.8	9.9	7.6
New Jersey	53.6	9.5	67.0	24.5	18.5	17.7	8.4	2.9
Pennsylvania	89.6	20.3	101.7	82.5	32.9	39.2	20.8	8.7
East North Central:								
Ohio	106.7	20.7	90.8	69.4	15.6	5.2	5.3	2.6
Indiana	32.1	8.6	23.2	20.3	4.1	8.1	3.9	6.6
Illinois	179.8	49.4	119.3	69.8	23.5	22.7	8.4	8.7
Michigan	163.3	28.0	86.1	38.7	1.9	0.4	-1.2	1.6
Wisconsin	11.9	1.0	4.4	2.2	0.5	3.0	0.1	1.3
West North Central:								
Minnesota	2.7	1.0	0.6	2.1	2.3	5.9	1.5	1.5
Iowa	1.0	-0.4	-1.9	3.9	2.1	1.6	0.4	2.3
Missouri	25.7	19.2	35.9	27.2	1.0	[3]	-4.0	-4.3
North Dakota	0.1	-0.1	-0.1	0.3	4.9	4.9	[3,4]	0.3[4]
South Dakota	0.2	-0.1	-0.2	[3]	0.3	14.0	[3,4]	0.3[4]
Nebraska	3.0	0.6	[3]	5.2	1.6	-2.3	7.3	1.2
Kansas	2.3	-0.1	6.0	5.4	2.6	-0.6	2.7	14.7
South Atlantic:								
Delaware	2.4	2.4	0.5	-0.6	-0.4	-0.7	0.3	-1.4
Maryland	29.9	10.7	5.0	7.0	-11.4	-6.5	-7.5	-7.5
District of Columbia	61.2	47.5	16.0	18.3	9.8	8.7	13.4	6.2
Virginia	-30.6	-36.9	-117.2	-27.2	-49.3	-70.8	-53.4	-37.6
West Virginia	-16.7	-4.1	12.8	15.5	15.3	5.8	3.6	2.1
North Carolina	-127.3	-60.0	-15.7	-28.9	-28.4	-48.7	-38.4	-7.9
South Carolina	-159.0	-94.4	-204.3	-74.5	-72.0	-65.5	-18.6	15.7
Georgia	-191.2	-90.3	-260.0	-74.7	-16.2	-27.3	12.3	-20.3
Florida	7.2	49.9	54.2	3.2	40.7	23.4	15.8	1.4
East South Central:								
Kentucky	-22.8	-9.1	-16.6	-16.6	-22.3	-12.2	-22.4	18.1
Tennessee	-38.2	3.6	-14.0	-29.3	-34.3	-19.0	-18.7	-24.6
Alabama	-165.4	-63.8	-80.7	-70.8	-22.1	-1.7	-5.8	-36.1

[Continued]

★ 1828 ★

Internal Migration of Population Surviving from Preceding Census Date by States, 1870-1950

[Continued]

State	1940 to 1950	1930 to 1940	1920 to 1930	1910 to 1920	1900 to 1910	1890 to 1900	1880 to 1890	1870 to 1880
Mississippi	-258.2	-58.2	-68.8	-129.6	-30.9	-10.4	-13.2	17.6
West South Central:								
Arkansas	-116.1	-33.3	-46.3	-1.0	22.5	-7.9	44.7	25.4
Louisiana	-113.8	-8.4	-25.5	-51.2	-16.1	-21.6	3.3	-1.3
Oklahoma	-67.2	4.9	9.7	5.2	-10.2	7.1	12.6	21.0
Texas	-67.2	4.9	9.7	5.2	-10.2	7.1	12.6	21.0
Mountain:								
Montana	0.1	3	-0.2	-0.1	0.3	-	-	-
Idaho	0.3	3	-0.1	0.3	0.3	-	-	-
Wyoming	1.3	-0.2	-0.1	-0.6	1.2	-	-	-
Colorado	6.1	0.9	0.8	0.7	3.1	-	-	-
New Mexico	2.3	1.5	-2.9	4.1	3	-	-	-
Arizona	6.7	3.5	1.9	5.8	0.2	-	-	-
Utah	1.1	0.2	-0.3	0.4	0.5	-	-	-
Nevada	2.8	0.2	0.2	-0.1	0.4	-	-	-
Pacific:								
Washington	17.8	1.2	0.2	1.1	3.4	-	-	-
Oregon	6.9	0.5	0.2	1.1	3.4	-	-	-
California	258.9	41.2	36.4	16.1	9.8	-	-	-

Source: "Estimated Net Intercensal Migration of Total, Native White, Foreign- Born White, and Negro Population Surviving From the Preceding Census Date, by States: 1870-1950." U.S. Bureau of the Census, *Historical Statistics of the United States: Colonial Times to 1957*, pp. 45-46. *Notes:* 1. For 1870-1890, only white population in the 11 Western States; no estimates made for Negroes. 2. Not available. 3. Less than 50. 4. Data includes North and South Dakota.

★ 1829 ★

Migration

Interregional Migration of the Population: 1970-1975

Numbers in thousands. Minus sign (-) denotes decrease.

Migration status and race	South	Northeast	North Central	West
BLACK				
Inmigrants	302	118	150	153
Outmigrants	288	182	202	51
Net migration	14	-64	-52	102
WHITE				
Inmigrants	3,730	920	1,569	2,155

[Continued]

★ 1829 ★

Interregional Migration of the Population: 1970-1975

[Continued]

Migration status and race	South	Northeast	North Central	West
Outmigrants	1,939	2,160	2,714	1,561
Net migration	1,791	-1,240	-1,145	594

Source: "Interregional Migration of the Population 5 Years Old and Over: March 1970 to March 1975," U.S. Department of Commerce, Bureau of the Census. *The Social and Economic Status of the Black Population in the United States: An Historical View, 1790-1978*, p. 16. Primary source: U.S. Department of Commerce, Bureau of the Census.

★ 1830 ★

Migration

Migrants and Immigrants of Cities of 50,000 or More, Having 5,000 or More Blacks, 1910 - I

CITY[1]	POPUALTION: 1910						
	All classes	Negro					
		Total	Born in the state	Born in other states		Other native[2]	Foreign born
				Number	Percent		
All cities[1]	17,025,664	1,228,509	719,566	479,793	39.1	9,300	19,850
NORTHERN AND WESTERN CITIES:							
Total	14,123,471	456,653	155,046	278,066	60.9	5,414	18,127
New York, N.Y.	4,766,883	91,709	26,977	52,202	56.9	773	11,757
Mahattan Borough	2,331,542	60,534	14,309	37,001	61.1	485	8,739
Bronx Borough	430,980	4,117	1,484	2,266	55.0	23	344
Brooklyn Borough	1,634,351	22,708	8,768	11,182	49.2	254	2,504
Queens Borough	284,041	3,198	1,805	1,284	40.2	7	102
Richmond Borough	85,969	1,152	611	469	40.7	4	68
Philadelphia, Pa.	1,549,008	84,459	29,686	53,161	62.9	455	1,157
Chicago, Ill.	2,185,283	44,103	8,519	34,017	77.1	903	664
St. Louis, Mo.	687,029	43,960	20,782	22,593	51.1	465	120
Pittsburgh, Pa.	533,905	25,623	8,810	16,289	63.6	258	266
Kansas City, Mo.	248,381	23,566	12,887	9,976	42.3	653	50
Indianapolis, Ind.	233,650	21,816	7,200	14,434	62.2	151	31
Cincinnati, Ohio	363,591	19,639	5,575	13,658	69.5	361	45
Boston, Mass.	670,585	13,564	3,961	7,759	57.2	90	1,754
Columbus, Ohio	181,511	12,739	6,705	5,912	46.4	81	41
Newark, N.J.	347,469	9,475	3,931	5,331	56.3	66	147
Kansas City, Kans.	82,331	9,286	3,057	6,098	65.7	115	16
Cleveland, Ohio	560,663	8,448	3,015	4,885	57.8	256	292
Los Angeles, Cal.	319,198	7,599	1,050	6,341	83.4	103	105
Evansville, Ind.	69,647	6,266	2,010	4,235	67.6	19	2

[Continued]

★ 1830 ★

Migrants and Immigrants of Cities of 50,000 or More, Having 5,000 or More Blacks, 1910 - I

[Continued]

CITY[1]	POPUALTION: 1910 All classes	Negro Total	Negro Born in the state	Born in other states Number	Born in other states Percent	Other native[2]	Foreign born
Camden, N.J.	94,538	6,076	2,540	3,463	57.0	28	45
Jersey City, N.J.	267,779	5,960	1,500	4,278	71.8	27	155
East St. Louis, Ill.	58,547	5,882	1,933	3,907	66.4	35	7
Detroit, Mich.	465,766	5,741	1,850	2,575	44.9	412	904
Denver, Colo.	213,381	5,426	973	4,277	78.8	130	46
Providence, R.I.	224,326	5,316	2,085	2,675	50.3	33	523
SOUTHRN CITIES:							
Total	2,902,193	771,856	564,520	201,727	26.1	3,886	1,723
Washington, D.C.	331,069	94,446	40,459	53,058	56.2	691	238
New Orleans, La.	339,075	89,262	76,383	12,169	13.6	333	377
Baltimore, Md.	558,485	84,749	64,872	19,240	22.7	274	363
Memphis, Tenn.	131,105	52,441	26,044	25,595	48.8	778	24
Birmingham, Ala.	132,685	52,305	39,593	12,419	23.7	271	22
Atlanta, Ga.	154,839	51,902	45,683	6,071	11.7	114	34
Richmond, Va.	127,628	46,733	42,926	3,705	7.9	62	40
Louisville, Ky.	223,928	40,522	33,143	7,299	17.8	120	30
Nashville, Tenn.	110,364	36,523	33,443	2,991	8.2	73	16
Savannah, Ga.	65,064	33,246	21,614	11,499	34.6	45	88
Charleston, S.C.	58,833	31,056	30,423	579	1.9	23	31
Jacksonville, Fla.	57,699	29,293	13,430	15,630	53.4	81	152
Norfolk, Va.	67,452	25,039	16,728	8,204	32.8	38	69
Houston, Tex.	78,800	23,929	19,313	4,399	18.4	155	62
Mobile, Ala.	51,521	22,763	19,974	2,451	10.8	258	80
Dallas, Tex.	92,104	18,024	14,318	3,565	19.8	127	14
Fort Worth, Tex.	73,312	13,280	10,759	2,263	17.0	232	26
San Antonio, Tex.	96,614	10,716	9,219	1,324	12.4	141	32
Wilmington, Del.	87,411	9,081	5,107	3,932	43.3	28	14
Oklahoma City, Okla.	64,205	6,546	1,089	5,404	82.6	42	11

Source: "Migrants and Immigrants in Negro and White Population of Cities or 50,000 or More Inhabitants, Having 5,000 or More Negroes: 1910." U.S. Bureau of the Census, *Negro Population, 1790-1915,* p. 74. *Notes:* 1. Cities of 50,000 or more inhabitants having 5,000 or more Negroes. 2. Includes persons born in the United States, State of birth not reported; persons born in outlying possessions, at sea under the United States flag, and American citizens born abroad.

★ 1831 ★

Migration

Migrants and Immigrants of Cities of 50,000 or More, Having 5,000 or More Blacks, 1910 - II

CITY[1]	POPULATION: 1910						
	White						Indian, Chinese, Japanese, and other colored
	Total	Born in the state	Born in other states		Other native[2]	Foreign born	
			Number	Percent			
All cities[1]	15,774,773	8,580,586	2,420,968	15.3	66,138	4,707,081	22,382
NORTHERN AND WESTERN CITIES:							
Total	13,646,530	7,224,187	1,893,441	13.9	56,033	4,472,869	20,228
New York, N.Y.	4,669,162	2,414,318	311,477	6.7	15,664	1,927,703	6,012
Mahattan Borough	2,266,578	991,167	159,438	7.0	11,954	1,104,019	4,430
Bronx Borough	426,650	249,388	27,278	6.4	1,049	148,935	213
Brooklyn Borough	1,610,487	937,250	99,849	6.2	2,032	571,356	1,156
Queens Borough	280,691	184,628	16,502	5.9	446	79,115	152
Richmond Borough	84,756	51,885	8,410	9.9	183	24,278	61
Philadelphia, Pa.	1,463,371	951,780	126,692	8.7	2,321	382,578	1,178
Chicago, Ill.	2,139,057	1,008,868	337,253	15.8	11,719	781,217	2,123
St. Louis, Mo.	642,488	377,039	137,181	21.4	2,562	125,706	581
Pittsburgh, Pa.	508,008	323,773	42,093	8.3	1,706	140,436	274
Kansas City, Mo.	224,677	93,696	100,497	44.7	5,157	25,327	138
Indianapolis, Ind.	211,780	142,005	49,141	23.2	867	19,767	54
Cincinnati, Ohio	343,919	232,018	53,871	15.7	1,238	56,792	33
Boston, Mass.	655,696	342,995	69,827	10.6	2,152	240,722	1,325
Columbus, Ohio	168,709	128,314	22,979	13.6	1,131	16,285	63
Newark, N.J.	337,742	179,529	46,441	13.8	1,117	110,655	252
Kansas City, Kans.	72,996	27,159	34,743	47.6	750	10,344	49
Cleveland, Ohio	551,925	292,747	61,667	11.2	1,808	195,703	290
Los Angeles, Cal.	305,307	62,084	180,590	59.1	2,049	60,584	6,292
Evansville, Ind.	63,377	43,081	15,738	24.8	96	4,462	4
Camden, N.J.	88,391	45,229	27,339	30.9	141	15,682	71
Jersey City, N.J.	261,659	129,879	53,489	20.4	594	77,697	160
East St. Louis, Ill.	52,646	27,948	15,123	28.7	175	9,400	19
Detroit, Mich.	459,926	243,383	57,929	12.6	2,049	156,565	99
Denver, Colo.	207,071	53,781	112,193	54.2	2,156	38,941	884
Providence, R.I.	218,623	104,561	37,178	17.0	581	76,303	387
SOUTHRN CITIES:							
Total	2,128,243	1,356,390	527,527	24.8	10,105	234,212	2,094
Washington, D.C.	236,128	98,843	111,452	47.2	1,483	24,351	495
New Orleans, La.	249,403	193,787	25,539	10.2	2,391	27,686	410
Baltimore, Md.	473,387	347,168	48,359	10.2	817	77,043	349
Memphis, Tenn.	78,590	36,167	35,008	44.5	948	6,467	74

[Continued]

★ 1831 ★

Migrants and Immigrants of Cities of 50,000 or More, Having 5,000 or More Blacks, 1910 - II

[Continued]

CITY[1]	POPULATION: 1910						
	White						Indian, Chinese, Japanese, and other colored
	Total	Born in the state	Born in other states		Other native[2]	Foreign born	
			Number	Percent			
Birmingham, Ala.	80,369	45,744	28,621	35.6	304	5,700	11
Atlanta, Ga.	102,861	72,815	25,277	24.6	359	4,410	76
Richmond, Va.	80,879	67,177	9,448	11.7	169	4,085	16
Louisville, Ky.	183,390	135,577	30,086	16.4	291	17,436	16
Nashville, Tenn.	73,831	58,531	12,223	16.6	84	2,993	10
Savannah, Ga.	31,784	20,313	8,097	25.5	42	3,332	34
Charleston, S.C.	27,764	22,335	2,976	10.7	49	2,404	13
Jacksonville, Fla.	28,329	10,352	15,020	53.0	469	2,488	77
Norfolk, Va.	42,353	26,724	11,998	28.3	67	3,564	60
Houston, Tex.	54,832	30,467	17,628	32.1	419	6,318	39
Mobile, Ala.	28,737	19,791	6,623	23.0	115	2,208	21
Dallas, Tex.	74,043	38,283	30,147	40.7	394	5,319	37
Fort Worth, Tex.	59,960	31,559	23,552	39.3	640	4,209	72
San Antonio, Tex.	85,801	48,870	18,983	22.1	541	17,407	97
Wilmington, Del.	78,309	44,108	20,349	26.0	174	13,678	21
Oklahoma City, Okla.	57,493	7,788	46,141	80.3	350	3,214	166

Source: "Migrants and Immigrants in Negro and White Population of Cities or 50,000 or More Inhabitants, Having 5,000 or More Negroes: 1910." U.S. Bureau of the Census, *Negro Population, 1790-1915,* p. 74. *Notes:* 1. Cities of 50,000 or more inhabitants having 5,000 or more Negroes. 2. Includes persons born in the United States, State of birth not reported; persons born in outlying possessions, at sea under the United States flag, and American citizens born abroad.

★ 1832 ★

Migration

Migration of Blacks Out of and Into the South by States, 1870-1910

Section, Division, and State	1910	1900	1890[1]	1880[1]	1870	Increase[2]			
						1900-1910	1890-1900	1880-1890	1870-1880
	Negro Population Born in the South								
THE NORTH AND WEST	440,534	349,651	241,855	198,029	149,100	90,883	107,796	43,826	48,929
THE NORTH	415,533	336,076	230,931	194,630	146,490	79,457	105,145	36,301	48,140
New England	22,600	22,279	13,848	10,824	8,269	321	8,431	3,024	2,555
Middle Atlantic	198,501	150,399	78,579	48,332	33,754	48,102	71,820	30,247	14,578
East North Central	128,547	102,917	78,567	75,217	63,856	25,630	24,350	3,350	11,361
West North Central	65,885	60,481	59,937	60,257	40,611	5,404	544	-320	19,646
NEW ENGLAND:									
Maine	178	212	177	227	366	-34	35	-50	-139

[Continued]

★ 1832 ★

Migration of Blacks Out of and Into the South by States, 1870-1910

[Continued]

Section, Division, and State	1910	1900	1890[1]	1880[1]	1870	Increase[2]			
						1900-1910	1890-1900	1880-1890	1870-1880
New Hampshire	169	298	158	162	173	-129	140	-4	-11
Vermont	779	190	111	142	199	589	79	-31	-57
Massachusetts	13,064	13,080	7,744	5,851	4,347	-16	5,336	1,893	1,504
Rhode Island	3,191	3,423	2,558	2,013	1,385	-232	865	545	628
Connecticut	5,219	5,076	3,100	2,429	1,799	143	1,976	671	630
MIDDLE ATLANTIC:									
New York	60,494	42,985	21,694	14,373	8,146	17,509	21,291	7,321	6,226
New Jersey	40,987	29,491	14,669	7,401	5,166	11,496	14,822	7,268	2,235
Pennsylvania	97,020	77,923	42,216	26,558	20,441	19,097	35,707	15,658	6,117
EAST NORTH CENTRAL:									
Ohio	44,439	34,848	32,280	31,880	31,378	9,591	2,568	400	502
Indiana	30,123	27,711	21,315	20,355	13,459	2,412	6,396	960	6,896
Illinois	50,314	36,976	21,647	19,150	14,408	13,338	15,329	2,497	4,742
Michigan	2,897	2,647	2,725	3,282	3,752	250	-78	-557	-470
Wisconsin	774	735	600	550	859	39	135	50	-309
WEST NORTH CENTRAL:									
Minnesota	2,502	1,901	1,335	558	391	601	546	797	167
Iowa	4,452	3,690	3,512	2,919	2,258	762	178	593	661
Missouri	36,329	32,376	28,665	30,785	30,754	3,953	3,711	-2,120	31
North Dakota	223	110	105	120[3,5]	62[3,5]	113	5	199[5]	58[5]
South Dakota	249	171	214	120[3,5]	62[3,5]	78	-43	199[5]	58[5]
Nebraska	2,327	1,854	2,983	1,035	353	473	-1,129	1,948	682
Kansas	19,803	20,379	23,103	24,840	6,793	-576	-2,724	-1,737	18,047
THE WEST	25,001	13,575	10,924	3,309	2,610	11,426	2,651	7,525	789
Mountain	10,140	7,294	5,855	1,606	754	2,846	1,439	4,249	852
Pacific	14,861	6,281	5,069	1,793	1,856	8,580	1,212	3,276	-63
MOUNTAIN:									
Montana	682	652	795	80	71	30	-143	715	9
Idaho	248	109	77	22	26	139	32	55	-4
Wyoming	1,210	398	528	108	96	812	-130	420	12
Colorado	5,212	3,789	2,423	942	248	1,423	1,366	1,481	694
New Mexico	889	880	725	187	80	9	155	538	107
Arizona	1,251	1,054	989	65	18	197	65	924	47
Utah	397	356	233	60	38	41	123	173	23
Nevada	251	56	85	142	177	195	-29	-57	-35
PACIFIC:									
Washington	2,992	1,225	803	99	33	1,767	422	704	66
Oregon	620	419	278	63	102	201	141	215	-39
California	11,249	4,637	3,988	1,631	1,721	6,612	649	2,357	-90
Negro Population Born in the North and West									
THE SOUTH	41,489	30,397	23,268	22,039	15,583	11,092	7,129	1,229	6,456
South Atlantic	15,651	9,297	6,388	5,207	2,425	6,354	2,909	1,181	2,782
East South Central	9,808	8,008	6,686	7,017	4,564	1,710	1,412	-331	2,435
West South Central	16,030	13,002	10,194	9,815	8,594	3,028	2,808	379	1,221

[Continued]

★ 1832 ★

Migration of Blacks Out of and Into the South by States, 1870-1910

[Continued]

Section, Division, and State	1910	1900	1890[1]	1880[1]	1870	Increase[2] 1900-1910	1890-1900	1880-1890	1870-1880
SOUTH ATLANTIC:									
Delaware	1,397	1,167	919	772	429	230	248	147	343
Maryland	2,894	2,019	1,453	999	677	875	566	454	322
District of Columbia	2,542	1,781	1,529	960	279	761	252	569	681
Virginia	3,151	1,408	741	530	207	1,743	667	211	323
West Virginia	2,127	1,211	681	477	224	916	530	204	253
North Carolina	911	404	195	438	122	507	209	-243	316
South Carolina	429	202	174	231	127	227	28	-57	104
Georgia	1,146	573	319	390	211	573	254	-71	179
Florida	1,054	532	377	410	149	522	155	-33	261
EAST SOUTH CENTRAL:									
Kentucky	3,735	3,244	2,089	1,622	977	491	1,555	467	645
Tennessee	2,676	2,333	1,733	1,653	1,231	443	500	80	422
Alabama	1,412	691	869	1,455	358	721	-178	-586	1,097
Mississippi	1,985	1,930	1,995	2,287	1,998	55	-65	-292	289
WEST SOUTH CENTRAL:									
Arkansas	3,690	2,918	3,149	2,806	2,032	772	-231	343	774
Louisiana	2,086	1,818	1,975	2,686	2,497	268	-157	-711	189
Oklahoma	6,096	4,225	870	[4]	[4]	1,871	3,355	870	-
Texas	4,158	4,041	4,200	4,323	4,065	117	-159	-123	258

Source: "Migration of Negroes Out of and Into the South, by States: 1870-1910." U.S. Bureau of the Census, *Negro Population, 1790-1915*, p. 68. *Notes:* 1. Colored. 2. A minus sign (-) denotes decrease. 3. Dakota Territory in 1880 and 1870. 4. No enumeration of Oklahoma and Indian Territory in 1880 and 1870. 5. Data includes North and South Dakota.

★ 1833 ★

Migration

Migration of Blacks from and to the South by Sections, Divisions, and States, 1910 to 1930

Section, Division, and State of Residence	1930	1920	1910	Increase or Decrease (-) Number 1920 to 1930	Number 1910 to 1920	Percent 1920 to 1930	Percent 1910 to 1920	Percent Distribution 1930	1920	1910
				Negro Population Born in the South						
The North and West	1,426,213	780,794	440,534	645,419	340,260	82.7	77.2	100.0	100.0	100.0
THE NORTH	1,355,789	737,423	415,533	618,366	321,890	83.9	77.5	95.1	94.4	94.3
New England	31,323	26,010	22,600	5,313	3,410	20.4	15.1	2.2	3.3	5.1
Middle Atlantic	586,607	310,991	198,501	275,616	112,490	88.6	56.7	41.1	39.8	45.1
East North Central	593,273	299,298	1128,547	293,975	170,751	98.2	132.8	41.6	38.3	29.2
West North Central	144,586	101,124	43,462	35,239	43.0	53.5	10.1	13.0	15.0	
NEW ENGLAND:										
Maine	119	163	178	-44	-15	-27.0	-8.4	[1]	[1]	[1]
New Hampshire	197	139	169	58	-30	41.7	-17.8	[1]	[1]	[1]
Vermont	89	113	779	-24	-666	-21.2	-85.5	[1]	[1]	.2
Massachusetts	14,510	13,902	13,064	608	838	4.4	6.4	1.0	1.8	3.0
Rhode Island	2,331	2,723	3,191	-392	-468	-14.4	-14.7	.2	.3	.7
Connecticut	14,077	8,970	5,219	5,107	3,751	56.9	71.9	1.0	1.1	.12

[Continued]

★ 1833 ★

Migration of Blacks from and to the South by Sections, Divisions, and States, 1910 to 1930

[Continued]

Section, Division, and State of Residence	1930	1920	1910	Increase or Decrease (-): Number, 1920 to 1930	Increase or Decrease (-): Number, 1910 to 1920	Increase or Decrease (-): Percent, 1920 to 1930	Increase or Decrease (-): Percent, 1910 to 1920	Percent Distribution: 1930	Percent Distribution: 1920	Percent Distribution: 1910
MIDDLE ATLANTIC:										
New York	199,811	84,817	60,494	114,994	24,323	135.6	40.2	14.0	10.9	13.7
New Jersey	121,992	59,338	40,987	62,654	18,351	105.6	44.8	8.6	7.6	9.3
Pennsylvania	264,804	166,836	97,020	97,968	69,816	58.7	72.0	18.6	21.4	22.0
EAST NORTH CENTRAL:										
Ohio	190,048	105,084	44,439	84,964	60,645	80.9	136.5	13.3	13.5	10.1
Indiana	66,203	45,888	30,123	20,315	15,765	44.3	52.3	4.6	5.9	6.8
Illinois	213,862	108,670	50,314	105,192	58,356	96.8	116.0	15.0	13.9	11.4
Michigan	116,789	37,113	2,897	79,676	34,216	214.7	1,181.1	8.2	4.8	.7
Wisconsin	6,371	2,543	774	3,828	1,769	150.5	228.6	.4	.3	.2
WEST NORTH CENTRAL:										
Minnesota	3,386	3,268	2,502	118	766	3.6	30.6	.2	.4	.6
Iowa	5,016	6,137	4,452	-1,121	1,685	-18.3	37.8	.4	.8	1.0
Missouri	102,084	62,415	36,329	39,669	26,086	63.6	71.8	7.2	8.0	8.2
North Dakota	118	140	223	-22	-83	-15.7	-37.2	[1]	[1]	.1
South Dakota	160	176	249	-16	-73	-9.1	-29.3	[1]	[1]	.1
Nebraska	6,305	6,103	2,327	202	3,776	3.3	162.3	.4	.8	.5
Kansas	27,517	22,885	19,803	4,632	3,082	20.2	15.6	1.9	2.9	4.5
THE WEST	70,424	43,371	25,001	27,053	18,370	62.4	73.5	4.9	5.6	5.7
Mountain	17,691	17,702	10,140	-11	7,562	.1	74.6	1.2	2.3	2.3
Pacific	52,733	25,669	14,861	27,064	10,808	105.4	72.7	3.7	3.3	3.4
MOUNTAIN:										
Montana	448	584	682	-136	-98	-23.3	-14.4	[1]	.1	.2
Idaho	304	391	248	-87	143	-22.3	57.7	[1]	.1	.1
Wyoming	520	587	1,210	-67	-623	-11.4	-51.5	[1]	.1	.3
Colorado	5,752	5,383	5,212	369	171	6.9	3.3	.4	.7	1.2
New Mexico	1,912	4,203	889	-2,291	3,314	-54.5	372.8	.1	.5	.2
Arizona	7,996	5,783	1,251	2,213	4,532	38.3	362.3	.6	.7	.3
Utah	496	617	397	-121	220	-19.6	55.4	[1]	.1	.1
Nevada	263	154	251	109	-97	70.8	-38.6	[1]	[1]	.1
PACIFIC:										
Washington	2,668	2,840	2,992	-172	-152	-6.1	-5.1	.2	.4	.7
Oregon	1,060	942	620	118	322	12.5	51.9	.1	.1	.1
California	49,005	21,887	11,249	27,118	10,638	123.9	94.6	3.4	2.8	2.6
Negro Population Born in the North and West										
The South	54,716	47,223	41,489	7,493	5,734	15.9	13.8	100.0	100.0	100.0
South Atlantic	28,869	22,771	15,651	6,098	7,120	26.8	45.5	52.8	48.2	37.7
East South Central	11,813	9,649	9,808	2,164	-159	22.4	-1.6	21.6	20.4	23.6
West South Central	14,034	14,803	16,030	-769	-1,227	-5.2	-7.7	25.6	31.3	38.6
SOUTH ATLANTIC:										
Delaware	1,614	1,477	1,397	137	80	9.3	5.7	2.9	3.1	3.4
Maryland	5,152	4,189	2,894	963	1,295	23.0	44.7	9.4	8.9	7.0
District of Columbia	4,772	3,751	2,542	1,021	1,209	27.2	47.6	8.7	7.9	6.1
Virginia	5,457	4,872	3,151	585	1,721	12.0	54.6	10.0	10.3	7.6
West Virginia	4,341	3,152	2,127	1,188	1,026	37.7	48.2	7.9	6.7	5.1
North Carolina	2,204	1,581	911	623	670	39.4	73.5	4.0	3.3	2.2
South Carolina	871	923	429	-52	494	-5.6	115.2	1.6	2.0	1.0
Georgia	2,145	1,307	1,146	838	161	64.1	14.0	3.9	2.8	2.8

[Continued]

★ 1833 ★

Migration of Blacks from and to the South by Sections, Divisions, and States, 1910 to 1930

[Continued]

Section, Division, and State of Residence	1930	1920	1910	Increase or Decrease (-) Number 1920 to 1930	Number 1910 to 1920	Percent 1920 to 1930	Percent 1910 to 1920	Percent Distribution 1930	1920	1910
Florida	2,313	1,518	1,054	795	464	52.4	44.0	4.2	3.2	2.5
EAST SOUTH CENTRAL:										
Kentucky	4,667	3,939	3,735	728	204	18.5	5.5	8.5	8.3	9.0
Tennessee	3,267	2,593	2,676	674	-83	26.0	-3.1	6.0	5.5	6.4
Alabama	1,965	1,460	1,412	505	48	34.6	3.4	3.6	3.1	3.4
Mississippi	1,914	1,657	1,985	257	-328	15.5	-16.5	3.5	3.5	4.8
WEST SOUTH CENTRAL:										
Arkansas	3,765	3,859	3,690	-94	169	-2.4	4.6	6.9	8.2	8.9
Louisiana	1,704	1,795	2,086	-91	-291	-5.1	-14.0	3.1	3.8	5.0
Oklahoma	5,185	5,406	6,096	-221	-690	-4.1	-11.3	9.5	11.4	14.7
Texas	3,380	3,743	4,158	-363	-415	-9.7	-10.0	6.2	7.9	10.0

Source: "Migration of Negroes Out of and Into the South, by Sections, Divisions, and States: 1910 to 1930." U.S. Bureau of the Census, *Negroes in the United States, 1920-1932*, p. 25. *Note:* 1. Less than one-tenth of 1 percent.

★ 1834 ★

Migration

Migration of Males from the South

Numbers are in percent.

Year	Black	White
1940-50	26.3	1.8
1950-60	24.5	8.4
1960-70	19.3	3.3
1970-80	2.1	-1.3

Source: "Rates of Net Migration from the South of Men Ages 20-24," *The Economic Progress of Black Mean in America*, p. 79. Primary source: *"The Economic Progress of Black Men America.* Washington, DC: U.S. Commission on Civil Rights, 1986. Clearing House Publication 91. *Notes:* These rates were calculated by comparing the share of males 20-24 years old living in the South in year t to the share of males 30-34 years old living in the South in year t + 10.

★ 1835 ★

Migration

Migration of the Civilian Population by Race, April 1940 to April 1947

Migration Status and Type of Migration	White	Nonwhite
Total civilian population, April, 1947	127,044	15,017
Born on or before April 1, 1940	110,099	12,534
Nonmigrants	86,864	9,701
Same house	47,065	5,071
Different house in same county	49,799	4,630
Migrants	22,740	2,729
Within a state	12,117	964
Between contiguous states	4,396	578
Between noncontiguous states	6,227	1,187
Persons abroad on April 1, 1940	495	104
Born after April 1, 1940	16,945	2,483
Nonmigrants	13,185	2,008
Migrants	3,713	427
Persons born abroad	47	48

Source: "Migration of the Civilian Population, by Color, for the United States: April 1940, to April 1947." Murray, Florence, ed., *The Negro Handbook, 1949,* 13. Primary source: U.S. Bureau of the Census.

★ 1836 ★

Migration

Percent Distribution by Migration Status and Type of Migration of Population Born on or Before Migration Period

Migration Status and Type of Migration	April 1948 to April 1949		April 1940 to April 1947		April 1935 to April 1940	
	White	Nonwhite	White	Nonwhite	White	Nonwhite
Nonmigrants	93.8	95.1	78.9	77.4	86.2	90.4
Migrants	5.9	4.7	20.7	21.8	13.5	9.5
Within a state	2.8	2.8	11.0	7.7	7.9	5.6
Between states	3.1	1.9	9.7	14.1	5.6	3.9
Abroad	0.4	0.1	0.4	0.8	0.3	0.1

Source: "Per cent Distribution by Migration Status and Type of Migration of Population Born On or Before Beginning of Migration Period, by Color." Guzman, Jessie Parkhurst, ed. *Negro Year Book: A Review of Events Affecting Negro Life, 1941-1946,* p. 11. Primary source: Current Population Reports: *Population Characteristics,* "Internal Migration in the United States: April, 1948 to April, 1949," Series P-20, No. 28, Table I.

Native and Foreign Born Population

★ 1837 ★

Black Population Born in Division of Residence, Other Divisions, or Foreign-Born, 1930

GEOGRAPHIC DIVISION	Total Negro population[1]	BORN IN THE UNITED STATES, AND WITH STATE OF BIRTH REPORTED				FOREIGN BORN	
		Born in division of of residence		Born in other divisions			
		Number	Percent	Number	Percent	Number	Percent
United States	11,891,143	9,762,855	82.1	1,976,624	16.6	98,620	0.8
New England	94,086	44,991	47.8	36,579	38.9	11,786	12.5
Middle Atlantic	1,052,899	354,910	33.7	611,497	58.1	64,565	6.1
East North Central	930,450	278,327	29.9	640,218	68.8	5,157	.6
West North Central	331,784	171,547	51.7	157,098	47.3	528	.2
South Atlantic	4,421,388	4,296,766	97.2	104,217	2.4	12,584	.3
East South Central	2,658,238	2,315,498	94.6	137,805	5.2	532	-
West South Central	2,281,951	2,077,617	91.0	197,058	8.6	1,412	.1
Mountain	30,225	6,122	20.3	23,591	78.1	187	.6
Pacific	90,122	19,077	21.2	67,561	75.0	1,869	2.1

Source: "Negro Population Distributed as Born in Division of Residence, of Other Divisions, or in Foreign Countries, by Divisions: 1930." U.S. Bureau of the Census, *Negroes in the United States, 1920-1932*, p. 21. *Notes:* 1. Includes Negroes born in the United States, State of birth not reported; Negroes born in outlying possessions, and born abroad or at sea. The combined numbers of these classes are 53,044, or 4/10 of 1 percent of the Negro population.

★ 1838 ★

Native and Foreign Born Population

Black and Foreign-Born White Population by Sections, Southern Divisions, and States, 1900-1910

SECTION, DIVISION, AND STATE	POPULATION										FOREIGN-BORN WHITE TO 1,000 NEGROES	
	1910		1900		Increase, 1900-1910[1]				Percentage distribution, 1910			
					Number		Percent					
	Negro	Foreign-born white	Negro	Foreign-born white	Negro	Foreign-born white	Negro	Foreign-born white	Negro	Foreign-born white	1910	1900
United States	9,827,763	13,345,545	8,833,994	10,213,817	993,769	3,131,728	11.2	30.7	100.0	100.0	1,358	1,156
The South	8,749,427	726,171	7,922,969	562,575	826,458	163,596	10.4	29.6	89.0	5.4	83	71
South Atlantic division	4,112,488	290,555	3,729,017	208,883	383,471	81,672	10.3	39.1	41.8	2.2	71	56
East South Central division	2,652,513	86,857	2,499,886	89,682	152,617	-2,825	6.1	-3.2	27.0	0.7	33	36
West South Central division	1,984,426	348,759	1,694,066	264,010	290,360	84,749	17.1	32.1	20.2	2.6	176	156
The North	1,027,674	11,321,016	880,771	8,890,390	146,903	2,430,626	16.7	27.3	10.5	84.8	11,016	10,094
The West	50,662	1,298,358	30,254	760,852	20,408	537,506	67.5	70.6	0.5	9.7	25,628	25,149
THE SOUTH												
South Atlantic division:												
Delaware	31,181	17,420	30,697	13,729	484	3,691	1.6	26.9	0.3	0.1	559	447
Maryland	232,250	104,174	235,064	93,144	-2,814	11,030	-1.2	11.8	2.4	0.8	449	396
District of Columbia	94,446	24,351	86,702	19,520	7,744	4,831	8.9	24.7	1.0	0.2	258	225
Virginia	671,096	26,628	660,722	19,068	10,374	7,560	1.6	39.6	6.8	0.2	40	29
West Virginia	64,173	57,072	43,499	22,379	20,674	34,693	47.5	155.0	0.7	0.4	889	514
North Carolina	697,843	5,942	624,469	4,394	73,374	1,548	11.7	35.2	7.1	[2]	9	7
South Carolina	835,843	6,054	782,321	5,371	53,522	683	6.8	12.7	8.5	[2]	7	7
Georgia	1,176,987	15,072	1,034,813	12,021	142,174	3,051	13.7	25.4	12.0	0.1	13	12
Florida	308,669	33,842	230,730	19,257	77,939	14,585	33.8	75.7	3.1	0.3	110	83

[Continued]

★ 1838 ★

Black and Foreign-Born White Population by Sections, Southern Divisions, and States, 1900-1910

[Continued]

SECTION, DIVISION, AND STATE	POPULATION										FOREIGN-BORN WHITE TO 1,000 NEGROES	
	1910		1900		Increase, 1900-1910[1]				Percentage distribution, 1910			
					Number		Percent					
	Negro	Foreign-born white	Negro	Foreign-born white	Negro	Foreign-born white	Negro	Foreign-born white	Negro	Foreign-born white	1910	1900
East South Central division:												
Kentucky	261,656	40,053	284,706	50,133	-23,050	10,080	-8.1	-20.1	2.7	0.3	153	176
Tennessee	473,088	18,459	480,243	17,586	-7,155	873	-1.5	5.0	4.8	0.1	39	37
Alabama	908,282	18,956	827,307	14,338	80,975	4,618	9.8	32.2	9.2	0.1	21	17
Mississippi	1,009,487	9,389	907,630	7,625	101,857	1,764	11.2	23.1	10.3	0.1	9	8
West South Central division:												
Arkansas	442,891	16,909	366,856	14,168	76,035	2,723	20.7	19.2	4.5	0.1	38	39
Louisiana	713,874	51,782	650,804	51,853	63,070	-71	9.7	-0.1	7.3	0.4	73	80
Oklahoma	137,612	40,084	55,684	20,390	81,928	19,694	147.1	96.6	1.4	0.3	291	366
Texas	690,049	239,984	620,722	177,581	69,327	62,403	11.2	35.1	7.0	1.8	348	286

Source: "Negro and Foreign-Born White Population, by Sections, Southern Divisions, and States: 1900-1910." U.S. Bureau of the Census, *Historical Statistics of the United States: Colonial Times to 1970, Part I*, Bicentennial Edition, p. 39. *Notes:* 1. A minus sign (-) denotes decrease. 2. Less than one-tenth of 1 per cent.

★ 1839 ★

Native and Foreign Born Population

Black and Foreign-Born White Population by Sections, Southern Divisions, and States, 1920 and 1930

SECTION, DIVISION AND STATE	POPULATION										FOREIGN-BORN WHITES TO 1,000 NEGROES	
	1930		1920		Increase or decrease (-), 1920-30				Percent distribution, 1930			
					Number		Percent					
	Negro	Foreign-born white	Negro	Foreign-born white	Negro	Foreign-born white	Negro	Foreign-born white	Negro	Foreign-born white	1930	1920
United States	11,891,143	13,366,407	10,463,131	13,255,394	1,428,012	111,013	13.6	0.8	100.0	100.0	1,124	1,267
THE SOUTH	9,361,577	532,175	8,912,231	505,570	449,346	-63,395	5.0	-10.6	78.7	4.0	57	67
South Atlantic	4,421,388	304,278	4,325,120	315,676	96,268	-11,398	2.2	-3.6	37.2	2.3	69	73
East South Central	2,658,238	57,665	2,523,532	71,698	134,706	-14,033	5.3	-19.6	22.4	.4	22	28
West South Central	2,281,951	170,232	2,063,579	208,196	218,372	-37,964	10.6	-18.2	19.2	1.3	75	101
THE NORTH	2,409,219	11,386,553	1,472,309	11,348,336	936,910	38,217	63.6	.3	20.3	85.3	4,726	7,708
THE WEST	120,347	1,447,679	78,591	1,311,488	41,756	136,191	53.1	10.4	1.0	10.8	12,029	16,688
The South												
SOUTH ATLANTIC:												
Delaware	32,602	16,885	30,335	19,785	2,267	-2,900	7.5	-14.7	.3	.1	518	652
Maryland	276,379	95,093	244,479	102,144	31,900	-7,051	13.0	-6.9	2.3	.7	344	418
District of Columbia	132,068	29,932	109,966	28,522	22,102	1,410	20.1	4.9	1.1	.2	227	259
Virginia	650,165	23,820	690,017	30,760	-39,852	-6,940	-5.8	-22.6	5.5	.2	37	45
West Virginia	114,893	51,520	86,345	61,864	28,548	-10,344	33.1	-16.7	1.0	.4	448	716
North Carolina	918,647	8,788	763,407	7,092	155,240	1,696	20.3	23.9	7.7	.1	10	9
South Carolina	793,681	5,266	864,719	6,397	-71,038	-1,131	-8.2	-17.7	6.7	[1]	7	7
Georgia	1,071,125	13,917	1,206,365	16,163	-135,240	-2,246	-11.2	-13.9	9.0	.1	13	13
Florida	431,828	59,057	329,487	42,949	102,341	16,168	31.1	37.5	3.6	.4	137	130
EAST SOUTH CENTRAL:												
Kentucky	226,040	21,840	235,938	30,707	-9,898	-8,867	-4.2	-28.9	1.9	.2	97	130
Tennessee	477,646	13,066	451,758	15,443	25,888	-2,377	5.7	-15.4	4.0	.1	27	34
Alabama	944,834	15,710	900,652	17,617	44,182	-1,907	4.9	-10.8	7.9	.1	17	20
Mississippi	1,009,718	7,049	935,184	7,931	74,534	-882	8.0	-11.1	8.5	.1	7	8
WEST SOUTH CENTRAL:												
Arkansas	478,463	10,173	472,220	13,781	6,243	-3,608	1.3	-26.2	4.0	.1	21	29
Louisiana	776,326	34,910	700,257	42,976	76,069	-8,066	10.9	-18.8	6.5	.3	45	61
Oklahoma	172,198	26,753	149,408	33,655	72,790	-6,902	15.3	-20.5	1.4	.2	155	225
Texas	854,964	98,396	741,694	117,784	113,270	-19,388	15.3	-16.5	7.2	.7	115	159

Source: "Negro and Foreign-Born White Population, by Sections, and by Southern Divisions, and States: 1920 and 1930." U.S. Bureau of the Census, *Negroes in the United States, 1920-1932*, p. 8. *Note:* 1. Less than 1/10 of 1 percent.

★ 1840 ★

Native and Foreign Born Population

Country of Birth of Foreign-Born Blacks in the United States, 1920 and 1930

COUNTRY OF BIRTH	1930	1920
All foreign countries	98,620	73,803
American	87,094	63,684
Canada	5,817	5,651
Newfoundland	9	6
Cuba	2,362	1,934
Other West Indies	72,138	50,488
Mexico	915	3,123
Central America	2,662	816
South America	3,191	1,666
Europe	4,632	3,996
Asia	44	27
China	1	6
India	29	-
Other Asia	14	21
Africa	986	556
Australia	81	107
Azores	177	206
Other Atlantic islands	5,411	5,143
Pacific Islands	96	40
Born at sea or not specified	99	44

Source: "Country of Birth of the Foreign-Born Negro Population of the United States: 1930 and 1920." U.S. Bureau of the Census, *Negroes in the United States, 1920-1932*, p. 21.

★ 1841 ★

Native and Foreign Born Population

Country of Birth of the Foreign-Born Black Population, 1910

COUNTRY OF BIRTH	Foreign born Negroes 1910
All foreign countries	40,339
America	33,233
Canada and Newfoundland	6,775

[Continued]

★ 1841 ★

Country of Birth of the Foreign-Born Black Population, 1910

[Continued]

COUNTRY OF BIRTH	Foreign born Negroes 1910
Mexico	1,184
Central America	215
Cuba and other West Indies[1]	24,426
South America	633
Europe	3,861
Asia	100
China	10
Japan	2
All other	88
Africa	473
Australia	94
Atlantic Islands	2,478
Pacific Islands[2]	61
All other	39

Source: "Untitled Table." U.S. Bureau of the Census, *Historical Statistics of the United States: Colonial Times to 1970, Part I*, Bicentennial Edition, p. 63. *Notes:* 1. Except Porto Rico. 2. Except Hawaii and Philippine Islands.

★ 1842 ★

Native and Foreign Born Population

Foreign-Born Black Population 1910, 1920, and 1930

Division and State	Foreign-Born Negroes			Increase or Decrease(-)	
	1930	1920	1910	1920 to 1930	1910 to 1920
United States	98,620	73,803	40,339	24,817	33,464
GEOGRAPHIC DIVISIONS:					
New England	11,786	12,256	7,710	-470	4,565
Middle Atlantic	64,565	37,625	16,322	29,940	21,303
East North Central	5,157	4,262	3,384	895	878
West North Central	528	1,049	807	-521	242
South Atlantic	12,584	12,962	8,075	-378	4,887
East South Central	532	636	625	-104	11
West South Central	1,412	2,991	1,869 -	1,579	1,122
Mountain	187	581	373	-394	208
Pacific	1,869	1,441	1,174	428	267

[Continued]

★ 1842 ★

Foreign-Born Black Population 1910, 1920, and 1930

[Continued]

Division and State	Foreign-Born Negroes 1930	Foreign-Born Negroes 1920	Foreign-Born Negroes 1910	Increase or Decrease(-) 1920 to 1930	Increase or Decrease(-) 1910 to 1920
NEW ENGLAND:					
Maine	203	274	237	-71	37
New Hampshire	195	70	40	125	30
Vermont	13	16	40	-3	-24
Massachusetts	8,934	9,037	6,152	-130	2,885
Rhode Island	1,063	1,496	872	-433	624
Connecticut	1,378	1,363	369	15	994
MIDDLE ATLANTIC:					
New York	57,895	31,971	12,851	25,924	19,120
New Jersey	3,719	2,634	1,487	1,085	1,147
Pennsylvania	2,951	3,020	1,984	-69	1,036
EAST NORTH CENTRAL:					
Ohio	1,077	951	655	126	296
Indiana	200	184	97	16	87
Illinois	1,566	1,245	928	321	317
Michigan	2,262	1,769	1,640	493	129
Wisconsin	52	113	64	-61	49
WEST NORTH CENTRAL:					
Minnesota	105	154	200	-49	-46
Iowa	50	107	55	-57	52
Missouri	209	376	326	-167	50
North Dakota	7	21	2	-14	19
South Dakota	7	14	9	-7	5
Nebraska	55	140	97	-85	43
Kansas	95	237	118	-142	119
SOUTH ATLANTIC:					
Delaware	87	51	35	36	16
Maryland	872	606	451	176	245
District of Columbia	457	364	238	93	126
Virginia	330	656	2996	-326	360
West Virginia	119	127	82	-8	45
North Carolina	118	91	88	27	3
South Carolina	54	96	72	-42	24
Georgia	200	216	228	-16	-12
Florida	10,347	10,665	6,585	-318	4,080
EAST SOUTH CENTRAL:					
Kentucky	68	76	66	-8	10
Tennessee	100	111	99	-11	12
Alabama	268	313	282	-45	31

[Continued]

★ 1842 ★

Foreign-Born Black Population 1910, 1920, and 1930

[Continued]

Division and State	Foreign-Born Negroes			Increase or Decrease(-)	
	1930	1920	1910	1920 to 1930	1910 to 1920
Mississippi	96	136	178	-40	-42
WEST SOUTH CENTRAL:					
Arkansas	70	86	80	-16	6
Louisiana	809	1,217	575	-408	642
Oklahoma	67	156	123	-89	33
Texas	466	1,532	1,091	-1,066	441
MOUNTAIN:					
Montana	14	48	61	-34	-13
Idaho	15	34	28	-19	6
Wyoming	8	30	38	-22	-8
Colorado	61	132	130	-71	2
New Mexico	14	96	34	-82	62
Arizona	53	178	31	-125	147
Utah	12	56	32	-44	24
Nevada	10	7	19	3	-12
PACIFIC:					
Washington	167	271	239	-104	33
Oregon	50	47	62	3	-15
California	1,652	1,123	874	529	249

Source: "Foreign-Born Negro Population: 1930, 1920, and 1910." U.S. Bureau of the Census, *Negroes in the United States, 1920-1932*, p. 23.

★ 1843 ★

Native and Foreign Born Population

Foreign-Born Black Population, Divisions and Increase, 1900 and 1910

DIVISION AND STATE	FOREIGN-BORN NEGROES		
	1910	1900	Increase:[1] 1900-1910
UNITED STATES	40,339	20,336	20,003
GEOGRAPHIC DIVISIONS:			
New England	7,710	4,368	3,342
Middle Atlantic	16,322	4,875	11,447
East North Central	3,384	2,316	1,068
West North Central	807	412	395
South Atlantic	8,075	5,495	2,580

[Continued]

★ 1843 ★

Foreign-Born Black Population, Divisions and Increase, 1900 and 1910

[Continued]

DIVISION AND STATE	FOREIGN-BORN NEGROES		
	1910	1900	Increase:[1] 1900-1910
East South Central	625	512	113
West South Central	1,869	1,556	313
Mountain	373	217	156
Pacific	1,174	585	589
NEW ENGLAND:			
Maine	237	218	19
New Hampshire	40	29	11
Vermont	40	18	22
Massachusetts	6,152	3,475	2,677
Rhode Island	872	392	480
Connecticut	369	236	133
MIDDLE ATLANTIC:			
New York	12,851	3,552	9,299
New Jersey	1,487	459	1,028
Pennsylvania	1,984	864	1,120
EAST NORTH CENTRAL:			
Ohio	655	483	172
Indiana	97	64	33
Illinois	928	610	318
Michigan	1,640	1,103	537
Wisconsin	64	56	8
WEST NORTH CENTRAL:			
Minnesota	200	82	118
Iowa	55	39	16
Missouri	326	153	173
North Dakota	2	7	-5
South Dakota	9	14	-5
Nebraska	97	53	44
Kansas	118	64	54
SOUTH ATLANTIC:			
Delaware	35	29	6
Maryland	451	303	148
District of Columbia	238	174	64
Virginia	296	152	144
West Virginia	82	24	58
North Carolina	88	54	34
South Carolina	72	97	-25
Georgia	228	202	26
Florida	6,585	4,460	2,125

[Continued]

★ 1843 ★

Foreign-Born Black Population, Divisions and Increase, 1900 and 1910

[Continued]

DIVISION AND STATE	FOREIGN-BORN NEGROES		
	1910	1900	Increase:[1] 1900-1910
EAST SOUTH CENTRAL:			
Kentucky	66	72	-6
Tennessee	99	92	7
Alabama	282	195	87
Mississippi	178	153	25
WEST SOUTH CENTRAL:			
Arkansas	80	54	26
Louisiana	575	490	85
Oklahoma	123	41	82
Texas	1,091	971	120
MOUNTAIN:			
Montana	61	20	41
Idaho	28	9	19
Wyoming	38	9	29
Colorado	130	54	76
New Mexico	34	22	12
Arizona	31	84	-53
Utah	32	14	18
Nevada	19	5	14
PACIFIC:			
Washington	238	108	130
Oregon	62	44	18
California	874	433	441

Source: "Foreign-Born Negro Population: 1910 and 1900." U.S. Bureau of the Census, *Historical Statistics of the United States: Colonial Times to 1970, Part I*, Bicentennial Edition, p. 62. *Note:* 1. A minus sign (-) denotes decrease.

★ 1844 ★

Native and Foreign Born Population

Foreign-Born Population by Gender and Race, 1850-1970 - I

Year	Male						
	All races	White	Negro	Other races			
				Total[1]	Indian	Japanese	Chinese
1970[2]	4,403,687	3,982,797	115,406	305,484	7,153	39,375	105,907
1960[3]*	4,760,432	4,507,502	65,952	186,978	NA	40,709	59,083
1930[3]	4,714,545	4,500,434	214,111[6]	214,111[6]	NA	NA	NA
1950[4]	5,258,255	5,098,370[5]	159,885[6]	159,885[6]	[6]	[6]	[6]
1940	6,121,647	6,011,015	44,488	66,144	2,463	29,651	31,687

[Continued]

★ 1844 ★

Foreign-Born Population by Gender and Race, 1850-1970 - I

[Continued]

Year	Male						
	All races	White	Negro	Other races			
				Total[1]	Indian	Japanese	Chinese
1930	7,647,090	7,502,491	54,081	90,518	1,888	45,897	39,109
1920	7,675,435	7,528,322	42,641	104,472	3,539	57,213	40,573
1910	7,667,748	7,523,788	23,888	120,072	1,464	60,730	54,935
1900	5,630,190	5,515,285	11,829	103,076	1,207	23,185	78,684
1890[7]	5,067,130	4,951,858	[3]	[8]	[8]	[8]	[8]
1880	3,630,566	3,521,635	7,758	101,173	1,002	133	100,038
1870[9]	3,006,943	2,942,579	5,346	59,018	647	46	58,325
1860	-	2,192,230	3,512[10]	33,149	-	-	-
1850	-	1,239,434	2,015[10]	-	-	-	-

Source: "Foreign Born Population, by Sex and Race: 1850-1970." U.S. Bureau of the Census, *Historical Statistics of the United States: Colonial Times to 1970, Part I*, Bicentennial Edition, p. 14. *Notes:* * Denotes first year for which figures include Alaska and Hawaii. NA Not available. 1. Includes races not shown separately, of which Filipinos are most numerous. FIlipino males: 1960 (including Alaska and Hawaii,)- 66,226; 1970-101,051; Filipino females: 1960 (including Alaska Hawaii)- 22,579; 1870-77,919. 2. 15-percent sample data. These data vary in degree of comparability with data on total population by race. 3. 25-percent sample data. 4. 20-percent sample data. Complete-count data available only for the white population. 5. Complete-count data: Males-5,176,390; females-4,984,778. 6. Data for specific races in the Negro and Other races grouping are based on various samples are extremely unreliable. 7. Excludes population enumerated in the Indian Territory and on Indian reservations (totaling 325,464) which was not classified by nativity. Totals by race and sex: Males-169,221; females-156,243; white males-64,047; white females-53,321; Negro males-10,042; Negro females-8,594; Indian males-95,119; Indian females-94,328; Chinese males-13. 8. Data by sex not available. Totals for both sexes; Negro-19,979; Indian-1,235; Japanese-1,921; Chinese-104,545. 9. Excludes 1,260,078 persons for whom data on nativity are not available. 10. Free Negroes only. Data on nativity were not collected for slaves.

★ 1845 ★

Native and Foreign Born Population

Foreign-Born Population by Gender and Race, 1850-1970 - II

Year	Female						
	All races	White	Negro	Other races			
				Total[1]	Indian	Japanese	Chinese
1970[2]	5,215,615	4,750,973	138,052	326,590	7,335	83,125	98,325
1960[3]*	4,977,659	4,786,490	59,370	131,799	NA	60,947	34,205
1930[3]	4,946,422	4,778,835	167,587[6]	167,587[6]	NA	NA	NA
1950[4]	5,089,140	4,997,045[5]	92,095[6]	92,095[6]	[6]	[6]	[6]
1940	5,473,249	5,408,123	39,453	25,673	2,028	17,654	5,555
1930	6,557,059	6,480,914	44,539	31,606	1,664	24,580	4,977
1920	6,245,257	6,184,432	31,162	29,663	2,760	24,125	2,534
1910	5,848,138	5,821,757	16,451	9,930	1,289	6,925	1,661
1900	4,711,086	4,698,532	8,507	4,047	1,006	872	2,169
1890[7]	4,182,417	4,170,009	[8]	[8]	[8]	[8]	[8]
1880	3,049,377	3,038,044	6,259	5,074	818	12	4,244
1870[9]	2,560,286	2,551,133	4,299	4,854	489	8	4,357

[Continued]

★ 1845 ★

Foreign-Born Population by Gender and Race, 1850-1970 - II

[Continued]

Year	Female						
	All races	White	Negro	Other races			
				Total[1]	Indian	Japanese	Chinese
1860	-	1,904,523	3,499[10]	1,784	-	-	-
1850	-	1,001,101	2,052[10]	-	-	-	-

Source: "Foreign Born Population, by Sex and Race: 1850-1970." U.S. Bureau of the Census, *Historical Statistics of the United States: Colonial Times to 1970, Part I*, Bicentennial Edition, p. 14. *Notes:* * Denotes first year for which figures include Alaska and Hawaii. NA Not available. 1. Includes races not shown separately, of which Filipinos are most numerous. FIlipino males: 1960 (including Alaska and Hawaii,)- 66,226; 1970-101,051; Filipino females: 1960 (including Alaska Hawaii)- 22,579; 1870-77,919. 2. 15-percent sample data. These data vary in degree of comparability with data on total population by race. 3. 25-percent sample data. 4. 20-percent sample data. Complete-count data available only for the white population. 5. Complete-count data: Males-5,176,390; females-4,984,778. 6. Data for specific races in the Negro and Other races grouping are based on various samples are extremely unreliable. 7. Excludes population enumerated in the Indian Territory and on Indian reservations (totaling 325,464) which was not classified by nativity. Totals by race and sex: Males-169,221; females-156,243; white males-64,047; white females-53,321; Negro males-10,042; Negro females-8,594; Indian males-95,119; Indian females-94,328; Chinese males-13. 8. Data by sex not available. Totals for both sexes; Negro-19,979; Indian-1,235; Japanese-1,921; Chinese-104,545. 9. Excludes 1,260,078 persons for whom data on nativity are not available. 10. Free Negroes only. Data on nativity were not collected for slaves.

★ 1846 ★

Native and Foreign Born Population

Free-Black Population by State of Birth Foreign-Birth, or Unknown Place of Birth, 1850

STATE AND TERRITORY	FREE COLORED POPULATION: 1850							
	Born in the state		Born out of state and in the United States		Born in foreign countries		Unknown	
	Males	Females	Males	Females	Males	Females	Males	Females
Alabama	758	883	279	310	5	6	14	10
Arkansas	165	128	138	159	1	2	10	5
California	60	9	641	68	161	12	10	1
Connecticut	2,945	3,132	685	666	127	40	63	35
Delaware	8,467	8,465	559	570	7	3	2	-
District of Columbia	2,580	3,417	1,655	2,386	3	2	10	6
Florida	357	447	46	53	15	14	-	-
Georgia	1,223	1,358	133	170	12	24	7	4
Illinois	1,308	1,356	1,396	1,267	16	16	57	20
Indiana	2,593	2,556	3,073	2,958	19	16	30	17
Iowa	24	28	140	140	1	-	-	-
Kentucky	3,732	3,936	1,106	1,186	8	11	17	15
Louisiana	6,821	8,381	387	892	238	687	33	23
Maine	449	479	178	98	81	49	18	4
Maryland	34,485	38,871	571	531	103	95	33	34
Massachusetts	2,719	2,980	1,348	1,339	232	194	125	127

[Continued]

★ 1846 ★

Free-Black Population by State of Birth Foreign-Birth, or Unknown Place of Birth, 1850

[Continued]

STATE AND TERRITORY	FREE COLORED POPULATION: 1850							
	Born in the state		Born out of state and in the United States		Born in foreign countries		Unknown	
	Males	Females	Males	Females	Males	Females	Males	Females
Michigan	452	338	898	745	53	57	28	12
Mississippi	317	323	144	121	3	3	10	9
Missouri	842	788	492	451	15	7	12	11
New Hampshire	165	174	84	83	8	-	3	3
New Jersey	9,978	10,451	1,655	1,454	86	58	79	49
New York	17,680	19,895	5,089	5,277	379	326	304	119
North Carolina	12,939	13,879	333	275	13	3	13	8
Ohio	6,093	6,293	6,451	6,211	57	37	90	47
Pennsylvania	17,603	20,165	7,367	7,796	151	161	248	135
Rhode Island	1,129	1,377	563	520	42	28	4	7
South Carolina	3,994	4,623	68	74	69	130	-	2
Tennessee	2,500	2,640	584	634	7	8	26	23
Texas	92	71	79	92	39	22	1	1
Vermont	234	218	117	103	14	13	10	9
Virginia	25,710	28,090	266	218	15	17	11	6
Wisconsin	100	67	255	199	3	3	7	1
Territories:								
Minnesota	7	7	14	11	-	-	-	-
New Mexico	7	4	10	1	-	-	-	-
Oregon	47	62	23	12	50	13	-	-
Utah	2	2	12	8	-	-	-	-
Total	168,577	185,893	36,839	37,078	2,033	2,057	1,275	743

Source: "Untitled Table." U.S. Bureau of the Census, *Historical Statistics of the United States: Colonial Times to 1970, Part I*, Bicentennial Edition, p. 63.

★ 1847 ★

Native and Foreign Born Population

Migration of the Native Black Population, by Region of Birth and Region of Residence, 1870-1910

YEAR	NATIVE NEGRO POPULATION					
	Born in the South			Born in the North and West		
	Total	Living in the North and West		Total	Living in the South	
		Number	Percent		Number	Percent
1910	9,109,153	440,534	4.8	636,890	41,489	6.5
1900	8,216,458	349,651	4.3	570,089	30,397	5.3
1890[1]	6,908,869	241,855	3.5	481,101	23,268	4.8
1880[1]	6,121,351	198,029	3.2	442,357	22,039	5.0
1870	4,548,991	149,100	3.3	319,897	15,583	4.9

Source: "Untitled Table." U.S. Bureau of the Census, *Historical Statistics of the United States: Colonial Times to 1970, Part I*, Bicentennial Edition, p. 65. *Notes:* It is assumed that in 1890 two-thirds-approximately the proportion in 1880—of the foreign born Negro population of 19,979, lived in the North and West, and one—third in the South: that of the Indians, Chinese, and Japanese, the same proportion of the native as of the total in each class lived in the North and West,a nd in the South, respectively and the natives of these classes resident in the North and West were born in the North and West and the natives resident in the South were born in the South. As practically all—i.e. 55,571 out of 58,806—of the native civilized Indians included in the aggregate colored distributed by state of birth, were native, the error in the assumption that the same proportion of the natives as of the total lived in the South and in the North and West is immaterial. The great mass of the Indian population in 1890—189,447 out of 248,253—were specially enumerated and for these state of birth was not reported. They are included under "Other colored" in Table 9 [In original source]. The number of native Chinese and Japanese is so small—i.e. 2,930 Chinese and 119 Japanese—that any error in distributing them as living in and born in the North and West, or South, is immaterial in its effects upon the figures for the native Negro population of 7,468,697. In the 57,571 civilized native Indian population, 2,930 Chinese and 118 Japanese included in the aggregate colored population of 7,510,680 in 1890, there were undoubtedly a few migrants into the out of the South. These are not taken into account in the estimate, but their number could not have been sufficiently large materially to affect the figures for the aggregate Negro. Similar assumptions are made for 1880, except that for this year the number of native Negroes, Indians, and Chinese, and Japanese, living in each state is given in the report for 1880, except that for this year and number of native Negroes, Indians, Chinese, and Japanese, living in each state is given in the report for 1880, and the number living in the South and in other sections is, therefore not as regards natives in these classes an estimated number, as it is for 1890. For 1880, therefore, it is assumed in the estimate that the 6,269 native Indians, Chinese, and Japanese resident in the North and West were native of the North and West. 1. Figures in italics are estimates.

★ 1848 ★

Native and Foreign Born Population

Native Black Population Reporting State of Birth, 1910

DIVISION AND SECTION	NATIVE NEGRO POPULATION: 1910				
	Total	Born in the United States			Born in outlying possessions[3]
		Total	State of birth reported	State of birth not reported[1]	
United States	9,787,424	9,783,985	9,746,043	37,943	3,438
The South	8,738,858	8,738,162	8,710,108	28,054	696
South Atlantic	4,104,413	4,104,020	4,094,486	9,534	393
East South Central	2,651,888	2,651,797	2,643,722	8,075	91
West South Central	1,982,557	1,982,345	1,971,900	10,445	212
The North	999,451	997,017	988,126	8,891	2,434
The West	49,115	48,807	47,809	998	308

Source: "Untitled Table." U.S. Bureau of the Census, *Historical Statistics of the United States: Colonial Times to 1970, Part I*, Bicentennial Edition, p. 63. *Notes:* 1. Includes those for whom no report of place of birth was made. 2. Includes 4 persons born in Alaska, 1 in Guam, 58 in Hawaii, 119 in the Philippine Island, 173 in Port Rico, 217 born at sea under the United States flag, and 2,866 American citizens born abroad.

★ 1849 ★

Native and Foreign Born Population

Native Black Population by Division of Birth and Residence, 1930, and Change Through Interdivisional Migration, 1910, 1920, and 1930

Geographic division	Born in the Specified Division			Born in and living in the specified division	Living in the Specified Division			Gain (+) or Loss (-) Through Interdivisional Migration		
	Total	Living in other divisions			Total	Born in other divisions		1930	1920	1910
		Number	Percent			Number	Percent			
United States	11,739,479	1,976,624	16.8	9,762,855	11,739,479	1,976,624	16.8	-	-	-
New England	57,530	12,539	21.8	44,991	81,570	36,579	44.8	+24,040	+21,325	+20,310
Middle Atlantic	394,022	39,112	9.9	354,910	966,407	611,497	63.3	+572,385	+296,664	+186,384
East North Central	323,198	44,871	13.9	278,327	918,545	640,218	69.7	+595,347	+296,111	+119,649
West North Central	229,719	58,172	25.3	171,547	328,645	157,098	47.8	+98,926	+68,222	+40,497
South Atlantic	5,195,040	989,274	17.3	4,296,766	4,400,983	104,217	2.4	-794,057	-455,410	-392,827
East South Central	3,193,449	679,951	21.3	2,513,498	2,652,303	138,805	5.2	-541,146	-405,511	-200,876
West South Central	2,310,969	233,352	10.1	2,077,617	2,274,675	107,058	8.7	-36,294	+127,350	+194,658
Mountain	12,327	6,205	50.3	6,122	29,713	23,591	79.4	+17,386	+20,085	+13,229
Pacific	23,225	4,148	17.9	19,077	86,638	67,561	78.0	+63,413	+31,164	+18,976

Source: "Native Negro Population, by Division of Birth and Division of Residence, 1930, With Gain or Loss Through Interdivisional Migration, 1930, 1920, and 1910." U.S. Bureau of the Census, *Negroes in the United States, 1920-1932*, p. 23.

★ 1850 ★

Native and Foreign Born Population

Native Black Population by Region of Birth and Region of Residence and Net Gain, 1870-1910

YEAR	NATIVE NEGRO POPULATION					
	Born in the South and Living in the North and West		Born in the North West and living in the South		Net gain of the North and West and loss of the South	
	Number	Increase	Number	Increase	Number	Increase
1910	440,534	90,883	41,480	11,092	390,045	79,791
1900[1]	349,651	107,796	30,397	7,129	319,254	200,667
1890[1]	241,855	43,826	23,268	1,229	118,587	-57,403
1880[1]	198,029	48,929	22,039	6,456	175,990	42,475
1870	149,100	-	15,583	-	133,517	-

Source: "Untitled Table." U.S. Bureau of the Census, *Historical Statistics of the United States: Colonial Times to 1970, Part I*, Bicentennial Edition, p. 65. *Notes:* It is assumed that in 1890 two—thirds—approximately the proportion in 1880—of the foreign born Negro population of 19,979, lived in the North and West, and one-third in the South: that of the Indians, Chinese, and Japanese, the same proportion of the native as of the total in each class lived in the North and West, and in the South, respectively and the natives of these classes resident in the North and West were born in the North and West and the natives resident in the South were born in the South. As practically all—i.e. 55,571 out of 58,806—of the native civilized Indians included in the aggregate colored distributed by state of birth, were native, the error in the assumption that the same proportion of the natives as of the total lived in the South and in the North and West is immaterial. The great mass of the Indian population in 1890—189,447 out of 248,253—were specially enumerated and for these state of birth was not reported. They are included under "Other colored" in Table 9 [In original source]. The number of native Chinese and Japanese is so small—i.e. 2,930 Chinese and 119 Japanese—that any error in distributing them as living in and born in the North and West, or South, is immaterial in its effects upon the figures for the native Negro population of 7,468,697. In the 57,571 civilized native Indian population, 2,930 Chinese and 118 Japanese included in the aggregate colored population of 7,510,680 in 1890, there were undoubtedly a few migrants into the out of the South. These are not taken into account in the estimate, but their number could not have been sufficiently large materially to affect the figures for the aggregate Negro. Similar assumptions are made for 1880, except that for this year the number of native Negroes, Indians, and Chinese, and Japanese, living in each state is given in the report for 1880, except that for this year and number of native Negroes, Indians, Chinese, and Japanese, living in each state is given in the report for 1880, and the number living in the South and in other sections is, therefore not as regards natives in these classes an estimated number, as it is for 1890. For 1880, therefore, it is assumed in the estimate that the 6,269 native Indians, Chinese, and Japanese resident in the North and West were native of the North and West. 1. Figures in italics are estimates.

★ 1851 ★

Native and Foreign Born Population

Native Black Population by State of Birth and Residence, 1930, and Population Change Through Interstate Migration, 1910, 1920, and 1930

State	Native Negro Population, 1930							Gain (+) or Loss (-) Through Interstate Migration		
	Born in the specified State			Born in and and living in the specified State	Living in the specified State					
	Total	Living in other States			Total	Born in other States				
		Number	Percent			Number	Percent	1930	1920	1910
United States	11,739,479	2,964,725	25.3	8,774,754	11,739,479	2,964,725	25.3	-	-	-
NEW ENGLAND:										
Maine	1,334	675	50.6	659	871	212	24.3	-463	-479	-473
New Hampshire	494	271	54.9	223	583	360	61.7	+89	-41	+9
Vermont	853	506	59.3	347	544	197	36.2	-309	-799	+501
Massachusetts	32,009	7,651	23.9	24,358	43,021	18,663	43.4	+11,012	+12,617	+12,563
Rhode Island	7,468	2,226	29.8	5,242	8,798	3,556	40.4	+1,330	+1,864	+3,196

[Continued]

★ 1851 ★

Native Black Population by State of Birth and Residence, 1930, and Population Change Through Interstate Migration, 1910, 1920, and 1930

[Continued]

State	Native Negro Population, 1930							Gain (+) or Loss (-) Through Interstate Migration		
	Born in the specified State			Born in and and living in the specified State	Living in the specified State					
	Total	Living in other States			Total	Born in other States				
		Number	Percent			Number	Percent	1930	1920	1910
Connecticut	15,372	4,869	31.7	10,503	27,753	17,250	62.2	+12,381	+8,143	+4,514
MIDDLE ATLANTIC:										
New York	125,964	17,613	14.0	108,351	336,240	227,889	67.8	+210,276	+83,334	+58,449
New Jersey	80,937	16,585	20.5	64,352	203,536	139,184	68.4	+122,599	+59,923	+42,450
Pennsylvania	187,121	40,747	21.8	146,374	426,631	280,257	65.7	+239,510	+153,407	+85,485
EAST NORTH CENTRAL:										
Ohio	129,116	29,637	23.0	99,479	306,196	206,717	67.5	+177,080	+95,465	+33,599
Indiana	53,032	17,305	32.6	35,727	110,837	75,110	67.8	+57,805	+39,270	+25,018
Illinois	101,878	25,809	25.3	76,069	325,470	249,401	76.6	+223,592	+116,476	+57,577
Michigan	35,906	6,785	18.9	29,121	165,436	136,315	82.4	+129,530	+42,374	+2,940
Wisconsin	3,266	1,534	47.0	1,732	10,606	8,874	83.7	+7,340	+2,526	+515
WEST NORTH CENTRAL:										
Minnesota	3,990	1,606	40.3	2,384	9,218	6,834	74.1	+5,228	+5,189	+3,950
Iowa	12,410	5,811	46.8	6,599	17,184	10,585	61.6	+4,774	+7,038	+5,966
Missouri	159,113	52,385	32.9	106,728	222,194	115,466	52.0	+63,081	+29,463	+6,030
North Dakota	377	283	75.1	94	361	267	74.0	-16	-103	+295
South Dakota	504	329	65.3	175	633	458	72.4	+129	-30	+287
Nebraska	5,882	2,759	46.9	3,123	13,474	10,351	76.8	+7,592	+8,569	+4,551
Kansas	47,443	19,778	41.7	27,665	65,581	37,916	57.8	+18,138	+18,096	+19,418
SOUTH ATLANTIC:										
Delaware	32,184	10,873	33.8	21,311	32,482	11,171	34.4	+298	-892	-1,597
Maryland	275,093	73,849	26.8	201,244	283,870	72,626	26.5	-1,223	-20,915	-31,177
District of Columbia	72,018	19,505	27.1	52,513	130,450	77,937	59.7	+58,432	+46,518	+41,235
Virginia	908,551	331,963	36.5	576,588	649,234	72,646	11.2	-259,317	-195,515	-206,764
West Virginia	64,898	18,064	27.8	46,834	114,558	67,724	59.1	+49,660	+40,456	+27,316
North Carolina	1,028,538	220,240	21.4	808,298	917,739	109,441	11.9	-110,799	-113,716	-109,751
South Carolina	1,095,214	319,156	29.1	776,058	793,308	17,250	2.2	-301,906	-152,423	-121,479
Georgia	1,403,856	407,445	29.0	996,411	1,069,784	73,373	6.9	-334,072	-121,576	-75,274
Florida	314,688	55,053	17.5	259,635	419,558	159,923	38.1	+104,870	+62,653	+84,664
EAST SOUTH CENTRAL:										
Kentucky	292,365	167,314	36.7	185,051	225,376	40,325	17.9	-66,989	-68,432	-62,878
Tennessee	539,556	175,852	32.6	363,704	475,473	11,769	23.5	-64,083	-63,557	-46,194
Alabama	1,133,771	250,482	22.1	883,289	943,406	60,117	6.4	-190,365	-134,344	-65,365
Mississippi	1,227,757	288,846	23.5	938,911	1,008,048	69,137	6.9	-219,709	-139,178	-26,439
WEST SOUTH CENTRAL:										
Arkansas	449,451	109,269	24.3	340,182	476,496	136,314	28.6	+27,045	+106,639	+105,516
Louisiana	882,024	171,130	19.4	710,894	774,596	63,702	8.2	-107,428	-52,784	-15,741
Oklahoma	115,284	29,524	25.6	85,760	171,250	85,490	49.9	+55,966	+69,994	+85,062
Texas	864,210	109,193	12.6	755,017	852,333	97,316	11.4	-11,877	+3,501	+19,321
MOUNTAIN:										
Montana	937	638	68.1	299	1,218	919	75.5	+281	+712	+1,041
Idaho	372	262	70.4	110	643	533	82.9	+271	+540	+140
Wyoming	596	418	70.1	178	1,232	1,054	85.6	+636	+902	+1,832
Colorado	6,062	3,170	52.3	2,892	11,673	8,781	75.2	+5,611	+6,332	+7,583
New Mexico	1,293	778	60.2	515	2,792	2,277	81.6	+1,499	+4,318	+636
Arizona	2,265	1,152	50.9	1,113	10,582	9,469	89.5	+8,317	+6,454	+1,407
Utah	627	337	60.1	250	1,078	828	76.8	+451	+675	+482
Nevada	175	128	73.1	47	495	448	90.5	+320	+152	+108
PACIFIC:										
Washington	2,998	1,518	50.6	1,480	6,457	4,977	77.1	+3,459	+3,582	+4,045

[Continued]

★ 1851 ★

Native Black Population by State of Birth and Residence, 1930, and Population Change Through Interstate Migration, 1910, 1920, and 1930

[Continued]

State	Native Negro Population, 1930							Gain (+) or Loss (-) Through Interstate Migration		
	Born in the specified State			Born in and living in the specified State	Living in the specified State					
	Total	Living in other States			Total	Born in other States				
		Number	Percent			Number	Percent	1930	1920	1910
Oregon	746	395	52.9	351	2,130	1,779	83.5	+1,384	+11,449	+989
California	19,481	2,967	15.2	16,514	61,537	78,051	78.8	+58,570	+26,133	+13,942

Source: "Native Negro Population, by State of Birth and State of Residence, 1930, with Gain or Loss Through Interstate Migration, 1930, 1920, and 1910." U.S. Bureau of the Census, *Negroes in the United States, 1920-1932,* p. 26.

★ 1852 ★

Native and Foreign Born Population

Native Black Population of Each Division and State by Division and State of Birth, 1930 - I

Division and State	Negro Population Born In- New England division					
	Maine	New Hampshire	Vermont	Massachusetts	Rhode Island	Connecticut
United States	1,334	494	853	32,009	7,468	15,372
GEOGRAPHIC DIVISIONS:						
New England	907	372	538	25,731	5,976	11,467
Middle Atlantic	245	64	210	4,034	1,037	2,776
East North Central	68	14	36	683	115	344
West North Central	12	4	16	104	16	30
South Atlantic	58	28	30	999	236	599
East South Central	12	3	1	83	15	36
West South Central	5	3	1	91	24	24
Mountain	2	-	5	38	9	20
Pacific	25	6	16	246	40	76
NEW ENGLAND:						
Maine	659	3	-	51	2	8
New Hampshire	4	223	26	64	-	9
Vermont	2	17	347	33	4	1
Massachusetts	211	116	119	24,358	545	732
Rhode Island	7	5	14	538	5,242	214
Connecticut	24	8	32	687	183	10,503
MIDDLE ATLANTIC:						
New York	140	42	169	2,830	710	1,932
New Jersey	42	10	25	569	172	481
Pennsylvania	63	12	16	635	155	363
EAST NORTH CENTRAL:						
Ohio	24	5	12	189	27	92
Indiana	9	1	2	38	8	20

[Continued]

★ 1852 ★

Native Black Population of Each Division and State by Division and State of Birth, 1930 - I

[Continued]

Division and State	Negro Population Born In- New England division					
	Maine	New Hampshire	Vermont	Massachusetts	Rhode Island	Connecticut
Illinois	18	4	12	287	50	122
Michigan	16	4	10	161	23	108
Wisconsin	1	-	-	17	7	2
WEST NORTH CENTRAL:						
Minnesota	1	2	5	18	3	10
Iowa	1	1	1	9	-	1
Missouri	3	1	3	53	7	11
North Dakota	1	-	1	2	-	-
South Dakota		-	-	-	-	-
Nebraska	1	-	-	3	2	1
Kansas	5	-	6	19	4	7
SOUTH ATLANTIC:						
Delaware	1	-	2	29	5	24
Maryland	5	1	4	165	56	101
District of Columbia	22	6	9	254	72	122
Virginia	14	13	6	210	62	140
West Virginia	1	-	4	39	3	22
North Carolina	7	1	2	92	10	64
South Carolina	-	-	-	33	9	9
Georgia	1	3	3	72	8	61
Florida	7	4	-	105	11	56
EAST SOUTH CENTRAL:						
Kentucky	6	-	-	11	3	9
Tennessee	3	2	-	26	6	12
Alabama	3	1	-	26	5	15
Mississippi	-	-	1	20	1	-
WEST SOUTH CENTRAL:						
Arkansas	-	-	-	10	9	3
Louisiana	2	-	1	23	9	17
Oklahoma	-	1	-	14	3	-
Texas	3	2	-	44	3	4
MOUNTAIN:						
Montana	1	-	-	1	2	2
Idaho	-	-	-	1	-	1
Wyoming	-	-	-	2	-	1
Colorado	-	-	1	18	4	8
New Mexico	-	-	-	2	-	1
Arizona	1	-	4	11	3	4
Utah	-	-	-	3	-	3
Nevada	-	-	-	-	-	-
PACIFIC:						
Washington	7	-	1	18	4	10

[Continued]

★ 1852 ★

Native Black Population of Each Division and State by Division and State of Birth, 1930 - I

[Continued]

Division and State	Negro Population Born In- New England division					
	Maine	New Hampshire	Vermont	Massachusetts	Rhode Island	Connecticut
Oregon	-	-	1	5	1	1
California	18	6	14	223	35	65

Source: "Native Negro Population of Each Division and State, by Division and State of Birth." U.S. Bureau of the Census, *Negroes in the United States, 1920-1932*, pp. 28-31.

★ 1853 ★

Native and Foreign Born Population

Native Black Population of Each Division and State by Division and State of Birth, 1930 - II

Division and State	Negro Population Born In- Middle Atlantic division			East North Central division				
	New York	New Jersey	Pennsylvania	Ohio	Indiana	Illinois	Michigan	Wisconsin
United States	125,964	80,937	187,121	129,116	53,032	101,878	35,906	3,266
GEOGRAPHIC DIVISIONS:								
New England	2,214	838	1,221	281	75	163	74	13
Middle Atlantic	115,876	75,646	163,388	6,747	1,287	2,483	998	114
East North Central	2,422	984	9,097	111,681	46,458	85,265	32,342	2,581
West North Central	301	111	579	1,401	1,198	6,638	471	227
South Atlantic	3,967	2,977	10,763	4,251	713	1,123	742	87
East South Central	268	124	709	2,438	1,980	2,510	497	68
West South Central	251	75	44	782	501	1,756	321	73
Mountain	97	44	212	338	206	471	80	30
Pacific	568	138	708	1,197	614	1,469	381	73
NEW ENGLAND:								
Maine	3	3	14	1	-	2	-	2
New Hampshire	17	5	9	4	7	13	-	-
Vermont	35	5	1	4	-	1	-	-
Massachusetts	851	362	646	143	52	97	53	6
Rhode Island	195	82	123	20	1	5	5	-
Connecticut	1,113	381	428	109	15	45	16	5
MIDDLE ATLANTIC:								
New York	108,351	6,354	8,310	2,545	556	1,402	498	73
New Jersey	5,149	64,352	8,704	682	160	292	134	11
Pennsylvania	2,376	4,940	146,374	3,520	571	789	366	30
EAST NORTH CENTRAL:								
Ohio	803	330	4,891	99,479	3,184	2,483	1,197	84
Indiana	95	37	503	2,296	35,727	2,962	550	55

[Continued]

★ 1853 ★

Native Black Population of Each Division and State by Division and State of Birth, 1930 - II

[Continued]

Division and State	Negro Population Born In-							
	Middle Atlantic division			East North Central division				
	New York	New Jersey	Pennsylvania	Ohio	Indiana	Illinois	Michigan	Wisconsin
Illinois	817	334	1,753	4,631	4,885	76,069	1,360	541
Michigan	673	276	1,881	5,050	2,473	3,027	29,121	169
Wisconsin	34	7	69	225	189	724	105	1,732
WEST NORTH CENTRAL:								
Minnesota	56	14	76	184	169	392	75	107
Iowa	24	6	61	98	99	683	32	26
Missouri	126	46	261	688	632	4,667	193	47
North Dakota	1	2	4	14	1	13	3	2
South Dakota	5	-	2	8	2	24	14	1
Nebraska	26	7	67	101	62	263	42	13
Kansas	63	36	108	308	233	596	112	31
SOUTH ATLANTIC:								
Delaware	93	282	1,064	32	16	11	5	4
Maryland	626	683	2,638	312	80	123	57	2
District of Columbia	756	513	1,633	439	117	233	83	10
Virginia	1,062	697	2,234	456	72	121	92	15
West Virginia	116	120	1,369	1,822	137	199	99	5
North Carolina	473	263	670	288	54	53	74	6
South Carolina	215	87	236	115	14	39	41	3
Georgia	274	132	438	433	109	180	154	20
Florida	352	200	481	354	114	164	137	22
EAST SOUTH CENTRAL:								
Kentucky	62	20	199	1,180	1,503	808	128	11
Tennessee	67	38	189	572	244	835	155	20
Alabama	94	54	245	465	133	322	149	17
Mississippi	45	12	76	221	100	545	70	20
WEST SOUTH CENTRAL:								
Arkansas	38	12	89	202	158	726	85	29
Louisiana	85	18	116	188	75	365	74	14
Oklahoma	33	10	76	178	125	346	70	8
Texas	95	35	163	214	143	319	92	23
MOUNTAIN:								
Montana	7	4	20	36	14	47	7	2
Idaho	2	1	4	13	7	15	2	-
Wyoming	6	1	5	35	17	31	3	4
Colorado	27	15	72	126	73	212	28	7
New Mexico	5	3	9	11	12	28	3	1
Arizona	43	18	89	98	61	100	24	13
Utah	2	1	7	12	13	25	8	2
Nevada	5	1	6	7	9	13	5	1
PACIFIC:								
Washington	55	10	82	174	100	224	45	18

[Continued]

★ 1853 ★

Native Black Population of Each Division and State by Division and State of Birth, 1930 - II

[Continued]

Division and State	Negro Population Born In-							
	Middle Atlantic division			East North Central division				
	New York	New Jersey	Pennsylvania	Ohio	Indiana	Illinois	Michigan	Wisconsin
Oregon	14	7	28	43	19	49	18	2
California	499	121	598	980	495	1,196	318	53

Source: "Native Negro Population of Each Division and State, by Division and State of Birth." U.S. Bureau of the Census, *Negroes in the United States, 1920-1932*, pp. 28-31.

★ 1854 ★

Native and Foreign Born Population

Native Black Population of Each Division and State by Division and State of Birth, 1930 - III

Division and State	Negro Population Born In- West North Central division						
	Minnesota	Iowa	Missouri	North Dakota	South Dakota	Nebraska	Kansas
United States	3,990	12,410	159,113	377	504	5,882	47,443
GEOGRAPHIC DIVISIONS:							
New England	23	16	134	3	13	11	34
Middle Atlantic	136	293	1,916	51	27	165	553
East North Central	677	2,751	22,222	52	77	808	4,340
West North Central	2,643	8,191	121,165	158	288	3,949	35,153
South Atlantic	80	157	857	19	17	100	277
East South Central	58	152	2,070	12	13	80	269
West South Central	111	263	5,061	20	5	226	2,823
Mountain	51	194	1,953	30	25	190	1,533
Pacific	211	393	2,735	32	39	353	2,461
NEW ENGLAND:							
Maine	-	-	3	-	-	-	-
New Hampshire	-	-	-	-	-	1	2
Vermont	1	-	2	-	-	1	-
Massachusetts	15	10	82	1	3	4	15
Rhode Island	-	-	-	-	1	-	1
Connecticut	7	6	47	2	9	5	16
MIDDLE ATLANTIC:							
New York	83	138	1,010	34	12	82	282
New Jersey	22	35	243	9	5	14	102
Pennsylvania	31	120	663	8	10	69	169
EAST NORTH CENTRAL:							
Ohio	89	193	1,973	11	22	90	523
Indiana	63	171	1,481	2	4	68	366

[Continued]

★ 1854 ★

Native Black Population of Each Division and State by Division and State of Birth, 1930 - III

[Continued]

Division and State	Negro Population Born In- West North Central division						
	Minnesota	Iowa	Missouri	North Dakota	South Dakota	Nebraska	Kansas
Illinois	352	1,694	14,885	22	30	432	2,246
Michigan	116	393	3,414	13	20	177	1,014
Wisconsin	57	300	469	4	1	41	191
WEST NORTH CENTRAL:							
Minnesota	2,384	432	1,105	41	36	130	457
Iowa	67	6,599	3,500	8	26	189	648
Missouri	81	527	106,728	6	22	242	5,215
North Dakota	23	17	39	94	5	5	11
South Dakota	23	47	104	-	175	28	29
Nebraska	27	342	1,762	2	11	3,123	1,128
Kansas	38	227	7,927	7	13	232	27,665
SOUTH ATLANTIC:							
Delaware	-	3	22	-	-	1	4
Maryland	7	26	110	1	3	8	26
District of Columbia	27	28	185	5	4	30	73
Virginia	3	17	68	3	4	7	40
West Virginia	6	61	168	2	2	14	55
North Carolina	11	7	51	1	-	5	20
South Carolina	8	1	32	-	-	2	4
Georgia	11	6	103	-	2	13	23
Florida	7	8	118	7	2	20	32
EAST SOUTH CENTRAL:							
Kentucky	9	48	479	3	5	22	76
Tennessee	23	42	798	2	2	15	89
Alabama	11	23	205	1	2	28	50
Mississippi	15	39	588	6	4	15	54
WEST SOUTH CENTRAL:							
Arkansas	20	56	1,934	7	1	33	184
Louisiana	16	38	417	3	-	24	63
Oklahoma	23	94	1,590	6	2	106	2,162
Texas	52	75	1,120	4	2	63	414
MOUNTAIN:							
Montana	21	18	137	19	5	10	55
Idaho	4	4	51	-	-	7	39
Wyoming	1	23	175	1	6	27	89
Colorado	9	103	1,146	3	4	92	875
New Mexico	4	10	74	-	3	6	97
Arizona	9	23	262	6	5	30	284
Utah	2	9	78	-	2	11	62
Nevada	1	4	30	1	-	7	32
PACIFIC:							
Washington	72	71	508	19	12	33	281

[Continued]

★ 1854 ★

Native Black Population of Each Division and State by Division and State of Birth, 1930 - III

[Continued]

Division and State	Negro Population Born In- West North Central division						
	Minnesota	Iowa	Missouri	North Dakota	South Dakota	Nebraska	Kansas
Oregon	8	18	193	-	2	19	111
California	131	304	3,034	13	25	301	2,069

Source: "Native Negro Population of Each Division and State, by Division and State of Birth." U.S. Bureau of the Census, *Negroes in the United States, 1920-1932*, pp. 28-31.

★ 1855 ★

Native and Foreign Born Population

Native Black Population of Each Division and State by Division and State of Birth, 1930 - IV

Division and State	Negro Population Born In- South Atlantic division								
	Delaware	Maryland	District of Columbia	Virginia	West Virginia	North Carolina	South Carolina	Georgia	Florida
United States	32,184	275,093	72,018	980,551	64,898	1,028,538	1,095,214	1,403,856	314,688
GEOGRAPHIC DIVISIONS:									
New England	133	1,452	891	9,223	152	5,881	4,269	5,982	1,002
Middle Atlantic	9,242	43,076	9,446	171,693	5,684	84,268	100,179	84,685	22,475
East North Central	205	2,596	1,506	22,490	6,104	18,073	27,009	110,423	8,939
West North Central	20	367	267	2,377	296	1,456	1,446	4,262	776
South Atlantic	22,507	226,557	59,291	691,711	51,399	902,275	946,447	1,122,715	273,864
East South Central	24	289	145	5,993	801	8,138	7,754	57,456	5,261
West South Central	10	302	110	2,877	182	6,943	6,610	12,381	1,611
Mountain	6	116	91	598	87	316	277	762	134
Pacific	37	338	271	1,589	193	1,188	1,133	5,190	626
NEW ENGLAND:									
Maine	3	12	3	41	-	19	13	9	3
New Hampshire	1	12	10	68	-	26	16	14	9
Vermont	1	10	3	19	3	10	10	5	1
Massachusetts	81	700	504	4,607	73	3,032	1,860	2,030	445
Rhode Island	7	301	110	1,141	14	267	176	167	60
Connecticut	40	417	261	3,347	62	2,527	2,194	3,757	484
MIDDLE ATLANTIC:									
New York	847	8,133	3,929	58,919	1,048	33,961	41,866	23,776	9,598
New Jersey	2,529	9,473	1,741	36,635	613	19,010	16,540	22,380	5,011
Pennsylvania	5,866	25,470	3,776	76,139	4,023	31,297	41,863	38,529	7,866
EAST NORTH CENTRAL:									
Ohio	73	1,184	565	13,892	4,384	9,939	11,831	48,847	3,102
Indiana	13	99	70	971	181	1,110	669	4,350	323
Illinois	55	695	526	3,726	568	2,760	5,533	24,902	1,888
Michigan	63	586	329	3,711	943	4,155	8,921	31,054	3,553
Wisconsin	2	32	16	190	28	109	145	1,270	73

[Continued]

★ 1855 ★

Native Black Population of Each Division and State by Division and State of Birth, 1930 - IV

[Continued]

Division and State	Negro Population Born In- South Atlantic division								
	Delaware	Maryland	District of Columbia	Virginia	West Virginia	North Carolina	South Carolina	Georgia	Florida
WEST NORTH CENTRAL:									
Minnesota	1	39	29	200	33	64	71	255	38
Iowa	1	34	14	638	49	134	88	220	51
Missouri	9	155	77	977	120	848	791	2,729	337
North Dakota	-	1	2	6	3	1	7	9	1
South Dakota	1	4	-	10	2	1	-	20	1
Nebraska	3	23	19	131	20	76	66	203	257
Kansas	5	111	126	415	69	332	423	826	91
SOUTH ATLANTIC:									
Delaware	21,311	5,340	113	2,152	38	620	329	430	206
Maryland	906	201,244	3,562	37,090	949	12,616	7,593	2,248	682
District of Columbia	87	16,346	52,513	30,236	751	8,026	10,166	3,383	626
Virginia	95	2,311	2,347	576,588	2,958	44,354	8,711	2,479	593
West Virginia	16	548	222	31,401	46,834	8,304	2,441	2,905	334
North Carolina	31	311	239	9,578	426	808,298	79,368	13,272	1,074
South Carolina	8	87	51	617	31	6,913	776,058	6,924	793
Georgia	24	131	151	1,682	140	5,208	32,695	996,411	9,921
Florida	29	239	93	2,367	172	7,936	29,086	94,663	259,635
EAST SOUTH CENTRAL:									
Kentucky	1	68	37	1,965	456	1,005	916	3,390	321
Tennessee	10	81	54	1,985	141	3,492	3,403	21,886	557
Alabama	10	95	38	1,123	166	1,444	2,258	28,374	3,667
Mississippi	3	45	16	920	38	2,197	1,177	3,806	716
WEST SOUTH CENTRAL:									
Arkansas	5	51	26	704	38	3,336	3,926	4,987	190
Louisiana	-	110	26	815	42	1,117	725	2,060	805
Oklahoma	2	37	13	401	46	859	821	1,868	133
Texas	3	104	45	957	56	1,631	1,138	3,466	483
MOUNTAIN:									
Montana	-	10	6	47	3	17	9	22	2
Idaho	-	3	3	13	2	16	5	11	4
Wyoming	-	4	5	37	7	10	6	27	11
Colorado	-	36	24	267	37	96	74	253	38
New Mexico	-	2	3	32	6	22	21	56	5
Arizona	6	43	38	166	26	133	148	353	66
Utah	-	7	9	18	2	15	12	19	6
Nevada	-	11	3	18	4	7	2	21	2
PACIFIC:									
Washington	7	48	29	229	42	151	79	170	39
Oregon	2	18	13	51	7	30	34	57	22
California	28	272	229	1,309	144	1,007	1,020	4,963	565

Source: "Native Negro Population of Each Division and State, by Division and State of Birth." U.S. Bureau of the Census, *Negroes in the United States, 1920-1932*, pp. 28-31.

★ 1856 ★

Native and Foreign Born Population

Native Black Population of Each Division and State by Division and State of Birth, 1930 - V

Division and State	Negro Population Born In-							
	East South Central division				West South Central division			
	Kentucky	Tennessee	Alabama	Mississippi	Arkansas	Louisiana	Oklahoma	Texas
United States	292,365	539,556	1,133,771	1,227,757	449,451	882,024	115,284	884,210
GEOGRAPHIC DIVISIONS:								
New England	332	421	854	172	91	226	61	181
Middle Atlantic	5,764	8,193	26,626	4,613	1,797	4,148	779	3,939
East North Central	76,888	81,082	86,314	76,972	29,111	27,983	5,098	12,390
West North Central	8,493	21,590	9,044	35,741	27,622	8,375	9,863	12,591
South Atlantic	4,639	8,899	50,648	4,758	887	2,904	557	2,056
East South Central	190,406	391,009	929,666	1,002,417	15,722	22,419	711	2,279
West South Central	3,017	24,124	26,292	98,565	369,785	805,262	92,488	810,082
Mountain	924	1,263	1,203	1,028	1,187	1,747	2,301	5,651
Pacific	1,902	2,975	3,124	3,491	3,249	8,960	3,425	15,041
NEW ENGLAND:								
Maine	-	2	4	1	-	4	2	3
New Hampshire	4	10	8	9	6	1	2	1
Vermont	6	9	6	3	1	-	1	1
Massachusetts	184	210	378	97	54	128	24	103
Rhode Island	11	25	25	4	-	7	4	12
Connecticut	127	165	433	58	30	86	28	61
MIDDLE ATLANTIC:								
New York	2,011	3,051	5,023	1,819	766	2,662	349	2,053
New Jersey	553	870	5,043	487	234	393	124	446
Pennsylvania	3,200	4,272	16,560	2,307	797	1,093	306	1,440
EAST NORTH CENTRAL:								
Ohio	27,177	19,222	34,366	7,588	3,377	2,096	739	1,667
Indiana	25,317	13,728	6,205	7,428	2,819	1,630	436	854
Illinois	17,280	34,844	24,958	50,851	16,425	19,867	2,315	6,669
Michigan	6,627	12,478	20,216	9,869	5,931	3,988	1,451	2,914
Wisconsin	487	810	569	1,236	559	402	157	286
WEST NORTH CENTRAL:								
Minnesota	465	439	314	331	277	224	214	392
Iowa	392	522	568	820	433	304	335	413
Missouri	4,957	16,836	5,966	31,363	21,559	5,680	3,468	6,212
North Dakota	15	17	6	11	8	13	3	15
South Dakota	26	21	12	21	8	10	7	16
Nebraska	325	486	840	615	730	441	717	1,353
Kansas	2,313	3,269	1,338	2,580	4,607	1,703	5,119	4,190
SOUTH ATLANTIC:								
Delaware	34	34	146	28	7	21	18	41
Maryland	254	316	508	213	90	164	64	219
District of Columbia	386	613	874	639	136	312	86	498
Virginia	526	1,507	1,493	234	66	183	51	181
West Virginia	2,467	2,794	10,560	796	126	211	107	151
North Carolina	196	821	1,206	340	82	125	50	118
South Carolina	40	199	435	119	29	75	12	46

[Continued]

★ 1856 ★

Native Black Population of Each Division and State by Division and State of Birth, 1930 - V

[Continued]

Division and State	Negro Population Born In-							
	East South Central division				West South Central division			
	Kentucky	Tennessee	Alabama	Mississippi	Arkansas	Louisiana	Oklahoma	Texas
Georgia	346	1,514	17,587	812	173	480	68	296
Florida	390	1,101	17,839	1,577	178	1,333	101	506
EAST SOUTH CENTRAL:								
Kentucky	185,051	16,752	7,589	1,761	587	442	110	258
Tennessee	4,297	333,704	13,551	48,320	7,412	2,393	242	678
Alabama	545	4,282	883,289	13,425	594	1,485	183	463
Mississippi	513	6,271	25,237	938,911	7,129	18,099	176	880
WEST SOUTH CENTRAL:								
Arkansas	877	16,432	9,142	57,229	340,182	28,886	1,554	5,166
Louisiana	401	1,047	5,925	30,515	8,706	710,894	447	9,257
Oklahoma	957	3,873	4,903	5,550	12,935	7,265	85,760	40,642
Texas	782	2,772	6,322	5,271	7,962	58,217	4,727	755,017
MOUNTAIN:								
Montana	59	68	28	29	33	17	22	71
Idaho	14	37	20	14	22	29	27	84
Wyoming	59	55	56	34	32	34	50	93
Colorado	450	644	516	434	500	386	524	1,473
New Mexico	62	67	107	89	141	171	277	851
Arizona	227	330	422	382	402	1,029	1,330	2,895
Utah	37	44	36	32	49	45	53	112
Nevada	16	18	18	14	8	36	13	72
PACIFIC:								
Washington	250	281	197	191	147	218	131	459
Oregon	51	76	76	63	75	143	74	268
California	1,601	2,618	2,851	3,237	3,027	8,599	3,221	14,314

Source: "Native Negro Population of Each Division and State, by Division and State of Birth." U.S. Bureau of the Census, *Negroes in the United States, 1920-1932*, pp. 28-31.

★ 1857 ★

Native and Foreign Born Population

Native Black Population of Each Division and State by Division and State of Birth, 1930 - VI

Division and State	Negro Population Born In-							
	Mountain division							
	Montana	Idaho	Wyoming	Colorado	New Mexico	Arizona	Utah	Nevada
United States	937	372	596	6,062	1,293	2,265	627	175
GEOGRAPHIC DIVISIONS:								
New England	7	2	7	23	2	7	5	-
Middle Atlantic	108	30	34	261	39	121	33	11
East North Central	115	44	91	681	117	140	49	12

[Continued]

★ 1857 ★

Native Black Population of Each Division and State by Division and State of Birth, 1930 - VI

[Continued]

Division and State	Negro Population Born In- Mountain division							
	Montana	Idaho	Wyoming	Colorado	New Mexico	Arizona	Utah	Nevada
West North Central	75	27	102	580	105	79	37	7
South Atlantic	55	11	22	126	29	75	13	-
East South Central	19	7	10	90	23	30	28	1
West South Central	27	34	22	349	91	107	30	8
Mountain	345	144	252	3,190	669	1,156	308	58
Pacific	186	73	56	762	218	550	124	78
NEW ENGLAND:								
Maine	-	-	-	-	-	-	-	-
New Hampshire	-	-	1	-	-	-	-	-
Vermont	1	-	-	-	-	-	-	-
Massachusetts	2	1	3	19	1	5	3	-
Rhode Island	1	-	-	1	-	-	1	-
Connecticut	3	1	3	3	1	2	1	-
MIDDLE ATLANTIC:								
New York	63	23	15	128	15	49	18	3
New Jersey	17	3	6	45	7	19	5	1
Pennsylvania	28	4	13	88	17	53	10	7
EAST NORTH CENTRAL:								
Ohio	29	6	28	103	23	41	8	3
Indiana	12	5	12	49	8	9	2	1
Illinois	46	22	25	355	60	54	28	4
Michigan	21	11	24	152	23	34	10	4
Wisconsin	7	-	2	22	3	2	1	-
WEST NORTH CENTRAL:								
Minnesota	26	1	4	29	7	4	5	1
Iowa	4	3	3	35	5	7	2	2
Missouri	23	16	31	226	30	34	50	4
North Dakota	1	-	-	1	1	1	-	-
South Dakota	-	-	4	6	-	-	-	-
Nebraska	5	5	41	72	12	6	8	-
Kansas	16	2	19	211	50	27	7	-
SOUTH ATLANTIC:								
Delaware	-	-	-	1	1	3	-	-
Maryland	8	1	2	13	10	10	1	-
District of Columbia	8	4	3	33	4	24	2	-
Virginia	16	-	4	13	1	11	1	-
West Virginia	3	1	7	26	9	7	2	-
North Carolina	1	1	1	12	-	-	-	-
South Carolina	1	1	1	2	2	1	-	-
Georgia	11	1	3	11	2	8	2	-
Florida	7	2	1	15	-	11	5	-

[Continued]

★ 1857 ★

Native Black Population of Each Division and State by Division and State of Birth, 1930 - VI

[Continued]

Division and State	Negro Population Born In- Mountain division							
	Montana	Idaho	Wyoming	Colorado	New Mexico	Arizona	Utah	Nevada
EAST SOUTH CENTRAL:								
Kentucky	3	-	5	18	2	8	9	-
Tennessee	6	6	4	26	7	8	3	1
Alabama	5	1	1	26	11	3	14	-
Mississippi	5	-	-	20	3	11	2	-
WEST SOUTH CENTRAL:								
Arkansas	5	12	4	57	6	6	4	-
Louisiana	9	7	3	25	8	6	6	2
Oklahoma	3	11	5	119	29	25	8	2
Texas	10	4	10	148	48	70	12	4
MOUNTAIN:								
Montana	299	6	8	17	1	4	1	3
Idaho	8	110	2	17	3	3	23	1
Wyoming	6	1	178	78	3	1	6	-
Colorado	13	5	42	2,892	53	15	18	1
New Mexico	4	1	2	49	5151	18	1	-
Arizona	6	4	10	78	89	1,113	3	3
Utah	7	7	9	46	4	1	250	3
Nevada	2	10	1	13	1	1	6	47
PACIFIC:								
Washington	87	31	16	117	18	18	14	3
Oregon	16	9	5	28	2	6	10	1
California	83	33	35	617	198	526	100	74

Source: "Native Negro Population of Each Division and State, by Division and State of Birth." U.S. Bureau of the Census, *Negroes in the United States, 1920-1932,* pp. 28-31.

★ 1858 ★

Native and Foreign Born Population

Native Black Population of Each Division and State by Division and State of Birth, 1930 - VII

Division and State	Negro Population Born In-			
	Pacific division			United States, State not reported
	Washington	Oregon	California	
United States	2,998	746	19,481	32,384
GEOGRAPHIC DIVISIONS:				
New England	31	3	56	319

[Continued]

★ 1858 ★

Native Black Population of Each Division and State by Division and State of Birth, 1930 - VII

[Continued]

Division and State	Negro Population Born In-			
	Pacific division			United States, State not reported
	Washington	Oregon	California	
Middle Atlantic	595	32	490	5,324
East North Central	248	40	718	5,317
West North Central	80	24	288	2,395
South Atlantic	123	15	320	7,153
East South Central	24	7	176	5,245
West South Central	53	29	424	5,488
Mountain	69	25	278	226
Pacific	1,775	571	16,731	917
NEW ENGLAND:				
Maine	1	-	-	13
New Hampshire	-	-	1	9
Vermont	-	-	-	1
Massachusetts	16	3	37	155
Rhode Island	6	-	5	30
Connecticut	8	-	13	111
MIDDLE ATLANTIC:				
New York	264	19	279	2,885
New Jersey	145	8	75	1,232
Pennsylvania	186	5	136	1,207
EAST NORTH CENTRAL:				
Ohio	52	3	151	1,762
Indiana	20	-	49	881
Illinois	124	19	336	1,605
Michigan	49	15	165	1,003
Wisconsin	3	3	17	66
WEST NORTH CENTRAL:				
Minnesota	25	2	31	70
Iowa	9	-	19	138
Missouri	32	8	132	1,365
North Dakota	-	-	1	5
South Dakota	-	-	1	3
Nebraska	5	2	30	205
Kansas	9	12	74	609
SOUTH ATLANTIC:				
Delaware	6	-	5	25
Maryland	30	5	38	1,482
District of Columbia	15	3	55	1,048
Virginia	25	4	46	504
West Virginia	14	2	26	191
North Carolina	12	-	25	758
South Carolina	5	1	9	295

[Continued]

★ 1858 ★

Native Black Population of Each Division and State by Division and State of Birth, 1930 - VII

[Continued]

Division and State	Negro Population Born In-			
	Pacific division			United States, State not reported
	Washington	Oregon	California	
Georgia	7	-	54	1,097
Florida	9	-	62	1,753
EAST SOUTH CENTRAL:				
Kentucky	10	2	33	574
Tennessee	8	3	55	2,035
Alabama	4	1	50	1,110
Mississippi	2	1	38	1,526
WEST SOUTH CENTRAL:				
Arkansas	7	7	61	1,878
Louisiana	13	4	73	773
Oklahoma	15	9	112	819
Texas	18	9	178	2,018
MOUNTAIN:				
Montana	12	3	8	15
Idaho	8	5	8	3
Wyoming	7	1	4	8
Colorado	12	6	41	75
New Mexico	3	-	18	40
Arizona	18	7	167	64
Utah	2	2	11	12
Nevada	7	1	21	9
PACIFIC:				
Washington	1,480	102	159	108
Oregon	45	351	58	35
California	250	118	16,514	774

Source: "Native Negro Population of Each Division and State, by Division and State of Birth." U.S. Bureau of the Census, *Negroes in the United States, 1920-1932*, pp. 28-31.

★ 1859 ★

Native and Foreign Born Population

Native Black Population of Each Division and State by Division and State of Birth, 1930 - VIII

Division and State	Negro Population Born In- Outlying possessions									American citizens born at sea	American citizens born abroad
	Total	Alaska	American Samoa	Guam	Hawaii	Panama Canal Zone	Phillipine Islands	Puerto Rico	Virgin Islands of the U.S.		
United States	17,625	42	30	48	217	594	402	11,132	5,160	39	2,996
GEOGRAPHIC DIVISIONS:											
New England	271	-	-	1	8	25	26	107	104	3	137
Middle Atlantic	15,863	5	-	13	44	426	135	10,389	4,851	12	728
East North Central	264	2	2	2	13	41	34	135	35	10	1,157
West North Central	61	4	2	-	7	4	22	17	5	0	155
South Atlantic	421	16	-	25	19	24	31	228	78	5	242
East South Central	97	-	9	-	8	7	12	49	12	-	61
West South Central	171	1	14	-	4	20	12	87	33	2	203
Mountain	52	3	1	1	8	3	24	9	3	-	47
Pacific	425	11	2	6	106	44	106	111	39	7	266
NEW ENGLAND:											
Maine	5	-	-	-	-	-	-	2	3	-	4
New Hampshire	3	-	-	-	-	1	-	2	-	-	-
Vermont	4	-	-	-	-	-	4	-	-	-	6
Massachusetts	150	-	-	1	7	21	20	53	48	2	103
Rhode Island	7	-	-	-	-	-	1	4	2	1	14
Connecticut	102	-	-	-	1	3	1	46	51	-	10
MIDDLE ATLANTIC:											
New York	15,305	1	-	12	22	385	82	10,145	4,658	6	483
New Jersey	247	3	-	-	6	11	18	96	113	1	93
Pennsylvania	311	1	-	1	16	30	35	148	80	5	152
EAST NORTH CENTRAL:											
Ohio	57	-	1	1	3	7	9	31	5	3	209
Indiana	22	1	-	-	3	-	4	8	6	2	40
Illinois	97	-	1	1	3	14	14	55	9	4	230
Michigan	85	1	-	-	4	20	7	38	15	1	666
Wisconsin	3	-	-	-	-	-	-	3	-	-	12
WEST NORTH CENTRAL:											
Minnesota	5	1	-	-	2	-	1	1	-	-	47
Iowa	2	1	-	-	1	-	-	-	-	-	6
Missouri	22	2	2	-	1	1	2	12	2	-	50
North Dakota	1	-	-	-	-	-	1	-	-	-	3
South Dakota	-	-	-	-	-	-	-	-	-	-	3
Nebraska	6	-	-	-	1	1	3	1	-	-	12
Kansas	25	-	-	-	2	2	15	3	3	-	34
SOUTH ATLANTIC:											
Delaware	5	-	-	-	1	1	-	3	-	-	3
Maryland	128	1	-	1	1	8	10	70	37	2	25
District of Columbia	74	13	-	2	7	1	11	30	10	-	39
Virginia	69	2	-	2	2	4	6	39	14	1	27
West Virginia	11	-	-	-	1	1	1	8	-	-	14
North Carolina	23	-	-	8	1	1	-	10	3	-	9
South Carolina	18	-	-	7	-	1	-	7	3	-	6
Georgia	31	-	-	2	4	2	-	20	3	-	13
Florida	62	-	-	3	2	5	3	41	8	2	106
EAST SOUTH CENTRAL:											
Kentucky	9	-	1	-	2	-	2	4	-	-	13
Tennessee	16	-	6	-	1	1	2	4	2	-	22
Alabama	41	-	2	-	2	4	5	24	4	-	9
Mississippi	31	-	-	-	3	2	3	17	6	-	17

[Continued]

★ 1859 ★

Native Black Population of Each Division and State by Division and State of Birth, 1930 - VIII

[Continued]

Division and State	Negro Population Born In- Outlying possessions									American citizens born at sea	American citizens born abroad
	Total	Alaska	American Samoa	Guam	Hawaii	Panama Canal Zone	Phillipine Islands	Puerto Rico	Virgin Islands of the U.S.		
WEST SOUTH CENTRAL:											
Arkansas	8	-	1	-	-	1	2	4	-	1	10
Louisiana	98	-	2	-	-	19	1	56	20	-	50
Oklahoma	9	-	1	-	1	-	3	3	1	-	53
Texas	56	1	10	-	3	-	6	24	12	1	90
MOUNTAIN:											
Montana	3	2	-	-	-	-	-	-	1	-	6
Idaho	3	1	-	-	-	-	-	2	-	-	4
Wyoming	1	-	-	-	-	-	-	1	-	-	1
Colorado	5	-	-	-	-	3	1	1	-	-	14
New Mexico	-	-	-	-	-	-	-	-	-	-	4
Arizona	36	-	1	1	6	-	22	5	1	-	14
Utah	4	-	-	-	2	-	1	-	1	-	2
Nevada	-	-	-	-	-	-	-	-	-	-	2
PACIFIC:											
Washington	31	5	-	-	6	-	12	7	1	3	74
Oregon	6	1	-	-	4	-	1	-	-	-	13
California	388	5	2	6	96	44	93	104	38	4	179

Source: "Native Negro Population of Each Division and State, by Division and State of Birth." U.S. Bureau of the Census, *Negroes in the United States, 1920-1932*, pp. 28-31.

★ 1860 ★

Native and Foreign Born Population

Native Black Population of Each Division and State, by Division and State of Birth, Summary Table, 1930 - I

Division and State	Total native Negro population	Negro Population Born In-					
		United States	Geographic divisions				
			New England	Middle Atlantic	East North Central	West North Central	South Atlantic
United States	11,792,523	11,771,863	57,530	394,022	323,198	299,719	5,195,040
GEOGRAPHIC DIVISIONS:							
New England	82,300	81,889	44,991	4,273	606	234	28,985
Middle Atlantic	988,334	971,731	8,366	354,910	11,629	3,141	530,748
East North Central	925,293	923,862	1,260	12,503	278,327	30,927	197,435
West North Central	331,256	331,040	182	991	9,935	171,547	11,267
South Atlantic	4,408,804	4,408,136	1,950	17,707	6,919	1,507	4,296,766
East South Central	2,657,706	2,657,548	150	1,101	7,493	2,654	85,861
West South Central	2,280,539	2,280,163	148	770	3,433	8,509	31,026
Mountain	30,038	29,939	74	353	1,125	3,976	2,387
Pacific	88,253	87,555	409	1,414	3,734	7,224	10,565

[Continued]

★ 1860 ★

Native Black Population of Each Division and State, by Division and State of Birth, Summary Table, 1930 - I

[Continued]

Division and State	Total native Negro population	Negro Population Born In-					
		United States	Geographic divisions				
			New England	Middle Atlantic	East North Central	West North Central	South Atlantic
NEW ENGLAND:							
Maine	893	884	723	20	5	3	103
New Hampshire	595	592	326	31	24	3	156
Vermont	555	545	404	41	5	4	62
Massachusetts	43,431	43,176	26,081	1,859	351	130	13,332
Rhode Island	8,850	8,828	6,020	400	31	24	2,243
Connecticut	27,976	27,864	11,437	1,922	190	92	13,089
MIDDLE ATLANTIC:							
New York	354,919	339,125	5,823	123,015	5,074	1,641	182,077
New Jersey	205,109	204,766	1,299	78,205	1,279	430	113,842
Pennsylvania	428,306	427,838	1,244	153,690	5,276	1,070	234,829
EAST NORTH CENTRAL:							
Ohio	308,227	307,958	349	6,024	106,427	2,901	93,816
Indiana	111,782	111,718	78	635	41,599	2,155	7,786
Illinois	327,406	327,075	484	2,904	87,486	19,661	40,653
Michigan	167,191	166,439	322	2,830	39,840	5,147	53,315
Wisconsin	10,687	10,672	27	110	2,975	1,063	1,865
WEST NORTH CENTRAL:							
Minnesota	9,340	9,288	39	146	927	4,585	730
Iowa	17,330	17,322	13	91	938	11,037	1,229
Missouri	223,631	223,559	78	433	6,227	112,821	6,043
North Dakota	379	366	4	7	33	194	30
South Dakota	639	636	-	7	49	406	39
Nebraska	13,697	13,679	7	100	481	5,395	798
Kansas	66,249	66,190	41	207	1,280	36,100	2,398
SOUTH ATLANTIC:							
Delaware	32,515	32,507	61	1,539	68	30	30,539
Maryland	275,507	275,352	332	3,947	574	181	266,890
District of Columbia	131,611	131,498	485	2,902	882	352	122,134
Virginia	649,835	649,738	445	3,993	756	142	639,536
West Virginia	114,774	114,749	69	1,605	2,262	308	93,005
North Carolina	918,529	918,497	176	1,406	475	95	912,597
South Carolina	793,627	793,603	51	538	212	47	791,492
Georgia	1,070,925	1,070,881	148	844	896	158	1,046,363
Florida	421,481	421,311	183	1,033	791	194	304,220
EAST SOUTH CENTRAL:							
Kentucky	252,972	225,950	29	281	3,625	642	8,159

[Continued]

★ 1860 ★

Native Black Population of Each Division and State, by Division and State of Birth, Summary Table, 1930 - I

[Continued]

Division and State	Total native Negro population	Negro Population Born In-						
		United States	Geographic divisions					
			New England	Middle Atlantic	East North Central	West North Central	South Atlantic
Tennessee	477,546	477,508	49	294	1,826	971	31,609
Alabama	944,566	944,516	50	393	1,086	320	37,175
Mississippi	1,009,622	1,009,574	22	133	956	721	8,918
WEST SOUTH CENTRAL:							
Arkansas	478,393	478,374	22	139	1,200	2,235	13,263
Louisiana	775,517	775,369	52	219	716	561	5,700
Oklahoma	172,131	172,069	18	119	727	2,983	4,180
Texas	854,498	854,351	56	293	790	1,730	7,883
MOUNTAIN:							
Montana	1,242	1,233	6	31	106	265	116
Idaho	653	646	2	7	37	105	57
Wyoming	1,242	1,240	3	12	90	322	107
Colorado	11,767	11,748	31	114	446	2,232	825
New Mexico	2,836	2,832	3	17	55	194	147
Arizona	10,696	10,646	23	150	296	619	979
Utah	1,096	1,090	6	10	60	164	88
Nevada	506	504	-	12	35	75	68
PACIFIC:							
Washington	6,673	6,565	40	147	561	996	794
Oregon	2,184	2,165	8	49	131	351	234
California	79,396	78,825	361	1,218	3,042	5,877	9,537

Source: "Native Negro Population of Each Division and State, by Division and State of Birth." U.S. Bureau of the Census, *Negroes in the United States, 1920-1932,* p. 27. *Notes:* 1. Includes persons born in outlying possessions and American citizens born abroad or at sea.

★ 1861 ★

Native and Foreign Born Population

Native Black Population of Each Division and State, by Division and State of Birth, Summary Table, 1930 - II

Division and State	Negro Population Born In-					Other native Negro population[1]
	Geographic divisions				United States, State not reported	
	East South Central	West South Central	Mountain	Pacific		
United States						
GEOGRAPHIC DIVISIONS:						
New England	3,193,449	2,310,969	12,327	23,225	32,384	20,660
Middle Atlantic	1,779	559	53	90	319	411
East North Central	45,196	10,663	637	1,117	5,324	16,603
West North Central	321,256	74,582	1,249	1,006	5,317	1,431
South Atlantic	74,868	58,451	1,012	392	2,395	216
East South Central	68,944	6,404	331	438	7,153	668
West South Central	2,513,498	41,131	208	207	5,245	158
Mountain	151,998	2,077,617	668	506	5,488	376
Pacific	4,418	10,886	6,122	372	226	99
NEW ENGLAND:						
Maine	7	9	-	1	13	9
New Hampshire	31	10	1	1	9	3
Vermont	24	3	1	-	1	10
Massachusetts	869	309	34	56	155	255
Rhode Island	65	23	3	11	30	22
Connecticut	783	205	14	21	111	112
MIDDLE ATLANTIC:						
New York	11,904	5,830	314	562	2,885	15,791
New Jersey	6,953	1,197	103	228	1,233	341
Pennsylvania	26,339	3,636	220	327	1,207	468
EAST NORTH CENTRAL:						
Ohio	88,353	7,879	241	206	1,762	269
Indiana	52,678	5,739	98	69	881	64
Illinois	127,933	45,276	594	479	1,605	331
Michigan	49,190	14,284	279	229	1,003	752
Wisconsin	3,102	1,404	37	23	66	15
WEST NORTH CENTRAL:						
Minnesota	1,549	1,107	77	58	70	52
Iowa	2,302	1,485	61	28	138	8
Missouri	59,122	36,919	379	172	1,365	72
North Dakota	49	39	4	1	5	4
South Dakota	80	41	10	1	3	3
Nebraska	2,266	3,241	149	37	205	18
Kansas	9,500	15,619	332	95	609	59

[Continued]

★ 1861 ★

Native Black Population of Each Division and State, by Division and State of Birth, Summary Table, 1930 - II

[Continued]

Division and State	Negro Population Born In- Geographic divisions: East South Central	West South Central	Mountain	Pacific	United States, State not reported	Other native Negro population[1]
SOUTH ATLANTIC:						
Delaware	242	87	5	11	25	8
Maryland	1,291	537	45	73	1,482	155
District of Columbia	2,512	1,032	78	73	1,048	113
Virginia	3,760	481	46	75	504	97
West Virginia	16,617	595	55	42	191	25
North Carolina	2,563	375	15	37	758	32
South Carolina	793	162	8	15	295	24
Georgia	20,259	1,017	38	61	1,097	44
Florida	20,907	2,118	41	71	1,753	170
EAST SOUTH CENTRAL:						
Kentucky	211,153	1,397	45	45	574	22
Tennessee	429,872	10,725	61	66	2,035	38
Alabama	901,541	2,725	61	55	1,110	50
Mississippi	970,932	26,284	41	41	1,526	48
WEST SOUTH CENTRAL:						
Arkansas	83,080	375,788	94	75	1,878	19
Louisiana	37,888	729,304	66	90	773	148
Oklahoma	15,283	146,602	202	136	819	62
Texas	15,147	825,923	306	205	2,018	147
MOUNTAIN:						
Montana	184	148	339	23	15	9
Idaho	85	162	167	21	3	7
Wyoming	204	209	273	12	8	2
Colorado	2,044	2,883	3,039	59	75	19
New Mexico	325	1,440	590	21	46	4
Arizona	1,361	5,656	1,306	192	64	50
Utah	149	259	327	15	12	6
Nevada	66	129	31	9	2	
PACIFIC:						
Washington	919	955	304	1,741	108	108
Oregon	266	560	77	454	35	19
California	10,307	29,161	1,0666	16,882	774	571

Source: "Native Negro Population of Each Division and State, by Division and State of Birth." U.S. Bureau of the Census, *Negroes in the United States, 1920-1932,* p. 27. *Notes:* 1. Includes persons born in outlying possessions and American citizens born abroad or at sea.

★ 1862 ★

Native and Foreign Born Population

Native Population by Race and Section of Birth, 1930

Section of Residence	Total		Born In- The South		Born In- The North		Born In- The West		State of Birth Not Reported, or Born in Outlying Possessions[1]	
	Negro	White	Negro	White	Negro	White	Negro	White	Negro	White
	Number									
United States	11,792,523	95,497,800	10,699,458	27,891,047	1,004,469	61,783,174	35,552	5,425,014	53,044	398,565
The South	9,347,049	27,141,704	9,273,245	25,172,567	52,338	1,821,678	2,378	96,234	19,088	51,225
The North	2,327,183	59,001,814	1,355,789	1,931,799	933,822	56,551,965	5,556	269,818	32,016	248,232
The West	118,291	9,354,282	70,424	786,681	18,309	3,409,531	27,618	5,058,962	1,940	99,108
	Percent Distribution by Section of Birth									
United States	1.000	100.0	90.7	29.3	8.5	64.7	0.3	5.7	0.4	0.4
The South	100.0	100.0	99.2	92.7	0.6	6.7	[2]	.4	.2	.2
The North	100.0	100.0	58.3	3.3	40.1	94.8	.2	.5	1.4	.4
The West	100.0	100.0	59.5	8.4	15.5	36.4	23.3	54.1	1.6	1.1
	Percent Distribution by Section of Residence									
United States	100.0	100.0	100.0	100.0	100.0	100.0	100.0	100.0	100.0	100.0
The South	79.3	28.4	86.7	90.3	5.2	2.9	6.7	1.8	36.0	12.9
The North	19.7	61.8	12.7	6.9	93.0	91.5	15.6	5.0	60.4	62.3
The West	1.0	9.8	0.7	2.8	1.8	5.5	77.7	93.3	3.7	24.9

Source: "Native Negro and White Population Classified by Section of Residence, and by Section of Birth: 1930." U.S. Bureau of the Census, *Negroes in the United States, 1920-1932*, p. 22. *Notes:* 1. Includes American citizens born abroad or at sea. 2. Less than 1/10 of 1 percent.

★ 1863 ★

Native and Foreign Born Population

Native Population by Race, Section of Residence, and Section of Birth, 1910

SECTION OF RESIDENCE	NATIVE POPULATION: 1910 — Total		Born in- The South		Born in- The North		Born in- The West		State of birth not reported, or born in outlying possessions[1]	
	Negro	White	Negro	White	Negro	White	Negro	White	Negro	White
	NUMBER									
United States	9,787,424	68,386,412	9,109,153	19,814,860	621,286	45,488,942	15,604	2,766,492	41,381	316,118
The South	8,738,858	19,821,249	8,668,619	18,326,236	39,077	1,407,262	2,412	34,523	28,750	53,228
The North	999,451	43,319,193	415,533	1,110,245	570,298	41,891,353	2,295	116,939	11,325	200,656
The West	49,115	5,245,970	25,001	378,379	11,911	2,190,327	10,897	2,615,030	1,306	62,234
	PERCENTAGE DISTRIBUTION BY SECTION OF BIRTH									
United States	100.0	100.0	93.1	29.0	6.3	66.5	0.2	4.0	0.4	0.5
The South	100.0	100.0	99.2	92.5	0.4	7.1	[2]	0.2	0.3	0.3
The North	100.0	100.0	41.6	2.6	57.1	96.7	0.2	0.3	1.1	0.5
The West	100.0	100.0	50.9	7.2	24.3	41.8	22.3	49.8	2.7	1.2

[Continued]

★ 1863 ★

Native Population by Race, Section of Residence, and Section of Birth, 1910

[Continued]

SECTION OF RESIDENCE	NATIVE POPULATION: 1910									
	Total		Born in- The South		Born in- The North		Born in- The West		State of birth not reported, or born in outlying possessions[1]	
	Negro	White	Negro	White	Negro	White	Negro	White	Negro	White
	PERCENTAGE OF DISTRIBUTION BY SECTION OF RESIDENCE									
United States	100.0	100.0	100.0	100.0	100.0	100.0	100.0	100.0	100.0	100.0
The South	89.3	29.0	95.2	92.5	6.3	3.1	15.5	1.2	69.5	16.8
The North	10.2	63.3	4.6	5.6	91.8	92.1	14.7	4.2	27.4	63.5
The West	0.5	7.7	0.3	1.9	1.9	4.8	69.8	94.5	3.2	19.7

Source: "Native Negro and White Population Classified by Section of Residence, and by Section of Birth: 1910." U.S. Bureau of the Census, *Historical Statistics of the United States: Colonial Times to 1970, Part I,* Bicentennial Edition, p. 67. *Notes:* 1. Includes also persons born at sea under the United States flag and American citizens born abroad. 2. Less than one-tenth of 1 per cent.

★ 1864 ★

Native and Foreign Born Population

Native and Foreign-Born Population, Number and Percentage, 1850-1910

YEAR	NEGRO POPULATION				WHITE POPULATION	
	Total	Native[1]	Foreign born		Number foreign born	Percentage foreign born
			Number	Percent		
1910	9,827,763	9,787,424	40,339	0.4	13,345,545	16.3
1900	8,833,994	8,813,658	20,336	0.2	10,213,817	15.3
1890	7,488,676	7,468,697	19,979	0.3	9,121,867	16.6
1880	6,580,793	6,566,776	14,017	0.2	6,559,679	15.1
1870	4,830,009	4,870,364	9,645	0.2	5,493,712	16.4
1860	4,441,830	4,437,467[1]	4,363	0.1	4,099,401	15.2
1850	3,638,808	3,634,741[1]	4,067	0.1	2,240,535	11.5

Source: "Untitled Table." U.S. Bureau of the Census, *Historical Statistics of the United States: Colonial Times to 1970, Part I,* Bicentennial Edition, p. 61. *Note:* 1. Includes all slaves and native free colored.

★ 1865 ★

Native and Foreign Born Population

Nativity and Parentage of the Black and White Population by Area of Enumeration, 1910

NATIVITY AND PARENTAGE CLASS	POPULATION: 1910						Percentage in each class				
	Area of enumeration	United States	Porto Rico	Hawaii	Alaska	Military and naval service abroad	Area of enumeration	United States	Porto Rico	Hawaii	Alaska
	NEGRO										
All classes	10,215,482	9,827,763	385,437	695	209	1,378	100.0	100.0	100.0	100.0	100.0
Native[1]	10,172,974	9,787,424	383,451	602	168	1,329	99.6	99.6	99.5	86.6	80.4
Both parents native	10,127,805	9,748,439	377,547	387	154	1,278	99.1	99.2	98.0	55.7	73.7
One parent foreign born	28,969	24,425	4,388	107	9	40	0.3	0.2	1.1	15.4	4.3
Both parents foreign born	16,200	14,560	1,516	108	5	11	0.2	0.1	0.4	15.5	2.4
Foreign born	42,506	40,339	1,986	93	41	49	0.4	0.4	0.5	13.4	19.6
	WHITE										
All classes	82,598,168	81,731,957	732,555	44,048	36,400	53,208	100.0	100.0	100.0	100.0	100.0
Native[1]	69,203,955	68,386,412	722,791	28,930	18,426	47,396	83.8	83.7	98.7	65.7	50.6
Both parents native	50,239,453	49,488,575	696,699	10,689	10,993	32,497	60.8	60.5	95.1	24.3	30.2
One parent foreign born	6,014,468	5,981,526	21,838	3,380	2,673	5,051	7.3	7.3	3.0	7.7	7.3
Both parents foreign born	12,950,034	12,916,311	4,254	14,861	4,760	9,848	15.7	15.8	0.6	33.7	13.1
Foreign born	13,394,213	13,345,545	9,764	15,118	17,974	5,812	16.2	16.3	1.3	34.3	49.4

Source: "Nativity and Parentage of the Negro and the White Population by Areas of Enumeration: 1910." U.S. Bureau of the Census, *Negro Population, 1790- 1915*, p. 23. *Note:* 1. Born in the United States or in any of its outlying possessions.

★ 1866 ★

Native and Foreign Born Population

Number and Percent Native and Foreign-Born in the Total Black Population, with State of Birth Reported, 1910 to 1930 - I

CENSUS YEAR	Total Negro population	NATIVE NEGRO POPULATION						
		Total		With State of birth reported				
				Born in State of residence		Born in other States		
		Number	Percent of total Negro population	Number	Percent of total Negro population	Number	Percent of total Negro population	Percent of native Negro population
1930	11,891,143	11,792,523	99.2	8,774,754	73.8	2,964,725	24.9	25.1
1920	10,463,131	10,389,328	99.3	8,288,492	79.2	2,054,242	19.6	19.8
1910	9,827,763	9,787,424	99.6	8,129,435	82.7	1,616,608	16.4	16.5

Source: "Number and Percent Native and Foreign Born in the Total Negro Population, With Classification of Native According to Whether Born in State of Residence or Elsewhere, for the United Stated: 1910 to 1930." U.S. Bureau of the Census, *Negroes in the United States, 1920-1932*, p. 21.

★ 1867 ★

Native and Foreign Born Population

Number and Percent Native and Foreign-Born in the Total Black Population, with State of Birth Reported, 1910 to 1930 - II

CENSUS YEAR	NATIVE NEGRO POPULATION				FOREGIN-BORN NEGRO POPULATION	
	State of birth not reported	Born in outlying possessions	American citizens born at sea	American citizens born abroad	Number	Percent of total Negro population
1930	32,384	17,625	39	2,996	98,620	0.8
1920	38,575	4,846	34	3,139	73,803	.7
1910	37,943	355	217	2,866	40,339	.4

Source: "Number and Percent Native and Foreign Born in the Total Negro Population, With Classification of Native According to Whether Born in State of Residence or Elsewhere, for the United Stated: 1910 to 1930." U.S. Bureau of the Census, *Negroes in the United States, 1920-1932,* p. 21.

★ 1868 ★

Native and Foreign Born Population

Parentage of the Black and White Population, 1930 and 1920

Nativity and Parentage	Population: Number, 1930		Number, 1920		Percent distribution, 1930		Percent distribution, 1920		Increase: Number		Increase: Percent	
	Negro	White	Negro	White	Negro	White	Negro	White	Negro	White	Negro	White
Total	11,891,143	108,864,207	10,463,131	94,120,374	100.0	100.0	100.0	100.0	1,428,012	14,743,833	13.6	15.7
Native	11,792,523	95,497,800	10,389,328	80,864,980	99.2	87.7	99.3	85.9	1,403,195	14,632,820	13.5	18.1
Both parents native	11,709,162	70,136,614	10,334,151	58,421,957	98.5	64.4	98.8	62.1	1,375,011	11,714,657	13.3	20.1
1 or both parents foreign born	83,361	25,361,186	55,177	22,443,023	.7	23.3	.5	23.8	28,184	2,918,163	51.1	13.0
1 parent foreign born, 1 native	39,909	8,361,965	29,334	6,921,188	.3	7.7	.3	7.4	10,575	1,440,777	36.1	20.8
Father foreign born	26,310	5,459,530	18,193	[1]	.2	5.0	.2	[1]	8,117	[1]	44.6	[1]
Mother foreign born	13,599	2,902,435	11,141	[1]	.1	2.7	.1	[1]	2,458	[1]	22.1	[1]
Both parents foreign born	43,452	16,999,221	25,843	15,521,835	.4	15.6	.2	16.5	17,609	1,477,386	68.1	9.5
Foreign born	98,620	13,366,407	73,803	13,255,394[2]	.8	12.3	.7	14.1	24,817	111,013	33.6	.8

Source: "Parentage of the Negro and White Population of the United States: 1930 and 1920." U.S. Bureau of the Census, *Negroes in the United States, 1920-1932*, p. 22. *Notes:* 1. Adjusted figures not available. 2. Figures for white population in 1920 and 1910 are adjusted by deducting the estimated number of Mexicans.

★ 1869 ★

Native and Foreign Born Population

Percentage Distribution of Native and Foreign-Born Population by Divisions, 1910

SECTION AND DIVISION	NEGRO POPULATION: 1910			PERCENTAGE DISTRIBUTION: 1910		PERCENTAGE FOREIGN BORN: 1910	
	Total	Native	Foreign born	Foreign-born Negro population	Foreign-born white population	Negro population	White population
United States	9,827,763	9,787,424	40,339	100.0	100.0	0.4	16.3
The South	8,749,427	8,738,858	10,569	26.2	5.4	0.1	3.5
South Atlantic	4,112,488	4,104,413	8,075	20.0	2.2	0.2	3.6
East South Central	2,652,513	2,651,888	625	1.5	0.7	[1]	1.5
West South Central	1,984,426	1,982,557	1,869	4.6	2.6	0.1	5.2
The North	1,027,674	999,451	28,223	70.0	84.8	2.7	20.7
New England	66,306	58,596	7,710	19.1	13.6	11.6	28.0
Middle Atlantic	417,870	401,548	16,322	40.5	36.2	3.9	25.6
East North Central	300,836	297,452	3,384	8.4	23.0	1.1	17.1
West North Central	242,662	241,855	807	2.0	12.1	0.3	14.2
The West	50,662	49,115	1,547	3.8	9.7	3.1	19.8
Mountain	29,195	28,021	1,174	2.9	6.5	4.0	21.4
Pacific	29,195	28,021	1,174	2.9	6.5	4.0	21.4

Source: "Untitled Table." U.S. Bureau of the Census, *Historical Statistics of the United States: Colonial Times to 1970, Part I*, Bicentennial Edition, p. 61. *Note:* 1. Less than one-tenth of 1 per cent.

★ 1870 ★

Native and Foreign Born Population

Proportion of Migrants in the South, North and West of the Native Black Population, 1910

YEAR	NATIVE NEGRO POPULATION						
	Total	Born in the South	Born in the North and West	Other[1]	Percentage: Born in the South	Percentage: Born in the North and West	Percentage: Other[1]
	LIVING IN THE SOUTH						
1910	8,738,858	8,668,619	41,489	28,750	99.2	0.5	0.3
1900	7,915,406	7,866,807	30,397	18,202	99.4	0.4	0.2
1890[2]	6,753,917	6,667,014	23,268	63,635	98.7	0.5	0.9
1880[2]	5,948,406	5,926,322	22,039	45	99.6	0.4	[3]
1870	4,416,788	4,400,132	15,583	1,073	99.6	0.4	[3]

[Continued]

★ 1870 ★

Proportion of Migrants in the South, North and West of the Native Black Population, 1910

[Continued]

YEAR	NATIVE NEGRO POPULATION						
	Total	Born in the South	Born in the North and West	Other[1]	Percentage		
					Born in the South	Born in the North and West	Other[1]
	LIVING IN THE NORTH AND WEST						
1910	1,048,566	440,534	595,401	12,631	42.0	56.8	1.2
1900	898,252	349,651	539,692	8,909	38.9	60.1	1.0
1890[2]	714,780	241,855	457,833	15,092	33.8	64.1	2.1
1880[2]	618,370	198,029	420,318	23	32.1	68.0	[3]
1870	453,576	149,100	304,073	403	32.9	67.0	[3]

Source: "Untitled Table." U.S. Bureau of the Census, *Historical Statistics of the United States: Colonial Times to 1970, Part I*, Bicentennial Edition, p. 66. *Notes:* Figures in italics are estimates. It is assumed that in 1890 two-thirds-approximately the proportion in 1880-of the foreign born Negro population of 19,979, lived in the North and West, and one-third in the South: that of the Indians, Chinese, and Japanese, the same proportion of the native as of the total in each class lived in the North and West, and in the South, respectively and the natives of these classes resident in the North and West were born in the North and West and the natives resident in the South were born in the South. As practically all-i.e. 55,571 out of 58,806-of the native civilized Indians included in the aggregate colored distributed by state of birth, were native, the error in the assumption that the same proportion of the natives as of the total lived in the South and in the North and West is immaterial. The great mass of the Indian population in 1890-189,447 out of 248,253-were specially enumerated and for these state of birth was not reported. They are included under "Other colored" in Table 9 [In original source]. The number of native Chinese and Japanese is so small-i.e. 2,930 Chinese and 119 Japanese-that any error in distributing them as living in and born in the North and West, or South, is immaterial in its effects upon the figures for the native Negro population of 7,468,697. In the 57,571 civilized native Indian population, 2,930 Chinese and 118 Japanese included in the aggregate colored population of 7,510,680 in 1890, there were undoubtedly a few migrants into the out of the South. These are not taken into account in the estimate, but their number could not have been sufficiently large materially to affect the figures for the aggregate Negro. Similar assumptions are made for 1880, except that for this year the number of native Negroes, Indians, and Chinese, and Japanese, living in each state is given in the report for 1880, except that for this year and number of native Negroes, Indians, Chinese, and Japanese, living in each state is given in the report for 1880, and the number living in the South and in other sections is, therefore not as regards natives in these classes an estimated number, as it is for 1890. For 1880, therefore, it is assumed in the estimate that the 6,269 native Indians, Chinese, and Japanese resident in the North and West were native of the North and West.

★ 1871 ★

Native and Foreign Born Population

Summary Data on Migration of the Native Population by Race and Division, 1920 to 1930

SECTION	NEGRO		WHITE	
	1930	1920	1930	1920
Born in the South and living in the North	1,355,789	737,423	1,931,799	1,412,779
Born in the North and living in the South	52,338	44,536	1,821,678	1,675,085
Net gain of the North	1,303,451	692,887	110,121	-
Net gain of the South	-	-	-	262,306
Born east and living west of the Mississippi River[1]	320,589	342,931	4,820,182	4,882,520

[Continued]

★ 1871 ★

Summary Data on Migration of the Native Population by Race and Division, 1920 to 1930

[Continued]

SECTION	NEGRO		WHITE	
	1930	1920	1930	1920
Born west and living east of the Mississippi River[1]	177,158	96,110	1,458,154	939,017
Net gain of the West	143,431	246,821	3,362,028	3,943,503
Net gain of the East	-	-	-	-

Source: "Summary of Data Indicating Results of the Migration of the Native Negro and White Population North and South, East and West: 1920 to 1930." U.S. Bureau of the Census, *Negroes in the United States, 1920-1932,* p. 21. *Notes:* 1. In the preparation of this table the entire States of Minnesota and Louisiana have been treated as living west of the Mississippi River.

★ 1872 ★

Native and Foreign Born Population

Year of Immigration of the Foreign-Born Black Population in the United States by Gender, 1911-1919 and 1920-1930

SEX	Total foreign born negroes	YEAR OF IMMIGRATION							
		1920 to 1930			1911 to 1919			1901 to 1910	1900 or earlier
		Total	1925 to 1930	1920 to 1924	Total	1915 to 1919	1911 to 1914		
Total	98,620	39,515	8,576	30,939	33,012	20,597	12,415	17,453	8,640
Male	54,081	19,944	4,414	15,530	18,215	11,248	6,967	10,644	5,278
Female	44,539	19,571	4,162	14,409	14,797	9,349	5,448	6,809	3,362

Source: "Year of Immigration of the Foreign-Born Negro Population of the United States, by Sex." U.S. Bureau of the Census, *Negroes in the United States, 1920-1932,* p. 21.

Property Holdings and Values

★ 1873 ★

Property Assessed to Blacks in Counties in Maryland, 1793-1860

County	1793	1804	1813	1825-26	1832-33	1836-38	1841-42	1846	1852-53	1860
Allegany	[2] 180.66	-	-	-	[3] 181	-	-	-	[15] 5501	[17] 6656
Anne Arundel	[8] 1066.66 (1783)	-	-	-	-	-	-	-	-	[98] 58274[1]
Baltimore Co.	-	-	[10] 571							

[Continued]

★ 1873 ★

Property Assessed to Blacks in Counties in Maryland, 1793-1860

[Continued]

County	1793	1804	1813	1825-26	1832-33	1836-38	1841-42	1846	1852-53	1860
			(1818)	[15] 2830.46	[44] 13884	-	[62] 16843	-	[129] 37801	-
Baltimore City	-	-	[59] 7843	[234] 12178	-	[201] 157100	-	[264] 150135	[338] 289492.37	[348] 449138
Calvert	-	-	-	-	-	-	-	-	-	-
Caroline	-	-	[14] 930	[19] 4406	[66] 6100	-	[98] 20984	-	[185] 53308	[184] 59291
Carroll	-	-	-	-	-	-	[29] 9867	-	[40] 8579	[35] 8140.50
Cecil	-	[11] 2245.33	[29] 3347	[16] 2279	[32] 3031	-	[41] 19401	[67] 19520 (1842)	[133] 42367	[145] 37411
Charles	[3] 237.33 (1783)	-	-	-	-	-	-	-	-	-
Dorchester	-	-	-	-	-	-	-	-	[178] 53859.16[3]	-
Frederick	[2] 49.66 (1798)	-	[4] 221 (1816)	[47] 1025	[81] 3625 (1835)	-	-	-	[275] 81712	[291] 86765
Harford	-	-	-	-	-	-	-	-	-	[167] 45350
Howard	-	-	-	-	-	-	[16] 5436	-	[26] 10056	[32] 10664
Kent	-	[49] 3794.88	[52] 7134	[85] 9152	[76] 7731	-	[127] 28937	-	[228] 58326	[282] 70702
Montgomery	[7] 349.33	-	-	-	[22] 1773	-	[31] 5371	-	[43] 9999	[51] 17142
Prince George's	-	-	-	-	-	-	-	-	-	-
Queen Anne's	[2] 143.185	-	-	[29] 5175 (1824)	[96] 4827	-	[105] 26588	-	[237] 66015	[215] 65227
St. Mary's	-	-	-	-	-	-	-	-	-	-
Somerset	[13] 1333.33 (1798)	-	[15] 1315	[73] 8009	[88] 12655	-	[137] 25498	-	[201] 54757	[205] 57298
Talbot	[18] 1766.30	[88] 6132.57	[102] 5141.50	[54] 3188.58	[56] 3550.05	-	[49] 11615.40	-	[169] 31364	[184] 36133
Washington	-	-	-	-	-	-	-	-	-	-
Worcester	[5] 762.66 (1783)	-	-	-	-	-	-	-	-	-

Source: "Table Showing Property Assessed to Negroes in the Counties of Maryland," James M. Wright, *The Free Negro in Maryland*, 1634-1860, p. 184. *Notes:* Small numbers in upper left hand corners of spaces indicate numbers of property-holders counted. 1. Three districts not accounted for. 2. Including estimates for counties of Baltimore and Dorchester. 3. Two districts not accounted for.

★ 1874 ★

Property Holdings and Values

Property Holdings in Counties in Maryland, 1859-1860

County	Totals	Holders of minima of $--each			
		$500	$1000	$2000	$5000
Allegany	17	-	-	-	-
Anne Arundel	98	31	14	5	1
Baltimore Co.	125	18	7	1	-
Baltimore City	348	274	137	40	10
Caroline	184	24	11	2	1
Carroll	35	1	-	-	-
Cecil	145	11	4	-	-
Charles	-	-	-	-	-
Dorchester	178	7	3	1	-
Frederick	291	31	7	2	-
Harford	167	19	7	-	-

[Continued]

★ 1874 ★

Property Holdings in Counties in Maryland, 1859-1860

[Continued]

County	Totals	Holders of minima of $--each			
		$500	$1000	$2000	$5000
Howard	32	3	1	-	-
Kent	283	14	6	2	-
Montgomery	51	4	2	1	-
Prince George's	-	-	-	-	-
Queen Anne's	215	28	7	1	-
St. Mary's	-	-	-	-	-
Somerset	205	27	6	2	-
Talbot	184	13	-	-	-
Washington	-	-	-	-	-
Worcester	-	-	-	-	-

Source: "Negro Property Holders in Various Counties, 1859-1860," James M. Wright, *The Free Negro in Maryland*, 1634-1860, p. 186. *Notes:* 1. In Dorchester and Anne Arundel no allowance has been made for the fact that certain districts in each were not represented in the records used in compiling the data.

★ 1875 ★

Property Holdings and Values

Property Holdings in Maryland, 1860

County	Negro holdings	Total holdings	White holdings	No. of free Negroes	No. of white population	Per capita holdings		No. of Negro holders	Total holders
						Negro	White		
Allegany	$6,656	$5,532,040	$5,525,384	467	27,215	$14.25	$203.02[1]	17	-
Anne Arundel	58,274	7,523,161	7,464,887	4,864	11,704	11.98	637.80	98	-
Baltimore Co. (1852)	37,801	20,579,170	20,541,369	4,231	46,822	8.93	438.71	125	-
Baltimore City	449,138	127,899,370	127,450,232	25,680	184,520	17.49	690.71	348	-
Caroline	59,291	2,059,050	1,999,759	2,786	7,604	21.28	263	184	-
Carroll	8,140.50	8,425,298	8,417,158	1,225	22,525	6.64	373	35	3556
Cecil	37,411	7,784,770	7,747,359	2,918	19,994	12.82	387	145	-
Charles	-	4,615,380	-	1,068	5,796	-	-	-	-
Dorchester (1852)	53,859.16	5,191,732	5,137,873	3,848	10,747	13.99	478[1]	178	-
Frederick	86,765	21,314,727	21,227,962	4,957	38,391	17.50	552	291	-
Harford	45,350	7,186,029	7,140,679	3,644	17,971	12.44	397	167	3310
Howard	10,664	4,213,408	4,202,844	1,395	9,081	7.64	462	32	-
Kent	70,702	4,982,750	4,912,048	3,411	7,347	20.72	668	283	-
Montgomery	17,142	5,571,747	5,554,605	1,552	11,349	11.04	489	51	-
Prince George's	-	9,101,755	-	1,198	9,650	-	-	-	-
Queen Anne's	65,227	5,348,479	5,283,252	3,372	8,415	19.34	627	215	-
Somerset	57,298	5,376,265	5,318,967	4,571	15,332	12.53	346	205	-
Talbot	36,133	5,227,011	5,190,878	2,964	8,106	12.19	641	184	-
Washington	-	14,171,725	-	1,677	28,305	-	-	-	-
Worcester	-	4,788,921	-	3,571	13,442	-	-	-	-

Source: "Table Comparing Property Holdings of Negroes and Whites, 1860," James M. Wright, *The Free Negro in Maryland*, 1634-1860, p. 185. *Notes:* 1. In Dorchester and Anne Arundel no allowance has been made for the fact that certain districts in each were not represented in the records used in compiling the data.

Racial Composition

★ 1876 ★

Black and Classes of the White Population by Age, Sections, and Southern Divisions, 1910 - I

SECTION, DIVISION, AND RACIAL CLASS	POPULATION: 1910 All ages	Under 5 years	5 to 9 years	10 to 14 years	15 to 19 years	20 to 24 years	25 to 29 years
UNITED STATES							
All classes	91,972,266	10,631,364	9,760,632	9,107,140	9,063,603	9,058,984	8,180,003
Negro	9,827,763	1,263,288	1,246,553	1,155,266	1,060,416	1,030,795	881,227
Native white:							
Native parentage	49,488,575	6,546,282	5,801,015	5,324,283	5,089,055	4,682,922	4,049,074
Foreign or mixed parentage	18,897,837	2,764,125	2,315,649	2,235,795	2,205,575	1,873,108	1,545,366
Foreign-born white	13,345,545	102,507	298,509	358,380	673,761	1,430,381	1,662,696
THE SOUTH							
All classes	29,389,330	4,053,348	3,750,535	3,381,932	3,141,631	2,873,464	2,426,387
Negro	8,749,427	1,176,331	1,164,557	1,073,980	970,716	911,603	749,782
Native white:							
Native parentage	18,561,146	2,702,147	2,413,795	2,139,915	1,992,684	1,768,938	1,488,071
Foreign or mixed parentage	1,260,103	149,410	136,803	131,669	130,289	117,061	103,990
Foreign-born white	726,171	8,910	21,550	25,087	38,081	67,654	77,929
SOUTH ATLANTIC							
All classes	12,194,805	1,657,219	1,524,850	1,396,058	1,289,792	1,193,525	1,000,453
Negro	4,112,488	570,516	555,030	513,239	457,053	426,876	341,665
Native white:							
Native parentage	7,341,205	1,027,812	915,529	830,589	773,565	696,449	587,969
Foreign or mixed parentage	439,843	54,686	45,386	42,842	42,599	37,848	33,944
Foreign-born white	290,555	2,575	7,593	8,259	15,526	31,373	36,047
EAST SOUTH CENTRAL							
All classes	8,409,901	1,160,471	1,070,852	969,343	905,052	814,177	685,911
Negro	2,652,513	347,803	343,812	320,476	294,183	274,935	230,624
Native white:							
Native parentage	5,452,492	796,697	709,965	629,684	588,058	514,065	428,451
Foreign or mixed parentage	214,977	15,048	15,158	17,025	19,622	19,353	19,306
Foreign-born white	86,857	426	1,538	1,812	2,882	5,548	7,290
WEST SOUTH CENTRAL							
All classes	8,784,534	1,235,658	1,154,833	1,016,531	946,787	865,762	740,023
Negro	1,984,426	258,012	265,709	240,265	219,480	209,792	177,493
Native white:							
Native parentage	5,767,449	877,638	788,301	679,642	631,061	558,424	472,651
Foreign or mixed parentage	605,283	79,676	76,259	71,802	68,068	59,860	50,659
Foreign-born white	348,759	5,909	12,419	15,016	19,673	30,733	34,592

[Continued]

★ 1876 ★

Black and Classes of the White Population by Age, Sections, and Southern Divisions, 1910 - I

[Continued]

SECTION, DIVISION, AND RACIAL CLASS	POPULATION: 1910						
	All ages	Under 5 years	5 to 9 years	10 to 14 years	15 to 19 years	20 to 24 years	25 to 29 years
THE NORTH							
All classes	55,757,115	5,900,586	5,403,840	5,163,075	5,330,302	5,486,602	5,041,380
Negro	1,027,674	83,729	78,892	78,205	86,126	113,925	124,832
Native white:							
Native parentage	27,352,035	3,412,551	3,069,248	2,847,255	2,762,466	2,555,907	2,219,762
Foreign or mixed parentage	15,967,158	2,320,380	1,994,384	1,922,670	1,884,564	1,576,243	1,279,302
Foreign-born white	11,321,016	83,593	252,672	306,632	588,705	1,232,780	1,412,085
THE WEST							
All classes	6,825,821	668,430	606,257	562,133	591,670	696,918	709,236
Negro	50,662	3,228	3,104	3,081	3,574	5,269	6,613
Native white:							
Native parentage	3,575,394	431,584	377,972	337,113	333,905	358,077	341,241
Foreign or mixed parentage	1,670,576	204,335	184,462	181,456	190,722	179,804	162,155
Foreign-born white	1,298,358	10,004	24,287	26,611	46,975	129,944	171,782

Source: "Negro Population and Classes of the White Population, Classified by Age Periods, by Sections and Southern Divisions: 1910." U.S. Bureau of the Census, *Negro Population, 1790-1915*, p. 176.

★ 1877 ★

Racial Composition

Black and Classes of the White Population by Age, Sections, and Southern Divisions, 1910 - II

SECTION, DIVISION, AND RACIAL CLASS	POPULATION: 1910					
	30 to 34 years	35 to 44 years	45 to 54 years	55 to 64 years	65 years and over	Age unknown
UNITED STATES						
All classes	6,972,185	11,657,687	8,369,988	5,054,101	3,949,524	159,055
Negro	668,089	1,088,862	711,979	396,124	294,124	31,040
Native white:						
Native parentage	3,401,601	5,495,766	4,022,103	2,717,897	2,201,068	97,509
Foreign or mixed parentage	1,359,960	2,304,783	1,522,857	594,529	255,586	10,504
Foreign-born white	1,505,715	2,711,568	2,071,415	1,321,103	1,183,349	26,211
THE SOUTH						
All classes	1,974,660	3,158,691	2,208,197	1,382,388	983,394	54,703
Negro	557,466	910,025	607,895	343,958	256,694	26,420
Native white:						
Native parentage	1,240,902	1,922,185	1,352,355	896,745	618,974	24,435

[Continued]

★ 1877 ★

Black and Classes of the White Population by Age, Sections, and Southern Divisions, 1910 - II

[Continued]

SECTION, DIVISION, AND RACIAL CLASS	POPULATION: 1910					
	30 to 34 years	35 to 44 years	45 to 54 years	55 to 64 years	65 years and over	Age unknown
Foreign or mixed parentage	98,288	178,884	129,647	56,445	26,573	1,125
Foreign-born white	72,754	138,926	112,362	81,608	78,902	2,408
SOUTH ATLANTIC						
All classes	815,946	1,325,796	932,819	597,751	489,628	21,058
Negro	253,860	421,374	279,676	162,623	119,140	11,430
Native white:						
Native parentage	495,892	780,597	562,293	383,224	278,967	8,319
Foreign or mixed parentage	33,291	61,634	49,143	23,029	12,072	366
Foreign-born white	32,259	57,896	40,630	23,377	29,089	931
EAST SOUTH CENTRAL						
All classes	555,365	893,208	640,396	402,681	297,289	15,156
Negro	171,477	278,306	191,801	108,199	82,481	8,416
Native white:						
Native parentage	355,933	559,019	402,393	268,356	193,484	6,387
Foreign or mixed parentage	20,476	40,152	30,572	12,431	5,654	180
Foreign-born white	7,290	15,393	15,391	13,550	15,567	170
WEST SOUTH CENTRAL						
All classes	603,349	939,687	634,982	381,956	246,477	18,489
Negro	132,129	210,345	136,418	73,136	55,073	6,574
Native white:						
Native parentage	389,077	582,569	387,669	245,165	146,523	9,729
Foreign or mixed parentage	44,518	74,098	49,932	20,985	8,847	579
Foreign-born white	33,205	65,637	56,341	39,681	34,246	1,307
THE NORTH						
All classes	4,379,440	7,499,249	5,463,289	3,291,788	2,697,624	87,940
Negro	104,600	169,052	98,341	49,737	35,973	4,264
Native white:						
Native parentage	1,871,954	3,118,453	2,352,731	1,638,504	1,445,947	57,254
Foreign or mixed parentage	1,120,325	1,904,513	1,260,412	489,416	206,889	8,060
Foreign-born white	1,275,677	2,294,388	1,742,027	1,108,770	1,004,699	18,085
THE WEST						
All classes	618,085	999,747	698,502	379,925	268,506	26,412
Negro	6,023	9,785	5,743	2,429	1,457	356

[Continued]

★ 1877 ★

Black and Classes of the White Population by Age, Sections, and Southern Divisions, 1910 - II

[Continued]

SECTION, DIVISION, AND RACIAL CLASS	POPULATION: 1910					
	30 to 34 years	35 to 44 years	45 to 54 years	55 to 64 years	65 years and over	Age unknown
Native white:						
Native parentage	288,745	455,128	317,014	182,648	136,147	15,820
Foreign or mixed parentage	141,347	221,386	132,798	48,668	22,124	1,319
Foreign-born white	157,284	278,254	217,026	130,725	99,748	5,718

Source: "Negro Population and Classes of the White Population, Classified by Age Periods, by Sections and Southern Divisions: 1910." U.S. Bureau of the Census, *Negro Population, 1790-1915*, p. 176.

★ 1878 ★

Racial Composition

Black and White Population of States Classified by Number of Blacks Per 100,000 Whites, 1900 and 1910

NEGROES TO 100,000 WHITES	STATES HAVING SPECIFIED NUMBER OF NEGROES TO 100,000 WHITES IN THE POPULATION									
	Number of states		Population							
			1910		1900		Percentage distribution			
							1910		1900	
	1910	1900	Negro	White	Negro	White	Negro	White	Negro	White
Total	49	49	9,827,763	81,731,957	8,833,994	66,809,196	100.0	100.0	100.0	100.0
Under 1,000	18	18	89,708	18,661,465	64,733	14,769,385	0.9	22.8	0.7	22.1
1,000 to 5,000	13	14	831,176	39,388,140	728,557	33,488,231	8.5	48.2	8.2	50.1
5,000 to 10,000	3	2	359,237	5,736,280	216,918	3,615,047	3.7	7.0	2.5	5.4
10,000 to 20,000	2	2	292,837	2,190,053	315,403	2,016,286	3.0	2.7	3.6	3.0
20,000 to 30,000	3	2	1,395,387	5,978,919	855,786	3,379,093	14.2	7.3	9.7	5.1
30,000 to 40,000	2	2	537,337	1,367,154	847,099	2,484,766	5.5	1.7	9.6	3.7
40,000 to 50,000	2	2	1,368,939	2,890,320	711,171	1,455,135	13.9	3.5	8.1	2.2
50,000 to 75,000	2	1	1,216,951	1,672,466	660,722	1,192,855	12.4	2.0	7.5	1.8
75,000 to 100,000	2	4	1,890,861	2,372,888	2,743,654	3,209,391	19.2	2.9	31.1	4.8
100,000 and over	2	2	1,845,330	1,465,272	1,689,951	1,199,007	18.8	1.8	19.1	1.8
Total	49	49	9,827,763	81,731,957	8,833,994	66,809,196	100.0	100.0	100.0	100.0
Under 1,000	18	18	89,708	18,661,465	64,733	14,769,385	0.9	22.8	0.7	22.1
1,000 or more	31	31	9,738,055	63,070,492	8,769,261	52,039,811	99.1	77.2	99.3	77.9
Under 5,000	31	32	920,884	58,049,605	793,290	48,257,616	9.4	71.0	9.0	72.2
5,000 or more	18	17	8,906,879	23,682,352	8,040,704	18,551,580	90.6	29.0	91.0	27.8
Under 10,000	34	34	1,280,121	63,785,885	1,010,208	51,872,663	13.0	78.0	11.4	77.6
10,000 or more	15	15	8,547,642	17,946,072	7,823,786	14,936,533	87.0	22.0	88.6	22.4
Under 20,000	36	36	1,572,958	65,984,938	1,325,611	53,888,949	16.0	80.7	15.0	80.7
20,000 or more	13	13	8,254,805	15,747,019	7,508,383	12,920,247	84.0	19.3	85.0	19.3

[Continued]

★ 1878 ★

Black and White Population of States Classified by Number of Blacks Per 100,000 Whites, 1900 and 1910

[Continued]

NEGROES TO 100,000 WHITES	STATES HAVING SPECIFIED NUMBER OF NEGROES TO 100,000 WHITES IN THE POPULATION									
	Number of states		Population							
			1910		1900		Percentage distribution			
							1910		1900	
	1910	1900	Negro	White	Negro	White	Negro	White	Negro	White
Under 30,000	39	38	2,968,345	71,963,857	2,181,397	57,268,042	30.2	88.0	24.7	85.7
30,000 or more	10	11	6,859,418	9,768,100	6,652,597	9,541,154	69.8	12.0	75.3	14.3
Under 40,000	41	40	3,505,682	73,331,011	3,028,496	59,752,808	35.7	89.7	34.3	89.4
40,000 or more	8	9	6,322,081	8,400,946	5,805,498	7,056,388	64.3	10.3	65.7	10.6
Under 50,000	43	42	4,874,621	76,221,331	3,739,667	61,207,943	49.6	93.3	42.3	91.6
50,000 or more	6	7	4,953,142	5,510,626	5,094,327	5,601,253	50.4	6.7	57.7	8.4
Under 75,000	45	43	6,091,572	77,893,797	4,400,389	62,400,798	62.0	95.3	49.8	93.4
75,000 or more	4	6	3,736,191	3,838,160	4,433,605	4,408,398	38.0	4.7	50.2	6.6
Under 100,000	47	47	7,982,433	80,266,685	7,144,043	65,610,189	81.2	98.2	80.9	98.2
100,000 or more	2	2	1,845,330	1,465,272	1,689,951	1,199,007	18.8	1.8	19.1	1.8

Source: "Negro and White Population of States Classified According to Number of Negroes Per 100,000 Whites: 1910 and 1900." U.S. Bureau of the Census, *Negro Population, 1790-1915*, p. 50.

★ 1879 ★

Racial Composition

Black, White, and Other Population at Each Census, and Changes Each Decade, 1790-1910

YEAR	POPULATION[1]										
	All classes	Negro		White	All other	Increase during preceding 10 years					
						Number			Per cent		
		Number	Percent			All classes	Negro	White	All classes	Negro	White
1910	91,972,266	9,827,763	10.7	81,731,957	412,546	15,977,691	993,769	14,922,761	21.0	11.2	22.3
1900	75,994,575	8,833,994	11.6	66,809,196	351,385	13,046,861	1,345,318	11,707,938	20.7	18.0	21.2
1890	62,947,714	7,488,676	11.9	55,101,258	357,780	12,791,931	907,883	11,698,288	25.5	13.8	27.0
1880	50,155,783	6,580,793	13.1	43,402,970	172,020	11,597,412	1,700,784	9,813,593	30.1	34.9	29.2
1870	38,558,371	4,880,009	12.7	33,589,377	88,985	7,115,050	438,179	6,666,840	22.6	9.9	24.8
1860	31,443,321	4,441,830	14.1	26,922,537	78,954	8,251,445	803,022	7,369,469	35.6	22.1	37.7
1850	23,191,876	3,638,808	15.7	19,553,068	-	6,122,423	765,160	5,357,263	35.9	26.6	37.7
1840	17,069,453	2,873,648	16.8	14,195,805	-	4,203,433	545,006	3,658,427	32.7	23.4	34.7
1830	12,866,020	2,328,642	18.1	10,537,378	-	3,227,567	556,986	2,670,581	33.5	31.4	33.9
1820	9,638,453	1,771,656	18.4	7,866,797	-	2,398,572	393,848	2,004,724	33.1	28.6	34.2
1810	7,239,881	1,377,808	19.0	5,862,073	-	1,931,398	375,771	1,555,627	36.4	37.5	36.1

[Continued]

★ 1879 ★

Black, White, and Other Population at Each Census, and Changes Each Decade, 1790-1910

[Continued]

YEAR	POPULATION[1]										
	All classes	Negro		White	All other	Increase during preceding 10 years					
						Number			Per cent		
		Number	Percent			All classes	Negro	White	All classes	Negro	White
1800	5,308,483	1,002,037	18.9	4,306,446	-	1,379,269	244,829	1,134,440	35.1	32.3	35.8
1790	3,929,214	757,208	19.3	3,172,006	-	-	-	-	-	-	-

Source: "Negro, White, and Other Population At Each Census, and Decennial Increase in Each Decade: 1790-1910." U.S. Bureau of the Census, *Negro Population, 1790-1915*, p. 25.

★ 1880 ★

Racial Composition

Increase in Population by Race, Divisions, and States, 1900-1910, and 30-Year Periods, 1790-1910

DIVISION AND STATE	INCREASE OF NEGRO AND WHITE POPULATION											
	1900-1910				1880-1910		1850-1880		1820-1850		1790-1820	
	Negro		White									
	Number	Percent	Number	Percent	Negro	White	Negro	White	Negro	White	Negro	White
UNITED STATES	993,769	11.2	14,922,761	22.3	3,246,970	38,328,987	2,941,985	23,849,902	1,867,152	11,686,271	1,014,448	4,694,791
GEOGRAPHIC DIVISIONS:												
New England	7,207	12.2	953,488	17.3	26,381	2,511,725	16,904	1,263,694	2,094	1,065,951	3,940	646,723
Middle Atlantic	91,949	28.2	3,769,590	24.9	228,378	8,575,397	62,751	4,533,061	36,944	3,161,946	39,360	1,701,853
East North Central	42,994	16.7	2,217,569	14.1	117,538	6,915,575	138,103	6,533,982	37,504	3,693,037	7,691	785,028
West North Central	4,753	2.0	1,285,804	12.8	40,339	5,402,245	111,911	5,159,453	79,843	733,906	10,569	56,017
South Atlantic	383,471	10.3	1,365,545	20.4	1,171,286	3,417,491	1,080,331	1,835,893	587,472	1,030,555	599,937	609,320
East South Central	152,627	6.1	709,479	14.1	727,517	2,096,733	802,206	1,417,112	834,733	1,338,049	271,735	809,386
West South Central	290,360	17.1	1,950,426	40.9	896,721	4,477,769	719,168	1,672,008	287,321	485,250	81,216	86,464
Mountain	5,877	37.7	940,600	59.5	16,445	1,905,634	4,950	541,966	72	72,855	-	-
Pacific	14,531	99.1	1,730,260	75.4	22,365	3,026,418	5,661	892,733	1,169	104,722	-	-
NEW ENGLAND:												
Maine	44	3.3	47,769	6.9	-88	93,143	95	65,039	427	284,407	391	201,404
New Hampshire	-98	-14.8	19,115	4.7	-121	83,677	165	28,773	-266	74,081	-2	102,278
Vermont	795	96.2	11,527	3.4	564	23,080	339	17,816	-185	78,324	632	149,924
Massachusetts	6,081	19.0	555,162	20.0	19,358	1,561,144	9,633	778,332	2,324	468,903	1,277	143,223
Rhode Island	437	4.8	113,442	27.1	3,041	262,553	2,818	126,064	68	64,418	-753	14,987
Connecticut	-52	-0.3	206,473	23.1	3,627	488,128	3,854	247,670	-273	95,818	2,395	34,907
MIDDLE ATLANTIC:												
New York	34,959	35.2	1,809,964	25.3	69,087	3,950,823	16,035	1,967,697	9,702	1,714,880	13,389	1,019,303
New Jersey	19,916	28.5	633,577	35.0	50,907	1,353,877	14,807	626,508	4,029	207,951	5,832	87,604
Pennsylvania	37,074	23.6	1,326,049	21.6	108,384	3,270,697	31,909	1,938,856	23,213	1,239,115	20,139	594,946
EAST NORTH CENTRAL:												
Ohio	14,551	15.0	594,693	14.6	31,552	1,536,977	54,621	1,162,870	20,556	1,378,339	4,723	576,711
Indiana	2,815	4.9	181,459	7.4	21,092	701,163	27,966	961,644	9,842	831,396	1,420	145,758
Illinois	23,971	28.2	792,089	16.7	62,681	2,495,811	40,932	2,185,117	4,062	792,197	1,374	53,837
Michigan	1,299	8.2	386,684	16.1	2,015	1,170,687	12,517	1,219,489	2,409	386,349	174	8,722
Wisconsin	358	14.1	262,644	12.8	198	1,010,937	2,067	1,004,862	635	304,756	-	-
WEST NORTH CENTRAL:												
Minnesota	2,125	42.9	322,191	18.5	5,520	1,282,343	1,525	770,846	39	6,038	-	-
Iowa	2,280	18.0	-9,476	-0.4	5,457	594,591	9,183	1,422,719	333	191,881	-	-
Missouri	-3,782	-2.3	190,089	6.5	12,102	1,112,106	55,310	1,430,822	79,471	535,987	10,569	56,017
North Dakota	331	115.7	258,143	82.8	504	533,663			-	-	-	-
South Dakota	352	75.7	183,057	48.1	529	466,816						
Nebraska	1,420	22.7	123,767	11.7	5,304	730,529	2,385	449,764	-	-	-	-
Kansas	2,927	3.9	218,033	15.4	10,923	682,197	43,107	952,155	-	-	-	-

[Continued]

★ 1880 ★

Increase in Population by Race, Divisions, and States, 1900-1910, and 30-Year Periods, 1790-1910

[Continued]

DIVISION AND STATE	INCREASE OF NEGRO AND WHITE POPULATION													
	1900-1910				1880-1910		1850-1880		1820-1850		1790-1820	
	Negro		White									
	Number	Percent	Number	Percent	Negro	White	Negro	White	Negro	White	Negro	White
SOUTH ATLANTIC:												
Delaware	484	1.6	17,125	11.1	4,739	50,942	6,079	48,991	2,896	15,887	4,681	8,972
Maryland	-2,814	-1.2	110,215	11.6	22,020	337,946	45,139	306,750	17,964	157,720	36,048	51,574
District of Columbia	7,744	8.9	44,596	23.3	34,850	118,122	45,850	80,065	3,321	15,327	10,425	22,614
Virginia	10,374	1.6	196,954	16.5	39,480	508,951	104,755	-13,942	64,830	291,465	156,538	161,218
West Virginia	20,674	47.5	241,584	26.4	38,287	564,280	25,886	592,537	-	-	-	-
North Carolina	73,374	11.7	236,908	18.7	166,566	633,269	215,266	314,214	96,382	133,828	114,082	130,996
South Carolina	53,522	6.8	121,354	21.8	231,511	288,056	210,388	116,542	128,643	37,123	156,406	97,262
Georgia	142,174	13.7	250,508	21.2	451,854	614,896	340,520	295,334	233,194	332,002	121,757	136,684
Florida	77,939	33.8	146,301	49.2	181,979	301,029	86,448	95,402	40,242	47,203	-	-
EAST SOUTH CENTRAL:												
Kentucky	-23,050	-8.1	165,642	8.9	-9,795	650,772	50,459	615,766	91,501	326,587	116,947	373,693
Tennessee	-7,155	-1.5	171,246	11.1	69,937	572,601	157,270	381,995	163,037	416,857	79,066	308,066
Alabama	80,975	9.8	227,680	22.7	308,179	566,647	254,994	235,671	302,659	341,063	42,450	85,451
Mississippi	101,857	11.2	144,911	22.6	359,196	306,713	339,483	183,680	277,536	253,542	33,272	42,176
WEST SOUTH CENTRAL:												
Arkansas	76,035	20.7	186,446	19.7	232,225	539,495	162,958	429,342	182,731	181,624	1,676	12,597
Louisiana	63,070	9.7	211,474	29.0	230,219	486,132	221,384	199,463	46,032	149,592	79,540	73,867
Oklahoma	81,928	147.1	774,327	115.5	137,612	1,444,531	-	-	-	-	-	-
Texas	69,327	11.2	778,179	32.1	296,665	2,007,611	334,826	1,043,203	58,558	154,034	-	-
MOUNTAIN:												
Montana	311	20.4	134,297	59.3	1,488	325,195	346	35,385	-	-	-	-
Idaho	358	122.2	164,726	106.6	598	290,208	53	29,013	-	-	-	-
Wyoming	1,295	137.8	51,267	57.6	1,937	120,881	120,298	19,437	-	-	-	-
Colorado	2,883	33.6	254,369	48.1	9,018	592,289	2,435	191,126	-	-	-	-
New Mexico	18	1.1	124,387	69.0	613	195,873	993	47,196	23	61,525	-	-
Arizona	161	8.7	78,565	84.6	1,854	136,308	155	35,160	-	-	-	-
Utah	472	70.2	94,118	34.5	912	224,160	182	131,093	50	11,330	-	-
Nevada	379	282.8	38,871	109.8	25	20,720	488	53,556	-	-	-	-
PACIFIC:												
Washington	3,544	141.0	612,807	123.5	5,733	1,041,912	325	67,190	-	-	-	-
Oregon	387	35.0	260,508	66.0	1,005	492,015	280	149,988	207	13,087	-	-
California	10,600	96.0	856,945	61.1	15,627	1,492,491	5,056	675,546	962	91,635	-	-

Source: "Negro and White Increase, by Divisions and States: Decennial, 1900- 1910, and by 30-Year Periods, 1790-1910." U.S. Bureau of the Census, *Negro Population, 1790-1915*, p. 37. *Note:* 1. Dakota Territory.

★ 1881 ★

Racial Composition

Number of Blacks to 100,000 Whites, at Each Census, by Divisions and States, 1790-1910 - I

DIVISION AND STATE	NUMBER OF NEGROES TO 100,000 WHITES						
	1910	1900	1890	1880	1870	1860	1850
UNITED STATES	12,024	13,223	13,591	15,162	14,528	16,499	18,610
GEOGRAPHIC DIVISIONS:							
New England	1,023	1,069	958	1,006	918	794	851
Middle Atlantic	2,213	2,157	1,807	1,839	1,709	1,792	2,196
East North Central	1,678	1,641	1,562	1,665	1,452	929	1,009
West North Central	2,138	2,364	2,588	3,401	3,842	5,896	11,446

[Continued]

★ 1881 ★

Number of Blacks to 100,000 Whites, at Each Census, by Divisions and States, 1790-1910 - I

[Continued]

DIVISION AND STATE	NUMBER OF NEGROES TO 100,000 WHITES						
	1910	1900	1890	1880	1870	1860	1850
South Atlantic	50,950	55,607	58,344	63,196	60,978	62,273	66,030
East South Central	46,096	49,553	49,233	52,630	49,820	53,091	50,114
West South Central	29,524	35,507	41,316	48,478	57,403	58,463	64,462
Mountain	852	987	1,161	817	515	143	99
Pacific	726	639	804	685	793	1,098	1,116
NEW ENGLAND:							
Maine	184	191	181	224	257	212	233
New Hampshire	131	161	163	198	183	152	164
Vermont	458	241	283	319	280	226	229
Massachusetts	1,144	1,154	1,000	1,060	966	786	920
Rhode Island	1,790	2,170	2,188	2,404	2,347	2,316	2,551
Connecticut	1,381	1,706	1,677	1,891	1,833	1,911	2,119
MIDDLE ATLANTIC:							
New York	1,497	1,387	1,183	1,298	1,203	1,279	1,610
New Jersey	3,670	3,854	3,411	3,558	3,502	3,918	5,166
Pennsylvania	2,597	2,554	2,090	2,038	1,889	1,999	2,375
EAST NORTH CENTRAL:							
Ohio	2,394	2,387	2,430	2,563	2,429	1,593	1,293
Indiana	2,285	2,339	2,106	2,023	1,483	854	1,153
Illinois	1,973	1,797	1,513	1,530	1,145	448	643
Michigan	614	659	734	935	1,015	924	654
Wisconsin	125	124	145	206	201	151	208
WEST NORTH CENTRAL:							
Minnesota	344	285	284	201	173	153	646
Iowa	678	572	562	589	485	159	174
Missouri	5,022	5,475	5,940	7,185	7,365	11,143	15,209
North Dakota	108	92	204				
South Dakota	145	122	165				
Nebraska	651	593	851	530	646	286	-
Kansas	3,306	3,672	3,611	4,527	4,939	589	-
SOUTH ATLANTIC:							
Delaware	18,224	19,936	20,266	22,006	22,299	23,874	28,612
Maryland	21,856	24,681	26,093	29,010	28,966	33,170	39,501
District of Columbia	39,998	45,268	48,852	50,503	49,167	23,560	36,230
Virginia	48,287	55,390	62,290	71,705	72,019	52,412	58,880
West Virginia	5,547	4,753	4,478	4,369	4,240	-	-
North Carolina	46,507	49,420	53,158	61,261	57,725	57,390	57,142
South Carolina	123,070	140,249	149,117	154,519	143,549	141,545	143,480
Georgia	82,203	87,600	87,781	88,766	85,322	78,725	73,741
Florida	69,577	77,600	73,875	88,840	95,453	80,618	85,253

[Continued]

★ 1881 ★

Number of Blacks to 100,000 Whites, at Each Census, by Divisions and States, 1790-1910 - I

[Continued]

DIVISION AND STATE	NUMBER OF NEGROES TO 100,000 WHITES						
	1910	1900	1890	1880	1870	1860	1850
EAST SOUTH CENTRAL:							
Kentucky	12,902	15,288	16,855	19,711	20,225	25,685	29,024
Tennessee	27,643	31,181	32,221	35,400	34,433	34,234	32,488
Alabama	73,914	82,636	81,381	90,625	91,201	83,183	80,914
Mississippi	128,415	141,552	136,287	135,647	116,011	123,596	105,103
WEST SOUTH CENTRAL:							
Arkansas	39,158	38,838	37,755	35,614	33,738	34,324	29,415
Louisiana	75,856	89,199	100,143	106,309	100,592	98,018	102,654
Oklahoma[2]	9,526	8,309	12,523	-	-	-	-
Texas	21,531	25,579	27,960	32,858	44,887	43,460	38,016
MOUNTAIN:							
Montana	509	673	1,167	978	1,000	-	-
Idaho	204	190	245	183	565	-	-
Wyoming	1,593	1,056	1,554	1,533	2,097	-	-
Colorado	1,462	1,620	1,536	1,274	1,163	134	-
New Mexico	534	893	1,369	934	190	103	36
Arizona	1,172	1,989	2,435	441	271	-	-
Utah	312	247	286	163	137	147	441
Nevada	691	378	619	911	916	661	-
PACIFIC:							
Washington	546	567	470	484	933	269	-
Oregon	228	280	393	299	398	245	1,582
California	958	787	1,018	784	855	1,264	1,050

Source: "Number of Negroes to 100,000 Whites, At Each Census, by Divisions and States: 1790-1910." U.S. Bureau of the Census, *Negro Population, 1790- 1915*, p. 52. *Notes:* 1. Dakota Territory. 2. Includes Indian Territory in 1900 and 1890.

★ 1882 ★

Racial Composition

Number of Blacks to 100,000 Whites, at Each Census, by Divisions and States, 1790-1910 - II

DIVISION AND STATE	NUMBER OF NEGROES TO 100,000 WHITES					
	1840	1830	1820	1810	1800	1790
UNITED STATES	20,252	22,110	22,521	23,504	23,268	23,872
GEOGRAPHIC DIVISIONS:						
New England	1,024	1,106	1,277	1,371	1,536	1,712
Middle Atlantic	2,716	2,980	3,440	4,261	4,814	5,554
East North Central	1,014	1,092	980	1,285	1,261	-

[Continued]

★ 1882 ★

Number of Blacks to 100,000 Whites, at Each Census, by Divisions and States, 1790-1910 - II

[Continued]

DIVISION AND STATE	NUMBER OF NEGROES TO 100,000 WHITES					
	1840	1830	1820	1810	1800	1790
West North Central	16,358	22,353	18,867	21,002	-	-
South Atlantic	68,614	72,256	71,233	67,800	60,253	57,153
East South Central	47,578	38,161	31,920	25,829	21,190	17,542
West South Central	90,970	113,815	93,930	123,124	-	-
Mountain	-	-	-	-	-	-
Pacific	-	-	-	-	-	-
NEW ENGLAND:						
Maine	271	299	312	425	542	560
New Hampshire	189	226	323	454	470	558
Vermont	251	315	384	345	362	318
Massachusetts	1,189	1,168	1,305	1,448	1,549	1,463
Rhode Island	3,071	3,822	4,553	5,077	5,630	6,755
Connecticut	2,691	2,787	2,981	2,650	2,567	2,398
MIDDLE ATLANTIC:						
New York	2,103	2,399	2,952	4,392	5,616	8,270
New Jersey	6,177	6,846	7,772	8,240	8,658	8,346
Pennsylvania	2,859	2,926	2,984	2,960	2,776	2,423
EAST NORTH CENTRAL:						
Ohio	1,155	1,031	819	830	748	-
Indiana	1,056	1,070	974	2,637	5,577	-
Illinois	832	1,537	2,552	6,791	-	-
Michigan	334	935	1,995	3,118	-	-
Wisconsin	637	-	-	-	-	-
WEST NORTH CENTRAL:						
Minnesota	-	-	-	-	-	-
Iowa	438	-	-	-	-	-
Missouri	18,467	22,353	18,867	21,002	-	-
North Dakota	-	-	-	-	-	-
South Dakota	-	-	-	-	-	-
Nebraska	-	-	-	-	-	-
Kansas	-	-	-	-	-	-
SOUTH ATLANTIC:						
Delaware	33,340	33,241	31,596	31,273	28,928	27,610
Maryland	47,710	53,565	56,539	61,954	57,886	53,237
District of Columbia	42,584	44,520	46,100	49,406	40,006	-
Virginia	67,321	74,479	76,580	76,714	71,152	69,098
West Virginia	-	-	-	-	-	-
North Carolina	55,386	56,074	52,392	47,578	41,549	36,622
South Carolina	129,423	125,385	111,734	93,801	76,093	77,683
Georgia	69,586	74,128	79,875	73,596	59,089	56,087

[Continued]

★ 1882 ★

Number of Blacks to 100,000 Whites, at Each Census, by Divisions and States, 1790-1910 - II

[Continued]

DIVISION AND STATE	NUMBER OF NEGROES TO 100,000 WHITES					
	1840	1830	1820	1810	1800	1790
Florida	94,958	88,904	-	-	-	-
EAST SOUTH CENTRAL:						
Kentucky	32,118	32,857	29,780	25,375	22,839	20,519
Tennessee	29,437	27,281	24,367	21,240	15,140	11,838
Alabama	76,248	62,562	49,678	-	-	-
Mississippi	109,774	93,945	78,888	75,261	70,882	-
WEST SOUTH CENTRAL:						
Arkansas	26,434	18,375	13,305	-	-	-
Louisiana	122,402	141,208	107,680	123,124	-	-
Oklahoma[2]	-	-	-	-	-	-
Texas	-	-	-	-	-	-
MOUNTAIN:						
Montana	-	-	-	-	-	-
Idaho	-	-	-	-	-	-
Wyoming	-	-	-	-	-	-
Colorado	-	-	-	-	-	-
New Mexico	-	-	-	-	-	-
Arizona	-	-	-	-	-	-
Utah	-	-	-	-	-	-
Nevada	-	-	-	-	-	-
PACIFIC:						
Washington	-	-	-	-	-	-
Oregon	-	-	-	-	-	-
California	-	-	-	-	-	-

Source: "Number of Negroes to 100,000 Whites, At Each Census, by Divisions and States: 1790-1910." U.S. Bureau of the Census, *Negro Population, 1790- 1915*, p. 52. *Notes:* 1. Dakota Territory. 2. Includes Indian Territory in 1900 and 1890.

★ 1883 ★

Racial Composition

Percent Black in the Population 21 Years of Age and Over by Divisions and States, 1900 and 1910

DIVISION AND STATE	PERCENTAGE NEGRO AMONG MALES 21 YEARS OF AGE AND OVER	
	1910	1900
UNITED STATES	9.1	9.7
GEOGRAPHIC DIVISIONS:		
New England	1.1	1.1
Middle Atlantic	2.3	2.3
East North Central	1.9	1.8
West North Central	2.4	2.4
South Atlantic	31.1	32.7
East South Central	30.6	31.6
West South Central	21.6	24.3
Mountain	1.0	1.2
Pacific	0.7	0.6
NEW ENGLAND:		
Maine	0.2	0.2
New Hampshire	0.1	0.2
Vermont	0.9	0.3
Massachusetts	1.2	1.2
Rhode Island	1.9	2.2
Connecticut	1.4	1.6
MIDDLE ATLANTIC:		
New York	1.6	1.4
New Jersey	3.7	3.9
Pennsylvania	2.8	2.8
EAST NORTH CENTRAL:		
Ohio	2.6	2.6
Indiana	2.5	2.5
Illinois	2.3	2.1
Michigan	0.7	0.7
Wisconsin	0.2	0.2
WEST NORTH CENTRAL:		
Minnesota	0.5	0.4
Iowa	0.8	0.7
Missouri	5.4	5.4
North Dakota	0.2	0.1
South Dakota	0.2	0.2
Nebraska	0.9	0.8
Kansas	3.5	3.6
SOUTH ATLANTIC:		
Delaware	14.6	15.5
Maryland	17.4	18.8
District of Columbia	26.6	27.5
Virginia	30.5	32.6
West Virginia	6.7	6.0

[Continued]

★ 1883 ★

Percent Black in the Population 21 Years of Age and Over by Divisions and States, 1900 and 1910

[Continued]

DIVISION AND STATE	PERCENTAGE NEGRO AMONG MALES 21 YEARS OF AGE AND OVER	
	1910	1900
North Carolina	29.0	30.4
South Carolina	50.5	54.0
Georgia	43.0	44.5
Florida	41.9	44.0
EAST SOUTH CENTRAL:		
Kentucky	12.5	13.7
Tennessee	21.6	23.0
Alabama	41.7	43.8
Mississippi	54.7	56.7
WEST SOUTH CENTRAL:		
Arkansas	28.1	27.8
Louisiana	42.0	45.2
Oklahoma	8.2	6.8
Texas	16.6	18.6
MOUNTAIN:		
Montana	0.5	0.7
Idaho	0.3	0.2
Wyoming	2.1	1.3
Colorado	1.6	1.7
New Mexico	0.7	1.4
Arizona	1.0	2.5
Utah	0.5	0.5
Nevada	0.6	0.4
PACIFIC:		
Washington	0.7	0.6
Oregon	0.3	0.4
California	0.9	0.7

Source: "Percentage Negro in the Population 21 Years of Age and Over, by Divisions and States: 1910 and 1900." U.S. Bureau of the Census, *Negro Population, 1790-1915*, p. 190.

★ 1884 ★

Racial Composition

Percent Black of Population Inside and Outside Metropolitan Areas: 1960, 1970, 1975

Data shown according to the definition and size of metropolitan area in 1970.

Type of residence	1960	1970	1975
United States	10.6	11.1	11.3
Metropolitan areas[1]	10.7	11.9	12.5
Central cities	16.4	20.5	22.6
Central cities in metropolitan areas of-			
1,000,000 or more	18.8	25.2	27.6
Less than 1,000,000	13.2	14.9	16.8
Suburbs	4.8	4.6	5.0
Suburbs in metropolitan areas of-			
1,000,000 or more	4.0	4.5	5.1
Less than 1,000,000	5.9	4.8	4.8
Nonmetropolitan areas	10.3	9.1	8.8
In counties designated metropolitan since 1970	(X)	7.7	(NA)

Source: "Black as a Percent of Total Population Inside and Outside Metropolitan Areas, by Size of Metropolitan Area: 1960, 1970, and 1975," U.S. Department of Commerce, Bureau of the Census. *The Social and Economic Status of the Black Population in the United States: An Historical View, 1790-1978,* p. 15. Primary source: U.S. Department of Commerce, Bureau of the Census. Current Population Survey. *Notes:* X Not applicable. NA Not available. Standard metropolitan areas as a statistical concept were first used in the 1950 census. However, data for 1950 have not been reconstructed according to the 1970 definition of metropolitan areas. 1. Excludes Middlesex and Somerset Counties in New Jersey.

★ 1885 ★

Racial Composition

Percent Distribution of the Population by Race, Section, and Division, 1920 and 1930

STATE	Negro percentage of total population	NEGRO POPULATION			WHITE POPULATION		
		Number	Cumulated by States		Number	Cumulated by States	
			Number	Percent		Number	Percent
Mississippi	50.2	1,009,718	1,009,718	8.5	996,856	996,856	0.9
South Carolina	45.6	793,681	1,803,399	15.2	944,040	1,940,896	1.8
Louisiana	36.9	776,326	2,579,725	21.7	1,318,160	3,259,056	3.0
Georgia	36.8	1,071,125	3,650,850	30.7	1,836,974	5,096,030	4.7
Alabama	35.7	944,834	4,595,684	38.6	1,700,775	6,796,805	6.2
Florida	29.4	431,828	5,027,512	42.3	1,035,205	7,832,010	7.2
North Carolina	29.0	918,647	5,946,159	50.0	2,234,948	10,066,958	9.2

[Continued]

★ 1885 ★

Percent Distribution of the Population by Race, Section, and Division, 1920 and 1930

[Continued]

STATE	Negro percentage of total population	NEGRO POPULATION			WHITE POPULATION		
		Number	Cumulated by States		Number	Cumulated by States	
			Number	Percent		Number	Percent
District of Columbia	27.1	132,068	6,078,227	51.1	353,914	10,420,872	9.6
Virginia	26.8	650,165	6,728,392	56.6	1,779,406	12,191,277	11.2
Arkansas	25.8	478,463	7,206,855	60.6	1,374,906	13,566,183	12.5
Tennessee	18.3	477,646	7,684,501	64.6	2,138,619	15,704,802	14.4
Maryland	16.9	276,379	7,960,880	66.9	1,354,170	17,058,972	15.7
Texas	14.7	854,964	8,815,844	74.1	4,283,491	21,342,463	19.6
Delaware	13.7	32,602	8,848,446	74.4	205,694	21,548,157	19.8
Kentucky	8.6	226,040	9,074,486	76.3	2,388,364	23,936,521	22.0
Oklahoma	7.2	172,198	9,246,684	77.8	7,123,424	26,059,945	23.9
West Virginia	6.6	114,893	9,361,577	78.7	1,613,934	27,673,879	25.4
Missouri	6.2	223,840	9,585,417	80.6	3,398,887	31,072,766	28.5
New Jersey	5.2	208,828	9,794,245	82.4	3,829,209	34,901,975	32.1
Ohio	4.7	309,304	10,103,549	85.0	6,331,136	41,233,111	37.9
Pennsylvania	4.5	431,257	10,534,806	88.6	9,192,602	50,425,713	46.3
Illinois	4.3	328,972	10,863,778	91.4	7,266,361	57,692,074	53.0
Indiana	3.5	111,982	10,975,760	92.3	3,116,136	60,808,210	55.9
Kansas	3.5	66,344	11,042,104	92.9	1,792,847	62,601,057	57.5
Michigan	3.5	169,453	11,211,557	94.3	4,650,171	67,251,228	61.8
New York	3.3	412,814	11,624,371	97.8	12,150,293	79,401,521	72.9
Arizona	2.5	10,749	11,635,120	97.8	264,378	79,665,899	73.2
Connecticut	1.8	29,354	11,664,474	98.1	1,576,673	81,242,572	74.6
California	1.4	81,048	11,745,522	98.8	5,040,247	86,282,819	79.3
Rhode Island	1.4	9,913	11,755,435	98.9	677,016	86,959,835	79.9
Massachusetts	1.2	52,365	11,807,800	99.3	4,192,926	91,152,761	83.7
Colorado	1.1	11,828	11,819,628	99.4	961,117	92,113,878	84.6
Nebraska	1.0	13,752	11,833,380	99.5	1,353,702	93,467,580	85.9
Iowa	.7	17,380	11,850,760	99.7	2,448,382	95,915,962	88.1
New Mexico	.7	2,850	11,853,610	99.7	331,755	96,247,717	88.4
Nevada	.6	516	11,854,126	99.7	81,425	96,329,142	88.5
Wyoming	.6	1,250	11,855,376	99.7	214,067	96,543,209	88.7
Minnesota	.4	9,445	11,864,821	99.8	2,538,973	90,082,182	91.0
Washington	.4	6,840	11,871,661	99.8	1,521,099	100,603,281	92.4
Wisconsin	.4	10,739	11,882,400	99.9	2,913,859	103,517,140	95.1
Idaho	.2	668	11,883,068	99.9	437,562	103,954,702	95.5
Montana	.2	1,256	11,884,324	99.9	517,327	104,472,029	96.0
New Hampshire	.2	790	11,885,114	99.9	464,350	104,936,379	96.4
Oregon	.2	2,234	11,887,348	100.0	937,029	105,873,408	97.3

[Continued]

★ 1885 ★

Percent Distribution of the Population by Race, Section, and Division, 1920 and 1930

[Continued]

STATE	Negro percentage of total population	NEGRO POPULATION			WHITE POPULATION		
		Number	Cumulated by States		Number	Cumulated by States	
			Number	Percent		Number	Percent
Utah	.2	1,108	11,888,456	100.0	495,955	106,369,363	97.7
Vermont	.2	568	11,889,024	100.0	358,965	106,728,328	98.0
Maine	.1	1,096	11,890,120	100.0	795,183	107,523,511	96.8
North Dakota	.1	377	11,890,497	100.0	671,243	108,194,754	99.4
South Dakota	.1	646	11,891,143	100.0	669,453	108,864,207	100.0

Source: "Percent Distribution, by Racial Classes, for Sections, and Divisions: 1930 and 1920." U.S. Bureau of the Census, *Negroes in the United States, 1920-1932*, p. 14.

★ 1886 ★

Racial Composition

Percentage Black in the Population At Each Census by Divisions and States, 1790-1910 - I

DIVISION AND STATE	PERCENTAGE NEGRO IN THE POPULATION						
	1910	1900	1890	1880	1870	1860	1850
UNITED STATES	10.7	11.6	11.9	13.1	12.7	14.1	15.7
GEOGRAPHIC DIVISIONS:							
New England	1.0	1.1	0.9	1.0	0.9	0.8	0.8
Middle Atlantic	2.2	2.1	1.8	1.8	1.7	0.8	2.1
East North Central	1.6	1.6	1.6	1.6	1.4	0.9	1.0
West North Central	2.1	2.3	2.5	3.3	3.7	5.6	10.3
South Atlantic	33.7	35.7	36.8	38.7	37.9	38.4	39.8
East South Central	31.5	33.1	33.0	34.5	33.2	34.7	33.4
West South Central	22.6	25.9	29.1	32.6	36.4	36.9	39.2
Mountain	0.8	0.9	1.1	0.8	0.5	0.1	0.1
Pacific	0.7	0.6	0.7	0.6	0.7	1.0	1.1
NEW ENGLAND:							
Maine	0.2	0.2	0.2	0.2	0.2	0.2	0.2
New Hampshire	0.1	0.2	0.2	0.2	0.2	0.2	0.2
Vermont	0.5	0.2	0.3	0.3	0.3	0.2	0.2
Massachusetts	1.1	1.2	1.0	1.1	1.0	0.8	0.9
Rhode Island	1.8	2.1	2.1	2.4	2.3	2.3	2.5
Connecticut	1.4	1.7	1.6	1.8	1.8	1.9	2.1
MIDDLE ATLANTIC:							
New York	1.5	1.4	1.2	1.3	1.2	1.3	1.6
New Jersey	3.5	3.7	3.3	3.4	3.4	3.8	4.9
Pennsylvania	2.5	2.5	2.1	2.0	1.9	2.0	2.3

[Continued]

★ 1886 ★

Percentage Black in the Population At Each Census by Divisions and States, 1790-1910 - I

[Continued]

DIVISION AND STATE	PERCENTAGE NEGRO IN THE POPULATION						
	1910	1900	1890	1880	1870	1860	1850
EAST NORTH CENTRAL:							
Ohio	2.3	2.3	2.4	2.5	2.4	1.6	1.3
Indiana	2.2	2.3	2.1	2.0	1.5	0.9	1.1
Illinois	1.9	1.8	1.5	1.5	1.1	0.4	0.6
Michigan	0.6	0.6	0.7	0.9	1.0	0.9	0.6
Wisconsin	0.1	0.1	0.1	0.2	0.2	0.2	0.2
WEST NORTH CENTRAL:							
Minnesota	0.3	0.3	0.3	0.2	0.2	0.1	0.6
Iowa	0.7	0.6	0.6	0.6	0.5	0.2	0.2
Missouri	4.8	5.2	5.6	6.7	6.9	10.0	13.2
North Dakota	0.1	0.1	0.2				
South Dakota	0.1	0.1	0.2				
Nebraska	0.6	0.6	0.9	0.5	0.6	0.3	-
Kansas	3.2	3.5	3.5	4.3	4.7	0.6	-
SOUTH ATLANTIC:							
Delaware	15.4	16.6	16.9	18.0	18.2	19.3	22.2
Maryland	17.9	19.8	20.7	22.5	22.5	24.9	28.3
District of Columbia	28.5	31.1	32.8	33.6	33.0	19.1	26.6
Virginia	32.6	35.7	38.4	41.8	41.9	34.4	37.1
West Virginia	5.3	4.5	4.3	4.2	4.1	-	-
North Carolina	31.6	33.0	34.7	37.9	36.6	36.4	36.4
South Carolina	55.2	58.4	59.9	60.7	58.9	58.6	58.9
Georgia	45.1	46.7	46.7	47.0	46.0	44.0	42.4
Florida	41.0	43.6	42.4	47.0	48.8	44.6	46.0
EAST SOUTH CENTRAL:							
Kentucky	11.4	13.3	14.4	16.5	16.8	20.4	22.5
Tennessee	21.7	23.8	24.4	26.2	25.6	25.5	24.5
Alabama	42.5	45.2	44.8	47.5	47.7	45.4	44.7
Mississippi	56.2	58.5	57.6	57.5	53.7	55.3	51.2
WEST SOUTH CENTRAL:							
Arkansas	28.1	28.0	27.4	26.3	25.2	25.6	22.7
Louisiana	43.1	47.1	50.0	51.5	50.1	49.5	50.7
Oklahoma	8.3	7.0[2]	8.4[2]	-	-	-	-
Texas	17.7	20.4	21.8	24.7	31.0	30.3	27.5
MOUNTAIN:							
Montana	0.5	0.6	1.1	0.9	0.9	-	-
Idaho	0.2	0.2	0.2	0.1	0.4	-	-
Wyoming	1.5	1.0	1.5	1.4	2.0	-	-
Colorado	1.4	1.6	1.5	1.3	1.1	0.1	-
New Mexico	0.5	0.8	1.2	0.9	0.2	0.1	[2]

[Continued]

★ 1886 ★

Percentage Black in the Population At Each Census by Divisions and States, 1790-1910 - I

[Continued]

DIVISION AND STATE	PERCENTAGE NEGRO IN THE POPULATION						
	1910	1900	1890	1880	1870	1860	1850
Arizona	1.0	1.5	1.5	0.4	0.3	-	-
Utah	0.3	0.2	0.3	0.2	0.1	0.2	0.4
Nevada	0.6	0.3	0.5	0.8	0.8	0.7	-
PACIFIC:							
Washington	0.5	0.5	0.5	0.4	0.9	0.2	-
Oregon	0.2	0.3	0.4	0.3	0.4	0.3	1.6
California	0.9	0.7	0.9	0.7	0.8	1.1	1.0

Source: "Percentage Negro in the Population At Each Census, by Divisions and States: 1790-1910." U.S. Bureau of the Census, *Negro Population, 1790- 1915*, p. 51. *Notes:* 1. Dakota Territory. 2. Includes population of Indian Territory for 1900 and 1890. 3. Less than one-tenth of 1 per cent.

★ 1887 ★

Racial Composition

Percentage Black in the Population At Each Census by Divisions and States, 1790-1910 - II

DIVISION AND STATE	PERCENTAGE NEGRO IN THE POPULATION					
	1840	1830	1820	1810	1800	1790
UNITED STATES	16.8	18.1	18.4	19.0	18.9	19.3
GEOGRAPHIC DIVISIONS:						
New England	1.0	1.1	1.3	1.4	1.5	1.7
Middle Atlantic	2.6	2.9	3.3	4.1	4.6	5.3
East North Central	1.0	1.1	1.0	1.3	1.2	-
West North Central	14.1	18.3	15.9	17.4	-	-
South Atlantic	40.7	41.9	41.6	40.4	37.6	36.4
East South Central	32.2	27.6	24.2	20.5	17.5	14.9
West South Central	47.6	53.2	48.4	54.4	-	-
Mountain	-	-	-	-	-	-
Pacific	-	-	-	-	-	-
NEW ENGLAND:						
Maine	0.3	0.3	0.3	0.4	0.5	0.6
New Hampshire	0.2	0.2	0.3	0.5	0.5	0.6
Vermont	0.3	0.3	0.4	0.3	0.4	0.3
Massachusetts	1.2	1.2	1.3	1.4	1.5	1.4
Rhode Island	3.0	3.7	4.3	4.8	5.3	6.3
Connecticut	2.6	2.7	2.9	2.6	2.5	2.3
MIDDLE ATLANTIC:						
New York	2.1	2.3	2.9	4.2	5.3	7.6

[Continued]

★ 1887 ★

Percentage Black in the Population At Each Census by Divisions and States, 1790-1910 - II

[Continued]

DIVISION AND STATE	PERCENTAGE NEGRO IN THE POPULATION					
	1840	1830	1820	1810	1800	1790
New Jersey	5.8	6.4	7.2	7.6	8.0	7.7
Pennsylvania	2.8	2.8	2.9	2.9	2.7	2.4
EAST NORTH CENTRAL:						
Ohio	1.1	1.0	0.8	0.8	0.7	-
Indiana	1.0	1.1	1.0	2.6	5.3	-
Illinois	0.8	1.5	2.5	6.4	-	-
Michigan	0.3	0.9	2.0	3.0	-	-
Wisconsin	0.6	-	-	-	-	-
WEST NORTH CENTRAL:						
Minnesota	-	-	-	-	-	-
Iowa	0.4	-	-	-	-	-
Missouri	15.6	18.3	15.9	17.4	-	-
North Dakota	-	-	-	-	-	-
South Dakota	-	-	-	-	-	-
Nebraska	-	-	-	-	-	-
Kansas	-	-	-	-	-	-
SOUTH ATLANTIC:						
Delaware	25.0	24.9	24.0	23.8	22.4	21.6
Maryland	32.3	34.9	36.1	38.2	36.7	34.7
District of Columbia	29.9	30.8	31.6	33.1	28.6	-
Virginia	40.2	42.7	43.4	43.4	41.6	40.9
West Virginia	-	-	-	-	-	-
North Carolina	35.6	35.9	34.4	32.2	29.4	26.8
South Carolina	56.4	55.6	52.8	48.4	43.2	43.7
Georgia	41.0	42.6	44.4	42.4	37.1	35.9
Florida	48.7	47.1	-	-	-	-
EAST SOUTH CENTRAL:						
Kentucky	24.3	24.7	22.9	20.2	18.6	17.0
Tennessee	22.7	21.4	19.6	17.5	13.2	10.6
Alabama	43.3	38.5	33.2	-	-	-
Mississippi	52.3	48.4	44.1	42.9	41.5	-
WEST SOUTH CENTRAL:						
Arkansas	20.9	15.5	11.7	-	-	-
Louisiana	55.0	58.5	51.8	55.2	-	-
Oklahoma	-	-	-	-	-	-
Texas	-	-	-	-	-	-
MOUNTAIN:						
Montana	-	-	-	-	-	-
Idaho	-	-	-	-	-	-

[Continued]

★ 1887 ★

Percentage Black in the Population At Each Census by Divisions and States, 1790-1910 - II

[Continued]

DIVISION AND STATE	PERCENTAGE NEGRO IN THE POPULATION					
	1840	1830	1820	1810	1800	1790
Wyoming	-	-	-	-	-	-
Colorado	-	-	-	-	-	-
New Mexico	-	-	-	-	-	-
Arizona	-	-	-	-	-	-
Utah	-	-	-	-	-	-
Nevada	-	-	-	-	-	-
PACIFIC:						
Washington	-	-	-	-	-	-
Oregon	-	-	-	-	-	-
California	-	-	-	-	-	-

Source: "Percentage Negro in the Population At Each Census, by Divisions and States: 1790-1910." U.S. Bureau of the Census, *Negro Population, 1790- 1915,* p. 51. *Notes:* 1. Dakota Territory. 2. Includes population of Indian Territory for 1900 and 1890. 3. Less than one-tenth of 1 per cent.

★ 1888 ★

Racial Composition

Racial Composition of the Population Each Census Year, 1790-1930

Census Year	Number				Per Cent			Per cent increase of white and Negro population	
	Total Population	White	Negro	Indian, Chinese and Japanese and all Others[1]	White	Negro	Indian, Chinese and Japanese and all Others[1]	White	Negro
1930	122,775,046	108,864,207	11,891,143	2,019,696	88.7	9.7	1.6	15.7	13.6
1920	105,710,620	94,120,374	10,463,131	1,127,115	89.7	9.9	0.4	15.7	6.5
1910	91,972,266	81,364,447	9,827,763	78,056	88.9	10.7	0.4	21.8	11.5
1900	75,994,575	66,809,196	8,833,994	351,385	87.9	11.6	0.5	21.2	18.0
1890	62,947,714	55,101,258	7,488,676	357,780	87.5	11.9	0.6	27.0	13.8
1880	50,155,783	43,402,970	6,580,793	172,020	86.5	13.1	0.3	29.2	22.0
1870	38,558,371	33,589,377	4,880,009	88,985	87.1	12.7	0.2	24.8	21.4
1860	31,443,321	26,922,537	4,441,830	78,954	85.6	14.1	0.3	37.7	22.1
1850	23,191,876	19,553,068	3,638,808	-	84.3	15.7	-	37.7	26.6
1840	17,069,453	14,195,805	2,873,648	-	83.2	16.8	-	34.7	23.4
1830	12,866,020	10,537,378	2,328,642	-	81.9	18.1	-	33.9	31.4
1820	9,638,453	7,866,797	1,771,656	-	81.6	18.4	-	34.2	28.6
1810	7,239,881	5,862,073	1,377,808	-	81.0	19.0	-	36.1	37.5

[Continued]

★ 1888 ★

Racial Composition of the Population Each Census Year, 1790-1930

[Continued]

Census Year	Number				Per Cent			Per cent increase of white and Negro population	
	Total Population	White	Negro	Indian, Chinese and Japanese and all Others[1]	White	Negro	Indian, Chinese and Japanese and all Others[1]	White	Negro
1800	5,308,483	4,306,446	1,002,037	-	81.1	18.9	-	35.8	32.3
1790	3,929,214	3,172,006	757,208	-	80.7	19.3	-	-	-

Source: "Population Each Census Year, 1790-1930." Work, Monroe N., ed, *Negro Year Book: An Annual Encyclopedia of the Negro, 1925-26.* p. 245. Primary source: U.S. Bureau of the Census. *Notes:* 1. A total of 1,422,533 Mexicans in 1930; 700,541 in 1920; and 367,510 in 1910 were excluded from the white population. For census years prior to 1910 the white population includes Mexicans.

★ 1889 ★

Racial Composition

Racial Composition of the Population by Divisions and States, 1940

Region, Division, and State	White	Negro
United States	118,214,870	12,865,518
Regions:		
The North	73,206,738	2,790,193
The South	31,658,578	9,904,619
The West	13,349,554	170,706
The North:		
New England	8,329,146	101,509
Middle Atlantic	26,237,622	1,268,366
East North Central	25,528,451	1,069,326
West North Central	13,111,519	350,992
The South:		
South Atlantic	13,095,227	4,698,863
East South Central	7,993,755	2,780,635
West South Central	10,569,596	2,425,121
The West:		
Mountain	3,978,913	36,411
Pacific	9,370,641	134,295
New England:		
Maine	844,543	1,304
New Hampshire	490,989	414
Vermont	358,806	384
Massachusetts	4,257,596	55,391

[Continued]

★ 1889 ★

Racial Composition of the Population by Divisions and States, 1940

[Continued]

Region, Division, and State	White	Negro
Rhode Island	701,805	11,024
Connecticut	1,675,407	32,992
Middle Atlantic:		
New York	12,879,546	571,221
New Jersey	3,931,087	226,973
Pennsylvania	9,426,989	470,172
East North Central:		
Ohio	6,566,531	339,461
Indiana	3,305,323	121,916
Illinois	7,504,202	387,446
Michigan	5,039,643	208,345
Wisconsin	3,112,752	12,158
West North Central:		
Minnesota	2,768,982	9,928
Iowa	2,520,691	16,694
Missouri	3,539,187	244,386
North Dakota	631,464	201
South Dakota	619,075	474
Nebraska	1,297,624	14,171
Kansas	1,734,496	65,138
South Atlantic:		
Delaware	230,528	35,876
Maryland	1,518,481	301,931
District of Columbia	474,326	187,266
Virginia	2,015,583	661,449
West Virginia	1,784,102	117,754
North Carolina	2,567,635	981,298
South Carolina	1,084,308	814,164
Georgia	2,033,278	1,084,927
Florida	1,381,986	514,198
East South Central:		
Kentucky	2,631,425	214,031
Tennessee	2,406,906	508,736
Alabama	1,849,097	983,290
Mississippi	1,106,327	1,074,578
West South Central:		
Arkansas	1,466,084	482,578
Louisiana	1,511,739	849,303
Oklahoma	2,104,228	168,849
Texas	5,487,545	924,391

[Continued]

★ 1889 ★

Racial Composition of the Population by Divisions and States, 1940

[Continued]

Region, Division, and State	White	Negro
Mountain:		
Montana	540,468	1,120
Idaho	519,292	595
Wyoming	246,597	956
Colorado	1,106,502	12,176
New Mexico	492,312	4,672
Arizona	426,792	14,993
Utah	542,920	1,235
Nevada	104,030	664
Pacific:		
Washington	1,698,147	7,424
Oregon	1,075,731	2,565
California	6,596,763	124,306

Source: "Population, White and Negro, for the United States, by Divisions and States: 1940." Murray, Florence, ed., *The Negro Handbook*, p. 188. Primary source: U.S. Bureau of the Census.

Size of the Population

★ 1890 ★

Number of Blacks Per 100,000 Whites at Each Census by Sections, Divisions, and States, 1790-1930 - I

SECTION, DIVISION, AND STATE	1930	1920[1]	1910[1]	1900	1890	1880	1870	1860
United States	10,923	11,117	12,079	13,223	13,591	15,162	14,528	16,499
The North	3,423	2,371	1,881	1,898	1,796	1,969	1,825	1,759
The South	33,828	37,554	43,066	47,954	51,242	59,406	56,221	58,247
The West	1,114	947	789	781	943	735	701	814
GEOGRAPHIC DIVISIONS:								
New England	1,167	1,081	1,023	1,069	958	1,006	918	794
Middle Atlantic	4,183	2,774	2,213	2,157	1,807	1,839	1,709	1,792
East North Central	3,833	2,458	1,678	1,641	1,562	1,665	1,452	929
West North Central	2,577	2,283	2,140	2,364	2,588	3,401	3,842	5,896
South Atlantic	38,957	44,827	50,951	55,607	58,344	63,196	60,978	62,273
East South Central	36,794	39,634	46,097	49,553	49,233	52,630	49,820	53,091
West South Central	25,076	26,744	30,574	35,507	41,816	48,478	57,403	58,463
Mountain	915	1,003	878	987	1,161	817	515	143
Pacific	1,202	914	734	639	804	685	793	1,098

[Continued]

★ 1890 ★

Number of Blacks Per 100,000 Whites at Each Census by Sections, Divisions, and States, 1790-1930 - I

[Continued]

SECTION, DIVISION, AND STATE	1930	1920[1]	1910[1]	1900	1890	1880	1870	1860
NEW ENGLAND:								
Maine	138	171	184	191	181	224	257	212
New Hampshire	170	140	131	161	163	198	183	152
Vermont	158	163	458	241	283	319	280	226
Massachusetts	1,249	1,195	1,145	1,154	1,000	1,060	966	786
Rhode Island	1,464	1,690	1,790	2,170	2,188	2,404	2,347	2,316
Connecticut	1,862	1,549	1,381	1,706	1,677	1,891	1,833	1,911
MIDDLE ATLANTIC:								
New York	3,398	1,952	1,497	1,387	1,183	1,298	1,203	1,279
New Jersey	5,454	3,857	3,670	3,854	3,411	3,558	3,502	3,918
Pennsylvania	4,691	3,375	2,597	2,554	2,090	2,038	1,889	1,999
EAST NORTH CENTRAL:								
Ohio	4,885	3,342	2,394	2,387	2,430	2,563	2,429	1,593
Indiana	3,594	2,837	2,285	2,339	2,106	2,023	1,483	854
Illinois	4,527	2,896	1,973	1,797	1,513	1,530	1,145	448
Michigan	3,644	1,669	615	659	734	935	1,015	924
Wisconsin	369	199	125	124	145	206	201	151
WEST NORTH CENTRAL:								
Minnesota	372	372	344	285	284	201	173	153
Iowa	710	798	678	572	562	589	485	159
Missouri	6,586	5,533	5,025	5,475	5,940	7,185	7,365	11,143
North Dakota	56	73	108	92	204	] 301	729	-
South Dakota	96	134	145	122	165			
Nebraska	1,016	1,037	652	593	851	530	646	286
Kansas	3,700	3,422	3,323	3,672	3,611	4,527	4,939	589
SOUTH ATLANTIC:								
Delaware	15,850	15,751	18,224	19,936	20,266	22,006	22,299	23,874
Maryland	20,409	20,294	21,856	24,681	26,093	29,010	28,966	33,170
District of Columbia	37,316	33,647	40,000	45,268	48,852	50,503	49,167	23,560
Virginia	36,724	42,650	48,287	55,390	62,290	71,705	72,019	52,412
West Virginia	7,119	6,270	5,547	4,753	4,478	4,369	4,240	-
North Carolina	41,104	42,797	46,507	49,420	53,158	61,261	57,725	57,390
South Carolina	84,073	105,643	123,070	140,249	149,117	154,519	143,549	141,545
Georgia	58,309	71,422	82,204	87,600	87,781	88,766	85,322	78,725
Florida	41,714	51,641	69,588	77,600	73,875	88,840	95,453	80,618
EAST SOUTH CENTRAL:								
Kentucky	9,464	10,821	12,903	15,288	16,855	19,711	20,225	25,685
Tennessee	22,334	23,954	27,643	31,181	32,221	35,400	34,433	34,234
Alabama	55,553	62,245	73,917	82,636	81,381	90,625	91,201	83,183
Mississippi	101,290	109,531	128,430	141,552	136,287	135,647	116,011	123,596

[Continued]

★ 1890 ★

Number of Blacks Per 100,000 Whites at Each Census by Sections, Divisions, and States, 1790-1930 - I

[Continued]

SECTION, DIVISION, AND STATE	1930	1920[1]	1910[1]	1900	1890	1880	1870	1860
WEST SOUTH CENTRAL:								
Arkansas	34,800	36,907	39,163	38,838	37,755	35,614	33,738	34,324
Louisiana	58,895	64,009	75,961	89,199	100,143	106,309	100,592	98,018
Oklahoma[2]	8,109	8,240	9,546	8,309	12,523	-	-	-
Texas	19,960	21,014	23,169	25,579	27,960	32,858	44,887	43,460
MOUNTAIN:								
Montana	243	310	509	673	1,167	978	1,000	-
Idaho	153	217	204	190	245	183	565	-
Wyoming	584	731	1,597	1,056	1,554	1,533	2,097	-
Colorado	1,231	1,244	1,468	1,620	1,536	1,274	1,163	134
New Mexico	859	1,899	574	893	1,369	934	190	103
Arizona	4,066	3,944	1,642	1,989	2,435	441	271	-
Utah	223	328	312	247	286	163	137	147
Nevada	634	499	698	378	619	911	916	661
PACIFIC:								
Washington	450	522	546	507	470	484	933	269
Oregon	238	279	228	280	393	299	398	245
California	1,608	1,233	979	787	1,018	784	855	1,264

Source: "Number of Negroes Per 100,000 Whites at Each Census, by Sections, Divisions, and States: 1790 to 1930." U.S. Bureau of the Census, *Negroes in the United States, 1920-1932,* p. 16. *Notes:* 1. Figures for white population in 1920 and 1910 are adjusted by deducting the estimated number of Mexicans. 2. Includes Indian Territory in 1900 and 1890.

★ 1891 ★

Size of the Population

Number of Blacks Per 100,000 Whites at Each Census by Sections, Divisions, and States, 1790-1930 - II

SECTION, DIVISION, AND STATE	1850	1840	1830	1820	1810	1800	1790
United States	18,610	20,252	22,110	22,521	23,504	23,268	23,872
The North	2,076	2,345	2,387	2,534	2,978	3,216	3,547
The South	59,537	61,317	60,968	59,162	57,882	53,907	54,254
The West	699	-	-	-	-	-	-
GEOGRAPHIC DIVISIONS:							
New England	851	1,024	1,106	1,277	1,371	1,536	1,712
Middle Atlantic	2,196	2,716	2,980	3,440	4,261	4,814	5,554
East North Central	1,009	1,014	1,092	980	1,285	1,261	-
West North Central	11,446	16,358	22,353	18,867	21,002	-	-
South Atlantic	66,030	68,614	72,256	71,233	67,800	60,253	57,153
East South Central	50,114	47,578	38,161	31,920	25,829	21,190	17,542
West South Central	64,462	90,970	113,815	93,930	123,124	-	-

[Continued]

★ 1891 ★

Number of Blacks Per 100,000 Whites at Each Census by Sections, Divisions, and States, 1790-1930 - II

[Continued]

SECTION, DIVISION, AND STATE	1850	1840	1830	1820	1810	1800	1790
Mountain	99	-	-	-	-	-	-
Pacific	1,116	-	-	-	-	-	-
NEW ENGLAND:							
Maine	233	271	299	312	425	542	560
New Hampshire	164	189	226	323	454	470	558
Vermont	229	251	315	384	345	362	318
Massachusetts	920	1,189	1,168	1,305	1,448	1,549	1,463
Rhode Island	2,551	3,071	3,822	,4533	5,077	5,630	6,755
Connecticut	2,119	2,691	2,787	2,981	2,650	2,567	2,398
MIDDLE ATLANTIC:							
New York	1,610	2,103	2,399	2,952	4,392	5,616	8,270
New Jersey	5,166	6,177	6,846	7,772	8,240	8,658	8,346
Pennsylvania	2,375	2,859	2,926	2,984	2,960	2,776	2,423
EAST NORTH CENTRAL:							
Ohio	1,293	1,155	1,031	819	830	748	-
Indiana	1,153	1,056	1,070	974	2,637	5,557	-
Illinois	643	832	1,537	2,552	6,791	-	-
Michigan	654	334	935	1,995	3,118	-	-
Wisconsin	208	637	-	-	-	-	-
WEST NORTH CENTRAL:							
Minnesota	646	-	-	-	-	-	-
Iowa	174	438	-	-	-	-	-
Missouri	15,209	18,467	22,353	18,867	21,002	-	-
North Dakota							
South Dakota							
Nebraska	-	-	-	-	-	-	-
Kansas	-	-	-	-	-	-	-
SOUTH ATLANTIC:							
Delaware	28,612	33,340	33,241	31,596	31,273	28,928	27,610
Maryland	39,501	47,710	53,565	56,539	61,854	57,886	53,237
District of Columbia	36,230	42,584	44,520	46,109	49,406	40,006	-
Virginia	58,880	67,321	74,479	76,580	76,714	71,152	69,098
West Virginia	-	-	-	-	-	-	-
North Carolina	57,142	55,386	56,074	52,392	47,578	41,549	36,622
South Carolina	143,480	129,423	125,385	111,734	93,801	76,093	77,683
Georgia	73,741	69,586	74,128	79,875	73,596	59,089	56,087
Florida	85,253	94,958	88,904	-	-	-	-
EAST SOUTH CENTRAL:							
Kentucky	29,024	32,118	32,857	29,780	25,375	22,839	20,519
Tennessee	32,488	20,437	27,281	24,367	21,240	15,149	11,838

[Continued]

★ 1891 ★

Number of Blacks Per 100,000 Whites at Each Census by Sections, Divisions, and States, 1790-1930 - II

[Continued]

SECTION, DIVISION, AND STATE	1850	1840	1830	1820	1810	1800	1790
Alabama	80,914	76,248	62,562	49,678	-	-	-
Mississippi	105,103	109,774	93,945	78,888	75,261	70,882	-
WEST SOUTH CENTRAL:							
Arkansas	29,415	26,434	18,375	13,305	-	-	-
Louisiana	102,654	122,402	141,208	107,680	123,124	-	-
Oklahoma[3]	-	-	-	-	-	-	-
Texas	38,016	-	-	-	-	-	-
MOUNTAIN:							
Montana	-	-	-	-	-	-	-
Idaho	-	-	-	-	-	-	-
Wyoming	-	-	-	-	-	-	-
Colorado	-	-	-	-	-	-	-
New Mexico	36	-	-	-	-	-	-
Arizona	-	-	-	-	-	-	-
Utah	441	-	-	-	-	-	-
Nevada	-	-	-	-	-	-	-
PACIFIC:							
Washington	-	-	-	-	-	-	-
Oregon	1,582	-	-	-	-	-	-
California	1,050	-	-	-	-	-	-

Source: "Number of Negroes Per 100,000 Whites at Each Census, by Sections, Divisions, and States: 1790 to 1930." U.S. Bureau of the Census, *Negroes in the United States, 1920-1932,* p. 16. *Notes:* 1. Figures for white population in 1920 and 1910 are adjusted by deducting the estimated number of Mexicans. 2. Dakota Territory. 3. Includes Indian Territory in 1900 and 1890.

★ 1892 ★

Size of the Population

Percent Black in Total Population at Each Census by Divisions and States, 1790-1930 - I

SECTION, DIVISION, AND STATE	1930	1920[1]	1910[1]	1900	1890	1880	1870	1860
United States	9.7	9.9	10.7	11.6	11.9	13.1	12.7	14.1
GEOGRAPHIC DIVISIONS:								
New England	1.2	1.1	1.0	1.1	0.9	1.0	0.9	0.8
Middle Atlantic	4.0	2.7	2.2	2.1	1.8	1.8	1.7	1.8
East North Central	3.7	2.4	1.6	1.6	1.5	1.6	1.4	.9
West North Central	2.5	2.2	2.1	2.3	2.5	3.3	3.7	5.6
South Atlantic	28.0	30.9	33.7	35.7	36.8	38.7	37.9	38.4
East South Central	26.9	28.4	31.5	33.7	33.0	34.5	33.2	34.7
West South Central	18.7	20.1	22.6	25.9	29.1	32.6	36.4	36.9

[Continued]

★ 1892 ★

Percent Black in Total Population at Each Census by Divisions and States, 1790-1930 - I

[Continued]

SECTION, DIVISION, AND STATE	1930	1920[1]	1910[1]	1900	1890	1880	1870	1860
Mountain	.8	.9	.8	.9	1.1	.8	.5	.1
Pacific	1.1	.9	.7	.6	.7	.6	.7	1.0
NEW ENGLAND:								
Maine	.1	.2	.2	.2	.2	.2	.3	.2
New Hampshire	.2	.1	.1	.2	.2	.2	.2	.2
Vermont	.2	.2	.5	.2	.3	.3	.3	.2
Massachusetts	1.2	1.2	1.1	1.1	1.0	1.0	1.0	.8
Rhode Island	1.4	1.7	1.8	2.1	2.1	2.3	2.3	2.3
Connecticut	1.8	1.5	1.4	1.7	1.6	1.9	1.8	1.9
MIDDLE ATLANTIC:								
New York	3.3	1.9	1.5	1.4	1.2	1.3	1.2	1.3
New Jersey	5.2	3.7	3.5	3.7	3.3	3.4	3.4	3.8
Pennsylvania	4.5	3.3	2.5	2.5	2.0	2.0	1.9	2.0
EAST NORTH CENTRAL:								
Ohio	4.7	3.2	2.3	2.3	2.4	2.5	2.4	1.6
Indiana	3.5	2.8	2.2	2.3	2.1	2.0	1.5	.9
Illinois	4.3	2.8	1.9	1.8	1.5	1.5	1.1	.5
Michigan	3.5	1.6	.6	.7	.7	.9	1.0	.9
Wisconsin	.4	.2	.1	.1	.1	.2	.2	.2
WEST NORTH CENTRAL:								
Minnesota	.4	.4	.3	.3	.3	.2	.2	.2
Iowa	.7	.8	.7	.6	.6	.6	.5	.2
Missouri	6.2	5.2	4.8	5.2	5.6	6.7	6.9	10.0
North Dakota[1]	.1	.1	.1	.1	.2	.3	.7	-
South Dakota[1]	.1	.1	.1	.1	.2	.3	.7	-
Nebraska	1.0	1.0	.6	.6	.8	.5	.6	.3
Kansas	3.5	3.3	3.2	3.5	3.5	4.3	4.7	.6
SOUTH ATLANTIC:								
Delaware	13.7	13.6	15.4	16.6	16.8	18.0	18.2	19.3
Maryland	16.9	16.9	17.9	19.8	20.7	22.5	22.5	24.9
District of Columbia	27.1	25.1	28.5	31.1	32.8	33.6	33.0	19.1
Virginia	26.8	29.9	32.6	35.6	38.4	41.8	41.9	34.4
West Virginia	6.6	5.9	5.3	4.5	4.3	4.2	4.1	34.4
North Carolina	29.0	29.8	31.6	33.0	34.7	38.0	36.6	36.4
South Carolina	45.6	51.4	55.2	58.4	59.8	60.7	58.9	58.6
Georgia	36.8	41.7	45.1	46.7	46.7	47.0	46.0	44.1
Florida	29.4	34.0	41.0	43.7	42.5	47.0	48.8	44.6
EAST SOUTH CENTRAL:								
Kentucky	8.6	9.8	11.4	13.3	14.4	16.5	16.8	20.4
Tennessee	18.3	19.3	21.7	23.8	24.4	26.1	25.6	25.5

[Continued]

★ 1892 ★

Percent Black in Total Population at Each Census by Divisions and States, 1790-1930 - I

[Continued]

SECTION, DIVISION, AND STATE	1930	1920[1]	1910[1]	1900	1890	1880	1870	1860
Alabama	25.7	38.4	42.5	45.2	44.8	47.5	47.7	45.4
Mississippi	50.2	52.2	56.2	58.5	57.6	57.5	53.7	55.3
WEST SOUTH CENTRAL:								
Arkansas	25.8	27.0	28.1	28.0	27.4	26.3	25.2	25.6
Louisiana	36.9	38.9	43.1	47.1	50.0	51.5	50.1	49.5
Oklahoma[3]	7.2	7.4	8.3	7.0[2]	8.4[2]	-	-	-
Texas	14.7	15.9	17.7	20.4	21.8	24.7	31.0	30.3
MOUNTAIN:								
Montana	.2	.3	.5	.6	1.0	.9	.9	-
Idaho	.2	.2	.2	.2	.2	.2	.4	-
Wyoming	.6	.7	1.5	1.0	1.5	1.4	2.0	-
Colorado	1.1	1.2	1.4	1.6	1.5	1.3	1.1	.1
New Mexico	.7	1.6	.5	.8	1.2	.8	.2	.1
Arizona	2.5	2.4	1.0	1.5	1.5	.4	.3	-
Utah	.2	.3	.3	.2	.3	.2	.1	.2
Nevada	.6	.4	.6	.3	.5	.8	.8	.7
PACIFIC:								
Washington	.4	.5	.5	.5	.4	.4	.9	.3
Oregon	.2	.3	.2	.3	.4	.3	.4	.2
California	1.4	1.1	.9	.7	.9	.7	.8	1.1

Source: "Percent Negro in Total Population at Each Census, Divisions, and States: 1790 to 1930." U.S. Bureau of the Census, *Negroes in the United States, 1920-1932*, p. 15. *Notes:* 1. Dakota Territory. 2. Includes population of Indian Territory. 3. Less than 1/10 of 1 percent.

★ 1893 ★

Size of the Population

Percent Black in Total Population at Each Census by Divisions and States, 1790-1930 - II

SECTION, DIVISION, AND STATE	1850	1840	1830	1820	1810	1800	1790
United States	15.7	16.8	18.1	18.4	19.0	18.9	19.2
GEOGRAPHIC DIVISIONS:							
New England	0.8	1.0	1.1	1.3	1.4	1.5	1.7
Middle Atlantic	2.1	2.6	2.9	3.3	4.1	4.6	5.3
East North Central	1.0	1.0	1.1	1.0	1.3	1.2	-
West North Central	10.3	14.1	18.3	15.9	17.4	-	-
South Atlantic	39.8	40.7	41.9	41.6	40.4	37.6	36.4
East South Central	33.4	32.2	27.6	24.2	20.5	17.5	14.9
West South Central	39.2	47.6	53.2	48.4	54.4	-	-

[Continued]

★ 1893 ★

Percent Black in Total Population at Each Census by Divisions and States, 1790-1930 - II

[Continued]

SECTION, DIVISION, AND STATE	1850	1840	1830	1820	1810	1800	1790
Mountain	.1	-	-	-	-	-	-
Pacific	1.1	-	-	-	-	-	-
NEW ENGLAND:							
Maine	.2	.3	.3	.3	.4	.5	.6
New Hampshire	.2	.2	.2	.3	.5	.5	.6
Vermont	.2	.3	.3	.4	.3	.4	.3
Massachusetts	.9	1.2	1.2	1.3	1.4	1.5	1.4
Rhode Island	2.5	3.0	3.7	4.3	4.8	5.3	6.3
Connecticut	2.1	2.6	2.7	2.9	2.6	2.5	2.3
MIDDLE ATLANTIC:							
New York	1.6	2.1	2.3	2.9	4.2	5.3	7.6
New Jersey	4.9	5.8	6.4	7.2	7.6	8.0	7.7
Pennsylvania	2.3	2.8	2.8	2.9	2.9	2.7	2.4
EAST NORTH CENTRAL:							
Ohio	1.3	1.1	1.0	.8	.8	.7	-
Indiana	1.1	1.0	1.1	1.0	2.6	5.3	-
Illinois	.6	.8	1.5	2.5	6.4	-	-
Michigan	.7	.3	.9	2.0	3.0	-	-
Wisconsin	.2	.6	-	-	-	-	-
WEST NORTH CENTRAL:							
Minnesota	.6	-	-	-	-	-	-
Iowa	.2	.4	-	-	-	-	-
Missouri	13.2	15.6	18.3	15.9	17.4	-	-
North Dakota							
South Dakota							
Nebraska	-	-	-	-	-	-	-
Kansas	-	-	-	-	-	-	-
SOUTH ATLANTIC:							
Delaware	22.3	25.0	24.9	24.0	23.8	22.4	21.6
Maryland	28.3	32.3	34.9	36.1	38.2	36.7	34.7
District of Columbia	26.6	29.9	30.8	31.6	33.1	28.6	-
Virginia	37.1	40.2	42.7	43.4	43.3	41.6	40.9
West Virginia	37.1	40.2	42.7	43.4	43.3	41.6	40.9
North Carolina	36.4	35.6	35.9	34.4	32.2	29.4	26.8
South Carolina	58.9	56.4	55.6	52.8	48.4	43.2	43.7
Georgia	42.4	41.0	42.6	44.4	42.4	37.1	35.9
Florida	46.0	48.7	47.1	-	-	-	-
EAST SOUTH CENTRAL:							
Kentucky	22.5	24.3	24.7	22.9	20.2	18.6	17.0
Tennessee	24.5	22.7	21.4	19.6	17.5	13.2	10.6

[Continued]

★ 1893 ★

Percent Black in Total Population at Each Census by Divisions and States, 1790-1930 - II

[Continued]

SECTION, DIVISION, AND STATE	1850	1840	1830	1820	1810	1800	1790
Alabama	44.7	43.3	38.5	33.2	-	-	-
Mississippi	51.2	52.3	48.4	44.1	42.9	41.5	-
WEST SOUTH CENTRAL:							
Arkansas	22.7	20.9	15.5	11.7	-	-	-
Louisiana	50.7	55.0	58.5	51.8	55.2	-	-
Oklahoma[3]	-	-	-	-	-	-	-
Texas	27.5	-	-	-	-	-	-
MOUNTAIN:							
Montana	-	-	-	-	-	-	-
Idaho	-	-	-	-	-	-	-
Wyoming	-	-	-	-	-	-	-
Colorado	-	-	-	-	-	-	-
New Mexico	[3]	-	-	-	-	-	-
Arizona	-	-	-	-	-	-	-
Utah	.4	-	-	-	-	-	-
Nevada	-	-	-	-	-	-	-
PACIFIC:							
Washington	-	-	-	-	-	-	-
Oregon	1.6	-	-	-	-	-	-
California	1.0	-	-	-	-	-	-

Source: "Percent Negro in Total Population at Each Census, Divisions, and States: 1790 to 1930." U.S. Bureau of the Census, *Negroes in the United States, 1920-1932*, p. 15. *Notes:* 1. Dakota Territory. 2. Includes population of Indian Territory. 3. Less than 1/10 of 1 percent.

★ 1894 ★

Size of the Population

Percentage Distribution of Blacks at Each Census, Ranged in Order According to Percentage by State, 1910

STATE	Percentage Negro	POPULATION, 1910					
		Negro			White		
		Number	Cumulated by states		Number	Cumulated by states	
			Number	Percent		Number	Percent
Mississippi	56.2	1,009,487	1,009,487	10.3	786,111	786,111	1.0
South Carolina	55.2	835,843	1,845,330	18.8	679,161	1,465,272	1.8
Georgia	45.1	1,176,987	3,022,317	30.8	1,431,802	2,897,074	3.5
Louisiana	43.1	713,874	3,736,191	38.0	941,086	3,838,160	4.7
Alabama	42.5	908,282	4,644,473	47.3	1,228,832	5,066,992	6.2
Florida	41.0	308,669	4,953,142	50.4	443,634	5,510,626	6.7

[Continued]

★ 1894 ★

Percentage Distribution of Blacks at Each Census, Ranged in Order According to Percentage by State, 1910

[Continued]

STATE	Percentage Negro	POPULATION, 1910					
		Negro			White		
		Number	Cumulated by states		Number	Cumulated by states	
			Number	Percent		Number	Percent
Virginia	32.6	671,096	5,624,238	57.2	1,389,809	6,900,435	8.4
North Carolina	31.6	697,843	6,322,081	64.3	1,500,511	8,400,946	10.3
Dist. Columbia	28.5	94,446	6,416,527	65.3	236,128	8,637,074	10.6
Arkansas	28.1	442,891	6,859,418	69.8	1,131,026	9,786,100	12.0
Tennessee	21.7	473,088	7,332,506	74.6	1,711,432	11,479,532	14.0
Maryland	17.9	232,250	7,654,756	77.0	1,062,639	12,542,171	15.3
Texas	17.7	690,049	8,254,805	84.0	3,204,848	15,747,019	19.3
Delaware	15.4	31,181	8,285,986	84.3	171,102	15,918,121	19.5
Kentucky	11.4	261,656	8,547,642	87.0	2,027,951	17,946,072	22.0
Oklahoma	8.3	137,612	8,685,254	88.4	1,444,531	19,390,603	23.7
West Virginia	5.3	64,173	8,749,427	89.0	1,156,817	20,547,420	25.1
Missouri	4.8	157,452	8,906,879	90.6	3,134,932	23,682,352	29.0
New Jersey	3.5	89,760	8,996,639	91.5	2,445,894	26,128,246	32.0
Kansas	3.2	54,030	9,050,609	92.1	1,634,352	27,762,598	34.0
Pennsylvania	2.5	193,919	9,244,588	94.1	7,467,713	35,230,311	43.1
Ohio	2.3	111,542	9,356,040	95.2	4,654,897	39,885,208	48.8
Indiana	2.2	60,320	9,416,360	95.8	2,639,961	42,525,169	52.0
Illinois	1.9	109,049	9,525,409	96.9	5,526,962	48,052,131	58.8
Rhode Island	1.8	9,529	9,534,938	97.0	532,492	48,584,623	59.4
New York	1.5	134,191	9,669,129	98.4	8,966,845	57,551,468	70.4
Wyoming	1.5	2,235	9,671,364	98.4	140,318	57,691,786	70.6
Colorado	1.4	11,453	9,682,817	98.5	783,415	58,475,201	71.5
Connecticut	1.4	15,174	9,697,991	98.7	1,098,897	59,574,098	72.9
Massachusetts	1.1	38,055	9,736,046	99.1	3,324,926	62,899,024	77.0
Arizona	1.0	2,009	9,738,055	99.1	171,468	63,070,492	77.2
California	0.9	21,645	9,759,700	99.3	2,259,672	65,330,164	79.9
Iowa	0.7	14,973	9,774,673	99.5	2,209,191	67,539,355	82.6
Michigan	0.6	17,115	9,791,788	99.6	2,785,247	70,324,602	86.0
Nebraska	0.6	7,689	9,799,477	99.7	1,180,293	71,504,895	87.5
Nevada	0.6	513	9,799,990	99.7	74,276	71,579,171	87.6
Montana	0.5	1,834	9,801,824	99.7	360,850	71,939,751	88.0
New Mexico	0.5	1,628	9,803,452	99.8	304,594	72,244,345	88.4
Vermont	0.5	1,621	9,805,073	99.8	354,298	72,598,643	88.8
Washington	0.5	6,058	9,811,131	99.8	1,109,111	73,707,754	90.2
Minnesota	0.3	7,084	9,818,215	99.9	2,059,227	75,766,981	92.7
Utah	0.3	1,144	9,819,359	99.9	366,583	76,133,564	93.2

[Continued]

★ 1894 ★

Percentage Distribution of Blacks at Each Census, Ranged in Order According to Percentage by State, 1910

[Continued]

STATE	POPULATION, 1910						
	Percentage Negro	Negro			White		
		Number	Cumulated by states Number	Cumulated by states Percent	Number	Cumulated by states Number	Cumulated by states Percent
Idaho	0.2	651	9,820,010	99.9	319,221	76,452,785	93.5
Maine	0.2	1,363	9,821,373	99.9	739,995	77,192,780	94.4
Oregon	0.2	1,492	9,822,865	100.0	655,090	77,847,870	95.2
New Hampshire	0.1	564	9,823,429	100.0	429,906	78,277,776	95.8
North Dakota	0.1	617	9,824,046	100.0	569,855	78,847,631	96.5
South Dakota	0.1	817	9,824,863	100.0	563,771	79,411,402	97.2
Wisconsin	0.1	2,900	9,827,763	100.0	2,320,555	81,731,957	100.0

Source: Untitled Table. U.S. Bureau of the Census, *Negro Population, 1790-1915*, p. 49.

★ 1895 ★

Size of the Population

Percentage of the Black Population by Marital Status and Age Period, 1890-1910

AGE PERIOD AND YEAR	PERCENTAGE							
	Single		Married		Widowed		Divorced	
	Negro population	White population	Negro population	White population	Negro population	White population	Negro population	White population
				MALE				
All ages:								
1910	59.6	57.8	35.8	38.5	3.9	3.0	0.4	0.3
1900	63.5	60.1	32.4	36.4	3.5	3.0	0.3	0.2
1890	65.7	61.7	31.6	35.4	2.5	2.6	0.1	0.2
Under 15 years of age:								
1910	100.0	100.0	[1]	[1]	[1]	[1]	[1]	[1]
1900	100.0	100.0	[1]	[1]	[1]	[1]	[1]	[1]
1890	100.0	100.0	[1]	[1]	[1]	[1]	[1]	[1]
15 years of age and over:								
1910	35.4	39.0	57.2	55.7	6.2	4.4	0.7	0.5
1900	39.2	40.2	54.0	54.6	5.8	4.5	0.4	0.3
1890	39.8	41.7	55.5	53.9	4.3	3.9	0.2	0.3
				FEMALE				
All ages:								
1910	53.9	52.5	36.0	40.1	9.3	6.8	0.7	0.4
1900	57.7	54.8	32.5	37.8	9.3	7.0	0.5	0.3
1890	59.3	55.8	31.7	37.1	8.6	6.8	0.3	0.2
Under 15 years of age:								
1910	100.0	100.0	[1]	[1]	[1]	[1]	[1]	[1]

[Continued]

★ 1895 ★

Percentage of the Black Population by Marital Status and Age Period, 1890-1910

[Continued]

AGE PERIOD AND YEAR	PERCENTAGE							
	Single		Married		Widowed		Divorced	
	Negro population	White population	Negro population	White population	Negro population	White population	Negro population	White population
1900	100.0	100.0	1	1	1	1	1	1
1890	100.0	100.0	1	1	1	1	1	1
15 years of age and over:								
1910	26.6	30.1	57.2	59.9	14.8	10.1	1.1	0.6
1900	29.9	31.4	53.7	57.3	15.4	10.7	0.8	0.4
1890	30.0	32.0	54.6	57.0	14.7	10.5	0.5	0.4

Source: "Untitled Table." U.S. Bureau of the Census, *Negro Population, 1790- 1915*, p. 238. *Note:* 1. Less than one-tenth of 1 per cent.

★ 1896 ★

Size of the Population

Population 15 Years of Age and Over by Race, 1910

RACIAL CLASS	POPULATION 15 YEARS OF AGE AND OVER: 1910					
	Male			Female		
	The South	The North	The West	The South	The North	The West
	PERCENTAGE SINGLE					
Negro	34.8	39.1	45.5	26.4	27.6	23.0
White	36.8	38.7	45.8	28.1	31.2	26.9
Native born	37.2	42.4	46.5	28.7	35.4	30.1
Foreign born	30.1	30.2	44.0	15.1	18.8	14.6
	PERCENTAGE MARRIED					
Negro	57.9	52.7	46.6	57.6	54.7	56.6
White	58.2	56.0	48.2	61.5	57.9	61.9
Native	58.0	52.6	47.7	61.3	55.0	59.9
Foreign born	62.2	63.8	49.4	65.7	66.4	69.1
	PERCENTAGE WIDOWED					
Negro	6.2	6.6	5.5	14.6	16.2	17.3
White	4.3	4.4	4.1	9.8	10.2	9.9
Native	4.1	4.0	3.8	9.4	8.7	8.5
Foreign born	6.8	5.4	4.7	18.9	14.4	15.2
	PERCENTAGE DIVORCED					
Negro	0.6	0.9	1.6	1.1	1.1	2.6
White	0.3	0.4	1.0	0.4	0.5	1.1
Native	0.3	0.5	1.0	0.4	0.5	1.2

[Continued]

★ 1896 ★

Population 15 Years of Age and Over by Race, 1910

[Continued]

RACIAL CLASS	POPULATION 15 YEARS OF AGE AND OVER: 1910					
	Male			Female		
	The South	The North	The West	The South	The North	The West
Foreign born	0.4	0.3	0.7	0.4	0.3	0.9
	PERCENTAGE MARRIED, WIDOWED, OR DIVORCED					
Negro	64.7	60.3	53.7	73.2	72.1	76.5
White	62.8	60.9	53.2	71.7	68.6	72.9
Native	62.4	57.2	52.5	71.1	64.4	69.6
Foreign born	69.4	69.5	54.8	84.7	81.1	85.2

Source: "Population 15 Years of Age and Over: 1910." U.S. Bureau of the Census, *Negro Population, 1790-1915*, p. 248.

★ 1897 ★

Size of the Population

Population Growth by Regions, Divisions, and States, 1940 and 1950

Region, Division and State	White		Nonwhite	
	1940	1950	1940	1950
North	73,206,738	79,671,283	2,913,371	4,267,196
New England	8,329,146	9,175,652	108,144	138,287
Maine	844,543	910,847	2,683	2,927
New Hampshire	490,989	532,275	535	967
Vermont	358,806	377,188	425	559
Massachusetts	4,257,596	4,626,000	59,125	64,000
Rhode Island	701,805	777,015	11,541	14,881
Connecticut	1,675,407	1,952,327	33,835	54,953
Middle Atlantic	26,327,622	28,303,000	1,301,865	1,860,000
New York	12,879,546	13,902,000	599,596	928,000
New Jersey	3,931,087	4,557,000	229,078	278,000
Pennsylvania	9,426,989	9,844,000	472,191	654,000
East North Central	15,528,451	28,632,130	1,097,891	1,767,669
Ohio	6,566,531	7,476,000	341,081	470,000
Indiana	3,305,323	3,753,439	122,473	175,785
Illinois	7,504,202	8,085,000	393,039	628,000
Michigan	5,039,643	5,920,000	216,463	452,000
Wisconsin	3,112,752	3,392,691	24,835	41,884
West North Central	13,111,519	13,560,501	405,471	501,240
Minnesota	2,768,982	2,953,678	23,318	28,805
Iowa	2,520,691	2,599,566	17,577	21,507

[Continued]

★ 1897 ★

Population Growth by Regions, Divisions, and States, 1940 and 1950

[Continued]

Region, Division and State	White		Nonwhite	
	1940	1950	1940	1950
Missouri	3,539,187	3,640,000	245,477	315,000
North Dakota	631,464	608,448	10,471	11,188
South Dakota	619,075	628,504	23,886	24,236
Nebraska	1,297,624	1,301,344	18,210	24,166
Kansas	1,734,496	1,828,961	66,532	76,338
South	31,658,578	36,877,791	10,007,323	10,249,103
East South Central	7,993,755	8,700,109	2,784,470	2,707,072
Kentucky	2,631,425	2,741,930	214,020	202,876
Tennessee	2,406,906	2,760,250	508,935	531,468
Alabama	1,849,097	2,079,500	983,864	982,243
Mississippi	1,106,327	1,118,429	1,077,469	990,485
South Atlantic	13,095,227	16,042,071	4,727,924	5,140,264
Delaware	230,528	273,878	35,977	44,207
Maryland	1,518,481	1,954,987	302,763	388,014
District of Columbia	474,326	518,147	188,765	284,031
Virginia	2,015,583	2,581,642	662,190	737,038
West Virginia	1,784,102	1,890,284	117,872	115,268
North Carolina	2,567,635	2,983,110	1,003,988	1,078,819
South Carolina	1,084,308	1,293,403	815,496	823,624
Georgia	2,038,278	2,380,573	1,085,445	1,064,005
Florida	1,381,986	2,166,047	515,428	605,258
West South Central	10,569,596	12,135,611	2,494,929	2,401,767
Arkansas	1,466,084	1,481,508	483,303	428,003
Louisiana	1,511,739	1,796,548	852,141	886,968
Oklahoma	2,104,228	2,032,555	232,206	200,796
Texas	5,487,545	6,825,000	927,279	886,000
West	13,349,554	18,606,256	533,711	955,046
Mountain	3,978,913	4,845,633	171,090	229,365
Montana	540,468	572,038	18,988	18,986
Idaho	519,292	581,395	5,581	7,242
Wyoming	246,597	284,009	4,145	6,520
Colorado	1,106,502	1,296,653	16,794	28,436
New Mexico	492,312	630,211	39,506	50,976
Arizona	426,792	654,511	72,469	95,076
Utah	542,920	676,909	7,390	11,953
Nevada	104,030	149,907	6,217	10,176
Pacific	9,370,641	13,760,623	362,621	725,681
Washington	1,698,147	2,316,495	38,044	62,468
Oregon	1,075,731	1,497,128	13,953	24,213

[Continued]

★ 1897 ★

Population Growth by Regions, Divisions, and States, 1940 and 1950

[Continued]

Region, Division and State	White		Nonwhite	
	1940	1950	1940	1950
California	6,596,763	9,947,000	310,624	639,000
Total	118,214,870	135,155,330	13,454,405	15,471,345

Source: "White and Nonwhite Population, by Regions, Divisions, and States, 1940 and 1950." Jessie Parkhurst Guzman, *Negro Yearbook, 1952,* p. 3. Primary source: U.S. Bureau of the Census.

★ 1898 ★

Size of the Population

Population Increase by Classes, 1900-1910

CLASS	POPULATION: 1910					
	Area of enumeration	United States	Porto Rico	Hawaii	Alaska	Military and naval service abroad
	NUMBER IN EACH CLASS					
All classes	93,402,151	91,972,266	1,118,012	191,909	64,356	55,608
Negro	10,215,482	9,827,763	385,437	695	209	1,378
White	82,598,168	81,731,957	732,555	44,048	36,400	53,208
Indian	291,018	265,683	-	-	25,331	4
Chinese	94,648	71,531	12	21,674	1,209	222
Japanese	152,956	72,157	8	79,675	913	203
Other	49,879	3,175	-	45,817	294	593
	PERCENTAGE IN EACH CLASS					
All classes	100.0	100.0	100.0	100.0	100.0	100.0
Negro	10.9	10.7	34.5	0.4	0.3	2.5
White	88.4	88.9	65.5	23.0	56.6	95.7
Indian	0.3	0.3	-	-	39.4	[1]
Chinese	0.1	0.1	[1]	11.3	1.9	0.4
Japanese	0.2	0.1	[1]	41.5	1.4	0.4
Other	0.1	[1]	-	23.9	0.5	1.1
	PERCENTAGE IN EACH AREA, BY CLASSES					
All classes	100.0	98.5	1.2	0.2	0.1	0.1
Negro	100.0	96.2	3.8	[1]	[1]	[1]
White	100.0	99.0	0.9	0.1	[1]	0.1
Indian	100.0	91.3	-	-	8.7	[1]
Chinese	100.0	75.6	[1]	22.9	1.3	0.2

[Continued]

★ 1898 ★

Population Increase by Classes, 1900-1910

[Continued]

CLASS	POPULATION: 1910					
	Area of enumeration	United States	Porto Rico	Hawaii	Alaska	Military and naval service abroad
Japanese	100.0	47.2	1	52.1	0.6	0.1
Other	100.0	6.4	-	91.9	0.6	1.2

Source: "Population Increase by Classes: 1900-1910." U.S. Bureau of the Census, *Negro Population, 1790-1915*, p. 22. *Note:* 1. Less than one-tenth of 1 per cent.

★ 1899 ★

Size of the Population

Population Increase by Number and Percent and by Race, 1790-1910

YEAR	NEGRO POPULATION					White population increase percent within area enumerated at preceding census	Percentage Negro in the total population	Negroes per 1,000 white population
	Number	Increase during preceding 10 years						
		Total	Population of area enumerated first in year specified	Increase within area enumerated at preceding census				
				Number	Percent			
1910	9,827,763	993,769	-	993,769	11.2	22.3	10.7	120
1900[1]	8,833,994	1,075,994	-	1,073,994	13.8	21.2	11.6	132
1890[1]	7,760,000	1,179,207	18,636	1,160,571	17.6	26.7	12.3	142
1880[1]	6,580,793	1,188,621	-	1,188,621	22.0	26.4	13.1	152
1870[1]	5,392,172	950,342	-	950,342	21.4	27.5	13.5	157
1860	4,441,830	803,022	800	802,222	22.0	36.8	14.1	165
1850	3,638,808	765,160	59,799	705,361	24.5	35.4	15.7	186
1840	2,873,648	545,006	188	544,818	23.4	34.3	16.8	202
1830	2,328,642	556,986	16,345	540,641	30.5	33.7	18.1	221
1820	1,771,656	393,848	-	393,848	28.6	34.2	18.4	225
1810	1,377,808	375,771	45,863	329,908	32.9	34.9	19.0	235
1800	1,002,037	244,829	4,480[2]	240,349	31.7	34.0	18.9	233
1790	757,208	-	-	-	-	-	19.3	239

Source: "Untitled Table." U.S. Bureau of the Census, *Negro Population, 1790- 1915*, p. 29. *Notes:* 1. Figures in italics are estimates. 2. Includes slaves only for western Georgia.

★ 1900 ★

Size of the Population

Population Increase by Race at Specific Periods, 1790-1910

PERIOD	POPULATION AT BEGINNING OF PERIOD		INCREASE DURING PERIOD				Negroes per 1,000 whites in the increase
			Number		Per cent		
	Negro	White	Negro	White	Negro	White	
1910	9,827,763	81,731,957	-	-	-	-	-
36-year periods:							
1880-1910	6,580,793	43,402,970	3,246,970	38,328,987	49.3	88.3	85
1850-1880	3,638,808	19,553,068	2,941,985	23,849,902	80.9	122.0	123
1820-1850	1,771,656	7,866,797	1,867,152	11,686,271	105.4	148.6	160
1790-1820	757,208	3,172,006	1,014,448	4,694,791	134.0	148.0	216
50-year periods:							
1860-1910	4,441,830	26,922,537	5,385,933	54,809,420	121.3	203.6	98
1810-1860	1,377,808	5,862,073	3,064,022	21,060,464	222.4	359.3	145
60-year periods:							
1850-1910	3,638,808	19,553,068	6,188,955	62,178,889	170.1	318.0	100
1790-1850	757,208	3,172,006	2,881,600	16,381,062	380.6	516.4	176

Source: "Untitled Table." U.S. Bureau of the Census, *Negro Population, 1790- 1915*, p. 30.

★ 1901 ★

Size of the Population

Population Increase, 1900-1910

CLASS	POPULATION INCREASE: 1900-1910[1]				
	Area of enumeration[2]	United States	Porto Rico	Hawaii	Alaska
	NUMBER				
All classes	16,145,521	15,977,691	164,769	37,908	764
Negro	1,010,951	993,769	21,695	462	41
White	15,056,025	14,922,761	143,129	15,229	5,907
Indian	24,258	28,487	-	-	-4,205
Chinese	-24,477	-18,332	-63	-4,093	-1,907
Japanese	66,956	47,831	8	18,564	634
Other	11,808	3,175	-	7,746	294
	PER CENT				
All classes	20.9	21.0	17.3	24.6	1.2
Negro	11.0	11.2	6.0	198.3	24.4
White	22.3	22.3	24.3	52.8	19.4
Indian	9.1	12.0	-	-	-14.2

[Continued]

★ 1901 ★

Population Increase, 1900-1910

[Continued]

CLASS	POPULATION INCREASE: 1900-1910[1]				
	Area of enumeration[2]	United States	Porto Rico	Hawaii	Alaska
Chinese	-20.5	-20.4	[3]	-15.9	-61.2
Japanese	77.9	196.6	-	30.4	227.2

Source: "Population Increase: 1900-1910." U.S. Bureau of the Census, *Negro Population, 1790-1915*, p. 22. *Notes:* 1. A minus sign (-) denotes decrease. 2. Includes military and naval service abroad. 3. Percentage not shown, base being less than 100.

★ 1902 ★

Size of the Population

Rank of States According to Black Population, 1790-1930 - I

STATE	1930	1920	1910	1900	1890	1880	1870	1860
Alabama	3	3	3	3	4	5	3	3
Arizona	33	35	38	37	39	46	47	-
Arkansas	9	9	10	10	10	11	12	13
California	25	27	27	30	29	30	30	26
Colorado	32	32	31	32	33	32	37	39
Connecticut	29	29	29	28	28	27	27	23
Delaware	28	28	26	26	24	23	22	19
District of Columbia	22	21	20	18	17	18	18	20
Florida	11	11	11	13	13	14	14	14
Georgia	1	1	1	1	1	1	1	2
Idaho	45	44	46	47	49	48	46	-
Illinois	14	17	19	19	19	19	20	24
Indiana	24	23	23	21	22	21	21	21
Iowa	30	30	30	29	30	28	28	30
Kansas	26	25	24	23	20	20	24	32
Kentucky	17	14	12	11	11	10	10	9
Louisiana	7	7	5	6	7	7	7	7
Maine	43	43	43	40	40	35	32	28
Maryland	16	13	13	12	12	12	11	11
Massachusetts	27	26	25	25	25	25	25	22
Michigan	21	24	28	27	27	26	26	25
Minnesota	36	34	24	34	34	34	35	34
Mississippi	2	2	2	2	2	2	4	4
Missouri	18	18	15	14	14	13	13	12
Montana	40	40	39	39	38	41	41	-
Nebraska	31	31	33	33	31	33	34	37
Nevada	48	49	49	49	48	39	38	40
New Hampshire	44	46	48	45	44	38	36	33
New Jersey	29	20	21	20	21	22	19	18

[Continued]

★ 1902 ★

Rank of States According to Black Population, 1790-1930 - I

[Continued]

STATE	1930	1920	1910	1900	1890	1880	1870	1860
New Mexico	38	37	40	38	36	37	43	36
New York	13	15	17	16	18	17	17	16
North Carolina	4	5	6	7	6	6	6	6
North Dakota	49	48	47	48	47	47[1]	45[1]	-
Ohio	15	16	18	17	16	16	16	17
Oklahoma	20	19	16	22	26	-	-	-
Oregon	39	39	42	41	41	40	39	35
Pennsylvania	12	12	14	15	15	15	15	15
Rhode Island	35	33	32	31	32	29	29	27
South Carolina	6	4	4	4	3	4	5	5
South Dakota	46	45	45	46	46	44[1]	45[1]	-
Tennessee	10	10	9	9	9	8	8	8
Texas	5	6	7	8	8	9	9	10
Utah	42	41	44	44	45	45	44	38
Vermont	47	47	41	43	42	36	33	31
Virginia	8	8	8	5	5	3	2	1
Washington	37	36	35	36	37	42	40	41
West Virginia	23	22	22	24	23	24	23	-
Wisconsin	34	38	36	35	35	31	31	29
Wyoming	41	42	37	42	43	43	42	-

Source: "Rank of States According to Negro Population: 1790-1930." U.S. Bureau of the Census, *Negroes in the United States, 1920-1932*, p. 6. *Note:* 1. Dakota Territory.

★ 1903 ★

Size of the Population

Rank of States According to Black Population, 1790-1930 - II

STATE	1850	1840	1830	1820	1810	1800	1790
Alabama	4	5	9	9	-	-	-
Arizona	-	-	-	-	-	-	-
Arkansas	15	16	21	21	-	-	-
California	28	-	-	-	-	-	-
Colorado	-	-	-	-	-	-	-
Connecticut	23	21	19	17	15	13	11
Delaware	19	17	15	14	13	10	8
District of Columbia	20	19	17	16	14	14	-
Florida	16	14	16	-	-	-	-
Georgia	3	3	4	4	5	5	5
Idaho	-	-	-	-	-	-	-
Illinois	24	23	24	23	22	-	-

[Continued]

★ 1903 ★

Rank of States According to Black Population, 1790-1930 - II

[Continued]

STATE	1850	1840	1830	1820	1810	1800	1790
Indiana	21	22	22	22	24	21	-
Iowa	32	30	-	-	-	-	-
Kansas	-	-	-	-	-	-	-
Kentucky	9	8	5	5	6	6	9
Louisiana	7	7	8	8	8	-	-
Maine	27	25	25	24	21	18	16
Maryland	10	10	6	5	4	4	2
Massachusetts	22	20	20	18	16	12	12
Michigan	26	27	28	27	25	-	-
Minnesota	35	-	-	-	-	-	-
Mississippi	6	6	10	11	12	16	-
Missouri	11	11	13	15	18	-	-
Montana	-	-	-	-	-	-	-
Nebraska	-	-	-	-	-	-	-
Nevada	-	-	-	-	-	-	-
New Hampshire	31	28	27	26	20	17	15
New Jersey	18	15	14	13	11	8	7
New Mexico	36	-	-	-	-	-	-
New York	14	12	11	10	9	7	6
North Carolina	5	4	3	3	3	3	4
North Dakota	-	-	-	-	-	-	-
Ohio	17	18	18	19	19	20	-
Oklahoma	-	-	-	-	-	-	-
Oregon	33	-	-	-	-	-	-
Pennsylvania	13	13	12	12	10	9	10
Rhode Island	25	24	23	20	17	15	13
South Carolina	2	2	2	2	2	2	3
South Dakota	-	-	-	-	-	-	-
Tennessee	8	9	7	7	7	11	14
Texas	12	-	-	-	-	-	-
Utah	34	-	-	-	-	-	-
Vermont	29	26	26	25	23	19	17
Virginia	1	1	1	1	1	1	1
Washington	-	-	-	-	-	-	-
West Virginia	-	-	-	-	-	-	-
Wisconsin	30	29	-	-	-	-	-
Wyoming	-	-	-	-	-	-	-

Source: "Rank of States According to Negro Population: 1790-1930." U.S. Bureau of the Census, *Negroes in the United States, 1920-1932*, p. 6. *Note:* 1. Dakota Territory.

★ 1904 ★

Size of the Population

Rank of States in Black, White, and Total Population, 1930

STATE	Negro population, 1930	RANK OF STATE IN-			NEGRO POPULATION, 1930, CUMULATED BY STATES	
		Negro population	White population	Total population	Number	Percent
United States	11,891,143	-	-	-	11,891,143	100.0
Georgia	1,071,125	1	19	14	1,071,125	9.0
Mississippi	1,009,718	2	31	23	2,080,843	17.5
Alabama	944,834	3	22	15	3,025,677	25.4
North Carolina	918,647	4	16	12	3,944,324	33.2
Texas	854,964	5	7	5	4,799,288	40.4
South Carolina	793,681	6	33	26	5,592,969	47.0
Louisiana	776,326	7	29	22	6,369,295	53.6
Virginia	650,165	8	21	20	7,019,460	59.0
Arkansas	478,463	9	26	25	7,497,923	63.1
Tennessee	477,646	10	17	16	7,975,569	67.1
Florida	431,828	11	30	31	8,407,397	70.7
Pennsylvania	431,257	12	2	2	8,838,654	74.3
New York	412,814	13	1	1	9,251,468	77.8
Illinois	328,972	14	3	3	9,580,440	80.6
Ohio	309,304	15	4	4	9,889,744	83.2
Maryland	276,379	17	15	28	10,166,123	87.4
Kentucky	226,040	17	15	17	10,392,163	85.4
Missouri	223,840	18	10	10	10,616,003	89.3
New Jersey	208,828	19	9	9	10,824,831	91.0
Oklahoma	172,198	20	18	21	10,997,029	92.5
Michigan	169,453	21	6	7	11,166,482	93.9
District of Columbia	132,068	22	44	41	11,298,550	95.0
West Virginia	114,893	23	23	27	11,413,443	96.0
Indiana	111,982	24	11	11	11,525,425	96.9
California	81,048	25	5	6	11,606,473	97.6
Kansas	66,344	26	20	24	11,672,817	98.2
Massachusetts	52,365	27	8	8	11,725,182	98.6
Delaware	32,602	28	48	47	11,757,784	98.9
Connecticut	29,354	29	24	29	11,787,138	99.1
Iowa	17,380	30	14	19	11,804,518	99.3
Nebraska	13,752	31	28	32	11,818,270	99.4
Colorado	11,828	32	32	33	11,830,098	99.5
Arizona	10,749	33	46	44	11,840,847	99.6
Wisconsin	10,739	34	12	13	11,851,586	99.7
Rhode Island	9,913	35	36	37	11,861,499	99.8
Minnesota	9,445	36	13	18	11,870,944	99.8
Washington	6,840	37	25	30	11,877,784	99.9
New Mexico	2,850	38	45	45	11,880,634	99.9
Oregon	2,234	39	34	34	11,882,868	99.9
Montana	1,256	40	39	39	11,884,124	99.9

[Continued]

★ 1904 ★

Rank of States in Black, White, and Total Population, 1930

[Continued]

STATE	Negro population, 1930	RANK OF STATE IN-			NEGRO POPULATION, 1930, CUMULATED BY STATES	
		Negro population	White population	Total population	Number	Percent
Wyoming	1,250	41	47	48	11,885,374	100.0
Utah	1,108	42	40	40	11,886,482	100.0
Maine	1,096	43	35	35	11,887,578	100.0
New Hampshire	790	44	41	42	11,888,368	100.0
Idaho	668	45	42	43	11,889,036	100.0
South Dakota	646	46	38	36	11,889,682	100.0
Vermont	568	47	43	46	11,890,250	100.0
Nevada	516	48	49	49	11,890,766	100.0
North Dakota	377	49	37	38	11,891,143	100.0

Source: "Rank of States in Negro, White, and Total Population: 1930." U.S. Bureau of the Census, *Negroes in the United States, 1920-1932*, p. 6.

★ 1905 ★

Size of the Population

Resident Population: 1790-1975

Year	Millions of persons		Percent Black of total	Average annual rate of of increase[1]	
	Total	Black		Total	Black
1790	3.9	0.8	19.3	(X)	(X)
1860	31.4	4.4	14.1	2.97	2.53
1870[2]	39.8	5.4	13.5	2.36	1.94
1890	62.9	7.5	11.9	2.29	1.64
1900	76.2	8.8	11.6	1.91	1.79
1910	92.2	9.8	10.7	1.91	1.07
1920	106.0	10.5	9.9	1.39	0.94
1930	123.2	11.9	9.7	1.50	1.28
1940	132.2	12.9	9.7	0.70	0.79
1950	151.3	15.0	9.9	1.35	1.56
1960	179.3	18.9	10.5	1.70	2.29
1970	203.2	22.6	11.1	1.25	1.77
1971	205.7	23.0	11.2	1.21	1.78
1972	207.8	23.4	11.3	1.03	1.69
1973	209.5	23.7	11.3	0.80	1.43

[Continued]

★ 1905 ★

Resident Population: 1790-1975

[Continued]

Year	Millions of persons		Percent Black of total	Average annual rate of of increase[1]	
	Total	Black		Total	Black
1974	211.0	24.0	11.4	0.74	1.36
1975	212.6	24.4	11.5	0.76	1.34

Source: "Total Resident Population for Selected Years: 1790 to 1975," U.S. Department of Commerce, Bureau of the Census. *The Social and Economic Status of the Black Population in the United States: An Historical View, 1790-1978*, p. 9. Primary source: U.S. Department of Commerce, Bureau of the Census. *Notes:* X Not applicable. The 1930 census and subsequent decennial censuses were conducted as of April 1 of the respective year; prior to 1930, the month of enumeration varied. In this section, the data for 1975 are from different sources. the 1975 data shown in table is an estimate of the population. 1. Computed by the formula for continuous compounding, $p_1 = p_o e^{rt}$. 2. Revised to include adjustment of 1,260,078 persons (512,163 Black and 747,915 White) for underenumeration in the Southern States, Unrevised census count is 38,558,371 for the total population and 4,880,009 for the Black population. Unadjusted data are used in subsequent tables because revised figures for States, age, etc., are not available.

★ 1906 ★

Size of the Population

Total Black and White Population at Each Census by Sections and Southern Divisions, 1790-1910 - I

SECTION AND DIVISION	POPULATION AT EACH CENSUS					
	1910	1900	1890	1880	1870	1860
	TOTAL					
United States	91,972,266	75,994,575	62,947,714	50,155,783	38,558,371	31,443,321
The South	29,389,330	24,523,527	20,028,059	16,516,568	12,288,020	11,133,361
South Atlantic	12,194,895	10,443,480	8,857,922	7,597,197	5,853,610	5,364,703
East South Central	8,409,901	7,547,757	6,429,154	5,585,151	4,404,445	4,020,991
West South Central	8,784,534	6,534,290	4,740,983	3,334,220	2,029,965	1,747,667
The North	55,757,115	47,379,699	39,817,386	31,871,518	25,279,841	19,690,984
The West	6,825,821	4,091,349	3,102,269	1,767,697	990,510	618,976
	NEGRO					
United States	9,827,763	8,833,994	7,488,676	6,580,793	4,880,009	4,441,830
The South	8,749,427	7,922,969	6,760,577	5,953,903	4,420,811	4,097,111
South Atlantic	4,112,488	3,729,017	3,262,690	2,941,202	2,216,705	2,058,198
East South Central	2,652,513	2,499,886	2,119,797	1,924,996	1,464,252	1,394,360
West South Central	1,984,426	1,694,066	1,378,090	1,087,705	739,854	644,553
The North	1,027,674	880,771	701,018	615,038	452,818	340,240
The West	50,662	30,254	27,081	11,852	6,380	4,479

[Continued]

★ 1906 ★

Total Black and White Population at Each Census by Sections and Southern Divisions, 1790-1910 - I

[Continued]

SECTION AND DIVISION	POPULATION AT EACH CENSUS					
	1910	1900	1890	1880	1870	1860
	WHITE					
United States	81,731,957	66,809,196	55,101,258	43,402,970	33,589,377	26,922,537
The South	20,547,420	16,521,970	13,193,453	10,555,427	7,863,209	7,033,973
South Atlantic	8,071,603	6,706,058	5,592,149	4,654,112	3,635,238	3,305,107
East South Central	5,754,326	5,044,847	4,305,668	3,657,593	2,939,091	2,626,376
West South Central	6,721,491	4,771,065	3,295,636	2,243,722	1,288,880	1,102,490
The North	54,640,209	46,413,758	39,035,798	31,235,267	24,815,772	19,337,997
The West	6,544,328	3,873,468	2,872,007	1,612,276	910,396	550,567

Source: "Total, Negro, and White Population at Each Census, by Sections and Southern Divisions: 1790-1910." U.S. Bureau of the Census, *Negro Population, 1790-1915,* p. 33. *Notes:* 1. Includes white persons (6,100 in 1840 and 5,318 in 1830) on public ships in the service of the United States, not credited to any division or state.

★ 1907 ★

Size of the Population

Total Black and White Population at Each Census by Sections and Southern Divisions, 1790-1910 - II

SECTION AND DIVISION	POPULATION AT EACH CENSUS						
	1850	1840	1830	1820	1810	1800	1790
	TOTAL						
United States	23,191,876	17,069,453[1]	12,866,020[1]	9,638,453	7,239,881	5,308,483	3,929,214
The South	8,982,612	6,950,729	5,707,848	4,419,232	3,461,099	2,621,901	1,961,174
South Atlantic	4,679,090	3,925,299	3,645,752	3,061,063	2,674,891	2,286,494	1,851,806
East South Central	3,363,271	2,575,445	1,815,969	1,190,489	708,590	335,407	109,368
West South Central	940,251	449,985	246,127	167,680	77,618	-	-
The North	14,030,446	10,112,624	7,152,854	5,219,221	2,778,782	2,686,582	1,968,040
The West	178,818	-	-	-	-	-	-
	NEGRO						
United States	3,638,808	2,873,648	2,328,642	1,771,656	1,377,808	1,002,037	757,208
The South	3,352,198	2,641,977	2,161,885	1,642,672	1,268,499	918,336	689,784
South Atlantic	1,860,871	1,597,317	1,529,283	1,273,399	1,080,800	859,690	673,462
East South Central	1,122,790	830,306	501,587	288,057	145,454	58,646	16,322
West South Central	368,537	214,354	131,015	81,216	42,245	-	-

[Continued]

★ 1907 ★

Total Black and White Population at Each Census by Sections and Southern Divisions, 1790-1910 - II

[Continued]

SECTION AND DIVISION	POPULATION AT EACH CENSUS						
	1850	1840	1830	1820	1810	1800	1790
The North	285,369	231,671	166,757	128,984	109,309	83,701	67,424
The West	1,241	-	-	-	-	-	-
				WHITE			
United States	19,553,068	14,195,805[1]	10,537,378[1]	7,866,797	5,862,073	4,306,446	3,172,006
The South	5,630,414	4,308,752	3,545,963	2,776,560	2,191,538	1,703,565	1,271,390
South Atlantic	2,818,219	2,327,982	2,116,469	1,787,664	1,594,091	1,426,804	1,178,344
East South Central	2,240,481	1,745,139	1,314,382	902,432	563,136	276,761	93,046
West South Central	571,714	235,631	115,112	86,464	34,311	-	-
The North	13,745,077	9,880,953	6,986,097	5,090,237	3,670,535	2,602,881	1,900,616
The West	177,577	-	-	-	-	-	-

Source: "Total, Negro, and White Population at Each Census, by Sections and Southern Divisions: 1790-1910." U.S. Bureau of the Census, *Negro Population, 1790-1915*, p. 33.

Women and Children

★ 1908 ★

Women 15 to 44 Years of Age, Children Under 5, and Changes in Children Per 1,000 Women by Divisions and States, 1900 and 1910 - I

DIVISION AND STATE	WOMEN 15 TO 44 YEARS OF AGE				CHILDREN UNDER 5 YEARS OF AGE			
	Negro		White		Negro		White	
	1910	1900	1910	1900	1910	1900	1910	1900
UNITED STATES	2,435,189	2,087,324	19,270,619	15,576,952	1,263,288	1,215,655	9,322,914	7,919,952
GEOGRAPHIC DIVISIONS:								
New England	18,833	17,526	1,608,443	1,389,1119	5,876	5,382	634,679	548,678
Middle Atlantic	131,605	100,004	4,673,693	3,727,053	35,298	29,075	2,013,901	1,660,162
East North Central	81,994	66,806	4,254,070	3,692,487	23,428	21,827	1,881,855	1,750,302
West North Central	64,766	60,851	2,611,619	2,253,085	19,127	21,510	1,286,089	1,236,854
South Atlantic	989,583	865,498	1,842,406	1,514,406	570,516	545,284	1,085,073	901,325
East South Central	649,752	582,279	1,297,554	1,123,231	347,803	348,061	812,171	707,449
West South Central	484,697	386,666	1,496,266	1,021,310	258,012	242,448	963,223	706,797
Mountain	6,038	4,042	553,000	336,603	1,350	981	293,222	193,876
Pacific	7,921	3,652	933,568	519,658	1,878	1,087	352,701	214,509
NEW ENGLAND:								
Maine	332	316	165,072	157,723	117	118	71,637	65,480

[Continued]

★ 1908 ★

Women 15 to 44 Years of Age, Children Under 5, and Changes in Children Per 1,000 Women by Divisions and States, 1900 and 1910 - I

[Continued]

DIVISION AND STATE	WOMEN 15 TO 44 YEARS OF AGE				CHILDREN UNDER 5 YEARS OF AGE			
	Negro		White		Negro		White	
	1910	1900	1910	1900	1910	1900	1910	1900
New Hampshire	149	220	98,665	96,986	40	37	39,538	38,190
Vermont	252	189	77,676	75,914	102	75	34,065	32,776
Massachusetts	11,053	9,520	860,006	729,499	3,448	2,954	325,327	279,203
Rhode Island	2,592	2,672	135,988	108,598	862	793	53,191	42,657
Connecticut	4,455	4,609	271,036	220,399	1,307	1,405	110,921	90,372
MIDDLE ATLANTIC:								
New York	45,629	33,210	2,301,760	1,819,786	10,061	7,762	887,997	744,939
New Jersey	27,124	21,012	610,292	449,664	7,922	6,453	258,995	199,987
Pennsylvania	58,852	45,782	1,761,641	1,457,603	17,315	14,860	886,909	715,236
EAST NORTH CENTRAL:								
Ohio	29,632	24,703	1,116,496	974,221	8,921	8,566	470,533	423,236
Indiana	16,342	14,862	617,469	576,136	4,763	5,054	270,732	269,711
Illinois	30,823	22,680	1,350,430	1,135,080	8,248	6,744	589,677	543,273
Michigan	4,347	3,919	641,765	551,288	1,285	1,287	296,338	258,597
Wisconsin	850	642	527,910	455,762	211	176	254,575	255,485
WEST NORTH CENTRAL:								
Minnesota	1,889	1,330	466,546	376,833	382	323	225,165	226,418
Iowa	3,708	3,119	509,502	503,555	1,245	983	234,755	262,404
Missouri	43,156	42,012	750,965	686,947	12,299	14,797	348,159	349,224
North Dakota	147	59	121,503	61,961	37	18	81,414	46,725
South Dakota	216	93	123,104	78,074	60	37	70,860	52,212
Nebraska	2,213	1,770	269,703	231,608	477	422	139,142	132,940
Kansas	13,437	12,468	370,296	314,107	4,627	4,930	186,594	166,931
SOUTH ATLANTIC:								
Delaware	7,437	7,253	40,136	36,231	3,089	3,622	16,956	16,173
Maryland	58,631	58,267	259,462	230,869	25,987	28,116	111,724	106,463
District of Columbia	31,166	28,634	64,794	52,537	7,290	7,278	19,361	15,862
Virginia	158,798	152,045	315,526	268,651	86,555	90,332	182,181	158,692
West Virginia	15,050	9,325	254,080	201,247	6,974	4,793	162,140	130,672
North Carolina	162,377	143,744	331,856	274,530	107,297	96,945	224,088	185,901
South Carolina	196,806	176,021	153,969	124,336	128,712	125,254	99,685	78,373
Georgia	282,888	237,245	322,963	261,933	167,498	157,201	209,117	168,264
Florida	76,430	52,964	99,620	64,072	37,114	31,743	59,821	40,925
EAST SOUTH CENTRAL:								
Kentucky	66,986	69,889	461,544	419,961	25,511	31,706	268,918	252,507
Tennessee	120,951	114,644	390,451	345,711	56,580	62,388	237,978	212,515
Alabama	220,984	191,017	271,560	217,749	123,991	119,275	187,531	148,007
Mississippi	240,831	206,729	173,999	139,810	141,691	134,692	117,744	94,420
WEST SOUTH CENTRAL:								
Arkansas	108,391	83,932	247,596	200,906	57,330	51,255	173,298	138,549
Louisiana	175,313	149,619	214,828	163,446	92,439	92,759	131,491	106,531
Oklahoma	31,783	12,026	315,490	138,251	18,186	7,916	209,623	99,858
Texas	169,210	141,089	718,352	518,617	90,057	90,518	448,811	361,859

[Continued]

★ 1908 ★

Women 15 to 44 Years of Age, Children Under 5, and Changes in Children Per 1,000 Women by Divisions and States, 1900 and 1910 - I

[Continued]

DIVISION AND STATE	WOMEN 15 TO 44 YEARS OF AGE				CHILDREN UNDER 5 YEARS OF AGE			
	Negro		White		Negro		White	
	1910	1900	1910	1900	1910	1900	1910	1900
MOUNTAIN:								
Montana	485	398	75,329	44,959	105	95	36,754	25,292
Idaho	158	75	66,713	30,151	40	14	39,963	21,030
Wyoming	479	206	27,328	16,183	109	59	15,009	10,179
Colorado	3,407	2,541	186,200	123,005	708	575	81,601	56,287
New Mexico	429	360	65,952	37,737	150	95	41,754	25,329
Arizona	606	310	36,337	18,510	156	93	20,172	11,090
Utah	309	122	80,400	59,177	56	46	52,150	41,503
Nevada	165	30	14,741	6,881	26	4	5,819	3,166
PACIFIC:								
Washington	1,517	582	246,962	101,973	289	139	106,325	51,775
Oregon	375	289	147,375	87,377	70	39	59,327	40,339
California	6,029	2,781	539,231	330,308	1,519	909	187,049	122,395

Source: "Negro and White Women 15 to 44 Years of Age, Children Under 5 Years, and Number and Increase or Decrease of Children Per 1,000 Women, by Divisions and States: 1910 and 1900." U.S. Bureau of the Census, *Negro Population, 1790-1915*, p. 294.

★ 1909 ★

Women and Children

Women 15 to 44 Years of Age, Children Under 5, and Changes in Children Per 1,000 Women by Divisions and States, 1900 and 1910 - II

DIVISION AND STATE	CHILDREN UNDER 5 PER 1,000 WOMEN 15 TO 44 YEARS OF AGE					
	Negro		White		Increase (+) or decrease (-); 1900-1910	
	1910	1900	1910	1900	Negro	White
UNITED STATES	519	582	484	508	-63	-24
GEOGRAPHIC DIVISIONS:						
New England	312	307	395	395	+5	-
Middle Atlantic	268	291	431	445	-23	-14
East North Central	286	327	442	474	-41	-32
West North Central	295	353	492	549	-58	-57
South Atlantic	577	630	589	595	-53	-6
East South Central	535	598	626	630	-63	-4
West South Central	532	627	644	692	-95	-48
Mountain	224	243	530	576	-19	-46
Pacific	237	298	378	413	-61	-35
NEW ENGLAND:						
Maine	352	373	434	415	-21	+19
New Hampshire	268	168	401	394	+100	+7
Vermont	405	397	439	432	+8	+7

[Continued]

★ 1909 ★

Women 15 to 44 Years of Age, Children Under 5, and Changes in Children Per 1,000 Women by Divisions and States, 1900 and 1910 - II

[Continued]

DIVISION AND STATE	CHILDREN UNDER 5 PER 1,000 WOMEN 15 TO 44 YEARS OF AGE					
	Negro		White		Increase (+) or decrease (-); 1900-1910	
	1910	1900	1910	1900	Negro	White
Massachusetts	312	310	378	383	+2	-5
Rhode Island	333	297	391	393	+36	-2
Connecticut	293	305	409	410	-12	-1
MIDDLE ATLANTIC:						
New York	220	234	386	409	-14	-23
New Jersey	292	307	424	445	-15	-21
Pennsylvania	294	325	492	491	-31	+1
EAST NORTH CENTRAL:						
Ohio	301	347	421	434	-46	-13
Indiana	291	340	438	468	-49	-30
Illinois	268	297	437	479	-29	-42
Michigan	296	328	462	469	-32	-7
Wisconsin	248	274	482	561	-26	-79
WEST NORTH CENTRAL:						
Minnesota	202	243	483	601	-41	-118
Iowa	336	315	461	521	+21	-60
Missouri	285	352	464	508	-67	-44
North Dakota	252	305	670	754	-53	-84
South Dakota	278	398	576	669	-120	-93
Nebraska	216	238	516	574	-22	-53
Kansas	344	395	504	531	-51	-27
SOUTH ATLANTIC:						
Delaware	415	500	422	446	-85	-24
Maryland	443	483	431	461	-40	-30
District of Columbia	234	254	299	302	-20	-3
Virginia	545	594	577	591	-49	-14
West Virginia	463	514	638	649	-51	-11
North Carolina	661	674	675	677	-13	-2
South Carolina	654	712	647	630	-58	+17
Georgia	592	663	647	642	-71	+5
Florida	486	599	600	639	-113	-39
EAST SOUTH CENTRAL:						
Kentucky	381	454	583	601	-73	-18
Tennessee	468	544	609	615	-76	-6
Alabama	561	624	691	680	-63	+11
Mississippi	588	652	677	675	-64	+2

[Continued]

★ 1909 ★

Women 15 to 44 Years of Age, Children Under 5, and Changes in Children Per 1,000 Women by Divisions and States, 1900 and 1910 - II

[Continued]

DIVISION AND STATE	CHILDREN UNDER 5 PER 1,000 WOMEN 15 TO 44 YEARS OF AGE					
	Negro		White		Increase (+) or decrease (-); 1900-1910	
	1910	1900	1910	1900	Negro	White
WEST SOUTH CENTRAL:						
Arkansas	529	611	700	689	-82	+11
Louisiana	527	620	612	652	-93	-40
Oklahoma	572	658	664	722	-86	-58
Texas	532	642	625	698	-110	-73
MOUNTAIN:						
Montana	216	239	488	563	-23	-75
Idaho	253	187	599	697	+66	-98
Wyoming	228	286	549	629	-58	-80
Colorado	208	226	438	458	-18	-20
New Mexico	350	264	633	671	+86	-38
Arizona	257	300	555	599	-43	-44
Utah	181	377	649	701	-196	-52
Nevada	158	133	395	460	+25	-65
PACIFIC:						
Washington	190	239	431	508	-49	-77
Oregon	187	135	403	462	+52	-59
California	252	327	347	371	-75	-24

Source: "Negro and White Women 15 to 44 Years of Age, Children Under 5 Years, and Number and Increase or Decrease of Children Per 1,000 Women, by Divisions and States: 1910 and 1900." U.S. Bureau of the Census, *Negro Population, 1790-1915*, p. 294.

Chapter 15
THE PROFESSIONS

Dentistry

★ 1910 ★

Number/Percent: Employed Negro Male Dentists in Relations to 1940 Negro Population, by Divisions

Region, Division, and State	EMPLOYED (except on public emergency work)	Average Negro Population per Negro EMPLOYED male dentist (exc. on pub. emerg. work)
UNITED STATES	1,463	8,794
REGIONS:		
The North	711	3,924
The South	708	13,990
The West	44	3,880
THE NORTH:		
New England	49	2,072
Middle Atlantic	325	3,903
East North Central	265	4,035
West North Central	72	4,875
THE SOUTH:		
South Atlantic	375	12,530
East South Central	170	16,357
West South Central	163	14,878
THE WEST:		
Mountain	7	5,202
Pacific	37	3,630

Source: "Employed Negro Male Dentists (Except on Public Emergency Work), for the United States, by Divisions and States 1940)," Jessie Parkhurst Guzman (Ed.), *Negro Year Book: An Review of Events Affecting Negro Life, 1941- 1946,* p. 333. Primary source: Federal Census, 1940.

Law

★ 1911 ★

Attorneys: Black Lawyers in 1910

"The 1910 census reported 779 Negro lawyers in the country, two of whom were women."

Source: [Untitled text], *Negro Year Book and Annual Encyclopedia of the Negro*, 1912, p. 246. Primary source: 1910 U.S. Census.

Medicine

★ 1912 ★

Physicians: Black Physicians in Relation to 1942 Black Population in Selected Cities

City	Negro Population 1940	Percentage of Total Negro Population of State	No. of Negro Physicians 1942	Percentage of Total Negro Physicians in the State	Population per Physician
Atlanta, Ga.	104,533	9.6	43	28.3	2,431
Baltimore	165,843	54.9	83	70.9	1,998
Birmingham, Ala.	108,938	11.1	19	15.2	5,734
Chicago	277,731	71.7	264	84.9	1,052
Cincinnati	55,593	16.4	25	13.7	2,224
Cleveland	84,504	29.4	51	28.0	1,657
Dallas, Texas	50,407	5.4	19	11.4	2,653
Detroit	149,119	71.6	97	74.0	1,537
Houston, Texas	86,302	9.3	21	12.7	4,110
Indianapolis	51,142	41.9	25	35.7	2,046
Jacksonville, Fla.	61,782	12.0	17	20.0	3,634
Los Angeles	63,774	51.3	50	73.5	1,275
Memphis, Tenn.	121,498	23.9	58	23.6	2,095
New Orleans	149,034	17.5	54	55.1	2,760
New York	458,444	80.2	250	92.9	1,834
Philadelphia	250,880	53.4	131	59.5	1,915
Pittsburgh	62,216	13.2	32	14.5	1,944
Richmond, Va.	61,251	9.3	23	12.6	2,663

[Continued]

★ 1912 ★

Physicians: Black Physicians in Relation to 1942 Black Population in Selected Cities

[Continued]

City	Negro Population 1940	Percentage of Total Negro Population of State	No. of Negro Physicians 1942	Percentage of Total Negro Physicians in the State	Population per Physician
St. Louis	108,765	44.5	142	58.2	766
Washington, D.C.	187,266	...	252	...	743

Source: "Distribution of Negro Physicians and Population, and the Population Per Physician, in Cities with 50,000 or More Negroes: 1942," *Negro Year Book: A Review of Events Affecting Negro Life, 1941-1946*, 1947, p. 333. Primary source: Guzman, Jessie Parkhurst (Ed.), *Negro Year Book: A Review of Events Affecting Negro Life, 1941-1946*, Tuskegee Institute, Ala.: Department of Records and Research, 1947.

★ 1913 ★

Medicine

Physicians: Black Physicians, by Type of Practice and Geographic Area of Activity, 1969

[Coverage estimated at 83 percent of total number of Negro physicians. Represents National Medical Association membership which includes a very small percentage of white physicians (exact number unknown). Year given in source as 1967, but data were extracted from American Medical Association master physician file as of April 1969].

ITEM	Number	Percent	ITEM	Number	Percent
Total	4,805	100	Region in which located- Con.		
Professional activity:[1]			East South Central	275	6
Solo, groups, partnerships	3,427	73	West South Central	244	5
Other activity[2]	836	18	Mountain	29	1
Training programs[3]	447	9	Pacific	598	12
Region in which located:			Puerto Rico	11	(Z)
New England	93	2	Virgin Islands	11	(Z)
Middle Atlantic	976	20			
East North Central	921	19	Abroa[4]d	262	5
West North Central	197	4	Foreign countries	20	(Z)
South Atlantic	1,084	23	Address unknown	84	2

Source: "Negro Physicians: 1969," *Statistical Abstract of the United States, 1970*, p. 66. Primary source: American Medical Association, Chicago, Ill.; *JAMA (The Journal of the American Medical Association)*, Vol. 210, No. 1, Oct. 6, 1969. (Copyright.) *Notes:* Z Less than 0.5 percent. 1. Excludes 95 physicians with addresses unknown or professional category not available. 2. Full-time hospital physician staff, 521; medical school faculty, 152; administration, 52; research, 17; and unclassified, 94. 3. Includes interns, residents, and fellows. 4. Federal physicians located abroad temporarily.

★ 1914 ★

Medicine

Physicians: Increase in Number from 1932-1942

"With reference to Negro physicians, in the decade 1932-1942 there was a decrease of 5 per cent in the total number, while the Negro population increased by about 8 per cent. In 1942 there were 3,810 Negro physicians, or a rate of 1 for every 3,377 Negroes; as compared with a total of 176,191 physicians in the United States serving 132,000,000 persons, or a ratio of 1 to 750."

Source: "Negroes in the Medical Professions," *Negro Year Book: A Review of Events Affecting Negro Life, 1941-1946,* 1947, p. 331. Primary source: Guzman, Jessie Parkhurst (Ed.), *Negro Year Book: A Review of Events Affecting Negro Life, 1941-1946,* Tuskegee Institute, Ala.: Department of Records and Research, 1947.

Mixed Professions

★ 1915 ★

Average Number of Black Persons per Each Black in Major Professions by Region and Division, 1930

SECTION AND DIVISION	Clergyman	College president and professor[1]	Dentist	Lawyer, judge, and justice	Musician and teacher of music	Physician and surgeon	Teacher (school)	Trained nurse
United States	475	5,541	6,707	9,536	1,124	3,125	218	2,076
The North	423	12,747	2,605	3,141	392	1,582	403	1,251
The South	495	4,796	11,731	21,472	2,446	4,286	194	2,567
The West	289	24,069	2,407	2,735	196	1,228	665	971
New England	493	8,553	1,568	2,002	389	1,447	765	1,960
Middle Atlantic	495	30,968	2,543	5,484	339	2,013	518	970
East North Central	405	11,929	2,689	2,231	466	1,387	457	1,865
West North Central	307	5,027	3,160	2,989	416	1,257	186	1,024
South Atlantic	500	4,187	10,428	15,962	2,793	4,191	181	1,947
East South Central	536	5,960	14,686	43,578	3,102	4,365	219	2,967
West South Central	445	5,071	11,824	23,285	1,645	4,388	194	4,754
Mountain	250	7,556	3,778	10,075	236	1,119	364	2,015
Pacific	305	90,122	2,146	2,198	185	1,269	920	827

Source: "Average Number of Negroes to Each Negro Reported in the Principal Professional Occupations, by Divisions, and States: 1930," *Negroes in the United States, 1920-1932,* 1935, p. 292. Primary source: U.S. Bureau of the Census. *Negroes in the United States, 1920-1932.* Washington, D.C.: U.S. Government Printing Office, 1935.

★ 1916 ★

Mixed Professions

Number of Black Persons in the Major Professions by Region and Division, 1930

SECTION AND DIVISION	Total Negro population	NUMBER OF-							
		Clergymen	College presidents and Professors[1]	Dentists	Lawyers, judges, and justices	Musicians and teachers of music	Physicians and surgeons	Teachers (school)	Trained nurses
United States	11,891,143	25,034	2,146	1,773	1,247	10,583	3,805	54,439	5,728
The North	2,409,219	5,694	189	925	767	6,141	1,523	5,972	1,957
The South	9,361,577	18,924	1,952	798	436	3,827	2,184	48,286	3,647
The West	120,347	416	5	50	44	615	98	181	124
New England	94,086	191	11	60	47	242	65	123	48
Middle Atlantic	1,052,899	2,126	34	414	192	3,106	523	2,034	1,086
East North Central	930,450	2,297	78	346	417	1,996	671	2,035	499
West North Central	331,784	1,080	66	105	111	797	264	1,780	324
South Atlantic	4,421,388	8,842	1,056	424	277	1,583	1,055	24,375	2,271
East South Central	2,658,238	4,957	446	181	61	857	609	12,159	896
West South Central	2,281,951	5,125	450	193	98	1,387	520	11,752	480
Mountain	30,225	121	4	8	3	128	27	83	15
Pacific	90,122	295	1	42	41	487	71	98	109

Source: "Number of Negroes Engaged in Principal Professions, by Sections, Divisions, and States: 1930," *Negroes in the United States, 1920-1932,* 1935, p. 293. Primary source: U.S. Bureau of the Census. *Negroes in the United States, 1920-1932.* Washington, D.C.: U.S. Government Printing Office, 1935. *Note:* 1. Probably includes some teachers in schools below collegiate rank.

★ 1917 ★

Mixed Professions

Number/Percent: Black Physician and Dentist Population Ratios in the 1940s

Region	Total Number Persons Per Physician[1]	Total Number Persons Per Negro Physician[1]	Total Number Negro Physicians[1]	Total Number Negro Persons Per Negro Dentists[2]	Total Number Negro Dentists[2]
South	1,146	6,203	1,572	15,859	584
Border States and District of Columbia	691	1,808	425	5,142	125
New England	658	1,668	68	2,051	49
Middle Atlantic	520	2,564	533	3,837	330
East North Central	867	1,709	707	4,005	267
West North Central	850	1,265	294	4,875	72
Mountain	734	3,283	13	5,202	7

[Continued]

★ 1917 ★

Number/Percent: Black Physician and Dentist Population Ratios in the 1940s

[Continued]

Region	Total Number Persons Per Physician[1]	Total Number Persons Per Negro Physician[1]	Total Number Negro Physicians[1]	Total Number Negro Persons Per Negro Dentists[2]	Total Number Negro Dentists[2]
Pacific	624	1,374	141	3,629	37
United States	780	3,681	3,753	8,745	1,471

Source: "Total Population-Physician Ratios: Negro Population Ratios for Negro Physicians and Negro Dentists in U.S. for Selected Years," *1952 Negro Year Book: A Review of Events Affecting Negro Life,* 1952, p. 164. Primary source: *Journal of Negro Education,* Yearbook Number 18, Summer 1949. "The Health Status and Health Education of Negroes in the United States." *The Journal of the American Dental Association,* June 1, 1947, "Distribution of Negro Dentists in the United States." *Notes:* 1. Year 1948, latest figures available for comparison. 2. Year 1940, population Census figures and number of Negro dentists in 1940 are used for comparison. 1950 figures are not available; estimate of population ratios for 1950 is about the same as 1940 figures.

★ 1918 ★

Mixed Professions

Number/Percent: Black Physicians and Dentists, c. 1916

"The number of colored physicians, according to the United States Census of 1910, was 3,077; colored dentists were 478 in number. Each group is increasing rapidly."

Source: [Untitled text], *Negro Education: A Study of the Private and Higher Schools for Colored People in the United States,* vol. I. Bulletin, 1916, No. 38, 1917, p. 68. Primary source: U.S. Office of Education. *Negro Education: A Study of the Private and Higher Schools for Colored People in the United States*, vol. I. Bulletin, 1916, No. 38. Washington, D.C.: Government Printing Office, 1917.

★ 1919 ★

Mixed Professions

Number/Percent: Black Teachers, Ministers, Physicians, and Members of the Bar, 1890-1970

Subject	Teachers, except college[1]	Clergy	Physicians and surgeons	Lawyers and judges
TOTAL BLACK EMPLOYED				
1890	15,100	12,159	909	431
1910	29,432	17,495	3,077	798
1940	63,697	17,102	3,524	1,052
1960	122,163	13,955	4,706	2,180
1970	235,436	12,850	6,106	3,728

[Continued]

★ 1919 ★

Number/Percent: Black Teachers, Ministers, Physicians, and Members of the Bar, 1890-1970

[Continued]

Subject	Teachers, except college[1]	Clergy	Physicians and surgeons	Lawyers and judges
BLACK AS A PERCENT OF TOTAL POPULATION IN EACH OCCUPATION GROUP				
1890	4	14	1	-
1910	5	15	2	1
1940	6	13	2	1
1960	8	7	2	1
1970	8	6	2	1
PERCENT BLACK IN EACH OCCUPATION GROUP RESIDING IN THE SOUTH				
1890	88	84	64	70
1910	90	82	62	54
1940	85	78	53	31
1960	78	68	36	29
1970	64	57	32	33

Source: "Black Persons Employed in Selected Professional Occupations for Selected Years: 1890 to 1970," *The Social and Economic Status of the Black Population in the United States: An Historical View, 1790-1978*, 1979, p. 76. Primary source: U.S. Department of Commerce, Bureau of the Census. *Notes:* - Rounds to zero. Data are not strictly comparable from census to census due to changes in definition. 1. Includes professors in colleges and universities for 1890 and county agents for 1940.

★ 1920 ★

Mixed Professions

Number/Percent: Race and Gender Distribution of Persons in Selected professions in 1940

Profession	Total		White		Negro	
	Male	Female	Male	Female	Male	Female
Teachers (College)	55,123	20,097	53,664	19,146	1,408	941
Teachers (Other)	260,324	792,375	245,660	739,797	14,169	51,935
Physicians & Surgeons	157,648	7,715	153,388	7,546	3,401	129
Dentists	69,370	5,607[1]	67,757	5,467[1]	1,471	140[1]
Nurses & Trainees	8,072	361,215	7,931	353,701	126	7,065
Ministers	135,091	[2]	117,211	[2]	17,487	[2]
Lawyers & Judges	175,261	4,293	174,123	4,251	1,023	40

Source: "Distribution of Whites and Negroes in Selected Professions by Sex—1940," *Negro Year Book: A Review of Events Affecting Negro Life, 1941-1946*, 1947, p. 142. Primary source: Federal Census, 1940. *Notes:* 1. Includes female pharmacists, osetopaths and veterinarians. 2. Figures not available.

Nursing

★ 1921 ★

Employment: Black Nurses Working for Public Health Agencies in 1947

Number	Total Nurses	Department of Health	Boards of Education	Other Official Agencies	Nonofficial Agencies
Totals	1,104 (33)	745 (14)	108	52	199 (8)

Source: "Number of Negro Nurses Employed by Various Agencies for Public Health Work, January 1, 1947," *The Negro Handbook, 1949,* 1949, p. 46-47. Primary source: U.S. Public Health Service. *Notes:* The figures in parentheses represent the number of nurses in supervisory positions. They are not included in the totals.

★ 1922 ★

Nursing

Number/Percent: Black Trained and Student Nurses Working and Seeking Work in 1940

Regions	EMPLOYED (except on public emergency work)			SEEKING WORK (experienced)			Average Negro population per Negro employed trained nurse and student nurse (except on public emergency work)
	Total	Male	Female	Total	Male	Female	
UNITED STATES	6,801	121	6,680	391	6	385	1,892
REGIONS:							
The North	2,936	36	2,900	195	3	192	950
The South	3,718	82	3,636	177	2	175	2,664
The West	147	3	144	19	1	18	1,161
THE NORTH:							
New England	61	2	59	6	...	6	1,664
Middle Atlantic	1,919	22	1,897	119	1	118	661
East North Central	496	12	484	55	2	53	2,156
West North Central	460	...	460	15	...	15	763
THE SOUTH:							
South Atlantic	2,373	44	2,329	113	1	112	1,980
East South Central	878	24	854	28	1	27	3,167

[Continued]

★ 1922 ★

Number/Percent: Black Trained and Student Nurses Working and Seeking Work in 1940

[Continued]

Regions	EMPLOYED (except on public emergency work)			SEEKING WORK (experienced)			Average Negro population per Negro employed trained nurse and student nurse (except on public emergency work)
	Total	Male	Female	Total	Male	Female	
West South Central	467	14	453	36	...	36	5,193
THE WEST:							
Mountain	5	...	5	3	1	2	7,282
Pacific	142	3	139	16	...	16	946

Source: "Negro Employed Trained Nurses and Students Nurses (Except on Public Emergency Work) and Negro Trained Nurses and Student Nurses Seeking Work (Experienced) for the United States, by Regions: 1940," *Negro Year Book: A Review of Events Affecting Negro Life, 1941-1946*, 1947, p. 335. Primary source: Dr. Joseph R. Houchins, Specialist, Negro Statistics.

★ 1923 ★

Nursing

Training Facilities: Growth in Training Facilities for Black Nurses from 1939-1948

"For the past decade Negro nurses have waged a fight for more training facilities. Since 1939 the number of nursing schools at which Negroes could receive training increased from 41, of which 30 were all-Negro hospitals, to 274 in 1948, of which only 26 are all-Negro hospitals (except for Harlem Hospital in New York City, which is interracial)."

Source: "Nurses," *The Negro Handbook, 1949*, 9194, p. 46. Primary source: National League of Nursing Education, 1790 Broadway, New York, 19, N.Y.

Opportunities for Professionals

★ 1924 ★

Membership in Health and Medical Organizations with No Color Bar, 1946-47

Organization	Home Office	No. of Members	Negro Members
Health and Medical			
American Heart Association Inc.	New York	2,420	?
American Hospital Association	Illinois	3,200 institutional, 2,200 personal	?
American Osteopathic Association	Chicago	7,300	?
American Medical Women's Assn. Inc.	New York	2,000	?
American Pharmaceutical Association	Washington	6,500	?
American Physiotherapy Association	New York	2,100	2
American Psychiatric Association	New York	3,387	10
American Public Health Association	New York	1,872	?
Association of Military Surgeons	Washington	10,300	about 200

Source: "Class A Organizations—Health and Medical," *The Negro Handbook, 1946- 1947*, 1947, pp. 206-207. Primary source: Murray, Florence (Ed.), *The Negro Handbook, 1946-1947*. New York: Current Books, Inc., A.A. Wyn, Pub., 1947.

★ 1925 ★

Opportunities for Professionals

Membership in Professional and Scientific Organizations with No Color Bar, c. 1946-47

Organization	Home Office	No. of Members	Negro Members
Professional and Scientific			
Actuarial Society of America	New York	810	0
American Astronomical Society	Evanston, Ill.	620	0
American Chemical Society	Washington	41,000	?
American Economic Association	New York	5,000	?
American Genetic Association	Washington	3,500	?
American Institute of Chemists	New York	2,000	?
American Institute of Consulting Engineers	New York	130	0
American Institute of Electrical Engineers	New York	22,000	2-3
American Institute of Physics	New York	6,000	?

[Continued]

★ 1925 ★

Membership in Professional and Scientific Organizations with No Color Bar, c. 1946-47

[Continued]

Organization	Home Office	No. of Members	Negro Members
American Meteorological Society	Massachusetts	2,300	?
American Society of Agricultural Engineers	St. Joseph, Mich.	1,448	0
American Society of Agronomy	Morgantown, W. Va.	1,250	2
Federal Bar Association	Washington, D.C.	2,500	3
Geological Society of America	New York	814	0
Institute of Radio Engineers	New York	13,138	?
International Chiropractors Assn.	Iowa	950	1
National Academy of Sciences	Washington	350	?
National Assn. of Orthodontists	St. Paul	730	0
National Lawyers Guild	New York	3,000	100
National Shorthand Reporters Assn.	New York	1,500	0
Society of American Bacteriologists	Washington	2,500	about 3
Society of Motion Picture Engineers	New York	1,614	0

Source: "Class A Organizations—Professional and Scientific," *The Negro Handbook, 1946-1947*, 1947, pp. 206-207. Primary source: Murray, Florence (Ed.), *The Negro Handbook, 1946-1947*. New York: Current Books, Inc., A.A. Wyn, Pub., 1947.

★ 1926 ★

Opportunities for Professionals

Professional Associations: Associations "Open" to Black Professionals in the Early 1950s

	Lawyers	Teachers	Dentists	Doctors	Nurses	Librarians	Social Workers
Alabama	X				X	X	X
Arkansas		X			X		X
Florida	X			X	X		X
Georgia							X
Kentucky	X			X	X	X	X
Louisiana	X					X	X
Mississippi					X		X
North Carolina					X		X
Oklahoma					X	X	X
South Carolina	X						X
Tennessee					X		X
Texas						X	X
Virginia	X					X	X

Source: "Professional Associations Without Color Bar," *1952 Negro Year Book: A Review of Events Affecting Negro Life*, 1952, p. 315. Primary source: Guzman, Jessie Parkhurst (Ed.), *1952 Negro Year Book: A Review of Events Affecting Negro Life*. New York: Wm. H. Wise & Co., Inc., 1952.

Chapter 16
RELIGION

Associations and Organizations

★ 1927 ★

Young Men's Christian Association: Buildings, 1912-1928

City	Year opened	Population		Cost of plant including land and furnishings	Amount subscribed by colored people
		Entire	Colored		
Washington, DC	1912	369,282	100,601	$120,000	$41,000
Chicago, IL	1913	2,547,201	57,176	200,000	67,000
Indianapolis, IN	1913	283,622	29,798	105,000	20,000
Kansas City, MO	1914	305,816	27,943	110,000	31,000
Philadelphia, PA	1914	1,735,514	101,420	110,000	25,000
Cincinnati, OH	1916	414,248	22,413	120,000	29,540
Columbus, OH	1916	220,135	16,182	150,000	18,614
Brooklyn, NY	1918	1,976,103	26,922	215,000	22,000
Baltimore, MD	1919	594,637	89,009	115,000	30,700
New York, NY	1919	5,737,492	119,922	375,000	34,300
St. Louis, MO	1919	768,630	50,882	200,000	69,000
Atlanta, GA	1920	196,144	60,143	160,000	53,000
Pittsburgh, PA	1923	588,345	37,725	225,000	25,000
Detroit, MI	1925	993,678	40,838	531,000	40,000
Los Angeles, CA	1926	576,673	15,579	180,735	37,166
Buffalo, NY	1928	574,000	10,000	265,000	19,000
Dayton, OH	1928	184,000	15,000	175,000	31,000
Montclair, NJ	1928	35,000	5,000	150,000	13,000

Source: The Annals, Clyde L. King, ed., Vol. 140, *The American Negro*, p. 284. Published by permission. Primary source: 1920 Census.

★ 1928 ★

Associations and Organizations

Young Men's Christian Association: Buildings, 1918-1919

Cities	Total cost of land building and equipment	Gift of Mr. Julius Rosenwald	Gift by local whites	Gift by local Negroes	From other sources	Date of opening
Atlanta	123,609.00	25,000	39,348.45	30,797.69	28,462.86	1919
Baltimore	110,000.00	25,000	50,000.00	20,000.00	15,000.00	1918
Brooklyn	208,545.85	25,000	160,597.85	14,648.00	8,300.00	1918
Chicago	186,767.14	25,000	60,000.00	22,000.00	79,767.14	1913
Columbus	116,450.00	25,000	76,450.00	15,000.00	-	1914
Cincinnati	112,500.00	25,000	71,500.00	16,000.00	-	1916
Indianapolis	105,000.00	25,000	55,000.00	10,000.00	15,000.00	1913
Kansas City	104,014.51	25,000	44,526.43	25,183.85	9,304.23	1914
New York	358,000.00	25,000	113,713.43	11,286.57	208,000.00	1919
Philadelphia	110,000.00	25,000	62,000.00	13,000.00	10,000.00	1913
Pittsburgh	160,000.00	25,000	90,000.00	12,000.00	33,000.00	1919
St. Louis	185,000.00	25,000	102,500.00	57,500.00	-	1918
Washington	114,877.95	25,000	34,877.95	35,000.00	20,000.00	1912
Total	1,994,764.45	325,000	969,514.11	282,416.11	426,834.23	

Source: Monroe N. Work, ed., *Negro Year Book: An Annual Encyclopedia of the Negro, 1918-1919*, 1919, p. 252. Published by permission. *Notes:* 1. Of the above cities all except Pittsburgh have met the conditions of Mr. Rosenwald's gift. Pittsburgh has been granted an extension of time until January 1, 1920.

★ 1929 ★

Associations and Organizations

Young Men's Christian Association: Buildings, 1937-1938

Location of Y.M.C.A	Original cost of land building equipment	Year dedicated	Sources of funds: Julius Rosenwald	Sources of funds: Local Negro population	Sources of funds: Other	Property debt
Atlanta	141,516	1920	25,000	35,242	81,274	None
Baltimore	115,000	1918	25,000	12,500	77,500	19,000
Brooklyn	230,271	1917	25,000	15,000	190,271	None
Buffalo	280,308	1928	25,000	7,500	32,500	None[1]
Chicago	193,979	1913	25,000	22,000	146,979	7,309
Cincinnati	111,545	1916	25,000	15,808	70,737	1,579
Columbus	140,496	1918	25,000	No record	115,496	None
Dallas	183,156	1930	25,000	49,761	108,394	None[1]
Dayton	194,385	1928	25,000	8,643	160,741	None
Denver	100,262	1924	25,000	9,000	66,262	37,000

[Continued]

★ 1929 ★

Young Men's Christian Association: Buildings, 1937-1938

[Continued]

Location of Y.M.C.A	Original cost of land building equipment	Year dedicated	Sources of funds: Julius Rosenwald	Sources of funds: Local Negro population	Sources of funds: Other	Property debt
Detroit	515,685	1925	25,000	25,084	465,601	None
Evanston	134,569	1929	12,000	11,000	111,569	None
Harrisburg	170,629	1933	25,000	11,307	134,321	None[1]
Indianapolis	110,000	1913	25,000	10,000	75,000	8,500
Kansas City	104,000	1914	25,000	30,250	48,750	None
Los Angeles	200,000	1926	25,000	20,000	155,000	None
Montclair	164,000	1928	25,000	9,000	130,000	None[1]
New York	373,541	1919	25,000	23,763	324,778	None[1]
New York	1,036,297	1933	25,000	14,292	997,005	None
Orange	175,000	1932	25,000	4,340	145,659	1,000
Philadelphia	127,384	1912	25,000	14,011	88,373	None
Pittsburgh	276,499	1923	25,000	21,291	230,208	7,527
St. Louis	225,000	1919	25,000	57,600	142,400	None
Toledo	203,002	1930	25,000	7,927	170,075	None[1]
Washington	110,000	1912	25,000	35,000	50,000	10,800
Youngstown	199,445	1931	25,000	2,000[2]	172,000	None
Total	$5,815,969		$637,000	$472,319	$4,490,893	

Source: "Statistics of Y.M.C.A. Buildings Erected Through Rosenwald Aid," Monroe N. Work, ed., *Negro Year Book: An Annual Encyclopedia of the Negro, 1937-1938*, 1937, p. 236. Published by permission. Primary source: Arthur, George. "Life on the Negro Frontier." *Notes:* 1. Property debt assumed by the general association. 2. Contributed to furnishings and equipment only. 3. Page 252 of "Life on the Negro Frontier." (For details of operating costs, range of membership, etc., see appendix Tables 3-9 of "Life on the Negro Frontier," by George R. Arthur.).

★ 1930 ★

Associations and Organizations

Young Men's Christian Association: Status, 1913-1919

There are associations organized in 110 black educational associations. These include practically all of the more important boarding schools. Out of an enrollment of 9,194 young men in these institutions, 4,727 are members of the Young Men's Christian Association. There are fifty black city associations scattered over twenty-three states. The first building for a student association was dedicated at Hampton Institute on February 2, 1913.

The YMCA work has been established in a number of places in connection with large corporate industries in which numbers of blacks are employed. The company usually puts up the building and pays the secretary. Operating expenses are paid from annual and monthly dues.

[Continued]

★ 1930 ★

Young Men's Christian Association: Status, 1913-1919

[Continued]

The first rural YMCA for blacks was organized in Brunswick County, Virginia, in 1913.

Source: Monroe N. Work, ed., *Negro Year Book: An Annual Encyclopedia of the Negro, 1918-1919*, 1919, p. 252. Published by permission.

Church Value

★ 1931 ★

Average Value and Debt of Churches of Denominations Having 50,000 or More Members, 1926

Denomination	Average value of church edifice[1]			Average debt of church edifice[1]		
	Total	Urban	Rural	Total	Urban	Rural
All denominations	$5,510	$16,279	$2,115	$2,496	$4,959	$513
Selected denominations						
Negro Baptists	5,217	17,309	2,150	2,814	5,438	569
African Methodist Episcopal Church	5,506	16,850	1,838	1,747	3,822	466
African Methodist Episcopal Zion Church	7,813	21,873	2,886	3,575	6,542	872
Methodist Episcopal Church	5,332	17,037	2,156	2,182	5,551	470
Colored Methodist Episcopal Church	3,935	11,115	1,879	1,625	3,587	383
Roman Catholic Church	37,043	44,397	7,330	19,801	20,578	3,875
Protestant Episcopal Church	16,072	21,054	2,881	5,687	6,252	611

Source: "Negro Churches—Average Value of Church Edifices, and Average Debt, for Denominations Having 50,000 or More Members, for the United States: 1926," U.S. Bureau of the Census, *Negroes in the United States, 1920-1932*, p. 531. *Note:* 1. Averages based on number of churches reporting value and debt.

★ 1932 ★

Church Value

Value of Churches by Denomination, 1906

Division and state	Value of church property		Debt on church property		Parsonages	
	Number of organizations reporting	Value reported	Number of organizations reporting	Amount of debt reported	Number of organizations reporting	Value of parsonages reported
United States	34,660	$56,636,159	9,003	$5,005,905	4,779	$3,727,884
Geographic divisions						
New England	113	1,213,626	74	242,722	26	68,450
Middle Atlantic	788	7,150,336	484	1,342,853	207	505,000
East North Central	913	3,304,824	408	382,598	262	285,516
West North Central	959	2,519,402	356	298,896	300	213,589
South Atlantic	14,448	21,779,621	3,584	1,692,995	1,771	1,364,885
East South Central	9,922	11,922,173	2,274	546,513	1,097	669,680
West South Central	7,400	7,941,335	1,762	417,272	1,058	556,614
Mountain	41	284,655	26	27,712	27	35,150
Pacific	76	520,187	35	54,344	31	29,000
New England						
Maine	1	3,000	1	1,600	-	-
New Hampshire	-	-	-	-	-	-
Vermont	-	-	-	-	-	-
Massachusetts	52	646,425	35	159,508	8	22,050
Rhode Island	18	184,346	15	37,350	3	10,500
Connecticut	42	379,855	23	44,264	15	35,900
Middle Atlantic						
New York	169	2,366,796	93	513,412	52	162,250
New Jersey	239	1,289,335	145	231,632	57	94,050
Pennsylvania	380	3,494,205	246	597,809	98	248,700
East North Central						
Ohio	336	1,473,251	132	125,636	90	106,286
Indiana	191	596,625	105	73,680	70	70,650
Illinois	333	1,040,148	148	165,422	78	81,520
Michigan	43	167,950	19	17,009	24	27,060
Wisconsin	10	26,850	4	851	-	-
West North Central						
Minnesota	9	74,300	5	5,362	3	7,700
Iowa	61	167,125	30	25,711	25	18,700
Missouri	605	1,690,119	202	229,805	173	123,890
North Dakota	-	-	-	-	-	-
South Dakota	2	3,900	1	1,700	1	1,800
Nebraska	11	73,500	5	2,130	6	7,100
Kansas	271	510,458	113	34,188	92	54,399
South Atlantic						
Delaware	122	319,832	74	40,836	32	35,750
Maryland	592	1,979,408	277	314,861	188	189,350

[Continued]

★ 1932 ★

Value of Churches by Denomination, 1906

[Continued]

Division and state	Value of church property: Number of organizations reporting	Value of church property: Value reported	Debt on church property: Number of organizations reporting	Debt on church property: Amount of debt reported	Parsonages: Number of organizations reporting	Parsonages: Value of parsonages reported
District of Columbia	83	2,051,942	60	328,454	18	70,360
Virginia	1,874	3,562,930	440	308,680	172	165,435
West Virginia	209	496,946	76	42,282	39	48,050
North Carolina	2,610	3,238,735	511	127,879	232	162,988
South Carolina	2,808	3,366,223	666	145,878	353	227,963
Georgia	4,608	5,125,207	1,182	264,966	464	290,513
Florida	1,542	1,638,398	298	119,159	273	174,476
East South Central						
Kentucky	964	1,845,538	263	102,328	199	122,573
Tennessee	1,743	2,631,502	364	136,630	199	109,270
Alabama	3,474	3,920,253	790	168,554	360	224,196
Mississippi	3,741	3,524,880	857	139,001	339	213,641
West South Central						
Arkansas	1,992	1,628,303	417	77,810	251	106,405
Louisiana	2,032	2,796,242	559	158,708	345	224,112
Oklahoma	543	410,689	140	31,957	58	24,437
Texas	2,833	3,106,101	646	148,797	404	201,660
Mountain						
Montana	6	11,650	4	432	4	3,600
Idaho	-	-	-	-	-	-
Wyoming	1	10,000	-	-	1	1,000
Colorado	24	241,455	17	26,494	19	28,750
New Mexico	7	10,050	3	440	3	1,800
Arizona	2	7,500	1	130	-	-
Utah	1	4,000	1	216	-	-
Nevada	-	-	-	-	-	-
Pacific						
Washington	13	57,900	8	6,125	4	2,400
Oregon	3	44,000	3	3,950	2	3,000
California	60	418,287	24	44,269	25	23,600

Source: "Negro Church Organizations, Showing Communicants or Members, Places of Worship, Value of Church Property, Debt on Church Property, Parsonages, and Sunday Schools, by Geographical Division and States: 1906," U.S. Bureau of the Census, *Negroes in the United States*, Bulletin 129, 1915, pp. 204-205. Adapted by the editors.

★ 1933 ★

Church Value

Value of Churches by Geographical Division and State, 1906

Division and state	Value of church property		Debt on church property		Parsonages	
	Number of organizations reporting	Value reported	Number of organizations reporting	Amount of debt reported	Number of organizations reporting	Value of parsonages reported
United States	34,600	$56,636,159	9,003	$5,005,905	4,779	$3,727,884
Geographic divisions						
New England	113	1,213,626	74	242,722	26	68,450
Middle Atlantic	788	7,150,336	484	1,342,852	207	505,000
East North Central	913	3,304,824	408	382,598	262	285,515
West North Central	959	2,519,402	356	298,896	300	213,589
South Atlantic	14,448	21,779,621	3,584	1,692,995	1,771	1,364,885
East South Central	9,922	11,922,173	2,274	546,513	1,097	669,680
West South Central	7,400	7,941,335	1,762	417,272	1,058	556,614
Mountain	41	284,655	26	27,712	27	35,150
Pacific	76	520,187	35	54,344	31	29,000
New England						
Maine	1	3,000	1	1,600	-	-
New Hampshire	-	-	-	-	-	-
Vermont	-	-	-	-	-	-
Massachusetts	52	646,425	35	159,508	8	22,050
Rhode Island	18	184,346	15	37,350	3	10,500
Connecticut	42	379,855	23	44,264	15	35,900
Middle Atlantic						
New York	169	2,366,796	93	513,412	52	162,250
New Jersey	239	1,289,335	145	231,632	57	94,050
Pennsylvania	380	3,494,205	246	597,809	98	248,700
East North Central						
Ohio	336	1,473,251	132	125,636	90	106,286
Indiana	191	596,625	105	73,680	70	70,650
Illinois	333	1,040,148	148	165,422	78	81,520
Michigan	43	167,950	19	17,009	24	27,060
Wisconsin	10	26,850	4	851	-	-
West North Central						
Minnesota	9	74,300	5	5,362	3	7,700
Iowa	61	167,125	30	25,711	25	18,700
Missouri	605	1,690,119	202	229,805	173	123,890
North Dakota	-	-	-	-	-	-
South Dakota	2	3,900	1	1,700	1	1,800
Nebraska	11	73,500	5	2,130	6	7,100
Kansas	271	510,458	113	34,188	92	54,399
South Atlantic						
Delaware	122	319,832	74	440,836	32	35,750
Maryland	592	1,979,408	277	314,861	188	189,350

[Continued]

★ 1933 ★

Value of Churches by Geographical Division and State, 1906

[Continued]

Division and state	Value of church property		Debt on church property		Parsonages	
	Number of organizations reporting	Value reported	Number of organizations reporting	Amount of debt reported	Number of organizations reporting	Value of parsonages reported
District of Columbia	83	2,051,942	60	328,454	18	70,360
Virginia	1,874	3,562,930	440	308,680	172	165,435
West Virginia	209	496,946	76	42,282	39	48,050
North Carolina	2,610	3,238,735	511	127,879	232	162,988
South Carolina	2,808	3,366,223	666	145,878	353	227,963
Georgia	4,608	5,125,207	1,182	264,966	464	290,513
Florida	1,542	1,638,398	298	119,159	273	174,476
East South Central						
Kentucky	964	1,845,538	263	102,328	199	122,573
Tennessee	1,743	2,631,502	364	136,630	199	109,270
Alabama	3,474	3,920,253	790	168,554	360	224,196
Mississippi	3,741	3,524,880	857	139,001	339	213,641
West South Central						
Arkansas	1,992	1,628,303	417	77,810	251	106,405
Louisiana	2,032	2,796,242	559	158,708	345	224,112
Oklahoma	543	410,689	140	31,957	58	24,437
Texas	2,833	3,106,101	646	148,797	404	201,660
Mountain						
Montana	6	11,650	4	432	4	3,600
Idaho	-	-	-	-	-	-
Wyoming	1	10,000	-	-	1	1,000
Colorado	24	241,455	17	26,494	19	28,750
New Mexico	7	10,050	3	440	3	1,800
Arizona	2	7,500	1	130	-	-
Utah	1	4,000	1	216	-	-
Nevada	-	-	-	-	-	-
Pacific						
Washington	13	57,900	8	6,125	4	2,400
Oregon	3	44,000	3	3,950	2	3,000
California	60	418,287	24	44,269	25	23,600

Source: "Negro Church Organizations, Showing Communicants or Members, Places of Worship, Value of Church Property, Debt on Church Property, Parsonages, and Sunday Schools, by Geographical Division and States: 1906," U.S. Bureau of the Census, *Negroes in the United States*, Bulletin 129, 1915, pp. 206-207. Adapted by the editors.

Churches

★ 1934 ★

African Methodist Episcopal Churches in Atlanta, Georgia: Characteristics, 1902-1903

Serial No.	Membership Claimed	Active Members	Real Estate	Income
37	340	110	$9,200	$1,420.00
38	30	20	200	125.00
39	40	32	150	120.00
40	20	6	1,200	233.00
41	35	20	600	307.00
42	400	600	50,000	4,864.86
43	100	70	2,000	585.00
44	506	200	20,000	5,274.00
45	370	135	3,500	3,058.67
46	16	8	500	-
47	90	50	250	740.02
48	110	100	300	587.55
49	135	85	2,000	135.00
50	50	25	300	140.00
All	3,242	1,461	90,200	17,590.10

Source: "African Methodist Episcopal Churches." Atlanta University Publications. No. 6, *The Negro Church*, edited by W.E. Burghardt Du Bois. Atlanta: Atlanta University Press, 1903, p. 71.

★ 1935 ★

Churches

African Methodist Episcopal Churches: Norfolk, Portsmouth, Richmond, and Roanoke, ca 1900

Ministers	77
Members	9,126
Churches	108
Parsonages	38
Value churches and parsonages	$168,114.09
Present indebtedness	64,739.61
Money raised for	
Pastors' support	18,578.62
Missionary money	1,177.46
Charitable purposes	1,162.53
Educational purposes	512.40

[Continued]

★ 1935 ★

African Methodist Episcopal Churches: Norfolk, Portsmouth, Richmond, and Roanoke, ca 1900

[Continued]

Building and repairs	8,489.40
Current expenses	38,284.22
For all purposes	70,584.67

Source: "Untitled Table." Atlanta University Publications. No. 6, *The Negro Church*, edited by W.E. Burghardt Du Bois. Atlanta: Atlanta University Press, 1903, p. 83.

★ 1936 ★

Churches

African Methodist Episcopal Churches: Summary, States and Territories, 1890

States and Territories	Organizations	Church Edifices	Approximate Seating Capacity	Halls, etc.	Seating Capacity	Value of Church Property	Communicants or Members
The United States	2,481	4,124	1,160,838	31	2,200	$6,468,280	452,725
Alabama	145	274	77,600	4	200	242,765	30,781
Arkansas	173	333	77,585	-	-	233,425	27,956
California	13	15	2,929	-	-	24,300	772
Colorado	8	6	2,300	-	-	63,500	788
Connecticut	4	4	1,275	-	-	16,000	158
Delaware	16	33	7,025	-	-	39,500	2,603
District of Columbia	6	7	5,500	-	-	117,500	1,479
Florida	152	269	63,445	-	-	168,473	22,463
Georgia	334	654	184,592	7	250	601,287	73,248
Illinois	74	105	23,799	-	-	310,985	6,383
Indiana	36	51	16,450	-	-	138,280	4,435
Indian Territory	14	22	1,680	-	-	2,618	489
Iowa	29	29	7,115	-	-	87,365	1,820
Kansas	48	58	14,309	-	-	153,530	4,678
Kentucky	90	106	39,100	-	-	181,201	13,972
Louisiana	81	115	36,150	-	-	193,115	13,631
Maryland	58	93	29,881	-	-	266,370	12,359
Massachusetts	12	11	5,950	1	75	119,200	1,342
Michigan	21	26	7,155	-	-	72,185	1,836
Minnesota	6	6	2,350	-	-	30,000	489
Mississippi	122	255	59,833	1	50	226,242	25,439
Missouri	87	126	27,870	-	-	281,289	9,589
Montana	3	2	350	1	100	14,000	32
Nebraska	4	4	1,350	-	-	62,000	399
New Jersey	54	68	19,510	1	300	159,850	5,851
New Mexico	3	3	550	-	-	3,300	62
New York	34	29	12,900	6	325	231,500	3,124
North Carolina	61	147	42,350	-	-	112,998	16,156

[Continued]

★ 1936 ★

African Methodist Episcopal Churches: Summary, States and Territories, 1890

[Continued]

States and Territories	Organizations	Church Edifices	Approximate Seating Capacity	Halls, etc.	Seating Capacity	Value of Church Property	Communicants or Members
Ohio	111	113	40,965	1	50	318,250	10,025
Oregon	1	-	-	-	-	-	16
Pennsylvania	87	112	39,900	5	600	605,000	11,613
Rhode Island	4	3	2,050	1	-	95,000	595
South Carolina	229	491	125,945	-	-	356,362	88,172
Tennessee	144	236	61,800	-	-	461,305	23,718
Texas	138	208	82,850	-	-	233,340	23,392
Utah	1	-	-	1	50	-	7
Virginia	67	102	34,375	-	-	187,245	12,314
Washington	2	1	400	-	-	4,000	66
West Virginia	3	3	1,050	-	-	11,000	216
Wisconsin	3	3	400	-	-	40,000	118
Wyoming	3	1	200	2	200	4,000	139

Source: "African Methodist Episcopal Church: Summary by States and Territories. Atlanta University Publications. No. 6, *The Negro Church*, edited by W.E. Du Bois. Atlanta: Atlanta University Press, 1903, p. 43.

★ 1937 ★

Churches

African Methodist Episcopal Zion: Summary by States, 1890

States	Organizations	Church Edifices	Approximate Seating Capacity	Halls, etc.	Seating Capacity	Value of Church Property	Communicants or Members
The United States	1,704	1,587	565,577	114	15,520	$2,714,128	349,788
Alabama	336	315	118,800	17	2,500	305,350	79,231
Arkansas	29	23	8,800	6	750	17,250	3,601
California	13	6	2,600	7	1,950	37,200	2,627
Connecticut	12	10	2,900	2	150	79,350	1,012
Delaware	2	1	115	1	200	500	158
District of Columbia	6	6	3,400	-	-	298,800	2,495
Florida	61	61	23,589	-	-	90,745	14,791
Georgia	70	62	19,775	9	200	52,360	12,705
Illinois	5	5	2,000	-	-	13,400	434
Indiana	5	5	2,400	-	-	54,700	1,339
Kentucky	55	52	13,075	3	250	86,830	7,217
Louisiana	21	19	5,200	2	350	12,920	2,747
Maryland	13	10	2,375	3	400	17,350	1,211
Massachusetts	7	6	2,050	1	75	58,800	724
Michigan	6	4	650	2	500	3,200	702
Mississippi	64	50	22,350	14	2,375	22,975	8,519
Missouri	6	6	3,900	-	-	6,000	2,037

[Continued]

★ 1937 ★

African Methodist Episcopal Zion: Summary by States, 1890

[Continued]

States	Organizations	Church Edifices	Approximate Seating Capacity	Halls, etc.	Seating Capacity	Value of Church Property	Communicants or Members
New Jersey	25	24	7,400	1	150	107,700	2,954
New York	47	47	17,000	-	-	371,400	6,668
North Carolina	541	527	171,430	14	1,300	485,711	111,949
Ohio	8	5	1,160	3	-	13,000	194
Oregon	2	2	300	-	-	20,000	275
Pennsylvania	62	55	17,625	7	275	256,150	8,689
Rhode Island	3	1	400	2	870	2,000	401
South Carolina	130	128	66,770	2	250	126,395	45,880
Tennessee	55	52	21,093	3	250	78,813	12,434
Texas	47	38	11,500	9	1,775	26,450	6,927
Virginia	72	66	16,770	6	950	68,449	11,765
Wisconsin	1	1	150	-	-	400	102

Source: "African Methodist Episcopal Zion: Summary by States; and Territories." Atlanta University Publications. No. 6, *The Negro Church*, edited by W.E. Burghardt Du Bois. Atlanta: Atlanta University Press, 1903, p. 46.

★ 1938 ★

Churches

African Union Methodist Protestant Churches: Summary by States, 1890

States	African Union Methodist Protestant						
	Organizations	Church Edifices	Approximate Seating Capacity	Halls, etc.	Seating Capacity	Value of Church Property	Communicants or Members
The United States	40	27	7,161	13	1,883	$54,440	3,415
Delaware	6	4	1,250	2	270	9,600	368
Maine	1	-	-	1	150	-	45
Maryland	8	7	2,255	1	240	5,600	1,546
New Jersey	8	6	836	2	108	5,940	281
New York	3	-	-	3	568	-	60
Pennsylvania	8	8	2,140	-	-	32,100	852
Rhode Island	1	-	-	1	148	-	49
Virginia	5	2	680	3	399	1,200	214

Source: "African Union Methodist Protestant: Summary by States. Atlanta University Publications. No. 6, *The Negro Church*, edited by W.E. Burghardt Du Bois. Atlanta: Atlanta University Press, 1903, p. 44.

★ 1939 ★

Churches

Baptist Churches in Atlanta, Georgia: Characteristics, 1902-1903

Serial No.	Baptist churches			
	Membership Claimed	Active Members	Value of Buildings	Income
1	79	12	$125	$178.20
2	874	350	2,500	750.00
3	85	50	-	162.00
4	400	150	1,500	310.00
5	20	14	-	87.00
6	150	60	1,000	263.00
7	30	20	800	112.00
8	37	20	700	791.00
9	600	300	7,000	1,148.50
10	387	200	4,000	2,405.00
11	34	32	200	120.00
12	125	75	1,000	582.00
13	120	80	500	300.00
14	12	7	85	57.00
15	22	18	200	101.00
16	500	200	4,000	2,408.00
17	750	150	6,000	1,960.00
18	800	200	2,500	2,400.00
19	200	125	2,000	392.25
20	62	40	800	-
21	50	20	800	106.00
22	500	250	4,500	1,200.00
23	15	6	13	25.50
24	60	30	1,000	-
25	13	10	900	55.00
26	265	165	1,200	514.60
27	2,598	1,560	2,700	4,040.00
28	1,500	1,100	1,500	2,774.00
29	75	30	250	17.25
All	10,363	5,274	61,273	23,259.30

Source: "Baptist Churches." Atlanta University Publications. No. 6, *The Negro Church*, edited by W.E. Burghardt Du Bois. Atlanta: Atlanta University Press, 1903, p. 70.

★ 1940 ★

Churches

Black Branches of White Denominations: Urban and Rural, 1937-1938, Part I

Denomination	Number churches			Number	
	Total	Urban	Rural	Total	Urban
Total	6,080	1,960	4,120	644,692	377,785
Adventist bodies:					
Advent Christian Church	6	1	5	164	22
Seventh-Day Adventist Denomination	93	88	5	5,133	5,052
Baptist bodies:					
Regular Baptists	1	-	1	38	-
Christian and Missionary Alliance	10	9	1	535	510
Christian Church (General Convention of the Christian Church)	68	18	50	7,312	1,705
Church of Christ, Scientist	1	1	-	274	274
Church of God	29	7	22	887	318
Church of God (Headquarters, Anderson, Ind.)	98	54	44	3,165	2,404
Churches of Christ	214	80	134	8,155	3,580
Churches of God in North America (General Eldership)	7	2	5	274	55
Congregational Churches	155	96	59	16,000	13,139
Disciples of Christ	487	160	327	37,325	14,938
Independent Churches	7	7	-	1,542	1,542
Lutheran bodies:					
United Lutheran Church in America	1	1	-	126	126
Evangelical Lutheran Synodical Conference of America	-	-	-	-	-
Evangelical Lutheran Synod of Missouri, Ohio, and other states	69	33	36	5,871	3,596
Methodist bodies:					
Methodist Episcopal Church	3,743	805	2,938	323,347	149,559
Methodist Protestant Church	46	9	37	2,529	305
Wesleyan Methodist Connection (or church) of America	26	10	16	1,215	672
Moravian bodies:					
Moravian Church in America	1	1	-	694	694
The (Original) Church of God	1	1	-	12	12
Presbyterian bodies:					
Presbyterian Church in U.S.A.	450	195	255	37,090	21,503
United Presbyterian Church of North America	14	6	8	1,202	602
Presbyterian Church in the United States	52	17	35	2,134	907
Protestant Episcopal Church	287	205	82	51,502	46,201
Reformed Episcopal Church	36	7	29	2,753	1,158
Roman Catholic Church	147	117	30	124,324	106,839
Salvation Army	5	5	-	495	495
Spiritualists:					
National Spiritualists Association	17	17	-	904	904
Progressive Spiritual Church	1	1	-	500	500
National Spiritual Alliance of the U.S.A.	8	7	1	190	173

Source: "Negro Churches of White Denominations," Monroe N. Work, ed., *Negro Year Book: An Annual Encyclopedia of the Negro, 1925-26*, 1925, p. 222. Published by permission.

★ 1941 ★

Churches

Black Branches of White Denominations: Urban and Rural, 1937-1938, Part II

Denomination	Members rural	Number Sunday schools			Number scholars			Value church edifices		
		Total	Urban	Rural	Total	Urban	Rural	Total	Urban	Rural
Total	266,907	5,470	1,741	3,729	307,850	154,922	152,928	37,489,276	29,408,326	8,080,950
Adventist bodies:										
Advent Christian Church	142	4	1	3	94	15	79	4,950	4,000	950
Seventh-Day Adventist Denomination	81	67	63	4	3,402	3,321	81	789,400	785,100	4,300
Baptist bodies:										
Regular Baptists	38	-	-	-	-	-	-	-	-	-
Christian and Missionary Alliance	25	8	7	1	490	465	25	57,625	55,625	2,000
Christian Church (General Convention of the Christian Church)	5,607	64	16	48	3,348	955	2,393	285,100	168,000	117,100
Church of Christ, Scientist	-	1	1	-	395	395	-	254,061	254,061	-
Church of God	569	24	7	17	901	246	655	78,015	57,000	21,015
Church of God (Headquarters, Anderson, Ind.)	761	89	52	37	3,131	2,296	835	343,450	305,150	38,300
Churches of Christ	4,575	177	71	106	5,905	2,819	3,086	138,919	90,010	49,909
Churches of God in North America (General Eldership)	219	7	2	5	298	109	189	8,000	6,200	1,800
Congregational Churches	2,861	140	86	54	8,899	6,862	2,037	1,896,415	1,733,700	162,715
Disciples of Christ	22,387	397	133	264	14,848	6,179	8,669	1,495,568	1,058,900	436,668
Independent Churches	-	6	6	-	491	491	-	67,000	67,000	-
Lutheran bodies:										
United Lutheran Church in America	-	1	1	-	90	90	-	13,000	13,000	-
Evangelical Lutheran Synodical Conference of America	-	-	-	-	-	-	-	-	-	-
Evangelical Lutheran Synod of Missouri, Ohio, and other states	2,275	61	26	35	3,314	1,801	1,513	339,650	293,500	46,150
Methodist bodies:										
Methodist Episcopal Church	3,182,788	3,527	778	2,749	196,496	83,357	113,139	18,938,353	12,914,353	6,023,893
Methodist Protestant Church	2,224	42	7	34	1,283	203	1,080	91,650	26,000	65,650
Wesleyan Methodist Connection (or church) of America	543	26	10	16	1,084	578	506	83,100	67,300	15,800
Moravian bodies:										
Moravian Church in America	-	1	1	-	208	208	-	30,000	30,000	-
The (Original) Church of God	-	-	-	-	-	-	-	-	-	-
Presbyterian bodies:										
Presbyterian Church in U.S.A.	15,587	400	181	219	27,817	15,598	12,219	3,285,860	2,718,550	567,310
United Presbyterian Church of North America	600	14	6	8	1,587	764	823	189,300	126,000	63,300
Presbyterian Church in the United States	1,227	43	16	27	1,569	777	792	138,140	92,175	45,965
Protestant Episcopal Church	5,301	260	190	70	19,075	15,704	3,371	4,162,735	3,958,210	204,525
Reformed Episcopal Church	1,595	28	7	21	1,216	450	766	59,850	29,500	30,350
Roman Catholic Church	17,485	76	65	11	11,406	10,736	670	4,677,378	4,484,128	183,250
Salvation Army	-	5	5	-	470	470	-	67,064	67,064	-
Spiritualists:										
National Spiritualists Association	-	1	1	-	10	10	-	-	-	-
Progressive Spiritual Church	-	-	-	-	-	-	-	3,800	3,800	-
National Spiritual Alliance of the U.S.A.	17	1	1	-	23	23	-	-	-	-

Source: "Negro Churches of White Denominations," Monroe N. Work, ed., *Negro Year Book: An Annual Encyclopedia of the Negro, 1925-26*, 1925, p. 222- 223. Published by permission.

★ 1942 ★

Churches

Black Denominations and Membership, 1936

The Census of 1936 showed that at least 7,000,000 Negroes did not belong to any church. The largest membership of Negro Churches is found in the South. By size of state membership they are: Georgia, Alabama, Texas, North Carolina, Mississippi, Louisiana, South Carolina, Virginia, and Arkansas. The following northern and southern States have over 100,000 Negro members each: Pennsylvania, Tennessee, Florida, New York, Illinois, and Ohio. However, in the states of Georgia, Alabama, Mississippi, Louisiana, South Carolina, Arkansas, Kentucky, and Tennessee, Negro church membership is less than half the total Negro population, as is the case in all northern states. In Ohio, Church membership is about 40% of the Negro population; in Illinois and New York, approximately 25%.

Source: "Denominations Belonging to the "Negro Church," Jessie Parkhurst Guzman, ed., *Negro Year Book: A Review of Events Affecting Negro Life, 1941-1946*, 1952, p. 254. Published by permission. Primary source: U.S. Bureau of the Census, *Religious Bodies*, 1936.

★ 1943 ★

Churches

Black Members of White Denominations, 1918-1919

Denominations	Number churches	Number communicants	Number Sunday schools	Number scholars	Value of church property
Seventh Day Adventists	29	562	26	539	100,000
Baptists - Northern Convention	108	32,639	106	12,827	1,561,326
Free Baptists	197	10,876	177	5,732	186,130
Primitive Baptists	797	35,706	-	-	2,300
Christian (Christian Connection)	92	7,545	88	4,001	69,505
Churches of God in the North America, General Eldership of the	15	329	11	270	5,500
Congregationalists	156	11,960	174	10,339	459,497
Disciples of Christ	129	9,705	117	4,319	170,265
Churches of Christ	41	1,528	24	597	14,956
Independent Churches	12	490	13	435	2,750
General Synod of the Evangelical Lutheran Church in United States of America	1	15	1	25	5,000
Evangelical Lutheran Joint Synod of Ohio and other states	3	65	4	280	2,700
Evangelical Lutheran Synodical Conference of North America	50	1,714	50	2,510	60,000
Methodist Episcopal Church	3,688	348,477	3,642	234,000	8,211,850
Methodist Protestant Church	64	1,612	53	1,650	62,651
Wesleyan Methodist Connection of America	22	1,258	16	769	21,000
Moravian Church (Unitas Fratrum)	2	351	2	217	8,000
Presbyterian Church in the United States of America	438	29,005	434	22,703	752,387

[Continued]

★ 1943 ★

Black Members of White Denominations, 1918-1919

[Continued]

Denominations	Number churches	Number communicants	Number Sunday schools	Number scholars	Value of church property
Cumberland Presbyterian Church	1	50	1	75	1,000
Presbyterian Church in the United States	44	1,183	42	1,160	32,850
Associate Reformed Synod of the South	1	18	1	35	200
Protestant Episcopal Church	198	19,098	188	13,779	1,773,279
Reformed Church in America	2	59	1	52	-
Reformed Episcopal Church	35	3,086	28	1,357	45,000
Roman Catholic Church[1]	36	38,235	33	3,151	678,480
Church of the United Brethren in Christ	10	277	8	236	3,100
Total	6,171	556,848	5,240	300,628	14,229,726

Source: "Negro Members of White Denominations," Monroe N. Work, ed., *Negro Year Book: An Annual Encyclopedia of the Negro, 1918-1919*, 1919, p. 239. Published by permission. *Notes:* 1. The Catholic Encyclopedia estimates that there are from 200,000 to 225,000 colored Catholics in the United States.

★ 1944 ★

Churches

Blacks in White Denominations, 1912

Denominations	Number churches	Number communicants	Number Sunday schools	Number schools	Value of church property
Total	5,377	477,792	10,301	291,529	12,013,116
Advent Christian Church	2	72	2	27	3,800
Seventh Day Adventists	29	562	26	539	6,474
Baptists-Northern Convention	108	32,639	106	12,827	1,561,326
Free Baptists	197	10,876	177	5,732	186,130
Primitive Baptists	4	102	-	-	2,300
Christians (Christians Connection)	92	7,545	88	4,001	69,505
Churches of God in North America, General Eldership of the	15	329	11	270	5,500
Congregationalists	156	11,960	174	10,339	459,497
Disciples of Christ	129	9,705	117	4,319	170,265
Churches of Christ	41	1,528	24	597	14,956
Independent Churches	12	490	13	435	2,750
General Council of the Evangelical Lutheran Church in North America	1	15	1	25	5,000
Evangelical Lutheran Synodical Conference of America	6	224	5	254	10,000
Methodist Episcopal Church	3,750	308,551	3,745	204,810	6,104,379
Methodist Protestant Church	64	2,612	53	1,650	62,651
Wesleyan Methodist Connection of America	22	1,258	16	769	21,000
Moravian Church (Unitas Fratrum)	2	351	2	217	8,000
Presbyterian Church in the United States of America	417	27,799	433	24,904	752,387
Cumberland Presbyterian Church	1	50	1	75	1,000
Presbyterian Church in the United States	44	1,183	42	1,160	32,850

[Continued]

★ 1944 ★

Blacks in White Denominations, 1912

[Continued]

Denominations	Number churches	Number communicants	Number Sunday schools	Number schools	Value of church property
Associate Reformed Synod of the South	1	18	1	35	200
Protestant Episcopal Church	198	19,098	188	13,779	1,773,279
Reformed Church in America	2	59	1	52	-
Reformed Episcopal Church	38	2,252	34	1,326	28,287
Roman Catholic Church	36	38,235	33	3,151	678,480
Church of the United Brethren in Christ	10	277	8	236	3,100

Source: "Negro Members of White Denominations," Monroe N. Work, ed., *Negro Year Book and Annual Encyclopedia of the Negro*, 1912, p. 86. Published by permission.

★ 1945 ★

Churches

Catholic Church: Black Presence, 1937-1938

	Amount
Catholic Negroes in the United States	270,000
Exclusively colored parishes	221
Negro children in parochial schools	36,509
Catholic Negro schools in the United States	214
Catholic Negro high schools, complete	28
Catholic Negro high schools, incomplete	13
Catholic Negro industrial schools	9
Homes	10
Social service centers	9
Boarding schools	4
Sisterhoods represented in negro work	82
Number of sisters working exclusively in negro work	1,000
Lay teachers	279
Schools receiving aid from the Catholic board of mission work among colored people	95
Total number of Negro priests in United States	6
Total number of Negro Sisters oblates of providence	212
Sisters of the Holy Family, New Orleans, Louisiana, established 1842	191
Handmaids of the most pure heart of Mary, established Savannah, Georgia, 1912, now in New York City	28
Negro Catholic universities in the United States	1

Source: "The Negro and the Catholic Church," Monroe N. Work, ed., *Negro Year Book: An Annual Encyclopedia of the Negro, 1937-38*, 1937, p. 231. Published by permission.

★ 1946 ★

Churches

Catholic Church: Missions, 1916-1917

	Amount
Priests having charge of Missions exclusively for blacks	
Josephites	62
Diocesan	32
Religious	39
Subtotal	133
Priests who have schools attached to churches for whites	
Diocesan	43
Religious	12
Subtotal	55
Total	188

Source: "Catholic Church and Negro Education," Monreo N. Work, ed., *Negro Yearbook*, 1916-17, 1917, p. 201.

★ 1947 ★

Churches

Church Expenditures and Value by Denomination, 1906, 1916, 1926 - I

Percent not shown where base is less than 100.

Denomination	Expenditures during year							
	Churches reporting				Amount		Average per church	
	1926	1916	Percent of all churches 1926	Percent of all churches 1916	1926	1916	1926	1916
All denominations	39,245	37,660	92.2	95.1	$43,024,259	$18,529,827	$1,096	$492
Adventist bodies								
Advent Christian Church	4	6	-	-	240	2,310	60	385
Seventh-day Adventist Denomination	85	43	-	-	261,975	41,365	3,082	962
African Orthodox Church	13	-	-	-	19,368	-	1,490	-
African Orthodox Church of New York	2	-	-	-	18,900	-	9,450	-
Apostolic Overcoming Holy Church of God	16	-	-	-	17,198	-	1,075	-
Baptist bodies								
Northern Baptist Convention[1]	-	136	-	95.8	-	381,457	-	2,805
Negro Baptists[1]	20,209	19,988	91.5	94.9	19,475,981	8,361,919	964	418
Free Baptists[1]	-	-	-	-	-	-	-	-
United American Free Will Baptist Church[1]	158	168	95.2	99.4	67,773	36,647	429	218
Regular Baptists	-	1	-	-	-	1	-	-
Primitive Baptists	-	-	-	-	-	-	-	-
Colored Primitive Baptists[1]	111	170	12.0	50.6	39,419	22,881	355	135
Christian and Missionary Alliance	10	-	-	-	19,177	-	1,918	-
Christian Church (General Convention of the Christian Church)[1]	68	103	-	92.8	45,739	36,338	673	353
Church of Christ (Holiness) U.S.A.	64	-	-	-	48,968	-	765	-

[Continued]

★ 1947 ★

Church Expenditures and Value by Denomination, 1906, 1916, 1926 - I

[Continued]

Denomination	Expenditures during year							
	Churches reporting				Amount		Average per church	
	1926	1916	Percent of all churches					
			1926	1916	1926	1916	1926	1916
Church of Christ, Scientist	1	-	-	-	38,995	-	-	-
Church of God[1]	25	1	-	-	39,064	200	1,563	-
Church of God (Headquarters, Anderson, Ind.)	82	-	-	-	86,094	-	1,050	-
Church of God and Saints of Christ	100	45	89.3	-	137,345	18,674	1,373	415
Church of God in Christ	624	-	85.1	-	516,011	-	827	-
Churches of Christ	212	6	99.1	-	40,996	189	193	32
Churches of God, Holiness	26	-	-	-	35,878	-	1,380	-
Churches of God in North America (General Eldership)	7	7	-	-	2,380	1,088	340	155
Churches of the Living God								
Church of the Living God, Christian Workers for Fellowship[1]	144	62	96.6	40.3	50,515	18,812	351	303
Church of Christ in God[1]	-	-	-	-	-	-	-	-
Church of the Living God, "The Pillar and Ground in Truth"[1]	81	-	-	-	64,555	-	797	-
Church of the Living God[1]	-	27	-	-	-	6,199	-	230
Church of the Living God, General Assembly[1]	-	9	-	-	-	3,704	-	412
Congressional Churches[1]	144	139	92.9	90.3	316,444	99,503	2,198	716
Disciples of Christ	447	96	91.8	61.5	289,721	53,798	648	560
Evangelistic associations								
Voluntary Missionary Society in America[2]	-	4	-	-	-	2,199	-	550
Free Christian Zion Church of Christ	5	35	-	-	2,481	19,154	496	547
Free Church of God in Christ	18	-	-	-	19,540	-	1,086	-
Independent Churches	6	6	-	-	34,904	1,128	5,817	188
Lutherans								
United Lutheran Church in America[1]	1	-	-	-	306	-	-	-
General Council of the Evangelical Lutheran Church in North America	-	-	-	-	-	-	-	-
Evangelical Lutheran Synodical Conference of America								
Evangelical Lutheran Synod of Missouri, Ohio, and other states	67	27	-	-	72,197	13,134	1,078	486
Methodist bodies								
Methodist Episcopal Church	3,682	3,639	98.4	98.2	3,694,508	1,670,407	1,003	459
Methodist Protestant Church	44	47	-	-	11,495	9,282	261	197
Wesleyan Methodist Connection (or Church) of America	25	13	-	-	16,679	4,655	667	358
African Methodist Episcopal Church	6,492	6,316	96.8	98.2	7,600,161	3,413,395	1,171	524
African Methodist Episcopal Zion Church	2,464	2,641	99.9	97.2	4,757,066	1,700,737	1,931	644
Colored Methodist Protestant Church	3	23	-	-	6,685	12,129	2,228	527
Union American Methodist Episcopal Church	68	65	-	-	222,621	40,664	3,274	626
African Union Methodist Protestant Church	43	53	-	-	99,563	47,231	2,315	891
Colored Methodist Episcopal Church	2,477	2,613	98.4	99.7	2,428,234	1,736,692	980	665
Reformed Zion Union Apostolic Church	44	41	-	-	37,610	13,156	855	321
African American Methodist Episcopal Church[2]	-	28	-	-	-	13,455	-	481
Reformed Methodist Union Episcopal Church	24	26	-	-	17,282	3,420	720	132
Independent African Methodist Episcopal Church	27	-	-	-	11,704	-	433	-
Moravian bodies								
Moravian Church in America[1]	1	1	-	-	4,475	1,042	-	-
The (Original) Church of God	-	-	-	-	-	-	-	-
Presbyterian bodies								
Presbyterian Church in the United States of America[1]	438	414	97.3	95.4	604,179	204,044	1,379	495
Cumberland Presbyterian Church	-	-	-	-	-	-	-	-
Colored Cumberland Presbyterian Church	167	127	93.8	93.4	80,304	39,497	481	311
United Presbyterian Church of North America	12	-	-	-	20,211	-	1,684	-
Presbyterian Church in the United States	51	29	-	-	27,846	8,154	546	281
Associate Reformed Presbyterian Church[1]	-	-	-	-	-	-	-	-
Protestant Episcopal Church	272	200	94.8	92.6	572,108	218,912	2,103	1,095

[Continued]

★ 1947 ★

Church Expenditures and Value by Denomination, 1906, 1916, 1926 - I

[Continued]

Denomination	Expenditures during year							
	Churches reporting				Amount		Average per church	
	1926	1916	Percent of all churches					
			1926	1916	1926	1916	1926	1916
Reformed bodies								
Reformed Church in America	-	-	-	-	-	-	-	-
Reformed Episcopal Church	35	35	-	-	18,417	9,243	526	264
Roman Catholic Church	129	70	87.8	-	1,005,645	262,112	7,796	3,744
Salvation Army	5	-	-	-	15,118	-	3,024	-
Spiritualists								
National Spiritualist Association[1]	9	-	-	-	7,655	-	851	-
Progressive Spiritual Church[1]	1	-	-	-	2,125	-	-	-
National Spiritual Alliance of the United States of America	2	-	-	-	413	-	207	-
United Brethren bodies								
Church of the United Brethren in Christ	-	-	-	-	-	-	-	-

Source: "Negro Churches—Expenditures, 1926 and 1916, and Value of Church Edifices, 1926, 1916, and 1906, by Denominations, for the United States, 1926, 1916, and 1906 U.S. Bureau of the Census, *Negroes in the United States, 1920-1932*, pp. 553-554. *Notes:* 1. For changes in denomination, see text. 2. So far as can be learned organ denominational existence has ceased, any organization formerly belonging to this group being included among the independent churches.

★ 1948 ★

Churches

Church Expenditures and Value by Denomination, 1906, 1916, 1926 - II

Percent not shown where base is less than 100.

Denomination	Value of church edifices										
	Churches reporting					Amount			Average per church		
	Number			Percent of all churches							
	1926	1916	1906	1926	1916	1926	1916	1906	1926	1916	1906
All denominations	37,347	37,083	34,648	87.7	93.7	$205,782,628	$86,809,970	$56,636,159	$5,510	$2,341	$1,635
Adventist bodies											
Advent Christian Church	3	6	2	-	-	4,950	10,000	3,800	1,650	1,667	1,900
Seventh-day Adventist Denomination	78	29	9	-	-	789,400	108,755	6,474	10,121	3,750	719
African Orthodox Church	2	-	-	-	-	30,000	-	-	15,000	-	-
African Orthodox Church of New York	1	-	-	-	-	50,000	-	-	-	-	-
Apostolic Overcoming Holy Church of God	10	-	-	-	-	16,950	-	-	1,695	-	-
Baptist bodies											
Northern Baptist Convention[1]	-	138	97	-	97.2	-	2,779,199	1,561,326	-	20,139	16,096
Negro Baptists[1]	19,833	20,117	17,890	89.8	95.5	103,465,759	41,184,920	24,437,272	5,217	2,047	1,366
Free Baptists[1]	-	-	173	-	-	-	-	186,130	-	-	1,076
United American Free Will Baptist Church[1]	142	164	151	85.5	97.0	308,425	178,385	79,278	2,172	1,088	525
Regular Baptists	-	-	-	-	-	-	-	-	-	-	-
Primitive Baptists	-	-	4	-	-	-	-	2,300	-	-	575
Colored Primitive Baptists[1]	87	164	501	9.4	48.8	171,518	154,690	296,539	1,971	943	592
Christian and Missionary Alliance	6	-	-	-	-	57,625	-	-	9,604	-	-
Christian Church (General Convention of the Christian Church)[1]	56	107	90	-	96.4	285,100	156,226	69,505	5,091	1,460	772
Church of Christ (Holiness) U.S.A.	68	-	-	-	-	326,850	-	-	4,807	-	-
Church of Christ, Scientist	1	-	-	-	-	254,061	-	-	-	-	-
Church of God[1]	15	1	-	-	-	78,015	1,000	-	5,201	-	-
Church of God (Headquarters, Anderson, Ind.)	77	-	-	-	-	343,450	-	-	4,460	-	-
Church of God and Saints of Christ	48	26	1	42.9	-	149,210	43,746	6,000	3,109	1,683	-
Church of God in Christ	516	-	-	70.4	-	1,508,079	-	-	2,923	-	-
Churches of Christ	141	63	25	65.9	-	139,919	52,925	14,950	992	840	598
Churches of God, Holiness	16	-	-	-	-	159,700	-	-	9,981	-	-
Churches of God in North America (General Eldership)	3	5	5	-	-	8,000	4,185	5,500	2,667	837	1,100
Churches of the Living God											
Church of the Living God, Christian Workers for Fellowship[1]	139	60	27	93.3	39.0	368,935	78,955	23,175	2,654	1,316	858
Church of Christ in God[1]	-	-	6	-	-	-	-	9,700	-	-	1,617
Church of the Living God, "The Pillar and Ground in Truth"[1]	81	-	-	-	-	170,547	-	-	2,106	-	-
Church of the Living God[1]	-	27	-	-	-	-	23,875	-	-	884	-
Church of the Living God, General Assembly[1]	-	6	12	-	-	-	12,700	25,700	-	2,117	2,142

[Continued]

★ 1948 ★

Church Expenditures and Value by Denomination, 1906, 1916, 1926 - II

[Continued]

Denomination	Value of church edifices										
	Churches reporting					Amount			Average per church		
	Number			Percent of all churches							
	1926	1916	1906	1926	1916	1926	1916	1906	1926	1916	1906
Congressional Churches[1]	139	137	137	89.7	89.0	1,896,415	843,518	459,497	13,643	6,157	3,354
Disciples of Christ	411	95	115	84.4	60.9	1,495,568	246,730	170,265	3,639	2,597	1,481
Evangelistic associations											
Voluntary Missionary Society in America[2]	-	4	2	-	-	-	2,580	2,400	-	645	1,200
Free Christian Zion Church of Christ	4	35	13	-	-	22,000	35,900	5,975	5,500	1,026	460
Free Church of God in Christ	11	-	-	-	-	23,700	-	-	2,155	-	-
Independent Churches	2	4	12	-	-	67,000	8,130	2,750	33,500	2,033	229
Lutherans											
United Lutheran Church in America[1]	1	-	-	-	-	13,000	-	-	-	-	-
General Council of the Evangelical Lutheran Church in North America	-	-	1	-	-	-	-	5,000	-	-	-
Evangelical Lutheran Synodical Conference of America											
Evangelical Lutheran Synod of Missouri, Ohio, and other states	55	26	6	-	-	339,650	57,332	10,000	6,175	2,205	1,667
Methodist bodies											
Methodist Episcopal Church	3,552	3,601	3,585	94.9	97.2	18,938,246	8,047,197	6,104,379	5,332	2,235	1,703
Methodist Protestant Church	44	44	50	-	-	91,650	44,146	62,651	2,083	1,003	1,253
Wesleyan Methodist Connection (or Church) of America	22	14	14	-	-	83,100	33,100	21,000	3,777	2,364	1,500
African Methodist Episcopal Church	5,829	6,232	6,299	86.9	94.0	32,092,549	14,631,792	11,303,489	5,506	2,348	1,794
African Methodist Episcopal Zion Church	2,370	2,475	2,104	96.1	91.1	18,515,723	7,591,393	4,833,207	7,813	3,067	2,297
Colored Methodist Protestant Church	3	16	-	-	-	36,000	52,733	-	12,000	3,296	-
Union American Methodist Episcopal Church	64	59	59	-	-	478,951	182,305	170,150	7,484	3,090	2,884
African Union Methodist Protestant Church	40	53	68	-	-	476,269	205,825	183,697	11,907	3,883	2,701
Colored Methodist Episcopal Church	2,341	2,490	2,264	93.0	95.0	9,211,437	5,619,862	3,017,849	3,935	2,257	1,333
Reformed Zion Union Apostolic Church	45	47	41	-	-	184,075	79,325	37,875	4,091	1,688	924
African American Methodist Episcopal Church[2]	-	1	-	-	-	-	6,280	-	-	-	-
Reformed Methodist Union Episcopal Church	21	27	57	-	-	74,800	35,500	36,965	3,562	1,315	649
Independent African Methodist Episcopal Church	28	-	-	-	-	98,050	-	-	3,502	-	-
Moravian bodies											
Moravian Church in America[1]	1	-	1	-	-	30,000	-	8,000	-	-	-
The (Original) Church of God	-	-	-	-	-	-	-	-	-	-	-
Presbyterian bodies											
Presbyterian Church in the United States of America[1]	398	353	365	88.4	81.3	3,285,860	1,276,148	752,387	8,256	3,615	2,061
Cumberland Presbyterian Church	-	-	1	-	-	-	-	1,000	-	-	-
Colored Cumberland Presbyterian Church	162	130	192	91.0	95.6	353,825	230,426	203,778	2,184	1,773	1,061
United Presbyterian Church of North America	12	-	-	-	-	189,300	-	-	15,775	-	-
Presbyterian Church in the United States	46	32	33	-	-	138,140	43,185	32,850	3,003	1,350	995
Associate Reformed Presbyterian Church[1]	-	-	1	-	-	-	-	200	-	-	-
Protestant Episcopal Church	259	188	159	90.2	87.0	4,162,735	1,527,768	1,773,279	16,072	8,126	11,153
Reformed bodies											
Reformed Church in America	-	-	-	-	-	-	-	-	-	-	-
Reformed Episcopal Church	36	34	38	-	-	59,850	45,862	28,287	1,663	1,349	744
Roman Catholic Church	126	73	32	85.7	-	4,667,378	1,173,372	678,480	37,043	16,074	21,203
Salvation Army	1	-	-	-	-	67,064	-	-	-	-	-
Spiritualists											
National Spiritualist Association[1]	-	-	-	-	-	-	-	-	-	-	-
Progressive Spiritual Church[1]	1	-	-	-	-	3,800	-	-	-	-	-
National Spiritual Alliance of the United States of America	-	-	-	-	-	-	-	-	-	-	-
United Brethren bodies											
Church of the United Brethren in Christ	-	-	6	-	-	-	-	3,100	-	-	517

Source: "Negro Churches—Expenditures, 1926 and 1916, and Value of Church Edifices, 1926, 1916, and 1906, by Denominations, for the United States, 1926, 1916, and 1906," U.S. Bureau of the Census, *Negroes in the United States, 1920-1932*, pp. 553-554. *Notes:* 1. For changes in denomination, see text. 2. So far as can be learned organic denominational existence has ceased, any organization formerly belonging to this group being included among the independent churches.

★ 1949 ★

Churches

Church Membership by Gender with Number of Males per 100 Females for Denominations Having 50,000 or More Members, 1926

Figures to be used with due consideration of the number of members not reported by sex.

Denomination	Total	Male	Female	Sex not reported	Males per 100 females
Negro Baptists	3,196,623	1,050,062	1,661,183	485,378	63.2
African Methodist Episcopal Church	545,814	165,615	295,137	85,062	56.1
African Methodist Episcopal Zion Church	456,813	167,432	289,381	-	57.9
Methodist Episcopal Church	332,347	117,176	192,905	22,266	60.7
Colored Methodist Episcopal Church	202,713	65,781	107,807	29,125	61.0
Roman Catholic Church	124,324	50,732	64,523	9,069	78.6
Protestant Episcopal Church	51,502	17,846	26,422	7,234	67.5

Source: "Percent Distribution of Urban and Rural Negro Churches and Membership for Denominations Having 50,000 or More Members: 1926," U.S. Bureau of the Census, *Negroes in the United States, 1920-1932*, p. 531.

★ 1950 ★

Churches

Church Membership by Race and Gender, 1906, 1916, and 1926

United States	Adult males			Adult females		
	Population	Members in church	Percent	Population	Members in church	Percent
1906 Total	29,208,612	13,769,443	47.1	28,133,335	18,098,396	64.3
Negro	3,305,878	1,292,221	39.1	3,345,788	2,153,701	64.4
White	25,902,734	12,477,222	48.2	24,787,547	15,944,695	64.3
1916 Total	35,023,659	16,610,186	47.4	33,224,501	21,174,762	63.7
Negro	3,636,671	1,643,686	45.2	3,665,882	2,659,158	72.5
White	31,386,988	14,966,500	47.7	29,558,619	18,515,604	62.6
1926 Total	40,761,580	19,656,452	48.2	39,208,089	24,668,052	62.9
Negro	3,942,665	1,795,593	45.5	3,974,332	2,904,913	73.1
White	36,818,915	17,860,858	48.5	35,232,757	21,758,139	61.8

Source: "Percent of Negro and White Men and Women in Church, 1926, 1916, and 1906," Monroe N. Work, ed., *Negro Year Book: An Annual Encyclopedia of the Negro, 1937-1938*. 1937, p. 228. Published by permission.

★ 1951 ★

Churches

Church Membership in Illinois, ca 1900

African Methodist Episcopal	8,375
Baptist	8,812
African Methodist Episcopal Zion	100
Methodist Episcopal	360
Old Time Methodist Episcopal	100
Episcopal	380
Presbyterian	210
Cumberland Presbyterian	65
Christian	50
Catholics (not ascertained)	-
Adventists (estimated)	25
The total amount of church property owned in the state was about	$4454,000
The total expenses for 1902 were about	133,000

Source: "Untitled Table." Atlanta University Publications. No. 6, *The Negro Church*, edited by W.E. Burghardt Du Bois. Atlanta: Atlanta University Press, 1903, p. 83.

★ 1952 ★

Churches

Church Membership in Ohio, 1890

State	Organizations	Edifices	Seating Capacity	Halls	Seating Capacity	Value	Communicants	Population
Total for United States	23,462	23,770	6,800,035	1,358	114,644	$26,626,488	2,673,977	7,488,788
Ohio	250	214	66,516	34	1,750	576,425	19,827	87,113

Source: "Untitled Table." Atlanta University Publications. No. 6, *The Negro Church*, edited by W.E. Burghardt Du Bois. Atlanta: Atlanta University Press, 1903, p. 94.

★ 1953 ★

Churches

Churches and Memberships: by State, 1936

Section, division and state	Number of Negro churches	Number of members
United States	38,303	5,660,618
The North	4,672	1,090,822
The South	33,230	4,519,461
The West	401	50,335
New England	185	40,935
Maine	1	206
New Hampshire	1	70
Vermont	-	-
Massachusetts	83	22,051
Rhode Island	24	4,333
Connecticut	76	14,275
Middle Atlantic	1,836	476,784
New York	453	171,118
New Jersey	511	89,646
Pennsylvania	872	216,020
East North Central	1,712	438,593
Ohio	634	147,327
Indiana	303	59,610
Illinois	513	170,153
Michigan	241	57,589
Wisconsin	21	3,914
West North Central	939	134,510
Minnesota	19	3,763
Iowa	83	6,134
Missouri	517	90,648
North Dakota	1	10
South Dakota	5	128
Nebraska	28	4,746
Kansas	286	29,081
South Atlantic	15,533	2,103,587
Delaware	137	18,468
Maryland	416	69,312
District of Columbia	209	77,187
Virginia	1,783	308,779
West Virginia	453	38,989
North Carolina	2,562	434,951
South Carolina	2,158	330,479
Georgia	5,954	629,028
Florida	1,861	196,394

[Continued]

★ 1953 ★

Churches and Memberships: by State, 1936

[Continued]

Section, division and state	Number of Negro churches	Number of members
East South Central	9,875	1,320,143
Kentucky	780	107,005
Tennessee	1,446	212,223
Alabama	4,011	585,733
Mississippi	3,638	415,182
West South Central	7,822	1,095,731
Arkansas	1,939	217,123
Louisiana	2,028	330,990
Oklahoma	774	82,681
Texas	3,081	464,937
Mountain	154	11,265
Montana	11	218
Idaho	6	221
Wyoming	9	270
Colorado	46	6,459
New Mexico	28	1,080
Arizona	42	2,401
Utah	9	485
Nevada	3	95
Pacific	247	39,070
Washington	27	1,754
Oregon	5	754
California	215	36,562

Source: "Value of Church Edifices," Florence Murray, ed., *The Negro Handbook*, 1942, p. 98. Published by permission.

★ 1954 ★

Churches

Churches in Atlanta, Georgia, 1902-1903

Denomination	No. Churches	Membership Claimed	Active Membership	Value of Property	Income, 1902
Baptist	29	10,363	5,274	$61,273	$23,259.30
Methodist	21	5,015	2,571	149,235	23,101.75
Other denominations	4	883	578	42,000	5,451.79
Total	54	16,261	8,423	252,508	51,812.84

Source: "A Southern City." Atlanta University Publications. No. 6, *The Negro Church*, edited by W.E. Burghardt Du Bois. Atlanta: Atlanta University Press, 1903, p. 69.

★ 1955 ★

Churches

Churches in Chicago: Characteristics, 1902

Denomination	No. reporting	Membership	Active membership	Valuation of church property	Expenses last year
African Methodist Episcopal	9	3,549	2,080	$125,800[1]	$39,372.95
Baptist	11	3,097	2,140	16,500	12,674.74
African Methodist Episcopal Zion	1	500	300	20,000	-
Presbyterian	2	215	134	8,000	2,640.60
Christian	1	50	40	-	-
Episcopal	1	280	125	5,000	1,811.25
Methodist Episcopal	2	310	150	3,500	1,909.00
Adventist	1	-	-	-	-
Total	28	8,001	4,969	178,800	58,408.50

Source: "The Negro Churches in Chicago," W.E.B. Du Bois, ed., *The Negro Church*, p. 87. *Notes:* These totals are smaller than they really should be owing to the fact that some churches were only partially reported, while the "Adventist Church" has no report of statistics. Four of the Baptist Churches do not own property, but use rented buildings. One of the Presbyterian Churches owns no property. The Christian Church uses a rented building. One of the Methodist Episcopal Churches uses a rented building. 1. One of the African Methodist Episcopal Churches does not own property, but uses a rented building.

★ 1956 ★

Churches

Churches in Ohio: Financial Conditions, ca. 1900

Churches	Value of Property	Indebtedness	Salary of Pastor	Paid on Debt	Total Raised
M.E. Church	$79,050.09[1]	$10,439.00	$8,430.00	$9,074.00[2]	–
A.M.E.					
N.O. Conference	242,375.00	17,055.25	14,692.01	14,898.29	$37,878.57
Ohio Conference	108,570.00	10,364.53	13,116.25	10,806.64	28,522.43
Baptist					
Eastern Association	-	-	-	-	-
Western Association	-	-	13,380.00	13,510.00[4]	-
Zion Association	-	-	-	-	-
Providence Association	31,350.00	-	1,414.40[3]	-	-
Wesleyan	9,400.00	-	1,954.99	-	3,296.52

Source: "Untitled Table." Atlanta University Publications. No. 6, *The Negro Church*, edited by W.E. Burghardt Du Bois. Atlanta: Atlanta University Press, 1903, p. 9. *Notes:* 1. $12,200 for parsonages. 2. $5,628 for improvements, $3,466 on debt. 3. For six pastors only. 4. The total valuation of church property of the Baptists is estimated at $259,200.

★ 1957 ★

Churches

Churches in Philadelphia: Characteristics, 1838

Denominations	No. Churches	Members	Annual Expenses	Value of Property	Incumbrance
Episcopalian	1	100	$1,000	$36,000	-
Lutheran	1	10	120	3,000	$1,000
Methodist	8	2,860	2,100	50,800	5,100
Presbyterian	2	325	1,500	20,000	1,000
Baptist	4	700	1,300	4,200	-
Total	16	3,995	6,020	114,000	7,100

Source: "Untitled Table." Atlanta University Publications. No. 6, *The Negro Church*, edited by W.E. Burghardt Du Bois. Atlanta: Atlanta University Press, 1903, p. 108.

★ 1958 ★

Churches

Churches in Philadelphia: Characteristics, 1867

Name	Founded	No. of Members	Value of Property	Pastor's Salary
Protestant Episcopal				
St. Thomas	1792	-	-	-
Methodist				
Bethel	1794	1,100	$50,000	$600
Union	1827	467	40,000	850
Wesley	1817	464	21,000	700
Zoar	1794	400	12,000	-
John Wesley	1814	42	3,000	No regular salary
Little Wesley	1821	310	11,000	500
Pisgah	1831	116	4,600	430
Zion City Mission	1858	90	4,500	-
Little Union	1837	200	-	-
Baptist				
First Baptist	1809	360	5,000	-
Union Baptist	-	400	7,000	600
Shiloh	1842	405	16,000	600
Oak Street	1827	137	-	-
Presbyterian				
First Presbyterian	1807	200	8,000	-

[Continued]

★ 1958 ★

Churches in Philadelphia: Characteristics, 1867

[Continued]

Name	Founded	No. of Members	Value of Property	Pastor's Salary
Second Presbyterian	1824	-	-	-
Central Presbyterian	1844	240	16,000	-

Source: "Untitled Table." Atlanta University Publications. No. 6, *The Negro Church,* edited by W.E. Burghaardt Du Bois. Atlanta: Atlanta University Press, 1903, p. 109.

★ 1959 ★

Churches

Churches in Philadelphia: Characteristics, 1897

Denomination	Churches	Members claimed	Value of property	Expenses
African Methodist Episcopal	14	3,210	202,229	27,074
African Methodist Episcopal Zion	3	-	25,000	5,000
Union African Methodist Episcopal	1	-	-	-
Methodist Protestant	1	-	-	-
Methodist Episcopal	6	1,202	49,700	16,394
Baptist	17	5,583	296,800	30,000
Presbyterian	3	633	150,000	4,473
Protestant Episcopal	6	791	130,000	6,613
Roman Catholic	1	200	-	-

Source: "Untitled Table," W.E. Burghardt DuBois, ed., *The Negro Church,* p. 109.

★ 1960 ★

Churches

Churches in Philadelphia: Membership, 1813

Churches	Members
St. Thomas, Protestant Episcoppal	560
Bethel, African Methodist Episcopal	1,272
Zoar, Methodist Episcopal	80
Union, African Methodist Episcopal	74
Baptist, Race and Vine Streets	80

[Continued]

★ 1960 ★

Churches in Philadelphia: Membership, 1813

[Continued]

Churches	Members
Presbyterian	300
Total	2,366

Source: "Untitled Table." Atlanta University Publications. No. 6, *The Negro Church,* edited by W.E. Burghardt Du Bois. Atlanta: Atlanta University Press, 1903, p. 108.

★ 1961 ★

Churches

Churches, Membership, and Sunday Schools, by Denominations, 1906, 1916, 1926 - I

Denomination	Number of churches[1]			Number of members[2]			Average members per church		
	1926	1916	1906	1926	1916	1906	1926	1916	1906
All denominations	42,585	39,592	36,563	5,203,487	4,602,805	3,691,844[3]	122	116	101
Adventist bodies									
Advent Christian Church	6	10	2	164	317	72	27	32	36
Seventh-day Adventist Denomination	93	54	29	5,133	2,553	562	55	47	19
African Orthodox Church	13	-	-	1,568	-	-	121	-	-
African Orthodox Church of New York	3	-	-	717	-	-	239	-	-
Apostolic Overcoming Holy Church of God	16	-	-	1,047	-	-	65	-	-
Baptist bodies									
Northern Baptist Convention[4]	-	142	108	-	53,842	32,639	-	379	302
Negro Baptist[4]	22,061	21,071	18,492	3,196,623	2,938,579	2,261,607	145	139	122
Free Baptist[4]	-	-	195	-	-	10,876	-	-	56
United American Free Will Baptist Church[4]	166	169	241	13,396	13,362	14,489	81	79	59
Regular Baptists	1	1	-	38	23	-	-	-	-
Primitive Baptists	-	-	4	-	-	102	-	-	26
Colored Primitive Baptists[4]	925	336	787	43,978	15,144	35,076	48	45	45
Christian and Missionary Alliance	10	-	-	535	-	-	54	-	-
Christian Church (General Convention of the Christian Church)[4]	68	111	91	7,312	10,120	7,545	108	91	83
Church of Christ (Holiness) United States of America	82	-	-	4,919	-	-	60	-	-
Church of Christ, Scientist	1	[5]	-	274	[5]	-	-	-	-
Church of God[4]	29	1	-	887	24	-	31	-	-
Church of God (Headquarters, Anderson, Ind.)	98	-	-	3,165	-	-	32	-	-
Church of God and Saints of Christ	112	92	48	6,741	3,311	1,823	60	36	38
Church of God in Christ	733	-	-	3,263	-	-	41	-	-
Churches of Christ	214	87	41	8,155	2,813	1,528	38	32	37
Churches of God, Holiness	29	-	-	2,278	-	-	79	-	-
Churches of God in North America (General Eldership)	7	7	14	274	189	329	39	27	24
Churches of the Living God									
Church of the Living God, Christian Workers for Fellowship[4]	149	154	44	11,558	9,626	2,676	78	63	61
Church of Christ in God[4]	-	-	9	-	-	848	-	-	94
Church of the Living God, "The Pillar and Ground in Truth"	81	-	-	5,844	-	-	72	-	-
Church of the Living God[4]	-	28	-	-	1,743	-	-	62	-
Church of the Living God, General Assembly[4]	-	10	14	-	266	752	-	27	54
Congressional Churches[4]	155	154	156	16,000	13,209	11,960	103	86	77
Disciples of Christ	487	156	129	37,325	11,478	9,705	77	74	75
Evangelistic associations									
Voluntary Missionary Society in America	-	4	3	-	855	425	-	214	142
Free Christian Zion Church of Christ	5	35	14	187	6,225	1,835	37	178	131
Free Church of God in Christ	19	-	-	874	-	-	46	-	-
Independent Churches	7	6	12	1,542	428	490	220	71	41
Lutherans									
United Lutheran Church in America[4]	1	-	-	126	-	-	-	-	-
General Council of the Evangelical Lutheran Church in North America	-	-	1	-	-	15	-	-	-
Evangelical Lutheran Synodical Conference of America	-	-	-	-	-	-	-	-	-

[Continued]

★ 1961 ★

Churches, Membership, and Sunday Schools, by Denominations, 1906, 1916, 1926 - I

[Continued]

Denomination	Number of churches[1]			Number of members[2]			Average members per church		
	1926	1916	1906	1926	1916	1906	1926	1916	1906
Evangelical Lutheran Synod of Missouri, Ohio, and other states	69	31	6	5,871	1,525	224	85	49	37
Methodist bodies									
Methodist Episcopal Church	3,743	3,704	3,682	332,347	320,025	308,551	89	86	84
Methodist Protestant Church	46	49	62	2,529	2,869	2,612	55	59	42
Wesleyan Methodist Connection (or Church) of America	26	16	19	1,215	819	1,258	47	51	66
African Methodist Episcopal Church	6,708	6,633	6,608	545,814	548,355	494,777	81	83	75
African Methodist Episcopal Zion Church	2,466	2,716	2,197	456,813	257,169	184,542	185	95	84
Colored Methodist Protestant Church	3	26	-	533	1,967	-	178	76	-
Union American Methodist Episcopal Church	73	67	77	10,169	3,624	4,347	139	54	56
African Union Methodist Protestant Church	43	58	69	4,086	3,751	5,592	95	65	81
Colored Methodist Episcopal Church	2,518	2,621	2,365	202,713	245,749	172,996	81	94	73
Reformed Zion Union Apostolic Church	48	47	45	4,538	3,977	3,059	95	85	68
African American Methodist Episcopal Church[6]	-	28	-	-	1,310	-	-	47	-
Reformed Methodist Union Episcopal Church	25	27	57	2,265	2,196	4,397	91	81	77
Independent African Methodist Episcopal Church	729	-	-	1,003	-	-	35	-	-
Moravian bodies									
Moravian Church in America[4]	1	1	2	694	419	351	-	-	176
The (Original) Church of God	1	-	-	12	-	-	-	-	-
Presbyterian bodies									
Presbyterian Church in the United States of America[4]	450	434	417	37,090	31,957	27,799	82	74	67
Cumberland Presbyterian Church	-	-	1	-	-	50	-	-	50
Colored Cumberland Presbyterian Church	178	136	196	10,868	13,077	18,066	61	96	92
United Presbyterian Church of North America	14	-	-	1,202	-	-	86	-	-
Presbyterian Church in the United States	52	36	40	2,134	1,429	1,183	41	40	30
Associate Reformed Presbyterian Church[4]	-	-	1	-	-	18	-	-	-
Protestant Episcopal Church	287	216	193	51,502	23,775	19,098	179	110	99
Reformed bodies									
Reformed Church in America	-	-	2	-	-	59	-	-	30
Reformed Episcopal Church	36	35	38	2,753	3,017	2,252	76	86	59
Roman Catholic Church	147	83	36	124,324	51,688	44,982[3]	846	623	1,250
Salvation Army	5	-	-	495	-	-	99	-	-
Spiritualists									
National Spiritualist Association[4]	17	-	-	904	-	-	53	-	-
Progressive Spiritual Church[4]	1	-	-	500	-	-	-	-	-
National Spiritual Alliance of the United States of America	8	-	-	190	-	-	24	-	-
United Brethren bodies									
Church of the United Brethren in Christ	-	-	10	-	-	277	-	-	28

Source: "Number of Negro Churches, Membership, and Sunday Schools, by Denominations, for the United States, 1926, 1916, and 1906," U.S. Bureau of the Census, *Negroes in the United States, 1920-1932*, pp. 551-552. *Notes:* 1. Includes only organizations reporting members. 2. Membership as defined by the particular denomination. 3. Corrected figures; see explanation on p. 531 for change in the number of members of the Roman Catholic Church. 4. For changes in denominations for earlier census see text. 5. Not reported. 6. So far as can be learned organic denominational existence has ceased, any organization formerly belonging to this group being included among the independent churches.

★ 1962 ★

Churches

Churches, Membership, and Sunday Schools, by Denominations, 1906, 1916, 1926 - II

Denomination	Sunday schools[1]								
	Churches reporting			Number of scholars			Average scholars per church		
	1926	1916	1906	1926	1916	1906	1926	1916	1906
All denominations	36,378	36,797	33,538	2,144,553	2,153,843	1,740,099	59	59	52
Adventist bodies									
Advent Christian Church	4	8	2	94	248	27	24	31	14
Seventh-day Adventist Denomination	67	51	25	3,402	2,610	539	51	51	22
African Orthodox Church	11	-	-	445	-	-	40	-	-

[Continued]

★ 1962 ★

Churches, Membership, and Sunday Schools, by Denominations, 1906, 1916, 1926 - II

[Continued]

enomination	Sunday schools[1]								
	Churches reporting			Number of scholars			Average scholars per church		
	1926	1916	1906	1926	1916	1906	1926	1916	1906
frican Orthodox Church of New York	3	-	-	220	-	-	73	-	-
postolic Overcoming Holy Church of God	15	-	-	1,068	-	-	71	-	-
aptist bodies									
Northern Baptist Convention[2]	-	137	102	-	20,705	12,827	-	151	126
Negro Baptist[2]	18,755	19,909	17,478	1,121,362	1,181,270	924,665	60	59	53
Free Baptist[2]	-	-	168	-	-	5,732	-	-	34
United American Free Will Baptist Church[2]	144	87	100	5,077	4,168	3,307	35	48	33
Regular Baptists	-	-	-	-	-	-	-	-	-
Primitive Baptists	-	-	-	-	-	-	-	-	-
Colored Primitive Baptists[2]	24	87	166	2,278	3,201	6,224	95	37	37
Christian and Missionary Alliance	8	-	-	490	-	-	61	-	-
Christian Church (General Convention of the Christian Church)[2]	64	105	87	3,348	6,834	4,001	52	65	46
Church of Christ (Holiness) United States of America	72	-	-	2,511	-	-	35	-	-
Church of Christ, Scientist	1	-	-	395	-	-	-	-	-
Church of God[2]	24	1	-	901	25	-	38	-	-
Church of God (Headquarters, Anderson, Ind.)	89	-	-	3,131	-	-	35	-	-
Church of God and Saints of Christ	67	57	1	2,010	1,526	150	30	27	-
Church of God in Christ	585	-	-	19,282	-	-	33	-	-
Churches of Christ	177	59	23	5,905	2,127	597	33	36	26
Churches of God, Holiness	27	-	-	1,246	-	-	46	-	-
hurches of God in North America (General Eldership)	7	7	7	298	248	270	43	35	39
hurches of the Living God									
Church of the Living God, Christian Workers for Fellowship[2]	140	99	43	3,465	2,328	886	25	24	21
Church of Christ in God[2]	-	-	5	-	-	289	-	-	58
Church of the Living God, "The Pillar and Ground in Truth"	26	-	-	1,468	-	-	56	-	-
Church of the Living God[2]	-	26	-	-	491	-	-	19	-
Church of the Living God, General Assembly[2]	-	10	13	-	168	585	-	17	45
ongressional Churches[2]	140	148	150	8,899	10,352	10,339	64	70	69
isciples of Christ	397	149	111	14,848	7,219	4,319	37	48	39
vangelistic associations									
Voluntary Missionary Society in America	-	4	3	-	386	390	-	97	130
ree Christian Zion Church of Christ	5	35	7	97	3,411	340	19	97	49
ree Church of God in Christ	17	-	-	633	-	-	37	-	-
ndependent Churches	6	6	12	491	198	435	82	33	36
utherans									
United Lutheran Church in America[2]	1	-	-	90	-	-	-	-	-
General Council of the Evangelical Lutheran Church in North America	-	-	1	-	-	25	-	-	-
Evangelical Lutheran Synodical Conference of America	-	-	-	-	-	-	-	-	-
Evangelical Lutheran Synod of Missouri, Ohio, and other states	61	28	5	3,314	2,158	254	54	77	51
Methodist bodies									
Methodist Episcopal Church	3,527	3,490	3,522	196,496	214,982	204,810	56	62	58
Methodist Protestant Church	42	44	48	1,283	1,861	1,650	31	42	34
Wesleyan Methodist Connection (or Church) of America	26	14	16	1,084	688	769	42	49	48
African Methodist Episcopal Church	5,884	6,084	6,056	288,247	311,051	292,689	49	51	48
African Methodist Episcopal Zion Church	2,429	2,535	2,060	267,141	135,102	107,692	110	53	52
Colored Methodist Protestant Church	3	24	-	98	870	-	33	36	-
Union American Methodist Episcopal Church	69	54	76	4,240	1,982	3,372	61	37	44
African Union Methodist Protestant Church	42	49	66	2,851	2,813	5,266	68	57	80
Colored Methodist Episcopal Church	2,351	2,541	2,207	103,523	167,880	92,457	44	66	42
Reformed Zion Union Apostolic Church	42	42	35	2,882	2,505	1,508	69	60	43
African American Methodist Episcopal Church[3]	-	6	-	-	200	-	-	33	-
Reformed Methodist Union Episcopal Church	19	25	54	673	699	1,792	35	28	33

[Continued]

★ 1962 ★

Churches, Membership, and Sunday Schools, by Denominations, 1906, 1916, 1926 - II

[Continued]

Denomination	Sunday schools[1]								
	Churches reporting			Number of scholars			Average scholars per church		
	1926	1916	1906	1926	1916	1906	1926	1916	1906
Independent African Methodist Episcopal Church	26	-	-	663	-	-	26	-	-
Moravian bodies									
Moravian Church in America[2]	1	1	2	208	178	217	-	-	109
The (Original) Church of God	-	-	-	-	-	-	-	-	-
Presbyterian bodies									
Presbyterian Church in the United States of America[2]	400	414	405	27,817	27,618	24,904	70	67	61
Cumberland Presbyterian Church	-	-	1	-	-	75	-	-	-
Colored Cumberland Presbyterian Church	153	133	192	5,223	7,471	6,952	34	56	36
United Presbyterian Church of North America	14	-	-	1,587	-	-	113	-	-
Presbyterian Church in the United States	43	30	36	1,569	1,417	1,166	36	47	32
Associate Reformed Presbyterian Church[2]	-	-	1	-	-	35	-	-	-
Protestant Episcopal Church	260	194	180	19,075	15,932	13,779	73	82	77
Reformed bodies									
Reformed Church in America	-	-	1	-	-	52	-	-	-
Reformed Episcopal Church	28	30	33	1,216	1,266	1,326	43	42	40
Roman Catholic Church	76	74	30	11,406	9,655	3,151	150	130	105
Salvation Army	5	-	-	470	-	-	94	-	-
Spiritualists									
National Spiritualist Association[2]	1	-	-	10	-	-	-	-	-
Progressive Spiritual Church[2]	-	-	-	-	-	-	-	-	-
National Spiritual Alliance of the United States of America	1	-	-	23	-	-	-	-	-
United Brethren bodies									
Church of the United Brethren in Christ	-	-	8	-	-	236	-	-	30

Source: "Number of Negro Churches, Membership, and Sunday Schools, by Denominations, for the United States, 1926, 1916, and 1906," U.S. Bureau of the Census, *Negroes in the United States, 1920-1932*, pp. 551-552. *Notes:* 1. The statistics given relate only to the Sunday schools reported by individual churches and do not include undenominational or union Sunday schools; nor do they include the parochial or week-day schools that are maintained by a number of bodies, particularlt the Roman Catholic Church and certain Lutheran bodies. 2. For changes in denominations for earlier census see text. 3. So far as can be learned organic denominational existence has ceased, any organization formerly belonging to this group being included among the independent churches.

★ 1963 ★

Churches

Churches: Ranked by State, 1926-1936

States	1926		1936	
	Number	Rank	Number	Rank
Total	5,203,487	-	5,660,618	-
Georgia	538,093	2	629,028	1
Alabama	557,231	1	585,733	2
Texas	351,305	6	464,937	3
North Carolina	431,333	3	434,951	4
Mississippi	348,425	7	415,182	5
Louisiana	248,797	8	330,990	6
South Carolina	405,614	4	330,479	7
Virginia	378,742	5	308,779	8
Arkansas	201,240	10	217,123	9
Pennsylvania	177,532	12	216,020	10
Tennessee	226,823	9	212,223	11

[Continued]

★ 1963 ★

Churches: Ranked by State, 1926-1936

[Continued]

States	1926		1936	
	Number	Rank	Number	Rank
Florida	190,893	11	196,394	12
New York	114,543	16	171,118	13
Illinois	137,131	13	170,153	14
Ohio	119,529	15	147,327	15
Kentucky	127,126	14	107,005	16
Missouri	82,207	18	90,648	17
New Jersey	71,221	20	89,646	18
Oklahoma	68,379	21	82,861	19
District of Columbia	72,382	19	77,187	20
Maryland	97,025	17	69,312	21
Indiana	49,704	22	59,610	22
Michigan	46,231	23	57,589	23
West Virginia	32,754	24	38,989	24
California	25,763	26	36,562	25
Kansas	28,292	25	29,081	26
Massachusetts	13,882	27	22,051	27
Delaware	12,459	28	18,468	28
Connecticut	10,593	29	14,275	29
Colorado	6,188	31	6,495	30
Iowa	8,577	30	6,134	31
Nebraska	5,163	32	4,746	32
Rhode Island	3,465	35	4,333	33
Wisconsin	3,699	34	3,914	34
Minnesota	3,702	33	3,763	35
Arizona	2,199	37	2,401	36
Washington	2,280	36	1,754	37
New Mexico	710	39	1,080	38
Oregon	832	38	754	39
Utah	269	41	485	40
Wyoming	398	40	270	41
Idaho	205	43	221	42
Montana	228	42	218	43
Maine	45	47	206	44
South Dakota	142	44	128	45
Nevada	46	46	95	46
New Hampshire	63	45	70	47
North Dakota	27	48	10	48
Vermont	-	-	-	-

Source: "Membership of Negro Churches, Ranked by States: 1926, 1936," Jessie Parkhurst Guzman, ed., *Negro Year Book: A Review of Events Affecting Negro Life, 1941-1946*, 1947, p. 117. Published by permission. Primary source: United States Census of Religious Bodies, 1936.

★ 1964 ★

Churches

Colored Methodist Episcopal Churches in Atlanta, Georgia: Characteristics: 1902-1903

Serial No.	Membership Claimed	Active Members	Real Estate	Income
30	100	50	$4,000	$1,543.05
31	75	25	35	20.65
32	265	125	6,500	780.00
All	440	200	10,535	2,343.65

Source: "Colored Methodist Episcopal Churches." Atlanta University Publications. No. 6, *The Negro Church*, edited by W.E. Burghardt Do Bois. Atlanta: Atlanta University Press, 1903, p. 71.

★ 1965 ★

Churches

Colored Methodist Episcopal Churches: Summary by States and Territories, 1890

States and Territories	Organizations	Church Edifices	Approximate Seating Capacity	Halls, etc.	Seating Capacity	Value of Church Property	Communicants or Members
The United States	1,759	1,653	541,464	64	6,526	$1,713,366	129,383
Alabama	222	220	69,200	-	-	264,625	18,940
Arkansas	116	104	31,059	13	1,200	60,277	5,888
Delaware	6	3	430	3	100	1,125	187
District of Columbia	5	4	3,500	1	100	123,800	939
Florida	36	26	7,000	5	1,236	14,700	1,461
Georgia	266	256	100,495	7	1,075	167,145	22,840
Illinois	2	2	800	-	-	1,250	56
Indian Territory	13	9	2,850	-	-	2,975	291
Kansas	17	15	3,625	-	-	14,400	713
Kentucky	91	63	16,000	12	1,225	140,330	6,908
Louisiana	138	131	43,220	2	100	134,135	8,075
Maryland	2	2	205	-	-	475	44
Mississippi	293	292	72,150	-	-	230,490	20,107
Missouri	35	31	5,554	3	100	22,140	953
New Jersey	5	3	625	2	140	7,500	266
North Carolina	26	20	7,725	6	-	23,120	2,786
Pennsylvania	6	2	310	4	1,050	1,400	247
South Carolina	34	33	15,045	1	100	65,325	3,468
Tennessee	206	205	67,900	-	-	258,120	18,968
Texas	222	216	88,330	3	-	147,075	14,895
Virginia	18	16	4,850	2	100	33,150	1,351

Source: "Colored Methodist Episcopal: Summary by States; and Territories." Atlanta University Publications. No. 6, *The Negro Church*, edited by W.E. Burghardt Du Bois. Atlanta: Atlanta University Press, 1903, p. 48.

★ 1966 ★

Churches

Colored [Christian] Methodist Episcopal Church, Characteristics, 1872, 1896, 1900

	1872	1896	1900
Bishops	3	5	6
Itinerant preachers	635	1,400	-
Local preachers	583	2,500	-
Members	67,889	200,000	-

Source: "The Colored Methodists," W.E.B. Du Bois, ed., *The Negro Church*, p. 113.

★ 1967 ★

Churches

Congressional Churches, Characteristics, 1902

Number of churches	230
Ministers and missionaries	139
Church members	12,155
Total additions	1,429
Added on profession	1,190
Benevolent contributions	$2,813.68
Raised for church purposes	39,397.82
Sunday-school scholars	17,311

Source: Untitled table, W.E.B. Du Bois, ed., *The Negro Church*, p. 151.

★ 1968 ★

Churches

Congressional Methodist: Summary by States, 1890

States	Congressional Methodist (Colored)						
	Organizations	Church Edifices	Approximate Seating Capacity	Halls, etc.	Seating Capacity	Value of Church Property	Communicants or Members
The United States	9	5	585	4	450	$525	319
Alabama	7	5	585	2	250	525	215
Texas	2	-	-	2	200	-	104

Source: "Congressional Methodist (Colored): Summary by States." Atlanta University Publications. No. 6, *The Negro Church*, edited by W.E. Burghardt Du Bois. Atlanta: Atlanta University Press, 1903, p. 44.

★ 1969 ★

Churches

Cumberland Presbyterian Churches: Summary by States and Territories, 1890

States and Territories	Organizations	Church Edifices	Approximate Seating Capacity	Halls, etc.	Seating Capacity	Value of Church Property	Communicants or Members
The United States	224	183	52,139	34	3,570	$195,826	12,956
Alabama	44	38	9,574	7	475	26,200	3,104
Arkansas	2	-	-	2	300	-	255
Illinois	7	4	1,300	2	75	5,375	195
Kansas	6	3	650	3	150	15,000	190
Kentucky	36	31	7,730	2	-	31,645	1,421
Mississippi	4	4	950	-	-	1,825	278
Missouri	10	9	1,650	1	50	17,900	471
Oklahoma	4	-	-	3	270	-	100
Tennessee	81	72	24,125	7	825	88,660	5,202
Texas	30	22	6,160	7	1,425	9,221	1,740

Source: "Cumberland Presbyterian (Colored): Summary by States; and Territories." Atlanta University Publications. No. 6, *The Negro Church*, edited by W.E. Burghardt Du Bois. Atlanta: Atlanta University Press, 1903, p. 49.

★ 1970 ★

Churches

Distribution of Urban and Rural Churches and Membership of Denominations Having 50,000 or More Members, 1926

Denomination	Churches[1]		Membership[2]	
	Urban	Rural	Urban	Rural
Negro Baptists	20.0	80.0	39.0	61.0
African Methodist Episcopal Church	23.8	76.2	50.0	50.0
African Methodist Episcopal Zion Church	26.4	73.6	42.5	57.5
Methodist Episcopal Church	21.5	78.5	45.0	55.0
Colored Methodist Episcopal Church	22.5	77.5	39.1	60.9
Roman Catholic Church	79.6	20.4	85.9	14.1
Protestant Episcopal Church	71.4	28.6	89.7	10.3

Source: "Percent Distribution of Urban and Rural Churches and Membership for Denominations Having 50,000 or More Members: 1926," U.S. Bureau of the Census, *Negroes in the United States, 1920-1932*, p. 531. *Notes:* 1. Includes only organizations reporting members. 2. Membership as defined by the particular denomination.

★ 1971 ★

Churches

Expenditures of Thirty-two Churches in Chicago, 1902

Total membership	6,811
Active membership	4,329
Valuation of churches	$199,300.00
Salaries	17,895.13
Debt and interest	17,617.39
Running expenses	12,869.32
Charity	2,760.98
Missions	609.10
Support of connection	1,550.95
Other expenses	4,267.10
Total	$57,569.97

Source: "Thirty-two Churches in Chicago," W.E.B. Du Bois, ed., *The Negro Church*, p. 89.

★ 1972 ★

Churches

Growth of the African Methodist Episcopal Church, 1816-1901

	1816	1826	1836	1846	1866	1876	1880	1900	1901
Bishops	1	2	3	4	4	6	9	13	13
General officers	-	-	-	-	-	3	4	-	12
Presiding elders	-	-	-	-	-	-	-	-	264
Annual conferences	2	2	4	6	10	25	40	-	-
Itinerant preachers	14	17	27	40	185	1,418	1,837	-	6,079
Local preachers	-	-	-	-	-	3,168	9,760	-	9,749
Members	3,000	-	7,270	-	-	172,806	391,044	561,550	68,354
Total members	-	7,927	-	-	-	213,469	402,638	663,746	762,580
Churches	-	-	86	198	285	1,833	2,051	5,630	5,715
Value of property	-	-	$43,000.00	$90,000.00	$813,000	$3,064,911	-	$8,718,456	$10,360,131
Parsonages	-	-	-	-	-	218	402	1,390	2,075
Value of total property	-	-	-	-	-	$3,203,711	$2,448,671	$9,309,973	$11,044,663
Schools	-	-	-	3	-	-	88	-	41
Raised for support of schools	-	-	-	-	-	-	-	-	$125,650
Total money raised	-	$1,151.75	$1,385.88	$7,231.03	$91,593(?)	$447,624	-	-	-

Source: "Growth of the African Methodist Episcopal Church," W.E.B. Du Bois, ed, *The Negro Church*, p. 126.

★ 1973 ★

Churches

Independent Black Denominations, 1913

Denominations	Number churches	Number communicants	Number Sunday schools	Number scholars	Value of church property
Total	32,985	3,779,681	25,960	1,448,570	44,632,043
Baptists - National Convention	18,534	2,261,607	17,910	924,665	24,437,272
Colored Primitive Baptists in America	797	35,076	166	6,224	296,539
United American Freewill Baptists (colored)	251	14,489	100	3,307	79,278
Church of God and Saints of Christ	48	1,823	1	150	6,000
Church of the Living God (Christian Workers for Friendship)	44	2,676	43	886	23,175
Church of the Living God (Apostolic Church)	15	752	13	585	25,700
Church of Christ in God	9	848	6	289	9,700
Voluntary Missionary Society in America (colored)	3	425	3	390	2,400
Free Christian Zion Church of Christ (colored)	15	1,835	7	340	5,975
Union American Methodist Episcopal Church (colored)	77	4,347	78	3,372	170,150
African Methodist Episcopal Church	6,647	620,000	6,285	292,689	11,303,489
African Union Methodist Protestant Church	69	5,592	66	5,266	183,697
African Methodist Episcopal Zion Church	3,180	568,608	3,100	107,692	4,833,207
Colored Methodist Episcopal Church	2,997	236,077	2,900	92,457	3,017,849
Reformed Zion Union Apostolic Church (colored)	45	3,059	36	1,508	37,875

[Continued]

★ 1973 ★

Independent Black Denominations, 1913

[Continued]

Denominations	Number churches	Number communicants	Number Sunday schools	Number scholars	Value of church property
Reformed Methodist Union Episcopal Church (colored)	58	4,397	54	1,792	36,965
Colored Cumberland Presbyterian Church	196	18,066	92	6,952	203,778

Source: "Independent Negro Denominations," Monroe N. Work, ed., *Negro Year Book: An Annual Encyclopedia of the Negro*, 1913, p. 178. Published by permission.

★ 1974 ★

Churches

Independent Denominations: Urban, Rural, 1937-1938, Part I

Denomination	Number churches			Total	Number Urban
	Total	Urban	Rural		
African Orthodox Church	13	13	-	1,568	1,568
African Orthodox Church of New York	3	3	-	717	717
Apostolic Overcoming Holy Church of God	16	8	8	1,047	581
Baptist Bodies:					
Negro Baptist	22,081	4,409	17,672	3,196,623	1,246,327
United American Free-Will Baptist Church	166	11	155	13,396	1,804
Colored Primitive Baptists	925	76	849	43,978	4,637
Church of Christ (Holiness) U.S.A.	82	46	36	4,919	3,002
Church of God and Saints of Christ	112	101	11	6,741	6,055
Church of God in Christ	733	405	328	30,263	20,805
Churches of God, Holiness	29	24	5	2,278	1,929
Churches of the Living God:					
Church of the Living God, "The Pillar and Ground of Truth"	81	45	36	5,844	3,886
Church of Living God, Christian Workers for Fellowship	149	82	67	11,558	7,289
Free Christian Zion Church of Christ	5	1	4	187	60
Free Church of God in Christ	19	15	4	874	797
Methodist Bodies:					
African Methodist Episcopal Church	6,708	1,599	5,109	545,814	272,765
African Methodist Episcopal Zion Church	2,466	650	1,816	456,313	193,926
Colored Methodist Protestant Church	3	3	-	533	533
Union American Methodist Episcopal Church	73	37	36	10,169	7,043
African Union Methodist Protestant Church	43	23	20	4,086	2,707
Colored Methodist Episcopal Church	2,518	567	1,951	202,713	79,183
Reformed Zion Union Apostolic Church	48	5	43	4,538	651
Reformed Methodist Union Episcopal Church	25	7	18	2,265	486
Independent African Methodist Episcopal Church	29	8	21	1,003	424
Presbyterian bodies:					
Colored Cumberland Presbyterian Church	178	60	118	10,868	3,911
Total	36,505	8,198	28,307	4,558,795	1,861,086

Source: "Independent Negro Denominations," Monroe N. Work, ed., *Negro Year Book: An Annual Encyclopedia of the Negro, 1937-38*, 1937, p. 224. Published by permission.

★ 1975 ★

Churches

Independent Denominations: Urban, Rural, 1937-1938, Part II

Denomination	Members rural	Number Sunday schools			Number scholars			Value church edifice		
		Total	Urban	Rural	Total	Urban	Rural	Total	Urban	Rural
African Orthodox Church	-	11	11	-	445	445	-	30,000	30,000	-
African Orthodox Church of New York	-	3	3	-	220	220	-	50,000	50,000	-
Apostolic Overcoming Holy Church of God	466	15	7	8	1,068	583	485	16,950	12,100	4,850
Baptist Bodies:										
Negro Baptist	1,950,296	18,755	3,918	14,837	1,121,362	402,416	718,946	103,465,759	69,444,724	34,021,035
United American Free-Will Baptist Church	11,592	144	11	133	2,278	709	4,368	308,425	53,900	254,525
Colored Primitive Baptists	39,341	24	10	14	5,077	780	1,498	171,518	93,870	77,648
Church of Christ (Holiness) U.S.A.	1,917	72	40	32	2,511	1,482	1,029	326,850	274,750	52,100
Church of God and Saints of Christ	686	67	60	7	2,010	1,751	259	149,210	138,860	10,350
Church of God in Christ	9,458	585	331	254	19,282	12,666	6,616	1,508,079	1,274,353	233,726
Churches of God, Holiness	349	27	22	5	1,246	1,066	180	159,700	152,500	7,200
Churches of the Living God:										
Church of the Living God, "The Pillar and Ground of Truth"	1,958	26	19	7	1,468	1,177	291	170,547	126,665	43,882
Church of Living God, Christian Workers for Fellowship	4,269	140	77	63	3,465	2,171	1,294	368,935	268,750	100,185
Free Christian Zion Church of Christ	127	5	1	4	97	85	62	22,000	16,000	6,000
Free Church of God in Christ	77	17	14	3	633	568	65	23,700	23,200	500
Methodist Bodies:										
African Methodist Episcopal Church	273,049	5,884	1,454	4,430	288,247	139,608	148,639	32,092,549	23,994,224	8,098,325
African Methodist Episcopal Zion Church	262,887	2,429	640	1,789	267,141	103,542	163,599	18,515,723	13,451,618	5,064,150
Colored Methodist Protestant Church	-	3	3	-	98	98	-	36,000	36,000	-
Union American Methodist Episcopal Church	3,126	69	37	32	4,240	3,019	1,221	478,951	380,150	98,801
African Union Methodist Protestant Church	1,379	42	22	20	2,851	1,724	1,127	476,269	381,483	94,786
Colored Methodist Episcopal Church	123,530	2,351	540	1,811	103,523	34,571	68,952	9,211,437	5,791,115	3,420,322
Reformed Zion Union Apostolic Church	3,887	42	5	37	2,882	394	2,488	184,075	57,000	127,075
Reformed Methodist Union Episcopal Church	1,779	19	3	16	673	78	595	74,800	29,450	45,350
Independent African Methodist Episcopal Church	579	26	8	18	663	280	383	98,050	74,000	24,050
Presbyterian bodies:										
Colored Cumberland Presbyterian Church	6,957	152	51	101	5,223	1,763	3,460	353,825	167,920	185,905
Total	2,697,709	30,908	7,287	23,621	1,836,703	711,146	1,125,557	168,293,352	116,322,632	51,970,720

Source: "Independent Negro Denominations," Monroe N. Work, ed., *Negro Year Book: An Annual Encyclopedia of the Negro, 1937-38*, 1937, p. 224-225. Published by permission.

★ 1976 ★

Churches

Membership and Place of Worship by Denomination, 1906

Division and state	Number of organizations	Communicants or members					Places of worship				
		Number of organizations reporting	Total number reported	Sex			Number of organizations reporting		Number of church edifices reported	Seating capacity of church edifices	
				Number of organizations reporting	Male	Female	Church edifices	Halls, etc.		Number of organizations reporting	Seating capacity reported
United States	36,770	36,563	3,685,097	34,648	1,324,123	2,203,537	34,506	1,261	35,160	33,091	10,481,738
Geographic divisions											
New England	135	134	16,053	126	5,029	9,274	109	21	111	109	39,764
Middle Atlantic	891	887	118,658	854	39,319	70,945	780	98	800	768	258,973
East North Central	986	979	92,403	928	31,753	56,268	901	57	913	876	254,760
West North Central	1,037	1,033	73,953	999	23,817	44,872	949	63	968	928	242,905
South Atlantic	15,250	15,163	1,741,491	14,297	636,338	1,032,207	14,397	416	14,671	13,827	4,639,781
East South Central	10,497	10,438	1,045,671	9,834	372,395	631,170	9,911	286	10,117	9,484	3,006,212
West South Central	7,844	7,799	588,384	7,492	213,082	354,352	7,347	313	7,465	6,990	2,009,101
Mountain	45	45	3,146	42	964	1,986	40	2	40	38	9,117
Pacific	85	85	5,338	76	1,426	2,463	72	5	75	71	21,125
New England											
Maine	1	1	25	1	10	15	1	-	1	1	200
New Hampshire	1	1	20	1	8	12	-	-	-	-	-
Vermont	-	-	-	-	-	-	-	-	-	-	-
Massachusetts	64	64	9,402	60	2,905	5,347	50	11	51	50	20,060
Rhode Island	20	20	2,114	17	569	1,098	18	2	19	18	7,700
Connecticut	49	48	4,492	47	1,537	2,802	40	8	40	40	11,804
Middle Atlantic											
New York	203	202	30,482	187	9,782	17,854	169	27	173	163	59,542
New Jersey	259	257	28,015	255	8,924	18,430	234	20	240	233	72,443

[Continued]

★ 1976 ★

Membership and Place of Worship by Denomination, 1906

[Continued]

Division and state	Number of organizations	Communicants or members: Number of organizations reporting	Communicants or members: Total number reported	Sex: Number of organizations reporting	Sex: Male	Sex: Female	Places of worship: Number of organizations reporting: Church edifices	Places of worship: Number of organizations reporting: Halls, etc.	Places of worship: Number of church edifices reported	Seating capacity of church edifices: Number of organizations reporting	Seating capacity of church edifices: Seating capacity reported
Pennsylvania	429	428	60,161	412	20,613	34,661	377	51	387	372	126,988
East North Central											
Ohio	371	367	33,667	328	11,276	19,134	333	20	336	318	94,000
Indiana	202	200	23,133	197	8,100	14,548	190	10	192	186	56,515
Illinois	359	358	32,058	349	11,079	20,339	327	25	332	322	89,815
Michigan	43	43	3,235	43	1,188	2,047	42	-	44	41	12,470
Wisconsin	11	11	310	11	110	200	9	2	9	9	1,960
West North Central											
Minnesota	10	10	1,453	9	393	760	9	-	9	9	2,755
Iowa	72	72	4,108	72	1,481	2,627	61	10	63	59	14,955
Missouri	655	651	50,074	625	15,514	30,197	600	38	617	584	153,914
North Dakota	-	-	-	-	-	-	-	-	-	-	-
South Dakota	2	2	38	2	15	23	1	-	1	1	150
Nebraska	12	12	1,007	9	308	567	11	1	11	10	3,175
Kansas	286	286	17,273	282	6,106	10,698	267	14	267	265	67,956
South Atlantic											
Delaware	125	125	10,583	117	3,867	5,277	122	3	124	119	29,894
Maryland	624	620	71,797	541	23,265	36,299	595	14	612	552	154,672
District of Columbia	102	102	46,249	97	14,153	28,909	82	20	84	80	51,342
Virginia	1,983	1,974	307,374	1,817	116,271	175,333	1,875	62	1,916	1,808	621,808
West Virginia	271	268	14,949	251	6,377	7,839	200	58	200	187	50,765
North Carolina	2,813	2,797	283,707	2,580	105,067	165,644	2,565	52	2,593	2,510	860,675
South Carolina	2,860	2,853	394,149	2,769	142,868	240,626	2,801	32	2,853	2,724	995,462
Georgia	4,834	4,790	507,005	4,565	185,114	308,620	4,608	113	4,717	4,406	1,522,656
Florida	1,638	1,634	105,678	1,560	39,356	63,660	1,549	62	1,572	1,441	352,507
East South Central											
Kentucky	1,007	1,005	116,918	966	44,639	69,263	956	36	967	939	268,035
Tennessee	1,879	1,855	172,867	1,726	59,645	106,318	1,735	69	1,808	1,644	530,457
Alabama	3,734	3,715	397,178	3,485	146,186	234,680	3,476	107	3,542	3,313	1,114,305
Mississippi	3,877	3,863	358,708	3,657	121,925	220,909	3,744	74	3,800	3,588	1,093,415
West South Central											
Arkansas	2,094	2,081	146,319	2,042	56,895	86,742	1,974	61	2,017	1,925	551,131
Louisiana	2,085	2,067	185,918	1,950	62,985	111,937	2,017	40	2,035	1,856	573,281
Oklahoma	618	616	29,115	595	11,397	16,918	534	56	553	517	116,991
Texas	3,047	3,035	227,032	2,905	81,805	138,755	2,822	156	2,860	2,692	767,698
Mountain											
Montana	6	6	135	6	35	100	6	-	6	6	1,175
Idaho	-	-	-	-	-	-	-	-	-	-	-
Wyoming	1	1	45	1	12	33	1	-	1	1	150
Colorado	25	25	2,507	22	776	1,535	23	1	23	21	6,160
New Mexico	7	7	221	7	68	153	7	-	7	7	912
Arizona	5	5	208	5	66	142	2	1	2	2	420
Utah	1	1	30	1	7	23	1	-	1	1	300
Nevada	-	-	-	-	-	-	-	-	-	-	-
Pacific											
Washington	18	18	614	18	229	385	13	-	14	13	3,250
Oregon	4	4	160	4	45	115	3	1	3	3	900
California	63	63	4,564	54	1,152	1,963	56	4	58	55	16,975

Source: "Negro Church Organizations, Showing Communicants or Members, Places of Worship, Value of Church Property, Debt on Church Property, Parsonages, and Sunday Schools, by Geographical Division and States: 1906," U.S. Bureau of the Census, *Negroes in the United States*, Bulletin 129, 1915, pp. 204-205. Adapted by the editors.

★ 1977 ★

Churches

Membership and Place of Worship by Geographical Division and State, 1906

Division and state	Number of organizations	Number of organizations reporting	Total number reported	Sex: Number of organizations reporting	Sex: Male	Sex: Female	Number of organizations reporting: Church edifices	Number of organizations reporting: Halls, etc.	Number of church edifices reported	Seating capacity of church edifices: Number of organizations reporting	Seating capacity of church edifices: Seating capacity reported
United States	36,770	36,563	3,685,097	34,648	1,324,123	2,203,537	34,506	1,261	35,160	33,091	10,481,738
Geographic divisions											
New England	135	134	16,053	126	5,029	9,274	109	21	111	109	39,764
Middle Atlantic	891	887	118,658	854	39,319	70,945	780	98	800	768	258,973
East North Central	986	979	92,403	928	31,753	56,268	901	57	913	876	254,760
West North Central	1,037	1,033	73,953	999	23,817	44,872	949	63	968	928	242,905
South Atlantic	15,250	15,163	1,741,491	14,297	636,338	1,032,207	14,397	416	14,671	13,827	4,639,781
East South Central	10,497	10,438	1,045,671	9,834	372,395	631,170	9,911	286	10,117	9,484	3,006,212
West South Central	7,844	7,799	588,384	7,492	213,082	354,352	7,347	313	7,465	6,990	2,009,101
Mountain	45	45	3,146	42	964	1,986	40	2	40	38	9,117
Pacific	85	85	5,338	76	1,426	2,463	72	5	75	71	21,125
New England											
Maine	1	1	25	1	10	15	1	-	1	1	200
New Hampshire	1	1	20	1	8	12	-	-	-	-	-
Vermont	-	-	-	-	-	-	-	-	-	-	-
Massachusetts	64	64	9,402	60	2,905	5,347	50	11	51	50	20,060
Rhode Island	20	20	2,114	17	569	1,098	18	2	19	18	7,700
Connecticut	49	48	4,492	47	1,537	2,802	40	8	40	40	11,804
Middle Atlantic											
New York	203	202	30,482	187	9,782	17,854	169	27	173	163	59,542
New Jersey	259	257	28,015	255	8,924	18,430	234	20	240	233	72,443
Pennsylvania	429	428	60,161	412	20,613	34,661	377	51	387	372	126,988
East North Central											
Ohio	371	367	33,667	328	11,276	19,134	333	20	336	318	94,000
Indiana	202	200	23,133	197	8,100	14,548	190	10	192	186	56,515
Illinois	359	358	32,058	349	11,079	20,339	327	25	332	322	89,815
Michigan	43	43	3,235	43	1,188	2,047	42	-	44	41	12,470
Wisconsin	11	11	310	11	110	200	9	2	9	9	1,960
West North Central											
Minnesota	10	10	1,453	9	393	760	9	-	9	9	2,755
Iowa	72	72	4,108	72	1,481	2,627	61	10	63	59	14,955
Missouri	655	651	50,074	625	15,514	30,197	600	38	617	584	153,914
North Dakota	-	-	-	-	-	-	-	-	-	-	-
South Dakota	2	2	38	2	15	23	1	-	1	1	150
Nebraska	12	12	1,007	9	308	567	11	1	11	10	3,175
Kansas	286	286	17,273	282	6,106	10,698	267	14	267	265	67,956
South Atlantic											
Delaware	125	125	10,583	117	3,867	5,277	122	3	124	119	29,894
Maryland	624	620	71,797	541	23,265	36,299	595	14	612	552	154,672
District of Columbia	102	102	46,249	97	14,153	28,909	82	20	84	80	51,342
Virginia	1,983	1,974	307,374	1,817	116,271	175,333	1,875	62	1,916	1,808	621,808
West Virginia	271	268	14,949	251	6,377	7,839	200	58	200	187	50,765
North Carolina	2,813	2,797	283,707	2,580	105,067	165,644	2,565	52	2,593	2,510	860,675
South Carolina	2,860	2,853	394,149	2,769	142,868	240,626	2,801	32	2,853	2,724	995,462
Georgia	4,834	4,790	507,005	4,565	185,114	308,620	4,608	113	4,717	4,406	1,522,656
Florida	1,638	1,634	105,678	1,560	39,356	63,660	1,549	62	1,572	1,441	352,507
East South Central											
Kentucky	1,007	1,005	116,918	966	44,639	69,263	956	36	967	939	268,035
Tennessee	1,879	1,855	172,867	1,726	59,645	106,318	1,735	69	1,808	1,644	530,457
Alabama	3,734	3,715	397,178	3,485	146,186	234,680	3,476	107	3,542	3,313	1,114,305
Mississippi	3,877	3,863	358,708	3,657	121,925	220,909	3,744	74	3,800	3,588	1,093,415
West South Central											
Arkansas	2,094	2,081	146,319	2,042	56,895	86,742	1,974	61	2,017	1,925	551,131
Louisiana	2,085	2,067	185,918	1,950	62,985	111,937	2,017	40	2,035	1,856	573,281
Oklahoma	618	616	29,115	595	11,397	16,918	534	56	553	517	116,991
Texas	3,047	3,035	227,032	2,905	81,805	138,755	2,822	156	2,860	2,692	767,698
Mountain											
Montana	6	6	135	6	35	100	6	-	6	6	1,175
Idaho	-	-	-	-	-	-	-	-	-	-	-
Wyoming	1	1	45	1	12	33	1	-	1	1	150
Colorado	25	25	2,507	22	776	1,535	23	1	23	21	6,160
New Mexico	7	7	221	7	68	153	7	-	7	7	912
Arizona	5	5	208	5	66	142	2	1	2	2	420
Utah	1	1	30	1	7	23	1	-	1	1	300
Nevada	-	-	-	-	-	-	-	-	-	-	-
Pacific											
Washington	18	18	614	18	229	385	13	-	14	13	3,250

[Continued]

★ 1977 ★

Membership and Place of Worship by Geographical Division and State, 1906

[Continued]

Division and state	Number of organizations	Number of organizations reporting	Total number reported	Sex			Number of organizations reporting		Number of church edifices reported	Seating capacity of church edifices	
				Number of organizations reporting	Male	Female	Church edifices	Halls, etc.		Number of organizations reporting	Seating capacity reported
Oregon	4	4	160	4	45	115	3	1	3	3	900
California	63	63	4,564	54	1,152	1,963	56	4	58	55	16,975

Source: "Negro Church Organizations, Showing Communicants or Members, Places of Worship, Value of Church Property, Debt on Church Property, Parsonages, and Sunday Schools, by Geographical Division and States: 1906," U.S. Bureau of the Census, *Negroes in the United States*, Bulletin 129, 1915, pp. 206-207. Adapted by the editors.

★ 1978 ★

Churches

Methodist Churches in Atlanta, Georgia: Characteristics, 1902-1903

	No.	Membership Claimed	Active Members	Real Estate	Income
African Methodist Episcopal	14	3,242	1,461	$90,200	$13,831.10
Methodist Episcopal	4	1,333	910	48,500	6,927.00
Colored Methodist Episcopal	3	440	200	10,535	2,343.65
Total	21	5,015	2,571	149,235	23,101.75

Source: "Methodist Churches." Atlanta University Publications. No. 6, *The Negro Church*, edited by W.E. Burghardt Du Bois. Atlanta: Atlanta University Press, 1903, p. 70.

★ 1979 ★

Churches

Methodist Episcopal Church, Characteristics, 1902

Conferences	Full membership	Valuation	Monies raised
Central Missouri	6,909	$200,606	$34,994
Delaware	19,288	552,251	104,055
Florida	4,490	79,943	14,674
Liberia	2,832	75,520	3,346
Little Rock	5,018	85,148	15,543
Louisiana	14,178	314,820	65,356
Lexington	9,558	301,775	49,341
Mississippi	18,042	181,070	35,907
Upper Mississippi	19,721	161,149	38,927
Washington	26,980	988,193	98,065
Atlanta	13,028	181,138	28,017

[Continued]

★ 1979 ★

Methodist Episcopal Church, Characteristics, 1902

[Continued]

Conferences	Full membership	Valuation	Monies raised
Central Alabama	5,149	65,700	11,470
East Tennessee	4,700	111,380	16,298
Mobile	5,546	71,235	11,829
North Carolina	9,912	116,170	23,481
Savannah	7,648	77,442	15,297
South Carolina	39,490	408,834	60,548
Tennessee	8,598	97,622	22,377
Texas	13,045	273,700	35,940
West Texas	11,792	193,255	31,935
Total	245,954	4,566,951	717,400

Source: "Methodist Episcopal Church-Negro Membership," W.E.B. Du Bois, ed., *The Negro Church*, p. 134.

★ 1980 ★

Churches

Methodist Episcopal Churches in Atlanta, Georgia: Characteristics: 1902-1903

Serial No.	Membership Claimed	Active Members	Real Estate	Income
33	740	500	$40,000	$3,235.00
34	227	115	1,000	542.00
35	166	100	2,500	1,425.00
36	200	195	5,000	1,725.00
All	1,333	910	48,500	6,927.00

Source: "Methodist Episcopal Churches." Atlanta University Publications. No. 6, *The Negro Church*, edited by W.E. Burghardt Do Bois. Atlanta: Atlanta University Press, 1903, p. 71.

★ 1981 ★

Churches

Miscellaneous Churches in Atlanta, Georgia, Characteristics: 1902-1903

Serial No.	Membership Claimed	Active Members	Real Estate	Income
51	485	400	$25,000	$2,225.00
52	180	80	10,000	1,494.00
53	68	-	4,000	1,296.79
54	150	30	3,000	436.00
All	4,125	1,971	42,000	5,451.79

Source: "Untitled Table." Atlanta University Publications. No. 6, *The Negro Church*, edited by W.E. Burghardt Du Bois. Atlanta: Atlanta University Press, 1903, p. 71.

★ 1982 ★

Churches

National Baptist Convention: Reports, 1901, 1902

	Total
Sermons preached	1,550
Sunday schools addressed	905
Prayer-meetings attended	829
B.Y.P.U. meetings attended	478
Women's meetings addressed	261
Other addresses made	1,495
Total number addresses made	2,376
Conventions, Associations and women's meetings visited since last report	253
Number of letters and cards written	12,056
Number of circulars and tracts distributed	40,703
Number of books and tracts donated	1,019
Books sold	1,774.83
Money collected	3,538.37
Total amount of money received from all sources	5,114.02
Subscriptions to the Union	256
Money collected for same	57.20
Days of service rendered	2,223
Homes visited	1,661
Homes found without Bibles	84
Churches visited	1,323
Sunday-schools organized	7
Missionary societies organized	44
Baptisms	70
Miles traveled by railroad	99,612
Cost of travel	1,493.64
Miles traveled otherwise	5,491

[Continued]

★ 1982 ★

National Baptist Convention: Reports, 1901, 1902

[Continued]

	Total
Cost of same	188.30
Total traveling expense	1,681.94
Total amount of money sent to National Baptist Publishing Board	1,281.36
Amount of the money collected applied to salaries	281.35
Total amount of money collected and left with churches	79.80
Number of Missionary Conferences held	31
Paid on salaries	3,839.38
Total paid on salaries	4,174.73

Source: "Combined Reports," W.E. Burghardt Du Bois, ed., *The Negro Church*, p. 112.

★ 1983 ★

Churches

Number of Churches and Membership: by Denominations, 1936

Denomination	Total number of churches	Number of Negro churches	Negro members
Total	128,309	38,303	5,660,618
Adventist bodies:			
Seventh-day Adventists denomination	2,054	97	6,367
African Orthodox Church[2]	13	13	1,952
Apostolic Overcoming Holy Church of God[2]	23	23	863
Baptist bodies:			
Negro Baptists[2]	23,093	23,093	3,782,464
United American Free Will Baptist Church (colored)	226	226	19,616
Colored Primitive Baptists[2]	1,009	1,009	43,897
National Baptist Evangelical Life and Soul Saving Assembly of the United States of America	28	28	2,300
Northern Baptist Convention	6,254	32	45,821
Christian and Missionary Alliance	444	5	135
Christ's Sanctified Holy Church[2]	31	31	665
Church of Christ, (Holiness), U.S.A.	106	106	7,379
Church of Christ, Scientist	2,113	4	262
Church of God	1,081	42	1,405
Church of God, (Anderson, Ind.)	1,032	117	4,310
Church of God and Saints of Christ[2]	213	213	37,084
Church of God in Christ[2]	772	772	31,564
Churches of Christ	3,815	1	70
Churches of God, Holiness[2]	35	35	5,872
Churches of God in North America, (General Eldership)	352	1	204

[Continued]

★ 1983 ★

Number of Churches and Membership: by Denominations, 1936

[Continued]

Denomination	Total number of churches	Number of Negro churches	Negro members
Churches of the Living God:			
Church of the Living God, Christian Workers for Fellowship[2]	96	96	4,525
Church of the Living God, "The Pillar and Ground of Truth"[2]	119	119	4,838
Congregational and Christian Churches[1]	5,300	233	20,437
Disciples of Christ	5,566	189	21,950
Apostolic Episcopal Church (The Holy Eastern Catholic and Apostolic Orthodox Church)	12	3	161
Federated Churches	508	1	50
Fire Baptized Holiness Church of God of the Americas[2]	59	59	1,973
Free Christian Zion Church of Christ[2]	9	9	1,840
House of God, Holy Church of the Living God, the Pillar and Ground of Truth, House of Prayer for all People[2]	4	4	200
House of the Lord[2]	4	4	302
Independent Negro Churches[2]	50	50	12,337
International Church of the Four Square Gospel	205	1	28
Kodesh Church of Immanuel[2]	9	9	562
The Latter House of the Lord, Apostolic Faith[2]	2	2	29
Lutheran bodies:			
American Lutheran Church	1,803	1	82
Evangelical Lutheran Synodical Conference of North America: Negro Mission of the Syndocial Conference	4,926	81	8,985
Methodist bodies:			
Methodist Episcopal Church	18,349	1,730	193,761
Methodist Protestant Church	1,498	40	2,321
African Methodist Episcopal Church[2]	4,578	4,578	493,357
African Methodist Episcopal Zion Church[2]	2,252	2,252	414,244
Colored Methodist Protestant Church[2]	1	1	216
Union American Methodist Episcopal Church[2]	71	71	9,369
African Union Methodist Protestant Church[2]	45	45	4,239
Colored Methodist Episcopal Church[2]	2,063	2,063	269,915
Reformed Zion Union Apostolic Church[2]	54	54	5,035
Independent African Methodist Episcopal Church[2]	29	29	1,064
Reformed Methodist Union Episcopal Church[2]	25	25	1,836
Moravian bodies:			
Moravian Church in America	132	1	628
National David Spiritual Temple of Christ Church Union[2]	11	11	1,880
Presbyterian bodies:			
Presbyterian Church in the United States of America	7,789	16	2,971
Colored Cumberland Presbyterian Church[2]	145	145	10,668
United Presbyterian Church of North America	778	1	45
Presbyterian Church in the United States	2,967	5	279

[Continued]

★ 1983 ★

Number of Churches and Membership: by Denominations, 1936

[Continued]

Denomination	Total number of churches	Number of Negro churches	Negro members
Protestant Episcopal Church	6,407	145	29,738
Reformed Episcopal Church	67	36	2,434
Roman Catholic Church	18,400	178	137,684
Salvation Army	1,088	3	436
Progressive Spiritualist Church	21	1	365
Triumph, The Church and Kingdom of God in Christ[2]	2	2	69
United Holy Church of America, Incorporate[2]	162	162	7,535

Source: "Negro Churches: Number and Membership, by Denominations: 1936," Florence Murray, ed., *The Negro Handbook*, 1942, pp. 95-96. *Notes:* 1. Represents merger of Congregational Churches with General Convention of the Christian Church, since 1926. 2. Wholly Negro Denominations.

★ 1984 ★

Churches

Operations of Seven Annual Conferences, AME Church, 1902

	1816	1826	1836	1846	1866	1876	1880	1900	1901
Bishops	1	2	3	4	4	6	9	13	13
General officers	-	-	-	-	-	3	4	-	12
Presiding Elders	-	-	-	-	-	-	-	-	264
Annual Conferences	2	2	4	6	10	25	40	-	-
Itinerant preachers	14	17	27	40	185	1,418	1,837	-	6,079
Local preachers	-	-	-	-	-	3,168	9,760	-	9,749
Members	3,000	-	7,270	-	-	172,806	391,044	561,550	688,354
Total members	-	7,927	-	-	-	213,469	402,638	663,746	762,580
Churches	-	-	86	198	285	1,833	2,051	5,630	5,715
Value of property	-	-	$43,000.00	$90,000.00	$813,000	$3,064,911	-	$8,718,456	$10,360,131
Parsonages	-	-	-	-	-	218	402	1,390	2,075
Value of total property	-	-	-	-	-	$3,203,711	$2,448,671	$9,309,973	$11,044,663
Schools	-	-	-	3	-	-	88	-	41
Raised for support of schools	-	-	-	-	-	-	-	-	$125,650
Total money raised	-	$1,151.75	$1,385.88	$7,231.03	$91,593(?)	$447,624	-	-	-

Source: "Annual Conference Reports," W.E.B. Du Bois, ed., *The Negro Church*, p. 126.

★ 1985 ★

Churches

Presbyterian Churches, Characteristics, 1902

Ministers	209
Churches and missions	353
Added on examination	1,737
Added on certificate	206
Whole number	21,341
Sunday-schools	350
Sunday-school scholars	21,299
Number of schools	88
Number of teachers	272
Number of pupils	10,715
Ministers who preach only	149
Ministers who preach and teach	49
Ministers who teach only	11
Laymen who teach	24
Women who teach	188

Source: Untitled table, W.E.B. Du Bois, ed., *The Negro Church*, p. 144.

★ 1986 ★

Churches

Regular Baptists: States and Territories: 1890

State and Territories	Organizations	Church Edifices	Approximate Seating Capacity	Halls, etc.	Seating Capacity	Value of Church Property	Communicants or Members
The United States	12,533	11,987	3,440,970	663	45,570	$9,038,549	1,348,989
Alabama	1,374	1,341	376,839	50	3,365	795,384	142,437
Arkansas	923	870	243,395	51	3,310	585,947	63,786
District of Columbia	43	33	18,600	10	1,150	383,150	12,717
Florida	329	295	61,588	37	2,270	137,578	20,828
Georgia	1,818	1,800	544,540	58	3,460	1,045,310	200,516
Kentucky	378	359	109,030	26	2,025	406,949	50,245
Louisiana	865	861	191,041	13	1,480	609,890	68,008
Maryland	38	34	12,389	-	-	150,475	7,750
Mississippi	1,385	1,333	371,115	59	3,695	682,541	136,647
Missouri	234	212	60,015	26	1,225	400,518	18,613
North Carolina	1,173	1,164	362,946	14	750	705,512	134,445
South Carolina	860	836	275,529	37	3,685	699,961	125,572
Tennessee	569	534	159,140	41	1,860	519,923	52,183
Texas	1,464	1,288	282,590	180	12,000	664,286	111,138

[Continued]

★ 1986 ★

Regular Baptists: States and Territories: 1890

[Continued]

State and Territories	Organizations	Church Edifices	Approximate Seating Capacity	Halls, etc.	Seating Capacity	Value of Church Property	Communicants or Members
Virginia	1,001	977	358,032	32	1,955	1,192,035	199,871
West Virginia	79	50	14,175	29	3,340	50,090	4,233

Source: "Regular Baptists (Colored). Atlanta University Publications, No. 6, *The Negro Church*, edited by W.E. Burghardt Du Bois. Atlanta: Atlanta University Press, 1903, p. 41.

★ 1987 ★

Churches

The Baptist Church in the United States, 1901-1902

	1901	1902
State conventions	-	43
Associations	515	517
Churches	15,654	16,440
Ordained ministers	14,861	16,080
Present membership in the United States	1,975,538	2,038,427
Meeting houses	7,576	11,069
Valuation	$11,605,891	$12,196,130
Sunday-schools	7,466	13,707
Teachers and officers	36,736	41,537
Pupils in Sunday-schools	473,271	544,505
Total in Sunday-schools	510,007	586,042

Source: "The Baptist Churches in Chicago," W.E.B. Du Bois, ed., *The Negro Church*, p. 113.

★ 1988 ★

Churches

Value and Wealth of Churches, 1913

St. Philip's Protestant Episcopal Church of New York City is the richest black church in the world. It is an offshoot of Trinity Protestant Episcopal Church, which is the richest white church in America. St. Philip's was organized in 1818 and incorporated in 1820. Its real estate holdings, much of which is residence property, amount to about $1,000,000.

Source: "The Richest Negro Church in the World," Monroe N. Work, ed., *Negro Year Book: An Annual Encyclopedia of the Negro*, 1913, p. 120. Published by permission.

★ 1989 ★

Churches

Value and Wealth of Churches, 1926 - I

Section, division and state	Total number of churches	Number of church edifices	Value of church edifices			Debt on church edifices		Value of parsonages	
			Churches reporting	Amount	Average per church	Churches reporting	Amount	Churches reporting	Amount
United States	42,585	37,749	37,347	$205,782,628	$5,510	8,884	$22,178,581	6,543	$18,122,240
The North	4,442	3,746	3,665	70,328,433	19,189	1,739	11,267,594	1,445	6,932,994
The South	37,790	33,725	33,409	132,285,237	3,960	7,007	10,415,596	4,978	10,788,596
The West	353	278	273	3,168,958	11,608	138	459,391	120	400,650
New England	164	141	136	3,093,850	22,749	62	390,349	55	422,900
Maine	1	1	1	15,000	-	1	2,100	1	8,000
New Hampshire	1	1	1	10,000	-	-	-	-	-
Vermont	-	-	-	-	-	-	-	-	-
Massachusetts	72	61	60	1,201,100	20,018	27	175,129	22	174,500
Rhode Island	21	20	19	410,21,595	21,595	8	45,050	7	42,000
Connecticut	69	58	55	1,457,450	26,499	26	168,070	25	198,400
Middle Atlantic	1,470	1,233	1,200	34,197,990	28,498	675	5,419,901	499	3,410,294
New York	352	279	274	11,615,049	42,391	150	2,300,302	123	1,059,700
New Jersey	412	370	354	7,220,587	20,397	211	971,640	132	870,550
Pennsylvania	706	584	572	15,362,354	26,857	314	2,147,959	244	1,480,044
East North Central	1,676	1,385	1,361	24,119,779	17,722	664	4,205,558	485	2,089,204
Ohio	622	523	513	9,113,989	17,766	226	1,362,271	156	766,400
Indiana	326	281	278	3,568,814	12,837	140	679,821	107	270,108
Illinois	523	405	399	7,774,032	19,484	196	1,496,332	154	652,549
Michigan	186	160	155	3,362,044	21,691	92	606,184	62	375,147
Wisconsin	19	16	16	300,900	18,806	10	60,950	6	25,000
West North Central	1,132	987	968	8,916,814	9,212	338	1,251,786	406	1,010,596
Minnesota	23	24	20	289,001	13,450	9	26,656	14	73,306
Iowa	89	82	81	565,135	6,977	41	62,541	39	96,600
Missouri	645	541	533	5,112,613	9,592	153	807,321	198	520,625
North Dakota	3	2	2	3,250	1,625	1	150	1	750
South Dakota	4	3	2	6,500	3,250	1	90	1	2,000
Nebraska	40	35	33	474,215	14,370	23	77,087	18	68,985
Kansas	328	300	297	2,486,100	8,371	110	277,941	135	248,330
South Atlantic	17,023	14,903	14,726	73,377,432	4,983	3,302	5,867,373	2,253	6,137,036
Delaware	152	146	131	944,380	7,209	74	71,002	57	132,340
Maryland	654	629	617	5,765,535	9,344	250	1,021,392	253	750,015
District of Columbia	147	128	123	6,589,258	53,571	60	874,460	34	320,200
Virginia	2,255	2,148	2,137	14,134,101	6,614	397	1,253,979	240	827,721
West Virginia	480	321	309	2,434,526	7,879	100	166,183	67	258,140
North Carolina	3,203	2,936	2,914	13,670,308	4,691	643	662,086	337	1,071,815
South Carolina	2,838	2,729	2,699	9,005,446	3,337	514	617,231	369	771,305
Georgia	5,201	4,133	4,085	12,380,886	3,031	805	636,704	462	794,245
Florida	2,093	1,733	1,711	8,452,992	4,940	459	564,336	434	1,211,255
East South Central	11,379	10,411	10,332	34,227,172	3,313	1,515	1,946,977	1,289	2,410,042
Kentucky	1,103	994	985	6,602,894	6,703	205	480,883	230	495,631
Tennessee	1,958	1,763	1,745	7,752,853	4,443	302	443,325	240	497,461
Alabama	4,284	3,817	3,799	12,737,558	3,353	593	774,066	455	918,075
Mississippi	4,034	3,837	3,803	7,133,867	1,876	413	248,703	364	498,875
West South Central	9,388	8,411	8,351	24,680,633	2,955	2,190	2,637,246	1,436	2,241,518
Arkansas	2,411	2,125	2,117	5,340,465	2,523	479	406,647	263	356,293
Louisiana	2,077	1,888	1,877	6,514,176	3,471	389	633,819	356	660,305
Oklahoma	990	859	851	2,238,849	2,631	228	192,569	141	183,925
Texas	3,910	3,539	3,506	10,587,143	3,020	1,094	1,404,211	676	1,040,995

[Continued]

★ 1989 ★

Value and Wealth of Churches, 1926 - I

[Continued]

Section, division and state	Total number of churches	Number of church edifices	Value of church edifices			Debt on church edifices		Value of parsonages	
			Churches reporting	Amount	Average per church	Churches reporting	Amount	Churches reporting	Amount
Mountain	133	83	83	409,200	4,930	45	67,946	38	85,450
Montana	9	9	9	36,400	4,044	5	2,039	7	12,300
Idaho	5	4	4	12,500	3,125	2	1,450	2	5,900
Wyoming	11	5	5	21,000	4,200	5	4,200	1	500
Colorado	55	33	33	215,300	6,524	19	52,386	13	41,300
New Mexico	17	11	11	25,600	2,327	8	2,270	6	8,900
Arizona	30	18	18	76,900	4,272	5	5,351	7	14,250
Utah	4	2	2	16,500	8,250	1	250	2	2,300
Nevada	2	1	1	5,000	-	-	-	-	-
Pacific	220	195	190	2,759,758	14,525	93	391,445	82	315,200
Washington	23	21	21	172,700	8,224	10	9,185	11	41,100
Oregon	5	4	4	98,510	24,628	4	11,700	2	3,800
California	192	170	165	2,488,548	15,082	79	370,560	69	270,300

Source: "Value of Negro Church Property, Church Debt, Land Expenditures, by Sections, Divisions, and States: 1926," U.S. Bureau of the Census, *Negroes in the United States, 1920-1932*, p. 537.

★ 1990 ★

Churches

Value and Wealth of Churches, 1926 - II

Section, division and state	Debt of parsonages		Expenditures during year					
	Churches reporting	Amount	Churches reporting	Total amount	For current expenses and improvements	For benevolences, missions, etc.	Not classified	Average per church
United States	1,399	$1,824,255	39,245	$43,024,259	$35,749,951	$6,152,905	$1,121,403	$1,096
The North	429	948,028	4,141	13,132,873	11,154,281	1,564,873	413,719	3,171
The South	939	837,819	34,799	29,225,266	24,029,159	4,493,938	701,169	840
The West	31	38,408	305	666,120	566,511	94,094	5,515	2,184
New England	23	77,950	162	530,409	462,099	68,310	-	3,274
Maine	-	-	1	1,635	1,500	135	-	-
New Hampshire	-	-	1	2,150	2,109	41	-	-
Vermont	-	-	-	-	-	-	-	-
Massachusetts	12	49,300	71	251,967	221,349	30,618	-	3,549
Rhode Island	4	11,750	21	67,809	61,044	6,765	-	3,229
Connecticut	7	16,900	68	206,848	176,097	30,751	-	3,042
Middle Atlantic	184	525,306	1,396	6,389,469	5,486,782	768,382	134,305	4,577
New York	39	182,359	336	2,048,710	1,750,092	258,203	40,415	6,097
New Jersey	50	112,009	392	1,588,821	1,387,760	161,267	39,794	4,053
Pennsylvania	95	230,938	668	2,751,938	2,348,930	348,912	54,096	4,120
East North Central	142	263,534	1,549	4,689,535	3,919,940	569,482	200,113	3,027
Ohio	38	89,239	572	1,800,095	1,528,371	188,059	83,665	3,147
Indiana	35	38,761	297	652,558	556,797	70,186	25,575	2,197
Illinois	41	77,582	487	1,485,297	1,211,496	183,176	90,625	3,050
Michigan	25	51,452	178	691,181	571,774	119,159	248	3,883
Wisconsin	3	6,500	15	60,404	51,502	8,902	-	4,027

[Continued]

★ 1990 ★

Value and Wealth of Churches, 1926 - II

[Continued]

Section, division and state	Debt of parsonages		Expenditures during year					
	Churches reporting	Amount	Churches reporting	Total amount	For current expenses and improvements	For benevolences, missions, etc.	Not classified	Average per church
West North Central	80	81,238	1,034	1,523,460	1,285,460	158,699	79,301	1,473
Minnesota	5	10,500	23	72,790	61,976	8,014	2,800	3,165
Iowa	8	4,415	87	130,241	105,780	18,728	5,733	1,497
Missouri	37	36,928	580	846,458	741,794	85,533	19,131	1,459
North Dakota	1	150	1	258	-	-	258	-
South Dakota	-	-	4	3,579	2,081	261	1,237	895
Nebraska	6	11,855	36	90,489	74,754	11,054	4,681	2,514
Kansas	23	17,390	303	379,645	299,075	35,109	45,461	1,253
South Atlantic	449	482,742	14,985	14,642,047	11,920,310	2,291,398	430,339	977
Delaware	16	17,816	149	244,173	211,004	29,719	3,450	1,639
Maryland	75	83,430	641	1,199,001	975,869	183,642	39,490	1,871
District of Columbia	14	45,800	144	838,212	715,557	121,255	1,400	5,821
Virginia	58	97,462	2,188	2,289,137	1,896,073	354,991	38,073	1,046
West Virginia	22	27,237	449	499,104	414,546	63,266	21,292	1,112
North Carolina	72	104,340	2,862	3,060,556	2,517,798	450,267	92,491	1,069
South Carolina	51	24,312	2,783	1,943,809	1,621,003	302,382	20,424	698
Georgia	64	32,685	3,874	2,434,130	1,827,849	420,702	185,579	628
Florida	77	49,660	1,895	2,133,925	1,740,611	365,174	28,140	1,126
East South Central	189	111,104	10,851	8,176,840	6,776,926	1,288,737	111,177	754
Kentucky	43	39,252	1,051	1,178,944	1,044,500	125,985	8,459	1,122
Tennessee	43	22,989	1,831	1,647,742	1,426,234	208,383	13,125	900
Alabama	57	35,655	4,041	3,480,988	2,838,602	595,514	46,872	861
Mississippi	46	13,208	3,928	1,869,166	1,467,590	358,855	42,721	476
West South Central	301	243,973	8,963	6,406,379	5,331,923	913,803	160,653	715
Arkansas	43	22,320	2,320	1,512,378	1,267,026	215,762	29,590	652
Louisiana	58	72,799	1,966	1,539,644	1,295,678	219,082	24,884	783
Oklahoma	20	26,799	943	617,605	519,983	86,809	10,813	655
Texas	180	122,055	3,734	2,736,752	2,249,236	392,150	95,366	733
Mountain	12	9,383	95	136,400	108,658	22,242	5,500	1,436
Montana	1	93	8	7,125	5,669	1,456	-	891
Idaho	1	2,700	4	8,165	6,965	1,200	-	2,041
Wyoming	-	-	6	4,211	3,036	975	200	702
Colorado	4	4,200	40	71,853	57,377	12,906	1,570	1,796
New Mexico	3	1,000	11	8,968	7,872	1,096	-	815
Arizona	2	690	23	33,716	25,802	4,184	3,730	1,466
Utah	1	700	2	1,962	1,612	350	-	981
Nevada	-	-	1	400	325	75	-	-
Pacific	19	29,025	210	529,720	457,853	71,852	15	2,522
Washington	1	1,000	20	45,146	39,918	5,228	-	2,257
Oregon	-	-	5	17,175	13,295	3,880	-	3,435
California	18	28,025	185	467,399	404,640	62,744	15	2,526

Source: "Value of Negro Church Property, Church Debt, Land Expenditures, by Sections, Divisions, and States: 1926," U.S. Bureau of the Census, *Negroes in the United States, 1920-1932,* p. 537.

★ 1991 ★

Churches

Value of Buildings, 1936

Denomination	Number of Negro churches	Number of church edifices	Churches reporting	Value reported	Average per church
Total	38,303	34,896	34,250	$164,531,531	$4,804
Adventist bodies:					
Seventh-day Adventists Denomination	97	76	68	281,670	4,142
African Orthodox Church[1]	13	4	4	36,204	9,051
Apostolic Overcoming Holy Church of God[1]	23	12	12	16,040	1,337
Baptist bodies:					
Negro Baptists[1]	23,093	21,350	21,045	93,798,181	4,457
United American Free Will Baptist Church (colored)[1]	226	207	207	468,883	2,265
Colored Primitive Baptists[1]	1,009	889	876	1,643,804	1,876
National Baptist Evangelical Life and Soul Saving Assembly of the United States of America[1]	28	21	20	84,459	4,222
Northern Baptist Convention	32	30	30	1,617,800	53,927
Christian and Missionary Alliance	5	4	4	9,000	2,250
Christ's Sanctified Holy Church[1]	31	27	24	21,215	884
Church of Christ, (Holiness), U.S.A.[1]	106	91	88	305,152	3,468
Church of Christ, Scientists	4	1	1	8,000	-
Church of God	42	23	22	60,290	2,740
Church of God, (Anderson, Ind.)	117	82	78	251,865	3,229
Church of God and Saints of Christ[1]	213	79	78	544,270	6,978
Church of God in Christ[1]	772	523	604	1,453,128	2,883
Churches of Christ	1	1	1	2,000	-
Churches of God, Holiness[1]	35	17	17	116,900	6,876
Churches of God in North America, (General eldership)	1	1	1	25,000	-
Churches of the Living God:					
Church of the Living God, Christian Workers for Fellowship[1]	96	66	66	130,100	1,971
Church of the Living God, "The Pillar and Ground of Truth"[1]	119	86	86	115,426	1,342
Congregational and Christian Churches[2]	233	216	208	1,506,989	7,245
Disciples of Christ	189	165	158	873,978	5,532
Apostolic Episcopal Church (The Holy Eastern Catholic and Apostolic Orthodox Church)	3	-	-	-	-
Federated Churches	1	1	1	500	-
Fire Baptized Holiness Church of God of the Americans[1]	59	46	43	146,232	3,401
Free Christian Zion Church of Christ[1]	9	8	8	8,442	1,055
House of God, Holy Church of the Living God, the Pillar and Ground of Truth, House of Prayer for all People[1]	4	1	1	1,500	-
House of the Lord[1]	4	-	-	-	-
Independent Negro Churches[1]	50	22	19	180,300	9,489
International Church of the Four Square Gospel	1	-	-	-	-
Kodesh Church of Immanuel[1]	9	2	2	11,000	5,500
The Latter House of the Lord, Apostolic Faith[1]	2	2	2	2,400	1,200
Lutheran bodies:					
American Lutheran Church	1	1	1	4,000	-

[Continued]

★ 1991 ★

Value of Buildings, 1936

[Continued]

Denomination	Number of Negro churches	Number of church edifices	Churches reporting	Value reported	Average per church
Evangelical Lutheran Synodical Conference of North America: Negro Mission of the Synodical Conference	81	70	66	369,150	5,593
Methodist bodies:					
Methodist Episcopal Church	1,730	1,690	1,642	10,065,869	6,130
Methodist Protestant Church	40	38	38	42,615	1,121
African Methodist Episcopal Church[1]	4,578	4,218	4,078	20,710,623	5,079
African Methodist Episcopal Zion Church[1]	2,252	2,048	2,008	14,750,165	7,346
Colored Methodist Protestant Church[1]	1	1	1	7,000	-
Union American Methodist Episcopal Church[1]	71	69	69	516,630	7,487
African Union Methodist Protestant Church[1]	45	42	40	302,325	7,558
Colored Methodist Episcopal Church[1]	2,063	1,988	1,979	6,148,826	3,107
Reformed Zion Union Apostolic Church[1]	54	53	53	283,100	5,342
Independent African Methodist Episcopal Church[1]	29	21	18	16,789	9,327
Reformed Methodist Union Episcopal Church[1]	25	23	23	49,229	2,140
Moravian bodies:					
Moravian Church in America	1	1	1	75,000	-
National David Spiritual Temple of Christ Church Union	11	4	4	6,875	1,719
Presbyterian bodies:					
Presbyterian Church in the United States of America	16	12	10	362,600	36,260
Colored Cumberland Presbyterian Church[1]	145	126	126	359,125	2,580
United Presbyterian Church of North America	1	1	1	6,000	-
Presbyterian Church in the United States	5	5	5	11,800	2,360
Protestant Episcopal Church	145	126	123	2,777,060	2,258
Reformed Episcopal Church	36	36	36	58,220	1,617
Roman Catholic Church	178	156	148	3,432,416	2,319
Salvation Army	3	2	2	106,064	53,032
Progressive Spiritualist Church	1	1	1	3,500	-
Triumph, The Church and Kingdom of God in Christ[1]	2	2	2	1,100	550
United Holy Church of America, Incorporated[1]	162	109	101	344,722	3,413

Source: "Value of Church Edifices: 1936," Florence Murray, ed., *The Negro Handbook*, 1942, p. 97. *Notes:* 1. Wholly Negro denominations. 2. Represents merger of Congregational Churches with General Convention of the Christian Church, since 1926.

Denominations

★ 1992 ★

Churches and Membership in Urban and Rural Areas by Gender and Geographical Areas, 1926 - I

Urban territory includes all cities and other incorporated places which had 2,500 inhabitants or more in 1920; rural territory comprises the remainder of the country.

Sections, division, and state	Number of churches			Number of members[2]			Average members per church		
	Total	Urban	Rural	Total	Urban	Rural	Total	Urban	Rural
United States	42,585	10,158	32,427	5,203,487	2,238,871	2,964,616	122	220	91
The North	4,442	3,343	1,099	875,748	816,608	59,140	197	244	54
The South	37,790	6,515	31,275	4,288,621	2,385,148	2,903,473	113	213	93
The West	353	300	53	39,118	37,115	2,003	111	124	38
New England	164	153	11	28,048	27,395	653	171	179	59
Maine	1	1	-	45	45	-	-	-	-
New Hampshire	1	1	-	63	63	-	-	-	-
Massachusetts	72	70	2	13,882	13,806	76	193	197	38
Rhode Island	21	19	2	3,465	3,292	173	165	173	87
Connecticut	69	62	7	10,593	10,189	404	154	164	58
Middle Atlantic	1,470	1,142	328	363,296	338,710	24,586	247	297	75
New York	352	313	39	114,543	112,406	2,137	325	359	55
New Jersey	412	275	137	71,221	61,181	10,040	172	222	73
Pennsylvania	706	554	152	177,532	165,123	12,409	251	298	82
East North Central	1,676	1,368	308	356,294	340,255	16,039	213	249	52
Ohio	622	465	157	119,529	112,308	7,221	192	242	46
Indiana	326	280	46	49,704	46,751	2,953	152	167	64
Illinois	523	433	90	1137,131	132,033	5,098	262	305	57
Michigan	186	171	15	46,231	45,464	767	249	266	51
Wisconsin	19	19	-	3,699	3,699	-	195	195	-
West North Central	1,132	680	452	128,110	110,248	17,862	113	162	40
Minnesota	23	22	1	3,702	3,688	14	161	168	-
Iowa	89	81	8	8,577	8,102	475	96	100	59
Missouri	645	319	326	82,207	68,463	13,744	127	215	42
North Dakota	3	3	-	27	27	-	9	9	-
South Dakota	4	4	-	142	142	-	36	36	-
Nebraska	40	38	2	5,163	5,097	66	129	134	33
Kansas	328	213	115	28,292	24,729	3,563	86	116	31
South Atlantic	17,023	2,733	14,290	2,159,295	674,620	1,484,675	127	247	104
Delaware	152	43	109	12,459	6,702	5,757	82	156	53
Maryland	654	169	485	97,025	62,915	34,110	148	372	70
District of Columbia	147	147	-	72,382	72,382	-	492	492	-
Virginia	2,255	361	1,894	378,742	105,546	273,196	168	292	144
West Virginia	480	100	380	32,754	12,585	20,169	68	126	53
North Carolina	3,203	547	2,656	431,333	114,556	316,777	135	209	119
South Carolina	2,838	371	2,467	405,614	78,603	327,011	143	212	133

[Continued]

★ 1992 ★

Churches and Membership in Urban and Rural Areas by Gender and Geographical Areas, 1926 - I

[Continued]

Sections, division, and state	Number of churches			Number of members[2]			Average members per church		
	Total	Urban	Rural	Total	Urban	Rural	Total	Urban	Rural
Georgia	5,201	618	4,583	538,093	136,145	401,948	103	220	88
Florida	2,093	377	1,716	190,893	85,183	105,707	91	226	62
East South Central	11,379	1,788	9,591	1,259,605	374,129	885,476	111	209	92
Kentucky	1,103	311	792	127,126	71,583	55,543	115	230	70
Tennessee	1,958	536	1,422	226,823	112,981	113,842	116	211	80
Alabama	4,284	534	3,750	557,231	132,777	424,454	130	249	113
Mississippi	4,034	407	3,627	348,425	56,788	291,637	86	140	80
West South Central	9,388	1,994	7,394	869,721	336,399	533,322	93	169	72
Arkansas	2,411	292	2,119	201,240	44,395	156,845	83	152	74
Louisiana	2,077	405	1,672	248,797	98,398	150,399	120	243	90
Oklahoma	990	325	665	68,379	34,733	33,646	69	107	51
Texas	3,910	972	2,938	351,305	158,873	192,432	90	163	165
Mountain	133	106	27	10,243	9,137	1,106	77	86	41
Montana	9	9	-	228	228	-	25	25	-
Idaho	5	5	-	205	205	-	41	41	-
Wyoming	11	11	-	398	398	-	36	36	-
Colorado	55	42	13	6,188	5,711	477	113	136	37
New Mexico	17	14	3	710	548	162	42	39	54
Arizona	30	20	10	2,199	1,753	446	73	88	45
Utah	4	4	-	269	269	-	67	67	-
Nevada	2	1	1	46	25	21	23	-	-
Pacific	220	194	26	28,875	27,978	897	131	144	35
Washington	23	22	1	2,280	2,271	9	99	103	-
Oregon	5	5	-	832	832	-	166	166	-
California	192	167	25	25,763	24,875	888	134	149	36

Source: "Number of Negro Churches and Membership Classified in the Urban and Rural Areas, Membership Classified by Sex, and Sunday Schools, by Sections, Divisions, and States: 1926," U.S. Bureau of the Census, *Negroes in the United States, 1920-1932,* p. 536. *Notes:* 1. Includes only organizations reporting members. 2. Membership as defined by the participating denominations.

★ 1993 ★

Denominations

Churches and Membership in Urban and Rural Areas by Gender and Geographical Areas, 1926 - II

Urban territory includes all cities and other incorporated places which had 2,500 inhabitants or more in 1920; rural territory comprises the remainder of the country.

Sections, division, and state	Total membership by sex[1]			Sunday schools[2]		
	Male	Female	Sex not reported	Churches reporting	Officers and teachers	Scholars
United States	1,726,347	2,789,749	687,391	36,378	298,283	2,144,553
The North	267,354	420,953	187,441	3,769	40,970	337,957
The South	1,447,031	2,348,037	493,553	32,332	254,748	1,789,095
The West	11,962	20,759	6,397	277	2,565	17,501
New England	10,462	17,421	165	151	1,761	15,059
Maine	11	34	-	1	7	28
New Hampshire	13	50	-	1	9	49
Massachusetts	4,898	8,819	165	68	752	7,766
Rhode Island	1,374	2,091	-	19	265	1,800
Connecticut	4,166	6,427	-	62	728	5,416
Middle Atlantic	124,526	185,804	52,966	1,302	16,139	140,490
New York	42,000	65,720	6,823	320	4,361	38,692
New Jersey	24,049	39,437	7,735	367	3,588	30,985
Pennsylvania	58,477	80,647	38,408	615	8,190	70,813
East North Central	88,941	142,973	124,380	1,411	15,041	130,625
Ohio	19,874	32,513	67,142	483	5,596	46,996
Indiana	16,298	26,984	6,422	281	2,646	18,139
Illinois	35,292	56,744	45,095	466	4,779	48,116
Michigan	16,213	25,036	4,982	169	1,918	16,328
Wisconsin	1,264	1,696	739	12	102	1,046
West North Central	43,425	74,755	9,930	905	8,029	51,783
Minnesota	1,424	2,264	14	22	195	1,643
Iowa	2,987	5,443	147	79	797	5,083
Missouri	27,354	47,495	7,358	498	4,512	30,174
North Dakota	1	1	25	-	-	-
South Dakota	65	77	-	3	21	55
Nebraska	1,200	2,302	1,661	29	234	1,580
Kansas	10,394	17,173	725	274	2,270	13,248
South Atlantic	715,277	1,132,963	311,055	13,708	110,957	860,878
Delaware	4,126	6,532	1,801	138	960	7,687
Maryland	34,150	51,484	11,391	606	5,202	43,678
District of Columbia	24,455	38,662	9,265	138	1,889	20,953
Virginia	147,751	219,591	11,400	2,062	17,553	137,019
West Virginia	11,713	16,406	4,635	412	3,337	20,042
North Carolina	158,055	252,660	20,618	2,801	28,653	213,700
South Carolina	148,679	240,964	15,971	2,641	21,376	183,161
Georgia	119,791	195,411	222,891	3,172	19,466	141,582
Florida	66,557	111,253	13,083	1,738	12,521	93,056

[Continued]

★ 1993 ★

Churches and Membership in Urban and Rural Areas by Gender and Geographical Areas, 1926 - II

[Continued]

Sections, division, and state	Total membership by sex[1]			Sunday schools[2]		
	Male	Female	Sex not reported	Churches reporting	Officers and teachers	Scholars
East South Central	417,963	695,864	145,778	10,326	81,705	537,196
Kentucky	46,903	75,751	4,472	957	7,630	50,136
Tennessee	80,561	140,799	5,463	1,714	13,226	87,706
Alabama	155,249	269,112	132,870	3,864	31,467	237,265
Mississippi	135,250	210,202	2,973	3,791	29,382	162,089
West South Central	313,791	519,210	36,720	8,298	62,086	391,021
Arkansas	72,756	118,761	9,723	2,216	16,740	101,375
Louisiana	91,353	149,289	8,155	1,843	13,304	87,867
Oklahoma	25,352	42,132	895	863	5,745	34,586
Texas	124,330	209,028	17,947	3,376	26,297	167,193
Mountain	2,301	4,035	3,907	89	607	3,607
Montana	82	146	-	9	49	183
Idaho	90	115	-	4	24	123
Wyoming	60	111	227	4	18	108
Colorado	1,260	2,204	2,724	39	254	1,692
New Mexico	182	290	238	9	67	326
Arizona	575	1,069	555	21	176	1,056
Utah	38	68	163	2	15	101
Nevada	14	32	-	1	4	18
Pacific	9,661	16,724	2,490	188	1,958	13,894
Washington	812	1,468	-	21	178	1,207
Oregon	202	330	300	4	69	371
California	8,647	14,926	2,190	163	1,711	12,316

Source: "Number of Negro Churches and Membership Classified in the Urban and Rural Areas, Membership Classified by Sex, and Sunday Schools, by Sections, Divisions, and States: 1926," U.S. Bureau of the Census, *Negroes in the United States, 1920-1932*, p. 536. *Notes:* 1. Figures are to be used with due consideration of the number of members not so reported. 2. The statistics given relate only to the Sunday schools reported by individual churches and do not include undenominational or union Sunday schools; nor do they include the parochial or week-day schools that are maintained by a number of bodies, particularly the Roman Catholic Church and certain Lutheran bodies.

★ 1994 ★

Denominations

Church Denominations in Virginia: Characteristics, ca 1900

Denomination	No. of Churches	Memebrship Claimed	Active Members	Value of Church Property	Expenses of Last Year
African Methodist Episcopal	1	236	78	$25,000	$3,810.00
Methodist Episcopal	1	97	50	3,500	1,490.00
Baptist	19	14,802	6,949	291,400	40,653.29
Presbyterian	1	83	60	11,000	732.00
Episcopal	2	143	138	10,800	1,210.70
Totals	24	15,361	7,275	341,700	47,895.99

Source: "Virginia." Atlanta University Publications. No. 6, *The Negro Church*, edited by W.E. Burghardt Du Bois. Atlanta: Atlanta University Press, 1903, p. 80.

★ 1995 ★

Denominations

Church Denominations in Virginia: Expenses, ca 1900

Denomination	No. of Churches	Membership Claimed	Active Members	Value of Church Property	Expenses of Last Year
African Methodist Episcopal	1	236	78	$25,000	$3,810.00
Methodist Episcopal	1	97	50	3,500	1,490.00
Baptist	19	14,802	6,949	291,400	40,653.29
Presbyterian	1	83	60	11,000	732.00
Episcopal	2	143	138	10,800	1,210.70
Totals	24	15,361	7,275	341,700	47,895.99

Source: "Untitled Table." Atlanta University Publications. No. 6, *The Negro Church*, edited by W.E. Burghardt Du Bois. Atlanta: Atlanta University Press, 1903, p. 80.

★ 1996 ★

Denominations

Membership, Churches, and Communicants of Selected Denominations, 1903

Denominations	Ministers	Churches	Communicants
Baptists	10,729	15,614	1,625,330
Union American Methodists	180	205	16,500
African Methodists	6,500	5,800	785,000
African Union Methodist Protestants	68	68	2,930
African Zion Methodists	3,386	3,042	551,591
Congressional Methodists	5	5	319
Colored Methodists	2,159	1,497	207,723
Cumberland Presbyterians	450	400	39,000
Total	23,477	26,631	3,228,393

Source: Untitled table, W.E.B. Du Bois, ed., *The Negro Church*, p. 153.

★ 1997 ★

Denominations

Number of Churches and Membership by Gender, Denominations, Urban, and rural, 1926 - I

Urban territory includes all cities and other incorporated places which had 2,500 inhabitants or more in 1920, rural territory comprises the remainder of the country.

Denomination	Total number of churches[1] in denominations wholly or in part Negro	Number of Negro churches[1]			Number of members[2]		
		Total	Urban	Rural	Total	Urban	Rural
All denominations	141,753	42,585	10,158	32,427	5,203,487	2,238,871	2,964,616
Adventist bodies							
Advent Christian Church	444	6	1	5	164	22	142
Seventh-day Adventist Denomination	1,981	93	88	5	5,133	5,052	81
African Orthodox Church	13	13	13	-	1,568	1,568	-
African Orthodox Church of New York	3	3	3	-	717	717	-
Apostolic Overcoming Holy Church of God	16	16	8	8	1,047	581	466
Baptist bodies							
Negro Baptist	22,081	22,081	4,409	17,672	3,196,623	1,246,327	1,950,296
United American Free Will Baptist Church	166	166	11	155	13,396	1,804	11,592
Regular Baptist	349	1	-	1	38	-	38
Colored Primitive Baptists	925	925	76	849	43,978	4,637	39,341
Christian and Missionary Alliance	332	10	9	1	535	510	25
Christian Church (General Convention of the Christian Church)	1,044	68	18	50	7,312	1,705	5,607
Church of Christ (Holiness) United States of America	82	82	46	36	4,919	3,002	1,917
Church of Christ, Scientist	1,913	1	1	-	274	274	-
Church of God	644	29	7	22	887	318	569

[Continued]

★ 1997 ★

Number of Churches and Membership by Gender, Denominations, Urban, and rural, 1926 - I

[Continued]

Denomination	Total number of churches[1] in denominations wholly or in part Negro	Number of Negro churches[1]			Number of members[2]		
		Total	Urban	Rural	Total	Urban	Rural
Church of God (Headquarters, Anderson, Ind)	932	98	54	44	3,165	2,404	761
Church of God and Saints of Christ	112	112	101	11	6,741	6,055	686
Church of God in Christ	733	733	405	328	30,263	20,805	9,458
Churches of Christ	6,226	214	80	134	8,155	3,580	4,575
Churches of God, Holiness	29	29	24	5	2,278	1,929	349
Churches of god in North America (General Eldership)	428	7	2	5	274	55	219
Churches of the Living God							
Church of the Living God, Christian Workers for Fellowship	149	149	82	67	11,558	7,289	4,269
Church of the Living God, "The Pillar and Ground of Truth"	81	81	45	36	5,844	3,886	1,958
Congregational Churches	5,028	155	96	59	16,000	13,139	2,861
Disciples of Christ	7,648	487	160	327	37,325	14,938	22,387
Free Christian Zion Church of Christ	5	5	1	4	187	60	127
Free Church of God in Christ	19	19	15	4	874	797	77
Independent Churches							
Lutherans							
United Lutheran Church in America	3,650	1	1	-	126	126	-
Evangelical Lutheran Synodical Conference of America							
Evangical Lutheran Synodical of Missouri, Ohio, and other states	3,917	69	33	36	5,871	3,596	2,275
Methodist bodies							
Methodist Episcopal Church	26,130	3,743	805	2,938	332,347	149,559	182,788
Methodist Protestant Church	2,239	46	9	37	2,529	305	2,224
Wesleyan Methodist Connection (or Church) of America	619	26	10	16	1,215	672	543
African Methodist Episcopal Church	6,708	6,708	1,599	5,109	545,814	272,765	273,049
African Methodist Episcopal Zion Church	2,466	2,466	650	1,816	456,813	193,926	262,887
Colored Methodist Protestant Church	3	3	3	-	533	533	-
Union American Methodist Episcopal Church	73	73	37	36	10,169	7,043	3,126
African Union Methodist Protestant Church	43	43	23	20	4,086	2,707	1,379
Colored Methodist Episcopal Church	2,518	2,518	567	1,951	202,713	79,183	123,530
Reformed Zion Union Apostolic Church	48	48	5	43	4,538	651	3,887
Reformed Methodist Union Episcopal Church	25	25	7	18	2,265	486	1,779
Independent African Methodist Episcopal Church	29	29	8	21	1,003	424	579
Moravian bodies							
Moravian Church in America	127	1	1	-	694	694	-
The (Original) Church of God	50	1	1	-	12	12	-
Presbyterian bodies							
Presbyterian Church in the United States of America	8,947	450	195	255	37,090	21,503	15,587
Colored Cumberland Presbyterian Church	178	178	60	118	10,868	3,911	6,957
United Presbyterian Church of North America	901	14	6	8	1,202	602	600
Presbyterian Church in the United States	3,469	52	17	35	2,1354	907	1,227

[Continued]

★ 1997 ★

Number of Churches and Membership by Gender, Denominations, Urban, and rural, 1926 - I

[Continued]

Denomination	Total number of churches[1] in denominations wholly or in part Negro	Number of Negro churches[1]			Number of members[2]		
		Total	Urban	Rural	Total	Urban	Rural
Protestant Episcopal Church	7,299	287	205	82	51,502	46,201	5,301
Reformed Episcopal Church	69	36	7	29	2,753	1,158	1,595
Roman Catholic Church	18,940	147	117	30	124,324	106,839	17,485
Salvation Army	1,052	5	5	-	495	495	-
Spiritualists							
National Spiritualist Associations	543	17	17	-	904	904	-
Progressive Spiritual Church	9	1	1	-	500	500	-
National Spiritual Alliance of the United States of America	59	8	7	1	190	173	17

Source: "Number of Negro Churches and Membership Classified by Sex, with Separate Figures for Urban and Rural Churches, by Denominations: 1926," U.S. Bureau of the Census, *Negroes in the United States, 1920-1932,* p. 532. *Notes:* 1. Includes only organizations reporting members. 2. Membership as defined by the particular denomination.

★ 1998 ★

Denominations

Number of Churches and Membership by Gender, Denominations, Urban, and rural, 1926 - II

Urban territory includes all cities and other incorporated places which had 2,500 inhabitants or more in 1920, rural territory comprises the remainder of the country.

Denomination	Average members per church			Membership by sex[1]			
	Total	Urban	Rural	Male	Female	Sex not reported	Males per 100 females
All denominations	122	220	91	1,726,347	2,789,749	687,391	61.9
Adventist bodies							
Advent Christian Church	27	-	28	83	81	-	[2]
Seventh-day Adventist Denomination	55	57	16	1,272	3,831	30	33.2
African Orthodox Church	121	121	-	689	879	-	78.4
African Orthodox Church of New York	239	239	-	262	355	100	73.8
Apostolic Overcoming Holy Church of God	65	73	58	352	695	-	50.6
Baptist bodies							
Negro Baptist	145	283	110	1,050,062	1,661,183	485,378	63.2
United American Free Will Baptist Church	81	164	75	5,079	8,236	81	61.7
Regular Baptist	-	-	-	16	22	-	[2]
Colored Primitive Baptists	48	61	46	2,346	4,856	36,776	48.3
Christian and Missionary Alliance	54	57	-	198	337	-	58.8
Christian Church (General Convention of the Christian Church)	108	95	112	2,690	4,622	-	58.2
Church of Christ (Holiness) United States of America	60	65	53	1,589	2,942	388	54.0
Church of Christ, Scientist	-	-	-	70	204	-	34.3
Church of God	31	45	26	296	591	-	50.1
Church of God (Headquarters, Anderson, Ind)	32	45	17	1,072	2,093	-	51.2
Church of God and Saints of Christ	60	60	62	2,539	4,202	-	60.4

[Continued]

★ 1998 ★

Number of Churches and Membership by Gender, Denominations, Urban, and rural, 1926 - II

[Continued]

Denomination	Average members per church			Membership by sex[1]			
	Total	Urban	Rural	Male	Female	Sex not reported	Males per 100 females
Church of God in Christ	41	51	29	9,077	20,873	313	43.5
Churches of Christ	38	45	34	3,296	4,839	20	68.1
Churches of God, Holiness	79	80	70	830	1,410	38	58.9
Churches of god in North America (General Eldership)	39	28	44	103	171	-	60.2
Churches of the Living God							
Church of the Living God, Christian Workers for Fellowship	78	89	64	3,964	7,594	-	52.2
Church of the Living God, "The Pillar and Ground of Truth"	72	86	54	3,247	2,597	-	125.0
Congregational Churches	103	137	48	6,081	9,782	137	62.2
Disciples of Christ	77	93	68	12,016	18,459	6,850	65.1
Free Christian Zion Church of Christ	37	-	32	94	93	-	[2]
Free Church of God in Christ	46	53	19	300	574	-	52.3
Independent Churches	220	220	-	401	1,021	120	39.3
Lutherans							
United Lutheran Church in America	-	-	-	73	53	-	[2]
Evangelical Lutheran Synodical Conference of America							
Evangical Lutheran Synodical of Missouri, Ohio, and other states	85	109	63	2,480	3,308	83	75.0
Methodist bodies							
Methodist Episcopal Church	89	186	62	117,176	192,905	22,266	60.7
Methodist Protestant Church	55	34	60	725	1,164	640	62.3
Wesleyan Methodist Connection (or Church) of America	47	67	34	424	791	-	53.6
African Methodist Episcopal Church	81	171	53	165,615	295,137	85,062	56.1
African Methodist Episcopal Zion Church	185	298	145	167,432	289,381	-	57.9
Colored Methodist Protestant Church	178	178	-	194	339	-	57.2
Union American Methodist Episcopal Church	139	190	87	4,223	5,946	-	71.0
African Union Methodist Protestant Church	95	118	69	1,255	1,786	1,045	70.3
Colored Methodist Episcopal Church	81	140	63	65,781	107,807	29,125	61.0
Reformed Zion Union Apostolic Church	95	130	90	1,876	2,544	118	73.7
Reformed Methodist Union Episcopal Church	91	69	99	764	1,501	-	50.9
Independent African Methodist Episcopal Church	35	53	28	351	652	-	53.8
Moravian bodies							
Moravian Church in America	-	-	-	250	444	-	56.3
The (Original) Church of God	-	-	-	-	-	12	-
Presbyterian bodies							
Presbyterian Church in the United States of America	82	110	61	14,048	21,376	1,666	65.7
Colored Cumberland Presbyterian Church	61	65	59	4,410	6,373	85	69.2
United Presbyterian Church of North America	86	100	75	421	668	113	63.0
Presbyterian Church in the United States	41	53	35	817	1,303	14	62.7
Protestant Episcopal Church	179	225	65	17,846	26,422	7,234	67.5
Reformed Episcopal Church	76	165	55	926	1,827	-	50.7
Roman Catholic Church	846	913	583	50,732	64,523	9,069	78.6
Salvation Army	99	99	-	140	355	-	39.4

[Continued]

★ 1998 ★

Number of Churches and Membership by Gender, Denominations, Urban, and rural, 1926 - II

[Continued]

Denomination	Average members per church			Membership by sex[1]			
	Total	Urban	Rural	Male	Female	Sex not reported	Males per 100 females
Spiritualists							
National Spiritualist Associations	53	53	-	100	176	628	56.8
Progressive Spiritual Church	-	-	-	200	300	-	66.7
National Spiritual Alliance of the United States of America	24	25	-	64	126	-	50.8

Source: "Number of Negro Churches and Membership Classified by Sex, with Separate Figures for Urban and Rural Churches, by Denominations: 1926," U.S. Bureau of the Census, *Negroes in the United States, 1920-1932*, p. 532. *Notes:* 1. Figures are to be used with due consideration of the number of members not so reported. 2. Ratio not shown where number of females is less than 100.

★ 1999 ★

Denominations

Proportion of Baptist and Methodists of All Denominations, 1904

State	Total Negro population	Church communicants or members[1]						
		All denominations	Baptists		Methodists		Others	
			Number	Percent	Number	Percent	Number	Percent
United States	9,827,763	3,685,097	2,354,789	63.9	1,182,131	32.1	148,177	4.0
The South	8,749,427	3,375,546	2,198,078	65.1	1,051,972	32.1	125,496	3.1
Alabama	908,282	397,178	275,358	69.3	111,571	28.1	10,249	2.6
Arkansas	442,891	146,319	94,464	64.6	47,449	32.4	4,406	3.0
Delaware	31,181	10,583	707	6.7	7,982	74.6	1,894	18.8
District of Columbia	94,446	46,249	30,392	65.7	8,813	19.1	7,044	15.2
Florida	308,669	105,678	54,109	51.2	47,201	44.7	4,368	4.1
Georgia	1,176,987	507,005	342,154	67.5	158,102	31.2	6,749	1.3
Kentucky	261,656	116,918	77,487	66.3	31,154	26.6	8,277	7.1
Louisiana	713,874	185,918	134,163	72.2	41,748	22.5	10,007	5.4
Maryland	232,250	71,797	19,193	26.7	46,338	64.5	6,266	1.9
Mississippi	1,009,487	358,708	243,603	67.9	110,465	30.8	4,604	1.3
North Carolina	697,843	283,707	165,503	58.3	96,465	34.0	21,739	7.7
Oklahoma	137,612	29,115	17,102	58.7	10,841	37.2	1,172	4.0
South Carolina	835,843	394,149	219,841	55.8	162,143	41.1	12,165	3.1
Tennessee	473,088	172,867	97,003	56.1	64,112	37.1	11,752	6.8
Texas	690,049	227,032	146,158	64.4	72,848	32.1	8,026	3.5
Virginia	671,096	307,374	270,219	87.9	30,492	9.9	6,663	2.2
West Virginia	64,173	14,949	10,622	71.1	4,248	28.4	79	.5

Source: "Proportion of Baptists and Methodists of All Denominations," U.S. Department of the Interior, Bureau of Education, Bulletin 1916, No. 38, *Negro Education: A Study of the Private and Higher Schools for Colored People in the United States*, Vol. 1, p. 62. Primary source: 1910 Census; *Note:* 1. United States census of religious denominations, 1904.

Periodicals and Publications

★ 2000 ★

Baptist Periodicals Published, 1900-1902

Periodicals	1900	1901	1902
Teachers	84,800	136,000	139,000
Advanced Quarterlies	416,000	244,000	543,000
Intermediate Quarterlies	175,000	244,000	250,000
Primary Quarterlies	275,000	380,000	332,000
Leaflets and Gems	557,000	528,000	585,000
Picture Lesson Cards	1,560,000	2,340,000	2,500,000
Bible Lesson Pictures	33,800	41,600	50,000
National Baptist Concert Quarterly	259,000	800,000	850,000
Child's Gem	6,000	-	-
Davidson's Questions	-	-	85,000
Boyd's Questions	-	-	85,000
National Baptist Easy Lessons	-	-	90,000
Total	3,366,600	4,713,600	5,509,000

Source: Untitled table, W.E.B. Du Bois, ed., *The Negro Church*, p. 115.

Sunday Schools

★ 2001 ★

Sunday Schools by Denomination, 1906

Division and state	Sunday schools conducted by church organizations			
	Number of organizations reporting	Number of schools reported	Number of officers and teachers	Number of scholars
United States	33,538	34,681	210,148	1,740,099
Geographic divisions				
New England	122	122	1,281	9,444
Middle Atlantic	837	849	7,795	68,098
East North Central	924	940	6,913	46,341
West North Central	939	951	6,000	36,039
South Atlantic	13,904	14,430	92,395	808,219
East South Central	9,540	9,848	54,049	452,504
West South Central	7,154	7,420	40,922	314,544

[Continued]

★ 2001 ★

Sunday Schools by Denomination, 1906

[Continued]

Division and state	Sunday schools conducted by church organizations			
	Number of organizations reporting	Number of schools reported	Number of officers and teachers	Number of scholars
Mountain	42	44	285	1,680
Pacific	76	77	508	3,230
New England				
Maine	1	1	8	30
New Hampshire	1	1	3	24
Vermont	-	-	-	-
Massachusetts	58	58	613	5,069
Rhode Island	17	17	202	1,557
Connecticut	45	45	455	2,764
Middle Atlantic				
New York	186	189	1,745	15,045
New Jersey	247	252	2,308	17,287
Pennsylvania	404	408	3,742	35,766
East North Central				
Ohio	343	347	2,721	18,470
Indiana	192	197	1,415	9,562
Illinois	337	344	2,364	16,155
Michigan	42	42	363	1,910
Wisconsin	10	10	50	244
West North Central				
Minnesota	8	8	78	497
Iowa	65	65	410	2,323
Missouri	588	597	3,650	22,912
North Dakota	-	-	-	-
South Dakota	2	2	9	32
Nebraska	11	11	101	589
Kansas	265	268	1,752	9,686
South Atlantic				
Delaware	116	118	900	7,651
Maryland	585	605	4,976	42,193
District of Columbia	98	103	1,165	13,570
Virginia	1,802	1,926	12,616	113,727
West Virginia	247	257	1,533	11,246
North Carolina	2,519	2,601	19,142	148,248
South Carolina	2,779	2,896	19,808	188,497
Georgia	4,304	4,425	23,891	218,359
Florida	1,454	1,499	8,364	64,728

[Continued]

★ 2001 ★

Sunday Schools by Denomination, 1906

[Continued]

Division and state	Sunday schools conducted by church organizations			
	Number of organizations reporting	Number of schools reported	Number of officers and teachers	Number of scholars
East South Central				
Kentucky	920	939	5,841	43,863
Tennessee	1,677	1,729	9,513	76,021
Alabama	3,349	3,469	19,105	164,436
Mississippi	3,594	3,711	19,590	168,184
West South Central				
Arkansas	1,908	1,984	11,552	80,152
Louisiana	1,927	2,001	10,194	92,266
Oklahoma	557	590	2,964	19,326
Texas	2,762	2,845	16,212	122,800
Mountain				
Montana	5	5	30	134
Idaho	-	-	-	-
Wyoming	1	1	12	40
Colorado	23	24	176	1,220
New Mexico	7	8	33	135
Arizona	5	5	24	121
Utah	1	1	10	30
Nevada	-	-	-	-
Pacific				
Washington	15	15	87	514
Oregon	3	3	15	85
California	58	59	406	2,631

Source: "Negro Church Organizations, Showing Communicants or Members, Places of Worship, Value of Church Property, Debt on Church Property, Parsonages, and Sunday Schools, by Geographical Division and States: 1906," U.S. Bureau of the Census, *Negroes in the United States*, Bulletin 129, 1915, pp. 204-205. Adapted by the editors.

★ 2002 ★

Sunday Schools

Sunday Schools by Geographical Division and State, 1906

Division and state	Sunday schools conducted by church organizations			
	Number of organizations reporting	Number of schools reported	Number of officers and teachers	Number of scholars
United States	33,538	34,681	210,148	1,740,099
Geographic divisions				
New England	122	122	1,281	9,444

[Continued]

★ 2002 ★

Sunday Schools by Geographical Division and State, 1906

[Continued]

Division and state	Sunday schools conducted by church organizations			
	Number of organizations reporting	Number of schools reported	Number of officers and teachers	Number of scholars
Middle Atlantic	837	849	7,795	68,098
East North Central	924	940	6,913	46,341
West North Central	939	951	6,000	36,039
South Atlantic	13,904	14,430	92,395	808,219
East South Central	9,540	9,848	54,049	452,504
West South Central	7,154	7,420	40,922	314,544
Mountain	42	44	285	1,680
Pacific	76	77	508	3,230
New England				
Maine	1	1	8	30
New Hampshire	1	1	3	24
Vermont	-	-	-	-
Massachusetts	58	58	613	5,069
Rhode Island	17	17	202	1,557
Connecticut	45	45	455	2,764
Middle Atlantic				
New York	186	189	1,745	15,045
New Jersey	247	252	2,308	17,287
Pennsylvania	404	408	3,742	35,766
East North Central				
Ohio	343	347	2,721	18,470
Indiana	192	197	1,415	9,562
Illinois	337	344	2,364	16,155
Michigan	42	42	363	1,910
Wisconsin	10	10	50	244
West North Central				
Minnesota	8	8	78	497
Iowa	65	65	410	2,323
Missouri	588	597	3,650	22,912
North Dakota	-	-	-	-
South Dakota	2	2	9	32
Nebraska	11	11	101	589
Kansas	265	268	1,752	9,686
South Atlantic				
Delaware	116	118	900	7,651
Maryland	585	605	4,976	42,193
District of Columbia	98	103	1,165	13,570
Virginia	1,802	1,926	12,616	113,727
West Virginia	247	257	1,533	11,246

[Continued]

★ 2002 ★

Sunday Schools by Geographical Division and State, 1906

[Continued]

Division and state	Sunday schools conducted by church organizations			
	Number of organizations reporting	Number of schools reported	Number of officers and teachers	Number of scholars
North Carolina	2,519	2,601	19,142	148,248
South Carolina	2,779	2,896	19,808	188,497
Georgia	4,304	4,425	23,891	218,359
Florida	1,454	1,499	8,364	64,728
East South Central				
Kentucky	920	939	5,841	43,863
Tennessee	1,677	1,729	9,513	76,021
Alabama	3,349	3,469	19,105	164,436
Mississippi	3,594	3,711	19,590	168,184
West South Central				
Arkansas	1,908	1,984	11,552	80,152
Louisiana	1,927	2,001	10,194	92,266
Oklahoma	557	590	2,964	19,326
Texas	2,762	2,845	16,212	122,800
Mountain				
Montana	5	5	30	134
Idaho	-	-	-	-
Wyoming	1	1	12	40
Colorado	23	24	176	1,220
New Mexico	7	8	33	135
Arizona	5	5	24	121
Utah	1	1	10	30
Nevada	-	-	-	-
Pacific				
Washington	15	15	87	514
Oregon	3	3	15	85
California	58	59	406	2,631

Source: "Negro Church Organizations, Showing Communicants or Members, Places of Worship, Value of Church Property, Debt on Church Property, Parsonages, and Sunday Schools, by Geographical Division and States: 1906," U.S. Bureau of the Census, *Negroes in the United States*, Bulletin 129, 1915, pp. 206-207. Adapted by the editors.

Temperance

★ 2003 ★

Lincoln National Temperance Union: Membership, 1867

Division	Number	City and State	Membership
Lincoln Division	1	Washington, DC	95
Kennedy Division	2	Washington, DC	34
Newton Division	3	Washington, DC	82
Shaw Division	4	Washington, DC	88
Burton Division	5	Washington, DC	98
Pioneer Division	6	Washington, DC	60
Langston Division	7	Washington, DC	90
Colfax Division	8	Washington, DC	94
Frederick Douglas Division	9	Washington, DC	100
Whittier Division	10	Georgetown, DC	119
Garnett Division	11	Washington, DC	63
Adams Division	12	Geeenville, AL	101
Cheney Division	13	Gordonsville, VA	100
Lincoln Division	14	Baltimore, MD	45
Loveland Division	15	Washington, DC	60
Hewes Division	16	Washington County, DC	134
Kendall Division	17	Washington DC	132
Toer Division	18	Lake City, FL	28

Source: "Temperance Movement," Monroe N. Work, ed., *Negro Year Book: An Annual Encyclopedia of the Negro, 1916-1917*, 1918, p. 223. Published by permission.

★ 2004 ★

Temperance

Vanguard of Freedom Temperance Union: Membership, 1868

State	Division	Members
District of Columbia	17	1,490
Maryland	4	151
Virginia	7	433
West Virginia	2	115
North Carolina	59	3,897
South Carolina	-	-
Georgia	9	418
Florida	1	28
Alabama	2	228

[Continued]

★ 2004 ★

Vanguard of Freedom Temperance Union: Membership, 1868

[Continued]

State	Division	Members
Mississippi	3	235
Louisiana	3	154
Arkansas	1	89
Missouri	2	114
Kansas	1	75
Total	111	7,427

Source: "Temperance Movement," Monroe N. Work, ed., *Negro Year Book: An Annual Encyclopedia of the Negro, 1914-1915*, 1914, p. 210. Published by permission.

Chapter 17
SLAVERY AND THE SLAVE TRADE

Families

★ 2005 ★

Slave-holding and Non-slave-holding Families: by State, 1790-1850

Division and state	Number of slave-holding families		Number of slaves		Average per slave-holding family	
	1850	1790	1850	1790	1850	1790
United States	347,725	96,168	3,204,313	697,624	9.2	7.3
New England	-	2,147	-	3,763	-	1.8
Maine	-	-	-	-	-	-
New Hampshire	-	123	-	157	-	1.3
Vermont	-	-	-	-	-	-
Massachusetts	-	-	-	-	-	-
Rhode Island	-	461	-	958	-	2.1
Connecticut	-	1,563	-	2,648	-	1.7
Middle Atlantic	200	14,414	236	36,323	1.2	2.5
New York	-	7,796	-	21,193	-	2.7
New Jersey	200	4,760[1]	236	11,423	1.2	2.4
Pennsylvania	-	1,858	-	3,707	-	2.0
South Atlantic	169,264	77,242	1,663,397	641,691	9.8	8.3
Delaware	809	1,851[1]	2,290	8,887	2.8	4.8
Maryland	16,040	13,777	90,368	103,036	5.6	7.5
District of Columbia	1,477	-	3,687	-	2.5	-
Virginia[2]	55,063	34,026[1]	472,528	292,627	8.6	8.5
North Carolina	28,303	16,310	288,548	100,783	10.2	6.7
South Carolina	25,596	8,859	384,984	107,094	15.0	12.1
Georgia	38,456	2,419[1]	381,682	29,264	9.9	12.1
Florida	3,520	-	39,310	-	11.2	-
East South Central	124,660	2,365	1,103,162	15,847	8.8	6.7
Kentucky	38,385	1,855[1]	210,981	12,430	5.5	6.7
Tennessee	33,864	510[1]	239,459	3,417	7.1	6.7
Alabama	29,295	-	342,844	-	11.7	-

[Continued]

★ 2005 ★

Slave-holding and Non-slave-holding Families: by State, 1790-1850

[Continued]

Division and state	Number of slave-holding families		Number of slaves		Average per slave-holding family	
	1850	1790	1850	1790	1850	1790
Mississippi	23,116	-	309,878	-	13.4	-
West South Central	34,116	-	350,070	-	10.2	-
Arkansas	5,999	-	47,100	-	7.9	-
Louisiana	20,670	-	244,809	-	11.8	-
Texas	7,747	-	58,161	-	7.5	-
West North Central	19,185	-	87,422	-	4.6	-
Missouri	19,185	-	87,422	-	4.6	-
Mountain	[2]	-	26	-	-	-
Utah	[2]	-	26	-	-	-

Source: "Slave-holding and Non-slave-holding families: 1790 and 1850," U.S. Bureau of the Census, *Negro Population in the United States, 1790-1915*, p. 56. *Notes:* (-) Represents zero. A few slaves were, however, held in Utah, although the number of slave-holding families is not given. The figures given for 1790 in the table include estimates for certain areas for which data gathered in 1790 are not now available. 1. Estimated. 2. Includes area now West Virginia. 3. Data not available.

Growth and Size

★ 2006 ★

Population: Slave and Free, 1790-1860

Census year	Negro population							
	Total	Free		Slave	Decennial increase			
					Number		Percent	
		Number	Percent		Free	Slave	Free	Slave
1860	4,411,830	488,070	11.0	3,953,760	53,575	749,447	12.3	23.4
1850	3,638,808	434,495	11.9	3,204,313	48,202	716,958	12.5	28.3
1840	2,873,648	386,293	13.4	2,487,355	66,694	478,312	20.9	23.9
1830	2,328,642	319,599	13.7	2,009,043	85,965	471,021	36.8	30.6
1820	1,771,656	233,634	13.2	1,538,022	47,188	346,660	25.3	29.1
1810	1,377,808	186,446	13.5	1,191,362	78,011	297,760	71.9	33.3
1800	1,002,037	108,435	10.8	893,602	48,908	195,921	82.2	28.1
1790	757,181[1]	59,557	7.9	697,624	-	-	-	-

Source: "Number and Increase: 1790 and 1860." U.S. Bureau of the Census, *Negro Population in the United States, 1790-1915*, p. 53. *Notes:* (-) Represents zero. 1. In other sections of this report and in census reports generally the total negro population in 1790 is given as 757,208. The population in Table is taken from "A Century of Population Growth in the United States, 1790-1900," and is a revised figure.

Population

★ 2007 ★

Black and Mulatto Population: Slave and Free, 1850

Division and state	Negro population: 1850								
	Total	Black	Mulatto	Free			Slave		
				Total	Black	Mulatto	Total	Black	Mulatto
United States	3,638,808	3,233,057	405,751	434,495	275,400	159,095	3,204,313	2,957,657	246,656
Geographic divisions:									
New England	23,021	17,301	5,720	23,021	17,301	5,720	-	-	-
Middle Atlantic	126,741	99,560	27,181	126,505	99,328	27,177	236	232	4
East North Central	45,195	21,688	23,507	45,195	21,688	23,507	-	-	-
West North Central	90,412	76,068	14,344	2,990	1,881	1,109	87,422	74,187	13,235
South Atlantic	1,860,871	1,674,968	185,903	197,474	119,652	77,822	1,663,397	1,555,316	108,081
East South Central	1,122,790	1,022,631	100,159	19,628	10,889	8,739	1,103,162	1,011,742	91,420
West South Central	368,537	319,891	48,646	18,467	3,720	14,747	350,070	316,171	33,899
Mountain	72	30	42	46	21	25	26	9	17
Pacific	1,169	920	249	1,169	920	249	-	-	-
New England:									
Maine	1,356	895	461	1,356	895	461	-	-	-
New Hampshire	520	336	184	520	336	184	-	-	-
Vermont	718	512	206	718	512	206	-	-	-
Massachusetts	9,064	6,724	2,340	9,064	6,724	2,340	-	-	-
Rhode Island	3,670	2,939	731	3,670	2,939	731	-	-	-
Connecticut	7,693	5,895	1,798	7,693	5,895	1,798	-	-	-
Middle Atlantic:									
New York	49,069	40,930	8,139	49,069	40,930	8,139	-	-	-
New Jersey	24,046	20,345	3,701	23,810	20,113	3,697	236	232	4
Pennsylvania	53,626	38,285	15,341	53,626	38,285	15,341	-	-	-
East North Central:									
Ohio	25,279	11,014	14,265	25,279	11,014	14,265	-	-	-
Indiana	11,262	5,941	5,321	11,262	5,941	5,321	-	-	-
Illinois	5,436	2,930	2,506	5,436	2,930	2,506	-	-	-
Michigan	2,583	1,465	1,118	2,583	1,465	1,118	-	-	-
Wisconsin	635	338	297	635	338	297	-	-	-
West North Central:									
Minnesota	39	16	23	39	16	23	-	-	-
Iowa	333	178	155	333	178	155	-	-	-
Missouri	90,040	75,874	14,166	2,618	1,687	931	87,422	74,187	13,235
South Atlantic:									
Delaware	20,363	18,632	1,731	18,073	16,425	1,648	2,290	2,207	83
Maryland	165,091	143,588	21,503	74,723	61,109	13,614	90,368	82,479	7,889

[Continued]

★ 2007 ★

Black and Mulatto Population: Slave and Free, 1850

[Continued]

Division and state	Negro population: 1850								
	Total	Black	Mulatto	Free			Slave		
				Total	Black	Mulatto	Total	Black	Mulatto
District of Columbia	13,746	9,668	4,078	10,059	6,783	3,276	3,687	2,885	802
Virginia	526,861	447,086	79,775	54,333	18,857	35,476	472,528	428,229	44,299
North Carolina	316,011	281,991	34,020	27,463	10,258	17,205	288,548	271,733	16,815
South Carolina	303,944	377,070	16,874	8,960	4,588	4,372	384,984	372,482	12,502
Georgia	384,613	360,416	24,197	2,931	1,403	1,528	381,682	359,013	22,669
Florida	40,242	36,517	3,725	932	229	703	39,310	36,288	3,022
East South Central:									
Kentucky	220,992	188,633	32,359	10,011	7,381	2,630	210,981	181,252	29,729
Tennessee	245,881	221,749	24,132	6,422	2,646	3,776	239,459	219,103	20,356
Alabama	345,109	321,806	23,303	2,265	567	1,698	342,844	321,239	21,605
Mississippi	310,808	290,443	20,365	930	295	635	309,878	290,148	19,730
West South Central:									
Arkansas	47,708	40,940	6,768	608	201	407	47,100	40,739	6,361
Louisiana	262,271	228,353	33,918	17,462	3,379	14,083	244,809	224,974	19,835
Texas	58,558	50,598	7,960	397	140	257	58,161	50,458	7,703
Mountain:									
New Mexico	22	6	16	22	6	16	-	-	-
Utah	50	24	26	24	15	9	26	9	17
Pacific:									
Oregon	207	45	162	207	45	162	-	-	-
California	962	875	87	962	875	87	-	-	-

Source: "Black and Mulatto Population, Free and Slave, by Divisions, and States: 1850," U.S. Bureau of the Census, *Negro Population in the United States, 1790-1915*, p. 220. *Note:* (-) Represents zero.

★ 2008 ★

Population

Black and Mulatto Population: Slave and Free, 1860

Division and state	Negro population: 1860											
	Free						Slave					
	Both sexes		Male		Female		Both sexes		Male		Female	
	Black	Mulatto	Black	Mulatto	Black	Mulatto	Black	Mulatto	Black	Mulatto	Black	Mulatto
United States	311,331	176,739	150,599	83,521	160,732	93,218	3,542,147	411,613	1,785,716	196,909	1,756,431	214,704
Geographic divisions:												
New England	17,663	7,048	8,416	3,303	9,247	3,745	-	-	-	-	-	-
Middle Atlantic	100,896	30,376	48,050	13,914	52,846	16,462	9	9	3	3	6	6
East North Central	33,862	29,837	17,501	14,761	16,361	15,076	-	-	-	-	-	-
West North Central	2,876	2,716	1,419	1,291	1,457	1,425	93,024	21,924	47,130	10,236	45,894	11,688
South Atlantic	139,243	78,510	66,618	36,991	72,625	41,519	1,674,254	166,191	839,509	79,940	834,745	86,251
East South Central	10,379	11,068	5,111	5,154	5,268	5,914	1,221,098	151,815	614,130	72,316	606,968	79,499

[Continued]

★ 2008 ★

Black and Mulatto Population: Slave and Free, 1860

[Continued]

Division and state	Negro population: 1860											
	Free						Slave					
	Both sexes		Male		Female		Both sexes		Male		Female	
	Black	Mulatto	Black	Mulatto	Black	Mulatto	Black	Mulatto	Black	Mulatto	Black	Mulatto
West South Central	3,628	15,518	1,504	7,028	2,124	8,490	553,748	71,659	284,935	34,405	268,813	37,254
Mountain	134	72	81	49	53	23	14	15	9	9	5	6
Pacific	2,650	1,594	1,899	1,030	751	564	-	-	-	-	-	-
New England:												
Maine	693	634	351	308	342	326	-	-	-	-	-	-
New Hampshire	241	253	123	130	118	123	-	-	-	-	-	-
Vermont	517	192	276	95	241	97	-	-	-	-	-	-
Massachusetts	6,531	3,071	3,055	1,414	3,476	1,657	-	-	-	-	-	-
Rhode Island	2,955	997	1,369	462	1,586	535	-	-	-	-	-	-
Connecticut	6,726	1,901	3,242	894	3,484	1,007	-	-	-	-	-	-
Middle Atlantic:												
New York	41,224	7,781	19,491	3,687	21,733	4,094	-	-	-	-	-	-
New Jersey	21,856	3,453	10,718	1,595	11,147	1,858	9	9	3	3	6	6
Pennsylvania	37,807	19,142	17,841	8,632	19,966	10,510	-	-	-	-	-	-
East North Central:												
Ohio	19,982	16,691	10,271	8,171	9,711	8,520	-	-	-	-	-	-
Indiana	5,981	5,447	3,102	2,089	2,879	2,758	-	-	-	-	-	-
Illinois	4,041	3,587	2,031	1,778	2,010	1,809	-	-	-	-	-	-
Michigan	3,424	3,375	1,842	1,725	1,582	1,650	-	-	-	-	-	-
Wisconsin	434	737	255	398	179	339	-	-	-	-	-	-
West North Central:												
Minnesota	90	169	39	87	51	82	-	-	-	-	-	-
Iowa	501	568	275	291	226	277	-	-	-	-	-	-
Missouri	1,898	1,674	925	772	973	902	93,017	21,914	47,127	10,233	45,890	11,681
Nebraska	28	39	14	21	14	18	7	8	3	3	4	5
Kansas	359	266	166	120	193	146	-	2	-	-	-	2
South Atlantic:												
Delaware	16,933	2,896	8,439	1,450	8,494	1,446	1,715	83	822	38	893	45
Maryland	67,902	16,040	32,507	7,239	35,395	8,801	78,316	8,873	40,126	4,187	38,190	4,686
District of Columbia	6,631	4,500	2,847	1,855	3,784	2,645	2,252	933	861	351	1,391	582
Virginia	34,557	23,485	16,648	11,073	17,909	12,412	420,886	69,979	216,009	33,474	204,877	36,505
North Carolina	8,655	21,808	4,046	10,834	4,609	10,974	308,069	22,990	155,195	11,274	152,874	11,716
South Carolina	2,780	7,134	1,263	3,285	1,517	3,849	381,226	21,180	186,303	10,268	194,923	10,912
Georgia	1,496	2,004	732	937	764	1,067	425,298	36,900	211,432	17,761	213,866	19,139
Florida	289	643	136	318	153	325	56,492	5,253	28,761	2,587	27,731	2,666
East South Central:												
Kentucky	6,607	4,077	3,223	1,878	3,384	2,199	182,202	43,281	92,731	20,278	89,471	23,003
Tennessee	3,008	4,292	1,516	2,022	1,492	2,270	238,133	37,586	118,683	17,687	119,450	19,899
Alabama	592	2,098	292	962	300	1,136	400,750	34,330	201,258	16,508	199,492	17,822
Mississippi	172	601	80	292	92	309	400,013	36,618	201,458	17,843	198,555	18,775
West South Central:												
Arkansas	57	87	30	42	27	45	97,066	14,049	49,236	6,938	47,830	7,111
Louisiana	3,489	15,158	1,438	6,841	2,051	8,317	299,103	32,623	156,287	15,690	142,816	16,933
Texas	82	273	36	145	46	128	157,579	24,987	79,412	11,777	78,167	13,210
Mountain:												
Colorado	33	13	28	9	5	4	-	-	-	-	-	-
New Mexico	46	39	22	23	24	16	-	-	-	-	-	-
Utah	28	2	12	1	16	1	14	15	9	9	5	6
Nevada	27	18	19	16	8	2	-	-	-	-	-	-

[Continued]

★ 2008 ★

Black and Mulatto Population: Slave and Free, 1860

[Continued]

Division and state	Negro population: 1860											
	Free						Slave					
	Both sexes		Male		Female		Both sexes		Male		Female	
	Black	Mulatto	Black	Mulatto	Black	Mulatto	Black	Mulatto	Black	Mulatto	Black	Mulatto
Pacific:												
Washington	27	3	24	2	3	1	-	-	-	-	-	-
Oregon	66	62	44	32	22	30	-	-	-	-	-	-
California	2,557	1,529	1,831	996	726	533	-	-	-	-	-	-

Source: "Black and Mulatto Population, Free and Slave, Classified by Sex, by Divisions, and States: 1860," U.S. Bureau of the Census, *Negro Population in the United States, 1790-1915*, p. 220. *Note:* (-) Represents zero.

★ 2009 ★

Population

Mulattoes in the Slave and Free Black Population, 1850

STATE AND TERRITORY	MULATTOES TO 100 BLACKS IN THE NEGRO POPULATION: 1850		
	Total	Free	Slave
United States	12.55	58.13	8.34
STATES			
Alabama	7.24	299.47	6.73
Arkansas	16.53	202.49	15.61
California	9.94	9.94	-
Connecticut	30.51	30.51	-
Delaware	9.29	10.03	3.76
District of Columbia	42.18	48.30	27.80
Florida	10.20	306.99	8.33
Georgia	6.71	108.91	6.31
Illinois	85.53	85.53	-
Indiana	89.56	89.56	-
Iowa	87.08	87.08	-
Kentucky	17.15	35.63	16.40
Louisiana	14.85	416.78	8.82
Maine	51.51	51.51	-
Maryland	14.98	22.28	9.56
Massachusetts	34.80	34.80	-
Michigan	76.31	76.31	-
Mississippi	7.01	215.25	6.80
Missouri	18.69	55.19	78.40
New Hampshire	54.76	54.76	-
New Jersey	18.19	18.38	1.72
New York	19.89	19.89	-
North Carolina	12.06	167.72	6.19
Ohio	129.52	129.52	-

[Continued]

★ 2009 ★

Mulattoes in the Slave and Free Black Population, 1850

[Continued]

STATE AND TERRITORY	MULATTOES TO 100 BLACKS IN THE NEGRO POPULATION: 1850		
	Total	Free	Slave
Pennsylvania	40.07	40.07	-
Rhode Island	24.87	24.87	-
South Carolina	4.48	95.29	3.36
Tennessee	10.88	142.71	9.29
Texas	15.73	183.57	15.27
Vermont	40.23	40.23	-
Virginia	17.84	188.13	10.34
Wisconsin	87.87	87.87	-
TERRITORIES[1]			
Minnesota	143.75	143.75	-
New Mexico	266.67	266.67	-
Oregon	360.00	360.00	-
Utah	108.33	60.00	188.89

Source: Untitled table. U.S. Bureau of the Census, *Negro Population, 1790-1915*, p. 209. *Notes:* 1. The Negro population of the territories was as follows: Free Minnesota, black 16, mulatto 23; New Mexico, black 6, mulatto 16; Oregon, black 45, mulatto 162; Utah, black 15, mulatto 9; 26 slaves, 9 black and 17 mulatto, were reported from Utah, "on their way to California."

★ 2010 ★

Population

Nonwhite Population by Gender and Race, 1820 and 1950

Year	Male						Female					
	Negro[1]		Indian	Japanese	Chinese	All other	Negro[1]		Indian	Japanese	Chinese	All other
	Total	Slave					Total	Slave				
1950	7,298,722	-	178,824	76,649	77,008	72,844[2]	7,743,564	-	164,586	65,119	40,621	37,396[2]
1940	6,269,038	-	171,427	71,967	57,389	43,223	6,596,480	-	163,542	54,980	20,115	7,244
1930	5,855,669	-	170,350	81,771	59,802	46,960	6,035,474	-	162,047	57,063	15,152	4,018
1920	5,209,436	-	125,068	72,707	53,891	8,674	5,253,695	-	119,369	38,303	7,748	814
1910	4,885,881	-	135,133	68,070	66,856	3,092	4,941,882	-	130,550	9,087	4,675	83
1900	4,386,547	-	119,484	23,341	35,341	-	4,447,447	-	117,712	985	4,522	-
1890	3,735,608	-	125,719	1,780	103,620	-	3,753,073	-	125,719	1,780	103,620	-
1880	3,253,115	-	33,985[3]	134	100,686	-	3,327,678	-	32,422[2]	14	4,779	-
1870	2,393,263[4]	-	12,534[2]	47	58,633	-	2,486,746[4]	-	13,197[3]	8	4,566	-
1860	2,216,744	1,982,625	23,924[3]	-	33,149	-	2,225,086	1,971,135	20,097[3]	-	1,784	-
1850	1,811,258	1,602,535	-	-	-	-	1,817,550	1,601,778	-	-	-	-
1840	1,432,988	1,246,467	-	-	-	-	1,440,660	1,240,888	-	-	-	-

[Continued]

★ 2010 ★

Nonwhite Population by Gender and Race, 1820 and 1950

[Continued]

Year	Male						Female					
	Negro[1]		Indian	Japanese	Chinese	All other	Negro[1]		Indian	Japanese	Chinese	All other
	Total	Slave					Total	Slave				
1830	1,166,276	1,012,828	-	-	-	-	1,162,366	996,220	-	-	-	-
1820	898,892	786,022	-	-	-	-	872,764	752,000	-	-	-	-

Source: "Nonwhite Population, by Sex and Race: 1820 and 1950." U.S. Bureau of the Census, *Historical Statistics of the United States: Colonial Times to 1957*, p. 9. *Notes:* 1. Sex not reported before 1820. Total for both sexes from 1790 to 1810 is as follows: For 1810, total 1,377,808, slaves 1,191,362; 1800, total 1,002,037, slaves 898,602; and 1790, total 757,208, slaves 697,681. 2. Includes persons of mixed white, Negro, and Indian ancestry is certain communities in eastern United States. 3. Excludes Indians in Indian Territory and on Indian reservations. 4. Adjustment for undernumeration is Southern States shows 5,392,172 Negroes for both sexes combined.

★ 2011 ★

Population

Persons in Maryland under Fifteen Years of Age, Free and Slave, 1755 - I

County	Whites						Mulattoes			
	Free		Hired or indentured servants		Servant convicts		Free		Slaves	
	Boys	Girls	Boys	Girls	Boys	Girls	Boys	Girls	Boys	Girls
Anne Arundel	1913	1705	82	26	16	-	28	35	31	23
Baltimore	3115	2951	126	49	6	6	63	62	28	43
Calvert	861	745	48	28	-	-	30	31	15	17
Cecil	1506	1372	55	20	1	1	10	4	89	108
Charles	1681	1799	228	41	16	7	69	57	52	51
Dorset	2347	2222	54	17	-	2	12	22	35	32
Frederick	3246	3105	80	56	9	1	22	23	19	19
Kent	1527	1423	134	76	4	1	16	19	9	20
Prince George's	1840	1674	33	10	1	-	42	26	46	55
Queen Anne's	2037	1864	82	44	9	-	31	24	57	58
St. Mary's	1845	1765	29	24	5	3	24	22	94	98
Somerset	1230	1232	12	-	-	-	24	19	21	25
Talbot	1322	1197	57	9	-	-	20	19	74	81
Worcester	2067	2083	28	12	-	-	28	29	7	8
Totals	26637	25136	1048	412	67	21	(419)	(392)	577	638

Source: "Account of Maryland Population in 1755," James M. Wright, *The Free Negro in Maryland, 1634-1860*, p. 85.

★ 2012 ★

Population

Persons in Maryland under Fifteen Years of Age, Free and Slave, 1755 - II

County	Black				Free Negro totals
	Free		Slaves		
	Boys	Girls	Boys	Girls	
Anne Arundel	10	5	1314	1321	138
Baltimore	3	1	959	1041	212
Calvert	-	-	671	645	103
Cecil	5	-	275	252	37
Charles	7	-	1145	1197	252
Dorset	6	1	666	681	77
Frederick	3	1	465	473	157
Kent	8	3	650	653	94
Prince George's	-	-	1340	1239	122
Queen Anne's	2	4	621	603	122
St. Mary's	13	17	862	839	149
Somerset	1	1	875	891	93
Talbot	-	1	579	657	111
Worcester	13	6	561	511	150
Totals	(71)	(40)	10983	11003	1817

Source: "Account of Maryland Population in 1755," James M. Wright, *The Free Negro in Maryland, 1634-1860*, p. 85.

★ 2013 ★

Population

Population Census in the Colonies and States, Showing Slaves, Including Free Blacks, and Mulattoes, 1624-1786 - I

Year and age	CONNECTICUT							
	Total population	White						
		Total	Male			Female		
			Total	Married	Single	Total	Male	Single
1782	209,177	202,904[1]	-	-	-	-	-	-
1774	197,842	191,378[2]	96,182	30,524	65,658	94,296	30,636	63,660
Under 10 years	-	61,164	31,114	-	31,114	30,050	-	30,050
10-20 years	-	46,828	24,271	222	24,049	22,557	697	21,860
20-70 years	-	78,310	38,807	28,866	9,941	39,503	29,017	10,486

[Continued]

★ 2013 ★

Population Census in the Colonies and States, Showing Slaves, Including Free Blacks, and Mulattoes, 1624-1786 - I

[Continued]

Year and age	CONNECTICUT							
	Total population	White						
		Total	Male			Female		
			Total	Married	Single	Total	Male	Single
Over 70 years	-	4,176	1,900	1,436	554	2,186	922	1,264
1756	130,612	126,976	-	-	-	-	-	-

Source: "Population Census Taken in the Colonies and States During the Colonial and Pre-Federal Period: 1624-25 to 1786." U.S. Bureau of the Census, *Historical Statistics of the United States: Colonial Times to 1970, Part II,* Bicentennial Edition, pp. 1169-1171. *Notes:* - Represents zero. 1. Corrected total from Greene and Harrington, p. 61. Morse gives total 202,877 including 39,388 males between the ages of 16 and 50 and 103,735 females 2. Includes 900 not distributed by sex.

★ 2014 ★

Population

Population Census in the Colonies and States, Showing Slaves, Including Free Blacks, and Mulattoes, 1624-1786 - II

Year and age	CONNECTICUT					
	Negro			Indian		
	Total	Male	Female	Total	Male	Female
1782	6,273[1]	-	-	-	-	-
1774						
Under 10 years						
10-20 years						
20-70 years						
Over 70 years						
1756	3,019	-	-	617	-	-

Source: "Population Census Taken in the Colonies and States During the Colonial and Pre-Federal Period: 1624-25 to 1786." U.S. Bureau of the Census, *Historical Statistics of the United States: Colonial Times to 1970, Part II,* Bicentennial Edition, pp. 1169-1171. *Notes:* - Represents zero. 1. Including Indians.

★ 2015 ★

Population

Population Census in the Colonies and States, Showing Slaves, Including Free Blacks, and Mulattoes, 1624-1786 - III

Year and age	MAINE											
	Houses	Families	Total population	White			Negro and mulatto			French neutral		
				Total	Male	Female	Total	Male	Female	Total	Male	Female
1784	-	-	50,493	-	-	-	-	-	-	-	-	-
1776	-	-	47,767	47,279	-	-	488	-	-	-	-	-
1764-65	2,486	3,481	21,857[1]	21,451	10,870	10,581	344	192	152	62	27	35
Under 16 years	-											
16 years and over	-	-	-	10,742	5,338	5,404	-	-	-	26	11	15

Source: "Population Census Taken in the Colonies and States During the Colonial and Pre-Federal Period: 1624-25 to 1786." U.S. Bureau of the Census, *Historical Statistics of the United States: Colonial Times to 1970, Part II*, Bicentennial Edition, pp. 1169-1171. *Notes:* - Represents zero. 1. 24,020 total per Williamson with 23,685 whites and 332 Negroes. Also 2,789 houses and 3,572 families, not including estimates for the plantations.

★ 2016 ★

Population

opulation Census in the Colonies and States, Showing Slaves, Including Free Blacks, and Mulattoes, 1624-1786 - IV

ear, age, and sex	MARYLAND									
	Total population	White			Mulatto			Negro		
		Total	Free	Servant	Total	Free	Slave	Total	Negro	Slave
782	254,050	170,688[1]	-	-	-	-	-	83,362[2]	-	-
755	153,505[3]	108,193	99,352	8,841	3,608	1,460	2,148	41,704	357	41,347
Under 16 years (not taxable)	77,444	53,321	51,773	1,548	2,026	811	1,215	22,097	111	21,986
Male	39,802	27,752	26,637	1,115[4]	996	419	577	11,054	71	10,983
Female	37,642	25,569	25,136[5]	433[6]	1,030	392	638	11,043	40	11,003
16 years and over (taxable)	48,811	28,469	23,386	5,083	1,388	554	834	18,954	188	18,766
Male	40,165	28,469	23,386	5,083[7]	749	307	442	10,947	119	10,828
Female	8,646	-	-	-	639	247	392	8,007[8]	69	7,938
16 years and over (not taxable)	27,250	26,403	24,193	2,210	194	95	99	653	58[9]	595[9]
Male	-	672	672[10]	-	-	-	-	-	-	-
Female	-	25,731	23,521	2,210[11]	-	-	-	-	-	-
712	46,151	37,743	-	-	-	-	-	8,408	-	-
710	42,741	34,796	-	-	-	-	-	7,945	-	-
704	34,912	30,437	-	-	-	-	-	4,475[12]	-	-

urce: "Population Census Taken in the Colonies and States During the Colonial and Pre-Federal Period: 1624-25 to 1786." U.S. Bureau of the Census, *Historical Statistics of e United States: Colonial Times to 1970, Part II*, Bicentennial Edition, pp. 1169-1171. *Notes:* - Represents zero. 1. Including 35,268 free males above 18 years of age. 2. Including ,626 under 8 years of age; 13,399 males and females 8 to 14 years of age; 16,246 males from 14 to 45 years of age; 13,832 females from 14 to 36 years of age; and 12,259 males ove 45 years of age and females above 36 years of age. 3. 153,565 per Greene and Harrington, p. 126. 4. Including 1,048 hired or indented and 67 convicts. 5. 24,141 per Greene d Harrington, p. 126. 6. Including 412 hired or indented and 21 convicts. 7. Including 3,576 hired or indented and 1,507 convicts. 8. 9,007 per Greene and Harrington, p. 126. 9. st labor or cripples. 10. Including 35 clergy and 637 poor men. 11. Including 1,824 hired or indented and 386 convicts. 12. Slaves.

★ 2017 ★

Population

Population Census in the Colonies and States, Showing Slaves, Including Free Blacks, and Mulattoes, 1624-1786 - V

Year	MARYLAND White			
	Total	Masters and taxable men	Women	Children
1712	37,743	11,029	9,081	17,633
1710	34,796	11,091	8,294	15,411
1704	30,437	11,026[1]	7,163[2]	12,248

Source: "Population Census Taken in the Colonies and States During the Colonial and Pre-Federal Period: 1624-25 to 1786." U.S. Bureau of the Census, *Historical Statistics of the United States: Colonial Times to 1970, Part II,* Bicentennial Edition, pp. 1169-1171. *Notes:* - Represents zero. 1. Masters, freemen, and servants. 2. Freewomen and servants.

★ 2018 ★

Population

Population Census in the Colonies and States, Showing Slaves, Including Free Blacks, and Mulattoes, 1624-1786 - VI

Year and age	MASSACHUSETTS								
	Houses	Families	Total population	White			Negro and mulatto		
				Total	Male	Female	Total	Male	Female
1784	-	-	307,018	-	-	-	-	-	-
1776	-	-	290,900	286,139	-	-	4,761	-	-
1764-65	31,707	43,483	223,841	216,700	106,611	110,089	4,891	2,824	2,067
Under 16 years	-	-	-	103,447	52,859	50,588	-	-	-
16 years and over	-	-	-	113,253	53,752	59,501	-	-	-

Source: "Population Census Taken in the Colonies and States During the Colonial and Pre-Federal Period: 1624-25 to 1786." U.S. Bureau of the Census, *Historical Statistics of the United States: Colonial Times to 1970, Part II,* Bicentennial Edition, pp. 1169-1171. *Note:* - Represents zero.

★ 2019 ★

Population

Population Census in the Colonies and States, Showing Slaves, Including Free Blacks, and Mulattoes, 1624-1786 - VII

Year and age	MASSACHUSETTS					
	Indian			French neutral		
	Total	Male	Female	Total	Male	Female
1784	-	-	-	-	-	-
1776	-	-	-	-	-	-
1764-65	1,681	728	953	569	274	295
Under 16 years	-	-	-	261	133	128
16 years and over	-	-	-	308	141	167

Source: "Population Census Taken in the Colonies and States During the Colonial and Pre-Federal Period: 1624-25 to 1786." U.S. Bureau of the Census, *Historical Statistics of the United States: Colonial Times to 1970, Part II*, Bicentennial Edition, pp. 1169-1171. *Note:* - Represents zero.

★ 2020 ★

Population

Population Census in the Colonies and States, Showing Slaves, Including Free Blacks, and Mulattoes, 1624-1786 - VIII

Year and age	NEW HAMPSHIRE								
	Total population	Free white							Widowed
		Total	Male			Female			
			Total	Single	Married	Total	Single	Married	
1786	95,849	95,452	-	-	-	-	-	-	-
1775	81,300	80,644	41,016	-	-	39,628	-	-	-
Under 16 years	-	-	20,863	-	-	-	-	-	-
16-50 years	-	-	14,231	-	-	-	-	-	-
Over 50 years	-	-	3,436	-	-	-	-	-	-
In Army	-	-	2,486	-	-	-	-	-	-
1773	73,097	72,423	36,739	-	-	35,684	22,228	11,887	1,569
Under 16 years	-	-	18,334	18,334	-	-	-	-	-
16-60 years	-	-	16,867	6,263	10,604	-	-	-	-
60 years and over	-	-	1,538	-	-	-	-	-	-
1767	52,720	52,087	26,264	-	-	25,823	15,992	8,467	1,364
Under 16 years	-	-	12,924	12,924	-	-	-	-	-
16-60 years	-	-	12,180	4,510	7,670	-	-	-	-
60 years and over	-	-	1,160	-	-	-	-	-	-

Source: "Population Census Taken in the Colonies and States During the Colonial and Pre-Federal Period: 1624-25 to 1786." U.S. Bureau of the Census, *Historical Statistics of the United States: Colonial Times to 1970, Part II*, Bicentennial Edition, pp. 1169-1171. *Note:* - Represents zero.

★ 2021 ★

Population

Population Census in the Colonies and States, Showing Slaves, Including Free Blacks, and Mulattoes, 1624-1786 - IX

Year and age	NEW HAMPSHIRE			
	Slave			Other
	Total	Male	Female	
1786	46	-	-	351
1775	656[1]	-	-	-
Under 16 years	-	-	-	-
16-50 years	-	-	-	-
Over 50 years	-	-	-	-
In Army	-	-	-	-
1773	674	379	295	-
Under 16 years	-	-	-	-
16-60 years	-	-	-	-
60 years and over	-	-	-	-
1767	633	384	249	-
Under 16 years	-	-	-	-
16-60 years	-	-	-	-
60 years and over	-	-	-	-

Source: "Population Census Taken in the Colonies and States During the Colonial and Pre-Federal Period: 1624-25 to 1786." U.S. Bureau of the Census, *Historical Statistics of the United States: Colonial Times to 1970, Part II*, Bicentennial Edition, pp. 1169-1171. *Notes:* - Represents zero. 1. Reported as Negroes and slaves.

★ 2022 ★

Population

Population Census in the Colonies and States, Showing Slaves, Including Free Blacks, and Mulattoes, 1624-1786 - X

Year and age	NEW JERSEY						
	Total population	White			Negro		
		Total	Male	Female	Total	Male	Female
1784	149,435	138,934	-	-	10,501[1]	-	-
1772	122,003	-	-	-	-	-	-
1745	61,403	56,797[2]	29,339	27,458	4,606	2,588	2,018
Under 16 years	-	28,007	14,253	13,754	-	-	-
16 years and over	-	28,790	15,086	13,704	-	-	-
1738	46,676	42,695	22,270	20,425	3,981	2,208	1,773

[Continued]

★ 2022 ★

Population Census in the Colonies and States, Showing Slaves, Including Free Blacks, and Mulattoes, 1624-1786 - X

[Continued]

Year and age	NEW JERSEY						
	Total population	White			Negro		
		Total	Male	Female	Total	Male	Female
Under 16 years	21,963	20,339	10,639	9,700	1,624	849	775
16 years and over	24,713	22,356	11,631	10,725	2,357	1,359	998
1726	32,442	29,861	15,737	14,124	2,581	1,435	1,146
Under 16 years	15,585	14,506	7,558	6,948	1,079	563	516
16 years and over	16,857	15,355	8,179	7,176	1,502	872	630

Source: "Population Census Taken in the Colonies and States During the Colonial and Pre-Federal Period: 1624-25 to 1786." U.S. Bureau of the Census, *Historical Statistics of the United States: Colonial Times to 1970, Part II*, Bicentennial Edition, pp. 1169-1171. *Notes:* - Represents zero. 1. 1,959 were slaves. 2. Includes 9,736 Quakers and reported Quakers who are whites and distributed by sex and age.

★ 2023 ★

Population

Population Census in the Colonies and States, Showing Slaves, Including Free Blacks, and Mulattoes, 1624-1786 - XI

Year and age	NEW YORK						
	Total population	White			Negro		
		Total	Male	Female	Total	Male	Female
1786	238,897[1]	219,996	112,465	107,531	18,889	9,521	9,368
Under 16 years	-	106,573	54,807	51,766	-	-	-
16-60 years							
Over 60 years							
1771	163,348	143,474	73,990	69,484	19,874	10,623	9,251
Under 16 years	74,456	65,986	33,628	32,358	8,470	4,414	4,056
16-60 years							
Over 60 years							
1756	96,790	83,242	43,261	39,981	13,548	7,570	5,978
Under 16 years	45,713	39,653	20,669	18,984	6,060	3,280	2,780
16-60 years							
Over 60 years							
1749	73,348	62,756	32,355	30,401	10,592	5,696	4,896
Under 16 years	34,688	30,069	15,457	14,612	4,619	2,379	2,240
16-60 years							
Over 60 years							
1746	61,589	52,482	26,622	9,107	4,857	4,250	
Under 16 years	29,924	25,744	12,938	4,180	1,964	2,216	

[Continued]

★ 2023 ★

Population Census in the Colonies and States, Showing Slaves, Including Free Blacks, and Mulattoes, 1624-1786 - XI

[Continued]

Year and age	NEW YORK						
	Total population	White			Negro		
		Total	Male	Female	Total	Male	Female
16-60 years							
Over 60 years							
1737	60,437	51,496	25,740	25,756	8,941	4,948	3,993
Under 10 years	19,261	16,585	8,347	8,238	2,676	1,397	1,279
10 years and over	41,176	34,911	17,393	17,518	6,265	3,551	2,714

Source: "Population Census Taken in the Colonies and States During the Colonial and Pre-Federal Period: 1624-25 to 1786." U.S. Bureau of the Census, *Historical Statistics of the United States: Colonial Times to 1970, Part II*, Bicentennial Edition, pp. 1169-1171. *Notes:* - Represents zero. 1. Total includes 12 Indians who paid taxes.

★ 2024 ★

Population

Population Census in the Colonies and States, Showing Slaves, Including Free Blacks, and Mulattoes, 1624-1786 - XII

Year and age	NEW YORK						
	Total population	White			Negro		
		Total	Male	Female	Total	Male	Female
1731	50,286	43,055	24,853	18,202	7,231	4,334	2,897
Under 10 years	19,362	16,916	10,243	6,673	2,446	1,402	1,044
10 years and over	30,924	26,139	14,610	11,529	4,785	2,932	1,853
1723	40,564	34,393	17,583	16,810	6,171	3,364	2,807
Adults	21,842	17,846	9,083	8,763	3,996	2,186	1,810
Children	18,722	16,547	8,500	8,047	2,175	1,178	997
1712-1714	22,608[1]	16,979	8,601	8,378	2,425	1,334	1,091
Under 16 years	9,294	8,450	4,389	4,061	844	434	410
16-60 years		7,853	3,850	4,003			
Over 60 years		676	362	314			
1703	20,665	18,282	9,197	9,085	2,258	1,174	1,084
Under 16 years	10,483	9,634	4,710	4,924	849	467	382
16 years and over	10,182[2]	8,648	4,487	4,161	1,409	707	702
1698	18,067	15,897	-	-	2,170	-	-

[Continued]

★ 2024 ★

Population Census in the Colonies and States, Showing Slaves, Including Free Blacks, and Mulattoes, 1624-1786 - XII

[Continued]

Year and age	NEW YORK						
	Total population	White			Negro		
		Total	Male	Female	Total	Male	Female
Adults	-	9,743	5,066	4,677	-	-	-
Children	-	6,154	-	-	-	-	-

Source: "Population Census Taken in the Colonies and States During the Colonial and Pre-Federal Period: 1624-25 to 1786." U.S. Bureau of the Census, *Historical Statistics of the United States: Colonial Times to 1970, Part II*, Bicentennial Edition, pp. 1169-1171. *Notes:* - Represents zero. 1. Total includes 12 Indians who paid taxes. 2. Total includes 125 over 60 years of age not distributed by sex or race.

★ 2025 ★

Population

Population Census in the Colonies and States, Showing Slaves, Including Free Blacks, and Mulattoes, 1624-1786 - XIII

Year and age	RHODE ISLAND								
	Families	Total population	White			Negro			Indian
			Total	Male	Female	Total	Male	Femal	
1783	-	51,887	48,556	-	-	2,806	-	-	525
1774	9,450	59,607	54,460	26,763	27,697	3,668	-	-	1,479
Under 16 years	-	-	25,079	12,731	12,348	-	-	-	-
16 years and over	-	-	29,381	14,032	15,349	-	-	-	-
1775	-	40,536	35,839	17,860	17,979	4,697	2,387	2,310	-
Adults	-	-	18,121	9,177	8,944	2,542	1,277	1,265	-
Children	-	-	17,718	8,683	9,035	2,155	1,110	1,045	-
1748	-	34,128	29,755	-	-	3,101	-	-	1,272
1730	-	17,935	15,302	-	-	1,648	-	-	985
1708	-	7,181	-	2,432[1]	-	426	-	-	-

Source: "Population Census Taken in the Colonies and States During the Colonial and Pre-Federal Period: 1624-25 to 1786." U.S. Bureau of the Census, *Historical Statistics of the United States: Colonial Times to 1970, Part II*, Bicentennial Edition, pp. 1169-1171. *Notes:* - Represents zero. 1. Including 1,015 freemen, 1,362 militia, and 55 white servants.

★ 2026 ★

Population

Population Census in the Colonies and States, Showing Slaves, Including Free Blacks, and Mulattoes, 1624-1786 - XIV

Year and age	VERMONT[1]						
	Total population	White			Negro		
		Total	Male	Female	Total	Male	Female
1771	4,669	4,650	2,503	2,147	19	13	6
Under 16 years	2,389	2,838	1,249	1,134	6	2	4
16-60 years							
Over 60 years							

Source: "Population Census Taken in the Colonies and States During the Colonial and Pre-Federal Period: 1624-25 to 1786." U.S. Bureau of the Census, *Historical Statistics of the United States: Colonial Times to 1970, Part II,* Bicentennial Edition, pp. 1169-1171. *Notes:* - Represents zero. 1. These figures over Cumberland and Gloucester counties which were superseded after Vermont became a State.

★ 2027 ★

Population

Population Census in the Colonies and States, Showing Slaves, Including Free Blacks, and Mulattoes, 1624-1786 - XV

Year	VIRGINIA											
	Total population	White						Negro				Indians
		Total	Free		Servants		Children	Total	Male	Female	Children	
			Male	Female	Male	Female						
1701	57,596[1]	-	-	-	-	-	-	-	-	-	-	-
1699	58,040[2]	-	-	-	-	-	-	-	-	-	-	-
1634	4,909	-	-	-	-	-	-	-	-	-	-	-
1624-25	1,227	1,202	432	176	441	46	107	23	11	10	2	2

Source: "Population Census Taken in the Colonies and States During the Colonial and Pre-Federal Period: 1624-25 to 1786." U.S. Bureau of the Census, *Historical Statistics of the United States: Colonial Times to 1970, Part II,* Bicentennial Edition, pp. 1169-1171. *Notes:* - Represents zero. 1. Includes 21,712 tithables and 35,884 untihables. 2. Includes 21,606 tithables and 36,434 untithables.

★ 2028 ★

Population

Population by Free-Slave and Change in Slave Population: 1790-1860

Numbers in thousands. Minus sign (-) denotes decrease.

Area and year	Total Black population	Free	Slave			
			Number	Percent of total black population	Change over preceding date Number	Change over preceding date Percent
UNITED STATES						
1790	757	60	698	92	(X)	(X)
1800	1,002	108	894	89	196	28
1810	1,378	186	1,191	86	298	33
1820	1,772	234	1,538	87	347	29
1830	2,329	320	2,009	86	471	31
1840	2,874	386	2,487	87	478	24
1850	3,639	434	3,204	88	717	29
1860	4,442	488	3,954	89	749	23
SOUTH						
1790	690	33	658	95	(X)	(X)
1810	1,268	108	1,161	92	503	77
1830	2,162	182	1,980	92	820	71
1850	3,352	236	3,117	93	1,136	57
1860	4,097	258	3,839	94	722	23
NORTH AND WEST						
1790	67	27	40	60	(X)	(X)
1810	109	79	31	28	-10	-24
1830	167	138	29	17	-2	-6
1850	287	199	88	31	59	203
1860	345	230	115	33	27	31

Source: "Black Population by Free-Slave and Change in Slave Population, by Region: 1790 to 1860," U.S. Department of Commerce, Bureau of the Census. *The Social and Economic Status of the Black Population in the United States: An Historical View, 1790-1978*, p. 11. Primary source: U.S. Department of Commerce, Bureau of the Census. *Notes:* X Not applicable. The standard census definition of regions is used. In that definition, the South includes the States of the old Confederacy as well as Delaware, the District of Columbia, Kentucky, Maryland, Oklahoma and West Virginia.

★ 2029 ★

Population

Sectional Distribution of Blacks in Maryland, 1755, 1790, 1860 - I

	Totals						Percentages of					
	Negro population			Free Negroes			All Negroes free			All free Negroes of the State		
	1755	1790	1860	1755	1790	1860	1755	1790	1860	1755	1790	1860
Eastern Shore	17826	42498	53414	684	3907	28277	3.8	1.19	53.2	37.6	48.5	33.6
Southern Maryland	19210	50856	62689	764	2145	13784	3.9	4.1	21.9	42.	26.6	16.4
Baltimore County[1]	8275[2]	8059	385311	369[2]	927	29911	4.4[2]	11.5	84.7	20.4[2]	11.5	35.6
Western Maryland	8275[2]	9666	19717	369[2]	1064	11970	4.4[2]	11.0	59.7	20.4[2]	13.3	14.0

Source: "Table V, Showing Changes in Sectional Distribution of Negroes," James M. Wright, *The Free Negro in Maryland, 1634-1860*, p. 89. *Notes:* 1. The reason for n distinguishing Baltimore County in 1755 was that at that time it embraced much of what later became Harford and Carroll counties. Further its negro population was n metropolitan then, as it tended later to become. Other counties erected in that section were Washington, Allegany and Garrett. 2. Totals include Baltimore County and Weste Maryland.

★ 2030 ★

Population

Sectional Distribution of Blacks in Maryland, 1755, 1790, 1860 - II

	No. of Slaves			Percentage						Slave population	
				Of Negro slave			Of slaves in state			Gain	Loss
	1755	1790	1860	1755	1790	1860	1755	1790	1860	1755-90	1790-1860
Eastern Shore	17142	38591	24957	96.2	90.8	4638	39.4	37.4	28.6	125	34.6
Southern Maryland	18446	48711	48905	96.1	95.9	78.1	42.0	47.2	56.0	164	0.13[1]
Baltimore County	9723[2]	7132	5400	95.6[2]	88.5	15.3	18.6[2]	6.9	6.1	61.8[2]	24.2
Western Maryland	9723[2]	8602	7927	95.6[2]	89.0	40.3	18.6[2]	8.3	9.0	61.8[2]	7.7
Whole state	43494	103036	87189	96.0	87.4	50.95	-	-	-	136.8	15.3

Source: "Table V, Showing Changes in Sectional Distribution of Negroes," James M. Wright, *The Free Negro in Maryland, 1634-1860*, p. 89. *Notes:* 1. Gain. 2. Data includes Baltimore County and Western Maryland.

★ 2031 ★

Population

Slave Population in Maryland, 1790-1860

County	1860	1850	1840	1830	1820	1810	1800	1790
Allegany	666	724	812	818	795	620	499	258
Anne Arundel	7332	11249	9819	10347	10301	11693	9760	10130
Baltimore	5400	6718	7595	10653	11077	11369	9673	7132
Calvert	4609	4486	4170	3899	3668	3937	4101	4305
Caroline	739	808	752	1177	1574	1520	1865	1057

[Continued]

★ 2031 ★

Slave Population in Maryland, 1790-1860

[Continued]

County	1860	1850	1840	1830	1820	1810	1800	1790
Carroll	783	975	1122	-	-	-	-	-
Cecil	950	844	1352	1705	2342	2467	2103	3407
Charles	9653	9584	9182	10129	9419	11435	9558	10085
Dorchester	4123	4282	4227	5001	5168	5032	4566	5337
Frederick	3243	3913	4445	6370	6685	5671	4572	3641
Harford	1800	2166	2643	2947	3320	4431	4264	3417
Howard	2862	-	-	-	-	-	-	-
Kent	2509	2627	2735	3191	4071	4249	4474	5433
Montgomery	5421	5114	5377	6447	6396	7572	6288	6030
Prince George's	12479	11510	10636	11585	11185	9189	12191	11176
Queen Anne's	4174	4270	3960	4872	5588	6381	6517	6674
St. Mary's	6549	5842	5761	6183	6047	6000	6399	6985
Somerset	5089	5588	5377	6556	7241	6975	7432	7070
Talbot	3725	4134	3687	4173	4768	4878	4775	4777
Washington	1435	2090	2546	2909	3201	2656	2200	1286
Worcester	3648	3444	3539	4032	4551	4427	4398	3836

Source: "Slave Population of the State of Maryland, 1790-1860," James M. Wright, *The Free Negro in Maryland*, 1634-1860, p. 86.

★ 2032 ★

Population

Slave and Free Population by Age, 1820-1870 - I

Year	Under 5 years	5 to 9 years	10 to 14 years	15 to 19 years	20 to 24 years	25 to 29 years	30 to 34 years	35 to 39 years
1870	791,421	659,831	645,311	520,550	498,854	379,048	284,749	258,838
1860	719,084	637,806	601,647	501,593	783,603[1]	783,603[1]	500,598[2]	500,598[2]
Free colored	65,918	61,857	60,399	52,747	85,562[1]	85,562[1]	61,732[2]	61,732[2]
Slave	653,166	575,949	541,248	448,346	698,041[1]	698,041[1]	438,866[2]	438,866[2]
1850	601,315	537,140	488,500	401,076	649,757[1]	649,757[1]	408,880[2]	408,880[2]
Free colored	60,821	58,052	52,308	43,794	77,547[1]	77,547[1]	55,225[2]	55,225[2]
Slave	540,494	479,088	436,192	357,282	572,210[1]	572,210[1]	353,655[2]	353,655[2]
1840	955,395[3]	955,395[3]	890,720[4]	890,720[4]	552,114[6]	552,114[6]	552,114[6]	552,114[6]
Free colored	111,346[3]	111,346[3]	109,397[4]	109,397[4]	77,003[6]	77,003[6]	77,003[6]	77,003[6]
Slave	344,049[3]	344,049[3]	781,323[4]	781,323[4]	475,111[6]	475,111[6]	475,111[6]	475,111[6]
1830	797,167[3]	797,167[3]	712,554[4]	712,554[4]	431,562[6]	431,562[6]	431,562[6]	431,562[6]
Free colored	96,004[3]	96,004[3]	91,217[4]	91,217[4]	60,191[6]	60,191[6]	60,191[6]	60,191[6]
Slave	701,163[3]	701,163[3]	621,337[4]	621,337[4]	371,371[6]	371,371[6]	371,371[6]	371,371[6]
1820	763,747[7]	763,747[7]	763,747[7]	456,372[8]	456,372[8]	367,156[5]	367,156[5]	367,156[5]
Free colored	93,551[7]	93,551[7]	93,551[7]	52,848[8]	52,848[8]	50,741[5]	50,741[5]	50,741[5]
Slave	670,196[7]	670,196[7]	670,196[7]	403,524[8]	403,524[8]	316,415[5]	316,415[5]	316,415[5]

Source: "Population by Age, Sex, Race, and Nativity: 1790-1950." *Historical Statistics of the United States: Colonial Times to 1957*, p. 11. *Notes:* 1. Data includes persons 20 to 29 years old. 2. Data includes persons 30 to 39 years old. 3. Data includes persons under 5 years to 9 years old. 4. 10 to 23 years old. 5. 26 to 44 years old. 6. 24 to 35 years old. 7. Under 14 years old. 8. 14 to 25 years old.

★ 2033 ★

Population

Slave and Free Population by Age, 1820-1870 - II

Year	40 to 44 years	45 to 49 years	50 to 54 years	55 to 59 years	60 to 64 years	65 and over	Age unknown
1870	216,820	168,968	161,362	80,857	91,314	122,058	28
1860	324,519[1]	324,519[1]	183,693[2]	183,693[2]	163,029[3]	163,029[3]	26,258
Free colored	44,726[1]	44,726[1]	27,991[2]	27,991[2]	26,966[3]	26,966[3]	172
Slave	279,793[1]	279,793[1]	155,702[2]	155,702[2]	136,063[3]	136,063[3]	26,086
1850	257,872[1]	257,872[1]	151,369[2]	151,369[2]	183,921[3]	183,921[3]	3,978
Free colored	37,940[1]	37,940[1]	24,353[2]	24,353[2]	24,169[3]	24,169[3]	286
Slave	219,932[1]	219,932[1]	127,016[2]	127,016[2]	114,752[3]	114,752[3]	3,692
1840	343,099[1]	343,099[1]	343,099[1]	132,320[3]	132,320[3]	132,320[3]	-
Free colored	58,635[1]	58,635[1]	58,635[1]	24,912[3]	24,912[3]	24,912[3]	-
Slave	284,464[1]	284,464[1]	284,464[1]	102,408[3]	102,408[3]	102,408[3]	-
1830	277,365[1]	277,365[1]	277,365[1]	109,994[3]	109,994[3]	109,994[3]	-
Free colored	46,598[1]	46,598[1]	46,598[1]	25,589[3]	25,589[3]	25,589[3]	-
Slave	230,767[1]	230,767[1]	230,767[1]	84,405[3]	84,405[3]	84,405[3]	-
1820	367,156[5]	184,381[4]	184,381[4]	184,381[4]	184,381[4]	184,381[4]	-
Free colored	50,741[5]	36,494[4]	36,494[4]	36,494[4]	36,494[4]	36,494[4]	-
Slave	316,415[5]	147,887[4]	147,887[4]	147,887[4]	147,887[4]	147,887[4]	-

Source: "Population by Age, Sex, Race, and Nativity: 1790-1950." *Historical Statistics of the United States: Colonial Times to 1957*, p. 11. *Notes:* 1. Data includes persons 36 to 54 years old. 2. Data includes persons 50 to 59 years old. 3. Data includes persons 60 years old and over. 4. Data includes persons 55 years old and over. 5. Data includes persons 30 to 44 years old.

★ 2034 ★

Population

Slave, White, Foreign Born, and Other Races for Regions, 1790-1950 - I

Year	Northeast						
	Total	White			Negro		Other races
		Total	Native	Foreign born	Total	Slave	
1950	39,477,986	37,398,684	32,204,834	5,193,850	2,018,182	-	61,120
1940	35,976,777	34,566,768	28,545,927	6,020,841	1,369,875	-	40,134
1930	34,427,091	33,244,081	26,135,432	7,108,649	1,146,985	-	36,025
1920	29,662,058	28,957,919	22,174,690	6,783,229	679,234	-	24,900
1910	25,868,573	25,360,966	18,720,401	640,565	484,176	-	23,431
1900	21,046,695	20,637,888	15,898,900	4,738,988	385,020	-	23,787
1890	17,406,969	17,121,985	13,247,119	3,874,866	269,906	-	15,078
1880	14,507,407	14,273,844	11,465,448	2,808,396	229,417	-	4,146
1870	12,298,730	12,117,269	9,599,990	2,517,279	179,738	-	1,723
1860	10,594,268	10,438,028	8,419,243	2,018,785	156,001	18	239
1850	8,626,851	8,477,089	7,153,512	1,323,577	149,762	236	-

[Continued]

★ 2034 ★

Slave, White, Foreign Born, and Other Races for Regions, 1790-1950 - I

[Continued]

Year	Northeast						
	Total	White			Negro		Other races
		Total	Native	Foreign born	Total	Slave	
1840[1]	6,761,082	6,618,758	-	-	142,324	765	-
1830[1]	5,542,381	5,417,167	-	-	125,214	2,780	-
1820	4,359,916	4,249,192	-	-	110,724	18,001	-
1810	3,486,675	3,384,438	-	-	102,237	27,081	-
1800	2,635,576	2,552,510	-	-	83,066	36,370	-
1790	1,968,040	1,900,616	-	-	67,424	40,354	-

Source: "Population, by Race and Nativity, for Regions: 1790-1950." *Historical Statistics of the United States: Colonial Times to 1957*, p. 11. *Notes:* 1. Excludes persons (6,100 in 1840 and 5,318 in 1830) on public ships in the service of the United States, not credited to any region.

★ 2035 ★

Population

Slave, White, Foreign Born, and Other Races for Regions, 1790-1950 - II

Year	North Central						
	Total	White			Negro		Other races
		Total	Native	Foreign born	Total	Slave	
1950	44,460,762	42,119,334	39,407,638	2,711,746	2,227,876	-	113,502
1940	40,143,332	38,639,970	35,291,033	3,348,937	1,420,318	-	83,044
1930	38,594,100	37,249,272	32,902,458	4,346,814	1,262,234	-	82,594
1920	34,019,792	33,164,249	28,569,009	4,595,240	793,075	-	62,468
1910	29,888,542	29,279,243	24,598,792	4,680,451	543,498	-	65,801
1900	26,333,004	25,775,870	21,624,468	4,151,402	495,751	-	61,383
1890	22,410,417	21,913,813	17,860,356	4,058,457	431,112	-	65,492
1880	17,364,111	16,961,423	14,049,225	2,912,198	885,621	-	17,067
1870	12,981,111	12,698,503	10,367,625	2,330,878	273,080	-	9,528
1860	9,096,716	8,899,969	7,357,376	1,542,598	184,239	114,948	12,508
1850	5,403,595	5,267,988	4,617,913	650,075	135,607	87,422	-
1840[1]	3,351,542	3,262,195	-	-	89,347	58,604	-
1830[1]	1,610,473	1,568,930	-	-	41,543	25,879	-
1820	859,305	841,045	-	-	18,260	11,329	-
1810	292,107	285,173	-	-	6,934	3,304	-

[Continued]

★ 2035 ★

Slave, White, Foreign Born, and Other Races for Regions, 1790-1950 - II

[Continued]

Year	North Central						
	Total	White			Negro		Other races
		Total	Native	Foreign born	Total	Slave	
1800	51,006	50,371	-	-	635	135	-
1790	-	-	-	-	-	-	-

Source: "Population, by Race and Nativity, for Regions: 1790-1950." *Historical Statistics of the United States: Colonial Times to 1957*, p. 11. *Notes:* 1. Excludes persons (6,100 in 1840 and 5,318 in 1830) on public ships in the service of the United States, not credited to any region.

★ 2036 ★

Population

Slaves and Free Blacks: Distribution in Four Cities, 1790

City	Population 1790				
	Total	Negro			White
		Total	Free	Slave	
New York	32,305	3,262	1,078	2,184	29,043
Philadelphia	28,522	1,630	1,420	210	26,892
Boston	18,038	761	761	-	17,277
Baltimore	13,503	1,578	323	1,255	11,925

Source: "Free and Slave Population of Four Cities: 1790," U.S. Bureau of the Census. *Negro Population in the United States, 1790-1915*, p. 55. *Note:* (-) Represents zero.

★ 2037 ★

Population

Slaves and Free Blacks: Distribution, by Region, 1790-1860 - I

Census year	Negro population Number						
	United States	South				North	West
		Total	South Atlantic division	East South Central division	West South Central division		
Slave							
1860	3,953,760	3,838,765	1,840,445	1,372,913	625,407	114,966	29
1850	3,204,313	3,116,629	1,663,397	1,103,162	350,070	87,658	26
1840	2,487,355	2,427,986	1,425,539	814,060	188,387	59,369	-
1830	2,009,043	1,980,384	1,376,196	490,024	114,164	28,659	-
1820	1,538,022	1,508,692	1,156,479	281,532	70,681	29,330	-
1810	1,191,362	1,160,841	983,997	142,184	34,660	30,521	-
1800	893,602	857,097	799,681	57,416	-	36,505	-
1790	697,624	657,538	641,691	15,847	-	40,086	-
Free							
1860	488,070	258,346	217,753	21,447	19,146	225,274	4,450
1850	434,495	235,569	197,474	19,628	18,467	197,711	1,215
1840	386,203	213,991	171,778	16,246	25,967	172,302	-
1830	319,599	181,501	153,087	11,563	16,851	138,098	-
1820	233,634	133,980	116,920	6,525	10,535	99,654	-
1810	186,446	107,658	96,803	3,270	7,585	78,788	-
1800	108,435	61,239	60,009	1,230	-	47,196	-
1790	59,557	32,523	32,048	475	-	27,034	-

Source: "Slave and Free Colored Population at Each Census by Sections and Southern Divisions: 1790-1860," U.S. Bureau of the Census, *Negro Population in the United States, 1790-1915*, p. 55. *Note:* (-) Represents zero.

★ 2038 ★

Population

Slaves and Free Blacks: Distribution, by Region, 1790-1860 - II

Census year	Negro population Percentage distribution by area						
	United States	South				North	West
		Total	South Atlantic division	East South Central division	West South Central division		
Slave							
1860	100.0	97.1	46.5	34.7	15.8	2.9	[1]
1850	100.0	97.3	51.9	34.4	10.9	2.7	[1]
1840	100.0	97.6	57.3	32.7	7.6	2.4	-
1830	100.0	98.6	68.5	24.4	5.7	1.4	-
1820	100.0	98.1	75.2	18.3	4.6	1.9	-
1810	100.0	97.4	82.6	11.9	2.9	2.6	-
1800	100.0	95.9	89.5	6.4	-	4.1	-
1790	100.0	94.3	92.0	2.3	-	5.7	-
Free							
1860	100.0	52.9	44.6	4.4	3.9	46.2	0.9
1850	100.0	54.2	45.4	4.5	4.3	45.5	0.3
1840	100.0	55.4	44.5	4.2	6.7	44.6	-
1830	100.0	56.8	47.9	3.6	5.3	43.2	-
1820	100.0	57.3	50.0	2.8	4.5	42.7	-
1810	100.0	57.7	51.9	1.8	4.1	42.3	-
1800	100.0	56.5	55.3	1.1	-	43.5	-
1790	100.0	54.6	53.8	0.8	-	45.4	-

Source: "Slave and Free Colored Population at Each Census by Sections and Southern Divisions: 1790-1860," U.S. Bureau of the Census, *Negro Population in the United States, 1790-1915*, p. 55. *Notes:* (-) Represents zero. 1. Less than one-tenth of 1 percent.

★ 2039 ★

Population

Slaves and Free Blacks: Distribution, by States, 1790-1860 - I

Division and state	Negro population							
	1860		1850		1840		1830	
	Slave	Free	Slave	Free	Slave	Free	Slave	Free
United States	3,953,760	488,070	204,313	434,495	487,355	386,293	2,009,043	319,599
Geographic divisions:								
New England	-	24,711	-	23,021	23	22,634	48	21,331
Middle Atlantic	18	131,272	236	126,505	742	118,925	2,732	101,103
East North Central	-	63,699	-	45,195	348	28,997	788	15,095
West North Central	114,948	5,592	87,422	2,990	58,256	1,746	25,091	569
South Atlantic	1,840,445	217,753	1,663,397	197,474	1,425,539	171,778	1,376,196	153,087
East South Central	1,372,913	21,447	103,162	19,628	814,060	16,246	490,024	11,563
West South Central	625,407	19,146	350,070	18,467	188,387	25,967	114,164	16,851
Mountain	29	206	26	46	-	-	-	-
Pacific	-	4,244	-	1,169	-	-	-	-
New England:								
Maine	-	1,327	-	1,356	-	1,355	2	1,190
New Hampshire	-	494	-	520	1	537	3	604
Vermont	-	709	-	718	-	730	-	881
Massachusetts	-	9,602	-	9,064	-	8,669	1	7,048
Rhode Island	-	3,952	-	3,670	5	3,238	17	3,561
Connecticut	-	8,627	-	7,693	17	8,105	25	8,047
Middle Atlantic:								
New York	-	49,005	-	49,069	4	50,027	75	44,870
New Jersey	18	25,318	236	23,810	674	21,044	2,254	18,303
Pennsylvania	-	56,949	-	53,626	64	47,854	403	37,930
East North Central:								
Ohio	-	36,673	-	25,279	3	17,342	6	9,568
Indiana	-	11,428	-	11,292	3	7,165	3	3,629
Illinois	-	7,628	-	5,436	331	3,598	747	1,637
Michigan	-	6,799	-	2,583	-	707	32	261
Wisconsin	-	1,171	-	635	11	185	-	-
West North Central:								
Minnesota	-	259	-	39	-	-	-	-
Iowa	-	1,069	-	333	16	172	-	-
Missouri	114,931	3,572	87,422	2,618	58,240	1,574	25,091	569
North Dakota	-	-	-	-	-	-	-	-
South Dakota	-	-	-	-	-	-	-	-
Nebraska	15	67	-	-	-	-	-	-
Kansas	2	625	-	-	-	-	-	-
South Atlantic:								
Delaware	1,798	19,829	2,299	18,073	2,605	16,919	3,292	15,855
Maryland	87,189	83,942	90,368	74,723	89,737	62,078	102,994	52,938
District of Columbia	3,185	11,131	3,687	10,059	4,694	8,361	6,119	6,152

[Continued]

★ 2039 ★

Slaves and Free Blacks: Distribution, by States, 1790-1860 - I

[Continued]

Division and state	Negro population							
	1860		1850		1840		1830	
	Slave	Free	Slave	Free	Slave	Free	Slave	Free
Virginia	490,865	58,042	472,528	54,333	448,987	49,842	469,757	47,348
West Virginia	-	-	-	-	-	-	-	-
North Carolina	331,059	30,463	288,548	27,463	245,817	22,732	245,601	19,543
South Carolina	402,406	9,914	384,984	8,960	327,038	8,276	315,401	7,921
Georgia	462,198	3,500	381,682	2,931	280,944	2,753	217,531	2,486
Florida	61,745	932	39,310	932	25,717	817	15,501	844
East South Central:								
Kentucky	225,483	10,684	210,981	10,011	182,258	7,317	165,213	4,917
Tennessee	275,719	7,300	239,459	6,422	183,059	5,524	141,603	4,555
Alabama	435,080	2,690	342,844	2,265	253,532	2,039	117,549	1,572
Mississippi	436,631	773	309,878	930	195,211	1,366	65,659	519
West South Central:								
Arkansas	111,115	144	47,100	608	19,935	465	4,576	141
Louisiana	331,726	18,647	244,809	17,462	168,452	25,502	109,588	16,710
Oklahoma	-	-	-	-	-	-	-	-
Texas	182,566	355	58,161	397	-	-	-	-
Mountain:								
Montana	-	-	-	-	-	-	-	-
Idaho	-	-	-	-	-	-	-	-
Wyoming	-	-	-	-	-	-	-	-
Colorado	-	46	-	-	-	-	-	-
New Mexico	-	85	-	22	-	-	-	-
Arizona	-	-	-	-	-	-	-	-
Utah	29	30	26	24	-	-	-	-
Nevada	-	45	-	-	-	-	-	-
Pacific:								
Washington	-	30	-	-	-	-	-	-
Oregon	-	128	-	207	-	-	-	-
California	-	4,086	-	962	-	-	-	-

Source: "Negro Population, Slave and Free, at Each Census by Division and States: 1790-1960, U.S. Bureau of the Census, *Negro Population in the United States, 1790-1915*, p. 57. *Note:* (-) Represents zero.

★ 2040 ★

Population

Slaves and Free Blacks: Distribution, by States, 1790-1860 - II

Division and state	Negro population							
	1820		1810		1800		1790	
	Slave	Free	Slave	Free	Slave	Free	Slave	Free
United States	1,538,022	233,634	1,191,362	186,446	893,602	108,435	697,624	59,557
Geographic divisions:								
New England	145	20,782	418	19,488	1,339	17,313	3,763	13,059
Middle Atlantic	17,856	71,941	26,663	55,668	35,031	29,383	36,323	13,975
East North Central	1,107	6,584	429	3,025	135	500	-	-
West North Central	10,222	347	3,011	607	-	-	-	-
South Atlantic	1,156,479	116,920	983,997	96,803	799,681	60,009	641,691	32,043
East South Central	281,532	6,525	142,184	3,270	57,416	1,230	15,847	475
West South Central	70,681	10,535	34,660	7,585	-	-	-	-
Mountain	-	-	-	-	-	-	-	-
Pacific	-	-	-	-	-	-	-	-
New England:								
Maine	-	929	-	969	-	818	-	536
New Hampshire	-	786	-	970	8	852	157	630
Vermont	-	903	-	750	-	557	-	269
Massachusetts	-	6,740	-	6,737	-	6,452	-	5,369
Rhode Island	48	3,554	108	3,609	380	3,304	958	3,484
Connecticut	97	7,870	310	6,453	951	5,330	2,648	2,771
Middle Atlantic:								
New York	10,088	29,279	15,017	25,333	20,903	10,417	21,193	4,682
New Jersey	7,557	12,460	10,851	7,843	12,422	4,402	11,423	2,762
Pennsylvania	211	30,202	795	22,492	1,706	14,564	3,707	6,531
East North Central:								
Ohio	-	4,723	-	1,899	-	337	-	-
Indiana	190	1,230	237	393	135	163	-	-
Illinois	917	457	168	613	-	-	-	-
Michigan	-	174	24	120	-	-	-	-
Wisconsin	-	-	-	-	-	-	-	-
West North Central:								
Minnesota	-	-	-	-	-	-	-	-
Iowa	-	-	-	-	-	-	-	-
Missouri	10,222	347	3,011	607	-	-	-	-
North Dakota	-	-	-	-	-	-	-	-
South Dakota	-	-	-	-	-	-	-	-
Nebraska	-	-	-	-	-	-	-	-
Kansas	-	-	-	-	-	-	-	-
South Atlantic:								
Delaware	4,509	12,958	4,177	13,136	6,153	8,268	8,887	3,899
Maryland	107,397	39,730	111,502	33,927	105,635	19,587	103,036	8,043
District of Columbia	6,377	4,048	5,395	2,549	3,244	783	-	-

[Continued]

★ 2040 ★

Slaves and Free Blacks: Distribution, by States, 1790-1860 - II

[Continued]

Division and state	Negro population							
	1820		1810		1800		1790	
	Slave	Free	Slave	Free	Slave	Free	Slave	Free
Virginia	425,148	36,883	392,516	30,570	345,796	20,124	292,627	12,866
West Virginia	-	-	-	-	-	-	-	-
North Carolina	204,917	14,712	168,824	10,266	133,296	7,043	100,783	5,041
South Carolina	258,475	6,826	196,365	4,554	146,151	3,185	107,094	1,801
Georgia	149,656	1,763	105,218	1,801	59,406	1,019	29,264	398
Florida	-	-	-	-	-	-	-	-
East South Central:								
Kentucky	126,732	2,759	80,561	1,713	40,343	739	12,430	114
Tennessee	80,107	2,737	44,535	1,317	13,584	309	3,417	361
Alabama	41,879	571	-	-	-	-	-	-
Mississippi	32,814	458	17,088	240	3,489	182	-	-
West South Central:								
Arkansas	1,617	59	-	-	-	-	-	-
Louisiana	69,064	10,476	34,660	7,585	-	-	-	-
Oklahoma	-	-	-	-	-	-	-	-
Texas	-	-	-	-	-	-	-	-
Mountain:								
Montana	-	-	-	-	-	-	-	-
Idaho	-	-	-	-	-	-	-	-
Wyoming	-	-	-	-	-	-	-	-
Colorado	-	-	-	-	-	-	-	-
New Mexico	-	-	-	-	-	-	-	-
Arizona	-	-	-	-	-	-	-	-
Utah	-	-	-	-	-	-	-	-
Nevada	-	-	-	-	-	-	-	-
Pacific:								
Washington	-	-	-	-	-	-	-	-
Oregon	-	-	-	-	-	-	-	-
California	-	-	-	-	-	-	-	-

Source: "Negro Population, Slave and Free, at Each Census by Division and States: 1790-1960, U.S. Bureau of the Census, *Negro Population in the United States, 1790-1915*, p. 57. *Note:* (-) Represents zero.

Private Families

★ 2041 ★

Slave-holding and Non-slave-holding Families, 1790-1850

The average number of slaves per slaveholding family was 7.3 in 1790 and 9.2 in 1850. In the 60 years, 1790 to 1850, the number of slave-holding families in the United States increased from 96,168 to 347,725.

Source: "Slave-holding and Non-slave-holding Families: 1790 and 1850," U.S. Bureau of the Census. *Negro Population in the United States, 1790-1915*, p. 56.

★ 2042 ★

Private Families

Slave-holding and Non-slave-holding Private Families, 1790

Division and state	Private families: 1790[1]					
	Free colored			White		
	Total number	Slave-holding	Non-slave-holding	Total number	Slave-holding	Non-slave-holding
Area covered by 1790 schedules in existence	5,161	195	4,966	405,475	47,664	357,811
New England	1,634	6	1,628	172,383	2,141	170,242
Maine	37	-	37	16,972	-	16,972
New Hampshire	83	-	83	23,982	123	23,859
Vermont	23	-	23	14,969	-	14,969
Massachusetts	630	-	630	65,149	-	65,149
Rhode Island	442	-	442	10,584	461	10,393
Connecticut	419	6	413	40,457	1,557	38,900
Middle states	1,245	16	1,229	127,507	9,638	117,869
New York	693	9	634	54,185	7,787	46,398
Pennsylvania	552	7	545	73,322	1,851	71,471
Southern states	2,282	173	2,109	105,585	35,885	69,700
Maryland[2]	1,282	84	1,198	32,012	12,142	19,870
North Carolina[3]	680	28	652	48,021	14,945	33,076
South Carolina	320	61	259	25,552	8,798	16,754

Source: "Slave-holding and Non-slave-holding families: 1790 and 1850," U.S. Bureau of the Census, *Negro Population in the United States, 1790-1915*, p. 56. *Notes:* (-) Represents zero. 1. Data not available for New Jersey, Delaware, Virginia, Georgia, Kentucky, or Southwest Territory. 2. Data not available for Allegany, Calvert, or Somerset Counties. 3. Data not available for Caswell, Granville, or Orange Counties, except the total number of families.

Protests

★ 2043 ★

Slave Insurrections, 1619-1791

Approximately twenty-five insurrections of slaves took place in the United States prior to the American Revolution. This figure excludes the insurrections in Louisiana and in the Spanish, French, and English colonies in the West Indies. The slave uprising of 1791 on the Island of Haiti was the most important insurrection in the West Indies. By this method the slaves secured their independence and in 1904 established themselves as the Republic of Haiti.

Source: "Slave Insurrections," Monroe N. Work, ed., *Negro Year Book and Annual Encyclopedia of the Negro*, 1912, p. 47.

Slave Labor

★ 2044 ★

Prices for Best Field Hands, 1829-1990

Year	Price	Year	Price
1800	$500	1830	$450
1801	550	1831	475
1802	550	1832	500
1803	575	1833	525
1804	600	1834	650
1805	550	1835	750
1806	550	1836	1100
1807	525	1837	1200
1808	550	1838	1000
1809	500	1839	1000
1810	500	1840	800
1811	550	1841	650
1812	500	1842	600
1813	450	1843	500
1814	450	1844	500
1815	500	1845	550
1816	600	1846	650
1817	650	1847	750
1819	850	1848	700
1820	725	1849	650

[Continued]

★ 2044 ★

Prices for Best Field Hands, 1829-1990

[Continued]

Year	Price	Year	Price
1822	650	1850	700
1823	600	1851	750
1824	500	1852	800
1825	500	1853	900
1826	475	1855	900
1827	475	1858	950
1828	450	1859	1100
1829	475	1860	1200

Source: "Prices for Best Field Hands." Low and Clift, *Enclopedia of Black America*, p. 764.

Slave Prices

★ 2045 ★

Slave Prices in the Richmond and Augusta Markets, 1862-1865

Year	Quarter	Age	Price in currency	Corresponding value in gold	Average quarterly value of gold dollar
1861	4	20	$1,160	$1,050	1.2
1862	1	28	895	746	1.2
	2	18	850	570	1.5
	3	23	1,100	647	1.7
	4	21	1,230	473	2.6
1863	1	20	1,450	410	3.5
	2	20	1,630	291	5.6
	3				11.0
	4[1]	20	2,300	144	16.0

[Continued]

★ 2045 ★

Slave Prices in the Richmond and Augusta Markets, 1862-1865

[Continued]

Year	Quarter	Age	Price in currency	Corresponding value in gold	Average quarterly value of gold dollar
1864	1	20	5,850	266	22.0
	2				19.0
	3	Adult males	4,140	190	21.7
	4	22			31.3
1865[2]	Feb. 11	Adult males	5,000	100	
	Mar. 22	Adult males	10,000	100	

Source: Untitled table, Wiley, *Southern Negroes 1861-1865*, p. 89. *Notes:* 1. Figures for fourth quarter are taken from the Augusta market as reported by the Augusta *Chronicle and Sentinel*. 2. From the Richmond market as reported by J.B. Jones in his *Diary*. Both the currency prices and the gold values for 1865 are from the *Diary*.

Slave Trade

★ 2046 ★

Slave Prices – British American and West African, 1638-1775

Period	British-American slave prices		West-African slave prices	
	Number of observations	Price in pounds sterling	Number of observations	Price in pounds sterling
1773-1775	19	44.08	11	17.04
1768-1772	28	38.39	17	17.72
1763-1767	21	34.74	18	15.91
1758-1762	11	35.61	11	13.71
1753-1757	27	33.10	22	13.66
1748-1752	7	27.12	28	14.01
1743-1747	9	31.04	8	11.21
1738-1742	11	26.64	6	17.43
1733-1737	5	18.50	13	15.37
1728-1732	14	24.91	13	12.86
1723-1727	18	23.92	18	11.87
1718-1722	13	24.11	21	11.13
1713-1717	9	25.67	23	9.88
1708-1712	24	24.37	14	8.75

[Continued]

★ 2046 ★

Slave Prices – British American and West African, 1638-1775

[Continued]

Period	British-American slave prices		West-African slave prices	
	Number of observations	Price in pounds sterling	Number of observations	Price in pounds sterling
1703-1707	26	26.37	13	8.87
1698-1702	26	23.68	24	5.21
1693-1797	9	26.02	5	4.19
1688-1792	5	23.35	4	3.37
1683-1787	10	19.95	13	3.92
1678-1782	29	19.32	20	3.28
1673-1777	19	21.92	5	2.04
1668-1772	20	21.14	4	3.03
1663-1767	15	21.14	2	5.41
1658-1762	3	21.12	1	3.01
1653-1757	2	24.09	1	11.38
1648-1752	3	27.70	1	6.72
1643-1747	3	20.20	3	1.87
1638-1742	3	16.50	2	3.91

Source: "British-American and West African Slave Prices, "U.S. Bureau of the Census, *Historical Statistics of the United States, Colonial Times to 1970,"* *Part* 2, 1970, p. 1174.

★ 2047 ★

Slave Trade

Slave Trade in New York, 1701-1764

Year	Imported				Exported
	Year	Africa	Continental colonies	Elsewhere	
1764	35	-	-	35	1
1763	205	196	-	9	-
1754	65	65	-	-	41
1748	10[1]	-	-	10	0[1]
1743	7	-	-	7	0[1]
1742	14	-	2	12	-
1741	55	-	7	48	-
1740	56	-	4	52	5
1739	100	-	11	89	-
1738	118	3	51	64	-
1737	99	-	3	96	0[1]

[Continued]

★ 2047 ★

Slave Trade in New York, 1701-1764

[Continued]

Year	Imported				Exported
	Year	Africa	Continental colonies	Elsewhere	
1736	13[1]	-	-	13	0[1]
1735	121	-	2	119	-
1734	52	-	1	51	7
1733	257	100	1	156	5
1732	139[1]	0	1	138	3
1731	309[2]	130[2]	2[2]	177[2]	0[1]
1730	165	-	7	158	4[1]
1729	211	-	11	200	8
1728	130	-	4	126	14
1727	221	-	3	218	1
1726	176	-	32	144	6
1725	211	59	6	146	6
1724	64	-	8	56	5
1723	101	-	1	100	3
1722	96	-	-	96	-
1721	205	117	2	86	4
1720	77	-	11	66	4
1719	104	-	-	104	8[1]
1718	517	70	-	447	-
1717	334	266	-	68	-
1716	62	43	-	19	-
1715	55	38	-	17	-
1714	53	-	-	53	-
1712	77	77	-	-	-
1711	55	55	-	-	-
1710	53	53	-	-	-
1705	24	24	-	-	-
1704	8	-	-	8	-
1703	16	-	-	16	-
1702	165	-	-	165	-
1701	36	-	-	36	-

Source: "Slave Trade in New York: 1701 to 1764," U.S. Bureau of the Census, *Historical Statistics of the United States, Colonial Times to 1970, Part II*, p. 1173. *Notes:* (-) Represents zero. 1. Partial year. 2. Figures have been extended to basis of partial data.

★ 2048 ★

Slave Trade

Slave Trade in Virginia, 1619-1767

Year	Imported			Exported
	Total	Africa	Elsewhere	
1767	61	[1]	61	[1]
1766	112	108	4	4
1765	66	[1]	66	[1]
1764	967	922	45	10
1763	1,195	1,080	115	3
1762	1,810	1,787	23	92
1761	1,581	1,470	111	28
1760[2]	1,158	1,152	6	52
1758	43	-	43	-
1757	4	[1]	4	[1]
1756	1	[1]	1	2
1755[2]	565	456	109	2
1754[2]	399	249	150	[1]
1753	21	[1]	21	9
1752	3,515[2]	3,515[2]	[1]	11
1751[2]	1,194	982	212	[1]
1750	1,010	849	161	-
1749[2]	2,338	1,826	512	[1]
1747	28	[1]	28	[1]
1746	1,647	1,299	348	10
1745	654	512	142	-
1744	672	486	186	-
1743	1,428	1,320	108	-
1742	1,529	1,095	434	63
1741	947	687	260	36
1740	1,646	934	712	6
1739	1,710	1,623	87	7
1738	1,101	839	262	-
1737	2,174	2,044	130	263
1736[2]	3,222	3,166	56	52
1735	2,104	1,798	306	[1]
1734	1,587	1,231	356	47
1733[2]	1,720	1,245	475	21
1732	1,291	1,223	68	149
1731	184	130	54	[1]
1730	276[2]	276[2]	[1]	[1]
1729	4	[1]	4	[1]
1728	26	24	2	4
1727	735	-	735	24
1726	-	2,149	-	55
1725	-	781	-	142
1724	-	464	-	-
1723	-	694	-	-

[Continued]

★ 2048 ★

Slave Trade in Virginia, 1619-1767

[Continued]

Year	Imported			Exported
	Total	Africa	Elsewhere	
1722	-	239	-	-
1721	-	1,960	-	-
1720	-	1,368	-	-
1719	-	1,842	-	-
1710-1718[3]	552	233	319	-
1709	-	326	-	-
1708	-	593	-	-
1707	-	713	-	-
1706	-	1,013	-	-
1705	-	1,639	-	-
1704	-	987	-	-
1703	-	156	-	-
1702	-	481	-	-
1701	-	796	-	-
1700	-	229	-	-
1699[4]	349	-	-	-
1687	-	120	-	-
1685	191	190[5]	1	-
1684	-	34	-	-
1679	-	245	-	-
1678	-	120	-	-
1677	-	150[5]	-	-
1674	-	650[5]	-	-
1665[4]	59	-	-	-
1662[4]	30	-	-	-
1656[4]	30	-	-	-
1652[4]	7	-	-	-
1649[4]	17	-	-	-
1643[4]	18	-	-	-
1642[4]	7	-	-	-
1639[4]	46	-	-	-
1638[4]	30	-	-	-
1637[4]	22	-	-	-
1636[4]	7	-	-	-
1635[4]	26	-	-	-
1628	100	-	-	-
1623	1	-	-	-
1622	1	-	-	-

[Continued]

★ 2048 ★

Slave Trade in Virginia, 1619-1767

[Continued]

Year	Imported			Exported
	Total	Africa	Elsewhere	
1621	1	-	-	-
1619	21	-	21	-

Source: "Slave Trade in Virginia: 1619-1767," U.S. Bureau of the Census, *Historical Statistics of the United States, Colonial Times to 1970, Part II*, Bicentennial Edition, p. 1172. *Notes:* (-) Represents zero. 1. Information lacking or too incomplete to calculate. 2. Figures have been extended on basis of partial data. 3. Annual average. Source also shown 72 Indian slaves imported; 231 slaves died and 103 drawn back for exportation during the 9 years. 4. Number of headrights granted. 5. Number of negroes shipped, not those actually arrived.

★ 2049 ★

Slave Trade

Slaves Imported into Charleston, S.C., 1706-1745

Year	Total importations		From African ports		From Caribbean ports		From North American ports		From other locations	
	Slaves	Cargoes	Slaves	Cargoes	Slaves	Cargoes	Slaves	Cargoes	Slaves	Cargoes
1745	7	3	-	-	7	3	-	-	-	-
1744[4]	291	6	289	5	2	1	-	-	-	-
1742[4]	81	2	-	-	81	2	-	-	-	-
1741[4]	1	1	-	-	-	-	1	1	-	-
1740	740	12	714	6	26	6	-	-	-	-
1739	2,017	16	1,975	12	42	4	-	-	-	-
1738	2,508	20	2,495	18	13	2	-	-	-	-
1737	1,063	13	1,055	8	1	1	1	1	6	3
1736	3,526	24	3,500	19	25	4	1	1	-	-
1735	2,723	28	2,641	11	80	15	2	2	-	-
1734	1,805	39	1,319	7	480	29	6	3	-	-
1733	179	3	160[2]	1	19	2	-	-	-	-
1732	996	18	810	4	168	12	18	2	-	-
1731	1,766	25	1,611	9	144	13	11	3	-	-
1727	652	9	610[2]	3	42[2]	6	-	-	-	-
1726	1,751[5]	-	-	-	-	-	-	-	-	-
1725	433[5]	1	-	-	4[2]	1[2]	-	-	-	-
1724	800[6]	12	763	5	35	5	2	2	-	-
1723	436	4	192[2]	1	38	3	-	-	-	-
1722[4]	323	4	-	-	38[2]	4	-	-	-	-
1721[4]	165	-	-	-	-	-	-	-	-	-
1720[4]	601	-	-	-	-	-	-	-	-	-
1719[4]	541	19	221[2]	3	212[2]	16	-	-	-	-
1718	566[6]	17	392	4	174	13	-	-	-	-
1717	619[6]	19	394	6	225	13	-	-	-	-
1716	67	-	-	-	-	-	-	-	-	-
1715	81	-	-	-	-	-	-	-	-	-
1714	419	-	-	-	-	-	-	-	-	-
1713	159	-	-	-	-	-	-	-	-	-
1712	76	-	-	-	-	-	-	-	-	-
1711	170	-	-	-	-	-	-	-	-	-
1710	131	-	-	-	-	-	-	-	-	-

[Continued]

★ 2049 ★

Slaves Imported into Charleston, S.C., 1706-1745

[Continued]

Year	Total importations		From African ports		From Caribbean ports		From North American ports		From other locations	
	Slaves	Cargoes	Slaves	Cargoes	Slaves	Cargoes	Slaves	Cargoes	Slaves	Cargoes
1709	107	-	-	-	-	-	-	-	-	-
1708	53	-	-	-	-	-	-	-	-	-
1707	22	-	-	-	-	-	-	-	-	-
1706	24	-	-	-	-	-	-	-	-	-

Source: "Slaves Imported into Charleston, S.C., by Origin: 1706 to 1775." U.S. Bureau of the Census, *Historical Statistics of the United States, Colonial Times to 1970, Part II,* Bicentennial Edition, p. 1173. *Notes:* (-) Represents zero. 1. Total number of slaves imported is greater than sum of source of importation; detailed figures are incomplete for early years. 2. Incomplete; records missing. 3. A three year prohibition of external slave trade was in effect during 1766 to 1768. 4. A prohibitively high duty on slave importation was in effect during 1719 to 1722 and 1741 to 1744. 5. Totals for 1725 and 1726 were obtained from BPRO Transcripts, C.O. 5, p. 387, and Elizabeth Donnan, ed., Documents Illustrative of the History of the Slave Trade to America, vol. IV, p. 267. Detailed figures for the source inportation for these years and earlier are missing. 6. Data from the "Shipping Records" of the Naval Officer of Charleston.

★ 2050 ★

Slave Trade

Slaves Imported into the Americas by Importing Country, 1816-1843

Importing country	1817-1820		1821-1830		1831-1840		1841-1843		Total	
	Number	Percent	Number	Percent	Number	Percent	Number	Percent	Number	Percent
Brazil	44,100	96.3	277,200	81.2	147,500	75.4	48,500	69.2	517,300	79.2
Cuba	1,000	2.3	22,700	6.7	42,600	21.8	20,500	29.2	86,800	13.3
Bahamas	-	-	600	0.2	1,800	0.9	-	-	2,400	0.4
Danish WI	200	0.4	-	-	-	-	-	-	200	[1]
Puerto Rico	-	-	-	-	300	0.2	-	-	300	[1]
United States	-	-	100	[1]	-	-	-	-	100	[1]
Guadeloupe	-	-	300	0.1	-	-	-	-	300	[1]
Martinique	-	-	1,400	0.4	-	-	-	-	1,400	0.2
Uruguay	-	-	-	-	1,400	0.7	-	-	1,400	0.2
British Honduras	-	-	-	-	200	0.1	-	-	200	[1]
Surinam	500	1.1	600	0.2	-	-	-	-	1,100	0.2
Destination unknown	-	-	38,300	11.2	1,800	0.9	1,100	1.6	41,200	6.3
Total	45,800[2]	100.0[2]	341,300[2]	100.0[2]	195,600[2]	100.0[2]	70,100[2]	100.0[2]	652,800[2]	100.0[2]

Source: "Slaves Imported into the Americas by Ships Known to the British Foreign Office, 1817-43." Philip D. Curtin, *The Atlantic Slave Trade: A Census,* p. 237. *Notes:* (-) Represents zero. 1. Less than 0.5 percent. 2. Totals and percentages have been rounded.

★ 2051 ★

Slave Trade

Slaves: Origin and Destination, 1768-1772 - I

Year and origin or destination	Total	New Hampshire	Massachusetts	Rhode Island	Connecticut	New York
1772						
Imports	10,165	4	4	2	-	23
Africa	6,638	-	-	-	-	19
West Indies	3,146	4	-	2	-	4
Continental colonies	381	-	4	-	-	-
Exports	495	4	-	-	-	2
West Indies	3	-	-	-	-	2
Continental colonies	492	4	-	-	-	-
1771						
Imports	4,970	-	-	12	-	9
Africa	2,754	-	-	-	-	-
West Indies	2,020	-	-	7	-	8
Continental colonies	196	-	-	5	-	1
Exports	341	-	1	6	1	-
West Indies	3	-	-	-	-	-
Continental colonies	338	-	1	6	1	-
1770						
Imports	3,069	-	-	-	-	69
Africa	2,266	-	-	-	-	67
West Indies	600	-	-	-	-	2
Continental colonies	203	-	-	-	-	-
Exports	144	-	1	13	-	-
West Indies	27	-	-	-	-	-
Continental colonies	117	-	1	13	-	-
1769						
Imports	6,736	4	-	6	-	-
Africa	5,161	-	-	6	-	-
West Indies	1,222	4	-	-	-	-
Colonial colonies	353	-	-	-	-	-
Exports	336	-	-	4	-	-
West Indies	9	-	-	-	-	-
Continental colonies	327	-	-	4	-	-
1768						
Imports	2,496	12	-	70	14	19
West Indies[1]	2,204	12	-	59	14	19
Continental colonies	292	-	-	11	-	-
Exports	282	1	-	34	-	-

[Continued]

★ 2051 ★

Slaves: Origin and Destination, 1768-1772 - I

[Continued]

Year and origin or destination	Total	New Hampshire	Massachusetts	Rhode Island	Connecticut	New York
West Indies	107	-	-	8	-	-
Continental colonies	175	1	-	26	-	-

Source: "Slave Trade, by Origin and Destination," U.S. Bureau of the Census, *Historical Statistics of the United States, Colonial Times to 1970, Part II*, Bicentennial Edition, p. 1172. *Notes:* (-) Represents zero. 1. Includes Africa.

★ 2052 ★

Slave Trade

Slaves: Origin and Destination, 1768-1772 - II

Year and origin or destination	Pennsylvania	Maryland	Virginia	North Carolina	South Carolina	Georgia	Florida
1772							
Imports	-	175	2,104	155	7,201	328	169
Africa	-	86	1,271	-	5,145	117	-
West Indies	-	82	794	145	2,027	69	19
Continental colonies	-	7	39	10	29	142	150
Exports	20	-	-	5	463	1	-
West Indies	-	-	-	-	-	1	-
Continental colonies	20	-	-	5	463	-	-
1771							
Imports	-	227	762	82	3,100	758	20
Africa	-	194	13	7	2,051	489	-
West Indies	-	28	744	68	998	148	20
Continental colonies	-	6	5	7	51	121	-
Exports	1	2	-	-	297	5	28
West Indies	-	2	-	-	1	-	-
Continental colonies	1	-	-	-	296	5	28
1770							
Imports	-	532	905	115	123	1,144	181
Africa	-	517	631	-	-	875	176
West Indies	-	14	274	103	81	126	-
Continental colonies	-	1	-	12	42	143	5
Exports	-	1	-	19	88	22	-
West Indies	-	1	-	14	5	7	-
Continental colonies	-	-	-	5	83	15	-

[Continued]

★ 2052 ★

Slaves: Origin and Destination, 1768-1772 - II

[Continued]

Year and origin or destination	Pennsylvania	Maryland	Virginia	North Carolina	South Carolina	Georgia	Florida
1769							
Imports	10	203	493	169	4,888	687	276
Africa	-	180	234	36	4,138	448	119
West Indies	10	23	258	79	675	91	82
Colonial colonies	-	-	1	54	75	148	75
Exports	-	1	-	5	298	28	-
West Indies	-	1	-	5	3	-	-
Continental colonies	-	-	-	-	295	28	-
1768							
Imports	-	301	354	198	249	1,001	278
West Indies[1]	-	288	354	170	187	971	130
Continental colonies	-	13	-	28	62	30	148
Exports	-	14	-	14	39	61	119
West Indies	-	1	-	1	-	5	92
Continental colonies	-	13	-	13	39	56	27

Source: "Slave Trade, by Origin and Destination," U.S. Bureau of the Census, *Historical Statistics of the United States, Colonial Times to 1970, Part II*, Bicentennial Edition, p. 1172. *Notes:* (-) Represents zero. 1. Includes Africa.

★ 2053 ★

Slave Trade

Value of Slaves Imported, 1768

[In thousands of pounds sterling]

Overseas area of trade and major colonial region	Exports	Imports	Shipping earnings	Other invisible earnings	Value of slaves imported
All areas	2,403	3,489	561	171	83
Northern colonies	96	224	5	2	-
New England	416	714	296	82	3
Middle colonies	420	1,209	165	53	1
Upper south	929	825	94	33	24
Lower south	538	452	94	33	50
Florida, Bahama, and Bermuda Islands	4	65	1	1	5
Great Britain and Ireland	1,429	2,837	144	35	1
Northern colonies	20	208	1	-	1
New England	89	441	55	15	1
Middle colonies	155	1,005	61	11	1
Upper south	784	728	27	9	1
Lower south	380	399	27	9	1
Florida, Bahama, and Bermuda Islands	1	56	-	-	1

[Continued]

★ 2053 ★

Value of Slaves Imported, 1768

[Continued]

Overseas area of trade and major colonial region	Exports	Imports	Shipping earnings	Other invisible earnings	Value of slaves imported
Southern Europe and Wine Islands	378	78	109	33	1
Northern colonies	68	6	3	1	1
New England	62	15	39	12	1
Middle colonies	103	35	39	12	1
Upper south	72	15	28	8	1
Lower south	73	6	28	8	1
Florida, Bahama, and Bermuda Islands	-	1	-	-	1
West Indies	583	574	293	103	1
Northern colonies	8	10	1	1	1
New England	252	258	193	55	1
Middle colonies	162	169	62	30	1
Upper south	73	82	36	16	1
Lower south	85	47	36	16	1
Florida, Bahama, and Bermuda Islands	3	8	1	1	1
Africa	13	-	3	-	1
New England	13	-	3	-	1
Middle colonies	(Z)	-	-	-	1
Upper south	-	-	-	-	1
Lower south	-	-	-	-	1
Florida, Bahama, and Bermuda Islands	-	-	-	-	1

Source: "Value of Commodity Exports and Imports, Earnings, and Value of Slaves Imported into British North American Colonies: 1768 to 1772," U.S. Bureau of the Census. *Historical Statistics of the United States, Colonial Times to 1970*, Bicentennial Edition, p. 1183. *Notes:* (-) Represents zero. (Z) Less than 500 pounds sterling. 1. Imports of slaves in 1768 were not given in the source by place of origin.

★ 2054 ★

Slave Trade

Value of Slaves Imported, 1769

[In thousands of pounds sterling]

Overseas area of trade and major colonial region	Exports	Imports	Shipping earnings	Other invisible earnings	Value of slaves imported
All areas	2,947	3,014	607	224	240
Northern colonies	122	296	7	3	-
New England	464	616	313	97	(Z)
Middle colonies	553	645	176	76	(Z)
Upper south	1,238	892	110	47	226
Lower south	551	498	110	47	205
Florida, Bahama, and Bermuda Islands	19	67	1	1	8
Great Britain and Ireland	1,620	2,099	147	35	-

[Continued]

★ 2054 ★

Value of Slaves Imported, 1769

[Continued]

Overseas area of trade and major colonial region	Exports	Imports	Shipping earnings	Other invisible earnings	Value of slaves imported
Northern colonies	26	288	1	-	-
New England	90	228	62	16	-
Middle colonies	120	325	57	9	-
Upper south	990	774	27	10	-
Lower south	379	429	27	10	-
Florida, Bahama, and Bermuda Islands	15	55	-	-	-
Southern Europe and Wine Islands	604	81	145	56	-
Northern colonies	87	4	4	2	-
New England	70	26	46	14	-
Middle colonies	225	30	52	23	-
Upper south	153	14	43	17	-
Lower south	69	5	43	17	-
Florida, Bahama, and Bermuda Islands	-	2	-	-	-
West Indies	699	834	299	133	46
Northern colonies	9	4	2	1	-
New England	281	362	195	67	(Z)
Middle colonies	207	290	64	44	(Z)
Upper south	95	104	37	20	11
Lower south	103	64	37	20	32
Florida, Bahama, and Bermuda Islands	4	10	1	1	3
Africa	24	-	4	-	194
New England	23	-	4	-	(Z)
Middle colonies	1	-	-	-	-
Upper south	-	-	-	-	16
Lower south	(Z)	-	-	-	173
Florida, Bahama, and Bermuda Islands	-	-	-	-	4

Source: "Value of Commodity Exports and Imports, Earnings, and Value of Slaves Imported into British North American Colonies: 1768 to 1772," U.S. Bureau of the Census. *Historical Statistics of the United States, Colonial Times to 1970, Part I,* Bicentennial Edition, p. 1182. *Note:* (-) Represents zero. (Z) Less than 500 pounds sterling.

★ 2055 ★

Slave Trade

Value of Slaves Imported, 1770

[In thousands of pounds sterling]

Overseas area of trade and major colonial region	Exports	Imports	Shipping earnings	Other invisible earnings	Value of slaves imported
All areas	2,983	3,991	615	230	108
Northern colonies	155	439	8	3	-
New England	496	821	323	100	-
Middle colonies	609	1,067	188	84	3
Upper south	1,169	1,234	95	42	53
Lower south	534	362	95	42	45
Florida, Bahama, and Bermuda Islands	20	68	1	1	7
Great Britain and Ireland	1,582	3,038	151	35	-
Northern colonies	39	423	1	-	-
New England	96	457	66	16	-
Middle colonies	139	717	59	10	-
Upper south	951	1,117	25	9	-
Lower south	340	261	25	9	-
Florida, Bahama, and Bermuda Islands	17	63	-	-	-
Southern Europe and Wine Islands	565	76	126	50	-
Northern colonies	106	6	5	2	-
New England	62	14	42	13	-
Middle colonies	214	43	51	23	-
Upper south	116	5	28	12	-
Lower south	67	7	28	12	-
Florida, Bahama, and Bermuda Islands	-	1	-	-	-
West Indies	815	877	322	145	23
Northern colonies	10	10	2	1	-
New England	318	350	205	71	-
Middle colonies	255	307	75	51	(Z)
Upper south	102	112	39	21	10
Lower south	127	94	39	21	12
Florida, Bahama, and Bermuda Islands	3	4	1	1	(Z)
Africa	21	-	4	-	85
New England	20	-	4	-	-
Middle colonies	1	-	-	-	3
Upper south	-	-	-	-	43
Lower south	-	-	-	-	33
Florida, Bahama, and Bermuda Islands	-	-	-	-	7

Source: "Value of Commodity Exports and Imports, Earnings, and Value of Slaves Imported into British North American Colonies: 1768 to 1772," U.S. Bureau of the Census. *Historical Statistics of the United States, Colonial Times to 1970, Part I*, Bicentennial Edition, p. 1182. *Note:* (-) Represents zero. (Z) Less than 500 pounds sterling.

★ 2056 ★

Slave Trade

Value of Slaves Imported, 1771

[In thousands of pounds sterling]

Overseas area of trade and major colonial region	Exports	Imports	Shipping earnings	Other invisible earnings	Value of slaves imported
All areas	3,252	6,104	626	223	182
Northern colonies	332	375	14	6	-
New England	500	1,783	348	109	(Z)
Middle colonies	527	1,758	174	65	(Z)
Upper south	1,256	1,464	89	42	37
Lower south	593	632	89	42	141
Florida, Bahama, and Bermuda Islands	44	92	1	1	4
Great Britain and Ireland	1,866	5,346	158	39	-
Northern colonies	83	353	2	1	-
New England	88	1,446	60	18	-
Middle colonies	127	1,551	66	9	-
Upper south	1,081	1,339	30	11	-
Lower south	446	572	30	11	-
Florida, Bahama, and Bermuda Islands	41	85	-	-	-
Southern Europe and Wine Islands	557	67	117	47	-
Northern colonies	236	12	10	4	-
New England	78	15	55	21	-
Middle colonies	146	22	36	15	-
Upper south	65	10	16	7	-
Lower south	32	7	16	7	-
Florida, Bahama, and Bermuda Islands	-	1	-	-	-
West Indies	813	691	337	137	79
Northern colonies	13	10	2	1	-
New England	319	322	225	70	(Z)
Middle colonies	253	185	69	41	(Z)
Upper south	110	115	40	24	29
Lower south	115	53	40	24	46
Florida, Bahama, and Bermuda Islands	3	6	1	1	4
Africa	16	-	2	-	103
New England	15	-	2	-	-
Middle colonies	1	-	-	-	-
Upper south	-	-	-	-	8
Lower south	(Z)	-	-	-	96
Florida, Bahama, and Bermuda Islands	-	-	-	-	-

Source: "Value of Commodity Exports and Imports, Earnings, and Value of Slaves Imported into British North American Colonies: 1768 to 1772, " U.S. Bureau of the Census, *Historical Statistics of the United States, Colonial Times to 1970*. Bicentennial Edition, p. 1182. *Note:* (-) Represents zero. (Z) Less than 500 pounds sterling.

★ 2057 ★

Slave Trade

Value of Slaves Imported, 1772

[In thousands of pounds sterling]

Overseas area of trade and major colonial region	Exports	Imports	Shipping earnings	Other invisible earnings	Value of slaves imported
All areas	3,487	5,128	643	261	392
Northern colonies	229	417	12	4	-
New England	509	1,335	354	113	(Z)
Middle colonies	688	1,332	181	92	1
Upper south	1,219	1,244	95	51	89
Lower south	800	727	95	51	300
Florida, Bahama, and Bermuda Islands	42	73	1	1	1
Great Britain and Ireland	1,902	4,080	145	38	-
Northern colonies	40	394	2	-	-
New England	78	912	60	17	-
Middle colonies	105	979	55	8	-
Upper south	1,003	1,100	28	13	-
Lower south	637	635	28	13	-
Florida, Bahama, and Bermuda Islands	39	60	-	-	-
Southern Europe and Wine Islands	592	84	116	54	-
Northern colonies	168	12	8	3	-
New England	59	20	48	16	-
Middle colonies	237	32	40	24	-
Upper south	96	10	20	11	-
Lower south	32	9	20	11	-
Florida, Bahama, and Bermuda Islands	-	1	-	-	-
West Indies	964	964	365	169	126
Northern colonies	21	11	2	1	-
New England	347	403	235	80	(Z)
Middle colonies	344	321	83	60	(Z)
Upper south	120	134	44	27	35
Lower south	129	83	44	27	90
Florida, Bahama, and Bermuda Islands	3	12	1	1	1
Africa	29	-	5	-	266
New England	25	-	5	-	-
Middle colonies	2	-	-	-	1
Upper south	-	-	-	-	54
Lower south	2	-	-	-	210
Florida, Bahama, and Bermuda Islands	-	-	-	-	-

Source: "Value of Commodity Exports and Imports, Earnings, and Value of Slaves Imported into British North American Colonies: 1768 to 1772," U.S. Bureau of the Census. *Historical Statistics of the United States, Colonial Times to 1970, Part I*, Bicentennial Edition, p. 1182. *Note:* (-) Represents zero. (Z) Less than 500 pounds sterling.

Slaves Escaped

★ 2058 ★

Underground Railroad Networks, 1830-1860

Northern states, from Maine to Kansas, were dotted with underground railroad stations. Between 1830 and 1860 more than 9,000 slaves escaped through the Philadelphia route. During the same period in Ohio, 40,000 fugitives are said to have escaped by underground railroads. Some also escaped from Texas and the Southwest and settled in Mexico. A colony of about 300 blacks lived in Nacimiento Coahuila, Mexico, in 1913, and was said to have been made up to descendants of fugitive slaves and black American soldiers who fought with the United States Army to drive the French out of Mexico.

Source: "The Underground Railroad," Monroe N. Work, ed., *Negro Year Book: An Annual Encyclopedia of the Negro*, 1913, p. 69.

Taxable Persons

★ 2059 ★

Taxable Persons in Maryland, 1755 - I

Account of Maryland population in 1755[1].

County	Taxable persons over sixteen years of age										
	Whites			Mulattoes				[C4]Blacks			
	Free Men	Servants		Free		Slaves		Free		Slaves	
		Men hired or indentured	Men convicts	Men	Women	Men	Women	Men	Women	Men	Women
Anne Arundel[2]	1534	438	184	16	22	25	11	8	4	1472	1060
Baltimore	2630	595	472	36	21	25	16	2	2	1144	833
Calvert	609	124	-	24	8	-	4	-	1	550	519
Cecil	1345	390	47	2	12	120	86	-	2	256	216
Charles	1929	173	205	60	36	48	33	3	1	1196	950
Dorset	1950	172	7	9	7	9	22	7	3	624	514
Frederick	2775	216	94	23	4	10	24	45	26	437	314
Kent	1454	365	82	8	13	7	9	10	5	690	523
Prince George's	1515	255	73	17	21	37	43	3	3	1278	151
Queen Anne's	1745	284	287	18	20	33	32	8	9	643	572
St. Mary's	1561	194	29	16	17	38	27	16	5	822	761
Somerset	1348	31	1	23	16	15	15	4	3	637	571

[Continued]

★ 2059 ★

Taxable Persons in Maryland, 1755 - I

[Continued]

County	Taxable persons over sixteen years of age										
	Whites			Mulattoes				[C4]Blacks			
	Free Men	Servants		Free		Slaves		Free		Slaves	
		Men hired or indentured	Men convicts	Men	Women	Men	Women	Men	Women	Men	Women
Talbot	1223	294	25	24	18	72	63	12	3	647	595
Worcester	1768	45	1	31	32	3	7	1	2	401	359

Source: "Account of Maryland Population in 1755," James M. Wright, *The Free Negro in Maryland, 1634-1860*, p. 84. *Notes:* 1. Gentleman's Magazine, *1764*, p. 261. 2. Order of presentation is here changed to alphabetical.

★ 2060 ★

Taxable Persons

Taxable Persons in Maryland, 1755 - II

Account of Maryland population in 1755[1].

County	Persons not taxable								
	Whites					Mulattoes		Blacks	
	Clergy	Men poor	Women	Hired or indentured	Convicts	Free	Slaves	Free	Slaves
Anne Arundel[2]	3	64	1539	93	51	4	15	6	92
Baltimore	4	58	2587	200	87	14	4	8	47
Calvert	2	20	639	61	-	2	15	7	39
Cecil	1	33	1186	282	8	-	2	2	13
Charles	4	51	1777	106	78	17	5	2	32
Dorset	3	44	2097	126	-	8	8	2	44
Frederick	1	45	2213	163	32	6	2	4	13
Kent	2	34	1448	181	12	6	9	6	35
Prince George's	3	44	1680	55	27	8	7	2	88
Queen Anne's	3	31	1843	159	73	3	6	3	32
St. Mary's	3	61	1806	164	13	16	14	3	49
Somerset	3	61	1446	37	-	-	1	2	37
Talbot	2	34	1296	160	4	10	1	4	30
Worcester	1	57	1964	37	1	1	10	7	44

Source: "Account of Maryland Population in 1755," James M. Wright, *The Free Negro in Maryland, 1634-1860*, p. 84. *Notes:* 1. Gentleman's Magazine, *1764*, p. 261. 2. Order of presentation is here changed to alphabetical.

Chapter 18
SPORTS AND LEISURE

Amateur Sports

★ 2061 ★

Basketball: The Beginning of Amateur Basketball among Black Groups, 1906

"In 1906 basketball had invaded the black YMCAs and later the YWCAs. These were teams in the eastern cities of New York, Washington, Jersey City, and Philadelphia. The Smart Set Athletic Club of Brooklyn was the first organized black basketball team in 1906."

Source: "Chalk, *Black College Sport*, 1976, p. 72. Primary source: Chalk, Ocania, *Black College Sport*. New York: Dodd, Mead and Company, 1976. Published by permission.

★ 2062 ★

Amateur Sports

Golf: Black Golfers in a National Amateur Tournament, 1943

"Eight Negro golfers...were all eliminated in the All-American Amateur Golf Championship at the Tam O'Shanter Country Club by nightfall of the second day, Tuesday, July 20, 1943. [The] high scorer among the colored entrants [had] an 82 on the first and an 80 on the second day; just 2 strokes over the qualifying score."

Source: "Golf," *The Negro Handbook, 1944*, 1944, p. 244. Primary source: Compiled by Dr. Edwin B. Henderson. Published by permission.

College Sports

★ 2063 ★

Basketball: The Beginning of Basketball in Black Colleges, 1900

"It is not known when the first Negroes actually played basketball. Fisk University reports that its students were competing in basketball as early as 1900 at the intramural level."

Source: Chalk, *Black College Sports*, 1976, p. 71. Primary source: Chalk, Ocania, *Black College Sport*. New York: Dodd, Mead and Company, 1976. Published by permission.

★ 2064 ★

College Sports

Football: The Beginning of Football in Black Colleges, 1892

"The first Negro intercollegiate [football] game was played on Tuesday, December 27, 1892, between Biddle University and Livingstone College on the Livingstone campus in Salisbury, North Carolina."

Source: Chalk, *Black College Sport*, 1976, p. 197. Primary source: Chalk, Ocania, *Black College Sport*. New York: Dodd, Mead and Company, 1976. Published by permission.

★ 2065 ★

College Sports

Track: The Beginning of Track and Field in Black Colleges, 1920s

"It was in the 1920s that [track and field] meets comparable to those that had been held in the white colleges started in the black colleges. On May 4, 1921, the first big college meet by the Colored Intercollegiate Athletic Association was held at Howard University....It was not only the Negro colleges in the South, but Negro colleges throughout the country had established track athletics by the 1920s."

Source: Chalk, *Black College Sport*, 1976, pp. 318 and 322. Primary source: Chalk, Ocania, *Black College Sport*. New York: Dodd, Mead and Company, 1976. Published by permission.

Leisure

★ 2066 ★

Activities: Leisure Pursuits of Rural Black persons in the 1920s

Fishing	193
Hunting	175
Hunting and Fishing	92
Sitting Down	88
Church	77
Lodge	63
Reading	48
Doing Nothing	47
Visiting	47
Singing and playing musical instruments	23
Talking	19
Knocking About	16
Working Around House	15
Gambling	14
Card Games	13
Drinking Liquor	10
Living Around	24
No answer	36
Total	1,000

Source: "Chief Leisure Time Activities of Rural Negroes," *The Annals*, vol. 140, November, 1928, p. 272. Primary source: Washington, Forrester B., "Recreational Facilities for the Negro," in King, Clyde L. (Ed.), *The Annals*, vol., 140, November, 1928.

★ 2067 ★

Leisure

Facilities: Amusement Parks for Blacks, c. 1918-1919

City	Number	City	Number
Joplin, Mo.	1	Birmingham, Ala.	1
Lexington, Ky.	1	Atlanta, Ga.	1
Washington, D.C.	1	Macon, Ga.	1
Baltimore, Md.	1	Norfolk, Va.	2

Source: "Commercial Amusement Parks for Negroes," *The Annals*, vol., 140, November, 1928, p. 281. Primary source: Washington, Forrester B., "Recreational Facilities for the Negro," in King, Clyde L. (Ed.), *The Annals*, vol., 140, November, 1928.

★ 2068 ★

Leisure

Facilities: Country Clubs and Golf Courses for Black Persons in the 1920s

Name of City	Country Club	Country Club and Golf Course
Newark, N.J.	0	1
Indianapolis, Ind.	1	1
Baltimore, Md.	1	0
Detroit, Mich.	1	0
Washington, D.C.	1	0
Lexington, Ky.	0	1
Oakland, Cal.	1	0
Springfield, Ill.	0	1
Fort Wayne, Ind.	1	0
Jacksonville, Fla.	0	1
Philadelphia, Pa.	1	0
San Francisco, Cal.	1	1
Los Angeles, Cal.	1	0
Atlanta, Ga.	1	1
Columbus, Ga.	1	0

Source: [Untitled Table], *The Annals*, vol. 140, November, 1928, p. 280. Primary source: Washington, Forrester B., "Recreational Facilities for the Negro," in King, Clyde L. (Ed.), *The Annals*, vol., 140, November, 1928.

★ 2069 ★

Leisure

Facilities: Degree of Segregation in Commercial Facilities in 17 Southern and 40 Northern Cities in the 1920s

Commercial Amusement	Whites Only		Com. Segrega.		Some Segrega.		No. Segrega.		No Facilities	
	South. Cities	North. Cities	South. Cities	North. Cities	South. Cities	North. Cities	South. Cities	North. Cities	South. Cities	North. Cities
Moving picture theatres	4	0	3	0	10	33	0	7	0	0
Pictures and vaudeville houses	2	0	2	0	10	24	--	16	3	0
Outdoor amusement parks	2	3	10	0	0	19	0	11	5	7
Legitimate theatres	3	0	0	0	11	26	0	14	3	0

Source: Adapted by the editors from "Commercial Amusement in Seventeen Southern Cities" and "Commercial Amusement in Forty Northern Cities," *The Annals*, vol. 140, November, 1928, p. 276. Primary source: Washington, Forrester B., "Recreational Facilities for the Negro," in King, Clyde L. (Ed.), *The Annals*, vol., 140, November, 1928.

★ 2070 ★

Leisure

Facilities: Degree of Segregation in Private Recreation in 17 Southern and 40 Northern Cities in the 1920s

Commercial Amusement	Whites Only		Com. Segrega.		Some Segrega.		No. Segrega.		No Facilities	
	South. Cities	North. Cities	South. Cities	North. Cities	South. Cities	North. Cities	South. Cities	North. Cities	South. Cities	North. Cities
Recreation centers, settlements, community centers	7	5	3	24	[1]	6	[1]	5	7	--
Playgrounds	9	0	2	1	[1]	34	[1]	5	6	--
Y.M.C.A.	2	2	15	22	[1]	6	[1]	10	0	--
Boy Scouts	14	0	3	14	[1]	14	[1]	12	0	--
Summer Camps	12	--	5	13	[1]	9	[1]	18	--	--
Swimming Pools	10	--	6	4	[1]	30	[1]	6	1	--
Camp Fire Girls	15	--	2	18	[1]	22	[1]	10	0	--

Source: Adapted by the editors from "Private Recreation (Social Service) in Seventeen Southern Cities" and "Private Recreation (Social Service) in Forty Northern Cities," *The Annals*, vol. 140, November, 1928, p. 275. Primary source: Washington, Forrester B., "Recreational Facilities for the Negro," in King, Clyde L. (Ed.), *The Annals*, vol., 140, November, 1928. *Note:* 1. Column not provided for Southern cities.

★ 2071 ★

Leisure

Facilities: Degree of Segregation in Public Recreation in 17 Southern and 40 Northern Cities in the 1920s

Recreation/Region	Facilities for Whites Only	Complete Segregation of Whites and Negroes	Some Segregation	No Segregation	No Facilities for Either Race
17 Southern Cities					
Playgrounds	0	8	0	0	3
Parks	4	13	0	0	0
Recreation centers	3	3	0	0	11
Bathing beaches	3	11	0	0	4
Swimming pools	10	6	0	0	1
40 Northern pools					
Playgrounds	0	0	7	33	0
Parks	0	0	0	40	0
Recreation centers	0	2	23	12	3
Bathing beaches	5	11	12	0	12
Swimming pools	3	2	29	3	3

Source: Adapted by the editors from "Public Recreation in Seventeen Southern Cities" and "Public Recreation in Forty Northern Cities," *The Annals*, vol. 140, November, 1928, p. 274. Primary source: Washington, Forrester B., "Recreational Facilities for the Negro," in King, Clyde L. (Ed.), *The Annals*, vol., 140, November, 1928.

★ 2072 ★

Leisure

Organizations: Dates when Organized and Membership (c. 1913) of Black Fraternal Organizations

Organization	Date Organized	Membership
Masons	1808	App. 150,000
Odd Fellows	1843	463,430
Knights of Pythias of Europe, Asia, Africa, North and South America	1864	>100,000
Knights of Pythias (Eastern and Western Hemisphere)	[1]	[1]
Improved Benevolent and Protective Order of Elks of the World	1899	>1,500
United Order of True Reformers	1881	[1]
Grand United Order of Galilean Fishermen	1856	[1]
United Brothers of Friendship	1861	[1]
Grand United Order of Wise Men and Women	1901	[1]
United Order of Good Shepherds	1906	[1]
Royal Knights of King David	1884	[1]
National Order of Mosaic Templars of America	1882	[1]
Knights and Daughters of Tabor	1871	[1]
Independent Order of St. Luke	1867	[1]
Grand United Order of Brothers and Sisters, Sons and Daughters of Moses		
Grand United Order of Sons and Daughters of Peace	1900	[1]
Royal Circle of Friends of the World	1909	App. 25,000
General Grand Order of Brothers and Sisters of Love and Charity	[1]	[1]

Source: Adapted by the editors from "Fraternal Organizations," *Negro Year Book and Annual Encyclopedia of the Negro*, 1913, pp. 275-279. Primary source: Work, Monroe N. (Ed.), *Negro Year Book and Annual Encyclopedia of the Negro*. Tuskegee Institute, Ala.: Negro Year Book Co., 1913. *Note:* 1. Information not supplied.

Olympic Sports

★ 2073 ★

Participation: Black Participation in Olympics in 1904, 1928, 1932, and 1936

"The first Negro American to compete in Olympic competition [competed] in the 1904 games, which were held in St. Louis....Three American Negroes were members of the 1928 track and field team....When the [Olympic] tryouts were completed in 1932, four Negroes were on their way to Los Angeles. After the 1936 tryouts, ten Negroes were on their way to Berlin....Of the ten black athletes on the track and field team, nine won either a gold, bronze, or silver medal."

Source: Chalk, *Black College Sport,* 1976, pp. 342, 351, 356, and 363. Primary source: Chalk, Ocania, *Black College Sport*. New York: Dodd, Mead and Company, 1976. Published by permission.

Professional Sports

★ 2074 ★

Baseball: Baseball Trivia – RBI Producers with Few At Bats, 1929-1973, and Big Homer Producers With and Without the HR Title, 1927-1971

Item	Total number	Number Black Americans
Players with most RBIs and Fewer than 400 at bats (1929-1973)	6	1
Players with most homers in a season who failed to win HR title (1927-1971)		
Home run runners-up	12	4
Home run champions	12	3

Source: Compiled by the editors from "Players with Most RBIs and Fewer than 400 At Bats" and "Players with Most Homers in a Season who Failed to Win HR Title," *Baseball Digest,* September, 1993, p. 12 and p. 13. Primary source: *Baseball Digest*. Evanston, Ill: Century Publishing Co.

★ 2075 ★

Professional Sports

Baseball: Black League (East) Batting Champions, 1923-1948

Year	Player	G	AB	H	BA
1923	Biz Mackey, Hilldales	42	150	66	.440
1924	John Lloyd, Bacharachs	41	144	64	.444[1]
1925	Oscar Charleston, Harrisburg	52	179	77	.430
1926	Luther Farrell, Bacharachs	47	141	52	.369
1927	Jud Wilson, Baltimore	57	212	105	.495
1929	Chino Smith, Lincolns		237	110	.464
1930					
1931					
1932					
Crawfords	40 127 59 .464				
Crawfords	34 117 45 .384				
Crawfords	31 109 48 .440				
Crawfords	38 116 53 .457				
1937	Buck Leonard, Grays				.500[1]
1938	Buck Leonard, Grays		50	24	.480[1]
1939	Bill Wright, Baltimore	28	101	49	.488
1940	Pee Wee Butts, Baltimore	24	83	35	.391[1]
1941	Monte Irvin, Newark		76	30	.395
1942	Josh Gibson, Grays	42	126	57	.452
1943	Josh Gibson, Grays	49	149	75	.503
1944	Fred Austin, Philadelphia	34	136	53	.390
1945	Josh Gibson, Grays	44	145	57	.393
1946	Monte Irvin, Newark	59	213	84	.394
1947	Luis Marquez, Grays		230	96	.417
1948	Buck Leonard, Grays				.395

Source: Holway, *Voices from the Great Black Baseball Leagues*, "Negro League Batting Champions," pp. 19-20. Primary source: Holway, John. *Voices from the Great Baseball Leagues*. New York: Dodd, Mead & Company, 1975. *Note:* 1. Incomplete; based on available information.

★ 2076 ★

Professional Sports

Baseball: Black League (West) Batting Champions, 1923-1948

Year	Player	G	AB	H	BA
1921	Oscar Charleston, St. Louis		127	54	.425[1]
1927	Sandy Thompson, Chicago		247	109	.441
1929	Cool Papa Bell, St. Louis		102	39	.382[1]
1930	Willie Wells, St. Louis				.409[1]
1933[2]				Josh Gibson	

[Continued]

★ 2076 ★

Baseball: Black League (West) Batting Champions, 1923-1948

[Continued]

Year	Player	G	AB	H	BA
1934[2]				Josh Gibson	
1935[2]				Josh Gibson	
1936[2]				Josh Gibson	
1944	Sam Jethroe, Cleveland	68	275	97	.353
1945	Sam Jethroe, Cleveland	56	214	84	.393
1946	Buck O'Neil, Kansas City	51	173	61	.353
1947	Hank Thompson, Kansas City				.344
1948	Artie Wilson, Birminhgam				.402

Source: Holway, *Voices from the Great Black Baseball Leagues*, "Negro League Batting Champions," pp. 19-20. Primary source: Holway, John. *Voices from the Great Baseball Leagues*. New York: Dodd, Mead & Company, 1975. *Notes:* 1. Incomplete; based on available information. 2. Only a single National League operated 1933-36.

★ 2077 ★

Professional Sports

Baseball: Champions of the Black Baseball League, 1921-1950

[World Series winner, if any, in italics. Loser of Play-off, if any, is in parentheses].

Year	West	East
1921	Chicago	Bacharachs, Philadelphia Hilldale
1922		
1923	Kansas City	Hilldale
1924	Kansas City	Hilldale
1925	Kansas City (St. Louis)	Hilldale
1926	Chicago (Kansas City)	Bacharachs
1927	Chicago (Birmingham)	Bacharachs
1928	St. Louis (Chicago)	-
1929	Kansas City	Baltimore
1930	St. Louis (Detroit)	Homestead Grays (Lincoln Giants)
1931	St. Louis	-
1932	Chicago (Nashville)	-
1933	Chicago (Pittsburgh)[1]	-
1934	Philadelphia (Chicago)[1]	-
1935	Pittsburgh (Cubans)[1]	-
1936	Pittsburgh/Washington[1]	-
1937	Kansas City (Chicago)	Homestead Grays
1938	Memphis/Atlanta[2]	Homestead Grays
1939	Kansas City (St. Louis)	Baltimore, (Grays)[3]
1940	Kansas City	Homestead Grays
1941	Kansas City	Homestead Grays (Cubans)
1942	Kansas City	Homestead Grays
1943	Birmingham (Chicago)	Homestead Grays
1944	Birmingham	Homestead Grays
1945	Cleveland	Homestead Grays
1946	Kansas City	Newark

[Continued]

★ 2077 ★

Baseball: Champions of the Black Baseball League, 1921-1950

[Continued]

Year	West	East
1947	Cleveland	Cubans (Newark)
1948	Birmingham (Kansas City)	Homestead Grays (Baltimore)
1949	Chicago (Kansas City)	Baltimore
1950	Kansas City	Indianapolis

Source: Holway, *Voices from the Great Black Baseball Leagues*, "Negro League Pennant & Winners," p. 18. Primary source: Holway, John. *Voices from the Great Black Baseball Leagues*. New York: Dodd, Mead & Company, 1975. *Notes:* 1. Only a single National League operated 1933-36. 2. No play-offs were held 1936 and 1938; divided season produced two champions. 3. Homestead finished first in 1939 but lost play-off to third place Baltimore.

★ 2078 ★

Professional Sports

Baseball: Drawing Power of "The Negro League," 1942

"The Washington Homestead Grays put Negro baseball among the top-drawing sports when they attracted over 125,000 fans in ten appearances at Griffith Stadium in Washington, D.C. The Grays won the Negro National League Championship for the third straight year, but were beaten by the Kansas City Monarchs in four straight games of the Negro World Series."

Source: "Baseball," *The Negro Handbook, 1944*, 1944, pp. 238-239. Primary source: Compiled by Leon Hardwick and Arthur M. Carter. Published by permission.

★ 2079 ★

Professional Sports

Baseball: Early Black Baseball Players, 1872-1927

"Back in 1872 Bud Fowler, a Negro, broke the color line and became the first man of his race to play in organized ball. Other blacks followed, and in 1884 two brothers from Ohio, Welday and Moses Fleetwood Walker, briefly crashed the major leagues with Toledo of the old American Association.

The first organized Negro team we know of was formed in 1885 in Babylon, Long Island, by waiters of Babylon's Argyle Hotel...By 1886 they were strong enough to beat the Cincinnati Red Stockings of the National League. A year later they almost beat the champion Detroit Tigers, losing 6-4 in the ninth on an error.

[Continued]

★ 2079 ★

Baseball: Early Black Baseball Players, 1872-1927

[Continued]

[In February 1920] Rube Foster...called a meeting of several western club owners in Kansas City...and proposed a revolutionary idea, a Negro National League...And so the first black league was born. It included the American Giants, Indianapolis ABC's, St. Louis Giants, Detroit Stars, and Kansas City Monarchs—the old All Nations team but now all black...Down South the Birmingham Black Barons, a team of coal miners, joined the Negro National League in 1927, with their skinny rookie named Leroy "Satchel" Paige."

Source: Adapted by the editors from Holway, *Voices from the Great Black Baseball Leagues,* [Text], 1975, pp. 1-7. Primary source: Holway, John. *Voices from the Great Black Baseball Leagues.* New York: Dodd, Mead & Company, 1975.

★ 2080 ★

Professional Sports

Baseball: League Leaders, 1901-1975

CATEGORY	AMERICAN LEAGUE		NATIONAL LEAGUE	
	Number Black Americans	Earliest Year	Number Black Americans	Earliest Year
Batting average	6	1964	5	1949
Runs batted in	5	1954	12	1951
Home runs	6	1952	14	1955

Source: Compiled by the editors from "Year-By-Year Leaders, American and National Leagues, Records Since 1900," *Baseball Digest,* September, 1993, pp. 92-95. Primary source: *Baseball Digest.* Evanston, Ill: Century Publishing Co.

★ 2081 ★

Professional Sports

Baseball: Retired Uniform Numbers, through 1975

Team	AMERICAN LEAGUE			NATIONAL LEAGUE	
	Total Retired Numbers	Black American Retired Numbers	Team	Total Retired Numbers	Black American Retired Numbers
Baltimore	5	2	Atlanta	4	1
Boston	4	0	Chicago	2	2
California	3	1	Cincinnati	2	0
Chicago	7	1	Houston	4	1
Cleveland	4	0	Los Angeles	8	3
Detroit	3	0	Montral	2	0

[Continued]

★ 2081 ★

Baseball: Retired Uniform Numbers, through 1975

[Continued]

Team	AMERICAN LEAGUE Total Retired Numbers	AMERICAN LEAGUE Black American Retired Numbers	Team	NATIONAL LEAGUE Total Retired Numbers	NATIONAL LEAGUE Black American Retired Numbers
Kansas City	1	0	New York Mets	3	0
Milwaukee	2	1	Philadelphia	4	0
Minnesota	3	1	Pittsburgh	8	1
New York	13	1	St. Louis	5	2
			San Diego	1	0
			San Francisco/ New York Giants	6	2
Total	45	7		49	12

Source: Compiled by the editors from "Retired Major League Uniform Numbers," *Baseball Digest*, September, 1933, p. 10. Primary source: *Baseball Digest*. Evanston, Ill: Central Publishing Co.

★ 2082 ★

Professional Sports

Basketball: Record of the Renaissance Big Five ("Rens"), Early Black Professional Team, 1923-24 through 1934-35

Games	Won	Lost	Season
23	15	8	1923-1924
79	67	12	1924-1925
98	81	17	1925-1926
103	84	19	1926-1927
131	111	20	1927-1928
126	107	19	1928-1929
132	112	20	1929-1930
136	114	22	1930-1931
138	115	23	1931-1932
128	120	8	1932-1933
140	121	19	1933-1934
139	122	17	1934-1935

Source: Chalk, [Untitled Table], *Pioneers of Black Sport*, 1975, pp. 93-94. Primary source: Chalk, Ocania. *Pioneers of Black Sport*. New York: Dodd, Mead & Co., 1975. Published by permission.

★ 2083 ★

Professional Sports

Boxing: But Who Won the Fight? Black Boxers and "No Decision Bouts"

"Under the old boxing laws, when a bout was stipulated to be a 'no decision' contest, the referee—who was the only judge—was not permitted to render a verdict at the end of the fight.

In certain cities, such as Philadelphia, San Francisco, New York, and Baltimore, a fight ended with neither receiving the verdict unless a knockout was scored or a foul committed.

Jack Johnson fought thirteen no-decision bouts....Joe Walcott, the Barbados Demon, fought in fifteen no-decision contests....Sam Langford engaged in fifty-eight no-decision bouts....Joe Gans fought in eighteen no-decision fights."

Source: Chalk, "No-Decision Bouts," *Pioneers of Black Sport*, 1975, p. 284. Primary source: Chalk, Ocania. *Pioneers of Black Sport*. New York: Dodd, Mead & Co., 1975. Published by permission.

★ 2084 ★

Professional Sports

Boxing: Outstanding Black Boxers – World Heavyweight Champion Joe Louis' 1934-1942 Record

Year	Total bouts	Total won	Total knockouts
1934	12	12	10
1935	14	14	12
1936	6	6	6
1937	5	5	3
1938	3	3	3
1939	4	4	4
1940	4	4	4
1941	7	7	7
1942	2	2	2

Source: Compiled by the editors from "Boxing Records," *The Negro Handbook, 1944*, 1944, p. 244. Primary source: Compiled by Dr. Edwin B. Henderson. Published by permission.

★ 2085 ★

Professional Sports

Boxing: Outstanding Black Boxers – "Beau Jack's" 1940-1943 Record

Year	Total bouts	Total won	Total knockouts
1940	16	12	8
1941	21	17	11
1942	13	13	8
1943	7	5	1

Source: Compiled by the editors from "Boxing Records," *The Negro Handbook, 1944,* 1944, p. 245. Primary source: Compiled by Dr. Edwin B. Henderson. Published by permission.

★ 2086 ★

Professional Sports

Boxing: Outstanding Black Boxers – "Sugar" Ray Robinson's 1940-1943 Record

Year	Total bouts	Total won	Total knockouts
1940	6	6	5
1941	20	20	15
1942	14	14	9
1943	7	6	2

Source: Compiled by the editors from "Boxing Records," *The Negro Handbook, 1944,* 1944, p. 245. Primary source: Compiled by Dr. Edwin B. Henderson. Published by permission.

★ 2087 ★

Professional Sports

Golf: Black Golfers in a National Professional Tournament, 1943

"No one of the thirteen Negro golfers who entered the $10,000 Tam O'Shanter Open Golf Tournament was able to finish for the money prizes."

Source: "Golf," *The Negro Handbook, 1944,* 1944, p. 244. Primary source: Compiled by Dr. Edwin B. Henderson. Published by permission.

Chapter 19
VITAL STATISTICS

Births

★ 2088 ★

Age-Specific Birth Rates, for Women, by Age: Birth Rates 1920-1975

Rates are live births per 1,000 women in specific age group. Data for years prior to 1960 have been adjusted for underregistration.

Year and race	Total, 15 to 44 years[1]	Age of women					
		15 to 19 years	20 to 24 years	25 to 29 years	30 to 34 years	35 to 39 years	40 to 44 years
ALL RACES							
1920[2]	117.9	62.6	168.7	167.2	122.9	90.5	34.5
1930[2]	89.2	56.7	136.8	128.6	93.3	63.3	24.0
1940[2]	79.9	53.4	131.1	119.7	78.6	45.1	15.0
1950[2]	106.2	79.4	190.0	164.4	101.7	53.1	14.9
1960	118.0	89.1	258.1	197.4	112.7	56.2	15.5
1970	87.9	68.3	167.8	145.1	73.3	31.7	8.1
1975	66.7	56.3	114.7	110.3	53.1	19.4	4.6
BLACK AND OTHER RACES							
1920[2]	137.5	106.1	188.0	156.6	100.7	106.2	37.0
1930[2]	105.9	99.9	149.4	114.3	81.9	66.4	24.7
1940[2]	102.4	109.5	158.4	109.8	68.6	50.7	19.0
1950[2]	137.3	145.0	221.9	160.8	101.2	61.9	18.2
1960	153.6	158.2	294.2	214.6	135.6	74.2	22.0
1970	113.0	133.4	196.8	140.1	82.5	42.2	12.6
1975	89.3	108.6	143.5	112.1	59.7	27.6	7.6
BLACK							
1960	153.5	156.1	295.4	218.6	137.1	73.9	21.9
1970	115.4	147.7	202.7	136.3	79.6	41.9	12.5
1975	89.2	113.8	145.1	105.4	54.1	25.4	7.5

[Continued]

★ 2088 ★

Age-Specific Birth Rates, for Women, by Age: Birth Rates 1920-1975

[Continued]

Year and race	Total, 15 to 44 years[1]	Age of women					
		15 to 19 years	20 to 24 years	25 to 29 years	30 to 34 years	35 to 39 years	40 to 44 years
WHITE							
1920[2]	115.4	55.6	165.5	168.6	125.7	88.9	34.3
1930[2]	87.1	50.6	135.0	130.5	94.9	63.0	23.8
1940[2]	77.1	45.6	127.5	121.0	80.1	44.5	14.7
1950[2]	102.3	69.3	185.3	164.6	101.8	52.1	14.5
1960	113.2	79.4	252.8	194.9	109.6	54.0	14.7
1970	84.1	57.4	163.4	145.9	71.9	30.0	7.5
1975	63.0	46.8	109.7	110.0	52.1	18.1	4.1

Source: "Age-Specific Birth Rates for Women, by Age: 1920 to 1975," U.S. Department of Commerce, Bureau of the Census. *The Social and Economic Status of the Black Population in the United States: An Historical View, 1790-1978*, p. 127. Primary source: U.S. Department of Health, Education, and Welfare, National Center for Health Statistics. *Notes:* 1. Rate includes the relatively few births to women of ages 15 to 44. 2. Age-specific rates for 1920 to 1950 are derived by a different methodology than those for subsequent years.

★ 2089 ★

Births

Age-adjusted Birth Rates, 1940-1960

[Rates are live births per 1,000 population.]

Year	Total	White	Nonwhite
Registered births			
1960	31.2	30.2	38.8
1959	31.4	30.3	39.4
Births adjusted for underregistration			
1959	31.7	30.5	40.9
1958	31.6	30.4	40.5
1957	32.2	30.9	41.2
1956	31.5	30.3	40.5
1955	30.5	29.4	39.0
1954	30.2	29.1	38.3
1953	29.2	28.2	36.8
1952	28.6	27.7	35.6
1951	27.9	26.9	35.1
1950	26.3	25.3	33.7
1949	26.5	25.6	33.1
1948	26.5	25.7	32.2
1947	27.8	27.4	30.6
1946	24.9	24.5	27.6
1945	20.9	20.3	25.6
1944	21.6	21.0	26.2
1943	23.0	22.5	26.7
1942	22.3	21.8	25.9

[Continued]

★ 2089 ★

Age-adjusted Birth Rates, 1940-1960

[Continued]

Year	Total	White	Nonwhite
1941	20.3	19.7	25.3
1940	19.4	18.8	24.5

Source: "Age-adjusted Birth Rates by Color: United States, 1940-60." National Center for Health Statistics. *Vital Statistics Rates in the United State, 1940-60.* By Robert D. Grove and Alice M. Hetzel. Washington, D.C.: U.S. Department of Health, Education, and Welfare, Public Health Service, 1968, p. 115.

★ 2090 ★

Births

Attended Live Births and Birth Weight, 1950-1973

Prior to 1960, excludes Alaska and Hawaii. Represents registered births. For number of births, see table 68 in the original source.

Year	Births attended (1,000)			Median birth weight[2]		
	By physician		By midwife, other, and not			
	In hospital[1]	Not in hospital	not specified	Total	White	Negro and other
1950	3,126	252	177	7 lb.-5 oz.	7 lb.-5 oz.	7 lb.-3 oz.
1955	3,819	101	128	7 lb.-5 oz.	7 lb.-5 oz.	7 lb.-1 oz.
1960	4,114	49	94	7 lb.-5 oz.	7 lb.-5 oz.	6 lb.-15 oz.
1965	3,661	33	66	7 lb.-4 oz.	7 lb.-5 oz.	6 lb.-14 oz.
1970[3]	3,708	5	18	7 lb.-4 oz.	7 lb.-5 oz.	6 lb.-14 oz.
1971[3]	3,524	10	23	7 lb.-4 oz.	7 lb.-6 oz.	6 lb.-15 oz.
1972[3]	3,234	7	18	7 lb.-5 oz.	7 lb.-6 oz.	6 lb.-15 oz.
1973[3]	3,115	7	16	7 lb.-5 oz.	7 lb-5 oz.	6 lb.-15 oz.

Source: "Attended Live Births and Birth Weight: 1950to 1973." Bureau of the Census, *Statistical Abstract of the United States, 1975.* Washington, D.C.: U.S. Government Printing Office, 1975, p. 57. Primary source: U.S. National Center for Health Statistics, *Vital Statistics of the United States,* annual. *Notes:* 1. Includes all births in hospitals or institutions and in clinics. 2. For definition of median, see p. xii in original source. 3. Excludes births to nonresident aliens.

★ 2091 ★

Births

Birth Expectations at Certain Ages, 1967

Subject	Age of wife			
	18 to 24	25 to 29	30 to 34	35 to 39
Total number of wives:				
Negro	342	307	309	321
White	3,798	3,420	3,390	3,831
Average number of births to date:				
Negro	1.8	3.0	2.9	4.2
White	1.1	2.3	3.0	3.1
Average number of total children expected:				
Negro	2.8	3.4	4.3	4.2
White	2.9	3.0	3.2	3.2
Percent of expected children already born:				
Negro	64	88	92	98
White	39	75	93	97
Percent of wives expecting no more children:				
Negro	42	73	77	95
White	22	56	85	94

Source: "Selected Data on the Birth Expectations of Wives 18 to 39 Years Old, by Age, for Wives Reporting: 1967." U.S. Bureau of the Census. Current Population Reports, Special Studies, Series P-23, No. 38. *The Social and Economic Status of the Black Population in the United States, 1970.* Washington, D.C.: Government Printing Office, 1970, p. 116. Primary source: U.S. Department of Commerce, Bureau of the Census.

★ 2092 ★

Births

Birth Expectations for Wives, of Household Heads, 1971

Subject	Total 18 to 39 years	Age of wife			
		18 to 24	25 to 29	30 to 34	35 to 39
Total number of reporting wives:					
Negro (thousands)	1,172	363	303	255	251
White (thousands)	15,326	4,207	4,019	3,556	3,544
Average number of births to date:					
Negro	2.7	1.4	2.5	3.5	4.1
White	2.1	6.0	1.9	2.8	3.2
Average number of total children expected:					
Negro	3.3	2.6	3.1	3.8	4.2
White	2.7	2.4	2.6	2.9	3.2
Percent of expected children already born:					
Negro	82	54	81	94	98
White	78	40	74	94	99

[Continued]

★ 2092 ★

Birth Expectations for Wives, of Household Heads, 1971

[Continued]

Subject	Total 18 to 39 years	Age of wife			
		18 to 24	25 to 29	30 to 34	35 to 39
Percent of wives expecting no more children:					
Negro	65	36	61	85	94
White	65	26	58	87	97

Source: "Selected Data on Birth Expectations for Wives 18 to 39 Years Old, of Household Heads." U.S. Bureau of the Census. Current Population Reports, Special Studies, Series P-23, No. 42. *The Social and Economic Status of the Black Population in the United States, 1971.* Washington, D.C.: Government Printing Office, 1972, p. 107. Primary source: U.S. Department of Commerce, Social and Economic Statistics Administration, Bureau of the Census.

★ 2093 ★

Births

Birth Expectations of Wives, 1967 and 1974

Refers to wives 18 to 39 years old in the civillian noninstitutionalized population.

Item	1967, Feb.-Mar. Births expected by wives aged --				1974, June Births expected by wives aged --			
	18-24	25-29	30-34	35-39	18-24	25-29	30-34	35-39
Births expected per 1,000 wives	2,852	3,037	3,288	3,299	2,165	2,335	2,724	3,091
White	2,859	3,001	3,200	3,215	2,154	2,304	2,689	3,040
Negro	2,787	3,407	4,257	4,226	2,215	2,779	3,238	3,642
Total births expected - percent								
White, none	1.3	2.1	3.4	4.9	5.2	4.8	5.0	5.5
1	5.7	4.8	5.9	7.3	11.2	9.5	8.6	8.2
2	37.5	30.0	25.9	25.8	57.1	52.7	37.1	25.5
3	29.6	34.3	27.1	26.6	19.1	22.1	27.0	27.8
4	18.2	17.9	20.7	15.8	5.5	7.5	13.2	16.7
5 or more	7.7	11.0	17.1	19.5	1.9	3.4	9.0	16.3
Negro, none	0.9	2.4	6.1	6.9	4.0	4.1	5.0	5.4
1	9.7	9.1	5.4	13.1	21.9	8.7	10.9	13.1
2	33.1	22.1	18.6	14.7	42.0	36.2	25.8	17.9
3	32.0	27.7	14.9	15.3	20.8	24.3	21.1	17.6
4	18.2	13.3	15.1	10.8	6.6	15.5	11.5	14.8
5 or more	6.2	25.4	39.9	39.2	4.7	11.2	25.8	31.2

Source: "Birth Expectations of Wives, by Age and Race: 1967 and 1974.." Bureau of the Census, *Statistical Abstract of the United States, 1975.* Washington, D.C.: U.S. Government Printing Office, 1975, p. 56. Primary source: U.S. Bureau of the Census, *Current Population Reports,* series P-20, No. 277.

★ 2094 ★

Births

Birth Rate by Race and Ethnicity, 1940-1975

Race/ethnicity	1940	1950	1960	1965	1970	1975
Total	2.30	3.09	3.65	2.91	2.48	1.77
White	2.23	2.98	3.53	2.78	2.39	1.69
Non-White	2.87	3.93	4.52	3.81	3.07	2.28
Black	[3]	[3]	4.54	3.83	3.10	2.24
Total Hispanic[1]						
Mexican						
Puerto Rican						
Cuban						
Other Hispanic[2]						
Non-Hispanic						
White						
Black						

Source: "Average Number of Children Born per Woman, 1940-1986," *U.S. Children and Their Families*, 1989, p. 7. Primary source: National Center for Health Statistics, 1988, *Vital Statistics of the United States, 1986*, Vol. I, Natality, Table 1-6 and NCHS, S.J. Ventura, "Births of Hispanic Parentage, 1980," *Monthly Vital Statistics Report*, Vol. 32, No. 6, Supplement, Table 5. *Notes:* Total fertility rates show the number of children that would be born to 1,000 women if they were subject at each year to the observed age specific fertility rates in a given year. Dividing by 1,000 gives the average number of children that a typical woman would bear under the same assumptions. Because the total fertility rate is unaffected by the differences in the age composition of women 15-49, it is a useful statistic for comparing fertility across different populations. 1. Data on Hispanic origin were obtained from 22 reporting states, accounting for about 90 percent of all Hispanic origin births in the United States, but for only about 57% of all births in the nation. To calculate total fertility rates, it is necessary to know the number of women in each age and ethnicity category. For the states reporting Hispanic origin information on their birth certificates, such data are currently only available during census years. 2. Includes Central and South American and other and unknown Hispanics. 3. Not available.

★ 2095 ★

Births

Birth Rate for Women 14-44 Years Old, by Race, 1800-1970

Based on estimated live births per 1,000 population for specified group. Based on a 50-percent sample of births for 1951-1954, 1956-1966, and 1968- 1970; on 20- to 50-percent sample for 1967. Prior to 1959, births adjusted for underregistration; thereafter, registered live births.

Year	Rate, total population			Rate, women 15-44 years[1]		
	Total	White	Negro and other	Total	White	Negro and other
1970	18.4	17.4	25.1	87.9	84.1	113.0
1969	17.8	16.9	24.4	86.5	82.4	114.8
1968	17.5	16.6	24.2	85.7	81.5	114.9
1967[2]	17.8	16.8	25.0	87.6	83.1	119.8
1966	18.4	17.4	26.1	91.3	86.4	125.9
1965	19.4	18.3	27.6	96.6	91.4	133.9

[Continued]

★ 2095 ★

Birth Rate for Women 14-44 Years Old, by Race, 1800-1970

[Continued]

Year	Rate, total population			Rate, women 15-44 years[1]		
	Total	White	Negro and other	Total	White	Negro and other
1964	21.0	20.0	29.1	105.0	99.9	141.7
1963[3]	21.7	20.7	29.7	108.5	103.7	144.9
1962[3]	22.4	21.4	30.5	112.2	107.5	148.8
1961	23.3	22.2	31.6	117.2	112.2	153.5
1960[4]	23.7	22.7	32.1	118.0	113.2	153.6
1959[5]	24.0	22.9	32.9	118.8	113.9	156.0
1958	24.5	23.3	34.3	120.2	114.9	160.5
1957	25.3	24.0	35.3	122.9	117.7	163.0
1956	25.2	24.0	35.4	121.2	116.0	160.9
1955	25.0	23.8	34.7	118.5	113.8	155.3
1954	25.3	24.2	34.9	118.1	113.6	153.2
1953	25.0	24.0	34.1	115.2	111.0	147.3
1952	25.1	24.1	33.6	113.9	110.1	143.3
1951	24.9	23.9	33.8	111.5	107.7	142.1
1950	24.1	23.0	33.3	106.2	102.3	137.3
1949	24.5	23.6	33.0	107.1	103.6	135.1
1948	24.9	24.0	32.4	107.3	104.3	131.6
1947	26.6	26.1	31.2	113.3	111.8	125.9
1946	24.1	23.6	38.4	101.9	100.4	113.9
1945	20.4	19.7	26.5	85.9	83.4	106.0
1944	21.2	20.5	27.4	88.8	86.3	108.5
1943	22.7	22.1	28.3	94.3	92.3	111.0
1942	22.2	21.5	27.7	91.5	89.5	107.6
1941	20.3	19.5	27.3	83.4	80.7	105.4
1940	19.4	18.6	26.7	79.9	77.1	102.4
1939	18.8	18.0	26.1	77.6	74.8	100.1
1938	19.2	18.4	26.3	79.1	76.5	100.5
1937	18.7	17.9	26.0	77.1	74.4	99.4
1936	18.4	17.6	25.1	75.8	73.3	95.9
1935	18.7	17.9	25.8	77.2	74.5	98.4
1934	19.0	18.1	26.3	78.5	75.8	100.4
1933	18.4	17.6	25.5	76.3	73.7	97.3
1932	19.5	18.7	26.9	81.7	79.0	103.0
1931	20.2	19.5	26.6	84.6	82.4	102.1
1930	21.3	20.6	27.5	89.2	87.1	105.9
1929	21.2	20.5	27.3	89.3	87.3	106.1
1928	22.2	21.5	28.5	93.8	91.7	111.0
1927	23.5	22.7	31.1	99.8	97.1	121.7

[Continued]

★ 2095 ★

Birth Rate for Women 14-44 Years Old, by Race, 1800-1970

[Continued]

Year	Rate, total population			Rate, women 15-44 years[1]		
	Total	White	Negro and other	Total	White	Negro and other
1926	24.2	23.1	33.4	102.6	99.2	130.3
1925	25.1	24.1	34.2	106.6	103.3	134.0
1924	26.1	25.1	34.6	110.9	107.8	135.6
1923	26.0	25.2	33.2	110.5	108.0	130.5
1922	26.2	25.4	33.2	111.2	108.8	130.8
1921	28.1	27.3	35.8	119.8	117.2	140.8
1920	27.7	26.9	35.0	117.9	115.4	137.5
1919	26.1	25.3	32.4	111.2	(NA)	-
1918	28.2	27.6	33.0	119.8	(NA)	-
1917	28.5	27.9	32.9	121.0	(NA)	-
1916	29.1	28.5	-	123.4	121.8	-
1915	29.5	28.9	-	125.0	123.2	-
1914	29.9	29.3	-	126.6	124.6	-
1913	29.5	28.8	-	124.7	122.4	-
1912	29.8	29.0	-	125.8	123.3	-
1911	29.9	29.1	-	126.3	123.6	-
1910	30.1	29.2	-	126.8	123.8	-
1909	30.0	29.2	-	126.8	123.6	-
1900	32.3	30.1	-	-	130	-
1890	(NA)	31.5	-	-	137	-
1880	39.8	35.2	-	-	155	-
1870	(NA)	38.3	-	-	167	-
1860	44.3	41.4	-	-	184	-
1850	(NA)	43.3	-	-	194	-
1840	51.8	48.3	-	-	222	-
1830	(NA)	51.4	-	-	240	-
1820	55.2	52.8	-	-	260	-
1810	-	54.3	-	-	274	-
1800	-	55.0	-	-	278	-

Source: "Birth Rate—Total and for Women 15-44 Years Old, by Race: 1800 to 1970. *Historical Statistics of the United States: Colonial Times to 1970, Part I.* Bicentennial Edition. Washington, D.C.: Government Printing Office, 1975, p. 49. *Notes:* NA not available. 1. Computed by relating total births, regardless of age of mother, to women aged 15-44 years. 2. Based on 20- to 50-percent sample of births. 3. Figures by race exclude New Jersey; State did not require reporting of race. 4. Denotes first year for which figures include Alaska and Hawaii. 5. Includes Alaska.

★ 2096 ★

Births

Birth Rate, by Race and Live-Order, 1940 to 1970

Rates are live births per 1,000 women aged 15-44 years in specified race group. Live-birth order refers to number of children born alive to mother. Prior to 1959, births adjusted for underregistration; thereafter, registered live births. Figures for not stated birth order have been distributed. Based on 50-percent sample of births for 1951-1954, 1956-1966, and 1968-1970; on 20- to 50-percent sample for 1967.

Year and race	Total	Birth rate, by live-birth order						
		1st	2d	3d	4th	5th	6th and 7th	8th and over
Total								
1970	87.9	34.1	24.2	13.7	7.2	3.8	3.2	1.8
1969	86.5	32.8	23.4	13.4	7.4	4.0	3.5	2.0
1968	85.7	32.1	22.5	13.2	7.5	4.2	3.9	2.3
1967	87.6	30.8	22.6	13.9	8.3	4.8	4.5	2.7
1966	91.3	31.0	22.5	14.8	9.2	5.4	5.2	3.2
1965	96.6	29.8	23.4	16.6	10.7	6.4	6.0	3.7
1964	105.0	30.4	25.1	18.8	12.3	7.3	6.9	4.1
1963	108.5	29.9	26.1	19.9	13.1	7.8	7.3	4.3
1962	112.2	30.1	27.0	21.1	13.8	8.2	7.5	4.4
1961	117.2	31.1	28.4	22.4	14.6	8.5	7.8	4.5
1960[2]	118.0	31.1	29.2	22.8	14.6	8.3	7.6	4.3
1959	118.8	31.5	29.9	23.0	14.5	8.2	7.4	4.2
1958	120.2	32.2	30.6	23.3	14.4	8.1	7.3	4.2
1957	122.9	33.7	31.7	23.9	14.4	7.9	7.1	4.2
1956	121.2	33.5	31.9	23.6	13.9	7.6	6.8	4.0
1955	118.5	32.9	31.9	23.1	13.3	7.2	6.4	3.8
1954	118.1	33.6	32.4	22.7	12.8	6.8	6.0	3.8
1953	115.2	33.4	32.5	21.9	12.0	6.3	5.5	3.6
1952	113.9	34.0	32.7	21.3	11.3	5.8	5.2	3.6
1951	111.5	34.9	32.6	20.0	10.2	5.3	5.0	3.6
1950	106.2	33.3	32.1	18.4	9.2	4.8	4.7	3.6
1949	107.1	36.2	32.1	17.1	8.6	4.7	4.7	3.7
1948	107.3	39.6	30.9	16.1	8.0	4.5	4.6	3.6
1947	113.3	46.7	30.3	15.6	7.9	4.5	4.6	3.7
1946	101.9	38.5	27.9	14.5	7.8	4.5	4.7	3.8
1945	85.9	28.9	22.9	13.4	7.5	4.5	4.8	4.0
1944	88.8	30.2	23.8	13.8	7.6	4.5	4.9	4.0
1943	94.3	34.7	25.5	13.5	7.4	4.4	4.8	4.0
1942	91.5	37.5	22.9	11.9	6.6	4.1	4.6	3.9
1941	83.4	32.2	20.7	11.2	6.4	4.1	4.7	4.1
1940	79.9	29.3	20.0	10.9	6.4	4.1	4.8	4.3
White								
1970	84.1	32.8	23.7	13.3	6.8	3.4	2.7	1.2
1969	82.4	31.5	22.9	13.1	7.0	3.6	2.9	1.4
1968	81.5	30.9	22.1	12.8	7.1	3.8	3.2	1.6

[Continued]

★ 2096 ★

Birth Rate, by Race and Live-Order, 1940 to 1970

[Continued]

Year and race	Total	Birth rate, by live-birth order						
		1st	2d	3d	4th	5th	6th and 7th	8th and over
1967	83.1	29.7	22.1	13.5	7.9	4.3	3.7	1.8
1966	86.4	30.1	22.0	14.4	8.7	4.9	4.3	2.1
1965	91.4	28.9	23.0	16.2	10.2	5.8	5.0	2.4
1964	99.9	29.8	24.8	18.5	11.7	6.7	5.7	2.7
1963[1]	103.7	29.4	25.9	19.6	12.6	7.1	6.1	2.9
1962[1]	107.5	29.8	26.9	20.9	13.3	7.5	6.2	2.9
1961	112.2	30.7	28.3	22.2	14.0	7.7	6.4	2.9
1960[2]	113.2	30.8	29.2	22.7	14.1	7.5	6.1	2.8
1959	113.9	31.2	29.9	22.9	13.9	7.3	5.9	2.8
1958	114.9	31.9	30.6	23.1	13.8	7.2	5.7	2.7
1957	117.7	33.4	31.7	23.7	13.7	7.0	5.6	2.7
1956	116.0	33.2	31.9	23.4	13.1	6.6	5.2	2.6
1955	113.8	32.6	32.0	22.9	12.6	6.2	4.9	2.5
1954	113.6	33.3	32.8	22.6	12.0	5.9	4.6	2.5
1953	111.0	33.3	32.9	21.6	11.1	5.4	4.3	2.5
1952	110.0	34.1	33.1	21.0	10.4	5.0	4.0	2.5
1951	107.7	35.0	32.9	19.5	9.4	4.5	3.9	2.5
1950	102.3	33.3	32.3	17.9	8.4	4.1	3.7	2.5
1949	103.6	36.3	32.2	16.6	7.9	4.0	3.8	2.7
1948	104.3	39.9	31.1	15.7	7.4	3.9	3.7	2.6
1947	111.8	47.8	30.8	15.3	7.4	4.0	3.8	2.7
1946	100.4	39.5	28.5	14.4	7.3	4.0	3.9	2.8
1945	83.4	29.0	23.3	13.2	7.0	3.9	4.0	3.0
1944	86.3	30.4	24.2	13.6	7.1	4.0	4.1	3.1
1943	92.3	35.2	25.9	13.2	6.9	3.9	4.0	3.1
1942	89.5	38.3	23.1	11.5	6.1	3.6	3.8	3.1
1941	80.7	32.5	20.7	10.7	5.9	3.6	3.9	3.2
1940	77.1	29.4	20.0	10.5	5.9	3.6	4.1	3.5
Negro and other								
1970	113.0	42.4	26.9	15.9	9.7	6.2	6.7	5.3
1969	114.8	42.2	26.4	15.9	10.1	6.6	7.4	6.3
1968	114.9	40.6	25.3	15.7	10.4	7.0	8.5	7.4
1967	119.8	38.4	25.9	16.8	11.5	8.1	10.1	9.0
1966	125.9	37.4	26.0	18.0	12.8	9.4	11.6	10.7
1965	133.9	35.8	26.6	19.6	14.6	10.8	13.8	12.6
1964	141.7	34.8	27.4	21.1	16.0	12.1	15.8	14.4
1963[1]	144.9	33.8	27.6	21.8	16.9	13.1	16.6	15.1
1962[1]	148.8	33.1	28.0	22.8	17.8	13.7	17.6	15.7
1961	153.5	33.6	28.8	23.7	18.8	14.1	18.4	16.0

[Continued]

★ 2096 ★

Birth Rate, by Race and Live-Order, 1940 to 1970

[Continued]

Year and race	Total	Birth rate, by live-birth order						
		1st	2d	3d	4th	5th	6th and 7th	8th and over
1960[2]	153.6	33.6	29.3	24.0	18.6	14.1	18.4	15.6
1959	156.0	33.9	29.8	24.4	19.1	14.5	18.7	15.6
1958	160.5	34.7	31.0	25.4	19.5	14.9	19.1	15.9
1957	163.0	36.1	31.6	25.7	19.8	15.3	19.0	15.6
1956	160.9	35.9	31.7	25.2	19.7	15.0	18.7	15.0
1955	155.3	35.0	30.7	24.4	19.1	14.6	17.4	14.1
1954	153.2	35.6	29.7	24.4	19.1	14.2	16.5	13.5
1953	147.2	34.1	29.5	23.8	18.4	13.3	15.4	12.8
1952	143.3	33.1	29.2	24.0	18.1	12.4	14.2	12.4
1951	142.1	34.1	29.9	23.9	16.9	11.2	13.5	12.2
1950	137.3	33.8	30.3	22.9	15.3	10.4	12.6	12.0
1949	135.1	35.4	30.8	21.2	14.0	9.8	12.2	11.8
1948	131.6	37.3	29.5	19.4	12.9	9.2	11.7	11.6
1947	125.9	38.4	26.2	17.3	12.1	8.8	11.4	11.6
1946	113.9	31.1	23.4	16.0	11.8	8.7	11.3	11.7
1945	106.0	27.9	20.1	14.7	11.3	8.7	11.3	11.9
1944	108.5	28.7	21.1	15.6	11.7	8.6	11.3	11.6
1943	111.0	31.0	22.2	15.5	11.4	8.4	11.0	11.6
1942	107.6	31.0	21.1	14.9	10.8	8.1	10.5	11.1
1941	105.4	29.8	20.6	14.5	10.6	8.0	10.6	11.3
1940	102.4	28.6	19.6	14.1	10.5	7.8	10.4	11.3

Source: "Birth Rate, by Race, by Live-Order: 1940 to 1970." *Historical Statistics of the United States: Colonial Times to 1970, Part I.* Bicentennial Edition. Washington, D.C.: Government Printing Office, 1975, pp. 51-52. *Notes:* 1. Excludes New Jersey; State did not require reporting of race. 2. Denotes first year for which figures includes Alaska and Hawaii.

★ 2097 ★

Births

Birth Rates and Fertility Rates, 1909-1960

Year	Birth rate (births per 1,000 population)			Fertility rate (births per 1,000 women aged 15-44 years)		
	Total	White	Nonwhite	Total	White	Nonwhite
Registered births:						
1960	23.7	22.7	32.1	118.0	113.2	153.6
1959	24.0	23.0	32.7	118.8	113.9	156.0
Births adjusted for underregistration:[1]						
1959	24.3	23.1	34.0	120.2	114.6	162.2
1958	24.6	23.3	34.3	120.2	114.9	160.5
1957	25.3	24.0	35.3	122.9	117.7	163.0
1956	25.2	24.0	35.4	121.2	116.0	160.9
1955	25.0	23.8	34.7	118.5	113.8	155.3

[Continued]

★ 2097 ★

Birth Rates and Fertility Rates, 1909-1960

[Continued]

Year	Birth rate (births per 1,000 population)			Fertility rate (births per 1,000 women aged 15-44 years)		
	Total	White	Nonwhite	Total	White	Nonwhite
1954	25.3	24.2	34.9	118.1	113.6	153.2
1953	25.1	24.0	34.1	115.2	111.0	147.3
1952	25.1	24.1	33.7	113.9	110.1	143.3
1951	24.9	23.9	33.8	111.5	107.7	142.1
1950	24.1	23.0	33.0	106.2	102.3	137.3
1949	24.5	23.6	33.0	107.1	103.6	135.1
1948	24.9	24.0	32.4	107.3	104.3	131.6
1947	26.6	26.1	31.2	113.3	111.8	125.9
1946	24.1	23.6	28.4	101.9	100.4	113.9
1945	20.4	19.7	26.5	85.9	83.4	106.0
1944	21.2	20.5	27.4	88.8	86.3	108.5
1943	22.7	22.1	28.3	94.3	92.3	111.0
1942	22.2	21.5	27.7	91.5	89.5	107.6
1941	20.3	19.5	27.3	83.4	80.7	105.4
1940	19.4	18.6	26.7	79.9	77.1	102.4
1939	18.8	18.0	26.1	77.6	74.8	100.1
1938	19.2	18.4	26.3	79.1	76.5	100.5
1937	18.7	17.9	26.0	77.1	74.4	99.4
1936	18.4	17.6	25.1	75.8	73.3	95.9
1935	18.7	17.9	25.8	77.2	74.5	98.4
1934	19.0	18.1	26.3	78.5	75.8	100.0
1933	18.4	17.6	25.5	76.3	73.7	97.3
1932	19.5	18.7	26.9	81.7	79.0	103.0
1931	20.2	19.5	26.6	84.6	82.4	102.1
1930	21.3	20.6	27.5	89.2	87.1	105.9
1929	21.2	20.5	27.3	89.3	87.3	106.1
1928	22.2	21.5	28.5	93.8	91.7	111.0
1927	23.5	22.7	31.1	99.8	97.1	121.7
1926	24.2	23.1	33.4	102.6	99.2	130.3
1925	25.1	24.1	34.2	106.6	103.3	134.0
1924	26.1	25.1	34.6	110.9	107.8	135.6
1923	26.0	25.2	33.2	110.5	108.0	130.5
1922	26.2	25.4	33.2	111.2	108.8	130.8
1921	28.1	27.3	35.8	119.8	117.2	140.8
1920	27.7	26.9	35.0	117.9	115.4	137.5
1919	26.1	25.3	32.4	111.2	-	-
1918	28.2	27.6	33.0	119.8	-	-
1917	28.5	27.9	32.9	121.0	-	-

[Continued]

★ 2097 ★

Birth Rates and Fertility Rates, 1909-1960

[Continued]

Year	Birth rate (births per 1,000 population)			Fertility rate (births per 1,000 women aged 15-44 years)		
	Total	White	Nonwhite	Total	White	Nonwhite
1916	29.1	28.5	-	123.4	121.8	-
1915	29.5	28.9	-	125.0	123.2	-
1914	29.9	29.3	-	126.6	124.6	-
1913	29.5	28.8	-	124.7	122.4	-
1912	29.8	29.0	-	125.8	123.3	-
1911	29.9	29.1	-	126.3	123.6	-
1910	30.1	29.2	-	126.8	123.8	-
1909	30.0	29.2	-	126.8	123.6	-

Source: "Birth Rates and Fertility Rates by Color: United Ststes. 1909-1960." National Center for Health Statistics. *Vital Statistics Rates in the United State, 1940-60*. By Robert D. Grove and Alice M. Hetzel. Washington, D.C.: U.S. Department of Health, Education, and Welfare, Public Health Service, 1968, p. 114. *Notes:* 1. For 1915-32 rates are computed from births adjusted to include States not in the registration area; for years prior to 1915 from births estimated from registered births in the 10 original registration States. Estimates for 1909-34 were prepared by P.K. Whelpton: National Office of Vital Statistics, "Births and Birth Rates in the Entire United States, 1909 to 1948," *Vital Statistics—Special Reports*, vol. 33, No. 8, 1950.

★ 2098 ★

Births

Birth Rates at Ages 15-44, 1950-1975

Race of child and Year	Total	Live-birth order				
		1	2	3	4	5 or higher
	Live births per 1,000 women 15-44 years of age					
All Races						
1950	106.2	33.3	32.1	18.4	9.2	13.2
1955	118.3	32.8	31.8	23.1	13.3	17.3
1960	118.0	31.1	29.2	22.8	14.6	20.3
1965	96.6	29.8	23.4	16.6	10.7	16.1
1970	87.9	34.2	24.2	13.6	7.2	8.7
1975	66.0	28.1	20.9	9.4	3.9	3.7

Source: "Birth Rates for Women 15-44 Years of Age, according to Live Birth Order and Race of Child: United States, Selected Years 1950-86," *Health United States - 1988*, p. 43. Primary source: National Center for Health Statistics: *Vital Statistics of the United States*, 1986, Vol. 1, Natality. Public Health Service, DHHS, Hyattsville, Md. To be published. *Notes:* Data are based on births adjusted for underregistration for 1950 and 1955 and on registered births for all other years. Beginning in 1970, births to nonresidents of the United States are excluded. Figures for live- birth order not stated are distributed.

★ 2099 ★

Births

Births Out of Wedlock, 1940-1967

	Number (thousands)		Percent illegitimate of all live births	
	Negro and other races	White	Negro and other races	White
1940	49	40	16.8	2.0
1945	61	56	17.9	2.4
1950	88	54	18.0	1.8
1955	119	64	20.2	1.9
1960	142	83	21.6	2.3
1965	168	124	26.3	4.0
1966	170	133	27.7	4.4
1967	176	142	29.4	4.9

Source: "Illegitimate Births, 1940-1967." U.S. Bureau of the Census. Current Population Reports, Special Studies, Series P-23, No. 29. *The Social and Economic Status of the Black Population in the United States, 1969*. Washington, D.C.: Government Printing Office, 1969, p. 77. Primary source: U.S. Department of Health, Education, and Welfare. *Notes:* As stated in the source cited, "No estimates are included for misstatements on the birth record or for failure to register births... The decision to conceal the illegitimacy of births is likely conditioned by attitudes in the mother's social group towards her and towards children born out of wedlock. Also, the ability (economic or otherwise) to leave a community before the birth of the child is an important consideration. These factors probably result in proportionately greater understatement of illegitimacy in the white group than in Negro and other races..." Thirty-four states and the District of Columbia report legitimacy status on birth certificates. For the remaining states the illegitimacy ratio is estimated from the reporting states in each of the nine geographic divisions. The following states do not report legitimacy: Arizona, Arkansas, California, Colorado, Connecticut, Idaho, Maryland, Massachusetts, Nebraska, New Hampshire, New Mexico, New York, Oklahoma, Vermont, Georgia, and Montana. The last two states reported before 1957.

★ 2100 ★

Births

Births Out of Wedlock – 1930, 1931

Percent distribution of illegitimate births by age, color, and nativity of mother, in the registration area of continental United States[1]: 1931 and 1930.

Color, nativity of mother, and year	All ages	10 to 14 years	15 to 19 years	20 to 24 years	25 to 29 years	30 to 34 years	35 to 39 years	40 to 44 years	45 years and over	Unknown
Total										
1931	100.0	2.1	44.5	27.3	9.2	4.4	2.8	0.9	0.1	8.6
1930	100.0	2.4	45.1	26.9	8.8	4.1	2.7	.9	.2	8.9
Colored										
1931	100.0	2.7	43.6	23.5	9.3	4.9	3.0	.9	.2	12.0
1930	100.0	3.1	44.2	22.9	8.9	4.6	3.0	.9	.2	12.3
Negro										
1931	100.0	2.7	43.8	23.3	9.3	4.9	3.0	.9	.2	12.0
1930	100.0	3.2	44.4	22.7	8.8	4.5	2.9	.9	.2	12.3

[Continued]

★ 2100 ★

Births Out of Wedlock – 1930, 1931

[Continued]

Color, nativity of mother, and year	All ages	10 to 14 years	15 to 19 years	20 to 24 years	25 to 29 years	30 to 34 years	35 to 39 years	40 to 44 years	45 years and over	Unknown
Other colored										
1931	100.0	1.4	35.5	29.2	11.3	6.0	3.6	1.3	.3	11.4
1930	100.0	1.0	30.8	31.4	13.6	5.7	4.6	1.0	.3	11.6
White										
1931	100.0	1.6	45.4	31.5	9.0	3.9	2.6	.9	.1	4.9
1930	100.0	1.7	46.0	31.3	8.7	3.7	2.5	.9	.1	5.3
Native										
1931	100.0	1.6	47.1	31.8	8.8	3.7	2.4	.8	.1	3.7
1930	100.0	1.8	48.0	31.6	8.5	3.5	2.3	.8	.1	3.6
Foreign born										
1931	100.0	.4	23.0	38.4	17.5	9.1	8.0	2.6	.3	.7
1930	100.0	.4	25.2	38.8	16.3	8.0	6.9	2.9	.6	.9
Unknown										
1931	100.0	1.3	15.0	7.2	2.8	1.5	1.2	.3	-	70.8
1930	100.0	.4	9.1	5.7	1.7	.7	.8	.1	.1	81.4

Source: "Percent Distribution of Illegitimate Births by Age, Color, and Nativity of Mother, in the Registration Area of Continental United States: 1931 and 1930." U.S. Bureau of the Census. *Negroes in the United States: 1920-32.* Washington, D.C.: Government Printing Office, 1935, p. 364. *Notes:* 1. Exclusive of California and Massachusetts. These states do not require a statement concerning legitimacy of child.

★ 2101 ★

Births

Births Out of Wedlock: Estimated Ratios, 1940-1960

Color and year	15-44 years	Age of mother								
		10-14 years	15-19 years			20-24 years	25-29 years	30-34 years	35-39 years	40 years and over
			15-19	15-17	18-19					
Total										
1960	52.7	678.5	148.4	239.6	107.3	47.7	29.4	27.5	29.5	31.0
1959	52.0	678.9	148.0	242.4	105.5	47.9	29.1	27.1	28.9	29.5
1958	49.6	661.9	143.3	233.5	102.8	45.9	27.8	26.3	27.6	28.8
1957	47.4	660.9	138.9	230.8	97.8	44.4	26.1	24.9	25.7	29.1
1956	46.5	660.8	139.9	230.4	99.8	44.4	26.0	23.4	24.8	26.4
1955	45.3	662.9	142.3	231.8	102.3	43.7	25.0	22.3	24.0	25.9
1954	44.0	643.8	140.6	231.5	100.7	42.4	23.7	21.5	23.4	23.9
1953	41.2	639.6	134.9	223.0	96.4	40.0	22.1	19.4	21.5	23.8
1952	39.1	645.3	134.0	228.4	92.2	37.5	20.3	18.2	20.3	19.2
1951	39.1	638.0	129.4	217.6	91.2	36.6	20.5	18.6	20.3	23.0
1950	39.8	637.3	133.5	226.1	93.6	38.1	20.5	18.1	20.4	21.3
1949	37.4	618.0	123.1	211.0	85.8	34.9	19.4	16.7	19.2	20.1
1948	36.7	614.3	121.5	207.6	85.3	35.2	18.6	15.2	16.9	17.5
1947	35.6	651.1	124.2	-	-	35.4	17.4	14.1	15.7	18.1
1946	38.1	664.4	152.0	-	-	41.1	18.2	13.2	14.8	16.1

[Continued]

★ 2101 ★

Births Out of Wedlock: Estimated Ratios, 1940-1960

[Continued]

Color and year	15-44 years	Age of mother								
		10-14 years	15-19 years			20-24 years	25-29 years	30-34 years	35-39 years	40 years and over
			15-19	15-17	18-19					
1945	42.9	699.7	175.1	-	-	49.3	18.7	13.3	14.3	15.1
1944	37.6	645.2	151.1	-	-	38.9	16.1	12.5	14.0	14.7
1943	33.4	642.2	128.1	-	-	32.0	13.7	12.0	14.1	15.4
1942	34.4	645.0	126.6	-	-	31.8	14.3	12.8	15.4	15.2
1941	38.1	640.8	136.1	-	-	36.3	15.7	13.8	16.0	18.3
1940	37.9	644.8	134.7	-	-	36.8	16.3	13.0	14.9	15.0
White										
1960	22.9	475.4	71.6	115.8	54.2	21.9	11.4	10.2	12.7	15.8
1959	22.1	466.6	69.4	114.4	51.6	21.8	11.1	9.8	11.9	13.5
1958	20.9	453.2	65.9	108.5	49.2	20.6	10.4	9.9	11.3	13.7
1957	19.6	415.4	62.7	104.1	46.6	19.5	9.9	9.5	9.8	14.6
1956	19.0	425.9	62.6	101.6	47.8	19.6	9.6	8.5	10.4	13.5
1955	18.6	421.3	63.6	102.4	48.7	19.3	9.3	8.5	10.0	12.5
1954	18.2	368.3	63.1	102.2	48.5	19.1	9.1	8.2	10.2	12.6
1953	16.9	431.5	59.0	95.7	45.3	18.1	8.4	7.7	9.1	10.6
1952	16.3	381.8	58.4	96.3	44.1	17.6	7.9	7.2	9.3	9.7
1951	16.3	376.6	57.9	97.3	43.5	16.7	8.2	7.4	8.5	10.6
1950	17.5	419.4	62.4	102.2	47.5	18.3	8.7	7.9	9.0	10.2
1949	17.3	404.4	59.3	100.5	44.6	17.7	9.2	7.9	9.0	10.1
1948	17.8	399.3	61.4	103.4	46.4	18.8	9.3	7.1	8.2	8.5
1947	18.5	451.0	64.6	-	-	20.7	9.6	7.1	7.3	9.6
1946	21.1	524.0	82.4	-	-	26.6	10.9	7.1	7.5	8.5
1945	23.5	506.8	97.4	-	-	32.6	11.0	6.8	6.8	7.2
1944	20.2	495.5	82.0	-	-	25.0	9.3	6.2	6.4	7.6
1943	16.5	451.8	63.1	-	-	18.8	7.3	5.6	6.7	8.0
1942	16.9	404.9	62.0	-	-	18.5	7.5	6.2	7.1	8.6
1941	19.0	449.2	68.5	-	-	21.5	8.4	7.3	7.1	8.7
1940	19.5	443.7	69.7	-	-	22.7	8.9	6.0	7.3	8.5
Nonwhite										
1960	215.8	822.4	421.5	542.9	337.0	199.6	141.3	129.9	127.7	116.8
1959	218.0	808.8	426.5	550.4	339.1	202.3	143.4	133.4	130.1	124.4
1958	212.3	825.0	419.0	537.3	336.0	194.2	141.6	130.9	127.1	119.7
1957	206.7	811.7	409.1	530.8	321.7	190.5	135.9	125.6	127.6	117.4
1956	204.0	798.4	404.8	529.0	317.9	189.7	136.0	123.4	116.7	111.6
1955	202.4	800.6	406.6	523.6	323.6	189.4	133.4	119.9	117.1	108.6
1954	198.5	797.7	399.8	516.4	318.1	184.6	127.2	119.7	113.7	94.8
1953	191.1	779.9	389.0	501.0	309.6	177.3	122.1	108.7	108.7	103.4
1952	183.4	783.8	384.1	513.7	290.9	163.7	116.2	106.5	99.9	79.3
1951	182.8	771.4	365.5	472.5	289.1	162.6	117.4	109.4	102.5	98.5

[Continued]

★ 2101 ★

Births Out of Wedlock: Estimated Ratios, 1940-1960

[Continued]

Color and year	15-44 years	Age of mother								
		10-14 years	15-19 years			20-24 years	25-29 years	30-34 years	35-39 years	40 years and over
			15-19	15-17	18-19					
1950	179.6	745.8	358.4	475.7	275.1	159.0	114.7	102.4	98.5	92.9
1949	167.5	730.6	333.3	447.5	255.6	144.8	104.8	93.3	93.0	86.6
1948	164.7	734.6	327.4	438.1	250.6	144.6	101.2	88.1	83.1	81.6
1947	168.1	758.1	341.4	-	-	149.3	98.2	86.8	85.5	80.6
1946	170.1	776.9	378.0	-	-	153.1	93.5	78.8	81.2	71.8
1945	179.2	795.3	398.2	-	-	162.7	91.2	78.8	76.8	73.0
1944	163.5	764.7	361.7	-	-	137.4	82.3	74.3	79.2	68.0
1943	162.9	747.2	338.8	-	-	132.8	83.9	79.1	80.0	69.9
1942	169.2	729.3	342.6	-	-	137.1	89.7	81.5	82.7	74.6
1941	174.4	732.8	351.7	-	-	143.2	89.6	85.6	84.9	87.9
1940	168.2	751.2	344.4	-	-	136.4	88.3	80.1	75.3	77.4

Source: "Estimated Ratios of Illegitimate Live Births by Age of Mother and Color: United States, 1940-1960." National Center for Health Statistics. *Vital Statistics Rates in the United States, 1940-60.* By Robert D. Grove and Alice M. Hetzel. Washington, D.C.: U.S. Department of Health, Education, and Welfare, Public Health Service, 1968, pp, 183-184.

★ 2102 ★

Births

Births Out of Wedlock: Percent – 1950, 1960, 1970

Race	Percent of All Births Occurring Outside Marriage, by Race/Hispanic Origin						
	1950	1960	1970	1975	1980	1985	1986
White	1.8	2.3	5.7	7.3	11.0	14.5	15.7
Non-white	18.0	21.6	34.9	44.2	48.5	51.4	52.4
Black	2	2	37.6	48.8	55.3	60.1	61.2
Hispanic	2	2	2	2	23.6	29.5	31.6
Non-Hispanic	2	2	2	2	18.5	21.6	22.8
	Non-Marital Birth Rate[1]						
White	6.1	9.2	13.9	12.4	17.6	21.8	23.2
Non-white	71.2	98.3	89.9	79.0	77.2	73.2	74.8
Black	2	2	95.5	84.2	82.9	78.8	80.9
Hispanic	2	2	2	2	52.0	2	2
Non-Hispanic	2	2	2	2	27.7	2	2

Source: "Births to Unmarried Women, 1950-1986," *U.S. Children and Their Families,* 1989, p. 15. Primary source: National Center for Health Statistics, *Vital Statistics of the United States,* Annual Natality Volumes for 1950, 1960, 1970, 1975, 1980, 1985, and 1986; *Monthly Vital Statistics Report,* "Advance Report of Final Natality Statistics, 1986," Vol. 37, No. 3, Supplement, Table 27; *Monthly Vital Statistics Report,* "Births of Hispanic Parentage, 1985," Vol. 36, No. 11, Supplement, Table 6; *Monthly Vital Statistics Report,* "Births of Hispanic Parentage, 1980," Vol. 32, No. 6, Supplement, Tables 1 and 11. *Notes:* Data on Hispanic origin are based on information from 22 reporting states in 1980 and from 23 reporting states and the District of Columbia in 1985 and 1986. 1. Births per 1,000 unmarried women aged 15-44. 2. Not available.

★ 2103 ★

Births

Births Out of Wedlock: Ratios – 1930, 1931

Number of illegitimate births (exclusive of stillbirths) in the registration area of continental United States[1], with ratios to 1,000 total births, by age, color, and nativity of mother: 1931 and 1930.

Color, nativity of mother, and year	All years	10 to 14 years	15 to 19 years	20 to 24 years	25 to 29 years	30 to 34 years	35 to 39 years	40 to 44 years	45 years and over	Unknown
					Number					
Total										
1931	69,403	1,478	30,866	18,950	6,382	3,071	1,967	611	91	5,987
1930	66,991	1,620	30,191	18,052	5,888	2,765	1,820	582	112	5,961
Colored										
1931	36,418	966	15,879	8,549	3,401	1,781	1,099	325	58	4,360
1930	34,647	1,085	15,311	7,921	3,080	1,582	1,026	307	75	4,260
Negro										
1931	35,717	956	15,630	8,344	3,322	1,739	1,074	316	56	4,280
1930	34,020	1,079	15,118	7,724	2,995	1,546	997	301	73	4,187
Other colored										
1931	701	10	249	205	79	42	25	9	2	80
1930	627	6	193	197	85	36	29	6	2	73
White										
1931	32,985	512	14,987	10,401	2,981	1,290	868	286	33	1,627
1930	32,344	535	14,880	10,131	2,808	1,183	794	275	37	1,701
Native										
1931	30,942	497	14,572	9,831	2,725	1,156	751	249	29	1,132
1930	29,984	526	14,407	9,467	2,534	1,050	677	228	26	1,069
Foreign born										
1931	1,358	6	312	521	237	124	109	35	4	10
1930	1,602	6	404	621	261	128	111	46	10	15
Unknown										
1931	685	9	103	49	19	10	8	2	-	485
1930	758	3	69	43	13	5	6	1	1	617
					Ratio					
Total										
1931	35.4	615.3	129.0	32.7	12.9	9.3	9.3	8.6	12.9	222.1
1930	32.7	595.4	119.4	29.8	11.6	8.0	8.2	7.8	15.3	220.9
Colored										
1931	147.5	725.8	299.7	112.6	67.5	55.7	51.4	50.3	58.2	793.9
1930	138.2	713.8	281.3	102.3	61.0	50.0	47.0	46.1	70.1	757.3
Negro										
1931	153.9	730.9	306.5	116.3	71.1	59.0	54.5	53.2	62.5	811.1
1930	143.4	715.0	286.7	104.9	63.3	52.5	49.2	48.6	73.3	801.6
Other colored										
1931	47.2	434.8	125.1	49.4	21.7	16.9	14.6	17.3	19.8	372.1
1930	47.0	545.5	113.1	51.7	27.0	16.5	18.8	12.7	27.0	181.6
White										
1931	19.2	478.1	80.5	20.6	6.7	4.3	4.6	4.4	5.5	75.8
1930	18.0	445.5	75.0	19.2	6.2	3.7	4.0	4.1	5.9	79.6

[Continued]

★ 2103 ★

Births Out of Wedlock: Ratios – 1930, 1931

[Continued]

Color, nativity of mother, and year	All years	10 to 14 years	15 to 19 years	20 to 24 years	25 to 29 years	30 to 34 years	35 to 39 years	40 to 44 years	45 years and over	Unknown
Native										
1931	20.3	470.2	80.6	20.9	7.0	4.6	4.9	4.9	6.4	63.4
1930	19.1	442.8	75.3	19.5	6.4	4.0	4.2	4.4	5.6	61.0
Foreign born										
1931	7.1	600.0	60.5	15.5	4.6	2.7	3.1	2.5	2.7	3.4
1930	7.2	600.0	60.0	15.1	4.4	2.4	2.7	2.9	6.2	4.9
Unknown										
1931	320.7	[2]	351.5	125.6	57.8	43.3	47.6	35.1	-	741.6
1930	396.7	100.0	371.0	124.6	54.4	27.8	50.4	15.2	200.0	803.4

Source: "Number of Illegitimate Births (Exclusive of Stillbirths) in the Registration Area of Continental United States, with Ratios to 1,000 Total Births, by Age, Color, and Nativity of Mother: 1931 and 1930." U.S. Bureau of the Census. *Negroes in the United States: 1920-32.* Washington, D.C.: Government Printing Office, 1935, p. 364. *Notes:* 1. Exclusive of California and Massachusetts. These states do not require a statement concerning legitimacy of child. 2. Rate not computed.

★ 2104 ★

Births

Births and Deaths by State – 1920, 1930

Area and year	Enumerated Negro population	Births	Deaths	Rate per 1,000 Negro population	
				Births	Deaths
Birth registration area					
1930	11,035,533	239,275	182,009	21.7	16.5
1920	3,922,084	103,796	72,411	26.5	18.5
Alabama					
1930	944,834	22,969	14,407	24.3	15.2
1920	900,652	[1]	[1]	[1]	[1]
Arizona					
1930	10,749	131	206	12.2	19.2
1920	8,005	[1]	[1]	[1]	[1]
Arkansas					
1930	478,463	9,077	6,461	19.0	13.5
1920	472,220	[1]	[1]	[1]	[1]
California					
1930	81,048	1,003	1,157	12.4	14.3
1920	38,763	657	779	16.9	20.1
Colorado					
1930	11,828	136	302	11.5	25.5
1920	11,318	[1]	[1]	[1]	[1]
Connecticut					
1930	29,354	728	513	24.8	17.5
1920	21,046	554	491	26.3	23.3
Delaware					
1930	32,602	723	706	22.2	21.7
1920	30,335	[1]	[1]	[1]	[1]

[Continued]

★ 2104 ★

Births and Deaths by State – 1920, 1930

[Continued]

Area and year	Enumerated Negro population	Births	Deaths	Rate per 1,000 Negro population	
				Births	Deaths
District of Columbia					
1930	132,068	3,036	2,780	23.0	21.0
1920	109,966	2,498	2,289	22.7	20.8
Florida					
1930	431,828	8,385	7,166	19.4	16.6
1920	329,487	[1]	[1]	[1]	[1]
Georgia					
1930	1,071,125	23,392	17,182	21.8	16.0
1920	1,206,365	[1]	[1]	[1]	[1]
Idaho					
1930	668	8	13	12.0	19.5
1920	920	[1]	[1]	[1]	[1]
Illinois					
1930	328,972	5,917	5,824	18.0	17.7
1920	182,274	[1]	[1]	[1]	[1]
Indiana					
1930	111,982	1,977	2,185	17.7	19.5
1920	80,810	1,503	1,802	18.6	22.3
Iowa					
1930	17,380	277	298	15.9	17.1
1920	19,005	[1]	[1]	[1]	[1]
Kansas					
1930	66,344	999	1,082	15.1	16.3
1920	57,925	1,003	1,189	17.3	20.5
Kentucky					
1930	226,040	3,376	4,748	14.9	21.0
1920	235,938	4,137	4,560	17.5	19.3
Louisiana					
1930	776,326	16,668	12,036	21.5	15.5
1920	700,257	[1]	[1]	[1]	[1]
Maine					
1930	1,096	15	18	13.7	16.4
1920	1,310	6	31	4.6	23.7
Maryland					
1930	276,379	6,401	5,251	23.2	19.0
1920	244,479	6,753	5,198	27.6	21.3
Massachusetts					
1930	52,365	961	834	18.4	15.9
1920	45,466	1,234	993	27.1	21.8
Michigan					
1930	169,453	3,468	2,786	20.5	16.4
1920	60,082	1,324	1,529	22.0	25.4
Minnesota					
1930	9,445	114	196	12.1	20.8
1920	8,809	129	188	14.6	21.3

[Continued]

★ 2104 ★

Births and Deaths by State – 1920, 1930

[Continued]

Area and year	Enumerated Negro population	Births	Deaths	Rate per 1,000 Negro population	
				Births	Deaths
Mississippi					
1930	1,009,718	24,804	14,910	24.6	14.8
1920	935,184	1	1	1	1
Missouri					
1930	223,840	3,688	4,604	16.5	20.6
1920	178,241	1	1	1	1
Montana					
1930	1,256	16	28	12.7	22.3
1920	1,658	1	1	1	1
Nebraska					
1930	13,752	235	255	17.1	18.5
1920	13,242	185	228	14.0	17.2
Nevada					
1930	516	6	14	11.6	27.1
1920	346	1	1	1	1
New Hampshire					
1930	790	9	7	11.4	8.9
1920	621	6	11	9.7	17.7
New Jersey					
1930	208,828	4,955	3,519	23.7	16.9
1920	117,132	1	1	1	1
New Mexico					
1930	2,850	25	59	8.8	20.7
1920	5,733	1	1	1	1
New York					
1930	412,814	8,872	6,841	21.5	16.6
1920	198,483	4,791	3,938	24.1	19.8
North Carolina					
1930	918,647	22,785	13,976	24.8	15.2
1920	763,407	23,954	12,315	31.4	16.1
North Dakota					
1930	377	1	5	2.7	13.3
1920	467	1	1	1	1
Ohio					
1930	309,304	5,931	5,803	19.2	18.8
1920	186,187	3,889	4,010	20.9	21.5
Oklahoma					
1930	172,198	1,582	2,242	9.2	13.0
1920	149,408	1	1	1	1
Oregon					
1930	2,234	24	55	10.7	24.6
1920	2,144	28	33	13.1	15.4
Pennsylvania					
1930	431,257	9,443	7,459	21.9	17.3
1920	284,568	6,478	6,065	22.8	21.3

[Continued]

★ 2104 ★

Births and Deaths by State – 1920, 1930

[Continued]

Area and year	Enumerated Negro population	Births	Deaths	Rate per 1,000 Negro population	
				Births	Deaths
Rhode Island					
1930	9,913	239	219	24.1	22.1
1920	10,036	1	1	1	1
South Carolina					
1930	793,681	20,396	13,160	25.7	16.6
1920	864,719	23,946	14,338	27.7	16.6
Tennessee					
1930	477,646	8,105	8,744	17.0	18.3
1920	451,758	1	1	1	1
Utah					
1930	1,108	15	23	13.5	20.8
1920	1,446	29	29	20.1	20.1
Vermont					
1930	568	11	8	19.4	14.1
1920	572	1	6	1.7	10.5
Virginia					
1930	650,165	15,689	11,699	24.1	18.0
1920	690,017	20,515	12,130	29.7	17.6
Washington					
1930	6,840	62	144	9.1	21.1
1920	6,883	89	143	12.9	20.8
West Virginia					
1930	114,893	2,454	1,854	21.4	16.1
1920	86,345	1	1	1	1
Wisconsin					
1930	10,739	154	201	14.3	18.7
1920	5,201	87	116	16.7	22.3
Wyoming					
1930	1,250	13	29	10.4	23.2
1920	1,375	1	1	1	1

Source: "Negro Births and Deaths (Exclusive of Stillbirths) in Registration Area: 1930 and 1920." U.S. Bureau of the Census. *Negroes in the United States: 1920-32.* Washington, D.C.: Government Printing Office, 1935, p. 362. *Note:* 1. Not in birth registration area, 1920.

★ 2105 ★

Births

Births and Rates of Births Out of Wedlock, 1940 to 1970

Refers only to illegitimate births occurring within the United States. Rates are illegitimate live births per 1,000 unmarried females in specified group. Figures for age of mother not stated are distributed. Based on 50- percent sample of births for 1951-1954, 1956-1966, and 1968-1970; on 20- to 50-percent sample for 1967.

Year and race	Births (1,000)	Rate, all ages[1]	Rate, by age of mother[2]						35-44 years
			15-19 years	20-24 years	25-29 years	30-34 years	35-39 years	40-44 years	
Total									
1970	399	26.4	22.4	38.4	37.1	27.0	13.3	3.6	
1969	361	25.0	20.6	37.4	38.1	27.4	13.6	3.6	
1968	339	24.4	19.8	37.3	38.6	28.2	14.9	3.8	
1967	318	23.9	18.6	38.3	41.4	29.2	15.4	4.0	
1966	302	23.4	17.5	39.1	45.6	33.0	16.4	4.1	
1965	291	23.5	16.7	39.9	49.3	37.5	17.4	4.5	
1964	276	23.0	15.8	39.9	50.2	37.2	16.3	4.4	
1963	259	22.5	15.2	40.3	49.0	33.2	16.1	4.3	
1962	245	21.9	14.8	40.9	46.7	29.7	15.6	4.0	
1961	240	22.7	15.9	41.7	46.5	28.3	15.4	3.9	
1960[5]	224	21.6	15.3	39.7	45.1	27.8	14.1	3.6	
1959[3]	221	21.9	15.5	40.2	44.1	28.1	14.1	3.3	
1958	209	21.2	15.3	38.2	40.5	27.5	13.3	3.2	
1957	202	21.0	15.8	37.3	36.8	26.8	12.1	3.1	
1956	194	20.4	15.6	36.4	35.6	24.6	11.1	2.8	
1955	183	19.3	15.1	33.5	33.5	22.0	10.5	2.7	
1954	177	18.7	14.9	31.4	31.0	20.4	10.3	2.5	
1953	161	16.9	13.9	28.0	27.6	17.3	9.0	2.4	
1952	150	15.8	13.5	25.4	24.8	15.7	8.2	1.9	
1951	147	15.1	13.2	23.2	22.8	14.6	7.6	2.2	
1950	142	14.1	12.6	21.3	19.9	13.3	7.2	2.0	
1949	133	13.3	12.0	21.0	18.0	11.4	6.8	1.9	
1948	130	12.5	11.4	19.8	16.4	10.0	5.8	1.6	
1947	132	12.1	1.0	18.9	15.7	9.2	5.6	1.8	
1946	125	10.9	9.5	17.3	15.6	7.3	4.4	1.8	
1945	117	101.1	9.5	15.3	12.1	7.1	4.1	1.6	
1944	105	9.0	8.8	13.1	10.1	7.0	4.0	1.3	
1943	98	8.3	8.4	11.4	8.8	6.7	3.8	1.3	
1942	97	8.0	8.2	11.0	8.4	6.3	3.8	1.2	
1941	96	7.8	8.0	10.5	7.8	6.0	3.7	1.4	
1940	90	7.1	7.4	9.5	7.2	5.1	3.4	1.2	
White									
1970	175	13.8	10.9	22.5	21.1	14.2			4.4
1969	164	13.5	10.0	23.0	22.4	15.1			4.4
1968	155	13.2	9.8	23.1	22.1	15.1			4.7

[Continued]

★ 2105 ★

Births and Rates of Births Out of Wedlock, 1940 to 1970

[Continued]

Year and race	Births (1,000)	Rate, all ages[1]	Rate, by age of mother[2] 15-19 years	20-24 years	25-29 years	30-34 years	35-39 years	40-44 years	35-44 years
1967	142	12.5	9.0	23.1	22.7	14.0			4.7
1966	133	12.0	8.5	22.5	23.5	15.7			4.9
1965	124	11.6	7.9	22.1	24.3	16.6			4.9
1964	114	11.0	7.3	21.2	24.1	15.9			4.8
1963[4]	102	10.5	7.0	20.8	22.0	14.2			4.6
1962[4]	93	9.8	6.5	20.0	19.8	12.6			4.3
1961	91	10.0	7.0	19.7	19.4	11.3			4.2
1960[5]	83	9.2	6.6	18.2	18.2	10.8			3.9
1959[3]	80	9.2	6.5	18.3	17.6	10.7			3.6
1958	75	8.8	6.3	17.3	15.8	10.8			3.4
1957	71	8.6	6.4	16.6	14.6	10.5			3.0
1956	68	8.3	6.2	16.3	14.0	9.2			3.0
1955	64	7.9	6.0	15.0	13.3	8.6			2.8
1950	54	6.1	5.1	10.0	8.7	5.9			2.0
1940	40	3.6	3.3	5.7	4.0	2.5			1.2
Negro and other									
1970	224	89.9	90.8	120.9	93.7	69.9			21.6
1969	197	86.6	85.6	116.6	98.0	73.5			22.3
1968	184	86.6	82.8	118.3	104.4	80.6			25.2
1967	176	89.5	80.2	128.2	118.4	97.2			28.9
1966	170	92.8	76.9	139.4	143.8	119.4			33.8
1965	168	97.6	75.8	152.6	164.7	137.8			39.0
1964	161	97.2	74.0	164.2	168.7	132.3			34.5
1963[4]	151	97.1	73.8	161.8	171.5	124.3			34.4
1962[4]	147	97.5	74.1	163.6	172.7	115.2			35.5
1961	149	100.8	77.6	169.6	172.7	112.0			37.4
1960[5]	142	98.3	76.5	166.5	171.8	104.0			35.6
1959[3]	141	100.8	80.8	167.8	168.0	106.5			34.9
1958	134	97.8	80.4	153.2	161.2	110.5			32.5
1957	131	95.3	81.4	147.7	142.6	115.1			30.3
1956	126	92.1	79.6	143.5	132.7	113.7			27.0
1955	119	87.2	77.6	133.0	125.2	100.9			25.3

[Continued]

★ 2105 ★

Births and Rates of Births Out of Wedlock, 1940 to 1970

[Continued]

Year and race	Births (1,000)	Rate, all ages[1]	Rate, by age of mother[2] 15-19 years	20-24 years	25-29 years	30-34 years	35-39 years	40-44 years	35-44 years
1950	88	71.2	68.5	105.4	94.2	63.5			20.0
1940	49	35.6	42.5	46.1	32.5	23.4			9.3

Source: "Illegitimate Live Births and Birth Rates. by Age and Race of Mother: 1940 to 1970." *Historical Statistics of the United States: Colonial Times to 1970, Part I.* Bicentennial Edition. Washington, D.C.: Government Printing Office, 1975, p. 52. *Notes:* 1. Rates computed by relating total illegitimate births regardless of age of mother to women aged 15-44 years. 2. Rates for total computed by relating illegitimate births to mothers aged 40 and over to unmarried women aged 40-44 years. Rates for race detail computed by relating births to mothers aged 35 and over to women aged 35-44 years. 3. Includes Alaska. 4. Excludes New Jersey; State did not require reporting of race. 5. Denotes first year for which figures include Alaska and Hawaii.

★ 2106 ★

Births

Births and Rates of Births Out of Wedlock: Five-Year Averages, 1950 to 1959, and Yearly 1960 to 1968

Year	All races: Illegitimate births (thousands)	All races: Illegitimacy rate[1]	Negro and other races: Illegitimate births (thousands)	Negro and other races: Illegitimacy rate[1]	White: Illegitimate births (thousands)	White: Illegitimacy rate[1]
1940 to 1944	97	8.0	54	35.6[2]	43	3.6[2]
1945 to 1949	127	11.8	70		57	
1950 to 1954	155	16.1	99	71.2[3]	56	6.1[3]
1955 to 1959	202	20.8	130	94.6	71	8.6
1960	224	21.6	142	98.3	83	9.2
1961	240	22.7	149	100.8	91	10.0
1962	245	21.9	150	97.5	95	9.8
1963	259	22.5	155	97.1	105	10.5
1964	276	23.0	161	97.2	114	11.0
1965	291	23.5	168	97.6	124	11.6
1966	302	23.4	170	92.8	133	12.0
1967	318	23.9	176	89.5	142	12.5
1968	339	24.4	184	86.6	155	13.2
Percent change						
1940-1944 to 1955-1959	+108	+160	+141	+166[4]	+65	+139[4]

[Continued]

★ 2106 ★

Births and Rates of Births Out of Wedlock: Five-Year Averages, 1950 to 1959, and Yearly 1960 to 1968

[Continued]

Year	All races		Negro and other races		White	
	Illegitimate births (thousands)	Illegitimacy rate[1]	Illegitimate births (thousands)	Illegitimacy rate[1]	Illegitimate births (thousands)	Illegitimacy rate[1]
1955-1959 to 1968	+68	+17	+42	-8	+118	+53

Source: "Estimated Illegitimate Births and Illegitimacy Rates: 5-Year Averages. 1940 to 1959 and Single-Year Data, 1960 to 1968." U.S. Bureau of the Census. Current Population Reports, Special Studies, Series P-23, No. 42. *The Social and Economic Status of the Black Population in the United States, 1971.* Washington, D.C.: Government Printing Office, 1972, p. 110. Primary source: U.S. Department of Health, Education, and Welfare. *Notes:* As stated in the source cited, "No estimates are included for misstatements on the birth record or for failure to register births... The decision to conceal the illegitimacy of births is likely conditioned by attitudes in the mother's social group towards her and towards children born out of wedlock. Also, the ability (economic or otherwise) to leave a community before the birth of the child is an important consideration. These factors probably result in proportionately greater understatement of illegitimacy in the white group than in Negro and other races..." Thirty- four states and the District of Columbia report legitimacy status on birth certificates. For the remaining states the illegitimacy ratio is estimated from the reporting states in each of the nine geographic divisions. The following states do not report legitimacy: Arizona, Arkansas, California, Colorado, Connecticut, Idaho, Maryland, Massachusetts, Nebraska, New Hampshire, New Mexico, New York, Oklahoma, Vermont, Georgia, and Montana. The last two states reported before 1957. 1. Illegitimate births, regardless of age of mother, per 1,000 unmarried women 15 to 44 years old. 2. Illegitimacy rate for 1940. 3. Illegitimacy rate for 1950. 4. Percent change, 1940 to 1955-1959.

★ 2107 ★

Births

Births and Rates of Births Out of Wedlock: by Age of Mother – 1940, 1950, 1960, 1965, 1968

Rates per 1,000 unmarried women in specified group.

Age and race of mother	1940	1950	1960[1]	1965[1]	1968[1]
Negro and other races					
Total, 15 to 44 years[2]	35.6	71.2	98.3	97.6	86.6
15 to 19 years	42.5	68.5	76.5	75.8	82.8
20 to 24 years	46.1	105.4	166.5	152.6	118.3
25 to 29 years	32.5	94.2	171.8	164.7	104.4
30 to 34 years	23.4	63.5	104.0	137.8	80.6
35 to 39 years	13.2	31.3/	35.6[4]	39.0[4]	25.2[4]
40 to 44 years	5.0[3]	837[3]/			
White					
Total, 15 to 44 years[2]	3.6	6.1	9.2	11.6	13.2
15 to 19 years	3.3	5.1	6.6	7.9	9.8
20 to 24 years	5.7	10.0	18.2	22.1	23.1
25 to 29 years	4.0	8.7	18.2	24.3	22.1
30 to 34 years	2.5	5.9	10.8	16.6	15.1

[Continued]

★ 2107 ★

Births and Rates of Births Out of Wedlock: by Age of Mother – 1940, 1950, 1960, 1965, 1968

[Continued]

Age and race of mother	1940	1950	1960[1]	1965[1]	1968[1]
35 to 39 years	1.7	3.2/	3.9[4]	4.9[4]	4.7[4]
40 to 44 years	0.7[3]	0.9[3]/			

Source: "Estimated Illegitimacy Rates by Age of Mother: 1940, 1950, 1960, 1965, and 1968." U.S. Bureau of the Census. Current Population Reports, Special Studies, Series P-23, No. 38. *The Social and Economic Status of the Black Population in the United States, 1970.* Washington, D.C.: Government Printing Office, 1970, p. 115. Primary source: U.S. Department of Health, Education, and Welfare. *Notes:* 1. Based on a 50 percent sample of births. 2. Rates computed by relating total illegitimate births regardless of age of mother to unmarried women 15 to 44 years old. 3. Rates computed by relating illegitimate births to mothers aged 40 and over to unmarried women 40 to 44 years old. 4. Rates computed by relating illegitimate births to mothers aged 35 and over to unmarried women 35 to 44 years old.

★ 2108 ★

Births

Births by Sex and Age of Mother in Selected States, 1930

Colored births[1] (exclusive of stillbirths), by sex, and by age of mother, in selected registration states: 1930[2].

Area and sex	Total births	Births by age of mother									
		10 to 14 years	15 to 19 years	20 to 24 years	25 to 29 years	30 to 34 years	35 to 39 years	40 to 44 years	45 to 49 years	50 years and over	Unknown
Selected states											
Alabama	22,977	178	5,611	7,465	4,452	2,595	1,911	559	106	-	100
Male	11,595	88	2,836	3,755	2,297	1,305	928	283	53	-	50
Female	11,382	90	2,775	3,710	2,155	1,290	983	276	53	-	50
Arkansas	9,093	71	2,278	2,726	1,735	1,064	736	215	26	4	238
Male	4,602	30	1,165	1,358	896	525	390	101	13	2	122
Female	4,491	41	1,113	1,368	839	539	346	114	13	2	116
Connecticut	736	1	147	269	158	98	48	12	1	1	1
Male	375	1	73	140	84	56	15	6	-	-	-
Female	361	-	74	129	74	42	33	6	1	1	1
Delaware	728	4	197	182	134	95	71	30	5	-	10
Male	370	2	95	86	74	56	36	18	1	-	2
Female	358	2	102	96	60	39	35	12	4	-	8
District of Columbia	3,054	30	745	1,025	579	331	213	61	6	-	64
Male	1,605	15	389	564	277	170	120	36	4	-	30
Female	1,449	15	356	461	302	161	93	25	2	-	34
Florida	8,391	79	2,136	2,484	1,788	969	632	182	32	1	88
Male	4,293	41	1,089	1,273	903	489	337	100	20	1	40
Female	4,098	38	1,047	1,211	885	480	295	82	12	-	48
Georgia	23,404	211	6,430	7,310	4,179	2,510	1,971	604	136	4	49
Male	11,826	115	3,259	3,697	2,137	1,205	1,002	301	79	1	30
Female	11,578	96	3,171	3,613	2,042	1,305	969	303	57	3	19
Illinois	6,013	23	1,304	1,974	1,334	804	447	109	9	-	9
Male	3,080	10	677	982	687	423	235	57	4	-	5
Female	2,933	13	627	992	647	381	212	52	5	-	4
Indiana	1,985	16	488	547	445	269	165	48	7	-	-
Male	960	6	244	261	198	132	88	27	4	-	-
Female	1,025	10	244	286	247	137	77	21	3	-	-
Iowa	288	-	71	76	66	39	29	6	1	-	-

[Continued]

★ 2108 ★

Births by Sex and Age of Mother in Selected States, 1930

[Continued]

Area and sex	Total births	Births by age of mother									
		10 to 14 years	15 to 19 years	20 to 24 years	25 to 29 years	30 to 34 years	35 to 39 years	40 to 44 years	45 to 49 years	50 years and over	Unknown
Male	143	-	37	33	29	17	21	5	1	-	-
Female	145	-	34	43	37	22	8	1	-	-	-
Kansas	1,540	11	282	416	353	239	162	64	7	-	6
Male	791	7	136	206	196	127	82	30	4	-	3
Female	749	4	146	210	157	112	80	34	3	-	3
Kentucky	3,381	30	740	904	710	505	344	120	20	-	8
Male	1,691	11	386	457	342	249	176	56	10	-	4
Female	1,690	19	354	447	368	256	168	64	10	-	4
Louisiana	16,731	98	3,632	5,332	3,505	2,065	1,446	472	77	2	102
Male	8,455	49	1,852	2,645	1,794	1,040	744	238	37	1	55
Female	8,276	49	1,780	2,687	1,711	1,025	702	234	40	1	47
Maryland	6,417	55	1,548	1,787	1,299	896	573	206	35	1	17
Male	3,155	27	745	887	637	458	281	100	13	1	6
Female	3,262	28	803	900	662	438	292	106	22	-	11
Massachusetts	1,029	5	156	264	233	183	133	39	4	1	11
Male	511	4	76	136	110	86	74	19	-	1	5
Female	518	1	80	128	123	97	59	20	4	-	6
Michigan	3,907	9	707	1,273	951	567	306	59	6	-	29
Male	1,989	3	355	655	483	300	143	29	4	-	17
Female	1,918	6	352	618	468	267	163	30	2	-	12
Mississippi	24,880	206	5,945	8,104	4,515	3,013	2,013	645	115	9	315
Male	12,778	97	3,080	4,130	2,288	1,566	1,043	349	65	4	156
Female	12,102	109	2,865	3,974	2,227	1,447	970	296	50	5	159
Missouri	3,770	35	989	1,064	775	486	316	85	9	-	11
Male	1,935	17	527	515	391	266	158	50	5	-	6
Female	1,835	18	462	549	384	220	158	35	4	-	5
Nebraska	606	4	111	178	133	104	51	19	-	1	5
Male	283	2	50	89	65	45	26	6	-	-	-
Female	323	2	61	89	68	59	25	13	-	1	5
New Hampshire	10	-	1	3	2	1	2	1	-	-	-
Male	4	-	-	1	1	1	-	1	-	-	-
Female	6	-	1	2	1	-	2	-	-	-	-
New Jersey	4,991	19	945	1,672	1,190	655	379	116	11	1	3
Male	2,546	9	453	861	607	350	187	72	4	1	2
Female	2,445	10	492	811	583	305	192	44	7	-	1
New York	9,188	15	1,510	3,141	2,324	1,368	658	150	10	-	12
Male	4,676	7	765	1,614	1,164	705	327	84	6	-	4
Female	4,512	8	745	1,527	1,160	663	331	66	4	-	8
North Carolina	23,310	25	2,806	6,240	4,376	2,925	2,041	651	99	3	4,144
Male	11,877	16	1,440	3,137	2,235	1,509	1,015	329	51	1	2,144
Female	11,433	9	1,366	3,103	2,141	1,416	1,026	322	48	2	2,000
Ohio	5,992	29	1,305	1,863	1,268	830	514	167	13	1	2
Male	3,102	16	668	948	666	431	278	85	8	-	2
Female	2,890	13	637	915	602	399	236	82	5	1	-
Oklahoma	3,225	16	701	967	677	439	311	87	12	-	15
Male	1,660	7	369	500	360	223	154	35	6	-	6
Female	1,565	9	332	467	317	216	157	52	6	-	9
Pennsylvania	9,506	65	2,025	2,958	2,171	1,268	767	218	19	1	14
Male	4,819	32	1,002	1,520	1,077	667	389	115	8	1	8
Female	4,687	33	1,023	1,438	1,094	601	378	103	11	-	6
Rhode Island	244	1	39	58	62	37	33	11	-	-	3

[Continued]

★ 2108 ★

Births by Sex and Age of Mother in Selected States, 1930

[Continued]

Area and sex	Total births	Births by age of mother									
		10 to 14 years	15 to 19 years	20 to 24 years	25 to 29 years	30 to 34 years	35 to 39 years	40 to 44 years	45 to 49 years	50 years and over	Unknown
Male	114	1	14	22	31	20	20	4	-	-	2
Female	130	-	25	36	31	17	13	7	-	-	1
South Carolina	20,403	86	4,724	6,899	3,872	2,313	1,869	543	88	-	9
Male	10,365	43	2,350	3,486	2,024	1,158	967	287	47	-	3
Female	10,038	43	2,374	3,413	1,848	1,155	902	256	41	-	6
Tennessee	8,106	65	2,046	2,480	1,580	982	694	202	41	3	13
Male	4,219	31	1,047	1,281	818	522	390	101	21	-	8
Female	3,887	34	999	1,199	762	460	304	101	20	3	5
Vermont	11	-	3	3	2	1	2	-	-	-	-
Male	6	-	2	1	-	1	2	-	-	-	-
Female	5	-	1	2	2	-	-	-	-	-	-
Virginia	15,732	108	3,252	4,541	3,103	2,258	1,746	603	79	-	42
Male	7,869	63	1,597	2,292	1,585	1,109	882	292	30	-	19
Female	7,863	45	1,655	2,249	1,518	1,149	864	311	49	-	23
West Virginia	2,462	19	500	747	530	372	223	63	8	-	-
Male	1,274	8	248	383	292	181	126	33	3	-	-
Female	1,188	11	252	364	238	191	97	30	5	-	-

Source: "Colored Births (Exclusive of Stillbirths), by Sex, and Age of Mother, in Selected Registration States: 1930." U.S. Bureau of the Census. *Negroes in the United States: 1920-32.* Washington, D.C.: Government Printing Office, 1935, p. 425. *Notes:* 1. Includes Negro and other nonwhite races. 2. States in which the Negro population constitutes 55 percent or more of the total colored population.

★ 2109 ★

Births

Births out of Wedlock, by Age of Mother – 1940, 1950, 1960, 1965, 1968

Rates per 1,000 unmarried women in specified group.

Age and race of mother	1940	1950	1960[1]	1965[1]	1968[1]
Negro and other races					
Total, 15 to 44 years[2]	35.6	71.2	98.3	97.6	86.6
15 to 19 years	42.5	68.5	76.5	75.8	82.8
20 to 24 years	46.1	105.4	166.5	152.6	118.3
25 to 29 years	32.5	94.2	171.8	164.7	104.4
30 to 34 years	23.4	63.5	104.0	137.8	80.6
35 to 39 years	13.2	31.3/			
40 to 44 years	5.0[3]	8.7[3]/	35.6[4]	39.0[4]	25.2[4]
White					
Total, 15 to 44 years[2]	3.6	6.1	9.2	11.6	13.2
15 to 19 years	3.3	5.1	6.6	7.9	9.8
20 to 24 years	5.7	10.0	18.2	22.1	23.1
25 to 29 years	4.0	8.7	18.2	24.3	22.1
30 to 34 years	2.5	5.9	10.8	16.6	15.1

[Continued]

★ 2109 ★

Births out of Wedlock, by Age of Mother – 1940, 1950, 1960, 1965, 1968

[Continued]

Age and race of mother	1940	1950	1960[1]	1965[1]	1968[1]
35 to 39 years	1.7	3.2/			
40 to 44 years	0.7[3]	0.9[3]/	3.9[4]	4.9[4]	4.7[4]

Source: "Estimated Illegitimacy Rates by Age of Mother: 1940. 1950, 1960, 1965, and 1968." U.S. Bureau of the Census. Current Population Reports, Special Studies, Series P-23, No. 42. *The Social and Economic Status of the Black Population in the United States, 1971.* Washington, D.C.: Government Printing Office, 1972, p. 111. Primary source: U.S. Department of Health, Education, and Welfare. *Notes:* 1. Based on a 50 percent sample of births. 2. Rates computed by relating total illegitimate births regardless of age of mother to unmarried women 15 to 44 years old. 3. Rates computed by relating illegitimate births to mothers aged 40 and over to unmarried women 40 to 44 years old. 4. Rates computed by relating illegitimate births to mothers aged 35 and over to unmarried women 35 to 44 years old.

★ 2110 ★

Births

Births out of Wedlock, by Race and Age of Mother, 1950-1973

In thousands, except as indicated. Prior to 1960, excludes Alaska and Hawaii. Includes estimates for states in which legitimacy data were not reported. No estimates included for misstatements on birth records or failures to register births.

Race and age	1950	1955	1960	1965	1970[1]	1971[1]	1972[1]	1973[1]
Total	141.6	183.3	224.3	291.2	398.7	401.4	403.2	407.3
Percent of births[2]	3.9	4.5	5.3	7.7	10.7	11.3	12.4	13.0
Rate[3]	14.1	19.3	21.6	23.5	26.4	25.6	24.9	24.5
White	6.1	7.9	9.2	11.6	13.8	12.5	12.0	11.9
Negro and other	71.2	87.2	98.3	97.6	89.9	90.6	86.9	84.2
Race of mother:								
White	53.5	64.2	82.5	123.7	175.1	163.8	160.5	163.0
Negro and other	88.1	119.2	141.8	167.5	223.6	237.5	242.7	244.3
Percent of total	62.2	65.0	63.2	57.5	56.1	59.2	60.2	60.0
Age of mother:								
Under 15 years	3.2	3.9	4.6	6.1	9.5	9.5	9.9	10.9
15-19 years	56.0	68.9	87.1	123.1	190.4	194.1	202.3	204.9
20-24 years	43.1	55.7	68.0	90.7	126.7	125.2	119.6	119.1
25-29 years	20.9	28.0	32.1	36.8	40.6	40.9	41.2	43.1
30-34 years	10.8	16.1	18.9	19.6	19.1	19.3	19.0	18.5
35-39 years	6.0	8.3	10.6	11.4	9.4	9.4	8.6	8.2
40 years and over	1.7	2.4	3.0	3.7	3.0	3.0	2.7	2.6

Source: "Illegitimate Live Births, by Race and Age of Mother: 1950 to 1973." Bureau of the Census, *Statistical Abstract of the United States, 1975.* Washington, D.C.: U.S. Government Printing Office, 1975, p. 57. Primary source: U.S. National Center for Health Statistics, *Vital Statistics of the United States*, annual. *Notes:* 1. Excludes nonresident aliens. 2. Through 1955, based on data adjusted for underregistration; thereafter, registered births. For total birth figures used to derive these data, see table 67. 3. Rate per 1,000 unmarried (never married, widowed, and divorced) women aged 15-44 years enumerated as of April 1 for census years and estimated as of July 1 for all other years.

★ 2111 ★

Births

Births per 100 Deaths in Cities Having 25,000 or More Black Inhabitants – 1930, 1931

Number of colored[1] and white births (exclusive of stillbirths) per 100 deaths in the birth registration cities having 25,000 or more negro inhabitants: 1931 and 1930.

City	1931		1930	
	Colored	White	Colored	White
Atlanta, Ga	87	163	86	166
Baltimore, Md	108	128	116	139
Birmingham, Ala	105	190	111	189
Charleston, S. C.	86	155	94	156
Charlotte, N. C.	86	218	94	219
Chattanooga, Tenn	67	170	59	175
Chicago, Ill	119	151	117	171
Cincinnati, Ohio	80	122	92	131
Cleveland, Ohio	100	170	117	190
Columbus, Ohio	104	123	100	123
Detroit, Mich	133	228	133	238
Indianapolis, Ind	102	137	98	138
Jacksonville, Fla	81	175	75	175
Kansas City, Mo	64	128	67	134
Louisville, Ky	71	141	66	152
Memphis, Tenn	80	140	79	146
Miami, Fla	136	144	151	170
Montgomery, Ala	89	160	79	145
Nashville, Tenn	90	151	84	173
Newark, N. J.	165	191	145	194
New Orleans, La	100	134	96	130
New York, N. Y.	119	151	130	166
Bronx Borough	129	168	107	185
Brooklyn Borough	149	176	167	196
Manhattan Borough	116	122	126	133
Queens Borough	82	153	103	171
Richmond Borough	22	127	30	132
Norfolk, Va	87	166	83	175
Philadelphia, Pa	129	135	137	148
Pittsburgh, Pa	104	157	119	167
Richmond, Va	102	133	106	148
St. Louis, Mo	84	119	95	133
Savannah, Ga	66	152	68	146
Shreveport, La	90	135	72	140
Washington, D. C.	101	133	109	138
Winston-Salem, N. C.	116	259	109	231

Source: "Number of Colored and White Births (Exclusive of Stillbirths) Per 100 Deaths in the Birth Registration Cities Having 25,000 or More Negro Inhabitants: 1931 and 1930." U.S. Bureau of the Census. *Negroes in the United States: 1920-32*. Washington, D.C.: Government Printing Office, 1935, p. 365. *Note:* 1. Includes Negro, and other nonwhite races.

★ 2112 ★

Births

Children Born to Women 35 to 44 years Old: Marital Status and Characteristics, 1960-1974

Refers to total population as of April 1960 and April 1970, based on a 5-percent sample from 1960 to 1970 census; and to civilian noninstitutional population as of June 1973 and 1974, based on Current Population Survey.

Characteristic	Total women (including single)					Women ever married				
	Number of women, 1974 (1,000)	Children ever born per 1,000 women				Number of women, 1974 (1,000)	Children ever born per 1,000 women			
		1960	1970	1973	1974		1960	1970	1973	1974
Total	11,613	2,465	2,956	3,015	2,958	11,041	2,625	3,132	3,169	3,111
White	10,080	2,419	2,888	2,967	2,891	9,618	2,572	3,047	3,105	3,030
Negro	1,330	2,835	3,489	3,436	3,495	1,227	3,049	3,817	3,727	3,789
Metropolitan	8,102	2,267	2,855	2,917	2,853	7,655	2,431	3,037	3,086	3,020
Nonmetropolitan[1]	3,512	2,857	3,203	3,244	3,197	3,386	3,000	3,356	3,357	3,316
In labor force	6,313	1,946	2,620	2,755	2,694	5,856	2,191	2,858	2,957	2,904
Not in labor force	5,300	2,851	3,295	3,318	3,272	5,184	2,918	3,393	3,404	3,345
Years of school completed										
Elementary: Less than 8 years	697	3,205	3,575	3,710	3,778	620	3,478	4,037	4,093	4,247
8 years	658	2,717	3,366	3,447	3,622	640	2,861	3,552	3,627	3,723
High school: 1-3 years	2,038	2,548	3,230	3,557	3,460	1,960	2,658	3,357	3,679	3,598
4 years	5,517	2,243	2,820	2,852	2,834	5,290	2,373	2,952	2,965	2,956
College: 1-3 years	1,357	2,207	2,743	2,827	2,748	1,312	2,361	2,889	2,961	2,842
4 years or more	1,346	1,918	2,297	2,345	2,163	1,219	2,233	2,591	2,596	2,389

Source: "Children Ever Born to Women 35 to 44 Years Old, by Marital Status and Selected Characteristics: 1960 to 1974." Bureau of the Census, *Statistical Abstract of the United States, 1975.* Washington, D.C.: U.S. Government Printing Office, 1975, p. 56. Primary source: U.S. Bureau of the Census, U.S. *Census of Population, 1960, Women by Number of Children Ever Born*, PC(2)- 3A; *U.S. Census of Population, 1970, Women by Number of Children Ever Born*, PC(2)- 3A and *Detailed Characteristics*, PC(1)- D; and *Current Population Reports*, series P-20, No. 277. *Notes:* 1. 1960 data refer to 212 SMSA's as defined in 1960 census publications; beginning 1970, data refer to 243 SMSA's as defined in 1970 census publications.

★ 2113 ★

Births

Children Born to Women Ever Married, 1910 to 1970

Year and race	15-44 years	15-19 years	20-24 years	25-29 years	30-34 years	35-39 years	40-44 years	45-49 years	50-59 years
	Percent childless among women ever married, by age of women								
Total									
1970	16.4	50.9	35.7	15.8	8.3	7.3	8.6	10.6	15.6
1960	15.0	43.6	24.2	12.6	10.4	11.1	14.1	18.1	20.7
1950	22.8	52.8	33.3	21.1	17.3	19.1	20.0	20.4	18.1
1940	26.5	54.6	39.9	30.1	23.3	19.9	17.4	16.8	16.6
1910	16.2	42.7	24.2	17.2	13.7	11.6	10.4	9.5	8.7
White									
1970	16.7	53.7	37.5	16.1	8.1	6.9	8.1	9.9	14.7
1960	14.6	46.0	25.0	12.3	9.7	10.2	13.0	17.1	20.0
1950	21.8	55.4	34.0	20.1	15.8	17.5	18.9	19.5	17.5

[Continued]

★ 2113 ★

Children Born to Women Ever Married, 1910 to 1970

[Continued]

Year and race	15-44 years	15-19 years	20-24 years	25-29 years	30-34 years	35-39 years	40-44 years	45-49 years	50-59 years
1940	25.9	56.4	40.3	29.7	22.3	18.9	16.7	16.3	16.5
1910	15.9	43.5	24.2	16.8	13.4	11.5	10.4	9.6	8.8
Negro									
1970	13.8	32.2	20.7	12.6	9.4	9.8	13.0	17.9	24.4
1960	18.7	25.3	17.0	14.2	15.8	20.0	24.7	27.9	28.1
1950	30.8	38.0	28.9	30.0	30.8	32.3	30.1	28.4	25.1
1940	32.8	46.6	38.7	35.1	31.0	28.8	25.8	23.8	19.8
1910	18.7	39.7	24.2	19.6	16.5	13.3	10.5	8.6	7.4
	Children ever born per 1,000 women ever married, by age of women								
Total									
1970	2,360	636	1,071	1,984	2,806	3,170	3,097	2,854	2,520
1960	2,314	792	1,441	2,241	2,627	2,686	2,564	2,402	2,420
1950	1,859	604	1,082	1,654	2,059	2,247	2,364	2,492	2,822
1940	1,904	572	987	1,463	1,964	2,414	2,754	2,998	3,215
1910	2,866	725	1,407	2,180	2,956	3,781	4,383	4,744	5,076
White									
1970	2,285	579	1,006	1,922	2,734	3,086	3,012	2,791	2,470
1960	2,253	729	1,370	2,171	2,559	2,629	2,516	2,354	2,378
1950	1,828	548	1,028	1,620	2,034	2,218	2,329	2,456	2,786
1940	1,870	539	941	1,413	1,922	2,369	2,717	2,968	3,180
1910	2,806	699	1,344	2,099	2,880	3,683	4,263	4,594	4,929
Negro									
1970	2,976	1,026	1,631	2,541	3,395	3,839	3,795	3,394	2,938
1960	2,808	1,258	2,030	2,835	3,190	3,139	2,949	2,761	2,756
1950	2,089	921	1,474	1,931	2,250	2,450	2,619	2,767	3,175
1940	2,096	723	1,234	1,761	2,243	2,666	3,012	3,255	3,660
1910	3,237	834	1,696	2,645	3,532	4,515	5,484	6,162	6,709

Source: "Children Ever Born to Women Ever Married, by Race and Age of Women: 1910 to 1970." *Historical Statistics of the United States: Colonial Times to 1970, Part I.* Bicentennial Edition. Washington, D.C.: Government Printing Office, 1975, p. 54.

★2114★

Births

Children Born to Women Who Bore Children: Average – 1930, 1931

Average number of children ever born to women who bore children in 1931 and 1930, by age, and color of mother in the registration area in continental United States[1].

Color and year	All ages	Under 20	20 to 24	25 to 29	30 to 34	35 to 39	40 to 44	45 to 49	50 and over	Unknown
Total										
1931	3.1	1.3	1.9	2.9	4.2	5.8	7.4	9.0	7.3	2.6
1930	3.1	1.3	1.9	2.9	4.2	5.8	7.5	9.0	7.5	2.5
Colored										
1931	3.7	1.3	2.5	4.2	5.9	7.5	9.1	10.0	7.7	2.4
1930	3.7	1.3	2.5	4.2	5.9	7.5	9.2	10.2	8.2	2.3
Negro										
1931	3.6	1.3	2.5	4.2	5.9	7.5	9.2	10.1	8.0	2.3
1930	3.6	1.3	2.5	4.2	5.9	7.6	9.3	10.3	8.4	2.2
Other colored										
1931	4.2	1.4	2.5	4.2	5.9	7.5	8.6	9.3	6.6	3.8
1930	4.0	1.3	2.4	4.0	5.4	6.8	8.2	8.8	7.5	3.5
White										
1931	3.0	1.2	1.9	2.8	4.0	5.5	7.3	8.8	7.2	2.9
1930	3.1	1.2	1.9	2.8	4.0	5.6	7.3	8.8	7.2	2.8

Source: "Average Number of Children Ever Born to Women Who Bore Children in 1931 and 1930, by Age, and Color of Mother, in the Registration Area in Continental United States." U.S. Bureau of the Census. *Negroes in the United States: 1920-32.* Washington, D.C.: Government Printing Office, 1935, p. 364. *Notes:* 1. Exclusive of Colorado, Maine, Massachusetts, New Hampshire, and Rhode Island.

★2115★

Births

Children Born to Women by Specific Age and Characteristics, 1969

Subject	Negro		White	
	Children ever born per woman	Replacement index[1]	Children ever born per woman	Replacement index[1]
United States	3.6	175	2.9	142
Region				
South	4.0	191	2.9	138
Remainder of United States	3.3	160	3.0	143
Education				
Elementary, 0 to 8 years	4.5	215	3.6	172
High school, 1 to 4 years	3.5	167	2.9	139
College, 1 year or more	2.3	113	2.6	128

[Continued]

★ 2115 ★

Children Born to Women by Specific Age and Characteristics, 1969

[Continued]

Subject	Negro		White	
	Children ever born per woman	Replacement index[1]	Children ever born per woman	Replacement index[1]
Labor force status				
Labor force	3.2	153	2.6	125
Not in labor force	4.3	208	3.2	157

Source: "Children Ever Born to All Women 34 to 44 Years Old, by Specific Characteristics of Women, 1969." U.S. Bureau of the Census. Current Population Reports, Special Studies, Series P-23, No. 38. *The Social and Economic Status of the Black Population in the United States, 1970*. Washington, D.C.: Government Printing Office, 1970, p. 118. Primary source: U.S. Department of Commerce, Bureau of the Census. *Notes:* "All Women" includes those ever married and never married. 1. Index of 100 denotes that the women will have exactly the number of children ever born by age 45 needed for replacement of the women. Negro women 35 to 44 years old have have completed approximately 96 percent of their eventual lifetime childbearing and white women of this group have completed approximately 97 percent of their eventual lifetime childbearing.

★ 2116 ★

Births

Children Born to Women, by Age and Marital Status: Birth Rates, 1960-1971

Marital status and age of women	April 1960	June 1965	January 1969	June 1971
Total women[1]				
Total, 15 to 44 years	2.0	2.1	2.0	1.8
15 to 19 years	0.2	0.2	0.1	0.1
20 to 24 years	1.3	1.2	1.0	0.9
25 to 29 years	2.4	2.6	2.3	2.0
30 to 34 years	2.9	3.4	3.1	3.0
35 to 39 years	2.9	3.5	3.7	3.6
40 to 44 years	2.8	3.1	3.5	3.4
Women ever married				
Total, 15 to 44 years	2.8	3.1	3.1	3.0
15 to 19 years	1.3	(B)	1.1	0.9
20 to 24 years	2.0	1.8	1.8	1.6
25 to 29 years	2.8	3.0	2.8	2.6
30 to 34 years	3.2	3.9	3.5	3.5
35 to 39 years	3.1	3.8	4.0	3.9
40 to 44 years	2.9	3.4	3.6	3.7

Source: "Children Ever Born, Per Woman, by Age and Marital Status for Negro Women: 1960, 1965, 1969, and 1971." U.S. Bureau of the Census. Current Population Reports, Special Studies, Series P-23, No. 42. *The Social and Economic Status of the Black Population in the United States, 1971*. Washington, D.C.: Government Printing Office, 1972, p. 109. Primary source: U.S. Department of Commerce, Social and Economic Statistics Administration, Bureau of the Census. *Notes:* B Base too small for rate to be shown. 1. Includes single women.

★ 2117 ★

Births

Children Born to Women, by Age and Marital Status: Birth Rates, 1969

	Percent distribution of women ever married by children ever born				Children ever born	
	Total	0-1	2-4	5 and over	Per woman[1]	Per ever married woman
Negro						
15 to 44 years	100	33	42	25	2.0	3.1
15 to 19 years	100	73	27	(Z)	0.1	1.1
20 to 24 years	100	48	47	5	1.0	1.8
25 to 29 years	100	29	51	20	2.3	2.8
30 to 34 years	100	26	43	32	3.1	3.5
35 to 39 years	100	22	38	40	3.7	4.0
40 to 44 years	100	31	37	32	3.5	3.6
White						
15 to 44 years	100	33	56	11	1.7	2.4
15 to 19 years	100	91	9	(Z)	0.1	0.6
20 to 24 years	100	71	28	(Z)	0.7	1.0
25 to 29 years	100	34	62	4	1.8	2.0
30 to 34 years	100	18	69	13	2.7	2.9
35 to 39 years	100	17	64	19	3.0	3.1
40 to 44 years	100	18	64	18	2.9	3.0

Source: "Children Ever Born, by Age and Marital Status of Woman." U.S. Bureau of the Census. Current Population Reports, Special Studies, Series P-23, No. 29. *The Social and Economic Status of the Black Population in the United States, 1969.* Washington, D.C.: Government Printing Office, 1970, p. 79. Primary source: U.S. Department of Commerce, Bureau of the Census. *Notes:* Z Represents zero or rounds to zero. 1. Including single women.

★ 2118 ★

Births

Children Born to Women, by Age of Woman: Birth Rates, 1940-1969

	1940	1950	1960	1965	1969
Negro					
15 to 19 years	0.1	0.2	0.2	0.2	0.1
20 to 24 years	0.8	1.0	1.3	1.2	1.0
25 to 29 years	1.4	1.7	2.4	2.6	2.3
30 to 34 years	1.9	2.0	2.9	3.4	3.1
35 to 39 years	2.5	2.3	2.9	3.5	3.7
40 to 44 years	2.9	2.5	2.8	3.1	3.5
White					
15 to 19 years	0.0	0.1	0.1	0.1	0.1
20 to 24 years	0.5	0.7	1.0	0.9	0.6
25 to 29 years	1.0	1.4	2.0	2.1	1.8

[Continued]

★ 2118 ★

Children Born to Women, by Age of Woman: Birth Rates, 1940-1969

[Continued]

	1940	1950	1960	1965	1969
30 to 34 years	1.6	1.8	2.4	2.7	2.7
35 to 39 years	2.1	2.0	2.5	2.8	3.0
40 to 44 years	2.5	2.1	2.4	2.7	2.9

Source: "Children Ever Born by Age of Woman." U.S. Bureau of the Census. Current Population Reports, Special Studies, Series P-23, No. 29. *The Social and Economic Status of the Black Population in the United States, 1969.* Washington, D.C.: Government Printing Office, 1969, p. 81. Primary source: U.S. Department of Commerce, Bureau of the Census.

★ 2119 ★

Births

Children Ever Born, by Age and Marital Status of Mother, 1969

Age of woman	Number (thousands)	Percent distribution of women ever married by children ever born				Children ever born	
		Total	0 to 1	2 to 4	5 or more	Per woman[1]	Per ever married woman
Negro							
Total, 15 to 44 years	3,115	100	33	42	25	2.0	3.1
15 to 19 years	157	100	73	27	-	0.1	1.1
20 to 24 years	581	100	48	47	5	1.0	1.8
25 to 29 years	600	100	29	51	20	2.3	2.8
30 to 34 years	584	100	26	43	32	3.1	3.5
35 to 39 years	584	100	22	38	40	3.7	4.0
40 to 44 years	609	100	31	37	32	3.5	3.6
White							
Total, 15 to 44 years	25,021	100	33	56	11	1.7	2.4
15 to 19 years	925	100	91	9	-	0.1	0.6
20 to 24 years	4,411	100	71	28	-	0.7	1.0
25 to 29 years	4,802	100	34	62	4	1.8	2.0
30 to 34 years	4,611	100	18	69	13	2.7	2.9
35 to 39 years	4,931	100	17	64	19	3.0	3.1
40 to 44 years	5,340	100	18	64	18	2.9	3.0

Source: "Children Ever Born, by Age and Marital Status of Woman: 1969." U.S. Bureau of the Census. Current Population Reports, Special Studies, Series P-23, No. 38. *The Social and Economic Status of the Black Population in the United States, 1970.* Washington, D.C.: Government Printing Office, 1970, p. 117. Primary source: U.S. Department of Commerce, Bureau of the Census. *Notes:* - Represents zero or rounds to zero. 1. Including single women.

★ 2120 ★

Births

Children Living or Ever Born: Percentage, 1927-1931

Percent of children living to those ever born in registration area, by color, and nativity of mother: 1927 to 1931[1].

Color and nativity of mother	1931	1930	1929	1928	1927
Total	91.1	91.0	90.7	90.5	90.1
Colored	87.7	87.9	87.8	87.5	86.8
Negro	88.3	88.2	87.9	87.5	86.7
Other colored	83.6	85.2	87.5	87.5	88.2
White	91.8	91.5	91.1	91.0	90.6
Native	92.1	92.0	91.8	91.7	91.4
Foreign-born	89.4	88.5	87.9	87.8	87.3
Unknown	91.8	92.1	92.2	90.6	90.1

Source: "Percent of Children Living to Those Ever Born in Registration Area, by Color, and Nativity of Mother: 1927 to 1931." U.S. Bureau of the Census. *Negroes in the United States: 1920-32.* Washington, D.C.: Government Printing Office, 1935, p. 364. *Notes:* 1. Exclusive of Delaware, Maine, Massachusetts, New Hampshire, and Rhode Island in 1927; exclusive of Colorado, Maine, Massachusetts, New Hampshire, and Rhode Island in other years.

★ 2121 ★

Births

Estimated Births Out-of-Wedlock: 1940-1975

Rates per 1,000 unmarried women in specified group. Minus sign (-) denotes decrease.

Year	Black and other races[1]			White		
	Illegitimate births		Illegitimacy rate[2]	Illegitimate births		Illegitimacy rate[2]
	Number (thousands)	Percent of total births		Number (thousands)	Percent of total births	
1940	49	16.8	35.6	40	2.0	3.6
1950	88	18.0	71.2	54	1.8	6.1
1960	142	21.6	98.3	83	2.3	9.2
1970	215	37.6	95.5	175	5.7	13.8
1975	250	48.8	85.6	186	7.3	12.6
PERCENT CHANGE						
1940 to 1950	79.6	7.1	100.0	35.0	-10.0	69.4
1950 to 1960	61.4	20.0	38.1	53.7	27.8	50.8

[Continued]

★ 2121 ★

Estimated Births Out-of-Wedlock: 1940-1975

[Continued]

Year	Black and other races[1]			White		
	Illegitimate births		Illegitimacy rate[2]	Illegitimate births		Illegitimacy rate[2]
	Number (thousands)	Percent of total births		Number (thousands)	Percent of total births	
1960 to 1970	57.7	61.6	-8.5	110.8	147.8	50.0
1970 to 1975	16.3	29.8	-10.4	6.3	28.1	-8.7

Source: "Estimated Illegitimate Births and Illegitimacy Rates: 1940 to 1975," Department of Commerce, Bureau of the Census. *The Social and Economic Status of the Black Population in the United States: An Historical View, 1790-1978,* p. 130. Primary source: U.S. Department of Health, Education, and Welfare, National Center for Health Statistics. *Notes:* As stated in the source, "No estimates are included for misstatements on the birth record or for failure to register births...The decision to conceal the illegitimacy of births is likely conditioned by attitudes in the mother's social group towards her and towards children born out of wedlock. Also the ability (economic or otherwise) to leave a community before the birth of the child is an important consideration. These factors probably result in proportionately greater understatement of illegitimacy in the White group than in Negro and other races...." A small number of States do not report the legitimacy status of births. The number of illegitimate births occurring in the nonreporting States is estimated by the National Center for Health Statistics. For the extent of coverage of legitimacy status, and the method of estimation for nonreporting States, consult the annual natality volumes of *Vital Statistics of the United States.* Beginning in 1970, data exclude births to nonresidents of the United states. 1. Data for 1970 and 1975 are for Black only. 2. Rate computed by relating total illegitimate births, regardless of age of mother, to unmarried women 15 to 44 years old.

★ 2122 ★

Births

Estimated Rates of Births Out-of-Wedlock: by Age of Mother: 1940-1975

Rates per 1,000 unmarried women in specified group.

Age and race of mother	1940	1960	1970	1975
BLACK AND OTHER RACES[1]				
Total, 15 to 44 years[2]	35.6	98.3	85.5	85.6
15 to 19 years	42.5	76.5	96.9	95.1
20 to 24 years	46.1	166.5	131.5	109.9
25 to 29 years	32.5	171.8	100.9	78.1
30 to 34 years	23.4	104.0	71.8	51.0
35 to 39 years	13.2	35.6[4,5]	32.9	20.3
40 to 44 years	5.0[3]	35.6[4,5]	10.4	7.2[3]
WHITE				
Total, 15 to 44 years[2]	3.6	9.2	13.8	12.6
15 to 19 years	3.3	6.6	10.9	12.1
20 to 24 years	5.7	18.2	22.5	15.7
25 to 29 years	4.0	18.2	21.1	15.1
30 to 34 years	2.5	10.8	14.2	10.0

[Continued]

★ 2122 ★

Estimated Rates of Births Out-of-Wedlock: by Age of Mother: 1940-1975

[Continued]

Age and race of mother	1940	1960	1970	1975
35 to 39 years	1.7	3.9[4,5]	7.6	5.4
40 to 44 years	0.7[3]	3.9[4,5]	2.0	1.5[3]

Source: "Estimated Illegitimate Rates by Age of Mother: 1940, 1970, and 1975," Department of Commerce, Bureau of the Census. *The Social and Economic Status of the Black Population in the United States: An Historical View, 1790-1978,* p. 131. Primary source: U.S. Department of Health, Education, and Welfare, National Center for Health Statistics. *Notes:* 1. Data for 1970 and 1975 are for Black only. 2. Rates computed by relating total illegitimate births regardless of age of mother to unmarried women 15 to 44 years old. 3. Rates computed by relating illegitimate births to mothers aged 40 and over to unmarried women 40 to 44 years old. 4. Rate computed by relating illegitimate births to mothers aged 35 and over to unmarried women 35 to 44. 5. Data includes 35 to 44 years.

★ 2123 ★

Births

Lifetime Births Expected, by Characteristics of Wives, 1967

Based on Survey of Economic Opportunity, February-March 1967; for details, see source.

Characteristics	Age of wife (in years)	
	14-24	30-39
Total	2,848	3,294
Residence		
Metropolitan areas	2,892	3,206
Nonmetropolitan areas	2,769	3,478
Nonfarm	2,852	3,277
Farm	2,714	3,729
Poverty status		
Above poverty line	2,812	3,138
Below poverty line	3,169	5,069
Race		
White	2,856	3,209
Negro	2,862	4,248
Years of school completed		
Elementary: 0-8	2,938	4,170
High school: 1-3	2,882	3,598
4	2,789	3,059
College: 1 year or more	2,929	2,984
Income of husband in 1966		
Under $3,000	2,993	3,992
$3,000-$4,999	2,901	3,646
$5,000-$5,999	2,677	3,307
$6,000-$7,499	2,879	3,221

[Continued]

★ 2123 ★

Lifetime Births Expected, by Characteristics of Wives, 1967

[Continued]

Characteristics	Age of wife (in years)	
	14-24	30-39
$7,500-$9,999	2,767	3,222
$10,000 and over	2,708	3,069

Source: "Lifetime Births Expected, Per 1,000 Wives, by Selected Characteristics of Wives: 1967." Bureau of the Census, *Statistical Abstract of the United States, 1973.* Washington, D.C.: U.S. Government Printing Office, 1967, p. 52. Primary source: Dept. of Commerce, Bureau of the Census; *Current Population Reports*, Series P-20, No. 211, and unpublished data.

★ 2124 ★

Births

Live Births and Birth Rates, 1915-1932 and 1933-1970

Area and year	Number				Rate[1]			
	Total	White	All other		Total	White	All other	
			Total	Negro			Total	Negro
United States[2]								
1970[3]	3,731,386	3,091,264	640,122	572,362	18.4	17.4	25.1	25.3
1969[3]	3,600,206	2,993,614	606,592	543,132	17.8	16.9	24.4	24.0
1968[3]	3,501,564	2,912,224	589,340	531,152	17.5	16.6	24.2	23.9
1967[4]	3,520,959	2,922,502	598,457	543,976	17.8	16.8	25.0	24.9
1966[3]	3,605,274	2,993,230	613,044	558,244	18.4	17.4	26.1	25.9
1965[3]	3,760,358	3,123,860	636,498	581,126	19.4	18.3	27.6	27.5
1964[3]	4,027,490	3,369,160	658,330	607,556	21.0	20.0	29.1	29.3
1963[3,5]	4,098,020	3,326,344	638,928	580,658	21.7	20.7	29.7	-
1962[3,5]	4,167,362	3,394,068	641,580	584,610	22.4	21.4	30.5	-
1961[3]	4,268,326	3,600,864	667,462	611,072	23.3	22.2	31.6	-
1960[3]	4,257,850	3,600,744	657,106	602,264	23.7	22.7	32.1	31.9
1959[3]	4,244,796	3,597,430	647,366	605,962	24.0	22.9	32.9	-
1958[3]	4,203,812	3,572,306	631,506	594,500	24.3	23.2	33.0	-
1957[3]	4,254,784	3,621,456	633,328	596,050	25.0	23.9	33.9	-
1956[3]	4,163,090	3,545,350	617,740	584,572	24.9	23.8	33.9	-
1955	4,047,295	3,458,448	588,847	558,251	24.6	23.6	33.1	-
1954[3]	4,017,362	3,443,630	573,732	544,288	24.9	23.9	33.2	-
1953[3]	3,902,120	3,356,772	545,348	517,576	24.7	23.7	32.3	-
1952[3]	3,846,986	3,322,658	524,328	497,880	24.7	23.9	31.8	-
1951[3]	3,750,850	3,237,072	513,778	489,282	24.5	23.6	31.8	-
1950	3,554,149	3,063,627	490,522	466,718	23.6	22.7	31.1	31.0
1949	3,559,529	3,083,721	475,808	453,235	23.9	23.2	30.6	-
1948	3,535,068	3,080,316	454,752	434,174	24.2	23.5	29.8	-

[Continued]

★ 2124 ★

Live Births and Birth Rates, 1915-1932 and 1933-1970

[Continued]

Area and year	Number				Rate[1]			
	Total	White	All other		Total	White	All other	
			Total	Negro			Total	Negro
1947	3,699,940	3,274,620	425,320	406,957	25.8	25.5	28.3	-
1946	3,288,672	2,913,645	375,027	358,114	23.3	23.0	25.3	-
1945	2,735,456	2,395,563	339,893	324,264	19.5	19.1	23.2	-
1944	2,794,800	2,454,700	340,100	324,183	20.2	19.8	23.6	-
1943	2,934,860	2,594,763	340,097	324,865	21.5	21.2	24.1	-
1942	2,808,996	2,486,934	322,062	307,777	20.8	20.6	23.2	-
1941	2,513,427	2,204,903	308,524	294,554	18.8	18.4	22.6	-
1940	2,360,399	2,067,953	292,446	278,869	17.9	17.5	21.7	21.7
1939	2,265,588	1,982,671	282,917	270,060	17.3	16.9	21.2	-
1938	2,286,962	2,005,955	281,007	267,700	17.6	17.2	21.2	-
1937	2,203,337	1,928,437	274,900	262,462	17.1	16.7	20.9	-
1936	2,144,790	1,881,883	262,907	251,098	16.7	16.4	20.1	-
1935	2,155,105	1,888,012	267,093	255,124	16.9	16.5	20.6	-
1934	2,167,636	1,898,501	269,135	257,106	17.2	16.7	20.9	-
1933	2,081,232	1,823,531	257,701	246,277	16.6	16.2	20.2	-
Birth-registration states[6]								
1932	2,074,042	1,822,425	251,617	239,796	17.4	17.0	21.3	-
1931	2,112,760	1,867,245	245,515	234,203	18.0	17.7	21.0	-
1930	2,203,958	1,953,163	250,795	239,275	18.9	18.6	21.6	21.6
1929	2,169,920	1,924,475	245,445	235,133	18.8	18.5	21.3	-
1928	2,233,149	1,982,246	250,903	240,683	19.7	19.4	22.1	-
1927	2,137,836	1,925,585	212,251	202,672	20.5	20.2	23.6	-
1926	1,856,068	1,707,034	149,034	139,181	20.5	20.2	25.0	-
1925	1,878,880	1,731,669	147,211	136,499	21.3	21.0	25.4	-
1924	1,930,614	1,762,872	167,742	156,947	22.2	21.9	26.3	-
1923	1,792,646	1,644,034	148,612	137,654	22.1	21.9	25.3	-
1922	1,774,911	1,629,387	145,524	134,824	22.3	22.1	25.3	-
1921	1,714,261	1,565,446	148,815	138,495	24.2	23.9	27.6	-
1920	1,508,874	1,395,523	113,351	103,796	23.7	23.5	27.0	26.3
1919	1,373,438	1,269,363	104,075	95,516	22.4	22.3	24.9	-
1918	1,363,649	1,288,711	74,938	72,351	24.7	24.8	24.3	-
1917	1,353,792	1,280,288	73,504	71,139	24.5	24.5	24.3	-
1916	818,983	799,817	19,166	18,619	24.9	25.0	20.4	-
1915	776,304	763,899	12,405	11,931	25.0	25.1	18.4	-

Source: "Live Births and Birth Rates by Race: Birth-Registration States: 1915- 32, and Uited States, 1933-70." U.S. Department of Health, Education, and Welfare, Public Health Service, National Center for Health Statistics. Vital Statistics of the United States 1970. Vol. 1—Natility. Rockville, Md.: 1975. For sale by the Superintendent of Documents, Washington, D.C. *Notes:* 1. For 1941-46, based on population including Armed Forces abroad. 2. Alaska included beginning 1959, and Hawaii, 1960. Beginning 1970, excludes births to nonresidents of the United States. 3. Based on a 50-percent sample of births. 4. Based on a 20- to 50-percent sample of births. 5. Figures by race exclude data for residents of New Jersey; see Technical Appendix. 6. Increased in number from 10 States and the District of Columbia in 1915 to the entire conterminous United States in 1933; see Technical Appendix.

★ 2125 ★

Births

Live Births and Birth Rates, 1950-1975

Data are based on the National Vital Statistics System.

Race of child and year	Live birth	Crude birth rate[1]	Live birth per 1,000 women by age of woman								
			10-14 years	15-17 years	18-19 years	20-24 years	25-29 years	30-34 years	35-39 years	40-44 years	45-49 years
All races											
1950	3,632,000	24.1	1.0	40.7	132.7	196.6	166.1	103.7	52.9	15.1	1.2
1955	4,097,000	25.0	0.9	44.5	157.9	241.6	190.2	116.0	58.6	16.1	1.0
1960	4,257,850	23.7	0.8	43.9	166.7	258.1	197.4	112.7	56.2	15.5	0.9
1965	3,760,358	19.4	0.8	36.6	124.5	195.3	161.6	94.4	46.2	12.8	0.8
1970	3,731,386	18.4	1.2	38.8	114.7	167.8	145.1	73.3	31.7	8.1	0.5
1975	3,144,198	14.6	1.3	36.1	85.0	113.0	108.2	52.3	19.5	4.6	0.3
1980	3,612,258	15.9	1.1	32.5	82.1	115.1	112.9	61.9	19.8	3.9	0.2
1981	3,629,238	15.8	1.1	32.1	81.7	111.8	112.0	61.4	20.0	3.8	0.2
1982	3,680,537	15.9	1.1	32.4	80.7	111.3	111.0	64.2	21.1	3.9	0.2
1983	3,638,933	15.5	1.1	32.0	78.1	108.3	108.7	64.6	22.1	3.8	0.2
1984	3,669,141	15.5	1.2	31.1	78.3	107.3	108.3	66.5	22.8	3.9	0.2
1985	3,760,561	15.8	1.2	31.1	80.8	108.9	110.5	68.5	23.9	4.0	0.2
1986	3,756,547	15.6	1.3	30.6	81.0	108.2	109.2	69.3	24.3	4.1	0.2
White											
1950	3,108,000	23.0	0.4	31.3	120.5	190.4	165.1	102.6	51.4	14.5	1.0
1955	3,485,000	23.8	0.3	35.4	145.7	235.8	186.6	114.0	56.7	15.4	0.9
1960	3,600,744	22.7	0.4	35.5	154.6	252.8	194.9	109.6	54.0	14.7	0.8
1965	3,123,860	18.3	0.3	27.8	111.9	189.0	158.4	91.6	44.0	12.0	0.7
1970	3,091,264	17.4	0.5	29.2	101.5	163.4	145.9	71.9	30.0	7.5	0.4
1975	2,551,996	13.6	0.6	28.0	74.0	108.2	108.1	51.3	18.2	4.2	0.2
1980	2,898,732	14.9	0.6	25.2	72.1	109.5	112.4	60.4	18.5	3.4	0.2
1981	2,908,669	14.8	0.5	25.1	71.9	106.3	111.3	60.2	18.7	3.4	0.2
1982	2,942,054	14.9	0.6	25.2	70.8	105.9	110.3	63.3	20.0	3.5	0.2
1983	2,904,250	14.6	0.6	24.8	68.3	102.6	108.0	64.0	21.0	3.5	0.2
1984	2,923,502	14.5	0.6	23.9	68.1	101.4	107.7	66.1	21.7	3.5	0.2
1985	2,991,373	14.8	0.6	24.0	70.1	102.8	110.0	68.1	22.7	3.6	0.2
1986	2,970,439	14.5	0.6	23.4	69.8	101.5	108.3	68.9	23.3	3.7	0.2
Black											
1960	602,264	31.9	4.3	-	-	295.4	218.6	137.1	73.9	21.9	1.1
1965	581,126	27.7	4.3	99.3	227.6	243.1	180.4	111.3	61.9	18.7	1.4
1970	572,362	25.3	5.2	101.4	204.9	202.7	136.3	79.6	41.9	12.5	1.0
1975	511,581	20.7	5.1	85.6	152.4	142.8	102.2	53.1	25.6	7.5	0.5
1980	589,616	22.1	4.3	73.6	138.8	146.3	109.1	62.9	24.5	5.8	0.3
1981	587,797	21.6	4.1	70.6	135.9	141.2	108.3	60.4	24.2	5.6	0.3
1982	592,641	21.4	4.1	71.2	133.3	139.1	106.9	60.4	24.4	5.4	0.4
1983	586,027	20.9	4.1	70.1	130.4	137.7	103.4	59.2	24.7	5.2	0.3
1984	592,745	20.8	4.3	69.7	132.0	137.9	103.2	59.5	24.8	5.1	0.2

[Continued]

★ 2125 ★

Live Births and Birth Rates, 1950-1975

[Continued]

Race of child and year	Live birth	Crude birth rate[1]	Live birth per 1,000 women by age of woman								
			10-14 years	15-17 years	18-19 years	20-24 years	25-29 years	30-34 years	35-39 years	40-44 years	45-49 years
1985	608,193	21.1	4.5	69.8	137.1	140.8	105.1	60.7	25.5	4.9	0.3
1986	621,221	21.2	4.6	70.0	141.0	143.7	105.9	62.2	25.5	5.1	0.3

Source: "Live Births, Crude Birth Rates, and Birth Rates by Age of Mother according to Race of Child: United States, Selected Years 1950-86," *Health United States - 1988*, p. 42. Primary source: *Vital Statistics of the United States, 1986.* National Center for Health Statistics. *Notes:* Data are based on births adjusted for underregistration for 1950 and on registered births for all other years. Beginning in 1970, births to nonresidents of the United States are excluded. 1. Live births per 1,000 population.

★ 2126 ★

Births

Live Births by Person in Attendance, 1936-1945

Year	Percent of live births attended by					
	Physician (in hospital))		Physician (not in hospital)		Midwife, Other, and not specified	
	White	Nonwhite	White	Nonwhite	White	Nonwhite
1945	84.3	40.2	13.7	21.7	2.0	38.1
1944	81.0	37.0	16.9	23.1	2.1	39.9
1943	77.2	33.3	20.6	24.0	2.2	42.7
1942	72.7	30.6	24.8	24.0	2.5	45.3
1941	65.7	29.0	31.2	23.3	3.1	47.7
1940	59.9	26.7	36.5	24.1	3.6	49.2
1939	55.0	24.3	41.1	24.8	3.9	50.9
1938	51.6	22.7	44.2	25.0	4.2	52.3
1937	48.2	21.0	47.3	25.5	4.5	53.5
1936	43.9	19.5	50.4	25.5	5.7	55.0

Source: "Percent Distribution of Live Births, by Persons in Attendance and by Race: United States, 1936-45." Murray, Florence, ed. *The Negro Handbook, 1949.* New York: Macmillan, 1949, p. 19. Primary source: U.S. Office of Vital Statistics.

★ 2127 ★

Births

Median Interval Between Births, by Race, 1930 to 1969

Race and interval	Year of birth of child							
	1965-1969	1960-1964	1955-1959	1950-1954	1945-1949	1940-1944	1935-1939	1930-1934
White								
Median interval in months from								
First marriage of mother to birth of first child	15.5	14.5	16.2	17.7	18.4	20.2	20.1	20.3
Birth of first child to birth of second child	29.3	25.9	28.2	30.7	32.9	32.8	32.0	32.2
Birth of second child to birth of third child	33.1	31.6	33.0	31.3	33.1	34.0	34.2	31.8
Birth of third child to birth of fourth child	35.0	31.2	30.4	30.0	32.5	34.4	32.8	33.1
Negro and other								
Median interval in months from								
First marriage of mother to birth of first child	-	9.0	11.9	12.7	11.1	10.7	12.9	11.9
Birth of first child to birth of second child	-	23.3	23.4	23.3	24.9	27.3	22.8	27.6
Birth of second child to birth of third child	-	23.8	23.3	23.4	24.6	24.1	22.6	(B)
Birth of third child to birth of fourth child	-	22.1	22.9	22.4	23.8	24.0	(B)	(B)

Source: "Median Interval Between Births, by Race: 1930 to 1969." U.S. Bureau of the Census. *Historical Statistics of the United States: Colonial Times to 1970, Part I.* Bicentennial Edition. Washington, D.C.: Government Printing Office, 1975, p. 55. *Notes:* B not shown; base for estimate is too small (number of children reported by women surviving to 1969 is less than 150,000).

★ 2128 ★

Births

Mothers Having Born Specified Number of Children, and Number of Children Living, 1930 - I

Percents are shown in *italics* when the number of mothers having specified number of children living is less than 5.

Mother and number of children	Number of mothers	Average number of children living	Percent of mothers having specified number or more of children living									
			1	2	3	4	5	6	7	8	9	10
Negro mothers having born												
1 child	70,545	1.0	100.0	-	-	-	-	-	-	-	-	-
2 children	41,950	1.9	100.0	86.1	-	-	-	-	-	-	-	-
3 children	29,735	2.7	100.0	96.1	77.1	-	-	-	-	-	-	-
4 children	22,473	3.6	100.0	98.3	90.7	68.7	-	-	-	-	-	-
5 children	17,519	4.4	100.0	98.9	95.5	86.0	61.7	-	-	-	-	-
6 children	13,656	5.3	100.0	99.4	97.7	92.6	80.6	56.0	-	-	-	-
7 children	10,268	6.0	100.0	99.7	98.5	95.5	88.4	73.6	49.0	-	-	-
8 children	8,152	6.8	100.0	99.7	99.0	96.9	92.3	84.5	68.2	44.0	-	-
9 children	5,869	7.6	100.0	99.9	99.3	98.2	95.3	89.4	80.4	62.8	38.5	-
10 children	4,612	8.4	100.0	99.9	99.4	98.6	96.7	92.5	84.8	74.0	54.8	34.3
11 children	2,920	9.0	100.0	100.0	99.7	98.9	97.2	94.0	88.4	80.4	68.1	48.6
12 children	2,106	9.6	100.0	9.99	99.7	98.8	97.7	95.5	91.2	84.3	73.7	59.0
13 children	1,334	10.4	100.0	99.9	99.6	99.1	98.4	96.3	93.6	87.9	81.0	70.4
14 children	824	10.6	100.0	100.0	99.5	99.0	98.7	97.0	93.3	86.9	80.8	70.3
15 children	465	11.5	100.0	100.0	100.0	99.6	99.1	98.3	96.8	93.3	85.2	80.0
16 children	232	11.5	100.0	100.0	99.6	99.1	98.3	95.3	92.2	90.1	81.5	74.6
17 children	122	11.8	100.0	100.0	99.2	99.2	98.4	96.7	95.1	91.8	84.4	73.8
18 children	48	11.8	100.0	100.0	100.0	97.9	97.9	93.8	89.6	87.5	81.3	70.8
19 children	32	12.9	100.0	100.0	100.0	100.0	100.0	100.0	100.0	93.8	93.8	84.4
20 children	21	12.0	100.0	100.0	100.0	100.0	100.0	100.0	95.2	95.2	95.2	76.2
21 children	12	11.2	100.0	100.0	100.0	100.0	100.0	100.0	100.0	91.7	75.0	75.0

[Continued]

★ 2128 ★

Mothers Having Born Specified Number of Children, and Number of Children Living, 1930 - I

[Continued]

Mother and number of children	Number of mothers	Average number of children living	Percent of mothers having specified number or more of children living									
			1	2	3	4	5	6	7	8	9	10
22 children	6	12.8	100.0	100.0	100.0	100.0	100.0	100.0	100.0	100.0	100.0	100.0
23 children	2	10.0	100.0	100.0	100.0	100.0	100.0	100.0	100.0	100.0	50.0	50.0
24 children	3	15.0	100.0	100.0	100.0	100.0	100.0	100.0	100.0	100.0	100.0	100.0
25 children	3	13.0	100.0	100.0	100.0	100.0	100.0	100.0	100.0	100.0	100.0	100.0
27 children	1	21.0	100.0	100.0	100.0	100.0	100.0	100.0	100.0	100.0	100.0	100.0

Source: "Mothers of Negro Children Born in 1930 Having Specified Number of Children Ever Born, with the Average Number Living and the Percent of Mothers Having Specified Number Living, in the Registration Area in Continental United States: 1930." U.S. Bureau of the Census. *Negroes in the United States: 1920-32*. Washington, D.C.: Government Printing Office, 1935, p. 366. *Notes:* Exclusive of Colorado, Maine, Massachusetts, New Hampshire, and Rhode Island.

★ 2129 ★

Births

Mothers Having Born Specified Number of Children, and Number of Children Living, 1930 - II

Percents are shown in *italics* when the number of mothers having specified number of children living is less than 5.

Mother and number of children	Percent of mothers having specified number or more of children living								
	11	12	13	14	15	16	17	18	19
Negro mothers having born									
1 child	-	-	-	-	-	-	-	-	-
2 children	-	-	-	-	-	-	-	-	-
3 children	-	-	-	-	-	-	-	-	-
4 children	-	-	-	-	-	-	-	-	-
5 children	-	-	-	-	-	-	-	-	-
6 children	-	-	-	-	-	-	-	-	-
7 children	-	-	-	-	-	-	-	-	-
8 children	-	-	-	-	-	-	-	-	-
9 children	-	-	-	-	-	-	-	-	-
10 children	-	-	-	-	-	-	-	-	-
11 children	28.5	-	-	-	-	-	-	-	-
12 children	40.9	24.0	-	-	-	-	-	-	-
13 children	54.6	36.1	19.7	-	-	-	-	-	-
14 children	55.5	41.6	26.1	15.3	-	-	-	-	-
15 children	69.0	56.1	39.6	23.4	14.0	-	-	-	-
16 children	62.9	54.7	42.7	28.9	16.8	10.3	-	-	-
17 children	62.3	54.1	45.1	33.6	23.0	15.6	10.7	-	-
18 children	60.4	52.1	45.8	37.5	27.1	16.7	10.4	6.5	-
19 children	68.8	62.5	50.0	43.8	31.3	21.9	18.8	12.5	12.5
20 children	71.4	42.9	33.3	28.6	19.0	19.0	19.0	4.8	4.8
21 children	50.0	41.7	25.0	16.7	16.7	16.7	8.5	-	-
22 children	100.0	66.7	50.0	33.3	33.3	-	-	-	-
23 children	50.0	50.0	-	-	-	-	-	-	-
24 children	100.0	100.0	100.0	100.0	66.7	33.3	-	-	-

[Continued]

★ 2129 ★

Mothers Having Born Specified Number of Children, and Number of Children Living, 1930 - II

[Continued]

Mother and number of children	Percent of mothers having specified number or more of children living								
	11	12	13	14	15	16	17	18	19
25 children	100.0	100.0	66.7	33.3	-	-	-	-	-
27 children	100.0	100.0	100.0	100.0	100.0	100.0	100.0	100.0	100.0

Source: "Mothers of Negro Children Born in 1930 Having Specified Number of Children Ever Born, with the Average Number Living and the Percent of Mothers Having Specified Number Living, in the Registration Area in Continental United States: 1930." U.S. Bureau of the Census. *Negroes in the United States: 1920-32.* Washington, D.C.: Government Printing Office, 1935, p. 366. *Notes:* Exclusive of Colorado, Maine, Massachusetts, New Hampshire, and Rhode Island.

★ 2130 ★

Births

Multiple Births and Multiple Stillbirths Selected Registration States: 1930, 1931 - I

Number of Colored Plural Births and Plural Stillbirths in Selected Registration States: 1931 and 1930[1].

Area and year	Number of twins						
	Total	Living			Stillborn		
		Total	Both	One	Total	Both	One
Selected States[2]							
Alabama							
1931	702	628	598	30	74	44	30
1930	726	625	576	49	101	52	49
Arkansas							
1931	362	310	288	22	52	30	22
1930	418	366	338	28	52	24	28
Connecticut							
1931	20	18	18	-	2	2	-
1930	20	20	20	-	-	-	-
Delaware							
1931	24	19	18	1	5	4	1
1930	14	13	12	1	1	-	1
District of Columbia							
1931	76	73	72	1	3	2	1
1930	80	71	64	7	9	2	7
Florida							
1931	202	165	154	11	37	26	11
1930	300	252	234	18	48	30	18
Georgia							
1931	716	589	564	25	127	102	25
1930	740	610	568	42	130	88	42
Illinois							
1931	164	142	138	4	22	18	4
1930	164	151	144	7	13	6	7
Indiana							
1931	52	48	44	4	4	-	4
1930	66	64	62	2	2	-	2

[Continued]

★ 2130 ★

Multiple Births and Multiple Stillbirths Selected Registration States: 1930, 1931 - I

[Continued]

Area and year	Number of twins						
	Total	Living			Stillborn		
		Total	Both	One	Total	Both	One
Iowa							
1931	4	3	2	1	1	-	1
1930	4	4	4	-	-	-	-
Kansas							
1931	32	29	26	3	3	-	3
1930	46	43	40	3	3	-	3
Kentucky							
1931	94	81	78	3	13	10	3
1930	92	75	70	5	17	12	5
Louisiana							
1931	612	536	506	30	76	46	30
1930	584	512	484	28	72	44	28
Maryland							
1931	178	146	140	6	32	26	6
1930	192	157	146	11	35	24	11
Massachusetts							
1931	40	36	32	4	4	-	4
1930	22	19	18	1	3	2	1
Michigan							
1931	110	105	104	1	5	4	1
1930	110	99	98	1	11	10	1
Mississippi							
1931	608	538	516	22	70	48	22
1930	720	597	572	25	123	98	25
Missouri							
1931	120	109	102	7	11	4	7
1930	86	72	62	10	14	4	10
Nebraska							
1931	8	8	8	-	-	-	-
1930	10	10	10	-	-	-	-
New Jersey							
1931	100	96	94	2	4	2	2
1930	118	104	96	8	14	6	8
New York							
1931	214	190	188	2	24	22	2
1930	252	223	220	3	29	26	3
North Carolina							
1931	824	708	650	58	116	58	58
1930	836	722	672	50	114	64	50
Ohio							
1931	120	113	108	5	7	2	5
1930	158	132	128	4	26	22	4
Oklahoma							
1931	104	95	92	3	9	6	3

[Continued]

★ 2130 ★

Multiple Births and Multiple Stillbirths Selected Registration States: 1930, 1931 - I

[Continued]

Area and year	Number of twins						
	Total	Living			Stillborn		
		Total	Both	One	Total	Both	One
1930	126	114	110	4	12	8	4
Pennsylvania							
1931	310	268	248	20	42	22	20
1930	262	236	220	16	26	10	16
Rhode Island							
1931	8	8	8	-	-	-	-
1930	4	4	4	-	-	-	-
South Carolina							
1931	806	697	658	39	109	70	39
1930	804	685	642	43	119	76	43
Tennessee							
1931	240	202	184	18	38	20	18
1930	216	177	166	11	39	28	11
Virginia[3]							
1931	450	370	328	42	80	38	42
1930	528	449	410	39	79	40	39
West Virginia							
1931	60	51	48	3	9	6	3
1930	64	61	60	1	3	2	1

Source: "Number of Colored Plural Births and Plural Stillbirths in Selected Registration States: 1931 and 1930." U.S. Bureau of the Census. *Negroes in the United States: 1920-32.* Washington, D.C.: Government Printing Office, 1935, p. 429. *Notes:* 1. Includes Negro and other nonwhite races. 2. States in which the Negro population constitutes 55 percent or more of the total colored population. 3. 8 quadruplets were reported for 1930, 1 case all living; the other, all stillborn.

★ 2131 ★

Births

Multiple Births and Multiple Stillbirths Selected Registration States: 1930, 1931 - II

Number of Colored Plural Births and Plural Stillbirths in Selected Registration States: 1931 and 1930[1].

Area and year	Number of triplets								
	Total	Living			One	Total	Stillborn		
		Total	All	Two			All	Two	One
Selected States[2]									
Alabama									
1931	9	7	6	-	1	2	-	2	-
1930	21	9	3	-	6	12	-	12	-
Arkansas									
1931	6	1	-	-	1	5	3	2	-
1930	9	6	6	-	-	3	3	-	-

[Continued]

★ 2131 ★

Multiple Births and Multiple Stillbirths Selected Registration States: 1930, 1931 - II

[Continued]

Area and year	Number of triplets								
	Total	Living				Total	Stillborn		
		Total	All	Two	One		All	Two	One
Connecticut									
1931	-	-	-	-	-	-	-	-	-
1930	-	-	-	-	-	-	-	-	-
Delaware									
1931	-	-	-	-	-	-	-	-	-
1930	-	-	-	-	-	-	-	-	-
District of Columbia									
1931	3	3	3	-	-	-	-	-	-
1930	-	-	-	-	-	-	-	-	
Florida									
1931	3	-	-	-	-	3	3	-	-
1930	9	7	6	-	1	2	-	2	-
Georgia									
1931	19	9	9	-	-	9	9	-	-
1930	30	16	12	-	4	14	6	8	-
Illinois									
1931	6	4	3	-	1	2	-	2	-
1930	-	-	-	-	-	-	-	-	-
Indiana									
1931	3	2	-	2	-	1	-	-	1
1930	-	-	-	-	-	-	-	-	-
Iowa									
1931	-	-	-	-	-	-	-	-	
1930	3	3	3	-	-	-	-	-	-
Kansas									
1931	-	-	-	-	-	-	-	-	-
1930	-	-	-	-	-	-	-	-	-
Kentucky									
1931	-	-	-	-	-	-	-	-	-
1930	-	-	-	-	-	-	-	-	-
Louisiana									
1931	9	7	6	-	1	2	-	2	-
1930	12	5	3	2	-	7	6	-	1
Maryland									
1931	9	7	6	-	1	2	-	2	-
1930	-	-	-	-	-	-	-	-	-
Massachusetts									
1931	-	-	-	-	-	-	-	-	-
1930	-	-	-	-	-	-	-	-	-
Michigan									
1931	-	-	-	-	-	-	-	-	-
1930	6	6	6	-	-	-	-	-	-
Mississippi									
1931	15	12	12	-	-	3	3	-	-

[Continued]

★ 2131 ★

Multiple Births and Multiple Stillbirths Selected Registration States: 1930, 1931 - II

[Continued]

Area and year	Number of triplets								
	Total	Living				Total	Stillborn		
		Total	All	Two	One		All	Two	One
1930	15	9	6	2	1	6	3	2	1
Missouri									
1931	3	-	-	-	-	3	3	-	-
1930	-	-	-	-	-	-	-	-	-
Nebraska									
1931	-	-	-	-	-	-	-	-	-
1930	-	-	-	-	-	-	-	-	-
New Jersey									
1931	6	6	6	-	-	-	-	-	-
1930	6	5	3	2	-	1	-	-	1
New York									
1931	6	6	6	-	-	-	-	-	-
1930	3	3	3	-	-	-	-	-	-
North Carolina									
1931	24	20	15	4	1	4	-	2	2
1930	27	22	18	4	-	5	3	-	2
Ohio									
1931	6	1	-	-	1	5	3	2	-
1930	3	2	-	2	-	1	-	-	1
Oklahoma									
1931	3	3	3	-	-	-	-	-	-
1930	3	3	3	-	-	-	-	-	-
Pennsylvania									
1931	6	6	6	-	-	-	-	-	-
1930	6	3	-	2	1	3	-	2	1
Rhode Island									
1931	3	3	3	-	-	-	-	-	-
1930	-	-	-	-	-	-	-	-	-
South Carolina									
1931	15	9	6	2	1	6	3	2	1
1930	3	-	-	-	-	3	3	-	-
Tennessee									
1931	3	3	3	-	-	-	-	-	-
1930	9	6	6	-	-	3	3	-	-
Virginia[3]									
1931	3	3	3	-	-	-	-	-	-
1930	-	-	-	-	-	-	-	-	-

[Continued]

★ 2131 ★

Multiple Births and Multiple Stillbirths Selected Registration States: 1930, 1931 - II

[Continued]

Area and year	Number of triplets								
	Total	Living			One	Total	Stillborn		
		Total	All	Two			All	Two	One
West Virginia									
1931	-	-	-	-	-	-	-	-	-
1930	-	-	-	-	-	-	-	-	-

Source: "Number of Colored Plural Births and Plural Stillbirths in Selected Registration States: 1931 and 1930." U.S. Bureau of the Census. *Negroes in the United States: 1920-32.* Washington, D.C.: Government Printing Office, 1935, p. 429. *Notes:* 1. Includes Negro and other nonwhite races. 2. States in which the Negro population constitutes 55 percent or more of the total colored population. 3. 8 quadruplets were reported for 1930, 1 case all living; the other, all stillborn.

★ 2132 ★

Births

Multiple Births, Percent of Twin Cases by Occurrence in Hospital, 1944

Excludes cases in which both individuals were stillborn. Figures in parentheses are percentages to be expected in the absence of any association between hospitalization and number born alive.

Race	Total	Both living	One living
All races	100.0	94.2	5.8
In hospital	73.9	70.2	3.7
		(69.6)	(4.3)
Not in hospital	26.1	24.1	2.0
		(24.6)	(1.5)
White	100.0	94.8	5.2
In hospital	79.8	96.0	3.8
		(75.7)	(4.1)
Not in hospital	20.2	18.8	1.4
		(19.1)	(1.1)
Nonwhite	100.0	91.0	9.0
In hospital	38.8	35.5	3.3
		(35.3)	(3.5)
Not in hospital	61.2	55.5	5.7
		(55.7)	(5.5)

Source: "Percent of Twin Cases by Occurrence in Hospital and Number Born Alive, by Race: United States, 1944." Murray, Florence, ed. *The Negro Handbook, 1949.* New York: Macmillan, 1949, p. 21. Primary source: U.S. Office of Vital Statistics.

★ 2133 ★

Births

Reproduction Rate by Race, Net and Gross: 1940-1968

Prior to 1959, excludes Alaska, and 1960, Hawaii. Prior to 1960, based on births adjusted for underregistration; beginning 1960, on registered births. Rates computed using annual vital statistics life tables and population estimates by age, except as noted for earlier years. A net reproduction rate of 1,000 means that each generation would just replace itself, if birth and death rates of a specified period were to continue indefinitely, in the absence of net immigration. A rate above 1,000 implies a potentially gaining population, and a rate below 1,000, a potentially declining population. A gross reproduction rate of 1,000 means that if all women born at the beginning of a generation were to live through their reproductive period and continue birth rates existing at the time of their birth, they would barely reproduce themselves, assuming no migration from outside the area. A comparison of the net rate with the gross rate affords an indication of the loss sustained by the potential childbearing population through mortality. See also *Historical Statistics, Colonial Times to 1957*, series B 31-36.

Period or year	Net rate			Gross rate		
	Total	White	Negro and other	Total	White	Negro and other
1905-1910[1]	1,336	1,339	1,329	1,793	1,740	2,240
1930-1935[1]	984	972	1,074	1,108	1,080	1,336
1935-1940[1]	978	957	1,137	1,101	1,063	1,413
1940	1,027	1,002	1,209	1,121	1,082	1,422
1950	1,435	1,387	1,780	1,505	1,446	1,940
1955	1,676	1,617	2,101	1,745	1,675	2,255
1959 (adj.)	1,742	1,679	2,200	1,812	1,737	2,360
1959 (reg.)	1,722	1,667	2,118	1,791	1,725	2,271
1960	1,715	1,662	2,093	1,783	1,720	2,241
1965	1,376	1,314	1,802	1,428	1,357	1,919
1966	1,288	1,231	1,678	1,336	1,271	1,785
1967	1,213	1,158	1,582	1,255	1,193	1,676
1968	1,166	1,116	1,495	1,206	1,151	1,577

Source: "Net and Gross Reproduction Rate, by Race: 1905-1968." Bureau of the Census. *Statistical Abstract of the United States, 1973.* Washington, D.C.: U.S. Government Printing Office, 1967, p. 52. Primary source: Dept. of Health, Education, and Welfare, Public Health Service (except as noted); annual report, *Vital Statistics of the United States*. *Notes:* 1. Data based on census samples. See source: Dept. of Commerce, Bureau of the Census; special report of Sixteenth Census, *Differential Fertility, 1940 and 1910—Standard Fertility Rates and Reproduction Rates.*

★ 2134 ★

Births

Reproduction Rates, by Race: 1905-1910 to 1970

Based on 50-percent sample of estimated total live births for 1951-1954, 1956-1966, and 1968-1970; on 20- to 50-percent sample for 1967.

Year	Gross reproduction rate			Net reproduction rate		
	Total	White	Negro and other	Total	White	Negro and other
1970	1,207	1,158	1,509	1,168	1,125	1,433
1969	1,201	1,147	1,554	1,161	1,113	1,473
1968	1,206	1,151	1,577	1,166	1,116	1,495
1967	1,255	1,193	1,676	1,213	1,158	1,582
1966	1,336	1,271	1,785	1,288	1,231	1,678
1965	1,428	1,357	1,919	1,376	1,314	1,802
1964	1,564	1,495	2,051	1,507	1,447	1,923
1963[1]	1,623	1,556	2,102	1,564	1,506	1,973
1962[1]	1,695	1,630	2,170	1,633	1,577	2,033
1961	1,770	1,704	2,240	1,704	1,648	2,100
1960[3]	1,783	1,720	2,241	1,715	1,662	2,093
1959[2]	1,791	1,725	2,271	1,722	1,667	2,118
1958	1,807	1,735	2,339	1,736	1,675	2,178
1957	1,837	1,764	2,371	1,765	1,701	2,206
1956	1,798	1,724	2,339	1,729	1,665	2,184
1955	1,745	1,675	2,255	1,676	1,617	2,101
1954	1,727	1,660	2,216	1,657	1,601	2,062
1953	1,668	1,607	2,118	1,597	1,546	1,959
1952	1,637	1,579	2,062	1,563	1,516	1,897
1951	1,593	1,534	2,027	1,521	1,472	1,865
1950	1,505	1,446	1,940	1,435	1,387	1,780
1949	1,515	1,462	1,906	1,439	1,397	1,743
1948	1,514	1,469	1,845	1,430	1,400	1,679
1947	1,593	1,568	1,766	1,505	1,492	1,594
1946	1,430	1,406	1,600	1,344	1,331	1,435
1945	1,212	1,175	1,493	1,132	1,106	1,323
1944	1,249	1,214	1,520	1,163	1,139	1,334
1943	1,323	1,294	1,543	1,228	1,211	1,348
1942	1,277	1,250	1,487	1,185	1,171	1,293
1941	1,168	1,131	1,458	1,075	1,052	1,242
1940	1,121	1,082	1,422	1,027	1,002	1,209
1935	1,091	1,059	1,350	975	958	1,108
1935-40	1,101	1,063	1,413	978	957	1,137

[Continued]

★ 2134 ★

Reproduction Rates, by Race: 1905-1910 to 1970

[Continued]

Year	Gross reproduction rate			Net reproduction rate		
	Total	White	Negro and other	Total	White	Negro and other
1930-35	1,108	1,080	1,336	984	972	1,074
1905-10	1,793	1,740	2,240	1,336	1,339	1,329

Source: "Gross and Reproduction Rates, by Rate: 1905-10 to 1970." U.S. Bureau of the Census. *Historical Statistics of the United states: Colonial Times to 1970, Part I.* Bicentennial Edition. Washington, D.C.: Government Printing Office, 1975, p. 53. *Notes:* 1. Excludes New Jersey; State did not require reporting of race. 2. Includes Alaska. 3. Denotes first year for which figures include Alaska and Hawaii.

★ 2135 ★

Births

Single and Multiple Birth Rates, 1960-1975

As of June. Covers civilian noninstitutional population. Since the number of women who had a birth during the 12-month period was tabulated and not the actual numbers of births some small underestimation of fertility for this period may exist due to the omission of; (1)Multiple births (2)Two or more live births spaced within the 12-month period (the woman is counted only once), (3)Women who had births in the period and who did not survive to the survey date, (4)Women who were in institutions and therefore not in the survey universe. These losses may be somewhat offset by the inclusion in the CPS of births to immigrants who did not have their children born in the United States and births to nonresidential women. These births would not have been recorded in the vital registration system. Based on Current Population Survey (CPS).

Characteristic	Total 18 to 44 years old			18 to 29 years old			30 to 44 years old		
	Number of women (1,000)	Women who have had a child in the last year		Number of women (1,000)	Women who have had a child in the last year		Number of women (1,000)	Women who have had a child in the last year	
		Total births per 1,000 women	First births per 1,000 women		Total births per 1,000 women	First births per 1,000 women		Total births per 1,000 women	First births per 1,000 women
Total[1]	52,139	71.0	27.4	24,265	103.9	48.0	27,874	42.3	9.4
White	43,634	68.5	27.5	20,091	100.3	48.4	23,543	41.3	9.6
Black	6,734	83.2	24.8	3,402	123.0	44.6	3,331	42.5	4.6
Hispanic	4,296	95.8	24.4	2,239	126.7	40.2	2,057	62.1	7.3

Source: "Social ad Economic Characteristics of Women, 18-44 Years Old Who Have Had A Child in The Last Year: 1987." *Statistical Abstract*, 1989, p. 67. U.S. Bureau of the Census, *Current Population Reports*, series P-20, No. 427. *Notes:* 1. Includes women of other races and women with family income not reported, not shown separately. 2. Hispanic persons may be of any race.

★ 2136 ★

Births

Single and Multiple Births, 1940-1944

Cases in which all individuals were stillborn are shown in parentheses but are not included in the totals.

Cases of birth	White	Negro	Other
Total cases (single and plural)	11,694,427	1,521,654	72,313
Cases of single birth	11,574,367	1,493,392	71,605
Total plural cases	120,060	19,262	708
Cases of twins	118,908	19,008	703
Both living	112,753	17,164	657
One living	6,155	1,844	46
(Both stillborn)	(3,814)	(1,262)	(20)
Cases of triplets	1,135	243	4
Three living	950	183	4
Two living	131	40	-
One living	54	20	-
(Three stillborn)	(42)	(19)	(-)
Cases of quadruplets	17	11	1
Four living	13	4	1
Three living	1	5	-
Two living	1	2	-
One living	2	-	-
(Four stillborn)	(-)	(-)	(-)

Source: "Cases of Single and Plural Births by Race and Number Born Alive: United States: 1940-1944." Murray, Florence, ed. *The Negro Handbook, 1949*. New York: Macmillan, 1949, p. 22. Primary source: U.S. Office of Vital Statistics.

★ 2137 ★

Births

Single and Multiple Births, Percent Distribution, 1940-1960

Color and year	All live births	Percentage of live births in--			
		Single deliveries	Plural deliveries		
			Total	Twins	Other
Total					
1960	100.0	98.0	2.0	2.0	0.0
1959	100.0	97.9	2.1	2.0	0.0
1958	100.0	97.9	2.1	2.0	0.0
1957	100.0	98.0	2.0	2.0	0.0
1956	100.0	97.9	2.0	2.1	0.0

[Continued]

★ 2137 ★

Single and Multiple Births, Percent Distribution, 1940-1960

[Continued]

Color and year	All live births	Percentage of live births in--			
		Single deliveries	Plural deliveries		
			Total	Twins	Other
1955	100.0	97.9	2.1	2.1	0.0
1954	100.0	97.9	2.1	2.1	0.0
1953	100.0	97.9	2.1	2.1	0.0
1952	100.0	97.9	2.1	2.0	0.0
1951	100.0	98.0	2.0	2.0	0.0
1950	100.0	97.9	2.1	2.1	0.0
1949	100.0	98.0	2.0	2.0	0.0
1948	100.0	98.0	2.0	2.0	0.0
1947	100.0	98.0	2.0	2.0	0.0
1946	100.0	97.8	2.2	2.2	0.0
1945	100.0	97.9	2.1	2.0	0.0
1944	100.0	98.0	2.0	2.0	0.0
1943	100.0	98.0	2.0	2.0	0.0
1942	100.0	98.0	2.0	2.0	0.0
1941	100.0	97.9	2.1	2.0	0.0
1940	100.0	97.9	2.1	2.0	0.0
White					
1960	100.0	98.1	1.9	1.9	0.0
1959	100.0	98.0	2.0	1.9	0.0
1958	100.0	98.1	1.9	1.9	0.0
1957	100.0	98.1	1.9	1.9	0.0
1956	100.0	98.0	2.0	2.0	0.0
1955	100.0	98.0	2.0	2.0	0.0
1954	100.0	98.0	2.0	2.0	0.0
1953	100.0	98.0	2.0	2.0	0.0
1952	100.0	98.0	2.0	2.0	0.0
1951	100.0	98.0	2.0	1.9	0.0
1950	100.0	98.0	2.0	2.0	0.0
1949	100.0	98.0	2.0	1.9	0.0
1948	100.0	98.0	2.0	2.0	0.0
1947	100.0	98.0	2.0	2.0	0.0
1946	100.0	97.8	2.2	2.1	0.0
1945	100.0	98.0	2.0	2.0	0.0
1944	100.0	98.0	2.0	1.9	0.0
1943	100.0	98.1	1.9	1.9	0.0
1942	100.0	98.0	2.0	2.0	0.0
1941	100.0	98.0	2.0	2.0	0.0
1940	100.0	98.0	2.0	2.0	0.0

[Continued]

★ 2137 ★

Single and Multiple Births, Percent Distribution, 1940-1960

[Continued]

Color and year	All live births	Percentage of live births in--			
		Single deliveries	Plural deliveries		
			Total	Twins	Other
Nonwhite					
1960	100.0	97.4	2.6	2.6	0.0
1959	100.0	97.3	2.7	2.7	0.0
1958	100.0	97.3	2.7	2.7	0.0
1957	100.0	97.3	2.7	2.6	0.0
1956	100.0	97.3	2.7	2.6	0.0
1955	100.0	97.4	2.6	2.6	0.0
1954	100.0	97.4	2.6	2.6	0.0
1953	100.0	97.3	2.7	2.7	0.0
1952	100.0	97.4	2.6	2.5	0.0
1951	100.0	97.5	2.5	2.4	0.0
1950	100.0	97.5	2.5	2.5	0.0
1949	100.0	97.6	2.4	2.4	0.0
1948	100.0	97.7	2.3	2.3	0.0
1947	100.0	97.5	2.5	2.4	0.0
1946	100.0	97.4	2.6	2.5	0.0
1945	100.0	97.6	2.4	2.4	0.0
1944	100.0	97.6	2.4	2.3	0.1
1943	100.0	97.7	2.3	2.3	0.0
1942	100.0	97.6	2.4	2.4	0.0
1941	100.0	97.6	2.4	2.4	0.0
1940	100.0	97.6	2.4	2.4	0.0

Source: "Percent Distribution of Live Births by Plurality and Color: United States, 1940-60." National Center for Health Statistics. *Vital Statistics Rates in the United State, 1940-60.* By Robert D. Grove and Alice M. Hetzel. Washington, D.C.: U.S. Department of Health, Education, and Welfare, Public Health Service, 1968, pp. 180-181.

★ 2138 ★

Births

Single and Multiple Births, Percent Distribution: 1940, 1950, and 1960

Percentage distribution of live births by plurality, age of mother, and color: United States, 1940, 1950, and 1960.

Age of mother, color, and year	All live births	Percentage of live births in--			
		Single deliveries	Plural deliveries		
			Total	Twins	Other
White					
All ages:					
1960	100.0	98.1	1.9	1.9	0.0
1950	100.0	98.0	2.0	2.0	0.0
1940	100.0	98.0	2.0	2.0	0.0
Under 15 years					
1960	100.0	99.0	1.0	1.0	-
1950	100.0	98.8	1.2	1.2	-
1940	100.0	98.8	1.2	1.2	-
15-19 years					
1960	100.0	98.8	1.2	1.2	0.0
1950	100.0	98.8	1.2	1.2	0.0
1940	100.0	98.9	1.1	1.1	0.0
20-24 years					
1960	100.0	98.4	1.6	1.6	0.0
1950	100.0	98.4	1.6	1.6	0.0
1940	100.0	98.4	1.6	1.6	0.0
25-29 years					
1960	100.0	98.0	2.0	2.0	0.0
1950	100.0	97.9	2.1	2.1	0.0
1940	100.0	97.9	2.1	2.1	0.0
30-34 years					
1960	100.0	97.5	2.5	2.5	0.0
1950	100.0	97.4	2.6	2.6	0.0
1940	100.0	97.3	2.7	2.6	0.0
35-39 years					
1960	100.0	97.2	2.8	2.7	0.1
1950	100.0	97.0	3.0	3.0	0.1
1940	100.0	96.8	3.2	3.1	0.1
40-44 years					
1960	100.0	97.8	2.2	2.2	0.1
1950	100.0	97.6	2.4	2.4	0.0
1940	100.0	97.4	2.6	2.5	0.0
45 years and over					
1960	100.0	98.9	1.1	1.1	-
1950	100.0	99.1	0.9	0.9	-
1940	100.0	98.6	1.4	1.4	-
Nonwhite					
All ages:					
1960	100.0	97.4	2.6	2.6	00
1950	100.0	97.5	2.5	2.5	0.0
1940	100.0	97.6	2.4	2.4	0.0

[Continued]

★ 2138 ★

Single and Multiple Births, Percent Distribution: 1940, 1950, and 1960

[Continued]

Age of mother, color, and year	All live births	Percentage of live births in--			
		Single deliveries	Plural deliveries		
			Total	Twins	Other
Under 15 years					
1960	100.0	99.2	0.8	0.8	0.0
1950	100.0	99.0	1.0	1.0	-
1940	100.0	99.3	0.7	0.7	-
15-19 years					
1960	100.0	98.5	1.5	1.5	0.0
1950	100.0	98.5	1.5	1.5	0.0
1940	100.0	98.7	1.3	1.3	0.0
20-24 years					
1960	100.0	97.8	2.2	2.2	0.0
1950	100.0	97.9	2.1	2.1	0.0
1940	100.0	97.9	2.1	2.0	0.0
25-29 years					
1960	100.0	97.0	3.0	3.0	0.0
1950	100.0	97.1	2.9	2.9	0.1
1940	100.0	97.2	2.8	2.8	0.1
30-34 years					
1960	100.0	96.4	3.6	3.6	0.1
1950	100.0	96.3	3.7	3.6	0.1
1940	100.0	96.5	3.5	3.5	0.1
35-39 years					
1960	100.0	95.9	4.1	4.0	0.1
1950	100.0	95.8	4.2	4.1	0.1
1940	100.0	95.5	4.5	4.3	0.1
40-44 years					
1960	100.0	97.0	3.0	2.9	0.1
1950	100.0	96.8	3.2	3.1	0.1
1940	100.0	96.5	3.5	3.5	-
45 years and over					
1960	100.0	97.7	2.3	2.1	0.2
1950	100.0	98.2	1.8	1.8	
1940	100.0	96.7	3.3	3.3	

Source: "Percent Distribution of Live Births by Plurality, Age of Mother, and Color: United States, 1940, 1950, and 1960." National Center for Health Statistics. *Vital Statistics Rates in the United State, 1940-60*. By Robert D. Grove and Alice M. Hetzel. Washington, D.C.: U.S. Department of Health, Education, and Welfare, Public Health Service, 1968, pp. 181-183.

★ 2139 ★

Births

Women Ever Married by Number of Children Born, 1971

Age of woman	Number (thousands)	Percent distribution of women ever married by children ever born			
		Total	0 to 1	2 to 4	5 or more
Negro					
Total, 15 to 44 years	3,021	100	31.6	45.6	22.8
15 to 19 years	120	100	81.7	18.4	-
20 to 24 years	569	100	55.5	40.6	4.0
25 to 29 years	617	100	27.6	58.7	13.6
30 to 34 years	574	100	20.2	49.3	30.5
35 to 39 years	563	100	21.0	41.2	37.8
40 to 44 years	578	100	24.0	42.3	33.7
White					
Total, 15 to 44 years	26,337	100	35.3	55.1	9.5
15 to 19 years	1,007	100	93.2	6.9	-
20 to 24 years	5,092	100	72.7	27.1	0.2
25 to 29 years	5,623	100	38.0	58.7	3.3
30 to 34 years	4,900	100	19.0	70.0	11.1
35 to 39 years	4,675	100	14.5	66.8	18.7
40 to 44 years	5,039	100	18.1	63.9	17.9

Source: "Women Ever Married by Number of Children Ever Born, by Age: 1971." U.S. Bureau of the Census. Current Population Reports, Special Studies, Series P-23, No. 42. *The Social and Economic Status of the Black Population in the United States, 1971.* Washington, D.C.: Government Printing Office, 1972, p. 108. Primary source: U.S. Department of Commerce, Social and Economic Statistics Administration, Bureau of the Census. *Note:* - Represents zero or rounds to zero.

★ 2140 ★

Births

Women Ever Married by Race and Children Born, Censuses of 1910, 1940, 1950, 1960, and 1970

Year of birth of women	Census year	Age of women reporting (years)	Percent of women, by number of births						Children per 1,000 women
			None	1 and 2	3 and 4	5 and 6	7 to 9	10 or more	
Total									
1920-24	1970	45-49	10.6	39.9	32.8	10.7	4.5	1.5	2,701
1915-19	1970	50-54	13.8	43.1	28.9	8.8	3.9	1.4	2,854
1910-14	1960[1]	45-49	18.1	44.2	24.7	7.8	3.8	1.5	2,402
1905-09	1960[1]	50-54	20.8	43.2	22.3	7.8	4.2	1.7	2,355
1900-04	1950	45-49	20.4	41.5	22.4	8.4	5.0	2.2	2,492
1895-99	1950	50-54	18.6	39.0	23.9	10.0	5.8	2.6	2,706
1890-94	1940	45-49	16.8	35.3	25.0	12.2	7.7	3.1	2,998

[Continued]

★ 2140 ★

Women Ever Married by Race and Children Born, Censuses of 1910, 1940, 1950, 1960, and 1970

[Continued]

Year of birth of women	Census year	Age of women reporting (years)	Percent of women, by number of births						Children per 1,000 women
			None	1 and 2	3 and 4	5 and 6	7 to 9	10 or more	
1885-89	1940	50-54	16.6	33.1	25.1	13.1	8.6	3.6	3,146
1880-84	1940	55-59	16.7	30.7	24.7	14.1	9.6	4.2	3,301
1875-79	1940	60-64	15.0	30.5	25.2	14.4	10.3	4.7	3,462
1870-74	1940	65-69	13.9	28.4	25.1	15.2	11.6	5.8	3,700
1865-69	1940	70-74	12.3	26.6	26.1	16.0	12.5	6.4	3,901
1860-64	1910	45-49	9.5	22.4	22.0	17.3	17.6	11.2	4,744
1855-59	1910	50-54	8.9	20.6	21.3	17.9	19.0	12.3	4,972
1850-54	1910	55-59	8.3	18.8	20.8	17.8	20.4	13.9	5,218
1845-49	1910	60-64	8.2	18.5	20.3	18.3	20.8	14.0	5,266
1840-44	1910	65-69	7.9	17.9	20.1	18.1	21.6	14.3	5,364
1835-39	1910	70-74	7.7	17.3	20.0	18.7	21.6	14.7	5,395
White									
1920-24	1970	45-49	9.9	40.9	33.9	10.5	3.8	1.0	2,791
1915-19	1970	50-54	12.9	44.3	29.9	8.6	3.3	1.0	2,553
1910-14	1960[1]	45-49	17.1	45.4	25.6	7.6	3.3	1.1	2,354
1905-09	1960[1]	50-54	20.0	44.3	23.0	7.6	3.8	1.4	2,313
1900-04	1950	45-49	19.5	42.7	23.0	8.3	4.6	1.9	2,456
1895-99	1950	50-54	18.0	39.9	24.5	10.0	5.4	2.3	2,665
1890-94	1940	45-49	16.3	36.0	25.5	12.1	7.4	2.7	2,968
1885-89	1940	50-54	16.4	33.6	25.3	13.0	8.4	3.2	3,106
1880-84	1940	55-59	16.7	31.4	24.7	13.7	9.2	4.2	3,270
1875-79	1940	60-64	16.6	30.3	24.9	13.9	9.9	4.3	3,349
1870-74	1940	65-69	15.7	28.3	25.0	14.6	11.2	5.2	3,558
1865-69	1940	70-74	14.3	26.6	25.7	15.7	11.8	5.8	3,741
1860-64	1910	45-49	9.6	22.9	22.7	17.7	17.4	9.8	4,594
1855-59	1910	50-54	9.0	20.9	22.0	18.3	19.0	10.8	4,817
1850-54	1910	55-59	8.4	19.1	21.3	18.2	20.5	12.5	5,082
1845-49	1910	60-64	8.3	18.8	20.8	18.7	20.9	12.6	5,123
1840-44	1910	65-69	8.0	18.2	20.6	18.5	21.7	13.0	5,237
1835-39	1910	70-74	7.9	17.5	20.3	19.1	21.8	13.4	5,278
Negro									
1920-24	1970	45-49	17.9	31.3	21.4	13.1	10.5	5.8	3,394
1915-19	1970	50-54	23.0	33.0	18.9	10.9	8.8	5.4	3,030
1910-14	1960[1]	45-49	27.9	33.2	16.9	8.9	7.8	5.2	2,761
1905-09	1960[1]	50-54	28.5	34.0	16.0	8.9	7.6	5.0	2,696
1900-04	1950	45-49	28.4	31.9	17.6	9.2	8.0	4.9	2,767
1895-99	1950	50-54	25.5	30.9	17.4	10.9	8.8	6.5	3,085

[Continued]

★ 2140 ★

Women Ever Married by Race and Children Born, Censuses of 1910, 1940, 1950, 1960, and 1970

[Continued]

Year of birth of women	Census year	Age of women reporting (years)	Percent of women, by number of births						Children per 1,000 women
			None	1 and 2	3 and 4	5 and 6	7 to 9	10 or more	
1890-94	1940	45-49	23.8	28.1	19.5	12.6	9.9	6.1	3,255
1885-89	1940	50-54	20.1	25.6	22.1	14.2	10.7	7.3	3,594
1880-84	1940	55-59	19.3	25.5	21.4	14.1	10.9	8.8	3,751
1875-79	1940	60-64	17.0	23.0	21.3	16.5	13.0	9.2	4,046
1870-74	1940	65-69	14.5	22.1	20.9	17.5	14.1	11.0	4,347
1865-69	1940	70-74	12.8	18.1	22.6	15.1	17.6	13.8	4,892
1860-64	1910	45-49	8.6	17.9	15.5	13.8	18.7	25.5	6,162
1855-59	1910	50-54	7.8	16.4	14.0	13.6	19.5	28.7	6,580
1850-54	1910	55-59	7.2	16.1	14.5	12.7	18.7	30.8	6,910
1845-49	1910	60-64	5.9	13.9	13.8	14.2	21.3	30.9	6,883
1840-44	1910	65-69	6.9	16.3	14.1	14.0	18.4	30.3	7,035
1835-39	1910	70-74	5.4	12.4	14.1	11.3	21.4	35.4	6,947

Source: "Percent Distribution of Ever-Married Women (Survivors of Birth Cohorts of 1835-39 to 1920-24) by Race and by Number of Children Ever Born, as Reported in Census of 1910, 1940, 1960, and 1970." *Historical Statistics of the United States: Colonial Times to 1970, Part I.* Bicentennial Edition. Washington, D.C.: Government Printing Office, 1975, p. 53. *Note:* 1. Denotes first year for which figures include Alaska and Hawaii.

Deaths

★ 2141 ★

Accidental Deaths: 1930, 1931

This supplemental list is made in accordance with the requirements of the International Conference at Paris, 1920. The deaths shown in this tabulation are supplemental to those reported opposite titles 178 to 194, inclusive. Comparable figures for Titles shown in prior years will be found opposite the International List Titles. To obtain the total number of deaths in 1930 due to any of the accidental causes, the supplemental figures should be added to those reported opposite the International List numbers in the regular table.

Cause of death	1930			1931		
	Total	Male	Female	Total	Male	Female
Accidents in mines and quarries	238	238	-	172	172	-
Accidents from agricultural machinery	16	15	1	15	14	1
Elevator accidents	35	32	3	20	19	1
Accidents from machinery used for recreation	1	1	-	1	1	-
Other machinery accidents	120	116	4	102	98	4
Railroad and automobile collisions	90	67	23	65	46	19
Other railroad accidents	536	495	41	537	483	54
Street car and automobile collisions	21	15	6	16	8	8
Other street car accidents	41	30	11	54	40	14

[Continued]

★ 2141 ★

Accidental Deaths: 1930, 1931

[Continued]

Cause of death	1930			1931		
	Total	Male	Female	Total	Male	Female
Automobile accidents (primary)	2,228	1,749	479	2,381	1,819	562
Motorcycle accidents	13	12	1	10	8	2
Other land transportation accidents	113	100	13	114	102	12
Water transportation accidents	79	70	9	75	73	2
Air transportation accidents	3	3	-	2	2	-

Source: "Negro Deaths (Exclusive of Stillbirths) from Each Cause, by Sex, in Registration States (Including District of Columbia): 1930," and "Negro Deaths Exclusive of Stillbirths) From Each Cause, by Sex, in Registration States (Including District of Columbia: 1931." U.S. Bureau of the Census. *Negroes in the United States: 1920-32.* Washington, D.C.: Government Printing Office, 1935, pp. 465, 467. Adapted by the editors.

★ 2142 ★

Deaths

Age-Adjusted Causes of Death: Selected Causes – 1950, 1960, 1970

Data are based on the National Vital Statistics System.

Sex, race, and cause of death	1950[1]	1960[1]	1970
	Deaths per 100,000 resident population		
All races			
All causes	841.5	760.9	714.3
Diseases of heart	307.6	286.2	253.6
Cerebrovascular diseases	88.8	79.7	66.3
Malignant neoplasms	125.4	125.8	129.9
Respiratory system	12.8	19.2	28.4
Colorectal	19.0	17.7	16.8
Prostate[2]	13.4	13.1	13.3
Breast[3]	22.2	22.3	23.1
Chronic obstructive pulmonary diseases	4.4	8.2	13.2
Pneumonia and influenza	26.2	28.0	22.1
Chronic liver disease and cirrhosis	8.5	10.5	14.7
Diabetes mellitus	14.3	13.6	14.1
Accidents and adverse effects	57.5	49.9	53.7
Motor vehicle accidents	23.3	22.5	27.4
Suicide	11.0	10.6	11.8
Homicide and legal intervention	5.4	5.2	9.1
White Male			
All causes	963.1	917.7	893.4
Diseases of heart	381.1	375.4	347.6
Cerebrovascular diseases	87.0	80.3	68.8
Malignant neoplasms	130.9	141.6	154.3
Respiratory system	21.6	34.6	49.9
Colorectal	19.8	18.9	18.9
Prostate	13.1	12.4	12.3

[Continued]

★ 2142 ★

Age-Adjusted Causes of Death: Selected Causes – 1950, 1960, 1970

[Continued]

Sex, race, and cause of death	1950[1]	1960[1]	1970
Chronic obstructive pulmonary diseases	6.0	13.8	24.0
Pneumonia and influenza	27.1	31.0	26.0
Chronic liver disease and cirrhosis	11.6	14.4	18.8
Diabetes mellitus	11.3	11.6	12.7
Accidents and adverse effects	80.9	70.5	76.2
Motor vehicle accidents	35.9	34.0	40.1
Suicide	18.1	17.5	18.2
Homicide and legal intervention	3.9	3.9	7.3
Black male			
All causes	1,373.1	1,246.1	1,1318.6
Diseases of heart	415.5	381.2	375.9
Cerebrovascular diseases	146.2	141.2	124.2
Malignant neoplasms	126.1	158.5	198.0
Respiratory system	16.9	36.6	60.8
Colorectal	13.8	156.0	17.3
Prostate	16.9	22.2	25.4
Chronic obstructive pulmonary diseases	-	-	-
Pneumonia and influenza	63.8	70.2	53.8
Chronic liver disease and cirrhosis	8.8	14.8	33.1
Diabetes mellitus	11.5	16.2	21.2
Accidents and adverse effects	105.7	100.0	119.5
Motor vehicle accidents	39.8	38.2	50.1
Suicide	7.0	7.8	9.9
Homicide and legal intervention	51.1	44.9	82.1
White female			
All causes	645.0	555.0	501.7
Diseases of heart	223.6	197.1	167.8
Cerebrovascular diseases	79.7	68.7	56.2
Malignant neoplasms	119.4	109.5	107.6
Respiratory system	4.6	5.1	10.1
Colorectal	19.0	17.0	15.3
Breast	22.5	22.4	23.4
Chronic obstructive pulmonary diseases	2.8	3.3	5.3
Pneumonia and influenza	18.9	19.0	15.0
Chronic liver disease and cirrhosis	5.8	6.6	8.7
Diabetes mellitus	16.4	13.7	12.8
Accidents and adverse effects	30.6	25.5	27.2
Motor vehicle accidents	10.6	11.1	14.4
Suicide	5.3	5.3	7.2
Homicide and legal intervention	1.4	1.5	2.2
Black female			
All causes	1,106.7	916.9	814.4
Diseases of heart	349.5	292.6	251.7
Cerebrovascular diseases	155.6	139.5	107.9

[Continued]

★ 2142 ★

Age-Adjusted Causes of Death: Selected Causes – 1950, 1960, 1970

[Continued]

Sex, race, and cause of death	1950[1]	1960[1]	1970
Malignant neoplasms	131.9	127.8	123.5
Respiratory system	4.1	5.5	10.9
Colorectal	15.0	15.4	16.1
Breast	19.3	21.3	21.5
Chronic obstructive pulmonary diseases	-	-	-
Pneumonia and influenza	50.4	43.9	29.2
Chronic liver disease and cirrhosis	5.7	8.9	17.8
Diabetes mellitus	22.7	27.3	30.9
Accidents and adverse effects	38.5	35.9	35.3
Motor vehicle accidents	10.3	10.0	13.8
Suicide	1.7	1.9	2.9
Homicide and legal intervention	11.7	11.8	15.0

Source: "Age-Adjusted Death Rates for Selected Causes of Death, according to Sex and Race: United States, Selected Years 1950-86, *Health United States 1988*, March 1989, pp. 62-63. National Center for Health Statistics: *Vital Statistics Rates in the United States, 1940-1960*, by R. D. Grove and A. M. Hetzel, DHEW Pub. No. (PHS) 1677. Public Health Service, Washington. U.S. Government Printing Office, 1968; Unpublished data from the Division of Vital Statistics; *Vital Statistics of the United States*, Vol. II, Mortality, Part A, 1950-89, Public Health Service, Washington. U.S. Government Printing Office; Data computed by the Division of Analysis from data compiled by the Division of Vital Statistics. *Notes:* For data years shown, the code numbers for cause of death are based on the then current *International Classification of Diseases*, which are described in Appendix II, tables IV and V of original source. 1. Includes deaths of nonresidents of the United States. 2. Male only. 3. Female only.

★ 2143 ★

Deaths

Death Rate From Diseases of the Heart – 1920, 1930, 1931

Colored[1] and White death rate from diseases of the heart, in selected states and cities: 1931, 1930, and 1920.

Area and color	Rate per 100,000 estimated population July 1		
	1931	1930	1920
Selected states[2]			
Alabama	122.5	139.8	[3]
Colored	147.2	177.5	[3]
White	108.9	118.8	[3]
Arkansas	111.2	116.8	[3]
Colored	130.8	159.6	[3]
White	104.3	101.9	[3]
Connecticut	258.7	260.9	171.5
Colored	338.7	333.3	[4]
White	257.1	259.5	[4]
Delaware	277.5	264.4	174.7
Colored	348.5	339.4	[4]
White	266.2	252.4	[4]
Florida	188.5	193.8	113.3
Colored	187.0	210.1	105.6
White	189.1	187.0	119.6

[Continued]

★ 2143 ★

Death Rate From Diseases of the Heart – 1920, 1930, 1931

[Continued]

Area and color	Rate per 100,000 estimated population July 1		
	1931	1930	1920
Georgia	142.6	153.8	[3]
Colored	182.6	200.4	[3]
White	119.6	126.8	[3]
Illinois	232.1	223.1	161.9
Colored	283.3	282.9	[4]
White	229.4	220.1	[4]
Indiana	233.8	241.4	166.6
Colored	285.7	330.9	[4]
White	231.7	237.8	[4]
Iowa	189.6	192.3	[3]
Colored	187.0	217.4	[3]
White	189.6	192.0	[3]
Kansas	176.0	178.0	128.7
Colored	204.5	214.6	[4]
White	174.6	176.2	[4]
Kentucky	159.3	160.4	99.6
Colored	328.8	377.9	210.0
White	143.4	139.9	87.9
Louisiana	185.5	197.0	119.6
Colored	227.8	248.2	146.3
White	160.4	166.7	103.4
Maryland	259.8	255.9	181.7
Colored	296.1	304.7	232.5
White	252.3	245.9	171.5
Massachusetts	287.4	281.5	215.9
Colored	331.6	247.4	[4]
White	286.8	282.0	[4]
Michigan	211.3	209.7	176.1
Colored	228.4	249.2	[4]
White	210.5	208.0	[4]
Mississippi	123.5	135.6	93.2
Colored	127.7	147.7	110.1
White	119.2	123.4	75.9
Missouri	218.7	216.3	136.0
Colored	369.7	364.7	[4]
White	208.3	206.2	[4]
Nebraska	171.5	16.7	107.6
Colored	245.8	266.7	[4]
White	170.2	164.9	[4]
New Hampshire	295.5	297.9	240.2
Colored	100.0	200.0	[4]
White	295.9	298.1	[4]
New Jersey	253.0	245.6	178.5
Colored	278.2	275.7	[4]
White	251.6	243.9	[4]

[Continued]

★ 2143 ★

Death Rate From Diseases of the Heart – 1920, 1930, 1931

[Continued]

Area and color	Rate per 100,000 estimated population July 1		
	1931	1930	1920
New York	287.8	286.3	211.9
Colored	254.7	253.0	[4]
White	289.0	287.5	[4]
North Carolina	140.5	154.5	101.7
Colored	164.9	183.9	120.8
White	130.3	142.3	94.1
Ohio	221.5	225.3	160.6
Colored	268.3	285.0	[4]
White	219.1	222.3	[4]
Oklahoma	97.8	92.9	[3]
Colored	110.1	105.8	[3]
White	96.2	91.2	[3]
Pennsylvania	247.6	243.5	160.8
Colored	280.4	277.7	[4]
White	246.0	241.9	[4]
Rhode Island	251.4	260.6	182.1
Colored	363.6	581.8	[4]
White	249.6	255.4	[4]
South Carolina	164.7	177.9	109.0
Colored	189.9	206.2	113.0
White	143.9	154.3	104.0
Tennessee	128.1	129.2	96.1
Colored	206.7	221.8	154.4
White	110.7	108.6	82.5
Vermont	281.4	298.3	259.1
Colored	300.0	100.0	[4]
White	281.3	298.9	[4]
Virginia	202.6	202.6	138.1
Colored	277.3	283.7	176.7
White	175.4	172.8	121.1
West Virginia	116.8	128.0	[3]
Colored	165.8	195.7	[3]
White	113.3	123.1	[3]
Selected Cities of 100,000 population or more in 1930			
Akron	139.8	148.7	109.3
Colored	180.3	[4]	[4]
White	17.8	[4]	[4]
Atlanta	194.2	216.0	147.5
Colored	262.9	285.6	195.3
White	159.4	181.2	125.6
Baltimore	281.4	274.7	194.0
Colored	314.5	345.6	287.3
White	274.1	259.4	177.5

[Continued]

★ 2143 ★

Death Rate From Diseases of the Heart – 1920, 1930, 1931

[Continued]

Area and color	Rate per 100,000 estimated population July 1		
	1931	1930	1920
Birmingham	146.7	169.7	153.8
Colored	160.8	230.5	209.3
White	138.0	132.3	118.0
Boston	332.1	311.8	249.4
Colored	395.7	283.2	[4]
White	330.2	312.6	[4]
Buffalo	283.9	273.4	195.3
Colored	259.7	[4]	[4]
White	284.4	[4]	[4]
Camden	247.9	250.0	187.2
Colored	245.8	[4]	[4]
White	248.1	[4]	[4]
Chattanooga	130.1	169.9	162.4
Colored	166.7	270.3	226.5
White	116.3	131.3	131.6
Chicago	223.6	218.9	176.4
Colored	260.9	266.6	[4]
White	220.4	214.9	[4]
Cincinnati	284.3	273.0	210.3
Colored	292.8	329.9	257.9
White	283.2	266.2	206.4
Cleveland	195.7	197.2	120.8
Colored	224.1	236.9	[4]
White	193.1	193.6	[4]
Columbus, Ohio	239.5	276.8	161.1
Colored	268.2	322.3	228.0
White	235.7	271.0	154.1
Dallas	160.4	161.5	110.2
Colored	204.3	199.6	157.8
White	151.3	153.6	101.8
Dayton	240.5	252.1	149.1
Colored	275.3	[4]	[4]
White	237.1	[4]	[4]
Detroit	162.0	164.6	126.8
Colored	221.3	240.6	[4]
White	156.5	157.8	[4]
El Paso	126.7	142.9	[4]
Colored	103.3	113.3	[4]
White	161.5	185.7	[4]
Fort Worth	137.4	145.0	[3]
Colored	128.3	163.5	[3]
White	139.1	141.5	[3]
Gary	124.6	119.2	71.2
Colored	111.1	[4]	[4]
White	128.5	[4]	[4]

[Continued]

★ 2143 ★

Death Rate From Diseases of the Heart – 1920, 1930, 1931

[Continued]

Area and color	Rate per 100,000 estimated population July 1		
	1931	1930	1920
Houston	130.3	140.2	110.2
Colored	144.8	162.0	128.0
White	125.1	132.3	104.5
Indianapolis	282.6	292.1	190.5
Colored	358.4	367.9	266.8
White	272.0	231.6	181.0
Jacksonville, Fla	238.8	263.1	140.6
Colored	305.6	350.6	144.6
White	200.5	211.5	137.3
Jersey City	253.6	252.2	184.9
Colored	335.8	[4]	[4]
White	250.0	[4]	[4]
Kansas City, Kans	208.3	229.3	134.8
Colored	198.3	205.2	217.9
White	210.6	234.9	120.8
Kansas City, Mo	236.2	224.9	199.3
Colored	408.4	350.7	396.3
White	216.0	210.1	178.6
Knoxville	161.2	163.4	141.4
Colored	241.6	254.3	302.0
White	145.5	145.7	113.9
Louisville	287.1	282.6	183.1
Colored	406.7	482.1	305.5
White	265.2	246.2	158.1
Memphis	217.9	216.1	138.3
Colored	266.9	280.7	150.1
White	187.6	176.3	131.1
Miami	175.1	160.4	127.5
Colored	126.5	134.9	124.8
White	189.2	167.8	128.7
Nashville	249.5	209.5	201.0
Colored	361.3	321.7	314.1
White	206.9	166.2	152.5
Newark, N.J.	250.4	260.7	183.0
Colored	230.6	280.4	[4]
White	252.5	258.8	[4]
New Orleans	324.5	336.6	226.8
Colored	428.7	445.0	301.8
White	282.4	293.2	200.0
New York	264.6	266.5	186.4
Colored	251.8	253.2	[4]
White	265.3	267.2	[4]
Norfolk	292.2	288.3	163.5
Colored	425.4	445.8	210.9
White	223.4	207.0	135.0

[Continued]

★ 2143 ★

Death Rate From Diseases of the Heart – 1920, 1930, 1931

[Continued]

Area and color	Rate per 100,000 estimated population July 1		
	1931	1930	1920
Oklahoma City	126.0	130.6	4
Colored	215.1	169.7	4
White	117.5	126.8	4
Omaha	234.0	216.8	152.6
Colored	344.0	333.3	4
White	227.2	209.7	4
Philadelphia	316.6	303.1	206.0
Colored	274.6	286.2	213.1
White	322.3	305.3	205.4
Pittsburgh	230.0	228.9	146.6
Colored	221.8	266.5	4
White	230.8	225.5	4
Richmond, Va	263.7	250.5	177.7
Colored	313.8	324.5	185.0
White	243.5	220.4	174.3
St. Louis	318.3	309.5	177.5
Colored	414.3	423.2	251.9
White	305.4	294.6	169.9
San Antonio	145.8	167.2	107.4
Colored	4	4	4
White	4	4	4
Tampa	202.9	189.4	111.1
Colored	279.3	279.1	126.2
White	182.4	165.4	106.7
Toledo	217.1	279.8	160.0
Colored	246.7	4	4
White	215.5	4	4
Tulsa	109.7	116.9	3
Colored	44.9	109.2	3
White	118.8	118.0	3
Washington, D.C.	331.0	336.3	210.0
Colored	373.3	400.8	232.6
White	314.9	312.1	202.3
Wilmington, Del	261.7	274.9	140.9
Colored	370.7	321.3	184.3
White	247.7	268.9	136.2
Youngstown	155.6	170.7	92.2
Colored	195.0	4	4
White	151.6	4	4

Source: "Colored and White Death Rate From Diseases of the Heart,in Selected States and Cities: 1931, 1930, and 1920." U.S. Bureau of the Census. *Negroes in the United States: 1920-32.* Washington, D.C.: Government Printing Office, 1935, p. 453. *Notes:* 1. Includes Negro, nonwhite, and other races. 2. States in registration area whose Negro population represented 55 percent or more of the total colored population in 1930. 3. Not in registration area. 4. Death rates by color not available.

★ 2144 ★

Deaths

Death Rate From Puerperal Causes Per 1,000 Live Births in Selected States and Cities – 1920, 1930, 1931

Colored[1] and White death rate from puerperal causes per 1,000 live births, in selected states and cities: 1931, 1930, and 1920.

[Rates in italics are based on less than 5 deaths]

Area and color	All puerperal causes			Puerperal septicemia			Other puerperal causes		
	1931	1930	1920	1931	1930	1920	1931	1930	1920
Selected states[2]									
Alabama	8.1	9.0	[3]	2.7	2.8	[3]	5.4	6.3	[3]
Colored	10.1	11.7	[3]	3.1	3.6	[3]	7.0	8.1	[3]
White	7.0	7.6	[3]	2.5	2.3	[3]	4.5	5.3	[3]
Arkansas	7.1	9.4	[3]	2.7	3.0	[3]	4.5	6.4	[3]
Colored	10.1	14.5	[3]	3.5	5.3	[3]	6.7	9.2	[3]
White	6.2	7.9	[3]	2.4	2.3	[3]	3.8	5.6	[3]
Florida	10.4	10.2	[4]	3.4	3.1	[4]	7.0	7.1	[4]
Colored	15.4	14.1	[4]	6.0	5.4	[4]	9.4	8.7	[4]
White	8.1	8.5	[4]	2.3	2.1	[4]	5.8	6.4	[4]
Georgia	9.9	10.6	[3]	3.0	3.2	[3]	6.9	7.4	[3]
Colored	12.2	12.4	[3]	3.7	4.0	[3]	8.5	8.4	[3]
White	8.4	9.4	[3]	2.6	2.7	[3]	5.9	6.7	[3]
Kentucky	6.4	6.4	6.4	2.5	2.5	2.8	3.9	4.0	3.7
Colored	13.5	15.4	13.0	5.5	7.7	7.0	8.0	7.7	6.0
White	6.0	5.9	6.0	2.3	2.1	2.5	3.7	3.8	3.5
Louisiana	8.6	10.0	[4]	3.3	2.9	[4]	5.3	7.1	[4]
Colored	10.6	12.5	[4]	4.6	3.9	[4]	6.0	8.5	[4]
White	7.3	8.4	[4]	2.4	2.3	[4]	4.9	6.1	[4]
Maryland	6.1	5.6	7.6	2.3	1.9	2.4	3.8	3.7	5.2
Colored	8.3	6.7	11.8	3.2	2.8	5.0	5.1	3.9	6.8
White	5.5	5.3	6.6	2.1	1.7	1.8	3.5	3.6	4.8
Mississippi	8.0	9.6	[4]	2.5	2.6	[4]	5.5	7.0	[4]
Colored	9.4	12.1	[4]	3.1	3.6	[4]	6.3	8.4	[4]
White	6.5	7.0	[4]	1.9	1.6	[4]	4.6	5.4	[4]
North Carolina	8.0	8.3	10.0	2.2	2.1	2.1	5.8	6.3	7.9
Colored	11.6	12.1	13.2	3.7	3.0	3.1	7.9	9.1	10.1
White	6.4	6.7	8.6	1.5	1.7	1.7	4.9	5.0	6.9
Oklahoma	6.2	6.9	[3]	2.8	3.0	[3]	3.4	3.9	[3]
Colored	15.4	16.4	[3]	7.1	5.0	[3]	8.2	11.5	[3]
White	5.4	6.1	[3]	2.4	2.9	[3]	3.0	3.2	[3]
South Carolina	10.2	11.4	12.2	2.5	2.7	2.8	7.8	8.7	9.4
Colored	12.7	13.1	15.4	3.2	3.2	3.7	9.6	9.9	11.7
White	7.6	9.6	9.0	1.7	2.1	1.8	5.9	7.4	7.1
Tennessee	7.4	8.4	[4]	3.2	3.3	[4]	4.3	5.1	[4]
Colored	13.7	15.8	[4]	6.0	8.4	[4]	7.7	7.4	[4]
White	6.3	7.0	[4]	2.7	2.3	[4]	3.7	4.7	[4]
Virginia	7.5	7.1	8.6	2.4	2.4	2.3	5.1	4.7	6.4
Colored	11.5	11.7	11.1	3.8	3.6	3.1	7.7	8.1	8.0
White	5.9	5.2	7.5	1.9	1.9	1.9	4.0	3.3	5.6

[Continued]

★ 2144 ★

Death Rate From Puerperal Causes Per 1,000 Live Births in Selected States and Cities – 1920, 1930, 1931

[Continued]

Area and color	All puerperal causes			Puerperal septicemia			Other puerperal causes		
	1931	1930	1920	1931	1930	1920	1931	1930	1920
Selected Cities[2]									
Atlanta, Ga	9.5	10.4	[4]	4.6	5.1	[4]	5.0	5.3	[4]
Colored	14.8	14.9	[4]	8.5	8.3	[4]	6.3	6.6	[4]
White	6.9	8.0	[4]	2.6	3.4	[4]	4.3	4.6	[4]
Baltimore, Md	7.7	6.1	7.6	3.0	2.7	2.8	4.8	3.5	4.8
Colored	9.5	8.0	11.5	3.5	3.7	6.3	6.0	4.3	5.2
White	7.2	5.6	6.8	2.8	2.4	2.1	4.4	3.2	4.7
Birmingham, Ala	12.5	11.3	[4]	5.3	5.8	[4]	7.2	5.6	[4]
Colored	19.8	11.7	[4]	7.3	6.6	[4]	12.5	5.2	[4]
White	8.1	11.1	[4]	4.0	5.2	[4]	4.0	5.9	[4]
Chattanooga, Tenn	10.3	13.3	[4]	3.8	6.4	[4]	6.6	6.9	[4]
Colored	17.5	28.9	[4]	6.6	20.6	[4]	11.0	8.2	[4]
White	8.4	9.2	[4]	3.0	2.7	[4]	5.4	6.5	[4]
Cincinnati, Ohio	7.4	7.0	9.6	3.4	3.1	4.4	4.0	3.9	5.2
Colored	7.4	11.5	22.6	4.2	5.7	8.1	3.2	5.7	14.5
White	7.4	6.4	8.4	3.3	2.7	4.0	4.1	3.7	4.4
Columbus, Ohio	10.1	10.6	10.0	5.0	4.8	3.6	5.0	5.8	6.4
Colored	12.5	14.8	4.4	5.4	4.9	4.4	7.2	9.9	-
White	9.7	10.1	10.6	5.0	4.8	3.5	4.8	5.2	7.1
Indianapolis, Ind	9.7	6.9	9.6	4.9	2.5	5.3	4.9	4.4	4.4
Colored	8.7	8.2	17.2	5.0	4.7	10.6	3.7	3.5	6.6
White	9.9	6.7	8.7	4.8	2.2	4.6	5.0	4.5	4.1
Jacksonville, Fla	9.3	9.8	[4]	5.2	2.9	[4]	4.0	6.9	[4]
Colored	16.4	10.5	[4]	12.6	5.3	[4]	3.8	5.3	[4]
White	5.9	9.5	[4]	1.8	1.8	[4]	4.2	7.7	[4]
Kansas City, Kans	10.4	8.9	8.9	4.3	4.7	4.0	6.1	4.2	4.9
Colored	20.7	12.2	23.1	5.2	12.2	9.3	15.5	-	13.9
White	8.4	8.2	7.4	4.2	3.1	3.4	4.2	5.1	3.9
Kansas City, Mo	10.3	8.2	[4]	4.7	3.7	[4]	5.6	4.5	[4]
Colored	5.3	16.1	[4]	3.5	8.1	[4]	1.8	8.1	[4]
White	10.8	7.3	[4]	4.9	3.2	[4]	6.0	4.1	[4]
Knoxville, Tenn	14.0	10.4	[4]	3.8	2.9	[4]	10.1	7.5	[4]
Colored	15.0	11.2	[4]	5.0	7.4	[4]	10.0	3.7	[4]
White	13.8	10.3	[4]	3.7	2.3	[4]	10.1	8.0	[4]
Los Angeles, Calif	9.2	6.5	8.1	3.8	3.1	3.3	5.4	3.3	4.8
Colored	9.0	[5]	12.8	4.0	[5]	6.0	5.0	[5]	6.8
White	9.2	[5]	7.6	3.7	[5]	3.0	5.6	[5]	4.6
Louisville, Ky	8.2	7.7	9.3	3.9	3.1	4.4	4.3	4.5	4.9
Colored	10.8	12.4	20.1	5.4	6.9	14.6	5.4	5.5	5.5
White	7.8	7.0	7.9	3.7	2.6	3.1	4.1	4.4	4.8
Memphis, Tenn	10.8	11.4	[4]	7.2	4.3	[4]	3.6	7.1	[4]
Colored	13.6	16.1	[4]	5.9	7.2	[4]	7.7	8.9	[4]
White	9.2	8.7	[4]	7.9	2.6	[4]	1.3	6.1	[4]
Miami, Fla	8.8	9.9	[4]	4.4	3.5	[4]	4.4	6.4	[4]
Colored	7.9	17.4	[4]	4.0	3.5	[4]	4.0	3.9	[4]

[Continued]

★ 2144 ★

Death Rate From Puerperal Causes Per 1,000 Live Births in Selected States and Cities – 1920, 1930, 1931

[Continued]

Area and color	All puerperal causes			Puerperal septicemia			Other puerperal causes		
	1931	1930	1920	1931	1930	1920	1931	1930	1920
White	9.1	6.9	[4]	4.6	3.5	[4]	4.6	3.5	[4]
Nashville, Tenn	10.5	11.8	[4]	6.6	5.5	[4]	3.9	6.4	[4]
Colored	12.8	25.3	[4]	8.1	15.7	[4]	4.7	9.7	[4]
White	9.7	7.6	[4]	6.1	2.3	[4]	3.6	5.3	[4]
New Orleans, La	12.2	11.1	[4]	5.5	4.4	[4]	6.6	6.7	[4]
Colored	16.7	13.6	[4]	9.1	6.6	[4]	7.6	7.0	[4]
White	9.8	9.9	[4]	3.7	3.2	[4]	6.1	6.6	[4]
Norfolk, Va	8.7	12.4	10.8	4.1	5.3	3.1	4.6	7.1	7.7
Colored	13.6	20.0	16.6	9.5	6.7	5.8	4.1	13.3	10.7
White	6.3	8.6	7.6	1.4	4.7	1.6	4.9	4.0	6.0
Philadelphia, Pa	6.8	6.4	7.6	2.8	2.3	2.7	4.1	4.0	4.9
Colored	8.2	7.4	11.1	3.6	3.0	3.2	4.6	4.4	7.9
White	6.6	6.2	7.4	2.6	2.2	2.7	4.0	4.0	4.7
Richmond, Va	12.1	9.2	13.3	5.5	4.2	4.8	6.7	5.0	8.6
Colored	18.1	11.6	20.0	6.9	4.2	7.2	11.2	7.5	12.9
White	9.1	8.0	10.0	4.8	4.2	3.6	4.3	3.8	6.4
St. Louis, Mo	7.0	5.6	[4]	3.9	2.7	[4]	3.2	2.9	[4]
Colored	10.1	8.0	[4]	7.9	5.9	[4]	2.2	2.1	[4]
White	6.6	5.2	[4]	3.3	2.2	[4]	3.3	3.0	[4]
Tampa, Fla	7.3	7.1	[4]	2.8	3.8	[4]	4.5	3.3	[4]
Colored	12.1	6.1	[4]	3.0	6.1	[4]	9.1	-	[4]
White	6.2	7.3	[4]	2.8	3.3	[4]	3.5	4.0	[4]
Tulsa, Okla	6.5	10.1	[3]	4.4	5.1	[3]	2.2	5.1	[3]
Colored	27.6	30.5	[3]	11.0	12.2	[3]	16.6	18.3	[3]
White	4.7	8.6	[3]	3.8	4.5	[3]	.9	4.1	[3]
Washington, D.C.	7.1	9.0	8.8	4.1	4.1	2.8	3.0	4.9	6.0
Colored	10.1	17.7	14.4	5.4	7.5	5.2	4.7	10.2	9.2
White	5.7	4.7	6.6	3.5	2.4	1.9	2.2	2.4	4.7
Wilmington, Del	6.4	7.8	[4]	1.4	4.3	[4]	5.0	3.5	[4]
Colored	8.8	4.1	[4]	-	4.1	[4]	8.8	-	[4]
White	6.1	8.3	[4]	1.5	4.4	[4]	4.6	3.9	[4]

Source: "Colored and White Death Rate From Puerperal Causes Per 1,000 Live Births, in Selected States and Cities: 1931, 1930, and 1920." U.S. Bureau of the Census. *Negroes in the United States: 1920-32.* Washington, D.C.: Government Printing Office, 1935, p. 457. *Notes:* 1. Includes Negro, nonwhite, and other races. 2. States and cities for which death rates by color are available. 3. Not in either birth or death registration area. 4. Not in birth area. 5. Death rates by color not available.

★ 2145 ★

Deaths

Death Rates by Marital Status, Age, Race, and Sex – 1940, 1950, 1960

Marital status, color, sex, and year	Total	Under 20 years	20-24 years	25-34 years	35-44 years	45-54 years	55-59 years	60-64 years	65-69 years	70-74 years	75 years and over
White											
Total											
1960	9.5	2.0	1.1	1.2	2.6	6.9	13.0	20.2	30.4	46.5	107.4
1950	9.5	2.6	1.3	1.5	3.1	7.7	14.5	22.1	32.7	51.1	110.8
1940	10.4	3.6	2.0	2.5	4.4	9.5	17.3	25.8	38.7	60.8	130.1
Single											
1960	3.8	2.1	1.6	2.4	4.9	10.2	15.6	24.7	35.6	52.7	117.6
1950	4.4	2.6	1.6	2.5	5.2	11.0	19.5	27.9	38.9	58.0	117.9
1940	5.2	3.6	2.1	3.3	6.3	12.6	21.7	29.7	42.3	63.2	128.4
Married											
1960	9.1	0.7	0.7	1.0	2.2	6.2	11.8	19.2	29.5	45.5	91.3
1950	8.8	0.9	0.9	1.2	2.7	6.9	13.6	20.9	31.0	48.6	93.9
1940	10.1	2.2	1.7	2.1	3.8	8.5	15.8	23.7	35.8	56.5	108.1
Widowed											
1960	54.5	2.1	2.7	2.4	3.9	8.0	12.6	19.8	22.9	46.8	122.9
1950	49.1	3.2	3.5	3.3	5.0	9.1	14.9	22.2	32.3	50.7	117.7
1940	52.3	5.9	4.9	5.0	6.3	11.8	19.6	27.9	41.0	63.4	140.7
Divorced											
1960	19.1	1.1	2.3	3.3	6.6	14.1	23.4	34.1	47.6	68.8	129.8
1950	16.2	1.9	2.1	3.5	6.8	14.2	24.2	34.5	51.5	78.7	159.0
1940	18.9	3.2	3.7	5.0	8.8	17.6	28.7	41.8	62.8	104.8	210.4
White Male											
Total											
1960	11.0	2.3	1.7	1.6	3.3	9.3	17.8	27.5	40.5	59.1	120.2
1950	10.9	3.0	1.7	1.9	3.8	9.8	18.8	28.1	40.7	60.4	120.8
1940	11.6	4.1	2.3	2.8	5.1	11.4	20.9	30.6	44.6	67.8	137.8
Single											
1960	4.4	2.4	2.1	2.9	6.3	14.6	23.3	37.0	53.7	76.2	140.6
1950	5.1	3.0	2.0	3.1	7.2	15.8	28.1	39.8	54.1	78.5	138.4
1940	5.9	4.1	2.5	4.0	8.1	16.2	27.7	37.4	51.9	74.4	131.7
Married											
1960	12.9	1.1	1.1	1.3	2.8	8.0	15.6	24.7	36.8	53.5	102.1
1950	12.0	1.6	1.3	1.5	3.2	8.7	17.0	25.4	36.7	54.8	101.6
1940	12.9	2.1	1.7	2.2	4.2	9.8	18.3	27.1	39.4	60.5	114.5
Widowed											
1960	89.8	3.9	4.3	5.0	8.0	17.3	28.2	39.6	55.1	75.4	158.8
1950	71.6	07	6.0	6.0	9.4	16.9	26.0	36.0	48.1	68.1	141.1
1940	71.7	11.9	7.8	7.8	10.6	19.2	31.0	40.6	56.3	79.3	163.3
Divorced											
1960	32.2	1.8	3.8	5.1	11.4	25.1	40.2	56.1	73.5	97.3	161.8
1950	26.0	2.8	3.5	5.5	11.0	22.7	35.6	47.1	65.6	91.5	175.5
1940	29.5	6.1	4.8	7.8	13.4	25.1	38.3	51.9	73.4	114.2	215.9
White Female											
Total											
1960	8.0	1.6	0.6	0.9	1.9	4.6	8.3	13.6	21.5	35.8	97.9

[Continued]

★ 2145 ★

Death Rates by Marital Status, Age, Race, and Sex – 1940, 1950, 1960

[Continued]

Marital status, color, sex, and year	Total	Under 20 years	20-24 years	25-34 years	35-44 years	45-54 years	55-59 years	60-64 years	65-69 years	70-74 years	75 years and over
1950	8.0	2.2	0.8	1.1	2.4	5.5	10.2	16.2	25.2	42.6	102.5
1940	9.2	3.1	1.6	2.2	3.7	7.5	13.5	20.8	32.9	54.0	123.4
Single											
1960	3.2	1.7	0.8	1.6	3.2	5.8	8.7	13.9	20.6	34.7	103.7
1950	3.6	2.2	0.9	1.7	3.1	6.1	10.6	15.7	24.5	41.4	104.3
1940	4.3	3.1	1.5	2.4	4.0	7.9	14.0	20.9	32.0	52.1	125.6
Married											
1960	5.4	0.6	0.5	0.7	1.7	4.1	7.5	12.5	19.8	32.9	69.4
1950	5.6	0.8	0.7	1.0	2.2	5.1	9.5	15.2	23.2	38.7	76.6
1940	7.2	2.2	1.7	2.0	3.5	7.0	12.6	19.2	30.4	49.1	92.6
Widowed											
1960	45.4	1.4	2.2	1.7	3.1	6.3	9.7	15.7	24.2	38.9	110.4
1950	41.6	6.3	2.6	2.7	4.0	7.2	11.9	17.9	27.0	44.3	107.5
1940	44.9	4.6	4.1	4.1	9.3	15.6	23.4	35.3	56.8	129.8	
Divorced											
1960	9.8	0.9	1.4	2.0	3.4	6.4	10.6	16.4	25.3	41.6	96.0
1950	8.5	1.6	1.4	2.2	3.8	7.1	12.8	19.8	32.4	58.9	130.9
1940	10.7	2.8	3.3	3.5	5.5	10.5	17.7	28.5	46.7	86.9	197.8
Nonwhite											
Total											
1960	10.1	4.1	2.0	3.2	6.3	13.4	22.2	35.2	42.5	55.8	87.9
1950	11.2	4.9	3.1	4.4	8.1	17.1	29.6	39.3	39.6	57.7	92.0
1940	13.8	6.7	6.1	7.9	12.4	22.9	34.4	42.1	44.4	64.6	113.6
Single											
1960	5.2	4.3	2.5	5.4	11.7	19.5	21.5	40.7	45.8	64.5	90.3
1950	6.2	5.0	3.8	7.4	15.3	27.8	42.5	51.7	54.5	81.4	90.2
1940	8.4	6.7	6.9	11.1	17.3	28.6	42.2	51.8	53.9	80.9	133.5
Married											
1960	10.2	1.2	1.5	2.5	5.1	10.9	17.5	28.3	35.4	45.8	70.9
1950	10.6	2.1	2.4	3.5	6.6	13.8	23.9	31.4	32.5	48.2	77.5
1940	13.9	5.1	5.0	6.5	10.5	19.0	27.7	33.5	37.5	55.0	96.1
Widowed											
1960	47.3	2.3	3.6	6.5	10.9	21.5	31.6	46.3	50.1	63.2	98.3
1950	43.4	8.0	5.3	9.2	13.7	25.9	40.5	50.7	43.0	60.9	95.4
1940	44.6	9.5	11.4	13.4	17.8	32.5	46.7	53.0	48.7	67.4	115.3
Divorced											
1960	18.3	0.4	2.9	4.3	10.2	20.5	29.5	45.7	59.1	66.4	86.9
1950	17.0	2.8	3.0	6.9	11.1	23.0	37.1	49.0	54.9	73.7	128.4
1940	22.8	7.7	6.3	9.8	17.3	32.3	47.1	64.0	69.2	114.5	192.7
Nonwhite Male											
Total											
1960	11.5	4.6	2.7	3.9	7.3	15.5	25.0	40.5	51.0	64.9	98.0
1950	12.5	5.5	3.7	5.0	8.6	18.6	32.6	42.7	46.2	63.7	101.2
1940	15.1	7.3	6.5	8.5	13.2	24.5	36.0	44.2	49.0	70.2	126.5

[Continued]

★ 2145 ★

Death Rates by Marital Status, Age, Race, and Sex – 1940, 1950, 1960

[Continued]

Marital status, color, sex, and year	Total	Under 20 years	20-24 years	25-34 years	35-44 years	45-54 years	55-59 years	60-64 years	65-69 years	70-74 years	75 years and over
Single											
1960	6.1	4.8	3.2	6.3	13.9	23.5	26.3	48.5	55.2	77.7	106.0
1950	7.2	5.5	4.2	8.2	18.0	32.3	53.2	59.1	70.5	100.2	117.2
1940	9.5	7.3	7.1	12.1	18.8	30.5	43.6	54.2	58.0	89.6	137.9
Married											
1960	13.6	2.1	2.0	2.9	5.5	12.4	19.9	33.3	42.3	52.6	78.3
1950	13.4	2.4	2.8	3.8	6.7	14.9	26.5	34.0	36.6	50.8	80.4
1940	16.5	4.2	4.8	6.5	10.6	20.2	29.2	35.6	39.9	57.0	98.8
Widowed											
1960	72.1	4.0	8.7	11.2	17.3	33.2	46.7	67.3	75.0	90.4	128.4
1950	62.8	13.0	6.2	12.0	20.3	36.9	55.3	67.3	61.4	78.8	118.6
1940	65.2	25.6	19.6	21.6	26.1	46.8	62.0	65.7	66.2	84.4	147.6
Divorced											
1960	30.2	-	4.5	6.5	15.3	31.8	41.9	66.3	82.0	89.3	109.1
1950	25.9	6.5	3.8	10.4	14.8	30.8	46.6	56.0	68.6	77.2	164.1
1940	34.9	5.1	10.2	14.4	24.3	41.6	51.4	72.1	74.1	115.3	192.9
Nonwhite female											
Total											
1960	8.7	3.5	1.4	2.6	5.5	11.4	19.5	30.2	34.7	47.4	79.0
1950	9.9	4.4	2.5	3.9	7.5	15.5	26.3	35.7	33.5	51.6	83.5
1940	12.6	6.1	5.8	7.4	11.7	21.1	32.7	39.9	39.5	58.7	102.0
Single											
1960	4.2	3.7	1.6	4.0	8.5	13.8	14.2	28.5	31.8	46.8	71.7
1950	5.2	4.5	3.1	6.3	11.6	20.2	25.4	39.6	33.1	56.7	65.4
1940	7.2	6.1	6.6	9.6	14.4	24.4	38.9	47.1	46.2	65.1	126.5
Married											
1960	7.0	1.0	1.2	2.2	4.6	9.2	14.6	21.4	24.8	32.9	51.3
1950	8.0	2.0	2.2	3.3	6.4	12.4	20.1	27.1	25.6	41.9	68.0
1940	11.3	5.3	5.1	6.5	10.3	17.4	25.4	29.6	32.7	49.8	87.5
Widowed											
1960	39.8	1.6	2.4	5.5	9.4	18.5	27.4	40.3	42.5	53.9	86.3
1950	36.9	6.3	5.0	8.5	12.2	22.8	35.7	44.5	36.5	53.4	84.6
1940	37.7	8.0	9.6	11.6	15.9	28.1	41.2	48.0	41.8	59.8	100.6
Divorced											
1960	10.9	0.5	2.3	3.3	7.3	13.1	19.6	27.3	35.9	41.9	56.9
1950	11.3	2.1	2.7	5.2	8.8	16.8	26.1	39.8	39.0	68.2	71.2
1940	15.8	7.9	5.3	7.9	13.3	23.9	42.3	53.2	62.3	112.9	192.2

Source: "Death Rates by Marital Status, Age, Color, and Sex: United States, 1940, 1950, and 1960," National Center for Health Services. *Vital Statistics in the United States 1940-1960*. By Robert D. Grove and Alice M. Hetzel. Washington, D.C.: Government Printing Office, 1968, pp. 335-336.

★ 2146 ★

Deaths

Death Rates for Tuberculosis, 1940-1948

Death rates for tuberculosis (all forms) by race and sex, 1910-1948[1].

Year	Total	White			Nonwhite		
		Total	Male	Female	Total	Male	Female
1948	30.0	24.3	33.3	15.4	78.7	92.1	65.4
1944	41.3	33.7	45.0	23.3	106.2	122.7	91.3
1943	42.6	34.3	44.4	24.7	112.9	126.4	100.0
1942	43.1	34.4	43.3	25.6	118.4	131.4	106.0
1941	44.5	35.4	43.3	27.4	124.2	134.3	114.5
1940	45.8	36.5	44.7	28.2	127.6	138.7	116.9
1935	55.1	44.9	51.7	37.8	145.1	155.4	135.0
1930	71.1	57.7	63.4	51.9	192.0	194.3	189.8
1925	84.8	71.6	75.8	67.2	221.3	215.8	226.7
1920	113.1	99.5	104.1	94.8	262.4	255.4	269.6
1915	140.1	128.5	144.0	112.2	401.1	420.2	380.5
1910	153.8	145.9	158.2	445.5	479.3	406.8	

Source: "Death Rates for Tuberculosis (All Forms) by Race and Sex, 1910-1948." Guzman, Jessie Parkhurst, ed. *Negro Year Book: A Review of Events Affecting Negro Life, 1941-1946*. New York: William H. Weise, 1952, p. 161. Primary source: Division of Chronic Disease and Tuberculosis and National Office of Vital Statistics, U.S. Public Health Service. *Note:* 1. Rates for death registration states.

★ 2147 ★

Deaths

Death Rates for Tuberculosis: Urban and Rural Sites, 1940

Division and state	Total	White	Negro	Urban	Rural[1]
United States	45.9	36.6	123.5	49.8	42.4
New England	35.2	33.9	124.1	36.6	33.0
Maine	29.9	29.6	76.7	27.9	31.9
New Hampshire	21.2	21.0	0	22.7	23.3
Vermont	41.5	41.5	0	70.0	38.5
Massachusetts	37.7	36.5	113.7	37.6	34.8
Rhode Island	33.1	31.2	154.2	31.7	54.4
Connecticut	34.9	32.9	136.4	39.4	30.2
Middle Atlantic	44.5	37.0	194.5	46.0	41.5
New York	46.4	30.9	205.0	45.2	47.6
New Jersey	43.0	34.4	190.3	42.0	49.6
Pennsylvania	42.6	35.4	183.8	49.7	35.2
East North Central	39.1	32.2	200.5	45.5	32.1
Ohio	40.4	32.1	200.3	48.9	30.4
Indiana	40.2	35.2	175.5	46.0	36.6
Illinois	46.2	37.0	218.6	52.8	37.3
Michigan	33.6	27.4	178.6	37.1	30.1
Wisconsin	26.5	24.9	255.0	27.2	24.3

[Continued]

★ 2147 ★

Death Rates for Tuberculosis: Urban and Rural Sites, 1940

[Continued]

Division and state	Total	White	Negro	Urban	Rural[1]
West North Central	28.7	24.6	134.8	33.1	27.3
Minnesota	27.1	25.5	141.0	25.0	27.8
Iowa	17.1	16.4	89.9	19.4	16.8
Missouri	45.0	37.5	152.2	47.8	45.4
North Dakota	19.3	15.8	0	17.7	19.7
South Dakota	29.4	15.7	211.0	20.2	33.2
Nebraska	17.1	15.0	112.9	29.4	12.3
Kansas	24.9	22.5	84.4	30.8	22.4
South Atlantic	53.9	32.5	113.4	71.6	45.2
Delaware	46.9	32.1	142.2	40.0	57.8
Maryland	79.1	47.5	237.5	79.4	64.5
District of Columbia	64.4	33.3	142.6	85.8	..
Virginia	58.1	36.5	123.8	66.0	55.9
West Virginia	46.1	40.7	127.4	53.0	44.7
North Carolina	49.9	26.4	112.1	67.4	39.2
South Carolina	47.4	21.2	82.2	81.6	41.9
Georgia	50.0	26.9	90.4	82.9	38.5
Florida	50.6	27.7	111.8	57.9	45.8
East South Central	62.4	48.8	101.5	76.8	58.7
Kentucky	69.7	62.1	162.1	73.2	67.4
Tennessee	74.9	59.2	149.2	83.9	72.6
Alabama	52.9	31.1	93.8	78.8	45.5
Mississippi	48.8	24.2	74.0	58.6	48.7
West South Central	55.9	46.2	92.7	71.8	50.0
Arkansas	50.6	35.9	95.5	78.0	48.7
Louisiana	58.8	38.4	95.5	78.8	48.7
Oklahoma	48.2	35.8	124.4	56.0	46.5
Texas	59.2	55.2	83.0	73.3	52.3
Mountain	57.4	49.5	181.3	68.6	43.6
Montana	40.2	31.8	178.6	53.4	37.4
Idaho	18.1	15.2	0	14.4	19.2
Wyoming	16.8	13.8	104.6	17.9	18.0
Colorado	53.4	51.0	230.0	53.7	37.7
New Mexico	75.4	74.5	214.0	111.2	57.7
Arizona	170.9	145.5	160.1	311.1	99.5
Utah	16.2	14.9	81.0	22.4	13.5
Nevada	71.7	50.0	0	51.6	75.3
Pacific	50.3	45.0	153.4	49.1	51.4
Washington	40.7	35.1	161.6	39.2	40.4
Oregon	27.3	24.5	272.9	33.6	25.1
California	56.3	50.9	150.4	52.5	62.3

Source: "Death Rates (Number per 100,000 Enumerated Population) for Tuberculosis (All Forms), by Race, and by Urban and Rural Place of Residence, Division and State, 1940." *The Negro Handbook, 1944*, pp. 183-184. *Note:* 1. "Rural" includes areas having less than 10,000 population.

★ 2148 ★

Deaths

Death Rates from Tuberculosis, 1910-1941

Death rate per 100,000 population.

Year	Total	White	Colored
1910	160.3	148.3	447.7
1911	159.2	146.3	446.1
1912	149.7	137.5	418.1
1913	147.8	134.8	387.8
1914	147.2	133.4	401.7
1915	146.3	131.7	409.8
1916	142.1	127.9	335.0
1917	147.1	131.5	344.5
1918	150.0	133.9	347.0
1919	125.6	110.6	282.3
1920	114.0	100.0	262.2
1921	98.9	85.6	239.7
1922	96.4	83.3	220.0
1923	92.8	80.4	213.4
1924	89.7	76.4	219.3
1925	86.7	73.1	222.9
1926	87.3	73.4	224.8
1927	80.9	67.6	208.7
1928	79.3	65.9	199.7
1929	76.0	63.0	191.9
1934	56.7	45.1	147.8
1935	55.1	44.9	145.1
1936	55.9	45.0	151.6
1937	53.8	43.4	145.1
1938	49.1	39.1	136.8
1939	47.1	37.7	129.1
1940	45.8	36.6	128.0
1941	44.4	35.4	124.6

Source: "Death Rates From Tuberculosis by Race: 1910-1941. United States Death Registration Area." *The Negro Handbook, 1944*, pp. 182-183. Primary source: National Tuberculosis Association.

★ 2149 ★

Deaths

Death Rates, by Age: 1940-1975

Age-specific death rates per 1,000 population in specified group.

Age and race	1940	1960	1970	1974	1975
BLACK AND OTHER RACES					
Crude death rate[1]	13.8	10.1	9.4	8.7	8.3
Age adjusted[2]	19.0	12.7	12.0	11.0	10.4
Under 1 year	89.2	46.3	36.7	29.2	27.7
1 to 4 years	4.8	1.9	1.4	1.1	1.0
5 to 14 years	1.5	0.6	0.5	0.5	0.5
15 to 24 years	5.0	1.6	2.0	1.7	1.6
25 to 34 years	7.9	3.2	3.5	3.1	3.0
35 to 44 years	12.4	6.3	6.7	5.7	5.3
45 to 54 years	22.9	13.4	13.0	11.5	10.8
55 to 64 years	35.3	27.7	24.5	22.9	21.8
65 to 74 years	57.8	47.8	45.1	42.7	39.7
75 to 84 years	96.1	76.3	74.7	70.8	70.8
85 years and over	176.7	139.1	122.2	112.5	101.0
WHITE					
Crude death rate[1]	10.4	9.5	9.5	9.2	9.0
Age adjusted[2]	13.4	9.8	9.1	8.6	8.2
Under 1 year	50.3	23.6	18.5	15.2	14.1
1 to 4 years	2.6	1.0	0.8	0.7	0.6
5 to 14 years	1.0	0.4	0.4	0.4	0.3
15 to 24 years	1.7	1.0	1.1	1.1	1.1
25 to 34 years	2.5	1.2	1.3	1.2	1.2
35 to 44 years	4.4	2.6	2.7	2.4	2.3
45 to 54 years	9.5	6.9	6.6	6.2	6.0
55 to 64 years	21.1	16.3	15.7	14.7	14.2
65 to 74 years	47.7	37.4	34.7	32.3	31.0
75 to 84 years	113.0	88.3	79.8	77.0	73.8
85 years and over	242.0	203.5	176.8	170.6	157.1

Source: "Death Rates for the Population, by Age, for Selected Years: 1940 to 1975," U.S. Department of Commerce, Bureau of the Census. *The Social and Economic Status of the Black Population in the United States: An Historical View, 1790-1978,* p. 123. Primary source: U.S. Department of Health, Education, and Welfare, National Center for Health Statistics and U.S. Department of Commerce, Bureau of the Census. *Notes:* Rates for 1970 revised by the Bureau of the Census to be consistent with population estimates by age as published by the Bureau of the Census in *Current Population Reports*, Series P-25, No. 614. 1. Unadjusted for differences in age structure. 2. Standardized on the age distribution of the total population for 1970.

★ 2150 ★

Deaths

Death Rates, by Cities, 1900 and 1910

City	Number of deaths				Death rate per 1,000 population				Increase (+) or decrease (-) per 1,000 population: 1900-1910	
	1910		1900		1910		1900			
	Negro	White	Negro	White	Negro	White	Negro	White	Negro	White
Total for 57 cities[1]	33,803	270,546	30,658	236,516	27.8	15.9	31.2	18.4	-3.4	-2.5
Northern and western cities										
Total for 33 cities	12,483	237,421	9,891	205,868	25.1	15.7	27.1	18.2	-2.0	-2.5
Atlantic City, N.J.	172	627	106	375	17.3	17.1	16.3	17.6	+1.0	-0.5
Boston, Mass	317	11,224	312	11,100	23.3	17.1	26.9	20.3	-3.6	-3.2
Cambridge, Mass	75	1,501	105	1,466	15.9	15.0	27.0	16.7	-11.1	-1.7
Camden, N.J.	192	1,437	186	1,182	31.5	16.2	33.4	16.8	-1.9	-0.6
Chicago, Ill	1,075	32,130	712	25,337	24.3	15.0	23.6	15.2	+0.7	-0.2
Cincinnati, Ohio	569	5,750	430	5,496	28.9	16.7	29.7	17.6	-0.8	-0.9
Cleveland, Ohio	167	7,880	99	6,627	19.6	14.2	16.5	17.6	+3.1	-3.4
Columbus, Ohio	262	2,548	187	1,801	20.4	15.0	22.8	15.3	-2.4	-0.3
Dayton, Ohio	99	1,625	68	1,267	20.4	14.5	20.1	15.5	+0.3	-1.0
Denver, Colo	132	3,389	89	2,444	24.1	16.2	22.7	18.9	+1.4	-2.7
Detroit, Mich	146	7,305	103	4,552	25.2	15.8	25.1	16.2	+0.1	-0.4
Evansville, Ind	117	831	150	781	18.9	13.5	20.0	15.2	-1.1	-1.7
Harrisburg, Pa	98	842	104	800	21.5	14.1	25.3	17.4	-3.8	-3.3
Indianapolis, Ind	548	3,275	383	2,503	25.0	15.4	24.0	16.3	+1.0	-0.9
Jersey City, N.J.	123	4,278	83	4,191	20.5	16.3	22.4	20.7	-1.9	-4.4
Kansas City, Mo	644	3,317	438	2,236	27.1	14.7	24.9	15.3	+2.2	-0.6
Los Angeles, Cal	136	4,299	62	1,809	17.6	13.9	29.1	18.4	-11.5	-4.5
Minneapolis, Minn	56	3,681	22	2,286	21.5	12.2	14.2	11.4	+7.3	+0.8
Newark, N.J.	296	5,484	202	4,755	31.1	16.1	30.2	19.9	+0.9	-3.8
New Bedford, Mass	85	1,727	32	1,293	29.2	18.3	19.0	21.3	+10.2	-3.0
New Haven, Conn	91	2,126	82	1,886	25.5	16.3	28.4	18.0	-2.9	-1.7
New York, N.Y.	2,391	74,274	1,950	68,709	25.9	15.8	32.1	20.4	-6.2	-4.6
Manhattan Borough	1,473	37,129	1,242	38,146	24.2	16.3	34.3	21.1	-10.1	-4.8
Bronx Borough	208	6,755	75	3,674	50.0	15.7	31.6	18.6	+18.4	-2.9
Brooklyn Borough	598	25,070	533	22,932	26.2	15.5	29.0	20.0	-2.8	-4.5
Queens Borough	82	3,882	66	2,702	25.4	13.7	25.3	18.0	+0.1	-4.3
Richmond Borough	30	1,438	34	1,345	25.9	16.9	31.7	20.4	-5.8	-3.5
Oakland, Cal	52	1,791	19	1,031	16.8	12.5	18.5	15.9	+1.7	-3.4
Omaha, Nebr	105	1,769	67	1,141	23.6	14.7	19.5	11.5	-4.1	+3.2
Philadelphia, Pa	2,276	24,740	1,894	25,055	26.9	16.8	30.2	20.4	-3.3	-3.6
Pittsburgh, Pa[2]	601	8,993	526	8,290	23.4	17.7	25.8	19.2	-2.4	-1.5
Providence, R.I.	139	3,837	140	3,513	26.0	17.5	29.1	20.6	-3.1	-3.1
St. Joseph, Mo	98	957	68	701	23.0	13.0	10.9	7.2	+12.1	+5.8
St. Louis, Mo	1,149	9,733	1,096	9,223	26.0	15.1	30.9	17.1	-4.9	-2.0
St. Paul, Minn	49	2,508	30	1,601	15.5	11.8	13.3	10.0	+2.2	+1.8
Springfield, Ill	67	793	57	548	22.5	16.2	25.6	17.1	-3.1	-0.9
Terre Haute, Ind	67	864	40	557	25.7	15.5	26.3	15.8	-0.6	-0.3
Trenton, N.J.	89	1,886	49	1,222	34.3	19.9	23.4	17.2	+10.9	+2.7

[Continued]

★ 2150 ★

Death Rates, by Cities, 1900 and 1910

[Continued]

City	Number of deaths				Death rate per 1,000 population				Increase (+) or decrease (-) per 1,000 population: 1900-1910	
	1910		1900		1910		1900			
	Negro	White	Negro	White	Negro	White	Negro	White	Negro	White
Southern cities										
Total for 24 cities	21,320	33,125	20,767	30,648	29.6	16.9	33.6	19.8	-4.0	-2.9
Alexandria, Va	138	189	160	205	32.9	17.0	35.3	20.5	-2.4	-3.5
Annapolis, Md	97	83	126	110	30.5	15.3	42.0	20.0	-11.5	-4.7
Atlanta, Ga	1,328	1,609	977	1,006	25.4	15.5	27.3	18.6	-1.9	-3.1
Baltimore, Md	2,597	8,152	2,653	8,242	30.6	17.2	33.5	19.2	-2.9	-2.0
Charleston, S.C.	1,221	526	1,399	554	39.3	18.9	44.4	22.9	-5.1	-4.0
Covington, Ky	59	802	81	743	20.3	15.9	32.6	18.4	-12.3	-2.5
Jacksonville, Fla	710	482	532	324	24.0	16.8	32.8	26.6	-8.8	-9.8
Key West, Fla	147	301	147	271	26.6	20.8	26.4	23.5	+0.2	-2.7
Louisville, Ky	1,089	2,667	1,070	2,802	26.7	14.4	27.3	16.9	-0.6	-2.5
Lynchburg, Va	231	242	298	218	24.3	12.0	36.1	20.5	-11.8	-8.5
Memphis, Tenn	1,492	1,326	1,218	1,084	28.3	16.8	24.4	20.7	+3.9	-3.9
Mobile, Ala	673	512	564	481	29.4	17.7	33.1	22.5	-3.7	-4.8
Nashville, Tenn	950	1,113	965	956	26.0	15.0	32.1	18.8	-6.1	-3.8
Norfolk, Va	775	700	770	496	30.8	16.5	38.1	18.8	-7.3	-2.3
New Orleans, La	2,933	4,311	3,184	4,420	32.8	17.2	41.0	21.2	-8.2	-4.0
Paducah, Ky	164	274	224	323	27.0	16.3	38.5	23.7	-11.5	-7.4
Petersburg, Va	377	264	379	279	34.2	20.1	35.3	25.2	-1.1	-5.1
Raleigh, N.C.	247	290	227	183	33.4	24.4	39.7	23.1	-6.3	+1.3
Richmond, Va	1,416	1,470	1,214	1,251	30.2	18.1	37.7	23.7	-7.5	-5.6
San Antonio, Tex	233	1,917	171	1,038	21.5	22.1	22.7	22.7	-1.2	-0.6
Savannah, Ga	1,134	616	1,070	612	34.1	19.4	38.1	23.4	-4.0	-4.0
Washington, D.C.	2,759	3,744	2,685	3,511	29.1	15.8	31.0	18.3	-1.9	-2.5
Wilmington, Del	225	1,322	269	1,277	24.7	16.8	27.6	19.1	-2.9	-2.3
Wilmington, N.C.	325	213	384	262	26.7	15.6	36.9	24.8	-10.2	-9.2

Source: "Negro and White Deaths, and Death Rates, by Cities: 1910 and 1900." U.S. Bureau of the Census. *Negro Population in the United States, 1790- 1915.* Washington, D.C.: Government Printing Office, 1918, p. 320. *Notes:* 1. Includes all cities for which data were available for 1900 and for 1910 which reported a Negro population of 2,500 or more. 2. Includes Allegheny, 1900.

★ 2151 ★

Deaths

Death Rates, by Selected Causes: 1910-1974

Death rates per 100,000 population in specified group. Statistics prior to 1933 are exclusive of States not yet included in the death registration area.

Cause of death	1910	1920	1930	1940	1960	1970	1974
BLACK							
All causes	2,172.4	1,767.5	1,633.0	1,382.8	1,008.5	938.4	869.1
Tuberculosis, all forms	445.5	262.4	192.0	128.0	13.2	6.0	4.1

[Continued]

★ 2151 ★

Death Rates, by Selected Causes: 1910-1974

[Continued]

Cause of death	1910	1920	1930	1940	1960	1970	1974
Syphilis and its sequelae[1]	30.8	38.8	52.5	54.3	4.5	0.7	0.5
Typhoid and paratyphoid fever	33.6	19.6	14.8	3.2	-	-	-
Scarlet fever and streptococcal sore throat	4.0	0.8	0.6	0.3	0.1	-	-
Diphtheria	11.6	8.6	4.9	1.8	0.1	-	-
Whooping cough	35.9	20.6	11.1	5.9	0.4	-	-
Measles	9.4	4.1	3.3	0.8	0.5	0.1	-
Malignant neoplasms[2]	54.0	48.5	56.6	78.4	121.6	134.4	144.1
Diabetes mellitus	7.2	8.0	12.8	17.9	18.8	22.9	21.9
Diseases of heart	204.8	160.7	224.7	248.5	287.1	274.2	258.0
Hypertension	(NA)	(NA)	(NA)	(NA)	(NA)	7.6	5.3
Influenza and pneumonia[3]	273.6	304.4	175.9	125.4	62.0	39.1	25.7
Influenza	16.7	107.5	37.5	32.7	8.0	1.9	0.6
Pneumonia[3]	92.4	27.2	12.0	9.8	54.0	37.1	25.2
Cirrhosis of liver	11.0	6.8	6.7	5.8	10.2	19.4	20.4
Motor vehicle accidents[4]	1.0	5.3	22.1	23.8	21.9	28.5	22.0
All other accidents[5]	92.0	72.9	63.9	52.3	44.1	40.3	34.0
Suicide	11.8	3.6	5.0	4.6	4.5	5.6	6.5
Homicide	22.3	28.5	37.9	33.9	21.9	35.5	39.7
Certain diseases of early infancy	55.2	32.4	24.0	60.5	77.2	43.2	29.0
Bronchitis[6]	36.5	15.2	5.2	2.4	2.2	8.4	6.0
WHITE							
All causes	1,448.8	1,256.1	1,076.8	1,041.5	947.8	946.3	921.9
Tuberculosis, all forms	145.9	99.5	57.7	36.6	5.1	2.1	1.3
Syphilis and its sequelae[1]	13.0	14.5	11.7	9.9	1.3	0.2	0.1
Typhoid and paratyphoid fever	22.2	6.6	3.7	0.9	-	-	-
Scarlet fever and streptococcal sore throat	11.6	5.0	2.1	0.5	0.1	-	-
Diphtheria	21.4	16.0	4.9	1.0	-	-	-
Whooping cough	11.0	11.7	4.1	1.8	-	-	-
Measles	12.5	9.3	3.2	0.5	0.2	-	-
Malignant neoplasms[2]	76.9	86.5	101.9	125.0	152.8	166.8	174.4
Diabetes mellitus	15.5	16.9	19.8	27.6	16.4	18.3	17.0
Diseases of heart	157.6	159.5	213.1	297.6	379.6	374.5	362.7
Hypertension	(NA)	(NA)	(NA0	(NA)	(NA)	3.6	3.0
Influenza and pneumonia[3]	152.6	198.4	94.4	64.0	34.1	29.7	25.9
Influenza	14.1	67.1	17.4	13.3	3.9	1.8	1.1
Pneumonia[3]	49.7	7.7	2.6	2.8	30.1	27.9	24.8
Cirrhosis of liver	13.4	7.1	7.3	8.9	11.5	14.9	15.1
Motor vehicle accidents[4]	1.8	10.8	27.2	26.5	21.2	26.7	21.9
All other accidents[5]	82.5	59.6	52.6	46.4	29.4	28.0	26.6
Suicide	15.4	10.8	16.8	15.5	11.4	12.4	13.0
Homicide	4.1	4.8	5.6	3.2	2.5	4.4	5.8

[Continued]

★ 2151 ★

Death Rates, by Selected Causes: 1910-1974

[Continued]

Cause of death	1910	1920	1930	1940	1960	1970	1974
Certain diseases of early infancy	34.7	25.0	17.4	36.8	32.3	18.1	11.3
Bronchitis[6]	23.5	13.1	4.1	3.1	2.4	16.2	13.7

Source: "Death Rates for the Black Population, by Age, for Selected Causes for Selected Years: 1910 to 1974," and "Death Rates for the White Population, by Age, for Selected Causes for Selected Years: 1910 to 1974,"U.S. Department of Commerce, Bureau of the Census. *The Social and Economic Status of the Black Population in the United States: An Historical View, 1790-1978*, pp. 124-125. Primary source: U.S. Department of Health, Education and Welfare, National Center for Health Statistics. *Notes:* - Represents or rounds to zero. NA Not available. 1. Data for 1910 and 1920 exclude aneurysm of the aorta. 2. Includes neoplasms of lymphatic and hematopoietic tissues. 3. Data for all years exclude pneumonia of newborn; data for 1910 and 1920 exclude capillary bronchitis. 4. Data for 1910 and 1920 exclude automobile collisions with trains and streetcars, and motorcycle accidents. 5. Data for 1910 and 1920 include legal execution. 6. Data for 1970 and 1974 include emphysema and asthma.

★ 2152 ★

Deaths

Death Rates, by race and Sex, 1900-1970 - I

Year	Death rate						
	Total	White			Negro and other		
		Both sexes	Male	Female	Both sexes	Male	Female
1970	9.5	9.5	10.9	8.1	9.4	11.2	7.8
1969	9.5	9.5	10.9	8.2	9.6	11.3	8.0
1968	9.7	9.6	11.1	8.2	9.9	11.6	8.3
1967	9.4	9.4	10.8	8.0	9.4	10.9	7.9
1966	9.5	9.5	10.9	8.1	9.7	11.3	8.3
1965	9.4	9.4	10.8	8.0	9.6	11.1	8.2
1964	9.4	9.4	10.8	8.0	9.7	11.1	8.3
1963[1]	9.6	9.5	11.0	8.1	10.1	11.5	8.7
1962[1]	9.5	9.4	10.8	8.0	9.8	11.2	8.5
1961	9.3	9.3	10.7	7.8	9.6	10.9	8.4
1960[3]	9.5	9.5	11.0	8.0	10.1	11.5	8.7
1959[2]	9.4	9.3	10.8	7.9	9.9	11.3	8.6
1958	9.5	9.4	10.9	8.0	10.3	11.6	9.0
1957	9.6	9.5	11.0	8.0	10.5	11.9	9.1
1956	9.4	9.3	10.8	7.8	10.1	11.4	8.8
1955	9.3	9.2	10.7	7.8	10.0	11.3	8.8
1954	9.2	9.1	10.6	7.6	10.1	11.4	8.8
1953	9.6	9.4	11.0	8.0	10.8	12.3	9.4
1952	9.6	9.4	11.0	8.0	11.0	12.5	9.6
1951	9.7	9.5	11.0	8.0	11.1	12.5	9.8
1950	9.6	9.5	10.9	8.0	11.2	12.5	9.9
1949	9.7	9.5	11.0	8.1	11.2	12.5	10.0
1948	9.9	9.7	11.2	8.3	11.4	12.7	10.1
1947	10.1	9.9	11.4	8.5	11.4	12.5	10.3

[Continued]

★ 2152 ★

Death Rates, by race and Sex, 1900-1970 - I

[Continued]

Year	Death rate						
	Total	White			Negro and other		
		Both sexes	Male	Female	Both sexes	Male	Female
1946	10.0	9.8	11.2	8.5	11.1	12.2	10.0
1945	10.6	10.4	12.5	8.6	11.9	13.5	10.5
1944	10.6	10.4	12.2	8.8	12.4	13.8	11.1
1943	10.9	10.7	12.2	9.2	12.8	14.0	11.6
1942	10.3	10.1	11.4	8.7	12.7	14.0	11.4
1941	10.5	10.2	11.4	8.9	13.5	14.8	12.2
1940	10.8	10.4	11.6	9.2	13.8	15.1	12.6
1939	10.6	10.3	11.3	9.2	13.5	14.7	12.4
1938	10.6	10.3	11.3	9.2	14.0	15.2	12.9
1937	11.3	10.8	12.0	9.6	14.9	16.4	13.4
1936	11.6	11.1	12.3	9.9	15.4	16.9	13.9
1935	10.9	10.6	11.6	9.5	14.3	15.6	13.0
1934	11.1	10.6	11.7	9.6	14.8	16.0	13.5
1933	10.7	10.3	11.2	9.3	14.1	15.1	13.1
1932	10.9	10.5	11.3	9.6	14.5	15.4	13.5
1931	11.1	10.6	11.5	9.6	15.5	16.5	14.5
1930	11.3	10.8	11.7	9.8	16.3	17.4	15.3
1929	11.9	11.3	12.2	10.4	16.9	18.0	15.8
1928	12.0	11.4	12.3	10.5	17.1	18.0	16.2
1927	11.3	10.8	11.6	10.0	16.4	17.2	15.6
1926	12.1	11.6	12.3	10.8	17.8	18.7	16.9
1925	11.7	11.1	11.8	10.4	17.4	18.2	16.6
1924	11.6	11.0	11.8	10.3	17.1	17.9	16.3
1923	12.1	11.7	12.3	11.0	16.5	17.0	16.0
1922	11.7	11.3	11.9	10.7	15.2	15.7	14.8
1921	11.5	11.1	11.6	10.6	15.5	15.7	15.4
1920	13.0	12.6	13.0	12.1	17.7	17.8	17.5
1919	12.9	12.4	13.0	11.8	17.9	18.1	17.8
1918	18.1	17.5	19.3	15.8	25.6	26.7	24.4
1917	14.0	13.5	14.6	12.4	20.4	21.4	19.4
1916	13.8	13.4	14.4	12.4	19.1	19.9	18.4
1915	13.2	12.9	13.7	12.0	20.2	20.8	19.5
1914	13.3	13.0	13.9	12.1	20.2	20.9	19.4
1913	13.8	13.5	14.5	12.5	20.3	21.0	19.6
1912	13.6	13.4	14.3	12.4	20.6	21.3	19.7
1911	13.9	13.7	14.5	12.8	21.3	21.9	20.6
1910	14.7	14.5	15.4	13.6	21.7	22.3	21.0

[Continued]

★ 2152 ★

Death Rates, by race and Sex, 1900-1970 - I

[Continued]

Year	Death rate						
	Total	White			Negro and other		
		Both sexes	Male	Female	Both sexes	Male	Female
1909	14.2	14.0	14.9	13.2	21.8	22.3	21.2
1908	14.7	14.5	15.3	13.6	22.4	22.8	22.0
1907	15.9	15.7	16.8	14.5	24.3	25.0	23.5
1906	15.7	15.5	16.5	14.4	24.2	24.7	23.6
1905	15.9	15.7	16.5	14.8	25.5	26.8	24.3
1904	16.4	16.2	17.1	15.3	26.1	27.6	24.7
1903	15.6	15.4	16.2	14.6	24.5	25.5	23.4
1902	15.5	15.3	16.2	14.4	23.6	24.8	22.3
1901	16.4	16.2	17.1	15.4	24.3	25.6	23.1
1900	17.2	17.0	17.7	16.3	25.0	25.7	24.4

Source: "Death Rate, by Race and Sex: 1900 to 1970." U.S. Bureau of the Census. *Historical Statistics of the United States: Colonial Times to 1970, Part I.* Bicentennial Edition. Washington, D.C.: Government Printing Office, 1975, p. 59. *Notes:* 1. Excludes New Jersey; State did not require reporting of race. 2. Includes Alaska. 3. Denotes first year for which figures include Alaska and Hawaii.

★ 2153 ★

Deaths

Death Rates, by race and Sex, 1900-1970 - II

Year	Age-adjusted death rate						
	Total	White			Negro and other		
		Both sexes	Male	Female	Both sexes	Male	Female
1970	7.1	6.8	8.9	5.0	9.8	12.3	7.7
1969	7.3	6.9	9.0	5.2	10.5	13.0	8.3
1968	7.5	7.1	9.2	5.3	10.8	13.3	8.6
1967	7.3	6.9	9.0	5.2	10.2	12.4	8.2
1966	7.5	7.1	9.2	5.3	10.5	12.7	8.6
1965	7.4	7.1	9.1	5.3	10.3	12.4	8.5
1964	7.4	7.1	9.0	5.3	10.3	12.2	8.6
1963[1]	7.6	7.2	9.2	5.5	10.6	12.5	8.9
1962[1]	7.5	7.1	9.0	5.4	10.3	12.0	8.7
1961	7.4	7.0	8.9	5.4	10.0	11.6	8.6
1960[3]	7.6	7.3	9.2	5.6	10.5	12.1	8.9
1959[2]	7.5	7.2	9.0	5.5	10.3	11.9	8.8
1958	7.7	7.3	9.1	5.7	10.6	12.2	9.2
1957	7.8	7.4	9.2	5.8	10.8	12.4	9.4
1956	7.6	7.3	9.1	5.7	10.5	11.9	9.1
1955	7.7	7.4	9.1	5.7	10.4	11.9	9.1

[Continued]

★ 2153 ★

Death Rates, by race and Sex, 1900-1970 - II

[Continued]

Year	Age-adjusted death rate						
	Total	White			Negro and other		
		Both sexes	Male	Female	Both sexes	Male	Female
1954	7.6	7.3	9.0	5.8	10.6	12.0	9.2
1953	8.0	7.7	9.4	6.1	11.4	13.0	9.9
1952	8.1	7.8	9.5	6.2	11.7	13.2	10.2
1951	8.3	7.9	9.6	6.3	11.9	13.3	10.5
1950	8.4	8.0	9.6	6.5	12.3	13.6	10.9
1949	8.5	8.1	9.7	6.6	12.3	13.5	11.1
1948	8.8	8.3	10.0	6.8	12.5	13.8	11.2
1947	9.0	8.6	10.1	7.1	12.5	13.6	11.4
1946	9.1	8.8	10.2	7.3	12.4	13.5	11.3
1945	9.5	9.1	10.7	7.5	13.1	14.5	11.9
1944	9.7	9.3	10.8	7.8	13.8	14.9	12.6
1943	10.2	9.7	11.2	8.2	14.5	15.7	13.4
1942	9.9	9.4	10.9	8.0	14.5	15.8	13.3
1941	10.3	9.7	11.2	8.3	15.6	16.9	14.3
1940	10.8	10.2	11.6	8.8	16.3	17.6	15.0
1939	10.7	10.2	11.4	8.9	16.0	17.1	14.9
1938	10.9	10.3	11.5	9.1	16.6	17.7	15.5
1937	11.7	11.1	12.4	9.7	17.8	19.2	16.3
1936	12.2	11.5	12.8	10.1	18.5	20.1	17.0
1935	11.6	11.1	12.3	9.8	17.3	18.5	16.1
1934	11.9	11.3	12.5	10.0	17.9	19.0	16.7
1933	11.6	11.0	12.2	9.9	17.2	18.1	16.4
1932	11.9	11.3	12.3	10.2	17.8	18.6	17.0
1931	12.1	11.4	12.5	10.3	19.0	19.9	18.1
1930	12.5	11.7	12.8	10.6	20.1	21.0	19.2
1929	13.2	12.4	13.5	11.4	21.0	21.9	20.0
1928	13.4	12.6	13.6	11.5	20.9	21.7	20.2
1927	12.6	11.9	12.8	10.9	19.8	20.4	19.3
1926	13.5	12.7	13.6	11.8	21.4	22.1	20.8
1925	13.0	12.3	13.2	11.4	20.9	21.4	20.4
1924	12.9	12.2	13.1	11.3	20.5	21.1	20.0
1923	13.5	12.9	13.7	12.1	19.8	20.0	19.7
1922	13.0	12.6	13.3	11.8	18.3	18.4	18.4
1921	12.7	12.2	12.7	11.6	18.2	18.0	18.6
1920	14.2	13.7	14.2	13.1	20.6	20.4	21.0
1919	14.0	13.4	14.1	12.8	20.5	20.3	20.8
1918	19.0	18.4	20.2	16.6	28.0	28.9	27.1
1917	15.3	14.7	16.0	13.4	23.4	24.1	22.7

[Continued]

★ 2153 ★

Death Rates, by race and Sex, 1900-1970 - II

[Continued]

Year	Age-adjusted death rate						
	Total	White			Negro and other		
		Both sexes	Male	Female	Both sexes	Male	Female
1916	15.1	14.7	15.8	13.4	22.2	22.6	21.6
1915	14.4	14.1	15.1	13.0	23.1	23.5	22.6
1914	14.5	14.1	15.2	13.0	22.6	23.3	21.9
1913	15.0	14.6	15.8	13.4	22.7	23.3	22.0
1912	14.8	14.6	15.7	13.4	23.1	24.0	22.2
1911	15.2	14.9	15.9	13.8	23.7	24.4	22.9
1910	15.8	15.6	16.7	14.4	24.1	24.8	23.2
1909	15.3	15.0	16.1	14.0	24.1	24.8	23.3
1908	15.8	15.5	16.6	14.4	24.7	25.3	24.1
1907	17.1	16.8	18.2	15.4	26.6	27.5	25.7
1906	16.7	16.4	17.6	15.1	26.2	27.0	25.5
1905	16.7	16.5	17.6	15.4	28.3	29.7	26.9
1904	17.3	17.1	18.1	16.0	29.1	30.7	27.4
1903	16.5	16.2	17.2	15.3	27.2	28.5	25.9
1902	16.2	16.0	17.0	14.9	25.9	27.5	24.5
1901	17.2	17.0	18.0	16.0	26.9	28.4	25.5
1900	17.8	17.6	18.4	16.8	27.8	28.7	27.1

Source: "Death Rate, by Race and Sex: 1900 to 1970." U.S. Bureau of the Census. *Historical Statistics of the United States: Colonial Times to 1970, Part I.* Bicentennial Edition. Washington, D.C.: Government Printing Office, 1975, p. 59. *Notes:* 1. Excludes New Jersey; State did not require reporting of race. 2. Includes Alaska. 3. Denotes first year for which figures include Alaska and Hawaii.

★ 2154 ★

Deaths

Death Rates: Metropolitan and Nonmetropolitan Counties – 1950, 1960

Rates are deaths per 1,000 population in specified group.

Area, color, and year	Total	Under 1 year	1-4 years	5-14 years	15-24 years	25-34 years	35-44 years	45-54 years	55-64 years	65-74 years	75-84 years	85 years and over
United States												
Total												
1960	9.5	27.0	1.1	0.5	1.1	1.5	3.0	7.6	17.4	38.2	87.5	198.6
1950	9.6	33.0	1.4	0.6	1.3	1.8	3.6	8.5	19.0	41.0	93.3	202.0
White												
1960	9.5	23.6	1.0	0.4	1.0	1.2	2.6	6.9	16.3	37.4	88.3	203.5
1950	9.5	29.9	1.2	0.6	1.1	1.5	3.1	7.7	18.0	40.2	94.2	206.8
Nonwhite												
1960	10.1	46.3	1.9	0.6	1.6	3.2	6.3	13.4	27.7	47.8	76.3	139.1
1950	11.2	53.7	2.5	0.9	2.5	4.4	8.1	17.1	31.3	52.0	80.4	144.7

[Continued]

★ 2154 ★

Death Rates: Metropolitan and Nonmetropolitan Counties – 1950, 1960

[Continued]

Area, color, and year	Total	Under 1 year	1-4 years	5-14 years	15-24 years	25-34 years	35-44 years	45-54 years	55-64 years	65-74 years	75-84 years	85 years and over
Metropolitan counties												
1960	9.3	26.0	1.0	0.4	0.9	1.4	3.0	7.8	18.0	39.6	89.0	196.9
1950	9.7	30.3	1.2	0.5	1.1	1.6	3.6	9.0	20.4	43.1	95.2	197.4
White												
1960	9.3	22.9	0.9	0.4	0.9	1.1	2.6	7.1	17.0	38.9	89.8	201.7
1950	9.5	27.7	1.1	0.5	1.0	1.3	3.1	8.1	19.4	42.6	95.7	201.4
Nonwhite												
1960	9.6	43.4	1.7	0.6	1.4	3.0	6.2	13.6	28.0	49.2	77.5	134.0
1950	11.2	50.2	2.1	0.8	2.4	4.1	8.2	17.7	35.4	49.7	86.0	135.3
Nonmetropolitan counties												
1960	10.0	28.7	1.3	0.5	1.3	1.6	3.1	7.1	16.3	36.0	85.3	200.7
1950	9.6	36.2	1.6	0.7	1.5	2.0	3.6	7.9	17.2	37.7	91.2	206.9
White												
1960	9.8	24.7	1.1	0.5	1.2	1.4	2.7	6.5	15.2	35.1	86.2	206.0
1950	9.3	32.7	1.5	0.6	1.3	1.7	3.1	6.9	15.9	37.2	92.4	212.9
Nonwhite												
1960	11.0	51.4	2.3	0.8	1.9	3.7	6.8	13.0	27.3	46.1	74.9	144.4
1950	11.2	57.0	2.8	0.9	2.6	4.9	7.9	16.2	31.8	42.9	76.3	151.1

Source: "Death Rates by Age and Color for Metropolitan and Nonmetropolitan Counties: United States and Each Division, 1950 and 1960." National Center for Health Statistics. *Vital Statistics Rates in the United States, 1940- 60*. By Robert D. Grove and Alice M. Hetzel. Washington, D.C.: U.S. Department of Health, Education, and Welfare, Public Health Service, 1968, p. 341. Adapted by the editors. *Notes:* For effect of age-bias adjustments in the Nonwhite population at ages 55-69, see text.

★ 2155 ★

Deaths

Deaths From All Causes and Unknown or Ill-Defined Diseases in Cities Reporting 500 or More Black Deaths in 1930

Colored[1] and white deaths (exclusive of stillbirths) from all causes and from unknown or ill-defined diseases, in selected registration cities reporting 500 or more colored deaths in 1930.

Cities	All causes		Unknown or ill-defined diseases			
			Colored	White	Percent of total	
	Colored	White			Colored	White
Atlanta, Ga	2,106	2,099	43	18	2.0	0.9
Augusta, Ga	680	532	4	2	.6	.4
Baltimore, Md	2,815	8,424	-	1	-	[2]
Birmingham, Ala	1,925	1,623	218	58	11.3	3.6
Charleston, S. C	927	499	2	-	.2	-
Chattanooga, Tenn	825	1,058	62	59	7.5	5.6
Chicago, Ill	4,045	31,271	80	251	2.0	.8
Cincinnati, Ohio	1,139	5,866	2	4	.2	.1
Cleveland, Ohio	1,293	8,613	7	29	.5	.3
Columbia, S.C	554	669	1	2	.2	.3

[Continued]

★ 2155 ★

Deaths From All Causes and Unknown or Ill-Defined Diseases in Cities Reporting 500 or More Black Deaths in 1930

[Continued]

Cities	All causes		Unknown or ill-defined diseases			
			Colored	White	Percent of total	
	Colored	White			Colored	White
Columbus, Ohio	608	3,862	-	4	-	.1
Dallas, Tex	859	2,153	-	1	-	[2]
Detroit, Mich	2,037	12,692	1	6	[2]	[2]
Houston, Tex	1,495	2,103	293	144	19.6	6.8
Indianapolis, Ind	867	4,326	-	-	-	-
Jacksonville, Fla	1,014	963	6	6	.6	.6
Kansas City, Mo	922	4,379	3	6	.3	.1
Little Rock, Ark	693	1,157	15	7	2.2	.6
Los Angeles, Calif	822	13,206	3	24	.4	.2
Louisville, Ky	1,104	3,286	2	2	0.2	0.1
Macon, Ga	609	452	53	9	8.7	2.0
Memphis, Tenn	2,274	2,124	95	49	4.2	2.3
Mobile, Ala	587	656	2	1	.3	.2
Montgomery, Ala	664	474	20	-	3.0	-
Nashville, Tenn	990	1,520	49	39	4.9	2.6
Newark, N. J	759	4,504	-	2	-	[2]
New Orleans, La	3,289	4,741	1	2	[2]	[2]
New York, N.Y	5,630	69,283	-	27	-	[2]
Norfolk, Va	902	861	-	-	-	-
Philadelphia, Pa	3,620	20,896	7	10	.2	[2]
Pittsburgh, Pa	1,103	8,209	16	64	1.5	.8
Richmond, Va	1,132	1,605	39	9	3.4	.6
St. Louis, Mo	1,982	9,500	1	4	.1	[2]
Savannah, Ga	1,033	627	2	-	.2	-
Shreveport, La	874	795	7	2	.8	.3
Vicksburg, Miss	521	222	83	12	15.9	5.4
Washington, D.C	2,792	4,595	3	2	.1	[2]
Winston-Salem, N.C	620	447	39	6	6.3	1.3

Source: "Colored and White Deaths (Exclusive of Stillbirths) From All Causes and From Unknown or Ill-Defined Diseases, in Selected Registration Cities Reporting 500 or More Colored Deaths in 1930." U.S. Bureau of the Census. *Negroes in the United States: 1920-32.* Washington, D.C.: Government Printing Office, 1935, p. 459. *Notes:* 1. Includes Negro and other nonwhite races. 2. Less than 1/10 of 1 percent.

★ 2156 ★

Deaths

Deaths From All Causes and Unknown or Ill-Defined Diseases in Selected Areas, 1930

Colored[1] and white deaths (exclusive of stillbirths) from all causes and from unknown or ill-defined diseases, in registration area of Continental United States, and selected registration states: 1930.

Cities	All causes		Unknown or ill-defined diseases			
			Colored	White	Percent of total	
	Colored	White			Colored[1]	White
The registration area in continental United States	199,167	1,144,189	12,479	12,385	6.3	1.1
Selected States[2]	182,232	917,552	11,508	9,487	6.3	1.0
Alabama	14,412	16,010	1,649	670	11.4	4.2
Arkansas	6,466	12,484	654	635	10.1	5.1
Connecticut	523	16,764	2	50	.4	.3
Delaware	707	2,549	5	4	.7	.2
District of Columbia	2,792	4,595	3	2	.1	[3]
Florida	7,182	11,047	396	243	5.5	2.2
Georgia	17,190	17,993	1,403	683	8.2	3.8
Illinois	5,961	77,630	90	416	1.5	.5
Indiana	2,313	36,883	2	26	.1	.1
Iowa	363	25,865	4	130	1.1	.5
Kansas	1,102	18,403	5	131	.5	.7
Kentucky	4,750	24,812	42	395	.9	1.6
Louisiana	12,086	12,621	467	182	3.9	1.4
Maryland	5,264	16,303	43	43	.8	.3
Massachusetts	908	48,425	2	60	.2	.1
Michigan	3,090	48,530	4	162	0.1	0.3
Mississippi	14,961	9,138	2,560	561	17.1	6.1
Missouri	4,653	38,446	35	273	.8	.7
Nebraska	467	12,825	7	70	1.5	.5
New Jersey	3,552	40,045	7	37	.2	.1
New York	7,199	140,254	5	106	.1	.1
North Carolina	14,155	21,627	1,458	1,161	10.3	5.4
Ohio	5,839	70,387	30	241	.5	.3
Oklahoma	3,063	16,583	152	467	5.0	2.8
Pennsylvania	7,511	104,095	44	371	.6	.4
Rhode Island	231	7,775	2	23	.9	.3
South Carolina	13,162	9,271	1,234	259	9.4	2.8
Tennessee	8,752	21,235	752	1,550	8.6	7.3
Virginia	11,722	18,593	442	449	3.8	2.4
West Virginia	1,856	16,364	9	87	.5	.5

Source: "Colored and White Deaths (Exclusive of Stillbirths) From All Causes and From Unknown or Ill-Defined Diseases, in Selected Registration Area of Continental United States, and Selected Registration States: 1930." U.S. Bureau of the Census. *Negroes in the United States: 1920-32.* Washington, D.C.: Government Printing Office, 1935, p. 458. *Notes:* 1. Includes Negro and other nonwhite races. 2. States in the registration area reporting 100 or more colored deaths and whose Negro population in 1930 constituted 55 percent or more of the total colored population. 3. Less than 1/10 of 1 percent.

★ 2157 ★

Deaths

Deaths From Breast Malignancies – 1950, 1960, 1970

Data are based on the National Vital Statistics System.

Sex, race, and age	1950[1]	1960[1]	1970
	Deaths per 100,000 resident population		
All races			
All ages, age adjusted	22.2	22.3	23.1
All ages, crude	24.7	26.1	28.4
Under 25 years	0.1	0.1	0.0
25-34 years	3.8	3.8	3.9
35-44 years	20.8	20.2	20.4
45-54 years	46.9	51.4	52.6
55-64 years	70.4	70.8	77.6
65-74 years	94.0	90.0	93.8
75-84 years	139.8	129.9	127.4
85 years and over	195.5	191.9	157.9
White			
All ages, age adjusted	22.5	22.4	22.8
All ages, crude	25.7	27.2	29.9
Under 25 years	0.1	0.0	0.0
25-34 years	3.7	3.6	3.7
35-44 years	20.8	19.7	20.2
45-54 years	47.1	51.2	53.0
55-64 years	70.9	71.8	79.3
65-74 years	96.3	91.6	95.9
75-84 years	143.6	132.8	129.6
85 years and over	204.2	199.7	161.9
Black			
All ages, age adjusted	19.3	21.3	21.5
All ages, crude	16.4	18.7	19.7
Under 25 years	0.1	0.2	0.1
25-34 years	4.9	6.1	5.9
35-44 years	21.0	24.8	24.4
45-54 years	46.5	54.4	52.0
55-64 years	64.3	63.2	64.7
65-74 years	67.0	72.3	77.3
75-84 years	81.0	87.5	101.8
85 years and over		92.1	112.1

Source: "Death Rates for Malignant Neoplasms of Breast for Females, according to Race and Age: United States, Selected Years 1950-86," *Health United States - 1988*, March 1989, p. 70. Primary source: *Vital Statistics of the United States*. National Center for Health Statistics, U.S. Government Printing Office, Washington, D.C. *Notes:* For data years shown, the code numbers for cause of death are based on the then current *International Classification of Diseases*, which are described in Appendix II, tables IV and V. 1. Includes deaths of nonresidents of the United States.

★ 2158 ★

Deaths

Deaths From Cancers and Other Tumors – 1930, 1931

Cause of death	1930			1931		
	Total	Male	Female	Total	Male	Female
Cancers and other tumors	7,081	2,189	4,892	7,308	2,225	5,083
Cancer and other malignant tumors	6,280	2,092	4,188	6,528	2,150	4,378
Buccal cavity	141	86	55	154	97	57
Pharynx	33	13	20	48	28	20
Esophagus	64	48	16	70	55	15
Stomach and duodenum	1,335	716	619	1,299	709	590
Liver and biliary passages	370	193	177	410	188	222
Pancreas	103	77	26	104	57	47
Other digestive tract and peritoneum	606	249	357	646	253	393
Respiratory system	110	68	42	115	73	42
Uterus	1,782	-	1,782	1,864	-	1,864
Other female genital organs	94	-	94	114	-	114
Breast	626	6	620	626	8	618
Male genitourinary organs	377	377	-	422	422	-
Skin	93	50	43	84	41	43
Other or unspecified organs	546	209	337	572	219	353
Nonmalignant tumors, ovary	14	-	14	21	-	21
Nonmalignant tumors, uterus	576	-	576	561	-	561
Nonmalignant tumors, other female genital organs	5	-	5	-	-	-
Nonmalignant tumors, other organs	53	26	27	67	27	40
Tumors, ovary (nature unspecified)	5	-	5	4	-	4
Tumors, uterus (nature unspecified)	5	-	5	2	-	2
Tumors, other female genital organs (nature unspecified)	1	-	1	1	-	1
Tumors, other organs (nature unspecified)	142	71	71	124	48	76

Source: "Negro Deaths (Exclusive of Stillbirths) From Each Cause, by Sex, in Registration States (Including District of Columbia): 1930," and "Negro Deaths Exclusive of Stillbirths) from Each Cause, by Sex, in Registration States (Including District of Columbia: 1931." U.S. Bureau of the Census. *Negroes in the United States: 1920-32.* Washington, D.C.: Government Printing Office, 1935, pp. 464, 466. Adapted by the editors.

★ 2159 ★

Deaths

Deaths From Cerebrovascular Diseases – 1950, 1960, 1970

Data are based on the National Vital Statistics System.

Sex, race, and age	1950[1]	1960[1]	1970
	Deaths per 100,000 resident population		
All races			
All ages, age adjusted	88.8	79.7	66.3
All ages, crude	104.0	108.0	101.9
Under 1 year	5.1	4.1	5.0
1-4 years	0.9	0.8	1.0
5-14 years	0.5	0.7	0.7
15-24 years	1.6	1.8	1.6
25-34 years	4.2	4.7	4.5
35-44 years	18.7	14.7	15.6
45-54 years	70.4	49.2	41.6
55-64 years	195.3	147.3	115.8
65-74 years	549.7	469.2	384.1
75-84 years	1,499.6	1,491.3	1,254.2
85 years and over	2,990.1	3,680.5	3,234.6
White male			
All ages, age adjusted	87.0	80.3	68.8
All ages, crude	100.5	102.7	93.5
Under 1 year	5.9	4.3	4.5
1-4 years	1.1	0.8	1.2
5-14 years	0.5	0.7	0.8
15-24 years	1.6	1.7	1.6
25-34 years	3.4	3.5	3.2
35-44 years	13.1	11.3	11.8
45-54 years	53.7	40.9	35.6
55-64 years	182.2	139.0	119.9
65-74 years	569.7	501.0	420.0
75-84 years	1,556.3	1,564.8	1,361.6
85 years and over	3,127.1	3,734.8	3,317.6
Black male			
All ages, age adjusted	146.2	141.2	124.2
All ages, crude	122.0	122.9	108.7
Under 1 year	2.5	8.5	12.2
1-4 years		1.9	1.4
5-14 years	0.7	0.9	0.8
15-24 years	3.3	3.7	3.0
25-34 years	12.0	12.8	14.6
35-44 years	59.3	47.4	52.7
45-54 years	211.9	166.1	136.2
55-64 years	522.8	439.9	343.4
65-74 years	783.6	899.2	780.0
75-84 years	1,504.9	1,475.2	1,442.6
85 years and over		2,700.0	2,315.4

[Continued]

★ 2159 ★

Deaths From Cerebrovascular Diseases – 1950, 1960, 1970

[Continued]

Sex, race, and age	1950[1]	1960[1]	1970
White female			
All ages, age adjusted	79.7	68.7	56.2
All ages, crude	103.3	110.1	109.8
Under 1 year	2.9	2.6	3.2
1-4 years	0.6	0.5	0.6
5-14 years	0.4	0.6	0.6
15-24 years	1.2	1.4	1.1
25-34 years	2.9	3.4	3.4
35-44 years	13.6	10.1	11.5
45-54 years	55.0	33.8	30.5
55-64 years	156.9	103.0	78.1
65-74 years	498.1	383.3	303.2
75-84 years	1,471.3	1,444.7	1,176.8
85 years and over	3,017.9	3,795.7	3,316.1
Black female			
All ages, age adjusted	155.6	139.5	107.9
All ages, crude	128.3	127.7	112.1
Under 1 year	2.8	6.7	9.1
1-4 years		1.3	1.4
5-14 years	0.6	1.0	0.8
15-24 years	4.2	3.4	3.0
25-34 years	15.9	17.4	14.3
35-44 years	75.0	57.4	49.1
45-54 years	248.9	166.2	119.4
55-64 years	567.7	452.0	272.5
65-74 years	754.4	830.5	673.4
75-84 years	1,496.7	1,413.1	1,337.8
85 years and over		2,578.9	2,504.8

Source: "Death Rates for Cerebrovascular Diseases, according to Sex, Race, and Age: United States, Selected Years 1950-86," *Health United States - 1988*, March 1989, p. 67. Primary source: *Vital Statistics of the United States*. National Center for Health Statistics, U.S. Government Printing Office, Washington, D.C. *Notes:* For data years shown, the code numbers for cause of death are based on the then current *International Classification of Diseases*, which are described in Appendix II, tables IV and V. 1. Includes deaths of nonresidents of the United States.

★ 2160 ★

Deaths

Deaths From Chronic Poisonings and Intoxications – 1930, 1931

Cause of death	1930			1931		
	Total	Male	Female	Total	Male	Female
Chronic poisonings and intoxications	462	368	94	452	369	83
Alcoholism (acute or chronic)	435	351	84	428	350	78
Chronic poisoning by other organic substances	12	5	7	6	4	2
Chronic lead poisoning	8	8	-	11	11	-
Other chronic poisoning by mineral substances	7	4	3	7	4	3

Source: "Negro Deaths (Exclusive of Stillbirths) From Each Cause, by Sex, in Registration States (Including District of Columbia): 1930," and "Negro Deaths Exclusive of Stillbirths) From Each Cause, by Sex, in Registration States (Including District of Columbia: 1931." U.S. Bureau of the Census. *Negroes in the United States: 1920-32.* Washington, D.C.: Government Printing Office, 1935, pp. 464, 466. Adapted by the editors.

★ 2161 ★

Deaths

Deaths From Congenital Malformations – 1930, 1931

Cause of death	1930			1931		
	Total	Male	Female	Total	Male	Female
Congenital malformations	638	369	269	657	383	274
Congenital hydrocephalus	113	66	47	89	54	35
Spina bifida and meningocele	31	16	15	38	18	20
Congenital malformations of heart	301	164	137	321	194	127
Other congenital malformations	193	123	70	209	117	92

Source: "Negro Deaths (Exclusive of Stillbirths) From Each Cause, by Sex, in Registration States (Including District of Columbia): 1930," and "Negro Deaths Exclusive of Stillbirths) From Each Cause, by Sex, in Registration States (Including District of Columbia: 1931." U.S. Bureau of the Census. *Negroes in the United States: 1920-32.* Washington, D.C.: Government Printing Office, 1935, pp. 465, 467. Adapted by the editors.

★ 2162 ★

Deaths

Deaths From Diseases of Pregnancy, Childbirth, and the Puerperal State – 1930, 1931

Cause of death	1930			1931		
	Total	Male	Female	Total	Male	Female
Diseases of pregnancy, childbirth, and the puerperal state	2,844	-	2,844	2,634	-	2,634
Abortion with septic conditions	270	-	270	309	-	309
Abortion without mention of septic conditions (including hemorrhages)	111	-	111	113	-	113
Ectopic gestation, septic condition specified	17	-	17	20	-	20
Ectopic gestation, septic conditions not mentioned	70	-	70	74	-	74
Other accidents of pregnancy (hemorrhage not included)	24	-	24	14	-	14
Placenta praevia	72	-	72	64	-	64
Other puerperal hemorrhages	133	-	133	137	-	137
Puerperal septicemia and pyemia (abortion excluded)	695	-	695	627	-	627
Puerperal tetanus (abortion excluded)	2	-	2	3	-	3
Puerperal albuminuria and eclampsia	932	-	932	757	-	757
Other toxemias of pregnancy	85	-	85	80	-	80
Puerperal phlegmasia alba dolens, embolus, sudden death (not specified as septic)	61	-	61	55	-	55
Other accidents of childbirth	364	-	364	372	-	372
Other and unspecified conditions of puerperal state	8	-	8	9	-	9

Source: "Negro Deaths (Exclusive of Stillbirths) From Each Cause, by Sex, in Registration States (Including District of Columbia): 1930," and "Negro Deaths Exclusive of Stillbirths) From Each Cause, by Sex, in Registration States (Including District of Columbia: 1931." U.S. Bureau of the Census. *Negroes in the United States: 1920-32.* Washington, D.C.: Government Printing Office, 1935, pp. 465, 467. Adapted by the editors.

★ 2163 ★

Deaths

Deaths From Diseases of the Blood and Blood-making Organs – 1930, 1931

Cause of death	1930			1931		
	Total	Male	Female	Total	Male	Female
Diseases of the blood and blood-making organs	400	186	214	425	217	208
Hemorrhage conditions	40	28	17	57	32	25
Pernicious anemia	135	28	97	138	58	80
Other anemias	56	19	37	56	19	37
True lukemias	96	64	32	95	54	41
Pseudoleukemias (Hodgkin's disease)	57	34	23	59	41	18

[Continued]

★2163★

Deaths From Diseases of the Blood and Blood-making Organs – 1930, 1931

[Continued]

Cause of death	1930			1931		
	Total	Male	Female	Total	Male	Female
Diseases of the spleen	14	7	7	17	11	6
Other diseases of blood and blood-making organs	2	1	1	3	2	1

Source: "Negro Deaths (Exclusive of Stillbirths) From Each Cause, by Sex, in Registration States (Including District of Columbia): 1930," and "Negro Deaths Exclusive of Stillbirths) From Each Cause, by Sex, in Registration States (Including District of Columbia: 1931." U.S. Bureau of the Census. *Negroes in the United States: 1920-32.* Washington, D.C.: Government Printing Office, 1935, pp. 464, 466. Adapted by the editors.

★2164★

Deaths

Deaths From Diseases of the Bone and Organs of Locomotion – 1930, 1931

Cause of death	1930			1931		
	Total	Male	Female	Total	Male	Female
Diseases of the bone and organs of locomotion	139	81	58	175	115	60
Osteomyelitis	77	49	28	103	70	33
Other diseases of bones (tuberculosis excepted)	21	12	9	29	20	9
Diseases of joints, other organs of locomotion	41	20	21	43	25	18

Source: "Negro Deaths (Exclusive of Stillbirths) From Each Cause, by Sex, in Registration States (Including District of Columbia): 1930," and "Negro Deaths Exclusive of Stillbirths) From Each Cause, by Sex, in Registration States (Including District of Columbia: 1931." U.S. Bureau of the Census. *Negroes in the United States: 1920-32.* Washington, D.C.: Government Printing Office, 1935, pp. 465, 467. Adapted by the editors.

★2165★

Deaths

Deaths From Diseases of the Circulatory System – 1930, 1931

Cause of death	1930			1931		
	Total	Male	Female	Total	Male	Female
Diseases of the circulatory system	27,958	14,724	13,234	26,193	13,735	12,458
Pericarditis	213	109	104	190	116	74
Acute endocarditis	374	178	196	336	150	186
Endocarditis, unspecified (under 45 years)	161	70	91	137	67	70
Endocarditis, specified as chronic, and other valvular diseases	8,616	4,471	4,145	7,604	3,897	3,707
Endocarditis, unspecified (45 years and over)	531	278	253	473	222	251

[Continued]

★ 2165 ★

Deaths From Diseases of the Circulatory System – 1930, 1931

[Continued]

Cause of death	1930			1931		
	Total	Male	Female	Total	Male	Female
Acute myocarditis	540	285	255	559	270	289
Myocarditis, unspecified (under 45 years)	507	212	295	463	229	234
Chronic myocarditis and myocardial degeneration	4,972	2,628	2,344	4,801	2,612	2,189
Other diseases of mycardium	2,369	1,268	1,101	2,220	1,126	1,094
Angina pectoris	853	461	392	880	483	397
Diseases of coronary arteries	271	170	101	375	218	157
Functional diseases of heart	50	27	23	45	21	24
Other and unspecified disease of heart	6,071	3,255	2,816	5,844	3,085	2,759
Aneurysm (except of heart)	437	302	135	395	274	122
Arteriosclerosis (coronary arteries excepted)	1,439	738	701	1,326	686	640
Gangrene	186	77	109	158	84	74
Other diseases of arteries	78	46	32	68	38	30
Diseases of veins (varices, hemorrhoids, phlebitis etc.)	47	21	26	53	23	30
Diseases of lymphatic system (lymphangitis, etc.)	15	9	6	34	21	13
Idiopathic anomalies of blood-pressure	173	91	82	190	88	102
Other diseases of circulatory system	55	28	27	41	25	16

Source: "Negro Deaths (Exclusive of Stillbirths) From Each Cause, by Sex, in Registration States (Including District of Columbia): 1930," and "Negro Deaths Exclusive of Stillbirths) From Each Cause, by Sex, in Registration States (Including District of Columbia: 1931." U.S. Bureau of the Census. *Negroes in the United States: 1920-32.* Washington, D.C.: Government Printing Office, 1935, pp. 464, 466. Adapted by the editors.

★ 2166 ★

Deaths

Deaths From Diseases of the Digestive System – 1930, 1931

Cause of death	1930			1931		
	Total	Male	Female	Total	Male	Female
Diseases of the digestive system	12,186	6,412	5,774	11,257	5,991	5,266
Diseases of pharynx and tonsils	501	238	263	529	254	275
Diseases of buccal cavity and annexs	131	67	64	130	59	71
Diseases of esophagus	7	5	2	8	4	4
Ulcer of stomach	561	238	223	516	347	169
Ulcer of duodenum	118	86	32	116	88	28
Other diseases of stomach (cancer excepted)	1,361	649	712	1,188	570	618
Diarrhea, enteritis (under 2 years of age)	3,628	1,949	1,679	3,049	1,645	1,404
Diarrhea, enteritis (2 years and over)	1,143	547	596	989	486	503
Appendicitis	1,521	872	649	1,543	896	647
Hernia	375	281	94	393	304	89
Intestinal obstruction	1,016	459	557	1,057	479	578
Other diseases of intestines	183	92	91	178	89	98
Cirrhosis of liver	740	453	287	703	412	291
Yellow atrophy of liver	58	19	39	52	15	37
Other disease of liver	227	116	111	208	114	94

[Continued]

★ 2166 ★

Deaths From Diseases of the Digestive System – 1930, 1931

[Continued]

Cause of death	1930			1931		
	Total	Male	Female	Total	Male	Female
Biliary calculi	111	35	76	120	31	89
Other diseases of gall-bladder, biliary passages	206	83	123	199	75	124
Disease of pancreas	36	20	16	35	19	16
Peritonitis, cause not specified	263	103	160	244	104	140

Source: "Negro Deaths (Exclusive of Stillbirths) From Each Cause, by Sex, in Registration States (Including District of Columbia): 1930," and "Negro Deaths Exclusive of Stillbirths) From Each Cause, by Sex, in Registration States (Including District of Columbia: 1931." U.S. Bureau of the Census. *Negroes in the United States: 1920-32.* Washington, D.C.: Government Printing Office, 1935, pp. 464, 466. Adapted by the editors.

★ 2167 ★

Deaths

Deaths From Diseases of the Genitourinary System – 1930, 1931

Cause of death	1930			1931		
	Total	Male	Female	Total	Male	Female
Diseases of genitourinary system	17,975	9,757	8,218	16,590	9,037	7,553
Acute nephritis (including unspecified under 10 years)	1,498	793	705	1,229	653	576
Chronic nephritis	11,856	6,418	5,438	11,246	5,992	5,254
Nephritis, unspecified (10 years and over)	2,487	1,351	1,136	2,087	1,219	868
Other diseases of kidneys, ureters (puerperal diseases excepted)	498	290	208	523	304	219
Calculi of urinary passages	54	33	21	52	33	19
Diseases of bladder (tumors excepted)	143	113	30	118	93	25
Diseases of urethra, urinary abscess, etc.	176	169	7	195	193	2
Diseases of prostate	554	554	-	522	522	-
Diseases of male genital organs, not specified as venereal	36	36	-	28	28	-
Cysts of ovary	53	-	53	60	-	60
Other diseases of ovaries, diseases of tubes and parametrium	508	-	508	410	-	410
Diseases of uterus	81	-	81	86	-	86
Nonpuerperal diseases of breast (cancer excepted)	8	-	8	8	-	8
Other diseases of female genital organs	23	-	23	26	-	26

Source: "Negro Deaths (Exclusive of Stillbirths) From Each Cause, by Sex, in Registration States (Including District of Columbia): 1930," and "Negro Deaths Exclusive of Stillbirths) From Each Cause, by Sex, in Registration States (Including District of Columbia: 1931." U.S. Bureau of the Census. *Negroes in the United States: 1920-32.* Washington, D.C.: Government Printing Office, 1935, pp. 465, 467. Adapted by the editors.

★ 2168 ★

Deaths

Deaths From Diseases of the Nervous System and Special-Sense Organs – 1930, 1931

Cause of death	1930			1931		
	Total	Male	Female	Total	Male	Female
Diseases of the nervous system and of the organs of special sense	15,872	8,122	7,750	14,680	7,389	7,291
Encephalitis (nonepidemic)	141	83	58	142	73	69
Simple meningitis	370	226	144	339	201	138
Nonepidemic cerebrospinal meningitis	99	57	42	73	43	30
Progressive locomotor ataxia (tabes dorsalis)	100	72	28	104	77	27
Other diseases of spinal cord	255	122	133	223	116	107
Cerebral hemorrhage	10,848	5,248	5,600	10,263	4,827	5,436
Cerebral embolism and thrombosis	244	119	125	236	120	116
Softening of brain	27	16	11	24	16	8
Hemiplegia and other paralysis, cause unspecified	1,244	616	628	1,016	486	530
General paralysis of insane	915	653	262	867	651	216
Dementia praecox and other psychoses	268	137	131	244	110	134
Epilepsy	497	319	178	438	271	167
Convulsions (under 5 years of age)	298	161	137	224	129	95
Other diseases of nervous system	285	144	141	232	124	108
Diseases of organs of vision	11	6	5	5	3	2
Diseases of ear	175	95	80	159	94	65
Diseases of mastoid process	95	48	47	91	48	43

Source: "Negro Deaths (Exclusive of Stillbirths) From Each Cause, by Sex, in Registration States (Including District of Columbia): 1930," and "Negro Deaths Exclusive of Stillbirths) From Each Cause, by Sex, in Registration States (Including District of Columbia: 1931." U.S. Bureau of the Census. *Negroes in the United States: 1920-32.* Washington, D.C.: Government Printing Office, 1935, pp. 464, 466. Adapted by the editors.

★ 2169 ★

Deaths

Deaths From Diseases of the Respiratory System – 1930, 1931

Cause of death	1930			1931		
	Total	Male	Female	Total	Male	Female
Diseases of the respiratory system	17,079	9,950	7,129	16,734	9,772	6,962
Diseases of nasal fossas	162	91	71	147	87	87
Diseases of nasal fossae and annexae	48	30	18	50	28	22
Diseases of larynx	59	36	23	59	32	27
Acute bronchitis	242	115	127	201	94	107
Chronic bronchitis	136	63	73	115	62	53
Bronchitis, unspecified	208	95	113	161	91	70
Bronchopneumonia	5,268	2,868	2,400	5,000	2,756	2,244

[Continued]

★ 2169 ★

Deaths From Diseases of the Respiratory System – 1930, 1931

[Continued]

Cause of death	1930			1931		
	Total	Male	Female	Total	Male	Female
Capillary bronchitis	92	54	38	79	40	39
Lobar pneumonia	8,628	5,307	3,321	8,802	5,418	3,384
Pneumonia, unspecified	1,274	746	528	1,238	675	563
Pleurisy	354	213	141	329	182	147
Pulmonary embolism and thrombosis	27	19	8	24	13	11
Pulmonary congestion, edema, hemorrhagic infarct	99	48	51	86	48	38
Asthma	292	149	143	262	148	114
Pulmonary emphysema	18	10	8	11	7	4
Other diseases of respiratory system (tuberculosis excepted)	172	106	66	143	91	52

Source: "Negro Deaths (Exclusive of Stillbirths) From Each Cause, by Sex, in Registration States (Including District of Columbia): 1930," and "Negro Deaths Exclusive of Stillbirths) From Each Cause, by Sex, in Registration States (Including District of Columbia: 1931." U.S. Bureau of the Census. *Negroes in the United States: 1920-32.* Washington, D.C.: Government Printing Office, 1935, pp. 464, 466. Adapted by the editors.

★ 2170 ★

Deaths

Deaths From Diseases of the Skin and Cellular Tissue – 1930, 1931

Cause of death	1930			1931		
	Total	Male	Female	Total	Male	Female
Diseases of the skin and cellular tissue	228	120	108	218	105	113
Furuncle, carbuncle	28	17	11	50	27	23
Phlegmon, acute abscess	108	61	47	94	47	47
Other diseases of skin and annexa, and of cellular tissue	92	42	50	74	31	43

Source: "Negro Deaths (Exclusive of Stillbirths) From Each Cause, by Sex, in Registration States (Including District of Columbia): 1930," and "Negro Deaths Exclusive of Stillbirths) From Each Cause, by Sex, in Registration States (Including District of Columbia: 1931." U.S. Bureau of the Census. *Negroes in the United States: 1920-32.* Washington, D.C.: Government Printing Office, 1935, pp. 465, 467. Adapted by the editors.

★ 2171 ★

Deaths

Deaths From Heart Disease – 1950, 1960, 1970

Data are based on the National Vital Statistics System.

Sex, race, and age	1950[1]	1960[1]	1970
	Deaths per 100,000 resident population		
All races			
All ages, age adjusted	307.6	286.2	253.6
All ages, crude	355.5	369.0	362.0
Under 1 year	3.5	6.6	13.1
1-4 years	1.3	1.3	1.7
5-14 years	2.1	1.3	0.8
15-24 years	6.8	4.0	3.0
25-34 years	19.4	15.6	11.4
35-44 years	86.4	74.6	66.7
45-54 years	308.6	271.8	238.4
55-64 years	808.1	737.9	652.3
65-74 years	1,839.8	1,740.5	1,558.2
75-84 years	4,310.1	4,089.4	3,683.8
85 years and over	9,150.6	9,317.8	8,468.0
White male			
All ages, age adjusted	381.1	375.4	347.6
All ages, crude	433.0	454.6	438.3
Under 1 year	4.1	6.9	12.0
1-4 years	1.1	1.0	1.5
5-14 years	1.7	1.1	0.8
15-24 years	5.8	3.6	3.0
25-34 years	20.1	17.6	12.3
35-44 years	110.6	107.5	94.6
45-54 years	423.6	413.2	365.7
55-64 years	1,081.7	1,056.0	979.3
65-74 years	2,308.3	2,297.9	2,177.2
75-84 years	4,907.3	4,839.9	4,617.6
85 years and over	9,950.5	10,135.8	9,693.0
Black male			
All ages, age adjusted	415.5	381.2	375.9
All ages, crude	348.4	330.6	330.3
Under 1 year	4.8	13.9	33.5
1-4 years		3.8	3.9
5-14 years	6.4	3.0	1.4
15-24 years	18.0	8.7	8.3
25-34 years	51.9	43.1	41.6
35-44 years	198.1	168.1	189.2
45-54 years	624.1	514.0	512.8
55-64 years	1,434.0	1,236.8	1,135.4
65-74 years	2,140.1	2,281.4	2,237.8
75-84 years	4,107.9	3,533.6	3,783.4
85 years and over		6,037.9	6,330.8

[Continued]

★ 2171 ★

Deaths From Heart Disease – 1950, 1960, 1970

[Continued]

Sex, race, and age	1950[1]	1960[1]	1970
White female			
All ages, age adjusted	223.6	197.1	167.8
All ages, crude	289.4	306.5	313.8
Under 1 year	2.7	4.3	7.0
1-4 years	1.1	0.9	1.2
5-14 years	1.9	0.9	0.7
15-24 years	5.3	2.8	1.7
25-34 years	12.2	8.2	5.5
35-44 years	40.5	28.6	23.9
45-54 years	141.9	103.4	91.4
55-64 years	460.2	383.0	317.7
65-74 years	1,400.9	1,229.8	1,044.0
75-84 years	3,925.2	3,629.7	3,143.5
85 years and over	9,084.7	9,280.8	8,207.5
Black female			
All ages, age adjusted	349.5	292.6	251.7
All ages, crude	289.9	268.5	261.0
Under 1 year	3.9	12.0	31.3
1-4 years		2.8	4.2
5-14 years	8.8	3.0	1.8
15-24 years	19.8	10.0	6.0
25-34 years	52.0	35.9	24.7
35-44 years	185.0	125.3	99.8
45-54 years	526.8	360.7	290.9
55-64 years	1,210.7	952.3	710.5
65-74 years	1,659.4	1,680.5	1,553.2
75-84 years	3,499.3	2,926.9	2,964.1
85 years and over		5,650.0	5,669.8

Source: "Death Rates for Diseases of Heart, according to Sex, Race, and Age: United States, Selected Years 1950-86," *Health United States - 1988,* March 1989, p. 66. Primary source: *Vital Statistics of the United States.* National Center for Health Statistics, U.S. Government Printing Office, Washington, D.C. *Notes:* For data years shown, the code numbers for cause of death are based on the then current *International Classification of Diseases,* which are described in Appendix II, tables IV and V. 1. Includes deaths of nonresidents of the United States.

★ 2172 ★

Deaths

Deaths From Infectious and Parasitic Diseases – 1930, 1931

Cause of death	1930			1931		
	Total	Male	Female	Total	Male	Female
Total deaths (all causes)	182,021	95,696	86,325	174,023	91,587	82,436
Infectious and parasitic diseases	37,629	19,325	18,304	37,968	19,681	18,287
Typhoid fever	1,666	892	774	1,591	843	748
Paratyphoid fever	12	7	5	16	6	10
Typhus fever	-	-	-	4	1	3
Relapsing fever	-	-	-	-	-	-
Undulant fever	3	-	3	5	3	2
Smallpox	17	10	7	15	10	5
Measles	293	155	138	273	146	127
Scarlet fever	72	33	39	79	45	34
Whooping cough	1,201	562	639	909	408	501
Diphtheria	537	284	253	638	326	312
Influenza, respiratory complications specified	2,518	1,336	1,182	3,531	1,764	1,767
Influenza, respiratory complications not specified	1,710	833	877	2,027	972	1,055
Cholera	-	-	-	-	-	-
Dysentery	739	378	361	575	288	287
Plague	-	-	-	-	-	-
Erysipelas	97	52	45	107	63	44
Acute poliomyelitis, acute polioencephalitis	115	62	53	110	59	51
Lethargic or epidemic encephalitis	65	29	36	71	38	33
Epidemic cerebrospinal meningitis	783	511	272	494	309	185
Glanders	-	-	-	-	-	-
Anthrax (bacillus anthracis) malignant pustule	-	-	-	-	-	-
Rabies	10	5	5	4	2	2
Tetanus	287	196	91	296	200	96
Tuberculosis (all forms)	20,590	10,207	10,383	20,683	10,447	10,236
Respiratory system	18,309	8,978	9,331	18,511	9,226	9,285
Meninges and central nervous system	534	291	243	452	270	182
Intestines and peritoneum	747	360	387	684	350	334
Vertebral column	184	130	54	204	141	63
Bones (vertebral column excepted)	41	28	13	50	35	15
Joints	70	44	26	79	47	32
Skin and subcutaneous cellular tissue	4	4	-	6	2	4
Lymphathic system (bronchial, mesenteric, and retroperitoneal glands excepted)	66	34	32	54	29	25
Genitourinary system	51	30	21	57	29	28
Other organs	41	25	16	29	16	13
Acute disseminated tuberculosis	493	260	233	499	265	234
Other disseminated tuberculosis	50	23	27	58	37	21
Leprosy	1	1	-	3	2	1
Syphilis	4,516	2,747	1,769	4,657	2,939	1,718
Gonococcus infection and other venereal diseases	360	69	291	376	54	322
Purulent infection, septicemia (nonpuerperal)	170	70	100	112	53	59
Yellow fever	-	-	-	-	-	-
Malaria	1,699	795	904	1,195	593	602

[Continued]

★ 2172 ★

Deaths From Infectious and Parasitic Diseases – 1930, 1931

[Continued]

Cause of death	1930			1931		
	Total	Male	Female	Total	Male	Female
Other diseases due to protozoal parasites	2	2	-	7	2	5
Ankylostomiasis	8	6	2	5	2	3
Hydatid cysts, liver	-	-	-	2	1	1
Hydatid cysts, other organs	-	-	-	-	-	-
Other diseases caused by helminths	42	16	26	47	19	28
Mycoses	68	38	30	93	57	36
Other infectious and parasitic diseases	48	29	19	43	29	14

Source: "Negro Deaths (Exclusive of Stillbirths) From Each Cause, by Sex, in Registration States (Including District of Columbia): 1930," and "Negro Deaths Exclusive of Stillbirths) From Each Cause, by Sex, in Registration States (Including District of Columbia: 1931." U.S. Bureau of the Census. *Negroes in the United States: 1920-32.* Washington, D.C.: Government Printing Office, 1935, pp. 464, 466. Adapted by the editors.

★ 2173 ★

Deaths

Deaths From Malignant Neoplasms – 1950, 1960, 1970

Data are based on the National Vital Statistics System.

Sex, race, and age	1950[1]	1960[1]	1970
	Deaths per 100,000 resident population		
All races			
All ages, age adjusted	125.4	125.8	129.9
All ages, crude	139.8	149.2	162.8
Under 1 year	8.7	7.2	4.7
1-4 years	11.7	10.9	7.5
5-14 years	6.7	6.8	6.0
15-24 years	8.6	8.3	8.3
25-34 years	20.0	19.5	16.5
35-44 years	62.7	59.7	59.5
45-54 years	175.1	177.0	182.5
55-64 years	39.9	396.8	423.0
65-74 years	692.5	713.9	754.2
75-84 years	1,153.3	1,127.4	1,168.0
85 years and over	1,451.0	1,450.0	1,417.3
White male			
All ages, age adjusted	130.9	141.6	154.3
All ages, crude	147.2	166.1	185.1
Under 1 year	9.6	7.9	4.3
1-4 years	13.1	13.1	8.5
5-14 years	7.6	8.0	7.0
15-24 years	9.9	10.3	10.6
25-34 years	17.7	18.8	16.2
35-44 years	44.5	46.3	50.1

[Continued]

★ 2173 ★

Deaths From Malignant Neoplasms – 1950, 1960, 1970

[Continued]

Sex, race, and age	1950[1]	1960[1]	1970
45-54 years	150.8	164.1	172.0
55-64 years	409.4	450.9	498.1
65-74 years	798.7	887.3	997.0
75-84 years	1,367.6	1,413.7	1,512.7
85 years and over	1,732.7	1,791.4	1,948.1
Black male			
All ages, age adjusted	126.1	158.5	198.0
All ages, crude	106.6	136.7	171.6
Under 1 year	8.2	6.8	5.3
1-4 years		7.9	7.6
5-14 years	5.8	4.4	4.8
15-24 years	7.9	9.7	9.4
25-34 years	18.0	18.4	18.8
35-44 years	55.7	72.9	81.3
45-54 years	211.7	244.7	311.2
55-64 years	490.8	579.7	689.2
65-74 years	636.4	938.5	1,168.9
75-84 years	853.5	1,053.3	1,624.8
85 years and over		1,155.2	1,635.9
White female			
All ages, age adjusted	119.4	109.5	107.6
All ages, crude	139.9	139.8	149.4
Under 1 year	7.8	6.8	5.4
1-4 years	11.3	9.7	6.9
5-14 years	6.3	6.2	5.4
15-24 years	7.5	6.5	6.2
25-34 years	20.9	18.8	16.3
35-44 years	74.5	66.6	62.4
45-54 years	185.8	175.7	177.3
55-64 years	362.5	329.0	338.6
65-74 years	616.5	562.1	554.7
75-84 years	1,026.6	939.3	903.5
85 years and over	1,348.3	1,304.9	1,179.4
Black female			
All ages, age adjusted	131.9	127.8	123.5
All ages, crude	111.8	113.8	117.3
Under 1 year	7.0	6.7	3.3
1-4 years		6.9	5.7
5-14 years	3.9	4.8	4.0
15-24 years	8.8	6.9	6.4
25-34 years	34.3	31.0	20.9
35-44 years	119.8	102.4	94.6
45-54 years	277.0	254.8	228.6
55-64 years	484.6	442.7	404.8

[Continued]

★ 2173 ★

Deaths From Malignant Neoplasms – 1950, 1960, 1970

[Continued]

Sex, race, and age	1950[1]	1960[1]	1970
65-74 years	477.3	541.6	615.8
75-84 years	605.3	696.3	763.3
85 years and over		728.9	896.8

Source: "Death Rates for Malignant Neoplasms, according to Sex, Race, and Age: United States, Selected Years 1950-86," *Health United States - 1988*, March 1989, p. 68. Primary source: *Vital Statistics of the United States*. National Center for Health Statistics, U.S. Government Printing Office, Washington, D.C. *Notes:* For data years shown, the code numbers for cause of death are based on the then current *International Classification of Diseases*, which are described in Appendix II, tables IV and V. 1. Includes deaths of nonresidents of the United States.

★ 2174 ★

Deaths

Deaths From Motor Vehicle Accidents, 1940-1960

Cause, color, sex and year	All ages	Under 1 year	1-4 years	5-14 years	15-24 years	25-34 years	35-44 years	45-54 years	55-64 years	65-74 years	75-84 years	85 years and over
Total nonwhite												
1960	21.9	7.7	11.2	8.3	30.3	29.5	26.2	30.5	30.7	30.9	32.4	41.9
1959	22.5	5.7	10.3	9.1	29.8	31.2	28.5	32.6	30.6	29.7	26.6	30.9
1958	22.2	5.4	10.8	7.6	29.6	31.7	28.7	29.6	29.9	33.7	28.8	16.7
1957	24.7	7.7	11.2	8.5	30.8	36.5	29.7	33.1	37.1	32.9	45.0	34.4
1956	26.8	11.5	11.5	8.9	34.9	38.2	34.8	34.7	39.3	34.5	37.3	27.9
1955	25.7	9.1	12.3	7.9	34.2	36.6	31.6	33.5	36.5	35.6	35.5	37.9
1954	24.5	11.0	12.2	7.9	29.8	33.9	28.9	34.3	35.8	31.2	39.8	49.1
1953	27.2	10.9	13.6	9.5	32.8	38.3	33.8	35.9	34.9	35.4	49.1	44.2
1952	26.8	8.1	12.9	8.1	33.5	37.3	31.2	37.7	38.7	33.7	44.2	55.1
1951	26.4	7.9	11.3	9.4	31.0	35.5	32.8	34.2	38.0	38.5	45.2	42.6
1950	24.2	7.9	10.6	8.6	27.4	32.1	28.5	31.6	35.7	37.2	44.3	38.0
1949	21.6	5.0	10.8	9.1	23.7	27.2	24.5	29.3	28.0	38.3	44.4	37.2
1948	20.8	5.0	10.6	8.4	22.6	23.3	24.6	29.2	31.5	35.7	46.8	24.4
1947	19.9	4.1	9.3	8.0	22.4	21.3	22.7	27.8	30.8	38.9	40.4	35.0
1946	21.2	4.6	11.8	10.4	22.8	23.1	23.9	28.9	32.1	34.2	40.6	34.2
1945	18.6	4.4	8.8	8.0	18.4	20.5	22.9	25.9	29.4	34.8	40.1	18.9
1944	17.7	4.5	9.4	8.8	17.6	21.1	20.2	24.4	23.1	34.3	35.4	25.7
1943	16.9	2.0	9.1	7.5	16.6	19.1	19.3	24.1	27.0	32.8	31.3	22.9
1942	20.2	2.5	8.2	8.1	21.0	25.0	23.5	29.9	30.1	33.5	33.8	44.1
1941	29.4	9.7	9.6	11.8	31.0	34.1	35.1	41.0	46.6	58.7	60.0	41.2
1940	23.8	5.4	8.6	9.8	23.9	28.4	26.7	36.5	38.0	46.1	48.5	59.3
Nonwhite male												
1960	34.4	7.5	13.1	10.7	50.7	51.7	43.1	49.1	47.6	49.1	56.0	70.2
1959	35.4	6.0	12.0	12.5	49.5	53.2	47.2	52.9	49.5	44.4	42.4	65.5
1958	35.4	5.9	11.9	11.1	50.1	55.6	47.4	47.3	48.8	54.0	43.2	33.3
1957	38.4	8.7	13.3	11.2	50.3	62.1	48.4	51.9	57.0	51.2	73.3	69.2

[Continued]

★ 2174 ★

Deaths From Motor Vehicle Accidents, 1940-1960

[Continued]

Cause, color, sex and year	All ages	Under 1 year	1-4 years	5-14 years	15-24 years	25-34 years	35-44 years	45-54 years	55-64 years	65-74 years	75-84 years	85 years and over
1956	42.6	13.6	13.9	11.2	59.7	67.3	57.3	55.3	58.4	56.9	61.5	64.0
1955	40.1	10.0	13.7	10.3	57.4	63.1	51.3	53.1	55.8	54.4	52.8	70.8
1954	38.3	13.3	13.2	10.4	50.3	59.1	45.9	55.3	54.8	50.0	60.5	95.5
1953	43.4	10.7	17.4	12.7	55.6	66.7	54.5	57.8	56.1	59.9	79.8	81.0
1952	42.7	8.6	15.8	11.4	55.5	63.6	53.1	58.9	61.4	54.0	69.1	105.0
1951	41.7	6.4	13.5	13.1	50.5	62.1	53.7	52.9	57.6	60.9	73.6	78.9
1950	38.2	8.9	11.7	10.8	44.3	55.4	46.9	52.0	57.0	58.8	66.4	64.3
1949	34.8	6.4	12.6	13.0	40.3	46.9	42.3	45.8	43.6	59.6	72.4	83.3
1948	33.8	8.4	12.6	11.5	37.6	39.9	41.5	48.7	51.7	57.4	76.8	41.2
1947	32.4	4.4	11.3	11.2	37.5	35.9	40.0	44.8	48.7	65.9	65.9	68.8
1946	33.9	3.6	14.1	14.0	37.4	40.1	40.1	46.8	50.5	54.0	62.1	86.7
1945	31.2	3.4	11.1	11.4	33.5	39.1	40.5	42.2	48.8	51.7	69.5	46.7
1944	29.7	4.1	12.3	13.1	32.0	38.6	35.2	40.5	36.7	56.1	59.0	57.1
1943	28.7	2.0	12.9	11.3	29.7	33.0	34.2	42.3	43.5	55.3	56.2	57.1
1942	33.6	3.6	11.2	11.6	36.3	43.9	40.1	50.0	48.9	52.9	49.3	85.7
1941	48.3	10.0	12.0	17.2	52.7	59.4	60.6	66.8	73.4	93.5	90.9	71.4
1940	38.6	5.0	9.9	13.7	41.8	48.0	45.0	58.4	57.8	72.1	85.5	106.5
Nonwhite female												
1960	10.1	7.8	9.4	5.9	11.2	10.3	11.0	12.8	14.4	14.4	11.3	19.9
1959	10.2	5.3	8.6	5.7	11.5	12.2	11.3	13.5	12.3	16.2	12.4	5.1
1958	9.7	4.8	9.6	4.1	10.7	11.1	11.6	12.8	11.7	15.1	15.7	5.3
1957	11.8	6.6	9.1	5.9	13.2	14.4	12.5	15.1	17.7	16.1	18.6	10.8
1956	11.9	9.5	9.2	6.6	12.5	12.9	13.9	14.8	20.6	13.8	14.5	2.8
1955	12.1	8.4	10.9	5.5	13.5	13.6	13.3	14.4	17.4	18.3	18.9	14.7
1954	11.4	8.8	11.2	5.4	11.9	12.0	13.2	13.9	16.8	13.9	19.8	18.8
1953	11.9	11.1	9.8	6.2	13.3	13.6	14.5	14.3	13.3	12.5	19.8	19.4
1952	11.8	7.6	10.0	4.8	14.5	14.3	10.9	16.8	15.3	14.6	20.7	20.7
1951	12.0	9.5	9.1	5.6	13.8	12.0	13.5	15.6	17.7	17.3	18.0	17.9
1950	10.8	6.9	9.4	6.4	12.1	11.4	11.5	11.1	13.9	15.4	22.5	19.1
1949	8.9	3.5	9.0	5.2	8.8	9.4	7.9	12.7	11.9	16.7	17.0	4.0
1948	8.3	1.6	8.7	5.3	9.0	8.0	8.8	9.6	10.6	13.2	16.5	12.5
1947	7.7	3.8	7.3	4.9	8.6	7.7	6.4	10.5	11.9	10.5	15.1	12.5
1946	9.0	5.7	9.4	6.7	9.8	7.2	8.6	10.6	12.2	13.2	19.3	-
1945	7.1	5.4	6.6	4.6	7.0	6.7	7.0	9.2	8.3	16.9	11.9	-
1944	6.6	4.9	6.5	4.6	6.1	7.4	6.4	7.8	8.2	10.9	12.3	4.8
1943	5.6	2.1	5.2	3.8	5.2	7.0	5.4	5.4	8.9	8.7	7.8	-
1942	7.3	1.5	5.2	4.7	7.2	8.3	7.9	8.8	9.3	12.3	19.4	15.0

[Continued]

★ 2174 ★

Deaths From Motor Vehicle Accidents, 1940-1960

[Continued]

Cause, color, sex and year	All ages	Under 1 year	1-4 years	5-14 years	15-24 years	25-34 years	35-44 years	45-54 years	55-64 years	65-74 years	75-84 years	85 years and over
1941	11.0	9.3	7.2	6.4	11.2	11.4	11.1	13.9	16.9	20.9	30.4	20.0
1940	9.4	5.7	7.3	6.0	7.7	10.7	9.4	13.3	15.7	17.7	13.7	24.5

Source: "Death Rates for 35 Selected Causes by Age, Color, and Sex: United States, 1940-1960." National Center for Health Services. *Vital Statistics Rates in the United States 1940-1960.* By Robert D. Grove and Alice M. Hetzel. Washington, D.C.: Government Printing Office, 1968, pp. 527-528.

★ 2175 ★

Deaths

Deaths From Motor Vehicle Accidents – 1950, 1960, 1970

Data are based on the National Vital Statistics System.

Sex, race, and age	1950[1]	1960[1]	1970
	Deaths per 100,000 resident population		
White male			
All ages, age adjusted	35.9	34.0	40.1
All ages, crude	35.1	31.5	39.1
Under 1 year	9.1	8.8	9.1
1-4 years	13.2	11.3	12.2
5-14 years	12.0	10.3	12.6
15-24 years	58.3	62.7	75.2
25-34 years	39.1	38.6	47.0
35-44 years	30.9	28.4	35.2
45-54 years	31.6	29.7	34.6
55-64 years	41.9	34.4	39.0
65-74 years	59.1	45.5	46.2
75-84 years	86.4	66.8	69.2
85 years and over	79.3	61.9	72.0
Black male			
All ages, age adjusted	39.8	38.2	50.1
All ages, crude	37.2	33.1	44.2
Under 1 year	9.0	6.8	10.6
1-4 years		12.7	16.9
5-14 years	9.7	10.4	16.1
15-24 years	41.6	46.4	58.1
25-34 years	57.4	51.0	70.4
35-44 years	45.9	43.6	59.5
45-54 years	49.9	48.1	61.4
55-64 years	58.8	47.3	62.1
65-74 years	48.5	46.1	54.9
75-84 years	61.8	51.8	51.5
85 years and over		58.6	53.8

[Continued]

★ 2175 ★

Deaths From Motor Vehicle Accidents – 1950, 1960, 1970

[Continued]

Sex, race, and age	1950[1]	1960[1]	1970
White female			
All ages, age adjusted	10.6	11.1	14.4
All ages, crude	10.9	11.2	14.8
Under 1 year	7.8	7.5	10.2
1-4 years	10.1	8.3	9.6
5-14 years	5.6	5.3	6.9
15-24 years	12.6	15.6	22.7
25-34 years	9.0	9.0	12.7
35-44 years	8.1	8.9	12.3
45-54 years	10.8	11.4	14.3
55-64 years	15.0	15.3	16.1
65-74 years	20.9	19.3	22.1
75-84 years	25.4	23.8	28.1
85 years and over	22.3	22.2	18.9
Black female			
All ages, age adjusted	10.3	10.0	13.8
All ages, crude	10.2	9.7	13.4
Under 1 year	7.0	8.1	11.9
1-4 years		8.8	12.6
5-14 years	6.2	5.9	9.3
15-24 years	11.5	9.9	13.4
25-34 years	10.7	9.8	13.3
35-44 years	11.1	11.0	16.1
45-54 years	10.6	11.8	16.4
55-64 years	14.0	14.0	17.1
65-74 years	12.7	14.2	16.3
75-84 years	17.6	8.8	14.3
85 years and over		21.1	17.5

Source: "Death Rates for Motor Vehicle Accidents, according to Sex, Race, and Age: United States, Selected Years 1950-86," *Health United States - 1988*, March 1989, p. 72. Primary source: *Vital Statistics of the United States*. National Center for Health Statistics, U.S. Government Printing Office, Washington, D.C. *Notes:* For data years shown, the code numbers for cause of death are based on the then current *International Classification of Diseases*, which are described in Appendix II, tables IV and V. 1. Includes deaths of nonresidents of the United States.

★ 2176 ★

Deaths

Deaths From Rheumatic Diseases, Nutritional Diseases, Diseases of the Endocrine Glands, and Other General Diseases - 1930, 1931

Cause of death	1930			1931		
	Total	Male	Female	Total	Male	Female
Rheumatic diseases, nutritional diseases, diseases of the endocrine glands, and other general diseases	6,032	1,981	4,051	5,407	1,775	3,632
Acute rheumatic fever	469	205	264	411	178	233
Chronic rheumatism, osteoarthritis	109	48	61	110	47	63
Gout	1	-	1	-	-	-
Diabetes mellitus	1,425	506	902	1,465	527	938
Scurvy	8	4	4	10	4	6
Beriberi	-	-	-	-	-	-
Pellagra	3,368	951	2,417	2,832	801	2,031
Rickets	143	88	55	138	78	60
Osteomalacia	1	1	-	-	-	-
Diseases of pituitary body	1	-	1	1	1	-
Simple goiter	36	5	31	23	4	19
Exophthalmic goiter	221	31	190	224	41	183
Other diseases of thyroid and paratyphoid glands	37	13	19	32	18	14
Diseases of thymus gland	100	56	44	84	42	42
Diseases of adrenais (Addison's disease not specified as tuberculosis)	11	8	3	9	2	7
Other general diseases	101	60	41	68	32	36

Source: "Negro Deaths (Exclusive of Stillbirths) From Each Cause, by Sex, in Registration States (Including District of Columbia): 1930," and "Negro Deaths Exclusive of Stillbirths) From Each Cause, by Sex, in Registration States (Including District of Columbia: 1931." U.S. Bureau of the Census. *Negroes in the United States: 1920-32*. Washington, D.C.: Government Printing Office, 1935, pp. 464, 466. Adapted by the editors.

★ 2177 ★

Deaths

Deaths From Senility - 1930, 1931

Cause of death	1930			1931		
	Total	Male	Female	Total	Male	Female
Senility	2,431	1,128	1,303	2,014	1,009	1,005

Source: "Negro Deaths (Exclusive of Stillbirths) From Each Cause, by Sex, in Registration States (Including District of Columbia): 1930," and "Negro Deaths Exclusive of Stillbirths) From Each Cause, by Sex, in Registration States (Including District of Columbia: 1931." U.S. Bureau of the Census. *Negroes in the United States: 1920-32*. Washington, D.C.: Government Printing Office, 1935, pp. 465, 467. Adapted by the editors.

★ 2178 ★

Deaths

Deaths From Specified Causes, 1910

Cause of death	Number		Distribution per 1,000		Per 100,000 population	
	Southern cities[1]	Northern and western cities[1]	Southern cities[1]	Northern and western cities[1]	Southern cities[1]	Northern and western cities[1]
All causes	15,955	11,393	1,000	1,000	2,893	2,514
Tuberculosis	2,602	2,507	163	220	472	553
Pneumonia	1,410	1,022	88	90	256	226
Violent deaths, except suicide	927	569	58	50	168	126
Diarrhea and enteritis (under 2 years)	851	656	53	58	154	145
Bronchopneumonia	558	557	35	49	101	123
Congenital debility	309	169	19	15	56	37
Bronchitis	263	226	16	20	48	50
Typhoid	237	111	15	10	43	25
Diarrhea and enteritis (2 years and over)	206	74	13	6	37	16
Influenza	206	59	13	5	37	13
Malaria	131	9	8	1	24	2
Meningitis	131	61	8	5	24	14
Whooping cough	129	123	8	11	23	27
Measles	41	58	3	5	7	13
Diphtheria	40	80	3	7	7	18
Suicide	33	52	2	5	6	12
Scarlet fever	16	24	1	2	3	5
Other causes	7,865	5,036	493	442	1,426	1,111

Source: "Negro Deaths From Specified Causes: 1910." U.S. Bureau of the Census. *Negro Population, 1790-1915*. Washington, D.C.: Government Printing Office, 1918, p. 317. *Notes:* 1. Includes all registration cities of 100,000 or more population and having a Negro population of 2,500 or more in 1910.

★ 2179 ★

Deaths

Deaths From Tuberculosis, 1940-1945

Year	Whites		Negroes	
	Number	Rates per 100,000 population	Number	Rates per 100,000 population
1945	38,623	32.7	13,114	98.0
1944	39,958	33.7	13,538	101.8
1943	41,209	34.3	14,513	108.4
1942	41,306	34.4	15,107	114.2

[Continued]

★ 2179 ★

Deaths From Tuberculosis, 1940-1945

[Continued]

Year	Whites		Negroes	
	Number	Rates per 100,000 population	Number	Rates per 100,000 population
1941	42,283	35.4	15,702	120.2
1940	43,211	36.5	15,883	123.1

Source: "Number of Deaths and Death Rates for Tuberculosis (All Forms) for Whites and Negroes, United States: 1940-1945." Murray, Florence, ed. *The Negro Handbook, 1949.* New York: Macmillan, 1949, p. 27. Primary source: National Tuberculosis Association.

★ 2180 ★

Deaths

Deaths From Violence and Accidents – 1930, 1931

Cause of death	1930			1931		
	Total	Male	Female	Total	Male	Female
Violent and accidental deaths	14,236	10,801	3,435	14,236	10,801	3,435
Suicide	458	336	122	509	373	136
By solid or liquid poisons or by absorption of corrosive substances	97	42	55	106	42	64
By poisonous gas	42	30	12	27	22	5
By hanging or strangulation	30	25	5	44	38	6
By drowning	48	33	15	46	29	17
By firearms	179	159	20	206	180	26
By cutting or piercing instruments	34	26	8	37	32	5
By jumping from high places	19	14	5	23	17	6
By crushing	5	4	1	6	6	-
By other means	4	3	1	14	7	7
Homicide	4,306	3,460	846	4,573	3,708	865
By firearms	2,850	2,351	499	3,005	2,504	501
By cutting or piercing instruments	992	762	230	1,099	860	239
By other means	464	347	117	469	344	125
Accidental, other, or undefined	9,472	7,005	2,467	8,887	6,445	2,412
Attack by venomous animals	12	9	3	23	16	7
Poisoning by food	207	107	100	157	82	75
Absorption of poisonous gas	88	67	21	89	68	21
Supplemental	3	2	1	1	1	-
Other acute accidental poisonings (gas excepted)	248	161	87	252	143	109
Conflagration	330	187	143	264	156	108
Burns (conflagration excepted)	1,130	481	649	1,004	396	608
Supplemental	44	35	9	37	29	8
Mechanical suffocation	202	109	93	171	96	75
Supplemental	4	4	-	10	9	1
Drowning	906	821	85	779	705	74

[Continued]

★ 2180 ★

Deaths From Violence and Accidents – 1930, 1931

[Continued]

Cause of death	1930 Total	1930 Male	1930 Female	1931 Total	1931 Male	1931 Female
Supplemental	101	81	20	109	91	18
Traumatism						
By firearms (wounds of war excepted)	660	531	129	527	426	101
By cutting or piercing instruments (wounds of war excepted)	86	58	28	130	90	40
Supplemental	20	16	4	16	13	3
By fall	761	496	265	761	468	293
Supplemental	263	228	35	306	269	37
By crushing landslide	77	73	4	58	54	4
Supplemental	442	400	42	572	487	85
Cataclysm	25	12	13	11	8	3
Injuries by animals	52	45	7	42	38	4
Hunger and thirst	3	2	1	14	9	5
Excessive cold	89	70	19	19	15	4
Excessive heat	238	178	60	220	172	48
Lightning	79	59	20	104	71	33
Due to electric currents	28	26	2	32	29	3
Supplemental	13	13	-	15	14	1
Foreign bodies	73	48	25	54	25	29
Supplemental	-	-	-	-	-	-
Other accidents	587	466	121	541	422	119
Supplemental	2,644	2,164	480	2,498	1,972	526
Violent deaths of unknown nature	1	1	-	-	-	-
Wounds of war	-	-	-	2	2	-
Execution of civilians by belligerent armies	-	-	-	-	-	-
Legal executions	56	55	1	69	69	-

Source: "Negro Deaths (Exclusive of Stillbirths) From Each Cause, by Sex, in Registration States (Including District of Columbia): 1930," and "Negro Deaths Exclusive of Stillbirths) From Each Cause, by Sex, in Registration States (Including District of Columbia: 1931." U.S. Bureau of the Census. *Negroes in the United States: 1920-32.* Washington, D.C.: Government Printing Office, 1935, pp. 464, 466. Adapted by the editors.

★ 2181 ★

Deaths

Deaths Per 1,000 Population at Specified Ages – 1900, 1910

Age	Negro						White
	1910				1900		1910
	Number		Excess of male over female	Excess of female over male	Excess male over female	Excess of female over male	Excess of male over female
	Male	Female					
All ages	25.3	22.1	3.2	-	2.3	-	1.8
Under 1 year	280.3	243.2	37.1	-	70.3	-	27.8
1 to 4 years	32.6	29.4	3.2	-	0.9	-	1.2
5 to 9 years	6.0	6.0	0.0	0.0	0.0	0.0	0.3

[Continued]

★ 2181 ★

Deaths Per 1,000 Population at Specified Ages – 1900, 1910

[Continued]

Age	Negro						White
	1910				1900		1910
	Number		Excess of male over female	Excess of female over male	Excess male over female	Excess of female over male	Excess of male over female
	Male	Female					
10 to 14 years	5.2	6.1	-	0.9	-	5.2	0.2
15 to 19 years	9.5	10.7	-	1.2	-	0.2	0.5
20 to 24 years	42.9	10.9	2.0	-	1.3	-	0.7
25 to 44 years	17.2	14.2	3.0	-	0.5	-	1.4
45 to 64 years	33.5	31.1	2.4	-	1.6	-	3.8
65 to 84 years	86.6	78.5	8.1	-	6.2	-	6.3
85 years and over	213.2	214.9	-	1.7	55.6	-	10.0
Age unknown	13.5	7.2	6.3	-	6.6	-	3.4

Source: "Deaths in the Registration States per 1,000 Population at Age Specified." U.S. Bureau of the Census. *Negro Population, 1790-1915.* Washington, D.C.: Government Printing Office, 1918, p. 307.

★ 2182 ★

Deaths

Deaths and Death Rates by Class of Population, 1910. Part I, Southern Cities

City	Population: April 15, 1910				Deaths: Calendar year 1910				Deaths per 1,000 population			
	Negro	Native White		Foreign born white	Negro	Native white		Foreign born white	Negro	Native white		Foreign born white
		Of native parentage	Of foreign or mixed parentage			Of native parentage	Of foreign or mixed parentage			Of native parentage	Of foreign or mixed parentage	
All cities	1,367,054	6,224,355	6,109,198	5,104,866	37,791	100,431	88,353	87,661	27.6	16.1	14.5	17.2
Southern cities	850,590	1,500,403	458,264	235,699	24,886	24,431	5,843	6,513	29.3	16.3	12.8	27.6
Southern Cities												
Alabama												
Birmingham	52,305	66,312	8,357	5,700	1,391	993	102	111	26.6	15.0	12.2	19.5
Mobile	22,763	20,944	5,585	2,208	673	396	30	86	29.6	18.9	5.4	38.9
Montgomery	19,322	16,708	1,390	704	680	307	5	16	35.2	18.4	3.6	22.7
Delaware												
Wilmington	9,081	44,937	19,694	13,678	225	791	284	247	24.8	17.6	14.4	18.1
District of Columbia												
Washington	94,446	166,711	45,066	24,351	2,759	2,553	521	670	29.2	15.3	11.6	27.5
Florida												
Jacksonville	29,293	22,628	3,213	2,488	710	398	20	64	24.2	17.6	6.2	25.7
Key West	5,515	3,212	6,509	4,688	147	199	-	102	26.7	62.0	-	21.8
Georgia												
Atlanta	51,902	91,987	6,464	4,410	1,328	1,458	87	64	25.6	15.9	13.5	14.5
Savannah	33,246	22,634	5,818	3,332	1,134	493	-	123	34.1	21.8	-	36.9
Kentucky												
Covington	2,899	31,079	15,346	3,933	59	446	151	205	20.4	14.4	9.8	52.1
Louisville	40,522	113,543	52,411	17,436	1,089	1,755	384	528	26.9	15.5	7.3	30.3
Paducah	6,047	15,022	1,341	347	164	248	3	23	27.1	16.5	2.2	66.3
Louisiana												
New Orleans	89,262	147,473	74,244	27,686	2,933	2,023	1,165	1,123	32.9	13.7	15.7	40.6
Maryland												
Annapolis	3,184	4,160	791	457	97	56	19	8	30.5	13.5	24.0	17.5
Baltimore	84,749	261,474	134,870	77,043	2,597	4,421	1,868	1,863	30.6	16.9	13.9	24.2

[Continued]

★ 2182 ★

Deaths and Death Rates by Class of Population, 1910. Part I, Southern Cities

[Continued]

City	Population: April 15, 1910				Deaths: Calendar year 1910				Deaths per 1,000 population			
		Native White				Native white				Native white		
	Negro	Of native parentage	Of foreign or mixed parentage	Foreign born white	Negro	Of native parentage	Of foreign or mixed parentage	Foreign born white	Negro	Of native parentage	Of foreign or mixed parentage	Foreign born white
North Carolina												
Asheville	5,359	12,436	579	386	135	193	24	18	25.2	15.5	41.5	46.6
Charlotte	11,752	21,208	579	472	299	292	7	7	25.4	13.8	12.1	14.8
Durham	6,869	10,875	269	228	179	184	2	3	26.1	16.9	7.4	13.2
Greensboro	5,710	9,590	369	225	143	155	2	5	25.0	16.2	5.4	22.2
Raleigh	7,372	11,461	234	151	247	275	9	6	33.5	24.0	38.5	39.7
Wilmington	12,107	12,417	766	444	325	189	12	12	26.8	15.2	15.7	27.0
Winston	7,828	9,040	172	124	186	163	3	-	23.8	18.0	17.4	-
South Carolina												
Charleston	31,056	20,458	4,902	2,404	1,221	360	67	99	39.3	17.6	13.7	41.2
Tennessee												
Knoxville	7,638	26,300	1,623	783	203	384	22	26	26.6	14.6	13.6	33.2
Memphis	52,441	59,985	12,138	6,467	1,492	1,049	118	159	28.5	17.5	9.7	24.6
Nashville	36,523	63,687	7,151	2,993	950	945	90	78	26.0	14.8	12.6	26.1
Texas												
Galveston	8,036	12,643	10,088	6,164	183	170	91	156	22.8	13.4	9.0	25.3
San Antonio	10,716	44,629	23,765	17,407	233	851	563	503	21.7	19.1	23.7	28.9
Virginia												
Alexandria	4,188	9,923	889	320	138	182	-	7	33.0	18.3	-	21.9
Danville	6,207	12,387	241	183	167	213	4	4	26.9	17.2	16.6	21.9
Lynchburg	9,466	18,743	830	450	231	226	6	10	24.4	12.1	7.2	22.2
Norfolk	25,039	34,471	4,318	3,564	775	579	60	61	31.0	16.8	13.9	17.1
Petersburg	11,014	12,196	528	388	377	248	8	8	34.2	20.3	15.2	20.6
Richmond	46,733	69,130	7,664	4,085	1,416	1,236	116	118	30.3	17.9	15.1	28.9

Source: "Deaths and Death Rates, by Class of Population, for Selected Registration Cities: 1910." U.S. Bureau of the Census. *Negro Population, 1790-1915.* Washington, D.C.: Government Printing Office, 1918, p. 329.

★ 2183 ★

Deaths

Deaths and Death Rates by Class of Population, 1910. Part II, Northern and Western Cities

City	Population: April 15, 1910				Deaths: Calendar year 1910				Deaths per 1,000 population			
		Native White				Native white				Native white		
	Negro	Of native parentage	Of foreign or mixed parentage	Foreign born white	Negro	Of native parentage	Of foreign or mixed parentage	Foreign born white	Negro	Of native parentage	Of foreign or mixed parentage	Foreign born white
All cities	1,367,054	6,224,355	6,109,198	5,104,866	37,791	100,431	88,353	87,661	27.6	16.1	14.5	17.2
Northern and Western cities	516,464	4,723,952	5,650,994	4,869,167	12,905	76,000	82,510	81,148	25.0	16.1	14.6	16.7
Northern and Western cities												
California												
Los Angeles	7,599	169,967	74,756	60,584	136	2,303	892	1,104	17.9	13.5	11.9	18.2
Oakland	3,055	55,198	49,936	36,822	52	689	449	653	17.0	12.5	9.0	17.7
Colorado												
Denver	5,426	106,945	61,185	38,941	132	1,757	755	877	24.3	16.4	12.3	22.5
Connecticut												
New Haven	3,561	37,726	49,434	42,784	91	655	722	749	25.6	17.4	14.6	17.5
Indiana												
Evansville	6,266	41,945	16,970	4,462	117	485	190	156	18.7	11.6	11.2	35.0
Indianapolis	21,816	150,593	41,429	19,767	548	2,249	519	507	25.1	14.9	12.5	25.6
Terre Haute	2,593	42,586	9,164	3,796	67	640	95	129	25.8	15.0	10.4	34.0
Massachusetts												
Boston	13,564	157,870	257,104	240,722	317	3,106	3,963	4,155	23.4	19.7	15.4	17.3
Cambridge	4,707	25,615	39,794	34,608	75	412	522	567	15.9	16.1	13.1	16.4
New Bedford	2,885	18,738	32,336	42,625	85	377	880	470	29.5	20.1	27.2	11.0

[Continued]

★ 2183 ★

Deaths and Death Rates by Class of Population, 1910. Part II, Northern and Western Cities

[Continued]

City	Population: April 15, 1910				Deaths: Calendar year 1910				Deaths per 1,000 population			
	Negro	Native White		Foreign born white	Negro	Native white		Foreign born white	Negro	Native white		Foreign born white
		Of native parentage	Of foreign or mixed parentage			Of native parentage	Of foreign or mixed parentage			Of native parentage	Of foreign or mixed parentage	
Michigan												
Detroit	5,741	115,106	188,255	156,565	146	2,175	2,751	2,379	25.4	18.9	14.6	15.2
Minnesota												
Minneapolis	2,592	96,186	116,548	85,938	56	1,300	1,163	1,218	21.6	13.5	10.0	14.2
St. Paul	3,144	61,594	93,398	56,524	49	825	813	870	15.6	13.4	8.7	15.4
New Jersey												
Atlantic City	9,834	22,410	7,421	6,400	172	358	149	120	17.5	16.0	20.1	18.8
Camden	6,076	49,581	23,128	15,682	192	840	375	222	31.6	16.9	16.2	14.2
Jersey City	5,960	74,861	109,101	77,697	123	1,182	1,621	1,475	20.6	15.8	14.9	19.0
Newark	9,475	94,737	132,350	110,655	296	1,670	1,961	1,853	31.2	17.6	14.8	16.7
Trenton	2,581	38,679	29,209	26,310	89	800	613	473	34.5	20.7	21.9	18.0
New York												
New York City	91,709	921,318	1,820,141	1,927,703	2,391	15,990	29,344	28,940	26.1	17.4	16.1	15.0
Bronx Borough	4,117	92,569	185,146	148,935	208	1,251	2,689	2,815	50.5	13.5	14.5	18.9
Brooklyn Borough	22,708	375,548	663,583	571,356	598	5,720	10,208	9,142	26.3	15.2	15.4	16.0
Manhattan Borough	60,534	344,351	818,208	1,104,019	1,473	7,556	14,506	15,067	24.3	21.9	17.7	13.6
Queens Borough	3,198	80,607	120,969	79,115	82	994	1,485	1,403	25.6	12.3	12.3	17.7
Richmond Borough	1,152	28,243	32,235	24,278	30	469	456	513	26.0	16.6	14.1	21.1
Ohio												
Cincinnati	19,639	154,937	132,190	56,792	569	2,287	1,687	1,776	29.0	14.8	12.8	31.3
Cleveland	8,448	132,314	223,908	195,703	167	2,088	3,001	2,791	19.8	15.8	13.4	14.3
Columbus	12,739	116,846	35,578	16,285	262	1,742	401	405	20.6	14.9	11.3	24.9
Dayton	4,842	72,301	25,559	13,847	99	992	345	288	20.4	13.7	13.5	20.8
Springfield	4,933	30,577	8,243	3,156	78	418	57	68	15.8	13.7	6.9	21.5
Pennsylvania												
Chester	4,795	17,793	9,258	6,673	107	241	169	132	22.3	13.5	18.3	19.8
Harrisburg	4,535	49,576	5,926	4,134	98	654	109	79	21.6	13.2	18.4	19.1
Philadelphia	84,459	584,008	496,785	382,578	2,276	9,977	7,663	7,100	26.9	17.1	15.4	18.6
Pittsburgh	25,623	176,089	191,483	140,436	601	2,900	3,451	2,642	23.5	16.5	18.0	18.8
Rhode Island												
Providence	5,316	59,966	82,354	76,303	139	1,173	1,400	1,264	26.1	19.6	17.0	16.6
Illinois												
Chicago	44,103	445,139	912,701	781,217	1,075	7,073	12,240	12,817	24.4	15.9	13.4	16.4
Springfield	2,961	27,944	13,855	6,900	67	531	92	170	22.6	19.0	6.6	24.6
Kansas												
Kansas City	9,286	48,021	14,631	10,344	237	720	221	211	25.5	15.0	15.1	20.4
Missouri												
Kansas City	23,566	153,717	45,633	25,327	644	2,213	552	552	27.3	14.4	12.1	21.8
St. Joseph	4,249	50,316	14,699	8,113	98	651	146	160	23.1	12.9	9.9	19.7
St. Louis	43,960	269,836	246,946	125,706	1,149	3,689	2,803	3,241	26.1	13.7	11.4	25.8
Nebraska												
Omaha	4,426	52,917	39,595	27,068	105	838	396	535	23.7	15.8	10.0	19.8

Source: "Deaths and Death Rates, by Class of Population, for Selected Registration Cities: 1910." U.S. Bureau of the Census. *Negro Population, 1790-1915.* Washington, D.C.: Government Printing Office, 1918, pp. 329-330.

★ 2184 ★

Deaths

Deaths and Death Rates by Race, Sex, and Age – 1900, 1910 - I

Age period	Registration states[1]							
	Negro population[2]				Deaths[3] per 1,000 population of age specified			
	1910	1900	Deaths at age specified during calendar year		Negro population		White population	
			1910	1900	1910	1900	1910	1900
				Both sexes				
All ages	1,051,877	388,198	24,908	9,954	23.7	25.6	14.6	17.0
Under 5 years	92,690	33,216	7,398	3,637	79.8	109.5	38.0	49.0
Under 1 year	19,634	7,196	5,143	2,479	261.9	344.5	129.7	159.4
5 to 9 years	87,054	31,681	520	282	6.0	8.9	3.4	4.6
10 to 14 years	85,035	30,677	482	280	5.7	9.1	2.3	2.9
15 to 19 years	90,267	37,513	916	424	10.1	11.3	3.6	4.7
20 to 24 years	115,494	51,509	1,365	590	11.8	11.5	5.2	6.7
25 to 44 years	393,247	135,301	6,183	1,849	15.7	13.7	7.5	9.0
45 to 64 years	149,317	53,853	4,829	1,686	32.3	31.3	18.3	19.7
65 to 84 years	33,244	11,376	2,746	977	82.6	85.9	73.8	74.7
85 years and over	2,016	893	432	194	214.2	217.2	254.6	262.6
Age unknown	3,513	2,179	37	35	10.5	16.1	9.0	31.2
				Male				
All ages	519,973	185,211	13,151	4,972	25.3	26.8	15.4	17.8
Under 5 years	45,631	16,239	3,949	1,924	86.5	118.5	41.4	53.1
Under 1 year	9,933	3,563	2,784	1,354	280.3	380.0	143.4	175.8
5 to 9 years	12,555	15,424	254	138	6.0	8.9	3.6	4.6
10 to 14 years	41,121	14,604	213	94	5.2	6.4	2.4	2.8
15 to 19 years	41,746	16,721	396	187	9.5	11.2	3.8	4.7
20 to 24 years	53,590	22,815	692	278	12.9	12.2	5.5	6.9
25 to 44 years	198,630	65,624	3,415	912	17.2	13.9	8.1	9.3
45 to 64 years	77,329	26,994	2,593	866	33.5	32.1	20.1	20.7
65 to 84 years	16,767	5,266	1,453	470	86.6	89.2	77.0	78.0
85 years and over	755	316	161	80	213.2	253.2	260.2	270.2
Age unknown	1,849	1,208	25	23	13.5	19.0	10.1	29.4
				Female				
All ages	531,904	202,987	11,757	4,982	22.1	24.5	13.6	16.3
Under 5 years	47,059	16,977	3,449	1,713	73.0	100.9	34.6	44.8
Under 1 year	9,701	3,633	2,359	1,125	243.2	309.7	115.6	142.6
5 to 9 years	44,499	16,257	266	144	6.0	8.9	3.3	4.5
10 to 14 years	43,914	16,073	269	186	6.1	11.6	2.2	2.9
15 to 19 years	48,521	20,792	520	237	10.7	11.4	3.3	4.7
20 to 24 years	61,904	28,694	673	312	10.9	10.9	4.8	6.5
25 to 44 years	194,617	69,677	2,768	937	14.2	13.4	6.7	8.8

[Continued]

★ 2184 ★

Deaths and Death Rates by Race, Sex, and Age – 1900, 1910 - I

[Continued]

Age period	Registration states[1]							
	Negro population[2]				Deaths[3] per 1,000 population of age specified			
	1910	1900	Deaths at age specified during calendar year		Negro population		White population	
			1910	1900	1910	1900	1910	1900
45 to 64 years	71,988	26,859	2,236	820	31.1	30.5	16.3	18.7
65 to 84 years	16,477	6,110	1,293	507	78.5	83.0	70.7	71.6
85 years and over	1,261	577	271	114	214.9	197.6	250.2	257.0
Age unknown	1,664	971	12	12	7.2	12.4	6.7	35.0

Source: "Negro Population and Deaths in the Registration States, and Negro and White Death Rates, by Sex and Age Periods, with Percentage Distribution by Age Periods of Negro and White Population and Deaths: 1910 and 1900." U.S. Bureau of the Census. *Negro Population, 1790-1915.* Washington, D.C.: Government Printing Office, 1918, p. 308. *Notes:* 1. Includes the District of Columbia, but does not include North Carolina, 1910. 2. Population as of Apr. 15, 1910, and June 1, 1900. 3. Exclusive of stillbirths.

★ 2185 ★

Deaths

Deaths and Death Rates by Race, Sex, and Age – 1900, 1910 - II

Age period	Registration states[1] Percent distribution by age							
	Population				Deaths			
	Negro		White		Negro		White	
	1910	1900	1910	1900	1910	1900	1910	1900
Both sexes								
All ages	100.0	100.0	100.0	100.0	100.0	100.0	100.0	100.0
Under 5 years	8.8	8.6	10.3	10.4	29.7	36.5	27.1	30.0
Under 1 year	1.9	1.9	2.2	2.2	20.6	24.9	19.3	20.6
5 to 9 years	8.3	8.2	9.4	10.0	2.1	2.8	2.2	2.7
10 to 14 years	8.1	7.9	9.0	9.1	1.9	2.8	1.4	1.5
15 to 19 years	8.6	9.7	9.4	9.0	3.7	4.3	2.3	2.5
20 to 24 years	11.0	13.3	9.8	9.4	5.5	5.9	3.5	3.7
25 to 44 years	37.4	34.9	31.0	30.9	24.8	18.6	15.9	16.4
45 to 64 years	14.2	13.9	16.1	15.7	19.4	16.9	20.2	18.2
65 to 84 years	3.2	2.9	4.7	4.9	11.0	9.8	23.8	21.4
85 years and over	0.2	0.2	0.2	0.2	1.7	2.0	3.5	3.2
Age unknown	0.3	0.6	0.2	0.2	0.1	0.4	0.1	0.3
Male								
All ages	100.0	100.0	100.0	100.0	100.0	100.0	100.0	100.0
Under 5 years	8.8	8.8	10.2	10.5	30.0	38.7	27.3	31.4
Under 1 year	1.9	1.9	2.1	2.2	21.2	27.2	19.9	22.0
5 to 9 years	8.2	8.3	9.3	10.0	1.9	2.8	2.1	2.6

[Continued]

★ 2185 ★

Deaths and Death Rates by Race, Sex, and Age – 1900, 1910 - II

[Continued]

Age period	Registration states[1] Percent distribution by age							
	Population				Deaths			
	Negro		White		Negro		White	
	1910	1900	1910	1900	1910	1900	1910	1900
10 to 14 years	7.9	7.9	8.8	9.1	1.6	1.9	1.4	1.5
15 to 19 years	8.0	9.0	9.1	8.8	3.0	3.8	2.3	2.4
20 to 24 years	10.3	12.3	9.7	9.1	5.3	5.6	3.5	3.5
25 to 44 years	38.2	35.4	31.7	31.4	26.0	18.3	16.6	16.4
45 to 64 years	14.9	14.6	16.3	15.8	19.7	17.4	21.3	18.4
65 to 84 years	3.2	2.8	4.5	4.7	11.0	9.5	22.5	20.7
85 years and over	0.1	0.2	0.2	0.2	1.2	1.6	2.9	2.6
Age unknown	0.4	0.7	0.2	0.3	0.2	0.5	0.1	0.4
Female								
All ages	100.0	100.0	100.0	100.0	100.0	100.0	100.0	100.0
Under 5 years	8.8	8.4	10.5	10.3	29.3	34.4	26.7	28.5
Under 1 year	1.8	1.8	2.2	2.2	20.1	22.6	18.7	19.1
5 to 9 years	8.4	8.0	9.6	9.9	2.3	2.9	2.3	2.8
10 to 14 years	8.3	7.9	9.2	9.1	2.3	3.7	1.5	1.6
15 to 19 years	9.1	10.3	9.6	9.2	4.4	4.8	2.4	2.6
20 to 24 years	11.6	14.1	9.9	9.8	5.7	6.3	3.5	3.9
25 to 44 years	36.6	34.3	30.2	30.5	23.5	18.8	15.0	16.4
45 to 64 years	13.5	13.2	15.8	15.6	19.0	16.5	18.9	18.0
65 to 84 years	3.1	3.0	4.9	5.0	11.0	10.2	25.4	22.2
85 years and over	0.2	0.3	0.2	0.2	2.3	2.3	4.2	3.8
Age unknown	0.3	0.5	0.1	0.1	0.1	0.2	[2]	0.3

Source: "Negro Population and Deaths in the Registration States, and Negro and White Death Rates, by Sex and Age Periods, with Percentage Distribution by Age Periods of Negro and White Population and Deaths: 1910 and 1900." U.S. Bureau of the Census. *Negro Population, 1790-1915.* Washington, D.C.: Government Printing Office, 1918, p. 308. *Notes:* 1. Includes the District of Columbia, but does not include North Carolina, 1910. 2. Less than one-tenth of 1 percent.

★ 2186 ★

Deaths

Deaths and Deaths Per 1,000 Population by Sex and Age – South, North, and West, 1910

Section and age period	Registration cities of 25,000 or more population and of 2,500 Negroes: 19											
	Negro population			Negro deaths of age specified during calendar year: 1910			Deaths per 1,000 population of age specified					
							Both sexes		Male		Female	
	Both sexes	Male	Female	Both sexes	Male	Female	Negro	White	Negro	White	Negro	White
United States												
All ages	1,297,761	615,139	682,622	35,811	18,810	17,001	27.6	15.8	30.6	17.3	24.9	14.4
Under 5 years	99,850	49,193	50,657	9,501	5,071	4,430	95.2	45.2	103.1	49.0	87.5	41.3

[Continued]

★ 2186 ★

Deaths and Deaths Per 1,000 Population by Sex and Age – South, North, and West, 1910

[Continued]

Section and age period	Registration cities of 25,000 or more population and of 2,500 Negroes: 19											
	Negro population			Negro deaths of age specified during calendar year: 1910			Deaths per 1,000 population of age specified					
							Both sexes		Male		Female	
	Both sexes	Male	Female	Both sexes	Male	Female	Negro	White	Negro	White	Negro	White
Under 1 year	21,292	10,722	10,570	6,561	3,597	2,964	308.1	146.1	335.5	159.8	280.4	132.1
1 to 4 years	78,558	38,471	40,087	2,940	1,474	1,466	37.4	17.7	38.3	18.6	36.5	16.7
5 to 9 years	94,908	45,913	48,995	713	344	369	7.5	4.1	7.5	4.2	7.5	4.0
10 to 14 years	94,668	44,599	50,069	635	298	337	6.7	2.5	6.7	2.6	6.7	2.4
15 to 19 years	111,960	48,619	63,341	1,395	652	743	12.5	3.9	13.4	4.3	11.7	3.5
20 to 24 years	159,611	69,092	90,519	2,447	1,228	1,219	15.3	5.4	17.8	5.8	13.5	4.9
25 to 34 years	306,498	145,455	161,043	5,257	2,807	2,450	17.2	7.3	19.3	8.0	15.2	6.6
35 to 44 years	217,059	109,228	107,831	5,025	2,793	2,232	23.2	11.2	25.6	13.2	20.7	9.1
45 to 64 years	174,165	85,723	88,442	7,408	3,984	3,424	42.5	24.2	46.5	27.9	38.7	20.4
65 years and over	33,593	14,397	19,196	3,403	1,618	1,785	101.3	90.9	112.4	97.4	93.0	85.6
Age unknown	5,449	2,920	2,529	27	15	12	5.0	1.0	5.1	2.4	4.7	1.0
The South												
All ages	781,297	360,960	420,337	22,906	11,879	11,027	29.3	16.7	32.9	18.2	26.2	15.2
Under 5 years	63,100	31,061	32,039	5,953	3,168	2,785	94.3	40.5	102.0	43.4	86.9	37.5
Under 1 year	13,180	6,612	6,568	4,199	2,313	1,886	318.6	136.1	349.8	145.3	287.1	126.8
1 to 4 years	49,920	24,449	25,471	1,754	855	899	35.1	15.5	35.0	16.8	35.3	14.2
5 to 9 years	62,996	30,484	32,512	435	210	225	6.9	3.6	6.9	3.6	6.9	3.6
10 to 14 years	63,245	29,865	33,380	433	211	222	6.8	2.7	7.1	2.9	6.7	2.6
15 to 19 years	75,046	32,315	42,731	978	464	514	13.0	4.4	14.4	4.6	12.0	4.2
20 to 24 years	98,871	41,900	56,971	1,683	839	844	17.0	6.4	20.0	6.6	14.8	6.1
25 to 34 years	170,256	77,845	92,411	3,320	1,715	1,605	19.5	8.2	22.0	9.0	17.4	7.4
35 to 44 years	120,117	57,837	62,280	3,063	1,644	1,419	25.5	11.5	28.4	13.6	22.8	9.5
45 to 64 years	102,993	48,945	54,046	4,777	2,538	2,239	46.4	25.3	51.9	29.9	41.4	20.8
65 years and over	21,389	9,024	12,365	2,246	1,081	1,165	105.0	98.4	119.8	109.5	94.2	89.8
Age unknown	3,284	1,682	1,602	18	9	9	5.5	2.5	5.4	2.6	5.6	2.4
The North and West												
All ages	516,464	254,179	262,285	12,905	6,931	5,974	25.0	15.7	27.3	17.2	22.8	14.3
Under 5 years	36,750	18,132	18,618	3,548	1,963	1,645	96.5	45.8	105.0	49.7	88.4	41.8
Under 1 year	8,112	4,110	4,002	2,362	1,284	1,078	291.2	147.4	312.4	161.6	269.4	132.8
1 to 4 years	28,638	14,022	14,616	1,186	619	567	41.4	17.9	44.1	18.9	38.8	17.0
5 to 9 years	31,912	15,429	16,483	278	134	144	8.7	4.2	8.7	4.3	8.7	4.0
10 to 14 years	31,423	14,734	16,689	202	87	117	6.4	2.5	5.9	2.6	6.9	2.3
15 to 19 years	36,914	16,304	20,610	417	188	229	11.3	3.8	11.5	4.2	11.1	3.4
20 to 24 years	60,740	27,192	33,548	764	389	375	12.6	5.2	14.3	5.7	11.2	4.7
25 to 34 years	136,242	67,610	68,632	1,937	1,092	845	14.2	7.2	16.1	7.9	12.3	6.5
35 to 44 years	96,942	51,391	45,551	1,962	1,149	813	20.2	11.2	22.4	13.1	17.8	9.1
45 to 64 years	71,172	36,776	34,396	2,631	1,446	1,185	37.0	24.0	39.3	27.6	34.5	20.3
65 years and over	12,204	5,373	6,831	1,157	537	620	94.8	89.7	99.9	95.5	90.8	84.8
Age unknown	2,165	1,238	927	9	6	3	4.2	1.9	4.8	2.4	3.2	0.8

Source: "Negro Deaths and Deaths Per 1,000 Population, by Sex and Age Periods, for Selected Registration Cities: 1910." U.S. Bureau of the Census. *Negro Population, 1790-1915.* Washington, D.C.: Government Printing Office, 1918, p. 316.

★ 2187 ★

Deaths

Deaths at Ages Eighty-five and Over, 1975

Age	Total			White		All other	
	Both sexes	Male	Female	Male	Female	Male	Female
85 years and over	285,077	107,720	177,357	100,236	167,262	7,484	10,095
85 years	42,320	17,764	24,556	16,533	23,200	1,231	1,356
86 years	39,698	16,338	23,360	15,314	22,154	1,024	1,206
87 years	35,049	14,162	20,887	13,276	19,797	886	1,090
88 years	30,062	11,658	18,404	10,965	17,516	693	888
89 years	27,244	10,355	16,889	9,687	16,011	668	878
90 years	24,115	8,908	15,207	8,319	14,374	589	833
91 years	19,833	7,145	12,688	6,715	12,007	430	681
92 years	16,238	5,531	10,707	5,160	10,102	371	605
93 years	13,272	4,424	8,848	4,092	8,333	332	515
94 years	10,417	3,424	6,993	3,150	6,537	274	456
95 years	7,842	2,488	5,354	2,253	5,033	235	321
96 years	5,498	1,719	3,779	1,554	3,549	165	230
97 years	4,222	1,221	3,001	1,098	2,797	123	204
98 years	3,103	916	2,187	829	2,021	87	166
99 years	2,077	580	1,497	503	1,359	77	138
100 years	1,392	353	1,039	299	909	54	130
101 years	919	221	698	179	608	42	90
102 years	602	175	427	129	365	46	62
103 years	414	124	290	86	238	38	52
104 years	259	70	189	38	147	32	42
105 years	186	56	130	31	95	25	35
106 years	100	27	73	10	49	17	24
107 years	59	17	42	4	23	13	19
108 years	53	16	37	7	17	9	20
109 years	23	7	16	-	8	7	8
110 years	24	7	17	2	8	5	9
111 years	19	2	17	1	4	1	13
112 years	5	1	4	-	-	1	4
113 years	8	3	5	-	1	3	4
114 years	11	5	6	2	-	3	6
115 years	4	1	3	-	-	1	3
116 years	1	-	1	-	-	-	1
117 years	3	2	1	-	-	2	1
118 years	-	-	-	-	-	-	-
119 years	1	-	1	-	-	-	1
120 years	2	-	2	-	-	-	2
121 years	1	-	1	-	-	-	1
122 years	-	-	-	-	-	-	-
123 years	1	-	1	-	-	-	1

[Continued]

★ 2187 ★

Deaths at Ages Eighty-five and Over, 1975

[Continued]

Age	Total			White		All other	
	Both sexes	Male	Female	Male	Female	Male	Female
124 years	-	-	-	-	-	-	-
125 years	-	-	-	-	-	-	-

Source: "Deaths at Age 85 Years and Over, by Single Years of Age, Color, and Sex: United States, 1975." National Center for Health Statistics. *Vital Statistics of the United States.* Vol. II—Mortality, Part A. Hyattsville, Md. U.S. Department of Health, Education, and Welfare. Public Health Service, 1979, p. 1-6.

★ 2188 ★

Deaths

Deaths at All Ages – 1900, 1910-1915 - I

Sex and year	Negro deaths in the registration area							
	Total at all ages	Number at age specified per 1,000 at all ages[1]						
		All ages	Under 1 year	1 year	2 years	3 years	4 years	5 to 9 years
Male								
1915	38,567	1,000	157	35	14	8	5	18
1914	36,846	1,000	171	36	16	9	7	19
1913	35,267	1,000	174	38	17	10	7	21
1912	29,600	1,000	164	36	16	10	6	19
1911	29,386	1,000	173	45	20	11	8	22
1910	25,840	1,000	196	46	20	10	7	19
1900	17,772	1,000	239	61	26	16	10	28
Female								
1915	35,796	1,000	139	36	15	9	6	20
1914	33,583	1,000	156	38	18	11	7	24
1913	31,999	1,000	163	39	18	11	7	24
1912	26,450	1,000	159	39	18	10	7	21
1911	27,045	1,000	162	46	21	12	8	23
1910	23,659	1,000	181	48	22	12	8	22
1900	17,223	1,000	213	58	28	16	10	32

Source: "Negro Deaths at All Ages, and Number at Age Specified Per 1,000 At All Ages, in the Registration Area, by Sex: For Each Year, 1910-1915, and in 1900." U.S. Bureau of the Census. *Negro Population, 1790-1915.* Washington, D.C.: Government Printing Office, 1918, p. 303. *Notes:* 1. For number of deaths in each age for the years specified (except 1915) see Table 39, p. 356.

★ 2189 ★

Deaths

Deaths at All Ages – 1900, 1910-1915 - II

Sex and year	Negro deaths in the registration area							
	10 to 14 years	Number at age specified per 1,000 at all ages[1]						
		15 to 19 years	20 to 24 years	25 to 44 years	45 to 64 years	65 to 84 years	85 years and over	Age unknown
Male								
1915	17	36	61	277	229	121	18	5
1914	17	36	63	270	218	114	17	5
1913	16	38	63	269	214	111	15	7
1912	16	37	64	282	222	110	15	5
1911	18	37	63	272	210	103	14	5
1910	17	35	62	274	204	95	12	2
1900	21	40	69	227	169	77	12	5
Female								
1915	22	50	72	264	216	123	25	3
1914	21	50	69	258	206	112	26	4
1913	22	52	69	252	203	110	24	6
1912	21	51	69	259	207	112	23	4
1911	23	51	72	252	200	102	26	3
1910	22	47	69	256	193	99	21	1
1900	31	52	72	213	162	88	20	3

Source: "Negro Deaths at All Ages, and Number at Age Specified Per 1,000 At All Ages, in the Registration Area, by Sex: For Each Year, 1910-1915, and in 1900." U.S. Bureau of the Census. *Negro Population, 1790-1915.* Washington, D.C.: Government Printing Office, 1918, p. 303. *Notes:* 1. For number of deaths in each age for the years specified (except 1915) see Table 39, p. 356.

★ 2190 ★

Deaths

Deaths by Age and Sex – 1929, 1930, 1931

Age	Negro				Native White				Foreign white			
	Total	Male	Female	Males per 100 females	Total	Male	Female	Males per 100 females	Total	Male	Female	Males per 100 females
							1931					
Total	177,358	93,349	84,009	111.1	861,973	468,822	392,451	119.5	249,545	141,002	108,543	129.9
Under 1 year	22,020	12,221	9,799	124.7	106,558	60,969	45,589	133.7	51	35	16	218.8
1 to 4 years	7,573	4,033	3,540	113.9	35,912	19,555	16,357	119.6	128	81	47	172.3
5 to 9 years	2,911	1,520	1,391	109.3	18,127	10,155	7,972	127.4	227	128	99	129.3
10 to 14 years	2,975	1,496	1,479	101.1	13,664	7,889	5,775	136.6	290	152	138	110.1
15 to 19 years	7,239	3,272	3,967	82.5	20,803	11,798	9,005	131.0	749	422	327	129.1
20 to 24 years	10,714	5,094	5,620	90.6	26,109	13,552	12,557	107.9	1,980	1,018	962	105.8
25 to 29 years	10,658	5,190	5,468	94.9	25,000	12,751	12,249	104.1	3,222	1,755	1,467	119.6
30 to 34 years	10,882	5,517	5,365	102.8	26,439	13,899	12,540	110.8	4,862	2,737	2,125	128.8
35 to 39 years	12,240	6,438	5,802	111.0	30,697	16,664	14,033	118.7	8,649	5,322	3,327	160.0

[Continued]

★ 2190 ★

Deaths by Age and Sex – 1929, 1930, 1931

[Continued]

Age	Negro				Native White				Foreign white			
	Total	Male	Female	Males per 100 females	Total	Male	Female	Males per 100 females	Total	Male	Female	Males per 100 females
40 to 44 years	12,334	6,465	5,869	110.2	34,084	18,928	15,156	124.9	12,846	8,336	4,510	184.8
45 to 49 years	13,110	6,978	6,132	113.8	39,938	22,667	17,271	131.2	16,543	10,635	5,908	180.0
50 to 54 years	14,157	7,675	6,482	118.4	47,271	27,047	20,224	133.7	19,897	12,296	7,601	161.8
55 to 59 years	11,164	6,212	4,952	125.4	56,007	32,368	23,639	136.9	22,514	13,372	9,142	146.3
60 to 64 years	10,145	5,569	4,576	121.7	65,553	36,985	28,568	129.5	28,238	16,190	12,048	134.4
65 to 69 years	8,415	4,527	3,888	116.4	70,972	39,222	31,750	123.5	32,457	18,401	14,056	130.9
70 to 74 years	6,765	3,718	3,047	122.0	83,454	45,245	38,209	118.4	31,365	17,222	14,143	121.8
75 to 79 years	4,997	2,785	2,212	125.9	72,479	37,928	34,551	109.8	26,289	13,845	12,444	111.3
80 to 84 years	3,886	2,098	1,788	117.3	50,368	24,610	25,758	95.5	21,320	10,694	10,626	100.6
85 to 89 years	2,238	1,186	1,052	112.7	26,417	12,027	14,390	83.6	12,343	5,964	6,379	93.5
90 years and over[1]	2,935	1,355	1,580	85.8	11,421	4,563	6,858	66.5	5,575	2,397	3,178	75.4
1930												
Total	185,503	97,524	87,979	110.8	877,018	475,591	401,427	118.5	249,423	141,003	108,420	130.1
Under 1 year	24,178	13,397	10,781	124.3	117,738	67,142	50,596	132.7	92	57	35	162.9
1 to 4 years	8,430	4,489	3,941	113.9	39,588	21,624	17,964	120.4	184	95	89	106.7
5 to 9 years	3,182	1,692	1,490	113.6	18,926	10,669	8,257	129.2	319	175	144	121.5
10 to 14 years	3,066	1,512	1,554	97.3	13,842	7,994	5,848	136.7	325	190	135	140.7
15 to 19 years	7,704	3,348	4,356	76.9	21,543	11,916	9,627	123.8	994	507	487	104.1
20 to 24 years	10,868	5,158	5,710	90.3	27,168	14,137	13,031	108.5	2,418	1,319	1,099	120.0
25 to 29 years	11,031	5,333	5,698	93.6	25,826	13,139	12,687	103.6	3,924	2,206	1,718	128.4
30 to 34 years	10,757	5,555	5,202	106.8	26,503	13,785	12,718	108.4	5,486	3,136	2,350	133.4
35 to 39 years	12,343	6,282	6,061	103.6	30,604	16,258	14,346	113.3	9,160	5,682	3,478	163.4
40 to 44 years	12,564	6,579	5,985	109.9	33,729	18,585	15,144	122.7	13,106	8,445	4,661	181.2
45 to 49 years	13,908	7,475	6,433	116.2	39,180	22,007	17,173	128.1	16,310	10,352	5,958	173.7
50 to 54 years	14,831	8,125	6,706	121.2	47,167	27,051	20,116	134.5	19,632	12,174	7,458	163.2
55 to 59 years	11,445	6,351	5,094	124.7	55,257	31,616	23,641	133.7	22,401	13,299	9,102	146.1
60 to 64 years	10,501	5,787	4,714	122.8	65,286	37,064	28,222	131.3	28,490	16,265	12,225	133.0
65 to 69 years	8,610	4,746	3,864	122.8	73,156	40,425	32,731	123.5	31,636	17,921	13,715	130.7
70 to 74 years	7,020	3,845	3,175	121.1	82,703	44,715	37,988	117.7	30,274	16,676	13,598	122.6
75 to 79 years	5,120	2,800	2,320	120.7	71,151	36,977	34,174	108.2	26,451	13,987	12,464	112.2
80 to 84 years	4,013	2,161	1,852	116.7	50,067	24,397	25,670	95.0	20,922	10,401	10,521	98.9
85 to 89 years	2,396	1,287	1,109	116.1	26,600	11,732	14,868	78.9	11,956	5,799	6,157	94.2
90 years and over[1]	3,536	1,602	1,934	82.8	10,984	4,358	6,626	65.8	5,343	2,317	3,026	76.6
1929												
Total	189,915	99,836	90,079	110.8	907,969	488,351	419,618	116.4	261,647	147,110	114,537	128.4
Under 1 year	24,191	13,479	10,712	125.8	123,191	70,081	53,110	132.0	129	80	49	163.3
1 to 4 years	9,368	4,945	4,423	111.8	46,557	25,023	21,534	116.2	261	141	120	117.5
5 to 9 years	3,475	1,808	1,667	108.5	20,761	11,583	9,178	126.2	407	235	172	136.6
10 to 14 years	2,969	1,556	1,413	110.1	15,133	8,703	6,430	135.3	358	198	160	123.8
15 to 19 years	7,811	3,394	4,417	76.8	23,023	12,652	10,371	122.0	1,278	673	605	111.2
20 to 24 years	11,550	5,476	6,074	90.2	28,603	14,484	14,119	102.6	3,051	1,629	1,422	114.6
25 to 29 years	11,887	5,714	6,173	92.6	27,353	13,800	13,553	101.8	4,653	2,587	2,066	125.2
30 to 34 years	10,749	5,451	5,298	102.9	27,972	14,166	13,806	102.6	6,453	3,667	2,786	131.6
35 to 39 years	12,761	6,444	6,317	102.0	31,903	16,833	15,070	111.7	10,468	6,414	4,054	158.2
40 to 44 years	13,008	6,801	6,207	109.6	34,602	19,094	15,508	123.1	14,169	9,128	5,041	181.1
45 to 49 years	13,781	7,422	6,359	116.7	39,869	22,183	17,686	125.4	17,132	10,999	6,133	179.3

[Continued]

★ 2190 ★

Deaths by Age and Sex – 1929, 1930, 1931

[Continued]

Age	Negro				Native White				Foreign white			
	Total	Male	Female	Males per 100 females	Total	Male	Female	Males per 100 females	Total	Male	Female	Males per 100 females
50 to 54 years	14,629	8,027	6,602	121.6	47,288	26,752	20,536	130.3	19,800	12,136	7,664	158.4
55 to 59 years	11,223	6,245	4,978	125.5	55,892	32,027	23,865	134.2	23,201	13,657	9,544	143.1
60 to 64 years	10,370	5,688	4,682	121.5	63,545	35,648	27,897	127.8	29,028	16,648	12,380	134.5
65 to 69 years	8,341	4,634	3,707	125.0	75,661	41,425	34,236	121.0	32,624	18,310	14,314	127.9
70 to 74 years	7,094	3,971	3,123	127.2	82,551	44,334	38,217	116.0	30,522	16,798	13,724	122.4
75 to 79 years	5,715	3,228	2,487	129.8	72,625	37,451	35,174	106.5	28,066	14,709	13,357	110.1
80 to 84 years	4,471	2,351	2,120	110.9	51,906	25,271	26,635	94.9	21,854	10,777	11,077	97.3
85 to 89 years	2,697	1,441	1,256	114.7	27,928	12,345	15,583	79.2	12,729	5,991	6,738	88.9
90 years and over[1]	3,825	1,761	2,064	85.3	11,606	4,496	7,110	63.2	5,464	2,333	3,131	74.5

Source: "Negro and White Deaths (Exclusive of Stillbirths), by Age, and Sex, in the Registration Area in Continental United States: 1931, 1930, and 1929." U.S. Bureau of the Census. *Negroes in the United States: 1920-32*. Washington, D.C.: Government Printing Office, 1935, p. 451. *Note:* 1. Includes persons of unknown age.

★ 2191 ★

Deaths

Deaths by Age, Sex, Race, and Nativity of White, 1931 - I

Native white includes native born of both parents native, of one or both foreign, and of both unknown or one unknown and one native Mexicans are included with "other races."

Area and age	All deaths		Negro		White					
					Native		Foreign		Unknown	
	Males	Females	Males	Females	Males	Females	Males	Females	Males	Females
The Registration Area in Continental United States										
All ages	126,132	596,455	93,349	84,009	468,822	392,451	141,002	108,543	12,936	4,274
Under 1 year	75,558	57,316	12,221	9,799	60,969	45,589	35	16	116	89
1 to 4 years	24,700	20,963	4,033	3,540	19,555	16,357	81	47	72	82
5 to 9 years	12,120	9,768	1,520	1,391	10,155	7,972	128	99	42	49
10 to 14 years	9,790	7,644	1,496	1,479	7,889	5,775	152	138	40	36
15 to 19 years	15,993	13,731	3,272	3,967	11,798	9,005	422	327	139	48
20 to 24 years	20,429	19,631	5,094	5,620	13,552	12,557	1,018	962	237	115
25 to 29 years	20,513	19,613	5,190	5,468	12,751	12,249	1,755	1,467	319	121
30 to 34 years	23,043	20,485	5,517	5,365	13,899	12,540	2,737	2,125	382	133
35 to 39 years	29,560	23,619	6,438	5,802	16,664	14,033	5,322	3,327	668	167
40 to 44 years	34,991	26,010	6,465	5,869	18,928	15,156	8,336	4,510	805	193
45 to 49 years	41,925	29,793	6,978	6,132	22,667	17,271	10,635	5,908	1,074	210
50 to 54 years	48,800	34,797	7,675	6,482	27,047	20,224	12,296	7,601	1,284	245
55 to 59 years	53,625	38,245	6,212	4,952	32,368	23,639	13,372	9,142	1,174	266
60 to 64 years	60,626	45,753	5,569	4,576	36,985	28,568	16,190	12,048	1,444	349
65 to 69 years	63,946	50,351	4,527	3,888	39,222	31,750	18,401	14,056	1,392	416
70 to 74 years	67,965	56,056	3,718	3,047	45,245	38,209	17,222	14,143	1,409	449
75 to 79 years	55,800	49,836	2,785	2,212	37,928	34,551	13,845	12,444	935	464

[Continued]

★ 2191 ★

Deaths by Age, Sex, Race, and Nativity of White, 1931 - I

[Continued]

Area and age	All deaths		Negro		White					
					Native		Foreign		Unknown	
	Males	Females	Males	Females	Males	Females	Males	Females	Males	Females
80 to 84 years	38,264	38,717	2,098	1,788	24,610	25,758	10,694	10,626	664	405
85 to 89 years	19,587	22,144	1,186	1,052	12,027	14,390	5,964	6,379	292	225
90 to 94 years	6,123	8,582	565	611	3,574	5,331	1,834	2,492	88	85
95 to 99 years	1,324	2,042	237	300	639	1,149	407	539	17	20
100 years and over	410	709	201	382	93	155	81	125	11	9
Unknown	1,040	650	352	287	257	223	75	22	332	98
Registration States of 1920[1]										
All ages	622,020	513,273	70,888	63,536	401,628	339,422	132,483	102,941	10,293	3,150
Under 1 year	61,660	46,643	9,337	7,564	50,823	37,867	32	15	95	79
1 to 4 years	19,842	16,737	3,079	2,718	16,071	13,429	76	43	45	50
5 to 9 years	10,056	8,099	1,188	1,077	8,533	6,738	122	95	28	30
10 to 14 years	8,039	6,216	1,112	1,100	6,629	4,824	139	131	23	20
15 to 19 years	12,971	10,958	2,342	2,904	9,921	7,509	381	302	93	28
20 to 24 years	16,561	15,826	3,731	4,129	11,320	10,514	958	904	180	63
25 to 29 years	16,901	16,024	3,936	4,083	10,697	10,275	1,670	1,392	240	86
30 to 34 years	19,189	16,984	4,230	3,997	11,682	10,669	2,601	2,030	305	93
35 to 39 years	25,166	19,781	4,981	4,372	14,196	11,903	5,078	3,200	567	118
40 to 44 years	30,376	22,020	5,082	4,389	16,264	12,990	8,013	4,335	683	137
45 to 49 years	36,380	25,521	5,324	4,620	19,542	14,908	10,181	5,685	909	146
50 to 54 years	42,468	30,262	5,819	4,928	23,432	17,709	11,773	7,316	1,088	184
55 to 59 years	46,959	33,752	4,761	3,801	28,102	20,807	12,759	8,775	971	206
60 to 64 years	53,420	40,783	4,258	3,504	32,328	25,271	15,358	11,614	1,166	265
65 to 69 years	56,405	45,184	3,422	3,039	34,319	28,260	17,288	13,407	1,083	345
70 to 74 years	59,575	50,095	2,840	2,363	39,337	33,841	16,048	13,452	1,091	331
75 to 79 years	48,501	44,272	2,106	1,713	32,832	30,516	12,692	11,594	687	355
80 to 84 years	33,206	34,220	1,540	1,320	21,274	22,617	9,761	9,905	502	301
85 to 89 years	16,987	19,602	882	789	10,419	12,750	5,390	5,840	230	171
90 to 94 years	5,273	7,560	411	450	3,117	4,711	1,652	2,289	61	70
95 to 99 years	1,108	1,772	162	231	546	1,017	372	490	13	18
100 years and over	293	534	126	268	73	131	76	106	5	5
Unknown	684	418	219	177	171	166	63	21	228	49
Registration states[2]										
All ages	717,630	589,643	91,587	82,436	463,871	388,626	140,179	107,902	12,643	4,180
Under 1 year	74,485	56,426	12,049	9,669	60,270	44,999	35	16	115	87
1 to 4 years	24,301	20,639	3,967	3,501	19,303	16,147	80	46	72	82
5 to 9 years	11,977	9,632	1,504	1,376	10,047	7,879	127	98	41	47
10 to 14 years	9,669	7,544	1,472	1,451	7,803	5,716	149	135	40	36
15 to 19 years	15,767	13,489	3,209	3,901	11,672	8,870	403	316	138	45
20 to 24 years	20,071	19,283	4,987	5,514	13,363	12,384	995	935	231	110
25 to 29 years	20,143	19,222	5,072	5,342	12,561	12,046	1,738	1,442	311	115

[Continued]

★ 2191 ★

Deaths by Age, Sex, Race, and Nativity of White, 1931 - I

[Continued]

Area and age	All deaths		Negro		White					
					Native		Foreign		Unknown	
	Males	Females	Males	Females	Males	Females	Males	Females	Males	Females
30 to 34 years	22,646	20,126	5,397	5,213	13,683	12,402	2,717	2,092	373	128
35 to 39 years	29,049	23,240	6,270	5,647	16,412	13,866	5,276	3,297	653	162
40 to 44 years	34,493	25,611	6,308	5,727	18,666	14,984	8,297	4,463	794	192
45 to 49 years	41,310	29,349	6,779	5,983	22,369	17,063	10,571	5,867	1,055	202
50 to 54 years	48,178	34,369	7,518	6,354	26,717	20,015	12,228	7,556	1,254	236
55 to 59 years	52,980	37,872	6,083	4,853	32,000	23,446	13,286	9,092	1,137	257
60 to 64 years	60,023	45,344	5,479	4,506	36,613	28,327	16,103	11,988	1,412	341
65 to 69 years	63,398	49,992	4,458	3,834	38,890	31,530	18,309	14,000	1,356	410
70 to 74 years	67,436	55,657	3,673	3,003	44,898	37,948	17,131	14,085	1,377	442
75 to 79 years	55,387	49,487	2,763	2,189	37,648	34,303	13,780	12,386	909	456
80 to 84 years	38,029	38,470	2,081	1,770	24,468	25,583	10,639	10,585	649	401
85 to 89 years	19,454	21,995	1,176	1,039	11,950	14,302	5,929	6,342	288	220
90 to 94 years	6,090	8,527	562	602	3,555	5,298	1,828	2,480	86	84
95 to 99 years	1,317	2,027	237	300	636	1,142	404	537	16	20
100 years and over	403	699	197	381	93	154	80	122	10	9
Unknown	1,024	643	346	281	254	222	74	22	326	98

Source: "Deaths (Exclusive of Stillbirths), by Age, Sex, Color, and Nativity of White: 1931." U.S. Bureau of the Census. *Negroes in the United States: 1920-32*. Washington, D.C.: Government Printing Office, 1935, p. 450. *Notes:* 1. See table 3. 2. Includes the District of Columbia.

★ 2192 ★

Deaths

Deaths by Age, Sex, Race, and Nativity of White, 1931 - II

Native white includes native born of both parents native, of one or both foreign, and of both unknown or one unknown and one native. Mexicans are included with "other races."

Area and age	Indian		Chinese		Japanese		Other races	
	Males	Females	Males	Females	Males	Females	Males	Females
The Registration Area in Continental United States								
All ages	2,597	2,453	1,153	148	756	297	5,517	4,280
Under 1 year	543	467	51	28	75	53	1,548	1,275
1 to 4 years	299	312	20	17	54	43	586	565
5 to 9 years	93	91	15	8	27	20	140	138
10 to 14 years	84	91	4	4	24	10	101	111
15 to 19 years	142	158	16	9	21	14	183	203
20 to 24 years	132	150	28	11	16	5	352	211
25 to 29 years	98	102	34	11	21	19	345	176
30 to 34 years	82	99	56	10	38	20	332	193
35 to 39 years	66	80	74	8	28	39	300	163
40 to 44 years	70	81	75	6	53	23	259	172
45 to 49 years	86	70	81	9	107	16	297	177

[Continued]

★ 2192 ★

Deaths by Age, Sex, Race, and Nativity of White, 1931 - II

[Continued]

Area and age	Indian		Chinese		Japanese		Other races	
	Males	Females	Males	Females	Males	Females	Males	Females
50 to 54 years	94	83	86	4	108	13	210	145
55 to 59 years	101	81	96	3	89	11	213	151
60 to 64 years	126	70	102	4	52	4	158	134
65 to 69 years	125	106	125	7	24	1	130	127
70 to 74 years	125	105	126	4	12	-	108	99
75 to 79 years	124	84	72	-	6	6	105	75
80 to 84 years	93	86	51	-	1	-	53	54
85 to 89 years	51	49	19	-	-	-	48	49
90 to 94 years	29	40	15	3	-	-	18	20
95 to 99 years	11	17	3	-	-	-	10	17
100 years and over	12	17	3	-	-	-	9	21
Unknown	11	14	1	2	-	-	12	4
Registration States of 1920[1]								
All ages	1,228	1,083	1,083	137	719	288	3,698	2,716
Under 1 year	239	218	43	25	72	50	1,019	825
1 to 4 years	131	105	20	16	52	42	368	334
5 to 9 years	50	43	13	8	25	20	97	88
10 to 14 years	38	44	4	4	22	10	72	83
15 to 19 years	71	57	15	9	21	14	127	145
20 to 24 years	59	61	26	11	15	5	272	139
25 to 29 years	40	48	33	11	21	19	264	110
30 to 34 years	34	36	55	9	38	18	244	132
35 to 39 years	33	34	74	7	27	37	210	110
40 to 44 years	37	33	75	6	47	23	175	107
45 to 49 years	44	31	79	9	102	15	199	107
50 to 54 years	43	32	83	4	96	13	134	76
55 to 59 years	43	43	92	2	88	11	143	107
60 to 64 years	61	39	95	4	51	4	103	82
65 to 69 years	73	43	119	5	23	1	78	84
70 to 74 years	71	55	111	4	12	-	65	49
75 to 79 years	59	41	67	-	6	6	52	47
80 to 84 years	49	49	45	-	1	-	34	28
85 to 89 years	31	22	16	-	-	-	19	30
90 to 94 years	10	25	13	1	-	-	9	14
95 to 99 years	5	10	3	-	-	-	7	6
100 years and over	6	12	2	-	-	-	5	12
Unknown	1	2	-	2	-	-	2	1
Registration states[2]								
All ages	2,595	2,453	1,146	148	752	297	4,857	3,601
Under 1 year	543	467	50	28	75	53	1,348	1,107
1 to 4 years	299	312	20	17	54	43	506	491

[Continued]

★ 2192 ★

Deaths by Age, Sex, Race, and Nativity of White, 1931 - II

[Continued]

Area and age	Indian		Chinese		Japanese		Other races	
	Males	Females	Males	Females	Males	Females	Males	Females
5 to 9 years	93	91	14	8	27	20	124	113
10 to 14 years	84	91	4	4	24	10	93	101
15 to 19 years	142	158	16	9	21	14	166	176
20 to 24 years	132	150	28	11	16	5	319	174
25 to 29 years	98	102	33	11	21	19	309	145
30 to 34 years	82	99	56	10	38	20	300	162
35 to 39 years	66	80	74	8	28	39	270	141
40 to 44 years	70	81	75	6	52	23	231	135
45 to 49 years	86	70	79	9	106	16	265	139
50 to 54 years	94	83	85	4	106	13	176	108
55 to 59 years	101	81	96	3	89	11	188	129
60 to 64 years	125	70	102	4	52	4	137	104
65 to 69 years	125	106	125	7	24	1	111	104
70 to 74 years	125	105	125	4	12	-	95	70
75 to 79 years	124	84	72	-	6	6	85	63
80 to 84 years	92	86	51	-	1	-	48	45
85 to 89 years	51	49	19	-	-	-	41	43
90 to 94 years	29	40	15	3	-	-	15	20
95 to 99 years	11	17	3	-	-	-	10	11
100 years and over	12	17	3	-	-	-	8	16
Unknown	11	14	1	2	-	-	12	4

Source: "Deaths (Exclusive of Stillbirths), by Age, Sex, Color, and Nativity of White: 1931." U.S. Bureau of the Census. *Negroes in the United States: 1920-32.* Washington, D.C.: Government Printing Office, 1935, p. 450. *Notes:* 1. See table 3. 2. Includes the District of Columbia.

★ 2193 ★

Deaths

Deaths by Age, Sex, and Race in Continental United States – 1920, 1930

Age	Number					
	1930				1920	
	Negro			White		
	Total	Male	Female		Negro	White
All ages	185,503	97,524	87,979	1,144,189	130,147	1,007,117
Under 1 year	24,178	13,397	10,781	118,134	22,456	151,284
1 to 4 years	8,430	4,489	3,941	39,906	9,052	64,118
5 to 9 years	3,182	1,692	1,490	19,308	3,139	23,750
10 to 14 years	3,066	1,512	1,554	14,232	2,980	16,338
15 to 19 years	7,704	3,348	4,356	22,702	6,340	24,724
20 to 24 years	10,868	5,158	5,710	29,928	9,275	34,327
25 to 29 years	11,031	5,333	5,698	30,205	8,399	41,060

[Continued]

★ 2193 ★

Deaths by Age, Sex, and Race in Continental United States – 1920, 1930

[Continued]

Age	Number					
	1930				1920	
	Negro			White		
	Total	Male	Female		Negro	White
30 to 34 years	10,757	5,555	5,202	32,573	7,432	42,314
35 to 39 years	12,343	6,282	6,061	40,661	8,663	43,138
40 to 44 years	12,564	6,579	5,985	47,861	7,217	40,110
45 to 49 years	13,908	7,475	6,433	56,777	7,551	44,185
50 to 54 years	14,831	8,125	6,706	68,404	7,194	50,634
55 to 59 years	11,445	6,351	5,094	79,146	5,264	56,153
60 to 64 years	10,501	5,787	4,714	95,600	5,308	67,183
65 to 69 years	8,610	4,746	3,864	106,714	4,978	71,349
70 to 74 years	7,020	3,845	3,175	114,833	4,629	74,780
75 to 79 years	5,120	2,800	2,320	99,083	3,471	70,398
80 to 84 years	4,013	2,161	1,852	72,007	2,671	50,708
85 to 89 years	2,396	1,287	1,109	39,078	1,577	27,759
90 to 94 years	1,363	624	739	12,869	915	9,425
95 to 99 years	622	276	346	2,743	411	2,032
100 years and over	745	264	481	411	601	341
Unknown	806	438	368	1,014	624	1,007
	Number per 1,000 deaths at all ages					
All ages	1,000	1,000	1,000	1,000	1,000	1,000
Under 1 year	130	137	123	103	173	150
1 to 4 years	45	46	45	35	70	64
5 to 9 years	17	17	17	17	24	24
10 to 14 years	17	16	18	12	23	16
15 to 19 years	42	34	50	20	49	25
20 to 24 years	59	53	65	26	71	34
25 to 29 years	59	55	65	26	65	41
30 to 34 years	58	57	59	28	57	42
35 to 39 years	67	64	69	36	67	43
40 to 44 years	68	67	68	42	55	40
45 to 49 years	75	77	73	50	58	44
50 to 54 years	80	83	76	60	55	50
55 to 59 years	62	65	58	69	40	56
60 to 64 years	57	59	54	84	41	67
65 to 69 years	46	49	44	93	38	71
70 to 74 years	38	39	36	100	36	74
75 to 79 years	28	29	26	87	27	70
80 to 84 years	22	22	21	63	21	50

[Continued]

★ 2193 ★

Deaths by Age, Sex, and Race in Continental United States – 1920, 1930

[Continued]

Age	Number					
	1930				1920	
	Negro			White	Negro	White
	Total	Male	Female			
85 to 89 years	13	13	13	34	12	28
90 to 94 years	7	6	8	11	7	9
95 to 99 years	3	3	4	2	3	2
100 years and over	4	3	5	1	5	1
Unknown	4	4	4	1	5	1

Source: "Deaths (Exclusive of Stillbirths) of Negro, by Age, and Sex, and White by Age, 1920; and of Negro and White, by Age, 1920, Registration Area in Continental United States." U.S. Bureau of the Census. *Negroes in the United States: 1920-32.* Washington, D.C.: Government Printing Office, 1935, p. 445. *Note:* 1. Less than 1.

★ 2194 ★

Deaths

Deaths by Month of Mortality in Two Southern Cities and in Registration Cities, 1910 - I

Area	Total	January	February	March	April	May	June
Southern states							
Maryland	5,343	507	473	427	426	379	440
North Carolina	3,024	246	256	257	227	261	240
Registration cities of 100,000 or more population and of 2,500 Negroes in 1910							
Total	27,348	2,519	2,237	2,478	2,338	2,304	2,353
Southern cities	15,955	1,478	1,295	1,337	1,306	1,341	1,399
Northern and western cities	11,393	1,041	942	1,101	1,032	963	951
Southern cities							
Atlanta, Ga	1,328	104	108	121	135	126	113
Baltimore, Md	2,597	272	237	200	199	192	223
Birmingham, Ala	1,391	117	113	115	99	149	111
Louisville, Ky	1,089	104	94	89	94	101	99
Memphis, Tenn	1,492	134	118	153	122	124	134
Nashville, Tenn	950	98	72	63	68	74	79
New Orleans, La	2,933	265	231	232	272	255	258
Richmond, Va	1,416	131	108	105	110	128	146
Washington, D.C.	2,759	253	214	299	207	192	236

[Continued]

★ 2194 ★

Deaths by Month of Mortality in Two Southern Cities and in Registration Cities, 1910 - I

[Continued]

Area	Total	January	February	March	April	May	June
Northern and western cities							
Boston, Mass	317	34	29	30	28	20	31
Cambridge, Mass	75	4	2	7	15	8	9
Chicago, Ill	1,075	102	86	105	80	105	85
Cincinnati, Ohio	569	39	66	53	59	40	46
Cleveland, Ohio	167	14	19	18	17	12	13
Columbus, Ohio	262	17	17	32	20	23	14
Dayton, Ohio	99	9	5	6	13	11	9
Denver, Colo	132	10	11	15	10	11	9
Detroit, Mich	146	15	19	21	14	12	12
Indianapolis, Ind	548	45	37	54	46	46	53
Jersey City, N. J	123	14	10	5	10	12	13
Kansas City, Mo	644	51	58	65	63	59	66
Los Angeles, Cal	136	17	9	15	14	6	13
Minneapolis, Minn	56	5	8	1	5	4	4
Newark, N. J	296	24	16	26	21	22	21
New Haven, Conn	91	6	8	6	7	17	10
New York City	2,391	215	188	213	190	186	205
Bronx Borough	208	17	24	16	13	34	18
Brooklyn Borough	598	62	41	58	58	42	58
Manhattan Borough	1,473	125	116	130	115	102	123
Queens Borough	82	8	4	6	3	5	5
Richmond Borough	30	3	3	3	1	3	1
Oakland, Cal	52	4	5	3	6	2	3
Philadelphia, Pa	2,276	215	199	213	231	188	187
Pittsburgh, Pa	601	61	47	70	72	44	30
Providence, R. I	139	17	10	18	9	9	8
St. Louis, Mo	1,149	99	90	120	97	120	109
St. Paul, Minn	49	4	3	5	5	6	4

Source: "Negro Deaths by Month of Mortality in Two Southern States and in Registration Cities: 1910." U.S. Bureau of the Census. *Negro Population, 1790-1915.* Washington, D.C.: Government Printing Office, 1918, p. 303.

★ 2195 ★

Deaths

Deaths by Month of Mortality in Two Southern Cities and in Registration Cities, 1910 - II

Area	July	August	September	October	November	December
Southern states						
Maryland	535	453	414	447	426	416
North Carolina	267	247	229	289	243	262
Registration cities of 100,000 or more population and of 2,500 Negroes in 1910						
Total	2,386	2,207	1,934	2,680	2,196	2,316
Southern cities	1,384	1,313	1,126	1,249	1,336	1,351
Northern and western cities	1,002	894	808	831	860	965
Southern cities						
Atlanta, Ga	98	107	76	112	114	114
Baltimore, Md	238	217	178	218	210	213
Birmingham, Ala	123	107	109	109	109	130
Louisville, Ky	90	94	71	85	86	82
Memphis, Tenn	124	119	100	110	120	134
Nashville, Tenn	93	89	71	72	75	96
New Orleans, La	236	231	213	219	263	258
Richmond, Va	129	124	98	113	115	109
Washington, D.C.	253	225	210	211	244	215
Northern and western cities						
Boston, Mass	19	23	32	19	31	21
Cambridge, Mass	8	3	2	5	8	4
Chicago, Ill	78	111	68	62	98	95
Cincinnati, Ohio	45	35	30	41	42	53
Cleveland, Ohio	9	13	18	9	10	15
Columbus, Ohio	25	25	20	20	27	22
Dayton, Ohio	11	3	5	9	7	11
Denver, Colo	10	14	6	8	9	19
Detroit, Mich	14	7	5	5	15	7
Indianapolis, Ind	43	41	48	46	43	46
Jersey City, N. J	11	9	10	9	11	9
Kansas City, Mo	55	46	37	49	43	52
Los Angeles, Cal	16	11	5	8	12	10
Minneapolis, Minn	8	4	1	6	5	5
Newark, N. J	37	24	27	26	20	32
New Haven, Conn	7	7	5	10	5	3
New York City	228	191	209	182	174	210
Bronx Borough	8	16	10	20	17	15

[Continued]

★ 2195 ★

Deaths by Month of Mortality in Two Southern Cities and in Registration Cities, 1910 - II

[Continued]

Area	July	August	September	October	November	December
Brooklyn Borough	53	50	44	36	38	58
Manhattan Borough	151	111	137	123	112	128
Queens Borough	13	10	14	3	7	4
Richmond Borough	3	4	4	-	-	5
Oakland, Cal	5	5	5	2	8	4
Philadelphia, Pa	233	172	137	161	147	193
Pittsburgh, Pa	50	49	36	53	48	41
Providence, R. I	6	21	9	10	9	13
St. Louis, Mo	79	75	93	86	83	98
St. Paul, Minn	5	5	-	5	5	2

Source: "Negro Deaths by Month of Mortality in Two Southern States and in Registration Cities: 1910." U.S. Bureau of the Census. *Negro Population, 1790-1915.* Washington, D.C.: Government Printing Office, 1918, p. 303.

★ 2196 ★

Deaths

Deaths by Suicide – 1950, 1960, 1970

Data are based on the National Vital Statistics System.

Sex, race, and age	1950[1]	1960[1]	1970
	Deaths per 100,000 resident population		
All races			
All ages, age adjusted	11.0	10.6	11.8
All ages, crude	11.4	10.6	11.6
Under 1 year	-	...	...
1-4 years	-	...	...
5-14 years	0.2	0.3	0.3
15-24 years	4.5	5.2	8.8
25-34 years	9.1	10.0	14.1
35-44 years	14.3	14.2	16.9
45-54 years	20.9	20.7	20.0
55-64 years	27.0	23.7	21.4
65-74 years	29.3	23.0	20.8
75-84 years	31.1	27.9	21.2
85 years and over	28.8	26.0	20.4
White male			
All ages, age adjusted	18.1	17.5	18.2
All ages, crude	19.0	17.6	18.0
Under 1 year	-	...	...
1-4 years	-	...	...
5-14 years	0.3	0.5	0.5

[Continued]

★ 2196 ★

Deaths by Suicide – 1950, 1960, 1970

[Continued]

Sex, race, and age	1950[1]	1960[1]	1970
15-24 years	6.6	8.6	13.9
25-34 years	13.8	14.9	19.9
35-44 years	22.4	21.9	23.3
45-54 years	34.1	33.7	29.5
55-64 years	45.9	40.2	35.0
65-74 years	53.2	42.0	38.7
75-84 years	61.9	55.7	45.5
85 years and over	61.9	61.3	50.3
Black male			
All ages, age adjusted	7.0	7.8	9.9
All ages, crude	6.3	6.4	8.0
Under 1 year	-	...	...
1-4 years		...	...
5-14 years	-	0.1	0.1
15-24 years	4.9	4.1	10.5
25-34 years	9.3	12.4	19.2
35-44 years	10.4	12.8	12.6
45-54 years	10.4	10.8	13.8
55-64 years	16.5	16.2	10.6
65-74 years	10.0	11.3	8.7
75-84 years	6.2	6.6	8.9
85 years and over		6.9	10.3
White female			
All ages, age adjusted	5.3	5.3	7.2
All ages, crude	5.5	5.3	7.1
Under 1 year	-	...	...
1-4 years	-	...	...
5-14 years	01	0.1	0.1
15-24 years	2.7	2.3	4.2
25-34 years	5.2	5.8	9.0
35-44 years	8.2	8.1	13.0
45-54 years	10.5	10.9	13.5
55-64 years	10.7	10.9	12.3
65-74 years	10.6	8.8	9.6
75-84 years	8.4	9.2	7.2
85 years and over	8.9	6.1	6.1
Black female			
All ages, age adjusted	1.7	1.9	2.9
All ages, crude	1.5	1.6	2.6
Under 1 year	-	...	...
1-4 years		...	...
5-14 years	-	0.0	0.2
15-24 years	1.8	1.3	3.8
25-34 years	2.6	3.0	5.7

[Continued]

★ 2196 ★

Deaths by Suicide – 1950, 1960, 1970

[Continued]

Sex, race, and age	1950[1]	1960[1]	1970
35-44 years	2.0	3.0	3.7
45-54 years	3.5	3.1	3.7
55-64 years	1.1	3.0	2.0
65-74 years	1.9	2.3	2.9
75-84 years	2.4	1.3	1.7
85 years and over		-	3.2

Source: "Death Rates for Suicide, according to Sex, Race, and Age: United States, Selected Years 1950-86," *Health United States - 1988*, March 1989, p. 74. Primary source: *Vital Statistics of the United States*. National Center for Health Statistics, U.S. Government Printing Office, Washington, D.C. *Notes:* For data years shown, the code numbers for cause of death are based on the then current *International Classification of Diseases*, which are described in Appendix II, tables IV and V. 1. Includes deaths of nonresidents of the United States.

★ 2197 ★

Deaths

Deaths from Specified Causes, Sex and Race – 1910, 1913

Cause of death	Negro deaths in the registration area from specified causes				Deaths from specified causes per 1,000 deaths from all causes						Deaths from specified causes per 100,000 population: 1910	
	1913			1910	1913				1910			
	Both sexes	Male	Female		Negro: Both sexes	Negro: Male	Negro: Female	White	Negro	White	Negro	White
All causes	67,266	35,267	31,999	49,499	1,000	1,000	1,000	1,000	1,000	1,000	2,546	1,457
Tuberculosis	11,851	6,241	5,610	8,998	176	177	175	98	182	102	463	148
Pneumonia	6,702	3,783	2,919	5,796	100	107	91	94	117	98	298	142
Organic diseases of the heart	6,030	3,120	2,910	4,120	90	88	91	99	83	95	212	139
Nephritis, Bright's disease	5,239	2,873	2,366	3,533	78	81	74	73	71	66	182	96
Violent deaths, except suicide	4,413	3,403	1,010	2,609	66	96	32	66	53	61	134	88
Congenital debility and malformations	3,059	1,621	1,438	2,140	45	46	45	60	43	51	110	74
Diarrhea and enteritis (under 2 years)	2,750	1,465	1,285	2,792	41	42	40	54	56	68	144	99
Cerebral hemorrhage and softening	2,567	1,161	1,406	1,705	38	33	45	56	34	52	88	76
Cancer	1,767	510	1,257	1,100	26	14	39	59	22	53	57	77
Typhoid	1,190	637	553	798	18	18	17	12	16	16	41	23
Bronchitis	878	442	436	793	13	13	14	13	16	16	41	23
Puerperal fever and affections	796	-	796	532	12	-	25	11	11	10	27	15
Whooping cough	691	319	372	588	10	9	12	7	12	7	30	11
Influenza	587	270	317	511	9	8	10	9	10	10	26	14
Meningitis	532	319	213	369	8	9	7	7	7	10	19	14
Malaria	501	235	266	413	7	7	8	1	8	1	21	1
Hernia, intestinal obstruction	449	256	193	316	7	7	6	8	6	8	16	12
Cirrhosis of the liver	417	260	157	265	6	7	5	10	5	10	14	14
Diphtheria and croup	342	161	181	231	5	5	6	14	5	15	12	22
Measles	334	163	171	181	5	5	5	9	4	8	9	12
Appendicitis	318	177	141	225	5	5	4	9	5	8	12	11
Rheumatism	299	113	186	208	4	3	6	5	4	5	11	7
Diabetes	258	129	129	142	4	4	4	11	3	10	7	15
Suicide	207	144	63	162	3	4	2	12	3	11	8	16
Erysipelas	63	38	25	83	1	1	1	3	2	3	4	5
Scarlet fever	55	28	27	71	1	1	1	7	1	8	4	12
Smallpox	16	9	7	12	[1]	[1]	[1]	[1]	[1]	[1]	1	[1]
All other and unknown causes	14,955	7,390	7,565	10,806	222	210	236	192	218	198	556	289

Source: "Negro and White Deaths from Specified Causes: 1913 and 1910." U.S. Bureau of the Census. *Negro Population, 1790-1915*. Washington, D.C.: Government Printing Office, 1918, p. 314. *Note:* 1. Less than 1 per 1,000.

★ 2198 ★

Deaths

Deaths in Cities and Rural Districts by Race, 1930

Area	Total	Negro		Indian	Chinese	Japanese	Other colored
		Number	Percent of total				
Registration states	194,082	182,021	93.79	5,384	1,331	1,109	4,237
Cities	87,316	83,739	95.90	454	1,025	682	1,416
Rural	106,766	98,282	92.05	4,930	306	427	2,821
Alabama							
Cities	4,516	4,515	99.98	-	1	-	-
Rural	9,896	9,892	99.96	4	-	-	-
Arizona							
Cities	602	131	21.76	39	4	5	423
Rural	2,397	75	3.13	790	11	5	1,516
Arkansas							
Cities	1,344	1,344	100.0	-	-	-	-
Rural	5,122	5,117	99.90	-	4	-	1
California							
Cities	2,095	844	40.29	53	430	475	293
Rural	1,542	313	20.30	381	206	291	351
Colorado							
Cities	362	217	59.94	1	5	15	124
Rural	689	85	12.34	23	2	12	567
Connecticut							
Cities	435	429	98.62	1	1	-	4
Rural	88	84	-	3	1	-	-
Delaware							
Cities	280	280	100.0	-	-	-	-
Rural	427	426	99.7	-	-	-	1
Florida							
Cities	2,939	2,930	99.69	1	4	1	3
Rural	4,243	4,236	99.84	4	-	2	1
Georgia							
Cities	6,088	6,085	99.95	-	3	-	-
Rural	11,102	11,097	99.95	3	2	-	-
Idaho							
Cities	16	7	-	3	2	3	1
Rural	145	6	4.14	122	3	10	4
Illinois							
Cities	4,951	4,834	97.64	6	77	7	27
Rural	1,010	990	98.02	1	6	1	12
Indiana							
Cities	1,931	1,812	93.84	1	4	-	114
Rural	382	373	97.64	-	-	-	9
Iowa							
Cities	276	243	88.04	-	-	-	33
Rural	87	55	-	11	-	-	21
Kansas							
Cities	765	758	99.08	6	-	-	1
Rural	337	324	96.14	10	-	-	3

[Continued]

★ 2198 ★

Deaths in Cities and Rural Districts by Race, 1930

[Continued]

Area	Total	Negro		Indian	Chinese	Japanese	Other colored
		Number	Percent of total				
Kentucky							
Cities	2,190	2,189	99.95	-	1	-	-
Rural	2,560	2,559	99.96	1	-	-	-
Louisiana							
Cities	4,937	4,919	99.64	-	10	1	7
Rural	7,149	7,117	99.55	25	4	-	3
Maine							
Cities	12	8	-	2	2	-	-
Rural	29	10	-	19	-	-	-
Maryland							
Cities	3,053	3,041	99.61	-	9	-	3
Rural	2,211	2,210	99.95	-	1	-	-
Massachusetts							
Cities	789	721	91.38	4	49	4	11
Rural	119	113	94.96	2	3	-	1
Michigan							
Cities	2,560	2,408	94.06	16	19	1	116
Rural	530	378	71.32	128	2	-	22
Minnesota							
Cities	190	167	87.89	12	8	2	1
Rural	285	29	10.18	252	1	-	3
Mississippi							
Cities	2,610	2,607	99.89	-	2	-	1
Rural	12,351	12,303	99.61	27	2	-	19
Missouri							
Cities	3,313	3,269	98.67	4	6	1	33
Rural	1,340	1,335	99.63	2	-	-	3
Montana							
Cities	30	10	-	5	10	1	4
Rural	333	18	5.41	300	8	3	4
Nebraska							
Cities	267	230	86.14	3	1	1	32
Rural	200	25	12.50	1	6	78	
Nevada							
Cities	24	7	-	10	7	-	-
Rural	132	7	5.30	108	9	3	5
New Hampshire							
Cities	6	5	-	-	1	-	-
Rural	3	2	-	1	-	-	-
New Jersey							
Cities	2,588	2,559	98.88	2	23	1	3
Rural	964	960	99.59	1	1	1	1
New Mexico							
Cities	30	22	-	7	-	1	-
Rural	381	37	9.71	341	1	-	2

[Continued]

★ 2198 ★

Deaths in Cities and Rural Districts by Race, 1930

[Continued]

Area	Total	Negro		Indian	Chinese	Japanese	Other colored
		Number	Percent of total				
New York							
Cities	6,568	6,296	95.86	35	177	27	33
Rural	631	545	86.37	75	6	2	3
North Carolina							
Cities	3,959	3,957	99.95	1	1	-	-
Rural	10,196	10,019	176	1	-	-	
North Dakota							
Cities	5	2	-	2	-	1	-
Rural	143	3	2.10	137	1	1	1
Ohio							
Cities	4,812	4,783	99.40	2	16	4	7
Rural	1,027	1,020	99.32	1	2	-	4
Oklahoma							
Cities	1,254	1,055	84.13	154	5	-	40
Rural	1,809	1,187	65.62	581	-	1	40
Oregon							
Cities	142	46	32.39	10	46	30	10
Rural	166	9	5.42	118	13	16	10
Pennsylvania							
Cities	6,136	6,092	99.28	2	34	1	7
Rural	1,375	1,367	99.42	4	2	-	2
Rhode Island							
Cities	203	194	95.57	6	3	-	-
Rural	28	25	-	3	-	-	-
South Carolina							
Cities	2,580	2,579	99.96	-	-	1	-
Rural	10,582	10,581	99.99	1	-	-	-
South Dakota							
Cities	9	5	-	2	1	-	1
Rural	543	7	1.29	530	1	-	5
Tennessee							
Cities	4,620	4,616	99.91	-	3	-	1
Rural	4,132	4,128	99.90	4	-	-	-
Utah							
Cities	63	22	-	2	6	10	23
Rural	51	1	-	13	-	14	23
Vermont							
Cities	3	3	-	-	-	-	-
Rural	6	5	-	-	-	-	1
Virginia							
Cities	4,001	3,994	99.83	1	3	1	2
Rural	7,721	7,705	99.79	12	2	1	1
Washington							
Cities	307	105	34.20	34	44	85	39
Rural	394	39	9.90	286	8	49	12

[Continued]

★ 2198 ★

Deaths in Cities and Rural Districts by Race, 1930

[Continued]

Area	Total	Negro		Indian	Chinese	Japanese	Other colored
		Number	Percent of total				
West Virginia							
Cities	479	478	99.79	-	-	-	1
Rural	1,377	1,376	99.93	1	-	-	-
Wisconsin							
Cities	158	131	82.91	25	1	-	1
Rural	344	70	269	1	-	4	
Wyoming							
Cities	26	10	-	-	2	-	14
Rural	187	19	10.16	70	1	9	88
District of Columbia	2,792	2,780	99.57	2	4	3	3

Source: "Deaths of Colored Persons (Exclusive of Stillbirths), in Cities and Rural Districts of Registration States, by Race: 1930." U.S. Bureau of the Census. *Negroes in the United States: 1920-32.* Washington, D.C.: Government Printing Office, 1935, p. 448.

★ 2199 ★

Deaths

Deaths in Registration Area by Age and Sex – 1900, 1915

Age	Number						Number per 1,000 deaths at all ages					
	1915				1900		1915				1900	
	Negro			White			Negro			White		
	Total	Male	Female		Negro	White	Total	Male	Female		Negro	White
All ages	74,363	38,567	35,796	831,181	34,995	503,569	1,000	1,000	1,000	1,000	1,000	1,000
Under 1 year	11,034	6,052	4,982	136,866	7,914	103,662	148	157	139	165	226	206
1 year	2,637	1,354	1,283	26,131	2,082	24,616	35	35	36	31	59	49
2 years	1,097	559	538	11,257	950	11,166	15	14	15	14	27	22
3 years	635	296	339	7,018	555	7,249	9	8	9	8	16	14
4 years	432	210	222	5,201	339	5,435	6	5	6	6	10	11
5 to 9 years	1,436	711	724	16,203	1,062	14,587	19	18	20	19	30	29
10 to 14 years	1,412	640	772	11,106	909	8,218	19	17	22	13	26	16
15 to 19 years	3,155	1,373	1,782	17,918	1,608	12,851	42	36	50	22	46	26
20 to 24 years	4,935	2,371	2,564	27,473	2,461	19,710	66	61	72	33	70	39
25 to 29 years	5,022	2,512	2,510	30,387	2,221	22,237	68	65	70	37	63	44
30 to 34 years	4,712	2,466	2,246	31,411	1,826	21,780	63	64	63	38	52	43
35 to 39 years	5,477	3,023	2,454	35,083	1,891	22,567	74	78	69	42	54	45
40 to 44 years	4,895	2,664	2,231	36,423	1,764	21,448	66	69	62	44	50	43
45 to 49 years	4,555	2,487	2,068	40,036	1,626	20,758	61	64	58	48	46	41
50 to 54 years	4,712	2,519	2,193	44,992	1,653	22,501	63	65	61	54	47	45
55 to 59 years	3,702	1,947	1,755	49,289	1,289	23,662	50	50	49	59	37	47

[Continued]

★ 2199 ★

Deaths in Registration Area by Age and Sex – 1900, 1915

[Continued]

Age	Number						Number per 1,000 deaths at all ages					
	1915				1900		1915				1900	
	Negro			White			Negro			White		
	Total	Male	Female		Negro	White	Total	Male	Female		Negro	White
60 to 64 years	3,591	1,869	1,722	53,974	1,237	26,343	48	48	48	65	35	52
65 to 69 years	3,032	1,557	1,475	59,238	1,037	28,041	41	40	41	71	30	56
70 to 74 years	2,772	1,498	1,274	62,979	820	28,190	37	39	36	76	23	56
75 to 79 years	1,890	960	930	55,794	579	24,857	25	25	26	67	17	49
80 to 84 years	1,359	646	713	40,727	459	18,380	18	17	20	49	13	36
85 to 89 years	728	353	375	21,537	251	9,385	10	9	10	26	7	19
90 to 94 years	414	162	252	7,332	148	3,216	6	4	7	9	4	6
95 to 99 years	197	75	122	1,666	167	940	3	2	3	2	5	2
100 years and over	239	86	153	291	-	-	3	2	4	[1]	-	-
Age unknown	294	177	117	836	147	1,770	4	8	3	1	4	4

Source: "Deaths in Registration Area." U.S. Bureau of the Census. *Negro Population, 1790-1915.* Washington, D.C.: Government Printing Office, 1918, p. 303. *Note:* 1. Less than 1.

★ 2200 ★

Deaths

Deaths in the Registration Area of Continental United States – 1920, 1930, 1931

State	1931			1930			1920		
	Total	Male	Female	Total	Male	Female	Total	Male	Female
The registration area in continental United States	177,358	93,349	84,009	185,503	97,524	87,979	130,147	65,426	64,721
Alabama	13,306	6,871	6,435	14,407	7,376	7,031	2,723[1]	1,410[1]	1,313[1]
Arizona	208	139	69	206	120	86	[2]	[2]	[2]
Arkansas	5,680	2,983	2,697	6,461	3,344	3,117	[2]	[2]	[2]
California	1,239	681	558	1,157	637	520	779	437	342
Colorado	278	151	127	302	178	124	303	172	131
Connecticut	514	254	260	513	290	223	491	253	238
Delaware	696	394	302	706	391	315	668	337	331
District of Columbia	2,958	1,542	1,416	2,780	1,424	1,356	2,289	1,040	1,249
Florida	7,032	3,915	3,117	7,166	4,031	3,135	5,134	2,748	2,386
Georgia	15,994	8,225	7,769	17,182	8,806	8,376	3,388[1]	1,619[1]	1,769[1]
Idaho	23	14	9	13	9	4	[2]	[2]	[2]
Illinois	6,191	3,453	2,738	5,824	3,210	2,614	3,925	2,057	1,868
Indiana	1,959	1,053	906	2,185	1,150	1,035	1,802	944	858
Iowa	293	158	135	298	170	128	[2]	[2]	[2]
Kansas	1,123	611	512	1,082	538	544	1,189	619	570
Kentucky	4,548	2,487	2,061	4,784	2,573	2,175	4,560	2,262	2,298
Louisiana	11,219	5,838	5,381	12,036	6,313	5,723	10,722	5,258	5,464
Maine	13	10	3	18	12	6	31	10	12

[Continued]

★ 2200 ★

Deaths in the Registration Area of Continental United States – 1920, 1930, 1931

[Continued]

State	1931			1930			1920		
	Total	Male	Female	Total	Male	Female	Total	Male	Female
Maryland	5,386	2,893	2,493	5,251	2,808	2,443	5,198	2,585	2,613
Massachusetts	832	449	383	834	432	402	993	495	498
Michigan	2,670	1,482	1,188	2,786	1,571	1,215	1,529	925	604
Minnesota	162	89	73	196	107	89	188	110	78
Mississippi	13,296	6,713	6,583	14,910	7,577	7,333	14,092	6,794	7,298
Missouri	4,643	2,506	2,137	4,604	2,538	2,066	3,761	1,808	1,893
Montana	24	14	10	28	17	11	41	25	16
Nebraska	271	145	126	255	151	104	228	138	90
Nevada	17	9	8	14	8	6	[2]	[2]	[2]
New Hampshire	5	1	4	7	4	3	11	6	5
New Jersey	3,526	1,908	1,618	3,519	1,904	1,615	2,460	1,211	1,249
New Mexico	71	45	26	59	34	25	[2]	2,009	[2]
New York	7,137	3,790	3,347	6,841	3,634	3,207	3,938	6,018	1,929
North Carolina	12,797	6,343	6,454	13,976	6,928	7,048	12,315	2[1]	6,297
North Dakota	4	2	2	5	4	1	2[1]	2,254	[2]
Ohio	5,787	3,304	2,483	5,803	3,267	2,536	4,010	86[1]	1,756
Oklahoma	2,106	1,127	979	2,242	1,204	1,038	170[1]	16	84[1]
Oregon	37	26	11	55	36	19	33	3,343	17
Pennsylvania	7,664	4,195	3,469	7,459	4,057	3,402	6,065	151	2,722
Rhode Island	181	98	83	219	125	94	270	7,095	119
South Carolina	12,368	6,198	6,170	13,160	6,683	6,477	14,338	[2]	7,243
South Dakota	6	2	4	12	7	5	[2]	3,971	[2]
Tennessee	8,013	4,217	3,796	8,744	4,600	4,144	8,169	952	4,198
Texas[3]	3,335	1,762	1,573	3,482	1,828	1,654	1,866	21	914
Utah	20	8	12	23	18	5	29	6	8
Vermont	7	3	4	8	3	5	6	[2]	[2]
Virginia	11,541	5,939	5,602	11,699	6,074	5,625	12,130	5,985	6,145
Washington	124	74	50	144	82	62	143	85	58
West Virginia	1,871	1,112	759	1,854	1,106	748	42[1]	25[1]	17[1]
Wisconsin	163	104	59	201	124	77	116	75	41
Wyoming	20	12	8	29	21	8	[2]	[2]	[2]

Source: "Deaths of Negroes (Exclusive of Stillbirths) in the Registration Area of Continental United States: 1931, 1930, 1920." U.S. Bureau of the Census. *Negroes in the United States: 1920-32*. Washington, D.C.: Government Printing Office, 1935, p. 446. *Notes:* 1. Nonregistration state; data for only those cities with satisfactory registration of deaths. 2. Not in registration area. 3. Not a registration state; covers data for 8 cities in 1931 and 1930, and for only 6 cities in 1920.

★ 2201 ★

Deaths

Homicides and Related Deaths – 1950, 1960, 1970

Deaths are based on the National Vital Statistics System.

Sex, race, and age	1950[1]	1960[1]	1970
	Deaths per 100,000 resident population		
All Races			
All ages, age justified	5.4	5.2	9.1
All ages, crude	5.3	4.7	8.3
Under 1 year	4.4	4.8	4.3
1-4 years	0.6	0.7	1.9
5-14 years	0.5	0.5	0.9
15-24 years	6.3	5.9	11.7
25-34 years	9.9	9.7	16.6
35-44 years	8.8	8.1	13.7
45-54 years	6.1	6.2	10.1
55-64 years	4.0	4.2	7.1
65-74 years	3.2	2.8	5.0
75-84 years	2.6	2.4	4.0
85 years and older	2.3	2.4	4.5
White male			
All ages, age justified	3.9	3.9	7.3
All ages, crude	3.9	3.6	6.8
Under 1 year	4.3	3.8	2.9
1-4 years	0.4	0.6	1.4
5-14 years	0.4	0.4	0.5
15-24 years	3.7	4.4	7.9
25-34 years	5.4	6.2	13.0
35-44 years	6.4	5.5	11.0
45-54 years	5.5	5.0	9.0
55-64 years	4.4	4.3	7.7
65-74 years	4.1	3.4	5.6
75-84 years	3.5	2.7	5.1
85 years and older	1.8	2.7	7.0
Black male			
All ages, age justified	51.1	44.9	82.1
All ages, crude	47.3	36.6	67.5
Under 1 year	1.8	10.3	14.3
1-4 years		1.7	5.1
5-14 years	1.8	1.4	4.2
15-24 years	58.9	46.4	102.5
25-34 years	110.5	92.0	158.5
35-44 years	83.7	77.5	126.2
45-54 years	54.6	54.8	100.6
55-64 years	35.7	31.8	59.8
65-74 years	18.7	19.1	40.6
75-84 years	11.5	16.1	18.9
85 years and older		10.3	23.1

[Continued]

★ 2201 ★

Homicides and Related Deaths – 1950, 1960, 1970

[Continued]

Sex, race, and age	1950[1]	1960[1]	1970
White female			
All ages, age justified	1.4	1.5	2.2
All ages, crude	1.4	1.4	2.1
Under 1 year	3.9	3.5	2.9
1-4 years	0.6	0.5	1.2
5-14 years	0.4	0.3	0.5
15-24 years	1.3	1.5	2.7
25-34 years	1.9	2.0	3.4
35-44 years	2.2	2.2	3.2
45-54 years	1.6	1.9	2.2
55-64 years	1.3	1.5	2.0
65-74 years	1.1	1.1	1.7
75-84 years	1.2	1.2	2.5
85 years and older	1.9	1.5	2.0
Black female			
All ages, age justified	11.7	11.8	15.0
All ages, crude	11.5	10.4	13.2
Under 1 year	2.6	13.8	10.7
1-4 years		1.7	6.3
5-14 years	1.2	1.0	2.0
15-24 years	16.5	11.9	17.7
25-34 years	26.6	24.9	25.6
35-44 years	17.8	20.5	25.1
45-54 years	8.5	12.7	17.5
55-64 years	3.6	6.8	8.1
65-74 years	3.4	3.3	7.7
75-84 years	4.0	2.5	5.7
85 years and older		2.6	11.1

Source: "Death Rates for Homicide and Legal Intervention, according to Sex, Race, and Age: United States, Selected Years 1950-86," *Health United States - 1988*, March 1989, p. 73. Primary source: National Center for Health Statistics, *Vital Statistics of the United States*: Vol. II, Mortality, Part A 1950-86, U.S. Government Printing Office, Washington, DC. *Notes:* For data years shown, the code numbers for cause of death are based on the then current *International Classification of Diseases*, which are described in Appendix II, tables IV and V. 1. Includes deaths of nonresidents of the United States.

★ 2202 ★

Deaths

Homicides by Race in Cities Having 25,000 or More Black Inhabitants, 1930

	Total	Colored[1]	White	Percent of total		Percent colored[1] population of total population
				Colored	White	
Atlanta, Ga	143	115	28	80.4	19.6	33.4
Baltimore, Md	72	41	31	56.9	43.1	17.8
Birmingham, Ala	127	106	21	83.5	16.5	38.1
Charleston, S.C.	17	16	1	94.1	5.9	45.1
Charlotte, N.C.	31	29	2	93.5	6.5	30.4
Chattanooga, Tenn	64	48	16	75.0	25.0	27.7
Chicago, Ill	488	174	314	35.7	64.3	7.7
Cincinnati, Ohio	87	48	39	55.2	44.8	10.7
Cleveland, Ohio	148	65	83	43.9	56.1	8.2
Columbus, Ohio	34	16	18	47.1	52.9	11.4
Dallas, Tex	66	35	31	53.0	47.0	17.2
Detroit, Mich	207	96	111	46.4	53.6	8.3
Houston, Tex	78	48	30	61.5	38.5	26.5
Indianapolis, Ind	39	19	20	48.7	51.3	12.1
Jacksonville, Fla	45	31	14	68.9	31.1	37.1
Kansas City, Mo	91	50	41	54.9	45.1	10.5
Los Angeles, Calif	87	20	67	23.0	77.0	13.3
Louisville, Ky	54	37	17	68.5	31.5	15.4
Memphis, Tenn	149	121	28	81.2	18.8	38.1
Miami, Fla	42	30	12	71.4	28.6	22.7
Montgomery, Ala	23	17	6	73.9	26.1	45.4
Nashville, Tenn	59	42	17	71.2	28.8	27.8
Newark, N.J.	54	27	27	50.0	50.0	9.1
New Orleans, La	107	64	43	59.8	40.2	28.6
New York, N.Y	525	131	394	25.0	75.0	5.0
Norfolk, Va	40	29	11	72.5	27.5	34.1
Philadelphia, Pa	142	68	74	47.9	52.1	11.5
Pittsburgh, Pa	64	23	41	35.9	64.1	8.3
Richmond, Va	29	23	6	79.3	20.7	28.9
St. Louis, Mo	143	68	75	47.6	52.4	11.6
Savannah, Ga	31	29	2	93.5	6.5	45.8
Shreveport, La	36	27	9	75.0	25.0	35.4
Washington, D.C.	65	44	21	67.7	32.3	27.3
Winston-Salem, N.C.	16	15	1	93.8	6.3	43.3

Source: "Deaths from Homicide, by Color, in Cities Having 25,000 or More Negro Inhabitants: 1930." U.S. Bureau of the Census. *Negroes in the United States: 1920-32.* Washington, D.C.:Government Printing Offices, 1935, p. 457. *Note:* 1. Includes Negro, and other nonwhite races.

★ 2203 ★

Deaths

Ill-defined Causes of Deaths – 1930, 1931

Cause of death	1930			1931		
	Total	Male	Female	Total	Male	Female
Ill-defined causes of death	11,407	6,039	5,368	10,483	5,464	5,019
Sudden death	919	483	436	763	414	349
Cause of death ill-defined	2,080	1,132	948	1,934	1,012	922
Cause of death not specified or unknown	8,408	4,424	3,984	7,786	4,038	3,748

Source: "Negro Deaths (Exclusive of Stillbirths) From Each Cause, by Sex, in Registration States (Including District of Columbia): 1930." and "Negro Deaths Exclusive of Stillbirths) From Each Cause, by Sex, in Registration States (Including District of Columbia: 1931." U.S. Bureau of the Census. *Negroes in the United States: 1920-32.* Washington, D.C.: Government Printing Office, 1935, pp. 465, 467. Adapted by the editors.

★ 2204 ★

Deaths

Maternal Mortality Rates by Pregnancy and Other Complications – 1950, 1960, 1970

Data are based on the National Vital Statistics System.

Race and age	1950[1]	1960[1]	1970	1980	1983	1984	1985	1986
	Deaths per 100,000 live births							
All races								
All ages, age adjusted	73.8	32.2	21.5	9.6	8.0	7.4	7.9	7.0
All ages, crude	83.3	37.1	21.5	9.2	8.0	7.8	7.8	7.2
Under 20 years	70.7	22.7	18.9	7.6	5.4	6.3	6.9	5.9
20-24 years	47.6	20.7	13.0	5.8	7.5	4.3	5.4	5.7
25-29 years	63.5	29.8	17.0	7.7	6.6	6.9	6.4	5.8
30-34 years	107.7	50.3	31.6	13.6	9.1	11.5	8.9	7.8
35 years and over[2]	222.0	104.3	81.9	36.3	20.7	21.9	25.0	21.4
White								
All ages, age adjusted	53.2	22.4	14.5	7.0	5.9	5.0	5.1	4.7
All ages, crude	61.1	26.0	14.4	6.7	5.9	5.4	5.2	4.9
Under 20 years	44.9	14.8	13.9	5.9	4.4[3]	4.3[3]	4.3[3]	4.1[3]
20-24 years	35.7	15.3	8.4	4.3	4.9	2.0[3]	3.4	3.7
25-29 years	45.0	20.3	11.2	5.5	5.2	5.7	4.7	3.6
30-34 years	75.9	34.3	18.8	9.4	6.0	7.8	5.2	5.2
35 years and over[2]	174.1	73.9	59.6	25.8	17.3	16.0	17.8	16.1
Black								
All ages, age adjusted	-	92.1	64.2	24.0	19.3	20.9	22.2	19.3
All ages, crude	-	103.6	59.8	21.5	18.3	19.7	20.4	18.8
Under 20 years	-	54.8	31.8	12.8	7.0[3]	11.4[3]	12.1[3]	10.6[3]

[Continued]

★ 2204 ★

Maternal Mortality Rates by Pregnancy and Other Complications – 1950, 1960, 1970

[Continued]

Race and age	1950[1]	1960[1]	1970	1980	1983	1984	1985	1986
20-24 years	-	56.9	41.0	13.4	20.2	15.2	14.0	13.9
25-29 years	-	92.8	63.8	21.4	16.0	15.6	18.4	19.3
30-34 years	-	150.6	115.6	41.9	31.1	37.9	35.8	29.0
35 years and over[2]	-	299.5	204.7	96.5	41.4[3]	67.6[3]	72.6	58.6[3]

Source: "Maternal Mortality Rates for Complications of Pregnancy, Childbirth, and the Puerperium, according to Race and Age: United States, Selected Years 1950-86," *Health United States - 1988*, March 1989, p. 71. Primary source: Vital *Statistics of the United States; Current Population Reports*. National Center for Health Statistics, U.S. Government Printing Office, Washington, DC. *Notes:* For data years shown, the code numbers for cause of death are based on the then current *International Classification of Diseases*, which are described in Appendix II, tables IV and V. 1. Includes deaths of nonresidents of the United States. 2. Rates computed by relating deaths of women 35 years and over to live births to women 35-49 years. 3. Based on fewer than 20 deaths.

★ 2205 ★

Deaths

Maternal Mortality Rates, 1973-75

Maternal deaths are those assigned to complications of pregnancy, childbirth, and the puerperium, category numbers 630-678 of the Eighth Revision International Classification of Diseases, Adapted, 1965. Rates per 100,000 live births in specific group, 1973-75.

Division and state	Total	White	All other
United States	14.2	9.9	32.9
Geographic divisions			
New England	5.3	4.5[1]	15.4[1]
Middle Atlantic	14.4	10.0	34.0
East North Central	11.8	8.5	28.7
West North Central	12.9	11.0	32.7
South Atlantic	17.6	9.7	36.3
East South Central	22.8	13.7	46.7
West South Central	17.6	12.1	38.0
Mountain	11.8	11.1	18.5[1]
Pacific	11.1	9.7	18.4
New England			
Maine	2.2[1]	2.2[1]	-
New Hampshire	2.9[1]	3.0[1]	-
Vermont	-	-	-
Massachusetts	2.8[1]	2.6[1]	6.5[1]
Rhode Island	5.8[1]	6.2[1]	-
Connecticut	12.7[1]	10.3[1]	29.7[1]
Middle Atlantic			
New York	17.6	11.7	39.6
New Jersey	13.8	11.0	24.8[1]

[Continued]

★ 2205 ★

Maternal Mortality Rates, 1973-75

[Continued]

Division and state	Total	White	All other
Pennsylvania	9.7	6.8	28.6[1]
East North Central			
Ohio	11.0	8.7	26.0[1]
Indiana	11.6	8.5[1]	36.6[1]
Illinois	13.6	10.0	25.7
Michigan	13.8	8.6	37.0
Wisconsin	4.7[1]	4.5[1]	7.0[1]
West South Central			
Minnesota	6.6[1]	5.0[1]	44.9[1]
Iowa	9.1[1]	8.5[1]	29.1[1]
Missouri	16.4	11.0[1]	43.9[1]
North Dakota	23.1[1]	25.1[1]	-
South Dakota	18.1[1]	20.9[1]	-
Nebraska	12.8[1]	12.1[1]	23.5[1]
Kansas	16.2[1]	16.6[1]	11.3[1]
South Atlantic			
Delaware	12.1[1]	10.4[1]	18.1[1]
Maryland	11.2[1]	6.9[1]	22.9[1]
District of Columbia	26.1[1]	-	30.1[1]
Virginia	12.7	5.5[1]	35.6[1]
West Virginia	12.0[1]	11.3[1]	27.5[1]
North Carolina	20.3	14.0	34.1
South Carolina	21.5	8.0[1]	42.2
Georgia	24.5	9.9[1]	51.8
Florida	15.7	10.9	29.5
East South Central			
Kentucky	16.1	12.2[1]	54.5[1]
Tennessee	28.3	19.5	59.3
Alabama	24.3	9.5[1]	51.9
Mississippi	21.1	11.6[1]	31.4
West South Central			
Arkansas	13.6[1]	5.2[1]	38.1[1]
Louisiana	16.5	4.1[1]	35.3
Oklahoma	14.3[1]	10.7[1]	30.5[1]
Texas	19.3	15.1	41.8
Mountain			
Montana	8.4[1]	6.2[1]	27.2[1]
Idaho	4.3[1]	4.4[1]	-
Wyoming	20.4[1]	21.3[1]	-
Colorado	11.0[1]	11.8[1]	-
New Mexico	20.6[1]	20.8[1]	19.4[1]

[Continued]

★ 2205 ★

Maternal Mortality Rates, 1973-75

[Continued]

Division and state	Total	White	All other
Arizona	10.2[1]	6.1[1]	32.7[1]
Utah	12.3[1]	12.7[1]	-
Nevada	11.3[1]	13.3[1]	-
Pacific			
Washington	6.7[1]	5.9[1]	15.1[1]
Oregon	3.1[1]	3.3[1]	-
California	12.8	10.7	24.4
Alaska	-	-	-
Hawaii	12.9[1]	46.8[1]	-

Source: "Maternal Mortality Rates by Color: United States, Each Division and States, 1973-75 (3 Year Average)." National Center for Health Statistics. *Vital Statistics of the United States*. Vol. II—Mortality, Part A. Hyattsville, Md. U.S. Department of Health, Education, and Welfare. Public Health Service, 1979, p. 1-74. *Note:* 1. Rate based on a frequency of less than 20.

★ 2206 ★

Deaths

Maternal and Infant Mortality Rates, 1940-1970

Per 1,000 live births.

Year	Maternal		Infant			
			Under 28 days		28 days to 11 months	
	Negro and other races	White	Negro and other races	White	Negro and other races	White
1940	7.6	3.2	39.7	27.2	34.1	16.0
1950	2.2	0.6	27.5	19.4	16.9	7.4
1960	1.0	0.3	26.9	17.2	16.4	5.7
1965	0.8	0.2	25.4	16.1	14.9	5.4
1966	0.7	0.2	24.8	15.6	14.0	5.0
1967	0.7	0.2	23.8	15.0	12.1	4.7
1968	0.6	0.2	23.0	14.7	11.6	4.5
1969	(NA)	(NA)	21.6	14.1	10.0	4.4
1970	(NA)	(NA)	21.6	13.5	9.8	3.9

Source: "Maternal and Infant Mortality Rates: 1940, 1950, 1960, and 1965 to 1970." U.S. Bureau of the Census. Current Population Reports, Special Studies, Series P-23, No. 42. *The Social and Economic Status of the Black Population in the United States, 1971*. Washington, D.C.: Government Printing Office, 1972, p. 113. Primary source: U.S. Department of Health, Education, and Welfare. *Note:* NA Not available. 1969 and 1970 data are provisional.

★ 2207 ★

Deaths

Maternal and Infant Mortality Rates: 1916-1975

Per 1,000 live births. Statistics prior to 1933 are exclusive of States not yet included in the death registration area.

Year	Maternal		Infant					
			Under 1 year		Under 28 days		28 days to 11 months	
	Black and other races	White	Black and other races	White	Black and other races	White	Black and other races	White
1916	11.7	6.1	184.9	99.0	68.9	43.5	116.0	55.5
1940	7.6	3.2	73.8	43.2	39.7	27.2	34.1	16.0
1960	1.0	0.3	43.2	22.9	26.9	17.2	16.4	5.7
1970	0.6	0.1	30.9	17.8	21.4	13.8	9.5	4.0
1974	0.4	0.1	24.9	14.8	17.2	11.1	7.7	3.7
1975	0.3	0.1	24.2	14.2	16.8	10.4	7.5	3.8

Source: "Maternal and Infant Mortality Rates for Selected Years: 1916 to 1975," U.S. Department of Commerce, Bureau of the Census. *The Social and Economic Status of the Black Population in the United States: An Historical View, 1790-1978,* p. 122. Primary source: U.S. Department of Health, Education, and Welfare, National Center for Health Statistics.

★ 2208 ★

Deaths

Mortality Trends for Specific Causes, 1919-1948

Cause of death	Nonwhite				White			
	1919-21	1929-31	1939-41	1948	1919-21	1929-31	1939-41	1948
Diphtheria	8.7	5.6	1.9	.75	16.7	5.4	1.1	.35
Scarlet fever	.82	.70	.26	.03	4.57	2.25	.53	.05
Whooping cough	17.7	11.2	6.7	2.55	8.2	4.3	2.0	.55
Tuberculosis (all forms)	250.9[2]	191.7	126.4	78.7	92.1	58.1	36.5	24.3
Cancer and other malignant tumors	48.9	56.9	76.2	98.4	87.7	101.9	124.0	139.1
Cancer of digestive organs and peritoneum	20.0[2]	22.8	30.4	40.5	47.5	51.8	57.7	60.4
Cancer of the breast	9.9[2]	10.6	13.6	8.0	16.1	19.3	24.0	13.6
Cancer of female genital organs	30.8[2]	33.8	37.8	38.3	24.5	27.5	31.2	30.8
Pneumonia (all forms)	160.7	140.1	91.4	66.4	107.7	79.1	49.7	35.4
Disease of the heart	160.7	217.6	239.2	263.3	157.7	212.4	290.8	330.1
Intracranial lesions of vascular origin	86.7	104.9	109.7	108.9	91.5	87.1	86.8	87.4
Nephritis (all forms)	110.5	133.5	120.3	84.4	84.3	85.0	75.0	49.3
Syphilis (all forms)	40.9	51.6	52.3	27.1	14.9	11.6	9.9	5.7
Diabetes mellitus	7.5	12.7	17.3	18.3	16.7	20.2	26.8	27.3
Pellagra	18.2	28.9	6.3	.95	1.3	2.4	1.1	.40
Malaria	22.4	13.8	5.6	.50	1.9	1.6	.60	.10
Puerperal causes (total)	12.0	11.6	7.4	17.4	7.0	6.1	3.1	4.2
Premature birth	24.3	19.5	17.6	43.0	18.4	16.3	13.2	24.8
Injury at birth	2.2	3.1	3.6	-	3.9	5.0	4.5	-

[Continued]

★ 2208 ★

Mortality Trends for Specific Causes, 1919-1948

[Continued]

Cause of death	Nonwhite				White			
	1919-21	1929-31	1939-41	1948	1919-21	1929-31	1939-41	1948
Congenital malformations	3.1	2.3	2.3	10.9	6.5	5.8	5.0	13.4
Diarrhea, enteritis, ulceration of intestines	18.3	10.6	6.4	10.4	14.4	6.8	3.4	5.5
Hernia and intestinal obstruction	12.1	12.7	11.3	8.4	10.3	10.1	8.7	6.7
Ulcer of the stomach and duodenum	4.1	6.0	6.2	4.4	4.0	6.2	6.8	6.1
Suicide	4.1	5.0	4.3	4.1	12.0	16.6	14.9	12.1
Motor vehicle accidents	5.2	22.0	25.3	20.9	10.8	26.9	27.1	22.3
Other accidents	70.2	62.4	51.0	50.3	59.0	52.3	45.9	44.4
Homicide	-	40.0	34.2[3]	30.6	-	5.6	3.2[3]	3.0

Source: "Mortality Trends for Specific Causes, by Race, 1919-1948." Guzman, Jessie Parkhurst, ed. *Negro Year Book: A Review of Events Affecting Negro Life, 1941-1946.* New York: William H. Wise, 1952, p. 160. Primary source: Office of Vital Statistics, U.S. Public Health Service. *Notes:* 1. Average of rates for males and females. 2. For 1920-21, except for digestive organs (1921). 3. For 1939.

★ 2209 ★

Deaths

Population, Deaths, and Death Rates in Cities, Incorporated Places, and Rural Districts, 1930

Area	Population				Deaths: Total		Deaths: Cities		Deaths: Incorporated places		Deaths: Rural	
	Total	Cities	Incorporated places	Rural	Number	Rate per 1,000 population	Number	Rate per 1,000 population	Number	Rate per 1,000 population	Number	Rate per 1,000 population
The registration area in continental United States	11,221,472	4,396,775	652,602	6,172,095	185,503	16.5	37,221	19.3	10,424	16.0	87,858	14.2
Alabama	944,834	222,177	46,273	676,384	14,407	15.2	4,515	20.3	1,082	23.4	8,810	13.0
Arizona	10,749	3,369	1,778	5,602	206	19.2	131	38.9	45	25.3	30	5.4
Arkansas	478,463	50,611	38,551	389,301	6,461	13.5	1,344	26.6	828	21.5	4,289	11.0
California	81,048	67,421	3,098	10,529	1,157	14.3	844	12.5	70	22.6	243	23.1
Colorado	11,828	9,829	642	1,357	302	25.5	217	22.1	11	17.1	74	54.5
Connecticut	29,354	24,125	406	4,823	513	17.5	429	17.8	13	32.0	71	14.7
Delaware	32,602	12,080	2,957	17,565	706	21.7	280	23.2	74	25.0	352	20.0
District of Columbia	132,068	132,068	-	-	2,780	21.0	2,780	21.0	-	-	-	-
Florida	431,828	156,397	53,895	221,536	7,166	16.6	2,930	18.7	1,290	23.9	2,946	13.3
Georgia	1,071,125	244,711	71,926	754,488	17,182	16.0	6,085	24.9	[1]	[1]	11,097[1]	13.4[1]
Idaho	668	348	154	166	13	19.5	7	20.1	6	39.0	-	-
Illinois	328,972	289,644	14,392	24,936	5,824	17.7	4,834	16.7	246	17.1	744	29.8
Indiana	111,982	99,324	3,718	8,940	2,185	19.5	1,812	18.2	89	23.9	284	31.8
Iowa	17,380	13,657	1,528	2,195	298	17.1	243	17.8	19	12.4	36	16.4
Kansas	66,344	46,155	5,126	15,063	1,082	16.3	758	16.4	73	14.2	251	16.7
Kentucky	226,040	87,015	29,546	109,479	4,748	21.0	2,189	25.2	[1]	[1]	2,559[1]	18.4[1]
Louisiana	776,326	202,896	54,567	518,863	12,036	15.5	4,919	24.2	1,502	27.5	5,615[1]	10.8[1]
Maine	1,096	574	129	393	18	16.4	8	13.9	[1]	[1]	10	25.4
Maryland	276,379	151,465	8,189	116,725	5,251	19.0	3,041	20.1	248	30.3	1,962	16.8
Massachusetts	52,365	44,194	2,129	6,042	834	15.9	721	16.3	19	8.9	94	15.6
Michigan	169,453	155,889	3,815	9,749	2,786	16.4	2,408	15.4	48	12.6	330	33.8
Minnesota	9,445	8,739	371	335	196	20.8	167	19.1	14	37.7	15	44.8
Mississippi	1,009,718	94,756	39,231	875,731	14,910	14.8	2,607	27.5	[1]	[1]	12,303[1]	13.4[1]
Missouri	223,840	151,985	17,969	53,886	4,604	20.6	3,269	21.5	388	21.6	947	17.6
Montana	1,256	856	171	229	28	22.3	10	11.7	4	23.4	14	61.1
Nebraska	13,752	12,512	600	640	255	18.5	230	18.4	12	20.0	13	20.3
Nevada	516	123	241	152	14	27.1	7	56.9	4	16.6	3	19.7
New Hampshire	790	567	27	196	7	8.9	5	8.8	-	-	2	10.2
New Jersey	208,828	158,151	16,834	33,843	3,519	16.9	2,559	16.2	361	21.4	599	17.7
New Mexico	2,850	857	861	1,132	59	20.7	22	25.7	19	22.1	18	15.9
New York	412,814	381,798	8,701	22,315	6,841	16.6	6,296	16.5	123	14.1	422	18.9
North Carolina	918,647	194,436	51,801	672,410	13,976	15.2	3,957	20.4	959	18.5	9,060	13.5
North Dakota	377	168	48	161	5	13.3	2	11.9	1	20.8	2	12.4
Ohio	309,304	256,424	15,548	37,332	5,803	18.8	4,783	18.7	264	17.0	756	20.3
Oklahoma	172,198	52,588	15,213	104,397	2,242	13.0	1,055	20.1	440	28.9	747	7.2
Oregon	2,234	1,727	163	344	55	24.6	46	26.6	4	24.5	5	14.5
Pennsylvania	431,257	354,667	18,913	57,677	7,459	17.3	6,092	17.2	290	15.3	1,077	18.7

[Continued]

★ 2209 ★

Population, Deaths, and Death Rates in Cities, Incorporated Places, and Rural Districts, 1930

[Continued]

Area	Population				Deaths							
					Total		Cities		Incorporated places		Rural	
	Total	Cities	Incorporated places	Rural	Number	Rate per 1,000 population	Number	Rate per 1,000 population	Number	Rate per 1,000 population	Number	Rate per 1,000 population
Rhode Island	9,913	8,982	97	834	219	22.1	194	21.6	9	92.8	16	19.2
South Carolina	793,681	89,245	49,109	655,327	13,160	16.6	2,579	28.9	1,033	21.0	9,548	14.6
South Dakota	646	251	86	309	12	18.6	5	19.9	2	23.3	5	16.2
Tennessee	477,646	201,252	38,916	237,478	8,744	18.3	4,616	22.9	[1]	[1]	4,128[1]	14.9[1]
Texas	185,293[2]	185,293[2]	[2]	[2]	3,482[2]	18.8[2]	3,482[2]	18.8[2]	-	-	-	-
Utah	1,108	913	31	164	23	20.8	22	24.1	1	32.3	-	-
Vermont	568	131	82	355	8	14.1	3	22.9	[1]	[1]	5[1]	11.4[1]
Virginia	650,165	187,636	25,765	436,764	11,699	18.0	3,994	21.3	490	19.0	7,215	16.5
Washington	6,840	5,600	218	1,022	144	21.1	105	18.8	11	50.5	28	27.4
West Virginia	114,893	23,040	8,184	83,669	1,854	16.1	478	20.7	316	38.6	1,060	12.7
Wisconsin	10,739	9,678	195	866	201	18.7	131	13.5	4	20.5	66	76.2
Wyoming	1,250	451	408	391	29	23.2	10	22.2	12	29.4	7	17.9

Source: "Population, Deaths (Exclusive of Stillbirths), and Death Rates of Negroes in Registration Area of Continental United States, Cities, Incorporated Places, and Rural Districts, and in Cities of Nonregistration States: 1930." U.S. Bureau of the Census. *Negroes in the United States: 1920-32*. Washington, D.C.: Government Printing Office, 1935, p. 447. *Notes:* 1. "Incorporated places" included in "Rural". 2. Nonregistration State in 1930. Statistics given relate to 8 registration cities only: Beaumont, Dallas, El Passo, Fort Worth, Galveston, Houston, San Antonio, and Waco.

★ 2210 ★

Deaths

Specific Death Rates by Age and Race, 1900-1940

Exclusive of stillbirths. By place of occurrence. Rates are the number of deaths in a specified group per 1,000 population of that group. Population of the death-registration States was estimated as of July 1 for 1900, 1910, 1920, and 1930, and enumerated as of Apr. 1 for 1940. Population of each State was enumerated for each census year as of June 1, Apr. 15, Jan. 1, Apr. 1, and Apr. 1, respectively. Rates for frequencies less than 20 are shown in italics.

Area, race, and year	All ages[1]	Under 1 year	1-4 years	5-14 years	15-24 years	25-34 years	35-44 years	45-54 years	55-64 years	65-74 years	75-84 years	85 years and over
Registration states												
All races												
1940	10.8	54.9	2.9	1.0	2.0	3.1	5.2	10.6	22.3	48.0	112.6	228.9
1930	11.3	69.0	5.6	1.7	3.3	4.7	6.8	12.2	24.0	51.4	112.7	228.0
1920	13.0	92.3	9.9	2.6	4.9	6.8	8.1	12.2	23.6	52.5	118.9	248.3
1910	14.7	131.8	14.0	2.9	4.5	6.5	9.0	13.7	26.2	55.6	122.2	250.3
1900	17.2	162.4	19.8	3.9	5.9	8.2	10.2	15.0	27.2	56.4	123.3	260.9
White												
1940	10.4	50.3	2.6	1.0	1.7	2.5	4.4	9.5	21.1	47.7	113.5	235.0
1930	10.8	63.9	5.2	1.6	2.8	3.8	5.9	10.8	22.8	50.6	113.2	230.5
1920	12.6	87.3	9.4	2.5	4.3	6.2	7.5	11.5	23.0	52.1	119.3	249.8
1910	14.5	129.3	13.7	2.9	4.4	6.3	8.7	13.5	26.0	55.4	122.5	252.5
1900	17.0	159.4	19.4	3.8	5.7	8.1	10.1	14.8	27.0	56.2	123.3	262.0
All other races												
1940	13.8	89.2	4.8	1.5	5.0	7.9	12.4	22.9	37.7	51.6	96.8	172.0
1930	16.3	110.0	9.3	2.6	8.0	11.6	16.1	25.8	40.8	63.9	104.2	204.9
1920	17.7	149.2	14.6	3.8	10.4	12.8	15.2	21.5	33.2	60.2	111.2	232.3

[Continued]

★ 2210 ★

Specific Death Rates by Age and Race, 1900-1940

[Continued]

Area, race, and year	All ages[1]	Under 1 year	1-4 years	5-14 years	15-24 years	25-34 years	35-44 years	45-54 years	55-64 years	65-74 years	75-84 years	85 years and over
1910	21.7	239.8	28.3	5.7	10.3	12.2	17.0	24.6	38.5	64.3	103.2	176.4
1900	25.0	333.9	43.5	9.0	11.5	12.1	14.8	24.3	42.1	68.9	120.9	215.2

Source: Specific Death Rates by Age and Race: Death Registration States and Each State, 1900, 1910, 1920, 1930, and 1940." U.S. Bureau of the Census. *Vital Statistics Rates in the United States 1900-1940*. By Forrest E. Linder and Robert D. Grove. Washington, D.C.: Government Printing Office, 1943, p. 150. *Note:* 1. Includes ages not stated.

★ 2211 ★

Deaths

Specific Death Rates for Selected Causes, Five-year Intervals, 1900-1940 - I

Exclusive of stillbirths. By place of occurrence. Rates are the number of deaths in a specified group per 100,000 population of that group, estimated as of July 1 for 1900-1935, and enumerated as of Apr. 1 for 1940. Rates for frequencies less than 20 are shown in italics.

Area, race, and year	All causes[1]	Typhoid and paratyphoid fever 1, 2	Cerebrospinal (meningo -coccus) meningitis 6	Scarlet fever 8	Whooping cough 9	Diphtheria 10	Tuberculosis All forms 13-22	Tuberculosis Of respiratory system 13	Tuberculosis Other forms 14-22	Dysentery 27	Malaria 28
All races											
1940	1,076.4	1.1	0.5	0.5	2.2	1.1	45.9	42.2	3.7	1.9	1.1
1935	1,094.5	2.8	2.1	2.1	3.7	3.1	55.1	49.9	5.2	1.9	3.5
1930	1,132.1	4.8	3.6	1.9	4.8	4.9	71.1	63.0	8.1	2.8	2.9
1925	1,168.1	7.8	1.0	2.7	6.7	7.8	84.8	74.1	10.7	3.1	2.0
1920	1,298.9	7.6	1.6	4.6	12.5	15.3	113.1	99.8	13.4	4.0	3.4
1915	1,317.6	11.8	1.4	3.6	8.2	15.2	140.1	122.6	17.5	3.4	1.6
1910	1,468.0	22.5	0.3	11.4	11.6	21.1	153.8	133.3	20.6	6.0	1.1
1905	1,588.9	22.4	-	6.8	8.9	23.5	179.9	157.1	22.9	8.3	2.5
1900	1,719.1	31.3	-	9.6	12.2	40.3	194.4	174.5	19.9	12.0	6.2
White											
1940	1,941.5	0.9	0.5	0.5	1.8	1.0	36.6	33.7	2.8	1.6	0.6
1935	1,056.4	2.2	2.0	2.3	3.2	3.0	44.9	40.8	4.1	1.7	2.3
1930	1,076.8	3.7	3.2	2.1	4.1	4.9	57.7	51.1	6.6	2.4	1.6
1925	1,113.1	6.2	1.0	2.9	5.9	7.9	71.6	62.2	9.3	2.6	1.1
1920	1,256.1	6.6	1.6	5.0	11.7	16.0	99.5	87.1	12.4	3.3	1.7
1915	1,286.3	11.1	1.4	3.7	7.7	15.4	128.5	112.0	16.5	3.1	1.4
1910	1,448.8	22.2	0.3	11.6	11.0	21.4	145.9	126.2	19.7	6.0	1.1
1905	-	-	-	-	-	-	-	-	-	-	-
1900	-	-	-	-	-	-	-	-	-	-	-
All other races											
1940	1,382.8	3.2	0.6	0.3	5.9	1.8	128.0	116.6	11.4	4.3	5.6
1935	1,430.2	8.2	3.3	0.6	8.3	3.6	145.1	130.5	14.7	4.1	14.3
1930	1,633.0	14.8	7.0	0.6	11.1	4.9	192.0	170.3	21.7	6.8	14.7
1925	1,735.9	24.9	1.0	0.7	15.2	6.3	221.3	196.7	24.6	8.4	11.9
1920	1,767.5	19.6	1.6	0.8	20.6	8.6	262.4	238.0	24.4	11.5	22.1
1915	2,021.3	26.9	1.7	1.4	17.9	9.9	401.1	360.7	40.4	8.4	7.4
1910	2,172.4	33.6	0.6	4.0	35.9	11.6	445.5	393.7	51.8	5.8	3.1
1905	-	-	-	-	-	-	-	-	-	-	-
1900	-	-	-	-	-	-	-	-	-	-	-

Source: Specific Death Rates for Selected Causes, by Race: Death-Registration States and Each State, 1900-1940, Every Fifth Year." U.S. Bureau of the Census. *Vital Statistics Rates in the United States 1900-1940*. By Forrest E. Linder and Robert D. Grove. Washington, D.C.: Government Printing Office, 1943, pp. 330-331. *Notes:* Numbers under causes of death are those of 1938 revision of the detailed International List. 1. Includes all causes shown in International List, see table 12, Section E.

★ 2212 ★

Deaths

Specific Death Rates for Selected Causes, Five-year Intervals, 1900-1940 - II

Exclusive of stillbirths. By place of occurrence. Rates are the number of deaths in a specified group per 100,000 population of that group, estimated as of July 1 for 1900-1935, and enumerated as of Apr. 1 for 1940. Rates for frequencies less than 20 are shown in italics.

Area, race, and year	Syphilis					Measles 35	Cancer and other malignant tumors				
	All forms[1] 30	Locomotor ataxia (tabes dorsalis) 30a	General paralysis of insane 30b	Aneurysm of aorta[2] 30d	Other forms 30c, e-g		All sites 45-55	Of digestive organs peritoneum[3] 46	Of female genital organs 48, 49	Of breast 50	Other sites[4] 45, 47, 51-55
All races											
1940	14.4	0.6	3.4	2.8	7.8	0.5	120.3	55.2	16.0	11.8	37.2
1935	15.4	0.7	3.6	1.9	9.1	3.1	108.2	52.2	15.1	10.4	30.5
1930	15.7	1.1	4.1	1.8	8.8	3.2	97.4	48.9	13.8	9.2	25.4
1925	17.3	1.6	5.8	1.8	8.0	2.3	92.0	47.8	13.4	8.2	22.6
1920	16.5	1.8	5.8	-	8.9	8.8	83.4	44.0	12.2	7.6	19.5
1915	17.7	2.6	7.5	-	7.6	5.2	80.7	-	11.7	7.7	-
1910	13.5	2.7	5.6	-	5.3	12.4	76.2	40.8	11.0	7.1	17.4
1905	13.8	2.5	8.0	-	3.3	7.4	73.4	35.3	10.4	6.3	21.4
1900	12.0	2.0	7.4	-	2.7	13.3	64.0	28.3	8.2	5.1	22.3
White											
1940	9.9	0.6	2.6	2.1	4.6	0.5	125.0	58.0	15.6	12.3	39.2
1935	11.0	0.7	3.0	1.7	5.5	3.0	113.0	55.1	14.8	10.9	32.2
1930	11.7	1.1	3.6	1.5	5.4	3.2	101.9	51.8	13.6	9.7	26.9
1925	14.1	1.6	5.6	1.5	5.4	2.4	95.5	50.2	13.1	8.5	23.7
1920	14.5	1.9	5.8	-	6.8	9.3	86.5	-	11.9	7.9	-
1915	16.3	2.6	7.3	-	6.4	5.3	81.7	-	11.6	7.7	-
1910	13.0	2.7	5.5	-	4.8	12.5	76.9	41.2	10.9	7.1	17.6
1905	-	-	-	-	-	-	-	-	-	-	-
1900	-	-	-	-	-	-	-	-	-	-	-
All other races											
1940	54.3	0.6	9.9	8.2	35.6	0.8	78.4	31.3	19.7	7.3	20.1
1935	54.0	0.7	8.6	4.1	40.8	3.6	65.8	27.0	17.8	6.0	14.9
1930	52.5	0.9	8.1	3.8	39.6	3.3	56.6	22.9	16.4	5.4	11.9
1925	49.8	1.3	8.3	4.7	35.5	1.8	56.5	23.0	17.1	5.5	10.9
1920	38.8	1.1	6.3	-	31.4	4.1	48.5	-	15.4	5.1	-
1915	49.3	2.0	11.7	-	35.6	4.2	58.3	-	15.2	6.8	-
1910	30.8	2.0	7.9	-	20.9	9.4	54.0	25.4	12.9	6.5	9.1
1905	-	-	-	-	-	-	-	-	-	-	-
1900	-	-	-	-	-	-	-	-	-	-	-

Source: Specific Death Rates for Selected Causes, by Race: Death-Registration States and Each State, 1900-1940, Every Fifth Year." U.S. Bureau of the Census. *Vital Statistics Rates in the United States 1900-1940*. By Forrest E. Linder and Robert D. Grove. Washington, D.C.: Government Printing Office, 1943, pp. 330-331. *Notes:* Numbers under causes of death are those of 1938 revision of the detailed International List. 1. Includes "Aneurysm (except of heart)" for 1925-1935, inclusive; aneurysm of the aorta for 1940. 2. Tabulated with "Aneurysm (except for heart)," for 1925-1935, inclusive. 3. Excludes cancer of the pancreas for 1900-1910, inclusive. 4. Excludes cancer of the pancreas for 1915-1940, inclusive.

★ 2213 ★

Deaths

Specific Death Rates for Selected Causes, Five-year Intervals, 1900-1940 - III

Exclusive of stillbirths. By place of occurrence. Rates are the number of deaths in a specified group per 100,000 population of that group, estimated as of July 1 for 1900-1935, and enumerated as of Apr. 1 for 1940. Rates for frequencies less than 20 are shown in italics.

Area, race, and year	Diabetes mellitus 61	Exophthalmic goiter 63b	Pellagra (except alcoholic) 69	Alcoholism (ethylism) 77	Intracranial lesions of vascular origin[1] 83	Diseases of heart[2] 90-95	Bronchitis[3] 105
All races							
1940	26.6	2.8	1.6	1.9	90.9	292.5	3.0
1935	22.3	2.8	2.8	2.6	85.7	245.4	3.1
1930	19.1	3.4	5.2	3.5	89.0	214.2	4.2
1925	16.8	3.4	3.0	3.6	89.5	184.8	6.4
1920	16.1	1.8	2.5	1.0	93.0	159.6	13.2
1915	17.6	1.5	1.1	4.4	94.5	163.9	17.5
1910	15.3	1.2	0.1	5.5	95.8	158.9	23.9
1905	14.1	0.7	0	5.9	105.9	161.9	32.7
1900	11.0	0.05	0.0	5.3	106.9	137.4	45.2
White							
1940	27.6	2.9	1.1	1.8	88.6	297.6	3.1
1935	23.3	3.0	1.7	2.5	83.8	248.7	3.1
1930	19.8	3.5	2.6	3.5	86.9	213.1	4.1
1925	17.4	3.5	1.5	3.5	88.5	182.9	6.3
1920	16.9	2.0	1.2	1.0	93.4	159.5	13.1
1915	17.9	1.5	0.9	4.4	93.7	161.5	17.1
1910	15.5	1.3	0.1	5.5	95.6	157.6	23.5
1905	-	-	-	-	-	-	-
1900	-	-	-	-	-	-	-
All other races							
1940	17.9	1.9	6.3	2.6	111.7	248.5	2.4
1935	13.6	1.8	12.2	3.8	102.9	217.0	2.9
1930	12.8	2.0	29.0	4.0	108.2	224.7	5.2
1925	10.6	1.6	18.5	3.8	99.8	204.7	7.3
1920	8.0	0.7	16.5	0.9	87.7	160.7	15.2
1915	10.9	1.0	7.3	4.3	111.1	217.4	25.2
1910	7.2	0.8	0.2	5.4	102.3	204.8	36.5
1905	-	-	-	-	-	-	-
1900	-	-	-	-	-	-	-

Source: Specific Death Rates for Selected Causes, by Race: Death-Registration States and Each State, 1900-1940, Every Fifth Year." U.S. Bureau of the Census. *Vital Statistics Rates in the United States 1900-1940.* By Forrest E. Linder and Robert D. Grove. Washington, D.C.: Government Printing Office, 1943, pp. 330-331. *Notes:* Numbers under causes of death are those of 1938 revision of the detailed International List. 1. Excludes diseases of coronary arteries for 1900-1925, inclusive, and for 1940 certain terms relating combined cardiorenal conditions, transferred to nephritis. 2. Excludes capillary bronchitis for 1925-1940, inclusive. 3. Rates are shown for only those years during which the State was in the registration system.

★ 2214 ★

Deaths

Suicides, 1940-1960

Cause, color, sex, and year	All ages	Under 1 year	1-4 years	5-14 years	15-24 years	25-34 years	35-44 years	45-54 years	55-64 years	65-74 years	75-84 years	85 years and over
Suicide												
Total nonwhite												
1960	4.5	-	-	0.1	3.4	7.9	8.3	7.9	10.0	8.0	7.6	9.8
1959	4.6	-	-	0.1	4.3	8.7	6.7	8.2	9.4	8.6	11.8	5.9
1958	4.4	-	-	0.1	3.5	7.8	7.3	7.8	9.0	8.0	7.2	7.6
1957	4.0	-	-	0.0	3.4	7.4	6.3	6.4	7.9	9.3	8.6	9.4
1956	3.8	-	-	0.1	3.4	6.4	6.6	6.4	7.7	6.2	6.5	4.9
1955	3.8	-	-	0.1	4.0	6.0	5.5	6.6	7.6	6.5	7.0	6.9
1954	4.1	-	-	0.0	3.4	7.4	6.1	7.1	7.5	7.9	7.0	3.6
1953	3.8	-	-	0.2	3.0	5.8	5.8	7.2	7.0	7.0	11.1	5.8
1952	3.7	-	-	0.2	2.7	6.5	5.5	5.7	8.3	5.5	5.8	10.2
1951	4.1	-	-	0.2	3.7	6.4	6.6	6.8	7.5	6.1	8.3	2.1
1950	4.3	-	-	0.1	3.4	6.3	6.6	7.9	9.1	8.7	5.4	6.7
1949	4.3	-	-	0.1	3.1	6.0	6.8	7.1	9.4	8.8	8.6	7.0
1948	4.1	-	-	0.0	3.3	6.0	7.1	8.1	6.0	8.1	6.3	2.4
1947	4.1	-	-	0.2	3.8	5.9	6.6	5.5	7.8	7.7	8.2	5.0
1946	3.9	-	-	0.1	3.6	6.0	5.7	6.6	7.7	6.2	6.3	2.6
1945	3.5	-	-	-	3.4	5.5	5.4	5.4	5.3	6.5	8.4	5.4
1944	3.0	-	-	0.1	2.8	4.5	4.5	4.9	6.3	4.7	5.1	5.7
1943	3.0	-	-	0.2	3.1	4.5	4.4	4.2	6.3	3.8	6.0	2.9
1942	3.9	-	-	0.2	3.9	6.5	6.2	5.1	8.2	5.3	4.9	-
1941	4.1	-	-	0.1	3.8	6.3	6.0	7.8	7.2	6.8	7.4	5.9
1940	4.6	-	-	0.2	4.2	7.3	6.7	9.2	7.3	8.2	3.9	8.5
Nonwhite male												
1960	7.2	-	-	0.1	5.3	12.9	13.5	12.8	16.9	12.6	11.3	15.9
1959	7.5	-	-	0.2	6.6	14.4	11.0	13.9	14.8	14.9	22.9	10.3
1958	7.1	-	-	0.2	5.4	12.6	12.3	12.8	15.3	14.2	11.5	14.8
1957	6.8	-	-	0.0	5.6	13.0	10.6	11.8	11.9	17.4	15.6	11.5
1956	6.1	-	-	0.1	5.8	10.8	10.5	9.8	12.2	10.0	11.5	12.0
1955	6.1	-	-	0.1	6.5	9.6	9.6	10.5	12.7	10.8	12.8	16.7
1954	6.8	-	-	0.1	5.5	12.8	10.6	11.4	12.2	13.6	13.4	4.5
1953	6.4	-	-	0.1	4.2	10.1	10.3	12.6	12.0	12.2	21.9	14.3
1952	6.1	-	-	0.3	4.5	10.7	8.9	9.9	14.3	11.0	10.9	20.0
1951	6.6	-	-	0.3	5.2	10.7	10.8	11.4	12.0	10.1	15.1	5.3
1950	7.0	-	-	0.1	5.3	10.1	11.3	11.7	16.8	15.0	7.9	16.1
1949	7.1	-	-	0.1	4.6	9.9	11.3	12.0	16.4	15.8	15.3	16.7
1948	6.9	-	-	-	5.0	9.1	12.2	14.1	10.9	14.5	12.6	5.9
1947	6.5	-	-	0.3	5.0	8.9	11.1	9.1	13.8	14.3	16.5	12.5
1946	6.1	-	-	0.2	5.0	9.4	8.8	9.9	12.8	10.7	12.6	6.7

[Continued]

★ 2214 ★

Suicides, 1940-1960

[Continued]

Cause, color, sex, and year	All ages	Under 1 year	1-4 years	5-14 years	15-24 years	25-34 years	35-44 years	45-54 years	55-64 years	65-74 years	75-84 years	85 years and over
1945	5.7	-	-	-	5.1	9.1	8.8	9.1	9.1	12.2	14.6	13.3
1944	4.8	-	-	0.1	3.9	7.6	7.2	8.0	11.1	6.7	7.7	7.1
1943	4.8	-	-	0.4	4.9	7.8	6.2	6.9	10.3	6.5	8.2	7.1
1942	6.0	-	-	0.2	5.0	9.3	9.7	8.0	14.5	9.2	10.1	-
1941	6.6	-	-	0.1	5.1	10.3	10.5	12.5	11.7	11.3	12.1	7.1
1940	7.2	-	-	0.4	5.1	11.5	10.6	14.8	12.6	13.5	6.5	13.3
Nonwhite female												
1960	2.0	-	-	0.0	1.5	3.5	3.7	3.2	3.4	3.8	4.2	5.0
1959	1.9	-	-	0.1	2.2	3.7	2.7	2.9	4.3	3.0	1.9	2.6
1958	1.8	-	-	0.0	1.7	3.6	2.8	3.1	2.9	2.4	3.3	2.6
1957	1.4	-	-	-	1.4	2.5	2.3	1.3	4.0	1.9	2.1	8.1
1956	1.6	-	-	0.1	1.2	2.6	3.0	3.0	3.3	2.7	1.4	-
1955	1.5	-	-	-	1.8	2.8	1.7	2.8	2.6	2.5	1.5	-
1954	1.5	-	-	-	1.5	2.8	2.0	2.8	2.9	2.6	0.8	3.1
1953	1.3	-	-	0.2	2.0	2.1	1.6	1.8	1.9	2.2	0.8	-
1952	1.3	-	-	0.1	1.3	2.7	2.5	1.6	2.2	0.3	0.9	3.4
1951	1.7	-	-	-	2.4	2.6	2.7	2.3	2.9	2.3	1.8	-
1950	1.7	-	-	0.1	1.7	2.8	2.2	4.0	1.2	2.5	2.9	-
1949	1.5	-	-	0.2	1.7	2.5	2.6	2.1	2.2	1.8	2.0	-
1948	1.5	-	-	0.1	1.8	3.1	2.4	2.2	0.8	1.5	-	-
1947	1.6	-	-	0.1	2.6	3.1	2.5	1.7	1.5	0.8	-	-
1946	1.8	-	-	-	2.3	2.8	2.8	3.4	2.2	1.6	-	-
1945	1.5	-	-	-	2.2	2.8	2.3	1.5	1.1	0.4	2.4	-
1944	1.4	-	-	0.1	2.0	2.1	2.0	1.8	1.2	2.5	2.5	4.8
1943	1.3	-	-	0.1	1.6	1.7	2.7	1.4	1.9	0.9	3.9	-
1942	2.0	-	-	0.1	2.8	4.0	2.9	2.1	1.3	0.9	-	-
1941	1.7	-	-	0.1	2.5	2.6	1.8	2.9	2.3	1.9	2.9	5.0
1940	2.1	-	-	-	3.3	3.5	3.0	3.2	1.4	2.5	1.5	4.9

Source: "Death Rates for 35 Selected Causes by Age, Color, and Sex: United States, 1940-1960." National Center for Health Services. *Vital Statistics Rates in the United States 1940-1960.* By Robert D. Grove and Alice M. Hetzel. Washington, D.C.: Government Printing Office, 1968, pp. 536-538.

★ 2215 ★

Deaths

Total Deaths, Deaths of Residents, and Death Rates in Cities Having 25,000 or More Inhabitants, 1930

Total colored[1] and white deaths (exclusive of stillbirths), deaths of residents, and death rates, in cities having 25,000 or more Negro inhabitants: 1930.

City and color	Total deaths		Deaths of residents[2]	
	Number	Rate per 1,000 estimated population July 1, 1930	Number	Rate per 1,000 estimated population July 1, 1930
Atlanta, Ga	4,205	15.5	3,945	14.5
Colored	2,106	23.2	2,058	22.8
White	2,099	11.6	1,877	10.4
Baltimore, Md	11,239	13.9	10,447	13.0
Colored	2,815	19.6	2,712	18.9
White	8,424	12.7	7,735	11.7
Birmingham, Ala	3,548	13.6	3,251	12.4
Colored	1,925	19.3	1,841	18.4
White	1,623	10.0	1,410	8.7
Charleston, S.C.	1,426	22.9	[3]	-
Colored	927	33.0	[3]	-
White	499	14.6	[3]	-
Charlotte, N.C.	1,065	12.8	970	11.7
Colored	481	19.1	474	18.8
White	584	10.1	496	8.6
Chattanooga, Tenn	1,883	15.7	1,841	15.3
Colored	825	24.8	826	24.8
White	1,058	12.2	1,015	11.7
Chicago, Ill	35,316	10.4	35,545	10.5
Colored	4,045	15.4	4,060	15.5
White	31,271	10.0	31,485	10.1
Cincinnati, Ohio	7,005	15.5	6,439	14.2
Colored	1,139	23.5	1,106	22.8
White	5,866	14.5	5,333	13.2
Cleveland, Ohio	9,906	11.0	9,597	10.6
Colored	1,293	17.4	1,292	17.4
White	8,613	10.4	8,305	10.0
Columbus, Ohio	4,470	15.3	4,002	13.7
Colored	608	18.3	593	17.9
White	3,862	15.0	3,409	13.2
Dallas, Tex	3,012	11.5	2,625	10.0
Colored	859	19.0	782	17.3
White	2,153	9.9	1,843	8.5
Detroit, Mich	14,729	9.3	14,947	9.4
Colored	2,037	15.6	2,138	16.3
White	12,692	8.7	12,809	8.8
Houston, Tex	3,598	12.2	3,382	11.5
Colored	1,495	19.1	1,440	18.5
White	2,103	9.7	1,933	8.9
Indianapolis, Ind	5,193	14.2	4,926	13.5

[Continued]

★ 2215 ★

Total Deaths, Deaths of Residents, and Death Rates in Cities Having 25,000 or More Inhabitants, 1930

[Continued]

City and color	Total deaths		Deaths of residents[2]	
	Number	Rate per 1,000 estimated population July 1, 1930	Number	Rate per 1,000 estimated population July 1, 1930
Colored	867	19.6	876	19.8
White	4,326	13.5	4,050	12.6
Jacksonville, Fla	1,977	15.2	1,802	13.9
Colored	1,014	21.0	987	20.3
White	963	11.8	824	10.1
Kansas City, Mo	5,301	13.2	4,987	12.4
Colored	922	21.8	930	22.0
White	4,3798	12.2	4,057	11.3
Los Angeles, Calif	14,028	11.2	13,953	11.1
Colored	[4]	[4]	[3]	[3]
White	[4]	[4]	[3]	[3]
Louisville, Ky	4,390	14.3	[3]	[3]
Colored	1,104	23.2	[3]	[3]
White	3,286	12.6	[3]	[3]
Memphis, Tenn	4,398	17.3	3,897	15.3
Colored	2,274	23.5	2,159	22.3
White	2,124	13.5	1,738	11.1
Miami, Fla	1,232	11.1	1,087	9.8
Colored	382	15.2	372	14.8
White	850	9.9	715	8.3
Montgomery, Ala	1,138	17.2	1,002	15.1
Colored	664	22.1	633	21.0
White	474	13.1	369	10.2
Nashville, Tenn	2,510	16.3	2,238	14.5
Colored	990	23.1	935	21.8
White	1,520	13.7	1,303	11.7
Newark, N.J.	5,263	11.9	5,210	11.8
Colored	759	18.8	821	20.4
White	4,504	11.2	4,389	10.9
New Orleans, La	8,030	17.4	6,804	14.8
Colored	3,289	25.0	2,737	20.8
White	4,741	14.4	4,067	12.4
New York, N.Y	74,913	10.8	75,341	10.8
Colored	5,630	16.2	5,572	16.0
White	69,283	10.5	69,769	10.5
Norfolk, Va	1,763	13.6	1,602	12.4
Colored	902	20.4	849	19.2
White	861	10.1	753	8.8
Philadelphia, Pa	24,516	12.5	24,692	12.6
Colored	3,620	16.1	3,636	16.2
White	20,896	12.1	21,056	12.2

[Continued]

★ 2215 ★

Total Deaths, Deaths of Residents, and Death Rates in Cities Having 25,000 or More Inhabitants, 1930

[Continued]

City and color	Total deaths		Deaths of residents[2]	
	Number	Rate per 1,000 estimated population July 1, 1930	Number	Rate per 1,000 estimated population July 1, 1930
Pittsburgh, Pa	9,312	13.9	9,002	13.4
Colored	1,103	19.7	1,094	19.6
White	8,209	13.3	7,908	12.9
Richmond, Va	2,737	14.9	2,439	13.3
Colored	1,132	21.4	1,054	19.9
White	1,605	12.3	1,385	10.6
St. Louis, Mo	11,482	13.9	10,842	13.2
Colored	1,982	20.7	1,963	20.5
White	9,500	13.1	8,879	12.2
Savannah, Ga	1,660	19.5	1,453	17.1
Colored	1,033	26.5	948	24.3
White	627	13.6	505	11.0
Shreveport, La	1,669	21.7	993	12.9
Colored	874	32.1	490	18.0
White	795	16.0	503	10.1
Washington, D.C	7,387	15.1	6,982	14.3
Colored	2,792	21.0	2,657	20.0
White	4,595	12.9	4,325	12.2
Winston-Salem, N.C	1,067	14.1	1,019	13.5
Colored	620	18.9	616	18.8
White	447	10.4	403	9.4

Source: "Total Colored and White Deaths (Exclusive of Stillbirths), Deaths of Residents, and Death Rates, in Cities Having 25,000 or More Negro Inhabitants: 1920." U.S. Bureau of the Census. *Negroes in the United States: 1920-32.* Washington, D.C.: Government Printing Office, 1935, p. 453. *Notes:* 1. Includes Negro, nonwhite, and other races. 2. The term "residents" excludes all nonresidents and includes residents who died elsewhere in the registration area. 3. Reliable data for nonresidents are not available. 4. Deaths and death rates by color not available.

★ 2216 ★

Deaths

Tuberculosis Death Rates in Large Cities – 1940, 1941

Tuberculosis death rates among residents of each racial group in 22 large cities[1]: 1941 and 1940.

City	1941 Tuberculosis death rates			1940 Tuberculosis death rates		
	All residents	White	Negro	All residents	White	Negro
Atlanta	105	26	255	88	30	197
Baltimore	90	48	261	95	57	253
Birmingham	81	30	153	72	25	141
Chicago	58[2]			61	45	241

[Continued]

★ 2216 ★

Tuberculosis Death Rates in Large Cities – 1940, 1941

[Continued]

City	1941 Tuberculosis death rates			1940 Tuberculosis death rates		
	All residents	White	Negro	All residents	White	Negro
Cincinnati	68[2]			68	42	255
Cleveland	61	35	297	58	44	196
Columbus	67	42	255	56	38	193
Dallas	55	42	114	56	42	124
Detroit	51	37	183	51	36	196
Houston	70[2]			68	54	115
Indianapolis	61	46	158	65	45	201
Kansas City, Mo	43	28	167	51	38	166
Los Angeles	49	43	138	50	45	143
Louisville	64	41	199	64	43	185
Memphis	93	45	159	82	39	142
Newark	62	39	255	71	43	300
New Orleans	78[2]			81	61	128
New York City	55	44	214	54	43	214
Philadelphia	65	43	204	65	45	200
Pittsburgh	54	41	177	54	40	188
St. Louis	65	42	215	57	35	198
Washington	77	36	178	90	38	219

Source: "Tuberculosis Death Rates Among Residents of Each Racial Group in 22 Large Cities: 1941 and 1940." Murray, Florence, ed., *The Negro Handbook, 1944*, p. 184. NY: Current Pubs, 1944. *Notes:* 1. Includes only those cities in which more than one-tenth of the population is Negro and those in which total Negro population exceeds 50,000. 2. Data for residents dying outside the city in 1941 are not available; figures include an estimate based on average of previous years.

★ 2217 ★

Deaths

Tuberculosis Mortality: Select Cities, 1938

Cities	Population 1938		Tuberculosis deaths[3]		Death rate[2]	
	White[1]	Negro	White[1]	Negro	White[1]	Negro
New York City	7,137,578	354,212	3,374	956	47	270
Chicago	3,357,143	249,857	1,434	724	43	290
Philadelphia	1,822,205	231,122	792	555	44	240
Detroit	1,523,709	126,291	616	332	40	263
Los Angeles	1,391,129	45,127	943	92	68	204
Cleveland	870,094	75,506	372[4]	218	43	289
Baltimore	709,854	152,205	404	344	57	226
St. Louis	763,385	98,068	358	242	47	247
Boston	787,208	21,296	456[4]	29[5]	58	136
Pittsburgh	644,262	57,617	294	150	46	260
San Francisco	688,849	4,151	418	15	61	361
Washington, D.C.	456,920	170,080	197	419	43	246
Milwaukee	611,959	8,041	260	39	42	485
Buffalo	585,089	14,184	306	68	52	479

[Continued]

★ 2217 ★

Tuberculosis Mortality: Select Cities, 1938

[Continued]

Cities	Population 1938		Tuberculosis deaths[3]		Death rate[2]	
	White[1]	Negro	White[1]	Negro	White[1]	Negro
New Orleans	375,216	147,784	241	302[5]	64	204
Minneapolis	487,689	4,424	177	10	36	226
Cincinnati	423,248	50,173	229	151[5]	54	301
Newark	417,742	40,258	156	131	37	325
Kansas City, Mo	382,727	40,873	153	92	40	225
Seattle	383,873	3,498	201	5	52	143
Indianapolis	327,173	44,927	175	88	53	196
Houston	281,552	77,864	173	122	61	157
Louisville	297,415	54,085	150	115	50	213
Rochester, N.Y.	336,792	2,771	141	6	42	217
Jersey City	322,663	13,339	189[4]	21[5]	59	157
Portland, Ore	332,787	1,729	137	0	41	0
Columbus	296,014	37,632	149	59	50	157
Atlanta	217,501	108,665	121	277	56	255
Oakland	305,310	8,282	126	12	41	145
Toledo	297,246	14,205	158	30[5]	53	211
Denver	302,241	7,759	172	19[5]	57	245
St. Paul	301,493	4,507	101[4]	5[5]	33	111
Dallas	259,571	45,355	139	77	54	170
Birmingham	181,704	112,096	48	197	26	176
Memphis	180,972	111,579	103	241	57	216
San Antonio	244,425	20,575	357	28	146	136
Akron	238,183	10,817	72	20	30	185
Providence	237,744	5,256	129	12	54	228
Dayton	207,712	19,288	73	45	35	233
Oklahoma City	206,453	17,731	91	34	44	192
Omaha	210,664	11,551	64	18	30	156
Syracuse	218,808	2,003	80	2	37	100
Worcester	190,644	1,356	78[4]	2[5]	41	147
Paterson	137,017	2,983	66	8	48	268
Kansas City, Kan	109,637	21,363	34	19	31	89
Elizabeth	124,093	5,378	41	4	33	74

Source: "Tuberculosis Mortality by Race of 46 American Cities in 1938, Including Their Residents Dying Out of Town." Murray, Florence, ed. *The Negro Handbook.* New York: Wendell Malliet, 1942, p. 151. Primary source: Division of Negro Health, U.S. Public Health Service. *Notes:* 1. Includes a small number of "other colored" groups. 2. Per 100,000 population. 3. Inclusive of known out-of-town deaths of white and Negro residents. 4. Includes known out-of-town deaths of white residents and probably a few unqualified as to color. 5. Out-of-town deaths unknown.—Compiled by G.J. Drolet, New York Tuberculosis and Health Association, from preliminary reports by courtesy of Health Commissioners of each city and other authorities.

Fertility

★ 2218 ★

Black Women Aged 15 to 44, Black Children Under Age 5, and Number of Black Children Per 1,000 Women, in Cities of 5,000 or More Black Inhabitants, 1930

City	Women 15 to 44 years of age	Children under 5 years	
		Number	Per 1,000 women 15 to 44 years of age
Alabama			
Anniston	2,152	710	330
Bessemer	3,625	1,096	302
Birmingham	32,283	8,717	270
Dothan	1,840	648	352
Fairfield	1,923	683	355
Gadsden	1,864	600	322
Mobile	7,914	2,016	255
Montgomery	9,963	2,384	239
Selma	3,097	795	257
Tuscaloosa	2,331	641	275
Arkansas			
Little Rock	6,608	1,323	200
NorthLittle Rock	1,822	526	289
Pine Bluff	2,066	419	203
California			
Los Angeles	12,174	2,435	200
Oakland	2,124	417	196
Colorado			
Denver	2,086	464	222
Connecticut			
Hartford	1,778	691	389
New Haven	1,317	483	367
Delaware			
Wilmington	3,404	833	245

[Continued]

★ 2218 ★

Black Women Aged 15 to 44, Black Children Under Age 5, and Number of Black Children Per 1,000 Women, in Cities of 5,000 or More Black Inhabitants, 1930

[Continued]

City	Women 15 to 44 years of age	Children under 5 years	
		Number	Per 1,000 women 15 to 44 years of age
District of Columbia			
Washington	39,745	10,006	252
Florida			
Daytona Beach	1,795	425	237
Jacksonville	16,394	3,543	216
Miami	8,195	2,639	322
Orlando	2,554	649	254
Pensacola	3,039	760	250
St. Petersburg	2,561	616	241
Tampa	7,019	1,636	233
West Palm Beach	3,076	720	234
Georgia			
Albany	2,499	581	232
Athens	1,987	514	259
Atlanta	30,443	7,090	233
Augusta	7,978	1,775	222
Brunswick	1,964	428	218
Columbus	4,739	1,216	257
La Grange	1,726	535	310
Macon	7,560	1,896	251
Savannah	13,719	2,660	194
Thomasville	1,896	433	228
Valdosta	2,008	484	241
Waycross	1,849	528	286
Illinois			
Chicago	74,982	17,529	234
East St. Louis	3,354	1,163	347
Indiana			
East Chicago	1,494	526	352
Evansville	1,888	399	211
Gary	5,260	1,672	318
Indianapolis	12,542	3,457	276

[Continued]

★ 2218 ★

Black Women Aged 15 to 44, Black Children Under Age 5, and Number of Black Children Per 1,000 Women, in Cities of 5,000 or More Black Inhabitants, 1930

[Continued]

City	Women 15 to 44 years of age	Children under 5 years	
		Number	Per 1,000 women 15 to 44 years of age
Iowa			
Des Moines	1,407	483	343
Kansas			
Kansas City	5,364	1,632	304
Topeka	1,481	452	305
Wichita	1,658	450	271
Kentucky			
Lexington	3,525	854	242
Louisville	13,952	3,101	222
Paducah	1,902	417	219
Louisiana			
Alexandria	2,993	819	274
Baton Rouge	3,683	736	200
Lafayette	1,381	545	395
Lake Charles	1,727	621	360
Monroe	3,498	681	195
New Orleans	40,521	11,518	284
Shreveport	9,535	1,930	202
Maryland			
Baltimore	40,751	12,274	301
Massachusetts			
Boston	5,525	1,582	286
Cambridge	1,342	497	370
Michigan			
Detroit	37,377	10,618	284
Flint	1,599	574	359
Mississippi			
Clarksdale	1,881	256	136

[Continued]

★ 2218 ★

Black Women Aged 15 to 44, Black Children Under Age 5, and Number of Black Children Per 1,000 Women, in Cities of 5,000 or More Black Inhabitants, 1930

[Continued]

City	Women 15 to 44 years of age	Children under 5 years	
		Number	Per 1,000 women 15 to 44 years of age
Greenville	2,693	550	204
Greenwood	1,960	378	193
Hattiesburg	2,213	659	298
Jackson	6,319	1,616	256
Laurel	2,261	681	301
Meridian	3,767	1,023	272
Natchez	2,310	489	212
Vicksburg	3,871	791	204
Missouri			
Kansas City	12,311	2,154	175
St. Louis	29,273	6,634	227
Nebraska			
Omaha	3,171	878	277
New Jersey			
Atlantic City	4,996	942	189
Camden	3,079	1,139	370
Jersey City	3,581	1,239	346
Montclair	2,350	563	240
Newark	11,881	3,821	322
Orange	1,478	469	317
Trenton	2,094	880	420
New York			
Buffalo	4,114	1,287	313
New York	111,230	26,920	242
North Carolina			
Asheville	4,889	1,238	253
Charlotte	8,283	2,140	258
Durham	6,134	1,765	288
Fayetteville	1,721	567	329
Goldsboro	1,998	719	360
Greensboro	4,548	1,244	274
High Point	2,316	722	312
Kinston	1,538	489	318

[Continued]

★ 2218 ★

Black Women Aged 15 to 44, Black Children Under Age 5, and Number of Black Children Per 1,000 Women, in Cities of 5,000 or More Black Inhabitants, 1930

[Continued]

City	Women 15 to 44 years of age	Children under 5 years	
		Number	Per 1,000 women 15 to 44 years of age
New Bern	1,791	583	326
Raleigh	3,858	1,042	270
Rocky Mount	2,593	891	344
Wilmington	3,973	1,215	306
Wilson	1,928	603	313
Winston-Salem	10,861	2,915	268
Ohio			
Akron	3,159	1,086	344
Cincinnati	14,190	4,003	282
Cleveland	21,911	6,458	295
Columbus	8,719	2,612	300
Dayton	4,701	1,576	335
Springfield	2,014	729	362
Toledo	3,869	1,115	288
Youngstown	3,969	1,659	418
Oklahoma			
Muskogee	1,991	490	246
Oklahoma City	4,895	1,033	211
Tulsa	5,427	1,034	191
Pennsylvania			
Chester	2,485	842	339
Harrisburg	1,730	522	302
Philadelphia	67,185	18,658	278
Pittsburgh	15,665	4,934	315
Rhode Island			
Providence	1,237	569	460
South Carolina			
Charleston	9,446	2,768	293
Columbia	6,679	1,436	215
Florence	1,996	496	248
Greenville	3,596	968	269
Spartanburg	3,086	921	298
Sumter	1,682	428	254

[Continued]

★ 2218 ★

Black Women Aged 15 to 44, Black Children Under Age 5, and Number of Black Children Per 1,000 Women, in Cities of 5,000 or More Black Inhabitants, 1930

[Continued]

City	Women 15 to 44 years of age	Children under 5 years	
		Number	Per 1,000 women 15 to 44 years of age
Tennessee			
Chattanooga	10,503	2,618	249
Jackson	2,384	539	226
Knoxville	5,282	1,314	249
Memphis	31,743	7,062	222
Nashville	13,116	3,083	235
Texas			
Austin	3,070	750	244
Beaumont	5,884	1,690	287
Dallas	13,412	2,751	205
Fort Worth	7,343	1,488	203
Galveston	4,428	945	213
Houston	21,524	4,588	213
Marshall	2,129	577	271
Port Arthur	3,212	937	292
San Antonio	6,177	1,098	178
Waco	2,922	688	235
Virginia			
Danville	1,713	525	306
Lynchburg	2,861	831	290
Newport News	3,833	1,216	317
Norfolk	13,270	3,378	255
Petersburg	3,665	1,047	286
Portsmouth	5,303	1,510	285
Richmond	15,816	4,576	289
Roanoke	3,795	1,144	301
West Virginia			
Charleston	2,099	509	242
Wisconsin			
Milwaukee	2,109	574	272

Source: "Negro Women 15 to 44 Years of Age, and Negro Children Under 5 Years, With Number of Negro Children Per 1,000 Women in the 147 Cities Having 5,000 or More Negro Inhabitants: 1930." U.S. Bureau of the Census. *Negroes in the United States: 1920-32*. Washington, D.C.: Government Printing Office, 1935, p. 207.

★ 2219 ★

Fertility

Children Under Age 5 Per 1,000 Women Aged 15 to 44, by Geographic Area, 1900 to 1930

Division, state, and racial class	1930	1920	1910	1900	Increase or decrease (-) 1920-30	1910-20	1900-16
South Atlantic							
Delaware							
Negro	363	381	415	500	-18	-34	-85
White	353	458	422	446	-105	36	-24
Maryland							
Negro	394	391	443	483	3	-52	-40
White	372	432	431	461	-60	1	-30
District of Columbia							
Negro	252	222	234	254	30	-12	-20
White	235	228	299	302	7	-71	-3
Virginia							
Negro	466	493	545	594	-27	-52	-49
White	461	540	577	591	-79	-37	-14
West Virginia							
Negro	416	409	463	514	7	-54	-51
White	550	631	638	649	-81	-7	-11
North Carolina							
Negro	507	596	661	674	-89	-65	-13
White	530	636	675	677	-106	-39	-2
South Carolina							
Negro	493	568	654	712	-75	-86	-58
White	495	601	647	630	-106	-46	17
Georgia							
Negro	414	485	592	663	-71	-107	-71
White	461	565	647	642	-104	-82	5
Florida							
Negro	332	383	486	599	-51	-103	-113
White	413	500	600	639	-87	-100	-39
East South Central							
Kentucky							
Negro	335	343	381	454	-8	-38	-73
White	522	562	583	601	-40	-21	-18
Tennessee							
Negro	346	391	468	544	-45	-77	-76
White	477	547	609	615	-70	-62	-6
Alabama							
Negro	443	468	561	624	-25	-93	-63
White	522	604	691	680	-82	-87	11
Mississippi							
Negro	465	468	588	652	-3	-120	-64
White	506	568	677	675	-62	-9	2

[Continued]

★ 2219 ★

Children Under Age 5 Per 1,000 Women Aged 15 to 44, by Geographic Area, 1900 to 1930

[Continued]

Division, state, and racial class	1930	1920	1910	1900	Increase or decrease (-)		
					1920-30	1910-20	1900-16
West South Central							
Arkansas							
Negro	402	426	529	611	-24	-103	-82
White	511	608	700	689	-97	-92	11
Louisiana							
Negro	420	432	527	620	-12	-95	-93
White	456	515	612	652	-59	-97	-40
Oklahoma							
Negro	386	438	572	658	-52	-134	-86
White	466	558	664	722	-92	-106	-58
Texas							
Negro	373	406	532	642	-33	-126	-110
White	407	500	625	698	-93	-125	-73

Source: "Number of Negro and White Children Under 5 Years Per 1,000 Women 15 to 44 Years of Age, by Southern Divisions, and States: 1900 to 1930." U.S. Bureau of the Census. *Negroes in the United States: 1920-32.* Washington, D.C.: Government Printing Office, 1935, p. 203.

★ 2220 ★

Fertility

Fertility Rate and Birth Rate: Age of Mother and Race, 1940 to 1970

Total fertility rates are the sum of birth rates, by age of mother, multiplied by 5. Birth rates are live births per 1,000 women in specified group. Prior to 1959, births adjusted for underregistration; thereafter, registered live births. Based on 50-percent sample of births for 1951-1954, 1956-1966, and 1968-1970; on 20- to 50-percent sample for 1967.

Year and race	Total fertility rate	Birth rate, by age of mother							
		10-14 years	15-19 years	20-24 years	25-29 years	30-34 years	35-39 years	40-44 years	45-49 years
Total									
1970	2,480	1.2	68.3	167.8	145.1	73.3	31.7	8.1	0.5
1969	2,465	1.0	66.1	166.0	143.0	74.1	33.4	8.8	.5
1968	2,477	1.0	66.1	167.4	140.3	74.9	35.6	9.6	.6
1967	2,573	.9	67.9	174.0	142.6	79.3	38.5	10.6	.7
1966	2,736	.9	70.6	185.9	149.4	85.9	42.2	11.7	.7
1965	2,928	.8	70.4	196.8	162.5	95.0	46.4	12.8	.8
1964	3,208	.9	72.8	219.9	179.4	103.9	50.0	13.8	.8
1963	3,333	.9	76.4	231.2	185.8	106.2	51.3	14.2	.9
1962	3,474	.8	81.2	243.7	191.7	108.9	52.7	14.8	.9
1961	3,629	.9	88.0	253.7	197.9	113.3	55.6	15.6	.9
1960	3,654	.8	89.1	258.1	197.4	112.7	56.2	15.5	.9

[Continued]

★ 2220 ★

Fertility Rate and Birth Rate: Age of Mother and Race, 1940 to 1970

[Continued]

Year and race	Total fertility rate	Birth rate, by age of mother 10-14 years	15-19 years	20-24 years	25-29 years	30-34 years	35-39 years	40-44 years	45-49 years
1959	3,670	.9	89.1	257.5	198.6	114.4	57.3	15.3	.9
1958	3,701	.9	91.4	258.2	198.3	116.2	58.3	15.7	.9
1957	3,767	1.0	96.3	260.6	199.4	118.9	59.9	16.3	1.1
1956	3,689	1.0	94.6	253.7	194.7	117.3	59.3	16.3	1.0
1955	3,580	.9	90.5	242.0	190.5	116.2	58.7	16.1	1.0
1954	3,543	.9	90.6	236.2	188.4	116.9	57.9	16.2	1.0
1953	3,424	1.0	88.2	224.6	184.1	113.4	56.6	15.8	1.0
1952	3,358	.9	86.1	217.6	182.0	112.6	555.8	15.5	1.3
1951	3,269	.9	87.6	211.6	175.3	107.9	54.1	15.4	1.1
1950	3,091	1.0	81.6	196.6	166.1	103.7	52.9	15.1	1.2
1949	3,110	1.0	83.4	200.1	165.4	102.1	53.5	15.3	1.3
1948	3,109	1.0	81.8	200.3	163.4	103.7	54.5	15.7	1.3
1947	3,274	.9	79.3	209.7	176.0	111.9	58.9	16.6	1.4
1946	2,943	.7	59.3	181.8	161.2	108.9	58.7	16.5	1.5
1945	2,491	.8	51.1	138.9	132.2	100.2	56.9	16.6	1.6
1944	2,568	.8	54.3	151.8	136.5	98.1	54.6	16.1	1.4
1943	2,718	.8	61.7	164.0	147.8	99.5	52.8	15.7	1.5
1942	2,628	.7	61.1	165.1	142.7	91.8	47.9	14.7	1.6
1941	2,399	.7	56.9	145.4	128.7	85.3	46.1	15.0	1.7
1940	2,301	.7	54.1	135.6	122.8	83.4	46.3	15.6	1.9
White									
1970	2,385	.5	57.4	163.4	145.9	71.9	30.0	7.5	.4
1969	2,360	.4	55.2	161.4	142.8	72.0	31.6	8.1	.5
1968	2,368	.4	55.3	162.6	139.7	72.5	33.8	8.9	.5
1967	2,453	.3	57.3	168.8	140.7	76.5	36.6	9.8	.6
1966	2,609	.3	60.8	179.9	146.6	82.7	40.0	10.8	.7
1965	2,790	.3	60.7	189.8	158.8	91.7	44.1	12.0	.7
1964	3,074	.3	63.2	213.1	176.2	100.5	47.7	13.0	.7
1963[1]	3,201	.3	68.1	224.7	181.5	102.6	48.9	13.4	.8
1962[1]	3,348	.4	73.1	238.0	187.7	105.2	50.2	14.1	.8
1961	3,502	.4	78.8	247.9	194.4	110.1	53.2	14.8	.9
1960	3,533	.4	79.4	252.8	194.9	109.6	54.0	14.7	.8
1959	3,544	.4	79.2	251.7	195.5	111.3	55.1	14.7	.9
1958	3,560	.5	81.0	251.4	194.8	113.0	55.8	14.8	.8
1957	3,625	.5	85.2	253.8	195.8	115.9	57.4	15.4	.8
1956	3,546	.3	83.2	247.1	190.6	114.4	57.0	15.4	.8
1955	3,446	.3	79.2	236.0	186.8	114.1	56.7	15.4	.9
1954	3,415	.4	79.0	230.7	185.0	115.1	56.2	15.4	.9

[Continued]

★ 2220 ★

Fertility Rate and Birth Rate: Age of Mother and Race, 1940 to 1970

[Continued]

Year and race	Total fertility rate	Birth rate, by age of mother 10-14 years	15-19 years	20-24 years	25-29 years	30-34 years	35-39 years	40-44 years	45-49 years
1953	3,306	.4	77.2	219.6	181.5	111.9	55.1	15.0	.9
1952	3,250	.4	75.0	212.5	180.5	111.4	54.4	14.8	.9
1951	3,157	.4	75.9	206.0	174.2	106.5	52.6	14.6	1.0
1950	2,977	.4	70.0	190.4	165.1	102.6	51.4	14.5	1.0
1949	3,009	.4	72.1	194.6	165.2	101.5	52.2	14.6	1.1
1948	3,022	.4	71.1	195.5	163.9	103.6	53.5	15.2	1.1
1947	3,230	.4	69.8	207.9	179.1	113.0	58.4	16.1	1.2
1946	2,901	.3	50.6	179.8	164.0	110.0	58.4	15.9	1.3
1945	2,421	.3	42.1	134.7	133.1	100.5	56.3	16.0	1.4
1944	2,501	.3	45.3	147.9	137.7	98.2	54.1	15.5	1.2
1943	2,664	.3	52.1	161.1	150.7	100.2	52.2	15.0	1.3
1942	2,577	.3	51.8	162.9	145.6	92.3	47.2	14.1	1.3
1941	2,328	.2	47.6	141.6	130.1	85.2	45.1	14.3	1.4
1940	2,229	.2	45.3	131.4	123.6	83.4	45.3	15.0	1.6
Negro and other									
1970	3,067	4.8	133.4	196.8	140.1	82.5	42.2	12.6	.9
1969	3,148	4.6	133.3	197.8	144.2	88.9	45.9	13.9	1.0
1968	3,197	4.4	133.3	200.8	144.8	91.2	48.6	15.0	1.2
1967	3,385	4.1	135.2	212.1	155.9	99.1	52.4	16.8	1.2
1966	3,615	4.0	135.5	228.9	169.3	107.9	57.7	18.4	1.4
1965	3,891	4.0	136.1	247.3	188.1	118.3	63.8	19.2	1.5
1964	4,153	4.0	138.7	268.6	202.0	127.5	67.5	20.9	1.5
1963[1]	4,269	4.0	139.9	277.3	211.8	129.3	68.9	21.0	1.5
1962[1]	4,396	3.9	144.6	285.7	217.4	132.4	72.0	21.7	1.5
1961	4,533	4.0	152.8	292.9	221.9	136.2	74.9	22.3	1.5
1960	4,522	4.0	158.2	294.2	214.6	135.6	74.2	22.0	1.7
1959	4,595	4.2	160.5	297.9	220.2	138.1	75.0	21.2	1.8
1958	4,727	4.3	167.3	305.2	224.2	142.3	78.4	21.8	1.9
1957	4,798	5.6	172.8	307.0	228.1	143.5	78.7	23.5	2.0
1956	4,730	4.7	172.5	299.1	225.9	139.4	78.8	23.6	2.0
1955	4,550	4.8	168.3	283.4	219.6	133.5	75.4	22.1	2.1
1954	4,474	4.9	170.3	274.7	215.7	131.3	72.9	22.5	2.1
1953	4,283	5.1	165.4	261.4	206.4	125.7	70.0	23.0	2.2
1952	4,147	5.2	162.9	254.0	194.2	122.0	66.6	21.9	2.2
1951	4,091	5.4	166.7	252.5	184.2	117.9	66.5	22.6	2.2
1950	3,928	5.1	163.5	242.6	173.8	112.6	64.3	21.2	2.6
1949	3,855	5.1	162.8	241.3	167.0	107.3	63.9	21.1	2.5
1948	3,742	4.9	157.3	237.0	159.6	104.1	62.5	20.4	2.8

[Continued]

★ 2220 ★

Fertility Rate and Birth Rate: Age of Mother and Race, 1940 to 1970

[Continued]

Year and race	Total fertility rate	Birth rate, by age of mother							
		10-14 years	15-19 years	20-24 years	25-29 years	30-34 years	35-39 years	40-44 years	45-49 years
1947	3,575	4.6	146.6	223.7	150.6	102.4	62.7	21.4	3.1
1946	3,238	3.7	121.9	197.3	139.2	99.3	61.0	21.8	3.5
1945	3,017	3.9	117.5	172.1	125.4	97.1	61.3	22.3	3.7
1944	3,075	3.9	121.5	182.4	126.8	97.3	58.4	21.5	3.2
1943	3,128	4.0	133.4	187.2	125.1	93.9	56.9	21.5	3.7
1942	3,022	3.9	131.8	182.3	119.6	88.1	54.0	20.8	4.0
1941	2,956	4.0	128.3	175.0	118.1	86.2	54.1	21.5	4.1
1940	2,870	3.7	121.7	168.5	116.3	83.5	53.7	21.5	5.2

Source: "Fertility Rate and Birth Rate, by Age of Mother, by Race: 1940 to 1970." *Historical Statistics of the United States: Colonial Times to 1970, Part I.* Bicentennial Edition. Washington, D.C.: Government Printing Office, 1975, p. 50. *Note:* 1. Excludes New Jersey; State did not require reporting of race.

★ 2221 ★

Fertility

Fertility Rate and Intrinsic Rate of Increase, 1940-1944 through 1975

Excludes Alaska prior to 1959 and Hawaii prior to 1960. Prior to 1960, based on births adjusted for underregistration; thereafter, registered births only. Beginning 1970, excludes births to nonresidents of United States. The total fertility rate is the number of births that 1,000 women would have in their lifetime if, at each year of age, they experienced the birth rates occurring in the specified year. A total fertility rate of 2,110 represents "replacement level" fertility for the total population under current mortality conditions (assuming no net immigration). The intrinsic rate of natural increase is the rate that would eventually prevail if a population were to experience at each year of age, the birth rates and death rates occurring in the specified year and if those rates remained unchanged over a long period of time. Minus sign (-) indicates decrease.

Annual average and year	Total fertility rate		Intrinsic rate of natural increase	
	White	Black and other	White	Black and other
1940-1944	2,460	3,010	3.9	9.8
1945-1949	2,916	3,485	10.9	17.2
1950-1954	3,221	4,185	15.4	25.7
1955-1959	3,549	4,716	19.5	30.7
1960-1964	3,326	4,326	17.1	27.7
1965-1969	2,512	3,362	6.4	18.6
1970-1974	1,997	2,680	-2.5	9.1
1965	2,783	3,808	10.3	23.1
1966	2,603	3,532	7.9	20.4
1967	2,447	3,299	5.6	18.2

[Continued]

★ 2221 ★

Fertility Rate and Intrinsic Rate of Increase, 1940-1944 through 1975

[Continued]

Annual average and year	Total fertility rate		Intrinsic rate of natural increase	
	White	Black and other	White	Black and other
1968	2,366	3,108	4.2	16.0
1969	2,360	3,061	4.1	15.4
1970	2,385	3,067	4.5	14.4
1971	2,161	2,920	.8	12.6
1972	1,907	2,628	-3.9	8.6
1973	1,783	2,444	-6.5	5.7
1974	1,749	2,339	-7.2	4.0
1975	1,686	2,276	-8.6	3.0

Source: "Total Fertility Rate and Intrinsic Rate of Natural Increase: 1940 to 1986." *Statistical Abstract*, 1989, p. 64.

★ 2222 ★

Fertility

Fertility Rate, 1955-1968

Year	Negro and other races	Negro	White
1955	4.55	(NA)	3.45
1956	4.73	(NA)	3.55
1957	4.80	(NA)	3.63
1958	4.73	(NA)	3.56
1959	4.77	(NA)	3.57
1960	4.52	(NA)	3.53
1961	4.53	(NA)	3.50
1962[1]	4.40	(NA)	3.35
1963[1]	4.27	(NA)	3.20
1964	4.15	(NA)	3.07
1965	3.89	(NA)	2.79
1966	3.61	3.58	2.61
1967	3.39	3.35	2.45
1968	3.20	3.13	2.37

Source: "Total Fertility Rates: 1955 to 1968." U.S. Bureau of the Census. Current Population Reports, Special Studies, Series P-23, No. 42. *The Social and Economic Status of the Black Populations in the United States, 1971.* Washington, D.C.: Government Printing Office, 1972, p. 106. Primary source: U.S. Department of Health, Education and Welfare and U.S. Depart of Commerce, Social and Economic Statistics Administration, Bureau of the Census. *Notes:* Total fertility rate is defined as the number of births that 1,000 women would have in their lifetime if, at each year of age, they experienced the birth rates occurring in the specified calendar year. Births 1955-59 adjusted for underregistration of births. NA Not available. 1. Excludes data for New Jersey.

★ 2223 ★

Fertility

Fertility Rate, 1960-1974

Year	All races	Black and other races	Black	White
1960	3.65	4.52	(NA)	3.53
1961	3.63	4.53	(NA)	3.50
1962	3.47	4.40[1]	(NA)	3.35[1]
1963	3.33	4.27[1]	(NA)	3.20[1]
1964	3.21	4.15	(NA)	3.07
1965	2.93	3.89	(NA)	2.79
1966	2.74	3.61	3.58	2.61
1967	2.57	3.39	3.35	2.45
1968	2.48	3.20	3.13	2.37
1969	2.47	3.15	3.07	2.36
1970	2.48	3.07	3.10	2.39
1971	2.27	2.93	2.91	2.17
1972	2.02	2.65	2.62	1.92
1973	1.90	2.47	2.44	1.80
1974	1.86[2]	(NA)	(NA)	(NA)

Source: "Total Fertility Rates: 1960 to 1974." U.S. Bureau of the Census. Current Population Reports, Special Studies, Series P-23, No. 54. *The Social and Economic Status of the Black Population in the United States, 1974.* Washington, D.C.: Government Printing Office, 1975, p. 115. Primary source: U.S. Department of Health, Education, and Welfare, and U.S. Department of Commerce, Social and Economic Statistics Administration, Bureau of the Census. *Notes:* A total fertility rate is defined as the average number of births that each woman in a synthetic cohort of women would have in their lifetime if, at each year of age, the women experienced the birth rates occurring in the specified calendar year. NA Not available. 1. Excludes data for residents of New Jersey. 2. Bureau of the Census estimate.

★ 2224 ★

Fertility

Fertility Rates: 1920-1975

Minus sign (-) denotes decrease.

Year	All races	Black and other races		White	Ratio: Black and other races to White
		Total	Black		
1920[1]	3.26	3.56	(NA)	3.22	1.11
1930[1]	2.53	2.73	(NA)	2.514	1.09
1940[1]	2.23	2.62	(NA)	2.18	1.20
1950[1]	3.03	3.58	(NA)	2.95	1.21
1960	3.65	4.52	4.54	3.53	1.28
1970	2.48	3.09	3.10	2.39	1.28
1974	1.86	2.38	2.33	1.77	1.34
1975	1.80	2.32	2.28	1.71	1.36

[Continued]

★ 2224 ★

Fertility Rates: 1920-1975

[Continued]

Year	All races	Black and other races		White	Ratio: Black and other races to White
		Total	Black		
PERCENT CHANGE					
1920 to 1930	-22	-23	(NA)	-22	(X)
1930 to 1940	-12	-4	(NA)	-13	(X)
1940 to 1950	+36	+37	(NA)	+35	(X)
1950 to 1960	+20	+26	(NA)	+20	(X)
1960 to 1970	-32	-32	-32	-32	(X)
1970 to 1975	-27	-24	-26	-28	(X)

Source: "Total Fertility Rates, for Selected Years: 1920 to 1975," U.S. Department of Commerce, Bureau of the Census. *The Social and Economic Status of the Black Population in the United STates: An Historical View, 1790-1978*, p. 126. *Notes:* NA Not available. X Not applicable. The total fertility rate shows the average number of births each woman would have in her lifetime if, at each year of age, women experienced the birth rates occurring in the specified calendar year. 1. Fertility rates for 1920 to 1950 are derived by a different methodology than those for subsequent years.

★ 2225 ★

Fertility

Number, Increase, and Proportion of Black and White Women Age 15 to 44 and Children at Specific Ages, 1900-1930

Census Year and decade	Total population		Women 15 to 44 years of age		Children: Under 10 years of age		Children: Under 5 years of age		Children: Under 1 year of age	
	Negro	White[1]	Negro	White[1]	Negro	White[1]	Negro	White[1]	Negro	White[1]
Number										
1930	11,891,143	108,864,207	3,131,885	25,702,404	2,598,587	20,883,540	1,230,206	9,927,396	232,378	1,896,730
1920	10,463,131	94,820,915	2,663,269	22,017,601	2,409,906	20,461,166	1,143,699	10,373,921	227,660	2,017,767
1910	9,827,763	81,731,957	2,435,189	19,270,619	2,509,841	17,798,087	1,263,288	9,322,914	252,386	1,955,605
1900	8,833,994	66,809,196	2,087,324	15,576,952	2,418,413	15,558,278	1,215,655	7,919,952	244,510	1,665,007
Percent in each group										
1930	100.0	100.0	26.3	23.6	21.9	19.2	10.3	9.1	2.0	1.7
1920	100.0	100.0	25.5	23.2	23.0	21.6	10.9	10.9	2.2	2.1
1910	100.0	100.0	24.8	23.6	25.5	21.8	12.9	11.4	2.6	2.4
1900	100.0	100.0	23.6	23.3	27.4	23.3	13.8	11.9	2.8	2.5
Increase or decrease (-)										
1920-30	1,428,012	14,043,292	468,616	3,684,803	188,681	422,374	86,507	-446,525	4,718	-121,037
1910-20	635,368	13,088,958	228,080	2,746,982	-99,935	2,663,079	-119,589	1,051,007	-24,726	62,162
1900-10	993,769	14,922,761	347,865	3,693,667	91,428	2,239,809	47,633	1,402,962	7,876	290,598
Percent increase or decrease (-)										
1920-30	13.6	14.8	17.6	16.7	7.8	2.1	7.6	-4.3	2.1	-6.0
1910-20	6.5	16.0	9.4	14.3	-4.0	15.0	-9.5	11.3	-9.8	3.2
1900-10	11.2	22.3	16.7	23.7	3.8	14.4	3.9	17.7	3.2	17.5

Source: "Number, Increase, and Proportion of Negro and White Women 15 to 44 Years of Age, and of Children 10 Years of Age, Under 5, and Under 1, for the United States: 1900 to 1930." U.S. Bureau of the Census. *Negroes in the United States: 1920-32*. Washington, D.C.: Government Printing Office, 1935, p. 201. *Note:* 1. Includes Mexicans prior to 1930.

★ 2226 ★

Fertility

Total Number of Children Under Age 5 Per 1,000 Women Aged 15 to 44 by Age, Race, and Geographical Area, 1900-1930

Number of children under 5 years per 1,000 women 15 to 44 years of age, by color, sections,and southern divisions: 1900 to 1930.

Section, division, and racial class	1930	1920	1910	1900	Increase or decrease (-)		
					1920-1930	1910-1920	1900-1910
United States							
Negro	393	429	519	582	-36	-90	-63
White[1]	386	471	484	508	-85	-13	-24
Other races	703	737	721	679	-34	16	42
The South							
Negro	423	463	554	619	-40	-91	-65
White[1]	468	547	617	633	-79	-70	-16
Other races	644	748	906	795	-104	-158	111
South Atlantic							
Negro	438	496	577	630	-58	-81	-53
White[1]	464	547	589	595	-83	-42	-6
Other races	738	872	860	629	-134	12	231
East South Central							
Negro	424	442	535	598	-18	-93	-63
White[1]	506	568	626	630	-62	-58	-4
Other races	688	729	940	716	-41	-211	224
West South Central							
Negro	396	422	532	627	-26	-110	-95
White[1]	443	531	644	692	-88	-113	-48
Other races	641	721	911	817	-80	-190	94
The North							
Negro	295	263	282	317	32	-19	-35
White[1]	364	449	442	470	-85	7	-28
Other races	796	685	645	678	111	40	-33
The West							
Negro	239	236	231	269	3	5	-38
White[1]	326	423	434	477	-97	-11	-43
Other races	742	748	645	600	-6	103	45

Source: "Children Under 5 Years Per 1,000 Women 15 to 44 Years of Age, by Color, Sections, and Southern Divisions: 1900 to 1930." U.S. Bureau of the Census. *Negroes in the United States: 1920-32.* Washington, D.C.: Government Printing Office, 1935, p. 202. *Note:* 1. Includes Mexicans prior to 1930.

★ 2227 ★

Fertility

Total Women Aged 15 to 44, Children Under Age 5 and Number of Children Per 1,000 Women, by Urban and Rural Areas, 1930

Section and area	Women 15 to 44 years of age		Children under 5 years of age		Children under 5 years per 1,000 women 15 to 44 years of age	
	Negro	White	Negro	White	Negro	White
United States						
Urban	1,592,847	16,065,798	427,607	5,074,431	268	316
Rural	1,539,038	9,636,606	802,599	4,852,965	521	504
Rural-farm	1,037,704	4,978,751	588,846	2,665,005	567	535
Rural-nonfarm	501,334	4,657,855	213,753	2,187,960	426	470
The South						
Urban	928,088	2,552,570	242,220	833,229	261	326
Rural	1,473,837	3,901,225	774,359	2,184,120	525	560
Rural-farm	1,023,402	2,337,472	581,424	1,364,575	568	584
Rural-nonfarm	450,435	1,563,753	192,935	819,545	428	524
The North						
Urban	636,144	11,880,182	179,197	3,818,598	282	321
Rural	60,854	4,835,152	26,556	2,265,770	436	469
Rural-farm	13,065	2,258,768	6,746	1,115,915	516	494
Rural-nonfarm	47,789	2,576,384	19,810	1,149,855	415	446
The West						
Urban	28,615	1,633,046	6,190	422,604	216	259
Rural	4,347	900,229	1,684	403,075	387	448
Rural-farm	1,237	382,511	676	184,515	546	482
Rural-nonfarm	3,110	517,718	1,008	218,560	324	422

Source: "Negro Women 15 to 44 Years of Age, Negro Children Under 5 Years, and Number of Negro Children Per 1,000 Women, for Urban, Rural-Farm, and Rural Non-Farm Areas, by Sections, Divisions, and States: 1930." U.S. Bureau of the Census. *Negroes in the United States: 1920-32*. Washington, D.C.: Government Printing Office, 1935, p. 202.

★ 2228 ★

Fertility

Unwanted Fertility: 1970

Based on data from the 1970 National Fertility Study for currently married women under 45 years of age.

Race and education	Most likely number of births per woman	Percent of births, 1966-1970[1]		Theoretical births per woman[2]
		Unwanted	Unplanned	
White	2.9	13	42	2.6
College				
4 years or more	2.5	7	32	2.4
1-3 years	2.8	10	39	2.6
High school				
4 years	2.8	13	42	2.6
1-3 years	3.2	18	44	2.8
Less	3.5	25	53	2.9
Negro	3.7	27	61	2.9
College				
4 years or more	2.3	3	21	2.2
1-3 years	2.6	21	46	2.3
High school				
4 years	3.3	19	62	2.8
1-3 years	4.2	31	66	3.2
Less	5.2	55	68	3.1

Source: "Unwanted Fertility: 1970." Bureau of the Census, *Statistical Abstract of the United States, 1975.* Washington, D.C.: U.S. Government Printing Office, 1975, p. 57. Primary source: U.S. Commission on Population Growth and the American Future, *Population and the American Future, 1970. Notes:* 1. Unplanned births included in unwanted births. 2. Excluding unwanted births.

★ 2229 ★

Fertility

Women Aged 15 to 44, Children Under Age 5 and Number of Children Per 1,000 Women, by Geographical Area: 1920, 1930 - I

Children per 1,000 women not shown where base is less than 100.

Division, and state	Women 15 to 44 years of age				Children under 5 years of age			
	Negro		White		Negro		White	
	1930	1920	1930	1920[1]	1930	1920	1930	1920[1]
United States	3,131,885	2,663,269	25,702,404	22,017,601	1,230,206	1,143,699	9,927,396	10,373,921
Geographic divisions								
New England	23,275	21,108	1,899,813	1,734,977	8,915	7,415	680,321	745,273
Middle Atlantic	317,861	182,939	6,140,080	5,173,535	93,251	47,306	2,118,758	2,305,998
East North Central	266,545	144,246	5,712,978	4,854,556	78,446	36,991	2,118,764	2,180,743

[Continued]

★ 2229 ★

Women Aged 15 to 44, Children Under Age 5 and Number of Children Per 1,000 Women, by Geographical Area: 1920, 1930 - I

[Continued]

Division, and state	Women 15 to 44 years of age				Children under 5 years of age			
	Negro		White		Negro		White	
	1930	1920	1930	1920[1]	1930	1920	1930	1920[1]
West North Central	89,317	75,581	2,962,463	2,814,701	25,141	19,689	1,166,525	1,316,245
South Atlantic	1,119,800	1,062,848	2,633,006	2,194,342	490,017	527,394	1,221,643	1,199,524
East South Central	679,862	628,839	1,648,498	1,426,127	288,162	277,670	834,129	810,201
West South Central	602,263	528,011	2,172,291	1,853,979	238,400	222,582	961,577	984,778
Mountain	7,546	6,636	742,709	713,555	2,084	1,540	325,009	383,287
Pacific	25,416	13,061	1,790,566	1,251,829	5,790	3,112	500,670	447,872
New England								
Maine	204	306	168,746	166,544	107	113	74,806	74,917
New Hampshire	127	127	101,046	98,138	48	72	39,294	41,316
Vermont	102	118	74,661	74,796	75	52	33,150	34,487
Massachusetts	12,822	12,470	1,013,210	930,542	4,708	4,308	344,605	381,284
Rhode Island	2,216	2,464	163,446	144,318	1,008	997	58,581	61,338
Connecticut	7,804	5,623	378,704	320,639	2,969	1,873	129,885	151,931
Middle Atlantic								
New York	136,164	67,188	3,064,202	2,522,447	34,116	14,726	953,331	994,584
New Jersey	59,409	33,940	941,160	727,887	19,790	10,171	309,662	328,481
Pennsylvania	122,288	81,811	2,134,718	1,923,201	39,345	22,409	855,765	982,933
East North Central								
Ohio	84,409	50,018	1,480,130	1,289,972	27,845	14,227	544,568	571,861
Indiana	30,076	21,910	703,001	649,096	9,142	5,922	274,618	283,247
Illinois	99,252	54,271	1,792,182	1,513,891	25,378	12,333	585,645	642,616
Michigan	49,900	16,709	1,075,214	808,571	15,231	4,141	445,235	399,700
Wisconsin	2,908	1,338	662,451	593,026	850	368	268,698	283,319
West North Central								
Minnesota	2,321	2,421	591,227	547,226	615	522	228,025	259,487
Iowa	4,128	4,843	550,207	548,048	1,391	1,550	217,991	249,267
Missouri	62,804	49,999	803,107	761,866	16,830	11,956	288,099	315,916
North Dakota	84	102	146,933	137,601	30	20	74,259	89,964
South Dakota	147	169	149,342	137,672	47	70	68,095	77,431
Nebraska	3,785	3,707	313,861	293,743	1,046	878	127,622	141,831
Kansas	16,048	14,340	407,786	388,545	5,182	4,693	162,434	182,349
South Atlantic								
Delaware	7,681	7,283	46,727	44,021	2,787	2,776	16,492	20,152
Maryland	68,548	61,777	316,357	284,332	27,006	24,145	117,544	122,844
District of Columbia	39,745	35,055	94,806	99,385	10,006	7,774	22,240	22,632
Virginia	151,720	164,978	404,117	362,720	70,662	81,263	186,341	195,765
West Virginia	29,077	21,662	354,698	296,481	12,104	8,854	194,935	187,071
North Carolina	226,053	178,722	516,478	393,422	114,695	106,460	273,807	250,294
South Carolina	195,225	206,813	219,692	184,526	96,300	117,526	108,642	110,992

[Continued]

★ 2229 ★

Women Aged 15 to 44, Children Under Age 5 and Number of Children Per 1,000 Women, by Geographical Area: 1920, 1930 - I

[Continued]

Division, and state	Women 15 to 44 years of age				Children under 5 years of age			
	Negro		White		Negro		White	
	1930	1920	1930	1920[1]	1930	1920	1930	1920[1]
Georgia	279,911	299,681	434,970	385,626	116,016	145,332	200,353	217,864
Florida	121,840	86,877	245,161	143,829	40,441	33,264	101,289	71,910
East South Central								
Kentucky	55,558	59,610	525,148	482,330	18,587	20,468	274,257	271,143
Tennessee	128,059	116,858	498,329	429,518	44,304	45,653	237,483	235,079
Alabama	243,502	222,670	394,837	323,084	107,836	104,155	205,960	195,290
Mississippi	252,743	229,701	230,184	191,195	117,435	107,394	116,429	108,689
West South Central								
Arkansas	124,172	120,425	310,288	278,693	49,957	51,274	158,614	169,520
Louisiana	202,304	179,057	316,743	255,811	84,986	77,296	144,541	131,745
Oklahoma	44,867	37,035	500,048	408,006	17,337	16,214	232,821	227,798
Texas	230,920	191,494	1,045,212	911,469	86,120	77,798	425,601	455,715
Mountain								
Montana	261	382	112,353	119,013	66	109	46,518	65,500
Idaho	157	192	94,243	91,145	30	55	45,010	53,832
Wyoming	297	335	47,795	41,798	63	59	20,917	22,099
Colorado	3,196	3,112	222,403	210,407	773	693	84,371	95,639
New Mexico	731	747	74,819	73,043	249	181	39,904	43,773
Arizona	2,518	1,390	62,647	66,418	793	333	24,495	35,764
Utah	253	391	111,363	97,208	89	95	57,698	60,517
Nevada	133	87	17,086	14,523	21	15	6,096	6,163
Pacific								
Washington	1,473	1,686	351,201	302,579	400	399	110,514	121,807
Oregon	550	541	216,759	177,289	107	117	67,200	69,885
California	23,393	10,834	1,222,606	771,961	5,283	2,596	322,956	256,180

Source: "Negro and White Women 15 to 44 Years of Age, Children Under 5 Years, and Number of Children Per 1,000 Women, by Divisions, and States: 1930 and 1920." U.S. Bureau of the Census. *Negroes in the United States: 1920-32*. Washington, D.C.: Government Printing Office, 1935, p. 204. *Note:* 1. Includes Mexicans.

★ 2230 ★

Fertility

Women Aged 15 to 44, Children Under Age 5 and Number of Children Per 1,000 Women, by Geographical Area: 1920, 1930 - II

Children per 1,000 women not shown where base is less than 100.

Division, and state	Children under 5 per 1,000 women 15 to 44 years of age					
	Negro		White		Increase or decrease (-) 1920-30	
	1930	1920	1930	1920[1]	Negro	White[1]
United States	393	429	386	471	-36	-85
Geographic divisions						
New England	383	351	358	430	32	-72
Middle Atlantic	293	259	345	446	34	-101
East North Central	294	256	371	449	38	-78
West North Central	281	261	394	468	20	-74
South Atlantic	438	496	464	547	-58	-83
East South Central	424	442	506	568	-18	-62
West South Central	396	422	443	531	-26	-88
Mountain	276	232	438	537	44	-99
Pacific	228	238	280	358	-10	-78
New England						
Maine	525	369	443	450	156	-7
New Hampshire	378	567	389	421	-189	-32
Vermont	735	441	444	461	294	-17
Massachusetts	367	345	340	410	22	-70
Rhode Island	455	405	358	425	50	-67
Connecticut	380	333	343	474	47	-131
Middle Atlantic						
New York	251	219	311	394	32	-83
New Jersey	333	300	329	451	33	-122
Pennsylvania	322	274	401	511	48	-110
East North Central						
Ohio	330	284	368	443	46	-75
Indiana	304	270	391	436	34	-45
Illinois	256	227	327	424	29	-97
Michigan	305	248	414	494	57	-80
Wisconsin	292	275	406	478	17	-72
West North Central						
Minnesota	265	216	386	474	49	-88
Iowa	337	320	376	455	17	-59
Missouri	268	239	359	415	29	-56
North Dakota	-	196	505	654	-	-149
South Dakota	320	414	456	562	-94	-106
Nebraska	276	237	407	483	39	-76
Kansas	323	327	398	469	-4	-71

[Continued]

★ 2230 ★

Women Aged 15 to 44, Children Under Age 5 and Number of Children Per 1,000 Women, by Geographical Area: 1920, 1930 - II

[Continued]

Division, and state	Children under 5 per 1,000 women 15 to 44 years of age					
	Negro		White		Increase or decrease (-) 1920-30	
	1930	1920	1930	1920[1]	Negro	White[1]
South Atlantic						
Delaware	363	381	353	458	-18	-105
Maryland	394	391	372	432	3	-60
District of Columbia	252	222	235	228	30	7
Virginia	466	493	461	540	-27	-79
West Virginia	416	409	550	631	7	-81
North Carolina	507	596	530	636	-89	-106
South Carolina	493	568	495	601	-75	-106
Georgia	414	485	461	565	-71	-104
Florida	332	383	413	500	-51	-87
East South Central						
Kentucky	335	343	522	562	-8	-40
Tennessee	346	391	477	547	-45	-70
Alabama	443	468	522	604	-25	-82
Mississippi	465	468	506	568	-3	-62
West South Central						
Arkansas	402	426	511	608	-24	-97
Louisiana	420	432	456	515	-12	-59
Oklahoma	386	438	466	558	-52	-92
Texas	373	406	407	500	-33	-93
Mountain						
Montana	253	285	414	550	-32	-136
Idaho	191	286	478	591	-95	-113
Wyoming	212	176	438	529	36	-91
Colorado	242	223	379	455	19	-76
New Mexico	341	242	533	599	99	-66
Arizona	315	240	391	538	75	-147
Utah	352	243	518	623	109	-105
Nevada	158	-	357	424	-	-67
Pacific						
Washington	272	237	315	403	35	-88
Oregon	195	216	310	394	-21	-84
California	226	240	264	332	-14	-68

Source: "Negro and White Women 15 to 44 Years of Age, Children Under 5 Years, and Number of Children Per 1,000 Women, by Divisions, and States: 1930 and 1920." U.S. Bureau of the Census. *Negroes in the United States: 1920-32*. Washington, D.C.: Government Printing Office, 1935, p. 204. *Note:* 1. Includes Mexicans.

★ 2231 ★

Fertility

Women Aged 15 to 44, Children Under Age 5 and Number of Children Per 1,000 Women, by Urban and Rural Areas, 1930 - I

Section, division, and state	Women 15 to 44 years of age					Children under 5 years of age				
	Total	Urban	Rural			Total	Urban	Rural		
			Total	Rural-farm	Rural-nonfarm			Total	Rural-farm	Rural-nonfarm
United States	3,131,885	1,592,347	1,539,038	1,037,704	501,334	1,230,206	427,607	802,599	588,846	213,753
The North	696,998	636,144	60,854	13,065	47,789	205,753	179,197	26,556	6,746	19,810
The South	2,401,925	928,088	1,473,837	1,023,402	450,435	1,016,579	242,220	774,359	581,424	192,935
The West	32,962	28,615	4,347	1,237	3,110	7,874	6,190	1,684	676	1,008
New England	23,275	20,530	2,745	208	2,537	8,915	7,637	1,278	91	1,187
Maine	204	147	57	18	39	107	71	36	14	22
New Hampshire	127	91	36	8	28	48	27	21	3	18
Vermont	102	43	59	13	46	75	22	53	20	33
Massachusetts	12,822	11,654	1,168	72	1,096	4,708	4,042	666	38	628
Rhode Island	2,216	2,047	169	20	149	1,008	937	71	3	68
Connecticut	7,804	6,548	1,256	77	1,179	2,969	2,538	431	13	418
Middle Atlantic	317,861	291,171	26,690	2,079	24,611	93,251	81,640	11,611	1,113	10,498
New York	136,164	130,397	5,767	430	5,337	34,116	32,080	2,036	221	1,815
New Jersey	59,409	51,570	7,839	852	6,987	19,790	16,363	3,427	485	2,942
Pennsylvania	122,288	109,204	13,084	797	12,287	39,345	33,197	6,148	407	5,741
East North Central	266,545	250,250	16,295	3,252	13,043	78,446	71,581	6,865	1,700	5,165
Ohio	84,409	76,816	7,593	1,307	6,286	27,845	24,363	3,482	740	2,742
Indiana	30,076	28,464	1,612	435	1,177	9,142	8,521	621	218	403
Illinois	99,252	94,196	5,056	1,074	3,982	25,378	23,381	1,997	503	1,494
Michigan	49,900	48,017	1,883	383	1,500	15,231	14,551	680	186	494
Wisconsin	2,908	2,757	151	53	98	850	765	85	53	32
West North Central	89,317	74,193	15,124	7,526	7,598	25,141	18,339	6,802	3,842	2,960
Minnesota	2,321	2,259	62	33	29	615	592	23	13	10
Iowa	4,128	3,722	406	89	317	1,391	1,223	168	59	109
Missouri	62,804	51,059	11,745	6,498	5,247	16,830	11,353	5,477	3,348	2,129
North Dakota	84	58	26	12	14	30	10	20	14	6
South Dakota	147	85	62	47	15	47	24	23	23	-
Nebraska	3,785	3,656	129	28	101	1,046	1,019	27	13	14
Kansas	16,048	13,354	2,694	819	1,875	5,182	4,118	1,064	372	692
South Atlantic	1,119,800	453,353	666,447	416,158	250,289	490,017	123,670	366,347	250,479	115,868
Delaware	7,681	4,078	3,603	1,290	2,313	2,787	1,072	1,715	720	995
Maryland	68,548	45,470	23,078	8,077	15,001	27,006	13,720	13,286	5,304	7,982
District of Columbia	39,745	39,745	-	-	-	10,006	10,006	-	-	-
Virginia	151,720	62,368	89,352	49,625	39,727	70,662	18,107	52,555	31,736	20,819
West Virginia	29,077	9,005	20,072	723	19,349	12,104	2,500	9,604	409	9,195
North Carolina	226,053	76,917	149,136	105,988	43,148	114,695	23,120	91,575	69,759	21,816
South Carolina	195,225	44,311	150,914	109,732	41,182	96,300	12,403	83,897	64,563	19,334
Georgia	279,911	103,354	176,557	124,072	52,485	116,016	25,260	90,756	69,651	21,105
Florida	121,840	68,105	53,735	16,651	37,084	40,441	17,482	22,959	8,337	14,622
East South Central	679,862	235,637	444,225	335,708	108,517	288,162	60,705	227,457	184,773	42,684
Kentucky	55,558	32,270	23,288	9,630	13,658	18,587	7,856	10,731	5,135	5,596
Tennessee	128,059	74,831	53,228	37,995	15,233	44,304	18,024	26,280	20,536	5,744
Alabama	243,502	85,135	158,367	110,447	47,920	107,836	23,920	83,916	63,473	20,443
Mississippi	252,743	43,401	209,342	177,636	31,706	117,435	10,905	106,530	95,629	10,901
West South Central	602,263	239,098	363,165	271,536	91,629	238,400	57,845	180,555	146,172	34,383
Arkansas	124,172	28,809	95,363	77,408	17,955	49,957	6,362	43,595	37,783	5,812
Louisiana	202,304	81,054	121,250	83,907	37,343	84,986	22,004	62,982	47,637	15,345
Oklahoma	44,867	21,645	23,222	17,295	5,927	17,337	5,135	12,202	9,845	2,357
Texas	230,920	107,590	123,330	92,926	30,404	86,120	24,344	61,776	50,907	10,869

[Continued]

★ 2231 ★

Women Aged 15 to 44, Children Under Age 5 and Number of Children Per 1,000 Women, by Urban and Rural Areas, 1930 - I

[Continued]

Section, division, and state	Women 15 to 44 years of age					Children under 5 years of age				
	Total	Urban	Rural			Total	Urban	Rural		
			Total	Rural-farm	Rural-nonfarm			Total	Rural-farm	Rural-nonfarm
Mountain	7,546	5,723	1,823	495	1,328	2,084	1,374	710	264	446
Montana	261	225	36	11	25	66	59	7	4	3
Idaho	157	137	20	10	10	30	22	8	3	5
Wyoming	297	216	81	13	68	63	41	22	5	17
Colorado	3,196	2,904	292	76	216	773	677	96	34	62
New Mexico	731	494	237	99	138	249	137	112	62	50
Arizona	2,518	1,433	1,085	278	807	793	349	444	153	291
Utah	253	214	39	5	34	89	71	18	3	15
Nevada	133	100	33	3	30	21	18	3	-	3
Pacific	25,416	22,892	2,524	742	1,782	5,790	4,816	974	412	562
Washington	1,473	1,314	159	43	116	400	325	75	21	54
Oregon	550	480	70	6	64	107	85	22	-	22
California	23,393	21,098	2,295	693	1,602	5,283	4,406	877	391	486

Source: "Negro Women 15 to 44 Years of Age, Negro Children Under 5 Years, and Number of Negro Children Per 1,000 Women, for Urban, Rural-Farm, and Rural Non-Farm Areas, by Sections, Divisions, and States: 1930." U.S. Bureau of the Census. *Negroes in the United States: 1920-32*. Washington, D.C.: Government Printing Office, 1935, p. 205.

★ 2232 ★

Fertility

Women Aged 15 to 44, Children Under Age 5 and Number of Children Per 1,000 Women, by Urban and Rural Areas, 1930 - II

Section, division, and state	Children under 5 per 1,000 women 15 to 44 years of age				
	Total	Urban	Rural		
			Total	Rural-farm	Rural-nonfarm
United States	393	268	521	567	426
The North	295	282	436	516	415
The South	423	261	525	568	428
The West	239	216	387	546	324
New England	383	372	466	438	468
Maine	525	483	-	-	-
New Hampshire	378	-	-	-	-
Vermont	735	-	-	-	-
Massachusetts	367	347	570	-	573
Rhode Island	455	458	420	-	456
Connecticut	380	388	343	-	355
Middle Atlantic	293	280	435	535	427
New York	251	246	353	514	340
New Jersey	333	317	437	569	421
Pennsylvania	322	304	470	511	467
East North Central	294	286	421	523	396

[Continued]

★ 2232 ★

Women Aged 15 to 44, Children Under Age 5 and Number of Children Per 1,000 Women, by Urban and Rural Areas, 1930 - II

[Continued]

Section, division, and state	Children under 5 per 1,000 women 15 to 44 years of age				
	Total	Urban	Rural		
			Total	Rural-farm	Rural-nonfarm
Ohio	330	317	459	566	436
Indiana	304	299	385	501	342
Illinois	256	248	395	468	375
Michigan	305	303	361	486	329
Wisconsin	292	277	563	-	-
West North Central	281	247	450	510	390
Minnesota	265	262	-	-	-
Iowa	337	329	414	-	344
Missouri	268	222	466	515	406
North Dakota	-	-	-	-	-
South Dakota	320	-	-	-	-
Nebraska	276	279	209	-	139
Kansas	323	308	395	454	369
South Atlantic	438	273	550	602	463
Delaware	363	263	476	558	430
Maryland	394	302	576	657	532
District of Columbia	252	-	-	-	
Virginia	466	290	588	640	524
West Virginia	416	278	478	566	475
North Carolina	507	301	614	658	506
South Carolina	493	280	556	588	469
Georgia	414	244	514	561	402
Florida	332	257	427	501	394
East South Central	424	258	512	550	393
Kentucky	335	243	461	533	410
Tennessee	346	241	494	540	377
Alabama	443	281	530	575	427
Mississippi	465	251	509	538	344
West South Central	396	242	497	538	375
Arkansas	402	221	457	488	324
Louisiana	420	271	519	568	411
Oklahoma	386	237	525	569	398
Texas	373	226	501	548	357
Mountain	276	240	389	533	336
Montana	253	262	-	-	-
Idaho	191	161	-	-	-
Wyoming	212	190	-	-	-
Colorado	242	233	329	-	287
New Mexico	341	277	473	-	362

[Continued]

★ 2232 ★

Women Aged 15 to 44, Children Under Age 5 and Number of Children Per 1,000 Women, by Urban and Rural Areas, 1930 - II

[Continued]

Section, division, and state	Children under 5 per 1,000 women 15 to 44 years of age				
	Total	Urban	Rural		
			Total	Rural-farm	Rural-nonfarm
Arizona	315	244	409	550	361
Utah	352	332	-	-	-
Nevada	158	180	-	-	-
Pacific	228	210	386	555	315
Washington	272	247	472	-	466
Oregon	195	177	-	-	-
California	226	209	382	564	303

Source: "Negro Women 15 to 44 Years of Age, Negro Children Under 5 Years, and Number of Negro Children Per 1,000 Women, for Urban, Rural-Farm, and Rural Non-Farm Areas, by Sections, Divisions, and States: 1930." U.S. Bureau of the Census. *Negroes in the United States: 1920-32*. Washington, D.C.: Government Printing Office, 1935, p. 205.

★ 2233 ★

Fertility

Women Aged 15 to 44, Children Under Age 5, and Number of Children Per 1,000 Women, in Cities of Over 50,000 Having in 1930 a Black Population of 10,000 or More – 1920, 1930 - I

City	Women 15 to 44 years of age				Children under 5 years of age			
	Negro		White		Negro		White	
	1930	1920	1930	1920[1]	1930	1920	1930	1920[1]
Akron, Ohio	3,159	1,421	64,377	48,420	1,086	306	22,915	20,572
Asheville, N. C.	4,889	2,369	10,320	5,944	1,238	679	3,217	2,211
Atlanta, Ga.	30,443	21,088	51,744	39,481	7,090	4,544	13,835	12,589
Atlantic City, N. J.	4,996	3,722	13,505	10,364	942	591	2,961	3,153
Augusta, Ga.	7,978	7,327	9,607	8,029	1,775	1,527	3,144	2,728
Baltimore, Md.	40,751	33,224	165,625	158,300	12,274	8,366	52,146	60,981
Beaumont, Tex	5,884	4,215	10,742	7,136	1,690	1,085	3,456	2,784
Birmingham, Ala	32,283	22,127	44,752	29,411	8,717	5,617	14,026	10,901
Boston, Mass	5,525	4,895	191,416	185,637	1,582	1,212	60,669	69,573
Buffalo, N. Y.	4,114	1,345	141,552	127,202	1,287	277	46,319	51,802
Camden, N. J.	3,079	2,323	26,295	25,815	1,139	750	8,946	12,208
Charleston, S. C.	9,446	10,514	8,684	9,008	2,768	2,761	3,144	3,512
Charlotte, N. C.	8,283	4,605	16,591	8,674	2,140	1,358	5,689	3,695
Chattanooga, Tenn	10,503	5,972	23,703	11,035	2,618	1,253	7,976	3,235
Chicago, Ill	74,982	35,574	833,662	666,698	17,529	6,404	234,641	265,943
Cincinnati, Ohio	14,190	9,183	103,500	96,394	4,003	1,995	28,960	28,736
Cleveland, Ohio	21,911	10,540	214,882	190,317	6,458	2,371	63,942	86,050
Columbus, S. C.	6,679	4,879	9,126	6,599	1,436	1,071	2,520	2,181

[Continued]

★ 2233 ★

Women Aged 15 to 44, Children Under Age 5, and Number of Children Per 1,000 Women, in Cities of Over 50,000 Having in 1930 a Black Population of 10,000 or More – 1920, 1930 - I

[Continued]

City	Women 15 to 44 years of age				Children under 5 years of age			
	Negro		White		Negro		White	
	1930	1920	1930	1920[1]	1930	1920	1930	1920[1]
Columbus, Ohio	8,719	6,266	66,259	56,056	2,612	1,638	19,521	17,671
Dallas, Tex	13,412	7,954	63,502	39,393	2,751	1,458	17,021	11,340
Dayton, Ohio	4,701	2,513	47,365	36,407	1,576	704	14,281	13,320
Detroit, Mich	37,377	12,212	373,787	236,514	10,618	2,482	134,938	109,603
Durham, N. C.	6,134	2,371	9,236	4,038	1,765	676	3,475	1,482
East St. Louis, Ill	3,354	2,108	16,240	14,716	1,163	669	5,282	5,921
Forth Worth, Tex	7,343	5,268	38,402	24,433	1,488	1,009	10,867	7,529
Galveston, Tex	4,428	3,160	9,337	8,419	945	573	2,771	2,988
Gary, Ind	5,260	1,502	19,501	10,882	1,672	378	7,464	6,914
Greensboro, N. C.	4,548	1,760	11,065	3,972	1,244	561	4,180	1,478
Houston, Tex	21,524	11,294	60,925	29,029	4,588	2,067	17,083	8,990
Indianapolis, Ind	12,542	10,174	83,886	74,283	3,457	2,480	24,183	23,023
Jacksonville, Fla	16,394	13,522	22,488	13,909	3,543	3,067	7,069	4,922
Jersey City, N. J.	3,581	2,247	77,113	71,887	1,239	677	25,037	32,697
Kansas City, Kans	5,364	4,038	24,733	21,160	1,632	1,120	8,532	9,072
Kansas City, Mo	12,311	10,123	100,230	82,009	2,154	1,462	23,454	22,529
Knoxville, Tenn	5,282	3,421	24,429	18,121	1,314	801	8,734	6,985
Little Rock, Ark	6,608	5,721	17,996	13,568	1,323	1,186	4,396	4,087
Los Angeles, Calif	12,174	4,897	285,740	144,359	2,435	988	59,046	34,910
Louisville, Ky	13,952	12,542	68,044	51,855	3,101	2,353	21,627	15,718
Macon, Ga	7,560	7,425	8,623	8,201	1,896	1,563	2,433	2,779
Memphis, Tenn	31,743	20,744	44,465	28,421	7,062	3,630	12,649	8,427
Miami, Fla	8,195	2,920	22,208	5,162	2,639	1,103	6,681	1,811
Mobile, Ala	7,914	7,610	11,384	9,678	2,016	1,796	3,573	3,425
Montgomery, Ala	9,963	6,621	10,055	6,525	2,384	1,433	3,240	2,170
Nashville, Tenn	13,116	11,241	30,500	22,752	3,083	2,424	9,293	7,205
Newark, N. J.	11,881	5,233	102,182	98,812	3,821	1,467	32,286	43,086
New Orleans, La	40,521	31,871	86,938	74,305	11,518	7,798	26,961	24,564
New York, N. Y.	111,230	54,348	1,775,935	1,431,670	26,920	11,147	507,846	549,402
Norfolk, Va	13,270	13,536	21,752	18,899	3,378	3,271	6,261	6,388
Oklahoma City, Okla	4,895	2,618	48,057	23,376	1,033	561	15,007	6,898
Omaha, Nebr	3,171	3,031	53,184	46,813	878	652	16,456	15,846
Philadelphia, Pa	67,185	42,959	434,912	420,350	18,658	9,769	129,548	168,828
Pittsburgh, Pa	15,665	10,949	156,162	138,240	4,934	2,732	52,120	59,262
Port Arthur, Tex	3,212	1,212	10,324	4,614	937	416	4,354	2,003
Richmond, Va	15,816	17,341	36,386	32,754	4,576	4,587	9,490	10,981
Roanoke, Va	3,795	2,906	15,788	11,006	1,144	903	5,270	4,707

[Continued]

★ 2233 ★

Women Aged 15 to 44, Children Under Age 5, and Number of Children Per 1,000 Women, in Cities of Over 50,000 Having in 1930 a Black Population of 10,000 or More – 1920, 1930 - I

[Continued]

City	Women 15 to 44 years of age				Children under 5 years of age			
	Negro		White		Negro		White	
	1930	1920	1930	1920[1]	1930	1920	1930	1920[1]
St. Louis, Mo	29,273	21,793	196,212	190,118	6,634	4,143	51,672	54,541
San Antonio, Tex	6,177	4,720	35,424	38,994	1,098	965	9,030	13,819
Savannah, Ga	13,719	13,347	12,437	11,684	2,660	2,584	3,663	4,405
Shreveport, La	9,535	5,899	14,221	7,306	1,930	1,210	4,255	2,223
Tampa, Fla	7,019	3,853	21,343	9,976	1,636	788	6,756	4,326
Toledo, Ohio	3,869	1,667	69,279	59,767	1,115	346	21,894	22,390
Tulsa, Okla	5,427	2,840	36,169	18,040	1,034	730	10,816	5,610
Washington, D.C.	39,745	35,055	94,806	99,385	10,006	7,774	22,240	22,632
Wilmington, Del	3,404	3,010	23,125	24,095	833	679	7,104	10,861
Winston-Salem, N. C.	10,861	6,764	12,172	7,618	2,915	1,695	4,741	3,115
Youngstown, Ohio	3,969	1,848	37,818	29,953	1,659	443	14,371	16,030

Source: "Negro and White Women 15 to 44 Years of Age, Children Under 5 Years, and Number of Children Per 1,000 Women, in the 65 Cities of 50,000 or More Inhabitants HAving in 1930 a Negro Population of 10,000 or More: 1930 and 1920." U.S. Bureau of the Census. *Negroes in the United States: 1920-32.* Washington, D.C.: Government Printing Office, 1935, p. 206. *Note:* 1. Includes Mexicans.

★ 2234 ★

Fertility

Women Aged 15 to 44, Children Under Age 5, and Number of Children Per 1,000 Women, in Cities of Over 50,000 Having in 1930 a Black Population of 10,000 or More – 1920, 1930 - II

City	Children under 5 per 1,000 women 15 to 44 years of age					
	Negro		White		Increase or decrease (-) 1920-30	
	1930	1920	1930	1920[1]	Negro	White[1]
Akron, Ohio	344	215	356	425	129	-69
Asheville, N. C.	253	287	312	372	-34	-60
Atlanta, Ga.	233	215	267	319	18	-52
Atlantic City, N. J.	189	159	219	304	30	-85
Augusta, Ga.	222	208	327	340	14	-13
Baltimore, Md.	301	252	315	385	49	-70
Beaumont, Tex	287	257	322	390	30	-68
Birmingham, Ala	270	254	313	371	16	-58
Boston, Mass	286	248	317	375	38	-58
Buffalo, N. Y.	313	206	327	407	107	-80
Camden, N. J.	370	323	340	473	47	-133
Charleston, S. C.	293	263	362	390	30	-28
Charlotte, N. C.	258	295	343	426	-37	-83
Chattanooga, Tenn	249	210	336	293	39	43

[Continued]

★ 2234 ★

Women Aged 15 to 44, Children Under Age 5, and Number of Children Per 1,000 Women, in Cities of Over 50,000 Having in 1930 a Black Population of 10,000 or More – 1920, 1930 - II

[Continued]

City	Children under 5 per 1,000 women 15 to 44 years of age					
	Negro		White		Increase or decrease (-) 1920-30	
	1930	1920	1930	1920[1]	Negro	White[1]
Chicago, Ill	234	180	281	399	54	-118
Cincinnati, Ohio	282	217	280	298	65	-18
Cleveland, Ohio	295	225	298	452	70	-154
Columbus, S. C.	215	220	276	331	-5	-55
Columbus, Ohio	300	261	295	315	39	-20
Dallas, Tex	205	183	268	288	22	-20
Dayton, Ohio	335	280	302	366	55	-64
Detroit, Mich	284	203	361	463	81	-102
Durham, N. C.	288	285	376	367	3	9
East St. Louis, Ill	347	317	325	402	30	-77
Forth Worth, Tex	203	192	283	308	11	-25
Galveston, Tex	213	181	297	355	32	-58
Gary, Ind	318	252	383	635	66	-252
Greensboro, N. C.	274	319	378	372	-45	6
Houston, Tex	213	183	280	310	30	-30
Indianapolis, Ind	276	244	288	310	32	-22
Jacksonville, Fla	216	227	314	354	-11	-40
Jersey City, N. J.	346	301	325	455	45	-130
Kansas City, Kans	304	277	345	429	27	-84
Kansas City, Mo	175	144	234	275	31	-41
Knoxville, Tenn	249	234	358	385	15	-27
Little Rock, Ark	200	207	244	301	-7	-57
Los Angeles, Calif	200	202	207	242	-2	-35
Louisville, Ky	222	188	318	303	34	15
Macon, Ga	251	211	282	339	40	-57
Memphis, Tenn	222	175	284	297	47	-13
Miami, Fla	322	378	301	351	-56	-50
Mobile, Ala	255	236	314	354	19	-40
Montgomery, Ala	239	216	322	333	23	-11
Nashville, Tenn	235	216	305	317	19	-12
Newark, N. J.	322	280	316	436	42	-120
New Orleans, La	284	245	310	331	39	-21
New York, N. Y.	242	205	286	384	37	-98
Norfolk, Va	255	242	288	338	13	-50
Oklahoma City, Okla	211	214	312	295	-3	17
Omaha, Nebr	277	215	309	338	62	-29

[Continued]

★ 2234 ★

Women Aged 15 to 44, Children Under Age 5, and Number of Children Per 1,000 Women, in Cities of Over 50,000 Having in 1930 a Black Population of 10,000 or More – 1920, 1930 - II

[Continued]

City	Children under 5 per 1,000 women 15 to 44 years of age					
	Negro		White		Increase or decrease (-) 1920-30	
	1930	1920	1930	1920[1]	Negro	White[1]
Philadelphia, Pa	278	227	298	402	51	-104
Pittsburgh, Pa	315	250	334	429	65	-95
Port Arthur, Tex	292	343	422	434	-51	-12
Richmond, Va	289	265	261	335	24	-74
Roanoke, Va	301	311	334	428	-10	-94
St. Louis, Mo	227	190	263	287	37	-24
San Antonio, Tex	178	204	255	354	-26	-99
Savannah, Ga	194	194	295	377	-	-82
Shreveport, La	202	205	299	304	-3	-5
Tampa, Fla	233	205	317	434	28	-117
Toledo, Ohio	288	208	316	375	80	-59
Tulsa, Okla	191	257	299	311	-66	-12
Washington, D.C.	252	222	235	228	30	7
Wilmington, Del	245	226	307	451	19	-144
Winston-Salem, N. C.	268	251	390	409	17	-19
Youngstown, Ohio	418	240	380	535	178	-155

Source: "Negro and White Women 15 to 44 Years of Age, Children Under 5 Years, and Number of Children Per 1,000 Women, in the 65 Cities of 50,000 or More Inhabitants HAving in 1930 a Negro Population of 10,000 or More: 1930 and 1920." U.S. Bureau of the Census. *Negroes in the United States: 1920-32.* Washington, D.C.: Government Printing Office, 1935, p. 206. *Note:* 1. Includes Mexicans.

Fetal and Infant Deaths

★ 2235 ★

Deaths From Diseases of Early Infancy: 1930, 1931

Cause of death	1930			1931		
	Total	Male	Female	Total	Male	Female
Diseases of early infancy	7,424	4,144	3,280	6,859	3,794	3,065
Congenital debility	1,036	601	435	952	537	415
Premature birth	4,791	2,551	2,240	4,481	2,394	2,087

[Continued]

★ 2235 ★

Deaths From Diseases of Early Infancy: 1930, 1931

[Continued]

Cause of death	1930			1931		
	Total	Male	Female	Total	Male	Female
Injury at birth	778	491	287	759	458	301
Other diseases peculiar to early infancy	819	501	318	667	405	262

Source: "Negro Deaths (Exclusive of Stillbirths) From Each Cause, by Sex, in Registration States (Including District of Columbia): 1930," and "Negro Deaths Exclusive of Stillbirths) From Each Cause, by Sex, in Registration States (Including District of Columbia: 1931." U.S. Bureau of the Census. *Negroes in the United States: 1920-32.* Washington, D.C.: Government Printing Office, 1935, pp. 465, 467. Adapted by the editors.

★ 2236 ★

Fetal and Infant Deaths

Deaths Under One Year of Age by Cause – 1930, 1931

Cause of death and year	Detailed international list no.	Total	Negro	Other colored	White
All causes					
1931		130,134	21,716	3,565	104,853
1930		142,413	23,812	2,517	116,084
Measles	7				
1931		753	67	54	632
1930		816	87	46	683
Scarlet fever	8				
1931		113	9	2	102
1930		111	7	-	104
Whooping-cough	9				
1931		2,633	496	113	2,024
1930		3,378	650	88	2,640
Diphtheria	10				
1931		393	81	5	307
1930		458	88	5	365
Influenza	11				
1931		3,800	723	132	2,945
1930		2,924	590	64	2,270
Dysentery	13				
1931		620	177	32	411
1930		853	218	35	600
Erysipelas	15				
1931		635	32	14	589
1930		708	29	13	666
Epidemic cerebrospinal meningitis	18				
1931		366	41	9	316
1930		476	60	6	410
Tetanus	22				
1931		127	66	1	60
1930		136	64	3	69

[Continued]

★ 2236 ★

Deaths Under One Year of Age by Cause – 1930, 1931

[Continued]

Cause of death and year	Detailed international list no.	Total	Negro	Other colored	White
Tuberculosis of the respiratory system	23				
1931		358	103	35	220
1930		421	135	30	256
Tuberculosis of the meninges, etc.	24				
1931		377	54	24	299
1930		444	54	20	370
Other forms of tuberculosis	25-32				
1931		184	47	15	122
1930		196	41	13	142
Syphilis	34				
1931		1,738	774	68	896
1930		1,810	831	42	937
Convulsions	86				
1931		710	179	12	519
1930		913	246	11	656
Bronchitis	106				
1931		773	141	13	619
1930		941	188	11	742
Bronchopneumonia	107				
1931		13,461	2,149	556	10,756
1930		14,142	2,343	363	11,436
Lobar and unspecified pneumonia	108, 109				
1931		5,062	1,221	197	3,644
1930		5,427	1,238	148	4,041
Diseases of the stomach	117, 118				
1931		558	153	24	411
1930		766	180	26	560
Diarrhea and enteritis	119				
1931		14,024	2,266	797	10,961
1930		17,292	2,686	502	14,104
Intestinal obstruction	122b				
1931		906	103	19	784
1930		892	96	19	777
Congenital malformations	157				
1931		11,494	557	139	10,798
1930		11,749	530	62	11,157
Congenital debility, icterus, sclerema	158, 161 b, c				
1931		5,283	1,088	185	4,010
1930		5,584	1,175	113	4,296
Premature birth	159				
1931		33,72	4,418	503	28,851
1930		36,756	4,787	346	31,623
Injury at birth	160				
1931		10,048	769	97	9,182
1930		10,626	778	75	9,773

[Continued]

★ 2236 ★

Deaths Under One Year of Age by Cause – 1930, 1931

[Continued]

Cause of death and year	Detailed international list no.	Total	Negro	Other colored	White
Other diseases of early infancy	161 a, d				
1931		4,160	536	91	3,533
1930		4,873	684	80	4,109
External causes	172-198, 201-214				
1931		2,070	395	79	1,596
1930		2,343	463	61	1,819
Unknown or ill-defined diseases	199, 200				
1931		7,875	3,917	176	3,782
1930		8,804	4,304	207	4,293
All other causes					
1931		7,811	1,154	173	6,484
1930		8,574	1,260	128	7,186

Source: "Deaths Under 1 Year of Age (Exclusive of Stillbirths) From Important Causes, by Color, in the Birth Registration Area in Continental United States: 1931 and 1930." U.S. Bureau of the Census. *Negroes in the United States: 1920-32.* Washington, D.C.: Government Printing Office, 1935, p. 367.

★ 2237 ★

Fetal and Infant Deaths

Fetal Death Ratio: Neonatal, Infant, and Maternal Mortality Rates, 1915-1970

Prior to 1933, for registration area only.

Year	Fetal death ratio per 1,000 live births[1]			Neonatal mortality rate per 1,000 live births			Infant mortality rate per 1,000 live births			Maternal mortality rate per 10,000 live births		
	Total	White	Negro and other	Total	White	Negro and other	Total	White	Negro and other	Total	White	Negro and other
1970	14.2	12.4	22.6	15.1	13.8	21.4	20.0	17.8	30.9	2.2	1.4	5.6
1969	14.1	12.4	22.5	15.6	14.2	22.5	20.9	18.4	32.9	2.2	1.5	5.6
1968	15.8	13.8	25.6	16.1	14.7	23.0	21.8	19.2	34.5	2.5	1.7	6.4
1967	15.6	13.5	25.8	16.5	15.0	23.8	22.4	19.7	35.9	2.8	2.0	7.0
1966	15.7	13.6	26.1	17.2	15.6	24.8	23.7	20.6	38.8	2.9	2.0	7.2
1965	16.2	13.9	27.2	17.7	16.1	25.4	24.7	21.5	40.3	3.2	2.1	8.4
1964	16.4	14.1	28.2	17.9	16.2	26.5	24.8	21.6	41.1	3.3	2.2	9.0
1963[2]	15.8	13.7	26.7	18.2	16.7	26.1	25.2	22.2	41.5	3.6	2.4	9.7
1962[2]	15.9	13.9	26.7	18.3	16.9	26.1	25.3	22.3	41.4	3.5	2.4	9.6
1961	16.1	14.1	27.0	18.4	16.9	26.2	25.3	22.4	40.7	3.7	2.5	10.1
1960[5]	16.1	14.1	26.8	18.7	17.2	26.9	26.0	22.9	43.2	3.7	2.6	9.8
1959[3]	16.2	14.2	27.3	19.0	17.5	27.7	26.4	23.2	44.0	3.7	2.6	10.2
1958	16.5	14.5	27.5	19.5	17.8	29.0	27.1	23.8	45.7	3.8	2.6	10.2
1957	16.3	14.5	26.8	19.1	17.5	27.8	26.3	23.3	43.7	4.1	2.8	11.8
1956	16.5	14.6	27.2	18.9	17.5	27.0	26.0	23.2	42.1	4.1	2.9	11.1
1955	17.1	15.2	28.4	19.1	17.7	27.2	26.4	23.6	42.8	4.7	3.3	13.0
1954	17.5	15.5	28.9	19.1	17.8	27.0	26.6	23.9	42.9	5.2	3.7	14.4
1953	17.8	15.9	29.6	19.6	18.3	27.4	27.8	25.0	44.7	6.1	4.4	16.6

[Continued]

★ 2237 ★

Fetal Death Ratio: Neonatal, Infant, and Maternal Mortality Rates, 1915-1970

[Continued]

Year	Fetal death ratio per 1,000 live births[1]			Neonatal mortality rate per 1,000 live births			Infant mortality rate per 1,000 live births			Maternal mortality rate per 10,000 live births		
	Total	White	Negro and other	Total	White	Negro and other	Total	White	Negro and other	Total	White	Negro and other
1952	18.3	16.1	32.2	19.8	18.5	28.0	28.4	25.5	47.0	6.8	4.9	18.8
1951	18.8	16.7	32.1	20.0	18.9	27.3	28.4	25.8	44.8	7.5	5.5	20.1
1950	19.2	17.1	32.5	20.5	19.4	27.5	29.2	26.8	44.5	8.3	6.1	22.2
1949	19.8	17.5	34.6	21.4	20.3	28.6	31.3	28.9	47.3	9.0	6.8	23.5
1948	20.6	18.3	36.5	22.2	21.2	29.1	32.0	29.9	46.5	11.7	8.9	30.1
1947	21.1	18.7	39.6	22.8	21.7	31.0	32.2	30.1	48.5	13.5	10.9	33.5
1946	22.8	20.4	40.9	24.0	23.1	31.5	33.8	31.8	49.5	15.7	13.1	35.9
1945	23.9	21.4	42.0	24.3	23.3	32.0	38.3	35.6	57.0	20.7	17.2	45.5
1944	27.0	24.5	45.4	24.7	23.6	32.5	39.8	36.9	60.3	22.8	18.9	50.6
1943	26.7	24.2	46.2	24.7	23.7	32.9	40.4	37.5	62.5	24.5	21.1	51.0
1942	28.2	25.5	49.3	25.7	24.5	34.6	40.4	37.3	64.6	25.9	22.2	54.4
1941	29.9	26.5	54.0	27.7	26.1	39.0	45.3	41.2	74.8	31.7	26.6	67.8
1940	31.3	27.7	56.7	28.8	27.2	39.7	47.0	43.2	73.8	37.6	32.0	77.4
1939	32.0	28.2	59.0	29.3	27.8	39.6	48.0	44.3	74.2	40.4	35.3	76.2
1938	32.1	28.1	61.1	29.6	28.3	39.1	51.0	47.1	79.1	43.5	37.7	84.9
1937	33.4	29.2	63.2	31.3	29.7	42.1	54.4	50.3	83.2	48.9	43.6	85.8
1936	34.4	29.8	66.9	32.6	31.0	43.9	57.1	52.9	87.6	56.8	51.2	97.2
1935	35.8	31.1	68.7	32.4	31.0	42.7	55.7	51.9	83.2	58.2	53.1	94.6
1934	36.2	31.4	70.1	34.1	32.3[4]	45.3[4]	60.1	54.5[4]	94.4[4]	59.3	54.4[4]	89.7[4]
1933	37.0	32.2	71.1	34.0	32.1[4]	45.8[4]	58.1	52.8[4]	91.3[4]	61.9	56.4[4]	96.7[4]
1932	37.8	32.7	74.4	33.5	32.0[4]	43.7[4]	57.6	53.3[4]	86.2[4]	63.3	58.1[4]	97.6[4]
1931	38.2	33.4	74.1	34.6	33.2	45.2	61.6	57.4	93.1	66.1	60.1	111.4
1930	39.2	34.0	79.9	35.7	34.2	47.4	64.6	60.1	99.9	67.3	60.9	117.4
1929	39.5	34.4	79.7	36.9	35.6	47.3	67.6	63.2	102.2	69.5	63.1	119.9
1928	40.2	35.0	81.5	37.2	35.7	48.8	68.7	64.0	106.2	69.2	62.7	121.0
1927	38.8	34.8	74.8	36.1	35.0	46.1	64.6	60.6	100.1	64.7	59.4	113.3
1926	38.1	35.1	73.0	37.9	37.1	48.0	73.3	70.0	111.8	65.6	61.9	107.1
1925	38.1	35.1	73.1	37.8	36.8	49.5	71.7	68.3	110.8	64.7	60.3	116.2
1924	39.3	35.8	76.2	38.6	37.4	51.2	70.8	66.8	112.9	65.6	60.7	117.9
1923	38.9	35.9	71.8	39.5	38.6	49.9	77.1	73.5	117.4	66.5	62.6	109.5
1922	39.4	36.4	73.4	39.7	38.8	49.9	76.2	73.2	110.0	66.4	62.8	106.8
1921	-	-	-	39.7	38.7	50.3	75.6	72.5	108.5	68.2	64.4	107.7
1920	-	-	-	41.5	40.4	55.0	85.8	82.1	131.7	79.9	76.0	128.1
1919	-	-	-	41.5	40.3	55.2	86.6	83.0	130.5	73.7	69.6	124.4
1918	-	-	-	44.2	43.3	60.5	100.9	97.4	161.2	91.6	88.9	139.3
1917	-	-	-	43.4	42.6	58.0	93.8	90.5	150.7	66.2	63.2	117.7
1916	-	-	-	44.1	43.5	68.9	101.0	99.0	184.9	62.2	60.8	117.9
1915	-	-	-	44.4	-	-	99.9	98.6	181.2	60.8	60.1	105.6

Source: "Fetal Death Ratio; Neonatal, Infant, and Maternal Mortality Rates, by Race: 1915 to 1970." U.S. Bureau of the Census. *Historical Statistics of the United States: Colonial Times to 1970, Part I.* Bicentennial Edition. Washington, D.C.: Government Printing Office, 1975, p. 57. *Notes:* 1. For 1945-1970, includes only deaths for which the period of gestation was given as 20 weeks or more or not stated. For earlier years, includes all fetal deaths, regardless of gestation. In 1945 ratios based on all fetal deaths, regardless of gestation, were: Total, 26.6; white, 24.1; Negro and other, 44.6 2. Figures by race exclude New Jersey; State did not require reporting of race. 3. Includes Alaska. 4. Mexicans included with Negro and other. 5. Denotes first year for which figures include Alaska and Hawaii.

★ 2238 ★

Fetal and Infant Deaths

Fetal Mortality Ratios and Rates by Race, 1933-1960

Includes all fetal deaths regardless of period of gestation.

Year	Ratio per 1,000 live births			Rates per 1,000 live births and fetal deaths		
	Total	White	Nonwhite	Total	White	Nonwhite
1960	22.2	19.2	38.6	21.7	18.8	37.1
1959	21.8	18.9	38.0	21.3	18.5	36.6
1958	22.1	19.3	37.9	21.6	18.9	36.5
1957	21.8	19.2	36.6	21.3	18.8	35.3
1956	22.2	19.5	37.3	21.7	19.2	36.0
1955	22.7	20.0	38.6	22.2	19.6	37.2
1954	22.9	20.3	38.5	22.4	19.9	37.1
1953	22.1	19.6	37.9	21.6	19.2	36.5
1952	22.2	19.5	39.8	21.8	19.1	38.2
1951	22.6	20.0	39.1	22.1	19.6	37.6
1950	22.9	20.3	39.2	22.4	19.9	37.7
1949	22.9	20.3	39.7	22.4	19.9	38.2
1948	23.5	20.9	41.3	22.9	20.4	39.6
1947	23.7	21.1	44.2	23.2	20.6	42.4
1946	25.6	23.2	44.2	25.0	22.7	42.4
1945	26.6	24.1	44.6	25.9	23.5	42.7
1944	27.0	24.5	45.4	26.3	23.9	43.4
1943	26.7	24.2	46.2	26.0	23.6	44.2
1942	28.2	25.5	49.3	27.4	24.8	47.0
1941	29.9	26.5	54.0	29.0	25.8	51.3
1940	31.3	27.7	56.7	30.3	26.9	53.7
1939	32.0	28.2	59.0	31.0	27.4	55.8
1938	32.1	28.1	61.1	31.1	27.3	57.6
1937	33.4	29.2	63.2	32.3	28.3	59.4
1936	34.4	29.8	66.9	33.2	29.0	62.7
1935	35.8	31.1	68.7	34.5	30.2	64.3
1934	36.2	31.4	70.1	35.0	30.5	65.5
1933	37.0	32.2	71.1	35.7	31.2	66.3
1932	37.8	32.7	74.4	36.4	31.7	69.2
1931	38.2	33.4	74.1	36.8	32.3	69.0
1930	39.2	34.0	79.9	37.8	32.9	73.9
1929	39.5	34.4	79.7	38.0	33.2	73.8
1928	40.2	35.0	81.5	38.6	33.8	75.4
1927	38.8	34.8	74.8	37.3	33.7	69.6
1926	38.1	35.1	73.0	36.7	33.9	68.0
1925	38.1	35.1	73.1	36.7	33.9	68.1
1924	39.3	35.8	76.2	37.8	34.5	70.8

[Continued]

★ 2238 ★

Fetal Mortality Ratios and Rates by Race, 1933-1960

[Continued]

Year	Ratio per 1,000 live births			Rates per 1,000 live births and fetal deaths		
	Total	White	Nonwhite	Total	White	Nonwhite
1923	38.9	35.9	71.8	37.5	34.7	67.0
1922	39.4	36.4	73.4	37.9	35.1	68.4

Source: "Fetal Mortality Ratios and Rates by Color: Birth-registration States, 1922-32, and United States 1933-60," National Center for Health Services. *Vital Statistics Rates in the United States 1940-1960.* By Robert D. Grove and Alice M. Hetzel. Washington, D.C.: Government Printing Office, 1968, p. 190.

★ 2239 ★

Fetal and Infant Deaths

Fetal Mortality Ratios, 20 Weeks or More, 1945-1960

Ratios are fetal deaths per 1,000 live births in specified group. Includes only fetal deaths for which the period of gestation was given as 20 weeks or more or was not stated.

Year	Total			White			Nonwhite		
	Both sexes	Male	Female	Both sexes	Male	Female	Both sexes	Male	Female
1960	16.1	16.9	15.2	14.1	14.7	13.5	26.8	29.1	24.4
1959	16.2	17.0	15.3	14.2	14.8	13.5	27.3	29.6	25.0
1958	16.5	17.4	15.6	14.5	15.1	13.9	27.5	30.1	24.9
1957	16.3	17.3	15.4	14.5	15.2	13.8	26.8	29.2	24.4
1956	16.5	17.4	15.5	14.6	15.4	13.9	27.2	29.4	24.9
1955	17.1	18.0	16.2	15.2	15.8	14.5	28.4	31.0	25.8
1954	17.5	18.4	16.4	15.5	16.3	14.7	28.9	31.2	26.5
1953	17.8	18.7	16.8	15.9	16.6	15.1	29.6	32.2	27.0
1952	18.3	19.4	17.2	16.1	16.8	15.3	32.2	35.6	28.9
1951	18.8	20.0	17.6	16.7	17.6	15.8	32.1	35.4	28.7
1950	19.2	20.5	17.9	17.1	18.0	16.1	32.5	36.0	28.9
1949	19.8	21.1	18.5	17.5	18.5	16.6	34.6	38.0	31.2
1948	20.6	21.8	19.3	18.3	19.3	17.2	36.5	39.6	33.3
1947	21.1	22.5	19.6	18.7	19.8	17.4	39.6	43.1	36.0
1946	22.8	24.3	21.2	20.4	21.7	19.1	40.9	44.6	37.2
1945	23.9	25.5	22.3	21.4	22.6	20.1	42.0	46.3	37.6

Source: "Fetal Mortality Ratios (20 Weeks or More) by Color and Sex: United States, 1945-60." National Center for Health Services. *Vital Statistics Rates in the United States 1940-1960.* By Robert D. Grove and Alice M. Hetzel. Washington, D.C.: Government Printing Office, 1968, p. 191.

★ 2240 ★

Fetal and Infant Deaths

Fetal Mortality Ratios, 28 Weeks or More, 1950-1960

Ratios are fetal deaths per 1,000 live births in specified group. Includes only fetal deaths for which the period of gestation was given as 28 weeks or more or was not stated.

Year	Total			White			Nonwhite		
	Both sexes	Male	Female	Both sexes	Male	Female	Both sexes	Male	Female
1960	12.7	13.2	12.1	11.3	11.6	11.0	20.2	21.9	18.5
1959	12.7	13.2	12.2	11.3	11.7	10.9	20.7	22.1	19.2
1958	13.0	13.5	12.5	11.6	12.0	11.3	20.9	22.6	19.2
1957	12.9	13.5	12.4	11.6	12.0	11.2	20.5	22.1	18.8
1956	13.0	13.6	12.4	11.7	12.2	11.2	20.8	22.3	19.2
1955	13.5	14.0	12.9	12.1	12.5	11.7	21.5	23.1	20.0
1954	13.8	14.4	13.2	12.4	12.9	11.9	22.3	23.9	20.7
1953	14.3	14.9	13.6	12.8	13.3	12.3	23.4	25.2	21.5
1952	14.7	15.4	14.0	13.0	13.5	12.6	25.3	27.9	22.7
1951	15.2	16.0	14.4	13.6	14.1	13.0	25.4	28.1	22.8
1950	15.6	16.5	14.7	13.9	14.6	13.2	26.1	28.7	23.4

Source: "Fetal Mortality Ratios (28 Weeks or More) by Color and Sex: United States, 1950-1960." National Center for Health Services. *Vital Statistics Rates in the United States 1940-1960.* By Robert D. Grove and Alice M. Hetzel. Washington, D.C.: Government Printing Office, 1968, p. 191.

★ 2241 ★

Fetal and Infant Deaths

Infant Deaths by States, 1940 to 1965

By place of residence. Deaths of infants under 1 year old; rates per 1,000 live births.

State	1940	1950	1960		1965		Rate					
							1940	1950	1960		1965	
			White	Nonwhite	White	Nonwhite			White	Nonwhite	White	Nonwhite
United States[1]	110,984	103,825	82,479	28,394	67,198	25,668	47.0	29.2	22.9	43.2	21.5	40.3
New England	5,196	4,729	4,941	320	4,3000	404	39.2	24.3	21.7	35.2	21.2	37.5
Maine	810	650	588	4	438	8	53.2	30.9	25.7	12.9	22.5	32.5
New Hampshire	341	282	326	1	274	1	40.9	24.5	23.7	10.6	21.2	10.9
Vermont	309	221	227	-	178	-	44.5	24.5	24.2	-	22.0	-
Massachusetts	2,458	2,240	2,343	147	2,056	171	37.5	23.3	21.1	34.4	21.4	38.5
Rhode Island	410	450	395	33	357	33	37.9	27.8	22.4	44.4	21.6	42.0
Connecticut	868	886	1,062	135	997	191	34.0	21.8	20.0	36.9	20.3	36.9
Middle Atlantic	16,822	16,022	14,139	3,707	11,477	4,043	39.9	25.8	22.0	41.4	20.3	40.6
New York	7,297	7,429	6,735	1,938	5,676	2,172	37.2	24.7	21.5	41.6	20.2	39.5
New Jersey	2,121	2,467	2,516	735	2,007	897	35.5	25.2	21.9	41.7	19.2	43.5
Pennsylvania	7,404	6,126	4,888	1,034	3,794	974	44.7	27.6	22.6	40.6	21.0	40.4
East North Central	17,815	18,729	17,244	3,834	14,086	3,670	39.2	26.3	22.1	39.4	21.3	40.1
Ohio	4,744	4,990	4,593	954	3,572	777	41.4	26.8	22.2	39.4	20.5	37.0
Indiana	2,595	2,520	2,335	354	1,991	318	42.1	27.0	22.6	37.7	22.2	38.5
Illinois	4,398	4,868	4,453	1,515	3,652	1,688	35.3	25.6	22.2	39.6	21.4	44.5
Michigan	4,032	4,230	3,833	871	3,164	779	40.7	26.3	22.1	40.4	21.6	37.8

[Continued]

★ 2241 ★

Infant Deaths by States, 1940 to 1965

[Continued]

State	1940	1950	1960		1965		Rate					
							1940	1950	1960		1965	
			White	Nonwhite	White	Nonwhite			White	Nonwhite	White	Nonwhite
Wisconsin	2,046	2,121	2,030	140	1,707	108	37.3	25.7	21.2	35.3	21.6	28.7
West North Central	9,236	8,806	7,514	977	5,725	847	39.2	26.3	21.7	42.5	20.8	38.7
Minnesota	1,758	1,889	1,853	37	1,384	51	33.2	25.1	21.6	22.6	20.0	30.1
Iowa	1,636	1,555	1,369	35	1,024	25	36.5	24.8	21.7	35.2	20.5	26.0
Missouri	2,885	2,510	1,810	610	1,531	533	46.9	29.2	21.4	45.4	22.3	42.2
North Dakota	593	453	386	27	252	28	45.1	26.6	24.1	43.3	20.2	40.2
South Dakota	466	473	394	102	242	73	38.7	26.6	24.2	76.0	19.5	48.8
Nebraska	792	796	697	52	577	51	36.0	25.0	21.3	34.3	22.0	35.2
Kansas	1,106	1,130	1,005	114	715	86	38.3	25.7	21.3	33.4	19.7	29.2
South Atlantic	21,200	17,997	10,469	8,752	8,993	7,288	57.1	33.7	23.6	47.2	22.4	41.9
Delaware	217	235	168	108	171	89	47.7	30.7	17.8	50.6	20.1	40.8
Maryland	1,590	1,465	1,336	772	1,248	575	49.1	27.0	22.3	44.6	21.8	34.9
District of Columbia	554	603	182	541	97	480	49.3	30.4	29.4	39.6	24.5	34.1
Virginia	3,335	2,836	1,767	1,084	1,489	876	58.5	34.6	24.6	45.5	22.2	39.7
West Virginia	2,269	1,822	933	72	794	68	53.7	36.1	24.8	37.7	26.1	41.6
North Carolina	4,631	3,674	1,677	1,807	1,464	1,512	57.6	34.5	22.3	52.4	22.1	48.3
South Carolina	3,042	2,220	828	1,223	694	965	68.2	38.6	23.9	48.5	22.7	43.3
Georgia	3,744	3,064	1,584	1,706	1,303	1,431	57.8	33.5	24.6	48.1	21.7	41.6
Florida	1,818	2,078	1,994	1,439	1,733	1,292	53.8	32.1	23.6	46.1	22.4	44.0
East South Central	13,080	11,006	5,318	4,183	4,314	3,585	55.7	36.2	25.6	48.4	23.7	47.3
Kentucky	3,387	2,616	1,713	302	1,331	225	53.1	34.9	26.0	48.3	23.7	42.6
Tennessee	2,954	2,961	1,618	791	1,345	699	53.5	36.4	25.3	43.5	23.8	42.0
Alabama	3,870	3,044	1,266	1,350	1,043	1,131	61.5	36.8	24.9	45.0	23.3	43.8
Mississippi	2,869	2,385	721	1,740	595	1,530	54.4	36.7	26.6	54.3	24.5	54.4
West South Central	15,991	12,992	8,464	4,032	6,525	3,446	61.2	34.6	24.9	44.3	22.5	40.6
Arkansas	1,810	1,209	637	473	531	414	47.0	26.5	22.5	38.7	20.6	37.7
Louisiana	3,268	2,639	1,251	1,637	1,046	1,382	64.3	34.6	22.6	46.9	22.0	43.1
Oklahoma	2,238	1,514	995	303	787	203	49.9	30.2	22.7	42.8	21.7	30.7
Texas	8,675	7,630	5,581	1,619	4,161	1,447	68.3	37.4	26.3	43.9	23.1	41.1
Mountain	5,664	5,095	4,452	725	3,310	565	62.0	36.2	25.7	51.7	22.8	37.7
Montana	537	441	392	44	301	40	46.5	28.2	24.2	34.5	24.3	32.2
Idaho	506	434	383	11	318	9	42.9	27.1	22.7	33.3	24.5	24.6
Wyoming	232	247	226	14	133	12	44.7	32.5	27.5	48.6	21.2	42.3
Colorado	1,270	1,167	1,110	70	837	58	60.4	34.4	26.9	44.0	24.0	30.8
New Mexico	1,488	1,211	846	173	535	120	100.6	54.8	30.9	52.8	25.6	35.4
Arizona	983	953	823	351	605	256	85.5	45.8	26.6	60.8	21.6	43.0
Utah	539	503	485	30	385	31	40.4	23.7	18.8	54.0	17.8	47.8
Nevada	109	139	187	32	196	39	51.7	37.9	29.6	33.9	23.7	32.7
Pacific[1]	5,980	8,449	9,938	1,864	8,468	1,820	37.8	25.1	22.6	30.5	21.1	28.8
Washington	992	1,522	1,398	131	1,010	122	35.2	27.3	22.7	36.7	20.4	36.4
Oregon	585	812	852	39	659	36	33.2	22.5	23.0	29.2	20.8	28.2
California	4,403	6,115	7,429	1,248	6,581	1,263	39.2	25.0	22.5	29.7	21.2	28.1
Alaska	(NA)	193[2]	145	161	113	156	(NA)	51.8[2]	27.9	68.2	24.0	66.1
Hawaii	421[2]	337[2]	114	285	105	243	44.7[2]	24.0[2]	21.5	24.0	20.9	21.5

Source: "Deaths of Infants: Total and Rate, by States: 1940 to 1945." Bureau of the Census, *Statistical Abstract of the United States, 1967*. Washington, D.C.: U.S. Government Printing Office, 1967, p. 61. Primary source: Dept. of Health, Education, and Welfare, Public Health Service; annual report, *Vital Statistics of the United States*. *Notes:* - Represents zero. NA Not Available. 1. Prior to 1960, excludes Alaska and Hawaii. 2. By place of occurrence.

★ 2242 ★

Fetal and Infant Deaths

Infant Mortality (Under One Year) in Selected Cities – 1910, 1914

Age	Negro deaths under 1 year in selected registration cities[1]			
	Number		Distribution per 1,000	
	Southern cities	Northern and western cities	Southern cities	Northern and western cities
	1914			
Total under 1 year	2,286	2,355	1,000	1,000
Under 1 day	252	275	110	117
1 day, under 1 week	318	309	139	131
1 week, under 1 month	295	279	129	118
1 month, under 6 months	869	860	380	365
6 months and over	552	632	241	268
	1910			
Total under 1 year	2,833	2,735	1,000	1,000
Under 1 day	214	213	76	78
1 day, under 1 week	364	343	128	125
1 week, under 1 month	368	317	130	116
1 month, under 6 months	1,197	1,023	423	374
6 months and over	690	839	244	307

Source: "Negro Deaths Under 1 Year in Selected Registration Cities." U.S. Bureau of the Census. *Negro Population, 1790-1915*. Washington, D.C.: Government Printing Office, 1918, p. 317. *Notes:* 1. Includes all registration cities of 100,000 or more population having a Negro population of 2,500 or more in 1910.

★ 2243 ★

Fetal and Infant Deaths

Infant Mortality Rate by Cause – 1930, 1931

Infant mortality rate (deaths[1] under 1 year of age per 1,000 live births) from important cause, in the birth registration area in the continental United States: 1931 and 1930.

Cause of death and year	Detailed international list no.	Total	Negro	Other colored	White
All causes					
1931		61.6	92.7	117.8	56.7
1930		64.6	99.5	141.1	59.6
Measles	7				

[Continued]

★ 2243 ★

Infant Mortality Rate by Cause – 1930, 1931

[Continued]

Cause of death and year	Detailed international list no.	Total	Negro	Other colored	White
1931		0.4	0.3	1.8	0.4
1930		.4	.4	2.6	.4
Scarlet fever	8				
1931		.1	[2]	.1	.1
1930		.1	[2]	-	.1
Whooping-cough	9				
1931		1.2	2.1	3.7	1.1
1930		1.5	2.7	4.9	1.4
Diphtheria	10				
1931		.2	.3	.2	.2
1930		.2	.4	.3	.2
Influenza	11				
1931		1.8	3.1	4.4	1.6
1930		1.3	2.5	3.6	1.2
Dysentery	13				
1931		.3	.8	1.1	.2
1930		.4	.9	2.0	.3
Erysipelas	15				
1931		.3	.1	.5	.3
1930		.3	.1	.7	.3
Epidemic cerebrospinal meningitis	18				
1931		.2	.2	.3	.2
1930		.2	.3	.3	.2
Tetanus	22				
1931		.1	.3	[2]	[2]
1930		.1	.3	.2	[2]
Tuberculosis of the respiratory system	23				
1931		.2	.4	1.2	.1
1930		.2	.6	1.7	.1
Tuberculosis of the meninges, etc.	24				
1931		.2	.2	.8	.2
1930		.2	.2	1.1	.2
Other forms of tuberculosis	25 to 32				
1931		.1	.2	.5	.1
1930		.1	.2	.7	.1
Syphilis	34				
1931		.8	3.3	2.2	.5
1930		.8	3.5	2.4	.5
Convlusions	86				
1931		.3	.8	.4	.3
1930		.4	1.0	.6	.3
Bronchitis	106				
1931		0.4	0.6	0.4	0.3
1930		.4	.8	.6	.4
Bronchopneumonia	107				

[Continued]

★ 2243 ★

Infant Mortality Rate by Cause – 1930, 1931

[Continued]

Cause of death and year	Detailed international list no.	Total	Negro	Other colored	White
1931		6.4	9.2	18.4	5.8
1930		6.4	9.8	20.3	5.9
Lobar and unspecified pneumonia	108, 109				
1931		2.4	5.2	6.5	2.0
1930		2.5	5.2	8.3	2.1
Diseases of the stomach	117, 118				
1931		.3	.7	.8	.2
1930		.3	.8	1.5	.3
Diarrhea and enteritis	119				
1931		6.6	9.7	26.3	5.9
1930		7.8	11.2	28.1	7.2
Intestinal obstruction	122b				
1931		.4	.4	.6	.4
1930		.4	.4	1.1	.4
Congenital malformations	157				
1931		5.4	2.4	4.6	5.8
1930		5.3	2.2	3.5	5.7
Congenita debility, icterus, sclerma	158, 161 b, c				
1931		2.5	4.6	6.1	2.2
1930		2.5	4.9	6.3	2.2
Premature birth	159				
1931		16.0	18.9	16.6	15.6
1930		16.7	20.0	19.4	16.2
Injury at birth	160				
1931		4.8	3.3	3.2	5.0
1930		4.8	3.3	4.2	5.0
Other diseases of early infancy	161 a, b				
1931		2.0	2.3	3.0	1.9
1930		2.2	2.9	4.5	2.1
External causes	172-198, 201-214				
1931		1.0	1.7	2.6	.9
1930		1.1	1.9	3.4	.9
Unknown or ill-defined diseases	199, 200				
1931		3.7	16.7	5.8	2.0
1930		4.0	18.0	11.6	2.5
All other causes					
1931		3.7	4.9	5.7	3.2
1930		3.9	5.3	7.1	3.7

Source: "Infant Mortality Rate (Deaths Under 1 Year of Age Per 1,000 Live Births) From Important Cause, in the Birth Registration Area in Continental United States: 1931 and 1930." U.S. Bureau of the Census. *Negroes in the United States: 1920-32*. Washington, D.C.: Government Printing Office, 1935, p. 368. *Notes:* 1. Exclusive of stillbirths. 2. Less than 1/10 of 1 per 1,000 births.

★ 2244 ★

Fetal and Infant Deaths

Infant Mortality Rates by Age and Race, 1915-1940 - I

Infant mortality rates by age and race: birth registration states and states of 1915[1,2] for 1915-1940. Exclusive of stillbirths. By place of occurrence. Rates are the number of deaths under 1 year of age in a specified race group per 1,000 live births in that group.

Area, race, and age	1915	1916	1917	1918	1919	1920	1921	1922	1923	1924	1925
All races											
Under 1 year	99.9	101.0	93.8	100.9	86.6	85.8	75.6	76.2	77.1	70.8	71.7
Under 1 day	15.0	14.8	15.0	15.4	14.5	14.8	14.5	14.9	14.7	14.8	15.0
1 day	4.9	4.9	4.6	5.0	4.5	4.6	4.4	4.4	4.4	4.2	4.2
2 days	3.5	3.6	3.5	3.6	3.4	3.4	3.4	3.3	3.3	3.3	3.2
3 to 6 days	6.7	6.9	6.7	6.5	6.3	6.4	6.3	6.4	6.1	6.2	5.8
1 week	6.0	5.8	6.0	6.0	5.9	5.4	5.0	4.9	4.9	4.6	4.4
2 weeks	4.6	4.5	4.2	4.3	3.8	3.8	3.4	3.3	3.4	2.9	2.9
3 weeks	3.7	3.6	3.4	3.4	3.1	3.1	2.7	2.6	2.7	2.5	2.3
Under 1 month	44.4	44.1	43.4	44.2	41.5	41.5	39.7	39.7	39.5	38.6	37.8
1 month	9.0	9.1	8.4	8.5	7.3	7.3	6.3	6.2	6.4	5.8	5.8
2 months	7.6	7.3	6.6	6.9	5.9	5.7	4.9	4.8	4.9	4.4	4.6
3 months								4.1	4.2	3.6	4.0
4 months	16.9	16.9	15.1	16.3	13.7	13.1	10.9	3.5	3.6	3.2	3.4
5 months								3.2	3.3	2.7	2.9
6 months								2.9	3.0	2.5	2.7
7 months	12.5	13.0	11.1	13.6	10.3	10.0	7.8	2.7	2.8	2.2	2.5
8 months								2.6	2.6	2.2	2.3
9 months								2.4	2.5	2.0	2.1
10 months	9.5	10.6	9.2	11.4	7.9	8.3	6.0	2.2	2.1	1.8	1.9
11 months								2.0	2.2	1.8	1.8
White[3]											
Under 1 year	-	99.0	90.5	97.4	83.0	82.1	72.5	73.2	73.5	66.8	68.3
Under 1 day	-	14.7	14.9	15.4	14.4	14.7	14.4	14.8	14.7	14.7	14.9
1 day	-	4.8	4.5	4.9	4.3	4.4	4.3	4.3	4.3	4.1	4.1
2 days	-	3.6	3.4	3.5	3.3	3.3	3.3	3.2	3.2	3.2	3.1
3 to 6 days	-	6.8	6.6	6.2	6.0	6.1	6.0	6.2	5.9	5.9	5.5
1 week	-	5.7	5.8	5.7	5.6	5.2	4.7	4.7	4.7	4.3	4.2
2 weeks	-	4.4	4.2	4.2	3.8	3.6	3.3	3.2	3.3	2.8	2.8
3 weeks	-	3.5	3.3	3.3	3.0	3.0	2.6	2.5	2.6	2.4	2.2
Under 1 month	-	43.5	42.6	43.3	40.3	40.4	38.7	38.8	38.6	37.4	36.8
1 month	-	8.9	8.1	8.2	7.0	6.9	6.0	5.9	6.1	5.4	5.5
2 months	-	7.1	6.3	6.6	5.7	5.4	4.7	4.6	4.6	4.1	4.3
3 months	-							3.8	3.9	3.4	3.7
4 months	-	16.4	14.4	15.5	12.9	12.3	10.3	3.3	3.3	2.9	3.1
5 months	-							2.9	3.0	2.5	2.7
6 months	-							2.7	2.7	2.2	2.5
7 months	-	12.7	10.6	12.9	9.6	9.3	7.2	2.5	2.5	2.0	2.3
8 months	-							2.4	2.4	2.0	2.1

[Continued]

★ 2244 ★

Infant Mortality Rates by Age and Race, 1915-1940 - I

[Continued]

Area, race, and age	1915	1916	1917	1918	1919	1920	1921	1922	1923	1924	1925
9 months	-							2.2	2.3	1.8	2.0
10 months	-	10.4	8.7	10.9	7.5	7.8	5.6	2.1	2.0	1.6	1.7
11 months	-							1.9	2.0	1.6	1.7
All other races[3]											
Under 1 year	-	184.9	150.7	161.2	130.5	131.7	108.5	110.0	117.4	112.9	110.8
Under 1 day	-	20.6	16.8	15.2	15.8	15.5	15.0	15.4	15.3	15.7	16.4
1 day	-	9.6	6.6	6.9	6.3	6.6	5.9	5.4	5.8	5.7	5.4
2 days	-	5.9	4.8	5.0	4.7	4.8	4.1	4.3	4.4	4.5	4.4
3 to 6 days	-	11.7	9.4	11.5	10.0	10.2	9.4	9.6	8.8	9.5	8.3
1 week	-	9.9	9.9	10.2	9.4	8.5	7.9	7.3	7.3	7.7	7.2
2 weeks	-	6.3	5.7	6.4	4.8	5.1	4.5	4.2	4.6	4.4	4.4
3 weeks	-	4.9	4.9	5.2	4.2	4.3	3.6	3.8	3.7	3.7	3.4
Under 1 month	-	68.9	58.0	60.5	55.2	55.0	50.3	49.9	49.9	51.2	49.5
1 month	-	15.2	13.5	13.1	11.1	11.7	9.7	9.7	9.6	10.0	9.6
2 months	-	13.9	11.6	10.7	9.2	8.7	7.4	7.7	8.0	7.6	7.3
3 months	-							6.5	7.8	6.5	6.9
4 months	-	37.4	28.4	30.5	23.3	23.4	17.8	5.9	6.7	6.3	6.3
5 months	-							5.7	6.3	5.4	5.6
6 months	-							5.5	6.4	5.5	5.7
7 months	-	28.2	21.3	25.2	18.6	18.6	13.4	4.8	5.3	4.4	4.6
8 months	-							4.0	4.9	4.4	4.6
9 months	-							3.9	4.8	4.3	4.2
10 months	-	21.3	17.9	21.2	13.0	14.3	9.9	3.3	3.9	3.6	3.2
11 months	-							3.3	3.8	3.7	3.2

Source: "Infant Mortality Rates by Age and Race: Birth-Registration States and States of 1915 for 1915-1940." U.S. Bureau of the Census. *Vital Statistics Rates in the United States 1900-1940.* By Forrest E. Linder and Robert D. Grove. Washington, D.C.: Government Printing Office, 1943, pp. 574-75. *Notes:* 1. Excludes Rhode Island. 2. Data not available by race. 3. Mexicans included with white each year except 1932, 1933, and 1934.

★ 2245 ★

Fetal and Infant Deaths

Infant Mortality Rates by Age and Race, 1915-1940 - II

Infant mortality rates by age and race: birth registration states and states of 1915[1,2] for 1915-1940. Exclusive of stillbirths. By place of occurrence. Rates are the number of deaths under 1 year of age in a specified race group per 1,000 live births in that group.

Area, race, and age	1926	1927	1928	1929	1930	1931	1932	1933	1934	1935	1936
Registration states											
All races											
Under 1 year	73.3	64.6	68.7	67.6	64.6	61.6	57.6	58.1	60.1	55.7	57.1
Under 1 day	15.2	15.1	15.3	15.3	15.0	15.0	15.0	15.1	15.4	15.0	15.1

[Continued]

★ 2245 ★

Infant Mortality Rates by Age and Race, 1915-1940 - II

[Continued]

Area, race, and age	1926	1927	1928	1929	1930	1931	1932	1933	1934	1935	1936
1 day	4.2	4.1	4.4	4.4	4.2	4.0	3.8	3.8	3.9	3.7	3.9
2 days	3.2	3.0	3.1	3.0	2.9	2.7	2.6	2.7	2.6	2.4	2.5
3 to 6 days	5.7	5.3	5.4	5.3	5.1	4.7	4.7	4.7	4.6	4.4	4.3
1 week	4.3	3.9	4.1	3.9	3.9	3.6	3.4	3.5	3.4	3.1	3.0
2 weeks	3.0	2.6	2.6	2.6	2.5	2.4	2.2	2.2	2.3	2.0	2.0
3 weeks	2.4	2.2	2.3	2.3	2.1	2.0	1.8	1.9	1.9	1.8	1.8
Under 1 month	37.9	36.1	37.2	36.9	35.7	34.6	33.5	34.0	34.1	32.4	32.6
1 month	6.0	5.1	5.5	5.6	5.3	5.0	4.7	4.5	4.8	4.4	4.4
2 months	4.7	4.0	4.4	4.3	4.2	4.0	3.6	3.5	3.8	3.5	3.6
3 months	4.0	3.4	3.6	3.6	3.5	3.1	2.9	2.8	3.1	2.9	3.1
4 months	3.4	2.8	3.0	3.0	2.8	2.6	2.3	2.3	2.5	2.3	2.5
5 months	3.0	2.4	2.7	2.6	2.4	2.2	2.0	2.0	2.2	2.0	2.1
6 months	2.8	2.3	2.5	2.4	2.3	2.1	1.8	1.9	2.0	1.8	1.9
7 months	2.6	2.0	2.2	2.2	2.0	1.8	1.6	1.6	1.7	1.6	1.7
8 months	2.5	1.7	2.2	2.0	1.8	1.8	1.5	1.5	1.6	1.4	1.5
9 months	2.3	1.7	1.9	1.8	1.7	1.6	1.4	1.4	1.5	1.3	1.4
10 months	2.1	1.5	1.8	1.6	1.5	1.4	1.2	1.3	1.4	1.1	1.2
11 months	2.1	1.5	1.7	1.6	1.4	1.4	1.2	1.3	1.3	1.1	1.1
White[3]											
Under 1 year	70.0	60.6	64.0	63.2	60.1	57.4	53.3	52.8	54.5	51.9	52.9
Under 1 day	15.1	15.0	15.2	15.2	14.8	14.8	14.8	14.9	15.2	14.8	14.9
1 day	4.1	4.0	4.2	4.2	3.9	3.8	3.7	3.6	3.7	3.6	3.7
2 days	3.1	2.9	3.0	2.9	2.8	2.6	2.4	2.5	2.4	2.3	2.4
3 to 6 days	5.5	5.1	5.0	5.0	4.8	4.4	4.4	4.3	4.1	4.0	3.9
1 week	4.1	3.6	3.8	3.6	3.6	3.3	3.1	3.0	3.0	2.8	2.7
2 weeks	2.8	2.4	2.5	2.5	2.3	2.3	2.0	2.0	2.0	1.9	1.8
3 weeks	2.3	2.0	2.1	2.1	2.0	1.9	1.7	1.8	1.8	1.6	1.6
Under 1 month	37.1	35.0	35.7	35.6	34.2	33.2	32.0	32.1	32.3	31.0	31.0
1 month	5.7	4.8	5.0	5.1	4.8	4.6	4.2	4.0	4.3	4.0	4.1
2 months	4.4	3.7	4.0	3.9	3.8	3.6	3.2	3.1	3.3	3.2	3.3
3 months	3.7	3.0	3.2	3.2	3.1	2.8	2.5	2.4	2.6	2.5	2.7
4 months	3.1	2.5	2.7	2.6	2.5	2.3	2.0	1.9	2.1	2.0	2.2
5 months	2.7	2.2	2.4	2.4	2.1	2.0	1.7	1.7	1.8	1.7	1.8
6 months	2.5	2.0	2.2	2.0	2.0	1.9	1.6	1.6	1.7	1.6	1.7
7 months	2.4	1.8	2.0	1.9	1.7	1.6	1.4	1.4	1.5	1.4	1.5
8 months	2.3	1.5	1.9	1.8	1.6	1.6	1.3	1.3	1.4	1.3	1.3
9 months	2.1	1.5	1.7	1.6	1.5	1.4	1.2	1.2	1.2	1.2	1.2
10 months	2.0	1.4	1.6	1.5	1.3	1.2	1.1	1.1	1.2	1.0	1.1
11 months	1.9	1.3	1.6	1.5	1.3	1.3	1.1	1.1	1.1	1.0	1.0
All other races[3]											
Under 1 year	111.8	100.1	106.2	102.2	99.9	93.1	86.2	91.3	94.4	83.2	87.6

[Continued]

★ 2245 ★

Infant Mortality Rates by Age and Race, 1915-1940 - II

[Continued]

Area, race, and age	1926	1927	1928	1929	1930	1931	1932	1933	1934	1935	1936
Under 1 day	15.8	16.0	16.5	16.5	16.6	16.6	16.3	16.6	16.3	16.2	16.4
1 day	5.6	5.4	5.7	5.6	5.8	5.3	4.8	4.9	5.1	4.6	5.1
2 days	4.0	3.6	4.2	3.8	3.9	3.6	3.7	3.8	3.4	3.4	3.4
3 to 6 days	7.9	7.3	8.4	7.7	7.7	7.0	7.1	7.4	7.5	6.8	7.1
1 week	7.0	6.6	6.7	6.3	6.3	5.9	5.5	6.3	6.2	5.4	5.6
2 weeks	4.2	3.8	3.9	3.9	3.9	3.8	3.4	3.7	3.6	3.3	3.4
3 weeks	3.4	3.4	3.5	3.5	3.2	3.1	3.0	3.1	3.1	3.0	2.8
Under 1 month	48.0	46.1	48.8	47.3	47.4	45.2	43.7	45.8	45.3	42.7	43.9
1 month	9.5	8.6	8.9	9.1	9.0	8.5	7.9	7.8	8.4	7.0	7.1
2 months	7.7	7.2	7.5	7.2	7.1	6.9	6.1	6.0	6.9	5.8	6.2
3 months	7.2	6.4	6.4	6.5	6.5	5.6	5.3	5.5	6.1	5.0	5.6
4 months	6.7	5.4	5.9	5.9	5.5	5.1	4.3	4.8	5.0	4.3	4.8
5 months	5.8	4.7	5.3	4.9	4.7	4.3	3.7	4.1	4.4	3.7	4.2
6 months	5.5	4.9	5.3	4.8	4.6	3.9	3.5	3.8	4.2	3.5	3.8
7 months	5.2	4.2	4.3	4.2	3.8	3.2	2.8	3.2	3.3	2.8	3.1
8 months	4.8	3.5	4.2	3.5	3.4	3.2	2.5	2.9	3.0	2.7	2.8
9 months	4.2	3.3	3.7	3.3	3.0	2.7	2.3	2.7	2.9	2.2	2.5
10 months	3.7	2.8	3.0	2.6	2.5	2.3	2.1	2.4	2.6	1.7	1.9
11 months	3.6	2.9	3.0	2.8	2.7	2.3	2.0	2.3	2.4	1.9	1.8

Source: "Infant Mortality Rates by Age and Race: Birth-Registration States and States of 1915 for 1915-1940." U.S. Bureau of the Census. *Vital Statistics Rates in the United States 1900-1940*. By Forrest E. Linder and Robert D. Grove. Washington, D.C.: Government Printing Office, 1943, pp. 574-75. *Notes:* 1. Excludes Rhode Island. 2. Data not available by race. 3. Mexicans included with white each year except 1932, 1933, and 1934.

★ 2246 ★

Fetal and Infant Deaths

Infant Mortality Rates by Age and Race, 1915-1940 - III

Infant mortality rates by age and race: birth registration states and states of 1915[1,2] for 1915-1940. Exclusive of stillbirths. By place of occurrence. Rates are the number of deaths under 1 year of age in a specified race group per 1,000 live births in that group.

Area, race, and age	1937	1938	1939	1940
Registration states				
All races				
Under 1 year	54.4	51.0	48.0	47.0
Under 1 day	14.7	14.1	14.1	13.9
1 day	3.7	3.6	3.7	3.5
2 days	2.3	2.3	2.3	2.2
3 to 6 days	4.0	3.7	3.7	3.6
1 week	2.9	2.6	2.5	2.4
2 weeks	1.9	1.8	1.6	1.6
3 weeks	1.7	1.5	1.4	1.4

[Continued]

★ 2246 ★

Infant Mortality Rates by Age and Race, 1915-1940 - III

[Continued]

Area, race, and age	1937	1938	1939	1940
Under 1 month	31.3	29.6	29.3	28.8
1 month	4.3	3.9	3.5	3.5
2 months	3.5	3.2	2.8	2.9
3 months	2.8	2.6	2.3	2.4
4 months	2.3	2.2	1.9	1.9
5 months	2.0	1.8	1.7	1.6
6 months	1.8	1.7	1.5	1.4
7 months	1.5	1.4	1.3	1.2
8 months	1.4	1.3	1.1	1.0
9 months	1.2	1.2	1.0	0.9
10 months	1.1	1.0	0.9	0.8
11 months	1.1	1.0	0.9	0.7
White[3]				
Under 1 year	50.3	47.1	44.3	43.2
Under 1 day	14.5	13.9	13.8	13.6
1 day	3.6	3.5	3.6	3.4
2 days	2.1	2.2	2.2	2.1
3 to 6 days	3.6	3.4	3.3	3.3
1 week	2.6	2.3	2.2	2.1
2 weeks	1.7	1.6	1.5	1.4
3 weeks	1.5	1.4	1.2	1.3
Under 1 month	29.7	28.3	27.8	27.2
1 month	3.9	3.5	3.1	3.1
2 months	3.1	2.9	2.5	2.6
3 months	2.5	2.3	2.0	2.1
4 months	2.1	1.9	1.7	1.7
5 months	1.8	1.6	1.5	1.4
6 months	1.5	1.4	1.2	1.2
7 months	1.4	1.2	1.1	1.0
8 months	1.3	1.2	1.0	0.9
9 months	1.1	1.0	0.9	0.8
10 months	1.0	0.9	0.8	0.7
11 months	0.9	0.9	0.8	0.7
All other races[3]				
Under 1 year	83.2	79.1	74.2	73.8
Under 1 day	16.1	15.8	16.2	16.0
1 day	4.8	4.5	4.5	4.7
2 days	3.3	3.2	3.1	3.3
3 to 6 days	6.6	5.6	5.8	5.7
1 week	5.5	4.7	4.5	4.6
2 weeks	3.1	2.8	2.8	2.9

[Continued]

★ 2246 ★

Infant Mortality Rates by Age and Race, 1915-1940 - III

[Continued]

Area, race, and age	1937	1938	1939	1940
3 weeks	2.7	2.4	2.5	2.5
Under 1 month	42.1	39.1	39.6	39.7
1 month	7.3	6.9	6.1	6.3
2 months	5.9	5.5	4.8	5.0
3 months	4.9	4.8	4.3	4.5
4 months	4.2	4.2	3.8	3.6
5 months	3.8	3.6	3.1	3.1
6 months	3.6	3.6	3.1	2.7
7 months	2.9	2.8	2.4	2.2
8 months	2.6	2.5	2.0	2.1
9 months	2.2	2.3	1.9	1.8
10 months	1.9	1.9	1.5	1.4
11 months	2.0	1.9	1.6	1.3

Source: "Infant Mortality Rates by Age and Race: Birth-Registration States and States of 1915 for 1915-1940." U.S. Bureau of the Census. *Vital Statistics Rates in the United States 1900-1940.* By Forrest E. Linder and Robert D. Grove. Washington, D.C.: Government Printing Office, 1943, pp. 574-75. *Notes:* 1. Excludes Rhode Island. 2. Data not available by race. 3. Mexicans included with white each year except 1932, 1933, and 1934.

★ 2247 ★

Fetal and Infant Deaths

Infant Mortality Rates by Detailed Age, Race, and Sex – 1940, 1950, 1960

Rates are infant deaths per 100,000 live births in specified color-sex group.

Age and year	Total			White			Nonwhite		
	Both sexes	Male	Female	Both sexes	Male	Female	Both sexes	Male	Female
Total under 1 year									
1960	2,604.0	2,933.2	2,258.6	2,290.6	2,600.5	1,963.8	4,321.1	4,788.0	3,845.6
1950	2,921.2	3,275.3	2,548.1	2,677.2	3,021.3	2,312.9	4,445.7	4,887.1	3,993.4
1940	4,701.9	5,245.3	4,128.7	4,323.4	4,832.5	3,783.8	7,378.5	8,221.3	6,519.4
Under 28 days									
1960	1,872.6	2,123.7	1,609.3	1,724.2	1,965.8	1,469.5	2,685.7	3,004.1	2,361.6
1950	2,049.9	2,334.5	1,750.0	1,937.2	2,217.6	1,640.4	2,753.6	3,076.0	2,423.3
1940	2,875.2	3,256.0	2,473.5	2,720.2	3,085.2	2,333.3	3,971.0	4,486.6	3,445.4
Under 1 day									
1960	1,034.2	1,163.1	898.9	960.7	1,085.6	829.0	1,436.6	1,595.4	1,274.9
1950	1,015.0	1,147.9	875.0	969.5	1,097.1	834.5	1,299.0	1,469.9	1,123.9
1940	1,392.6	1,567.8	1,207.7	1,362.7	1,533.6	1,181.5	1,603.7	1,814.2	1,389.2
1 day									
1960	271.2	314.7	225.6	253.3	294.7	209.6	369.5	426.2	311.7
1950	311.8	362.6	258.2	302.1	353.7	247.5	372.1	418.9	324.0
1940	351.8	406.8	293.7	335.5	391.9	275.6	467.1	514.2	419.1
2 days									
1960	176.9	208.5	143.8	172.0	203.2	139.1	203.9	237.7	169.5

[Continued]

★ 2247 ★

Infant Mortality Rates by Detailed Age, Race, and Sex – 1940, 1950, 1960

[Continued]

Age and year	Total			White			Nonwhite		
	Both sexes	Male	Female	Both sexes	Male	Female	Both sexes	Male	Female
1950	204.1	241.5	164.7	200.1	236.9	161.2	229.1	270.7	186.6
1940	224.5	268.1	178.6	209.5	251.0	165.6	330.7	390.9	269.3
3 days									
1960	82.6	97.3	67.2	77.7	91.0	63.7	109.4	132.4	86.0
1950	106.4	125.4	86.3	101.7	122.3	79.9	135.8	145.4	125.9
1940	-	-	-	-	-	-	-	-	-
4 days									
1960	46.3	51.6	40.8	41.3	45.2	37.3	73.8	87.5	59.9
1950	62.8	71.2	54.0	58.6	67.6	49.1	88.9	93.9	83.8
1940	-	-	-	-	-	-	-	-	-
5 days									
1960	34.2	38.5	29.7	30.4	35.1	25.3	55.4	57.3	53.4
1950	48.6	53.9	43.0	42.8	48.5	36.8	84.8	87.8	81.7
1940	-	-	-	-	-	-	-	-	-
6 days									
1960	25.0	27.3	22.5	22..5	24.8	20.1	38.3	41.6	35.0
1950	35.6	40.4	30.6	30.8	35.2	26.1	65.8	73.7	57.8
1940	-	-	-	-	-	-	-	-	-
3-6 days									
1960	188.1	214.8	160.2	171.9	196.1	146.4	277.0	318.8	234.3
1950	253.4	290.9	213.9	233.9	273.5	191.9	375.3	400.8	349.2
1940	360.4	415.1	302.6	330.4	378.6	279.2	572.4	678.1	464.7
7-13 days									
1960	99.0	107.0	90.6	85.3	93.6	76.6	173.9	181.6	166.2
1950	134.6	148.1	120.3	117.5	130.6	103.6	241.4	259.4	222.9
1940	243.8	269.8	216.3	213.9	236.3	190.2	455.1	511.5	397.7
14-20 days									
1960	58.2	64.7	51.4	46.2	52.9	39.0	124.3	130.6	117.9
1950	74.8	80.8	68.5	64.8	69.9	59.5	137.0	149.9	123.
1940	160.0	168.3	151.3	141.0	149.1	132.3	294.8	306.2	283.1
21-27 days									
1960	45.0	50.9	38.7	34.8	39.6	29.8	100.4	113.7	86.9
1950	56.2	62.7	49.3	49.2	55.9	42.2	99.7	106.3	92.9
1940	142.2	160.1	123.3	127.3	144.6	109.0	247.2	271.6	222.3
28-59 days									
1960	170.8	192.2	148.3	133.8	153.1	113.5	373.5	410.5	335.7
1950	182.9	205.3	159.4	155.0	174.8	134.1	357.2	398.8	314.5
1940	349.3	396.6	299.5	309.4	352.2	264.0	631.9	716.7	545.5
2 months									
1960	132.9	152.8	112.0	103.4	120.9	84.9	294.8	330.9	258.0
1950	136.7	150.5	122.1	115.7	130.2	100.4	267.3	279.2	255.1
1940	286.8	313.7	258.4	256.6	280.3	231.4	500.3	554.1	445.4
3 months									
1960	100.7	111.9	89.0	78.6	89.0	67.7	221.7	239.5	203.6
1950	115.5	126.1	104.2	98.9	108.0	89.2	219.0	240.9	196.5
1940	235.3	250.7	219.0	205.1	221.0	188.3	448.6	464.7	432.2

[Continued]

★ 2247 ★

Infant Mortality Rates by Detailed Age, Race, and Sex – 1940, 1950, 1960

[Continued]

Age and year	Total			White			Nonwhite		
	Both sexes	Male	Female	Both sexes	Male	Female	Both sexes	Male	Female
4 months									
1960	77.2	83.9	70.3	57.3	62.0	52.5	186.3	206.3	165.9
1950	91.3	96.6	85.8	77.4	83.0	71.6	178.2	183.3	172.9
1940	193.1	207.7	177.7	169.8	180.3	158.7	357.7	405.1	309.3
5 months									
1960	57.4	63.7	50.8	43.2	47.8	38.3	135.6	152.6	118.2
1950	73.6	78.1	68.9	61.7	65.8	57.4	148.0	156.3	139.5
1940	159.4	170.6	147.6	137.5	148.4	125.9	314.6	330.6	298.3
6 month									
1960	47.2	51.3	43.0	35.2	38.8	31.3	113.2	120.7	105.7
1950	64.2	67.1	61.1	53.2	55.7	50.5	132.9	139.0	126.7
1940	139.7	144.6	134.5	120.8	126.5	114.9	272.9	275.0	270.7
7 months									
1960	39.2	42.1	36.3	30.4	32.7	28.0	87.5	94.1	80.8
1950	55.4	58.9	51.8	47.2	49.6	44.7	106.8	118.0	95.3
1940	118.5	132.0	104.2	103.4	113.3	92.8	225.0	266.2	183.0
8 months									
1960	33.2	34.7	31.7	26.4	27.7	25.1	70.5	73.9	67.0
1950	46.9	48.8	44.9	40.5	42.7	38.2	86.8	87.4	86.3
1940	104.0	115.4	92.0	89.3	98.3	79.7	208.2	238.5	177.5
9 months									
1960	26.7	28.9	24.4	21.3	23.2	19.3	56.3	60.6	51.9
1950	40.8	43.0	38.4	34.8	36.6	33.0	77.9	83.8	71.8
1940	88.8	94.6	82.7	76.4	82.0	70.4	176.4	184.9	167.8
10 months									
1960	23.0	23.7	22.2	18.4	19.3	17.3	48.2	48.0	48.5
1950	33.9	34.2	33.5	29.4	29.9	28.8	62.0	61.6	62.3
1940	77.7	85.4	69.6	69.3	75.9	62.4	137.1	153.8	120.1
11 months									
1960	22.9	24.3	21.4	18.3	20.3	16.3	47.8	46.8	48.8
1950	30.2	32.3	28.1	26.1	27.5	24.7	56.1	62.8	49.1
1940	74.1	78.1	69.9	65.5	68.8	62.1	134.7	145.0	124.3

Source: "Infant Mortality Rates by Detailed Age, Color, and Sex: United States, 1940, 1950, and 1960." National Center for Health Services. *Vital Statistics Rates in the United States 1940-1960*. By Robert D. Grove and Alice M. Hetzel. Washington, D.C.: Government Printing Office, 1968, pp. 210-11.

★ 2248 ★

Fetal and Infant Deaths

Infant Mortality Rates for Selected Causes by Age and Race, 1916-1940, Part 1A

Infant mortality rates for selected causes, by race[1]: birth- registration states, 1916-1940.Exclusive of stillbirths. By place of occurrence. Rates are the number of deaths under 1 year of age in a specified group per 1,000 live births in that group. Rates for frequencies less than 20 are shown in italics.

Cause of death and race	1916	1917	1918	1919	1920	1921	1922	1923	1924	1925	1926	1927
All causes												
All races	101.0	93.8	100.9	86.6	85.8	75.6	76.2	77.1	70.8	71.7	73.3	64.6
White	99.0	90.5	97.4	83.0	82.1	72.5	73.2	73.5	66.8	68.3	70.0	60.6
All other races	184.9	150.7	161.2	130.5	131.7	108.5	110.0	117.4	112.9	110.8	111.8	100.1
Cerebrospinal (meningococcous) meningitis (6)												
All races	0.2	0.3	0.2	0.2	0.2	0.1	0.1	0.1	0.1	0.1	0.1	0.1
White	-	-	-	-	-	0.2	0.1	0.1	0.1	0.1	0.1	0.1
All other races	-	-	-	-	-	0.1	0.1	0.1	0.1	0.1	0.1	0.2
Scarlet fever (8)												
All races	0.1	0.1	0.1	0.1	0.1	0.1	0.1	0.1	0.1	0.1	0.1	0.1
White	0.1	0.1	0.1	0.1	0.1	0.1	0.1	0.1	0.1	0.1	0.1	0.1
All other races	0.1	0	0.0	0.0	0.0	0.1	0.0	0.0	0.0	0.0	0.1	0.0
Whooping cough (9)												
All races	2.2	2.4	3.3	1.4	3.0	2.2	1.4	2.4	2.1	1.8	2.3	1.9
White	2.2	2.2	3.1	1.2	2.9	2.0	1.3	2.1	1.8	1.6	2.1	1.7
All other races	5.4	5.8	8.2	3.0	4.7	4.3	2.8	5.1	4.9	3.2	3.8	4.2
Diphtheria (10)												
All races	0.5	0.5	0.4	0.5	0.5	0.4	0.5	0.4	0.3	0.3	0.2	0.2
White	0.5	0.5	0.4	0.4	0.4	0.4	0.5	0.4	0.3	0.3	0.2	0.2
All other races	1.2	0.9	0.7	0.6	0.6	0.7	0.6	0.7	0.4	0.4	0.4	0.3
Erysipelas (11)												
All races	0.6	0.5	0.4	0.4	0.4	0.4	0.4	0.4	0.4	0.3	0.4	0.4
White	0.6	0.5	0.4	0.4	0.4	0.4	0.4	0.4	0.4	0.4	0.4	0.4
All other races	0.5	0.2	0.2	0.1	0.2	0.2	0.2	0.2	0.2	0.2	0.3	0.1
Tetanus (12)												
All races	0.1	0.1	0.1	0.1	0.1	0.1	0.1	0.1	0.1	0.1	0.1	0.1
White	0.1	0.1	0.1	0.1	0.1	0.1	0.1	0.1	0.0	0.0	0.0	0.1
All other races	0.4	0.7	0.6	0.6	0.6	0.4	0.5	0.5	0.5	0.4	0.4	0.5
Tuberculosis of respiratory system (13)												
All races	0.5	0.6	0.5	0.4	0.4	0.3	0.3	0.2	0.2	0.2	0.2	0.2
White	0.5	0.5	0.4	0.4	0.3	0.2	0.2	0.2	0.2	0.2	0.2	0.1
All other races	2.3	1.6	1.7	1.2	1.0	0.8	0.7	0.7	0.7	0.7	0.6	0.7
Tuberculosis of meninges and central nervous system (14)												
All races	0.8	0.7	0.7	0.6	0.5	0.4	0.4	0.4	0.3	0.3	0.3	0.3

[Continued]

★ 2248 ★

Infant Mortality Rates for Selected Causes by Age and Race, 1916-1940, Part 1A

[Continued]

Cause of death and race	1916	1917	1918	1919	1920	1921	1922	1923	1924	1925	1926	1927
White	0.8	0.7	0.7	0.6	0.5	0.4	0.4	0.4	0.3	0.3	0.3	0.2
All other races	1.9	0.8	0.6	0.6	0.6	0.5	0.5	0.6	0.4	0.4	0.5	0.4
Tuberculosis (other forms) (15-22)												
All races	0.2	0.2	0.2	0.2	0.1	0.2	0.2	0.1	0.1	0.1	0.1	0.1
White	0.2	0.2	0.2	0.2	0.1	0.2	0.1	0.1	0.1	0.1	0.1	0.1
All other races	0.3	0.3	0.2	0.2	0.2	0.2	0.3	0.3	0.3	0.3	0.2	0.2
Dysentery (27)												
All races	0.2	0.3	0.4	0.4	0.4	0.4	0.3	0.3	0.3	0.3	0.3	0.3
White	0.2	0.3	0.3	0.3	0.3	0.3	0.2	0.2	0.2	0.3	0.2	0.2
All other races	0.4	1.8	1.9	1.9	1.7	1.1	1.2	1.1	1.0	0.9	0.8	0.8
Syphilis (30c, e-g)												
All races	1.4	1.2	1.0	0.9	0.9	0.9	0.8	0.8	0.7	0.7	0.6	0.7
White	1.2	1.0	0.8	0.8	0.7	0.7	0.7	0.6	0.5	0.5	0.5	0.5
All other races	7.9	3.9	3.4	2.6	2.7	2.8	2.6	2.8	2.7	2.9	2.8	3.1
Measles (35)												
All races	1.4	1.2	1.0	0.5	1.0	0.5	0.6	1.2	0.8	0.3	1.1	0.4
White	1.4	1.2	1.0	0.5	1.0	0.5	0.6	1.2	0.7	0.3	1.1	0.4
All other races	1.5	2.3	0.8	0.2	0.5	0.4	0.4	1.7	1.5	0.2	1.0	0.6
Convulsions (86)												
All races	1.3	1.1	1.2	1.0	1.0	0.9	0.8	0.7	0.7	0.7	0.6	0.5
White	1.2	1.0	1.1	0.9	0.9	0.7	0.7	0.6	0.6	0.6	0.5	0.4
All other races	3.1	2.8	2.7	2.2	2.0	1.9	2.0	1.7	1.7	1.2	1.2	1.1
Pneumonia (all forms) and influenza (107-109, 33)												
All races	14.3	13.3	20.6	15.2	13.8	9.3	12.5	12.9	10.9	11.2	13.3	9.5
White	13.9	12.7	19.6	14.3	12.8	8.7	11.8	11.8	9.9	10.4	12.2	8.6
All other races	29.9	24.4	38.8	26.3	26.6	15.1	20.0	23.9	21.1	21.5	25.3	18.2

Source: "Infant Mortality Rates for Selected Causes, by Race: Birth-Registration States, 1915 for 1916-1940." U.S. Bureau of the Census. *Vital Statistics Rates in the United States 1900-1940*. By Forrest E. Linder and Robert D. Grove. Washington, D.C.: Government Printing Office, 1943, pp. 608-609. *Notes:* 1. Mexicans included with white for each year except 1932, 1933, and 1934.

★ 2249 ★

Fetal and Infant Deaths

Infant Mortality Rates for Selected Causes by Age and Race, 1916-1940, Part 1B

Infant mortality rates for selected causes, by race[1]: birth- registration states, 1916-1940. Exclusive of stillbirths. By place of occurrence. Rates are the number of deaths under 1 year of age in a specified group per 1,000 live births in that group. Rates for frequencies less than 20 are shown in italics.

Cause of death and race	1928	1929	1930	1931	1932	1933	1934	1935	1936	1937	1938
All causes											
All races	68.7	67.6	64.6	61.6	57.6	58.1	60.1	55.7	57.1	54.4	51.0
White	64.0	63.2	60.1	57.4	53.3	52.8	54.5	51.9	52.9	50.3	47.1
All other races	106.2	102.2	99.9	93.1	86.2	91.3	94.4	83.2	87.6	83.2	79.1
Cerebrospinal (meningococcous) meningitis (6)											
All races	0.2	0.3	0.2	0.2	0.1	0.1	0.1	0.1	0.1	0.1	0.1
White	0.2	0.3	0.2	0.2	0.1	0.1	0.1	0.1	0.1	0.1	0.1
All other races	0.2	0.2	0.2	0.2	0.1	0.1	0.1	0.1	0.1	0.1	0.1
Scarlet fever (8)											
All races	0.1	0.1	0.1	0.1	0.0	0.0	0.0	0.1	0.0	0.0	0.0
White	0.1	0.1	0.1	0.1	0.0	0.0	0.0	0.1	0.0	0.0	0.0
All other races	0.0	0.0	0.0	0.0	0.0	0.0	0.0	0.0	0.0	0.0	0.0
Whooping cough (9)											
All races	1.6	1.9	1.5	1.2	1.5	1.3	2.1	1.4	0.8	1.4	1.4
White	1.4	1.7	1.4	1.1	1.4	1.0	1.8	1.2	0.7	1.3	1.2
All other races	2.9	3.3	2.8	2.2	2.8	2.7	4.2	2.3	1.4	2.3	2.6
Diphtheria (10)											
All races	0.3	0.2	0.2	0.2	0.2	0.2	0.2	01	0.1	0.1	0.1
White	0.3	0.2	0.2	0.2	0.2	0.2	0.1	0.1	0.1	0.1	0.1
All other races	0.4	0.4	0.4	0.3	0.2	0.3	0.2	0.2	0.3	0.2	0.1
Erysipelas (11)											
All races	0.3	0.4	0.3	0.3	0.3	0.3	0.2	0.3	0.2	0.1	0.1
White	0.4	0.4	0.3	0.3	0.3	0.3	0.3	0.3	02	0.1	0.1
All other races	0.2	0.2	0.1	0.2	0.1	0.1	0.1	0.1	0.1	0.1	0.1
Tetanus (12)											
All races	0.1	0.1	0.1	0.1	0.1	0.1	0.1	0.1	0.1	0.1	0.1
White	0.1	0.0	0.0	0.0	0.0	0.1	0.0	0.1	0.0	0.0	0.0
All other races	0.5	0.3	0.3	0.3	0.2	0.3	0.4	0.2	0.3	0.3	0.2
Tuberculosis of respiratory system (13)											
All races	0.2	0.2	0.2	0.2	0.1	0.2	0.1	0.1	0.1	0.1	0.1
White	0.1	0.1	0.1	0.1	0.1	0.1	0.1	0.1	0.1	0.1	0.1
All other races	0.7	0.4	0.6	0.5	0.5	0.5	0.4	0.5	0.4	0.4	0.3
Tuberculosis of meninges and central nervous system (14)											
All races	0.2	0.2	0.2	0.2	0.2	0.1	0.1	0.1	0.1	0.1	0.1

[Continued]

★ 2249 ★

Infant Mortality Rates for Selected Causes by Age and Race, 1916-1940, Part 1B

[Continued]

Cause of death and race	1928	1929	1930	1931	1932	1933	1934	1935	1936	1937	1938
White	0.2	0.2	0.2	0.2	0.1	0.1	0.1	0.1	0.1	0.1	0.1
All other races	0.3	0.2	0.3	0.3	0.2	0.2	0.3	0.2	0.2	0.2	0.2
Tuberculosis (other forms) (15-22)											
All races	0.1	0.1	0.1	0.1	0.1	0.1	0.1	0.1	0.1	0.1	0.1
White	0.1	0.1	0.1	0.1	0.1	0.0	0.0	0.0	0.1	0.0	0.0
All other races	0.3	0.3	0.2	0.2	0.3	0.2	0.2	0.2	0.2	0.2	0.1
Dysentery (27)											
All races	0.3	0.3	0.4	0.3	0.2	0.4	0.4	0.4	0.5	0.5	0.5
White	0.3	0.2	0.3	0.2	0.2	0.3	0.3	0.3	0.5	0.4	0.5
All other races	1.0	0.8	0.9	0.8	0.5	1.0	1.1	0.6	0.8	0.9	0.9
Syphilis (30c, e-g)											
All races	0.8	0.8	0.8	0.8	0.8	0.8	0.7	0.7	0.7	0.7	0.6
White	0.5	0.5	0.5	0.5	0.4	0.4	0.4	0.4	0.4	0.4	0.3
All other races	3.2	3.3	3.4	3.3	3.1	3.0	2.8	2.8	3.1	3.0	2.8
Measles (35)											
All races	0.6	0.3	0.4	0.4	0.2	0.3	0.7	0.4	0.1	0.2	0.3
White	0.6	0.3	0.4	0.4	0.2	0.2	0.6	0.3	0.1	0.1	0.3
All other races	1.0	0.2	0.4	0.4	0.2	0.5	1.3	0.5	0.1	0.2	0.4
Convulsions (86)											
All races	0.5	0.4	0.4	0.3	0.3	0.3	0.3	0.3	0.3	0.2	0.2
White	0.4	0.4	0.3	0.3	0.3	0.2	0.2	0.2	0.2	0.2	0.1
All other races	1.1	1.0	1.0	0.8	0.8	0.7	0.6	0.6	0.7	0.6	0.5
Pneumonia (all forms) and influenza (107-109, 33)											
All races	12.4	12.5	10.2	10.6	9.7	9.4	9.5	9.2	9.9	9.2	7.9
White	11.3	11.3	9.2	9.6	8.7	8.2	8.2	8.2	8.8	8.2	7.0
All other races	21.7	21.5	17.7	17.9	16.5	16.7	17.7	16.0	17.6	16.5	14.7

Source: "Infant Mortality Rates for Selected Causes, by Race: Birth-Registration States, 1915 for 1916-1940." U.S. Bureau of the Census. *Vital Statistics Rates in the United States 1900-1940.* By Forrest E. Linder and Robert D. Grove. Washington, D.C.: Government Printing Office, 1943, pp. 608-609. *Notes:* 1. Mexicans included with white for each year except 1932, 1933, and 1934.

★ 2250 ★

Fetal and Infant Deaths

Infant Mortality Rates for Selected Causes by Age and Race, 1916-1940, Part 1C

Infant mortality rates for selected causes, by race[1]: Birth- registration states, 1916-1940. Exclusive of stillbirths. By place of occurrence. Rates are the number of deaths under 1 year of age in a specified group per 1,000 live births in that group. Rates for frequencies less than 20 are shown in italics.

Cause of death and race	1939	1940
All causes		
All races	48.0	47.0
White	44.3	43.2
All other races	74.2	73.8
Cerebrospinal (meningococcous) meningitis (6)		
All races	0.1	0.1
White	0.1	0.1
All other races	0.1	0.1
Scarlet fever (8)		
All races	0.0	0.0
White	0.0	0.0
All other races	0.0	0.0
Whooping cough (9)		
All races	0.9	0.9
White	0.7	0.7
All other races	2.1	1.7
Diphtheria (10)		
All races	0.1	0.1
White	0.1	0.1
All other races	0.1	0.1
Erysipelas (11)		
All races	0.0	0.0
White	0.0	0.0
All other races	0.0	0.0
Tetanus (12)		
All races	0.1	0.1
White	0.0	0.0
All other races	0.2	0.2
Tuberculosis of respiratory system (13)		
All races	0.1	0.1
White	0.1	0.1
All other races	0.4	0.3

[Continued]

★ 2250 ★

Infant Mortality Rates for Selected Causes by Age and Race, 1916-1940, Part 1C

[Continued]

Cause of death and race	1939	1940
Tuberculosis of meninges and central nervous system (14)		
All races	0.1	0.1
White	0.1	0.1
All other races	0.1	0.2
Tuberculosis (other forms) (15-22)		
All races	0.0	0.0
White	0.0	0.0
All other races	0.2	0.1
Dysentery (27)		
All races	0.4	0.4
White	0.4	0.4
All other races	0.8	0.8
Syphilis (30c, e-g)		
All races	0.6	0.5
White	0.3	0.2
All other races	2.6	2.5
Measles (35)		
All races	0.1	0.1
White	0.1	0.1
All other races	0.2	0.1
Convulsions (86)		
All races	0.2	0.2
White	0.2	0.1
All other races	0.5	0.4
Pneumonia (all forms) and influenza (107-109, 33)		
All races	7.1	7.4
White	6.2	6.5
All other races	13.4	14.0

Source: "Infant Mortality Rates for Selected Causes, by Race: Birth-Registration States, 1915 for 1916-1940." U.S. Bureau of the Census. *Vital Statistics Rates in the United States 1900-1940.* By Forrest E. Linder and Rovbert D. Grove. Washington, D.C.: Government Printing Office, 1943, pp. 608-609. *Notes:* 1. Mexicans included with white for each year except 1932, 1933, and 1934.

★ 2251 ★

Fetal and Infant Deaths

Infant Mortality Rates for Selected Causes by Age and Race, 1916-1940, Part 2A

Infant mortality rates for selected causes, by race[1]: birth- registration states, 1916-1940.Exclusive of stillbirths. By place of occurrence. rates are the number of deaths under 1 year of age in a specified group per 1,000 live births in that group. Rates for frequencies less than 20 are shown in italics.

Cause of death and race	1916	1917	1918	1919	1920	1921	1922	1923	1924	1925	1926	1927
Pneumonia (all forms) (107-109)												
All races	13.4	12.6	13.9	11.0	11.1	8.7	10.8	10.6	9.8	9.5	10.8	8.1
White	13.1	12.0	13.2	10.6	10.4	8.1	10.2	9.8	8.9	8.7	10.0	7.3
All other races	28.7	23.4	25.8	16.1	19.9	14.0	17.0	19.4	18.8	18.2	20.6	15.6
Influenza (33)												
All races	0.8	0.8	6.7	4.2	2.7	0.6	1.7	2.2	1.1	1.8	2.4	1.4
White	0.8	0.8	6.4	3.7	2.3	0.6	1.6	2.0	1.0	1.6	2.2	1.3
All other races	1.2	1.0	13.0	10.2	6.8	1.1	3.0	4.6	2.4	3.4	4.7	2.6
Diseases of the stomach (117, 118)												
All races	1.4	1.2	1.4	1.4	1.2	1.0	0.8	0.8	0.7	0.6	0.5	0.5
White	1.4	1.2	1.4	1.3	1.1	0.9	0.7	0.7	0.6	0.5	0.5	0.4
All other races	1.1	1.9	2.0	2.3	2.0	1.6	1.6	1.5	1.5	0.9	0.9	0.8
Diarrhea, enteritis, ulceration of intestines (119)												
All races	24.1	20.0	19.0	15.7	14.9	13.5	11.7	11.5	9.2	11.2	9.7	7.8
White	23.7	19.5	18.6	15.4	14.6	13.3	11.4	11.2	8.8	10.7	9.3	7.3
All other races	41.0	28.8	24.9	19.4	19.4	16.1	14.8	15.2	14.2	16.8	14.4	12.2
Congenital malformations (157)												
All races	6.8	6.3	6.5	6.3	6.2	6.1	6.3	6.3	6.1	6.2	6.2	5.6
White	6.8	6.4	6.6	6.5	6.5	6.4	6.7	6.6	6.4	6.5	6.5	6.0
All other races	6.7	3.7	3.9	3.1	3.2	3.0	2.8	3.0	3.0	3.3	3.2	2.4
Congenital debility (158)[2]												
All races	6.8	5.9	6.3	5.4	4.8	4.4	3.9	4.0	3.5	3.5	3.3	2.8
White	-	-	-	-	-	4.1	3.7	3.7	3.3	3.2	3.1	2.6
All other races	-	-	-	-	-	7.1	6.4	6.7	5.9	6.1	5.9	4.9
Premature birth (159)												
All races	19.3	19.1	20.2	19.2	19.4	17.9	18.1	17.8	17.7	17.2	17.7	16.8
White	19.1	19.0	20.1	18.6	18.9	17.6	17.8	17.5	17.2	16.9	17.4	16.6
All other races	31.0	21.9	21.2	25.8	25.4	21.7	21.5	21.4	22.9	20.7	20.9	18.9
Injury at birth (160)												
All races	4.2	3.8	3.3	3.4	3.7	4.2	4.5	4.6	4.8	4.9	4.9	4.8
White	4.2	3.9	3.4	3.5	3.9	4.4	4.7	4.8	5.0	5.1	5.1	5.0
All other races	4.3	2.5	2.5	2.2	2.2	2.2	2.6	2.7	2.9	3.2	3.1	3.2
All other causes												
All races	14.6	15.0	14.2	13.5	13.3	12.4	12.4	12.1	11.7	11.5	11.4	11.4
White[3]	21.0	19.7	19.1	17.5	16.7	10.9	11.0	10.7	10.3	10.1	10.1	9.7
All other races[3]	45.8	46.4	47.0	38.0	38.0	28.1	28.3	27.7	26.7	27.3	26.1	27.2

Source: "Infant Mortality Rates for Selected Causes, by Race: Birth-Registration States, 1915 for 1916-1940." U.S. Bureau of the Census. *Vital Statistics Rates in the United States 1900-1940*. By Forrest E. Linder and Robert D. Grove. Washington, D.C.: Government Printing Office, 1943, pp. 610-11. *Notes:* Numbers after cause of death are those of the 1938 revision of the detailed International List. 1. Mexicans included with white for each year except 1932, 1933, and 1934. 2. Includes icterus and sclerema for 1916-1936, inclusive. 3. Includes cerebrospinal meningitis and congenital debility for 1916- 1920, inclusive.

★ 2252 ★

Fetal and Infant Deaths

Infant Mortality Rates for Selected Causes by Age and Race, 1916-1940, Part 2B

Infant mortality rates for selected causes, by race[1]: birth- registration states, 1916-1940.Exclusive of stillbirths. By place of occurrence. rates are the number of deaths under 1 year of age in a specified group per 1,000 live births in that group. Rates for frequencies less than 20 are shown in italics.

Cause of death and race	1928	1929	1930	1931	1932	1933	1934	1935	1936	1937	1938
Pneumonia (all forms) (107-109)											
All races	9.7	9.1	8.9	8.8	7.9	7.5	8.3	7.7	8.3	7.5	7.0
White	8.7	8.3	8.1	8.0	7.0	6.6	7.1	6.9	7.4	6.7	6.2
All other races	16.9	15.3	15.2	14.7	13.5	13.2	15.4	13.3	14.2	13.2	12.8
Influenza (33)											
All races	2.8	3.4	1.3	1.8	1.8	1.9	1.2	1.5	1.6	1.7	0.9
White	2.5	3.0	1.2	1.6	1.6	1.6	1.0	1.3	1.4	1.5	0.8
All other races	4.8	6.1	2.4	3.2	3.1	3.5	2.4	2.8	3.4	3.2	1.9
Diseases of the stomach (117, 118)											
All races	0.5	0.4	0.3	0.3	0.2	0.3	0.3	0.2	0.2	0.2	0.2
White	0.4	0.4	0.3	0.2	0.2	0.2	0.2	0.2	0.2	0.2	0.1
All other races	0.9	0.7	0.8	0.6	0.6	0.7	0.6	0.6	0.5	0.5	0.4
Diarrhea, enteritis, ulceration of intestines (119)											
All races	7.7	7.1	7.8	6.6	5.2	5.6	6.1	4.9	5.7	5.3	5.0
White	7.2	6.7	7.4	6.2	4.7	4.8	5.3	4.6	5.3	4.9	4.5
All other races	11.7	10.7	11.4	9.8	8.5	10.3	11.0	7.2	8.7	8.0	8.3
Congenital malformations (157)											
All races	5.4	5.5	5.3	5.4	5.3	5.1	5.2	4.8	4.9	4.6	4.5
White	5.8	5.9	5.7	5.8	5.7	5.6	5.6	5.2	5.2	5.0	4.8
All other races	2.3	2.3	2.2	2.4	2.4	2.4	2.6	2.1	2.3	2.2	2.2
Congenital debility (158)[2]											
All races	3.0	2.8	2.5	2.5	2.3	2.4	2.4	2.1	2.1	1.6	1.4
White	2.6	2.5	2.2	2.2	2.0	2.0	2.0	1.8	1.8	1.3	1.1
All other races	5.6	5.3	4.9	4.6	4.4	4.7	5.1	4.3	4.4	3.6	3.3
Premature birth (159)											
All races	17.6	17.5	16.7	16.0	15.8	15.8	16.2	15.4	15.7	15.3	14.3
White	17.2	17.1	16.3	15.6	15.3	15.3	15.8	15.0	15.3	14.8	13.8
All other races	20.2	20.3	19.7	18.6	18.7	19.2	18.7	17.9	18.7	18.7	17.6
Injury at birth (160)											
All races	4.7	4.8	4.8	4.8	4.6	4.6	4.5	4.5	4.5	4.4	4.4
White	4.9	5.0	5.0	5.0	4.8	4.8	4.7	4.7	4.7	4.5	4.5
All other races	3.0	2.8	3.3	3.3	3.0	3.4	3.4	3.1	3.3	3.1	3.2
All other causes											
All races	12.1	11.9	12.0	11.2	10.4	10.8	10.7	10.6	10.8	10.2	9.8
White[3]	10.0	9.9	9.8	9.1	8.5	8.6	8.6	8.8	8.9	8.4	8.2
All other races[3]	29.0	27.9	29.3	26.6	23.3	24.4	23.5	23.6	24.3	22.4	20.9

Source: "Infant Mortality Rates for Selected Causes, by Race: Birth-Registration States, 1915 for 1916-1940." U.S. Bureau of the Census. *Vital Statistics Rates in the United States 1900-1940*. By Forrest E. Linder and Robert D. Grove. Washington, D.C.: Government Printing Office, 1943, pp. 610-11. *Notes:* Numbers after cause of death are those of the 1938 revision of the detailed International List. 1. Mexicans included with white for each year except 1932, 1933, and 1934. 2. Includes icterus and sclerema for 1916-1936, inclusive. 3. Includes crebrospinal meningitis and congenital debility for 1916- 1920, inclusive.

★ 2253 ★

Fetal and Infant Deaths

Infant Mortality Rates for Selected Causes by Age and Race, 1916-1940, Part 2C

Infant mortality rates for selected causes, by race[1]: birth- registration states, 1916-1940.Exclusive of stillbirths. By place of occurrence. rates are the number of deaths under 1 year of age in a specified group per 1,000 live births in that group. Rates for frequencies less than 20 are shown in italics.

Cause of death and race	1939	1940
Pneumonia (all forms) (107-109)		
All races	6.1	6.3
White	5.4	5.6
All other races	11.2	11.4
Influenza (33)		
All races	1.0	1.1
White	0.9	0.9
All other races	2.2	2.5
Diseases of the stomach (117, 118)		
All races	0.1	0.1
White	0.1	0.1
All other races	0.3	0.2
Diarrhea, enteritis, ulceration of intestines (119)		
All races	4.0	3.5
White	3.7	3.2
All other races	6.3	5.8
Congenital malformations (157)		
All races	4.6	4.7
White	4.9	5.0
All other races	2.1	2.2
Congenital debility (158)[2]		
All races	1.2	1.2
White	0.9	0.9
All other races	3.4	3.5
Premature birth (159)		
All races	14.2	13.7
White	13.7	13.2
All other races	17.7	17.3
Injury at birth (160)		
All races	4.5	4.5
White	4.6	4.6
All other races	3.5	3.7
All other causes		
All races	9.5	9.4
White[3]	8.0	7.8
All other races[3]	20.1	20.5

Source: "Infant Mortality Rates for Selected Causes, by Race: Birth-Registration States, 1915 for 1916-1940." U.S. Bureau of the Census. *Vital Statistics Rates in the United States 1900-1940*. By Forrest E. Linder and Robert D. Grove. Washington, D.C.: Government Printing Office, 1943, pp. 610-11. *Notes:* Numbers after cause of death are those of the 1938 revision of the detailed International List. 1. Mexicans included with white for each year except 1932, 1933, and 1934. 2. Includes icterus and sclerema for 1916-1936, inclusive. 3. Includes crebrospinal meningitis and congenital debility for 1916- 1920, inclusive.

★ 2254 ★

Fetal and Infant Deaths

Infant Mortality Rates, Including Blacks and Other Minorities, 1950-1975

	1950	1960	1970	1975
All Races	29.2	26.0	20.0	16.1
Whites	26.8	22.9	17.8	14.2
Blacks	43.9	44.3	32.6	26.2
Hispanics				
Mexican				
Puerto Rican				
Cuban				
Other Hispanic				

Source: "Infant Deaths Per 1,000 Live Births, 1950-1988," *U.S. Children and Their Families*, 1989, p. 171. Primary source: Hispanic rates are based on data from 18 reporting states and the District of Columbia. National Center for Health Statistics, "Advance Report of Final Mortality Statistics, 1986," *Monthly Vital Statistics Reports*, Vol. 37, No. 6, Supplement, Table 13 and 20; "Annual Summary, 1987," *Monthly Vital Statistics Report*, Vol. 36, No. 13, Table 11; "Births, Marriages, Divorces, and Deaths for 1988," *Monthly Vital Statistics Report*, Vol. 37, No. 12. *Notes:* The infant mortality rate is the number of deaths of children under age 1 per 1,000 live births. It is not a percentage.

★ 2255 ★

Fetal and Infant Deaths

Infant Mortality and Fetal Death Rates, 1950-1975

Data based on the National Vital Statistics System.

Race and year	Infant mortality rate[1] Deaths per 1,000 live births				Fetal death rate[2]	Late fetal death rate[3]	Peri-natal mortality rate[4]
	Total	Neonatal		Post neo-natal			
		Under 28 days	Under 7 days				
All races							
1950[5]	29.9	20.5	17.8	8.7	18.4	14.9	32.5
1960[5]	26.0	18.7	16.7	7.3	15.8	12.1	28.6
1970	20.0	15.1	13.6	4.9	14.0	9.5	23.0
1975	16.1	11.6	10.0	4.5	10.6	7.8	17.7
Provisional data							
1985[5]	10.6	6.9	-	3.6	-	-	-
1986[5]	10.4	6.7	-	3.7	-	-	-
1987[5]	10.0	6.5	-	3.4	-	-	-
White							
1950[5]	26.8	19.4	17.1	7.7	16.6	13.3	30.1
1960[5]	22.9	17.2	15.6	5.7	13.9	10.8	26.2
1970	17.8	13.8	12.5	4.0	12.3	8.6	21.1
1975	14.2	10.4	9.0	3.8	9.4	7.1	16.0

[Continued]

★ 2255 ★

Infant Mortality and Fetal Death Rates, 1950-1975

[Continued]

Race and year	Infant mortality rate[1] Deaths per 1,000 live births				Fetal death rate[2]	Late fetal death rate[3]	Peri-natal mortality rate[4]
	Total	Neonatal		Post neo-natal			
		Under 28 days	Under 7 days				
Black							
1950[5]	43.9	27.8	23.0	16.1	32.1	-	-
1960[5]	44.3	27.8	23.7	16.5	-	-	-
1970	32.6	22.8	20.3	9.9	23.2	-	-
1975	26.2	18.3	15.7	7.9	16.8	11.4	26.9

Source: "Infant Mortality Rates, Fetal Death Rates, and Perinatal Mortality Rates, According to Race: United States, Selected Years 1950-1987," *Health United States - 1988*, March 1989, p. 54. Primary source: National Center for Health Statistics: *Vital Statistics of the United States*, Vol. II, Mortality, Part A, 1950-83. Public Health Service. Washington. U.S. Government Printing Office. 1984-86, to be published; Annual summary of births, marriages, divorces, and deaths, United States, 1985. *Monthly Vital Statistics Report*. Vol. 34, No. 13. DHHS Pub. No. (PHS) 86-1120. Sept. 19, 1986; Annual summary of births, marriages, divorces, and deaths, United States, 1987. *Monthly Vital Statistics Report*. Vol, 36, No. 13. DHHS Pub. No. (PHS) 87-1120. July 29, 1988. Public Health Service. Hyattsville, MD; Data computed by the Division of Analysis from data compiled by the Division of Vital Statistics. *Notes:* 1. Infant mortality is number of deaths of infants under 1 year per 1,000 live births. Neonatal deaths occur within 28 days of birth; postneonatal deaths occur 28-365 days after birth. Deaths within 7 days are early neonatal deaths. 2. Number of deaths of fetuses of 20 weeks or more gestation per 1,000 live births plus fetal deaths. 3. Number of fetal deaths of 28 weeks or more gestation per 1,000 live births plus late fetal deaths. 4. Number of late fetal deaths plus infant deaths within 7 days of birth per 1,000 live births plus late fetal deaths. 5. Includes births and deaths of nonresidents of the United States.

Life Expectancy

★ 2256 ★

Life Expectancy at 5-Year Age Intervals by Race and Sex – 1939-41, 1949-51, 1959-61

Expectation of life ($^{o}e_{x}$) at 5-year intervals, by color and sex: United States, 1939-41, 1949-51, and 1959-61. In years. See text for definition and interpretation.

Age and sex	Total			White			Nonwhite		
	1959-61	1949-51	1939-41	1959-61	1949-51	1939-41	1959-61	1949-51	1939-41
Both sexes									
0	69.89	68.07	63.62	70.73	69.02	64.92	63.91	60.73	-
1	70.75	69.16	65.76	71.38	69.95	66.84	65.75	62.65	-
5	67.04	65.54	62.49	67.64	66.29	63.52	62.21	59.25	-
10	62.19	60.74	57.82	62.79	61.48	58.83	57.41	54.50	-
15	57.33	55.91	53.10	57.92	56.65	54.09	52.57	49.73	-
20	52.58	51.20	48.54	53.16	51.91	49.47	47.88	45.19	-
25	47.89	46.56	44.09	48.44	47.22	44.92	43.35	40.85	-
30	43.18	41.91	39.67	43.69	42.52	40.40	38.89	36.59	-
35	38.51	37.31	35.30	38.97	37.86	35.93	34.56	32.44	-

[Continued]

★ 2256 ★

Life Expectancy at 5-Year Age Intervals by Race and Sex – 1939-41, 1949-51, 1959-61

[Continued]

Age and sex	Total			White			Nonwhite		
	1959-61	1949-51	1939-41	1959-61	1949-51	1939-41	1959-61	1949-51	1939-41
40	33.92	32.81	31.03	34.33	33.29	31.54	30.39	28.48	-
45	29.50	28.49	26.90	29.84	28.88	27.29	26.46	24.75	-
50	25.29	24.40	22.98	25.57	24.70	23.26	22.74	21.38	-
55	21.37	20.57	19.31	21.58	20.77	19.47	19.45	18.41	-
60	17.71	17.04	15.91	17.84	17.15	15.98	16.53	15.87	-
65	14.39	13.83	12.80	14.44	13.86	12.80	13.96	13.59	-
70	11.38	10.92	10.00	11.37	10.89	9.96	11.63	11.48	-
75	8.71	8.40	7.62	8.65	8.34	7.55	9.52	9.48	-
80	6.39	6.34	5.73	6.33	6.27	5.64	7.28	7.62	-
85	4.58	4.69	4.31	4.53	4.62	4.20	5.27	5.79	-
Male									
0	66.80	65.47	61.60	67.55	66.31	62.81	61.48	58.91	52.33
1	67.80	66.73	64.00	68.34	67.41	64.98	63.50	61.06	56.05
5	64.10	63.12	60.76	64.61	63.77	61.68	59.98	57.69	53.13
10	59.27	58.35	56.12	59.78	58.98	57.03	55.19	52.96	48.54
15	54.43	53.56	51.43	54.93	54.18	52.33	50.39	48.23	43.95
20	49.77	48.92	46.91	50.25	49.52	47.76	45.78	43.73	39.74
25	45.19	44.36	42.51	45.65	44.93	43.28	41.38	39.49	35.94
30	40.56	39.78	38.13	40.98	40.29	38.80	37.05	35.31	32.25
35	35.94	35.23	33.79	36.31	35.68	34.36	32.81	31.21	28.67
40	31.42	30.79	29.57	31.73	31.17	30.03	28.72	27.29	25.23
45	27.09	26.55	25.52	27.34	26.87	25.87	24.89	23.59	22.02
50	23.02	22.59	21.72	23.22	22.83	21.96	21.28	20.25	19.18
55	19.32	18.96	18.20	19.45	19.11	18.34	18.11	17.36	16.67
60	15.94	15.68	14.99	16.01	15.76	15.05	15.29	14.91	14.38
65	12.95	12.74	12.07	12.97	12.75	12.07	12.84	12.75	12.18
70	10.33	10.11	9.46	10.29	10.07	9.42	10.81	10.74	10.06
75	7.99	7.83	7.22	7.92	7.77	7.17	8.93	8.83	8.09
80	5.95	5.94	5.44	5.89	5.88	5.38	6.87	7.07	6.46
85	4.39	4.41	4.11	4.34	4.35	4.02	5.08	5.38	5.08
Female									
0	73.24	70.96	65.89	74.19	72.03	67.29	66.47	62.70	55.51
1	73.93	71.84	67.73	74.68	72.77	68.93	68.10	64.37	58.47
5	70.21	68.21	64.43	70.92	69.09	65.57	64.54	60.93	55.47
10	65.35	63.38	59.73	66.05	64.26	60.85	59.72	56.17	50.83
15	60.45	58.52	54.97	61.15	59.39	56.07	54.85	51.36	46.22
20	55.60	53.73	50.37	56.29	54.56	51.38	50.07	46.77	42.14
25	50.79	48.99	45.87	51.45	49.77	46.78	45.40	42.35	38.31
30	46.00	44.28	41.41	46.63	45.00	42.21	40.83	38.02	34.52

[Continued]

★ 2256 ★

Life Expectancy at 5-Year Age Intervals by Race and Sex – 1939-41, 1949-51, 1959-61

[Continued]

Age and sex	Total			White			Nonwhite		
	1959-61	1949-51	1939-41	1959-61	1949-51	1939-41	1959-61	1949-51	1939-41
35	41.27	39.63	37.01	41.84	40.28	37.70	36.41	33.82	30.83
40	36.61	35.06	32.68	37.13	35.64	33.25	32.16	29.82	27.31
45	32.09	30.64	28.46	32.53	31.12	28.90	28.14	26.07	24.00
50	27.71	26.40	24.40	28.08	26.76	24.72	24.31	22.67	21.04
55	23.53	22.33	20.54	23.81	22.58	20.73	20.89	19.62	18.44
60	19.52	18.50	16.92	19.69	18.64	17.00	17.83	16.95	16.14
65	15.80	14.95	13.57	15.88	15.00	13.56	15.12	14.54	13.95
70	12.37	11.71	10.56	12.38	11.68	10.50	12.46	12.29	11.81
75	9.33	8.94	8.01	9.28	8.87	7.92	10.10	10.15	9.80
80	6.72	6.67	5.99	6.67	6.59	5.88	7.66	8.15	8.00
85	4.71	4.90	4.47	4.66	4.83	4.34	5.44	6.15	6.38

Source: "Expectation of Life ($^{o}e_{x}$) at 5-Year Age Intervals, by Color and Sex: United States, 1939-41, 1949-51, 1959-61." U.S. Bureau of the Census. *Vital Statistics Rates in the United States 1900-1940.* By Forrest E. Linder and Robert D. Grove. Washington, D.C.: Government Printing Office, 1943, p. 308.

★ 2257 ★

Life Expectancy

Life Expectancy at Birth, 1900-1970

Prior to 1929, for death-registration area only.

Year	Total			White			Negro and other		
	Both sexes	Male	Female	Both sexes	Male	Female	Both sexes	Male	Female
1970	70.9	67.1	74.8	71.7	68.0	75.6	65.3	61.3	69.4
1969	70.5	66.8	74.3	71.3	67.8	75.1	64.3	60.5	68.4
1968	70.2	66.6	74.0	71.1	67.5	74.9	63.7	60.1	67.5
1967	70.5	67.0	74.2	71.3	67.8	75.1	64.6	61.1	68.2
1966	70.1	66.7	73.8	71.0	67.6	74.7	64.0	60.7	67.4
1965	70.2	66.8	73.7	71.0	67.6	74.7	64.1	61.1	67.4
1964	70.2	66.9	73.7	71.0	67.7	74.6	64.1	61.1	67.2
1963[1]	69.9	66.6	73.4	70.8	67.5	74.4	63.6	60.9	66.5
1962[1]	70.0	66.8	73.4	70.9	67.6	74.4	64.1	61.5	66.8
1961	70.2	67.0	73.6	71.0	67.8	74.5	64.4	61.9	67.0
1960[3]	69.7	66.6	73.1	70.6	67.4	74.1	63.6	61.1	66.3
1959[2]	69.9	66.8	73.2	70.7	67.5	74.2	63.9	61.3	66.5
1958	69.6	66.6	72.9	70.5	67.4	73.9	63.4	61.0	65.8
1957	69.5	66.4	72.7	70.3	67.7	73.7	63.0	60.7	65.5
1956	69.7	66.7	72.9	70.5	67.5	73.9	63.6	61.3	66.1

[Continued]

★ 2257 ★

Life Expectancy at Birth, 1900-1970

[Continued]

Year	Total			White			Negro and other		
	Both sexes	Male	Female	Both sexes	Male	Female	Both sexes	Male	Female
1955	69.6	66.7	72.8	70.5	67.4	73.7	63.7	61.4	66.1
1954	69.6	66.7	72.8	70.5	67.5	73.7	63.4	61.1	65.9
1953	68.8	66.0	72.0	69.7	66.8	73.0	62.0	59.7	64.5
1952	68.6	65.8	71.6	69.5	66.6	72.6	61.4	59.1	63.8
1951	68.4	65.6	71.4	69.3	66.5	72.4	61.2	59.2	63.4
1950	68.2	65.6	71.1	69.1	66.5	72.2	60.8	59.1	62.9
1949	68.0	65.2	70.7	68.8	66.2	71.9	60.6	58.9	62.7
1948	67.2	64.6	69.9	68.0	65.5	71.0	60.0	58.1	62.5
1947	66.8	64.4	69.7	67.6	65.2	70.5	59.7	57.9	61.9
1946	66.7	64.4	69.4	67.5	65.1	70.3	59.1	57.5	61.0
1945	65.9	63.6	67.9	66.8	64.4	69.5	57.7	56.1	59.6
1944	65.2	63.6	66.8	66.2	64.5	68.4	56.6	55.8	57.7
1943	63.3	62.4	64.4	64.2	63.2	65.7	55.6	55.4	56.1
1942	66.2	64.7	67.9	67.3	65.9	69.4	56.6	55.4	58.2
1941	64.8	63.1	66.8	66.2	64.4	68.5	53.8	52.5	55.3
1940	62.9	60.8	65.2	64.2	62.1	66.6	53.1	51.5	54.9
1939	63.7	62.1	65.4	64.9	63.3	66.6	54.5	53.2	56.0
1938	63.5	61.9	65.3	65.0	63.2	66.8	52.9	51.7	54.3
1937	60.0	58.0	62.4	61.4	59.3	63.8	50.3	48.3	52.5
1936	58.5	56.6	60.6	59.8	58.0	61.9	49.0	47.0	51.4
1935	61.7	59.9	63.9	62.9	61.0	65.0	53.1	51.3	55.2
1934	61.1	59.3	63.3	62.4	50.6	64.6	51.8	50.2	53.7
1933	63.3	61.7	65.1	64.3	62.7	66.3	54.7	53.5	56.0
1932	62.1	61.0	63.5	63.2	62.0	64.5	53.7	52.8	54.6
1931	61.1	59.4	63.1	62.6	60.8	64.7	50.4	49.5	51.5
1930	59.7	58.1	61.6	61.4	59.7	63.5	48.1	47.3	49.2
1929	57.1	55.8	58.7	58.6	57.2	60.3	46.7	45.7	47.8
1928	56.8	55.6	58.3	58.4	57.0	60.0	46.3	45.6	47.0
1927	60.4	59.0	62.1	62.0	60.5	63.9	48.2	47.6	48.9
1926	56.7	55.5	58.0	58.2	57.0	59.6	44.6	43.7	45.6
1925	59.0	57.6	60.6	60.7	59.3	62.4	45.7	44.9	46.7
1924	59.7	58.1	61.5	61.4	59.8	63.4	46.6	45.5	47.8
1923	57.2	56.1	58.5	58.3	57.1	59.6	48.3	47.7	48.9
1922	59.6	58.4	61.0	60.4	59.1	61.9	52.4	51.8	53.0
1921	60.8	60.0	61.8	61.8	60.8	62.9	51.5	51.6	51.3
1920	54.1	53.6	54.6	54.9	54.4	55.6	45.3	45.5	45.2
1919	54.7	53.5	56.0	55.8	54.5	57.4	44.5	44.5	44.4
1918	39.1	36.6	42.2	39.8	37.1	43.2	31.1	29.9	32.5

[Continued]

★ 2257 ★

Life Expectancy at Birth, 1900-1970

[Continued]

Year	Total			White			Negro and other		
	Both sexes	Male	Female	Both sexes	Male	Female	Both sexes	Male	Female
1917	50.9	48.4	54.0	52.0	49.3	55.3	38.8	37.0	40.8
1916	51.7	49.6	54.3	52.5	50.2	55.2	41.3	39.6	43.1
1915	54.5	52.5	56.8	55.1	53.1	57.5	38.9	37.5	40.5
1914	54.2	52.0	56.8	54.9	52.7	57.5	38.9	37.1	40.8
1913	52.5	50.3	55.0	53.0	50.8	55.7	38.4	36.7	40.3
1912	53.5	51.5	55.9	53.9	51.9	56.2	37.9	35.9	40.0
1911	52.6	50.9	54.4	53.0	51.3	54.9	36.4	34.6	38.2
1910	50.0	48.4	51.8	50.3	48.6	52.0	35.6	33.8	37.5
1909	52.1	50.5	53.8	52.5	50.9	54.2	35.7	34.2	37.3
1908	51.1	49.5	52.8	51.5	49.9	53.3	34.9	33.8	36.0
1907	47.6	45.6	49.9	48.1	46.0	50.4	32.5	31.1	34.0
1906	48.7	46.9	50.8	49.3	47.3	51.4	32.9	31.8	33.9
1905	48.7	47.3	50.2	49.1	47.6	50.6	31.3	29.6	33.1
1904	47.6	46.2	49.1	48.0	46.6	49.5	30.8	29.1	32.7
1903	50.5	49.1	52.0	50.9	49.5	52.5	33.1	31.7	34.6
1902	51.5	49.8	53.4	51.9	50.2	53.8	34.6	32.9	36.4
1901	49.1	47.6	50.6	49.4	48.0	51.0	33.7	32.2	35.3
1900	47.3	46.3	48.3	47.6	46.6	48.7	33.0	32.5	33.5

Source: "Expectation of Life (in Years) at Birth, by Race and Sex: 1900 to 1970." U.S. Bureau of the Census. *Historical Statistics of the United States: Colonial Times to 1970, Part I.* Bicentennial Edition. Washington, D.C.: Government Printing Office, 1975, p. 55. *Notes:* 1. Excludes New Jersey; State did not require reporting of race. 2. Includes Alaska. 3. Denotes first year for which figures include Alaska and Hawaii.

★ 2258 ★

Life Expectancy

Life Expectancy at Birth, by Gender: 1900-1961, 1970-1974

Years of life expected at birth. Statistics prior to 1933 are exclusive of States not yet included in the death registration area. Minus sign (-) denotes Black and other races less than White.

Year and sex	Black and other races	White	Difference in years	Percent Black and other races of White
MALE				
1900-1902	32.5	48.2	-15.7	67.4
1909-1911	34.1	50.2	-16.1	67.9
1919-1921	47.1	56.3	-9.2	83.7
1929-1931	47.6	59.1	-11.5	80.5
1939-1941	52.3	62.8	-10.5	83.3

[Continued]

★ 2258 ★

Life Expectancy at Birth, by Gender: 1900-1961, 1970-1974

[Continued]

Year and sex	Black and other races	White	Difference in years	Percent Black and other races of White
1949-1951	58.9	66.3	-7.4	88.8
1959-1961	61.5	67.6	-6.1	91.0
1970	61.3	68.0	-6.7	90.1
1974	62.9	68.9	-6.0	91.3
Increase in Expectation of Life at Birth (Years)				
1900-1902 to 1974	30.4	20.7	9.7	(X)
1900-1902 to 1939-1941	19.8	14.6	5.2	(X)
1939-1941 to 1970	9.0	5.2	3.8	(X)
1970 to 1974	1.6	0.9	0.7	(X)
FEMALE				
1900-1902	35.0	51.1	-16.1	68.5
1909-1911	37.7	53.6	-15.9	70.3
1919-1921	46.9	58.5	-11.6	80.2
1929-1931	49.5	62.7	-13.2	78.9
1939-1941	55.5	67.3	-11.8	82.5
1949-1951	62.7	72.0	-9.3	87.1
1959-1961	66.5	74.2	-7.7	89.6
1970	69.4	75.6	-6.2	91.8
1974	71.2	76.6	-5.4	93.0
Increase in Expectation of Life at Birth (Years)				
1900-1902 to 1974	36.2	25.5	10.7	(X)
1900-1902 to 1939-1941	20.5	16.2	4.3	(X)
1939-1941 to 1970	13.9	9.3	4.6	(X)
1970 to 1974	1.8	1.0	0.8	(X)

Source: "Life Expectancy at Birth, by Sex, for Selected 3-Year Averages, 1900 to 1961, and Single-Year Data, 1970 and 1974," U.S. Department of Commerce, Bureau of the Census. *The Social and Economic Status of the Black Population in the United States: An Historical View, 1790-1978,* p. 120. Primary source: U.S. Department of Health, Education, and Welfare, National Center for Health Statistics. *Note:* X Not applicable.

★ 2259 ★

Life Expectancy

Life Expectancy at Selected Ages: 1900-1961, 1970-1974

Years of life expected at birth. Minus sign (-) denotes Black and other races less than White.

Age and year	Male			Female		
	Black and other races	White	Difference in years of life	Black and other races	White	Difference in years of life
1939-1941[1]						
0 years (at birth)	52.3	62.8	-10.5	67.3	-11.8	
1 year	56.1	65.0	-8.9	58.5	68.9	-10.4
15 years	44.0	52.3	-8.3	46.2	56.1	-9.9
25 years	35.9	43.3	-7.4	38.3	46.8	-8.5
40 years	25.2	30.0	-4.8	27.3	33.3	-6.0
65 years	12.2	12.8	-0.6	14.0	13.6	+0.4
1959-1961[1]						
0 years (at birth)	61.5	67.6	-6.1	66.5	74.2	-7.7
1 year	63.5	68.3	-4.8	74.7	-6.6	
15 years	50.4	54.9	-4.5	54.9	61.2	-6.3
25 years	41.4	45.7	-4.3	45.4	51.5	-6.1
40 years	28.7	31.7	-3.0	32.2	37.1	-4.9
65 years	12.8	13.0	-0.2	15.1	15.9	-0.8
1970						
0 years (at birth)	61.3	68.0	-6.7	69.4	75.6	-6.2
1 year	62.5	68.4	-5.9	70.4	75.8	-5.4
15 years	49.2	54.9	-5.7	57.0	62.2	-5.2
25 years	40.6	45.8	-5.2	47.5	52.5	-5.0
40 years	28.6	31.9	-3.3	34.2	38.3	-4.1
65 years	13.3	13.1	+0.2	16.4	17.1	-0.7
1974						
0 years (at birth)	62.9	68.9	-6.0	71.2	76.6	-5.4
1 year	63.7	69.1	-5.4	71.8	76.6	-4.8
15 years	50.3	55.6	-5.3	58.3	62.9	-4.6
25 years	41.5	46.5	-5.0	48.8	53.3	-4.5
40 years	29.3	32.6	-3.3	35.3	38.9	-3.6
65 years	13.4	13.4	-	16.7	17.6	-0.9

Source: "Life Expectancy at Selected Ages, by Sex, for Selected 3-Year Averages, 1939-1941 and 1959-1961, and Single-Year Data, 1970 and 1974," U.S. Department of Commerce, Bureau of the Census. *The Social and Economic Status of the Black Population in the United States: An Historical View, 1790-1978*, p. 121. Primary source: U.S. Department of Health, Education, and Welfare, National Center for Health Statistics. *Notes:* - Represents zero. 1. 3-year average.

★ 2260 ★

Life Expectancy

Life Expectancy at Specified Ages, 1900-1970

In years.

Year or period[1]	At birth		Age 20		Age 40		Age 60		Age 70	
	Male	Female	Male	Female	Male	Female	Male	Female	Male	Female
White										
1970	68.0	75.6	50.3	57.4	31.9	38.3	16.2	21.0	10.5	13.6
1969	67.8	75.1	50.1	56.9	31.8	37.8	16.0	20.5	10.4	13.0
1968	67.5	74.9	49.9	56.7	31.6	37.6	15.8	20.2	10.2	12.9
1967	67.8	75.1	50.2	56.9	31.8	37.8	16.1	20.4	10.4	13.0
1966	67.6	74.7	50.1	56.7	31.6	37.5	15.9	20.2	10.3	12.8
1965	67.6	74.7	50.2	56.6	31.7	37.5	16.0	20.1	10.3	12.8
1964	67.7	74.6	50.2	56.6	31.8	37.5	16.0	20.1	10.4	12.8
1963[2]	67.5	74.4	50.1	56.4	31.6	37.3	15.8	19.9	10.2	12.5
1962[2]	67.6	74.4	50.2	56.4	31.7	37.3	16.0	19.9	10.3	12.5
1961	67.8	74.5	50.4	56.6	31.9	37.4	16.1	20.0	10.4	12.6
1960[5]	67.4	74.1	50.1	56.2	31.6	37.1	15.9	19.7	10.2	12.4
1959[3]	67.6	74.2	50.3	56.3	31.8	37.2	16.1	19.7	10.4	12.5
1958	67.2	73.7	50.0	55.9	31.5	36.7	15.7	19.2	10.1	12.0
1957	67.1	73.5	49.9	55.7	31.4	36.6	15.7	19.2	10.1	12.1
1956	67.3	73.7	50.1	55.9	31.6	36.7	15.9	19.3	10.3	12.2
1955	67.3	73.6	50.1	55.8	31.7	36.7	16.0	19.3	10.3	12.2
1949-51	66.3	72.0	49.5	54.6	31.2	35.6	15.8	18.6	10.1	11.7
1939-41	62.8	67.3	47.8	51.4	30.0	33.3	15.1	17.0	9.4	10.5
1929-31	59.1	62.7	46.0	48.5	29.2	31.5	14.7	16.1	9.2	10.0
1919-21	56.3	58.5	45.6	46.5	29.9	30.9	15.3	15.9	9.5	9.9
1909-11	50.2	53.6	42.7	44.9	27.4	29.3	14.0	14.9	8.8	9.4
1901-10	49.3	52.5	42.4	44.4	27.6	29.3	14.2	15.1	(NA)	(NA)
1900-02	48.2	51.1	42.2	43.8	27.7	29.2	14.4	15.2	9.0	9.6
Negro and other										
1970	61.3	69.4	44.7	52.2	28.6	34.2	15.7	19.4	11.2	13.7
1969	60.5	68.4	43.9	51.2	27.8	33.3	14.9	18.5	10.9	13.7
1968	60.1	67.5	43.6	50.5	27.4	32.7	14.5	17.9	10.5	13.2
1967	61.1	68.2	44.8	51.3	28.3	33.4	15.3	18.7	11.2	13.9
1966	60.7	67.4	44.6	50.7	28.0	32.8	14.9	18.1	11.0	13.4
1965	61.1	67.4	45.1	50.8	28.3	32.8	15.1	18.2	11.2	13.5
1964	61.1	67.2	45.3	50.6	28.5	32.7	15.2	18.1	11.4	13.4
1963[2]	60.9	66.5	45.1	50.0	28.1	32.1	14.6	17.5	10.7	12.8
1962[2]	61.5	66.8	45.6	50.2	28.6	32.4	15.0	17.7	10.9	12.9
1961	61.9	67.0	46.0	50.5	29.0	32.6	15.3	18.0	11.2	13.0
1960[5]	61.1	66.3	45.5	49.9	28.4	32.1	14.9	17.7	10.7	12.7
1959[3]	61.4	66.5	45.8	50.2	28.8	32.4	15.5	18.2	11.2	13.0
1958	60.6	65.5	45.0	49.3	28.0	31.5	14.5	17.4	10.9	13.1
1957	60.3	65.2	44.7	48.9	27.8	31.3	14.5	17.4	11.1	13.2

[Continued]

★ 2260 ★

Life Expectancy at Specified Ages, 1900-1970

[Continued]

Year or period[1]	At birth		Age 20		Age 40		Age 60		Age 70	
	Male	Female	Male	Female	Male	Female	Male	Female	Male	Female
1956	61.1	65.9	45.4	49.4	28.5	31.8	15.2	17.9	11.5	13.6
1955	61.2	65.9	45.5	49.6	28.6	32.0	15.4	18.1	11.7	13.8
1949-51	58.9	62.7	43.7	46.8	27.3	29.8	14.9	17.0	10.7	12.3
1939-41[4]	52.3	55.5	39.7	42.1	25.2	27.3	14.4	16.1	10.1	11.8
1929-31[4]	47.6	49.5	36.0	37.2	23.4	24.3	13.2	14.2	8.8	10.4
1919-21[4]	47.1	46.9	38.4	37.2	26.5	25.6	14.7	14.7	9.6	10.3
1909-11[4]	34.1	37.7	33.5	36.1	21.6	23.3	11.7	12.8	8.0	9.2
1900-02[4]	32.5	35.0	35.1	36.9	23.1	24.4	12.6	13.6	8.3	9.6

Source: "Expectations of Life at Specified Ages, by Sex and Race: 1900 to 1970." U.S. Bureau of the Census. *Historical Statistics of the United States: Colonial Times to 1970, Part I.* Bicentennial Edition. Washington, D.C.: Government Printing Office, 1975, p. 56. *Notes:* NA Not available. 1. Data for 1929-31 to 1958 are for conterminous United States; those for 1919-21, for death-registration States of 1920 (34 States and the District of Columbia); those for earlier years, for death-registration States of 1900 (20 States and the District of Columbia). 2. Excludes New Jersey; State did not require reporting race. 3. Includes Alaska. 4. Negroes only. 5. Denotes first year for which figures include Alaska and Hawaii.

★ 2261 ★

Life Expectancy

Life Expectancy in Prime Working Years, 1960 and 1968

Additional years of life expected.

Age	1960			1968		
	Negro and other races	White	Difference	Negro and other races	White	Difference
25	43.1	48.3	-5.2	42.6	48.6	-6.0
35	34.3	38.8	-4.5	34.0	39.1	-5.1
45	26.2	29.7	-3.5	26.2	30.0	-3.8
55	19.3	21.5	-2.2	19.2	21.8	-2.6

Source: "Life Expectancy in Prime Working Years: 1960 and 1968." U.S. Bureau of the Census. Current Population Reports, Special Studies, Series P-23, No. 38. *The Social and Economic Status of the Black Population in the United States, 1970.* Washington, D.C.: Government Printing Office, 1970, p. 97. Primary source: U.S. Department of Health, Education, and Welfare.

★ 2262 ★

Life Expectancy

Persons Alive at Beginning of Age Interval Dying during Interval – 1939-41, 1949-51, 1959-61

Interval and sex	Total			White			Nonwhite		
	1959-61	1949-51	1939-41	1959-61	1949-51	1939-41	1959-61	1949-51	1939-41
Both sexes									
0-1	0.02593	0.02976	0.04710	0.02286	0.02722	0.04315	0.04268	0.04593	-
1-5	.00420	.00559	.01123	.00369	.00502	.01016	.00711	.00970	-
5-10	.00240	.00316	.00541	.00228	.00298	.00512	.00322	.00447	-
10-15	.00221	.00304	.00507	.00209	.00284	.00463	.00301	.00440	-
15-20	.00456	.00541	.00858	.00433	.00483	.00720	.00614	.00970	-
20-25	.00618	.00724	.01190	.00563	.00620	.00971	.01017	.01528	-
25-30	.00641	.00800	.01376	.00547	.00665	.01115	.01319	.01902	-
30-35	.00802	.01004	.01671	.00673	.00831	.01364	.01803	.02436	-
35-40	.01147	.01428	.02171	.00979	.01210	.01805	.02532	.03345	-
40-45	.01812	.02198	.02979	.01594	.01910	.02546	.03720	.04701	-
45-50	.02869	.03395	.04261	.02615	.03013	.03760	.05123	.06870	-
50-55	.04557	.05099	.06125	.04208	.04634	.05571	.07832	.09758	-
55-60	.06663	.07612	.08779	.06222	.07094	.08224	.10959	.13401	-
60-65	.10017	.11019	.12417	.09540	.10524	.11958	.14829	.16971	-
65-70	.14463	.15644	.17743	.14046	.15263	.17462	.18923	.20623	-
70-75	.20847	.22960	.26020	.20592	.22810	.25985	.24394	.24984	-
75-80	.30297	.33232	.37708	.30460	.33379	.37902	.27760	.30948	-
80-85	.44776	.46150	.51610	.45191	.46649	.52106	.38195	.37844	-
85 and over	1.00000	1.00000	1.00000	1.00000	1.00000	1.00000	1.00000	1.00000	-
Male									
0-1	0.02913	0.03339	0.05238	0.02592	0.03069	0.04812	0.04699	0.05089	0.08304
1-5	.00457	.00604	.01201	.00403	.00545	.01090	.00767	.01043	.01937
5-10	.00277	.00365	.00609	.00265	.00346	.00583	.00355	.00498	.00789
10-15	.00278	.00376	.00587	.00264	.00355	.00547	.00382	.00522	.00890
15-20	.00641	.00704	.00963	.00617	.00652	.00855	.00816	.01101	.01863
20-25	.00901	.00955	.01345	.00836	.00852	.01140	.01378	.01801	.03129
25-30	.00851	.00992	.01522	.00741	.00854	.01259	.01693	.02169	.03795
30-35	.00999	.01186	.01840	.00860	.01012	.01531	.02148	.02702	.04551
35-40	.01418	.01692	.02432	.01242	.01480	.02066	.02929	.03616	.05643
40-45	.02271	.02647	.03414	.02049	.02381	.02987	.04279	.05005	.07299
45-50	.03680	.04169	.04958	.03434	.03821	.04466	.05892	.07365	.09995
50-55	.05986	.06389	.07191	.05675	.05964	.06663	.08918	.10658	.12999
55-60	.08825	.09564	.10306	.08462	.09099	.09805	.12341	.14722	.16073
60-65	.13142	.13587	.14378	.12785	.13162	.13988	.16665	.18614	.19063
65-70	.18594	.18868	.20059	.18241	.18580	.19837	.22334	.22523	.22901
70-75	.25446	.26414	.28537	.25301	.26348	.28531	.27183	.27260	.28617
75-80	.35045	.36780	.40387	.35352	.37001	.40546	.31207	.33637	.37504

[Continued]

★ 2262 ★

Persons Alive at Beginning of Age Interval Dying during Interval – 1939-41, 1949-51, 1959-61

[Continued]

Interval and sex	Total			White			Nonwhite		
	1959-61	1949-51	1939-41	1959-61	1949-51	1939-41	1959-61	1949-51	1939-41
80-85	.49229	.49434	.54235	.49736	.49948	.54617	.41883	.41446	.47439
85 and over	1.00000	1.00000	1.00000	1.00000	1.00000	1.00000	1.00000	1.00000	1.00000
Female									
0-1	0.02256	0.02594	0.04152	0.01964	0.02355	0.03789	0.03828	0.04087	0.06682
1-5	.00382	.00511	.01043	.00334	.00457	.00938	.00654	.00895	.01723
5-10	.00203	.00264	.00470	.00188	.00246	.00440	.00291	.00396	.00673
10-15	.00162	.00229	.00426	.00154	.00210	.00375	.00218	.00355	.00801
15-20	.00268	.00379	.00752	.00246	.00312	.00582	.00418	.00847	.02057
20-25	.00349	.00503	.01041	.00300	.00396	.00804	.00692	.01291	.02875
25-30	.00438	.00617	.01235	.00356	.00486	.00974	.00995	.01665	.03274
30-35	.00611	.00828	.01505	.00490	.00657	.01201	.01504	.02196	.03930
35-40	.00890	.01173	.01913	.00729	.00944	.01542	.02175	.03100	.04971
40-45	.01370	.01753	.02538	.01152	.01440	.02099	.03215	.04410	.06386
45-50	.02078	.02617	.03527	.01811	.02200	.03018	.04394	.06382	.08690
50-55	.03149	.03796	.04974	.02762	.03293	.04394	.06769	.08845	.11507
55-60	.04546	.05606	.07134	.04033	.05040	.06526	.09593	.12021	.14484
60-65	.07069	.08371	.10357	.06486	.07812	.09841	.13034	.15221	.17075
65-70	.10657	.12475	.15375	.10196	.12020	.15048	.15702	.18614	.19988
70-75	.16699	.19672	.23488	.16614	.19466	.23436	.20935	.22602	.24282
75-80	.26254	.29984	.35123	.26108	.30095	.35365	.25222	.28104	.30449
80-85	.41321	.43354	.49237	.41700	.43860	.49841	.34871	.34421	.37877
85 and over	1.00000	1.00000	1.00000	1.00000	1.00000	1.00000	1.00000	1.00000	1.00000

Source: "Proportion of Persons Alive at Beginning of Age Interval Dying During Interval ($_nq_x$), by Color and Sex: United States: 1939-41, 1949-51, 1959-61." National Center for Health Statistics. *Vital Statistics Rates in the United States, 1940-60.* By Robert D. Grove and Alice M. Hetzel. Washington, D.C.: U.S. Department of Health, Education, and Welfare, Public Health Service, 1968, p. 306.

★ 2263 ★

Life Expectancy

Survivors Out of 100,000 Born Alive, Life Tables – 1939-41, 1949-51, 1959-61

Age and sex	Total			White			Nonwhite		
	1959-61	1949-51	1939-41	1959-61	1949-51	1939-41	1959-61	1949-51	1939-41
Both sexes									
0	100,000	100,000	100,000	100,000	100,000	100,000	100,000	100,000	-
1	97,407	97,024	95,290	97,714	97,278	95,685	95,732	95,407	-
5	96,998	96,482	94,220	97,353	96,790	94,713	95,051	94,482	-
10	96,765	96,177	93,710	97,131	96,502	94,228	94,745	94,060	-
15	96,551	95,885	93,235	96,928	96,228	93,792	94,460	93,646	-

[Continued]

★ 2263 ★

Survivors Out of 100,000 Born Alive, Life Tables – 1939-41, 1949-51, 1959-61

[Continued]

Age and sex	Total			White			Nonwhite		
	1959-61	1949-51	1939-41	1959-61	1949-51	1939-41	1959-61	1949-51	1939-41
20	96,111	95,366	92,435	96,508	95,763	93,117	93,880	92,738	-
25	95,517	94,676	91,335	95,965	95,169	92,213	92,925	91,321	-
30	94,905	93,919	90,078	95,440	94,536	91,185	91,699	89,584	-
35	94,144	92,976	88,573	94,798	93,750	89,941	90,046	87,402	-
40	93,064	91,648	86,650	93,870	92,616	88,318	87,766	84,478	-
45	91,378	89,634	84,069	92,374	90,847	86,069	84,501	80,507	-
50	88,756	86,591	80,487	89,958	88,110	82,833	80,172	74,976	-
55	84,711	82,176	75,557	86,173	84,027	78,218	73,893	67,660	-
60	79,067	75,921	68,924	80,811	78,066	71,785	65,795	58,593	-
65	71,147	67,555	60,366	73,102	69,850	63,201	56,038	48,649	-
70	60,857	56,987	49,655	62,834	59,189	52,165	45,434	38,616	-
75	48,170	43,903	36,735	49,895	45,688	38,610	34,531	28,968	-
80	33,576	29,313	22,883	34,697	30,438	23,976	24,815	20,003	-
85	18,542	15,785	11,073	19,017	16,239	11,483	15,337	12,443	-
Male									
0	100,000	100,000	100,000	100,000	100,000	100,000	100,000	100,000	100,000
1	97,087	96,661	94,762	97,408	96,931	95,188	95,301	94,911	91,696
5	96,643	96,077	93,624	97,015	96,403	94,150	94,570	93,921	89,920
10	96,375	95,726	93,054	96,758	96,069	93,601	94,234	93,453	89,211
15	96,107	95,366	92,508	96,503	95,728	93,089	93,874	92,965	88,417
20	95,491	94,695	91,617	95,908	95,104	92,293	93,108	91,941	86,770
25	94,631	93,791	90,385	95,106	94,294	91,241	91,825	90,285	84,055
30	93,826	92,861	89,009	94,401	93,489	90,092	90,270	88,327	80,865
35	92,889	91,760	87,371	93,589	92,543	88,713	88,331	85,940	77,185
40	91,572	90,207	85,246	92,427	91,173	86,880	85,744	82,832	72,830
45	89,492	87,819	82,336	90,533	89,002	84,285	82,075	78,686	67,514
50	86,199	84,158	78,254	87,424	85,601	80,521	77,239	72,891	60,766
55	81,039	78,781	72,627	82,463	80,496	75,156	70,351	65,122	52,867
60	73,887	71,246	65,142	75,485	73,172	67,787	61,669	55,535	44,370
65	64,177	61,566	55,776	65,834	63,541	58,305	51,392	45,198	35,912
70	52,244	49,950	44,588	53,825	51,735	46,739	39,914	35,018	27,688
75	38,950	36,756	31,864	40,207	38,104	33,404	29,064	25,472	19,765
80	25,300	23,237	18,995	25,993	24,005	19,860	19,994	16,904	12,352
85	12,845	11,750	8,693	13,065	12,015	9,013	11,620	9,898	6,492
Female									
0	100,000	100,000	100,000	100,000	100,000	100,000	100,000	100,000	100,000
1	97,744	97,406	95,848	98,036	97,645	96,211	96,172	95,913	93,318
5	97,371	96,908	94,848	97,709	97,199	95,309	95,543	95,055	91,710
10	97,173	96,652	94,402	97,525	96,960	94,890	95,265	94,679	91,092
15	97,016	96,431	94,000	97,375	96,756	94,534	95,057	94,343	90,363

[Continued]

★ 2263 ★

Survivors Out of 100,000 Born Alive, Life Tables – 1939-41, 1949-51, 1959-61

[Continued]

Age and sex	Total			White			Nonwhite		
	1959-61	1949-51	1939-41	1959-61	1949-51	1939-41	1959-61	1949-51	1939-41
20	96,756	96,066	93,293	97,135	96,454	93,984	94,660	93,544	88,505
25	96,418	95,583	92,322	96,844	96,072	93,228	94,005	92,336	85,961
30	95,996	94,993	91,182	96,499	95,605	92,320	93,070	90,799	83,147
35	95,409	94,206	89,810	96,026	94,977	91,211	91,670	88,805	79,879
40	94,560	93,101	88,092	95,326	94,080	89,805	89,676	86,052	75,908
45	93,265	91,469	85,856	94,228	92,725	87,920	86,793	82,257	71,061
50	91,327	89,075	82,828	92,522	90,685	85,267	82,979	77,007	64,886
55	88,451	85,694	78,708	89,967	87,699	81,520	77,362	70,196	57,419
60	84,430	80,890	73,093	86,339	83,279	76,200	69,941	61,758	49,102
65	78,462	74,119	65,523	80,739	76,773	68,701	60,825	52,358	40,718
70	70,100	64,873	55,449	72,507	67,545	58,363	51,274	42,612	32,579
75	58,394	52,111	42,425	60,641	54,397	44,685	40,540	32,981	24,668
80	43,063	36,486	27,524	44,676	38,026	28,882	30,315	23,712	17,157
85	25,269	20,668	13,972	26,046	21,348	14,487	19,744	15,550	10,658

Source: "Number of Survivors Out of 100,000 Born Alive (l_x), by Color and Sex: United States, 1939-41, 1949-51, 1959-61." National Center for Health Statistics. *Vital Statistics Rates in the United States, 1940-60.* By Robert D. Grove and Alice M. Hetzel. Washington, D.C.: U.S. Department of Health, Education, and Welfare, Public Health Service, 1968, p. 307.

Marital Status

★ 2264 ★

Children Born Per Woman Married, 35 to 44 Years, by Educational Level: 1940-1975

Subject	1940[1]	1960[2]	1970	1975
BLACK				
Total, women ever married (thousands)	857	1,231	1,197	1,239
Years of School Completed by Women Ever Married				
Total, children ever born per woman ever married	2.9[3]	3.1	3.8	3.8
Elementary: 8 years or less	3.1	3.6	4.6	4.8
High school: 1 to 3 years	2.3	3.0	4.2	4.4
4 years	2.0	2.4	3.3	3.4
College: 1 to 3 years	1.7	2.1	2.9	3.5
4 years or more	1.2	1.7	1.8	2.1

[Continued]

★ 2264 ★

Children Born Per Woman Married, 35 to 44 Years, by Educational Level: 1940-1975

[Continued]

Subject	1940[1]	1960[2]	1970	1975
WHITE				
Total, women ever married (thousands)	6,266	10,356	9,824	9,659
Years of School Completed by Women Ever Married				
Total, children ever born per woman ever married	2.6[3]	2.6	3.0	3.1
Elementary: 8 years or less	3.1	3.1	3.6	3.9
High school: 1 to 3 years	2.3	2.6	3.2	3.5
4 years	1.8	2.4	2.9	3.0
College: 1 to 3 years	1.8	2.4	2.9	2.9
4 years or more	1.5	2.3	2.6	2.4

Source: "Children Ever Born Per Woman Ever Married 35 to 44 Years Old, by Years of School Completed: 1940, 1960, 1970, and 1975,"Department of Commerce, Bureau of the Census. *The Social and Economic Status of the Black Population in the United States: An Historical View, 1790-1978,* p. 129. Primary source: U.S. Department of Commerce, Bureau of the Census. *Notes:* Average number of children ever born per woman ever married for 1940 are based on women reporting number of children ever born; in 1960, 1970, and 1975, women who did not report the number of children ever born were allocated a number. 1. Data for White exclude foreign-born population. 2. Data for Black includes persons of "other" races. 3. Includes a small number of persons not reporting their educational attainment.

★ 2265 ★

Marital Status

Duration of Current Marriages for Women and Number of Times Married, 1971

As of June.

Item	Total	Duration in years of current marriage: 10 years and over	20 years and over	25 years and over	30 years and over	35 years and over	40 years and over	45 years and over	50 years and over	Median years[1]
All married women.....1,000	48,991	32,335	21,185	15,861	10,665	7,260	4,435	2,640	1,222	17.0
Percent married once	100.0	68.8	46.4	35.3	24.1	16.5	10.2	6.1	2.8	(x)
Percent more than once	100.0	48.5	23.7	14.2	7.4	4.2	2.1	1.1	0.4	(x)
Negro married women.....1,000	4,234	2,545	1,446	1,024	635	396	234	106	51	13.9
Percent married once	100.0	61.0	35.8	25.7	16.2	10.3	6.2	2.9	1.4	(x)
Percent more than once	100.0	55.9	26.8	17.3	9.7	4.9	2.3	0.8	0.5	(x)

Source: "Duration of Current Marriage for Married Women, by Number of Times Married: 1971." U.S. Bureau of the Census. *Statistical Abstract of the United States, 1975.* Washington, D.C.: Government Printing Office, 1975, p. 69. *Notes:* X Not applicable. Median: The value which divides the distribution into two equal parts—one-half the cases falling below this value and one-half exceeding it. In many tables, details will not add to the totals shown because of rounding.

★ 2266 ★

Marital Status

Marital Condition by Age Periods, Urban and Communities, 1910 - I

Age period and class of population	Total		Single		Married, widowed, or divorced			
					Total		Married	
	Male	Female	Male	Female	Male	Female	Male	Female
	Number							
15 years and over	3,059,312	3,103,344	1,083,472	823,996	1,959,344	2,269,066	1,749,228	1,775,949
Urban	947,605	1,058,325	350,598	292,992	590,757	761,658	519,740	544,179
Rural	2,111,707	2,045,019	732,874	531,004	1,368,587	1,507,408	1,229,488	1,231,770
15 to 19 years								
Urban	111,172	142,255	108,150	119,824	2,164	21,566	2,056	19,869
Rural	396,773	410,216	384,003	328,691	9,420	78,655	9,008	74,218
20 to 24 years								
Urban	142,067	182,805	93,923	78,189	47,131	103,980	44,847	92,407
Rural	340,090	365,833	194,071	113,207	143,948	251,445	137,263	231,366
25 to 34 years								
Urban	273,678	304,303	90,244	61,019	182,065	242,705	170,098	201,987
Rural	480,290	491,045	98,952	54,663	379,753	435,643	357,051	390,560
35 to 44 years								
Urban	203,931	203,462	36,765	20,414	166,444	182,746	149,729	132,356
Rural	346,199	335,270	30,438	17,691	315,059	317,210	290,172	268,713
45 to 64 years								
Urban	174,362	176,897	17,707	10,647	156,222	165,907	128,504	86,310
Rural	421,192	335,652	18,954	11,836	401,553	323,316	349,208	229,513
65 years and over								
Urban	34,973	42,462	2,046	1,790	32,796	40,501	21,174	8,872
Rural	117,509	99,180	4,239	3,453	112,764	95,324	81,496	33,532
Age unknown								
Urban	7,422	6,141	1,763	1,109	3,935	4,253	3,332	2,378
Rural	9,654	7,823	2,217	1,463	6,090	5,815	5,290	3,868
	Percentage distribution by marital class							
15 years and over	100.0	100.0	35.4	26.6	64.0	73.1	57.2	57.2
Urban	100.0	100.0	37.0	27.7	62.3	72.0	54.8	51.4
Rural	100.0	100.0	34.7	26.0	64.8	73.7	58.2	60.2
15 to 19 years								
Urban	100.0	100.0	97.3	84.2	1.9	15.2	1.8	14.0
Rural	100.0	100.0	96.8	80.1	2.4	19.2	2.3	18.1
20 to 24 years								
Urban	100.0	100.0	66.1	42.8	33.2	56.9	31.6	50.5
Rural	100.0	100.0	57.1	30.9	42.3	68.7	40.4	63.2
25 to 34 years								
Urban	100.0	100.0	33.0	20.1	66.5	79.8	62.2	66.4
Rural	100.0	100.0	20.6	11.1	79.1	88.7	74.3	79.5
35 to 44 years								
Urban	100.0	100.0	18.0	10.0	81.6	89.8	73.4	65.1
Rural	100.0	100.0	8.8	5.3	91.0	94.6	83.8	80.1

[Continued]

★ 2266 ★

Marital Condition by Age Periods, Urban and Communities, 1910 - I

[Continued]

Age period and class of population	Total		Single		Married, widowed, or divorced			
					Total		Married	
	Male	Female	Male	Female	Male	Female	Male	Female
45 to 64 years								
Urban	100.0	100.0	10.2	6.0	89.6	93.8	73.7	48.8
Rural	100.0	100.0	4.5	3.5	95.3	96.3	82.9	68.4
65 years and over								
Urban	100.0	100.0	5.9	4.2	93.8	95.4	60.5	20.9
Rural	100.0	100.0	3.6	3.5	96.0	96.1	69.4	33.8
Age unknown								
Urban	100.0	100.0	23.8	18.1	53.0	69.3	44.9	38.7
Rural	100.0	100.0	23.0	18.7	63.1	74.3	54.8	49.4

Source: "Marital Condition by Age Periods of Urban and Rural Negro Population: 1910." *Negro Population, 1790-1910.* Washington, D.C.: Government Printing Office, 1918, p. 253.

★ 2267 ★

Marital Status

Marital Condition by Age Periods, Urban and Communities, 1910 - II

Age period and class of population	Married, widowed, or divorced				Marital condition unknown	
	Widowed		Divorced			
	Male	Female	Male	Female	Male	Female
			Number			
15 years and over	189,970	459,831	20,146	33,286	16,496	10,282
Urban	63,075	202,182	7,942	15,297	6,250	3,675
Rural	126,895	257,649	12,204	17,989	10,246	6,607
15 to 19 years						
Urban	86	1,303	22	394	858	865
Rural	330	3,626	82	811	3,350	2,870
20 to 24 years						
Urban	1,727	9,156	557	2,417	1,013	636
Rural	5,433	16,620	1,252	3,459	2,071	1,181
25 to 34 years						
Urban	9,372	34,636	2,595	6,082	1,369	579
Rural	18,889	38,717	3,813	6,366	1,585	739
35 to 44 years						
Urban	14,222	46,362	2,493	4,028	722	302
Rural	21,922	44,477	2,965	4,020	702	369
45 to 64 years						
Urban	25,737	77,480	1,981	2,117	433	343
Rural	49,072	90,966	3,273	2,837	685	500
65 years and over						
Urban	11,392	31,460	230	169	131	171

[Continued]

★ 2267 ★

Marital Condition by Age Periods, Urban and Communities, 1910 - II

[Continued]

Age period and class of population	Married, widowed, or divorced				Marital condition unknown	
	Widowed		Divorced			
	Male	Female	Male	Female	Male	Female
Rural	30,499	61,396	769	396	506	403
Age unknown						
Urban	539	1,785	64	90	1,724	779
Rural	750	1,847	50	100	1,347	545
	Percentage distribution by marital class					
15 years and over	6.2	14.8	0.7	1.1	0.5	0.3
Urban	6.7	19.1	0.8	1.4	0.7	0.3
Rural	6.0	12.6	0.6	0.9	0.5	0.3
15 to 19 years						
Urban	0.1	0.9	[1]	0.3	0.7	0.6
Rural	0.1	0.9	[1]	0.2	0.8	0.7
20 to 24 years						
Urban	1.2	5.0	0.4	1.3	0.7	0.3
Rural	1.6	4.5	0.4	0.9	0.6	0.3
25 to 34 years						
Urban	3.4	11.4	0.9	2.0	0.5	0.2
Rural	3.9	7.9	0.8	1.3	0.3	0.2
35 to 44 years						
Urban	7.0	22.8	1.2	2.0	0.4	0.1
Rural	6.3	13.3	0.9	1.2	0.2	0.1
45 to 64 years						
Urban	14.8	43.8	1.1	1.2	0.2	0.2
Rural	11.7	27.1	0.8	0.8	0.2	0.1
65 years and over						
Urban	32.6	74.1	0.7	0.4	0.4	0.4
Rural	26.0	61.9	0.7	0.4	0.4	0.4
Age unknown						
Urban	7.3	29.1	0.9	1.5	23.2	12.7
Rural	7.8	23.6	0.5	1.3	14.0	7.0

Source: "Marital Condition by Age Periods of Urban and Rural Negro Population: 1910." *Negro Population, 1790-1910.* Washington, D.C.: Government Printing Office, 1918, p. 253. *Note:* 1. Less than one-tenth of 1 per cent.

★ 2268 ★

Marital Status

Marital Condition of Urban, Rural-Farm, and Rural-Nonfarm Black Population 15 Years Old and Over by Sex and Age, 1930. Part 1, New England

Area and age	Males 15 years old and over				Females 15 years old and over			
	Total	Single	Married	Widowed or divorced	Total	Single	Married	Widowed or divorced
Urban	29,085	10,211	16,735	2,063	29,753	7,503	16,794	5,414
15 to 19 years	2,916	2,876	39	-	3,283	2,871	406	6
20 to 24 years	2,919	2,033	852	23	3,371	1,571	1,718	75
25 to 34 years	7,010	2,483	4,298	218	7,133	1,364	5,171	592
35 to 44 years	6,828	1,466	4,943	407	6,743	739	4,865	1,130
45 to 54 years	5,292	843	3,911	530	4,908	511	3,056	1,337
55 to 64 years	2,601	325	1,876	399	2,546	267	1,175	1,102
65 and over	1,463	173	803	483	1,712	165	383	1,163
Rural-farm	505	248	213	44	318	97	188	33
15 to 19 years	56	56	-	-	46	39	7	-
20 to 24 years	52	48	3	1	34	20	14	-
25 to 34 years	89	49	39	1	59	14	41	4
35 to 44 years	109	41	63	5	69	11	54	4
45 to 54 years	87	24	52	11	62	7	49	6
55 to 64 years	67	19	39	9	24	3	14	7
65 and over	43	11	15	17	21	2	7	12
Rural-nonfarm	4,172	1,675	2,192	298	3,701	1,118	2,075	506
15 to 19 years	523	519	3	1	516	456	58	2
20 to 24 years	433	339	88	4	513	249	257	7
25 to 34 years	856	316	521	18	712	146	529	37
35 to 44 years	864	214	611	39	796	119	578	98
45 to 54 years	790	167	545	77	588	75	405	108
55 to 64 years	431	68	286	76	307	41	175	91
65 and over	265	49	133	83	264	30	71	163

Source: "Marital Condition of the Urban, Rural-Farm, and Rural-Nonfarm Negro Population 15 Years Old and Over, by Sex, and 5-Year Age Periods, by Geographic Divisions: 1930." U.S. Bureau of the Census. *Negroes in the United States: 1920-32*. Washington, D.C.: Government Printing Office, 1935, p. 170.

★ 2269 ★

Marital Status

Marital Condition of Urban, Rural-Farm, and Rural-Nonfarm Black Population 15 Years Old and Over by Sex and Age, 1930. Part 2, East North Central

Area and age	Males 15 years old and over				Females 15 years old and over			
	Total	Single	Married	Widowed or divorced	Total	Single	Married	Widowed or divorced
Urban	328,875	99,730	201,065	27,611	316,080	54,064	201,755	59,941
15 to 19 years	27,661	26,740	872	28	32,270	24,113	7,710	427
20 to 24 years	39,074	23,211	15,113	703	45,752	12,569	30,276	2,849
25 to 34 years	100,811	27,686	67,932	5,106	100,184	10,555	77,152	12,407
35 to 44 years	84,444	13,954	62,594	7,813	72,044	4,269	52,798	14,942
45 to 54 years	48,808	5,634	36,209	6,927	39,081	1,636	24,310	13,105
55 to 64 years	18,449	1,694	12,985	3,752	15,966	519	7,024	8,400
65 and over	8,818	602	4,968	3,237	10,138	310	2,171	7,639
Rural-farm	6,946	2,561	3,666	704	5,377	1,206	3,554	610
15 to 19 years	1,013	998	13	-	821	715	106	1
20 to 24 years	709	561	143	2	519	219	280	19
25 to 34 years	923	359	516	47	876	125	714	37
35 to 44 years	1,085	225	788	68	1,036	54	910	71
45 to 54 years	1,237	185	904	146	967	41	805	121
55 to 64 years	1,052	125	767	157	644	22	508	113
65 and over	925	107	535	283	509	27	231	247
Rural-nonfarm	28,509	11,099	14,297	2,995	18,990	3,782	12,090	3,085
15 to 19 years	3,144	3,077	63	3	2,542	2,071	441	29
20 to 24 years	3,392	2,380	956	51	2,191	706	1,383	100
25 to 34 years	7,001	2,761	3,797	427	4,366	446	3,565	353
35 to 44 years	5,928	1,379	3,955	576	3,944	237	3,191	513
45 to 54 years	4,417	786	2,982	635	2,884	142	2,114	624
55 to 64 years	2,473	419	1,552	491	1,588	91	946	545
65 and over	2,063	279	966	807	1,444	85	438	914

Source: "Marital Condition of the Urban, Rural-Farm, and Rural-Nonfarm Negro Population 15 Years Old and Over, by Sex, and 5-Year Age Periods, by Geographic Divisions: 1930." U.S. Bureau of the Census. *Negroes in the United States: 1920-32.* Washington, D.C.: Government Printing Office, 1935, p. 170.

★ 2270 ★

Marital Status

Marital Condition of Urban, Rural-Farm, and Rural-Nonfarm Black Population 15 Years Old and Over by Sex and Age, 1930. Part 3, Middle Atlantic

Area and age	Males 15 years old and over				Females 15 years old and over			
	Total	Single	Married	Widowed or divorced	Total	Single	Married	Widowed or divorced
Urban	349,615	119,782	210,534	18,431	364,276	88,991	217,474	56,999
15 to 19 years	29,742	28,895	739	18	37,662	30,683	6,675	214
20 to 24 years	44,755	28,047	16,229	315	56,249	21,540	33,097	1,470
25 to 34 years	11,566	35,146	73,762	2,458	115,303	21,789	84,204	9,104
35 to 44 years	86,742	17,413	64,462	4,731	81,957	8,968	57,865	14,995
45 to 54 years	49,957	7,247	37,543	5,074	45,040	3,862	26,247	14,850
55 to 64 years	18,453	2,162	13,130	3,124	17,358	1,302	7,086	8,936
65 and over	7,733	671	4,382	2,666	10,020	661	2,020	7,317
Rural-farm	4,612	2,115	2,148	339	2,965	750	1,934	276
15 to 19 years	758	751	6	-	461	402	59	-
20 to 24 years	643	502	137	4	369	160	208	-
25 to 34 years	873	352	495	20	640	91	531	16
35 to 44 years	848	217	575	56	609	32	527	50
45 to 54 years	755	161	508	85	487	30	392	64
55 to 64 years	442	80	288	74	233	15	161	57
65 and over	285	51	135	98	160	19	52	89
Rural-nonfarm	38,986	13,912	22,198	2,669	33,171	7,658	21,289	4,105
15 to 19 years	4,360	4,269	68	3	4,497	3,621	857	11
20 to 24 years	4,656	3,073	1,509	23	4,492	1,613	2,772	78
25 to 34 years	10,077	3,191	6,578	255	8,865	1,197	7,174	462
35 to 44 years	8,075	1,736	6,409	536	6,757	569	5,381	796
45 to 54 years	6,075	903	4,493	666	4,706	363	3,341	989
55 to 64 years	3,054	433	2,077	535	2,183	171	1,227	782
65 and over	1,915	256	1,005	640	1,570	103	486	971

Source: "Marital Condition of the Urban, Rural-Farm, and Rural-Nonfarm Negro Population 15 Years Old and Over, by Sex, and 5-Year Age Periods, by Geographic Divisions: 1930." U.S. Bureau of the Census. *Negroes in the United States: 1920-32*. Washington, D.C.: Government Printing Office, 1935, p. 170.

★ 2271 ★

Marital Status

Marital Condition of Urban, Rural-Farm, and Rural-Nonfarm Black Population 15 Years Old and Over by Sex and Age, 1930. Part 4, West North Central

Area and age	Males 15 years old and over				Females 15 years old and over			
	Total	Single	Married	Widowed or divorced	Total	Single	Married	Widowed or divorced
Urban	100,003	29,554	59,619	10,613	102,530	19,328	60,081	22,980
15 to 19 years	8,990	8,659	314	11	10,253	8,022	2,082	144
20 to 24 years	10,297	6,224	3,836	220	12,968	4,531	7,485	937
25 to 34 years	24,327	6,986	15,893	1,413	27,173	3,936	19,487	3,723
35 to 44 years	24,473	4,184	17,753	2,506	23,799	1,673	16,897	5,213
45 to 54 years	18,389	2,259	13,334	2,766	15,682	732	9,645	5,286
55 to 64 years	8,321	787	5,742	1,779	7,148	237	3,200	3,701
65 and over	4,931	374	2,662	1,886	5,202	161	1,221	3,908
Rural-farm	12,971	4,161	7,528	1,270	10,493	2,023	7,384	1,082
15 to 19 years	1,994	1,934	57	3	1,830	1,334	468	27
20 to 24 years	1,582	897	649	32	1,515	365	1,085	63
25 to 34 years	2,207	502	1,604	97	2,117	131	1,861	125
35 to 44 years	2,291	310	1,797	181	2,064	89	1,798	177
45 to 54 years	2,190	250	1,665	275	1,505	40	1,270	195
55 to 64 years	1,518	145	1,068	305	811	29	612	170
65 and over	1,180	119	684	376	644	31	289	323
Rural-nonfarm	15,619	5,615	7,845	2,026	12,103	2,501	7,154	2,433
15 to 19 years	1,598	1,552	44	2	1,582	1,285	274	22
20 to 24 years	1,668	1,173	429	60	1,353	519	769	65
25 to 34 years	3,306	1,276	1,735	267	2,358	319	1,795	243
35 to 44 years	3,214	792	2,053	318	2,305	137	1,831	337
45 to 54 years	2,510	432	1,676	382	1,954	123	1,369	462
55 to 64 years	1,667	204	1,095	359	1,264	63	705	496
65 and over	1,614	170	797	631	1,236	52	389	786

Source: "Marital Condition of the Urban, Rural-Farm, and Rural-Nonfarm Negro Population 15 Years Old and Over, by Sex, and 5-Year Age Periods, by Geographic Divisions: 1930." U.S. Bureau of the Census. *Negroes in the United States: 1920-32.* Washington, D.C.: Government Printing Office, 1935, p. 170.

★ 2272 ★

Marital Status

Marital Condition of Urban, Rural-Farm, and Rural-Nonfarm Black Population 15 Years Old and Over by Sex and Age, 1930. Part 5, South Atlantic

Area and age	Males 15 years old and over				Females 15 years old and over			
	Total	Single	Married	Widowed or divorced	Total	Single	Married	Widowed or divorced
Urban	481,169	155,476	288,468	36,025	582,457	148,143	308,894	124,237
15 to 19 years	62,207	59,821	2,249	87	83,484	67,392	15,016	1,007
20 to 24 years	69,379	39,066	29,096	1,063	97,125	37,644	53,493	5,860
25 to 34 years	124,364	31,360	87,844	4,985	154,166	25,800	106,810	21,368
35 to 44 years	103,153	14,789	80,031	8,165	118,578	9,738	78,103	30,560
45 to 54 years	71,999	6,855	55,687	9,336	73,645	4,488	39,289	29,752
55 to 64 years	31,245	2,266	22,745	6,173	31,147	1,648	11,580	17,851
65 and over	17,180	985	10,002	6,136	22,442	1,074	3,859	17,415
Rural-farm	549,725	203,342	315,447	30,483	552,623	166,909	319,580	65,658
15 to 19 years	135,547	130,927	4,370	147	130,274	109,288	19,895	1,040
20 to 24 years	80,640	45,290	34,015	1,197	86,100	34,738	47,890	3,378
25 to 34 years	84,017	15,517	65,559	2,880	103,454	13,778	82,193	7,403
35 to 44 years	78,789	5,580	69,059	4,123	96,330	4,577	80,175	11,499
45 to 54 years	80,742	3,201	71,031	6,478	73,636	2,325	57,156	14,094
55 to 64 years	54,048	1,663	45,803	6,554	35,021	1,109	22,557	11,316
65 and over	35,568	1,081	25,372	9,079	27,433	1,005	9,528	16,839
Rural-nonfarm	337,430	115,674	194,538	25,277	330,632	78,551	191,458	60,055
15 to 19 years	52,605	50,304	2,143	66	57,678	43,383	13,521	731
20 to 24 years	54,819	29,708	23,836	840	56,918	17,633	36,281	2,908
25 to 34 years	78,176	19,417	54,902	3,177	76,283	9,578	58,554	8,021
35 to 44 years	61,795	8,489	48,365	4,628	59,410	3,872	43,530	11,920
45 to 54 years	46,996	4,550	36,543	5,740	41,565	2,177	25,804	13,519
55 to 64 years	24,820	1,914	18,119	4,698	20,306	989	9,208	10,061
65 and over	17,681	1,162	10,361	6,085	18,038	829	4,380	12,771

Source: "Marital Condition of the Urban, Rural-Farm, and Rural-Nonfarm Negro Population 15 Years Old and Over, by Sex, and 5-Year Age Periods, by Geographic Divisions: 1930." U.S. Bureau of the Census. *Negroes in the United States: 1920-32.* Washington, D.C.: Government Printing Office, 1935, p. 171.

★ 2273 ★

Marital Status

Marital Condition of Urban, Rural-Farm, and Rural-Nonfarm Black Population 15 Years Old and Over by Sex and Age, 1930. Part 6, West South Central

Area and age	Males 15 years old and over				Females 15 years old and over			
	Total	Single	Married	Widowed or divorced	Total	Single	Married	Widowed or divorced
Urban	256,705	72,903	157,753	25,616	302,206	61,587	166,305	73,871
15 to 19 years	29,760	28,464	1,177	94	39,870	30,043	8,641	1,176
20 to 24 years	35,607	18,794	15,416	1,344	49,815	14,917	29,412	5,442
25 to 34 years	69,438	14,730	49,592	5,048	86,378	10,466	59,577	16,249
35 to 44 years	57,537	6,441	44,843	6,187	63,035	3,785	41,199	17,971
45 to 54 years	38,774	2,918	30,003	5,801	36,083	1,430	19,481	15,101
55 to 64 years	16,012	992	11,463	3,522	15,304	526	5,795	8,942
65 and over	9,066	461	5,003	3,578	11,204	320	1,987	8,854
Rural-farm	371,880	111,571	231,224	28,821	355,762	77,293	230,859	47,418
15 to 19 years	70,464	67,472	2,761	182	71,400	52,956	17,000	1,425
20 to 24 years	55,817	27,208	26,730	1,811	58,422	15,107	39,320	3,966
25 to 34 years	71,725	10,296	57,037	4,356	77,263	5,899	64,385	6,940
35 to 44 years	60,664	3,383	52,455	4,798	64,451	1,760	54,258	8,404
45 to 54 years	58,291	1,855	50,010	6,397	46,226	860	35,905	9,431
55 to 64 years	33,961	802	27,932	5,205	22,369	373	14,480	7,503
65 and over	20,742	503	14,176	6,045	15,462	303	5,428	9,706
Rural-nonfarm	124,120	37,317	73,800	12,762	122,185	22,445	72,335	27,127
15 to 19 years	15,670	14,969	645	50	18,181	12,779	4,885	511
20 to 24 years	18,800	10,119	8,057	599	19,807	4,903	12,933	1,952
25 to 34 years	30,198	6,951	21,063	2,137	30,128	2,879	22,617	4,575
35 to 44 years	24,552	3,002	18,876	2,629	23,513	1,002	17,074	5,372
45 to 54 years	18,840	1,422	14,628	2,744	15,466	494	9,456	5,451
55 to 64 years	9,224	531	6,645	2,017	7,913	200	3,592	4,092
65 and over	6,632	279	3,781	2,558	7,028	166	1,728	5,114

Source: "Marital Condition of the Urban, Rural-Farm, and Rural-Nonfarm Negro Population 15 Years Old and Over, by Sex, and 5-Year Age Periods, by Geographic Divisions: 1930." U.S. Bureau of the Census. *Negroes in the United States: 1920-32*. Washington, D.C.: Government Printing Office, 1935, p. 171.

★ 2274 ★

Marital Status

Marital Condition of Urban, Rural-Farm, and Rural-Nonfarm Black Population 15 Years Old and Over by Sex and Age, 1930. Part 7, East South Central

Area and age	Males 15 years old and over				Females 15 years old and over			
	Total	Single	Married	Widowed or divorced	Total	Single	Married	Widowed or divorced
Urban	257,371	76,397	155,781	24,766	310,162	68,104	164,071	77,515
15 to 19 years	31,402	29,957	1,294	91	41,105	31,419	8,547	1,093
20 to 24 years	35,156	18,898	15,038	1,140	49,604	16,733	27,756	5,020
25 to 34 years	63,596	15,028	44,408	4,078	81,669	11,816	54,981	14,783
35 to 44 years	54,637	7,000	42,181	5,398	63,259	4,615	40,833	17,746
45 to 54 years	41,715	3,560	32,157	5,959	41,332	2,110	22,238	16,933
55 to 64 years	19,121	1,239	13,995	3,865	18,557	803	6,942	10,782
65 and over	11,251	611	6,427	4,187	14,060	522	2,572	10,925
Rural-farm	446,642	135,274	279,636	31,356	451,523	104,374	281,096	65,707
15 to 19 years	91,584	87,071	4,188	245	90,769	68,372	20,707	1,641
20 to 24 years	64,602	29,205	33,328	1,957	72,221	20,630	46,570	4,954
25 to 34 years	79,463	11,205	63,962	4,248	92,591	9,031	74,194	9,312
35 to 44 years	64,333	3,617	56,250	4,435	80,127	3,178	65,440	11,456
45 to 54 years	72,070	2,210	63,136	6,695	62,081	1,679	47,078	13,286
55 to 64 years	45,228	1,137	38,159	5,905	30,253	773	19,207	10,247
65 and over	29,107	753	20,476	7,848	23,235	628	7,799	14,757
Rural-nonfarm	147,353	46,120	85,608	13,976	145,685	29,486	84,286	31,399
15 to 19 years	19,707	18,686	879	60	22,139	15,391	6,146	591
20 to 24 years	23,876	12,451	10,416	735	25,079	6,751	16,119	2,169
25 to 34 years	35,827	8,505	24,747	2,132	35,208	4,087	25,978	5,061
35 to 44 years	26,227	3,446	19,878	2,619	26,091	1,642	18,442	5,969
45 to 54 years	21,353	1,711	16,479	2,979	18,287	824	11,106	6,321
55 to 64 years	11,196	778	8,122	2,231	9,478	422	4,255	4,757
65 and over	8,692	496	4,950	3,190	9,005	338	2,160	6,476

Source: "Marital Condition of the Urban, Rural-Farm, and Rural-Nonfarm Negro Population 15 Years Old and Over, by Sex, and 5-Year Age Periods, by Geographic Divisions: 1930." U.S. Bureau of the Census. *Negroes in the United States: 1920-32.* Washington, D.C.: Government Printing Office, 1935, p. 171.

★ 2275 ★

Marital Status

Marital Condition of Urban, Rural-Farm, and Rural-Nonfarm Black Population 15 Years Old and Over by Sex and Age, 1930. Part 8, Mountain

Area and age	Males 15 years old and over				Females 15 years old and over			
	Total	Single	Married	Widowed or divorced	Total	Single	Married	Widowed or divorced
Urban	8,603	2,684	4,904	993	8,303	1,262	4,929	2,101
15 to 19 years	632	599	28	1	693	543	143	7
20 to 24 years	794	547	228	19	890	281	527	81
25 to 34 years	1,901	649	1,109	139	2,071	226	1,512	331
35 to 44 years	2,164	450	1,476	233	2,069	112	1,457	497
45 to 54 years	1,742	266	1,208	264	1,477	63	902	511
55 to 64 years	875	111	587	175	652	19	294	339
65 and over	472	56	257	159	429	13	89	327
Rural-farm	921	314	507	96	668	117	485	66
15 to 19 years	132	130	2	-	91	74	16	1
20 to 24 years	84	47	33	4	74	27	45	2
25 to 34 years	136	47	85	3	166	8	147	11
35 to 44 years	184	35	135	13	164	5	144	15
45 to 54 years	221	31	156	33	110	2	99	9
55 to 64 years	96	12	65	19	40	1	25	14
65 and over	67	12	30	24	22	-	8	14
Rural-nonfarm	3,693	1,833	1,507	343	1,777	274	1,226	275
15 to 19 years	301	291	9	-	206	146	58	2
20 to 24 years	531	458	66	5	194	46	135	13
25 to 34 years	915	513	356	46	475	36	385	53
35 to 44 years	970	370	514	83	453	23	371	59
45 to 54 years	566	117	367	81	273	11	201	61
55 to 64 years	252	52	138	62	97	4	51	41
65 and over	151	31	54	65	71	7	19	45

Source: "Marital Condition of the Urban, Rural-Farm, and Rural-Nonfarm Negro Population 15 Years Old and Over, by Sex, and 5-Year Age Periods, by Geographic Divisions: 1930." U.S. Bureau of the Census. *Negroes in the United States: 1920-32.* Washington, D.C.: Government Printing Office, 1935, p. 171.

★ 2276 ★

Marital Status

Marital Condition of Urban, Rural-Farm, and Rural-NonFarm Black Population 15 Years Old and Over by Sex and Age, 1930. Part 9, Pacific

Area and age	Males 15 years old and over				Females 15 years old and over			
	Total	Single	Married	Widowed or divorced	Total	Single	Married	Widowed or divorced
Urban	30,608	9,377	17,872	3,145	32,286	5,653	18,499	8,063
15 to 19 years	2,413	2,357	47	-	2,812	2,345	434	29
20 to 24 years	2,840	1,980	830	65	3,620	1,325	1,996	294
25 to 34 years	7,404	2,220	4,660	500	8,408	1,049	5,993	1,353
35 to 44 years	7,980	1,526	5,586	841	8,052	508	5,510	2,021
45 to 54 years	5,861	850	4,195	804	5,361	257	3,139	1,961
55 to 64 years	2,582	334	1,732	508	2,387	99	1,057	1,229
65 and over	1,327	127	784	415	1,560	56	346	1,154
Rural-farm	1,449	528	780	139	1,090	192	726	101
15 to 19 years	179	174	5	-	159	128	29	2
20 to 24 years	143	106	35	2	137	36	95	6
25 to 34 years	260	77	163	19	220	15	196	9
35 to 44 years	294	65	206	23	226	7	202	17
45 to 54 years	294	49	213	31	161	4	135	22
55 to 64 years	182	40	106	36	72	1	50	21
65 and over	97	17	52	28	43	1	18	24
Rural-nonfarm	3,900	1,477	1,956	447	2,506	395	1,623	474
15 to 19 years	288	286	2	-	258	193	61	4
20 to 24 years	354	241	104	8	237	64	158	13
25 to 34 years	923	381	486	51	646	60	509	76
35 to 44 years	991	261	619	109	641	42	484	114
45 to 54 years	723	165	448	105	394	23	271	100
55 to 64 years	346	81	188	75	182	7	96	79
65 and over	262	59	106	97	137	5	44	88

Source: "Marital Condition of the Urban, Rural-Farm, and Rural-Nonfarm Negro Population 15 Years Old and Over, by Sex, and 5-Year Age Periods, by Geographic Divisions: 1930." U.S. Bureau of the Census. *Negroes in the United States: 1920-32*. Washington, D.C.: Government Printing Office, 1935, p. 171.

★ 2277 ★

Marital Status

Marital Condition of the Black Population 15 Years Old and Over by Geographical Areas, 1930

Section, division, and state	Males 15 years old and over						Females 15 years old and over					
	Total	Single	Married	Widowed	Divorced	Unknown	Total	Single	Married	Widowed	Divorced	Unknown
United States	3,941,462	1,270,950	2,357,821	247,595	55,713	9,383	4,099,552	953,806	2,398,144	652,663	88,868	6,071
The North	919,998	300,663	548,040	54,586	14,477	2,132	899,757	189,021	551,772	140,032	17,432	1,500
The South	2,972,395	954,074	1,782,255	189,714	39,368	6,984	3,153,235	756,892	1,818,884	503,911	69,076	4,472
The West	49,169	16,213	27,526	3,295	1,868	267	46,560	7,893	27,488	8,720	2,360	99

[Continued]

★ 2277 ★

Marital Condition of the Black Population 15 Years Old and Over by Geographical Areas, 1930

[Continued]

Section, division, and state	Males 15 years old and over						Females 15 years old and over					
	Total	Single	Married	Widowed	Divorced	Unknown	Total	Single	Married	Widowed	Divorced	Unknown
New England	33,762	12,134	19,140	1,931	474	83	33,772	8,718	19,057	5,256	697	44
Maine	442	184	210	40	8	-	358	116	188	38	15	1
New Hampshire	457	192	237	18	9	1	192	57	112	19	4	-
Vermont	226	96	109	12	7	2	165	51	84	25	5	-
Massachusetts	18,702	7,006	10,304	1,056	283	53	18,956	5,186	10,311	3,064	363	32
Rhode Island	3,369	1,199	1,855	250	59	6	3,529	923	1,855	624	125	2
Connecticut	10,566	3,457	6,425	555	108	21	10,572	2,385	6,507	1,486	185	9
Middle Atlantic	393,213	135,809	234,880	19,020	2,419	1,085	400,412	97,399	240,697	57,591	3,789	936
New York	155,349	55,311	92,159	6,456	821	602	167,408	44,060	96,475	24,801	1,520	552
New Jersey	75,094	24,628	45,928	3,994	432	112	77,522	18,041	47,247	11,452	674	108
Pennsylvania	162,770	55,870	96,793	8,570	1,166	371	155,482	35,298	96,975	21,338	1,595	276
East North Central	364,330	113,390	219,028	23,148	8,162	602	340,447	59,052	217,399	54,214	9,422	360
Ohio	119,402	37,361	71,922	7,535	2,440	144	109,012	19,662	70,599	15,863	2,811	77
Indiana	43,369	13,259	25,823	3,019	1,146	122	41,027	7,320	25,491	7,018	1,127	71
Illinois	128,527	39,768	76,887	8,799	2,866	207	127,196	22,349	77,865	23,112	3,722	148
Michigan	68,493	21,408	41,891	3,492	1,587	115	59,610	9,153	41,061	7,707	1,630	59
Wisconsin	4,539	1,594	2,505	303	123	14	3,602	568	2,383	514	132	5
West North Central	128,593	39,330	74,992	10,487	3,422	362	125,126	23,852	74,619	22,971	3,524	160
Minnesota	4,033	1,304	2,261	283	178	7	3,510	596	2,141	642	126	5
Iowa	6,830	2,234	3,841	471	274	10	6,188	1,137	3,766	1,009	270	6
Missouri	86,100	26,201	50,784	7,221	1,698	196	86,046	16,788	50,988	16,176	1,976	118
North Dakota	200	95	70	21	13	1	111	22	68	17	4	-
South Dakota	279	119	131	22	7	-	212	48	125	30	9	-
Nebraska	5,502	1,662	3,159	454	212	15	5,173	845	3,130	967	219	12
Kansas	25,649	7,715	14,746	2,015	1,040	133	23,886	4,416	14,401	4,130	920	19
South Atlantic	1,368,324	474,492	798,453	81,096	10,689	3,594	1,465,712	393,603	819,932	230,957	18,993	2,227
Delaware	12,485	4,971	6,485	880	96	53	11,097	3,024	6,424	1,544	82	23
Maryland	99,951	37,113	55,258	6,376	782	422	94,231	24,295	55,009	13,466	1,006	455
District of Columbia	47,443	15,925	28,212	2,714	342	250	54,297	14,058	29,942	9,556	530	211
Virginia	204,713	75,076	114,672	12,630	2,008	327	210,823	59,134	116,842	31,848	2,834	165
West Virginia	43,429	15,492	24,969	2,302	636	30	36,048	7,602	23,838	4,045	544	19
North Carolina	266,001	98,885	152,237	13,023	1,418	438	290,045	90,894	157,643	38,356	2,773	379
South Carolina	218,367	76,557	130,007	10,999	629	175	251,595	74,892	135,531	39,385	1,579	208
Georgia	324,068	103,281	196,041	21,538	2,786	422	365,622	90,080	210,168	67,516	6,530	328
Florida	151,867	47,192	90,572	10,634	1,992	1,477	151,954	29,624	93,535	25,241	3,115	439
East South Central	851,366	257,791	521,025	57,094	13,004	2,452	907,370	201,964	529,453	150,767	23,854	1,332
Kentucky	83,165	26,864	47,225	7,242	1,722	112	82,174	17,585	47,137	15,349	2,007	96
Tennessee	161,503	49,752	96,330	11,862	2,903	656	173,319	38,962	98,188	30,642	4,924	603
Alabama	290,079	91,027	176,191	18,544	3,912	405	320,277	77,161	179,650	55,127	8,000	339
Mississippi	316,619	90,148	201,279	19,446	4,467	1,279	331,600	68,256	204,478	49,649	8,923	294
West South Central	752,705	221,791	462,777	51,524	15,675	938	780,153	161,325	469,499	122,187	26,229	913
Arkansas	158,239	42,866	100,470	11,773	3,002	128	162,123	30,171	101,199	25,927	4,743	83
Louisiana	248,678	76,739	153,916	14,833	2,855	335	264,780	59,127	157,360	42,049	5,871	373
Oklahoma	59,193	17,969	34,965	4,637	1,506	116	57,580	11,879	35,096	8,553	1,972	80
Texas	286,595	84,217	173,426	20,281	8,312	359	295,670	60,148	175,844	45,658	13,643	377
Mountain	13,217	4,831	6,918	952	480	36	10,748	1,653	6,640	2,024	418	13
Montana	601	237	276	50	32	6	437	65	267	78	25	2
Idaho	338	118	168	35	16	1	226	27	162	27	10	-
Wyoming	602	240	292	53	14	3	446	73	278	78	16	1
Colorado	4,621	1,240	2,757	438	173	13	4,902	798	2,778	1,135	185	6
New Mexico	1,141	364	661	75	40	1	938	158	618	128	32	2
Arizona	5,181	2,381	2,373	258	157	12	3,217	450	2,163	481	121	2
Utah	482	160	267	28	27	-	374	42	251	63	18	-
Nevada	251	91	124	15	21	-	208	40	123	34	11	-
Pacific	35,952	11,382	20,608	2,343	1,388	231	35,812	6,240	20,848	6,696	1,942	86
Washington	3,152	1,126	1,567	264	166	29	2,419	376	1,466	431	143	3

[Continued]

★ 2277 ★

Marital Condition of the Black Population 15 Years Old and Over by Geographical Areas, 1930

[Continued]

Section, division, and state	Males 15 years old and over						Females 15 years old and over					
	Total	Single	Married	Widowed	Divorced	Unknown	Total	Single	Married	Widowed	Divorced	Unknown
Oregon	1,051	367	551	85	47	1	827	134	512	142	38	1
California	31,749	9,889	18,490	1,994	1,175	201	32,566	5,730	18,870	6,123	1,761	82

Source: "Marital Condition of the Negro Population 15 Years Old and Over, by Sex, by Sections, Divisions, and States: 1930." U.S. Bureau of the Census. *Negroes in the United States: 1920-32.* Washington, D.C.: Government Printing Office, 1935, p. 150.

★ 2278 ★

Marital Status

Marital Condition of the Black Population 15 Years Old and Over by Sex for Cities With 5,000 to 10,000 Black Inhabitants, 1930

City	Males 15 years old and over						Females 15 years old and over					
	Total	Single	Married	Widowed	Divorced	Unknown	Total	Single	Married	Widowed	Divorced	Unknown
Albany, Ga	2,181	556	1,415	142	63	5	3,280	616	1,617	779	265	3
Alexandria, La	3,106	944	1,917	213	28	4	3,777	845	2,053	759	118	2
Anniston, Ala	2,277	651	1,406	176	44	-	2,731	614	1,452	581	84	-
Athens, Ga	1,848	594	1,088	155	11	-	2,672	777	1,157	716	22	-
Austin, Tex	3,159	879	1,854	224	127	75	4,307	938	2,056	831	348	134
Brunswick, Ga	2,098	583	1,308	169	34	4	2,506	540	1,414	513	36	3
Cambridge, Mass	1,736	588	1,029	92	26	1	2,005	546	1,104	326	29	-
Charleston, W. Va	2,431	892	1,362	148	29	-	2,717	681	1,526	437	73	-
Chester, Pa	3,592	1,426	1,914	188	33	31	3,187	764	1,958	409	44	12
Clarksdale, Miss	1,750	380	1,197	162	10	1	2,297	440	1,345	479	32	1
Danville, Va	1,588	424	1,029	112	16	7	2,332	626	1,115	553	30	8
Daytona Beach, Fla	1,754	489	1,111	130	24	-	2,245	491	1,230	481	42	1
Denver, Colo	2,730	674	1,694	255	102	5	3,133	488	1,746	778	116	5
Des Moines, Iowa	1,913	510	1,187	143	72	1	2,049	340	1,216	389	104	-
Dothan, Ala	1,845	665	1,010	113	51	6	2,223	598	1,037	429	156	3
East Chicago, Ind	2,051	660	1,271	71	45	4	1,702	235	1,227	192	47	1
Evansville, Ind	2,576	944	1,362	210	57	3	2,634	680	1,397	484	67	6
Fairfield, Ala	2,152	655	1,345	99	53	-	2,264	470	1,390	321	83	-
Fayetteville, N.C	1,567	596	883	75	11	2	2,146	754	975	384	29	4
Flint, Mich	2,321	727	1,458	77	57	2	1,894	227	1,427	181	58	1
Florence, S.C	1,681	493	1,085	78	25	-	2,437	661	1,216	493	66	1
Gadsden, Ala	2,214	675	1,293	137	108	1	2,251	442	1,290	390	128	1
Goldsboro, N.C	2,040	694	1,220	109	17	-	2,552	661	1,334	532	25	-
Greenville, Miss	2,996	993	1,807	143	47	6	3,602	1,035	1,950	558	53	6
Greenwood, Miss	1,776	457	1,216	94	8	1	2,397	488	1,392	455	60	2
Harrisburg, Pa	2,412	823	1,426	149	12	2	2,336	529	1,457	326	22	2
Hartford, Conn	2,172	648	1,386	105	28	5	2,321	459	1,461	349	48	4
Hattiesburg, Miss	2,091	507	1,375	114	94	1	2,701	509	1,537	403	251	1
High Point, N.C	2,482	927	1,426	117	11	1	2,659	784	1,513	337	24	1
Jackson, Tenn	2,528	759	1,528	211	30	-	3,167	706	1,613	762	81	5
Kinston, N.C	1,481	498	843	101	38	1	2,016	566	902	426	120	2
Lafayette, La	1,468	551	828	83	6	-	1,807	543	908	317	38	1
La Grange, Ga	1,661	530	939	189	3	-	2,116	547	988	565	15	1
Lake Charles, La	1,836	491	1,158	109	77	1	2,210	479	1,238	312	181	-
Laurel, Miss	2,192	532	1,444	193	23	-	2,684	472	1,582	575	55	-

[Continued]

★ 2278 ★

Marital Condition of the Black Population 15 Years Old and Over by Sex for Cities With 5,000 to 10,000 Black Inhabitants, 1930

[Continued]

City	Males 15 years old and over						Females 15 years old and over					
	Total	Single	Married	Widowed	Divorced	Unknown	Total	Single	Married	Widowed	Divorced	Unknown
Lynchburg, Va	2,854	924	1,682	205	43	-	4,077	1,288	1,834	876	73	6
Marshall, Tex	2,133	647	1,286	148	52	-	2,679	611	1,314	614	140	-
Milwaukee, Wis	3,156	1,060	1,798	215	78	5	2,548	353	1,740	365	88	2
Montclair, N.J	1,988	521	1,378	69	19	1	2,980	930	1,558	451	40	1
Muskogee, Okla	2,213	588	1,379	168	73	5	2,678	556	1,452	521	146	3
Natchez, Miss	2,147	639	1,341	133	30	4	3,270	858	1,638	651	122	1
New Bern, N.C	1,939	674	1,083	162	19	1	2,467	616	1,211	604	35	1
New Haven, Conn	1,935	617	1,174	119	23	2	1,957	404	1,204	305	42	2
North Little Rock, Ark	2,119	638	1,267	189	18	7	2,324	455	1,319	516	32	2
Oakland, Calif	3,050	956	1,724	159	155	56	3,019	510	1,735	574	181	19
Orange, N.J	1,682	584	1,032	59	7	-	1,996	528	1,104	342	21	1
Orlando, Fla	2,468	664	1,609	156	33	6	3,073	601	1,782	579	84	27
Paducah, Ky	2,502	812	1,397	265	25	3	2,767	618	1,390	704	52	3
Pensacola, Fla	3,208	923	2,009	222	51	3	3,965	851	2,195	795	114	10
Pine Bluff, Ark	1,986	491	1,267	167	61	-	2,738	517	1,398	646	177	-
Providence, R.I	1,827	621	1,029	146	27	4	1,970	508	1,016	372	73	1
Rocky Mount, N.C	2,549	808	1,568	164	8	1	3,214	877	1,683	625	22	7
St. Petersburg, Fla	2,296	701	1,492	95	8	-	3,039	711	1,690	574	63	1
Selma, Ala	2,671	802	1,610	231	27	1	4,126	1,099	1,748	1,184	94	1
Spartansburg, S.C	2,920	964	1,783	164	6	3	3,823	1,071	1,962	766	18	6
Springfield, Ohio	3,036	865	1,901	200	61	9	2,910	523	1,908	424	49	6
Sumter, S.C	1,417	422	939	47	9	-	2,112	539	1,127	422	24	-
Thomasville, Ga	1,806	557	1,099	123	27	-	2,588	633	1,195	675	85	-
Topeka, Kans	2,047	520	1,258	164	105	-	2,280	438	1,318	389	134	1
Trenton, N.J	3,062	1,029	1,807	203	20	3	2,580	640	1,548	371	14	7
Tuscaloosa, Ala	2,253	708	1,341	176	24	4	2,929	721	1,392	761	47	8
Valdosta, Ga	1,971	601	1,209	125	35	1	2,585	541	1,343	582	119	-
Waco, Tex	3,200	909	1,864	261	163	3	3,823	798	1,900	771	350	4
Waycross, Ga	1,746	465	1,149	116	12	4	2,328	531	1,256	495	44	2
West Palm Beach, Fla	3,262	918	2,116	198	23	7	3,594	647	2,327	569	46	5
Wichita, Kans	2,054	530	1,284	156	84	-	2,118	373	1,271	395	79	-
Wilson, N.C	1,808	658	1,000	104	46	-	2,418	730	1,065	478	138	7

Source: "Marital Condition of the Negro Population 15 Years Old and Over, by Sex, for Cities Having 5,000 to 10,000 Negro Inhabitants: 1930." U.S. Bureau of the Census. *Negroes in the United States: 1920-32.* Washington, D.C.: Government Printing Office, 1935, p. 184.

★ 2279 ★

Marital Status

Marital Condition of the Black Population 15 to 34 Years Old by Sex, 1930

Age	Total	Single		Married		Widowed		Divorced	Unknown
		Number	Percent	Number	Percent	Number	Percent		
Males									
Negro population									
15 years	117,062	116,867	99.8	183	0.2	9	[1]	3	-
16 years	123,890	123,333	99.6	531	.4	17	[1]	9	-
17 years	120,994	119,078	98.4	1,805	1.5	63	0.1	48	-
18 years	123,927	117,147	94.5	6,166	5.0	193	.2	116	305
19 years	109,773	95,409	86.9	13,332	12.1	369	.3	265	398
20 years	110,375	84,044	76.1	24,652	22.3	756	.7	541	382
21 years	113,774	70,804	62.2	40,823	35.9	1,077	.9	733	337
22 years	115,651	60,592	52.4	52,045	45.0	1,561	1.3	1,107	346
23 years	107,116	46,804	43.7	57,080	53.3	1,745	1.6	1,183	304
24 years	106,706	40,312	37.8	62,572	58.6	2,075	1.9	1,449	298
25 years	112,485	38,720	34.4	69,310	61.6	2,473	2.2	1,650	332
26 years	92,974	27,862	30.0	61,205	65.8	2,218	2.4	1,466	223
27 years	92,341	25,246	27.3	63,106	68.3	2,275	2.5	1,466	248
28 years	105,189	25,907	24.6	74,349	70.7	2,914	2.8	1,768	251
29 years	97,531	21,053	21.6	71,899	73.7	2,717	2.8	1,670	192
30 years	135,112	30,207	22.4	97,250	72.0	4,852	3.6	2,538	265
31 years	57,438	11,117	19.4	43,147	75.1	1,923	3.3	1,123	128
32 years	85,060	15,738	18.5	64,301	75.6	3,149	3.7	1,683	189
33 years	67,484	11,162	16.5	52,262	77.4	2,539	3.8	1,400	121
34 years	71,775	10,991	15.3	56,314	78.5	2,809	3.9	1,493	168
Females									
15 years	123,375	119,639	97.0	3,483	2.8	159	0.1	94	-
16 years	133,835	121,941	91.1	11,070	8.3	519	.4	305	-
17 years	123,991	100,744	81.3	21,667	17.5	983	.8	597	-
18 years	145,204	97,183	66.9	44,600	30.7	1,899	1.3	1,314	208
19 years	128,477	70,557	54.9	53,421	41.6	2,585	2.0	1,688	226
20 years	148,172	66,705	45.0	74,463	50.3	4,188	2.8	2,625	191
21 years	114,530	43,088	37.6	65,036	56.8	3,814	3.3	2,406	186
22 years	133,740	42,720	31.9	82,200	61.5	5,427	4.1	3,201	192
23 years	127,376	33,721	26.5	83,945	65.9	6,079	4.8	3,477	154
24 years	125,751	28,663	22.8	86,430	68.7	6,963	5.5	3,541	154
25 years	133,762	27,692	20.7	93,220	69.7	8,654	6.5	4,013	183
26 years	110,637	19,051	17.2	80,597	72.8	7,366	6.7	3,511	112
27 years	102,581	15,497	15.1	76,305	74.4	7,525	7.3	3,138	116
28 years	119,635	16,315	13.6	89,892	75.1	9,508	7.9	3,790	130
29 years	104,652	12,077	11.5	79,844	76.3	9,292	8.9	3,326	113
30 years	146,634	18,908	12.9	107,044	73.0	15,626	10.7	4,845	211

[Continued]

★ 2279 ★

Marital Condition of the Black Population 15 to 34 Years Old by Sex, 1930

[Continued]

Age	Total	Single		Married		Widowed		Divorced	Unknown
		Number	Percent	Number	Percent	Number	Percent		
31 years	59,006	5,506	9.3	45,861	77.7	5,689	9.6	1,881	69
32 years	92,580	8,563	9.2	70,744	76.4	10,210	11.0	2,962	101
33 years	73,106	5,602	7.7	57,032	78.0	8,178	11.2	2,224	70
34 years	76,319	5,626	7.4	59,716	78.2	8,559	11.2	2,351	67

Source: "Marital Condition of the Negro Population 15 to 34 Years Old, by Sex, and Single Years of Age, for the United States: 1930." U.S. Bureau of the Census. *Negroes in the United States: 1920-32.* Washington, D.C.: Government Printing Office, 1935, p. 148. *Note:* 1. Less than 1/10 of 1 percent.

★ 2280 ★

Marital Status

Marital Condition of the Black Population by Geographical Divisions, 1890-1910

Section, age period and marital class	Number						Percentage distribution by marital class					
	Male			Female			Male			Female		
	1910	1900	1890[1]	1910	1900	1890[1]	1910	1900	1890	1910	1900	1890
The South												
All ages	4,339,625	3,925,404	3,353,334	4,409,802	3,997,565	3,388,607	-	-	-	-	-	-
Under 15 years of age[2]	1,704,176	1,635,805	1,492,532	1,710,692	1,634,403	1,455,846	100.0	100.0	100.0	100.0	100.0	100.0
Single	1,704,047	1,635,589	1,492,501	1,709,978	1,633,579	1,455,563	100.0	100.0	100.0	100.0	100.0	100.0
Married, widowed, or divorced	129	152	12	714	734	276	[3]	[3]	[3]	[3]	[3]	[3]
15 years of age and over	2,635,449	2,289,599	1,860,802	2,699,110	2,363,162	1,932,761	100.0	100.0	100.0	100.0	100.0	100.0
Single	915,961	879,668	726,383	713,083	698,010	575,815	34.8	38.4	39.0	26.4	29.5	29.8
Married, widowed, or divorced	1,705,432	1,397,906	1,130,614	1,976,998	1,659,385	1,352,447	64.7	61.1	60.8	73.2	70.2	70.0
Married	1,527,069	1,258,611	1,047,668	1,554,357	1,278,965	1,062,932	57.9	55.0	56.3	57.6	54.1	55.0
Widowed	162,326	130,333	78,811	394,169	361,256	280,398	6.2	5.7	4.2	14.6	15.3	14.5
Divorced	16,037	8,962	4,135	28,472	19,164	9,117	0.6	0.4	0.2	1.1	0.8	0.5
Unknown	14,056	12,025	3,805	9,029	5,767	4,499	0.5	0.5	0.2	0.3	0.2	0.2
The North												
All ages	518,544	444,007	355,661	509,130	436,764	345,357	-	-	-	-	-	-
Under 15 years of age[2]	117,834	114,470	110,047	122,992	119,151	110,086	100.0	100.0	100.0	100.0	100.0	100.0
Single	117,824	114,442	110,041	122,955	119,117	110,074	100.0	100.0	100.0	100.0	100.0	100.0
Married, widowed, or divorced	10	15	1	37	32	11	[3]	[3]	[3]	[3]	[3]	[3]
15 years of age and over	400,710	329,537	245,614	386,138	317,610	235,271	100.0	100.0	100.0	100.0	100.0	100.0
Single	156,984	146,297	108,068	106,750	103,074	74,323	39.2	44.4	44.0	27.6	32.5	31.6
Married, widowed, or divorced	241,471	180,948	136,859	278,228	213,419	160,558	60.3	54.9	55.7	72.1	67.2	68.2
Married	211,363	158,918	123,500	211,347	159,650	120,487	52.7	48.2	50.3	54.7	50.3	51.2
Widowed	26,364	20,101	12,380	62,536	51,088	38,607	6.6	6.1	5.0	16.2	16.1	16.4
Divorced	3,744	1,929	979	4,345	2,681	1,464	0.9	0.6	0.4	1.1	0.8	0.6
Unknown	2,255	2,292	687	1,160	1,117	390	0.6	0.7	0.3	0.3	0.4	0.2
The West												
All ages	27,712	17,136	16,566	22,950	13,118	10,515	-	-	-	-	-	-
Under 15 years of age[2]	4,559	3,264	3,261	4,854	3,307	2,997	100.0	100.0	100.0	100.0	100.0	100.0
Single	4,559	3,264	3,261	4,849	3,303	2,995	100.0	100.0	100.0	99.9	99.9	99.9
Married, widowed, or divorced	-	-	-	5	4	2	[3]	[3]	[3]	01	0.1	0.1
15 years of age and over	23,153	13,872	13,305	18,096	9,811	7,518	100.0	100.0	100.0	100.0	100.0	100.0
Single	10,527	7,320	8,313	4,163	2,599	2,176	45.5	52.8	62.5	23.0	26.5	28.9
Married, widowed, or divorced	12,441	6,291	4,935	13,840	7,153	5,311	53.7	45.4	37.1	76.5	72.9	70.6
Married	10,796	5,357	4,345	10,245	5,202	4,015	46.6	38.6	32.7	56.6	53.0	53.4
Widowed	1,280	799	492	3,126	1,763	1,189	5.5	5.8	3.7	17.3	18.0	15.8

[Continued]

★ 2280 ★

Marital Condition of the Black Population by Geographical Divisions, 1890-1910

[Continued]

Section, age period and marital class	Number						Percentage distribution by marital class					
	Male			Female			Male			Female		
	1910	1900	1890[1]	1910	1900	1890[1]	1910	1900	1890	1910	1900	1890
Divorced	365	135	98	469	188	107	1.6	1.0	0.7	2.6	1.9	1.4
Unknown	185	261	57	93	59	31	0.8	1.9	0.4	0.5	0.6	0.4

Source: "Marital Condition of the Negro Population, by Sections: 1910, 1900, and 1980." *Negro Population, 1790-1910*. Washington, D.C.: Government Printing Office, 1918, p. 247. *Notes:* 1. Exclusive of persons specially enumerated in Indian Territory and on Indian reservations for whom statistics of marital condition are not available. 2. Totals include persons of unknown marital condition in 1900 and 1890. 3. Less than one-tenth of 1 per cent.

★ 2281 ★

Marital Status

Marital Condition of the Black Population, Sections and Southern Divisions, 1910

Sex and section and division	Under 15 years of age			15 years of age and over					
	Total	Single	Married widowed or divorced	Total[1]	Single	Married, widowed, or divorced			
						Total[1]	Married	Widowed	Divorced
				Number					
Male									
United States	1,826,569	1,826,430	139	3,059,312	1,083,472	1,959,344	1,749,228	189,970	20,146
The South	1,704,176	1,704,047	129	2,635,449	915,961	1,705,432	1,527,069	162,326	16,037
South Atlantic	816,738	816,680	58	1,213,070	431,943	773,945	701,837	67,831	4,277
East South Central	506,613	506,571	42	809,179	272,322	533,393	473,135	53,596	6,662
West South Central	380,825	380,796	29	613,200	211,696	398,094	352,097	40,899	5,098
The North	117,834	117,824	10	400,710	156,984	241,471	211,363	26,364	3,744
The West	4,559	4,559	-	23,153	10,527	12,441	10,796	1,280	365
				Percentage distribution by marital class					
United States	100.0	100.0	2	100.0	35.4	64.0	57.2	6.2	0.7
The South	100.0	100.0	2	100.0	34.8	64.7	57.9	6.2	0.6
South Atlantic	100.0	100.0	2	100.0	35.6	63.8	57.9	5.6	0.4
East South Central	100.0	100.0	2	100.0	33.7	65.9	58.5	6.6	0.8
West South Central	100.0	100.0	2	100.0	34.5	64.9	57.4	6.7	0.8
The North	100.0	100.0	2	100.0	39.2	50.3	52.7	6.6	0.9
The West	100.0	100.0	-	100.0	45.5	53.7	46.6	5.5	1.6
				Excess of males over females					
United States	-	-	-	-	259,476	-	-	-	-
The South	-	-	-	-	202,878	-	-	-	-
South Atlantic	-	-	-	-	76,631	-	-	-	-
East South Central	1,135	1,326	-	-	64,531	-	-	-	-
West South Central	-	-	-	5,960	61,716	-	-	-	-
The North	-	-	-	14,572	50,234	-	16	-	-
The West	-	-	-	5,057	6,364	-	551	-	-
				Number					
Female									
United States	1,838,538	1,837,782	756	3,103,344	823,996	2,269,066	1,775,949	459,831	33,286
The South	1,710,692	1,709,978	714	2,699,110	713,083	1,976,998	1,554,357	394,169	28,472
South Atlantic	822,053	821,725	328	1,260,627	355,312	901,033	716,955	176,715	7,363
East South Central	505,478	505,245	233	831,243	207,791	620,879	480,406	128,500	11,973

[Continued]

★ 2281 ★

Marital Condition of the Black Population, Sections and Southern Divisions, 1910

[Continued]

Sex and section and division	Under 15 years of age			15 years of age and over					
	Total	Single	Married widowed or divorced	Total[1]	Single	Married, widowed, or divorced			
						Total[1]	Married	Widowed	Divorced
West South Central	383,161	383,008	153	607,240	149,980	455,086	356,996	88,954	9,136
The North	122,992	122,955	37	386,138	106,750	278,228	211,347	62,536	4,345
The West	4,854	4,849	5	18,096	4,163	13,840	10,245	3,126	469
Percentage distribution by marital class									
United States	100.0	100.0	2	100.0	26.6	73.1	57.2	14.8	1.1
The South	100.0	100.0	2	100.0	26.4	73.2	57.6	14.6	1.1
South Atlantic	100.0	100.0	2	100.0	28.2	71.5	56.9	14.0	0.6
East South Central	100.0	100.0	2	100.0	25.0	74.7	57.8	15.5	1.4
West South Central	100.0	100.0	2	100.0	24.7	74.9	58.8	14.6	1.5
The North	100.0	100.0	2	100.0	27.6	72.1	54.7	16.2	1.1
The West	100.0	100.0	2	100.0	23.0	76.5	56.6	17.3	2.6
Excess of females over males									
United States	11,969	11,352	617	44,032	-	309,722	26,721	269,861	13,140
The South	6,516	5,931	585	63,661	-	271,566	27,288	231,843	12,435
South Atlantic	5,315	5,045	270	47,557	-	127,088	15,118	108,884	3,086
East South Central	-	-	191	22,064	-	87,486	7,271	74,904	5,311
West South Central	2,336	2,212	124	-	-	56,992	4,899	488,055	4,038
The North	5,158	5,131	27	-	-	36,757	-	36,172	601
The West	295	290	5	-	-	1,399	-	1,846	104

Source: "Marital Condition of the Negro Population, by Sections and Southern Divisions: 1910." *Negro Population, 1790-1910.* Washington, D.C.: Government Printing Office, 1918, p. 246. *Notes:* 1. Includes those of unknown marital condition. 2. Less than one-tenth of 1 per cent.

★ 2282 ★

Marital Status

Marital Condition of the Population, 1910 - I

Age period and racial class	Male						
	Total	Single	Married, widowed, or divorced				Marital condition unknown
			Total	Married	Widowed	Divorced	
Number							
All ages	47,332,277	27,455,607	19,721,146	18,093,498	1,471,472	156,176	155,524
Negro	4,885,881	2,909,902	1,959,483	1,749,359	189,976	20,148	16,496
White	42,178,245	24,379,558	17,664,375	16,254,696	1,274,464	135,215	134,312
Other	268,151	166,147	97,288	89,443	7,032	813	4,716
Under 15 years of age	14,906,472	14,905,478	994	898	82	14	-
Negro	1,826,569	1,826,430	139	131	6	2	-
White	13,020,120	13,019,276	844	756	76	12	-
Other	59,783	59,772	11	11	-	-	-

[Continued]

★ 2282 ★

Marital Condition of the Population, 1910 - I

[Continued]

Age period and racial class	Male						
	Total	Single	Married, widowed, or divorced				Marital condition unknown
			Total	Married	Widowed	Divorced	
15 years of age and over	32,425,805	12,550,129	19,720,152	18,092,600	1,471,390	156,162	155,524
Negro	3,059,312	1,083,472	1,959,344	1,749,228	189,970	20,146	16,496
White	29,158,125	11,360,282	17,663,531	16,253,940	1,274,388	135,203	134,312
Native	22,018,232	9,091,366	12,823,611	11,821,805	889,662	112,144	103,255
Native parentage	16,233,095	6,185,324	9,960,438	9,144,099	728,883	87,456	87,333
Mixed parentage	1,725,359	916,915	803,581	751,631	43,733	8,217	4,863
Foreign parentage	4,059,778	1,989,127	2,059,592	1,926,075	117,046	16,471	11,059
Foreign born	7,139,893	2,268,916	4,839,920	4,432,135	384,726	23,059	31,057
Indian	80,383	27,391	52,152	46,154	5,319	679	840
Chinese	64,394	34,330	27,633	26,449	1,139	45	2,431
Japanese	60,536	42,688	16,499	15,918	495	86	1,349
Other	3,055	1,966	993	911	79	3	96
Percentage distribution by marital class							
All ages	100.0	58.0	41.7	38.2	3.1	0.3	0.3
Negro	100.0	59.6	40.1	35.8	3.9	0.4	0.3
White	100.0	57.8	41.9	38.5	3.0	0.3	0.3
Other	100.0	62.0	36.3	33.4	2.6	0.3	1.8
Under 15 years of age	100.0	100.0	[1]	[1]	[1]	[1]	-
Negro	100.0	100.0	[1]	[1]	[1]	[1]	-
White	100.0	100.0	[1]	[1]	[1]	[1]	-
Other	100.0	100.0	[1]	[1]	-	-	-
15 years of age and over	100.0	38.7	60.8	55.8	4.5	0.5	0.5
Negro	100.0	35.4	64.0	57.2	6.2	0.7	0.5
White	100.0	39.0	60.6	55.7	4.4	0.5	0.5
Native	100.0	41.3	58.2	53.7	4.0	0.5	0.5
Native parentage	100.0	38.1	61.4	56.3	4.5	0.5	0.5
Mixed parentage	100.0	53.1	46.6	43.6	2.5	0.5	0.3
Foreign parentage	100.0	49.0	50.7	47.4	2.9	0.4	0.3
Foreign born	100.0	31.8	67.8	62.1	5.4	0.3	0.4
Indian	100.0	34.1	64.9	57.4	6.6	0.8	1.0
Chinese	100.0	53.3	42.9	41.1	1.8	0.1	3.8
Japanese	100.0	70.5	27.3	26.3	0.8	0.1	2.2
Other	100.0	64.4	32.5	29.8	2.6	0.1	3.1

Source: "Marital Condition of the Negro and Other Classes of the Population: 1910." U.S. Bureau of the Census. *Negro Population, 1790-1915.* Washington, D.C.: Government Printing Office, 1918, p. 237. *Note:* 1. Less than one-tenth of 1 percent.

★ 2283 ★

Marital Status

Marital Condition of the Population, 1910 - II

Age period and racial class	Female						
	Total	Single	Married, widowed, or divorced				Marital condition unknown
			Total	Married	Widowed	Divorced	
	Number						
All ages	44,639,989	23,522,121	21,049,696	17,688,169	3,176,426	185,101	68,172
Negro	4,941,882	2,661,778	2,269,822	1,776,643	459,889	33,290	10,282
White	39,553,712	20,784,712	18,711,714	15,854,757	2,706,127	150,830	57,286
Other	144,395	75,631	68,160	56,769	10,410	981	604
Under 15 years of age	14,592,664	14,588,951	3,713	3,482	198	33	-
Negro	1,838,538	1,837,782	756	694	58	4	-
White	12,696,375	12,693,463	2,912	2,746	137	29	-
Other	57,751	57,706	45	42	3	-	-
15 years of age and over	30,047,325	8,933,170	21,045,983	17,684,687	3,176,228	185,068	68,172
Negro	3,103,344	823,996	2,269,066	1,775,949	459,831	33,286	10,282
White	26,857,337	8,091,249	18,708,802	15,852,011	2,705,990	150,801	57,286
Native	21,411,031	7,097,139	14,264,145	12,228,008	1,905,878	130,259	49,747
Native parentage	15,523,900	4,644,122	10,842,998	9,219,385	1,523,560	100,053	36,780
Mixed parentage	1,794,559	792,897	997,647	880,458	105,970	11,219	4,015
Foreign parentage	4,092,572	1,660,120	2,423,500	2,128,165	276,348	18,987	8,952
Foreign born	5,446,306	994,110	4,444,657	3,624,003	800,112	20,542	7,539
Indian	76,982	16,324	60,125	49,095	10,071	959	533
Chinese	2,955	680	2,250	2,016	229	5	25
Japanese	6,648	908	5,694	5,581	96	17	46
Other	59	13	46	35	11	-	-
	Percentage distribution by marital class						
All ages	100.0	52.7	47.2	39.6	7.1	0.4	0.2
Negro	100.0	53.9	45.9	36.0	9.3	0.7	0.2
White	100.0	52.5	47.3	40.1	6.8	0.4	0.1
Other	100.0	52.4	47.2	39.3	7.2	0.7	0.4
Under 15 years of age	100.0	100.0	[1]	[1]	[1]	[1]	-
Negro	100.0	100.0	[1]	[1]	[1]	[1]	-
White	100.0	100.0	[1]	[1]	[1]	[1]	-
Other	100.0	100.0	0.1	0.1	[1]	-	-
15 years of age and over	100.0	29.7	70.0	58.9	10.6	0.6	0.2
Negro	100.0	26.6	73.1	57.2	14.8	1.1	0.3
White	100.0	30.1	69.7	59.0	10.1	0.6	0.2
Native	100.0	33.1	66.6	57.1	8.9	0.6	0.2
Native parentage	100.0	29.9	69.8	59.4	9.8	0.6	0.2
Mixed parentage	100.0	44.2	55.6	49.1	5.9	0.6	0.2
Foreign parentage	100.0	40.6	59.2	52.0	6.8	0.5	0.2
Foreign born	100.0	18.3	81.6	66.5	14.7	0.4	0.1

[Continued]

★ 2283 ★

Marital Condition of the Population, 1910 - II

[Continued]

Age period and racial class	Female						
	Total	Single	Married, widowed, or divorced				Marital condition unknown
			Total	Married	Widowed	Divorced	
Indian	100.0	21.2	78.1	63.8	13.1	1.2	0.7
Chinese	100.0	23.0	76.1	68.2	7.7	0.2	0.8
Japanese	100.0	13.7	85.6	84.0	1.4	0.3	0.7
Other	100.0	[2]	[2]	[2]	[2]	-	-

Source: "Marital Condition of the Negro and Other Classes of the Population: 1910." U.S. Bureau of the Census. *Negro Population, 1790-1915.* Washington, D.C.: Government Printing Office, 1918, p. 237. *Notes:* 1. Less than one-tenth of 1 percent. 2. Per cent not shown where base is less than 100.

★ 2284 ★

Marital Status

Marital Condition of the Total Population by Sex, Race, and Age-Periods, 1930

Racial class and age	Males						Females					
	Total	Single	Married	Widowed	Divorced	Unknown	Total	Single	Married	Widowed	Divorced	Unknown
All classes	62,137,080	33,208,947	26,327,870	2,025,078	489,499	85,686	60,637,966	29,102,964	26,174,997	4,734,374	573,246	52,385
Under 15 years old	18,256,059	18,255,235	761	42	21	-	17,800,817	17,796,311	4,241	167	98	-
15 years old and over	43,881,021	14,953,712	26,327,109	2,025,036	489,478	85,686	42,837,149	11,306,653	26,170,756	4,734,207	573,148	52,385
15 to 19 years	5,757,825	5,645,359	100,362	1,513	1,348	9,243	5,794,290	5,032,174	731,967	12,337	12,371	5,441
20 to 24 years	5,336,815	3,779,443	1,500,493	17,657	21,900	17,322	5,533,563	2,547,057	2,857,665	56,375	62,464	10,002
25 to 29 years	4,860,180	1,785,413	2,977,004	39,013	50,229	8,521	4,973,428	1,079,923	3,697,645	102,041	89,124	4,695
30 to 34 years	4,561,786	965,945	3,468,176	59,493	62,669	5,503	4,558,635	603,048	3,715,648	148,571	88,219	3,149
35 to 39 years	4,679,860	718,396	3,792,614	93,204	70,765	4,881	4,528,785	472,053	3,725,680	240,604	87,533	2,915
40 to 44 years	4,136,459	543,309	3,396,838	125,677	66,415	4,220	3,853,736	367,077	3,106,901	306,958	70,117	2,683
45 to 49 years	3,671,924	435,252	3,013,521	158,561	60,850	3,740	3,370,355	303,864	2,616,213	391,342	56,446	2,490
50 to 54 years	3,131,645	341,611	2,537,625	198,486	50,621	3,302	2,844,159	260,602	2,057,326	481,334	42,428	2,469
55 to 59 years	2,425,992	251,017	1,929,201	204,742	38,220	2,812	2,219,685	199,569	1,469,931	520,158	27,898	2,129
60 to 64 years	1,941,508	191,488	1,478,550	240,520	28,279	2,671	1,809,713	160,619	1,029,354	599,644	17,983	2,113
65 to 69 years	1,417,812	131,451	1,013,226	252,072	18,783	2,280	1,352,793	114,186	630,293	596,224	10,204	1,886
70 to 74 years	991,647	84,851	641,628	251,970	11,157	2,041	958,357	80,918	334,963	536,003	4,830	1,643
75 years and over	915,752	64,315	461,683	379,638	7,431	2,685	997,444	73,312	181,944	736,807	2,859	2,522
Unknown	51,816	15,862	16,188	2,490	811	16,465	42,206	12,251	15,226	5,809	672	8,248
Negro	5,855,669	3,185,005	2,357,954	247,610	55,717	9,383	6,035,474	2,888,607	2,399,171	652,721	88,904	6,071
Under 15 years old	1,914,207	1,914,055	133	15	4	-	1,935,922	1,934,801	1,027	58	36	-
15 years old and over	3,941,462	1,270,950	2,357,821	247,595	55,713	9,383	4,099,552	953,806	2,398,144	652,663	88,868	6,071
15 to 19 years	595,646	571,834	22,017	651	441	703	654,882	510,064	134,241	6,145	3,998	434
20 to 24 years	553,622	302,556	237,172	7,214	5,013	1,667	649,569	214,897	392,074	26,471	15,250	877
25 to 29 years	500,520	138,788	339,869	12,597	8,020	1,246	571,267	90,632	419,858	42,345	17,778	654
30 to 34 years	416,869	79,215	313,274	15,272	8,237	871	447,645	44,205	340,397	48,262	14,263	518
35 to 39 years	430,472	60,682	338,705	21,263	9,050	772	460,428	31,702	346,217	68,496	13,544	469
40 to 44 years	339,329	39,703	267,772	24,088	7,119	647	348,094	20,061	247,700	70,935	8,971	427
45 to 49 years	323,162	28,760	259,149	28,402	6,300	551	306,903	14,142	208,459	77,347	6,584	371
50 to 54 years	277,532	19,891	220,934	31,733	4,586	388	227,058	10,167	136,804	75,792	3,976	319
55 to 59 years	174,367	11,078	137,017	23,200	2,803	269	135,030	5,341	74,453	52,964	2,055	217
60 to 64 years	133,349	7,335	99,687	24,137	1,965	225	108,820	4,393	47,569	55,455	1,200	203
65 to 69 years	82,843	4,364	57,881	19,371	1,090	137	72,334	2,716	26,001	42,825	651	141
70 to 74 years	50,896	2,454	32,278	15,500	553	111	48,200	1,916	12,411	33,478	261	134
75 years and over	55,791	2,677	28,757	23,728	459	170	62,655	2,281	9,311	50,614	212	237
Unknown	7,064	1,613	3,309	439	77	1,626	6,667	1,289	2,649	1,534	125	1,070
White	55,163,854	29,313,557	23,603,919	1,745,239	428,090	73,049	53,700,353	25,706,178	23,447,330	4,023,477	477,684	45,684
Under 15 years old	15,949,698	15,949,048	607	26	17	-	15,480,124	15,476,872	3,087	105	60	-
15 years old and over	39,214,156	13,364,509	23,603,312	1,745,213	428,073	73,049	38,220,229	10,229,306	23,444,243	4,023,372	477,624	45,684
15 to 19 years	5,063,975	4,977,503	76,465	833	861	8,313	5,047,609	4,449,325	579,504	5,832	8,028	4,920
20 to 24 years	4,666,016	3,389,842	1,234,723	9,882	16,387	15,182	4,800,139	2,304,549	2,412,268	28,387	45,931	9,004
25 to 29 years	4,246,957	1,592,650	2,581,163	25,045	41,278	6,821	4,326,739	979,382	3,216,233	57,175	69,974	3,975

[Continued]

★ 2284 ★

Marital Condition of the Total Population by Sex, Race, and Age-Periods, 1930

[Continued]

Racial class and age	Males						Females					
	Total	Single	Married	Widowed	Divorced	Unknown	Total	Single	Married	Widowed	Divorced	Unknown
30 to 34 years	4,059,179	859,861	3,099,125	42,246	53,591	4,356	4,050,587	554,453	3,323,466	97,089	72,978	2,601
35 to 39 years	4,171,206	639,880	3,397,317	69,273	60,864	3,872	4,012,414	437,404	3,331,898	167,550	73,153	2,409
40 to 44 years	3,733,591	491,575	3,081,779	98,256	58,595	3,386	3,464,916	345,230	2,826,591	230,337	60,528	2,230
45 to 49 years	3,293,779	397,943	2,712,488	126,327	53,964	3,057	3,029,210	288,425	2,382,342	306,961	49,392	2,090
50 to 54 years	2,815,281	315,948	2,287,972	162,975	45,583	2,803	2,593,775	249,506	1,905,135	398,865	38,157	2,112
55 to 59 years	2,225,068	236,505	1,772,722	178,255	35,121	2,465	2,068,039	193,675	1,385,758	461,044	25,682	1,880
60 to 64 years	1,789,010	181,762	1,365,713	213,058	26,098	2,379	1,687,983	155,781	975,776	537,884	16,654	1,888
65 to 69 years	1,322,823	125,560	947,545	230,050	17,566	2,102	1,272,017	111,177	600,998	548,662	9,458	1,722
70 to 74 years	933,348	81,389	605,085	234,449	10,535	1,890	904,702	78,816	320,929	498,930	4,529	1,498
75 years and over	851,414	60,645	428,812	352,576	6,908	2,473	927,279	70,781	171,097	680,529	2,621	2,251
Unknown	42,509	13,446	12,403	1,988	722	13,950	34,820	10,802	12,248	4,127	539	7,104

Source: "Marital Condition of the Total Population, by Sex, and Racial Classes, and 5-Year Age Periods, for the United States: 1930." U.S. Bureau of the Census. *Negroes in the United States: 1920-32*. Washington, D.C.: Government Printing Office, 1935, p. 148.

★ 2285 ★

Marital Status

Marital Condition of the Urban, Rural-Farm, and Nonfarm Black Population by Age, 1930

Area and age	Total	Single		Married		Widowed		Divorced	Unknown
		Number	Percent	Number	Percent	Number	Percent		
				Males 15 years old and over					
Urban	1,842,029	576,114	31.3	1,112,731	60.4	118,454	6.4	30,809	3,921
15 to 19 years	195,723	188,368	96.2	6,759	3.5	179	0.1	151	266
20 to 24 years	240,821	138,750	57.6	96,638	40.1	2,684	1.1	2,208	541
25 to 29 years	271,191	84,425	31.1	175,977	64.9	6,071	2.2	4,318	400
30 to 34 years	239,226	51,863	21.7	173,521	72.5	8,527	3.6	5,029	286
35 to 39 years	242,537	40,903	16.9	183,389	75.6	12,201	5.0	5,713	331
40 to 44 years	185,421	26,320	14.2	140,480	75.8	13,984	7.5	4,383	254
45 to 49 years	162,055	18,564	11.5	124,057	76.6	15,567	9.6	3,632	235
50 to 54 years	120,482	11,868	9.9	90,190	74.9	15,864	13.2	2,398	162
55 to 59 years	69,921	6,208	8.9	51,390	73.5	10,889	15.6	1,330	104
60 to 64 years	47,738	3,702	7.8	32,865	68.8	10,265	21.5	813	93
65 to 69 years	28,505	2,037	7.1	18,084	63.4	7,899	27.7	432	53
70 to 74 years	16,563	1,022	6.2	9,413	56.8	5,888	35.5	197	43
75 years and over	17,173	1,001	5.8	7,791	45.4	8,168	47.6	163	50
Unknown	4,673	1,083	23.2	2,177	46.6	268	5.7	42	1,103
Rural-farm	1,395,651	460,114	33.0	841,149	60.3	79,452	5.7	13,800	1,136
15 to 19 years	301,727	289,513	96.0	11,402	3.8	358	0.1	219	235
20 to 24 years	204,272	103,864	50.8	95,073	46.5	3,135	1.5	1,875	325
25 to 29 years	135,841	26,710	19.7	102,894	75.7	4,040	3.0	2,095	102
30 to 34 years	103,852	11,694	11.3	86,566	83.4	3,872	3.7	1,664	56
35 to 39 years	113,332	8,008	7.1	98,550	87.0	5,082	4.5	1,645	47
40 to 44 years	95,265	5,465	5.7	82,778	86.9	5,682	6.0	1,293	47
45 to 49 years	105,737	4,276	4.0	92,429	87.4	7,577	7.2	1,412	43
50 to 54 years	110,150	3,690	3.3	95,246	86.5	9,953	9.0	1,209	52
55 to 59 years	74,602	2,251	3.0	63,672	85.3	7,762	10.4	881	36

[Continued]

★ 2285 ★

Marital Condition of the Urban, Rural-Farm, and Nonfarm Black Population by Age, 1930

[Continued]

Area and age	Total	Single		Married		Widowed		Divorced	Unknown
		Number	Percent	Number	Percent	Number	Percent		
60 to 64 years	61,992	1,772	2.9	50,555	81.6	8,920	14.4	701	44
65 to 69 years	38,742	1,148	3.0	29,905	77.2	7,254	18.7	405	30
70 to 74 years	23,700	704	3.0	16,752	70.7	6,014	25.4	213	17
75 years and over	25,572	802	3.1	14,818	57.9	9,740	38.1	172	40
Unknown	867	217	25.0	509	58.7	63	7.3	16	62
Rural-nonfarm	703,782	234,722	33.4	403,941	57.4	49,689	7.1	11,104	4,326
15 to 19 years	98,196	93,953	95.7	3,856	3.9	114	0.1	71	202
20 to 24 years	108,529	59,942	55.2	45,461	41.9	1,395	1.3	930	801
25 to 29 years	93,488	27,653	29.6	60,998	65.2	2,486	2.7	1,607	744
30 to 34 years	73,791	15,658	21.2	53,187	72.1	2,873	3.9	1,544	529
35 to 39 years	74,603	11,771	15.8	56,766	76.1	3,980	5.3	1,692	394
40 to 44 years	58,643	7,918	13.5	44,514	75.9	4,422	7.5	1,443	346
45 to 49 years	55,370	5,920	10.7	42,663	77.1	5,258	9.5	1,256	273
50 to 54 years	46,900	4,333	9.2	35,498	75.7	5,916	12.6	979	174
55 to 59 years	29,844	2,619	8.8	21,955	73.6	4,549	15.2	592	129
60 to 64 years	23,619	1,861	7.9	16,267	68.9	4,952	21.0	451	88
65 to 69 years	15,596	1,179	7.6	9,892	63.4	4,218	27.0	253	54
70 to 74 years	10,633	728	6.8	6,113	57.5	3,598	33.9	143	51
75 years and over	13,046	874	6.7	6,148	47.1	5,820	44.6	124	80
Unknown	1,524	313	20.5	623	40.9	108	7.1	19	461
Females 15 years and over									
Urban	2,048,053	454,635	22.2	1,158,802	56.6	376,331	18.4	54,790	3,495
15 to 19 years	251,432	197,431	78.5	49,654	19.7	2,320	0.9	1,783	244
20 to 24 years	319,394	111,111	34.8	185,760	58.2	13,661	4.3	8,367	495
25 to 29 years	325,239	57,645	17.7	229,027	70.4	26,518	8.2	11,667	382
30 to 34 years	257,246	29,356	11.4	185,860	72.2	32,059	12.5	9,666	305
35 to 39 years	255,528	21,399	8.4	179,590	70.3	45,077	17.6	9,179	283
40 to 44 years	184,008	13,008	7.1	119,937	65.2	45,143	24.5	5,676	244
45 to 49 years	154,535	9,075	5.9	92,940	60.1	48,255	31.2	4,059	206
50 to 54 years	108,074	6,014	5.6	55,367	51.2	44,340	41.0	2,182	171
55 to 59 years	63,019	3,103	4.9	28,100	44.6	30,639	48.6	1,072	105
60 to 64 years	48,046	2,317	4.8	16,053	33.4	29,011	60.4	560	105
65 to 69 years	32,028	1,431	4.5	8,398	26.2	21,821	68.1	306	72
70 to 74 years	20,087	908	4.5	3,565	17.7	15,446	76.9	99	69
75 years and over	24,752	943	3.8	2,685	10.8	20,953	84.7	77	94
Unknown	4,665	894	19.2	1,866	40.0	1,088	23.3	97	720
Rural-farm	1,380,749	352,961	25.6	845,806	61.3	161,530	11.7	19,421	1,031
15 to 19 years	295,851	233,308	78.9	58,286	19.7	2,637	0.9	1,500	120
20 to 24 years	219,391	71,302	32.5	135,507	61.8	8,114	3.7	4,274	194
25 to 29 years	155,559	20,483	13.2	122,559	78.8	9,009	5.8	3,414	94
30 to 34 years	121,827	8,609	7.1	101,703	83.5	8,964	7.4	2,470	81
35 to 39 years	134,987	5,737	4.3	113,856	84.3	13,058	9.7	2,261	75
40 to 44 years	110,089	3,976	3.6	89,652	81.4	14,567	13.2	1,807	87

[Continued]

★ 2285 ★

Marital Condition of the Urban, Rural-Farm, and Nonfarm Black Population by Age, 1930

[Continued]

Area and age	Total	Single		Married		Widowed		Divorced	Unknown
		Number	Percent	Number	Percent	Number	Percent		
45 to 49 years	104,141	2,767	2.7	83,329	80.0	16,622	16.0	1,361	62
50 to 54 years	81,094	2,221	2.7	59,560	73.4	18,244	22.5	1,001	68
55 to 59 years	49,002	1,195	2.4	34,366	70.1	12,837	26.2	569	35
60 to 64 years	40,465	1,131	2.8	23,248	57.5	15,661	38.7	381	44
65 to 69 years	26,007	719	2.8	12,644	48.6	12,408	47.7	204	32
70 to 74 years	17,700	575	3.2	6,249	35.3	10,755	60.8	83	38
75 years and over	23,822	722	3.0	4,467	18.8	18,478	77.6	83	72
Unknown	814	216	26.5	380	46.7	176	21.6	13	29
Rural-nonfarm	670,750	146,210	21.8	393,536	58.7	114,802	17.1	14,657	1,545
15 to 19 years	107,599	79,325	73.7	26,301	24.4	1,188	1.1	715	70
20 to 24 years	110,784	32,484	29.3	70,807	63.9	4,696	4.2	2,609	188
25 to 29 years	90,469	12,504	13.8	68,272	75.5	6,818	7.5	2,697	178
30 to 34 years	68,572	6,240	9.1	52,834	77.0	7,239	10.6	2,127	132
35 to 39 years	69,913	4,566	6.5	52,771	75.5	10,361	14.8	2,104	111
40 to 44 years	53,997	3,077	5.7	38,111	70.6	11,225	20.8	1,488	96
45 to 49 years	48,227	2,300	4.8	32,190	66.7	12,470	25.9	1,164	103
50 to 54 years	37,890	1,932	5.1	21,877	57.7	13,208	34.9	793	80
55 to 59 years	23,009	1,043	4.5	11,987	52.1	9,488	41.2	414	77
60 to 64 years	20,309	945	4.7	8,268	40.7	10,783	53.1	259	54
65 to 69 years	14,299	566	4.0	4,959	34.7	8,596	60.1	141	37
70 to 74 years	10,413	433	4.2	2,597	24.9	7,277	69.9	79	27
75 years and over	14,081	616	4.4	2,159	15.3	11,183	79.4	52	71
Unknown	1,188	179	15.1	403	33.9	270	22.7	15	321

Source: "Marital Condition of the Urban, Rural-Farm, and Rural Nonfarm Negro Population 15 Years Old and Over, by Sex, and 5-Year Age Periods, for the United States: 1930." U.S. Bureau of the Census. *Negroes in the United States: 1920-32.* Washington, D.C.: Government Printing Office, 1935, p. 149.

★ 2286 ★

Marital Status

Marital Status of Blacks by Divisions and States, 1890

Division and state	Negro population 15 years of age and over: 1890[1]											
	Male						Female					
	Total	Single	Married	Widowed	Divorced	Unknown	Total	Single	Married	Widowed	Divorced	Unknown
United States	2,119,721	842,764	1,175,513	91,683	5,212	4,549	2,175,550	652,314	1,187,434	320,194	10,688	4,920
Geographic divisions												
New England	15,924	6,774	8,263	778	65	44	16,807	5,779	8,028	2,880	93	27
Middle Atlantic	81,552	36,883	40,599	3,713	103	254	82,557	28,523	39,836	13,856	174	168
East North Central	74,601	32,395	37,437	4,179	435	155	66,130	19,357	35,620	10,446	627	80
West North Central	73,537	32,016	37,201	3,710	376	234	69,777	20,664	37,003	11,425	570	115
South Atlantic	892,567	355,956	499,573	34,594	1,153	1,291	942,587	298,713	510,127	128,239	2,714	2,794
East South Central	590,870	228,566	332,455	26,945	1,663	1,211	611,087	176,434	335,542	94,431	3,718	962
West South Central	377,365	141,861	215,640	17,272	1,319	1,273	379,087	100,668	217,263	57,728	2,685	743
Mountain	7,089	4,789	2,003	209	48	40	3,444	1,116	1,734	514	58	22
Pacific	6,216	3,524	2,342	283	50	17	4,074	1,060	2,281	675	49	9
New England												
Maine	448	207	211	25	2	3	417	150	190	74	1	2

[Continued]

★ 2286 ★

Marital Status of Blacks by Divisions and States, 1890

[Continued]

Division and state	Negro population 15 years of age and over: 1890[1]											
	Male						Female					
	Total	Single	Married	Widowed	Divorced	Unknown	Total	Single	Married	Widowed	Divorced	Unknown
New Hampshire	238	122	100	13	2	1	201	85	83	32	1	-
Vermont	350	147	173	26	3	1	295	92	151	51	1	-
Massachusetts	8,103	3,533	4,162	376	17	15	8,333	2,858	3,998	1,435	31	11
Rhode Island	2,492	975	1,360	143	12	2	2,986	1,024	1,375	550	33	4
Connecticut	4,293	1,790	2,257	195	29	22	4,575	1,570	2,231	738	26	10
Middle Atlantic												
New York	24,913	10,912	12,723	1,175	26	77	27,647	9,687	12,665	5,213	45	37
New Jersey	16,906	7,334	8,769	708	17	78	17,420	5,878	8,864	2,624	32	22
Pennsylvania	39,733	18,637	19,107	1,830	60	99	37,490	12,958	18,307	6,019	97	109
East North Central												
Ohio	31,071	13,535	15,659	1,675	151	51	28,242	8,639	14,959	4,393	218	33
Indiana	15,894	6,919	7,896	933	113	33	14,256	4,142	7,626	2,258	204	26
Illinois	21,087	9,221	10,497	1,190	140	39	17,997	4,928	9,962	2,950	150	7
Michigan	5,604	2,292	2,940	319	27	26	4,936	1,416	2,716	748	45	11
Wisconsin	945	428	445	62	4	6	699	232	357	97	10	3
West North Central												
Minnesota	1,802	965	755	61	12	9	1,144	299	675	161	7	2
Iowa	3,952	1,741	1,980	197	28	6	3,229	904	1,849	441	30	5
Missouri	47,595	20,613	24,175	2,452	199	156	47,585	14,404	24,429	8,291	372	89
North Dakota	162	101	53	7	-	1	93	29	49	15	-	-
South Dakota	294	173	102	18	1	-	122	29	73	17	1	2
Nebraska	3,921	2,242	1,485	125	21	48	2,461	824	1,316	291	27	3
Kansas	15,811	6,181	8,651	850	115	14	15,143	4,175	8,612	2,209	133	14
South Atlantic												
Delaware	9,355	4,097	4,806	434	9	9	8,764	2,749	4,905	1,096	7	7
Maryland	64,958	27,329	34,585	2,841	71	132	69,460	23,934	35,377	9,921	133	95
District of Columbia	22,628	9,330	12,240	980	33	45	30,075	11,689	12,805	5,444	99	38
Virginia	173,118	74,676	90,303	7,727	228	184	189,142	68,942	92,290	26,941	432	537
West Virginia	12,009	6,484	4,980	416	30	99	8,826	3,070	4,656	1,035	45	20
North Carolina	147,594	60,355	81,209	5,684	164	182	160,687	55,490	83,905	20,518	369	405
South Carolina	178,161	63,747	107,966	6,186	161	101	187,688	53,611	109,596	23,580	372	529
Georgia	236,036	90,689	136,228	8,436	289	394	240,498	66,170	138,833	33,575	901	1,019
Florida	48,708	19,249	27,256	1,890	168	145	47,447	13,058	27,760	6,129	356	144
East South Central												
Kentucky	80,843	34,248	41,620	4,320	310	345	82,412	25,684	41,868	13,910	690	260
Tennessee	121,910	48,472	66,709	5,990	423	316	128,003	38,017	67,521	21,237	1,049	179
Alabama	187,150	70,605	108,085	7,690	486	284	194,996	56,115	108,850	28,977	979	75
Mississippi	200,967	75,241	116,041	8,945	444	296	205,676	56,618	117,303	30,307	1,000	448
West South Central												
Arkansas	90,371	34,262	50,592	4,928	330	259	83,400	20,588	50,284	11,788	591	149
Louisiana	153,992	55,804	90,874	6,463	375	476	162,620	43,467	92,468	25,566	787	332
Oklahoma	1,048	330	653	55	6	4	872	198	582	83	3	6
Texas	131,954	51,465	73,521	5,826	608	534	132,195	36,415	73,929	20,291	1,304	256
Mountain												
Montana	977	767	189	12	-	9	334	118	160	48	1	7
Idaho	93	60	23	7	3	-	57	22	23	10	2	-
Wyoming	582	457	98	21	3	3	206	74	97	28	4	3
Colorado	2,941	1,653	1,132	111	23	22	1,983	628	992	319	39	5
New Mexico	923	590	300	27	6	-	531	180	280	64	7	-
Arizona	1,113	946	140	17	10	-	135	34	81	16	4	-
Utah	315	209	93	6	1	6	132	37	73	15	1	6
Nevada	145	107	28	8	2	-	66	23	28	14	-	1
Pacific												
Washington	980	640	279	48	8	5	396	108	235	46	7	-

[Continued]

★ 2286 ★

Marital Status of Blacks by Divisions and States, 1890

[Continued]

Division and state	Negro population 15 years of age and over: 1890[1]											
	Male						Female					
	Total	Single	Married	Widowed	Divorced	Unknown	Total	Single	Married	Widowed	Divorced	Unknown
Oregon	599	401	174	17	4	3	301	72	172	59	4	3
California	4,637	2,483	1,889	218	38	9	3,377	880	1,874	579	38	6

Source: "Marital Condition of the Negro Population, by Divisions and States: 1910, 1900, and 1890." U.S. Bureau of the Census. *Negro Population, 1790- 1910.* Washington, D.C.: Government Printing Office, 1918, p. 265. *Notes:* 1. Exclusive of persons specially enumerated in Indian Territory and on Indian reservations for whom statistics of marital conditions are not available.

★ 2287 ★

Marital Status

Marital Status of Blacks by Divisions and States, 1900

Division and state	Negro population 15 years of age and over: 1900											
	Male						Female					
	Total	Single	Married	Widowed	Divorced	Unknown	Total	Single	Married	Widowed	Divorced	Unknown
United States	2,633,008	1,033,285	1,422,886	151,233	11,026	14,578	2,690,583	803,683	1,443,817	414,107	22,033	6,943
Geographic divisions												
New England	21,671	9,373	10,799	1,247	92	160	23,063	8,245	10,795	3,759	166	98
Middle Atlantic	121,613	55,329	59,166	6,037	267	814	125,612	45,502	60,370	18,859	417	464
East North Central	100,537	44,036	47,806	7,026	927	742	88,333	25,310	46,879	14,683	1,189	272
West North Central	85,716	37,559	41,147	5,791	643	576	80,602	24,017	41,606	13,787	909	283
South Atlantic	1,063,554	414,861	584,372	55,150	2,542	6,629	1,116,171	349,621	597,272	160,817	5,637	2,824
East South Central	733,058	280,308	401,997	44,558	3,316	2,879	752,786	215,626	406,331	121,931	7,176	1,722
West South Central	492,987	184,499	272,242	30,625	3,104	2,517	494,205	132,763	275,362	78,508	6,351	1,221
Mountain	7,626	4,176	2,781	431	71	167	4,973	1,277	2,671	876	104	45
Pacific	6,246	3,144	2,576	368	64	94	4,838	1,322	2,531	887	84	14
New England												
Maine	521	232	243	29	7	10	457	164	210	78	3	2
New Hampshire	264	128	108	21	3	4	274	127	102	38	6	1
Vermont	348	165	151	19	3	10	258	97	120	38	3	-
Massachusetts	12,001	5,317	5,936	606	36	106	12,371	4,343	5,851	2,035	60	82
Rhode Island	3,198	1,329	1,653	187	17	12	3,689	1,298	1,696	647	43	5
Connecticut	5,339	2,202	2,708	385	26	18	6,014	2,216	2,816	923	51	8
Middle Atlantic												
New York	36,600	16,651	17,971	1,760	85	133	41,595	15,831	18,603	6,905	160	96
New Jersey	25,086	10,509	12,921	1,222	47	387	27,046	9,378	13,456	3,908	78	226
Pennsylvania	59,927	28,169	28,274	3,055	135	294	56,971	20,293	28,311	8,046	179	142
East North Central												
Ohio	36,781	15,785	17,967	2,549	274	206	33,251	10,139	17,597	5,091	346	78
Indiana	21,708	9,113	10,414	1,668	323	190	19,582	5,511	10,280	3,350	380	61
Illinois	34,748	15,992	15,909	2,280	268	299	29,183	7,807	15,631	5,248	376	121
Michigan	6,153	2,565	3,045	455	55	33	5,472	1,569	2,949	871	72	11
Wisconsin	1,147	581	471	74	7	14	845	284	422	123	15	1
West North Central												
Minnesota	2,376	1,218	985	113	24	36	1,619	475	869	237	31	7
Iowa	5,209	2,258	2,487	338	76	50	4,148	1,146	2,346	581	48	27
Missouri	56,932	25,347	27,079	3,812	375	319	55,340	16,804	27,825	9,955	582	174
North Dakota	132	79	37	14	1	1	75	28	36	11	-	-
South Dakota	215	125	76	9	3	2	129	33	76	18	2	-
Nebraska	2,710	1,455	1,082	141	20	12	2,171	736	1,047	354	25	9
Kansas	18,142	7,077	9,401	1,364	144	156	17,120	4,795	9,407	2,631	221	66
South Atlantic												
Delaware	10,360	4,479	5,108	657	22	94	9,766	3,154	5,197	1,353	21	41
Maryland	74,958	31,674	38,287	4,147	137	713	77,865	26,768	39,252	11,129	248	468
District of Columbia	27,726	11,354	14,570	1,683	90	29	36,922	14,321	15,501	6,854	212	34
Virginia	190,739	81,296	97,886	10,250	426	881	202,573	71,612	100,042	29,680	688	551

[Continued]

★ 2287 ★

Marital Status of Blacks by Divisions and States, 1900

[Continued]

Division and state	Negro population 15 years of age and over: 1900											
	Male						Female					
	Total	Single	Married	Widowed	Divorced	Unknown	Total	Single	Married	Widowed	Divorced	Unknown
West Virginia	18,484	9,967	7,232	786	83	416	11,740	3,735	6,419	1,459	71	56
North Carolina	169,613	66,719	93,001	8,512	311	1,070	186,782	66,244	95,908	23,642	641	347
South Carolina	207,960	74,754	122,688	9,615	195	708	222,456	65,676	125,905	29,912	673	290
Georgia	287,619	102,919	166,418	15,319	908	2,055	301,937	81,524	170,025	47,117	2,389	882
Florida	76,095	31,699	39,182	4,181	370	663	66,130	16,587	39,023	9,671	694	155
East South Central												
Kentucky	93,156	39,400	46,140	6,397	608	611	93,409	28,756	46,805	16,400	1,109	339
Tennessee	145,671	58,572	76,069	9,520	654	856	149,819	44,854	77,070	25,923	1,444	528
Alabama	236,223	87,863	133,009	13,622	1,078	651	247,480	70,805	134,299	39,735	2,338	303
Mississippi	258,008	94,473	146,779	15,019	976	761	262,078	71,211	148,157	39,873	2,285	552
West South Central												
Arkansas	110,886	40,700	61,002	8,000	630	554	106,208	27,036	61,110	16,631	1,203	228
Louisiana	187,585	69,053	106,535	10,830	752	415	194,210	52,281	108,306	31,689	1,667	267
Oklahoma	17,598	6,512	9,647	1,211	120	108	15,692	3,821	9,553	2,036	214	68
Texas	176,918	68,234	95,058	10,584	1,602	1,440	178,095	49,625	96,393	28,152	3,267	658
Mountain												
Montana	771	489	223	43	6	10	477	129	235	99	13	1
Idaho	144	89	50	5	-	-	93	26	49	14	3	1
Wyoming	539	351	149	32	4	3	234	102	116	11	3	2
Colorado	3,602	1,520	1,706	235	35	106	3,185	789	1,700	595	64	37
New Mexico	878	508	289	39	13	29	427	94	251	73	9	-
Arizona	1,216	888	253	56	9	10	357	80	215	54	7	1
Utah	403	285	93	15	4	6	153	34	89	23	4	3
Nevada	73	46	18	6	-	3	47	23	16	7	1	-
Pacific												
Washington	598	388	173	27	9	1	710	186	411	101	9	3
Oregon	1,362	796	462	72	13	19	345	138	142	57	8	-
California	4,286	1,960	1,941	269	42	71	3,783	998	1,978	729	67	11

Source: "Marital Condition of the Negro Population, by Divisions and States: 1910, 1890, and 1890." U.S. Bureau of the Census. *Negro Population, 1790- 1915.* Washington, D.C.: Government Printing Office, 1918, p. 264.

★ 2288 ★

Marital Status

Marital Status of Blacks by Divisions and States, 1910

Division and state	Negro population 15 years of age and over: 1900											
	Male						Female					
	Total	Single	Married	Widowed	Divorced	Unknown	Total	Single	Married	Widowed	Divorced	Unknown
United States	3,059,312	1,083,472	1,749,228	189,970	20,146	16,496	3,103,344	823,996	1,775,949	459,831	33,286	10,282
Geographic divisions												
New England	24,955	10,345	12,893	1,454	177	86	25,274	8,121	12,641	4,235	236	41
Middle Atlantic	156,872	61,537	85,523	8,673	500	639	165,026	50,736	87,989	25,087	787	427
East North Central	122,237	47,401	63,243	8,950	1,767	876	109,124	26,571	62,020	18,294	1,881	358
West North Central	96,646	37,701	49,704	7,287	1,300	654	86,714	21,322	48,697	14,920	1,441	334
South Atlantic	1,213,070	431,943	701,837	67,831	4,277	7,182	1,260,627	355,312	716,955	176,715	7,363	4,282
East South Central	809,179	272,322	473,135	53,596	6,662	3,464	831,243	207,791	480,406	128,500	11,973	2,573
West South Central	613,200	211,696	352,097	40,899	5,098	3,410	607,240	149,980	356,996	88,954	9,136	2,174
Mountain	9,819	4,308	4,673	574	179	85	7,650	1,718	4,333	1,341	224	34
Pacific	13,334	6,219	6,123	706	186	100	10,446	2,445	5,912	1,785	245	59
New England												
Maine	554	250	249	46	9	-	495	192	217	74	11	1
New Hampshire	229	95	111	18	4	1	211	84	97	26	1	3
Vermont	1,054	765	248	27	14	-	320	84	199	29	8	-
Massachusetts	14,237	5,941	7,391	753	87	65	14,576	4,783	7,232	2,447	100	14

[Continued]

★ 2288 ★

Marital Status of Blacks by Divisions and States, 1910

[Continued]

Division and state	Negro population 15 years of age and over: 1900											
	Male						Female					
	Total	Single	Married	Widowed	Divorced	Unknown	Total	Single	Married	Widowed	Divorced	Unknown
Rhode Island	3,510	1,404	1,860	208	32	6	3,689	1,108	1,841	673	53	14
Connecticut	5,371	1,890	3,034	402	31	14	5,983	1,870	3,055	986	63	9
Middle Atlantic												
New York	51,428	21,151	27,435	2,533	164	145	56,435	18,268	28,577	9,206	292	142
New Jersey	32,831	12,228	18,649	1,775	88	91	34,868	10,302	19,256	5,112	109	89
Pennsylvania	72,613	28,158	39,439	4,365	248	403	73,673	22,166	40,156	10,769	386	196
East North Central												
Ohio	44,894	17,774	23,210	3,162	558	190	40,052	10,596	22,641	6,138	564	113
Indiana	23,848	9,045	12,327	1,969	418	89	21,818	5,238	12,204	3,851	487	38
Illinois	45,199	17,441	23,361	3,232	635	530	39,961	8,860	23,051	7,172	690	188
Michigan	7,087	2,610	3,794	498	130	55	6,194	1,520	3,575	968	114	17
Wisconsin	1,209	531	551	89	26	12	1,099	357	549	165	26	2
West North Central												
Minnesota	3,657	1,772	1,618	187	38	42	2,334	641	1,328	322	31	12
Iowa	6,222	2,350	3,221	462	143	46	4,943	1,112	3,008	677	128	18
Missouri	61,645	23,967	31,714	4,811	742	411	57,550	14,240	31,613	10,553	926	218
North Dakota	331	190	107	15	5	14	185	56	106	16	7	-
South Dakota	373	170	176	21	6	-	262	79	152	27	4	-
Nebraska	3,541	1,541	1,702	237	54	7	2,746	643	1,627	417	55	4
Kansas	20,877	7,711	11,166	1,554	312	134	18,694	4,551	10,863	2,908	290	82
South Atlantic												
Delaware	11,015	4,518	5,621	791	34	51	10,222	3,145	5,579	1,423	35	40
Maryland	77,191	30,141	41,495	5,090	264	201	78,668	24,469	42,607	11,103	337	152
District of Columbia	32,156	12,132	17,863	1,880	183	98	40,597	13,443	19,065	7,665	284	140
Virginia	202,055	79,328	109,723	11,782	682	540	210,968	66,902	112,351	30,200	1,123	392
West Virginia	27,317	13,144	12,487	1,330	182	174	18,184	4,615	11,304	2,011	204	50
North Carolina	191,986	69,483	111,770	9,514	427	792	208,993	66,965	114,810	25,765	803	650
South Carolina	225,020	75,462	137,488	10,880	271	919	244,703	68,178	141,327	33,694	659	845
Georgia	338,942	109,458	206,386	20,017	1,281	1,800	355,224	87,461	210,607	53,229	2,726	1,201
Florida	107,388	38,277	59,004	6,547	953	2,607	93,068	20,134	59,305	11,625	1,192	812
East South Central												
Kentucky	92,230	35,239	48,538	7,019	1,050	384	90,814	24,849	48,951	15,245	1,476	293
Tennessee	150,860	52,874	85,020	11,029	1,282	655	156,459	40,455	86,908	26,243	2,344	509
Alabama	269,025	88,577	160,594	17,101	2,011	742	281,202	70,466	162,347	43,684	4,222	483
Mississippi	297,064	95,632	178,983	18,447	2,319	1,683	302,768	72,021	182,200	43,328	3,931	1,288
West South Central												
Arkansas	139,798	45,591	81,279	10,857	1,190	881	134,532	30,748	81,917	19,385	1,889	593
Louisiana	217,006	76,748	125,446	12,684	967	1,161	222,527	57,639	127,984	34,101	2,069	734
Oklahoma	45,671	16,170	25,345	3,428	460	268	39,278	8,566	25,136	4,871	555	150
Texas	210,725	73,187	120,027	13,930	2,481	1,100	210,903	53,027	121,959	30,597	4,623	697
Mountain												
Montana	911	454	393	41	15	8	627	163	360	82	22	-
Idaho	350	179	142	17	10	2	209	61	113	30	3	2
Wyoming	1,408	988	364	29	16	11	560	152	306	76	26	-
Colorado	4,761	1,722	2,608	317	95	19	4,422	936	2,529	828	111	18
New Mexico	718	283	357	61	14	3	520	107	305	90	17	1
Arizona	827	313	434	54	16	10	734	167	402	141	22	2
Utah	606	263	269	34	8	32	365	81	221	42	10	11
Nevada	238	106	106	21	5	-	213	51	97	52	13	-
Pacific												
Washington	3,336	1,819	1,296	126	50	45	1,907	437	1,133	242	48	47
Oregon	815	425	333	42	13	2	490	99	290	88	13	-
California	9,183	3,975	4,494	538	123	53	8,049	1,909	4,489	1,455	184	12

Source: "Marital Condition of the Negro Population, by Divisions and States: 1910, 1900, and 1890." U.S. Bureau of the Census. *Negro Population, 1790- 1915.* Washington, D.C.: Government Printing Office, 1918, p. 263.

★ 2289 ★

Marital Status

Marital Status of Blacks in Cities of 100,000 or More, 1890

City	Male						Female					
	Total	Single	Married	Widowed	Divorced	Marital condition unknown	Total	Single	Married	Widowed	Divorced	Marital condition unknown
Albany, N.Y.[1]	-	-	-	-	-	-	-	-	-	-	-	-
Atlanta, Ga.[1]	-	-	-	-	-	-	-	-	-	-	-	-
Baltimore, Md.	20,159	7,720	11,430	974	27	8	28,174	10,606	12,396	5,055	87	30
Birmingham, Ala.[1]	-	-	-	-	-	-	-	-	-	-	-	-
Boston, Mass.	3,362	1,643	1,581	128	2	8	3,101	1,045	1,466	572	11	7
Bridgeport, Conn.[1]	-	-	-	-	-	-	-	-	-	-	-	-
Buffalo, N.Y.	438	165	247	24	-	2	422	147	214	58	-	-
Cambridge, Mass.[1]	-	-	-	-	-	-	-	-	-	-	-	-
Chicago, Ill.	6,772	3,449	3,024	241	30	28	5,084	1,418	2,723	883	56	4
Cincinnati, Ohio	4,438	1,998	2,234	192	7	7	4,559	1,292	2,274	963	25	5
Cleveland, Ohio	1,278	584	624	57	7	6	1,070	313	565	178	11	3
Columbus, Ohio[1]	-	-	-	-	-	-	-	-	-	-	-	-
Dayton, Ohio[1]	-	-	-	-	-	-	-	-	-	-	-	-
Denver, Colo.	1,403	789	548	53	6	7	1,041	337	527	162	14	1
Detroit, Mich.	1,305	534	694	72	3	2	1,318	398	662	247	4	7
Fall River, Mass.[1]	-	-	-	-	-	-	-	-	-	-	-	-
Grand Rapids, Mich.[1]	-	-	-	-	-	-	-	-	-	-	-	-
Indianapolis, Ind.	3,285	1,380	1,688	191	22	4	3,282	930	1,671	619	57	5
Jersey City, N.J.	763	290	444	25	3	1	816	257	437	118	4	-
Kansas City, Mo.	5,173	2,455	2,477	219	12	10	5,174	1,627	2,636	844	62	5
Los Angeles, Cal.[1]	-	-	-	-	-	-	-	-	-	-	-	-
Louisville, Ky.	9,619	4,193	4,779	573	59	15	11,349	3,639	5,008	2,545	149	8
Lowell, Mass.[1]	-	-	-	-	-	-	-	-	-	-	-	-
Memphis, Tenn.[1]	-	-	-	-	-	-	-	-	-	-	-	-
Milwaukee, Wis.	202	97	94	7	-	4	140	40	76	21	3	-
Minneapolis, Minn.	669	377	253	26	6	7	407	95	243	67	2	-
Nashville, Tenn.[1]	-	-	-	-	-	-	-	-	-	-	-	-
New Haven, Conn.[1]	-	-	-	-	-	-	-	-	-	-	-	-
New Orleans, La.	18,577	6,683	10,959	890	29	16	25,186	7,334	11,740	5,955	139	18
New York, N.Y.[2]	11,466	4,904	6,043	504	6	9	14,912	5,337	6,432	3,108	15	20
Manhattan Borough	-	-	-	-	-	-	-	-	-	-	-	-
Bronx Borough	-	-	-	-	-	-	-	-	-	-	-	-
Brooklyn Borough	3,240	1,271	1,815	148	2	4	4,402	1,551	1,929	906	3	13
Queens Borough	-	-	-	-	-	-	-	-	-	-	-	-
Richmond Borough	-	-	-	-	-	-	-	-	-	-	-	-
Newark, N.J.	1,357	485	814	57	1	-	1,685	561	828	283	9	4
Oakland, Ca.[1]	-	-	-	-	-	-	-	-	-	-	-	-
Omaha, Nebr.	2,101	1,226	759	61	13	42	1,351	489	678	170	12	2
Paterson, N.J.[1]	-	-	-	-	-	-	-	-	-	-	-	-
Philadelphia, Pa.	13,768	6,041	7,042	603	15	67	16,606	6,267	7,154	3,078	35	72
Pittsburgh, Pa.[3]	4,561	2,398	1,977	174	6	6	3,155	909	1,737	492	16	1
Portland, Oreg.[1]	-	-	-	-	-	-	-	-	-	-	-	-
Providence, R.I.	1,343	477	780	80	5	1	1,570	483	775	291	19	2
Richmond, Va.[1]	-	-	-	-	-	-	-	-	-	-	-	-
Rochester, N.Y.	183	84	91	7	-	1	239	82	98	57	-	2
St. Louis, Mo.	9,488	4,009	4,901	491	35	52	10,071	2,777	5,002	2,201	72	19
St. Paul, Minn.	735	365	341	24	4	1	502	127	300	71	3	1
San Francisco, Cal.	807	448	313	38	6	2	624	160	307	149	7	1

[Continued]

★ 2289 ★

Marital Status of Blacks in Cities of 100,000 or More, 1890

[Continued]

City	Male						Female					
	Total	Single	Married	Widowed	Divorced	Marital condition unknown	Total	Single	Married	Widowed	Divorced	Marital condition unknown
Scranton, Pa.[1]	-	-	-	-	-	-	-	-	-	-	-	-
Seattle, Wash.[1]	-	-	-	-	-	-	-	-	-	-	-	-
Spokane, Wash.[1]	-	-	-	-	-	-	-	-	-	-	-	-
Syracuse, N.Y.[1]	-	-	-	-	-	-	-	-	-	-	-	-
Toledo, Ohio[1]	-	-	-	-	-	-	-	-	-	-	-	-
Washington, D.C.	22,628	9,330	12,240	980	33	45	30,075	11,689	12,805	5,444	99	38
Worcester, Mass.[1]	-	-	-	-	-	-	-	-	-	-	-	-

Source: "Marital Condition of the Negro Population, by Cities of 100,000 or More Inhabitants: 1910, 1900, and 1890." U.S. Bureau of the Census. *Negro Population, 1790-1915* Washington, D.C.: Government Printing Office, 1918, p. 275. *Notes:* 1. Population less than 100,000 in 1890. 2. Figures for 1890 are for the combined population of New York and Brooklyn cities as constituted at that census; statistics of marital condition of the population of the present area of New York city are not available. 3. Includes population of Allegheny.

★ 2290 ★

Marital Status

Marital Status of Blacks in Cities of 100,000 or More, 1900

City	NEGRO POPULATION 15 YEARS OF AGE AND OVER: 1900											
	Male						Female					
	Total	Single	Married	Widowed	Divorced	Marital condition unknown	Total	Single	Married	Widowed	Divorced	Marital condition unknown
Albany, N.Y.[1]	...	...	...	...	...	...	...	...	...	...	...	...
Atlanta, Ga.	...	...	...	...	...	...	...	...	...	...	...	...
Baltimore, Md.	25,510	10,334	13,510	1,510	57	99	33,438	12,791	14,461	5,929	142	115
Birmingham, Ala.	...	...	...	...	...	...	...	...	...	...	...	...
Boston, Mass.	4,885	2,305	2,286	225	10	59	4,467	1,417	2,178	817	23	32
Bridgeport, Conn.[1]	...	...	...	...	...	...	...	...	...	...	...	...
Buffalo, N.Y.	741	347	352	39	1	2	643	194	342	99	8	...
Cambridge, Mass.[1]	...	...	...	...	...	...	...	...	...	...	...	...
Chicago, Ill.	13,783	6,757	6,072	801	79	74	11,622	2,995	5,996	2,461	142	28
Cincinnati, Ohio	5,661	2,460	2,830	333	28	10	5,752	1,698	2,913	1,079	56	6
Cleveland, Ohio	2,626	1,232	1,236	132	16	10	2,193	637	1,214	311	30	1
Columbus, Ohio	3,416	1,672	1,508	188	19	29	2,926	990	1,410	482	32	12
Dayton, Ohio[1]	...	...	...	...	...	...	...	...	...	...	...	...
Denver, Colo.	1,488	611	726	110	17	24	1,621	447	797	338	29	10
Detroit, Mich.	1,563	646	811	95	9	2	1,630	506	801	308	13	2
Fall River, Mass.	90	42	47	1	...	...	172	78	66	26	...	2
Grand Rapids, Mich.[1]	...	...	...	...	...	...	...	...	...	...	...	...
Indianapolis, Ind.	6,041	2,322	3,048	449	112	110	6,092	1,604	3,112	1,163	186	27
Jersey City, N.J.	1,408	557	781	64	1	5	1,394	381	784	220	8	1
Kansas City, Mo.	6,764	2,910	3,315	456	78	5	7,097	2,051	3,450	1,451	139	6
Los Angeles, Cal.	731	262	415	35	10	9	804	198	429	160	14	3
Louisville, Ky.	14,557	6,685	6,595	1,066	113	98	15,797	5,013	6,896	3,581	260	47
Lowell, Mass.[1]	...	...	...	...	...	...	...	...	...	...	...	...
Memphis, Tenn.	17,420	8,106	7,638	1,435	82	159	18,366	5,711	7,936	4,378	212	129
Milwaukee, Wis.	398	205	171	10	1	11	313	99	156	47	10	1

[Continued]

★ 2290 ★

Marital Status of Blacks in Cities of 100,000 or More, 1900

[Continued]

City	NEGRO POPULATION 15 YEARS OF AGE AND OVER: 1900											
	Male						Female					
	Total	Single	Married	Widowed	Divorced	Marital condition unknown	Total	Single	Married	Widowed	Divorced	Marital condition unknown
Minneapolis, Minn.	690	319	324	37	9	1	550	146	292	97	15	...
Nashville, Tenn.[1]	...	...	...	...	...	...	...	...	...	...	...	...
New Haven, Conn.	1,011	359	562	83	5	2	1,165	341	587	226	11	...
New Orleans, La.	23,795	8,919	13,279	1,489	84	24	30,866	8,978	14,225	7,386	248	29
New York, N.Y.	21,401	9,380	11,067	865	45	44	27,263	10,376	11,968	4,771	96	52
Manhattan Borough] Bronx Borough	14,094	6,211	7,277	534	31	41	17,524	6,508	7,823	3,080	64	49
Brooklyn Borough	6,134	2,674	3,175	273	9	3	8,162	3,206	3,476	1,452	25	3
Queens Borough[2]	...	...	...	...	...	...	...	...	...	...	...	...
Richmond Borough[2]	...	...	...	...	...	...	...	...	...	...	...	...
Newark, N.J.	2,254	822	1,330	91	5	6	2,799	893	1,426	470	8	2
Oakland, Ca.[1]	...	...	...	...	...	...	...	...	...	...	...	...
Omaha, Nebr.	1,449	732	632	70	12	3	1,305	417	623	252	12	1
Paterson, N.J.	400	142	234	20	1	3	514	180	269	59	5	1
Philadelphia, Pa.	22,636	10,245	11,223	1,034	29	105	26,717	10,543	11,980	4,058	59	77
Pittsburgh, Pa.[3]	8,845	4,387	3,992	412	14	40	6,689	1,939	3,806	900	35	9
Portland, Oreg.	...	...	...	...	...	...	...	...	...	...	...	...
Providence, R.I.	1,720	651	944	112	9	4	1,942	617	936	360	28	1
Richmond, Va.[1]	...	...	...	...	...	...	...	...	...	...	...	...
Rochester, N.Y.	228	107	106	13	2	...	233	82	106	43	2	...
St. Louis, Mo.	13,603	5,972	6,619	862	65	85	14,089	4,040	6,899	2,996	105	49
St. Paul, Minn.	1,146	596	466	44	9	31	727	195	404	109	12	7
San Francisco, Cal.	690	325	279	49	6	31	628	183	295	131	17	2
Scranton, Pa.	227	94	115	12	4	3	171	35	113	21	1	1
Seattle, Wash.[1]	...	...	...	...	...	...	...	...	...	...	...	...
Spokane, Wash.[1]	...	...	...	...	...	...	...	...	...	...	...	...
Syracuse, N.Y.	390	138	234	17	1	...	421	134	220	61	6	...
Toledo, Ohio	669	255	359	45	4	6	700	223	352	115	7	3
Washington, D.C.	27,726	11,354	14,570	1,683	90	29	36,922	14,321	15,501	6,854	212	34
Worcester, Mass.	401	167	215	17	2	...	436	140	221	70	5	...

Source: "Marital Condition of the Negro Population, by Cities of 100,000 or More Inhabitants: 1910, 1900, and 1890." U.S. Bureau of the Census. *Negro Population, 1790-1915* Washington, D.C.: Government Printing Office, 1918, p. 274. *Notes:* 1. Population less than 100,000 in 1900. 2. Data not available for 1900. 3. Includes population of Allegheny.

★ 2291 ★

Marital Status

Marital Status of Blacks in Cities of 100,000 or More, 1910

City	Male						Female					
	Total	Single	Married	Widowed	Divorced	Marital condition unknown	Total	Single	Married	Widowed	Divorced	Marital condition unknown
Albany, N.Y.	415	171	208	32	4	-	445	146	214	82	3	-
Atlanta, Ga.	16,600	5,776	9,736	1,024	46	18	21,789	5,597	10,834	5,221	121	16
Baltimore, Md.	29,982	11,651	16,045	2,060	146	80	35,572	12,170	17,095	6,044	197	66
Birmingham, Ala.	19,092	6,436	10,821	1,679	109	47	19,706	3,964	11,103	4,387	234	18
Boston, Mass.	5,482	2,359	2,778	303	37	5	5,572	1,744	2,710	1,069	47	2

[Continued]

★ 2291 ★

Marital Status of Blacks in Cities of 100,000 or More, 1910

[Continued]

City	Male						Female					
	Total	Single	Married	Widowed	Divorced	Marital condition unknown	Total	Single	Married	Widowed	Divorced	Marital condition unknown
Bridgeport, Conn.	514	206	272	33	2	1	519	140	282	89	5	3
Buffalo, N.Y.	791	362	366	53	8	2	696	223	363	107	1	2
Cambridge, Mass.	1,585	520	964	91	7	3	1,814	539	1,000	266	9	-
Chicago, Ill.	19,372	7,631	10,076	1,232	279	154	17,962	3,800	9,978	3,746	355	83
Cincinnati, Ohio	8,246	3,268	4,284	550	81	63	8,002	2,054	4,305	1,482	126	35
Cleveland, Ohio	3,630	1,350	2,017	194	53	16	3,361	819	1,965	513	61	3
Columbus, Ohio	5,629	2,429	2,774	347	66	13	4,696	1,215	2,687	699	82	13
Dayton, Ohio	1,976	713	1,085	138	36	4	1,876	468	1,096	280	30	2
Denver, Colo.	2,203	787	1,233	128	48	7	2,278	504	1,249	447	72	6
Detroit, Mich.	2,465	938	1,343	130	27	27	2,261	545	1,286	388	34	8
Fall River, Mass.	143	59	77	7	-	-	146	43	69	33	1	-
Grand Rapids, Mich.	291	96	164	23	2	6	264	59	158	40	5	2
Indianapolis, Ind.	8,521	3,093	4,576	690	142	20	8,692	1,963	4,723	1,809	189	8
Jersey City, N.J.	2,335	861	1,353	111	7	3	2,206	500	1,344	352	7	3
Kansas City, Mo.	10,107	3,818	5,251	727	168	143	9,782	2,275	5,295	1,920	246	46
Los Angeles, Cal.	2,921	1,002	1,747	144	25	3	3,070	668	1,783	568	47	4
Louisville, Ky.	15,772	6,399	7,780	1,288	224	81	16,853	4,612	8,170	3,638	361	72
Lowell, Mass.	52	22	24	5	1	-	57	24	19	12	1	1
Memphis, Tenn.	20,012	7,371	10,586	1,633	366	56	21,510	4,951	11,234	4,587	706	32
Milwaukee, Wis.	422	175	203	29	9	6	431	144	198	76	13	-
Minneapolis, Minn.	1,321	588	601	83	14	35	907	235	516	130	16	10
Nashville, Tenn.	11,933	4,140	6,584	1,067	137	5	15,757	4,222	7,025	4,154	348	8
New Haven, Conn.	1,335	461	767	98	6	3	1,473	400	775	284	13	1
New Orleans, La.	29,692	10,783	16,879	1,634	113	283	36,392	10,179	18,100	7,597	293	223
New York, N.Y.	34,269	13,335	19,196	1,540	101	97	40,792	13,174	20,466	6,844	206	102
Manhattan Borough	23,495	9,472	12,885	979	74	85	27,348	8,800	13,688	4,612	159	89
Bronx Borough	1,436	460	883	87	2	4	1,700	493	927	273	5	2
Brooklyn Borough	7,869	2,869	4,573	398	21	8	9,950	3,251	4,985	1,665	39	10
Queens Borough	1,079	395	633	48	3	-	1,336	459	643	232	2	-
Richmond Borough	390	139	222	28	1	-	458	171	223	62	1	1
Newark, N.J.	3,414	1,115	2,117	163	10	9	3,848	1,045	2,196	591	11	5
Oakland, Ca.	1,357	617	650	72	17	1	1,168	241	665	231	29	2
Omaha, Nebr.	2,044	871	999	136	36	2	1,698	404	986	270	35	3
Paterson, N.J.	512	169	313	27	-	3	652	193	367	84	4	4
Philadelphia, Pa.	30,976	11,360	17,727	1,713	86	90	35,700	11,156	18,678	5,726	145	85
Pittsburgh, Pa.	10,374	4,070	5,594	645	32	33	9,224	2,313	5,547	1,269	80	15
Portland, Oreg.	550	263	253	26	8	-	376	65	236	63	12	-
Providence, R.I.	1,978	768	1,068	121	20	1	2,125	600	1,062	418	43	2
Richmond, Va.	15,778	6,552	8,229	907	62	28	19,210	6,842	8,459	3,752	121	36
Rochester, N.Y.	346	138	187	19	2	-	366	124	198	40	2	2
St. Louis, Mo.	18,318	7,271	9,415	1,421	169	42	17,689	3,916	9,607	3,860	276	30
St. Paul, Minn.	1,681	838	749	75	16	3	1,010	270	587	141	11	1
San Francisco, Cal.	911	526	308	55	13	9	504	152	254	76	22	-
Scranton, Pa.	242	114	117	11	-	-	200	64	107	28	-	1
Seattle, Wash.	1,256	677	498	35	17	29	776	175	446	102	17	36
Spokane, Wash.	339	122	196	15	5	1	283	46	193	35	7	2
Syracuse, N.Y.	478	192	250	28	7	1	434	124	239	68	2	1
Toledo, Ohio	790	306	412	56	15	1	756	212	432	100	11	1

[Continued]

★ 2291 ★

Marital Status of Blacks in Cities of 100,000 or More, 1910

[Continued]

City	Male						Female					
	Total	Single	Married	Widowed	Divorced	Marital condition unknown	Total	Single	Married	Widowed	Divorced	Marital condition unknown
Washington, D.C.	32,156	12,132	17,863	1,880	183	98	40,597	13,443	19,065	7,665	284	140
Worcester, Mass.	435	156	250	26	2	1	508	160	249	97	2	-

Source: "Marital Condition of the Negro Population, by Cities of 100,000 or More Inhabitants: 1910, 1900, and 1890." U.S. Bureau of the Census. *Negro Population, 1790-1915.* Washington, D.C.: Government Printing Office, 1918, p. 273.

★ 2292 ★

Marital Status

Marital Status of Blacks of the Population, 1890-1910 - I

Age period and marital class	Negro population											
	Male			Female			Percentage distribution by marital class					
							Male			Female		
	1910	1900	1890[1]	1910	1900	1890[1]	1910	1900	1890	1910	1900	1890
All ages	4,885,881	4,386,547	3,725,561	4,941,882	4,447,447	3,744,479	100.0	100.0	100.0	100.0	100.0	100.0
Single	2,909,902	2,786,580	2,448,567	2,661,778	2,559,682	2,220,946	59.6	63.5	65.7	53.9	57.6	59.3
Married, widowed, or divorced	1,959,483	1,585,312	1,272,421	2,269,822	1,880,727	1,518,605	40.1	36.1	34.2	45.9	42.3	40.5
Married	1,749,359	1,423,039	1,175,525	1,776,643	1,444,533	1,187,706	35.8	32.4	31.6	36.0	32.5	31.7
Widowed	189,976	151,245	91,683	459,889	414,151	320,205	3.9	3.4	2.5	9.3	9.3	8.6
Divorced	20,148	11,028	5,213	33,290	22,043	10,694	0.4	0.3	0.1	0.7	0.5	0.3
Unknown	16,496	14,655	4,573	10,282	7,038	4,928	0.3	0.3	0.1	0.2	0.2	0.1
Under 15 years	1,826,569	1,753,539	1,605,840	1,838,538	1,756,864	1,568,929	100.0	100.0	100.0	100.0	100.0	100.0
Single	1,826,430	1,753,295	1,605,803	1,837,782	1,755,999	1,568,632	100.0	100.0	100.0	100.0	100.0	100.0
Married, widowed, or divorced	139	167	13	756	770	289	[2]	[2]	[2]	[2]	[2]	[2]
Married	131	153	12	694	716	272	[2]	[2]	[2]	[2]	[2]	[2]
Widowed	6	12	-	58	44	11	[2]	[2]	[2]	[2]	[2]	[2]
Divorced	2	2	1	4	10	6	[2]	[2]	[2]	[2]	[2]	[2]
Unknown	-	77	24	-	95	8	-	[2]	[2]	-	[2]	[2]
15 years and over	3,059,312	2,633,008	2,119,721	3,103,344	2,690,583	2,175,550	100.0	100.0	100.0	100.0	100.0	100.0
Single	1,083,472	1,033,285	842,764	823,996	803,683	652,314	35.4	39.2	39.8	26.6	29.9	30.0
Married, widowed, or divorced	1,959,344	1,585,145	1,272,408	2,269,066	1,879,957	1,518,316	64.0	60.2	60.0	73.1	69.9	69.8
Married	1,749,228	1,422,886	1,175,513	1,775,949	1,443,817	1,187,434	57.2	54.0	55.5	57.2	53.7	54.6
Widowed	189,970	151,233	91,683	459,831	414,107	320,194	6.2	5.7	4.3	14.8	15.4	14.7
Divorced	20,146	11,026	5,212	33,286	22,033	10,688	0.7	0.4	0.2	1.1	0.8	0.5
Unknown	16,496	14,578	4,549	10,282	6,943	4,920	0.5	0.6	0.2	0.3	0.3	0.2

Source: "Marital Status of the Negro Population: 1910, 1900, 1890." *Negro Population, 1790-1915.* Washington, D.C.: Government Printing Office, p. 236. *Notes:* 1. Exclusive of 10,042 males and 8,594 females specially enumerated in 1890 in Indian Territory and on Indian reservations, for whom statistics of marital conditions are not available. 2. Less than one-tenth of 1 per cent.

★ 2293 ★

Marital Status

Marital Status of Blacks of the Population, 1890-1910 - II

Age period and marital class	Negro population Excess of males or females					
	1910		1900		1890	
	Of male	Of female	Of male	Of female	Of male	Of female
All ages	-	56,001	-	60,900	-	18,918
Single	248,124	-	226,898	-	227,621	-
Married, widowed, or divorced	-	310,339	-	295,415	-	246,184
Married	-	27,284	-	21,494	-	12,181
Widowed	-	269,913	-	262,906	-	228,522
Divorced	-	13,142	-	11,015	-	5,481
Unknown	6,214	-	7,617	-	-	355
Under 15 years	-	11,969	-	3,325	36,911	-
Single	-	11,352	-	2,704	37,171	-
Married, widowed, or divorced	-	617	-	603	-	276
Married	-	563	-	563	-	260
Widowed	-	52	-	32	-	11
Divorced	-	2	-	8	-	5
Unknown	-	-	-	18	16	-
15 years and over	-	44,032	-	57,575	-	55,829
Single	259,476	-	229,602	-	190,450	-
Married, widowed, or divorced	-	309,722	-	294,812	-	245,908
Married	-	26,721	-	20,931	-	11,921
Widowed	-	269,861	-	262,874	-	228,511
Divorced	-	13,140	-	11,007	-	5,476
Unknown	6,214	-	7,635	-	-	371

Source: "Marital Status of the Negro Population: 1910, 1900, 1890." *Negro Population, 1790-1915.* Washington, D.C.: Government Printing Office, p. 236.

★ 2294 ★

Marital Status

Marital Status of Men and Women in Urban and Rural Communities and Classes of Cities, 1910 - I

Section and class of community	Negro population 15 years of age and over: 1910			
	Total		Single	
	Male	Female	Male	Female
United States				
	Number			
Rural communities	2,111,707	2,045,019	732,874	531,004
Urban communities	947,605	1,058,325	350,598	292,992
Cities of 2,500 to 25,000	351,825	396,547	126,922	110,146
Cities of 25,000 to 100,000	214,737	239,683	78,619	63,924
Cities of 100,000 and over	381,043	422,095	145,057	118,922
The South				
Rural communities	2,015,851	1,970,640	692,530	510,627
Urban communities	619,598	728,470	223,431	202,456
Cities of 2,500 to 25,000	271,402	317,617	95,469	87,702
Cities of 25,000 to 100,000	157,179	183,467	56,722	48,774
Cities of 100,000 and over	191,017	227,386	71,240	65,980
The North				
Rural communities	89,891	71,583	37,004	19,731
Urban communities	310,819	314,555	119,980	87,019
Cities of 2,500 to 25,000	75,678	74,726	29,411	21,391
Cities of 25,000 to 100,000	54,652	53,575	20,746	14,537
Cities of 100,000 and over	180,489	186,254	69,823	51,091
The West				
Rural communities	5,965	2,796	3,340	646
Urban communities	17,188	15,300	7,187	3,517
Cities of 2,500 to 25,000	4,745	4,204	2,042	1,053
Cities of 25,000 to 100,000	2,906	2,641	1,151	613
Cities of 100,000 and over	9,537	8,455	3,994	1,851
	Percentage distribution by marital class			
United States				
Rural communities	100.0	100.0	34.7	26.0
Urban communities	100.0	100.0	37.0	27.7
Cities of 2,500 to 25,000	100.0	100.0	36.1	27.8
Cities of 25,000 to 100,000	100.0	100.0	36.6	26.7
Cities of 100,000 and over	100.0	100.0	38.1	28.2
The South				
Rural communities	100.0	100.0	34.4	25.9
Urban communities	100.0	100.0	36.1	27.8
Cities of 2,500 to 25,000	100.0	100.0	35.2	27.6
Cities of 25,000 to 100,000	100.0	100.0	36.1	26.6

[Continued]

★ 2294 ★

Marital Status of Men and Women in Urban and Rural Communities and Classes of Cities, 1910 - I

[Continued]

Section and class of community	Negro population 15 years of age and over: 1910			
	Total		Single	
	Male	Female	Male	Female
Cities of 100,000 and over	100.0	100.0	37.3	29.0
The North				
Rural communities	100.0	100.0	41.2	27.6
Urban communities	100.0	100.0	38.6	27.7
Cities of 2,500 to 25,000	100.0	100.0	38.9	28.6
Cities of 25,000 to 100,000	100.0	100.0	38.0	27.1
Cities of 100,000 and over	100.0	100.0	38.7	27.4
The West				
Rural communities	100.0	100.0	56.0	23.1
Urban communities	100.0	100.0	41.8	23.0
Cities of 2,500 to 25,000	100.0	100.0	43.0	25.0
Cities of 25,000 to 100,000	100.0	100.0	39.6	23.2
Cities of 100,000 and over	100.0	100.0	41.9	21.9

Source: "Marital Conditions of the Negro Population 15 Years of Age and Over, in Urban and Rural Communities and in Classes of Cities: 1910." *Negro Population, 1790-1915.* Washington, D.C.: Government Printing Office, 1918, p. 257.

★ 2295 ★

Marital Status

Marital Status of Men and Women in Urban and Rural Communities and Classes of Cities, 1910 - II

Section and class of community	Negro population 15 years of age and over: 1910									
	Married, widowed, or divorced								Marital condition unknown	
	Total		Married		Widowed		Divorced			
	Male	Female	Male	Female	Male	Female	Male	Female	Male	Female
United States										
	Number									
Rural communities	1,368,587	1,507,408	1,229,488	1,231,770	126,895	257,649	12,204	17,989	10,246	6,607
Urban communities	590,757	761,658	519,740	544,179	63,075	202,182	7,942	15,297	6,250	3,675
Cities of 2,500 to 25,000	221,404	284,740	194,605	203,764	23,672	74,289	3,127	6,687	3,499	1,661
Cities of 25,000 to 100,000	134,900	174,880	118,150	124,800	14,899	46,413	1,851	3,667	1,218	879
Cities of 100,000 and over	234,453	302,038	206,985	215,615	24,504	81,480	2,964	4,943	1,533	1,135
The South										
Rural communities	1,313,831	1,453,662	1,182,780	1,187,985	119,789	248,298	11,262	17,379	9,490	6,351
Urban communities	391,601	523,336	344,289	366,372	42,537	145,871	4,775	11,093	4,566	2,678
Cities of 2,500 to 25,000	172,958	228,549	152,527	161,633	18,240	61,390	2,191	5,526	2,975	1,366
Cities of 25,000 to 100,000	99,562	133,992	87,239	93,654	11,125	37,436	1,198	2,902	895	701
Cities of 100,000 and over	119,081	160,795	104,523	111,085	13,172	47,045	1,386	2,665	696	611

[Continued]

★ 2295 ★

Marital Status of Men and Women in Urban and Rural Communities and Classes of Cities, 1910 - II

[Continued]

Section and class of community	Negro population 15 years of age and over: 1910									
	Married, widowed, or divorced								Marital condition unknown	
	Total		Married		Widowed		Divorced			
	Male	Female	Male	Female	Male	Female	Male	Female	Male	Female
The North										
Rural communities	52,168	51,602	44,557	42,102	6,760	8,952	851	548	719	250
Urban communities	189,303	226,626	166,806	169,245	19,604	53,584	2,893	3,797	1,536	910
Cities of 2,500 to 25,000	45,772	53,050	39,783	39,879	5,146	12,154	843	1,017	495	285
Cities of 25,000 to 100,000	33,652	38,887	29,446	29,662	3,601	8,517	605	708	254	151
Cities of 100,000 and over	109,879	134,689	97,577	99,704	10,857	32,913	1,445	2,072	787	474
The West										
Rural communities	2,588	2,144	2,151	1,683	346	399	91	62	37	6
Urban communities	9,853	11,696	8,645	8,562	934	2,727	274	407	148	87
Cities of 2,500 to 25,000	2,674	3,141	2,295	2,252	286	745	93	144	29	10
Cities of 25,000 to 100,000	1,686	2,001	1,465	1,484	173	460	48	57	69	27
Cities of 100,000 and over	5,493	6,554	4,885	4,826	475	1,522	133	206	50	50
	Percentage distribution by marital class									
United States										
Rural communities	64.8	73.7	58.2	60.2	6.0	12.6	0.6	0.9	0.5	0.3
Urban communities	62.3	72.0	54.8	51.4	6.7	19.1	0.8	1.4	0.7	0.3
Cities of 2,500 to 25,000	62.9	71.8	55.3	51.4	6.7	18.7	0.9	1.7	1.0	0.4
Cities of 25,000 to 100,000	62.8	73.0	55.0	52.1	6.9	19.4	0.9	1.5	0.6	0.4
Cities of 100,000 and over	61.5	71.6	54.3	51.1	6.4	19.3	0.8	1.2	0.4	0.3
The South										
Rural communities	65.2	73.8	58.7	60.3	5.9	12.6	0.6	0.9	0.5	0.3
Urban communities	63.2	71.8	55.6	50.3	6.9	20.0	0.8	1.5	0.7	0.4
Cities of 2,500 to 25,000	63.7	72.0	56.2	50.9	6.7	19.3	0.8	1.7	1.1	0.4
Cities of 25,000 to 100,000	63.3	73.0	55.5	51.0	7.1	20.4	0.8	1.6	0.6	0.4
Cities of 100,000 and over	62.3	70.7	54.7	48.9	6.9	20.7	0.7	1.2	0.4	0.3
The North										
Rural communities	58.0	72.1	49.6	58.8	7.5	12.5	0.9	0.8	0.8	0.3
Urban communities	60.9	72.0	53.7	53.8	6.3	17.0	0.9	1.2	0.5	0.3
Cities of 2,500 to 25,000	60.5	71.0	52.6	53.4	6.8	16.3	1.1	1.4	0.7	0.4
Cities of 25,000 to 100,000	61.6	72.6	53.9	55.4	6.6	15.9	1.1	1.3	0.5	0.3
Cities of 100,000 and over	60.9	72.3	54.1	53.5	6.0	17.7	0.8	1.1	0.4	0.3
The West										
Rural communities	43.4	76.7	36.1	60.2	5.8	14.3	1.5	2.2	0.6	0.2
Urban communities	57.3	76.4	50.3	56.0	5.4	17.8	1.6	2.7	0.9	0.6
Cities of 2,500 to 25,000	56.4	74.7	48.4	53.6	6.0	17.7	2.0	3.4	0.6	0.2
Cities of 25,000 to 100,000	58.0	75.8	50.4	56.2	6.0	17.4	1.7	2.2	2.4	1.0
Cities of 100,000 and over	57.6	77.5	51.2	57.1	5.0	18.0	1.4	2.4	0.5	0.6

Source: "Marital Conditions of the Negro Population 15 Years of Age and Over, in Urban and Rural Communities and in Classes of Cities: 1910." *Negro Population, 1790-1915*. Washington, D.C.: Government Printing Office, 1918, p. 257.

★ 2296 ★

Marital Status

Marital Status of Men and Women in Urban and Rural Communities, 1910 - I

Age period and section	Number									
	Total		Single		Married		Widowed		Divorced	
	Male	Female	Male	Female	Male	Female	Male	Female	Male	Female
Urban communities										
15 years and over										
United States	947,605	1,058,325	350,598	292,992	519,740	544,179	63,075	202,182	7,942	15,297
The South	619,598	728,470	223,431	202,456	344,289	366,372	42,537	145,871	4,775	11,093
The North	310,819	314,555	119,980	87,019	166,806	169,245	19,604	53,584	2,893	3,797
The West	17,188	15,300	7,187	3,517	8,645	8,562	934	2,727	274	407
15 to 24 years										
United States	253,239	325,060	202,073	198,013	46,903	112,276	1,813	10,459	579	2,811
The South	180,588	237,458	141,987	142,473	35,194	82,838	1,470	8,772	422	2,231
The North	69,493	83,941	57,400	53,377	11,274	28,112	329	1,595	143	512
The West	3,158	3,661	2,686	2,163	435	1,326	14	92	14	68
25 to 44 years										
United States	477,609	507,765	127,009	81,433	319,827	334,343	23,594	80,998	5,088	10,110
The South	298,366	337,660	69,812	51,251	207,850	219,371	15,998	59,103	3,053	7,270
The North	169,546	161,889	53,527	29,018	106,518	109,335	7,251	20,767	1,852	2,575
The West	9,697	8,216	3,670	1,164	5,459	5,637	345	1,128	183	265
45 years and over										
United States	209,335	219,359	19,753	12,437	149,678	95,182	37,129	108,940	2,211	2,286
The South	135,434	148,822	10,412	7,885	98,672	62,408	24,674	76,613	1,257	1,525
The North	69,745	67,245	8,553	4,380	48,298	31,214	11,886	30,840	880	690
The West	4,156	3,292	788	172	2,708	1,560	569	1,487	74	71
Rural communities										
15 years and over										
United States	2,111,707	2,045,019	732,874	531,004	1,229,488	1,231,770	126,895	257,649	12,204	17,989
The South	2,015,851	1,970,640	692,530	510,627	1,182,780	1,187,985	119,789	248,298	11,262	17,379
The North	89,891	71,583	37,004	19,731	44,557	42,102	6,760	8,952	851	548
The West	5,965	2,796	3,340	646	2,151	1,683	346	399	91	62
15 to 24 years										
United States	736,863	776,049	578,074	441,898	146,271	305,584	5,763	20,246	1,334	4,270
The South	710,575	753,698	555,057	427,187	143,355	298,373	5,660	19,984	1,298	4,185
The North	24,936	21,679	21,799	14,314	2,794	6,951	99	253	35	79
The West	1,352	672	1,218	397	122	260	4	9	1	6
25 to 44 years										
United States	826,489	826,315	129,390	72,354	647,223	659,273	40,811	83,194	6,778	10,386
The South	786,031	795,216	115,724	68,010	622,820	635,140	39,066	81,012	6,327	10,021
The North	37,360	29,689	11,963	4,153	23,161	23,112	1,638	2,027	417	323
The West	3,098	1,410	1,703	191	1,242	1,021	107	155	34	42
45 years and over										
United States	538,701	434,832	23,193	15,289	430,704	263,045	79,571	152,362	4,042	3,233
The South	510,074	414,217	19,652	14,021	411,518	250,748	74,365	145,534	3,591	3,074

[Continued]

★ 2296 ★

Marital Status of Men and Women in Urban and Rural Communities, 1910 - I

[Continued]

Age period and section	Number									
	Total		Single		Married		Widowed		Divorced	
	Male	Female	Male	Female	Male	Female	Male	Female	Male	Female
The North	27,143	19,918	3,132	1,216	18,410	11,901	4,973	6,594	395	145
The West	1,484	697	409	52	776	396	233	234	56	14

Source: "Marital Condition in Urban and Rural Communities of Negro Males and Females 15 Years of Age and Over Classified by Age Periods, by Sections: 1910." *Negro Population, 1790-1915.* Washington, D.C.: Government Printing Office, 1918, p. 259.

★ 2297 ★

Marital Status

Marital Status of Men and Women in Urban and Rural Communities, 1910 - II

Age period and section	Percentage						Males to 1,000 females		
	Single		Married		Widowed				
	Male	Female	Male	Female	Male	Female	Single	Married	Widowed
				Urban communities					
15 years and over									
United States	37.0	27.7	54.8	51.4	6.7	19.1	1,197	955	312
The South	36.1	27.8	55.6	50.3	6.9	20.0	1,104	940	292
The North	38.6	27.7	53.7	53.8	6.3	17.0	1,379	986	366
The West	41.8	23.0	50.3	56.0	5.4	17.8	2,044	1,010	343
15 to 24 years									
United States	79.8	60.9	18.5	34.5	0.7	3.2	1,021	418	173
The South	78.6	60.0	19.5	34.9	0.8	3.7	997	425	168
The North	82.6	63.6	16.2	33.5	0.5	1.9	1,075	401	206
The West	85.1	59.1	13.8	36.2	0.4	2.5	1,242	328	[1]
25 to 44 years									
United States	26.6	16.0	67.0	65.8	4.9	16.0	1,560	957	291
The South	23.4	15.2	69.7	65.0	5.4	17.5	1,362	947	271
The North	31.6	17.9	62.8	67.5	4.3	12.8	1,845	974	349
The West	37.8	14.2	56.3	68.6	3.6	13.7	3,153	968	306
45 years and over									
United States	9.4	5.7	71.5	43.4	17.7	49.7	1,588	1,573	341
The South	7.7	5.3	72.9	41.9	18.2	51.5	1,320	1,581	322
The North	12.3	6.5	69.2	46.4	17.0	45.9	1,953	1,547	385
The West	19.0	5.2	65.2	47.4	13.7	45.2	4,581	1,736	383
				Rural communities					
15 years and over									
United States	34.7	26.0	58.2	60.2	6.0	12.6	1,380	998	493
The South	34.4	25.9	58.7	60.3	5.9	12.6	1,356	996	482
The North	41.2	27.6	49.6	58.8	7.5	12.5	1,875	1,058	755
The West	56.0	23.1	36.1	60.2	5.8	14.3	5,170	1,278	867

[Continued]

★ 2297 ★

Marital Status of Men and Women in Urban and Rural Communities, 1910 - II

[Continued]

Age period and section	Percentage						Males to 1,000 females		
	Single		Married		Widowed				
	Male	Female	Male	Female	Male	Female	Single	Married	Widowed
15 to 24 years									
United States	78.5	56.9	19.9	39.4	0.8	2.6	1,308	479	285
The South	78.1	56.7	20.2	39.6	0.8	2.7	1,299	480	283
The North	87.4	66.0	11.2	32.1	0.4	1.2	1,523	402	391
The West	90.1	59.1	9.0	38.7	0.3	1.3	3,068	469	[1]
25 to 44 years									
United States	15.7	8.8	78.3	79.8	4.9	10.1	1,788	982	491
The South	14.7	8.6	79.2	79.9	5.0	10.2	1,702	981	482
The North	32.0	14.0	62.0	77.8	4.4	6.8	2,881	1,002	808
The West	55.0	13.5	40.1	72.4	3.5	11.0	8,916	1,216	690
45 years and over									
United States	4.3	3.5	80.0	60.5	14.8	35.0	1,517	1,637	522
The South	3.9	3.4	80.7	60.5	14.6	35.1	1,402	1,641	511
The North	11.5	6.1	67.8	59.7	18.3	33.1	2,576	1,547	754
The West	27.6	7.5	52.3	56.8	15.7	33.6	[1]	1,960	996

Source: "Marital Condition in Urban and Rural Communities of Negro Males and Females 15 Years of Age and Over Classified by Age Periods, by Sections: 1910." *Negro Population, 1790-1915.* Washington, D.C.: Government Printing Office, 1918, p. 259. *Note:* 1. Ratio not shown, the number of females being less than 100.

★ 2298 ★

Marital Status

Marital Status of the Population 15 Years Old and Over by Sex and Race, 1910-1930 - I

Racial class and census year	Males 15 years old and over								
	Total	Single		Married		Widowed		Divorced	Unknown
		Number	Percent	Number	Percent	Number	Percent		
All classes									
1930	43,881,022	14,953,712	34.1	26,327,109	60.0	2,025,036	4.6	489,478	85,686
1920	36,920,663	12,967,565	35.1	21,849,266	59.2	1,758,308	4.8	235,284	110,240
1910	32,425,805	12,550,129	38.7	18,092,600	55.8	1,471,390	4.5	156,162	155,524
Negro									
1930	3,941,462	1,270,950	32.2	2,357,821	59.8	247,595	6.3	55,713	9,383
1920	3,393,211	1,104,877	32.6	2,050,407	60.4	200,734	5.9	26,689	10,504
1910	3,059,312	1,083,472	35.4	1,749,228	57.2	189,970	6.2	20,146	16,496
White									
1930	39,214,156	13,364,509	34.1	23,603,312	60.2	1,745,213	4.5	408,073	73,049
1920[1]	33,335,586	11,782,665	35.3	19,698,113	59.1	1,549,164	4.6	207,663	97,981
1910[1]	29,158,125	11,360,282	39.0	16,253,940	55.7	1,274,388	4.4	135,203	134,312
Other races[2]									
1930	725,403	318,253	43.9	365,976	50.5	32,228	4.4	5,692	3,254

[Continued]

★ 2298 ★

Marital Status of the Population 15 Years Old and Over by Sex and Race, 1910-1930 - I

[Continued]

Racial class and census year	Males 15 years old and over								
	Total	Single		Married		Widowed		Divorced	Unknown
		Number	Percent	Number	Percent	Number	Percent		
1920	191,866	80,023	41.7	100,746	52.5	8,410	4.4	932	1,755
1910	208,368	106,375	51.1	89,432	42.9	7,032	3.4	813	4,716

Source: "Marital Condition of the Population 15 Years Old and Over, by Sex, and Racial Classes, for the United States: 1910 to 1930." U.S. Bureau of the Census. *Negroes in the United States: 1920-32.* Washington, D.C.: Government Printing Office, 1935, p. 147. *Notes:* 1. Includes Mexicans. 2. Includes Mexicans (1930 only), Indians, Chinese, Japanese, Filipinos, and all other.

★ 2299 ★

Marital Status

Marital Status of the Population 15 Years Old and Over by Sex and Race, 1910-1930 - II

Racial class and census year	Females 15 years old and over								
	Total	Single		Married		Widowed		Divorced	Unknown
		Number	Percent	Number	Percent	Number	Percent		
All classes									
1930	42,837,149	11,306,653	26.4	26,170,756	61.1	4,734,207	11.1	573,148	52,385
1920	35,177,515	9,616,902	27.3	21,318,933	60.6	3,917,625	11.1	273,304	50,751
1910	30,047,325	8,933,170	29.7	17,684,687	58.9	3,176,228	10.6	185,068	68,172
Negro									
1930	4,099,552	953,806	23.3	2,398,144	58.5	652,663	15.9	88,868	6,071
1920	3,423,100	825,258	24.1	2,039,181	59.6	507,961	14.8	43,871	6,829
1910	3,103,344	823,996	26.6	1,775,949	57.2	459,831	14.8	33,286	10,282
White									
1930	38,220,229	10,229,306	26.8	23,444,243	61.3	4,023,372	10.5	477,624	45,684
1920[1]	31,654,841	8,772,732	27.7	19,210,238	60.7	3,399,662	10.7	228,565	43,644
1910[1]	26,857,337	8,091,249	30.1	15,852,011	59.0	2,705,990	10.1	150,801	57,286
Other races[2]									
1930	517,368	123,541	23.9	328,369	63.5	58,172	11.2	6,656	630
1920	99,574	18,912	19.0	69,514	69.8	10,002	10.0	868	278
1910	86,644	17,925	20.7	57,727	65.5	10,407	12.0	981	604

Source: "Marital Condition of the Population 15 Years Old and Over, by Sex, and Racial Classes, for the United States: 1910 to 1930." U.S. Bureau of the Census. *Negroes in the United States: 1920-32.* Washington, D.C.: Government Printing Office, 1935, p. 147. *Notes:* 1. Includes Mexicans. 2. Includes Mexicans (1930 only), Indians, Chinese, Japanese, Filipinos, and all other.

★ 2300 ★

Marital Status

Marriage Rates by Age and Race of Couple, 1950 and 1960

Rates are marriages per 1,000 unmarried population in specified group. By place of occurrence. Marriages for 1960 based on sample data.

Area, color, sex and year	14 years and over	Age										
		14-19 years	20-24 years	25-29 years	30-34 years	35-39 years	40-44 years	45-49 years	50-54 years	55-59 years	60-64 years	65 years and over
Bride												
Total												
Marriage-registration area 1960	64.1	76.6	277.1	175.9	111.2	74.5	54.8	39.8	20.5	12.8	7.6	2.3
10 reporting states[1]												
1960	63.4	77.9	265.0	177.3	108.5	74.8	53.7	36.4	21.5	12.3	8.8	2.6
1950	74.6	85.8	259.7	185.4	121.8	81.3	52.6	34.8	20.2	12.3	7.3	2.1
White												
Marriage-registration area 1960[2]	63.6	78.9	289.8	182.4	115.7	75.4	53.2	36.7	19.9	11.7	7.3	2.2
10 reporting states[1]												
1960	62.4	78.7	275.9	184.0	109.0	77.1	52.6	33.2	21.8	12.0	8.0	2.3
1950	74.0	85.9	268.1	186.6	119.6	79.4	51.0	34.5	20.2	12.0	7.4	2.1
Nonwhite												
Marriage-registration area 1960[2]	63.4	66.7	186.6	141.6	99.6	65.7	53.9	47.5	20.2	16.7	14.6	4.0
10 reporting states[1]												
1960	63.3	65.4	191.7	138.7	103.4	56.8	57.5	49.3	17.7	14.5	15.5	4.1
1950	78.6	85.1	207.9	178.5	135.2	91.2	61.5	36.6	19.6	14.1	6.0	2.3
Groom												
Total												
Marriage-registration area 1960	75.0	23.5	212.7	199.0	129.2	93.6	81.3	68.0	46.1	41.0	28.3	13.4
10 reporting states[1]												
1960	73.3	23.7	200.1	192.6	124.3	89.2	75.3	71.2	49.4	40.5	31.0	15.2
1950	81.2	16.2	187.8	198.1	153.9	113.7	85.7	64.9	49.5	37.8	26.7	12.5
White												
Marriage-registration area 1960[2]	74.6	23.8	215.0	206.1	130.9	93.0	76.1	64.6	44.8	37.4	27.4	12.1
10 reporting states[1]												
1960	72.7	23.7	203.0	196.8	123.7	91.1	72.2	69.7	46.8	37.4	30.3	13.4
1950	80.5	16.4	188.0	199.4	150.0	108.6	81.6	60.6	46.7	34.9	25.5	11.8
Nonwhite												
Marriage-registration area 1960[2]	72.0	21.8	173.4	158.4	118.2	85.7	89.0	75.6	58.0	53.9	39.5	28.4
10 reporting states[1]												
1960	71.0	21.3	166.4	157.5	121.1	73.7	87.8	70.5	59.9	56.1	36.4	28.8
1950	86.1	15.3	185.8	189.8	179.6	144.0	110.2	91.5	69.0	63.2	37.6	19.5

Source: "Marriage Rates by Age and Color of Bride and Groom: Reporting States, 1950 and 1960, and Marriage-Registration Area, 1960." National Center for Health Statistics. *Vital Statistics Rates in the United States, 1940-60.* By Robert D. Grove and Alice M. Hetzel. Washington, D.C.: U.S. Department of Health, Education, and Welfare, Public Health Service, 1968, p. 105. *Notes:* 1. Reporting States are: Alabama, California, Connecticut, Florida, Kansas, Michigan, Mississippi, New York (exl. New York City), Tennessee, Virginia. 2. Excludes Ohio.

★ 2301 ★

Marital Status

Percent Distribution by Marital Status of the Black Female Population 15 Years Old and Over by Geographical Area, 1900-1930 - I

Section, division, and state	Percent single				Percent married			
	1930	1920	1910	1900	1930	1920	1910	1900
United States	23.3	24.1	26.6	29.9	58.5	59.6	57.2	53.7
The North	21.0	22.2	27.6	32.5	61.3	60.9	54.7	50.3
The South	24.0	24.5	26.4	29.5	57.7	59.3	57.6	54.1
The West	17.0	17.1	23.0	26.5	59.0	61.7	56.6	53.0
New England	25.8	27.1	32.1	35.7	56.4	55.3	50.0	46.8
Maine	32.4	33.7	38.8	35.9	52.5	51.2	43.8	46.0
New Hampshire	29.7	27.9	39.8	46.4	58.3	59.0	46.0	37.2
Vermont	30.9	29.5	26.3	37.6	50.9	53.0	62.2	46.5
Massachusetts	27.4	28.0	32.8	35.1	54.4	54.1	49.6	47.3
Rhode Island	26.2	27.4	30.0	35.2	52.6	53.0	49.9	46.0
Connecticut	22.6	24.6	31.3	36.8	61.5	59.2	51.1	46.8
Middle Atlantic	24.3	25.7	30.7	36.2	60.1	58.8	53.3	48.1
New York	26.3	28.8	32.3	38.1	57.6	54.8	50.6	44.7
New Jersey	23.3	25.3	29.5	34.7	60.9	58.5	55.2	49.8
Pennsylvania	22.7	23.5	30.1	35.6	62.4	62.1	54.5	49.7
East North Central	17.3	18.2	24.3	28.7	63.9	64.6	56.8	53.1
Ohio	18.0	18.9	26.5	30.5	64.8	65.9	56.5	52.9
Indiana	17.8	18.6	24.0	28.1	62.1	62.1	55.9	52.5
Illinois	17.6	18.3	22.2	26.8	61.2	62.0	57.7	53.6
Michigan	15.4	15.2	24.5	28.7	68.9	72.7	57.7	53.9
Wisconsin	15.8	19.7	32.5	33.6	66.2	65.8	50.0	49.9
West North Central	19.1	20.1	24.6	29.8	59.6	60.6	56.2	51.6
Minnesota	17.0	17.0	27.5	29.3	61.0	65.2	56.9	53.7
Iowa	18.4	17.7	22.5	27.6	60.9	65.3	60.9	56.6
Missouri	19.5	20.8	24.7	30.4	59.3	59.3	54.9	50.3
North Dakota	19.8	22.1	30.3	-	61.3	60.7	57.3	-
South Dakota	22.6	22.1	30.2	25.6	59.0	62.1	58.0	58.9
Nebraska	16.3	15.5	23.4	33.9	60.5	67.5	59.2	48.2
Kansas	18.5	19.8	24.3	28.0	60.3	61.2	58.1	54.9
South Atlantic	26.9	26.2	28.2	31.3	55.9	58.6	56.9	53.5
Delaware	27.3	27.0	30.8	32.3	57.9	58.6	54.6	53.2
Maryland	25.8	26.1	31.1	34.4	58.4	58.5	54.2	50.4
District of Columbia	25.9	28.5	33.1	38.8	55.1	51.0	47.0	42.0
Virginia	28.0	27.9	31.7	35.4	55.4	57.1	53.3	49.4
West Virginia	21.1	20.9	25.4	31.8	66.1	67.1	62.2	54.7
North Carolina	31.3	29.8	32.0	35.5	54.4	56.8	54.9	51.3
South Carolina	29.8	28.1	27.9	29.5	53.9	57.9	57.8	56.6
Georgia	24.6	23.2	24.6	27.0	55.0	60.1	59.3	56.3

[Continued]

★ 2301 ★

Percent Distribution by Marital Status of the Black Female Population 15 Years Old and Over by Geographical Area, 1900-1930 - I

[Continued]

Section, division, and state	Percent single				Percent married			
	1930	1920	1910	1900	1930	1920	1910	1900
Florida	19.5	20.8	21.6	25.1	61.6	62.6	63.7	59.0
East South Central	22.3	23.4	25.0	28.6	58.4	59.2	57.8	54.0
Kentucky	21.4	22.7	27.4	30.8	57.4	57.5	53.9	50.1
Tennessee	22.5	22.9	25.9	29.9	56.7	58.6	55.5	51.4
Alabama	24.1	24.4	25.1	28.6	56.1	57.8	57.7	54.3
Mississippi	20.6	22.9	23.8	27.2	61.7	61.5	60.2	56.5
West South Central	20.7	22.6	24.7	26.9	60.2	60.9	58.8	55.7
Arkansas	18.6	20.6	22.9	25.5	62.4	63.5	60.9	57.5
Louisiana	22.3	24.1	25.9	26.9	59.4	59.9	57.5	55.8
Oklahoma	20.6	21.1	21.8	24.3	61.0	62.5	64.0	60.9
Texas	20.3	22.6	25.1	27.9	59.5	59.8	57.8	54.1
Mountain	15.4	15.7	22.5	25.7	61.8	64.2	56.6	53.7
Montana	14.9	15.6	26.0	27.0	61.1	63.0	57.4	49.3
Idaho	11.9	13.2	29.2	-	71.7	71.1	54.1	-
Wyoming	16.4	16.0	27.1	43.6	62.3	65.5	54.6	49.6
Colorado	16.3	17.9	21.2	24.8	56.7	58.8	57.2	53.4
New Mexico	16.8	13.2	20.6	22.0	65.9	73.2	58.7	58.8
Arizona	14.0	13.1	22.8	22.4	67.2	69.5	54.8	60.2
Utah	11.2	10.4	22.2	22.2	67.1	74.8	60.5	58.2
Nevada	19.2	20.2	23.9	-	59.1	62.1	45.5	-
Pacific	17.4	17.8	23.4	27.3	58.2	60.5	56.6	52.3
Washington	15.5	14.5	22.9	26.2	60.6	66.3	59.4	57.9
Oregon	16.2	14.9	20.0	40.0	61.9	67.9	59.2	41.2
California	17.6	18.4	23.7	26.4	57.9	59.2	55.8	52.3

Source: "Percent Distribution by Marital Condition of the Negro Female Population 15 Years Old and Over, by Sections, Divisions, and States: 1900 to 1930." U.S. Bureau of the Census. *Negroes in the United States: 1920-32.* Washington, D.C.: Government Printing Office, 1935, p. 152.

★ 2302 ★

Marital Status

Percent Distribution by Marital Status of the Black Female Population 15 Years Old and Over by Geographical Area, 1900-1930 - II

Section, division, and state	Percent widowed				Percent divorced			
	1930	1920	1910	1900	1930	1920	1910	1900
United States	15.9	14.8	14.8	15.4	2.2	1.3	1.1	0.8
The North	15.6	15.5	16.2	16.1	1.9	1.2	1.1	.8
The South	16.0	14.7	14.6	15.3	2.2	1.3	1.1	.8
The West	18.7	18.1	17.3	18.0	5.1	2.9	2.6	1.9
New England	15.6	16.4	16.8	16.3	2.1	1.0	.9	.7
Maine	10.6	13.5	14.9	17.1	4.2	1.6	2.2	.7
New Hampshire	9.9	8.2	12.3	13.9	2.1	4.4	.5	2.2
Vermont	15.2	15.7	9.1	14.7	3.0	1.8	2.5	1.2
Massachusetts	16.2	16.8	16.8	16.4	1.9	.9	.7	.5
Rhode Island	17.7	17.9	18.2	17.5	3.5	1.5	1.4	1.2
Connecticut	14.1	15.2	16.5	15.3	1.7	.9	1.1	.8
Middle Atlantic	14.4	14.8	15.2	15.0	.9	.5	.5	.3
New York	14.8	15.6	16.3	16.6	.9	.5	.5	.4
New Jersey	14.8	15.6	14.7	14.4	.9	.5	.3	.3
Pennsylvania	13.7	13.8	14.6	14.1	1.0	.5	.5	.3
East North Central	15.9	15.5	16.8	16.6	2.8	1.6	1.7	1.3
Ohio	14.6	13.6	15.3	15.3	2.6	1.5	1.4	1.0
Indiana	17.1	17.0	17.7	17.1	2.7	1.9	2.2	1.9
Illinois	18.2	18.1	17.9	18.0	2.9	1.6	1.7	1.3
Michigan	12.9	10.7	15.6	15.9	2.7	1.3	1.8	1.3
Wisconsin	14.3	11.7	15.0	14.6	3.7	2.5	2.4	1.8
West North Central	18.4	17.1	17.2	17.1	2.8	2.0	1.7	1.1
Minnesota	18.3	15.5	13.8	14.6	3.6	2.1	1.3	1.9
Iowa	16.3	14.1	13.7	14.0	4.4	2.6	2.6	1.2
Missouri	18.8	17.9	18.3	18.0	2.3	1.8	1.6	1.1
North Dakota	15.3	15.7	8.6	-	3.6	1.4	3.8	-
South Dakota	14.2	14.0	10.3	14.0	4.2	1.3	1.5	1.6
Nebraska	18.7	14.3	15.2	16.3	4.2	2.5	2.0	1.2
Kansas	17.3	16.2	15.6	15.4	3.9	2.6	1.6	1.3
South Atlantic	15.8	14.4	14.0	14.4	1.3	.7	.6	.5
Delaware	13.9	13.5	13.9	13.9	.7	.4	.3	.2
Maryland	14.3	14.6	14.1	14.3	1.1	.6	.4	.3
District of Columbia	17.6	19.5	18.9	18.6	1.0	.7	.7	.6
Virginia	15.1	14.0	14.3	14.7	1.3	.7	.5	.3
West Virginia	11.2	10.6	11.1	12.4	1.5	1.0	1.1	.6
North Carolina	13.2	12.6	12.3	12.7	1.0	.4	.4	.3
South Carolina	15.7	13.5	13.8	13.4	.6	.4	.3	.3
Georgia	18.5	15.6	15.0	15.6	1.8	.9	.8	.8

[Continued]

★ 2302 ★

Percent Distribution by Marital Status of the Black Female Population 15 Years Old and Over by Geographical Area, 1900-1930 - II

[Continued]

Section, division, and state	Percent widowed				Percent divorced			
	1930	1920	1910	1900	1930	1920	1910	1900
Florida	16.6	15.3	12.5	14.6	2.0	1.1	1.3	1.0
East South Central	16.6	15.6	15.5	16.2	2.6	1.6	1.4	1.0
Kentucky	18.7	17.8	16.8	17.6	2.4	1.9	1.6	1.2
Tennessee	17.7	16.6	16.8	17.3	2.8	1.8	1.5	1.0
Alabama	17.2	16.0	15.5	16.1	2.5	1.6	1.5	.9
Mississippi	15.0	14.0	14.3	15.2	2.7	1.4	1.3	.9
West South Central	15.7	14.2	14.6	15.9	3.4	2.1	1.5	1.3
Arkansas	16.0	13.8	14.4	15.7	2.9	2.0	1.4	1.1
Louisiana	15.9	14.4	15.3	16.3	2.2	1.3	.9	.9
Oklahoma	14.9	13.1	12.4	13.0	3.4	2.0	1.4	1.4
Texas	15.4	14.4	14.5	15.8	4.6	3.0	2.2	1.8
Mountain	18.8	17.2	17.5	17.6	3.9	2.7	2.9	2.1
Montana	17.8	18.1	13.1	20.8	5.7	3.3	3.5	2.7
Idaho	11.9	13.2	14.4	-	4.4	2.6	1.4	-
Wyoming	17.5	16.0	13.6	4.7	3.6	2.6	4.6	1.3
Colorado	23.2	20.0	18.7	18.7	3.8	3.1	2.5	2.0
New Mexico	13.6	11.8	17.3	17.1	3.4	1.2	3.3	2.1
Arizona	15.0	15.1	19.2	15.1	3.8	2.3	3.0	2.0
Utah	16.8	12.2	11.5	15.0	4.8	2.6	2.7	2.6
Nevada	16.3	13.7	24.4	-	5.3	3.2	6.1	-
Pacific	18.7	18.5	17.1	18.3	5.4	3.0	2.3	1.7
Washington	17.8	15.3	12.7	14.2	5.9	3.5	2.5	1.3
Oregon	17.2	13.1	18.0	16.5	4.6	4.0	2.7	2.3
California	18.8	19.3	18.1	19.3	5.4	2.9	2.3	1.8

Source: "Percent Distribution by Marital Condition of the Negro Female Population 15 Years Old and Over, by Sections, Divisions, and States: 1900 to 1930." U.S. Bureau of the Census. *Negroes in the United States: 1920-32.* Washington, D.C.: Government Printing Office, 1935, p. 152.

★ 2303 ★

Marital Status

Percent Distribution by Marital Status of the Black Male Population 15 Years Old and Over by Geographical Area, 1900-1930 - I

Section, division, and state	Percent single				Percent married			
	1930	1920	1910	1900	1930	1920	1910	1900
United States	32.2	32.6	35.4	39.2	59.8	60.4	57.2	54.0
The North	32.7	35.6	39.2	44.4	59.6	57.2	52.7	48.2
The South	32.1	31.7	34.8	38.4	60.0	61.3	57.9	55.0
The West	33.0	45.4	45.5	52.8	56.0	46.8	46.6	38.6
New England	35.9	38.9	41.5	43.3	56.7	54.9	51.7	49.8
Maine	41.6	43.2	45.1	44.5	47.5	47.0	44.9	46.6
New Hampshire	42.0	44.1	41.5	48.5	51.9	48.6	48.5	40.9
Vermont	42.5	46.4	72.6	47.4	48.2	47.2	23.5	43.4
Massachusetts	37.5	39.3	41.7	44.3	55.1	54.9	51.9	49.5
Rhode Island	35.6	40.1	40.0	41.6	55.1	52.6	53.0	51.7
Connecticut	32.7	36.9	35.2	41.2	60.8	56.8	56.5	50.7
Middle Atlantic	34.5	36.2	39.2	45.5	59.7	57.9	54.5	48.7
New York	35.6	36.6	41.1	45.5	59.3	57.7	53.3	49.1
New Jersey	32.8	32.9	37.2	41.9	61.2	60.6	56.8	51.5
Pennsylvania	34.3	37.2	38.8	47.0	59.5	57.0	54.3	47.2
East North Central	31.1	35.2	38.8	35.4	60.1	57.3	51.7	55.5
Ohio	31.3	36.2	39.6	42.9	60.2	56.8	51.7	48.8
Indiana	30.6	32.9	37.9	42.0	59.5	57.9	51.7	48.0
Illinois	30.9	34.1	38.6	46.0	59.8	57.7	51.7	45.8
Michigan	31.3	37.5	36.8	41.7	61.2	56.9	53.5	49.5
Wisconsin	35.1	39.7	43.9	50.7	55.2	52.5	45.6	41.1
West North Central	30.6	34.3	39.0	43.8	58.3	56.5	51.4	48.0
Minnesota	32.3	37.5	48.5	51.3	56.1	54.6	44.2	41.5
Iowa	32.7	33.7	37.8	43.3	56.2	56.7	51.8	47.7
Missouri	30.4	34.4	38.9	44.5	59.0	56.3	51.4	47.6
North Dakota	47.5	48.7	57.4	59.8	35.0	39.3	32.3	28.0
South Dakota	42.7	42.5	45.6	58.1	47.0	49.3	47.2	35.3
Nebraska	30.2	38.0	43.5	53.7	57.4	54.4	48.1	39.9
Kansas	30.1	32.6	36.9	39.0	57.5	58.0	53.5	51.8
South Atlantic	34.7	33.1	35.6	39.0	58.4	60.7	57.9	54.9
Delaware	39.8	38.0	41.0	43.2	51.9	54.2	51.0	49.3
Maryland	37.1	36.2	39.0	42.3	55.3	56.7	53.8	51.1
District of Columbia	33.6	34.3	37.7	41.0	59.5	58.6	55.6	52.5
Virginia	36.7	35.8	39.3	42.6	56.0	57.7	54.3	51.3
West Virginia	35.7	39.5	48.1	53.9	57.5	54.5	45.7	39.1
North Carolina	37.2	34.1	36.2	39.3	57.2	60.6	58.2	54.8
South Carolina	35.1	32.4	33.5	35.9	59.5	62.5	61.1	59.0
Georgia	31.9	29.9	32.3	35.8	60.5	63.6	60.9	57.9

[Continued]

★ 2303 ★

Percent Distribution by Marital Status of the Black Male Population 15 Years Old and Over by Geographical Area, 1900-1930 - I

[Continued]

Section, division, and state	Percent single				Percent married			
	1930	1920	1910	1900	1930	1920	1910	1900
Florida	31.1	31.9	35.6	41.7	59.6	60.0	54.9	51.5
East South Central	30.3	30.2	33.7	38.2	61.2	62.2	58.5	54.8
Kentucky	32.3	33.3	38.2	42.3	56.8	57.2	52.6	49.5
Tennessee	30.8	30.8	35.0	40.2	59.6	60.7	56.4	52.2
Alabama	31.4	30.5	32.9	37.2	60.7	62.2	59.7	56.3
Mississippi	28.5	28.7	32.2	36.6	63.6	64.5	60.3	56.9
West South Central	29.5	30.8	34.5	37.4	61.5	61.4	57.4	55.2
Arkansas	27.1	28.5	32.6	36.7	63.5	63.5	58.1	55.0
Louisiana	30.9	31.4	35.4	36.8	61.9	62.3	57.8	56.8
Oklahoma	30.4	31.1	35.4	37.0	59.1	59.8	55.5	54.8
Texas	29.4	31.8	34.7	38.6	60.5	59.7	57.0	53.7
Mountain	36.6	55.7	43.9	54.8	52.3	37.9	47.6	36.5
Montana	39.4	42.8	49.8	63.4	45.9	48.5	43.1	28.9
Idaho	34.9	47.0	51.1	61.8	49.7	45.2	40.6	34.7
Wyoming	39.9	48.7	70.2	65.1	48.5	43.0	25.9	27.6
Colorado	26.8	33.1	36.2	42.2	59.7	56.2	54.8	47.4
New Mexico	31.9	73.7	39.4	57.9	57.9	22.5	49.7	32.9
Arizona	46.0	67.8	37.8	73.0	45.8	28.2	52.5	20.8
Utah	33.2	36.1	43.4	70.7	55.4	57.4	44.4	23.1
Nevada	36.3	40.1	44.5	-	49.4	50.3	44.5	-
Pacific	31.7	36.6	46.6	50.3	57.3	54.4	45.9	41.2
Washington	35.7	40.6	54.5	58.4	49.7	48.6	38.8	33.9
Oregon	34.9	38.9	52.1	64.9	52.4	52.8	40.9	28.9
California	31.1	35.6	43.3	45.7	58.2	55.7	48.9	45.3

Source: "Percent Distribution by Marital Condition of the Negro Male Population 15 Years Old and Over, by Sections, Divisions, and States: 1900 to 1930." U.S. Bureau of the Census. *Negroes in the United States: 1920-32.* Washington, D.C.: Government Printing Office, 1935, p. 151.

★ 2304 ★

Marital Status

Percent Distribution by Marital Status of the Black Male Population 15 Years Old and Over by Geographical Area, 1900-1930 - II

Section, division, and state	Percent widowed				Percent divorced			
	1930	1920	1910	1900	1930	1920	1910	1900
United States	6.3	5.9	6.2	5.7	1.4	0.8	0.7	0.4
The North	5.9	5.8	6.6	6.1	1.6	1.0	.9	.6
The South	6.4	6.0	6.2	5.7	1.3	.7	.6	.4
The West	6.7	5.2	5.5	5.8	3.8	2.0	1.6	1.0
New England	5.7	5.2	5.8	5.8	1.4	.7	.7	.4
Maine	9.0	8.0	8.3	5.6	1.8	1.1	1.6	1.3
New Hampshire	3.9	5.3	7.9	8.0	2.0	2.0	1.7	1.1
Vermont	5.3	4.7	2.6	5.5	3.1	1.7	1.3	.9
Massachusetts	5.6	4.7	5.3	5.0	1.5	.7	.6	.3
Rhode Island	7.4	6.3	5.9	5.8	1.8	.9	.9	.5
Connecticut	5.3	5.6	7.5	7.2	1.0	.6	.6	.5
Middle Atlantic	4.8	5.0	5.5	5.0	.6	.4	.3	.2
New York	4.2	4.5	4.9	4.8	.5	.3	.3	.2
New Jersey	5.3	5.8	5.4	4.9	.6	.4	.3	.2
Pennsylvania	5.3	5.1	6.0	5.1	.7	.4	.3	.2
East North Central	6.4	6.0	7.3	8.2	2.2	1.3	1.4	.9
Ohio	6.3	5.5	7.0	6.9	2.0	1.3	1.2	.7
Indiana	7.0	7.1	8.3	7.7	2.6	1.6	1.8	1.5
Illinois	6.8	6.7	7.2	6.6	2.2	1.2	1.4	.8
Michigan	5.1	4.2	7.0	7.4	2.3	1.2	1.8	.9
Wisconsin	6.7	5.3	7.4	6.5	2.7	1.9	2.2	.6
West North Central	8.2	7.3	7.5	6.8	2.7	1.6	1.3	.8
Minnesota	7.0	5.8	5.1	4.8	4.4	1.9	1.0	1.0
Iowa	6.9	7.1	7.4	6.5	4.0	2.0	2.3	1.5
Missouri	8.4	7.5	7.8	6.7	2.0	1.4	1.2	.7
North Dakota	10.5	7.1	4.5	10.6	6.5	2.2	1.5	.8
South Dakota	7.9	5.5	5.6	4.2	2.5	1.9	1.6	1.4
Nebraska	8.3	5.7	6.7	5.2	3.9	1.6	1.5	.7
Kansas	7.9	7.2	7.4	7.5	4.1	1.9	1.5	.8
South Atlantic	5.9	5.5	5.6	5.2	.8	.4	.4	.2
Delaware	7.0	6.8	7.2	6.3	.8	.4	.3	.2
Maryland	6.4	6.4	6.6	5.5	.8	.5	.3	.2
District of Columbia	5.7	6.1	5.8	6.1	.7	.5	.6	.3
Virginia	6.2	5.6	5.8	5.4	1.0	.5	.3	.2
West Virginia	5.3	4.5	4.9	4.3	1.5	.9	.7	.4
North Carolina	4.9	4.8	5.0	5.0	.5	.2	.2	.2
South Carolina	5.0	4.6	4.8	4.6	.3	.1	.1	.1
Georgia	6.6	5.8	5.9	5.3	.9	.5	.4	.3

[Continued]

★ 2304 ★

Percent Distribution by Marital Status of the Black Male Population 15 Years Old and Over by Geographical Area, 1900-1930 - II

[Continued]

Section, division, and state	Percent widowed				Percent divorced			
	1930	1920	1910	1900	1930	1920	1910	1900
Florida	7.0	6.9	6.1	5.5	1.3	.7	.9	.5
East South Central	6.7	6.4	6.6	6.1	1.5	.9	.8	.5
Kentucky	8.7	7.8	7.6	6.9	2.1	1.5	1.1	.7
Tennessee	7.3	7.3	7.3	6.5	1.8	1.0	.8	.4
Alabama	6.4	6.1	6.4	5.8	1.3	.8	.7	.5
Mississippi	6.1	5.9	6.2	5.8	1.4	.7	.8	.4
West South Central	6.8	6.2	6.7	6.2	2.1	1.2	.8	.6
Arkansas	7.4	6.6	7.8	7.2	1.9	1.2	.9	.6
Louisiana	6.0	5.5	5.8	5.8	1.1	.6	.4	.4
Oklahoma	7.8	7.2	7.5	6.9	2.5	1.4	1.0	.7
Texas	7.1	6.5	6.6	6.0	2.9	1.7	1.2	.9
Mountain	7.2	4.3	5.8	5.7	3.6	1.6	1.8	.9
Montana	8.3	5.3	4.5	5.6	5.3	3.2	1.6	.8
Idaho	10.4	6.2	4.9	3.5	4.7	1.2	2.9	-
Wyoming	8.8	4.9	2.1	5.9	2.3	3.0	1.1	.7
Colorado	9.5	7.4	6.7	6.5	3.7	1.9	2.0	1.0
New Mexico	6.6	2.5	8.5	4.4	3.5	1.2	1.9	1.5
Arizona	5.0	2.7	6.5	4.6	3.0	1.2	1.9	.7
Utah	5.8	4.1	5.6	3.7	5.6	2.1	1.3	1.0
Nevada	6.0	5.6	8.8	-	8.4	1.1	2.1	-
Pacific	6.5	6.0	5.3	5.9	3.9	2.3	1.4	1.0
Washington	8.4	6.5	3.8	5.3	5.3	3.1	1.5	1.0
Oregon	8.1	4.9	5.2	4.5	4.5	2.7	1.6	1.5
California	6.3	5.9	5.9	6.3	3.7	2.1	1.3	1.0

Source: "Percent Distribution by Marital Condition of the Negro Male Population 15 Years Old and Over, by Sections, Divisions, and States: 1900 to 1930." U.S. Bureau of the Census. *Negroes in the United States: 1920-32.* Washington, D.C.: Government Printing Office, 1935, p. 151.

★ 2305 ★

Marital Status

Percent Distribution of the Married Population 15 Years Old and Over by Sex, Race, and Age Periods, 1930

Racial class and age	Males 15 years old and over				Females 15 years old and over			
	Single	Married	Widowed	Divorced	Single	Married	Widowed	Divorced
All classes	34.1	60.0	4.6	1.1	26.4	61.1	11.1	1.3
15 to 19 years	98.0	1.7	1	1	86.8	12.6	.2	.2
20 to 24 years	70.8	28.1	.3	.4	46.0	51.6	1.0	1.1
25 to 29 years	36.7	61.3	.8	1.0	21.7	74.3	2.1	1.8
30 to 34 years	21.2	76.0	1.3	1.4	13.2	81.5	3.3	1.9
35 to 39 years	15.4	81.0	2.0	1.5	10.4	82.3	5.3	1.9
40 to 44 years	13.1	82.1	3.0	1.6	9.5	80.6	8.0	1.8
45 to 49 years	11.9	82.1	4.3	1.7	9.0	77.6	11.6	1.7
50 to 54 years	10.9	81.0	6.3	1.6	9.2	72.3	16.9	1.5
55 to 59 years	10.3	79.5	8.4	1.6	9.0	66.2	23.4	1.0
60 to 64 years	9.6	76.2	12.4	1.5	8.9	65.9	33.1	1.3
65 to 69 years	9.3	71.5	17.8	1.3	8.4	46.6	44.1	.8
70 to 74 years	8.6	64.7	25.4	1.1	8.4	35.0	55.9	.5
75 years and over	7.0	50.4	41.5	.8	7.3	18.2	73.9	.3
Negro	32.2	59.8	6.3	1.4	23.3	58.5	15.9	2.2
15 to 19 years	96.0	3.7	.1	.1	77.9	20.5	.9	.6
20 to 24 years	54.7	42.8	1.3	.9	33.1	60.4	4.1	2.3
25 to 29 years	27.7	67.9	2.5	1.6	15.9	73.5	7.4	3.1
30 to 34 years	19.0	75.1	3.7	2.0	9.9	76.0	10.8	3.2
35 to 39 years	14.1	78.7	4.9	2.1	6.9	75.2	14.9	2.9
40 to 44 years	11.7	78.9	7.1	2.1	5.8	71.2	20.4	2.6
45 to 49 years	8.9	80.2	8.8	1.9	4.6	67.9	25.2	2.1
50 to 54 years	7.2	79.6	11.4	1.7	4.5	60.3	33.4	1.8
55 to 59 years	6.4	78.6	13.3	1.6	4.0	55.1	39.2	1.5
60 to 64 years	5.5	74.8	18.1	1.5	4.0	43.7	51.0	1.1
65 to 69 years	5.3	69.9	23.4	1.3	3.8	35.9	59.2	.9
70 to 74 years	4.8	63.4	30.5	1.1	4.0	25.7	69.5	.5
75 years and over	4.8	51.5	42.5	.8	3.6	14.9	80.8	.3
White	34.1	60.2	4.5	1.1	26.8	61.3	10.5	1.2
15 to 19 years	98.3	1.5	1	1	88.1	11.5	.1	.2
20 to 24 years	72.6	26.5	.2	.4	48.0	50.3	.6	1.0
25 to 29 years	37.5	60.8	.6	1.0	22.6	74.3	1.3	1.6
30 to 34 years	21.2	76.3	1.0	1.3	13.7	82.0	2.4	1.8
35 to 39 years	15.3	81.4	1.7	1.5	10.9	83.0	4.2	1.8
40 to 44 years	13.2	82.5	2.6	1.6	10.0	81.6	6.6	1.7
45 to 49 years	12.1	82.4	3.8	1.6	9.5	78.6	10.1	1.6
50 to 54 years	11.2	81.3	5.8	1.6	9.6	73.5	15.4	1.5
55 to 59 years	10.6	79.7	8.0	1.6	9.4	67.0	22.3	1.2
60 to 64 years	10.2	76.3	11.9	1.5	9.2	57.8	31.9	1.0
65 to 69 years	9.5	71.6	17.4	1.3	8.7	47.2	43.1	.7
70 to 74 years	8.7	64.8	25.1	1.1	8.7	35.5	55.1	.5
75 years and over	7.1	50.4	41.4	.8	7.6	18.5	73.4	.3

[Continued]

★ 2305 ★

Percent Distribution of the Married Population 15 Years Old and Over by Sex, Race, and Age Periods, 1930

[Continued]

Racial class and age	Males 15 years old and over				Females 15 years old and over			
	Single	Married	Widowed	Divorced	Single	Married	Widowed	Divorced
Other races	43.9	50.5	4.4	.8	23.9	63.5	11.2	1.3
15 to 19 years	97.8	1.9	1	1	79.3	19.8	.4	.4
20 to 24 years	74.3	24.4	.5	.4	32.9	63.6	1.8	1.5
25 to 29 years	47.9	49.7	1.2	.8	13.1	81.6	3.3	1.8
30 to 34 years	31.3	65.1	2.3	1.0	7.3	85.7	5.3	1.6
35 to 39 years	22.8	72.4	3.4	1.1	5.3	85.0	8.1	1.5
40 to 44 years	18.9	74.4	5.2	1.1	4.4	80.1	14.0	1.5
45 to 49 years	15.5	76.2	7.0	1.1	3.8	74.2	20.5	1.4
50 to 54 years	14.9	74.0	9.7	1.2	4.0	66.0	28.6	1.3
55 to 59 years	12.9	73.3	12.4	1.1	3.3	58.5	37.0	1.0
60 to 64 years	12.5	68.7	17.4	1.1	3.4	46.5	48.8	1.0
65 to 69 years	12.6	64.2	21.8	1.0	3.5	39.0	56.1	1.1
70 to 74 years	13.6	57.6	27.3	.9	3.4	29.8	65.9	.7
75 years and over	11.6	48.1	39.0	.7	3.3	20.5	75.4	.3

Source: "Percent Distribution of the Population 15 Years Old and Over, by Sex, Racial Classes, and 5-Year Age Periods for the United States: 1930." U.S. Bureau of the Census. *Negroes in the United States: 1920-32.* Washington, D.C.: Government Printing Office, 1935, p. 147. *Note:* 1. Less than 1/10 of 1 percent.

★ 2306 ★

Marital Status

Percent Married in Urban, Rural-Farm, and Rural Non-Farm Population 15 Years Old and Over by Sex and Age Periods, 1930 - I

Percent not shown where base is less than 100.

Area and age	New England		Middle Atlantic		East North Central		West North Central		South Atlantic	
	Male	Female	Male	Female	Male	Female	Male	Female	Male	Female
Urban	57.5	56.4	60.2	59.7	61.1	63.8	59.6	58.6	60.0	53.0
15 to 19 years	1.3	12.4	2.5	17.7	3.2	23.9	3.5	20.3	3.6	18.0
20 to 24 years	29.2	51.0	36.3	58.8	38.7	66.2	37.3	57.7	41.9	55.1
25 to 34 years	61.3	72.5	66.1	73.0	67.4	77.0	65.3	71.7	70.6	69.3
35 to 44 years	72.4	72.1	74.3	70.6	74.1	73.3	72.5	71.0	77.6	65.9
45 to 54 years	73.9	62.3	75.2	58.3	74.2	62.2	72.5	61.5	77.3	53.3
55 to 64 years	72.1	46.2	71.2	40.8	70.4	44.0	69.0	44.8	72.8	37.2
65 and over	54.9	22.4	56.7	20.2	56.3	21.4	54.0	23.0	58.2	17.2
Rural-farm	42.2	59.1	46.6	65.2	52.8	66.1	58.0	70.4	57.4	57.8
15 to 19 years	-	-	.8	12.8	1.3	12.8	2.9	25.6	3.2	15.3
20 to 24 years	-	-	21.3	56.4	20.2	53.9	41.0	71.6	42.2	55.6
25 to 34 years	-	-	56.7	83.0	55.9	81.5	72.7	87.9	78.0	79.4
35 to 44 years	57.8	-	67.8	86.5	72.6	87.8	78.4	87.1	87.7	83.2
45 to 54 years	-	-	67.3	80.5	73.1	83.2	76.0	84.4	88.0	77.6
55 to 64 years	-	-	65.2	69.1	72.9	78.9	70.4	75.5	84.7	64.4

[Continued]

★ 2306 ★

Percent Married in Urban, Rural-Farm, and Rural Non-Farm Population 15 Years Old and Over by Sex and Age Periods, 1930 - I

[Continued]

Area and age	New England		Middle Atlantic		East North Central		West North Central		South Atlantic	
	Male	Female	Male	Female	Male	Female	Male	Female	Male	Female
65 and over	-	-	47.4	32.5	57.8	45.4	58.0	44.9	71.3	34.7
Rural-nonfarm	52.5	56.1	56.9	64.2	50.1	63.7	50.2	59.1	57.7	57.9
15 to 19 years	.6	11.2	1.6	19.1	2.0	17.3	2.8	17.3	4.1	23.4
20 to 24 years	20.3	50.1	32.4	61.7	28.2	63.1	25.7	56.8	43.5	63.7
25 to 34 years	60.9	74.3	65.3	80.9	54.2	81.7	52.5	76.1	70.2	76.8
35 to 44 years	70.7	72.6	73.6	79.6	66.7	80.9	63.9	79.4	78.3	73.3
45 to 54 years	69.0	68.9	74.0	71.0	67.5	73.3	66.8	70.1	77.8	62.1
55 to 64 years	66.4	57.0	68.0	56.2	62.8	59.6	65.7	55.8	73.0	45.3
65 and over	50.2	26.9	52.5	31.0	46.8	30.3	49.4	31.5	58.6	24.3

Source: "Percent Married in the Urban, Rural-Farm, and Rural-Nonfarm Negro Population 15 Years Old and Over, by Sex, and 5-Year Age Periods, by Geographic Divisions: 1930." U.S. Bureau of the Census. *Negroes in the United States: 1920-32*. Washington, D.C.: Government Printing Office, 1935, p. 172.

★ 2307 ★

Marital Status

Percent Married in Urban, Rural-Farm, and Rural Non-Farm Population 15 Years Old and Over by Sex and Age Periods, 1930 - II

Percent not shown where base is less than 100.

Area and age	East South Central		West South Central		Mountain		Pacific	
	Male	Female	Male	Female	Male	Female	Male	Female
Urban	60.5	52.9	61.5	55.0	57.0	59.4	58.4	57.3
15 to 19 years	4.1	20.8	4.0	21.7	4.4	20.6	1.9	15.4
20 to 24 years	42.8	56.0	43.3	59.0	28.7	59.2	29.2	55.1
25 to 34 years	69.8	67.3	71.4	69.0	58.3	73.0	62.9	71.3
35 to 44 years	77.2	64.5	77.9	65.4	68.2	70.4	70.0	68.4
45 to 54 years	77.1	53.8	77.4	54.0	69.3	61.1	71.6	58.6
55 to 64 years	73.2	37.4	71.6	37.9	67.1	45.1	67.1	44.3
65 and over	57.1	18.3	55.2	17.7	54.4	20.7	59.1	22.2
Rural-farm	62.6	62.3	62.2	64.9	55.0	72.6	53.8	71.2
15 to 19 years	4.6	22.8	3.9	23.8	1.5	-	2.8	18.2
20 to 24 years	51.6	64.5	47.9	67.3	-	-	24.5	69.3
25 to 34 years	80.5	80.1	79.5	83.3	62.5	88.6	62.7	89.1
35 to 44 years	87.4	81.7	86.5	84.2	73.4	87.8	70.1	89.4
45 to 54 years	87.6	75.8	85.8	77.7	70.6	90.0	72.4	83.9
55 to 64 years	84.4	63.5	82.2	64.7	-	-	58.2	-
65 and over	70.3	33.6	68.3	35.1	-	-	-	-
Rural-nonfarm	58.1	57.9	59.5	59.2	40.8	69.0	50.2	64.8
15 to 19 years	4.5	27.8	4.1	26.9	3.0	28.2	.7	23.6
20 to 24 years	43.6	64.3	42.9	65.3	12.4	69.6	29.4	66.7

[Continued]

★ 2307 ★

Percent Married in Urban, Rural-Farm, and Rural Non-Farm Population 15 Years Old and Over by Sex and Age Periods, 1930 - II

[Continued]

Area and age	East South Central		West South Central		Mountain		Pacific	
	Male	Female	Male	Female	Male	Female	Male	Female
25 to 34 years	69.1	73.8	69.7	75.1	38.9	81.1	52.7	78.8
35 to 44 years	75.8	70.7	76.9	72.6	53.0	81.9	62.5	75.5
45 to 54 years	77.2	60.7	77.6	61.1	64.8	73.6	62.0	68.8
55 to 64 years	72.5	44.9	72.0	45.4	54.8	-	54.3	52.7
65 and over	56.9	24.0	57.0	24.6	35.8	-	40.5	32.1

Source: "Percent Married in the Urban, Rural-Farm, and Rural-Nonfarm Negro Population 15 Years Old and Over, by Sex, and 5-Year Age Periods, by Geographic Divisions: 1930." U.S. Bureau of the Census. *Negroes in the United States: 1920-32*. Washington, D.C.: Government Printing Office, 1935, p. 172.

★ 2308 ★

Marital Status

Percent of the Black Population Married, Single, Widowed or Divorced by Age, 1910

Age period	Population 15 years of age and older							
	Male				Female			
	Negro	White			Negro	White		
		Total	Native	Foreign born		Total	Native	Foreign born
				Percentage single				
Total	35.4	39.0	41.3	31.8	26.6	30.1	33.1	18.3
15 to 19 years	96.9	98.4	98.4	98.6	81.2	88.8	89.1	86.3
20 to 24 years	59.7	76.7	75.8	80.3	34.9	50.3	51.3	44.9
25 to 29 years	29.7	44.1	42.3	49.1	17.1	26.0	26.9	22.3
30 to 34 years	19.2	26.5	25.8	28.5	11.0	16.8	17.7	13.2
35 to 44 years	12.2	17.0	16.9	17.3	7.1	11.9	12.9	8.6
45 to 54 years	6.8	11.4	11.3	11.6	4.7	8.9	9.9	6.1
55 to 64 years	5.0	8.5	8.2	9.1	3.9	7.3	8.2	5.2
65 years and over	4.1	6.3	6.0	7.1	3.7	6.5	7.5	4.5
				Percentage married				
Total	57.2	55.7	53.7	62.1	57.2	59.0	57.1	66.5
15 to 19 years	2.2	1.0	1.0	0.8	17.0	10.5	10.3	13.4
20 to 24 years	37.8	22.4	23.3	19.0	59.0	48.4	47.3	54.3
25 to 29 years	65.9	54.5	56.1	59.9	73.2	71.5	70.5	75.9
30 to 34 years	75.1	71.2	71.7	69.9	76.3	79.3	78.2	83.5
35 to 44 years	80.0	79.3	79.1	79.7	74.4	80.7	79.7	84.1
45 to 54 years	81.4	81.7	81.5	82.1	66.4	75.6	75.0	77.4
55 to 64 years	78.1	79.2	79.6	78.2	52.8	62.9	63.6	61.1
65 years and over	67.3	65.5	67.1	62.5	29.9	35.4	35.7	34.7

[Continued]

★ 2308 ★

Percent of the Black Population Married, Single, Widowed or Divorced by Age, 1910

[Continued]

Age period	Population 15 years of age and older							
	Male				Female			
	Negro	White			Negro	White		
		Total	Native	Foreign born		Total	Native	Foreign born
Percentage widowed								
Total	6.2	4.4	4.0	5.4	14.8	10.1	8.9	14.7
15 to 19 years	0.1	[1]	[1]	[1]	0.9	0.1	0.1	0.1
20 to 24 years	1.5	0.3	0.3	0.2	4.7	0.7	0.8	0.5
25 to 29 years	3.2	0.8	0.9	0.5	7.9	1.7	1.8	1.4
30 to 34 years	4.5	1.5	1.7	1.1	11.0	3.1	3.2	2.8
35 to 44 years	6.6	2.9	3.1	2.4	16.9	6.5	6.4	6.8
45 to 54 years	10.6	6.0	6.2	5.6	27.7	14.6	14.2	15.9
55 to 64 years	15.9	11.3	11.1	11.9	42.4	29.0	27.4	33.1
65 years and over	27.5	27.1	25.9	29.6	65.6	57.5	56.2	60.4
Percentage divorced								
Total	0.7	0.5	0.5	0.3	1.1	0.6	0.6	0.4
15 to 19 years	[1]	[1]	[1]	[1]	0.2	0.1	0.1	[1]
20 to 24 years	0.4	0.1	0.1	[1]	1.1	0.4	0.4	0.1
25 to 29 years	0.8	0.3	0.4	0.1	1.5	0.6	0.7	0.3
30 to 34 years	0.9	0.5	0.6	0.2	1.6	0.8	0.8	0.4
35 to 44 years	1.0	0.7	0.8	0.4	1.5	0.8	0.9	0.5
45 to 54 years	0.9	0.8	0.9	0.5	1.1	0.8	0.9	0.5
55 to 64 years	0.8	0.8	0.9	0.6	0.7	0.6	0.7	0.5
65 years and over	0.7	0.7	0.7	0.5	0.4	0.3	0.4	0.3
Percentage married, widowed, divorced								
Total	64.0	60.6	58.2	67.8	73.1	69.7	66.6	81.6
15 to 19 years	2.3	1.0	1.0	0.8	18.1	10.7	10.5	13.2
20 to 24 years	39.6	22.8	23.8	19.2	64.8	49.5	48.5	54.9
25 to 29 years	69.8	55.6	57.4	50.5	82.7	73.8	72.9	77.6
30 to 34 years	80.5	73.2	74.0	71.2	88.9	83.2	82.2	86.7
35 to 44 years	87.5	82.8	83.0	82.5	92.8	88.0	87.0	91.4
45 to 54 years	93.0	88.5	88.6	88.2	95.2	91.0	90.1	93.8
55 to 64 years	94.8	91.4	91.6	90.7	95.9	92.6	91.7	94.7
65 years and over	55.5	93.3	93.7	92.6	95.9	93.2	92.2	95.3

Source: Untitled Table. *Negro Population, 1790-1910.* Washington, D.C.: Government Printing Office, 1918, p. 241. *Note:* 1. Less than one-tenth of 1 per cent.

★ 2309 ★

Marital Status

Percent of the Black Population Married, Single, Widowed, or Divorced by Sex, 1890-1910

Sex and year	Negro population 15 years of age and over						
	15 to 19 Total	20 to 24 years	25 to 34 years	35 to 44 years	45 to 64 years	65 years and over	
				Percentage single			
Male							
1910	35.4	96.9	59.7	25.1	12.2	6.2	4.1
1900	39.2	97.9	64.3	27.9	13.2	6.5	4.6
1890	39.8	99.0	65.7	25.1	11.3	6.2	5.4
Female							
1910	26.6	81.2	34.9	14.5	7.1	4.4	3.7
1900	29.9	83.2	39.8	17.4	8.0	4.7	4.3
1890	30.0	84.9	38.0	15.0	7.3	4.5	4.3
				Percentage married			
Male							
1910	57.2	2.2	37.8	69.9	80.0	80.2	67.3
1900	54.0	1.7	33.8	67.7	79.1	80.4	69.6
1890	55.5	0.9	33.4	71.8	82.9	84.4	74.4
Female							
1910	57.2	17.0	59.0	74.5	74.4	61.6	29.9
1900	53.7	15.6	54.6	71.0	72.3	60.7	28.9
1890	54.6	14.4	57.3	74.8	74.6	61.3	29.0
				Percentage widowed			
Male							
1910	6.2	0.1	1.5	3.7	6.6	12.6	27.5
1900	5.8	0.1	1.1	3.4	6.7	12.2	25.0
1890	4.3	[1]	0.7	2.6	5.2	9.2	19.6
Female							
1910	14.8	0.9	4.7	9.2	16.9	32.9	65.6
1900	15.4	0.9	4.7	10.1	18.3	33.7	66.0
1890	14.7	0.5	4.0	9.1	17.0	33.4	66.1
				Percentage divorced			
Male							
1910	0.7	[1]	0.4	0.8	1.0	0.9	0.7
1900	0.4	[1]	0.2	0.5	0.7	0.7	0.4
1890	0.2	[1]	0.1	0.3	0.4	0.4	0.3
Female							
1910	1.1	0.2	1.1	1.6	1.5	1.0	0.4
1900	0.8	0.1	0.8	1.3	1.2	0.7	0.3
1890	0.5	0.1	0.4	0.8	0.8	0.5	0.2

[Continued]

★ 2309 ★

Percent of the Black Population Married, Single, Widowed, or Divorced by Sex, 1890-1910

[Continued]

Sex and year	Negro population 15 years of age and over						
	15 to 19 Total	20 to 24 years	25 to 34 years	35 to 44 years	45 to 64 years	65 years and over	
	Percentage married, widowed, or divorced						
Male							
1910	64.0	2.3	39.6	74.5	87.5	93.7	95.5
1900	60.2	1.8	35.1	71.6	86.5	93.3	95.0
1890	60.0	0.9	34.2	74.7	88.5	93.9	94.3
Female							
1910	73.1	18.1	64.8	85.3	92.8	95.4	95.9
1900	69.9	16.6	60.0	82.4	91.9	95.1	95.2
1890	69.8	15.0	61.7	84.8	92.4	95.2	95.3

Source: Untitled Table. *Negro Population, 1790-1910.* Washington, D.C.: Government Printing Office, 1918, p. 240.
Note: 1. Less than one-tenth of 1 per cent.

★ 2310 ★

Marital Status

Percent of the Black Population Single, Married, and Widowed: Divisions and States: 1890-1910 - I

Division and state	Negro population 15 years of age and over Male								
	Percentage single			Percentage married			Percentage widowed		
	1910	1900	1890	1910	1900	1890	1910	1900	1890
United States	35.4	39.2	39.8	57.2	54.0	55.5	6.2	5.7	4.3
Geographic divisions									
New England	41.5	43.3	42.5	51.7	49.8	51.9	5.8	5.8	4.9
Middle Atlantic	39.2	45.5	45.2	54.5	48.7	49.8	5.5	5.0	4.6
East North Central	38.8	43.8	43.4	51.7	47.6	50.2	7.3	7.0	5.6
West North Central	39.0	43.8	43.5	51.4	48.0	50.6	7.5	6.8	5.0
South Atlantic	35.6	39.0	39.9	57.9	54.9	56.0	5.6	5.2	3.9
East South Central	33.7	38.2	38.7	58.5	54.8	56.3	6.6	6.1	4.6
West South Central	34.5	37.4	37.6	57.4	55.2	57.1	6.7	6.2	4.6
Mountain	43.9	54.8	67.6	47.6	36.5	28.3	5.8	5.7	2.9
Pacific	46.6	50.3	56.7	45.9	41.2	37.7	5.3	5.9	4.6
New England									
Maine	45.1	44.5	46.2	44.9	46.6	47.1	8.3	5.6	5.6
New Hampshire	41.5	48.5	51.3	48.5	40.9	42.0	7.9	8.0	5.5
Vermont	72.6	47.4	42.0	23.5	43.4	49.4	2.6	5.5	7.4
Massachusetts	41.7	44.3	43.6	51.9	49.5	51.4	5.3	5.0	4.6
Rhode Island	40.0	41.6	39.1	53.0	51.7	54.6	5.9	5.8	5.7

[Continued]

★ 2310 ★

Percent of the Black Population Single, Married, and Widowed: Divisions and States: 1890-1910 - I

[Continued]

Division and state	Negro population 15 years of age and over Male								
	Percentage single			Percentage married			Percentage widowed		
	1910	1900	1890	1910	1900	1890	1910	1900	1890
Connecticut	35.2	41.2	41.7	56.5	50.7	52.6	7.5	7.2	4.5
Middle Atlantic									
New York	41.1	45.5	43.8	53.3	49.1	51.1	4.9	4.8	4.7
New Jersey	37.2	47.9	43.4	56.8	51.5	51.9	5.4	4.9	4.2
Pennsylvania	38.8	47.0	46.9	54.3	47.2	48.1	6.0	5.1	4.6
East North Central									
Ohio	39.6	42.9	43.6	51.7	48.8	50.4	7.0	6.9	5.4
Indiana	37.9	42.0	43.5	51.7	48.0	49.7	8.3	7.7	5.9
Illinois	38.6	46.0	43.7	51.7	45.8	49.8	7.2	6.6	5.6
Michigan	36.8	41.7	40.9	53.5	49.5	52.5	7.0	7.4	5.7
Wisconsin	43.9	50.7	45.3	45.6	41.1	47.1	7.4	6.5	6.6
West North Central									
Minnesota	48.5	51.3	53.6	44.2	41.5	41.9	5.1	4.8	3.4
Iowa	37.8	43.3	44.1	51.8	47.7	50.1	7.4	6.5	5.0
Missouri	38.9	44.5	43.3	51.4	47.6	50.8	7.8	6.7	5.2
North Dakota	57.4	59.8	62.3	32.3	28.0	32.7	4.5	10.6	4.3
South Dakota	45.6	58.1	58.8	47.2	35.3	34.7	5.6	4.2	6.1
Nebraska	43.5	53.7	57.2	48.1	39.9	37.9	6.7	5.2	3.2
Kansas	36.9	39.0	39.1	53.5	51.8	54.7	7.4	7.5	5.4
South Atlantic									
Delaware	41.0	43.2	43.8	51.0	49.3	51.4	7.2	6.3	4.6
Maryland	39.0	42.3	42.1	53.8	51.1	53.2	6.6	5.5	4.4
District of Columbia	37.7	41.0	41.2	55.6	52.5	54.1	5.8	6.1	4.3
Virginia	39.3	42.6	43.1	54.3	51.3	52.2	5.8	5.4	4.5
West Virginia	48.1	53.9	54.0	45.7	39.1	41.5	4.9	4.3	3.5
North Carolina	36.2	39.3	40.9	58.2	54.8	55.0	5.0	5.0	3.9
South Carolina	33.5	35.9	35.8	61.1	59.0	60.6	4.8	4.6	3.5
Georgia	32.3	35.8	38.4	60.9	57.9	57.7	5.9	5.3	3.6
Florida	35.6	41.7	39.5	54.9	51.5	56.0	6.1	5.5	3.9
East South Central									
Kentucky	38.2	42.3	42.4	52.6	49.5	51.5	7.6	6.9	5.3
Tennessee	35.0	40.2	39.8	56.4	52.2	54.7	7.3	6.5	4.9
Alabama	32.9	37.2	37.7	59.7	56.3	57.8	6.4	5.8	4.1
Mississippi	32.2	36.6	37.4	60.3	56.9	57.7	6.2	5.8	4.5
West South Central									
Arkansas	32.6	36.7	37.9	58.1	55.0	56.0	7.8	7.2	5.5
Louisiana	35.4	36.8	36.2	57.8	56.8	59.0	5.8	5.8	4.2

[Continued]

★ 2310 ★

Percent of the Black Population Single, Married, and Widowed: Divisions and States: 1890-1910 - I

[Continued]

Division and state	Negro population 15 years of age and over Male								
	Percentage single			Percentage married			Percentage widowed		
	1910	1900	1890	1910	1900	1890	1910	1900	1890
Oklahoma	35.4	37.0	31.5	55.5	54.8	62.3	7.5	6.9	5.2
Texas	34.7	38.6	39.0	57.0	53.7	55.7	6.6	6.0	4.4
Mountain									
Montana	49.8	63.4	78.5	43.1	28.9	19.3	4.5	5.6	1.2
Idaho	51.1	61.8	1	40.6	34.7	1	4.9	3.5	1
Wyoming	70.2	65.1	78.5	25.9	27.6	16.8	2.1	5.9	3.6
Colorado	36.2	42.2	56.2	54.8	47.4	38.5	6.7	6.5	3.8
New Mexico	39.4	57.9	63.9	49.7	32.9	32.5	8.5	4.4	2.9
Arizona	37.8	73.0	85.0	52.5	20.8	12.6	6.5	4.6	1.5
Utah	43.4	70.7	66.3	44.4	23.1	29.5	5.6	3.7	1.9
Nevada	44.5	1	73.8	44.5	1	19.3	8.8	1	5.5
Pacific									
Washington	54.5	64.9	65.3	38.8	28.9	28.5	3.8	4.5	4.9
Oregon	52.1	58.4	66.9	40.9	33.9	29.0	5.2	5.3	2.8
California	43.3	45.7	53.5	48.9	45.3	40.7	5.9	6.3	4.7

Source: "Percent Single, Married, and Widowed in the Negro Population, by Divisions and States: 1910, 1900, and 1890." *Negro Population, 1790-1910*. Washington, D.C.: Government Printing Office, 1918, p. 252. *Note:* 1. Per cent not shown where bases is less than 100.

★ 2311 ★

Marital Status

Percent of the Black Population Single, Married, and Widowed: Divisions and States: 1890-1910 - II

Division and state	Negro population 15 years of age and over Female								
	Percentage single			Percentage married			Percentage widowed		
	1910	1900	1890	1910	1900	1890	1910	1900	1890
United States	26.6	29.9	30.0	57.2	53.7	54.6	14.8	15.4	14.7
Geographic divisions									
New England	32.1	35.7	34.4	50.0	46.8	47.8	16.8	16.3	17.1
Middle Atlantic	30.7	36.2	34.5	53.3	48.1	48.3	15.2	15.0	16.8
East North Central	24.3	28.7	29.3	56.8	53.1	53.9	16.8	16.6	15.8
West North Central	24.6	29.8	29.6	56.2	51.6	53.0	17.2	17.1	16.4
South Atlantic	28.2	31.3	31.7	56.9	53.5	54.1	14.0	14.4	13.6
East South Central	25.0	28.6	28.9	57.8	54.0	54.0	15.5	16.2	15.5
West South Central	24.7	26.9	26.6	58.8	55.7	57.3	14.6	15.9	15.2
Mountain	22.5	25.7	32.4	56.6	53.7	50.3	17.5	17.6	14.9

[Continued]

★ 2311 ★

Percent of the Black Population Single, Married, and Widowed: Divisions and States: 1890-1910 - II

[Continued]

Division and state	Negro population 15 years of age and over Female								
	Percentage single			Percentage married			Percentage widowed		
	1910	1900	1890	1910	1900	1890	1910	1900	1890
Pacific	23.4	27.3	26.0	56.6	52.3	56.0	17.1	18.3	16.6
New England									
Maine	38.8	35.9	36.0	43.8	46.0	45.6	14.9	17.1	17.7
New Hampshire	39.8	46.4	42.3	46.0	37.2	41.3	12.3	13.9	15.9
Vermont	26.3	37.6	31.2	62.2	46.5	51.2	9.1	14.7	17.3
Massachusetts	32.8	35.1	34.3	49.6	47.3	48.0	16.8	16.4	17.2
Rhode Island	30.0	35.2	34.3	49.9	46.0	46.0	18.2	17.5	18.4
Connecticut	31.3	36.8	34.3	51.1	46.8	48.8	16.5	15.3	16.1
Middle Atlantic									
New York	32.3	38.1	35.0	50.6	44.7	45.8	16.3	16.6	18.9
New Jersey	29.5	34.7	33.7	55.2	49.8	50.9	14.7	14.4	15.1
Pennsylvania	30.1	35.6	34.6	54.5	49.7	48.8	14.6	14.1	16.1
East North Central									
Ohio	26.5	30.5	30.6	56.5	52.9	53.0	15.3	15.3	15.6
Indiana	24.0	28.1	29.1	55.9	52.5	53.5	17.7	17.1	15.8
Illinois	22.2	26.8	27.4	57.7	53.6	55.4	17.9	18.0	16.4
Michigan	24.5	28.7	28.7	57.7	53.9	55.0	15.6	15.9	15.2
Wisconsin	32.5	33.6	33.2	50.0	49.9	51.1	15.0	14.6	13.9
West North Central									
Minnesota	27.5	29.3	26.1	56.9	53.7	59.0	13.8	14.6	14.1
Iowa	22.5	27.6	28.0	60.9	56.6	57.3	13.7	14.0	13.7
Missouri	24.7	30.4	30.3	54.9	50.3	51.3	18.3	18.0	17.4
North Dakota	30.3	[1]	[1]	57.3	[1]	[1]	8.6	[1]	[1]
South Dakota	30.2	25.6	23.8	58.0	58.9	59.8	10.3	14.0	13.9
Nebraska	23.4	33.9	33.5	59.2	48.2	53.5	15.2	16.3	11.8
Kansas	24.3	28.0	27.6	58.1	54.9	56.9	15.6	15.4	14.6
South Atlantic									
Delaware	30.8	32.3	31.4	54.6	53.2	56.0	13.9	13.9	12.5
Maryland	31.1	34.4	34.5	54.2	50.4	50.9	14.1	14.3	14.3
District of Columbia	33.1	38.8	38.9	47.0	42.0	42.6	18.9	18.6	18.1
Virginia	31.7	35.4	36.4	53.3	49.4	48.8	14.3	14.7	14.2
West Virginia	25.4	31.8	34.8	62.2	54.7	52.8	11.1	12.4	11.7
North Carolina	32.0	35.5	34.5	54.9	51.3	52.2	12.3	12.7	12.8
South Carolina	27.9	29.5	28.6	57.8	56.6	58.4	13.8	13.4	12.6
Georgia	24.6	27.0	27.5	59.3	56.3	57.7	15.0	15.6	14.0
Florida	21.6	25.1	27.5	63.7	59.0	58.5	12.5	14.6	12.9

[Continued]

★ 2311 ★

Percent of the Black Population Single, Married, and Widowed: Divisions and States: 1890-1910 - II

[Continued]

Division and state	Negro population 15 years of age and over Female								
	Percentage single			Percentage married			Percentage widowed		
	1910	1900	1890	1910	1900	1890	1910	1900	1890
East South Central									
Kentucky	27.4	30.8	31.2	53.9	50.1	50.8	16.8	17.6	16.9
Tennessee	25.9	29.9	29.7	55.5	51.4	52.7	16.8	17.3	16.6
Alabama	25.1	28.6	28.8	57.7	54.3	55.8	15.5	16.1	14.9
Mississippi	23.8	27.3	27.5	60.2	56.5	57.0	14.3	15.2	14.7
West South Central									
Arkansas	22.9	25.5	24.7	60.9	57.5	60.3	14.4	15.7	14.1
Louisiana	25.9	26.9	26.7	57.5	55.8	56.9	15.3	16.3	15.7
Oklahoma	21.8	24.3	22.7	64.0	60.9	66.7	12.4	13.0	9.5
Texas	25.1	27.9	27.5	57.8	54.1	55.9	14.5	15.8	15.3
Mountain									
Montana	26.0	27.0	35.3	57.4	49.3	47.9	13.1	20.8	14.4
Idaho	29.2	[1]	[1]	54.1	[1]	[1]	14.4	[1]	[1]
Wyoming	27.1	43.6	35.9	54.6	49.6	47.1	13.6	4.7	13.6
Colorado	21.2	24.8	31.7	57.2	53.4	50.0	18.7	18.7	16.1
New Mexico	20.6	22.0	33.9	58.7	58.8	52.7	17.3	17.1	12.1
Arizona	22.8	22.4	25.2	54.8	60.2	60.0	19.2	15.1	11.9
Utah	22.2	22.2	28.0	60.5	58.2	55.3	11.5	15.0	11.4
Nevada	23.9	[1]	[1]	45.5	[1]	[1]	24.4	[1]	[1]
Pacific									
Washington	22.9	26.2	27.3	59.4	57.9	59.3	12.7	14.2	11.6
Oregon	20.2	40.0	23.9	59.2	41.2	57.1	18.0	16.5	16.6
California	23.7	26.4	26.1	55.8	52.3	55.5	18.1	19.3	17.1

Source: "Percent Single, Married, and Widowed in the Negro Population, by Divisions and States: 1910, 1900, and 1890." *Negro Population, 1790-1910.* Washington, D.C.: Government Printing Office, 1918, p. 252. *Note:* 1. Per cent not shown where bases is less than 100.

★ 2312 ★

Marital Status

Percent of the Black Population, Marital Class and Sections, 1890-1910 - I

Class of population	Negro population 15 years of age and over							
	Total		15 to 19 years		20 to 24 years		25 to 34 years	
	Male	Female	Male	Female	Male	Female	Male	Female
	Percentage single							
The South								
1910	34.8	26.4	96.8	80.7	57.9	33.4	22.2	13.3
1900	38.4	29.5	97.8	82.7	62.3	38.0	25.0	16.3
1890	39.0	29.8	99.0	84.5	63.6	36.6	22.3	14.2
The North								
1910	39.2	27.6	98.1	86.7	73.2	46.9	39.1	21.8
1900	44.4	32.5	98.8	88.5	78.7	53.5	43.5	24.5
1890	44.0	31.6	99.5	89.6	80.4	50.0	39.9	20.9
The West								
1910	45.5	23.0	98.4	83.9	79.4	40.1	50.9	18.4
1900	52.8	26.5	98.5	85.7	87.3	46.4	58.5	22.1
1890	62.5	28.9	99.7	82.6	89.4	46.3	68.4	20.1
	Percentage married							
The South								
1910	57.9	57.6	2.3	17.5	39.5	60.3	72.6	75.5
1900	55.0	54.1	1.8	16.1	35.7	56.0	70.5	71.8
1890	56.3	55.0	1.0	14.9	35.4	58.6	74.5	75.6
The North								
1910	52.7	54.7	1.2	12.2	25.2	49.2	57.0	68.6
1900	48.2	50.3	0.9	10.8	20.2	43.0	53.1	65.6
1890	50.3	51.2	0.4	9.9	18.9	46.6	57.2	69.5
The West								
1910	46.6	56.6	1.2	15.1	19.1	53.1	45.4	69.2
1900	38.6	53.0	0.9	13.2	10.6	47.6	37.4	64.3
1890	32.7	53.4	0.3	16.6	10.0	49.5	29.3	68.4
	Percentage widowed							
The South								
1910	6.2	14.6	0.1	0.9	1.6	4.9	4.0	9.4
1900	5.7	15.3	0.1	0.9	1.2	4.9	3.6	10.4
1890	4.2	14.5	[1]	0.5	0.7	4.1	2.7	9.2
The North								
1910	6.6	16.2	0.1	0.4	0.8	2.8	2.7	7.9
1900	6.1	16.1	[1]	0.4	0.6	2.7	2.5	8.5
1890	5.0	16.4	[1]	0.4	0.4	2.8	2.3	8.5
The West								
1910	5.5	17.3	-	0.4	0.6	3.8	2.0	9.2
1900	5.8	18.0	-	0.7	0.5	4.6	2.2	10.7
1890	3.7	15.8	-	0.6	0.1	3.1	1.4	9.2
	Percentage divorced							
The South								
1910	0.6	1.1	[1]	0.2	0.4	1.1	0.8	1.6

[Continued]

★ 2312 ★

Percent of the Black Population, Marital Class and Sections, 1890-1910 - I

[Continued]

Class of population	Negro population 15 years of age and over							
	Total		15 to 19 years		20 to 24 years		25 to 34 years	
	Male	Female	Male	Female	Male	Female	Male	Female
1900	0.4	0.8	1	0.1	0.2	0.8	0.5	1.3
1890	0.2	0.5	1	0.1	0.1	0.4	0.3	0.8
The North								
1910	0.9	1.1	1	0.2	0.3	0.9	0.9	1.5
1900	0.6	0.8	1	0.1	0.1	0.7	0.5	1.2
1890	0.4	0.6	1	0.1	0.1	0.5	0.3	0.9
The West								
1910	1.6	2.6	0.1	0.4	0.5	2.7	1.3	3.1
1900	1.0	1.9	-	0.3	0.4	0.9	0.9	2.4
1890	0.7	1.4	-	0.3	1	0.9	0.5	2.1
	Percentage married, widowed, or divorced							
The South								
1910	64.7	73.2	2.4	18.6	41.5	66.3	77.4	86.5
1900	61.1	70.2	1.9	17.2	37.0	61.8	74.6	83.5
1890	60.8	70.0	1.0	15.4	36.2	63.1	77.5	85.6
The North								
1910	60.3	72.1	1.2	12.8	26.3	52.8	60.6	78.0
1900	54.9	67.2	1.0	11.3	20.9	46.3	56.1	75.3
1890	55.7	68.2	0.4	10.3	19.4	49.8	59.8	78.9
The West								
1910	53.7	76.5	1.3	15.9	20.2	59.6	48.7	81.5
1900	45.4	72.9	0.9	14.2	11.5	53.1	40.5	77.3
1890	37.1	70.6	0.3	17.4	10.2	53.4	31.2	79.7

Source: "Percentage of Each Marital Class, by Persons, for the Negro Population 15 Years of Age and Over, by Sections: 1910, 1900, and 1890." *Negro Population, 1790-1910.* Washington, D.C.: Government Printing Office, 1918, p. 249. *Note:* 1. Less than one-tenth of 1 per cent.

★ 2313 ★

Marital Status

Percent of the Black Population, Marital Class and Sections, 1890-1910 - II

Class of population	Negro population 15 years of age and over					
	35 to 44 years		45 to 64 years		65 years and over	
	Male	Female	Male	Female	Male	Female
	Percentage single					
The South						
1910	10.0	6.4	4.9	4.0	3.5	3.5
1900	11.2	7.4	5.5	4.5	4.1	4.1
1890	9.7	7.0	5.2	4.3	5.0	4.1

[Continued]

★ 2313 ★

Percent of the Black Population, Marital Class and Sections, 1890-1910 - II

[Continued]

Class of population	Negro population 15 years of age and over					
	35 to 44 years		45 to 64 years		65 years and over	
	Male	Female	Male	Female	Male	Female
The North						
1910	22.1	10.8	13.1	6.7	7.7	5.2
1900	22.9	11.2	12.5	6.7	7.8	6.0
1890	19.5	10.1	10.3	6.4	8.0	5.8
The West						
1910	30.9	8.3	21.8	5.8	17.7	4.6
1900	35.7	8.4	26.7	5.7	24.1	3.9
1890	43.2	10.8	31.0	6.1	28.5	6.6
	Percentage married					
The South						
1910	82.2	75.3	81.7	62.6	68.7	30.6
1900	81.2	73.0	81.7	61.5	70.7	29.5
1890	84.6	75.2	85.4	62.1	75.5	29.6
The North						
1910	70.0	69.9	71.3	55.5	58.2	25.6
1900	69.1	68.5	72.2	55.1	60.8	24.5
1890	74.0	70.5	77.7	55.6	66.3	24.9
The West						
1910	61.1	69.1	63.6	54.4	51.1	21.9
1900	56.3	68.1	58.2	53.1	42.1	22.4
1890	50.5	67.2	56.7	50.5	46.7	27.5
	Percentage widowed					
The South						
1910	6.6	16.7	12.3	32.3	26.8	65.1
1900	6.8	18.3	12.0	33.2	24.5	65.7
1890	5.2	16.9	8.9	32.9	19.0	65.7
The North						
1910	6.3	17.6	14.0	36.5	32.1	68.4
1900	6.8	18.8	14.0	37.2	30.0	68.8
1890	5.6	18.4	11.1	37.2	25.0	68.9
The West						
1910	5.5	19.0	11.8	37.4	28.9	72.3
1900	6.2	20.3	12.7	39.1	31.8	71.7
1890	4.6	19.6	10.4	42.3	23.7	65.1
	Percentage divorced					
The South						
1910	0.9	1.5	0.8	0.9	0.6	0.4
1900	0.6	1.2	0.6	0.7	0.4	0.3
1890	0.4	0.7	0.3	0.4	0.3	0.2
The North						
1910	1.4	1.5	1.4	1.1	1.1	0.4

[Continued]

★ 2313 ★

Percent of the Black Population, Marital Class and Sections, 1890-1910 - II

[Continued]

Class of population	Negro population 15 years of age and over					
	35 to 44 years		45 to 64 years		65 years and over	
	Male	Female	Male	Female	Male	Female
1900	0.9	1.3	1.0	0.8	0.8	0.3
1890	0.6	1.0	0.7	0.6	0.5	0.2
The West						
1910	2.1	3.3	2.4	2.3	1.5	1.2
1900	1.2	2.8	1.6	1.7	1.5	0.8
1890	1..3	2.2	1.6	1.0	1.1	0.8
	Percentage married, widowed, or divorced					
The South						
1910	89.7	93.5	94.9	95.9	96.1	96.1
1900	88.6	92.4	94.3	95.3	95.5	95.4
1890	90.2	92.8	94.6	95.5	94.7	95.5
The North						
1910	77.7	89.1	86.7	93.1	91.3	94.4
1900	76.8	88.6	87.2	93.1	91.5	93.5
1890	80.3	89.8	89.5	93.4	91.8	93.9
The West						
1910	68.7	91.4	77.8	94.1	81.4	95.4
1900	63.7	91.3	72.6	94.0	75.3	95.0
1890	56.4	89.0	68.7	93.7	71.5	93.4

Source: "Percentage of Each Marital Class, by Persons, for the Negro Population 15 Years of Age and Over, by Sections: 1910, 1900, and 1890." *Negro Population, 1790-1910.* Washington, D.C.: Government Printing Office, 1918, p. 249. *Note:* 1. Less than one-tenth of 1 per cent.

★ 2314 ★

Marital Status

Percentage Married in the Black Population: Southern and Northern Cities: 1910

City	Total	15 to 19 years	20 to 24 years	25 to 34 years	35 to 44 years	45 to 64 years	65 years and over
				Male			
Southern Cities							
Atlanta, Ga.	58.7	3.2	41.5	69.9	80.3	76.9	62.5
Baltimore, Md	53.5	1.1	30.3	57.8	70.4	70.6	60.8
Birmingham, Ala.	56.7	1.7	33.5	66.3	74.8	76.8	55.8
Louisville, Ky.	49.3	1.7	31.9	52.8	64.1	65.8	57.6
Memphis, Tenn.	52.9	2.8	32.3	60.7	71.1	69.1	61.3
Nashville, Tenn.	55.2	4.1	37.6	64.0	74.4	75.9	61.0
New Orleans, La.	56.8	2.0	35.0	67.7	75.7	72.6	57.8

[Continued]

★ 2314 ★

Percentage Married in the Black Population: Southern and Northern Cities: 1910

[Continued]

City	Total	15 to 19 years	20 to 24 years	25 to 34 years	35 to 44 years	45 to 64 years	65 years and over
Richmond, Va.	52.2	1.2	27.2	60.8	75.3	73.5	59.2
Washington, D.C.	55.6	1.5	29.6	63.2	75.5	73.6	59.1
Northern cities							
Boston, Mass.	50.7	1.2	18.9	49.3	66.1	66.5	48.0
Chicago, Ill.	52.0	1.8	24.5	53.4	66.0	66.3	55.0
Cincinnati, Ohio	52.0	1.4	29.4	56.4	66.1	65.0	51.5
Columbus, Ohio	49.3	1.5	25.0	51.0	64.9	67.4	54.0
Indianapolis, Ind.	53.7	2.9	27.0	58.1	68.8	70.1	58.4
Kansas City, Mo.	52.0	1.7	28.0	55.7	66.5	67.3	57.6
New York City, N.Y.	56.0	1.1	28.3	60.6	74.3	72.7	58.2
Philadelphia, Pa.	57.2	1.0	29.9	61.6	71.6	70.9	57.1
Pittsburgh, Pa.	53.9	1.2	22.0	58.2	69.1	69.1	56.7
St. Louis, Mo.	51.4	1.7	25.3	56.1	65.7	66.4	55.8
				Female			
Southern Cities							
Atlanta, Ga.	49.7	18.1	55.6	62.5	59.6	42.2	18.2
Baltimore, Md	48.1	8.4	42.2	61.8	63.9	49.1	20.2
Birmingham, Ala.	56.3	21.1	59.9	70.0	67.2	46.9	18.1
Louisville, Ky.	48.5	15.9	48.7	60.6	59.7	45.4	18.8
Memphis, Tenn.	52.2	20.1	54.1	65.6	60.9	45.4	18.7
Nashville, Tenn.	44.6	16.3	47.0	56.3	55.8	42.4	17.6
New Orleans, La.	49.7	15.7	52.2	67.5	62.7	41.3	15.6
Richmond, Va.	44.0	9.1	41.0	60.7	59.5	39.8	15.2
Washington, D.C.	47.0	9.3	43.9	61.7	61.2	42.7	19.2
Northern cities							
Boston, Mass.	48.6	7.9	43.4	60.5	59.5	42.3	15.7
Chicago, Ill.	55.6	15.2	54.0	68.3	65.0	44.9	15.1
Cincinnati, Ohio	53.8	17.5	50.0	66.1	67.4	46.8	20.0
Columbus, Ohio	57.2	16.7	51.8	72.8	73.0	53.2	22.5
Indianapolis, Ind.	54.3	15.6	52.2	66.3	65.7	53.4	23.5
Kansas City, Mo.	54.1	18.1	52.3	64.9	64.1	50.1	21.7
New York City, N.Y.	50.2	10.1	44.5	62.6	60.6	42.2	15.5
Philadelphia, Pa.	52.2	9.9	46.0	65.6	64.8	45.2	19.2
Pittsburgh, Pa.	60.1	11.4	52.0	73.8	74.6	55.5	18.0
St. Louis, Mo.	54.3	18.9	54.3	68.7	63.7	45.1	19.4

Source: "Percentage Married in the Negro Population 15 Years of Age and Over: 1910." U.S. Bureau of the Census. *Negro Population, 1790-1910*. Washington, D.C.: Government Printing Office, 1918, p. 260.

★ 2315 ★

Marital Status

Percentage of the Population Single, Married, Widowed, and Divorced, Urban and Rural, 1910 - I

Class of population	Male						
	Total	15 to 19 years	20 to 24 years	25 to 34 years	35 to 44 years	45 to 64 years	65 years and over
	Percentage single						
Urban							
Negro	37.0	97.3	66.1	33.0	18.0	10.2	5.9
White	40.1	98.8	79.3	38.7	18.2	10.6	6.2
Native	44.4	98.8	79.4	39.5	19.7	11.4	6.2
Foreign born	31.7	98.6	79.1	37.4	15.7	9.3	6.2
Rural							
Negro	34.7	96.8	57.1	20.6	8.8	4.5	3.6
White	37.8	98.1	73.9	32.5	15.6	10.0	6.4
Native	38.9	98.1	72.7	30.3	14.5	9.2	5.8
Foreign born	32.0	98.3	83.4	44.6	21.0	13.4	8.3
	Percentage married						
Urban							
Negro	54.8	1.8	31.6	62.2	73.4	73.7	60.5
White	54.8	0.7	19.9	59.5	78.0	80.3	64.4
Native	50.8	0.7	19.8	58.5	76.0	79.2	66.2
Foreign born	62.7	0.8	20.2	61.3	81.2	81.9	62.1
Rural							
Negro	58.2	2.3	40.4	74.3	83.8	82.9	69.4
White	56.7	1.3	25.1	65.6	80.7	81.2	66.3
Native	56.0	1.3	26.3	67.7	81.7	81.9	67.5
Foreign born	60.7	0.9	15.7	54.0	76.0	78.2	62.9
	Percentage widowed						
Urban							
Negro	6.7	0.1	1.2	3.4	7.0	14.8	32.6
White	4.1	[1]	0.2	1.0	2.9	8.2	28.7
Native	3.7	[1]	0.2	1.2	3.1	8.2	26.7
Foreign born	5.0	[1]	0.1	0.8	2.5	8.2	31.1
Rural							
Negro	6.0	0.1	1.6	3.9	6.3	11.7	26.0
White	4.6	[1]	0.4	1.3	2.9	7.8	26.1
Native	4.3	[1]	0.4	1.4	3.0	7.9	25.5
Foreign born	6.4	[1]	0.2	0.8	2.3	7.5	27.9

[Continued]

★ 2315 ★

Percentage of the Population Single, Married, Widowed, and Divorced, Urban and Rural, 1910 - I

[Continued]

Class of population	Male						
	Total	15 to 19 years	20 to 24 years	25 to 34 years	35 to 44 years	45 to 64 years	65 years and over
	Percentage divorced						
Urban							
Negro	0.8	[1]	0.4	0.9	1.2	1.1	0.7
White	0.5	[1]	0.1	0.4	0.7	0.8	0.6
Native	0.6	[1]	0.1	0.6	1.0	1.0	0.7
Foreign born	0.3	[1]	[1]	0.2	0.4	0.5	0.4
Rural							
Negro	0.6	[1]	0.4	0.8	0.9	0.8	0.7
White	0.4	[1]	0.1	0.4	0.6	0.8	0.7
Native	0.5	[1]	0.1	0.4	0.6	0.8	0.7
Foreign born	0.4	[1]	[1]	0.1	0.4	0.7	0.7
	Percentage married, widowed, or divorced						
Urban							
Negro	62.3	1.9	33.2	66.5	81.6	89.6	93.8
White	59.4	0.7	20.2	61.0	81.6	89.3	93.6
Native	55.0	0.7	20.1	60.3	80.1	88.4	93.6
Foreign born	67.9	0.8	20.3	62.2	84.0	90.6	93.6
Rural							
Negro	64.8	2.4	42.3	79.1	91.0	95.3	96.0
White	61.8	1.3	25.6	67.2	84.2	89.8	93.1
Native	60.8	1.3	26.8	69.5	85.4	90.6	93.7
Foreign born	67.4	0.9	15.9	54.9	78.7	86.4	91.4

Source: "Percent Single, Married, Widowed and Divorced Persons by Age Periods, in the Negro Population and in Classes of White Population, in Urban and Rural Communities: 1910." *Negro Population, 1790-1910.* Washington, D.C.: Government Printing Office, 1918, p. 255. *Note:* 1. Less than one-tenth of 1 per cent.

★ 2316 ★

Marital Status

Percentage of the Population Single, Married, Widowed, and Divorced, Urban and Rural, 1910 - II

Class of population	Female						
	Total	15 to 19 years	20 to 24 years	25 to 34 years	35 to 44 years	45 to 64 years	65 years and over
	Percentage single						
Urban							
Negro	27.7	84.2	42.8	20.1	10.0	6.0	4.2
White	33.2	92.1	57.0	26.6	14.9	10.1	7.3
Native	38.1	92.8	59.9	29.3	17.4	12.0	8.8
Foreign born	20.9	87.9	47.7	19.9	9.6	6.6	5.3
Rural							
Negro	26.0	80.1	30.9	11.1	5.3	3.5	3.5
White	26.7	85.8	42.3	15.7	8.2	6.4	5.8
Native	28.7	86.0	43.0	16.2	8.6	6.9	6.6
Foreign born	10.0	77.6	30.2	10.6	5.2	3.6	3.0
	Percentage married						
Urban							
Negro	51.4	14.0	50.5	66.4	65.1	48.8	20.9
White	54.9	7.3	41.7	69.8	76.2	65.0	30.0
Native	51.2	6.6	38.7	66.8	73.3	63.8	29.9
Foreign born	63.9	11.5	51.4	77.4	82.2	67.1	30.2
Rural							
Negro	60.2	18.1	63.2	79.5	80.1	68.4	33.8
White	63.7	13.5	56.3	81.7	86.4	77.0	40.3
Native	62.5	13.3	55.6	81.1	85.9	76.5	39.7
Foreign born	74.6	21.6	68.8	87.5	90.1	79.7	42.7
	Percentage widowed						
Urban							
Negro	19.1	0.9	5.0	11.4	22.8	43.8	74.1
White	11.1	0.1	0.7	2.6	7.8	24.0	62.2
Native	9.7	0.1	0.7	2.8	8.0	23.0	60.7
Foreign born	14.6	0.1	0.5	2.2	7.5	25.7	64.1
Rural							
Negro	12.6	0.9	4.5	7.9	13.3	27.1	61.9
White	8.9	0.2	0.8	2.0	4.8	15.9	53.2
Native	8.2	0.2	0.9	2.0	4.8	15.9	53.1
Foreign born	14.9	0.2	0.6	1.6	4.3	16.1	53.8

[Continued]

★ 2316 ★

Percentage of the Population Single, Married, Widowed, and Divorced, Urban and Rural, 1910 - II

[Continued]

Class of population	Female						
	Total	15 to 19 years	20 to 24 years	25 to 34 years	35 to 44 years	45 to 64 years	65 years and over
	Percentage divorced						
Urban							
Negro	1.4	0.3	1.3	2.0	2.0	1.2	0.4
White	0.7	0.1	0.4	0.8	1.0	0.8	0.3
Native	0.8	0.1	0.5	1.0	1.3	1.0	0.4
Foreign born	0.4	[1]	0.1	0.4	0.5	0.5	0.3
Rural							
Negro	0.9	0.2	0.9	1.3	1.2	0.8	0.4
White	0.4	0.1	0.3	0.5	0.6	0.6	0.4
Native	0.4	0.1	0.3	0.5	0.6	0.6	0.4
Foreign born	0.3	0.1	0.1	0.3	0.4	0.5	0.3
	Percentage married, widowed, or divorced						
Urban							
Negro	72.0	15.2	56.9	79.8	89.8	93.8	95.4
White	66.6	7.4	42.8	73.3	85.0	89.8	92.5
Native	61.6	6.7	39.9	70.5	82.6	87.9	91.0
Foreign born	78.9	11.6	52.1	80.0	90.3	93.3	94.5
Rural							
Negro	73.7	19.2	68.7	88.7	94.6	96.3	96.1
White	73.1	13.8	57.5	84.2	91.7	93.5	93.9
Native	71.1	13.6	56.8	83.7	91.3	93.0	93.1
Foreign born	89.8	21.9	69.6	89.3	94.8	96.3	96.8

Source: "Percent Single, Married, Widowed and Divorced Persons by Age Periods, in the Negro Population and in Classes of White Population, in Urban and Rural Communities: 1910." *Negro Population, 1790-1910.* Washington, D.C.: Government Printing Office, 1918, p. 255. *Note:* 1. Less than one-tenth of 1 per cent.

★ 2317 ★

Marital Status

Sex Ratio by Marital Condition, Totals, 1890-1910

Age period and marital class	Males to 1,000 females					
	Negro population			White population		
	1910	1900	1890	1910	1900	1890
Total	989	986	995	1,066	1,049	1,053
Under 15 years of age	993	998	1,024	1,025	1,024	1,032
Single	994	998	1,024	1,026	1,024	1,032
Married, widowed, or divorced	184	217	45	290	170	10
15 years of age and over	986	979	974	1,086	1,062	1,065
Single	1,315	1,286	1,292	1,404	1,360	1,387
Married, widowed, or divorced	864	843	838	944	921	910
Married	985	986	990	1,025	1,011	1,007
Widowed	413	365	286	471	445	394
Divorced	605	500	488	897	793	717
Unknown	1,604	2,100	925	2,345	2,663	3,527

Source: Untitled Table. *Negro Population, 1790-1910.* Washington, D.C.: Government Printing Office, 1918, p. 238.

★ 2318 ★

Marital Status

Single and Ever-Married Men and Women by Marital History, 1971

Item	Total	White	Negro	Other	Year of birth				
					1945-1954	1935-1944	1925-1934	1915-1924	1900-1914
Men									
Single men in 1971	23.2	22.4	29.2	30.9	67.2	12.2	6.4	5.4	5.5
Men ever married in 1971									
once	66.5	67.4	58.3	61.6	31.7	79.2	80.7	79.2	76.4
Twice or more	10.3	10.1	12.5	7.2	1.1	8.6	12.9	15.3	18.1
Women									
Single women in 1971	17.5	16.6	24.5	22.4	50.9	7.1	4.5	4.3	6.2
Women ever married in 1971									
Once	85.5	85.9	80.8	91.7	94.3	87.7	84.6	82.2	80.8
Twice or more	14.5	14.1	19.2	8.1	5.6	12.3	15.4	17.8	19.2
Never divorced or widowed	73.9	74.8	64.4	81.2	90.2	82.0	78.0	70.7	53.9
Divorced, total	14.9	14.3	21.1	9.4	9.2	16.2	17.2	17.0	13.9
After first marriage only	13.7	12.9	18.6	8.8	8.8	15.3	15.6	15.4	12.5
Widowed	12.3	11.8	16.9	9.5	0.7	2.0	5.3	13.7	36.1

Source: "Percent Distribution of Single and Ever-Married Men and Women, by Marital History, Year of Birth, and Race: 1971." U.S. Bureau of the Census. *Statistical Abstract of the United States, 1975.* Washington, D.C.: Government Printing Office, 1975, p. 69. Primary source: U.S. Bureau of the Census, *Current Population Reports,* series P-20, No. 239.

★ 2319 ★

Marital Status

Women Ever Married by Children Ever Born: 1910-1975

Age of woman and year	Total, women ever married (thousands)	Percent distribution by specified number of children ever born					Children ever born per woman ever married
		Total	0	1	2 to 4	5 or more	
1910							
Total, 15 to 49 years	1,820	100	18	18	33	31	3.5
15 to 19 years	103	100	40	42	18	-	0.8
20 to 24 years	356	100	24	28	43	5	1.7
25 to 29 years	378	100	20	19	41	21	2.6
30 to 34 years	299	100	16	16	33	35	3.5
35 to 39 years	292	100	13	13	29	45	4.5
40 to 44 years	212	100	11	11	26	52	5.5
45 to 49 years	180	100	9	10	24	58	6.2
1940							
Total, 15 to 49 years	2,655	100	29	21	32	18	2.3
15 to 19 years	127	100	42	41	17	-	0.8
20 to 24 years	405	100	35	28	34	2	1.3
25 to 29 years	491	100	32	21	36	11	1.8
30 to 34 years	454	100	29	20	32	18	2.3
35 to 39 years	476	100	27	18	32	23	2.7
40 to 44 years	381	100	24	16	33	27	3.1
45 to 49 years	322	100	22	15	34	29	3.3
1960							
Total, 15 to 49 years	3,312	100	20	19	39	22	2.8
15 to 19 years	125	100	25	41	33	1	1.3
20 to 24 years	413	100	17	25	51	7	2.0
25 to 29 years	536	100	14	17	47	22	2.8
30 to 34 years	597	100	16	16	41	28	3.2
35 to 39 years	599	100	20	17	36	27	3.1
40 to 44 years	540	100	25	18	33	25	2.9
45 to 49 years	502	100	28	19	31	22	2.8
1970							
Total, 15 to 49 years	3,639	100	14	19	43	24	3.0
15 to 19 years	141	100	32	43	24	1	1.0
20 to 24 years	536	100	21	33	43	4	1.6
25 to 29 years	608	100	13	20	52	15	2.5
30 to 34 years	598	100	9	14	48	29	3.4
35 to 39 years	596	100	10	12	42	35	3.8
40 to 44 years	604	100	13	14	38	34	3.8
45 to 49 years	557	100	18	16	36	29	3.4
1975							
Total, 15 to 49 years	3,841	100	12	20	46	21	2.9

[Continued]

★ 2319 ★

Women Ever Married by Children Ever Born: 1910-1975

[Continued]

Age of woman and year	Total, women ever married (thousands)	Percent distribution by specified number of children ever born					Children ever born per woman ever married
		Total	0	1	2 to 4	5 or more	
15 to 19 years	108	100	28	47	25	-	1.0
20 to 24 years	514	100	20	37	42	-	1.4
25 to 29 years	706	100	16	25	53	6	2.0
30 to 34 years	689	100	8	17	55	20	3.0
35 to 39 years	605	100	6	11	46	36	3.9
40 to 44 years	634	100	11	11	42	35	3.9
45 to 49 years	587	100	10	17	40	34	3.7

Source: "Black Women Ever Married by Number of Children Ever Born, by Age for Selected Years: 1910 to 1975," Department of Commerce, Bureau of the Census. *The Social and Economic Status of the Black Population in the United States: An Historical View, 1790-1978*, p. 128. Primary source: U.S. Department of Commerce, Bureau of the Census. *Notes:* - Represents or rounds to zero. For 1910 and 1940 percentages and average number of children ever born per woman ever married are based on women reporting number of children ever born; in 1960, 1970, and 1975, women who did not report the number of children ever born were allocated a number.

★ 2320 ★

Marital Status

Women Separated and Divorced, 1950-1971

Year	Separated[1]		Divorced	
	Negro and other races	White	Negro and other races	White
1950	11	2	3	3
1951	9	(NA)	3	(NA)
1952	10	1	3	3
1953	8	2	4	3
1954	14	1	4	3
1955	12	2	3	3
1956	11	2	4	3
1957	10	1	4	3
1958	12	2	3	3
1959	14	2	4	3
1960	11	2	5	3
1961	11	2	5	3
1962	11	2	5	3
1963	11	2	6	3
1964	12	2	5	4
1965	12	2	5	4
1966	11	2	5	4
1967	11	2	5	4
1968	12	2	6	4
1969	12	2	6	5

[Continued]

★ 2320 ★

Women Separated and Divorced, 1950-1971

[Continued]

Year	Separated[1]		Divorced	
	Negro and other races	White	Negro and other races	White
1970	13	2	6	4
1971	13	2	7	4

Source: "Percent of Ever-Married Women Not Living With Their Husbands Because of Marital Discord: 1950-1971." U.S. Bureau of the Census. Current Population Reports, Special Studies, Series P-23, No. 42. *The Social and Economic Status of the Black Population in the United States, 1971.* Washington, D.C.: Government Printing Office, 1972, p. 102. Primary source: U.S. Department of Commerce, Social and Economics Statistics Administration Bureau of the Census. *Notes:* Categories "Separated" and "Divorced" refer to marital status at time of enumeration. NA Not available. 1. Excludes separations for reasons such as spouse being in Armed Forces, employed and temporarily living considerable distance from home, or inmate of institution.

Reference Sources

Baseball Digest. Monthly. Century Publishing Co., 990 Grove Street, Evanston, Ill. 60201-4370.

Black Enterprise 3 (June 1973); 4 (June 1974) and 5 (June 1975). Monthly. Earl Graves Publishing Co., Inc., 130 Fifth Avenue, New York, N.Y. 10001.

Bloom, Gordon, and Fletcher, F. Marion. *The Negro in the Supermarket Industry*. Philadelphia: Industrial Research Unit, Department of Industry, Wharton School of Finance and Commerce, University of Pennsylvania, 1972.

Chalk, Ocania. *Black College Sport*. New York: Dodd, Mead and Co., 1976.

———. *Pioneers of Black Sports*. New York: Dodd, Mead and Company, 1975.

Du Bois, W. E. Burghardt, ed. *The Negro Church*. Atlanta University Publications No. 6. Atlanta: Atlanta University Press, 1903.

———, ed. *The Negro in Business*. Atlanta University Publications No. 4. Atlanta: Atlanta University Press, 1899.

The Ebony Handbook. Chicago: Johnson Publishing Co., 1974.

Favrot, Leo Mortimer. *A Study of County Training Schools for Negroes in the South*. Slater Fund Occasional Papers. Charlottesville, Va., 1923.

Frazier, E. Franklin. *The Free Negro Family*. Nashville: Fisk University Press, 1932.

Fulmer, William E. *The Negro in the Furniture Industry*. Industrial Research Unit, Wharton School. Philadelphia: University of Pennsylvania, 1973.

Goldman, Peter. *Report from Black America*. New York: Simon and Schuster, 1969.

Guzman, Jessie Parkhurst, ed. *Negro Year Book: A Review of Events Affecting Negro Life, 1941-1946*. Tuskegee Institute, Ala.: Department of Records and Research, 1947.

———, ed. *Negro Year Book: A Review of Events Affecting Negro Life, 1952.* New York: William H. Wise, 1952.

Hamilton, J. G. de Roulhac; Wagstaff, Henry McGilbert and Pierson, William Whatley, Jr. ''The Free Negro in North Carolina'' and ''Some Colonial History of Craven County.'' *The James Sprunt Historical Publications*, Vol. 17, No. 1. Chapel Hill: University of North Carolina Press, 1920.

Holway, John. *Voices from the Great Black Baseball Leagues.* New York: Dodd, Mead, 1975.

Jeffress, Philip W. *The Negro in the Urban Transit Industry.*

Philadelphia: Industrial Research Unit, Department of Industry, Wharton School of Finance and Commerce, University of Pennsylvania, 1970.

Joyce, Donald Franklin. *Gatekeepers of Black Culture: Black-owned Book Publishing in the United States, 1817-1981.* Westport, Conn.: Greenwood Press, 1983.

Linder, Forrest E., and Grove, Robert D. *Vital Statistics Rates in the United States 1900-1940.* Washington, D.C.: Government Printing Office, 1943.

Locke, Alain. *A Decade of Negro Self-Expression.* Slater Fund, Occasional Papers, 1928.

Low, W. Augustus, and Clift, Virgil A., eds. *Encyclopedia of Black America.* New York: McGraw-Hill, 1981.

Mitchell, Doris J., and Bell, Jewel H., eds. *The Black Woman: Myths and Realities.* Selected papers from the Radcliffe Symposium, ''The Black Woman: Myths and Realities,'' May 4-5, 1973. Cambridge, Mass.: Radcliffe College, 1975.

Murray, Florence, ed. *The Negro Handbook.* New York: Wendell Malliet, 1942.

———, ed. *The Negro Handbook, 1944.* New York: Current Reference Publications, 1944.

———, ed. *The Negro Handbook, 1947.* New York: Current Books, A. A. Wyn, Publisher, 1947.

———, ed. *The Negro Handbook, 1949.* New York: Macmillan, 1949.

Northrup, Herbert R. *The Negro in the Aerospace Industry.* Philadelphia: Industrial Research Unit, Wharton School of Finance and Commerce, University of Pennsylvania, 1968.

———; Thieblot, Armand J.,and Chernish, William N. *The Negro in the Air Transport Industry.* Philadelphia: Industrial Research Unit, Department of Industry, Wharton School of Finance and Commerce, University of Pennsylvania, 1971.

Perry, Charles R.; Kemp, Elsa and Keeney, Marie R. *The Negro in the Department Store Industry*. Philadelphia: Industrial Research Unit, Department of Industry, Wharton School of Finance and Commerce, University of Pennsylvania 1971.

Quay, William Howard, Jr., and Denison, Marjorie C. *Negro in the Chemical Industry*. Philadelphia: Industrial Research Unit, Department of Industry, Wharton School of Finance and Commerce, University of Pennsylvania, 1969.

Risher, Howard W., Jr., Denison, Marjorie C. *The Negro in the Railroad Industry*. Philadelphia: Industrial Research Unit, Department of Industry, Wharton School of Finance, University of Pennsylvania, 1971.

Robert, Charles Edwin. *Negro Civilization in the South: Educational, Social, and Religious Advancement of the Colored People*. Nashville, 1980.

Rubin, Lester, *The Negro in the Longshore Industry*. Philadelphia: Industrial Research Unit, Wharton School, University of Pennsylvania, 1974.

———. *The Negro in the Shipbuilding Industry*. Philadelphia: Industrial Research Unit, Department of Industry, Wharton School of Finance and Commerce, University of Pennsylvania, 1970.

The John F. Slater Fund. *Proceedings and Reports*. For the Year Ending September 30, 1931.

———. *Proceedings of the Trustees of the John F. Slater Fund for the Education of Freedmen*. 1901-1911.

Smythe, Mabel K., ed. *The Black American Reference Book*. Englewood Cliffs, N.J.: Prentice-Hall, 1976.

Southern Regional Education Board. *Readings for Mental Health and Human Service Workers in the Black Community*. The Community Clinical Psychology Project. Atlanta, 1980.

U.S. Bureau of Education. *Negro Education: A Study of the Private and Higher Schools for Colored People in the United States*. 2 vols. Bulletin 1916, Nos. 38, 39. Washington, D.C.: Government Printing Office, 1917.

———. *Survey of Negro Colleges and Universities*. Bulletin 1928, No. 7. Washington, D.C.: Government Printing Office, 1929.

U.S. Bureau of the Census. *Historical Statistics of the United States: Colonial Times to 1957*. Washington, D.C.: Government Printing Office, 1960.

———. *Historical Statistics of the United States: Colonial Times to 1970*. 2 parts. Bicentennial Edition. Washington, D.C.: Government Printing Office, 1975.

———. *Negro Population, 1790-1915.* Washington, D.C.: Government Printing Office, 1918.

———. *Negroes in the United States.* Bulletin 129. Washington, D.C.: Government Printing Office, 1915.

———. *Negroes in the United States, 1920-1932.* Washington, D.C.: Government Printing Office, 1935.

———. *1972 Survey of Minority Business Enterprises.* Special Report. *Minority Owned BusinessesBlack*, MB72-1. Washington, D.C.: Government Printing Office, 1974.

———. *The Social and Economic Status of the Black Population in the United States: An Historical View, 1790-1978.* Current Population Reports, Special Studies, Series P-23, No. 80. Washington, D.C.: Government Printing Office, 1979.

———. *The Social and Economic Status of the Black Population in the United States, 1969.* Current Population Reports, Special Studies, Series P-23, No. 29. Washington, D.C.: Government Printing Office, 1969.

———. *The Social and Economic Status of the Black Population in the United States, 1970.* Current Population Reports, Special Studies, Series P-23, No. 38. Washington, D.C.: Government Printing Office, 1970.

———. *The Social and Economic Status of the Black Population in the United States, 1971.* Washington, D.C.: Government Printing Office, 1972.

———. *The Social and Economic Status of the Black Population in the United States, 1972.* Current Population Reports, Special Studies, Series P-23, No. 42. Washington, D.C.: Government Printing Office, 1972.

———. *The Social and Economic Status of the Black Population in the United States, 1974.* Current Population Reports, Special Studies, Series P-23, No. 54. Washington, D.C.: Government Printing Office, 1975.

———. *Statistical Abstract of the United States, 1964.* Various editions. Washington, D.C.: Government Printing Office, 1964, 1966, 1967, 1970, 1971, 1973, 1975.

U.S. Commission on Civil Rights. *Social Indicators for Equality for Minorities and Women.* Washington, D.C.: Government Printing Office, 1978.

U.S. Department of Health, Education, and Welfare. National Center for Health Services. *Vital Statistics Rates in the United States 1940-1960.* Washington, D.C.: Government Printing Office, 1968.

Washington, Forrester B. "Recreational Facilities for the Negro." *The Annals* 140 (November 1928).

Wiley, Bell Irvin. *Southern Negroes 1861-1865.* New Haven, Conn.: Yale University Press, 1938.

Williams, W. T. B. *Report on Negro Universities and Colleges.* Slater Fund Occasional Papers, 1922.

Woodson, Carter G. *The Education of the Negro Prior to 1861: A History of the Colored People of the United States from the Beginning of Slavery to the Civil War.* New York: G. P. Putnam's Sons, 1915.

Work, Monroe N., ed. *Negro Year Book and Annual Encyclopedia of the Negro.* Tuskegee, Ala.: Tuskegee Normal and Industrial Institute, 1912.

———, ed. *Negro Year Book: An Annual Encyclopedia of the Negro.* Various years. Tuskegee Institute, Ala.: Negro Year Book Publishing Co., 1914, 1918, 1919, 1925, 1937-38.

Wright, James M. *The Free Negro in Maryland.* New York: Columbia University Press, 1921.

SUBJECT INDEX

The Subject Index holds nearly 1631 terms referring to topics, organization, and issues contained in *Historical Statistics of Black America*. Each term is followed by one or more page numbers, marked by the letter "p." The table numbers follow in brackets. For access to *HSBA* by year, please use the Index by Year.

Numbers following p. or pp. are page references. Numbers in [ ] are table references. Volumn two begins on page 1203.

Numbers following p. or pp. are page references. Numbers in [ ] are table references. Volumn two begins on page 1203.

Numbers following p. or pp. are page references. Numbers in [ ] are table references. Volumn two begins on page 1203.

Numbers following p. or pp. are page references. Numbers in [ ] are table references. Volumn two begins on page 1203.

Numbers following p. or pp. are page references. Numbers in [ ] are table references. Volumn two begins on page 1203.

Subject Index

Numbers following p. or pp. are page references. Numbers in [ ] are table references. Volumn two begins on page 1203.

Numbers following p. or pp. are page references. Numbers in [ ] are table references. Volumn two begins on page 1203.

Numbers following p. or pp. are page references. Numbers in [ ] are table references. Volumn two begins on page 1203.

Numbers following p. or pp. are page references. Numbers in [ ] are table references. Volumn two begins on page 1203.

Numbers following p. or pp. are page references. Numbers in [ ] are table references. Volumn two begins on page 1203.

Numbers following p. or pp. are page references. Numbers in [ ] are table references. Volumn two begins on page 1203.

Numbers following p. or pp. are page references. Numbers in [ ] are table references. Volumn two begins on page 1203.

Subject Index

Numbers following p. or pp. are page references. Numbers in [ ] are table references. Volumn two begins on page 1203.

Numbers following p. or pp. are page references. Numbers in [ ] are table references. Volumn two begins on page 1203.

Numbers following p. or pp. are page references. Numbers in [ ] are table references. Volumn two begins on page 1203.

Numbers following p. or pp. are page references. Numbers in [ ] are table references. Volumn two begins on page 1203.

Numbers following p. or pp. are page references. Numbers in [ ] are table references. Volumn two begins on page 1203.

Numbers following p. or pp. are page references. Numbers in [ ] are table references. Volumn two begins on page 1203.

Numbers following p. or pp. are page references. Numbers in [ ] are table references. Volumn two begins on page 1203.

Numbers following p. or pp. are page references. Numbers in [ ] are table references. Volumn two begins on page 1203.

INDEX BY YEAR

The Index by Year holds more than 1596 references arranged by year and major topic. Each reference is followed by one or more page numbers, marked by the letter "p." The table or entry numbers follow in brackets. For access to *Historical Statistics of Black America* by subject, please consult the Subject Index.

Numbers following p. or pp. are page references. Numbers in [ ] are table references. Volumn two begins on page 1203.

Numbers following p. or pp. are page references. Numbers in [ ] are table references. Volumn two begins on page 1203.

Numbers following p. or pp. are page references. Numbers in [ ] are table references. Volumn two begins on page 1203.

Numbers following p. or pp. are page references. Numbers in [ ] are table references. Volumn two begins on page 1203.

Index by Year

Numbers following p. or pp. are page references. Numbers in [ ] are table references. Volumn two begins on page 1203.

Numbers following p. or pp. are page references. Numbers in [ ] are table references. Volumn two begins on page 1203.

Numbers following p. or pp. are page references. Numbers in [ ] are table references. Volumn two begins on page 1203.

Numbers following p. or pp. are page references. Numbers in [ ] are table references. Volumn two begins on page 1203.

Numbers following p. or pp. are page references. Numbers in [ ] are table references. Volumn two begins on page 1203.

Numbers following p. or pp. are page references. Numbers in [ ] are table references. Volumn two begins on page 1203.

Numbers following p. or pp. are page references. Numbers in [ ] are table references. Volumn two begins on page 1203.

Numbers following p. or pp. are page references. Numbers in [ ] are table references. Volumn two begins on page 1203.

Numbers following p. or pp. are page references. Numbers in [ ] are table references. Volumn two begins on page 1203.

Numbers following p. or pp. are page references. Numbers in [ ] are table references. Volumn two begins on page 1203.

Numbers following p. or pp. are page references. Numbers in [ ] are table references. Volumn two begins on page 1203.

Numbers following p. or pp. are page references. Numbers in [ ] are table references. Volumn two begins on page 1203.

Numbers following p. or pp. are page references. Numbers in [ ] are table references. Volumn two begins on page 1203.

Numbers following p. or pp. are page references. Numbers in [ ] are table references. Volumn two begins on page 1203.